GENERAL INDEX

TO THE

COLONIAL RECORDS,

IN 16 VOLUMES,

AND TO THE

PENNSYLVANIA ARCHIVES,

IN 12 VOLUMES,

PREPARED AND ARRANGED BY

SAMUEL HAZARD,

UNDER AN ACT OF THE

GENERAL ASSEMBLY

OF

PENNSYLVANIA.

PHILADELPHIA:
PRINTED BY JOSEPH SEVERNS & CO.
1860.

PREFACE.

FREQUENT inquiries having been made of the Editor, during the preparation and printing of this work, as to the difference between the Colonial Records and Pennsylvania Archives, to which the present volume is a general index, it may be useful to state the following facts:

It is believed that the early Records or Minutes of the Provincial Councils, &c., were kept on loose sheets of paper, and not, at the time, recorded in books, as appears by frequent long intervals of dates, and blanks left for documents. Many of these loose sheets are in the handwriting of James Logan, the then Secretary, and after being for many years preserved in his family, were deposited among the archives of several societies; some having been recorded in the volumes in the State department, and some not being yet in print. At a subsequent period, it is believed, an attempt was made to collect and record in volumes as many of these loose sheets as could be obtained, but without entire success, though the collection from 1682 to 1790, now consists of 32 MS. volumes. As they were the only records in existence, and liable at any moment to be destroyed, the Philosophical and Historical Societies in 1836, directed the attention of the Legislature to the subject of their preservation by printing these volumes; which, in 1837, resulted in an Act authorizing the Secretary of the Commonwealth to cause a portion of them to

be printed. And again in 1838, another portion, so that in 1840, three volumes, bringing down the date to 1735, had been printed. Here the matter rested for several years, owing, it is understood, to financial difficulties. In 1851, the subject was again revived, and the Secretary was authorized to continue the printing of the minutes, to the adoption of the State Constitution in 1789–90. This was accordingly done, the proofs being revised by clerks in the Secretary's office, till the whole were printed in sixteen volumes, including the first three volumes, which, having become scarce, were reprinted uniformly with the rest. These are the *Colonial Records*.

In 1851, the Governor in his annual message stated that his "attention had been called to the large body of original papers in the State Department connected with the Colonial and Revolutionary History of the State," and recommended the employment of a suitable person to select and arrange them for publication. A committee of each body was appointed to consider the suggestion of the Governor, both of which made favorable reports, and the Assembly authorized the Governor to make such an appointment. The editor was honored with this selection; and after carefully examining all the papers of early date in pigeon-holes and bundles in the office, made his report as published, and presented by the Governor with his message to the Assembly, who by Act of March, 1852, appointed the person who had made the selection, to superintend the printing; but it was not till the 27th August, 1852, owing to various delays in making the contracts, that the publication was commenced. This collection containing about 11,000 distinct papers, from originals in the Secretary's office, and now forming twelve volumes, constitutes the *Pennsylvania Archives*.

As the two works make twenty-eight volumes, and the Records being without any other index than a meagre table of contents, from which but few facts could be ascertained,

and as there are twelve volumes of the Archives, which, though each volume contains a full index, yet requiring an examination of each, it was deemed advisable, for greater ease of reference, that a general index, embraced in one volume, should be prepared. The Assembly, perceiving this necessity, authorized the editor by Act to prepare it, and the present volume is the result of his labors.

So far as the Records are concerned, it is an entirely original index, made from the volumes themselves, with which the editor had before no more acquaintance than other persons. As he prepared those for the Archives, the subjects were more familiar to him, yet the combination of the twelve indices into one, became equally necessary and not less laborious.

It will be seen that the index is made very full and in detail, and it is believed that no important fact has escaped the notice of the editor. That so large a work, abounding with references to volumes and pages, should be entirely free from errors, cannot reasonably be expected or even hoped for; but, it is believed, from frequent references made, while in progress, that they will be found very few and unimportant. If any are met with, the means of correcting many may be found in the fact, that all important subjects are referred to under several heads, as well as the one adopted by the editor. For the Archives, in such cases, the several volumes may prove also available.

Some difficulty has been experienced in connecting events and names, from the circumstance that sometimes only the name, without the office; and at others the title without the Christian name, occur, not even allowing for changes by promotions; some confusion may, therefore, occur which could not well be avoided.

It is, however, believed that with all its imperfections the index will promote a more intimate acquaintance with the history of our State, as detailed in the Records and Archives, than could possibly be attained without it, and make every

one who chooses to consult and trace it, better acquainted with the occurrences of his own neighborhood at least. Indeed, the editor is satisfied that no better and fuller history of the State can be found, than in the sources referred to in this volume.

The volume has been so printed that it may be kept together or separated to suit the wishes of persons possessing either the Records or Archives; or both; and to one who has neither, it will possess an interest, as referring to subjects on which he may desire information; and obtain it from some library or neighbor, who has either one or both works.

The numerals refer to the volumes, and the figures to the pages.

INDEX

TO

COLONIAL RECORDS

OF

PENNSYLVANIA.

VOLUMES I. TO XVI. INCLUSIVE.

INDEX TO COLONIAL RECORDS.

VOLUMES I. TO XVI., INCLUSIVE.

Abercrombie, James, to inspect goods damaged, xiii., 773.

Abercrombie, Gen. James, letters to and from, vii., 193. Appointment of Sir Wm. Johnston as colonel, agent, and sole superintendent of Six nations, 193. Succeeds Lord Loudoun, viii., 26. Recommends embargo, &c., 38. Assembly in answer to, 52. Letters to and from, 37, 69, 74, 78, 97, 141. Order respecting capitulation of Fort William Henry, 141.

Abolition Society—memorial respecting negro Philip's bondage in Louisiana, to be demanded, xvi., 33, 34. Address, 210.[2]

Abraham, Noah, Justice, xi., 524; xiv., 567.

Abrams, Henry, Second Lieut., xii., 70.

Academy and College of Philadelphia, charter to be sent Council, xii., 39. Commencement postponed, 43. Attorney General's opinion asked on several points, 58. To confer with others, 62, 64. Views of, 98. Confiscated estates for, 189, 585.

Acquanushioony—Six nations of Indians, means confederate, v., 86.

Act for Advancement of Justice, &c., confirmed, iii., 71. Respecting elections, iii., 277. Proposed publication of Colonial Records, iv., 8. Passed by Assembly for ditto, 14. For vesting State house, &c., in trustees, for use of province, 46. Confirmed, 483–485. Repealed, 486.

Act of Assembly, Feb. 20, 1736, declaring State house a public green and walk, forever, xiii., 692.

Active, sloop, xi., 647, 657. Case of, xii., 144.

Adams, John, petition respecting goods seized at New Castle by sheriff, &c., i., 541.

Adams, John (pilot), attends lighthouse, xi., 574.

Adams, John (minister), letter on American Bishop, xiv., 399.

Adams, Robert, letter, vii., 43.

Adams, Solomon, surveyor to lay out a road, xv., 191.

Adams, Doctor William, Surgeon, xii., 215. Case of, as Surgeon of Pennsylvania Artillery, xiii., 572.

Addis, John, coroner, ix., 199.

Address proposed to King and Duke, on alarms and building forts, i., 109. Of Council to Governor, 402. Of Territories to Governor, ii., 128. Governor's answer, 130. Of Governor, 143. To King, on accession to the throne, iii., 226-291. Quakers object to style of it, 226, signed by Assembly, Governor and Council, 228. On Sugar Islands, 423. Of Assembly to Governor Thomas, v., 63. Of General Assembly, New York, to Governor Clinton, 465. To King, on death of Prince of Wales, 527. Of Assembly to King, against proprietary restrictions, vi., 448. Answer to, 504–510. Of Bethlehem Indians, 747, 750. Of Assembly to Governor, on enlistment of servants, vii., 37. Of Quakers, against war, 84. On Indian treaty, 311. Of Quakers, on militia bill, 405. Of Moravians at Bethlehem, 494. Commissioners, 498. From Friendly Association, 638. Answer, 647, 648. From Quaker meeting of sufferings on Indian complaints at Easton, viii., 239, 241. Answer to, 242. Another, 243. Gov. and Council to King, on repeal of Stamp Act, ix., 315. Of Assembly to Governor, 610.

To and from Governor Richard Penn, x., 12. Of Assembly against C. Jolly, a Justice, 31. To Governor, John Penn, 107. From Committee of Safety to people of Pennsylvania, 623. Of the Supreme Executive Council to the people, on taking active measures against approaching enemy, xi., 204. Of General Washington to inhabitants, 429. To Assembly, 685–690. Of Council to Sieur Gerard, on his departure, xii., 110. Of Council to Chev. de la Luzerne, on birth of a Dauphin, xiii., 284. And answer, 285.

Adjouquay, fort at, vii., 157. Three days above Shamokin, 157. Fourteen miles above Wyoming, 157, 159, 182, 184.

Adjutants appointed, x., 453, 494, 515.

Adjutant General, services dispensed with, xi., 400—xiv., 217.

Adlum, John, Sheriff, v., 597, 662—vi., 144, 638. Coroner, ix., 57, 199, 399. Surveyor to attend Commissioners to run north line, xv., 212. Applies for money to defray expenses of locating reserved lands, no money appropriated, xvi., 66. Surveys of reserved tracts on Erie, 161, 169. Commissioner to view Schuylkill, 178, 195. And Quittapœhilla, &c., 319.

Adlum, Joseph, Coroner, ix., 333, 548, 624, 689, 778—x., 56, 101, 212, 271—xi., 371—xii., 145, 161.

Admiralty Court, appointed, i., 121. Robert Webb, Marshal of, seizes goods, 539. Trial by, John Moore, deputy of Col. Quarry, Judge of, 580. Vice—Wm. Asheton, Judge, iii., 172. A. Hamilton appointed Judge, iv., 250. Decision by, necessary to a register for Dutch vessels brought in by privateers, viii., 155. Proceeding of "Stanwix" privateer, 172. Matthew Clarkson appointed Marshal, x., 538. Judge Ross, xi., 713. Andrew Robinson appointed Register, xii., 14. Death of Judge George Ross, 46. Cost of seal for, cut by Caleb Lownes, 102. Case of French claim, referred to Attorney General, 267. His and Council's opinion, 275. Judge F. Hopkinson, 307. Matthew Clarkson Marshal, Andrew Robinson, Register, 316, 351. Memorial, 409. Petition of Marshal, 477, 523, 531, 533, 537. Register, James Read, elected in place of A. Robinson, dec'd, xii., 745. Reference of Act for establishing Courts for trial of piracies, &c., xii., 702. Board of Supplies, 707. Francis Hopkinson reappointed, xv., 191.

Adultery, a Justice removed for, xii., 634.

Ætna, fire ship, William Gamble appointed Captain, x., 525. Resigns, 760.

Affirmation, Commissioners under dedimus, refuse to administer to Council, &c., ii., 93–96. Instead of oath, 168. Rejected, 170. Arguments in favor of, 227. Respecting, 615. Respecting, iv., 336, 629.

Afflick, Thomas, to be seized, xi., 284.

Agaghradarisha, Indian chief, vii., 154. "The Old Man," a noted friend of Pennsylvania, 156. Conference between Clapham and, at Armstrong, 157. Answer of Governor M. to, speech of, 158. Conference with, 182. Fort at Adjouquay, 184. At Fort Augusta, 281, 282.

Agency, Christy, Lieutenant, xii., 70.

Agent to be appointed for the Province, in London—Henry Goldney named, iii., 44.

Agnew, Edward, prisoner at Quebec, xi., 658.

Agnew, John, Prothonotary, xi., 365. Sub-Lieutenant, tenders resignation—not accepted, xii., 633. Resigns, 685. Justice, xiv,, 164.

Agreement with Indians, ii., 15. Between Lord Baltimore and Hannah Penn, iii., 232. Duplicate received, 233. Respecting division line, 461, 463, 464, 497. Report, 544. Penn and Indians, 601. Between agents, to receive money granted by Parliament, ix., 47.

Agricultural Society, addressed on subject of Hessian fly, xv., 524. Answer, 526.
Agriculture, donation to American Philosophical Society to encourage, xiv., 51.
Air-furnace of M. Bustead, x., 641.
Aitkin, John, receives pay for a hanger lost by President, at James Wilson's riot, xii., 341.
Aitkin, Robert, paid for paper, xii., 179. Secretary to Commissioners, for procuring flour, 227. To deliver salt, 241. Pays for, 316. Bill for printing, xiv., 75, 157, 206, 510, 643. Printer, xv., 69, 169, 251, 351, 460, 520, 648—xvi., 100, 411.
Aix-la-Chapelle, treaty of peace, or cessation of arms, signed at, v., 330. Proclamation, 331. Other papers respecting it, 359, 362, 553.
Akins—place, vii., 155.
Akoan, (Indian) on Indian Murders, vii., 357.
Alarm, false, by Governor Evans, 1706, ii., 433, 453. Committee, x., 549.
Albany, proceedings with Indians at, ii., 461. Conference with the Five nations at, iii., 193. Expenses provided for, 196. Governor's speech, &c., at, 198. Answer of Indians, 200. Surrender of land by Indians, 201. Governor's answer to Indians, 202. Respecting, 203 - 207. French erect fortifications near Albany, 419. Indian affairs at, iv., 770, 771, 774, 775. Treaty with Six nations, report of Commissioners at, v., 7-26. Message respecting, 329, 495. Meeting postponed, 524. Time of, 749. Commissioners to, vi., 23, 25, 47. Proceedings of the Congress at, 57-129. Rank of Colonies to be according to location, 65. Plan of union proposed, 66, 91. Committee on, 67. Draft of general speech to Six Nations, 69-71. Plans of union, 71, 72, 78, 87, 89, 93, 96, 100, 105-109. Stockbridge Indians attend—to be supported and addressed, 72. Mohawks deliver speech, 74. Answer of Six Nations, 79. Speeches from Governors, 85. Message of Commissioners to Governor, 91. Answer, 92. Indian lands, 93, 96. Plan of union presented by Franklin, 105-109. Report on necessary forts, 109. Meeting ends, 110. Report of John Penn and R. Peters, Commissioners to Governor H. of their proceedings at, 111-129. Deeds for lands, 119-129. Indians complain of, 286. Settlers north of, 420. Treaty at, viii., 641. Treaty at and Commissioners, x., 177. Chairman of Committee receives powder, 327. Lutheran Church at, asks for a brief to collect, xv., 14.
Alberson, Ricliff, Lieutenant, xi., 56.
Albion, ship, sunk in Delaware, seized by Navy Board and libelled, claimed by David Beveridge, &c., xi., 544.
Aldermen, of Philadelphia, xvi., 53.
Ale-houses, courts held in, ii., 409.
Alexander, Captain Charles, appointed to command the "Bull Dog," x., 290. Resigns, 540.
Alexander, James, letter to Governor M., on Connecticut claim, vi., 267. Letter from a Connecticut man, and answer, 270. From James Brown and answer, 271, 273.
Alexander, Joseph, resigns as Lieutenant, xii., 390.
Alexander, William, letters to and from, vi., 248, 262, 555. Conduct of Lydius, 248. Sends a minute of Council of New Jersey, respecting Connecticut, 555. Takes brig, x., 563. Assistance requested for, xi., 275, 528.
Alexander, Major William, recommended as Surveyor, xv., 49.
Alexandria, proceedings of meeting of General Braddock with Governors at, vi., 365.
Alfred, General Hopkins of the, to search vessels for seamen for public vessels, x., 435.
Algiers declares war against United States, xiv., 560.
Allaguipas, Old, his mother now alive near Raystown, son Kanuksusy present at conference at Philadelphia, vi., 588.

Allegheny County, Prothonotary, &c., James Bryson, xv., 548. Register and Recorder, S. Jones, Justices, 550. County Lieutenant, General R. Butler, 551. Justice, 560, 604, 606. Lands at Conewango to be reserved, 593. Proposals for purchase of reserved tract opposite Pittsburg, right of pre-emption to certain islands in, 598. Lots not to be sacrificed, 599. Valuation of by Council, 601. Committee to name streets in the new town, restrictions removed in part, 604. Appointment of justices rescinded, and others appointed, 606. Certain lots to be valued by a Committee, 606. Various petitions, &c., for lots and islands in, and patents, 609. Sales of lots to J. Robinson, 609. Report on names for streets, &c., in, sale of farm vacated, and islands, 611. Returns of all islands in, to be made, 612. Names of streets, 623. Reservation for State at Conewango in, xvi., 47. Islands in, surveyed, 97. Divided into Townships, 150, Collector of Excise, John Griffin, 162. Sheriff, 204. Coroner, 204. Huling's Island in, S. Huling has pre-emption right, 284. Island in, granted to William Todd, 289. Form of conveyance for, 301. Militia officers, 372. Justices, 377. General St. Clair's requisition of men, 424. Report on. Register and Record, 450. R. Butler resigns as Justice being elected to Assembly, 539.

Alleghany River, line run between Susquehanna—Ferry over, xii., 309, 317. ; xv., 5, 85. Islands in, for sale, 513. Islands in, sold to W. Wilson, xvi., 84.

Allegiance to King and fidelity, &c., to, William Penn promised, i., 80. To the Crown insisted on in a qualification, ii., 108. Question respecting, 385.

Aliens, rights of, viii., 355.

Allen, Andrew, member of Council, ix., 704. Attorney General, x., 53, Sent Commissioner to Virginia, 173, 174. Instructions, 175. Report, 181. Forfeited estate, sale of, xii., 88, 152. Continental money declined for, 248. Sold 340, 343, 344, 614, 745. Estate in Berks, Big Spring tract, xiii., 236, 286, 296, 303. Reconveyed to State, 766. Suit of children of, with State, xiv., 448, 459, 463, 589, 590, 592. Estate, xv., 4, 40, 43, 124, 237, 265.

Allen, Andrew, a forger delivered to New Jersey, xvi., 14.

Allen, Fort, vii., 15, 17, 189, 222, 267, 305, 309, 314, 429, 474, 476, 622, 723. Plan of, 18. Teedyuscung and his party at, perpetually drunk. Commander complained of for selling rum to Indians, 222. Sons at, 475, 476. Indians at, 478, viii., 98, 138, 143, 150, 167, 234, 513, 515. Agents for Indian trade appointed at, 234. A place of rendezvous for troops, xv., 295.

Allen, George, and others' examination, vii., 154. Appointed Indian agent, viii., 286.

Allen, Ira, of Vermont, on controversy between Vermont and New York, xii., 233.

Allen, Lieutenant James, x., 339.

Allen, John, Commissioner, to Fort Pitt to attend Indian treaty, ix., 491. Commission, 492. instructions, 493. Report 514–543. justice xii., 391.

Allen, Nathaniel, regulator of weights and measures, xiii., 633.

Allen, Sarah, removal postponed on account of sickness, xii., 386. petition, 743, 746.

Allen, William, appointed to try a negro for arson, iv., 243. Elected to Assembly by two counties, required to select which he will serve vii. 283. To hold Supreme Court, viii., 481. Chief Justice of Supreme Court, ix., 393. Chief Justice Salary, x., 53. Resigns, 173. Presents shot, 364. Appointed Lieutenant Colonel, 444, 445. Pass for his daughter Mrs. Delancey to visit him, xi., 593.

Allen, William, (Captain,) recommended to Congress as Lieutenant Colonel, x., 444. Appointed, 445.

Alles, Captain Henry, resigns Commission in Shee's battalion, x., 497.

Allibone, Captain, letter to, xii., 203.
Allibone, William, Commander for defence of Delaware River, xiii., 316.
Allison, Robert First Lieutenant, xi., 140. To have articles left by enemy secured, 534, and used at Billingsport, &c., 575, 584, 655, 682, 715. Take down spouts.
Allinson, William, to R. Peterson, condition of Braddock's road, vi., 434.
Atkinson, Wilson, Quarter Master, xi., 84
Allummappees, an Indian, iii., 297, 304, 315, 318. (al Sassoonan,) Delaware chief, in Philadelphia, iv., 53, 307. A special present to, from Governor, 309.
Almanac, printed in 1685, by William Bradford, "Lord Penn," to be stricken from, i., 165.
Almshouse, Philadelphia, iii., 588.
Alricks, Hermanus, resigns several offices in Cumberland County, his successor, ix., 671.
Alricks, Peter, elected councillor, i., 122, and Justice, 122. Alludes to historical account of Mohawks, in 1665, 300. Commissioned by Penn, Lieutenant and Commander-in-chief of Town and Fort of New Castle, 337, also names of persons enlisted, 337. Justice, 369.
Amazon, ship, Captain Floyd goes to Charleston, xiii., 521.
Amberson, William, Commissioner, xii., 371. Resigns, 465.
Amboy, camp at, powder for, x., 703, 704. Stores at, xi., 119.
America, the independence and sovereignty of United States acknowledged, xiii., 543. Proclamation of Congress on cessation of hostilities, 553.
America, North, his majesty's title to rests on discovery, vi., 100–105.
American Philosophical Society, donation to, to encourage Agriculture and Commerce, xiv., 51.
Amherst, General, Jeff., Letters to and from, viii., 236, 261, 262, 274, 283, 300, 316, 322, 331, 380, 381, 437, 448, 452, 454, 503, 504, 578, 581, 590, 592, 602, 622, 627, 628, 679, 687, 710. Appointed Commander in chief, 236. Pay for private arms, 274. Answer to Assembly's address to Governor on quarters, wagons, &c., 283. Appoints General Stanwix to succeed General Forbes, 298. Restoration of Fort Du Quesne, 316, 322. Names Commissioners to state account of expenses of expedition, 322. Objects to per diem pay, 323. In Philadelphia, 324. Supply bill, 331. Ticonderoga, 380. Exchange of prisoners, 381. Success at Isle Royal, &c., 503. Wants men, 578, 590, 602. Letters to and from, ix., 33, 34, 48, 62, 63, 74. Intelligence from Colonel Boquet, 34. Asks for troops, 74.
Ammunition removed, xi., 538.
Andaggyjunguah, a Conestoga chief, ii., 246.
Andrews, John, under Sheriff of Philadelphia, ii., 181.
Andrews, Major John, x., 683.
Andrews, Robert, Commissioner, on boundary with Virginia, xiv., 211, 236.
Andrews, Thomas, to take account of arms, ii., 241.
Andross, Sir Edmund, regulation respecting issue of patents, i., 86.
Ann, Princess of Denmark, made Queen of England, proclaimed, ii., 70.
Annaly, Indian, dies, viii., 163.
Annand, William, dedimus to, ii., 97.
Annapolis, General B. invites Governors to meet at, vi., 332. Congress adjourn from Princeton to, xiii., 746.
Anne, Queen, allusion to sale of province to, iii., 73. Act for continuing the Government in case of death of Governor, iv., 49.
Annuities to widows, &c., of officers, xvi., 140, 142.
Antes, Colonel Frederick, to rendezvous at Swedesford, xi., 301. Justice, xii. Resigns as Justice, xiv., 167, 169. Commissioner to examine rivers, xvi. 319.
Antes, Henry, Sheriff, xiii., 398,

751.; xiv., 256. Pay for services against Indians, 534, 603. Irregular returns, 726.
Antes, Lieutenant Henry.
Antis, William, Commissioner for taxes and levies, xi., 536.
Antille, Edward, i., 588.
Antitrinitarians to be discountenanced, iii., 64.
Apoquinimy and Upland Indians, willing to sell lands—Commissioners appointed, i., 156.
App, Michael, Coroner, xv., 570.
Appeals, iii., 278.
Apple-tree alley, between Third and Fourth, xii., 751.
Apprentice seized by Sheriff, ii., 148. An enlisted, discharged, x., 470.
Apty, Thomas, keeper of new gaol, x., 429. Rate of maintenance, 430. Declines victualing people in prison, 470. His account, 504, 699.
Arch street bridge and wharf, petition for, i., 330.
Archer, Lt. Henry W., xiv., 217.
Archives, Pennsylvania, Act authorizing Governor to select a competent person to arrange documents for publication, and also to have them printed, iv., 14.
Arentz, Baron de, case of, xii., 743.
Argus, armed boat, N. Galt, master, xiv., 10.
Armand, General, corps, petition for clothing, xii., 216, 568. List of his corps, xiii., 763. Letter, xiv., 12. Legion, 626.
Armitage, Benjamin, ii., 540.
Armitage, Shewbart, appointed Third Lieutenant, xi., 774.
Armour, Lt. James, recruits for Lancaster county, xi., 477.
Armourer, of boats, x., 490; xi., 408.
Arms, sent, vii., 107, 109. Required by General Forbes, order for, viii., 79, Not received, 84, 112. Disguised, forbid, ix., 546, 659; xi., 752, 756. From Mons. Penet, agreement with for, xii., 104. Of the State, to be worked on the standards for public use, 108.
Armstrong's, compact, vii., 154, 156, 172. Conference between Indians and Col. Clapham at, 157.
Armstrong, Alexander, writes letters to Indians, which create disturbance, iv., 680.
Armstrong, Edward, Chairman of Committee of H. R., reports in favor of publishing Colonial Records, iv., 10.
Armstrong, George, Commissioner to cut road west, vi., 318. Instructions to, vii., 535. Letter from, 556. Message from Yaughtanno, 558.
Armstrong, James, Coroner, iii., 615.
Armstrong, James, Quartermaster, x., 499.
Armstrong, John, an Indian trader, and three others, murdered by Delaware Indians, iv., 675, 678, 679. C. Weiser's report respecting, 680–684. Report to Governor M., of mission to Connecticut, vi., 259–261. Commission, &c., to survey road, 323, 377, 378, 401. Letter, Great Cove destroyed, 318, 676.
Armstrong, Lieutenant Colonel John, orders of Governor M., vii., 161. Letters to and from, 231, 259, 503, 594, 630. Arrived, his report, 257–263. Conference with Cherokees, 552. Murder at Great Cove, 599. Arrival of Cherokees at Fort Loudoun, destitute, viii., 77, 78. Letters to and from, 111. Letters to and from, ix., 181, 274, 444, 446, 448, 451, 461, 484. Instructions to, 451, in Philadelphia, 490, 510, 512.
Armstrong, Major General John, to remove troops from Billingsport, xi., 270. State of army, 396. Order, 475. To repair to city to command troops, 597. Paymaster at B., 618. In Philadelphia, 707. Pay for Billingsport, 757. Superintendent on Delaware, 759. Lieutenant, xi., 187. Resigns, 199. Appointed first Brigadier General, 199. Major General, 214. Attends Council —Resol'n of Congress, 248. Applies for a pass for L. Thompson, xii., 32, 63, 83, 120, 124, 130. Member of Congress, 172, 371. Letter, 322. Clothes for, 420. Commissioner of peace in Northumberland county, xiv., 168. Letter on Wyoming, 188. Commissioner to Wyoming, 202. Commiss'r to Wyoming paid, xiv., 638.

Armstrong, John, Jr., Secretary of Council, appointed in place of Timothy Matlack, xiii., 540. Secretary of Council, xiv., 10. Accounts, 118. Appointed Adjutant General, with rank of Brigadier General—President's opinion, 217, 219. Requests investigation into reports respecting him, 383. Appointed Commissioner, xv., 5. Commissioner to Commercial Convention, 82, 156. Member of Congress has leave of absence as Secretary, 195. His account of expenses of the Convention, paid, 250. Resigns as Secretary, 301. Delegate to Congress, 341, 418, 513.

Armstrong, Col. Joseph, respecting Braddock's road, vi., 425; x., 700; xi., 111, 113.

Armstrong, Thomas, Coroner, vi., 638; vii., 266.

Armstrong, Lieutenant, returned as belonging to Pennsylvania, xii., 235.

Armstrong, Lieutenant William, at Frederick, vii., 553.

Armstrong, William, paymaster at B., xi., 575, 578, 590, 618.

Armstrong, Major William, paymaster at Billingsport and Mud Island, xii., 10, 22, 40, 120, 150, 162, 186. His pay, &c., 283, 457, 570, 598, 667, 703. Appointed Commissary to Commissioners for running line with Virginia, xiii., 203. Pay to, 347. To pay workmen at forts, xi., 767. To run a north boundary line, xv., 22, 32. Stores for, 33. Pay, 120, 190, 204, 328, 605. Pay for labors, 356, 374. To report description of Erie lands, 382. Commissioner to Luzerne county, 452. His pay, 456, 595, 613. Late Deputy Adj. General of State Militia, paid for actions 1777, 1778, xvi., 261. Coroner, 542.

Army, rations, x., 500. Desertions, xii., 3, 322. New arrangements of, 500. Southern, 643. Continental, xvi., 214.[2]

Arndt, Hon. Jacob, money paid to, for purchase of provisions, xi., 422. Councilor, 652. Paid, xii., 180, 302. Letters, 317, 407, 502.

Arndt, John, xiii., 137. Censor, 723. Justice, xiv., 670.

"Arnold," name of floating battery, x., 525; xi., 138.

Arnold, Major General Benedict, to have command of militia at Bristol, and all east of Philadelphia, xi., 224. Letters to and from, 228. Why shops are to be shut on fourth July, his reasons, 523. Invites Council to dinner, 523. To furnish aid in quelling riot, 665. Sends wagons to Egg-harbor, 674. Pass to Miss Levy, 676, 679, 680. Leaves city before complaint about wagons sent to Egg-harbor is settled, xi., 684. Resolves respecting, sent to Delegates, 690. To be published, 692. Applies to Congress for court martial, 703. Proceedings against John Mitchell, 707, 708, 709. Complaint against proceedings, printed and sent to Congress, 720. Resigns command in Philadelphia, 725. His case resumed, 759. Depositions to be taken of his conduct when commanding city, xii., 225. Expenses of witnesses on trial of, to be charged to Congress, per resolve, 225. Objections to certificates of Geddis and Govett, 225, 226. Joins enemy at New York, 490. Papers to be seized, 490. Proclamation against, 496. Miss Hannah and nephew pass to Connecticut, 509. Baron Steuben to occupy his country-seat, 519. His wife to depart—sale of land in Northern Liberties, xiii., 80, 81. T. Matlack's accounts as prosecutor of, xiv., 605. Estate sold, xv., 640.

Arnold, Thomas, claim for estate to William Green, xvi., 307.

Arsenal ordered to be erected on Thirteenth and Juniper, xiv., 401, 458. Pay for, 469, 477, 588.

Arters, John, confesses a murder, x., 88.

Articles of agreement between Penn and Baltimore, proceedings of Court respecting, iv., 255. With Indians, 1701, 338.

Artificers, Colonel Baldwin's Regiment of, xii., 719.

Artillery Company, rules and regu-

lations for, x., 391–394. Men to be increased, 464. Officers, 584. Pay, 619. At Fort Island, xi., 1. Captain Strohbogh, 4, 265. Company and Officers commissioned, 223. Horses impressed, 301. Guards for, 302. Companies, at Forts on Delaware river, xii., 10. Petition for an Independent Company, 391. Proctors, 727. Officers appointed, xv., 437. Powder, 581. Articles ordered for, xvi., 24.

Arts and Sciences, a School of, proposed, i., 93.

Ash, James & Co., powder for privateer Rebecca, xi., 642.

Ash, James, contest with William Will, as Sheriff of Philadelphia, 567, 569, 570, 571, 572, 573, 574, 575, 576, 577, 578. Declared elected, 579. Sheriff of Philadelphia, xvi., 208, 211, 490.

Ash, Martha, to be imprisoned, x., 661.

Ashbridge, Justice of Chester county, complaint against, vii., 406.

Ashburn, William, Coroner, vii., 266; viii., 402.

Ashcomb, Charles, Deputy Surveyor of Chester county, complaints against, i., 151, 153, 154, 155, 163, 191, 193. Vexatious suit, 200.

Ashman, Colonel George, appointed Lieutenant of Bedford, xii., 549. xiii., 1, 150. Resigns as Lieutenant of Bedford county, xiv., 169, 207.

Ashton, Joseph, petitions for a road, ii., 10.

Ashton, Robert, Clerk of county, ii., 87. Asks for the records, 87. Dedimus to, 96. Clerk of city and county, 254. Complaint against his holding several offices, 456. Laws, 488, 571.

Ashton, Thomas, prisoner, not discharged from parol, xi., 625.

Assay bill, proposed, ix., 358.

Assembly, thank Governor for his kind speech, i., 65. To examine old laws, 67. Meeting made open, 86. To sit at New Castle, 96, 102. Members for Philadelphia, 99. Not to be arrested for debt, 102. Nicholas More, appointed speaker, 105. To have 8 days to peruse bills, 106. Dismissal of, power of Governor, &c., 107. Speaker charged with expressions against laws, 109. Old laws, 133. Alteration of style of bills proposed, 178, 180. Sit in the meeting-house, 179. Vacancies by suspension of Members of Council, 203. Governor's speech, 286. Speaker White imprisoned, 292. Adjournment, proceeding in Council on, 294. To meet at New Castle, 324. Under Fletcher, 366. Speaker, 399. Address to Governor, 402–6. Discussions with the Governor, 406–433. Answer of Council to remonstrance of Assembly, 423. To sit in Philadelphia, 437. Difficulty on an adjournment by Governor, 445. Governor asks to answer Queen's letter, 446. Returns of Members, 454, 482. David Lloyd appointed Speaker, 454. Respecting adjournment, 456. Remonstrance, 457. Address of Governor, 459. Grant of one penny to New York, 460, 462. Remonstrance in answer to Queen's letter, 469. Gov. Markham's addresses to, 480, 484, 488, 490, 494, 503, 505, 506, 519, 548. Edward Shippen, Speaker, 490. Answer to Governor's speech, 492. 506. Members elected, 502, 516, 518, 547, 567, 595, 601. John Simcock, Speaker, 503. Committee on answer to Queen's letter, 507. Markham proposes a new frame, 507. John Blunston, Speaker, 518, 568, 601. Phineas Pemberton, Speaker, 548. Address to King, 553, 554. Grand Committee of the Whole to inquire into absences, 569. To meet at New Castle, 588. Speech of Governor, 590. Advice of proprietary to, 596. Read charter and frame, 597, and laws, 598, 602. David Lloyd suspended, 604. Come to hear charter and frame read, 603, 604, 605, 611. Debate about oaths and tests, 606. Illegal arrest of David Lloyd, 607. And Robert Turner, 609. Differ about time of end of session, 610. Joseph Growden, Speaker, 615. Act of Union, 619.

Prorogued, ii., 11, 12. Called together, 25. Richard Wilson, dies, 27. Resolution of Council, 26. Convened on King's letter, 2, 28, 29, 30. Letter to Proprietary on defence of New York, 31. Answer to King's letter, 30. Called to consider proposed bill to annex proprietary governments to Crown, 32. Members, 34, 37. Governor's speech, 35. Joseph Growden, Speaker, 36, 206. Address to Governor, 36. Reply, 36. Conference with, 37. Address Governor, 37. Respecting privileges and property, 38, 43–45. To think of some person to represent Governor in his absence—Suggests Andrew Hamilton, 46. To consider further the laws of marriage, 48. Difficulties arising out of laws passed at New Castle, 50. Address of Governor to, and the secluding members, 50. Bill prepared for payment of £2,000 to Governor—Sent to them—Their action, 51. Message from Governor, 54. To Governor and 10 per cent. allowance on lands, 54. Charter of privileges signed —Number of members, &c., 58. Further prorogued for want of business, 69. Adjourn for a month, 75. Discussion on situation of Lower Counties, 71–75. Meeting at Samuel Peres, 76. Address of Representatives of Philadelphia, Bucks and Chester to Governor, 84. Meet — Inquiry, Why 8 members are returned?—Reply, 105. Debate on it, 105. Decision, 106. David Lloyd, Speaker, 106. Members, 109. Dispute between, and Council about future time of meeting, 110. Prorogued by Council, 111. To be called, 116, 119. Conference with territories, 120. Meeting to consider of union of territories and province, 123. Difficulties about meeting, 125. Address of Governor, 126. Address of Territories to Governor, 128. To meet at Joseph Shippen's, 129. Address of Governor, 130, 132. Meeting of, appointed, 130, 132. Separation in Legislation of Territories, 133. Governor advised not to meet at New Castle without new writs, 136. Commissions of peace issued, 136. Ask Governor for copies of orders respecting defence of New York, 138. Address to Governor on separation—Defence of New York, &c., 139. Answer to Governor, 140. Meeting of, with Council, 144. Ask Council's opinion in writing, 146. Answer, 146. Resolution on adjournment, 147. Send bill to prevent disputes concerning meetings of, 149. Message from Council on adjournment, 149. Resolution on right of Governor to dissolve or prorogue, 157, 158, 169. Separation from Territories, 163, 164. Send qualifications to Governor, 165. Speech of Governor to, 165, 168, 174. Address to Governor, 167, 175. Refusal to wait on Governor in a body, 173. Complains of their sending a remonstrance against him to proprietaries, 176. Address on candidates for Sheriff, 177. Governor's answer, 178. Remonstrance ordered back from New York, 178. Governor's message giving proprietaries' views on various matters, 187. Journal demanded, 186, 190, 191. Members deceased, 190. Answer to, 191, 193, 195-197, 198-200. Joseph Growden, Speaker, 206. Speech of Governor, 207. Send message to Governor on adjournment, 226. Address to Queen and Proprietary, 235, 236. Governor's address, 249. The answer, 249. On bills for establishing courts, 253–256. Message to Governor, 256. Governor's views, 256. Discussion about courts, 257, 261, 262. Objections of Governor and Council to bill establishing courts, 263–266. Answer to, 266–270. Answer of Governor and Council, 270–275. Answer to, 277–279. Charges against James Logan, Secretary, as one of his advisers on courts, ask for his removal from Council, 279. Governor goes to New Castle, 280. Resolution of Council sent to, 280.

Message of Governor, 281. Answer, 281, 282, 283. Logan's explanation of remark to S. Richardson, who took it as a joke, 284. Governor's reply to Assembly, 284–289. Governor's answer, 289–296. Adjourn without Governor's leave, 298. Called together by Governor at earlier day, 298. Governor's speech to, respecting courts and other subjects, 300–308. Conference with Governors subjects to be discussed, 309. Conference and discussion between Governor and, on their respective powers and duties, 311–315. Speaker and representatives affronted, depart suddenly, 314. Apologies, 315. Messages and speeches between them, 316–327. Remonstrance of, 328–336. Message, &c., 337–344. Articles of impeachment against James Logan, 344–348. Remonstrance of, on courts, 348–353. Adjourn themselves, called again by Governor, 353. Message of Governor to, 356. Answer to, 358. Governor to, 359–361. Answer to Governor, articles against Logan to be prosecuted, 361. Meeting of, to try the impeachment of James Logan, discussion of the right of Assembly to do so, 365–6, 372. James Logan's defence on each article, 367–372. Messages between Assembly and Governor on impeachment, 372–385. Jas. Logan's petition to Governor and Council, 376. Petition of Philadelphia against New Castle, 379. Action on, 379–383. Governor's message and answer, 384. D. Lloyd, speaker, Governor's message, reflections on, 398. Answer of, 399. Magistrates' courts held in ale-houses, 409. Message from Governor to, on French privateers, 413. Answer to, 415. Governor's reply, 417–420. Answer, 421-423. On quit rents, Assembly of New Castle, 424. Conference with, and Governor, on respective powers, as to meetings and adjournments, 432. Address to Governor Gookin, on his arrival, &c., 433. Governor's message to, 437. Answer, 441. Value of money and contracts, 445. Conference with Council on, 446. Governor's speech, 451. Answer, 452. Remonstrance of, 454. Address Council, 460. Governor's address, 461. Neglect to raise funds censured, 462. Reply, 463. Governor to, 465. Resolutions by, 466. Adjourns without Governor's consent, 467. Governor lets them alone, but removes embargo, 467. Called, 469. Governor's message, 472. Address to Governor, 475. Answer, 476. Message from, 478. Answer, 479, 480. Swedes' petition, 480. Message, Answer to Governor, 482. His answer, 483. Committee of conference, 483. Discussions about courts, 485. And message to Governor, 486. Ashton, (Robert,) makes alterations in court bill, and is blamed, 489, 490. Messages, 491. Remonstrance, 495. D. Lloyd, speaker, 503. Governor's address to, 503. Answer, 504. Issue a mittimus to jail, of James Logan, 507. Order to Sheriff, 507. Governor denies power of, to commit, 507. Governor gives order to protect him, 508. Remonstrance of, to Governor, 514. Change of members of three counties, 516. Richard Hill, speaker, 517. Addresses between Governor and Assembly, 517, 518. Discussion with Governor about laws, 520–529. Meet—Governor's address to, 535. Answer, 535, 536. Governor to, 537. Agree to £2000 for Queen's use, 538. Governor's speech, R. Hill, speaker, 541. Answer, 544. Several Acts sent to Governor, 548. Isaac Norris, speaker, Governor's speech, loses by coming here, 560. Answer, 560. Governor's mill creek, Nathaniel Pool's, road to William Coates's corner, 561. Governor's speech, 568. Answer, 568. Complain of having two Reg. Generals, 569. Address to Governor on too few members, 562. Governor to, and answer, 572. D. Lloyd, speaker, 575. Rumor of death of Queen, 574.

Summons to meet, 590. Governor's speech, 591. Answer, 592. Governor to, 594. Discussions on laws between Governor and Assembly, 590–597. Joseph Growden, speaker, 608. Governor's speech, 609. Discussions between, and Governor, 611. Richard Hill, speaker, 613. Governor's speech, 613. Resolutions adopted, 614. To Governor, 615. Representation of position of proprietary at first, with regard to Quakers and affirmation, 616. Vote Governor Gookin, £100, 630. Asks for £200, granted, 630.

Convened by Governor Keith, iii., 14. Address to King, 25. Governor's speeches to, 25, 27. Answers to, 27. At New Castle, 32. Appealed to by Governor in case of murderer, 40. Jonathan Dickinson, speaker, 56. Speech of Governor Keith, continuance of Government supplies, 63. New commission and instructions from William Penn, Jr., laid before, speech to, 65. Answer, 66. Their advice to delay publication of commission, 67. William Trent, speaker, 69. Governor's speech and answer, 70. Jeremiah Langhorn, speaker, 140. Speech to Governor, and answer, 141. Address to King, 226. Address to Governor Keith from, complaining of grievances and encroachments of New Castle county, upon Chester county, 234. Governor Gordon's speech to, 255. D. Lloyd, speaker, 261. Speech to Governor, and his answer, 261. Message of Governor, 262, 263. Speech of Governor to on bills of credit, iron works, 264. Prevented by heavy rains, from meeting, 267. Message of Governor on adulteration of bills of credit, designs of John French against proprietary's interests, William Till, Supreme Court, dams in Brandywine creek, 267–9. David Lloyd, speaker, 289. Address to King George II., 291. Speech of Governor to, 292. Withdrawal of eight members from, occasions want of a quorum, 298. Representation from speaker to Governor, respecting, 298. Names of the eight members, letter from, unopened by, 298. Their representation to Governor, 299. Objections to electing a member in place of Keith, 300. Governor's speech to, 305, 338. D. Lloyd, speaker, 337. Complain of rude treatment in Philadelphia, 340. Action of Council on, 340. Governor's speech on, 341. Recommends their course, 342. Agree to division of Chester county, 345. Act sent to Council to issue bills of credit, 346. Proclamation respecting riotous conduct in Philadelphia, 351. Speech of Governor on paper currency, 352. Answer, 353. Governor to, 354, 357. A. Hamilton, speaker, 371, 387. Govr.'s speech to, 373. Message of Governor on paper money, 377. Governor's speech, 390. Message of Governor on application of Sugar Islands, to Parliament, 401. Answer to Governor on, 406. Charges, 407. Message on Indian trade, 408. Andrew Hamilton, speaker, 417. Address to Governor, 420. On Sugar Islands, 420. Answer, 421. Address to King, &c., 423. Adjourn in consequence of small-pox, 426. Bill for paying wages of, 427, 434. Pay to Governor, object to his message, his reply, 427–8. Wait on Thos. Penn with an address, 433. His answer, 434. A. Hamilton, speaker, 466. Governor's speech, 493. Address to Governor, 493. To Governor, 509. Jeremiah Langhorne, speaker of, 528. Governor's speech, 531. Answer, 532. Message of Governor on appointment of Mr. Davis as agent, 539. On Act for small debts, 540. Resolves on, 541. Message to Governor respecting Maryland affairs, 566. A. Hamilton, speaker, 576, 615. Governor's speech to, 576. Address to proprietary, 582. And answer, 582. To Governor, 582. And answer, 583. Called to consider Lord Baltimore's application to the King for the territories, 594. Governor's speech to, 595. An-

swer to, 596. Address to Governor, 596. Petition to King, 596. Waits on John Penn, proprietary, prior to his departure for England and address to him, 611. Answer, 611. Message of Governor and answer, he being sick, 616.

Pass act for printing Colonial Records and Pennsylvania Archives, iv., 14. Message from Governor and Council, 18, 19. On wears, 20. Court of Chancery and Equity, 18, 20, 22. Message from Governor and Council on wears, 23. Petitions against Court of Chancery, 35, 36, 37. Message of Governor on do, 39. Answer, 41. James Logan assumes the government on death of Governor Gordon, and makes a speech, referring to the posture of affairs, 50. Address in reply, 51. A. Hamilton is Speaker, 53, 95, 97, 249. Message to, 95, 97. Message apprehended and corrected, 98. Position on account of Governor's death, 98, 99. Maryland affairs, 101, 151, Answer to President's message, 119, 120. Petition to King, 125. From Council to, 201. To Council, 202. Message to, 233. Answer, 236. Council object to certain expressions 237. Message to Council on Indian treaty, 238. Answer to, 239. Papers laid before, recommendation of Governor Thomas and petition of Lord Baltimore against, 249. Gov. Thomas arrives, and is proclaimed, 288. Appoints Thomas Lawrie, Secretary, 289. Message to, 290. Address from, to Governor, 292. Proceedings at Hampton Court, writ to, 301. Message of Governor on bills of credit, 303. Complimentary message to, 305. A. Hamilton, Speaker, 311, Message to, 305, 314, 319, 322, 331, 332, 333, 335, 354, 359, 380, 385, 387, 389, 398, 402, 405, 407, 587, 737, 754, 758, 773. From, 316, 321, 330, 333, 356, 360, 375, 387, 402, 754, 758, 773. On bills credit, 319–321, 330. A bill to regulate choice of inspectors of elections necessary, 335. Message on proprietary lands, 348. Dr. Græme's salary, 349. Speaker John Kinsey, 353, 470. Call of, 359. Papers submitted from Lords of trade, &c., on value of gold and silver coins and on bills of credit, 359. Reports on, 360, 365. On state of Province, 366–371. On liberty of conscience, 367, 375. Governor's message on raising money for Philadelphia, 385. Objects to it, 385. Answer to Governor, 389. Governor represents conduct of Is. Pemberton, 389. Messages of Governor to, reviewing various proceedings of, 398–402. Reasons for bill to raise money on Philadelphia, 408. Governor's answer to, 409–413. Answer to, 414. Governor's reply to, 419. Governor's speech in defence, 422. Asks for originals, received from England, 424, 425, 426. Governor to, on probable peace with Spain, 427. Adjourn abruptly, 430. Greater number are Quakers, 435. Resolution to pay £3000 for King's use, 459. Messages of Governor, 431, 438–443, 447, 461, 466, 473, 491, 495, 507, 510, 540, 558, 590–600, 602, 626, 627, 658, 672, 676, 677, 678, 685, 687, 737, 740, 749, 750, 763, 765, 772. Messages to Governor, 435–438, 448, 450–459, 466, 470, 491, 495, 509, 511, 549, 558, 602, 603–618, 628, 637, 659, 673, 676–679, 685, 740, 763, 773. Minute of Council, 459. Resolution respecting Drs. Græme and Zachary, health officers, 496. Governor asks for erection of a pest house, 507. Assembly's reply, 509. Governor's answer respecting funds, and his support, 510. Reply, 511. Report of a Committee on port physician, Dr. Græme, 515, –523. On powers of Government, &c., 519–559. Presents to Indians, 575. John Kinsey, Speaker, 618, 669, 749. Speech and Governor's answer, 619. Address to Governor, 619. Answer, 620. Address to Governor on election riots in Philadelphia, 620. Attorney General's opinion on, in reply to Mayor, 621. Governor's an-

swer to, 623. Message of Governor on Thomas McKee's deposition respecting Indians, 634. Answer, 637. Send orders for money, 638. Rupture with France, 672. Murders by Delaware Indians, 679. Proposed visit of Governor, &c., to Indians, 679. Pay Governor £500, 753. Expedition to Cape Breton, 754. Catawbas and Virginia, 758. Grant provisions for King's use, 769. The Governor objects, 769. Governor's pay, 770. Propose to Governor to visit Albany, appoints commissioners, 771. In view of Indians taking sides with French, 773. John Wright, Speaker, 782.

John Kinsey, Speaker, v., 4, 55, 123, 347, 411. Isaac Norris Speaker, 484, 558, 599, 662. Messages from Governor to, 4, 26, 30, 36, 44, 45, 46, 53, 62, 64, 124, 154, 156, 182, 230, 233, 270, 329, 339, 454, 484, 491, 493, 499, 502, 505, 511, 513, 524, 528, 540, 546, 564, 605. Do. to Governor, 31, 43, 44, 46, 48, 54, 56, 58, 63, 124, 159, 183, 184, 234, 237, 274, 333, 341, 347, 459, 484, 506, 526, 545, 547, 562. On instructions to commissioners to Albany, 26, 36. Conscientious scruples, 43, 49. Bills credit, 44, 46, 49. Funds, billeting soldiers, 54, 65. Pay of troops, 58. Death of Jno. Penn,—Gov'r, going to England for health, 62. Review of his nine years' administration, 62. Address to Governor in reply, 63. Sketch of John Penn, 63. Governor's reply, 64. Proposed call of, objected to, 73. Kinsey consulted, 74. Speech of Council to, 95, 96. Message to President and Council, 100. Council refuse to print, 105. Called together on important matters, 135. Account of money given for King's use, 160. Unexpected adjournment of, 163, 164, 165. Respecting Indians, 184. Message relative to capture by privateers, 233. Means of defence on the river, 271, 274. Adjourns, Resolutions of Council in consequence, passed, 277, 279. Peace between England and France, &c., 333. Disapproving Governor's course, 333. His reply to, 339. Expenses of treaty with Indians, 341. Messages of Governor James Hamilton, 365, 395, 412, 430, 456, 484, 491, 493, 499, 502, 505, 511, 513, 524, 528, 540, 546, 564, 578, 608, 638, 639, 652, 729, 737, 747, 751, 757, 764. Messages, &c. of, to Governor Hamilton, 367, 372, 412, 414, 427, 605, 613, 617, 648, 711, 763. Present Governor with £600, 368, 428, 461, 711. Presents to Indians, 403, 711. On bills of credit, 415. Report of committee on paper currency, 415. Do. of lower counties, 417. Address to Governor on public houses, 428. Governor's answer, 430. Relative to settlers on unpurchased lands, 459. Isaac Norris, Speaker, 484, 558, 599, 662. Indian affairs, 484, 485, 513. Informal call of, message, controversies between Gov. and Assembly, about the legality of the meeting, 491–494. On lighting and watching city, 506, 512, French claims—on Indians, &c., 528. Heavy expenses of Indian affairs, 545, 546. Proprietaries decline bearing a part of expenses of treaties with Indians, &c., 546. Bills credit, 562. Amendments to fee bills, 579. Serjeant at arms, 617. Bills credit, 638, 652, 723, 747. Affairs with French and Indians on Ohio, 705–722. Passionate treatment of Governor alluded to, 723. Extract from report of Committee on bills of credit, 723. Governor replies to their violent address, 737–746. On western boundary, 763.

Messages and speeches from Governor to, vi., 22, 23, 26, 37, 39, 41, 139, 166, 185, 188, 190, 206, 211, 221, 236, 243, 244, 247, 320, 322, 327, 330, 352, 386, 408, 425, 427, 438, 440, 502, 504, 525, 534, 536, 537, 550, 565, 612, 617, 670, 684, 689, 702, 706, 715, 728, 729, 733, 743. Messages to Governor, 40, 139, 167, 189, 191, 206, 211, 220, 226, 236, 243, 244, 325, 329, 384, 388, 425, 437, 441, 525, 536, 569–587, 597, 598, 605, 616, 624,

637, 677, 691. On defensive measures, 23. Expenses of Commissioners to Albany, 23. Wont raise men or money, 27. Money for King's use, 41. Governor lays before, proceedings of Congress at Albany, 57–129. Speaker chosen, 165, 639. Isaac Norris, 167, 639. Grant money, 167. Edward Warner, deceased, 176. Contagious fever, 190. Bills credit, 206. Discussion with Governor on, exhibit proprietary instructions, 220, 221–223. French troops at Ohio, 223. A very long message to Governor, relative to proprietary instructions, &c., 226–236, 617. Governor's Answer, 236–243. Arrival of Mohocks, 243–4. Passenger Bill, 243. Currency, discovery of Governor, &c., 244–246. His answer, 247. Conduct of, 295, 299, 302. Minutes of Assembly asked for by Governor, 305, 322, 331. Accused by General Braddock of pusillanimous and improper behavior, 307. Arrival of Braddock—Roads—Embargo—Post—common fund, &c., 320. Governor complains of publishing official letters, 322. Answer to Governor, 325. Letter, &c., of Massachusetts Commissioners, 330. Governor directs Secretary to make copy of minutes, 331, 339. Indian affairs, 352. German bill, 384. Access to Journals, 392. Governor calls it the Quaking Assembly, 409. Lower, presents to General Braddock, 415. Demand sight of a letter from, 424, 433. Troops from Canada, 427. Provisions go to New Foundland, 439. Power to call Assembly discussed with Governor, 441. Address of, to his Majesty, presented by proprietaries on restrictions, 448. Council blame, 461. Speech of Governor on Braddock's defeat, &c., 486. Answer to address by privy council, 505–510, Colonel Dunbar's request for winter quarters, &c., 513, 535. Tax on proprietary estate, 525–532, 715. Roman Catholics in Bucks County, 503, 533. Militia bill, 534, 598. Tax on proprietary estate, 537–546, 569–587, 604, 703, 707, 711, 715. Exposure of frontiers, 550, 565. General Shirley's orders to Dunbar, 586. Conduct of, complaint of Governor against Quaker preaching, Franklin, &c., 600. Supplies for Crown Point, 616. Long message of Governor to, 617–623. Long answer to, 624–637. Distribute arms and ammunition, 663, 677. French and Indian outrages, 677. Report to Council on arms, &c., 679. Messages to Governor, 707–710, 714, 743, 746. Remonstrance of Philadelphia militia bill, 735. Councils report on claims of Shawnees, 746.

Messages to, vii., 18, 19, 39, 55, 87, 91, 92, 120, 130, 131, 142, 143, 148, 178, 186, 195, 202, 246, 387, 413, 417, 453, 562, 569, 578, 582, 592, 605, 617. From, 18, 45, 91, 93, 125, 143, 183, 196, 201, 303, 384, 411, 413, 573, 579, 609. Vote sixty thousand pounds, 125. Address to Governor on enlisting servants, 37, 39. Conspiracy in back counties, 87, 91. Several members resign—new writs issued—by Speaker—Governor declines acting on the occasion, 148–151. Minute of, signed by William Franklin, (clerk,) on resignation of members, 150. Resolutions on various bills and Governor's course, 184. To lower counties on export of provision, 195. Acts of New York and New Jersey on embargo. 197. Proposed treaty, 203. Tax on proprietary estate, 204. Remarks of council on message, 204, Address to Governor Denny on arrival, give him £600—his answer, 227. Speech 229. Messages of Governor Denny, 235, 248, 304, 306, 342, 346, 350, 364, 365, 368, 370, 375, 718, 733, 736, 748, 751, 758, 763, 774, 779, 757, 779. Messages to Governor Denny, 236, 237, 246, 307, 313, 345, 352, 363, 364, 368, 369, 375, 379, 721, 727, 730, 742, 751, 759, 757, 758, 781. Western boundary, &c., 236. Instructions, 237, 238. Committee of conference on money bill, 249–250. Reasons offered to Governor, 251.

Committee to draw up reasons for his Majesty, 255. Various documents from privy council on affairs in the province, 272–278. Conduct of, 272. Speeches of Governor Denny, 280. Order to, Secretary Peters to issue writs of election for several members—letter from Richard Peters by order of Governor inquiring the reason of so many vacancies, 291. Answer of Speaker with letter of four members resigning—Ministers ask Quakers to allow seats to be filled by persons of other denominations, 292. Writs of elections issued, 293. Indian murders, 304. Indian trade, 307. Appointment of Samuel Kirk, as Sergeant-at-arms, 313. Number of public houses in Philadelphia, 352. Various proceedings respecting quartering of soldiers, 361–373. Meet on Sunday and send message to Governor, 364. Committee of Conference, proceedings, 370–374. Conestogo Indians want clothes, 379. On money for Mr. Croghan, 384. Remonstrance against Governor's message on supply bill, 401. His answer, 403. Asks right of his reasons to King —postponed, 406. Neutrals, 410. On quartering soldiers, 410, 411. On supply bill and answer, 413. Report on supply bill, 421. Answer to 437. Powers of, Assembly—Governor, &c., under constitution in reply to Lord Loudoun, 449. Answers of Speaker and Franklin to Lord Loudoun on money bill, 450. Governor agrees to, 453. Speaker on Indians at Lancaster, 497, Account of provincial forces, asked for, 565. Address to Governor on embargo, 567. Remonstrance to Governor on embargo, 571. Embargo and militia, 573. Roads, 592. Resolutions—militia, &c., 618. Committee wait on Governor to inspect minutes of council on purchase of land, 635. Refused, 636. Governor's speech to, on French and Indians, 718. Troops for New York, 721. Address to Governor's agent, William Moore, Esq,, 741. Pray his removal, 742. Militia bill and services of troops, 744, 751. Governor's answer, 748–750. Proceedings against Moore, 750. Governor asks for minutes, 751. J. Norris sick, resigns, 770. Thomas Leech, elected, 772.

Messages to Gov. Denny, viii., 4, 36, 39, 51, 53, 71, 102–110, 111, 112, 170, 229, 240, 323, 324, 330, 331, 354, 356, 363, 373, 374, 396, 446. Messages from Gov. Denny, 1, 12–17, 29, 41, 61, 62, 65, 66, 68, 72, 78, 81, 166, 169, 237, 240, 275, 291, 303, 317, 319, 327, 339, 349, 361, 369, 372, 382, 447. Impeachment of W. Moore, 1, 11. Indian trade, 19–24, 51, 240. Treaty at Easton referred to, 39. Duties, 41. Captives with Indians, 51, Answer to Gen. Abercrombie, 52. Letter from General Forbes, 61. Remonstrance to Governor, 74. Supply bill, 75. Condition of provinces, 102. Letter from Admiral Boscawen asking for men, 164. Answer, 164, 166. Councils opinion on, 165. Letter from General Forbes, 169, 170. Indian Affairs, 171. Isaac Norris, Speaker, 224, 407, 506, 671. Governor's speech, 227. Respecting General Forbes, &c., 229, 237, 240. Demand of General Schuyler for pay of prisoners, 240. Blankets for soldiers, 263. Dr. Franklin hands proprietaries a paper unsigned from, on which, as well as their rights, they remark, 276. Address delivered by eight members, 282. Two members apply for answer, 284. Letter, General Amherst, letter respecting, 284. Resolve of House of Representaiives respecting Wm. Moore of Chester Co., 287. Respecting appointment of Colonel Byrd of Virginia to succeed General Forbes, 299. Bills credit, taxes, 303. Supply bill, 331. Distressed situation of Lancaster, by quartering soldiers, 330. Supply bill, 331. Obstinacy of, 351. Reply to proposed amendments, respecting warrants, 354. Plays and lotteries, 356. Governor refuses to sign bill on warrants, &c., 361. Mr. Galloway's remarks on observa-

tions on bill for recording warrants, 363-369. Letter from General Stanwix, 373. On pay for wagons, 373. Bill for warrants, views of proprietary estate, 374. J. Norris resigns; Thomas Leech chosen Speaker, 396. Carriages, 397. Called on account of absence of great seal, 408. Messages to Governor Hamilton, 424, 425, 428, 447, 496, 510, 560, 572, 580, 584, 611, 692, 715. Messages from Governor Hamilton, 437, 446, 448, 449-478, 480, 481, 495, 509, 512, 559, 563, 577, 578, 579, 581, 593, 596, 603, 605-609, 662, 666, 674, 676, 681, 687, 688, 691, 693, 695, 710, 775. On Indian wars, 429. Military forces, 447. Reverend Wm. Smith serves an order of privy council against, 438, and other papers relating to him, 438-446. With report and Governor's message to, 446. Resolve to raise two thousand seven hundred men, arrears due, and estimated expense of raising, 458. Supply bill, 478, 480, 481. Grant £1000 to sufferers by fire at Boston, 483, Troops, 495, 496, 509. Council not a part of, 503. Answer to General Monckton for troops, 510. Appointment of Franklin and Charles as agents to England, 512. Letter of condolence of Governor on death King George II., 521. Exclusive nomination of officers, 533. Laws repealed, &c., 559. Condolence on King's death, 560. Governor presses answer to message, 563, 580. Acts of agents, 572. £1000 to Governor, 583. Tax on proprietary estate, 584. Money bills, 596. Supply bill, 603, 605. Indian treaty, 662. Fees of Attorney General, 667. Adjourns without Governor's consent, 685. War with Spain, 703, 706, 710. Report of committee on Governor's message, 716. Resolutions appointing committee on treaty with Indians, and asking inspection of Council minutes, 719. Declined, 720. Dissolves without notice to Governor, 776. Minutes of treaty at Lancaster, 775.

Meets—Isaac Norris, Speaker, ix., 158, 181, 200, 236. Conduct censured by Earl of Egremont, 16. Message from Governor, 2, 10, 16, 18, 19, 21, 37, 52, 53, 55-58, 94, 108, 113, 115, 116, 122, 131, 149, 158, 174, 179, 181, 183, 240, 244, 283, 290, 310, 323, 363, 394, 396. Messages to Governor, 20, 64, 97, 109, 116, 123-125, 134, 153, 155, 157, 180, 182, 185, 246, 284, 312, 324, 361, 369-374, 385, 407, 685. Resolution authorizing Governor to enlist soldiers on frontiers, 36. Will pay for them, 36. Pays Governor £800, 37. Surprise at General Amherst's letter, 64. Vote a reward to be offered against highway robbery about Philadelphia, 70. Take leave of Governor Hamilton, who is succeeded by John Penn, 73. Speech of Governor Penn, 91-93. Indian murders, 92, 97. Address to Governor, congratulatory, 97. Answer, 99. Reply of New York to application to protect Indians, 122, 123. Militia bill, 133. Remonstrance of Smith and Gibson on Indian affairs, 138. Declaration of frontier inhabitants, 142. Proceedings on, 146, 147. Governor's answer to committee of, on, 147. Supply bill, 149, 158, 161, 174, 284. Proprietary lands, 153, 155, 156, 161, 185. Charged by Governor with ill treatment of himself and proprietaries—history of supply bill, &c., 174. Supply bills, &c., 179, 180, 184. J. Norris resigns as Speaker, Benjamin Franklin chosen, 182, 236. Members, 201. Joseph Fox, Speaker, 236, 287, 590. Assessment on proprietary lands, 241. Money for Fort Augusta, 244. Advices respecting evacuation, &c., of Fort Augusta, 283, 284. Tie vote between two members for, new election ordered, 286. Writs to Sheriff, 288. Fire at Montreal, 290. John Fairlamb dies—election ordered, 301. Repeal of Stamp Act, 311, 312. Lands—troops quartered, 324. Present Governor £500, 327, 805. Joseph Galloway, Speaker, 335, 399, 551, 591, 625-691. Courts of judicature, 361, 369-

374. New member for Chester, in room of John Morton, 375. Salary to Governor, 392, 622. Messages from Governor to, 407, 408, 425, 427, 430, 434, 459, 466, 545, 554, 595, 622, 645, 682, 692, 708, 713, 720. Messages to Governor, 407, 432, 454, 465, 473–480, 568, 592, 594, 692, 709, 714, 721. Murders of Indians by F. Stump, 414–490. Poor Indians from Wyalusing, 423. Lottery asked for—also charter for Philadelphia Contributionship, 440. Reflecting on Governor, 454, 473. Raising money, 466. Answer of Governor, 473. Treaty at Fort Stanwix, 545. New member to be elected for Chester Co., 550. John Fairlamb died, 550. Indian trade, 557, 592. Indian boundary, 554, 568. Address on fisheries, 610. Lotteries, 622. Indian trade, 645. A member must be resident of city or county from which he is elected, 650. Arrest of Connecticut men, 682. Remonstrance from, on impressment of carriages, 684. Reward for Stewart, 685. Grant to Governor, 687. Money for Indians, 692. Improvement of rivers, 720, 721. Pay Governor, 730. Message from President and Council on Wyoming, 772.

Messages from Governor, x., 2, 17, 28, 31, 34, 60, 68, 71, 117, 142, 146, 195, 208, 214, 224, 233, 237, 249, 260. Messages to Governor, 1, 17, 28, 33, 35, 71, 74, 142, 209, 215, 225, 237, 252. Address to Gov. Richard Penn, 1. His answer, 2. Joseph Galloway, Speaker, 2. Present to Governor, 2. Members' views on offering a reward, 14. Carriages impressed by Colonel Wilkins, 17. Foreign evidence, 18, 20. Bills, credit, 33. Duties and excise, 33, 34, 35. Joseph Galloway, Speaker, 59, 105. Letter from Governor Payne, 60. Evacuation of Fort Pitt, 68, 70, 74. Address to Governor John, 96. Answer, 97. Present to Governor, 97. Support of Government, 96. Connecticut people, 117, 142. Fortifications in Philadelphia, 146. Vote an increase of pay, 148. Petition to call in account of Boston port bill, declined by Governor, 180. Called on account of Indian difficulties, 195. Virginia and Indians, 206. Continue troops, 209. Edward Biddle, Speaker, 213, 241. Pay of soldiers, 214, 215. Resolutions, pay of rangers, 215. Petition to King on affairs, 233. Petitions from the Colonies, 239. E. Biddle, sick—John Morton chosen Speaker, 241, 272. Resolutions of House of Commons, 251, 252. List of certificates, 260. Resolutions appointing Committee of Safety, &c., 279, 282. Charles Moore, clerk, 282. Resolution appointing new committee, 375. Benjamin Franklin, President. Order barracks to be repaired, 389. Resolution for purchase of clothing and accoutrements by an agent, Mathias Slough, 538. Complaint against Committee of, 573. Memorial on increase of Committee, 579. Memorial on Roebuck, 582. Ask what military preparations have been made, 586. Report on conduct of Committee of Safety, 611. Adjourn without raising flying camp, according to Congress, 611.

Memorial from Council on refusal of Continental Currency, xi., 2. Memorial to, on calling out militia, 15. Add seven members to Council of Safety, 45. Loan asked by Council of Safety, 117. Committee from, 208. Wait by Committee on Council, respecting quota to be furnished by this State, 210. Present complaints of officers against Colonel Bull and Major McCurry, 210. Pecuniary state of Board of War, referred to the, 211. Order on Council for money, 213. Petition of Walter Hall, a person about to abscond being in his debt, 214. Letter from Council on state of land forces, 215. Minute asking conference with Council on state of affairs, 217. Plan for removing citizens, 218. Representation from Council on present frame of Gov-

ernment, 220. Resolutions respecting probable attack of enemy, 227. Resolution on borrowing money, 227. On loan from Congress, 228. Resolution allowing Militia rum or whiskey, 230. With Council, elects President and Vice-president, 375. Elect delegates to Congress; their names, 385. Representation of Council respecting wagons, &c., impressed, 390. On calling out whole force on petition—conference, 394. Referred to Congress, 394. On recruits, 401. Council inform of J. P. Howell being Receiver General of clothing, 424. Interference of Board of War respecting provisions, 425. Representation of Supreme Executive Council to, on expenses of recruiting, 431. Conference on magazines, 434. Commissioners to Congress at Yorktown, 438. Wages of Executive Council and Navy department, 441. Appoint Lieutenant—Resolves respecting Colonel Hartley's enlisting soldiers for Congress, 452. Respecting the quota of the State, 454. Battalions and conference with Council, 456. Early call of—act regulating prices of goods, suspended, 525. Resolutions respecting Navy, &c., 554. Public offenders, 558. Resolution—embargo on provisions, 569. Petition of Ralph, (negro,) 570, 571. Summons by Justices to take oath of allegiance, 574. Order copies of acts, &c., 585. Plan of the river Delaware, 587. Speaker chosen, 617. Case of Charles Campbell, 618. General Lacey and Colonel Knox, Committee to Council on letter of General Wayne, 619, Letter from Colonel Hartley—March of troops, 621. Register and recorder of Bedford County. Public expression favor of Colonel Hartley—Letter from Massachus'ts on Tories–Provisions permitted to Bermuda, 629. Long address from Council to, on various subjects, 685–690. Resolutions of Virginia, 691. Application to Congress for money, 693. Conference on Constitution, 695, 699. Letter of Monsieur Holker, and message of Supreme Executive Council, 699, 711, 714. Distribution of provisions, &c., 711. Committee meets Council on finances, 717. Notice of Indian murders by Indians at Bushy Run, 718. Defence of frontiers, 719. Message sent from Council respecting Arnold, 721. Conference with Council respecting, 726, 727. Resolutions respecting officers, 727. Letter of Massachusetts, 729. Resolve, Rangers, 730. Conference, 730. Letter from Field officers of Pennsylvania Line, 731. Message of Council, 734. Resolution approving of acts of Council to borrow money, 739.

Resignations—Answers to Queries by Attorney General—Committee meets Council—Address of Council, xii. 95. Messages from President, 96, 124, 125, 167, 175, 176, 246, 254, 264, 285, 366, 474, 526, 545. Messages to the President, 555, 564, 569, 575, 624–626, 630, 637, 641, 644, 667, 675, 676, 738, 742, 749, 753, 759, 765. Resolution respecting confiscated property of Reynold Keen, 103. Address Mons. Gerard on his departure, 109. Act of Congress respecting arrival of Count D'Estaing, 114. Resolutions—Council to procure flour and salt, 117, 118. Thanks to Gen. Wayne and Pennsylvania Line, 124, 134. Bounty for wood, 125. New members elected, 129, 131, 134, 145. Vote of thanks to Gen. Wayne for affair at Stony Point, 135. Conference with Council, 156. Sale of ship Gen. Greene. Opening of Land Office, 160. Respecting boundaries with Virginia and Connecticut—Great seal of late province—papers sent to—regulation of prices, 176, 177. Archibald Thompson, deceased—Joseph Blewer elected, 188. Confiscated estates reserved for University—rules and regulations, 189. To decide about Great Seal of late Province, 205. Bills of

Credit ceased—Taxes—Property of Aliens, &c., 134. Receive reverse of Great Seal, 237. Conference with Council on defence of frontiers, 248. Pay of Mr. Bradford as Commissary, 253. Account of troops, 254, 255. Raising four companies, 258, 261. Memorial on Taxes in Philadelphia county, 263. Message on proprietary lands taken under old right–Case of Jehu Eyre for plank and timber taken by enemy—Army supplies, 264. Case of John Ensmenger, 267. H. and I. Ichelburg, 280. Papers, &c., 285. Act for paper moulds for money, 298. Meet Council on scarcity at camp, 351. Conference with Committee of Congress and Council on Loan Office Certificate —Their value—Amount from this State—Supplies, &c., 360. Respecting Mrs. Murray and Mrs. Ferguson, 366. James Hutchinson member in room of G. Bryan, 367. Letter of Congress—Quartermaster and Commissary Departments, 369. Delegate to Congress elected—Supplies, 371. Action under various subjects, 475. Decision of Virginia—Letter of Gen. W., 476. Conference on supplies, 478, 479. Conference on finances, 480. Respecting Virginia, 486. Order cattle bought, 488. Papers from Maryland and Virginia on confederation, &c., 491. New members, 506, 507, 508, 510, 513, 517, 518. Army—Virginia boundary—Supplies, 529, 530. Resolution to suspend sales of estates, 539. To prevent frauds in British vessels using American prize papers, 543. New members —Resolution, expenses of government—Clothing for army, 545. Appointments by 554. Finances, 555. Resolution, Loan Officer, 556. Resolution for purchase of corn—Rescinded, 561. Not to pay continental money to Commissioner, 567. Finances, 568. Loan, 571. Provisions, 575. Francis Hopkinson, 567, 573, 578. T. M'Kean to occupy J. Duche's house, 578. Case of Francis Hopkinson, 579, 580, 581, 582, 583. Acquit him, 584. Thomas Paine paid as Clerk, 594. Committee to inquire into causes of discontent in Pennsylvania Line, 632, 636. Account of provisions purchased, 638. Tender of flour exported, 644. Appropriation for infantry —Increase of auditors, 645. Conference on calling in old continental money, 649. Militia, 652. Gratuities to officers, 655. Dispute with Connecticut, 657. Defence of frontiers, 659. Hog Island, 661. Action towards traitors, 675. Lieutenants and Sub-Lieutenants, 676. State House Steeple to be taken down, 682. Order a fine on delinquent Commissioners, 686. Various resolutions calling in continental money—Floating bridge on Schuylkill, 691, 692. Report of Committee of Grievances, 694. Recall of Mr. Searle, 694. Powers disputed in case of Isaac Austin, 720. Complaint, Col. Hart, 737. Pennsylvania Line—Gen. Wayne—Militia prisoners, &c., 738. Conference, 740. Pay of labor, 752, Message, 763, 765. Recruit of Federal Army, 765. Resolutions on various matters—supplies, finances, &c., 770.

Resolution for money through R. Morris to Thos. Smith, xiii., 6. Resolutions respecting Connecticut claim, 10. Messages from Council, 58, 67, 107, 129, 258, 259, 262, 348, 363, 408, 425, 438, 483, 518, 537, 538, 647, 648, 666, 682, 683, 692. Messages to Council, 733, 761. Deficiency of recruits, 58. Resolutions respecting Connecticut claim, 123. On supplies to United States, 125. Sales of Province Island—Defence of frontiers, 127, 128. Expedition against Indians, 132. Various papers submitted to, 199. Conference with Council on Virginia line, 209. On militia fines and taxes, 236. May draw on State Treasury—Message, various complaints—On powers of Council, 258, 262. J. Dunlap for printing votes of, 277. Difficulties of officers, 308. Loans—Taxes—Robberies, British goods, 349. Estimate of supplies

required, 352. Council may draw—Damage by enemy, 363. Jno. Craig elected, 407. Disposal of funds for defence, 420. Powers, Commissioners to make levys—evils of debts to State, 438. Seizure of British good, 483. Pennsylvania and Virginia, 519. Minutes and resolutions on accounts, 525. T. Matlack's accounts, 537–8. Confirms appointment of Stille to settle accounts with United States—Letter Fred. Phile, 563. On peace, &c., &c., 647–666. Memorial of officers of Pennsylvania Line, 682. Virginia boundary, 685. Order State House lot to be a public green for ever, 692. List of officers entitled to benefit of Resolution 22d Sept., 712–718. On a public demonstration on account of peace, 748, 761. Vendue laws, 761. Conference with Council, 762.

Messages from Council, xiv., 11, 16, 39, 44, 45, 61, 163, 183, 185, 246, 269, 270, 275, 276, 284, 328, 342, 343, 348, 366, 380, 381, 388, 392, 564, 575, 645. Messages to Council, 289. Conference of Committee with Council, 25. Inundation at Wyoming, 61. Indian Affairs, 185. Resolutions on Wyoming, 202. Appoint Joseph Reed, Cad. Morris, W. Montgomery, J. Gardner and William Henry, delegates to Congress, 261. On Escheats, 269. Purchase from Six Nations, public debt, plans of payment, &c., 270, 274. Respecting Thomas Paine's services and his reward, 275. March of troops for Wyoming, 276. Sale of old jail, and money for Montgomery Court House, purchase of part of State House lot, 284. And improvement of, 286. Dismiss H. Shoemaker, a justice, 288. Council recommend a law for jail in Montgomery County, 313. Land Office, public debt, &c., 328, 342. Message on revenue, comptroller's taxes, foreigners, justices, prisons, &c., 349, 355. Resolutions on N. Boundary with N. Y., 363. Treaty with Indians at Fort Stanwix, 366. Improvement of State House lot, 369. N. Y. Boundary, Capt. Houston's demands, 381, 387. Case of Aaron Doane, 388, 392. Flour Inspector and Land Officers, 444. Various papers, 564. Letter from Council respecting Sick Keesar, &c., 569. Disturbances at Wyoming, 572. From Council relative to Test Law, 573. Taxes, Revenues, Test Laws, &c., 575. Message on affairs of State generally, 645. Letter and papers from Council, 647. State of representation, 652.

Messages from Council, xv., 70, 76, 106, 116, 167, 268, 276, 304, 314, 393, 400, 401, 408, 419, 528, 532, 536, 541, 547, 582, 592, 594, 605, 658. Messages to Council, send various papers, 71. Inspector-General, letter, Pres't Sullivan, proposition respecting arms, 78. Petition from Wyoming, 79. Various letters, &c., 106. Western Line—Lake Erie, 116. Conference with Council on pay of Inspector-General, 135. Election in Luzerne, T. Pickering, funded certificates, lower price of land, balances due, &c., 167. Various papers sent to, 268. Wm. Mitchell member, 302. Wyoming and Luzerne affairs, 304. Appointment of officers, 314. Measures to enforce laws in Luzerne Co., expulsion of comm'rs from Wyoming, &c., 315. Delegates to Congress, 341. Conference with Council on depreciation of paper money, 398. Letter of P. Bond, petition of and summons, and A. Betz's memorial against J. Weaver, 419. Supplement to Act of Assembly for raising by lottery funds to improve public roads, 448. Resolution of 1787 respecting reserved tract opposite Pittsburg, 504. Papers submitted by Council, 518. Capture of Col. Pickering—purchase of triangle, concerning prices of land, adulterated plate, powder magazine, pensioners, 529. Conference on purchase of Lake Erie triangle, petition respecting certain lots, 532. Conference respecting Jno. Franklin, 533. Powder magazine, 535. Memorial D. Lenton, 541. Council refer case

of Capt. Wm. Ross to, 543. Ask respite of Doane negatived, 544. Extension of time for settling accounts, 550. Prest. T. Mifflin, V. P. Geo. Ross, 584. Goods for Indians, 605. Members of Congress, electors, test law, bills of credit, Presq. isle roads, canals, &c., 658, 660.

Conference on payment of pensioners, xvi., 2. R. Peters, speaker, 39. Messages from Council, 16, 39, 141, 148, 204, 274, 277, 429, 437. Message to Council, 39. Lake Erie triangle, 39. Resolutions to call convention to examine constitution, 41. Resolutions respecting reservations at Presque Isle, De Bœuf, Conewango and Venango, 47. Acts to establish board of appeal, and for collection of fines and taxes, 73. Petition of D. Leet, 148. Call a convention to amend the constitution, proceedings of Council respecting, 159. To appoint commissioners to view rivers, 315. Pay to officers, 445. New members, 533. 537.

Assembly of Lower Counties meet at New Castle, and choose Jacob Kollock, Speaker, ix., 2, 71, 200, 289. Messages from Gov'or, 2, 10, 18, 25, 42, 108, 115, 122, 338, 597, 660. Message from Assembly, 109, 115, 116, 123, 598, 661. Courts, 18. Relating to Paxton riots at Lancaster, 89. Speech to, 166, 168. From to Governor, 167. Proceedings, 168. Laws, 168. Present to Governor, 169, 289. Members, 203. Repeal of Stamp Act, 313. Sundry laws, 314. John Vining chosen Speaker, 336, 400, 697. Laws, 337. Present Govern'r £200, 340, 601. Various laws, 599, 600. Cæsar Rodney, Speaker, 625. Give Governor £200, 627. Indian trade, 660, 661. Pay Gov'r £100. Gov. Hamilton meets at New Castle William Armstrong, Speaker. Justices, 742. John Vining dead, 713.

Elect David Hall, Speaker, x., 5. Address to and from Governor, 6. Acts passed by, 48, 79, 84, 109, 218, 244, 265, 272. Present to Governor, 49, 85. Thomas McKean, Speaker. Message from, 83. Answer of Gov. P., 84. Cæsar Rodney chosen Speaker, 106, 216, 272. Address to Gov. John Penn, 107. Answer, 108. Pay Governor £250, 110. Resignation of Gov. Read as Attorney-General, and appointment of Jacob Moore, 216. Message from Governor, 216, 243. Message to Governor. Boundary line with Maryland, 216.

Assessors, xii., 134, 136, 145, 506, 512, 513, 516, 518.

Assize of Bread, i., 576, 582, v., 565, 619, viii., 575., ix., 727, x., 18, 75, 243.

Aspden, Mathias, a house and lot in the city to be valued by W. Rush and B. Harbeson, xiii., 170. Report on, 209. Petition in favor of, xiv., 578. Respited, 625. His estate in Chester county to be sold, 663. Pardoned, xv., 4. Deed for his estate in Chester County, 72.

Assheton, Ralph, Member of Council iii., 333. Goes to Lancaster at request of Council, iv., 153.

Assheton, Robert, bill respecting Courts, ii., 491. Remonstrance against, 494. Member of Council, 536. Dep. clerk, 567. Administers oath to Governor Keith, iii., 13. Charges against him by Governor, 72. Pleads innocence, 72, 77. Suspended and restored to Council, 172. Recorder, 172. A judge, 187. Powder house referred to, 242. Invited over by Penn—his long and valued services, &c., 258. Appointed judge, declines, 258. A near relation of William Penn, 258. His powers as Recorder, 258. Dies, 270.

Assheton, William, Judge of Vice Admiralty and called to Council, iii., 172. A near relative of William Penn, 174.

Assheton, William, (merchant) to be seized, xi., 284.

Association, Friendly, Committee from, vii., 637, 638, 647, 648.

Associators formed for defence of city, v., 158. Declaration to, by Council, 168, 172. Form compa-

nies and elect officers, 174. Commissions, 181. Superior officers take oaths, 183. Officers of companies of several counties, 185. Officers of Chester county, 185. Of Philadelphia county, 193. Bucks, 193. Reviewed by President and Council, to their satisfaction, 223. Good effects as to security, 231. Artillery company formed, Captain Sibbald to command batteries, 267. New company and officers in Bucks county, 325, 326. And Commissioners, x., 279. Expenses of, 285. Returns to be made, 294. Form of commission for officers, 295. Of counties ask for pattern guns. Rules and regulations, 307. Articles of Association, 308–312, 315. Officers, 314, 315. Youngest companies, 315. Rank, 315. Resolution of Congress establishing, 316–321. Go to New York, 486. Rules and regulations printed, 548. To parade, 560. Cartridges, 579. Powder to, 622, 636. Rules printed for, 636. Families provided, 646, 680, 696. To join guard, 649. Colonel Lewis, 651. Pay to families, 671. March of, 673. Names of deserters to be reported, 687. City Guards, 691. Arms for, 706. Wages from Congress, 716. To make returns of arms, &c., 753. Families to be provided for, xi., 22, 23. To form a brigade, 27. To be supplied by shops—Not to be distressed by creditors, 30. Colonel and Lieutenant Colonel appointed, 31. Their tanners to have preference of hides, 58. Arms, 78, 198.

Aston, Captain, vi., 764.

Aston, George, petition, road, iii., 227, 230. Justice, left out, 381.

Atkins, Edmond, vii., 600, 622, 626. Letters to and from, 626.

Atkins, Samuel, prepares chronology of almanac—To blot out "Lord Penn," i., 165. Dispute, 341.

Atkins, Captain Christopher, arrives in the Bay, in an armed sloop—Stops vessels — Embargo — Permitted to proceed, viii., 58.

Atkinson, Joseph, confined for robbery, xi., 123.

Atkinson, Wilton, justice, xi., 528.

Atkinson, William, Coroner of Bucks, iii., 140, 416, 465, 520, 574, 614, iv., 247, 309, 352, 469.

Atlee, John, recommended to Congress as a Colonel, x., 442.

Atlee, Col. Samuel, recruiting, x., 538. His battalion, 673, 674, 734. to order battalion from Chester, 605. Paid, 649. Battalion, xi., 16, 116, 215. Paid, 568. His rank as Brigadier General in Continental army referred to General Washington, 673.

Atlee, Colonel Samuel John, battalion, x., 704. Delegate to Congress, xii., 138. Lieutenant of Lancaster, 436. Councillor, xiii., 722. Member of Council, xiv., 5. Commissioner to Indians, 40, 54.

Atlee, William, appointed Judge of Supreme Court, xi., 196. To inquire into case of Joseph Richardson, 202. Money to, to purchase blankets, 271, 319. A commissary of prisoners, 414, 560. Judge of Supreme Court, xii., 69. Account of Conestoga manor, 221.

Atlee, William Augustus, of Lancaster, appointed second Judge of Supreme Court, xi., 270. Paid, 694. Deputy Commissary General, pay to, xiii., 526. Resigns as second Justice of Supreme Court, but is immediately re-appointed, xiv., 175. Letter—Resignation as Deputy Commissary General, 314. Chairman and Treasurer of Committee of Inspection and Observation of Lancaster County, xv., 166. And Justice of Supreme Court, 167, 204. Travelling expenses paid, 262, 291, 398, 560, 579, 645. Of Supreme Court, Pay to, xvi., 17.

Atlee, William Richardson, Prothonotary of Delaware, xvi., 172.

Attachments, Act regulating, v., 619.

Attainder, Act of, and names of Commissioners under, xi., 479, 504.

Atterwancy's account of French building a ship at Cadaraghqui, v., 549.

Attorneys, Prosecuting, i., 167.

Sheriffs cannot act as, 170. Nor can the Clerk of the Court, 170.
Attorney Generals appointed, i., 174, 188. Fees, 199. Vacancy, 210. ii., 11. A. Hamilton, iii., 113. Resigns, 239. To be advised respecting discharge of prisoners, iv., 267. Tench Francis, is, 620. Opinion on riots, 623. Tench Francis, resigns, vi., 277. Benjamin Chew, appointed, 277; x., 216; xi., 254.
Attorney General answers to queries, xii., 94. Appointed, 550. Opinion on right to vote in a certain case, xv., 376. Fees, 537.
Attwood, Judge, 68. Chief Justice of New York, 68.
Auctioneer elected, xii., 185, 186.
Auctioneers, xv., 50, 52, 53, 166, 183, 197, 198, 321, 322, 324; xvi., 36, 155, 177, 235, 253, 315, 500, 541.
Audendried, Dr. Frederick, convicted of burglary, ix., 173.
Audibert, Philip, Deputy Paymaster General, U. S., xiii., 7.
Auditor General, Letter on Accounts, xii., 176.
Auditors to adjust pay of troops, provided, xii., 588, 600, 633, 646, 653, 654, 747; xiii., 242.
Aucquick, treaty at, vi., 145. Names of Indians present, 159. Governor notifies Indians of his appointment, 169. Tanacharisson arrives from, 192.
Augusta, Fort, vii., 281, 294, 302, 436, (See Shamokin,) 453, 512, 724, 760, 772. Store proposed at, 622, 736. Indian agent appointed at, viii., 99. A Delaware family of Indians settles near, 120. Francis Campbell declines as Indian Agent to, 128. N. Holland appointed, 129. Letter from, 458, 499. Troops at, 513, 515; ix., 42. Aid for support of garrison asked for, 244. Advice of Assembly—On evacuating, or reducing garrison, 246. Orders to evacuate, 283, 284. Road to, from Reading, 440. Conference at, 610. Road from, 651.
Auld, Jacob, Sub-Lieut., xiii., 262.
Auley, Cornelius, Coroner, xi., 363.
Austin, Thomas, Memorial of officers of boats against, x., 472, 473, 477, 485. Signs declaration and resigns as member of Committee of Inspection, &c., 485.
Avery, Cap. John, Jr., a pirate, i., 549, 580.
Awandoe Creek, ix., 554.
Awannameak Indian wounds Henry Webb, iv., 413, 420, 447.
Awnings for tents, x., 632, 642.
Ax, Jacob, convicted of regrating pork, xii., 240
Axtel, Capt. Thomas, xvi., 42.
Ayres, Col., xi., 278.

B.

Babbit, Samuel, allowance for taking, claimed, ii., 54.
Bache, Benjamin Franklin establishes a newspaper, The Daily Advertiser, xvi., 409.
Bache, Capt. L., applies to committee for guns, 287, 288.
Bache, Richard, mem. of Board of War, xi., 198, 201.
Backhouse, Richard, charged with sending public wagons on private account to Boston, xi., 453. Obtains deed for estate late of Joseph Galloway, xii., 104.
Bacon, Wm., an early purchaser of lands, xiii., 321.
Bader, Philip, petition—a prisoner taken on way to Du Quesne, vii., 398.
Badger, Edmond, Coroner, iv., 500, 602.
Bahl, Philip, appointed sub-lieutenant, xii., 317, resigns as sub-lieutenant, xii., 38, 384.
Bahringer, David, Coroner, ix., 333.
Bail, when to be taken, ii., 11.
Bail, Robert, coroner, x., 100.
Bayley, Francis, Coroner, xi., 191, 368.
Bayley, Francis, printer, xii., 186; xiv., 239; xv., 13, 185, 204, 366, 441; xvi., 7, 67, 200, 244. Pay for printing laws, xiii., 90, 93. And laws, 447, 496, 702. Deed to, 727.
Bailey, Jacob, Coroner, xi., 606. Sheriff, xii., 134.
Bailey, James, Justice, xiv., 653.
Bailey, John, member of Council, xi., 210. Account, 719.

Bailey, Jonathan, Sheriff of Sussex county, discharged, ii., 101. Justice of Lewis, complaint against, 465. Judge of Sussex, iii., 253. Judge of Supreme Court, 269.

Baily, Thomas, severe sentence, xiii., 314.

Bailey, Wm., Sheriff, xiii., 723, 745; xiv., 234, 557, 558.

Baird, George, Justice, xiv., 262.

Baird, Patrick, Surgeon of Philadelphia, appointed to visit sickly vessels, iii., 112. Clerk of Council, 216. Secretary to Governor, 322. Appointed Secretary of Council, in place of T. Lawrie, iv., 429. Resigns, 639. Omits to enter several messages, required to be entered by his successor, v., 67.

Baker, Hilary, tavern licenses, Philadelphia, xvi., 216.[2]

Baker, Hilary, Jr., Clerk of Court of Quarter Sessions, xi., 271, 547, 689. Renders account of fines collected, xii., 215. Asks opinion respecting a law of Assembly, xiii., 549.

Baker, Dr. John, petition for negroes, xii., 501, 502.

Baker, Lieutenant, vii., 603.

Bakers, to be kept at making bread, xi., 303.

Baldwin, Col., Regiment of artificers, xii., 719.

Baldwin, John, to keep ferry over Neshaming, i., 514. Refuses Continental bills—Declared an enemy, &c., x., 774.

Ball, John, Justice, xi., 379.

Ball, Lieutenant George, on parole, x., 575. Sent to Germantown, 580, 581. Sent to York, 601, 622, 627.

Ball, Thomond, Justice, xi., 528.

Ballet, James, Commander of Man-of-war Otter, arrives, v., 239. Meets Council and shows instructions, 241. Meets and fights a large ship, 243. An entertainment to, 243. Committee to consult with, 246. Sent for by Council—proposes raising a battery and placing his guns on it, 249. To consult with Hector, Man-of-war, off Virginia, 254. Fears desertion of seamen, 255. Fears for his ship if Captain Randolph's is taken at New Castle, 261. Orders her up, 264. Requested to fit his vessel as soon as possible, 269. Asks an assistant, 273. Can't sail for want of men—Proposes pressing—President advises a bounty, 282. Thinks it unsafe to proceed, 284. Captures French prizes, 324.

Ballew, Bennet, accompanies Indians on way to New York, xvi., 135.

Balliot, Captain Stephen, xi., 109; xiii., 177, 270, 316, 378, 449, 519.

Balliott, Stephen, Council of Censors, xiv., 170. A Commissioner to lay out road from Lehigh Water Gap to Wyoming, xv., 22. Commissioner of Claims in Luzerne, 222. Accounts, 595. Commands battalion of Northampton Co. militia, xvi., 364.

Ballot-box, in what cases to be used, i., 58. Not used excepting in Upland and Lower counties, 282.

Bancroft, Daniel, suspected as a spy from Jersey—committed to gaol, xi., 59.

Bank proposed to be set up, by Robert Turner and others, i., 236. Caution against counterfeits, 236.

Bank North America, xiii., 175. Letter from T. Willing, 200. Copy of rules, &c., sent to Council, xv., 192.

Banks, dams, &c., at Point-no-point, Act for keeping in order, viii., 480. And at Greenwich, 482, 484.

Bankson, Andrew, complaint against, for marrying persons illegally, ii., 114. Dismissed, 115.

Bankson, And., Jr., a Justice, ii., 159.

Bankson, Capt. John, xi., 510.

Baltimore, Lord, expected, Council ordered by Governor to attend him when Lord Baltimore arrives, i., 74. Abuse of his agents complained of to Governor of New York, 103. Commission sent to New York, 103. The conduct of his agents complained of, 103, 104, 106. High taxes complained of, 101—iii., 60, 223. Original agreement between Hannah Penn, Joshua Gue and Henry Gouldney, for mortgages respecting boundaries, 232. Letter of Governor Keith to Governor of Maryland, 232. Attempts to ob-

tain lower counties, 252. Letter to Governor on riots, 468, 479, 486. Claims territories, 594. Objects to George Thomas as Governor, iv., 249. Proceedings of Hampton Court, 256. Incapacity of guardians of heir of, to arrange respecting boundary with Pennsylvania, x., 220. Inhabitants, difficulty as to non-entry and clearance of vessels from New Castle, i., 101. Patents from, to Harman and Moll, 109. Visit of Colonel Talbot to Widow Ogles, 113. Commissioners to look into his conduct, 113. Declaration of Penn against, 113. His agents, 114, 115. Difference between his government and Penn's, 114. Hessian prisoners taken to, xi., 77, 104, 129. Merchants complain of annoyance from small privateers on coast, xi., 702. Seamen from gunboats induced to, 770, 771. Brought back, 783. Expenses divided, 783.

Baptists, Seventh Day, John Horn, a minister, released from militia fine, xiv., 568.

Barbadoes, claim from, for lands through Tretwell and Taylor, v., 551.

Barber, Lt. Col. Francis, xii., 711.

Barber, Robert, letters of remonstrance sent by, proceedings, ii., 186, 187, 192. Coroner of Chester county, iii., 140. Sheriff of Lancaster, 370.

Barber, William, a prisoner of war, asks to become a citizen, and Cap. Benj. Wickes, xii., 354. Released from parol, 385.

Barckley, Hugh, justice, xiii., 760.

Barclay, George, Secretary to Governor and to J. Logan, iii., 243.

Barclay, John, justice, xiii., 454.

Barclay, Thomas, appointed member of Navy Board, xi., 127. Paid for saltpetre, &c., 184. Imports a cargo of salt at $10 per bushel, 249.

Bard, Richard, justice, xiv., 657.

Bard, Dr. Samuel, xii., 36.

Barge, Jacob, warden, xi., 557. To distribute salt and flour, xii., 119.

Barkstead, Joshua, Coroner for Sussex. Resigns, i., 168. Attorney-General, 174. Letter from, Maryland. Council called, 298.

Barley, every man seated 3 years, to sow a bushel of, i., 98.

Barnes, John, a member of Council, to keep debates secret, i., 125. Appointed Ranger for Philadelphia county, 165, 166.

Barney, Capt. Joshua, commissioned with others on ship Gen. Washington, late "Monck," xiii., 283.

Barnhill, Robert, paid for gunpowder, &c., xv., 653.

Barnitz, Jacob, Register and Recorder, having vacated office of Collector of Excise, xiv., 584. Justice, 663.

Barony, the Welsh claim to be a distinct, i., 265.

Barr, James, Justice, iv., 605.

Barr, John, Sheriff, ix., 199, 285, 333.

Barr, Thos., fire worker to artillery, x., 3, 15, 16, 225, 389, 390, 395, 399, 408, 415, 419, 427, 428, 485, 529, 587.

Barracks, xiii., 128.

Barracks, at Carlisle, strange conduct of commissioners, vii., 737. Lord Loudon respecting, 756.

Barracks, at French Creek, xi., 58.

Barracks, at Lancaster, repairs, xii., 659. To be sold, xvi., 325.

Barracks, at Philadelphia, complained of, viii., 71. Officer at Philadelphia to place guard at Fort Wiccacoa, 147, 224, 262, 331, 333. Attack on, expected, ix., 132. Memorial of Indians in, 135. Sir W. Johnson to be consulted on their removal from—letter to him, 137. Indians to be removed from, 170. General Gage's troops quartered there, 323. Build'g middle house, west side, 461, 472. At Lancaster, 556. On Liberty Island, x., 490. Irregularities and destruction—quarrels among soldiers, complaints against, xii., 204. Committee to inquire about, 206. Their report, 208, 209, 211. Repairs, 613, 632. To be laid off into lots, xiv., 76, 456, 603. Lots, xv., 18, 21, 50, 256, 434.

Barrack Master to furnish battalion with bedding, x., 400. Wood and candles, 426. L. Nicola, order for arms, 517. John Reed appointed, 553, 568.

Barrack Masters, xi., 51.
Barrack Master General established, 1776. Abolished, 1778. Colonel Isaac Melchor, xvi., 301.
Barrel, dimensions of, iii., 277.
Barrett, Captain Lemuel, respecting Indian murder near Fort Cumberland, ix., 304.
Barrett, Philip, Sheriff, x., 270.
Barrington, an officer on parole, x., 698.
Barry, Captain John, commands brig Lexington, x., 526. Prisoners taken by, paroled, 545, 546. And others to be, prosecuted for seizing James M'Calmont, xv., 286, 389.
Bartholomew, Edward, commissioner of taxes and levies, xi., 536. Collector of Excise, Philadelphia, xiv., 311. Colonel, battalion Chester Co. militia, xvi., 251.
Barton, Rev. S., applies for and obtains a pass to New York, xi., 565.
Barton, Rev. Thomas, Letter on Indian depredations, vi., 675. Pass for self and wife to New York, xi., 579. Wife asks for pass from New York—rejected, xii., 339, 357.
Barton, William, pass to New York, xii., 47, 256, 339. Rejected, 314. Granted, 317. Notary Public, xiii., 20, 36. Prays for a stay of execution, xv., 66. Suspended for two years, 72. Petition, judgment suspended for five years, 542.
Bartram, Alexander, estate sold, xii., 329, 441.
Bartram, Mrs. Jane, pass for, xiii., 292.
Bass, Robert, orders for medicines, x., 292, 305. To deliver medicines to D. Rush, 489.
Bassett, Frances and family, authorized to hold lands, i., 538.
Bassini and Garrison agree to remove obstructions, xiii., 744.
Bastard child, case of a, xii., 77.
Bastardy, cases of, i., 440.
Battalions, x., 458. Officers of, xi., 179.
Battel, French, Coroner, v., 597, 662; vi., 638.
Batteries formed in Philadelphia, v., 158, 161, 172, 173, 205, 231, 249, 251, 267, 269, 284. Block house at, 269.
Battery Guns at Wiccacoa fired, in compliment to Governor John Penn, ix., 72. A floating, to be built, x., 437. Committee appointed, 437. Captain Samuel Davidson to command, 510. To be called Arnold, 525. Lt. Fitzsimons, 531. Lt. McFatridge, 536. Officers, pay, 634. Pay of Marines, 651.
Battery, Putnam, irons and handcuffs for, xi., 5, 8, 17.
Batwell, Rev. Mr., letters respecting his lands, xii., 297.
Bawcomb, Peter, Sheriff of Kent Co.
Bawer, Jacob, Sheriff, xv., 294.
Bayard and Hodge, buy cannon, xii., 279.
Bayard, John, member of Council of Safety, x., 717, 718. Councillor, xiii., 87, 152, 160. Auctioneer, xii., 524. Commissions, 313. Judge, 513. Major, asks for a pilot to cruise off the Capes, x., 469. Colonel, to guard State prisoners to Lancaster,, xi., 4. Surgeons appointed to his battalion, 24.
Bayard, Stephen, clerk to Dr. Kearsley, x., 374.
Bayard, Colonel Stephen, recruits, xi., 463.
Baynton, John, a provincial Commissioner, vii., 499. Secretary's Seal affixed, viii., 8, 335. Collector of tonnage, xiv., 654; xv., 321. Dies, 416, 417.
Baynton, Peter, wife's petition for his estate, i., 536.
Baynton, Wharton, & Co., advised of mischief intended to their goods, ix., 302.
Bay Verte, Fort on side of, captured by the English, vi., 447.
Baxter, Mrs. Elizabeth, pension, xv., 322, 413.
Baxter, Colonel Wm., of Flying Camp, xv., 10.
Baxter, Lt. Colonel, x., 766.
Beale, Thomas, Justice, xiii., 7.
Beans, Dr., Surgeon, xi., 123.
Beaton, John, paymaster, xi., 231.
Beaton, Major John, paid for ser-

vice] in purchase of wheat, &c., xii., 193. Commissioner of purchases, 334.

Beaton, John, justice, xiii., 316.

Beatty, Charles, appointed a Commissioner to Wyoming, vii., 754.

Beatty, Colonel. Letter on conduct of Lieutenant Benjamin Wilson, xii., 101. Commissary of prisoners in relation to Mr. Lynch, xii., 326.

Beatty, David, Justice, xii., 353.

Beatty, Ercurius, receiver of certificates for arrears of pay, xiv., 150, 173. Lieutenant, xv., 437.

Beatty, Captain John, made Major, x., 768.

Beatty, Reading, Surgeon, xii., 622. xiii. 115.

Beaver Creek, Indian town, v., 349; viii., 305.

Becker, Major Henry, x., 768.

Bedford, Col., at Barracks, x., 671.

Bedford County formed out of Cumberland, Justices appointed, ix., 730. Arthur St. Clair appointed Prothonotary, &c., 731. Sheriffs elected, 779. Coroners, 779. Lieutenant Hamilton charged with murder in, x., 7. Special Court to try, 8. Justices appointed, 8, 78, 162, 212. Sheriffs elected, 59, 101, 212, 271, Coroners elected, 59, 101, 271. Germans settled at the Glades, on Stony Creek, &c., in, 8. Boundary line, 27, 41. Division of, 32, 42, 72. Westmoreland formed, 77. Thos. Smith, Prothonotary of B. and St. Clair, of Westmoreland, 78. Act to lend money to build Court house and prison, 198. A special Court ordered, 265. Colonel Thomas Smith of, 672. Audit of Accounts, xi., 16. Lieutenant appointed, 187, 303. Prothonotary, 187, 718. A Councillor to be elected, 195. Sheriffs appointed, 234, 363. Justices, 301. Officers elected, 363, 572, 620, 716, 774, 781. Coroners, 363. Recorder refuses to deliver papers, imprisoned, 373. Incursions of Indians, call out militia, 382. Arms for, pay for provisions to Colonel Piper, 392. Letter from, exposed situation, men enlisted by Colonel Piper, Council answer him, 410. To be supplied with arms, 422. Horses, 493. Stockade, fort to be erected in, 555. Traitors in, 556. Sheriff, 608. Coroners, 608. Register and Recorder, 628, 646. Pay Master, 637. Militia to be paid off, 717. To be raised, 740. Justices, 781. Militia to be called out by Lieutenant in case of invasion, xii., 10. Justices, 19. Officers of militia commissioned, 70. Letter, Mr. Dougherty, respecting road to Fort Pitt, 72. Agents in, to receive proceeds of sales of horses taken by Colonel William Maloney, 115. Election Reports, Assessors, &c., 146, 544. Sheriffs, 147, 544. Coroners, 147, 544. Money to, 340, 342. Lieutenants, 372. Justices, 456, 459, 556, 615. Appointments, 554. Agents for confiscated estate appointed, 610. Complaints, sub-Lieutenant J. Martin, 647. Volunteers, 678. Lieutenants, xiii., 284, 367, 446. Justice resigns, 101, 118. Capt. Boyd's Rangers ordered to Yorktown, 121. Lieut. Richard Johnston, 121. Sheriffs, 134, 400, 730. Election, 729. Coroners, 134, 400, 730. Clothing for, 145. Pay for Capt. Boyd's company's conveyance, 151. Recruits, 168. Persons appointed to try cases in, 198. Militia—defence of frontiers, 203. Jno. Overholz, Jno. Reid, 204. Classmen Rangers, 257. Pay to troops, 265. Sale of land in, 300. Rations for, 359. Justices, 389, 400. Jos. Galloway's estate sold, 450. Harvey Gordon's estate, 701. Censors, 729. Justices Resign, 748, 761. Elected, 761. Provisions delivered to Militia at, xiv., 3. Justices, xv., 24, 209, 212, 666. Lieutenant Ashman resigns, 169. Rations, 181. Geo. Wood appointed Lieutenant, 207. Elections, 244, 563. Sheriffs, 244, 567. Representatives, 244. Coroner, 244, 567. Eighteen penny tax, 267. Fees in case of Charles Cessna, 266. Justices, 368, 602. Accounts, 628. Captain John Galloway, of the militia of, 637. Justices, 24, 26, 51, 58, 109, 189, 278, 450, 605. Justices

resigned, 109. Contested election, 26, 112, 126, 127, 132–133, 157, 160, 162, 170, 176, 298, 583. Sheriffs, 139, 298, 600. Coroner, 139, 298, 600. County Lieutenant, 184, 187. Collector of Excise, 222. Division of districts for election of Justices in, 270. Huntingdon county separated from, 278. Councillor, 298. W. Road to, confirmed, 330, 331–337. Witnesses paid. Lieutenant resigns, 339. Hugh Barclay appointed, 341. Road to Loyal Hanna, 346. Witnesses paid in contested election case, 351. Road, 358. Petition and order respecting, 359. Road from Ray's Hill, 431, 519. Completed by J. Skinner, 543. Road to Pittsburgh, 599, 635. Justices, xvi., 1. Road to Pittsburgh, 27, 51. Sureties, 32. Contested election, 36. For providing for militia at Morrison's Cove, 1778 and 1779, 45. Lieutenant, 52. Pay for a gun taken by savages in. Road from Frankstown Branch of Juniata to Conemaugh, 71. Contested election, 76. Complaint of military flour, 160. Returns of three Battalions, 163. Pay to orphans of their pensions, 184. Sheriffs, 212, 498. Coroners, 212, 498. Hugh Barclay, Lieutenant of, 223. Rations for, 262. Contested election, 280. Commissioners to settle Treasurer's accounts, 315. Justices, 319, 341, 407, 433, 448. Militia, 337. Excise received, 372. Death of Collector, 383, 385. Illegal election, 407, 448. Militia fines remitted, 461. Samuel Brady serves in militia in, 464. Specification of road to Pittsburgh, 466, 476, 531. Indians in, 515. D. Espy, Prothonotary, 517. Taxes received by B. Dougherty, Treasurer of, 520. Powder and lead for militia. Justice Cable elected to General Assembly; resigns, 533. Tavern licenses, 541. Capt'n McDonald's company, 547.

Bedford, Duke of, letter respecting treaty, v., 360, 379, 411. Letter to, on paper currency, 416. Act to encourage importation of iron from Colonies, 457.

Bedford, Fort, ix., 32, 34, 304, 386.

Bedford, Gunning, measurer of grain, xi., 546 Removed, 607. Appointed Measurer of grain and salt in Philadelphia, xi., 541. Receives pay for making a triumphal arch in Philadelphia for Federal procession, xv., 574.

Bedkin, Henry, Captain of Dragoons in Armand's Legion, xiv., 626.

Bedwell, Thomas, proposes to erect furnaces for refining sulphur, x., 519, 550.

Beer, good quality of, iii., 391. Sent to boats, x., 562.

Beeson, Henry, Coroner, xv., 121, 303, 584, xvi., 202, 232, 518.

Belcher, Jonathan, Governor of Massachusetts, requested to arrest a counterfeiter, iv., 225. Answer, 241.

Belcher, Governor Jonathan, of New Jersey, in Philadelphia, is applied to for aid against privateers in Bay, v., 110, 112. On privateers, 266. Alters destination of troops, vi., 410. Embargo, 463, 662. To be informed of suspension of hostilities with Indians, vii., 163. Letters to and from, 166, 359, 385, 467, 566, 606. Copy of minutes at Easton, sent to, 359. Militia, 566.

Bell, Robert, Lieutenant, xiv., 38.

Bell, Samuel and Mary Parrock, estate to be restored, xii., 315.

Bell, Captain Thomas, commands privateer Speedwell, xi., 2.

Bell, William, Justice, xiii., 7. Present at Riot at J. Wilson's; gives bail, xii., 130.

Belmont, Earl of, i., 578.

Bellamy, Charles, Petition, his vessel to be repaired, v., 597.

Bellamy, John, *vs.* Luke Watson, for lands, and being appeal from judgment in Sussex County, on prime hook, i., 77.

Belleu, Captain of the Liverpool, 595, 596.

Bells, to be removed from the City, xi., 306.

"Benefit of Clergy," how to be administered, ii., 86.

Benezet, Anthony, presents the case of the French neutrals, vii., 7, 17, 720.

Benezet, Daniel and James, attend to removal of sick, vi., 171.

Benezet, James, Prothonotary, xi., 187; Clerk of Orphans' Court, 194.

Benezet, Sam'l, Prothonotary of Bucks, in room of James B., resigned, xv., 271; Justice, xiv., 198.

Benham, Robert, Coroner, xv., 646.

Benjamin, a Mahakin Indian, living near Bethlehem, brings news, viii., 126.

Benkson, Andrew, offers to take up arms against French, i., 334.

Bennet, Abraham, pilot, commission granted to justify him on repelling and making reprisals on the enemy with an armed pilot boat called the Randolph, xii., 326.

Bennett, Caleb, Coroner, xvi, 494.

Bennett, Joshua, (a schoolmaster, convicted and fined for keeping school, not having taken oath of allegiance,) remitted, xi., 652, 653.

Bennett, Jacob, sheriff, xv., 566; xvi., 192.

Bennett, William, Sheriff, xiii., 392; Coroner, 720; xiv., 237.

Bensell, Dr. Charles, of Germantown, x., 547. Lieut. Ball sent to, 580. Draper and Budden, 596; to collect leaden weights, 637.

Bensill, George, pay as aid-de-camp, xii., 589.

Benson, Henry, Coroner, xiv., 567.

Benzier, Chris. Thos., a Moravian, sent to consult with Gov. M., vii., 190.

Bergen, Elizabeth, gives information respecting inhabitants of Elizabethtown and New York, xii., 206, 207.

Berkenbout, Dr., to be arrested, xi., 567; letter to R. H. Lee on making a treaty, 569, 570; sent to N. Y., 576.

Berker, Colonel, xi., 272.

Berks County, proposed, v. 560, 565; petition for road, 576; return of, 610. Sheriffs elected, 597, 662. Coroners, 597, 662. Act respecting Inspectors, 619. Road to Reading, 610. Sheriffs elected, vi. 144, 638. Coroners elected, 144, 638. Justices complain of Roman Catholics in, 503, 533. Persons coming to compel passage of law for defence, 729. Great body of Indians in, 772. New York troops sent to, 775. Instructions to their Captain, 775. Sheriffs elected, vii., 266. Coroners elected, 266. Indians invade, and murder, 302; murders in, 357. Petition from, respecting Indian ravages—troops ordered from General Forbes' regiment, viii. 99, 102. Indian murders in, 140. Coroners appointed, 223, 403, 506, 780. Sheriffs appointed, 223, 403, 506, 780. Inspectors, 400. Justices commissioned, 562. Coroners elected, ix., 57, 199, 285, 333, 398, 547, 623, 688, 778. Sheriffs elected, 57, 199, 285, 333, 398, 547, 632, 688, 778. Justices, 172, 340, 673, 680. Execution at, 192, 402. Lottery for Episcopal Church, 243. Deaths of two Justices—Jacob Levan and Wm. Maugridge, 340. Letter to Magistrates on murders, by F. Stump, 418. Petition for road to Fort Augusta, 440, 556. Authorized to elect two Members, 650. Execution, 678. D. Broadhead, Justice, 746. Division of, x., 32, 42. Sheriffs elected, 56, 101, 211, 270. Coroners elected, 56, 101, 211, 270. Justices, Letter to Committee, 654. Arms to be collected, 441; arms, 652. Estate of Daniel Andrews, 261. Powder for, 371. Muskets made in, 584, Declaration of Independence to be published, 635. Express to order militia to City, xi., 7. Militia under Colonel Morgan to be ready, 86. Troops refuse to march to General Washington; Commissioners to settle accounts of militia, and flying camp instructions, 146. Sheriffs elected, 187, 358, 363, 596. Coroners, 358, 363, 445. Justices, 195, 251, 300, 596, 598, 741. Prothonotary, 197, 341, 471. Arms for, 218. Paymasters, 277. Militia called out, 302, 360. Guard to be raised for defence of frontiers, 350. Officers elected, 358. Commissioners to buy supplies in for army, 404. Provisions purchased in, 423. Money for recruiting, 424. Mili-

tia, 200, to be at Reading, 446; Pay to, 450; rifles, 506. Aid asked for by Colonel Hunter, 531. Ammunition, 538. Disturbances at Reading, xii., 12. H. Haller receives subscriptions to Loan Office, 47. Elections, Assembly, 131, 508. Sheriffs. 131, 132, 508. Coroners, 131, 132, 508. Justices, 519. Estate of Andrew Allen in, forfeited, sale postponed, 152. Commissioners complain of being obstructed, 275, 357. Appointments, 554. Order favor of Henry Spicker, paymaster, 556. Militia to be paid off. Collection of taxes opposed in, 568. Petition for, 608. Justice Weaver removed, 635. Auditors, 646. Militia ordered out, 721. Deeds in, xiii., 12. Militia called out, 53, 204. Sale of confiscated estates, 57. Election, 88, 393, 720. Sheriff 88, 393, 720. Coroner, 88, 393, 720. Estate of A. Allen—Big Spring tract, 236. Petition of militia and soldiers, 299. Indians invade, 350. Militia called out, 357, 365, 368. Militia, 600. Division into election districts, 751. Justices, xiv., 170, 226, 321, 373, 442. To send fifty men to Wyoming, 217. Councillor, 231, 232. 554, Elections, 232, 554. Sheriffs, 232, Coroners, 232, 554. Representatives, 232, 554. Contested election, 321. Comptroller's reports on accounts, 382. Deed for land, late Andrew Allen's, xv., 40. Accounts of agents for confiscated estates, 62. Elections, 98, 294, 376, 439, 482. Sheriffs, 98, 294. 565. Coroners, 98, 294. 565, Representatives, 98. Estate of Christian Hack, 180, Justices, 202, 376, 419, 437, 439, 463, 520, 522, 577. Oley furnace in, 229. Agent for purchasing flour in, 249. M. Moore, Commissioner to repair road from Hamburg to county line, 252. Militia, 281. Called out to quell riots in Luzerne, 292. Val. Eckhart sent with instructions. M. Hollenback proposes to supply rations, 295. Contested election for Justice—settled by opinion of Attorney-General on right of a non-resident holding freehold estate in County. M. Richards elected, 396. Election for Justice set aside, 482. Petition of militia, 415. Pay to militia to Wyoming, 421; removal of J. Livergood, 428; contested election, 439, 482. Witnesses, 454. Burgesses of Reading, 462. D. Hunter, Justice, revoked, 482 Contested election, 546, 559. Justice Ludwig resigns, 577. Expense of prisoners, 1777, 641. Claim of widow of Rev. J. Rosenborough, referred to Judges, 643. Deputy Surveyor, xvi., 28. Sureties for Prothonotary, 31. Militia, 90. J. Diemer, appointed President of C. C. P., 125. H. Christ, clerk of Orphans' Court, dec'd—James Scull appointed, 144. Expense of wagons to Reading, 160. Return of militia officers, 171. Justices, 174. Sheriff, 192, 490. Coroner, 192, 490. Accounts of paymaster of militia, 195. Provisions, 230. Prisoners removed to Philada., 234. Militia paid, 319, 348, 523. Officers elected, 362, 418. N. Brosius dies, and Peter Feather, jr., elected, 372. Pensions, 412. Contested election, 435, 457, 460. Captain Robinson, 530, 536. Capts. Rheim and Spratts, 533. Col. Samuel Ely's battalion, 538. Militia, 542.

Bermudas, Governor of, applies for provisions, vii., 168, 202. Powder from, 321. Petition from, for provisions, granted, 413. Flag of Truce from, xii., 2, 29. Sloop Industry, Captain Harvey, from, ordered to depart, 34, 38. Suspends trade, 426, 428. Flour shipped to, xiii., 50. Flag of Truce from, 524.

Bernard, Governor Francis, of New Jersey. Letter announcing his arrival and taking possession, viii., 139. Complains of Indian barbarities—is invited to a conference—arrives and examines into Indian affairs, 140. Arrives in Philadelphia—invites Indians to Burlington, 140. Gov. Denny, &c., visit, 151. His return—conference with Indians, 156. Speech to Indians, 159. At Easton, 179, 193,

216. His protection asked for Waping Indians, 217.
Bernice, Lawrence, makes files, x., 612.
Berringer, David, Coroner, ix., 199, 285, 398.
Berry, Samuel, Coroner, iii., 332, 370.
Berry, William, appointed clerk of Kent, i., 170.
Berry's Place, vii., 154.
Bethlehem, Indians, address and answer, vi., 747, 750. Indians from Diahoga may be received at, vii., 170. Names of two Delaware families at, 174. Speech to Indians at, 174, 175. Indians arrive at from Diahoga, 187. Apprehended difficulty, 190. Two brethren sent to Gov. M., 190. Indians removed to Easton, 191. Number of Moravians in, by Spangenberg, 353. Petition for a watch, 459. Governor's answer, 460. Indians at, 461. Fears of Indians at, 478, Information received at, 478. Address of Moravians at, 494. Indians apply to minister of, for permission to hunt, 516. March from, to Fort Allen, 723. Benjamin, an Indian of Makin tribe, living near, brings news, viii., 126. Sisterhood present rags—thanks for, x., 553. Militia to guard, xi., 446.
Bevan, Aubrey, Coroner, iv., 309, 352, 469, 500, 601.
Bevan, Davis, Coroner, ix., 57, 199. xii., 62, 316. Caveat of, for city lots set aside, xv., 518.
Bevan, Wm., complains of Enoch Story, ii., 160.
Bewley, John, appointed Collector of Customs, i., 534. Seizes goods, 543. Called on by Council to administer oath under dedimus—he declines, ii., 95. Agrees to it, and administers both oath and affirmation to several members, 96. Receives a commission from Queen, 104. Invited to Council, but declines, 117.
Bible, latest quarto edition ordered by Supreme Executive Council, xv., 138.
Bicker, Henry, recommended to Congress as Major, x., 446. Appointed, 446; xii., 215. Lieut. Colonel, promoted, xii., 35.
Bickham, George, Quartermaster's Captain, xi., 21, 32, 113.
Bickley, Samuel, Sheriff, iv., 602, 748.
Biddle, Charles, pass to, xiii., 547. Councillor from Berks, xiv., 231, 269. Elected Vice President of Council, 553, 565; xv., 110. Vote of thanks to, for the faithful discharge of his duties as vice president, 292. Paid, 297. Chosen Secretary of Council, 301, 312, 592. Fees received by him, xvi., 286, 371.
Biddle, Clement, proposes to supply boats with liquors, x., 331. Contract ends, 418. To supply prisoners from St. Johns, 424, 427. To locate and contract for powder mills, 488, 497. To manufacture powder, x., 600. To have shot, 650. Quarter-Master General receives several articles for continental use, 638, 641. To receive blankets, 672; xi., 17; xii., 392. Appointed Marshal, 537. Appointed Quarter-Master General of militia, xiii., 53. Pay, 667. To receive stores, 71. Paid to, 136, 198, 296. To provide stores, 296. Supplies furnished, 386, 706. Notary Public, xiv., 571. Proposes to furnish rations to invalid guard, rates, xv., 17, 63, 115, 212. Marshal, 323. Rations, 349, 365, 381, 448, 503, 613. Justice, 541. For rations to invalid guard, xvi., 76. For pensions, 286. Time allowed him for paying debt due by him, 287. Fees, 523.
Biddle, Edward, on Indian murders at Tulpehocken, vi., 705. Speaker, x., 213. Sick, resigns, 241.
Biddle, Capt. James, x., 407. Elected Prothonotary of Philadelphia, xv., 595, 596. Justice, 607. Tax on writs received, xvi., 220.
Biddle, John, measurer of grain, xiv, 568; xv., 322. Dies, xvi., 204.
Biddle, Capt. Nicholas, appointed to command of boat Franklin, x., 296. Resigns commission to enter into continental service, 425, 426.
Biddle, Owen, Committee of Safety,

to have boats and machines constructed, who to employ, x., 283. To procure grape-shot, 287. Order for lead and flints, 305. To procure a seal for committee with motto, 328. To procure a special rifle, 332. Paid for pikes, 482. To buy shot, 592. To engage store-houses at Germantown, 596. Clothing, 673. Member Board of War, xi., 201. Appointed a Commissioner to run line between Virginia, xiii., 192.

Bigham, Lieutenant Jno., complains of Captain Gardener, xii., 316. To be prosecuted, 683. Writ against, xii., 618. Court martial, 675.

Bigland, Wm., invents a rowing wheel for the row boats, and thanks, x., 295.

Biles, John, Justice, xi., 760.

Biles, Samuel, Sheriff, x., 100, 270.

Biles, Capt. Thos., a prisoner, applies for certificate of rank, xi., 496.

Biles, Thos., Sheriff of Bucks, iii., 289.

Biles, William, member of first Council, i., 57. Appointed sub-Treasurer for Bucks, 111. A special Commissioner to try cases, 164. Road to New York, 514. Coroner of Bucks, iii., 31. Commissioner for building a new court house and prison, 241.

Billings, Joseph, counterfeits bills of credit, proclamation for arrest, ix., 647.

Billingsport, not suitable as Hog Island, for "frames," x., 294. Report of committee to survey Jersey Shore, views of defence, 474. Redoubt to be erected at, 601. Chev.-de-friese to be sunk, 603, 700. Survey to fort, x., 568. Fortifications, 572, 605. Engineer to give plan for works, lands to be bought, Congress to pay for, 619. Troops to and from, 627. Sheds at, Robert Smith appointed, Mons. Kermanvor, engineer, appointed at, 631. Timber for, 645. House purchased at, for fortifications, of Benjamin Weatherby by Congress, paid for, Robert Smith paid, 675. Redoubt, 660. Fortifications, 673. Committee on plan of, 678, 683, 700. Barracks at, 704. Fortifications, piers, 719, 729. Officers appointed to erect fortifications at, 730. Militia of city to be employed at, 734. Colonel John Bull, superintendent of works at, 737. Stores for, 745, 771. Sinking Chev-de-frieze, 753. Pay of J. Dundas as assistant superintendent, xi., 6. Chev.-de-friese built at, Rob't Smith, articles for, 5, 6, 19. Men sent down, 19. Respecting, 60. Colonel Bull to command and superintend, Blathwaite Jones, Chief Engineer, 125. Salt for provisions at, 135. Teams for, 139. Laborers to be employed, provisions and soldiers, 142. Troops from South Carolina may be employed at, 236, 242. The Boards visit, 243. General Du Coudray presents a plan for the fort at, tents for, 245, 246. Colonel Bull to procure carts and teams, 246. General Potter asks for boats to convey the militia from Chester to; Captain Downey ordered from; resolutions of Cong'ss on fortifications at, to be furnished General Armstrong, 248. Ordnance, 252. Removal of troops to Fort Island, 269. Boats to be furnished Major General Armstrong, to remove troops, 270. Work done at, by Colonel Bull, 399. Colonel B. Jones discharged as engineer, 486. Council visit, 570, 571. Cannon for, 572. Signal gun at, 573. Colonel Bull and Wm. Armstrong employed at, &c., 575. Provisions, 576, 578. Barracks, 575. Pay at, 607, 618, 629, 643. Men left to take care of cannon, xi., 636. James Dundas pay-master, garrison relieved, workmen paid, 756, 757. To stop vessels, 761. Workmen at, 767, 777. Wm. Armstrong, pay-master, xii., 10. Pay to Colonel Bull, 13. For workmen, time of service expiring, 26. A flag of truce arrives with prisoners, 29. Pay for work, 40. Supplies at, for United States, 41, 65, 66. Service of militia about to expire, others to be called out, 71. Claim

of Captain McGinley for work, pay for, 83, 86. James Loughead pay master at, 86. Provisions purchased for, 86. Sickly state of garrison, 117. Time expiring, persons to be left in charge by Captain Boys from galleys, 134. Workmen to be discharged when works are secured from weather, 146. Pay to Colonel Bull, 180. Major Wm. Armstrong paid for workmen, 186. Under Captain Boys, 627. Pay to Major Wm. Armstrong, 636. Pay to guard at, 718. Troops raised for defence of, 719. Pay for officers, &c., xiii., 14. Supplies, men to be discharged, 16. Overseer wanted, 30. Pay to, 43, 48. French Generals, view, 51. In charge of Wm. Smith, 54, 121. Pay of officers and workmen, 121, 149. Return of stores made by Wm. Smith, pay for sails of boat for, 272. For fencing in the State lands, 276, 325. Arms to be brought from, 334. Repair of boat, 383. Fencing, 405. Salary to cease, 429. Pay at, 444. Taxes, 449. Visit of Council to, 578. Report on account of Edward McKeggan, mason at, xiv., 465. Accounts, 581, 586, 617. B. Jones, engineer at, paid, xv., 24. Claim for a frame building, taken by British at, 37. Two broken cannon (French nine pounders) at, to be delivered to Henry Hill, 192. Paid Andrew Long for logs for chevaux-de-frieze in 1777, xvi., 45. Stores, &c., 1779, and hoisting flag, 456.

Bills of credit, proposed acts for, iii., 226, 227, 228. Approved by Governor for £30,000, 229. Re-emitted, 248. Governor's remarks on currency, 249. Sir Alfred Popple on issues of, 262. Speech of Governor on, 264. Adulterated, 268. Act of Assembly, for issue of, 346. And terms of, 346. Governor's views, 347, 348–350, 356, 360, 377, 393, 396. Counterfeited in Virginia by R. Jenkins, iv., 629. Instructions to Governor, 473. Lords of trade on, 476, 673. Respecting, 676. Merchants petition against, 750, 752. Counterfeited, iv., 273. Governor to Assembly, respecting, 303, 304, 315, 317, 318–336, 375. Lords of Trade on, 357, 358. Reports of Assembly on, 361. Respecting, v., 33, 35, 42–47, 375, 396, 412, 415, 416, 561, 562, 605, 613, 638, 723–728; vi., 39, 139, 191, 207, 209, 222, 231, 239, 246, 339, 340, 352, 353, 386, 388, 437, 439, 446, 505–510, 518, 521, 524, 537, 546, 587, 588, 597, 680, 682, 693, 696, 702, 711, 714, 720, 724, 736, 738, 743. Opinion of Council, 207, vii., 94, 196, 231, 238, 246, 247–257, 264, 396, 409, 413, 417, 430, 441, 442, 450, 453, 463, 565, 572, 618, 743; viii., 39, 66, 76, 80, 86, 299, 301, 318, 323, 332, 350, 357, 397, 399, 402, 460, 483, 502, 511, 515, 529, 535, 559, 584, 596, 605, 693, 715. Ratified in England, 39, 64, 68, 342. Passed, 86. Important omission in, for loss of quit rents, 350. Opinion of Privy Council on, 529; ix., 10, 12, 17, 19, 52–55, 115, 117, 148, 149, 177, 178, 197, 199, 240, 244, 245, 325, 389, 392, 575, 576, 589–592, 595, 597, 642, 651. Counterfeited, 647; x., 24, 27, 28, 31, 41, 67, 139, 148, 223, 263, 281, 485, 497, 637–774, 779, 780. Of 1769, counterfeited, proclamation, 88, 97–99, 256, 257. Refused by John Drinker and J. Fisher and sons —proceedings, 486. Exchanged, xi., 709. Mistake in printing the backs, proclamation to call in, 362. Old to be called in, issued by British Government, 382. Counterfeit, 397, 709, 735, 765. Called in by Congress, Commissioners appointed for each county, xi., 736. Called in, xii., 3, 67, 73, 108, 233, 299, 364, 369, 589, 707, 732, 745, 760, 770. Sale of Province Island to redeem, 671. Proclamation respecting, 726; xiii., 26, 28, 39, 45, 54, 56, 66, 109, 118, 142, 180, 190, 193, 218, 235, 236, 246, 250, 274, 305, 315, 316, 320, 325, 345, 366, 389, 395, 409, 505, 543, 552, 572, 576, 618, 729. Lots sold to redeem, xiv., 34, 35, 65, 333, 338, 457, 466, 476, 559, 572,

604, 631. Pay to signers of, 572, 573, 596, 621, 624, 631. Paper for, 580, 635; xv., 10, 155, 405. Depreciation on, 445. Pay to signers, 155.

Bills to be passed into laws by vote, i., 58; prepared, 61, 64, 66, 71, 72, 81, 97, 98; of Excise, 108. Alteration of style proposed by Assembly, 179.

Bingham, Wm., delegate to Congress, xv., 189, 341.

Bingley, Edw'd, appointed captain of Fire Brig, x., 609.

Binney, Dr. Barnabas, a physician and surgeon in hospital of U. S. applies for pay of depreciation, xiii., 122; city lot, xv., 46; dead, 621.

Birch, Matthew, appointed collector of customs, i. 534; and surveyor, 535; seizes goods, 543. Complaints against him, 559–61.

Bird, Colonel James, x., 601.

Bird, Mark, offers to make muskets in Berks county, x., 504, 696, 691, 697, 699; at Riot at James Wilson's, gives bail, xii., 139.

Birmingham, Richard, brother-in-law of Gov. Gookin, ii., 614, 630.

Bizalion, Louis and P., Indian traders, complained of, ii., 18, and confined, 19; give security, 100; wife interprets, 141; arrives, 145, 155, 186. Complained against, 403.

Bizalion, Peter, a French Roman Catholic Indian trader arrested, ii., 509; invites Governor to Conestoga, 537; in prison—gives bond, 539, asks to trade with Indians, 545. Indian Interpreter, iii., 19; iv., 53.

Blackberry Creek, xi., 699.

Blackfan, Edward, Sec'y, letter from proprietary by, called for, i., 230, 231; from, 340.

Blakiston, Wm., Coroner, v., 411.

Black Log, or Sleeping Place, v., 349.

Blacks' Gap, road through, xvi., 102, 484.

Blackwell, Captain John, Governor, arrives and produces commission, i., 228; takes his seat in Council, 229; his speech to Assembly, 286–289; sends a long letter of resignation, and two Commissions from Wm. Penn for successor, 313–315; instructions, 318, 319.

Blackwood, Marm'ke, Smith, x., 421.

Blaine, Ephraim, Sheriff, ix., 779; Sheriff, x., 56, 150; Lieut, appointed, xi., 199; Deputy Commissioner of purchases; Letter on scarcity of flour, xii., 112, 144; order of Congress for five million, 235, 359; returns of purchases, 411; Letter, xiv., 283, 286; claims a city lot, 469.

Blair, Captain James, commands a boat, x., 339.

Blair, Rev. Samuel, Chaplain, furnished with a suit of black clothes, xii., 358.

Blair, Wm., Jr., Coroner, xiv., 236, 567; xv., 102.

Blaithwaite, Secretary, Letter to Governor, i., 526.

Blakeney, Col., Adjutant General, iv., 430.

Blakeney, Gilbert, proposes to raise men at Fort Pitt, xiii., 454.

Blanchard, Colonel Joseph, Letter to commander at Albany, relative to battle, &c., at Lake George, vi., 623.

Blankets, housekeepers called on for, x., 400, 473, 508, 672; to be procured from Citizens, xi., 21, 23, 328, 334; Commissioners, 329; increased, 334.

Blewer, Cap. Joseph, x., 660, 661, 683, 689, 700, 726, 761. To fit out armed boat "Convention," xi., 2, 52; to sink gondolas, 470; orders, 475; sale of estates, 539; son pris'er, 571. Appointed member of Navy Board, 122, 397. Warden, xiii., 100.

Blond, Col., xi., 107.

Bloom, Stephen, Coroner, xv., 101.

Blue Anchor, in Philadelphia, ii., 9; its locality—used as a public landing, 10; papers respecting, noticed, —again considered, 12, 14, 19, 39, 54.

Blunston, John, member of Council, i., 331, 333; Speaker of Assembly, 518, 568, 601.

Blunston, Samuel, Justice, iii., 359; letters, 470; in Philadelphia Reports Germans going over Susquehanna, iv., 57, 147; letters from, 147, 149, 155, 190; on Maryland affairs. Indian outrage in Lancaster County, 280.

Blythe, Benjamin, Sub-Lieutenant, xi., 358, 564; xii., 323.
Blythe, William, deposition of murder of ten Indians by Frederick Stump, ix., 414.
Board of inspection on tea imported from Amsterdam xiv., 33.
Board of Property, establishment of a, proposed, xiii., 132; to meet, 296; meeting, 320, 442, 498, 621, 638, 704, 760, 761; xiv., 46, 139, 200, 374, 451, 452, 473, 494, 503, 518, 591, 616, 639, 652, 672; xv., 15, 31, 48, 61, 76, 93, 112, 128, 140, 161, 173, 189, 222, 223, 254, 261, 266, 270, 279, 310, 311, 326, 345, 346, 349, 362, 381, 383, 387, 401, 419, 420, 425, 466, 487, 524, 558, 612, 637, 652; xvi., 16, 46, 70, 86, 104, 124, 145, 177, 208, 220[2], 242, 269, 290, 316, 374, 394, 414, 434, 480, 509. Reports, xv., 379.
Board of Treas'y, letter from, xii., 55.
Board of War (State), x., 699, 719, 755; xi., 177, 181, 182, 188, 194, 198, 201, 211, 221, 243, 246, 250, 260, 303, 394, 411, 425, 497, 759. Ask for wagons, xii., 16; for key of Magazine, 32; information asked of, 67; letters, 85, 93, 94, 100, 116, 117, 174, 198, 240, 312, 433, 452, 454, 495, 741, 743; xiii., 96, 128, 449.*
Board of War (Continental), Rich'd Peters, Secretary, xi., 226. Instructions, 425, 497, 508, 509, 630, 627, 637.
Boats, models offered, x., 284, 285; guns for, 288; ordered to be built, 284, 285; a sail for, ordered, 285; names of, 289, 290, 296, 314, 328, 329, 335, 351, 404, 407, 408, 426, 437, 440, 488, 501, 505, 511, 554, 664; names of Commanders, 287, 290, 296, 328, 329, 330, 335, 352, 355, 362, 383, 396, 404, 407, 408, 423, 426, 427, 437, 440, 488, 490, 501, 505, 516, 521, 554, 592, 664, 725; failure and success in launching, 291; model of, 296; launch, 314; regulations for, 321; commission of Officers, 321; Committee to draw rules for, 327; for supplies of, 328; to be manned—pay of officers and men, 329; supplies for, 331; cartridge boxes for, 333; muster master, 338; to have handcuffs on board, 361; bounty, 361, 385; stores for, 362; general instructions for, 368; rations, 415; proposals for provisions, 418; number of men, 465; proposal for supplying, 423; Francis Wade obtains contract, 423; three to be at Liberty Island, 429; rules and regulations for men in Barracks, 428; number of men on board, 430; hands for, 462. Memorial of officers, 472. Committee to superintend, 480; officers to be convened, 489; crews to be well clothed, 498; rations, 500. Five guard boats to be built, 514; to act in concert with brig Lexington, 526; swivels for, 552; Commodore to distribute powder to, 610; flat bottom to be built to transport men from shore to shore, 612, 613; officers pay, 634; Commodore Caldwell, 650; in Darby creek, 656; John Peal, Court Martial on, 656; Camden, 689; to be built, 758. Armed—Delaware, xi., 5; "Convention" ordred to Cape May, 8; Delaware, 5, 10.
Boccalunce—at head of Ohio—fort at, v., 634; or Conewago Indians, viii., 270.
Bodie, William, of Bucks, charged with counterfeiting bills of credit, iv., 273–277.
Boehm, Philip, Paymaster, xi., 279. Appointed Justice; resigns as Paymaster, 588. Appointed Coroner, 597. To pay off militia, or give reasons, 718. Receives pay for, xii., 55. To render account, 243. Coroner, 506.
Boehm, Philip, Jr., Paymaster, xi., 767.
Bœufs, Fort aux, latitude, distances, &c., v., 761.
Boger, Lieutenant Richard, prisoner, x., 601, 622, ordered to York, 627.
Boggs, John, Lieutenant, xii., 489; Sheriff, 518; xiii., 134, 396. Agent for confiscated estates, xiv., 140. Justice, xv., 59.
Bond, Phineas, to be seized, xi., 284; released, 300, 525; on petition of his mother, his attainder was suspended, xv., 8; estate of,

* It is sometimes difficult to determine from the minutes which Board is intended.

claim of J. Weiss on, 187; British Consul, 215; suggests certain matters, 408, 410, 417, 419; complaint against, 517, 520.
Bond, Dr. Thomas, visits sickly vessels, iv., 498, 587, 674; with Dr. Graeme, visits sickly ships, vi., 170; their joint report, 171–173. To visit a vessel arrived with passengers, v., 100; to visit ship from Barbadoes, 109, 112, 121; to visit, 410. Coroner, vii., 266; to examine surgeons, x., 452, 458; asks for powder to burn in gaol, 512; to collect rags in store, 633;
Bond, Thomas, Jr., Purveyor of United States Hospital, xi., 168; xiii., 115.
Bonham, Ephraim, Sub-Lieutenant, xi., 218.
Bonsall, Justice, proceedings against, vii., 354, 356, 391.
Book, Law proposed for making several sorts of, for use of the people, i., 93.
Books, military, to be purchased, x., 500.
Boon, Captain Andrew, x., 669.
Boonbrack, Lieutenant Benjamin, leaves his colors, x., 694.
Boone, Captain Hawkins, a wounded soldier rewarded for his bravery, xi., 704.
Boone, William, Coroner, v., 597, 662; vi., 144, 638; sheriff, vii., 266.
Boquinville, Colonel, at Montreal, viii., 505.
Bordentown, troops sent to, x., 629.
Bordley—of Maryland, iv., 115.
Bore, Lassee, justice left out, iii., 531.
Boring Mill, erecting, near City, x., 641.
Bork, Lawrence, of Lancaster, viii., 143.
Boscawen, Admiral, on French fleet arrived, vi., 451. Captures three French vessels, 463, 465. Intelligence from, 592. Reported capture of French vessels, vii., 156. Letter asking men, viii., 163; Assembly decline, 164; opinion of Council, 165, 166; message from Assembly on, 170.
Boston, great fire at, Relief asked by Governor of Massachusetts for sufferers, viii., 483; donation by Assembly, 483.
Boston Port Bill, Governor petitioned to call Assembly on account of, declines, x., 177; Ministerial troops captured at, 409.
Botanist, appointed by French Minister, xii., 610.
Boucaloonce or Canawago Indians, viii., 270.
Bouchet, Cheval. Du, Letter, xiv., 173.
Boude, Dr. Samuel, collector, vi., 653.
Boude, Thomas, Coroner, vi., 144, 638.
Boudinot, Elias, elected President of Congress, xiii., 412.
Boundaries of Counties, i., 126, 129, 130, 154, 262, 265, 266, v., 502, 514; x., 273.
Boundaries between Maryland and Pennsylvania, ii., 362; iii., 232, 233, 461, 463, 464, 467–491; v., 422; x., 216, 220, 221, 240, 241.
Boundaries between Virginia, and Pennsylvania, v., 758–767; vi., 8, 81, 240; xii., 16, 224, 234, 250, 287, 303, 444, 476; xiii., 685, xiv., 56, 74, 104, 211, 236, 360, 402, 518.
Boundaries between Maryland, Virginia and Pennsylvania, v., 422.
Boundary, Northern, xiv., 362, 385, 655; xv., 12, 22, 33, 38, 190, 202, 204, 212, 220, 328, 374, 393, 401, 421, 456, 458, 614, 642.
Boundary, Western, xiv., 464, 507, 643; xv., 16, 19, 38, 106, 108.
Boundary Treaty with Indians at Fort Stanwix, ix., 545, 568, 586.
Boundary between Pennsylvania and New York, xvi., 225.
Bounties, xvi., 106.
Bounty of Lands offered to officers and soldiers, vi., 504.
Bouquet, Colonel Henry, demands quarters in Philadelphia for soldiers, vii., 358. Proceedings by Governor, Sheriff, &c., 359–78; viii., 234, 270. Letters to and from, ix., 35, 197, 247. Journal, 208–234. Posts cut off, 35. Good conduct of, 42. Peace with Indians on Ohio, 238.
Bourne—Health Officer, vi., 169.
Bowen, Major Thomas B., xi., 20;

receiver of certificates for arrears of pay, xiv., 151, 173, 401.
Bowles, Joseph, testifies against Col. Talbot, i., 115.
Bowles, Leonard, becomes a citizen from Bahama Islands, xii., 92.
Bowman, Captain W., x., 529.
Bowman, Henry, appointed Ranger for Sussex County, i., 166.
Bowman, John, Ensign, xii., 9.
Bowman, Martin, Commissioner, xii., 406.
Boyce, Nathan, Captain of a boat, x., 327, 423, 426.
Boyd, Major Alexander, Auctioneer, xii., 625, 659; to examine British goods, xiii., 491. Resigns as auctioneer of Philad'a, xv., 50, 53.
Boyd, Andrew, sub-lieutenant, xi., 318, 496, 511; wagon-master, 589. Col. xii., 445; resigns, 733.
Boyd, Captain Andrew, offers reward, xi., 511, 761.
Boyd, David, Coroner, ix., 689.
Boyd, Lieutenant John, xi., 511.
Boyd, Captain John, asks for pay, xiii., 729; Councillor, 751.
Boyd, Hon. John, Commissioner respecting peace in Northumberland, xiv., 168, ; Commissioner to Wyoming, 202; Justice, 237, 307.
Boyd, Samuel, Coroner, ix., 778; x., 56, 101, 211, 270; Paid for services, xiii. 44.
Boyd, Lieutenant Thomas, appointed, x., 678. Thomas, wagon master, dies, xi., 580.
Boyd, Captain, x., 708.
Boyd, Captain, with his company of rangers ordered to Yorktown, xiii., 121.
Boyd, Tho's, proclamation against, xi., 446.
Boyd, Wm., Justice, xiii., 542.
Boyer, Conrad, Coroner, xiv., 230.
Boyer, Jacob, Sheriff, xvi., 192.
Boyer, James, Justice, ix., 645.
Boyrie, Mons., and LeRoy, two Frenchmen arrested at Philadelphia, viii., 714.
Boys, Capt. Nathan, leaves men from galleys in charge of fortifications at Billingsport and Mud Island, xii., 134. To discharge men, 190. Pay for, 223, 250, 275, 314. Expense of boats, 354, 376, 392, 406, 452, 489, 627, 628, 657. To raise troops, 719. Pay for men at forts, xiii., 14, 43, 48, 121. Discharged from service, with compliments for his merits, 151. To order out a signal boat, xi., 692. Boats to Colonel Bull, 717. To make list of officers, &c., 727.
Braddock, General Edward, his arrival looked for, vi., 298. Arrives in Virginia, 303. Lord Halifax notices his appointment as Commander-in-Chief, 306. Letters to and from, 307, 331, 332, 335, 338, 371, 377, 380, 383, 394, 398, 399, 401, 406, 408, 461. Accuses Assembly of pusillanimous and improper behavior, 307. Flour for his army, 308. Wishes a post between Philadelphia and Winchester, 321. Troops arrive in Virginia, 331. Commissioners for laying out road, 318. Necessity of union of colonies, 332. Desires meeting of Governors at Annapolis, 332. Governors Shirley and Delancey arrive in Philadelphia on their way to, 358. Meeting with Governors at Alexandria, and proceedings, 365, 368. Proposals for a common fund, 365, Letter, Commissioners on road, 369, 374. Flour not arrived at Fort Cumberland, 373. Letter, R. Peters, to Commissioners on road, 376, 378, 398, 425, 466, 521. Wishes to contract for wagons, 378. Persons charged with supplying French, 380. Governor supplies money, 383. Letter, Sir Thomas Robinson on General Braddock's affairs, 394. R. Peters' reports on road, 395. Approves of Shirley taking Colonel Schuyler and men, 398. Proposes setting out for DuQuesne, what he intends to do if he takes the fort, &c., 399. Complains of Governor Dinwiddie and roguery of Assembly, 400. Proposals for provisions, 401. Letter from Wm. Shirley, secretary to, 404. On garrisoning fort, 406. Has begun his march, 413. Wagons, 414. Present to, from lower Assembly, 414. Supplies, 415. Letters to and from, 415, 424, 426, 428, 429, 430, 445, 461, 475, 476. Money wanted for road; soldiers'

wives sent home, 426. Remits bills to Governor, 426, 429. Is informed of French at Ohio, 431. Thanks to Governor Morris for provisions; sends a draft for Franklin; road, 446. Progress, 460, 463, 466, 475, 477. Colonel Burd's account of road, &c., 466. Murders near Fort Cumberland, 475. His defeat and death, 478–484, 487, 492, 495, 496, 498–502, 511–520, 548, 593, 599, 625, 700. Letter from Capt. Robert Orme, account of action, &c., 487. List of killed and wounded, 489–492, 499, 502. Retreat of Colonel Dunbar, 492. Wives of Indians from Aughwick, 494. Letter from General Shirley on, 548, 549. Payment of claims to Governor Morris, 643. From proprietaries on, 730, 733. Commissioners appointed to settle his accounts of wagoner, vii., 10. Succeeded by Lord Loudoun, 181. Effects of, 351. Sir Jno. St. Clair on his road, 592. Wagon account, viii., 284.

Bradford, Andrew, printer, ordered before Council for publishing a pamphlet, reflecting on the credit of the province, also in Weekly Mercury, iii., 143. Appears before Council; denies all knowledge of the pamphlet and charges his journeyman with the other; asks pardon and is forgiven by the Governor, and ordered to print nothing in future about government without permission, 145. Publishes in his paper "Brutus and Cassius;" ordered to be arrested for it; house searched for manuscript of it; found to be by Parson Campbell, 369. Committed and bound over to Court, 370.

Bradford, Joseph, xi., 408.

Bradford, Thomas, appointed agent for marine prisoners of war sent to Philadelphia, xii., 23. To receive prisoners from flag of truce, 29, 37, 44. Applies for officers, 53, 55, 495. Buys city lot, xiv., 34, 37. Paid for printing, 643. Newspaper, xv., 187, 366, 384. To be filed, 444, 639.

Bradford, Thomas and William, printers, x., 420. Newspapers ordered, xi., 654; xii., 197.

Bradford, William, prints almanac, 1685; required to blot out "Lord Penn," i., 165. Complains of his tools and letters being taken from him by late rulers, 366. Restored, 367. Printer, in case of Wm. Moore and Dr. Smith, viii., 440. Printer, xvi., 527.

Bradford, Capt. William, of Second Battalion, ordered to take British officers into custody, x., 302. To print rules and regulations, 321.

Bradford, Capt. William, Jr., xi., 2. Member of Navy Board, 127. Pay master of State Navy Board, 366.

Bradford, Wm. C., pay master of the fleet, xi., 387, 442, 448, 475, 588. Pay master, xii., 44, 48. Discharged, 192. Pay as Commissioner fixed, 253.

Bradford, Wm., Jr., appointed Attorney General, xii., 550. Counsel on Connecticut claim, xiii., 128. Retaining fee, 136. Also in case of Baron Hurst & Co., 137. Retained, 241, 281, 310. Case between State and General Roberdeau, 319. To remove a suit to another Court, 367, 496. Appointed agent on trial of private rights at Wyoming, xiv., 35. Fees on Connecticut claim, 141. Returns two threatening letters to Marbois, 143. Attorney General, pay to, 628. Opinion on pardoning power, xv., 329. Report on claim to a city lot, 71. Pay to, 227, 419; xvi., 21. Fees in four suits, 391. Settlement for fees, 546.

Bradin, Nath'l, Justice, xiv., 362.

Bradshall, John, appointed Attorney-General for Kent, i., 174.

Bradshaw, James, appointed Chief Surveyor and Register of New Castle, i., 157, 161, 164.

Bradshaw, William, Constable, complaint of Quakers against, vii., 405.

Bradstreet, Colonel John, letter to Governor M. on French sent to Ohio, vi., 412, 427. At Presque Isle, letter from, inclosing terms of peace with Indians, ix., 193.

Brady, John, Captain, x., 752.
Brady, John, wounded at Battle of Brandywine, loses a gun, for which he is paid, xvi., 288.
Brady, Lieutenant, appointed Captain, xii., 437.
Brady, Captain Joseph, petition, xi., 313.
Brady, Captain Samuel, reward to, for an Indian scalp, xii., 632. serves in Bedford county, xvi., 464.
Brandingham, Dr., a pirate, i., 578.
Brandt, Henry, vi., 291.
Brandywine Creek, a bridge, road and water-mill complained of, i., 199. Obstructions, 292. Roads, ii., 111; iii., 142. Indians complain against mill and dam hindering their fishing; sheriff to throw them down, 269. Fisheries, ix., 465, 472, 598, 638, 639. Marsh to be repaired, &c., x., 80.
Brandywine Shoal, man-of-war Roebuck aground on, x., 552.
Brandywine, Battle of, Captain William Mackay wounded at, xi., 667. William Russell loses a leg at, asks aid, xii., 107.
Brannon, Benjamin, Sub-Lieutenant of Chester county, applies for cannon, xi., 219, 242.
Brass to be purchased, x., 612. Cannons to be made by B. Loxley, 626.
Brassines, Monsieur de, debts paid —he to be delivered to French Consul, x., 235. To be delivered to Monsieur de Marbois to be sent to France, xv., 215.
Bratton, Captain William, xi., 569, 684. Justice, xiii., 666.
Bread, assize of, i., 576, 582; viii., 574; ix., 727; x., 18, 75, 243.
Bread and flour, exportation of Merchantable; law proposed, iii., 240, 391, 536–538; v., 565, 619. Not merchantable, not to be exported, viii., 172, 173, 407, 548. Bill for assize of, 574. Not merchantable export of, ix., 362, 364. Assize of, 727.
Bread, army, no want of, xi., 303.
Breading, Nathaniel, councillor, xvi., 202.
Brearly, David, C. J., xiii., 74.
Brecht, Peter, Coroner, x., 100, 211, 270.
Breinig, George, Justice, xiv., 629, 637.
Breintnall, Joseph, Sheriff, iv., 85, 247.
Breton, Cape, expedition against, from New England, iv., 753, 754, 762, 763.
Brett, Robert, Clerk of Market, Philadelphia, complained of, i., 442, 443, 444.
Bribery and corruption at elections, v., 564, 566, 619.
Brice, John, Lieutenant of "Warren," x., 501.
Bridge at Frankford out of repair, ii., 194, 406, 407, 658.
Bridge at Schuylkill, tolls to be paid, xi., 53. Floating at, 55. Guards for, 56. Pensawkin Creek, 104. Over Schuylkill nearly ready, 210. To be removed to Delaware, 305. In Delaware River, 310, 666, 711.
Bridges, iii., 246, 263, 426, 428, 481; ix., 284, 285, 658, 719, 729; x., 109; xi., 614.
Briefs, necessary before asking charity, iv., 259.
Brientnal, Joseph, Sheriff Philadelphia County, iii., 614.
Brigade, Expenses, xii., 510.
Brigadier Generals appointed, xi., 62, 199, 398.
Briggs, Samuel, of Philadelphia, petition, with a model of machine for making nails, screws and gimblets, xvi., 88. Model returned, 346.
Bright, Jacob, Com. made prisoner, xi., 536.
Brimstone, Bounty for, x., 530.
Brinkloe, Clerk of Kent, resigns, i., 170.
Bristol, (Buckingham,) to be laid out, i., 513. Ferry to Burlington, ii., 488. Petition about road, 549; iii., 43. Erected into a borough, 58. Ferry over Neshaminy creek, 233. Passed, 235. Act for erecting house of correction in, v., 34. Road from Philadelphia to, 59, 61. Election of Burgesses and Constable—dedimus to administer oath, 110. Petition of inhabitants complaining of an insult from a Captain Sims, xi., 254. Mr. De Normandie, 480. Election of Amos Gregg, Chief Burgess, xv.,

83, 273; and second Burgess, Thos. Pearson, 273.
Bristow, John, Councillor, i., 196.
British half pence, proclamation against importation or manufacture of, xiii., 4. Goods to be seized, 170, 317, 328. Deserters to report themselves to Council, 342. Prisoners on board ship at New York, 431. Goods seized at Lancaster, 453. Provisions sent to American prisoners, 459. Goods seized, 482, 483, 484, 525, 526, 563, 667. Prisoners allowed to pass through city to N. York, 572.
British Consul, complaint against, by Admiralty Court for a survey ordered, xv,, 517, 520.
Britton, John, plank, x., 672.
Brockden, Chas., Recorder of Deeds, Philadelphia, vii., 464. Master of Rolls, removed on account of age, ix., 397.
Brodhead, Charles, brings message from Indians of Wyomink, vi., 751. Commissioners to Indians, instructions, 754. Charges Teedyuscung with Indian murders, vii., 326, 328.
Brodhead, Daniel, a justice, v., 113. Letter from Northampton on disturbances, 757. Letter to Mr. Peters on Connecticut claim, vi., 253, 255. Removes from Northampton (where he acted as justice) to Berks, where he is now appointed a justice, ix., 746. Recommended to Congress as Lt. Colonel, x., 442, 444, 722, 767. Articles furnished, 722. Pay, 751.
Brodhead, Colonel, ordered with men to Bordentown, x., 629. Letter to, 743. Wants bayonets, xi., 457. Pay to, 400. Ask nothing for soldiers, 519, 531. Letters to and from, xii., 25, 31, 80, 84, 173, 215, 245, 435, 445, 498, 585, 743. Moravians recommended to, 346. Complaints against, at Fort Pitt, 747. Pass, xiii., 544. Report of Comptroller against, xvi., 44. Elected Surveyor General, 208, 210. Names of his deputies, 214. 222, 224, 222[2], 229, 257, 261, 280, 288, 292, 390, 461.
Brodhead, Garret, appointed justice, ix., 660. Information respecting, Connecticut settlers, x., 50.
Brooke, Henry, Collector of Lewes, ii., 98. Member of Council from Lewes, iii., 143. Judge of Supreme Court, 269. Brooks, Jas., to be arrested, x., 359. His friends may visit him, 371. Goes under escort to Lancaster, 380. At Lancaster, 385. Pay to guards, 403, 409, 503, 698. In gaol, 699.
Brooks, Edward, Frankford Bridge referred to, iii., 246.
Broonback, Lieut. Benjamin, charged with leaving colors, x., 694.
Brosius, Nicholas, collector of excise, dies, vi., 371.
Brothers, Ship, sails under sea letter from Council, from Philadelphia for China, Capt. Josiah, xvi., 224[4].
Broughton, Thomas, Governor of S. Carolina, letter on Spanish preparations at Havanna, iv., 165.
Brown, Andrew, prints Federal Gazette, and Council subscribes, xv., 566; xvi., 222[4], 493.
Brown, Colonel, battalion to defend frontiers of Cumberland, xiii., 222. Ammunition sent to, 247.
Brown, Lieut. David, on frontier, complains of want of clothing—is supplied, xi., 665.
Brown, Elijah, to be seized, xi., 283.
Brown, James, Letter to J. Alexander on Connecticut claim, vi., 271; and answer, 273.
Brown, John, arrested and imprisoned, his examination implicates Messrs. Morris and Willing, xi., 345. To be published with remarks by V. P. and Mr. Sergeant—no person to converse with him—proposals of General Howe, 347. Remarks on, 348. Permitted to go to Lancaster Co., 406, 407. Discharged, 452, 459. Seized by order of Congress—taken to Lancaster—his examination, 394. Resigns, but not accepted, 774.
Brown, John, case of, in Montgomery county, xv., 423, 432.
Brown, William, Captain of Marines, x., 488, 504, 606. To recruit men, 505. Sent with prisoners to be exchanged, 596, 688. To command floating battery; to raise men for, 725; xi., 278.

Brown, William, auctioneer, xii., 185, 186, 525. Justice, xiv., 344.
Bruner, George, xii., 70.
Brushes and priming wires, x., 314.
Bryan, George, tie vote for Assembly, new election ordered, ix., 286. Naval officer, x., 611, 728. Vice President, xi., 174, 375, 632, 634, 721. Extra pay, 387. Father-in-law dies, 721. Proclamation, 493, 513, 545, 610, 627. Resigns as Vice-President, another elected, xii., 127. Elected to Assembly, 129. His account, 211. Appointed Judge of Supreme Court, 303, 305. Opinion, case of William Hanks, xiii., 543; xiv., 668. Reappointed Judge Supreme Court, xv., 189, 190. Paid, xvi., 312.
Bryan, Jacob, pays Lydius for a share, vi., 293.
Bryan, John, Coroner, x., 100, 211, 273.
Bryant, Captain John, xii., 2.
Bryce, John, Ensign, x., 464. First Lieutenant, 501.
Buchannan, Colonel Arthur, battalion to be supplied with axes, &c., xi., 413. Sub-Lieutenant, xii., 322.
Buchannan, Robert, Sheriff, iii., 465, 520, 575. Attacked by rioters from Maryland, 612. Sheriff, iv., 309, 352, 470.
Buchannan, Thomas, Sub-Lieutenant, xii., 322. Sheriff, xvi., 194, 509.
Buchannan, William, Commissioner to cut road westward, vi., 318, 324, 377, 435. Commissary-General, letter to, on supplying provisions for the army—prices, xi., 334.
Buck, Dr. Henry, xi., 116.
Buckanon, William, Coroner, viii., 505.
Buckingham (Bristol) to be laid out as a market town, i., 513. Road to, 514.
Buckingham township, petition for road, ii., 520, 539.
Buckley, Samuel, and C. Pickering charged and tried for counterfeiting, i., 85.
Buckman, William, Coroner, viii., 781; ix., 57. Sheriff, 285, 333, 398.
Bucks County, Sheriffs of, i., 58, 186, 332, 368. Seal for, ordered; its device, 66. County Court of Philadelphia fined for deciding a case in jurisdiction of, 76. Sub-Treasurer appointed, 111. Division line between Philadelphia county, 126–130. Coroner, 162, 228. Trial for murder, 164. Special commissioners, 164. Petition of Jacob Hall, 194. Road from Philadelphia, 195, 298. Joseph Growden, member of Council, 196. Roads, ii., 67, 520. Road from King's road to be extended and surveyed, 67. Dedimus to Jeremiah Langhorn, 97. Commission to try a negro in, 112, 160. Claim John Tatham vs. Joseph Growdon, 179. Case of John Eastburn, 182, 209. William Biles, Sheriff, 182. Two members of Assembly die, 190. Complaint of John Eastburn against sheriff for not obtaining restitution, 209. Act to sell old court-house and building a new one and prison read, 214. Sheriff complains about tax-payers, 391. William Crasdell, Sheriff, 397. Case of J. Heaton and J. Growdon, 407. Petition of Thomas Fairman about land in, 434. Manner of laying in, complained of, 456. Case of David Bollard, 456. Extortion, 456. Two Justices appear before Council to explain, 458. Are acquitted, 459. Want ferry from Bristol to Burlington, 488. Mingo, an Indian slave, arrested, 489, 508. Sufferers from fire ask relief, 544. Road from opposite Reading's Landing, 561, 562. Justices, iii., 28. William Biles, Coroner, 31. John Hall, Sheriff, 31, 56, 108, 140. Ferry from Bristol to Burlington, 43. Mary Underwood under sentence of death for murder of her child, reprieved for twelve months, 45. John Cutler, Coroner, 56, 69. Bristol erected into a borough, 58. Abraham de Normandy, Sheriff, 69. Jeffry Pollard, Coroner, 108. Wm. Atkinson, Coroner, 140. Ferry at Solebury, 171, 174. Division line between Philadelphia and, 177-8. Thomas

Watson, charges against, 233. Ferry over Neshaminy Creek, 233, 235. Bill proposed and Commissioners named for building a new Court house and prison for, Governor's objections to, 241. Frankford bridge, 246. Thomas Biles, Sheriff and Jno. Woolston, Coroner, 210, 289, 332, 370, 387. Indian disturbances near Durham Iron Works, 329. T. Smith, Sheriff, 332, 387. Sheriffs, 416, 464, 520, 574. Coroners, 416, 465, 520, 574. Road petitioned for from Great Swamp; Commissioners appointed, 542. Return of, 584–587. Road to Macousic, 590. Coroner, 614. Sheriff, 614. Petition, respecting Court of Chancery; its history, 617. Petition against Court of Chancery, iv., 37. Sheriffs elected, 85, 247, 309, 352, 470, 500, 601, 669, 748, 782. Coroners elected, 85, 247, 309, 352, 601, 669, 748, 782. Lawrence Growden appointed by special commission Justice, 141. Special commissions for in, in consequence of sickness of Dr. Græme, 244. Wm. Bodie of, charged with counterfeiting bills of credit, 273. Examination of Robert Savery, 274. Justices appointed, 312, 482, 782. Coroners, 469, 500. Justices appointed, v., 3, 113, 388, 573. Road from Frankford to Bristol, 29. Sheriffs elected, 55, 120, 345, 411, 464, 550, 597, 662. Coroners elected, 55, 120, 345, 411, 464, 550, 597, 662. Road from Philadelphia to Bristol, 59, 61. Officers elected by associators, 193, 247, 325, 326. Commissions to, 209. French prisoners ordered to Newtown jail from privateer Trembleur, 264. Escort for, 267. Complaint against Sheriff at election; not sustained, 345. New county out of, 619. Members of Council appointed, v., 213. Justices, 320, 374. Amount of Poor tax, 462. Road from Dunk's ferry to Philadelphia, 498, 502, 510. Case of Edward Antill, 512. The town of Buckingham (Bristol) to be laid out as a market town, 513. Road to, 514. Sheriffs elected, vi., 144, 638. Coroners elected, 144, 638. Sheriffs elected, vii., 266. Coroners elected, 266, Justices appointed, 437. Negroes convicted and pardoned, viii., 58. Coroners appointed, 223, 403, 506, 781. Sheriffs appointed, 223, 403, 506, 781. Wagons furnished by, 376. Justices appointed, 576. Courts, ix., 22, 23, 663. Coroners elected, 57, 199, 285, 333, 398, 547, 623, 688, 778. Sheriffs elected, 57, 199, 285, 333, 398, 547, 623, 688, 778. An interior county, 138. Justices appointed, 205, 235, 583, 663, 672. Indians commit outrages on lands of Peter Tuck, 385, 388. Furnaces and forges, in 1750, 632–636. L. Growden dies and is succeeded by Wm. Hicks, 663. Road, 703. County road line between Philadelphia, 745, 750, 760. Records, preservation of, x., 23, 42. Sheriffs elected, 56, 101, 211, 270. Coroners elected, 56, 101, 211, 270. Justices, 47, 88, 162. Lottery in, 26, 41. Pigeon Swamp, 26, 41. Dogs, damage by, 32, 42. Convictions, executions and reprieves, 172, 225. Division of county, 224, 226. Associators of, 362. Coal mine to be sought for in, 428. Call of Committee on important business, 452. Committee to meet, 464. Powder in, 471. Saltpetre, knapsacks, 474. Firelocks, 537, 554. Troops to be ready, 647. Declaration of Independence to be read, 635. Arms, 638. Election suppressed, 764. To be ready at moment's warning, 781. Troops ordered from, xi., 43, 44, 55. House of Isaac Hicks searched; books, papers, records, &c.; magazine at Newtown to be cleared for the books, &c., 127. Sheriffs, 179, 372, 378, 596. Coroners, 179, 217, 372, 378, 596. Register, 187. Prothonotary, 187. Clerk of Orphans' Court, 194. Dedimus, 194. Justices, 248, 251, 282, 372. Joseph Hart, Councillor, 249. Committee for driving off cattle increased, 253. Lieutenants, 259. Discharge of soldiers, 266. Militia to be sent

down, 275. Troops now in barracks to guard neighborhood of city, 302. To guard prisoners to Reading, 302. Militia, 360. Justices, 379. Pay Master of, 390, 508. Goods seized by Colonels Smith and Keichlein, 392. John Kerr appointed to receive and collect clothing, instead of General Lacey, Brigadier General, 411. Lieutenant, 452. Goods found in swamp seized, 462. Robbery of G. Vansant, of Middletown, 512. Reward for robbers in, 518, Clothing purchased, 541. Agents, 556. B. Walton confined, 565. Militia, 626. Militia called out, 636. Justices, 708. Record of a road, 764. Jno. Hart receives subscriptions to Loan Office, xii., 47. Forfeited estates in, 73, 77. Militia called out, 129. Elections, 136, 510. Sheriffs, 136, 510. Coroners, 136, 510. Representatives, Assessors, Commiss'rs, Councillor, 136. Estate of Gilbert Hicks sold, 156. J. Galloway's estate, 104, 191, 256, 268. Hooper's trial, 250. Military officers appointed, 298. Commissioners of purchases, 301. Sale of Jno. Jones' estate, 350. Edward Jones, R. Swanwick, 381. Phineas Paxton, Tory, prohibited from keeping public house, 401, 403. Wm. Scott, Pay Master, 461. Appointments, 554. Justice Long resigns, 557. Pardon of J. Baldwin, 571. Andrew Allen's estate, 615. Auditors, 646. Estate of Daniel Williams, 671. Election of military officers, 720. Estate of Peter Perlie sold, 733. Wm. Thomas, 734. Complaint of Captain Joseph against Colonel Joseph Hart, 737. Recruits at Newtown to be provided for, xiii., 8. Militia to rendezvous at ,53. Informality in election of Lieutenant; money for supplies, 83. Elections, 86, 719. Justices, 454. Sheriff, 86, 391, 720. Censors, 719. Coroner, 86, 391, 720. Pay to militia, 90. Estate of John Meredith, 94. Treasury robbed, proclamation, 95. Justice Long resigns, 98. Robbery of Collector Barton; depositions, 139. D. Reeder convicted of misdemeanor at Court, 180. Estates of John Reid and Owen Roberts sold, 180, 183, 204. Evan Thomas, John Overholz, 204. Deed to Eben Carson for part of Tinicum, Jos. Paxson's estate, 236, 256, 266. J. Reid, 277. Robberies in, 338, 339. Militia called out, 369. Execution, 394. John Tomlinson apprehended, 431. Agents for forfeited estates, 441. A. Bartram's estate 498. Robberies, 515, 532. Israel Doan, 516. A. Long, 524. Accounts of Colonel Joseph Hart; damages from enemy, 574. Estate, S. Byles, 599. Banditti, 600. Proceedings against Doans, Dillon, &c.; depositions, 616. Estate, Joseph Doan, 623. Robberies by the Doans; depositions and proclamation, 630, 687. John Clark resigns as Justice, 732. Colonel F. Murray, Lieutenant, 746. Estate of Alexander Bartram, 748. Officers' lands in, 753. Justices, xiv., 139, 147, 197, 198, 200, 203, 212, 270, 313. Dedimus to administer oaths, 153. Contested election for Justices, 197, 207. To send fifty men to Wyoming, 215, 555. Elections, 237, 555. Sheriffs, 237, 555. Reports, 237, 555. Coroners, 237, 555. Council, 237, 555. Contested election decided by appointment of George Weickart as Justice, 270. Valentine Nelson's estate, 307. Militia, 374. Counterfeits, 383. Case of Aaron Doan, 178, 384, 385, 386, 387, 388, 392, 395. Of Solomon Vicars, 364, 393. Message to Assembly respecting, 395. Inspector of flour, 488. Murder and arson by John McDonald; inquest and proclamation, 489. J. Galloway's estate, 494. Robbery of Treasury; prisoner brought to Philadelphia, 516. Militia, 596. Excise Collector, 596. Attorney General to defend a suit for land late of John Overholtz, 657. Deed for land in, estate of E. Thomas, xv., 14. Justices, 30, 32, 104, 131, 437, 441, 644, 645. Elections, 98, 296. Representatives, 98, 296. Sher-

iffs, 98, 296, 566. Coroners, 98, 296, 566. Resignation of Justice and Collector of Excise; William Harvey chosen, 104. Thomas Wright assaults J. Thomas, 255, 256. Claim for land supposed of Peter Perlee, 260. Prothonotary, James Benezet, resigns, 269. Samuel Benezet appointed, 271. Burgesses of Bristol, 272. Councillors, 296. James Hanna, Register, &c., 406. Mrs. Elizabeth Baxter, receives pension, 322, 413. Sale of R. Robertson's estate postponed, xvi., 35. Receipts from tavern licenses, 83. Justices, 70, 105, 145, 153, 289. Sheriff, 192, 490. Coroner, 192, 490. Henry Wynkoop resigns as Judge and Justice, 105. Contested election, 129. Election of President Court Quarter Sessions; J. Barclay appointed, 133. Accounts of Collector of Excise, 136. Irregular election in, 142, 151, 153. Fees for defence of title in, 153. Estate of D. Kennedy, supposed escheat, 174. Report on contested election in, 200. Wm. Harvey, Collector of Excise, 271. Taxes; J. Chapman, Treasurer, 286. Patent for land to Martha Biles, 309, 320, 390. Repairs of arms, 400. Pensions, 412. Lieutenant-Colonel, Valentine Eckart, 418. Militia under General Lacey in, 457.

Budd, John, story of West Jersey Indians, i., 449.

Budd, Levi, xii., 112.

Budden, James, deed for part of Tinicum, xii., 256.

Budden, Captain William, and sons to be exchanged for Lieutenant Ball of Roebuck, x., 563, or Midshipman Draper, 595, 596.

Bull, Colonel John, to appoint guards for powder-magazine, x., 420; his battalion, 423, 436, to march for Canada—articles for, 454; second Lieutenant of, 457; Chaplain appointed, 458; pikes, 653; examine condition of associators, 673, 674; wagons, 675; superintendant, 737, at Norrington, 784; Store at Norrington, xi., 6, 48; commands at Billingsport, 125, 142; officers complain against, 210; to procure teams, &c., 246; arms should be packed, 399; account of work done at Red Bank and Billingsport, 399; services dispensed with as Adjutant-General, 400; employed to direct the works at Billingsport and Mud Island—his pay, 575; rations, 636, 637; to make repairs at Fort Island, 725, 728, 777; to secure plank, &c., at Sullivan's Bridge, 709; to have boats, 717; paid, 743, 757; pay to, xii., 13, 66; claim of McGinley, 83, 105; pay to, 180; commissioner of purchases, 301, 372, 403; paid for expense of dispatches from Wyoming, xv., 276; purchases a negro, part of Ed. Stiles' confiscated property, 277.

Bull, John, a Moravian Missionary, pass to, xiii., 570.

Bull, William, Governor of South Carolina, letter respecting peace with Indian tribes, ix., 775.

"Bull-Dog," Gunboat, x., 290, 291, 353, 506; Lieutenant Webb, 643.

"Bull-Dog," Galley, xi., 510.

Bulla, Thomas, to be seized as inimical, xi., 344.

Bullock, Joseph, Warden, xiv., 150.

Bullocks, price of, xii., 385.

Bull's-head, Philadelphia, ii., 134, 491.

Bunner, Andrew, owns privateer, xi., 543.

Bunner, Jacob, a Captain, x., 634.

Bunthurst, (al. Bunter) convicted of murder, xi., 608; sentenced, 609.

Buott, Pont Du, captured and described, vi., 447.

Buoys, proposed in the Delaware River, i., 82, 204, 205; iii., 493.

Burd, Edward, Prothonotary Supreme Court, xi., 566; petition to be continued prothonotary of Supreme Court, xiv., 628; is appointed, 629; prothonotary of Court paid their expenses, xv., 226; xvi., 17.

Burd, Major, Letters to and from, vii., 436, 453, 619, 622, 734, 736, 772; to furnish supplies, 550.

Burd, Fort, xvi., 223[2].

Burd, Colonel James, Commissioner to cut road westward, vi., 317,

318, 377, 403; letters to and from, 377, 433, 435, 436, 466, 485; for escorts, 435, 436; on road, 466; on Braddock's defeat, vi., 499; letter from Wm. Trent on murders on Patterson's Creek, 641; letter on blowing up Fort Du Quesne, viii., 234; commissioner with J. Davenport to receive Ind'n prisoners, 776, 777; sent with Thomas McKee, under instructions, to Wyoming, ix., 29; appointed Commissioner to Wyoming, 59.

Burd, John, xi., 493, 773.

Burgesses elected, xv., 83, 273, 463.

Burglars convicted by Supreme Court, v., 155; one reprieved, 163.

Burglary, iii., 109, 110.

Burinol—commands, viii., 311.

"Burk," Gunboat, x., 351, 585.

Burk, Lawrence, sells English child to French at Fort Niagara, reasons for—his character, viii., 147.

Burkhard, Captain Daniel, x., 634, 649.

Burley, Henry, xii., 53.

Burlington, N. J., a general meeting at., ii., 253; ferry to Bristol, 488; road to—return of, iii., 218; Indian conference at, viii., 156; called an "Island," 177; prisoners sent from, to York Town, by order of Congress, 645.

Burney, Thomas, ordered to Philadelphia to be examined, v., 600; a counterfeiter, xii., 89, 272; a notorious counterfeiter apprehended, 267.

Burns, James, Justice, xiii., 647.

Burns, Larry, a soldier in Pennsylvania line, arrested for stealing—excuses himself, xii., 275, 276; released, 276.

"Burnt Cabins," road to, xv., 121, 322, 371, 395.

Burrall, Jonathan, commissioner to settle accounts of Commissary department, xiv., 28.

Burrows, John, petition for release, iii., 81.

Burt, John, Indian trader, concerned in murder, by Indians of Thomas Wright, iii., 285, 313, 326.

Bush, David, Justice of New Castle Company, complained of, by meeting of sufferings, vii., 405, 559.

Bush, Captain George Bush, xi., 488.

Bush, Henry, Sheriff, xv., 640.

Bush, Major Solomon, appointed Deputy Adjutant-General, xi., 240; petition, interesting recital of his services, &c., xii., 140; deputy Adjutant, referred to Board of War, as Lieutenant-Colnel, 151.

Bush-Hill, (Philadelphia,) Indian conference at, viii., 667.

Bushy Run, murders by Indians, xi., 718.

Busse, Captain Christian, at Augusta and Fort Hunter, vii., 302; a great want of clothes, 302.

Busse, Captain Jacob, of Northampton, petition of, and other Captains, and resolutions of Council, xii., 141.

Bustead, Morgan, to cast heavy cannon, 412, 438, 439, 462; his furnace to be examined by Captain Loxley, 622; his air furnace taken, 641.

Butler, Anthony, appointed Quarter-Master, xi., 279.

Butler, Mr.—to be furnished with boats for wounded, xi., 303.

Butler, Colonel, xi., 493.

Butler, Charles, petition against David Lloyd, i., 383, 386.

Butler, Lord, sheriff, xv., 193, 300, 577; xvi., 17; Councillor, 204.

Butler, Colonel Richard, recommends officers, xii., 10; return of his regiment, 37; recommends ensign, 37; xiii., 418; letters and papers delivered by officers to Congress, 608; Lieutenant of Allegheny county, xv., 551; Commissioner with Gen. Gibson on Erie triangle, 554; and others propose purchase of lots opposite Pittsburg, 598; goods for Indians, 604, 618; Commissioner for purchase from Indians triangle on Lake Erie, xvi., 36; paid, 95; value of lots in reserved tract, opposite Pittsburg, 45, 176; Lieutenant of Allegheny county, requisition for men, 422; report on, 424; elected to Assembly, 537.

Butler, Simon, Coroner, vi., 638.

Butler, Walter, letter from, v., 624.

Butler, William, ferry on depreciated lands, opposite to, and other privileges, xv., 42.
Butler, Zebulon, terms on delivery of Fort at Wyoming, by Amos Ogden, ix., 677; order for arrest, 682; circulates advertisements—proclamation of Governor Penn against, x., 153; committed, xiii., 760; Lieutenant of Luzerne county, xv., 264; xvi., 29; Letter from, on division of militia, 317.
Buttons for soldiers to be made out of lead and tin, xi., 440.
Buyers, John, Justice, xii., 491.
Byers, John, Member of Congress, xiii., 120, 152.
Byrd, Colonel, of Virginia, fears of Assembly respecting his appointment to succeed Forbes, viii., 297.

C.

Cable, Abraham, Justice, xi., 716. Justice, xv., 241.
Cackawatchky, a Shawnese Chief, present to, v., 351, 530.
Cadaraghqui, fort at, v., 549. French building a ship at, 547. French building a fort at, vi., 10.
Cadenhead, John, memorial respecting goods, &c., xiii, 760, 764.
Cadwalader, General, xiv., 634.
Cadwalader, Colonel John, member of Committee of Safety, to procure patterns of muskets, &c., x., 282. To inspect ordnance, &c., 283. Committee to wait on, 754. To command a brigade, xi., 27. Brigadier General, 62. Appointed Second Brigadier General, 199.
Cadwalader, Lambert, recommended as Lieutenant-Colonel, x., 444. 445. Receives muskets, 548. Made Colonel, 767; respecting, xi., 110, 114, 131, 494.
Cadwalader, Robert, recommended to Congress as a Colonel, x., 443.
Cadwalader, Dr. Thomas, member of Council, vi., 666. To examine Surgeons, x., 452, 458.
Cage, a, ordered to be built in Philadelphia, i., 92. Claim for building, ii., 26.
Caghnawaga Indians, v., 643.
Cahectodo, a French Interpreter, iii. 439.
Caldwell, Andrew, appointed Commander-in-Chief of the Navy of Pennsylvania, x., 255. Commodore of fleet, 459, 480. To call together officer of boats, 489, 651. Resigns as Commodore, 581, 587. Member of Council of Safety, xi., 45. Appointed member of Navy Board, 122. A Warden, 538; xiii., 100. Deed to, xii., 326.
Caldwell, Charles, apprehended, ii., 488.
Caldwell, James, Sheriff, ix., 689, 778.
Caldwell, Robert, taken prisoner at Mount Washington; exchanged; appointed Captain of marines on ship, General Greene, xi., 751, 758.
Caldwell, Samuel, to purchase shoes, hats, &c., x., 402, 408. Buys a part of Hog Island, xiii., 281, 325, 328. Appointed Collector of tonnage duty, xv., 417, 435. Claim to Hog Island, 481. Collector of Tonnage; certificate to, xvi., 114.
Calhoun, Captain George, xi., 2. Appointed Lieutenant, xii., 16.
Calico, printing by Jno. Hewson, encouraged by Council, xvi., 85. payments, 116, 254.
Callahan, David, discharged, x., 465.
Callender, William, resigns as member of Assembly, vii., 148. Asks to examine minutes, 394–397.
Callender, Captain, ix., 269.
Callender, Colonel, x., 737.
Callender, Robert, letter to Baynton, Wharton & Co.; intended mischief to their goods, ix., 302.
Calumet pipe, meaning of ceremony with, v., 313.
Calvert, Benedict, of Maryland, disputes and riots, iii., 484.
Calvert, Colonel, Governor of Maryland, iii., 180. Letter from Governor Keith to, 180–222, 224.
Camden, armed boat, x., 351, 506, 689.
Cameron, Allen, and Dr. Conolly and servants, imprisoned in Philadelphia, x., 445. In room with General McDonald, 595.
Campbell, an Episcopal clergyman of dissolute character, writes

Brutus and Cassius, on throwing off subjection to powers of Governor, iii.. 369.
Campbell, Charles, Sub-Lieutenant, xi., 618. Commissioner to lay out a road, xv., 191.
Campbell, Captain Duncan, of ship stranded on New Jersey; orders respecting, x., 386.
Campbell, Francis, letter, on Indian affairs, vi., 699. Appointed Indian agent at Fort Augusta, viii., 99. Declines, 128.
Campbell, George, member of Council of Safety, xi., 45. Prothonotary for Philadelphia county, 190. Declines taking oath, 195. Register of Wills, xiii., 253.
Campbell, James, goes to Steele's fort, vi., 675.
Campbell, Captain James, of man-of-war Nightingale, for men, viii., 290.
Campbell, James, Ensign, xii., 8.
Campbell, John, Braddock's defeat, vi., 481.
Campbell, Mary, pass for, xi., 597.
Campbell, Michael, pension to his children, xv., 430.
Campbell, Thomas, Captain, xi., 17, 740. Of company of Rangers, xii., 16, 65.
Canachquasy, Indian, v., 166.
Canada, proposed expedition from New York, ii., 449. Queen's letter respecting, 449. Governor of, name given to him by Indians, iv., 732. Expedition against, v., 127, 130, 132, 134, 140–145, 148, 152, 159, 168, 296, 553. Letter from Governor Clinton to Governor of, 553, 554. Governor Vaudievil, letter of General Abercrombie to, on capitulation of Fort William Henry, viii., 141, 504. Col. Boquinville, 505. Falls into hands of English by peace treaty of 1763; proclamation by Governor Penn, ix., 80. Colonel Bull to march for, x., 454, 480, 483.
Cannasatego, Indian chief—speech to Delawares about lands, iv., 579. Dies and is buried, v., 467.
Canasatagy, the chief town of the Senecas, viii., 118.
Canasoragy, an Indian town, vi., 444.
Candles, price of, xii., 175.
Caniadarogon, an Indian, v., 84.
Cann, James, appointed Register of Newcastle, i., 121.
Cann, John, member of Council, i., 369.
Cannon requested from England, Massachusetts and New York, v., 173. Answer from Governor Clinton, 189. Governor Shirley, 198. From Cape Breton, 203. From Governor Clinton, 205. Governor Shirley, 206. Admiral Knowles, 207. Furnished by Governor Clinton, 215. To be asked of Governor Trelawney, 228. Received, 231. Placed on batteries, 249, 250. Cost of, x., 373. Committee on, 548. Heavy, to be cast by persons named, 412, 462, 500. Timber for carriages, 470. Brass, B. Loxley's proposition, 627. Brass, xi., 5, 6, 7, 20. Arrived in prize vessels, 20. To be cast, 73.
Cannon, John, appointed Sub-Lieutenant of Washington county, xii., 681.
Cannon, Capt. Newton, of a schooner from West Indies, petition to sell cargo, xii., 11. Depositions and proceedings, 12, 13.
Canowarookary, an Indian village, viii., 118.
Canteens ordered, x., 628.
Canterbury Township, Kent county, formed, i., 556.
Cantwell, Edmund, Sheriff of Newcastle county, i., 57. Member of first Council, 65.
Cape Breton, expedition against, from New England, iv., 753, 754, 762. Commander of, written to for cannon, v., 203.
Cape de Verd Islands, deposition respecting Gov. of, &c., iv., 289, 296.
Cape May, wrecked goods arrive from; proceedings, iii., 238.
Capitulation, articles of, at Fort Necessity to Captain Villier, vi., 52. Articles of, at Blockhouse, Wyoming, ix., 771.
Captains recommended to or by Congress, x., 634. Appointed, xi., 2, 4, 17, 18, 20, 21, 32, 37, 62, 74, 578, 740. Chosen, xii., 2, 88, 89, 338, 374, 662; xiii., 160, 275; xiv., 181.

Carberry, Captain, case of, xii., 348.
Carberry, Henry, Captain in Pennsylvania line, to be arrested, xiii., 616. Trial, xiv., 105, 106, 240.
Carey, Matthew, & Co., paid for newspapers, xv., 25, 139.
Carey, Nathan, Sheriff, xv., 193. Coroner, 300, 577.
Cariljas, Don Francisco, Governor of Monte Cristo, respecting privateers, viii., 235.
Carleton, General, letter to, xiii., 680.
Carlisle, great distance from Philadelphia, v., 657. Commissioners appointed to hold conference with Indians at, 665, 684, 719. Distances to Shanoppens town, 750. Suffering from Indians, vi., 675. Fort at, 732. Indian conference at, 776, 778–784. Conference with Indians at, vii., 1–6. Colonel Stanwix at, 714. Barracks at, 737. Post through, to Winchester, to be continued, viii., 71. Barracks complained of, 71. Fort at, 224. Murder of Doctor John, &c., at, 455. Proclamation respecting, 456. Colonel Bouquet at, ix., 35. Order of General Gage for troops at, 118. Letter of Governor Penn to Captain William Murray at, for troops to Lancaster, 127. Lottery for Episcopal church in, 243, 325. Frederick Stump in gaol at, 438. Ordered from, to Philadelphia, 441. Rescue of Stump, 448. Convictions, 513, 632. Lottery for Steele's church, 622. Conviction and execution, 743. Prisoners at, x., 688. Dr. John Kearsley removed to, 773. Return of election of Burgesses, &c.—expenses of stores to, xiii., 575. Election for Chief Burgess and other officers, xv., 216. Burgess of, 463. Gazette paid for printing, 518. Entitled to a third Justice, 520.
Carlisle, Abraham, transcript of record of Court of Oyer and Terminer, xi., 600. Order for execution, 606. Petition to delay execution till meeting of Assembly, 607, 613. Of his wife, 613. Condemned, 614. Costs in case of, xii., 36. Estate in Philadelphia sold to R. Bethell, xii., 687; xiii., 6.
Carlisle, Alexander, is rewarded for arresting two persons, xiv., 666. Pardoned for extortion, xv., 33.
Carnaghan, John, Sheriff, x., 212, 273. Deposition, 235.
Carondowana, alias Robert Hunter (an Indian), marries Mrs. Montour, a French woman, iii., 295, 337.
Carothers, Col., Lieutenant, request to resign; not accepted, xii., 4. Resignation accepted, 94. Letter from, 100, 721.
Carothers, John, Lieut.-Colonel, xi., 272, 444, 489, 491. Intelligence of Indian murders in Cumberland, 489, 506, 520, 538. Return of militia, 772. Resigns, xii., 93, 721.
Carpenter, Sub-Lieutenant, resigns, xii., 395.
Carpenter, Emanuel, Justice, xiii., 290. Resigns, xiv., 563.
Carpenter, Lieutenant John, appointed, x., 678.
Carpenter, Joshua, a Justice, i., 382.
Carpenter, Samuel, has execution against Society of Free Traders, i., 146, 149. Succeeds Claypoole in Council, 210. With others proposes to set up a bank, 236. Appointed by W. Penn, assistant to Governor Markham, 475. Appointed Treasurer, 576. Member of new Council, 580. Proposes to settle claims for Blue Anchor Landing, and take Walnut street wharf, ii., 19. Asks allowance for taking Babbit, 55. Affirmed, 96. Provincial Treasurer, 122. Produces his accounts, 153. Goes to New Castle about powder money, 351. Treasurer, 530.
Carpenters' Hall, militia to meet at, to protect Congress from insult, xiii., 664. Rooms spoken of for public offices, xvi., 486.
Carr, Jno., Sheriff, xii., 510; xiii., 87.
Carriages, for majesty's service hire, vii., 433. 443. Hire of, in majesty's service, viii., 171, 333, 342, 344, 373, 397, 549. Bill proposed for regulating hire of, 66.
Carrough and Fullerton, build and launch boat "Effingham," x., 314.
Carson, Andrew, pilot, xiv., 49, 53, 68, 69, 183.

Carson, Ebenezer, deed to, at Tinicum, xiii., 236, 623.
Carson, James, bond to J. Molesworth, xiii., 385.
Carson, John, Indian trader, arrives at Fort Augusta, vii., 773.
Carson, John, of Carlisle, to attend to repairs of muskets, xi., 739.
Carson, John, letters to and from, xii., 8, 16. Clothes for a wounded officer, 318.
Carson, Lieutenant, arrives with prize to the ship General Greene; mast required, xii., 19.
Carson, Joseph, Paymaster succeeded, xi., 23, 27. To appraise an armed boat, 670. Paid for goods seized in Bucks, 392, 397, 413, 462, 476. Asks for cannon, 636, 696. Deed for part of Tinicum, xii., 256. Fine remitted, 506. Deed to, for land on Hollander's Creek, xiii., 52. In N. L., 126.
Carson, Samuel, Lieutenant, xi., 751. Applies for clothing, xii., 687.
Carter, Christopher, taken into custody, x., 360. May be visited in jail, 371. Released on bond, 372. Friends may visit, 397. To be released, on leaving the country, 455.
Carter, Henry, traitor, xii., 273.
Carter, James, to superintend making firelocks, x., 650.
Carter, John, appointed Regulator of Weights and Measures, iii., 372.
Carter, William, Sheriff of Philadelphia county, i., 195. Term expires, 211.
Carthagena, letter from Commandant, respecting citizens returned from thence, xvi., 381.
Cartledge, John, informs about disturbances at Conestogoe, iii., 15. Interprets, 45. His accounts for treaty with Indians, 81. Sent with wampum to Conestogoe Indians, 114. Suspected of Indian murder, 146, 148-156, 157. Left off as Justice, 157. Committed to Sheriff till legally discharged, 162. Admitted to habeas corpus, 162. Delivered to magistrates for trial, 165. Message respecting, 167. Petition for trial, 186. Indians ask for his pardon, 189, 200. Trial deferred, 191.
Cartledge, Edmund, suspected of murdering an Indian, iii., 146, 148-156. Petition; bailed, 156. Committed to Sheriff till legally discharged, 162. Habeas corpus, 162. Delivered to magistrates, 165, 167. Petition for trial, 187. Trial deferred, 191. Pardon asked for by Indians, 189, 200.
Cartridges, certificate, x., 577. Weight of powder to ball, 587. Sizes of muskets, 588. Paper for, 701. To have buckshot in, 626.
Cartridge paper, x., 701.
Cartwright, Richard, on bounds of Connecticut, 1664, vi., 263.
Casdrop, Major, to have bridge over Schuylkill removed to the Delaware, &c., xi., 298, 305. Called into service; Richard Dennis to supply his place at Schuylkill, 310. To replace bridge at, 536.
Cash, Caleb, Coroner, ix., 57, 199, 286, 333, 398, 547, 623, 689, 777; x., 56. Dies, 78.
Caswell, Governor of North Carolina, letter on refugee, xii., 314. Letter on Convention, xv., 159.
Catawba Indians, murder of, iii., 21. Aid in settling peace between Virginia and, requested, iv., 755. Complaint against North Indians by South Carolina, v., 346. Unfriendly — wampum returned in consequence by other Indians, 402. At Fort Loudoun, viii., 111.
Cathcart, John, asks relief, respecting goods sold him by Sheriff, iii., 241.
Catholics, Roman, letter from Justices of Berks Co. respecting, vi., 503, 533.
Cattle, only one half of stock to be killed, ii., 27. Certain days, between which none to be killed, 27. To be driven from shores of river, xi., 4, 266, 281, 310. Stock to be preserved and fed; proclamation, 429.
Cauffmann, Joseph, refused right to hold land, being a Roman Catholic, 596.
Cavenaugh, William, Notary Public, xiv., 287.
Caves, in Philadelphia, dwellers in, ordered before Council, i., 160.

Letter from Governor Penn, respecting, 163, William Frampton petitions for removal, from before his door, 167, 199. To be cleared by a certain day, 201.

Cayuga Indians, Scaienties, a noted man among, at Chamber's Mill, v., 83. Indians in Philadelphia, x., 255.

Cecil, Charles, claim for city lots, xv., 379, 387, 436, 459, 480, 481.

Celeron, Captain, a French officer on the Ohio — extraordinary letters from, v., 425. Speech to Indians, 530. Leaden plates on Ohio, 634.

Censors elected, xiii., 673, 719, 720, 721, 722, 723, 726, 729, 730. F. A. Muhlenberg, President, 744.

Censors, council of, F. A. Muhlenberg, President, receives his pay, xiv., 2, 8. S. Davidson, 140. W. Irvine, 160. St. Clair, 163. A Wayne, 166. Pay for, 170, 176, 184. Doorkeeper paid, 196, 203, 210, 212. Pay to, 213, 229, 231. Report of, 335.

Census, United States, xvi., 401.

Cesna, Charles, xiii., 298. Complaints against, 509. To be prosecuted for forgery and perjury, xiii., 683. His sureties, letter of Thos. Smith on, xiv., 29. Fees paid in case of, 266.

Cesna, John, Coroner, x., 101, 212. Sheriff, xii., 147, 547 ; xiii., 134. Expenses as, xvi.

Cesna, Major, xi., 123. Sheriff, 363. Takes arms from individuals, xii., 575.

Chalkley, Thomas, iii., 246.

Challenge, Captain Young confined for giving a, xii., 62, 67.

Chaloner, John, Commissary—report purchase of flour by agent of Maryland, xi., 767. Deputy Commissary of purchases, xii., 253. Deed for part of Tinicum, 256. Appointed auctioneer for N. L., xvi., 315, 316. Auctioneer at Philadelphia, receipts for duties on sales, 500.

Chamberlain, Edward, appointed Master at Arms, &c. Resigns, x., 512.

Chamberlain, Maj. James, appointed Wagon Master, xii., 393.

Chamberlaine, Samuel, appointed to run line between Maryland and Pennsylvania, iv., 313.

Chamberlain, Peter, road to, i., 387.

Chambers, Benjamin, appointed to keep order in public houses, i., 74. As High Sheriff, to summon juries, 86. Appointed a Sub-Treasurer for Philadelphia county, 111. Debt against, 152. Petition, 189, 190. For a road to Bucks county, 298. Petition for Arch street bridge and Front, 330. Water Bailiff, 342. Complains of two Swedes ministers setting up a boat at Schuylkill ferry, ii., 137. Case of Rudman and Sandal, 147, 149, 150. President of Free Society of Traders, 154, 163. Invents a boat, 258. Objects to other ferries, 258. Attacked by Swedes, 477. Petition about ferry, 525. Intelligence about Great Cove, &c., vi., 675.

Chambers, Colonel, xii., 8.

Chambers, James, applies to be Prothonotary, xiii., 324.

Chambers, Joseph, at house at Paxton, memorandum of message to Indians, v., 84, 87.

Chambers' mill at Paxton, Indians at, v., 83.

Chambers, Lieutenant John, account, xiii., 702.

Chambers, Stephen, present at riot at J. Wilson's, gives bail, xii., 137. Censor, xiii., 722.

Chambers, Thomas, appointed Ensign, xiii., 215.

Chambly and St. John, forts, prisoners taken at, released on parole, x., 410.

Chambou, Monsieur Du, commands Fort Du Buott, vi., 447.

Chancellor, William, xvi., 456.

Chancery Courts proposed, iii., 91, 105. Assembly and Council recommend Governor Keith to hold, 105. Members of Council to sit on bench with Governor, 106. Proclamation for holding at Philadelphia, 106. Held by Governor Gordon, 266. Persons appointed to draw up rules, 266. Petitions respecting—history of, 617. ; iv., 19, 21, 22, 27, 32, 33, 34, 35, 36, 37, 38, 40–46.

Chandler, Rev. Dr. Thomas B., letter to, x., 359.
Chaplains to Battalions, x., 452, 457, 550.
Chapman, Abraham, Commissioner for building new court-house and prison for Bucks county, iii., 241.
Chapman, Benjamin, Sheriff, vi., 638; vii., 266.
Chapman, John, Coroner, v., 55. Justice, xi., 708; xv., 30. Resigns, 104.
Chapman, Joseph, Coroner, iv., 669, 748, 782.
Chapman, Samuel, imprisoned, xii., 540.
Charles, Robert, appointed clerk of Council at suggestion of Governor Gordon, iii., 257. Minutes to be under inspection of James Logan, iii., 257. Commissioner to Maryland, 544. Appointed agent with Benjamin Franklin to England, viii., 512. Agent in England, ix., 10.
Charles II., King, death of, i., 132.
Charleston, S. C., yellow fever at, vessels from, examined and stopped at Mud Island, xii., 457, 483.
Charlestown — exchanged prisoners arrive in Philadelphia in distress and are provided for, xiii., 1.
Charter — number of members to stand, i., 71. To be enrolled, 71. Read, signed, sealed and delivered, and old one returned with hearty thanks, 72. Of liberty, 111. Amended, 111. Members to be elected according to charter, 324, 577.
Charter for Bristol, iii., 102.
Charter of Pennsylvania, i., 17. New preferred to old, 63. Alterations proposed, 68. To be transcribed, 68. Committee to draw up, 69, 70. Under great seal, 276.
Charter of Philadelphia, signed, ii., 61. Version respecting Justices being Aldermen, 66. Bill for confirmation proposed, 153.
Charter of Privileges read, ii., 46. Of property, also of Philadelphia, read, 53. Signed, 56. Copy of it, 56–60. Sent for, by Council, 103. Bill for confirming, 155, 156, 157, 158, 170, 171, 172.
Charter of Property read, ii., 54. A, prepared by D. Lloyd, 61. Signed under conditions, 62. Instrument asked for and sent to Assembly, 109, 110, 157, 199, 252.
Charter of Liberty to be kept by Master of Rolls, i., 111. For Philadelphia to be drawn up, 117. Old charter taken, 573. Old and new, 573, 580. Out of settlement, 597.
Chartier's Island, in Ohio, sale of ordered, xvi., 284,
Chartier, Peter, accepts a commission under French, iv., 757, 759. Fears from, v., 1. Goes over to French, 167. Seduces Ind'ns, 311.
Chartier, Martin, sent on message to Indians, ii., 390. Complaint, 403. Indian interpreter, iii., 22.
Chastenoy, Monsieur, Lieutenant-General of Leeward Islands, relative to English prisoners taken by French privateer, and also some free negroes, v., 71, 122. Letter to, with Spanish prisoners, 131. Reported capture of a French ship from, 347.
"Chatham," galley—man paid for loss of arm, xi., 464. Lieutenants Meyers and McClaner, 576. Captain Roach, 578.
"Chatham," gunboat, x., 305.
Chatham, John, Coroner, xiii., 398.
Chatham, Lieutenant John, of a boat, x., 339.
Cheaver, Peter, an Indian trader, iii., 501.
Cheltenham, road to Philadelphia, i., 379, 384, 387. Petition about road, ii., 549.
Chenastry, on Susquehanna, iii., 295.
Cheny, Colonel Thomas, sub-Lieutenant of Chester, xi., 321, 507.
Cherokees, oppose the French, vii., 31. Conference with, 552. Chiefs answer, 558. Message from, 528, 599, 600, 603. Arrive destitute at Fort Loudoun, viii.; Sir J. St. Clair's opinion of them, 77. He and Mr. Hockly refuse supplies, 77. March from Fort Loudoun, 111. Engaged to aid in defence, 112. Arrive from Virginia, 126. Deputy attacked wlth pleurisy, 128. Message of, to Delawares, 135. Sick recovers, 141.

Chestnut Hill, action at, xiv., 637.
Chester Co., Sheriff of, i., 58, 174. Seal for, ordered; its device, 66. Sub-Treasurer appointed for, 111. Division line between Philadelphia and, 126, 154, 265, 266. Refusal to survey lands in, 151, 153. Deputy Surveyor of, 151, 154, 193. A Justice complained of, 157. Request of clerk, 182. Members of Council, 196, 213. Complaint against Sheriff, 200. Which of the members to attend Council, 234. Welsh Tract, 263–265, 266. Petition to extend it, 263. Deposition of John Blunston, 264. Thomas Usher, 264. Election disputed, 268. Taxes for New Castle to be paid in, till division is made. 311. Justices, 320, 374. J. Blunston, member of Council, 331. Resigns, 333. Successor elected, and declines, 335. Sheriff, 368. Petition to divide, from New Castle co., 379, 388. Jn. Bristow, Ranger of, called to account for a marked horse, 438. Amount of one penny tax, 462. Trial of a vessel seized, to be in, 475. Petition for a ferry at the rock, 478. Bridge over Chester creek, 522, 526. Sale of old Court house, 525. Petition, Ann Baynton, 536. Bridge over Chester creek, 525, 624. Andrew Job, Sheriff, ii., 22. Roads, 33. Commission for a Court to be held extra, 105. Jno. Hoskins, Sheriff, 105, 397. Taxes, 150. Road, 239. Wm. Davis, a Justice, removed, 561. Trial for murder, 612, 613, 616, 629. Justices, iii., 28, 50. Sheriffs, 31, 56, 69, 108, 140, 260, 332. Coroners, 31, 56, 69, 108, 140, 260, 332. Petition of murderers, 41. Justices complain of grievances in commissions to Justices; action of Council on, 57. Township of New Garden, 91. Rocks and mountains between, and Philadelphia, 111. Petition for a division between Philadelphia and, 111. Uninhabited and unsettled lands in, 142. Petition for roads, 142. Difficulties in paying taxes for want of division line; Secretary's report on original proprietary line, and action and decision of Council, 144, 158. Line of 1688 referred to, 159. Papers of Record in hands of Pat Robinson's widow, 159. Search for evidence of division line, 160. To pay expenses of messenger to Maryland, 175. Petition for respite of Mary Woolvin, 186, 193. And for Wm. Hill, 189, 193. Wm. Battin, to be hung in chains, 193. Isaac Taylor, Surveyor, and Elisha Gatchell, made prisoners by Maryland, 212, 214. Road to Swede's Ford, 225, 230. Road near Thomas Moore's mill, 227. Confirmed, 231. Complains of encroachments and grievances from New Castle county, 234, 236. Division line, 234. Old Court house and prison to be sold, 235. Justices, 256. Jno. Taylor, Sheriff, Jno. Mendenhall, Coroner, 260, 289. Road through Pequea, 263. Commissioners appointed, 263. Send Justices left out, James James, commissioned, 282. John Burt, an Indian trader from, 286. Daniel Williamson, a member of Assembly, dies, 228. Conviction for murder of Indians in, 327. R. Parke, Coroner, 332. Jno. Taylor, Sheriff, 332. Proposes a division of the county; inconveniently large; no jail at, 343. Reference to Assembly, 344. Division agreed to, and persons appointed to it, 345. And lines, 345. Complaint from Governor of Maryland, 347. Division; Lancaster county taken from it, 355. Sheriff and Coroner, 370, 387. Regulator of Weights and Measures appointed, 372. New Justices to be elected, in lieu of those declined, 381. John Karnanghan, a Justice, 412. Sheriffs, 416, 464, 520, 574. Coroners, 416, 464, 520, 574. Bridge to be built over Cobb's creek, 426, 428. Persons to build; their report, 431. History of division line, 470. Justices, 531, 533. Sheriffs, 614. Coroner, 614. Petition, respecting Court of Chancery; its history, 617. Petition against Court of Chancery, iv., 37. Sheriffs, 86, 247, 309, 352, 469, 500, 602,

669, 748, 782. Coroners, 86, 247, 309, 352, 469, 500, 601, 669, 748, 782. Difficulties with Maryland; numerous documents, 101–151. Road from Lancaster to Coventry Iron Works, on French creek, 152, 266. Road from Susquehanna; laid out, 181. Case of Elisha Gatchell attached by persons from Maryland, 227. Justices, 259, 312, 481, 482. Roads, 278, 282, 284, 495, 503. Juror set aside for declining to take affirmation, 482. Standard weights and measures purchased by; Regulator appointed, 507. Justices appointed, v., 3, 387, 547, 572. Sheriffs elected, 55, 120, 345, 411, 464, 550, 597, 662. Coroners elected, 55, 120, 345, 411, 464, 550, 597, 662. Complaint against Justice Ruston, 78, 95, 378. Road to Cobb's creek, &c. complained of by George Gray, 99, 100, 202. Officers chosen by companies of Associators, 185, 186, 247. Commissions to, 209, 325. Sheriff complained of by Governor Ogle, case of Samuel England, 376, 382. Justices Ruston and Emmet complained of by inhabitants; proceedings respecting them; Presbyterians involved, 378. New county out of, 619. Act respecting Inspectors, 619. Sheriffs elected, vi., 144, 638. Coroners elected, 144, 638. Law for chosing Inspectors, 623, 624. Danger from Indians, 670. A large number of persons coming from, to compel Governor and Assembly to pass certain laws, 729. Sheriffs elected, vii., 266. Coroners elected, 266. Complaint of Justice Ashbridge, 406. Justices elected, 417. Mordecai Moore, C. Burgess, 417. Number of Roman Catholics in, 448. Address of Assembly against William Moore, Justice, to Governor, 741. Proceedings, 776. Coroners appointed, viii., 223, 403, 506, 781. Sheriffs appointed, 223, 403, 506, 781. Case of William Moore, Justice of, 1, 11, 17, 162, 282, 287. Wagons furnished by, 376. Respecting choice of Inspectors, 400. Trial and execution of John Lewis, 496. Justices, 573. Dams, &c., 683. Banks, dams, &c., ix., 24. Coroners elected, 57, 199, 285, 333, 398, 547, 623, 689, 777. Sheriffs elected, 57, 199, 285, 333, 398, 547, 623, 689, 777, Justices appointed, 205, 673, 750. Conviction, 235. Execution, 236, 545, 678. Lottery for Episcopal churches in, 243. Writ for election of new member of Assembly, in room of John Fairlamb, deceased, 301. New member of Assembly, in room of John Morton, 375. Sheriff to receive Stump and his servant from Lancaster, and send them to Philadelphia, 442. Act for embankments, 470, 472, 576, 658. John Fairlamb dies, 550. Division of, 556, 563–579, 729. Road to Philadelphia, 623, 627, 692. Forges and furnaces in 1750, 632–636. Special Court, for trial of a negro in, for rape, 648. Embankments, x., 26, 42. Estate of Samuel Phipps, &c., 40, 42. Sheriffs elected, 56, 100, 211, 270. Coroners elected, 56, 100, 211, 270. Justices; convictions; executions, &c, 43, 65, 94, 92, 265, 268. "Chester County man" demands money from J. Galloway, 44. Alleged error in road to Lancaster, 65, 69. Estate of Wm. Martin, 72. Complaint against Sheriff, &c., for not aiding custom house officer in seizing a vessel, 230. Decision of Governor, that the jurisdiction of the county does not extend into the river, 232. Estate John Taylor, 259, 261. Proclamation for murderer of John Faughnar, 269. Colonel Wayne of, 288. Manufacture of arms in, 356. Letter to Committee to be prepared, 507. Powder for, 526. Battalion ordered from Chester, 605. Troops to be ready, 627. Declaration of Independence to be published, 635, 677, 753. Election contrary to Convention; Sheriff Vernon arraigned, 742. Prothonotary, xi., 188. Register and Recorder of Deeds, 190. Prothonotary 197, 230, 244. Justices, 198, 251, 274, 759. Recorder to be

written to respecting papers, 216. Artillery company applies for cannon, 219. Lieutenants, 229, 257, 318. Paymaster, 230. Records detained from Prothonotary, C. Davis; John Evans, Judge Supreme Court, 270. Militia sent to, from Philadelphia, 275. Wagons to be impressed; militia called out, 302, 318. Committee to collect blankets, 328. Militia, 360. John Temple seized and imprisoned, 362. Pay to horsemen, 387. Case of Charles Dingee, 402. Purchase of provisions in, 423. Paymaster, Beaton, 444. Complaint against, for bringing to Philadelphia, provisions, 445. Traitors in, 496. Militia, 497. Murder of William Hammon, and proclamation, 446. Flag at, 591. Ravages of enemy in; expenses of prisoners; guard to aid in collecting militia fines in, 507. Justices, 541. Disputed election of representatives, 621, 622, 623. Claim and payment of reward for arrest of James Fitzpatrick, a noted robber, 616, Sheriff, 624. Commissioners and Assessors' election illegal, 662. Elections, 729, 760, 772. Militia officers chosen, xii., 2. Justices, 15, 285. W. Clingham receives subscriptions to Loan Office, 47. Militia called out, 129. Councillor, 131, 148. Justices, 752. Assembly, 131, 512. Sheriff, 131, 151, 512. Coroners, 131, 151, 512. Militia; resolution respecting, 142. Election of D. Gardner confirmed, 146. Estate of Christian Wilson, 246. Military officers appointed, 298. Commissioner of purchases, 301. Murder of Wm. Boyd in, by Jno. and Robert Smith; reward offered by State, 349. Paid, 362. Military election, 379. Militia duty, 456. Estate David Dawson, 463. Justices and Treasurer resign, 526. Appointments, 554. Pay for soldiers, 600. Auditors, 647. Agents not to receive money for sales at Hogg Island, xiii., 14. False returns of election, 43. Militia called out, 53. Sales of confiscated estates, 56, 57. Elections, 87, 392, 722. Sheriffs, 87, 392, 722. Censors, 722. Coroners, 87, 392, 722. Justices, 633. John Hannum as Justice resigns, 105, and Agent, 106. Robbery of collectors, 129. Depositions, 139. Justices, 140. Wm. Armstrong's estate, 182. Justices, 219, 316. Estate of Wm. Maddock, 251. Military officers elected, 282. Robberies in, 338. British goods seized, 482, 525, 526, 563. Robberies, proclamations, 339, 533. Isaac Pyle pardoned, 577. Justices, xiv., 138, 217, 226, 228, 567. Prothonotary, complaint against, 204, 209. Election, 238, 555. Sheriffs, 238, 555. Represen'ives, 238, 558. Coroner, 238, 555. Commissioner, 238, 555. Execution ordered, 240. Contested election, 260. Collector of excise, 445. Adam Grubb, flour inspector, 487. Lieutenant, 486. Appeal of Lieut. Thomas Levis, 522. Militia, 584. Execution of Eliz. Wilson ordered, 586. Postponed, 591. Execution of Robert Elliott ordered, 622. Pardoned, 635. Abuses and irregularities, 647. Lieut'nt R. Smith removed, 650. Restored as Lieut. of County—further proceedings, 658, 660, 661, 664, 665, 666, 670. Sales of confiscated lands ordered of A. Matthias, Aspden, &c., 663. Successor to R. Smith, 666. Chas. Dilworth appointed, 670. Pardon of several persons, 671. P. Frazer, Recorder and Register, xv., 4; and Justice, 38. Sale of P. Bulla's property postponed, 6. F. & W. Armstrong's do., 9. Orders for executions of McDonough and Shirtliffe, the latter to be reprieved under the gallows, 31. Militia, 32, 37, 40, 98, 105. Justices, 38, 39, 41, 96, 359, 450. Sale of R. Young's property postponed, 61. Contested election, 62, 131. Deed for late estate of M. Aspden in, 72. Sheriffs, 98, 296, 566. Coroner, 98, 296, 566. Sale of estate of Peter Bell postponed, 120. Petition of tax collectors; Capt. David Hayes's Co., 141. Treas.'s acc't, 179. Contested elections, 182. J. McClelland, County Lieutenant, in room of C. Dilworth, resigned,

197. Account of D. Cloyd, Treasurer of, for taxes, &c., 227. Captain Rudolph's company, 261. Negro of John Bell, fine remitted, 267. Election set aside, 326. Fines, 327, 328, 413. Reduced, 371. Complaints against Cabel Davis, prothonotary, 404, 405, 406, 410. Petition of Quakers to Council respecting militia fines and order of Council on it, 418. Contested election, 450. R. Willing, councillor, 566. Justices, xvi., 6, 38, 52, 88, 96, 200, 433. Militia, 8, 18, 251. Accounts in, 30, 34. Sureties for prothonotary, 31. Contested election, 38. Children of John L. Shumann called on to pursue a claim in Germany, 49. Accounts of John Christie, collector of excise, 50. Amount of tavern and marriage licenses, 61. Contested election, 68. Confirmed, 88. Tavern licenses, 166. Opinion of Attorney-General in regard to Justices and Judges, on division of the county, 187. Sheriff, 190, 232, 492. Coroner, 190, 232, 492. Part erected into new county-surety increased, 194. Report on contested election—it is confirmed and Justice R. Cooper elected, 200. Doctr. Thomas Ruston claims his seat in Council over Colonel R. Willing—decision, 202. Tavern licenses, 272. Excise received by J. Christie, 355. Militia battalion of Colonel John McDowell, 372. Tavern and marriage licenses, 380. Repairs of arms, 416. Militia officers elected, 419. Pay of Captain David Crosby's company, 424. Andrew Boyd, wagon-master, 533.

Chester, town or borough, complaint of Robert Wade against authorities for laying out a street and wharf on his property, i., 440, 477. Bridge over Chester creek, 522, 526, 624. D. Lloyd's lots in the green—claim of Church, 556. Petition and order respecting fairs, ii., 40. Proposed act to confirm to Ralph Fishbourn the old court-house of, 218. Asks to be a free port, 546. Act proposed to sell old court-house and prison in, iii., 233. Passed, 235. Not room for troops at, x., 540. Colonel Moses Moore, Colonel R. Thomas of county, arms to, 672.

Cheston, Daniel, runs off with Governor's negroes from Cape de Verde—proceedings against him, iv., 289. Released on bail, 296.

Chevalier, James, clerk in Register's office, xvi., 445.

Chevaux-de-frise to be sunk opposite the Fort, x., 334. Committee to attend to it, 334. Certain persons only to act as pilots, 372, 376. Logs for a third tier, 390. To be connected by chains, 399. Commissioners to buy logs, 404. More to be sunk, 404. Views of committee on defending, 474. A. Donaldson to launch at Gloucester—John Coburn to take them to their places near Fort Island, 513; and Captain Rice, 514, 616. Sunk at Fort Island to be examined, 519. Boom to be sunk, 525. Two more, 535. What vessels may pass, 540. Pay of men at, 556, 567, 598. To be sunk—Robert Smith, 603, 606, 645. Pilots through, 611. Workmen, 636. Timber for, 645. Piers—Captain Whyte, 648, 650, 682, 700. J. Coburn, 722. S. Morris, 753. Vessels to be inspected, 779. To raise, 781. No vessels to pass, xi., 4, 25. Samuel Wheeler works at, 5. Relating to, 60. Under charge of Navy Board, 122. Pilots not subject to fine, 233. To be discharged, 281. A. Donaldson, 558. New ones ordered, 725. Building by Francis McClester, 752. Removal of, xiii., 637. On Jersey shore to be sold, 590, 671. Proposal De Bartine and G., 739. Removal, xiv., 58, 73, 78, 104, 153, 200, 241, 501.

Chew, Benjamin, appointed Attorney-General, vi., 277. Commissioner to Lancaster, vii., 93, 96. Goes to Easton with Governor, vii., 204. Speaker of Assembly at Newcastle, 295. To draw up message to Assembly, 433, 441, 442, 716. Attorney-General Supreme Court, viii., 66. Gives opinion on registers for Dutch

vessels, 155. Testimony respecting land office, 338, 342. Report, 345. Opinion on rights of aliens, 355. Second report on warrants, 361. Protests against Governor on bill for commission, viii., 357. Objections to bill on warrants, 361. Attorney-General asks for fees—Governor's message, 666. To draw for money granted by Parliament, ix., 2, 4. Appointed Chief Justice of Supreme Court, x., 173. Chief Justice, Register-General of Wills, &c., and one of Governor's Council, prisoner, to be removed by Congress—refuses signing parole, xi., 264. Escort for, 265, 266. Rev. Dr. Ewing apologizes for, and declares his willingness to sign the parole, 267. Papers of Land Office to be demanded of, xiii., 434. Deposition, xiv., 463. Charter returned to, 513. Agent for Proprietaries, xiv., 624.

Chew, John, a Justice, x., 9.

Chew, Richard, x., 694.

Chew, Sam'l, M. D., befriends Wm. Rumsey, of Maryland, iii., 591. Sam. Chew, a Justice, x., 9. Third Justice of Supreme Court, 108.

Chichester, weekly market and fair, i., 558. Petition for a fair and market; established, ii., 12. Lottery for Episcopal Ch. in, ix., 243.

Chickasalary, John, (Indian) at Augusta, desires a conference with C. Weiser, viii., 458.

Chief Justice appointed, Jeremiah Langhorne, in room J. Logan, iv., 348. Death of, 640; v., 433. Appointed, xi., 186, 195, 202, 249, 254. McKean opinion on characters of prisoners, xii., 75. McKean re-appointed, xiv., 167.

Chillaway, Job, (Indian), complains of being cheated in a horse, viii., 489.

China Factory, xii., 204.

China, ship Brothers, Captain Josiah, sails—under sea letter from Council—for, xvi., 224[2].

Cheverie, Captain De, to be arrested, v., 168.

Chorley, Joseph, ferry at, i., 514.

Chovet, Dr., gives certificate in favor S. Fisher, xii., 221.

Christ Church, Philadelphia, vestry to be informed of proposed bill to alienate lands, ii., 222. Certificate of Robert Jenny, rector &c., of Governor's having taken Sacrament, vii., 741. Bells rung, for peace between France and Spain, ix., 42. In compliment to Governor John Penn, 72. Representation from Wardens, &c. respecting Rev. Mr. Comb, xi., 296, 300. Bells rung on capture of Cornwallis; pay to ringers, xiii., 143. Joseph Dolby receives pay for, 423, 559, 563. Bells rung on La Fayette's arrival, xiv., 176. On anniversary of Independence, 494. Pay for ringing bells of, 4th July, xv., 60. On proclamation of President and Vice President, 121, 344, 363, 597. Bells rung, xvi., 224[2], 410.

Christ, Henry, Sheriff, viii., 780. Respecting Reading, xii., 780. Justice, xiv., 170.

Christ, John, Register and Recorder, xvi., 143.

Christian Religion, religious worship restricted to the, ii., 220.

Christiana, fort at, reinforced by Marylanders, i., 188.

Christiana, Fort, Virginia, murder of Catawba Indians at, iii., 21.

Christie, Captain, vii., 714.

Christie, Dr. David, buys city lots, xvi., 95.

Christie, John, Second Lieutenant, x., 488.

Christy, William, releases prisoners from jail, x., 227.

Church of England complains against law about marriages, ii., 26, 48. On alienation of lands, 222. Clergy to be protected, William Penn, Jr. being a member, iii., 64. Proportion of, to Quakers in Council observed, 143. Frequent absence of, 143. Equal on Supreme Court, 158. Petition of Wardens of Christ Church respecting Keithian meeting house, 394.

Churches in City; troops to be quartered in, if not provided for elsewhere, x., 673.

Civility, or Tagodrancy, Indian Chief, ii., 553, 565. In Philadelphia, 566. Indian Chief, iii., 15.

At Philadelphia conference, 45, 163. Meeting of Governors and Indians at his cabin, 121, Visit of Governor to, and presents, 302. Loses child, 332. At Philadelphia, 361.

Clapham, Colonel William, on cessation of Indian hostilities, vii., 117. Letters to and from, 155, 157, 161. Conferences with Indians, 157. Answer of Governor Morris to Indians, 158.

Clarke, George, Coroner, xv., 589; xvi., 210, 495, 516.

Clark, James, Coroner, iv., 602.

Clarke, John, Sheriff, x., 270. Resigns as Justice of Bucks, xiii., 732.

Clark, Samuel, Coroner, xvi., 212, 514, 537.

Clark, Thomas, a lawyer, opinion on bill for Courts, ii., 254.

Clark, Thomas, a traitor, to be arrested, xi., 539, 542.

Clarke, William, member of First Council, i., 57. Has leave of absence, 78. A Judge, 324, 331. Complaint, 339. Collector of Customs; seizes goods, 450. Member of new Council, 580. A provincial Judge, ii., 87. Takes affirmation, 96. Member of Council, 117. Complaint against claims of boundary between Maryland and Pennsylvania, 362. Applies to be measure sealer, v., 280; x., 688, 699, 735; xi., 496, 508; xii., 31.

Clarkson, Matthew, Justice and Notary; may take acknowledgements, ix., 760. A Justice, x., 48. Quarter-master, 314. Appointed by Committee of Safety Marshal of Court of Admiralty, 538. To superintend troops going to Trenton in shallops with oars, xi., 24. Petition, 176. To be Marshal, 576, 657, 760. Case of sloop Active, 657. Marshal memorial, xii., 105. Obstructed by a merchant; advice, 105, 155, 316, 351. On currency, 353. Marshal answer to memorial, 482. Complaints against, 523, 531. Exonerated but superceded, 533. And case of F. Hopkinson, 579, 584. Late Marshal; to pay forfeited money to Treasurer, xiii., 341. Manager of State Lottery, xiv., 286, 652. Marshal; accounts called for, xv., 397.

Clarkson, Major Matthew, A. D. C., letter from, respecting Miss Levy, xi., 676. Summoned before C. denies their right, 677. Aid to General Arnold, 709.

Clause, Daniel, letters to and from, vi., 181, 292. Lives with Hendrick, the Mohawk Chief, 182. Letter on Lydius' deed, 249. To Onondago, 291. At Albany, 293. Conference with Indians at Colonel Johnson's, 468–475. Statement of designs of French and Indians, vii., 43. Letters to and from, 155.

Claypoole, James, answers to execution against the Society of Free Traders; appeal to England, i., 146, 149. Appointed Judge, 153, 156. Applies to be Register General, 185. Complaint against Clerk of County Court, 190. Appointed Register General, 195. Member of Council, 196. Dies, 208. His successor, 210. Seal to be delivered as clerk, 250. D. Lloyd refused to deliver papers, 256, 265, 333, 341. Division of estate, 341, 537. Clerk of New Castle; to deliver up records, ii., 97. Applies to be Sheriff of Philadelphia county, xi., 217. Appointed, 223, 502, 511, 512. Sheriff, 595, 599, 614.

Claypoole, John, Appointed Sheriff of Philadelphia county, i., 211. Not to continue in office as others, 321. Collector of monies, 384. Fees, 388. Seizes goods from Marshal, 543. Complaint against, 555. Sheriff, complaint against, ii., 21.

Claypoole, John, upholsterer, xv., 598.

Clayton, Ashur, deposition respecting Wyoming, ix., 767.

Clayton, John, Jr., Sheriff, v., 597, 662.

Clayton, John, invents a machine for threshing wheat, ix., 698.

Clayton, William, claim for building the Cage in Philadelphia, ii., 26.

Clement, Jacob, patent for land, xvi., 220[2].

Clerk of a Court cannot act as attorney in it, i., 170.
Clerke, Colonel William, Paymaster, xi., 272.
Clerkship, errors of, how amended, i., 461.
Clifford, Thomas, messenger of Council, obtains aid from counties, i., 212. Door-keeper to Council, 298.
Clift, Benjamin, i., 435.
Clifton, William, asks for money to search for coal in Bucks county, x., 427.
Cline, Sergeant, asks to be promoted, xi., 774.
Clingan, William, Justice, xv., 41.
Clingham, William, Member of Congress, xi., 385; xii., 47.
Clinton, Governor George, of New York, letter on position of French and Indians, iv., 772. Letter on French and Indian affairs, v., 30. To furnish account of payments to troops, &c., 131. Letter to and from, for information, 133, 135, 164. Cannon requested from, 173. Letter to and from, 178 to 189, 205, 215, 265, 284, 297, 305, 462. Address of Assembly to, 465. Letter, 495, 517, 548, 553. Letter to Governor of Canada, 553. To Governor H., 553. Answer to, 554. Letters, 573, 575, 607, 625, 639, 642. Proceedings of Council at Fort George, 640–667. Very ill, 647. Provision by the State for officers, xii., 305. Letter on boundary, xiv., 457. Letter, &c., respecting rioters in Luzerne county, xv., 497. Ratification of Constitution by New York, 506. Asked for letters of John Franklin, 571. Amendments of Constitution, xvi., 103.
Clothes, law proposed for two sorts only, one for winter and one for summer, i., 93.
Clothier, State, app'd, xii., 56, 87.
Clothing, v., 53, 56. To be purchased by an agent, x., 538. Applications for, xi., 772. Receiver-General of, 407, 588, 591; xii., 92, 94, 174, 267, 622.
Cloughan, William, Justice, xi., 759.
Clowes, John, Coroner, iii., 416. Justice, ix., 203. Dies, 581.
Clowes, Peter, Coroner, iv., 500, 602. Sheriff, v., 411.
Club, Mrs. Margaret, pass for, xiii., 567.
Cluggage, Captain of Rangers, xii., 32.
Cluggage, Robert, Justice, xiii., 367. Resigns, 748.
Cluggage, Thomas, Captain, xi., 740.
Clunie, James, Sheriff, xv., 570; xvi., 195, 498, 499.
Clunn, Captain John, to be arrested, convicted and imprisoned for treason, xii., 199. Conspiracy with enemy from Elizabethtown, 206. Discharged, 207. Trunks delivered to Gov. of New Jersey, 224.
Clymer, Daniel, present at riot at J. Wilson's—surrenders and gives bail, xii., 128. Deeds to, 323, 348. Applies to be naval officer, xiii., 735.
Clymer, George, Continental Treasurer, to have battery built, x., 401. Appointed Commissioner, xv., 5.
Clymer, William, member of Assembly from Philadelphia, deceased, v., 516.
Coal to be taken up out of the river, x., 421. To be purchased, 422. Thrown into river, 423. Quantity, 423. Quantity in Philadelphia, 425. Brought from Virginia, 707. Ordered from Jamaica, 428. Mine searched for in Bucks county, 428.
Coart, Rev. Mr., letter to—murders by Indians, vi., 658.
Coates, Dr. John, commands boat, xi., 2; xii., 142.
Coates, William, appointed Lieut. Colonel, xi., 31. Lieutenant of County Philadelphia, 207, 221, 257, 258, 261, 275, 318, 390. A prisoner, 419. Prisoner on parole—exchange, xii., 51. Assembly, 131. To muster militia, 220. Appointed Lieutenant, 298. Memorial respecting pay of men, xiii., 503; xv., 13, 373. Paid, 209. Justice, 520.
Cobeas, Lieutenant John—recruits, xi., 424.
Cobey, John, Second Lieutenant, x., 457.
Coblehill, Indian disabled at, x., 435.

Cobb's creek, near Darby, the first dividing line between Chester county and Philadelphia county, iii., 144. Bridge to be built over, 426, 428, 431. Road to, very ancient, in use before grant of Province, v., 100, 202.

Coburn, John, to take chevaux-de-frise from Gloucester, near Fort Island, x., 513, 539. Pay for sinking chevaux-de-frise, 567, 598, 645, 648, 672, 682, 722.

Coburn, Thomas, pay for attending flag at Chester, xi., 590.

Cochran, Captain, company to be paid, xi., 15, 424.

Cochran, William, Sub-Lieutenant, xi., 379.

Cock, Captain Lasse, asks leave of absence to attend to Society's business, i., 65. Member of first Council, 57. Offers to take up arms—proposes visit to Indians, 334. Interpreter, 435.

Cock, Lawrence, a councillor, i., 365.

Codorus river, fisheries in, ix., 719, 720.

Cœur, Jean, a French officer on Ohio, sent to Ohio for Indians, v., 462. Leaden plate stolen from, 508. Speech, 531.

Coffin, Stephen, deposition respecting his being made prisoner by French and Indians on Ohio, vi., 9.

Cohen, Benjamin, Attorney-General and member of Council, vi., 666.

Cohen, Solomon Myers, deed for city lot, xiii., 598.

Cohongoruton, Indian name for Potowmac river, iv., 719.

Coin, too much taken to East Jersey to pay cattle, ii., 27. Rates at which foreign, are to pass proclaimed, 179. Exportation of, 529. Gold and silver, value of, iv., 357, 358, 361–2.

Coiners, two convicted, vii., 725.

Colden, Alexander, Deputy Postmaster in New York, v., 647.

Colden, Governor Cad'r, of New York—letters to and from, ix., 113, 120. Protection of Indians refused, 121. Minutes of New York Council, 121. Administers oath to Governor Penn, 630. Indian trade, 656.

Cole, Colonel Philip, x., 744, 746; xi., 83.

Coleman, William, appointed third Judge, viii., 77, 481. Committee on warrants, 342. Report, 345. Reference of warrants to, 342, 361. Judge, 481, 592. Judge of Supreme Court, ix., 393.

Collectors of customs, ii., 121, 123, 127; xiv., 52.

Collectors of excise, xiv., 445, 573, 620.

College, Academy and Charity Sch'ls of Philadelphia, condition and usefulness—act for suppressing lotteries and plays levelled against them—vindication—statistics, &c., viii., 339. Imprisonment of Provost Smith, 443. Charter for, 40. Commencement postponed, xii., 43, 98. [See University.]

College at Princeton, pay for damage done to, by militia, xiii., 64.

Collier, James, Captain, xi., 750.

Collier, Joseph, makes saltpetre, x., 480.

Collier, Richard, Quartermaster, x., 480.

Collings, Robert, commands privateer, xi., 3.

Collins, Thomas, Sheriff, ix., 199, 286, 333.

Colonels—recommended to Congress as, x., 442. Appointed, 443. Lieutenant, 444. Appointed, 445. xi., 31: xii., 71.

Colonial Records, respecting publication, i., 9–16. Message of Governor Johnston recommending publication of, iv., 1. Report of Committee of Senate, 1. Act proposed, providing for, 8. Report of select committee of House of Representat'es recommending, 10. Act passed by Assembly for, 14.

Colonies, petition from, &c., x., 238, 248, 250, 251.

Colony vessel, estimate of equipment of a, v., 272.

Colt, Arnold, Collector of Excise, xvi., 308,

Colville, Lord, Commander of fleet in North America, asks for seamen, vii., 772, 775. Of naval forces in America, ix., 299.

Commerce, donation by Assembly to encourage, xiv., 51.

Commercial Convention, xv., 82. Letter and papers from Fench Coxe, Commissioner to, 86. Expenses paid, 250.
Commissary's office in Philadelphia, x., 698; xi., 448.
Commissary of provisions, x., 510.
Commission of provincial Judges, i., 121. Of Collector of Customs, 148. To Markham, Goodson and Ellis, 205. For successor to Blackwell, 315. For Benjamin Fletcher, as Governor, 345–364. For officers of Customs, 534–539. For trials, &c., ii., 112, 123. Style of, iii., 256. For Justices, 28. Style of, 62, 175. To military officers in the counties, v., 209. To Colonel Taylor to command battery, 251. To Abraham Wiltbank, 266. To Captain Sibbald, 267. Military, vi., 754. Colonel James Burd and Josiah Davenport, to receive prisoners from Indians, viii., 776. To James Searle, xii., 414, 418.
Commissioner to receive public aid, i., 111. To purchase lands from Indians, 156. To regulate Water Courses appointed, ii., 23. Report, 24. Under dedimus to administer oaths, 62, 92.
Commissioners of property, their commission and names, ii., 61.
Commissioners for Indian Affairs at Albany; proposal, iii., 82.
Commissioners on line with Maryland, iii., 464, 497, 544. Report and oath, 544.
Commissioners to treaty at Albany report, v., 27, 36, 296, 299. Instructions to, 300. At Lancaster, report of, 306.
Commissioners to run line between Maryland and Pennsylvania, iv., 313, 329.
Commissioners for laying out a road from Philadelphia through several counties to Easton, v., 577, 610. To hold conference with Indians at Carlisle, 658. Report of, 664.
Commissioners, provincial letter to, vi., 744.
Commissioners to Albany, vi., 25. Their commission, 47. Of wagons, 775,
Commissioners to Indians, B. Franklin, J. Mifflin, J. Fox, E. Morgan and J. Hughes; Letter from; meet Council; examination of several persons, vii., 153. Letter to Governor, 773.
Commissioners, provincial, letter to, respecting quarters for troops, vii., 380. And answer, 380. Applied to by Governor; their answer, 383. To Governor, 498, 636, 657, 671, 694, 733. Governor to, 671, 672. Governor complains of, viii., 64, 66.
Commissioners appointed to remove settlers from Indian lands, ix., 481. Instructions, 483. Letter, Governor John Penn to, 237. Names of, 237, 240. Answer to circular, 240. For making road from Lancaster to Philadelphia appointed, 657.
Commissioners to settle accounts of militia and flying camp of Berks county; and instructions, xi., 146.
Commissioners, under Act of Attainder; their names, and instructions, xi., 479.
Commissioners elected, xii., 134 136, 506; xiii., 719–723.
Commissioners of purchases, Appointed, xii., 301, 302. List of, 302, 305, 306. More pay, 362, 370, 371, 372, 393, 405, 406, 434, 660. xiii., 7, 18. Controversy between S. Lyons and Major Smith, 222.
Commissioners, xiv., 230, 256, 490, 504, 555, 602. Of taxes for Philadelphia, 4, 9, 151. For settling account of Commissary's department, 28, 386. For treaty with Indians, 40, 45, 51, 72, 186, 205, 452, 514, 518, 658. On boundary with Virginia, 56, 59, 60. Their pay, 60, 69, 74, 211, 286. Report, 288, 518. To examine Susquehanna river, 182. To proceed to Wyoming; on claims, 202, 204, 235. Of streets, 230. Roads, 442. On islands in Delaware, 345, 460, 505. On northern and western line, 363, 380, 385, 399, 445, 454, 460, 507, 514, 655.
Commissioners for improving Susquehanna river, xiv., 485.
Commissioners appointed, xv., 2, 5. Northern boundary, 12, 16, 22,

190, 212, 340, 356, 382, 464. North-western boundary, 16, 19, 38, 39. Man killed while in service, 285. Laying out road from Millers' Spring to Pittsburg, 13. To Wyoming, 22. To examine River Delaware, 19. For inland navigation, 60, 135. For islands in Delaware river, 65. To lay out road between Juniata and Conemaugh, 191. On claims in Luzerne county, 214, 217, 237, 453, 470, 471, 472. To Wyoming, 314. Between New York and Pennsylvania, report it finished, 340, 356, 554. To lay out roads in Northampton and Luzerne, 425. To view Jones' lane, 448.

Commissioners for ascertaining claims of settlers at Wyoming, xvi., 16. To ascertain quantity and quality of land at and near Wyoming, 22. To purchase triangle at Lake Erie Report, 36. On boundary line of Huntingdon county, 46. For Indian affairs, 63, 178. To view Delaware, Schuylkill, Susquehanna and Juniata, 178. Instructions to, 181. J. Sellers resigns; B. Rittenhouse appointed, 194. Instructions to, 208, 347. Letter from, 222[2], 260, 279. Pay, 384, 462, 513. To examine Quittapahilla and Swatara and other rivers, 315. T. Matlack, J. Adlum and Samuel Maclay; also F. Antes, R. Howell and William Dean, 319. Pay, 321. Instructions, 337. Order to, 347, 407, 429, 525, 544, 547. On road to Pittsburgh, report, 466–476, 530.

Committee of Inspection and Observation, x., 497; 645.

Committee of Safety, minutes of, x., 279–652. And regulations, 283. Resolutions of Assembly; Associators; Commissioners and Assessors; minute men; fire-locks; saltpetre; names of Committee of Safety; duties, 280. Bills of credit; signers—amounts; Treasurer; tax sinking bills, &c., 281. Benjamin Franklin, president, William Govett, clerk; patterns of muskets to be provided Colonel John Cadwalader and S. Moore; committee to procure powder and saltpetre, 282. Model of a pike to be procured, 283, 284. Committee visit Red Bank and Mud fort and examine river; they deem it impracticable to lay a boom across, 283. Committee for construction of boats, &c.; one for inspecting ordnance, &c., 283. Commissary of stores, 284. Plan for building a boat or calevat, 284. Various committees appointed, 282, 284, 289. Thanks to author of a plan, 284. Order on Captain Loxley for guns, &c., 285. Plan for stopping the channel rewarded, 286. Members of Continental Congress paid, 286. Ground to be viewed, for a proposed battery, 286. Grape shot to be procured, 286. Boats to be built, and carpenters, &c. to be employed, 287. Inhabitants of New Jersey to be asked for aid in defence of river, 287. Military guard to be appointed at State House; commanders appointed for boats; New Jersey will furnish logs, &c. for obstructing channel, 287. Minute men, and arms for boats, 287 Committee to borrow money provincial Treasurer, 286. Medicines for use of hospitals, 288. Offer to take charge of powder, 288. Keeper of stores and cannon, 288. Account of logs from New Jersey, 289. Names of boats, 287, 290, 296. Account of logs furnished by New Jersey, 289. Committee to inquire respecting damaged gunpowder and saltpetre at Long Island, 289, 291. Teams to be furnished New Jersey, 289. Workmen for fire arms to be procured, 289. Joel Ferree makes guns at Lancaster, 290. To attend the launch of the "Bull Dog," 290, 291. Names of commanders of boats, 287, 290, 296. Model presented of a boat, 291. List of medicines; orders for, 292. Plan of Captain John McPherson's for defence of this country; thanks to, 292. Resolutions of Congress, recommending active measures, 292. Advertisement in consequence, 294. Committee report Hog Island rather than Billings-

port for the "frames," 294. "A "rowing wheel" invented, 295. Borrow money from Wardens, 295, 296, 297. Form of a commission for officers of military association, 295. Model of a boat, 296. Guard for powder in new jail at night and on Sundays, 296. Cannon balls to be purchased, 297. Memorial from committee of city, &c., 297. Committee appointed to draw up rules and regulations for associators, 297. Dr. Franklin applies for powder for General Schuyler, 300. Robert Towers, keeper of Magazine, 300. Military associations of York, Cumberland, &c. apply for pattern guns, &c., 300. Inquire what quantity of lead may be had in city; can find only five hundred weight, 300. Three ministerial officers arrive from Cork, 302. Captain William Bradford to take them in custody and bring them before the, 302. Proceedings against them, as coming to enlist with General Gage in Boston; required to sign an instrument of writing that they will not serve against the Colonies, 303. List of packages of goods arrived with them for use of the army under General Gage; proceedings against them, 304, 305, 306. Articles of association, 308–312, 315. Recommendations as to rank, 315–321. Various committees, 328. Order a seal, with device and motto, 328. Chevaux-de-frise to be sunk opposite fort, 334. Committee to see it done, 334. Regulation of pilots, 337, Watch at the Capes, 356. Buoys to be taken up; cannon lent to Lewes, 338. Comm'tee to examine knapsacks, &c.; resolution of Congress respecting Major Rogers, 342. Funds sent to counties for arms and ammunition, 346. Cartridges reduced, 347. Memorial to Assembly on state of affairs, 348. Estimate of monies, 350. Arms called in, 351. Lewes and Pilot Town to be supplied with ammunition, 352. Offer of carbines by Congress accepted, 354. Warrant, &c. for Jno. Ross, 355. And Jno. M. Nesbitt, 356. Report of arms, being made, 356. Resolution of Congress for arrest of dangerous persons going at large, 357. Proceedings; papers and persons arrested, &c., 358, 360. Order to jailor, 359. Carpenters to be employed to make floats for machines for Fort Island, 360. Lend Congress powder, 361. Agree upon a list of military stores, 362. Order pilots for chevaux-de-frise, 363. Send powder to Northampton, 363. Wm. Allen presents cannon shot; thanks to, 364. Instructions to Peter Long as ship-husband, 364. Resolve of Congress to raise a battalion for general defence, 365. Firelocks and bayonets to be collected, 366. Hospital requested for use of sick, 366. Granted gratis except for venereal patients, 366. Cases of Dr. Kearsley and Brooks laid before Congress, 367. Accommodations provided at Fort Island, 367. Instructions for armed boats, 368. For defence at Fort Island, 368. Hulk to be sunk in river, 368. May erect works on Province Island, 371. An English deserter receives aid, 372. Proposals of pilots, 372. Christopher Carter released, 372. Re-appointed by Assembly, 373. Grant Dr. Kearsley a clerk, 374. Riots; arms, 375. Gunsmiths, 376. Pilots enter into an agreement, 376. Oaths taken by them, 376. Vessel cast away on Jersey coast, with men and ammunition; statement, &c., 377. Order Dr. Kearsley to Yorktown jail, 378. Order to R. Morris for expenses, 381. Appoint Thos. Proctor Capt'n, and David Rittenhouse, engineer, 383. Engage person from York to make saltpetre, 384. Correction of minutes, 385. Export provisions to West Indies, to be returned in arms, &c., 385. Orders for confinement of officers and men stranded on New Jersey, 385–387. Defence of city, 390. Captain Proctor's company to be received into barracks, 390. Rules and regulations for artillery company,

391. Resolution respecting Capt. Proctor's company, 394. Loan of powder to Congress, 395. Inquire if a master of arms is necessary, 395. Turpentine to be purchased, 395. Quantity of sulphur in city, 395. Committee to contract for building and equipping a ship of war for river service, 396. Regulations for pilots, 396. Pilot between Philadelphia and Chester, 397. Agree to purchase powder and lead from Cumberland county, 398. Fire rafts, 399. Officers, pro tem., 406. Resolutions of Congress; prisoners to be released on parole, 410. Apply to Westmoreland respecting arms, 411. Committee to apply to Congress for export of produce, 411. Condition of soldiers in jail, 411. Authority to John Wilcocks to load a vessel with produce, to procure powder for province, 413, 421. Heavy cannon to be cast, 412. Order removal of coal from river, 421. Respecting coal thrown into, 423. Dismiss two officers on complaints against them. 323. Committees to ascertain quantity of coal in city, 423. Make contract for supplying boats, 423, 424. Congress requests supplies to women and children of soldiers taken at St, Johns, 424. Prisoners secured, 424. Return of coal in city, 425. Direct a vessel to be loaded with produce, on their account under Act of Congress, 426. Furnish money to search for coal in Bucks county, 428. Order coal from Jamaica, 428. Orders for removal of prisoners to new gaol, 429. Rule for supplying Congress with powder, &c., 431. Committee to visit Fort Island, inquire what further defences are necessary, 432. To recommend to Congress field officers for battalion, 432. Action on resolution of Congress respecting powder, &c., 433. Order boats up to city and men into the barracks, 434. Authorize Gen. Hopkins of the Alfred, &c., to search outward bound vessels for seamen; recommend a discreet use of this privilege, 435. Order artillery company to Fort Island; fire-rafts; a battery to be built, 437. Restore Captain Proctor, 438. Files ordered, 438. Order for Russia sheeting; inquiry what goods of Joshua Fisher & Son are in possession of Committee of Inspection, 439, 449, 451, 453, 454. Resolutions respecting city and liberties, respecting powder, 440. Congress may employ three pilots, 441. And men from the boats, 441. Choice of Colonels for battalions to be recommended to Congress, 442, 444, 446. Chosen, 443, 446, 447. Resolutions of Congress respecting D. Conolly, A. Cameron and servants, 444. Order of commitment, 445. Parole required of Andrew Ellicott and Lord Drummond, 445. Recommendations to Congress for Captains, 447. Appointed, 448; and other officers appointed, 442–451. Surgeons to be examined; Captain Proctor to command artillery at Fort Island; a call of Bucks County Committee to choose Lieutenants and Captains, &c.; places for Magazines, 452. Resolution of Congress for supplies to Colonel Bull for Canada, 454. Apply to City Committee to procure certain articles, 454. Committee to procure copies of all petitions, &c., presented by this Colony to the throne since 1762, 455, 461. Release of Carter and Snowden, 455. Committee to procure spades, &c.; letters to assessors and counties for arms and saltpetre, 455. Andrew Caldwell appointed Commander-in-Chief of navy, 456. Returns of men in service; Second Lieutenants chosen, 457. Appoint surgeon and chaplain, 458. Authorize a shipment of produce; offer to loan money to persons who will erect powder mills; also for firelocks, 459. Order for sale of J. Fisher & Son's goods, 460. Dr. John Smith imprisoned; order for iron for gunbarrels, and brass; report of Committee on copies of petitions, &c., 461. Works on Liberty Island, 462. Hands for navy; contract

for cannon; resolution of Congress, money for recruiting, &c., 463. Orders, 464. Ensigns for Colonel Bull's battalion, 464. Number of hands on boats; survey of Jersey coast, 464. Purchase of arms by counties, 465. Release of Campbell and Snowden; increase of men in service for defence; powder-mills to be employed, 467. Export of produce; Dr. Smith examined and remanded to prison; pilot to cruise for vessel with arms, &c., 469, 470. Lieutenant Cameron convicted and remanded; minutes to be read; leave of absence to be asked; officers to be appointed; timber for carriages to be procured; rags and lint to be advertised for, and saltpetre, 470, 471. Dr. Conolly examined and remanded, 472. Memorial against T. Austen, &c., 473, 477. R. Seward, Lieutenant, 473. Ammunition to be imported, 473. Offer to buy blankets of Mr. Gratz, 473. Committee on survey of Jersey shore report, 474. Purchase of Oznaburgs, 474. Dr. Conolly's servant sent from gaol to workhouse, 476. Two prisoners discharged, also steward of a boat; pay of Captain of boats increased; share of prize-money, 477. Offer to Maryland to instruct in art of making saltpetre; appoint Dr. Hugh Hodge a surgeon, 476. Bernard Romans, Captain of Mattrosses; T. Hanson, Quartermaster; powder mills, 479. Insure a vessel against seizure for bringing powder, 479. Quartermasters appointed; four boats; officers of Mattrosses; pay for recruiting; Captain Campbell; gun locks, &c., 481. Proposals for gunpowder, 482. Men to be raised, by request of Congress, for New York, 483. Congress to be applied to replace arms, 483. Congress furnish, through "Secret Committe," fifty tons saltpetre, 484. To place soldiers in pest-house and gaol, 485. Order papers and stores of John Drinker and J. Fisher & Sons to be locked up, they refusing to take Continental bills, 486. Appoint Rev. William Linn chaplain, 487. Changes of officers on navy, 488. powder mills and survey of river, 489. Officers of boats to be convened by Com. Caldwell, 489. Erection of barracks on Liberty Island, 490. Saltpetre; armourer of boats; removal of prisoner from Lancaster, 490. Pest-house—ask for two thousand men; meet every day; key of old gaol; powder mills, 491. Address memorial to Assembly to raise two thousand men; Dr. Robert Harris borrows money for building powder magazine, 493. And to others, sailcloth for Pennsylvania ship, 493. Notice for volunteers, 493. Rooms at Province Island; signals for vessels on river; flag-staff for fort; smith's shop and forge on; First Lieutenant, 494. Building of ship to be hastened; powder mill necessary, 495. Letter to Committee of Inspection, respecting T. Rogers and J. Sermon; raise salary of R. Towers; payment for site of powder mill, 497, 499. Purchase military books; call for volunteers; M. Bunstead to be prosecuted, 500. Powder mill; Abel Morris resigns as Ensign; George Ross appointed; experiments on rifling cannon, &c., 501. May distribute prisoners; commit H. Y. Price as a tory, 503. Order to raise men; regulations; officers to boats appointed, 505. Survey of river between Reedy Point and Pea Patch; a pilot; committee on gun-locks, 506. Boats to be sent to Fort Island; pilot-boats to survey, 507. Order call on citizens for blankets; pay stopped for clothing; pay for goods shipped for powder, 508. Decline loaning arms on account of their scarcity; give a hat to each man, 509. Resolution of Congress respecting arms; signals; appointments, 510. Riot in prison, call on military; prisoners of war to repair to places named by Congress; chevaux-de-frise; pay to seamen in navy; guards for gaol; State House, &c., 512. Appointments; pay and bounty; chevaux-de-frise; guard

boats to be built; discovery of sulphur ore; recruits; prisoners of war, 514. Signals; officers; chevaux-de-frise; arms; L. Nicola, Barrackmaster; recruits; no indented servants, 516. Pay to officers; chevaux-de-frise, report on; sulphur refining, 519. Recruits; armourer at Fort Island; pay of pilots; floating battery; city battalions; signals, 520. Officers of provincial ship; muskets for Congress; naval stores; timber for carriages, 522. Fitting out brig Lexington; arms taken from Custom House officer; Mattrosses; release of Henry Price; fortifications on Delaware; names for vessels; sinking piers at Fort Island, 525. A man-of-war and tender arrive in Delaware Bay; pay to H. Fisher; saltpetre; provincial ship, 526. Proceedings for defence, 526. Guns, locks, rifles; cannon; vessels to sink in river; logs for piers; officers; McBean runs off with pilot-boat, 531, 533. Congress send information respecting Samuel Sample's art of boring and grinding gun-barrels, to be purchased, 534. Vessel to cruise in Delaware Bay; gaol to have iron doors; arms for pilot-boat at Bombay Hook; pilot-boats to stay below Chester, 535. Two more chevaux-de-frise to be sunk, 535. Officers appointed; brig to be purchased for a fire vessel; three new members added, 537. Assembly authorize agent to buy clothing, 538. Appoint M. Clarkson Marshal of Court of Admiralty, 538. Barracks to be provided; Continental troops; orders for officers, &c.; quarters at Chester, &c.; surgeon for provincial ship; powder magazine; resolves of Congress, 540. Various committees, 543. Prisoners paroled, 545. Prisoners removed from Reading, 546. Defence of river; floating battery to be built; two prisoners on parole sent to Germantown, 547. Two men deserted from Lord Dunmore, sent to their families; order printing of rules and regulations of associators; Drs. Rush and Duffield have charge of hospital and pest-house, 549. Send memorial to Congress asking cannon taken by Commodore Hopkins at Providence; write to several counties for fire-locks, &c.; powder magazine to be built at French Creek; examination of prisoners by Court of Admiralty; David Jones appointed chaplain, 551. Orders to vessels to attack man-of-war Roebuck, aground; cause of boats returning; John Reed, commissary, &c.; medicines; sisterhood at Bethlehem present rags; boats stationed in Bay; order respecting prisoners on parole, 553. Order of business; boats to cruise in river, 554. Men, &c., at Fort Island to prepare for action, 557. Express from Port Penn; vessels in sight from; orders to Captain Reed, 557. Orders for ammunition; enlistment of apprentices; inhabitants to supply lead from houses; committee go to Fort Island; expresses, 559. Old hulks to be purchased for covering gondolas; beer to be sent to gondolas; resolution of Congress on prisoners to be exchanged, 563. And cannon, 564, 565. Shot; pay for chevaux-de-frise; call on important business; Lieutenant appointed; two vessels to be purchased for special purposes; fire rafts; survey of river; resolution of Congress respecting gaoler, 567. Instructions to John Read, Barrackmaster, 568. Two gallies to be built, &c.; sale of Joshua Fisher & Son's rigging at auction; sick men to hospital; to fortify part of Jersey shore; write to Committee of Delaware; officers of boats to attend, 571. Memorial to Congress on fortifications at Billingsport; sulphur and lead, 573. Committee to procure carriages; beef and pork; list of necessaries; complain of committee of Assembly, 573. Fascines to be cut; removal of a prisoner of war; survey of river; memorial to Congress on defence, 575. Survey of river, 575. Instructions to Wm. Richards, as ship's husband, 576.

One hundred men for Fort Island; salt removed to Germantown; certificate of committee on cartridges, 577; Lieutenant Ball on parole; powder from Congress; memorial to Assembly for increase of committee; floating battery; flats; cartridges; cargoes, 579. Prisoners from North Carolina committed to gaol; gaol secured; guard for; Com. Caldwell resigns, 581. Stores for saltpetre in Germantown, 581. Ask Congress how to treat prisoners in gaol; reply, 582, 584. Memorial to Assembly respecting engagement with the Roebuck, &c., 582. Accept of proposals for muskets from Berks county, 584. Appointments; vessels to be equipped for service; order various articles; resolve of Assembly inquiring what preparations have been made; committee to draw up an account of them; the fire sloop to be manned, 585. Instructions to Captain Read for better government of navy; pay of officers; two shallops to be fitted up to attend guard-boats; officers appointed; Captain Montgomery called to answer; prisoner on parole; cartridges, proportion of powder to ball, 587. Sizes of muskets; order for purchase of formers, &c.; men sent to pilot-boat; sulphur, &c.; representation from Committee of Bucks, 589. Resolution of Congress respecting privateers; disposition of prisoners from North Carolina; timber for carriages, 591. Cannon ordered from Newport, &c.; guard-boats to be built; lead to be purchased; cannon shot; guard-boats sent to Lewes T.; alteration in galleys; appointment of a Commodore for Navy considered; brimstone; hulks to be fitted out, 593. Pay; two gondolas to be built; victualling of navy; saltpetre; Captain Read resigns; prisoners; bedcases; resolution of Congress, exchange of prisoners, 595. Send prisoners with Captain Brown; his instructions; commanding officer of fleet ordered to allow marine company to be under its own officers, 596. Rifle guns; purchases; chevaux-de-frise; saltpetre; gondolas; guards for powder house, 599. Prisoners to be removed from Germantown; arms; lead; fire rafts; fortifications on Delaware river; redoubt to be erected at Billingsport, 601. And boom; fire brig at Fort Island; gun-barrels; chevaux-de-frise to be moored at lower and middle buoy; John McLean, a tory, committed; Samuel Davidson to be Commodore; rifle company of Westmoreland, under command of Captain Vansweringen and Colonel Proctor; chevaux-de-frise to be sunk at Billingsport, under Robt. Smith; cartridges to be made up for ship Montgomery, 603. Write to General Washington for an engineer to erect fortifications at Billingsport; Dr. Rush to procure surgical instruments for use of Province; desist from building at Fort Island; battalion ordered up from Chester; privateer brig Hancock; exchange of rifles for muskets, 604. Exchange of prisoners with Liverpool man-of-war; S. Davidson appointed Commodore; officers of boats resist his authority, 606. Hog Island to be laid under water, 607. Ask loan; flying camp; Congress except to exchange of prisoners; instructions to Commodore Davidson; Capt. Bingley appointed, 609. Order purchases of brass—plank; building of flat-bottom boats; what stores are wanted; copper, ammunition to be delivered, 613. Agree with Thomas Savage to make salt in Jersey; Drs. Rush and Duffield to make list of medicines, &c., wanted; Marine Committee of Congress ask for lead for four frigates building; rum for rifle company; to confine Commodore Davidson's command to ship of war, &c., 615. Transactions to be laid before public, 615. Traitor allowance to officers in gaol, 615. Instructions to Capt. Henry Dougherty, 617. Orders for discharge of R. Saunderson, &c.; against seducing men from boats;

appointments; engineer to make draft of fortifications at Billingsport; to purchase land there; pay, 619. Appointments; H. Fisher's receipt for guard-boat; resolution of Congress to raise companies; send money to Committee and Convention, 621. Gunpowder to be distributed to associators; battalion of Germans; prisoners to be escorted to Yorktown; powder to Commiss'rs of Jersey; address to inhabitants of Pennsylvania, explanatory of its course with regard to Commodore Davidson, 623. Title papers of land at Billingsport; battalion ordered to Jersey; erection of fortifications; allowance of rum; proposals for casting brass cannon; privateer; battalion ordered back; troops in counties to be in readiness; guard-house at old powder-house to be removed to new magazine; laboratory enclosed with fence; sails for gondola; refusal of Lieutenants to give parole, to be conveyed to York, 627. Colonel Miles to order troops to Philadelphia and Jersey; resolutions of Congress; officers, prisoners, to wear their uniforms; prisoners on parole; provincial troops to receive Continental pay; appointments; five hundred riflemen to be got ready to proceed to Bordentown, under command of Colonel Brodhead; six shallops to transport troops, 629. Reward offered for cutting loose pier at Fort Island; rough sheds at Billingsport; New London cannon sent down to Fort; patroles for city; awnings bought up for tents; conference with committee of Congress, &c.; Monsieur Kermanvor appointed engineer at Billingsport, 631. Dr. Dunlap, surgeon; arrival of cannon; flints; value of arms taken from non-associators to be paid for; linen for bandages and lint, and awnings for tents, 633. Surgeon's mate; pay of officers; Captains; resolution of Congress sending copies of Declaration of Independence; orders to proclaim it, 634. Rules and regulations of army; employment of soldiers, &c., by iron-masters; Dr. Kuhn appointed physician and Director-General of hospital for troops in New Jersey, and adjust a plan; persons employed by Committee not to be enlisted; printing bills of credit; leaden weights to be collected; Dr. Dunlap to purchase medicines, &c., 637. Loan from Congress; arms, &c., in Bucks to be repaired; Dr. John Davis may purchase instruments; prisoners of North Carolina, in gaol, may write to friends under inspection: L. Kaigher seeks redress; order to C. Biddle for sundry articles, and to Colonel Thomas McKean; resolution of Congress for parole of A. McDonald; bandages; prisoners discharged, 639. Offer a reward for apprehension of Major Rogers; all provincial arms to be delivered to General Roberdeau's order; prisoners of war sent to Yorktown; awnings for tents; M. Bustead's air furnace to be taken for public use; a boring mill near city; intrenching tools; orders for various payments, 641. Payment for brig Nancy, lost; plan for supporting families of poor associators; privateer Venus; pay of artillery company increased; Major Potts resigns; Lieutenant Webb suspended and restored; Ensigns and Lieutenants recommended to Congress; arms from non-associators, 643. Sundry orders; appointments; cartridges sent to New Jersey; land at Billingsport; prisoners to York, &c., 645. British officers, prisoners, required to leave city; the families of poor associators to be provided for; brig Dolphin's freight money paid; old scow for hulk, &c., paid for; discharge of McDonald, by order of Congress, on parole, 647, 648. Gun-barrels; chevaux-de-frise; pay for Mrs. Conolly; leaden weights; guard; associators, 649. Pay of marines; saltpetre; firelocks; rank; exchange of copper; purchase of rifles; provisions for troops; arms to be repaired, 651. Required by

Convention to lay accounts and proceedings before them; payment to, 674.

Committee of Safety—their accounts to be settled by a committee appointed, xi., 643.

Committee of all the Counties meet in Philadelphia; delegates to General Congress, x., 200.

Committee, Secret, to furnish Committee of Safety fifty tons saltpetre, 484.

Committee to fix signals at Cape Henlopen, 510. Alarm, 548.

Committee, Marine, of Congress, x., 648.

Commodities, price to be according to value of money, ii., 445, 446.

Commodore of fleet to be appointed; his pay, to have clerk, x., 379.

Commodores, of Navy, x., 593, 603.

Comptroller General, Reports, xiii., 509, 511, 517, 532, 534, 536, 546, 552, 553, 557, 561, 563, 566, 567, 570, 573, 574, 576, 579, 580, 583, 584, 586, 589, 590, 593, 596, 598, 601, 603, 604, 607, 611, 613, 615, 617, 619, 620, 622, 623, 624, 628, 631, 632, 634, 636, 638, 640, 643, 647, 668, 673, 674, 676, 679, 680, 682, 683, 690, 692, 694, 696, 701, 702, 703, 706, 708, 711, 731, 736, 741, 743, 746, 751, 753, 755, 768, 775, 777; xiv., 4, 9, 13, 15, 29, 33, 34, 37, 38, 39, 41, 45, 50, 53, 55, 60, 61–64, 67, 69, 71, 73, 75, 80–103, 107, 110, 118, 123–134, 141, 151, 153, 159, 160, 164, 165, 169, 176, 177, 178, 179, 183, 189–196, 199, 202, 207, 211, 215, 216, 217, 224, 225, 228, 229, 230, 231, 234, 235, 236, 237, 238, 239, 240, 243, 244, 255, 261, 262, 263, 264, 265, 273, 276, 278, 287, 289, 292–300, 309, 311, 312, 314, 318, 320, 322, 324, 342, 346, 347, 348, 356, 357, 359, 361, 364, 366, 370, 374, 376, 380, 382, 395, 396, 400, 402, 406–440, 446, 448, 452, 458, 462, 463, 464, 467, 473, 477, 478, 480, 482, 487, 492, 500, 503, 507, 509, 511, 512, 514, 519, 520, 522, 551, 553, 557, 558, 562, 570, 574, 578, 579, 581, 583, 587, 590, 592, 601, 604, 606, 607–615, 617, 631, 632, 633, 634, 636, 639, 643, 653, 655, 659, 662, 679; xv., 1, 8, 13, 24, 25, 27, 33, 37, 40, 45, 54, 57, 60, 64, 74, 76, 80, 83, 95, 97, 98, 103, 107, 122, 125, 105, 133, 135, 142, 144, 149, 152, 164, 168, 180, 185, 186, 193, 196, 205, 206, 212, 215, 219, 221, 225, 226, 238, 245, 246, 248, 249, 250, 261, 267, 282, 286, 374, 401, 406, 411, 413, 432, 519, 546, 560, 566, 595, 635, 640, 643, 644; xvi., 7, 10, 17, 18, 21, 22, 23, 24, 30, 35, 39, 41, 44, 50, 61, 63, 80, 82, 86, 89, 92, 94, 101, 127, 148, 154, 161, 166–201, 217, 222, 210^{2}, 214^{4}, 216^{2}, 227, 228, 234, 236, 253, 267, 291, 315, 317, 326, 328, 359, 373, 381, 407, 419, 420, 427, 459, 432, 434, 481, 515. To appoint an invalid corps, xiv., 666. Controversy between Comptroller and Board of Treas'y, xv., 54. To have balance in Treasury transferred to State Treasury, 54, 60. Expenses of office, 225. To pay specie, 324. Instructions to, xvi., 80. Additional instructions to, and opinion of judges on manner of settling accounts, 90. Vote on, 91. Accounts examined by Receiver, 272. Report of Committee on, 314. Alters warrants, 320, 323. Resolutions respecting, 331.

Conarroe, Thomas, agrees to build piers at Marcus Hook, xiv., 479. Claim for building piers at Marcus Hook, xv., 228. Report of Wardens on, 233.

Conditions or Concessions of Pennsylvania, i., 26.

Conestoga, attack of Indians on families at, ii., 121, 122, 131, 138, 141. Indians from, 186. Indians alarmed by threats from Maryland, 191. Indian Harry and brother, 204. Indians in Philadelphia, 245. Present large wampum belt, 246. Treaty with, 299. Message to and from, 467. Suspected of murder, 70. In Philadelphia, 246. Message from, 403. Conference with Indians at, 511, 513, 516, 531, 533, 574, 594–600. Death of Old Queen, 574. Move off, 603. Chiefs arrive in Philadelphia, 606. Disturbance among Indians, iii., 15, 17, 18. Conference at, 19–24. Trespassers from Maryland on lands, 37. Petition for a road to

Brandywine, 43. Civility or Tagotolessa and other chiefs visit Philadelphia Conference, 45. Letter from, on Indian murders, 66. Col. John French sent to, makes his report, 77–81. Report of Conference with Indians at, 92. Presents from Virginia to Indians, 114. Visit of Five Nations and Governor, &c. to, 120. Conference at, 121–130. Murder of Indians by Cartledge reported, 146. Proceedings, 146–7. Indians from, at Philadelphia, 163. Governor's message to Assembly, 167. Governor holds council with Indians, 178, 181–184. Lands near, surrendered by Indians to Governor Keith at Albany, 201, 202. Governor going to, 225. Indians killed by Shawnese, 302. Governor visits, 302. Proposed treaty, 302. Message sent to, to convene Indians, 305. Council at, 309–314. Disturbances, 331. Treaty at, 337; vii., 7, 59, 282. Want clothing, 379. At Lancaster, 479. Deputies from, 484. About to remove, complain of Governor, viii., 113. Propose to to build beyond Fort Augusta, 113. Intelligence from; Sewaise their head man, 115. Letter from James Wright respecting, 116. At Lancaster not well taken care of; conference with them, 457. Indians' address to Governor Jno. Penn, ix., 88. Letter, E. Shippen on, 89. Action of Council, 90. Governor Penn's letter to magistrates on, 92. To be brought to a place of safety, 97. Second murder, E. Shippen's account, 100. On Province Island, 100. E. Shippen sent to, for intelligence; also Rev. Jno. Elder and Colonel Armstrong, 101. List of papers and effects, 102. Of murdered Indians, 103. Proclamation, 107. Paxton Boys preparing to march to Philadelphia to kill Indians at Province Island, 108. Message of Governor Penn, 109. From Assembly, 109. To be sent to Governor Johnson, 110, 111. Letters to, by Indians and Captain Robinson of Highlanders, 111. To Governor of New York, 112. Governor Franklin of New Jersey, 113. Council of New York will not allow them to pass through, 119, 120, 121. Return from Amboy to Trenton under Captain Schlosser, 124. Sheriff and Magistrate of Lancaster to give information, 124, 128, 352. Deposition of Benjamin Kendal of Lancaster, 125–6. Letter, Magistrates of Lancaster, 131. Act for preventing tumults, &c., 132. Body preparing to come to Philadelphia, 132. Public meeting called at State House, 132. Memorial from Philadelphia barracks, 135. Letter to Sir William Johnson on their removal, 137. Memorial of Matthew Smith and James Gibson, &c., respecting Indians, 138–142. Declaration of frontier inhabitants, 142. To be removed from barracks, 170. Message of Assembly respecting massacre, 410–412. Of Governor, 460. Indians, murder of, at Lancaster, complaint, x., 255. Manor, 257.

Conewago, river fisheries, ix., 719, 720.

Conewango (Alleghany Co.), lands adjacent to the mouth to be reserved for Commonw'th, xv., 593.

Confederacy frigate, xii., 85. Requires double-headed shot, 106. Impresses seamen, 148.

Confederation, copy of the, received from Congress, xi., 379. Maryland on, xii., 491, 492. Ratified by all the States, 649.

Conferences with Indians in Philadelphia, viii., 9, 29, 30, 32, 42–49–51, 54, 86.

Confirmation of laws passed at New Castle, ii., 46, 49. Of public landings, Blue Anchor and Penny Pot, 39.

Congress of Governors at New York, vi., 751.

"Congress," gunboat, x., 335, 488, 504.

"Congress," armed boat, xi., 3.

Congress, privateer sloop, x., 605.

Congress, privateer, x., 740.

Congress, proceedings, x., 240.

Congress, Continental, members from Pennsylvania receive pay, x., 286.

Resolutions of, 292, 316. Carbines offered, 354 Provincial, of New York, asks for loan of powder, 312, 315. State of account between Pennsylvania and, 340. Resolution to arrest all dangerous persons going at large, 357. Recommend export of provisions to West Indies and import of arms, 385. Decision respecting officers, &c. stranded in New Jersey, 386. Offer to buy ship Sally, 407. Resolutions respecting British officers, 410. Respecting export of provisions to Bermuda, 413. Resolutions of, 432, 433, 439, 453, 463, 484, 485, 502, 510, 591, 592, 595, 612. Ask for pilots and men to navigate the public vessels to Reedy Island, 442. Recommendations as Colonels to, 442. Resolutions respecting Dr. Conolly and Allen Cameron and servants, 444. To replace arms, 483. Order respecting soldiers and barracks, 485. Order return of arms and powder, 508. Resolution respecting prisoners, 541, 563, 565—and cannon at Providence, 564, 565, 567. Order muskets, 522. Trade, 541, 546. Build magazine on French Creek, 552. Loan money, 638. Cannon Committee, Marine Committee, xi., 7. Send State $40,000, 7. Loan to Council, 12, Resolutions of, 31. Fast Day. 175. Loan money, 177, 199. Conference with Council respecting General Howe, 198. Resolutions on steps to be taken to oppose the enemy if they approach, 203. Resolution for Board of War to furnish arms to Pennsylvania militia, 212. Appoint General Arnold commander of militia East of Philadelphia, 224. Resolutions respecting Billingsport, 248. Resolution calling for four thousand militia, 254. Arrest of Thomas Lightfoot ordered, 269. To be consulted on discharge of militia, 272. Resolution to seize persons, &c., 283. Arrest and examination of John Brown, 345. Copy of Confederation, 379. Recommend calling in old bills of credit issued by G. B., and abolishing substitutes, 382. Election of delegates by Assembly, 385. Resolution of, on proposed attack on Philadelphia, 404. Resolutions respecting officers' oaths, 417. Resolutions respecting accoutrements, 460. Money from, 466. Treaty with France, and other papers received from, to be read in churches, 487. Respecting further purchases of clothing, 507. Troops, &c., 509. Indecent application of Secretary to G. Bryan respecting a house, 531. Grant money to Council, 534. Resolutions in case of evacuation of city, 539. Protest against their laying embargo on provisions in Pennsylvania, 546. Invite Council to attend public reception of French Minister, 548. Ask for a galley at Cape May, 556. Asked for commissions, 564. Money, 580. Appealed to, on requisition for eight hundred wagons, 589. Joseph Reed resigns seat in, 594. Attempt of British to spread seditious papers, 596. Resolutions, 636. Commissions for vessels; Commissary of Naval stores, 649. Case of C. J. McKean and General Thompson, 653, 660. Resolutions respecting money bills, 661. Money, 669. Resolution for persons going within enemy's lines, 704. Respecting officers, 727. Resolution respecting meaning of department, 758. Respecting soldiers, in room of Colonel Proctor's men, 766. Commissary Trumbull's account, 775. Resolution to ship some corn, 782. Letters to and from, xii., 3. Call in bills of credit, 3. Resolution on exchange of prisoners, relative to appeals, 6. Conference with delegates in, on wagons, 19. Claim for purchases; Indian affairs; wagon service, 25. Resolution on wagons, 26. Conduct of J. McAllister, 31. Recommend completing battalions, &c., 36. Papers and resolutions; shipment of flour, 61. Illegal capture of a Portuguese ship, 63. Paper of Mons. Gerard sent to Council, 67. Mr. Holker and flour, 54, 56, 67,

68. Request militia to be placed at Sunbury, 74. Circular; expected enemy at New York; and necessary operations of army; Act respecting John Douglass of privateer, 75. Continuance of embargo, 82. Provision for officers, 85. On public credit; embargo; restrictions on internal trade; clothing for troops, 108. Act, on arrival of Count D'Estaing, 114. Samuel Huntingdon elected Speaker, 116. Letter from Commercial Committee of, to export provisions, 130. Appoint a fast, 145. Resolutions, 147. Impressment of Pennsylvanians on board of Confederacy, 148. King of France to be received through his minister, 170. Members from Pennsylvania elected, 172. Resolution respecting artificers and court martial, 176. Regulation of prices, 177. Fast Day, 183, 282. On supplies for army, 197, 198. Order expenses of witnesses in case of Arnold to be charged to them, 225, Various papers from, 227. Prisoners of war; estates of French subjects, 230. Draw bill for a million, 232. Troops to be raised, 250. Laws sent to, by State, 251. Requisition to supply Mr. Holker with flour, 275. Continental bills; finance, 286. Letter and resolutions of Council on state of frontiers, 289–292. Represent scarcity of meat in camp, 349, 351. Case of Richard Wells' lot on Arch street, 353. Draw on Council, 359. Conference with Assembly and Council on loan office certificates; their value; quota of supplies, &c., 360. Embargo to be continued; order for money, 363. On Quarter-Masters' debts, 369. Jared Ingersoll and Tim. Matlack new delegates; letter from committee at camp, 370, 371. Order for money, 395. Action, under various laws, &c., 398. Commissions for capture, 399. Supplies, 403. Furnish exchange, 420, 423. Wagons, 433. Call in bills, 459. Draw bills, 462. Resolutions respecting officers, 471–473. Supplies, 483. Resolutions, new arrangement of army, 500. Fast Day, 518. Increase of companies, 520. Supplies, 546. Names of agents for supply of southern army; live stock, 562. Wyoming garrison, 569. Meeting of Pennsylvania line, 593. Ill-treatment of prisoners; money for, 597. Clothier-General and deputy to be prosecuted, 599. Ask for men, 615. Removal of convention troops, 648. Articles of confederation ratified by all the States, 649. Fast, 675. Money required, 675. Capture of prizes, 683. Resolutions on soldiers; and Continental money, 692. Fast Day, 697. Act for Court to try piracies, &c., 702. Pay to officers; circular; naval officer's duty, 733. Convention troops; liquidation of debts; heavy expenses, 737. Persons to sign bills of credit, 740. Call for men, 742, 743. Thomas McKean, Speaker, 782. Respecting French sailors, xiii., 5. Drafts for money, 3–7. Petition to, for settlement of Connecticut claim, 10. Delegates on do., 16. Leaden spouts, 42. Resolution to Pennsylvania and New Jersey to embody three thousand men; French seamen, 53, 55. Conference on defence, 61. Connecticut claim, 79. General Wm. Irvine, Brigadier Gen., appointed to command at Fort Pitt, 79. Fast Day, 101, 124. John Hanson, president, 105. Money for, 110. Respecting Connecticut claim, 123. Requisition for supply of federal army, 144. Quota of troops, 148. What captures are lawful, 154. Reward for prisoners, 256. Fast Day, 267. Audience with French Minister on birth of a Dauphin, 282, 284. Resolutions of Council on treaty power of, 286. Conference on pursuing war with vigor, 291. Letters of General Irvine on emigration, 297. On robbery of mail, 311. Congress advise Pennsylvania and Virginia to send each one hundred and fifty men to Fort Pitt, 348. Proclamation for thanksgiving, 396, 400. Resolu-

tions; estimates; quotas of States, 406. Elias Boudinot, president, 412. Conference on British goods, 482. Proclamation on cessation of hostilities, 555. Letter on literary property, 574. Address on finances, 576. Proposals of New York and Maryland fixing federal city, 599. Conference of committee with Council relative to troops at Lancaster, 603. Complain of insults by an armed body of soldiers; conference on, 604, 606, 609. Report on late disturbances, 619. Papers respecting claim of Shallus and Sallaway referred to land office; city lots, 636. Propose to return to city, 637. Mode of corresponding with Council; adjourn from Princeton to Annapolis; choose president, 747. Ratify peace; proclamation, 749. Interest on money loaned United States, xiv., 7. Resolutions, 25. Private right to Wyoming lands, 31. Resolutions, 38. States unrepresented; Mons. Marbois, French Consul, 43. Petition of settlers at Wyoming; resolution on place of meeting of Commissioners to Indians, 51. Preference to States which comply with resolutions of 1782, 119. On raising troops for western posts; and for commissioners to Indians, 143. Acts of, 144. Cession of lands to United States; Acts of Connecticut and North Carolina, 162. Case of Robert Shewell, 162. Quota required for protection of north-west frontiers, 177. Delegates to, 261. Richard Henry Lee, president, 270. Delay of public accounts, 283. Council on powers of; public debt, 328–342. Resolution and proclamation on counterfeiting certificates, 347. Resolution, Commissioners for settling accounts; list of deputies to issue certificates, 372. Resolutions, 384. Order to raise troops, &c., 406. Delegates commissioned to, 442. Propose to lay off into States the western territory, 471. Acts of, 473. Birth of Duke of Normandie, 480. Recognize Mons. Marbois as Vice Consul of Pennsylvania, 491. Ask for attendance of delegates, &c., 517. John Hancock elected president, 587. Form of cession by Connect't, xv., 19. Have accepted the cession of lands by Connecticut, 28. Disturbances in Wyoming, 37. Papers relating to infractions of treaty, 50. Increase of federal troops; establishment of a mint, 105, 106. Act for reducing expenses of civil list, 192. Resolution, Phineas Bond, British Consul, 205. Send to Council the Report of convention in Philadelphia, 286. Delegates to, 339. Ratification of Federal Constitution, 351. Act to grant sea letters, 392. State of representation, 455. Act, settlement of accounts, 458. Fix price of triangle on Erie, 472. Settlement of accounts, 480. Mode of disposing of lands in western territory, 496. Agree to send troops to Easton, 502. Call on Virginia and Pennsylvania for troops against Indians, 515. Requisition of, for 1788, 521. Proposals for sale and purchase of triangle on Erie, 524. Act relinquishing to Pennsylvania, 530. Act putting in operation the Constitution; now adopted by eleven States, 535. Recommend prevention of importation of convict malefactors into this country, 542. Returns of elections in this State for members of, 636, 638. Proclamation of, 638. Act respecting oaths, and transmitting acts of Governor, xvi., 96. Laying duty on goods, 112, On tonnage, 119. Several Acts; department of Foreign Affairs established, 126. Act providing for expenses of Indian treaties, 141. Acts of, establishing Treasury department; registering and clearing vessels; coast'g trade, &c., 154. Acts for salaries; safe keeping of Records, 167, 175. Act respecting North Carolina, 289. Indian difficulties in Washington county, 306. Act to promote useful arts; and collection of duties, 347. Various Acts, 374, 381, 384, 392. Act for census United States, 402. Seat of gov-

ernment; invalid pensioners, 408. Light houses, &c.; trade and treaties with Indians; seamen; time of holding seats of president, &c., 423. Acts—of temporary establishment of post office, &c., 428, 433. Terms of members, 438. Journals sent, 439. Arrangements for accomodating Congress in State House, 486.

Connecticut, to raise troops for Canada expedition, ii., 450. Represented at treaty with Indians at Albany, v., 7. Settlers from, show symptoms of disturbance in Northampton county on account of pretended claim to lands, 734. Letter, D. Brodhead, 757. From Governor H. to Governor of, 758. Relative to dispute with, 767–777. Influence of Lydius, &c., with Indians in purchase of lands, vi., 117. Message from Jno. Shekelalmy on designs of settlers from, 215. Speech to Scaroyady, 217. Various papers relating to claim, 247–275, 286–293. Bounds described in 1664, 263. Proceedings at Court at Kensington on do. 264 Invalidation of Lydius' deed, 284. Minutes of Council of New Jersey respecting, 555–558. Lotteries, forbidden in, vii., 113. Settlers in Northampton county, viii., 563, 598, 646. Report of Sheriff and Justices on, 564. Governor's proclamation against, 566. Letter to Governor Fitch, 568. To Sir Wm. Johnson, 570. Number of families, 595. At Cushietunck, 612. Opinion of Attorney General, 620. Letters, &c., 621. Letters to and from Governor, 568, 570, 620, 627. Proclamation against settlers, 663. Settlers at Wyomink, ix., 7, 27, 602, 606. Proclamation against, 27. Instructions to Burd & McKee, agents, 29. Instructions to Governor H. 60. To Colonel Burd, 61. Proceedings and resolutions of Susquehanna Company, 569. Letters from L. Gordon, Chas. Stewart and John Jennings respecting New England settlers, 573. Governor P.'s proclamation, 588. Letters of Governor, 602. Letters from Governor P. to several persons respecting, 606. Riots at Wyoming, 663. Depositions, Amos and Nathan Ogden and Zebulon Butler, 674. Proclamation against settlers at Wyoming, 679. Depositions respecting, 710. People on their way to Wyoming armed; proclamation of Governor Hamilton, 747. Depositions, 751, 767. Proceeding of Council, 753. Letters respecting Wyoming, 754, 756. Letter to Governor Trumbull, 777. Letters to and from Governors, x., 3, 117, 151, 162, 163. People settling on proprietary lands, 50. Letters respecting, 86. Petition against people from Northumberland, 111. Eliphalet Dyer, Wm. S. Johnson and Secretary Strong arrive from, 118. Letter of Governor Trumbull, and resolutions of Assembly, 119–139, 143, 151. From John Penn to Governor 152. Proclamation against settlers, 153. Governor Trumbull's account of affairs, 163. History of Indian deed to Susquehanna Company, 177. People refuse to submit to laws of Pennsylvania, 275. Governor's letter to magistrates, 275. Boundaries, xii., 177. Letter from Governor declining to refer dispute on principles of confederation, 287. Proceedings of Convention, 585. Respecting dispute, 657. Claims—resolutions of Assembly and petition of Sup. Exec. Council for settlement of, xiii., 10. Letter from delegates of Pennsylvania in Congress on, 16. Proceedings, 79. In Congress and Assembly, 123. Counsel appointed, 215. Law for raising troops—counsel inquire respecting it, 217. H. Osburne solicitor, 266. Counsel appointed, counsellors appointed by Council, 310. Suit to be brought to a speedy close, 313. Agents to have use of papers, 314, 332. Papers to be examined, 361. Expenses attending suit against, 366. Conference respecting evidence, 417. Indian deeds, &c., 418, 420, 434. Expenses attending suit, 421. Court at Trenton, 430.

Papers demanded and delivered over by Jno. Penn, 437. Journal at Fort Stanwix, counsellors appointed, 441. Witnesses, 442. Pay on account, 446, 452. Decree in favor of Pennsylvania proclamation, 475. H. Osburne discharged, 596. Letter from Governor Jona. Trumbull, xiv., 2. Petition of settlers, 51. Fees to counsel, 141. Reports of Wm. Bradford, Jr., and James Wilson, 159. Act of Legislature and letter, S. Hardy, 162. Resolutions of Council respecting Wyoming, 169. Conference relative to settlers driven off in May, 188. Copies of Indian deeds taken, 240. List of papers relating to Wyoming, 318–320. Form of cession by, xv., 19. Cession of lands by, 28. Claims in Luzerne County, 279, 280, 355. Governor Huntington interposes for Jno. Franklin, 385, 386. Letter to Comptroller of, 546. Laws against settlers to be enforced, xvi., 317, 322, 352, 364.

Connell, William, commands privateer General Thompson, x., 793.

Connelly, Captain Robert, of Pennsylvania Regiment, xiv., 655.

Conner, Michael, complains of being in fear of his life from several persons, x., 723.

Conococheague—murders at, vii., 479, 503.

Conogocheague — evil intentions at —towards goods, ix., 302, 303.

Conolloway Indians, vi., 675.

Conolly, Dr. John, letters to and from, x., 140. His advertisement and conduct, &c., 140, 141, 146, 148, 164, 165. Lord D.'s views of his commitment, 161. Address to magistrates of Westmoreland, 167. Deposition of Henry Reed, 168. Answer of magistrates, 167. Murders in Westmoreland county—His conduct complained of, 180. Releases prisoners from gaol, 227. Proclamation against tax collectors, &c., from "Fort Dunmore," 227. Certificate respecting collectors, 228. Resolutions of Congress respecting his confinement in prison at Philadelphia with Allen Cameron and their servants, 444. Order from Committee of Safety to the gaoler, 445. Examined and remanded, 472. His servant, John Brown, sent to workhouse, 476. Person may visit on business, in presence of another, 482. A supposed accomplice, 533. Wife's allowance, 648, 696. Asks permission to retire to a plantation—Allowed, he to give bond, xi., 196. Enlarged on bond, 200. A British officer, to be arrested—Violates parole, imprisoned, xiii., 161. His servant committed, 163.

Conoy Indians, letter at their instance to Governor, iv., 656. Move higher up Susquehanna, 747. Claim lands where their town stood, v., 393; viii., 730.

Conoy Town, conference with Indians at, iii., 188.

Conshocken—Delaware Indians declare war against Senecas, xii., 586.

Conscience, rights of, declared, ii., 57. Liberty of, and Sabbath, 210. Liberty of, to be observed, iii., 64. On liberty of, views of Assembly and Governor, iv., 366–371.

Constable, William, to be arrested, xii., 495. To give security, 496.

Constitution, dissatisfaction with—Convention—Sense of people to be taken, xi., 221. Federal, order of procession on ratification of, by Pennsylvania, xv., 350. By Virginia, 498. By New York, 506.

Constitution of Pennsylvania, call of Convention to amend the, by Assembly—Proceedings of Assembly, xvi., 41, 159.

Continental Board of War, informed of great number of prisoners in new gaol, xi., 298. Bakers to be kept at making bread, 303.

Continental Navy Board to purchase 12 fireships, xi., 255. To have pilots furnished for their ships, 260.

Continental Army, rules and regulations printed by John Dunlap, x., 636.

Continental Bills, refusal of, xi., 2. Persons to be punished who re-

fused to take—Letter on, from J. Dickinson, 92.

Continental-Money tendered in payment for a redeemable ground-rent forfeited by Andrew Allen, xii., 249. Teams to pass bridge free, 271. Moulds for, 298. Exchanged, 429, 430, 434, 448, 552. Scale of depreciation to be published, 612, 648, 684. To be called in, 649, 692, 724.

Continental-Treasury, x., 401.

Contrecœur, Capt'n, summons from, to surrender, vi., 29.

"Convention," galley, x., 702. Armed boat to be fitted out, xi., 2. Captain Rice ordered to Cape May, 9, 107. Captain Richard Eyre appointed to command of, 543, 557.

"Convention," brig, to be commanded by Captain Thomas Houstons, and to be fitted out, xi., 555. Takes prizes—Expense of fitting out, 592.

Convention in Philadelphia, minutes sent Council, xv., 286. Order of procession in Philadelphia, 351.

Conveyances, act to prevent disputes in, v., 619.

Convictions, &c., x., 60, 92, 172, 225, 226, 256.

Conway, Henry Seymour, Rt. Hon., letters to and from, ix., 298, 299, 309, 310. Stamp Acts, 298, 307. Repeal of, 310.

Conway, George, discharged, x., 465.

Conwell, William, Justice, ix., 272.

Coogler, John and wife, to be arrested for aiding British, xii., 301, 308. He and wife released on conditions, 384.

Cook, Arthur, appointed judge, i., 153, 156, 324. Appointed special Commissioner, 164. A Councillor, 169. To act as Lieutenant Governor, 212. Judge, 324, 331. Guardian to J. Taylor, 331. Assistant to Governor, 505. Deceased, 607.

Cook, Benjamin, Coroner, iv., 602, 748, 782.

Cook, George, ordered out of the State, xii., 293.

Cook, Jacob, resigns as Justice, xii., 556; xiv., 45.

Cook, John, Sheriff, x., 56, 100, 211.

Cook, Richard, accomplice of L. Stewart, to be arrested, ix., 717.

Cook, William, Sheriff, x., 59, 101, 212; xi., 84, 112, 126, 131, 270.

Cooke, Edward, Lieut., xiii., 167.

Cookson, Thomas, writes letter to Governor at instance of Conoy Indians, iv., 656; murders by Delaware Indians, 675, 678; a Justice v., 3. Prothonotary of Lancaster county—Letter on death of Adam Furney, 377. A Justice, 600.

Coombe, Thomas, appointed by Governor Collector of light money, ix., 197.

Coombe, Major, xi., 123.

Coombe, Rev. Thomas, to be seized, xi., 284, 299, 300, 525, 527. His wife applies for a pass for his son John to New York, xiii., 122.

Cooper, William, Ensign, xiii., 53.

Copper mine sought for on Susquehanna—a subterfuge for annoyance of Indians, iii., 160. Perkiomen, proposed sale of, x., 23, 41.

Copper, to be purchased, x., 612.

Coppock, Bartholomew, member of Council for Chester, i., 213.

Corbin, Margaret, order in favor of, for her bravery, she having been wounded and utterly disabled by three grape shop, while filling the post of her husband, who was killed by her side at Fort Washington, xii., 34.

Coren, Captain Isaac, applies for articles, xii., 55.

Cornbury, Lord, letter from, ii., 78. To be addressed on decease of Governor, 91. Vice Admiral of the Jerseys, issues a commission to arrest a vessel, 99. Said to have issued a marriage license, 115. Asks Governor to urge means of defence for New York, 136. Address of merchants to, on privateers, 411. Vice Admiral, 421.

Cornish, Andrew, Governor, &c., arrive at his house, iii., 309. Justice, 358. Justice left out, 531.

Cornwell, Frank, Sheriff of Sussex county, i., 213.

Cornplanter, Indian Chief, grant of land to, xvi., 38. In Philadelphia, 497, 498, 499. And other Indian Chiefs, petition, 353. In Philadelphia, speeches to and from, 497. Letter to, 510. Speeches to and from Council, terms of sale and purchase at Fort Stanwix, of lands on Lake Erie, 500–509. And Half-town, remain in city till arrival of President of the United States, 513. Interpreter paid, 534. Expenses paid in Philadelphia, 547.

Cornwallis, Lord, surrenders to General Washington at Yorktown, news brought by his aid, Colonel Tilghman, to Philadelphia, xiii., 94. Christ Church bells rung, 143.

Coroners for each county proposed, i., 65, 187. Organized, appointed, 343. A deputy pro tem. appointed, 158. Appointed, 162, 174, 286; ii., 163. Is a Justice's inquest in absence of, valid? 184; iii., 30, 56, 69, 108, 139, 140, 260, 289, 332, 359, 370, 387, 521, 574, 614. Inquest, when necessary, 150. Elected, iv., 85, 86, 247, 309, 352, 469, 500, 601, 669, 748, 782; v., 55, 120, 345, 551, 597, 662; vi., 144, 637; vii., 267, 753; viii., 223, 403, 781; ix., 57, 199, 285, 333, 398, 547, 623, 624, 689, 691, 777, 778; x., 56, 78, 100, 211, 212, 270, 273; xi., 179, 191, 217, 235, 363, 365, 366, 372, 373, 378, 593, 596, 606, 638; xii., 131, 134, 136, 145, 146, 147, 161, 166, 182, 506, 507, 508, 510, 512, 518, 540–544; xiii., 85, 86, 87, 88, 92, 133, 134, 158, 391, 393, 395, 397, 398, 400, 419, 719–723, 726, 730, 740, 751; xiv., 230, 232, 234, 236, 237, 238, 244, 248, 256, 267, 268, 289, 554, 557, 558, 563, 597; xv., 98, 100, 102, 109, 116, 120, 125–139, 193, 294, 296, 298, 300, 301, 565, 566, 570, 580, 586, 589, 646; xvi., 191, 193, 195, 208, 212, 215, 490, 492, 493, 494, 496, 498, 499, 509, 514, 518, 527, 542.

Correction, a house of, in each county, proposed, i., 61.

Corsey Col., Battalion to rendezvous at Swedes' ford, xi., 301.

Coskosky, Indian town, v., 349.

Cotnam, Lieutenant George, permitted to raise recruits for Lieutenant General Philips's regiment at Annapolis Royal, v., 269.

Cottringer, John, refused right to hold land, being a Catholic, ix., 596.

Coultas, James, Sheriff, vi. 638. vii., 266. Breach of confidence in, 362. Of Philadelphia, order to arrest and imprison Dr. Wm. Smith, for libel, viii., 442;

Coulter, Thomas, Justice, xiv., 602.

Council—first meeting of, i., 56. Names of members, 58. Rules of, 56, 59, 60. Number of members returned by Sheriffs, not agreeing with charter; pray Governor that it may not operate against; W. Penn's reply, that it should not, 58. Member elect, sent for, 65. Nicholas Moore appointed Secretary, 73. Propose that magistrates provide for the sustenance of the people, 78. Debates to be kept secret, 96. Proposed to double the number of members for Philadelphia, 98. To be always with Governor, 98. Persons not serving when elected to be fined, 101. Members not to be arrested for debt, 102. List of members to be kept, 103. Members sent for to Kent county, 103. Sheriff may attach goods, &c., of members not paying their fines, 107. President, how chosen, 120, 146. To define jurisdiction of Courts, 124. Debates in, to be kept secret, 125. Refuse a collector's oath, but take his attestation, 148. Counties not to suffer by suspension of members, 203. Sheriff to summon member, 146. Notice of meeting to be set up "at the gate," 157. Supervise the press, 165. Refuse to sign a minute in President Lloyd's time, for want of his reasons for refusing, 165. Counsellors appointed, 168, 169, 552. A member charged with fornication retires, 176, 178, 180. Etiquette towards Assembly, 177. Early meetings of, 176. Adjourn to Quaker meeting house, 178, 224,

226. Members dismissed, 211. Members attend, as Deputy to Governor, 212. Claim papers and copies, 230, 231, Member to attend on Governor, 231, 232, 238, 239. Days of meeting, 231. Decide that keeper of great seal has a right to absent himself, 234. Difficulty between, and the keeper of seal, 235, 236. T. Lloyd's letter to, 236. Authority of certain papers required, 239. Question as to right of election of a member serving seven years without intermission of one year, 267. Jno. Eckley's election disputed, 268. Also Thomas Lloyd's, 269. Stormy debates in, 277. Discussion about laws and adjournment of Assembly, 290, 294. Debate between Assembly and, on imprisonment of Speaker White, 292. Tumultuous proceedings, 297. Extra meeting called on receipt of a letter from Maryland, 298, 299. Governor Blackwell resigns, 313. Thomas Lloyd elected President, 317, 323. Penn's instructions, 318. Returns of members, 322, 323, 324. Members sign declaration of allegiance, 321, 450. Member objected to on account of debauchery, 323, New mode of election of members, 324. New Council under Fletcher, 365, 369, 567. Nominate officers, 366. Day appointed for considering government affairs, 367. A fixed day for meeting, 572. Number of members, 577. New, formed by proprietary-members, 580. Fixed time for meeting, 581. Records missing, 589. Difficulty in election, 590.

Days of meeting fixed, ii., 66. To have cognizance of affairs of individuals, 67. Administer oath to Governor Hamilton, 69. Joseph Growden's speech to, 78. Reply of Governor, 78. Oath taken by members, 90. Present themselves before Commissioners to take oath, —Colonel Quarry's remarks on detention of dedimus, 92, 93. Difficulties suggested by Colonel Quarry respecting the oath and affirmation, 93. Proposal as to where the dedimus is to be kept, 93. Oath and affirmation administered to, by John Bewley, Collector, 96. Commission to William Markham as Register-General, 96. Times of meeting, 96, 97. Debate about meeting of Assembly prorogued by, 110. Power of Legislation affected by death of Governor H., 114. Commission read, 116. New members, 117. Proprietary's son, and Collector Bewley invited, 117. Address of Governor to, 141. Message to Assembly on adjournment, 149. Remonstrance of Philadelphia against licenses, &c., 161. Answer to, 161. Addresses to and from Governor, 164, 167. Assembly ask removal of James Logan from, 279. Resolution sent to Assembly, 280. Debate about sheriffs, 297. Discussions on impeachment of James Logan, 365–385. Mayor and Recorder of Philadelphia appear before, 407. Petition of Philadelphia to, on tax for court-house, 410. On French privateers, 413. Order about change in money, 435. Complaint to Governor about his address, 435. Colonel Evans's (late Governor) address to, on Assembly's address to Governor G., 436. Action on, 437. Address of nine members of late Governor's Council to Governor G., 439. Receive no compensation, 440. Answer of Assembly, 442. Discussion on value of money, contracts, &c., 445, 446. Assembly's Address in answer to Governor and Council, false alarm, &c., 453. Address from Assembly, 460. Case of A. Sandall, Swedish minister, 484, 500, on Queen's order to Governor to meet at New York, 532. Receive complaints from Indians, 554. Answer to, 555. Demand from Governor Hunter of New York for £2000—decision, 557. Presents to Indians, 561. Robert Asheton appointed deputy clerk, 567. Letters on repeal of laws by Queen—Proclamation on peace with Spain, &c., 571. Meet weekly without summons, 597. Governor attends for the last time, 629.

Governor Keith attends and

qualifies members, iii., 14. Names magistrates for Lower Counties, 15. Accusation of Governor Gookin against sundry persons, 15. Meet to hear Colonel Gookin's charges—who confesses he has none to make, 17. Colonel John French a member, 18. Governor's speech, and discussion on mode of issuing commissions, 33–35. To meet every week, 56. New commission and instructions from William Penn, jr., laid before, 64. Agree with Assembly in advising delay, 68. Governor's charges against Robert Asheton, 72, 77. Letter and Report on Governor's position, 73. Order of Privy Council for repeal of certain laws, 75. New members, 113. Governor attends, after return from Virginia, 115. Views on demand of New York for contribution to fortifications, 134. Not satisfied with powers of Court respecting a road, 142. Jasper Yeates dies—Henry Brookes succeeds him, as Collecter of Lewes, 143. Proportion in members between Church of England and Quakers observed, 314. Decision about dividing line between Chester and Philadelphia Counties and taxes, 144. Preceding minutes to be read and examined, 147. Proceedings in case of Indian murder by J. & E. Cartledge, 148–156. To receive message from Five Nations, 163. Robert and William Asheton called to Council, 173. Vote of thanks and £500 to Governor, 174. Write to Governor at Conestogo—lands on Susquehanna—Indians—Maryland title, 178, 180. Decline ordering provisions, 180. Various proceedings respecting treaties with Indians at Conestogo, 203. Message to Indians on treaty with Virginia—runaway negroes, &c., 209. Advice to Governor Keith as to his course with Maryland, 214. William Fishbourne and Josiah Rolfe, 225. Thomas Masters dies, 232. Francis Rawle elected in his place, 232. John Ramsey, chamber-keeper, 233. Business without a quorum, 247. Address to King George II., 271. New members, 333. Assembly complain to, on rude treatment in Philadelphia, 340. Governor's speech to Assembly on, 341. Rank of members, 384. Thomas Griffitts and Charles Reed chosen members, 529. Ask Governor how the Court of Chancery is constituted—petition respecting, 617.

On Court of Chancery or Equity, iv., 19, 21, 22, 27. Can Governor be Chancellor? 23. Report of James Logan on Court of Chancery, 27. James Logan becomes president on death of Governor Gordon, 47. Have under consideration affairs with Maryland, 63–73. Letter to Governor Ogle, 76. Relative position of, and Assembly with regard to powers arising from death of late Governor—explanations, &c., 99. On Maryland affairs, 101—151. Petition to King, 125. Proceedings on Maryland affairs, 197, 232, 237. Message to Assembly on do., 201. Answer, 233. Expressions objected to, 236. Clerk asks for salary, 237. Message from Assembly, 238. Answer to, 239. Clerk justified in his claims, 240. Two prisoners apply for trial—referred to Supreme Court, 250. Proceedings respecting discharge of prisoners under proceedings at Hampton Court, 264. Governor Thomas arrives, 288. Appoints Thomas Lawrie, clerk, 289. Governor inquires why A. Hamilton and Dr. Græme do not attend, 292. Repeats the inquiry, and receives answers not satisfactory, 295. Proceedings in England for quieting Maryland and Pennsylvania, 298—301. Proclamation to be made, 301. On value of gold and silver coin, and bills of credit, 365. Petition from Mayor, &c., of Philadelphia, to raise money, 376. Order for appearance of petitioners, 379. Proceedings against Israel Pemberton, Jr., 389—394. Thomas Lawrie resigns, and P. Baird appointed secretary, 429. Minute to Assembly, 460. Petition of seven companies of soldiers,

466. Action on, 469. Discussion respecting health officer, 496—498. Rights of, and Assembly respecting, 498. Pest-house—report of Assembly—Messages, &c., on controversy between Governor and Assembly, 507—559. P. Baird resigns as Secretary, and Richard Peters appointed, 639.

James Hamilton, a member, v., 1. Benjamin Shoemaker, do., 3. Address to King on successes in Scotland, 51. Joseph Turner, Thomas Hopkinson, and Lawrence Growden become members of, 65. List of members according to priority, 67. William Logan becomes a member, 68. Richard Peters, Clerk, 68. Course of business settled, 69. Form of licenses changed, 69. Chamber to be in State-house, 69. Governor replies to Governor Shirley respecting supplies, 76. Proceedings relative to robberies by French and Spaniards, 90. Letter to Proprietaries on robberies, 92. Speech to Assembly, 95, 96. Message from Assembly, 101. Governor Shirley and Indians, 102. Refuse to print address to Assembly, and their answer, 104, 105. Relative to forces raised for expedition to Canada, 130–145. Letter to Governor Shirley, 143. Message to Assembly, 154, 156. Letter to Proprietaries on defenceless state of province and city, 160. Declaration to Associators, encouraging them to proceed in choosing officers, 168. Letters to Governors Clinton and Shirley, for loan of cannon till those ordered from England should arrive, 172, 173. Send Messrs. Lawrence and Taylor to New York for cannon, 206. Higginbotham and Perie appear before, 218. Review the Associators, 222. Message to Assembly, 230. Captain Ballet meets, and shows his instructions, 241. Sits every morning, City Court-house, 246. Resolutions of, for defence of city, 250. Orders to ferrymen respecting seamen from Otter sloop, 256. Message to Assembly on means of defence, and estimate of charge of equipment of a colony vessel and smart money, 270–273. Several messages received from Assembly—Anxious to adjourn, 276. Remarks on, 276. Assembly adjourn, and a series of resolutions is passed by Council, 277–279. Letters to Governors Gooch and Clinton, on privateers, 283, 284. Answer Governor Gooch, 301. Letter to Proprietaries, 319. Decision respecting Bucks county Associators and officers, 326. Message to Assembly, 329. Message from Assembly disapproving of resolutions, 338. Reply to, 339. Governor James Hamilton meets Council, 362. Richard Peters appointed Clerk and Secretary of Province, 365. Governor goes to New Castle and leaves members in charge, 488. John Penn arrives—Made a member, with rank of Eldest Councillor, 606. Is present, 618.

Various papers relative to Connecticut claim, vi., 247–275. Advice to Governor M., 274. Road from Shippensburg to Du Quesne, 317. Opinion of, on publishing papers by Assembly, 328. Governor informs of appointment of Mr. Quincey as Commissioner, 329. Governor informs of French fleet and troops for North America, 353. Lynford Lardner a member, 414. Opinion of, on saving clause in Colonel Evans's commission—Tax on proprietary estate, 520. New Members—B. Cohen, John Mifflin, and Dr. Thomas Cadwalader, 666. Advise Governor and some members to proceed to frontiers, 676. Report of Committee on distribution of arms, &c., by Assembly, 679. On defenceless state of province, 680. Petitions for defence from all parts, 680. Advise Governor not to assent to bill for taxing proprietary estates, 680, 692, 696. Advice to Governor, 705. Advice to Governor respecting French neutrals, 711. Proceedings, 713. Extracts from old Minutes of Council, 1709–1746, 720–724.

Advise Governor towards Qua-

kers on war against Delaware Indians, vii., 103, 107. B. Franklin and other Commissioners meet, 153. Letter to Governor Belcher, 166. Proceedings on Assembly's message on tax on proprietary estate, 204 Governor Morris retires, and William Denny presents his commission as Governor, and order clearance of vessels, 221. Governor Denny asks advice of Council, 236. Appoint Hamilton, Shoemaker, Logan, and Secretary Peters to investigate proprietary purchases from Indians, 354. Quartering soldiers, 359–378. G. Croghan attends in, and gives his opinion on Indian affairs, 382. W. Callender and Israel Pemberton ask permission to examine minutes of Council respecting Indian claims to lands, 394. Answer to, 397. Answer to remarks of Assembly on supply bill, 437. Chew and Peters to draw up proposition to Assembly on money bill, 441. Report, 442. Lord Loudon sends answers to money bill, 451. Address of Moravians, 494. Discussion on building fort and houses at Wyoming for Delawares, 734. Proceedings in case of William Moore, 741, 750, 764, 776, 781.

W. Peters, Secretary pro tem., viii., 19. Governor complains of insult from Commissioners, 31. Affairs with Teedyuscung and his clerk, 31. Communication from Governor respecting bills, &c., 70. Convened at request of General Forbes on Indian affairs, 126. Opinion of proper treatment of French prisoners, 148. Governor asks advice of, in case of Dutch vessels brought in by privateers, 155. Proceedings in case of William Moore, 161. Acquittal, 162. Opinion on Assembly's rejection of Admiral Boscowen's request for men, 165. Addresses of meetings of sufferings on Indian land claims, and proceedings on, 239, 241, 243–245. Report of Committee on complaints of Indians at Easton, respecting claims for land by Teedyuscung, 246–261. Opinions on supply bill and Assembly, 325. Objections of, to bill for remission of bills of credit, respecting quit rents, 350. Governor's insinuations against—Their reply—Protest of Mr. Chew, 357. Protest against Governor for assenting to a bill of credit, 358. Allusion to Governor Keith, 359. John Moland, a member, 360. Discussion continued on bill, 361. Proposals of Lardner and Logan to send bill on warrants to proprietary, 362. Mr. Galloway's remarks on bill, 363–369. New bill proposed by Mr. Moland sent to Assembly, 369. Speech of Governor on bill—Rights of property—Of Secretary and Surveyor-General, 375. Not a part of the Legislature, 503. Take oaths of allegiance, &c., to King George III., 520. Address of Governor and Council to George III., 561. Governor sick — Transmits message and report respecting Connecticut settlers in Northampton county, 564. R. Peters resigns as Secretary, and Joseph Shippen, Jun'r, elected, 671. Decline exhibiting to Committee of Assembly their minutes, 719, 720.

Joseph Shippen, Jr., continued Secretary and Clerk—reception of John Penn as Governor, ix., 74. Action in relation to murder of Conestoga Indians, 90, 100. Richard Penn admitted as a member, 101, 104. Relating to murder of Conestoga Indians, 88–128. Advice about their removal from barracks, 135. Action on remonstrance of Smith & Gibson, 146. Various letters submitted on the Indians in barracks, 170. Address to King on repeal of Stamp Act, 315. William Till dies—James Tilghman elected in his place, 354. Murders of Indians by F. Stump, 414–490. Examination of James Cunningham respecting rescue of Stump, 450. Colonel Armstrong to be written to, to regain him, 451. Proceedings respecting shooting Indian George, 603. New Members, 704. James Hamilton as President succeeds John Penn

on his going to England, 733. Joseph Shippen, Jr., is continued Clerk, 733. Alteration in forms, 734. Take oaths, 734. Order men to be raised for Wyoming, 753. Letter to proprietaries respecting, 727, 779. Proclamation respecting approval or annulling of laws by King, 766.

Minutes, x., 1 to 276. William Hicks added to, 12. In absence of Richard Penn—the President, James Hamilton acts as Governor, 90. John Penn arrives as Governor, and is present, 91. Action respecting Connecticut claim, 118–139. Dr. Conolly, 140, 145, 169, 170. Recommend petition to the King in the present posture of affairs, 232. Message to Assembly, 233.

Council—Privy—Acts confirmed or repealed by, iv., 483–486. On state of the province, &c., vii., 272–278. On various Acts, 275.

Council of Safety. (See also Committee of Safety, x., 279–652.) Appointed by Convention of State—meet—names of members, 653. Declaration read subscribed—Mr. Rittenhouse, chairman—Colonel Miles' men sick-Dr. Thomas Parke to attend them—stage in State House yard fitted up for guard—doorkeeper appointed — Colonel Bull to procure pikes and Tomahawks, 653. Resolutions respecting flying camp and letter to Committee of Berks—Jacob S. Howell appointed Secretary—Resolution of Convention—defence of frontiers—new members, 655. Petition from boats at Darby Creek—S. Morris to supply them —Court martial on John Peal—Captain Loxly ordered to city—William Nisbett, Treas'rer, orders, 659. Major Bell—Colonel Montgomery new members—allowance to associators' families—sinking piers—flying camp—Colonel Rankin command of fleet, 659. Powder—return of stores—redoubt at Billingsport—salt for navy—Congress order cannon to General Mercer for flying camp—combustibles—persons and papers to be arrested, 661. Men employed not to be enlisted—order for powder for Maryland, Ind. Co.—deposition of John Walker—and Martha Ash, 663. Compliance with rules and regulat'ns of Assembly for associators—arms—letters from boats, resignation J. and A. Arthur—J. and J. Hatton to be apprehended-letter to Salem-Colonel Kirkland—apprehension of Tories, 667, 670. Orders for sail cloth, &c.—pay for families of associators—letter to delegates in Congress on militia, 669. Orders for arms-Committee on complaints of families, 671. Thomas Wharton, Jr., chosen President, and David Rittenhouse Vice President —furnish Lancaster with arms—blankets—workmen not to be enlisted—troops to be quartered in places of worship—wardens and deacons to be informed of this order—flying camp to be raised—condition of companies of associators to be examined—assistance—sloop to J. Coburn—clothing—Billingsport—Ensign Kirk resigns, 673. New member—clothing for Col. Atlee's battalion — supplies for families, 675. Workmen not to serve in militia—insult at Philadelphia—William Sutton from New York, confined as Tory—poor associators of Bucks county—man from Chester county confined—militia quartered in private houses —George Gray a new member—battalion short of officers to be passed by Muster Master, 677. Appointment of officers—committee on plan of fortifications at Billingsport—German lieutenants recommended to Congress—flying camp—arms to be repaired—officers' account, 679. Cannon sent to camp in New Jersey—Congress resolve that paper makers do not go with associators to New Jersey —deserters from Continental army in custody of Colonel Haslett—dissatisfaction in naval department —relief of poor families of associators—sick soldier of Continental army provided with a physician—William Sutton—sash weights—various orders, 681. Maryland

money to be changed—fortifications at Billingsport, 683. Various orders and payments for arms, &c.—troops under Captain Proctor increased—recommend to Congress another lieutenant, 685. Sundry payments—deserters from associators to be reported, 687. Permission granted to prisoners confined at Lancaster, 688. State cannon foundry and boring mill—Aid to Captain Mathew Smith—wages to a slave to be paid, 689. Sundry orders—pay for arms taken from non-associators—bounty to soldiers in Bucks County—pay for shot cast by G. Taylor—Captain Opp's company to march to Jersey, 690. Orders for city guards, 691. Order to Commodore Davison, 693. Respecting enlargement of James McConneaughy—forged deeds for land by George Crows are to be taken, 693. Money found in his trunk, 695, 696. Reward offered on account of riot, 701. Loan to Congress, 703. Urgent order to troops to depart for Amboy, 704. Publish handbills denying reports respecting number of troops in New Jersey, 706. Guard for Reading, 714. Blankets, &c., to be purchased—apply to Congress to pay wages &c., of associators—four members added by convention, 717. F. Gurney a member—piers to be finished, 718. Hospital for sick soldiers—Dr. Gerardus Clarkson physician—fortifications at Billingsport—various orders, 719. Fast sailing sloops or schooners to be engaged, 719. Guards for frigates, prison and powder—prisoners discharged, 720. Regimental paymaster—enlistments—report on Chevaux de frise, &c.,—complaint of Michael Conner—committee to inspect arms, &c.—pilot through Chevaux de frise appointed—servants and apprentices not to be enlisted, 723. Barracks—S. Mifflin declines being Commodore—purchase of arms and commander of floating battery, 724. Appoint T. Seymour Commodore—instructions to, 731. Visit Fort Island, 732. Militia of city to be employed at Billingsport—Dr. Wm. Currie resigns as Surgeon—Prisoner enlarged on parole—Change of officers of Flying Camp—Congress agree to provide for disabled men, 735. Order on Congress for money—L. Nicola continued as Barrack-Master—Various accounts—Return of arms to be made—12 recruiting sergeants, 737. Persons to buy blankets—New commissions to Captains of Galleys, 739. Privateer commissioned—Regulars for Continental service—Exchange of cannon in ship Montgomery — Officers appointed, 741. New arrangement of battalions—Letter to Colonel Brodhead—To General McKinley—Men to be sent to Fort Montgomery, 743. Raise pay of pilots—Ship Montgomery be fitted out—Various orders, 744. Resolutions respecting pay, stores, associators—Guard for city, 747. Monopoly of salt, 748. Lists of clothing, 749. Orders respecting chain and boom in river—General Howe expected, 747, 750. Salt—Pay to Colonel Brodhead, 750. Order arms to be distributed—Associators to report—Letter from General Lee respecting Hessians approaching—Complaint of Sharp Delancy, 753. Offer bounty—Committee to view avenues to city—Brass cannon from Jersey—Articles for Billingsport—Send expresses, 755. Appoint officers of foot—Proposals to Board of War for defence—No persons of military experience—General Stevens proposed, 757. No persons to view the works at Fort Island, nor sound Channel—Salt to be sent and sold at Trenton—A Captain appointed—Pay increased of men in fleet, 759. Magazine for military stores, 763. Officers appointed—Boats to be built—A fire to be erected, and nails made at Fort Island, 765. Arrangements in Battalion, officers commanding companies, promotions, &c., 766. Orders, 769. Men to be enlisted, 773. Privateers, 773. Various orders, 783.

Minutes, xi., 1 to 170. Artillery to be paraded at Fort Island, —Fleet to be manned and rendezvous at Philadelphia—Store for clothing, &c., 1. Memorial to Assembly on continental currency, 2. Arrival of transports at New York, 3. Appointments, 2, 17. Privateers, 3. Captain Strohbogh's company of artillery to be sent for—no vessels to pass chevaux-de-frise —orders to Commodore Seymour —removal of cattle from shores—Putnam Battery—prisoners of war under care of S. C. Morris—S. Wheeler works at chevaux-de-frise, 5. Order troops from Berks, pay at Billingsport—brass cannon, money from Congress, 7. Pay of officers of armed boats—Captain Rice ordered to Cape May—his instructions, 8. Orders to Chester militia to march to city, 9. Order troops from counties, 10. Borrow from Congress, 12. Captain Cochran's Company to be paid—Memorial to Assembly on calling out militia, 15. Various orders, 17. Authority to collect blankets and stockings in city, 18. Will provide for Associators' families—Salt for Philadelphia County—no vessels to depart except already cleared—William Parr to remove records to Lancaster—supply for families of Associators, 23. Field Officers to be nominated—Surgeons appointed—Troops sent to Trenton—and to General W., 25. No person to pass ferries with fire arms without permit—L. Nicola, Town Major—duty—guards for city—volunteers——shops to be shut up, and schools broken up—Brigade formed—armed boat, 27. Ferrymen on Delaware to transport Maryland flying camp to the city—troop of horse to be formed to proceed to General W.—wagoners needed—not to be impressed—paymaster—Associators to be supplied from stores, 29. Port opens —vessels may pass—loan from Congress—appointments, 37.—Schools opened—prisoners removed under guard to Newtown—medicines—resolutions on defence, 38. General Howe advancing—boats sent to Trenton ferries to be in order—Commodore Seymour to be under General Washington—expresses, 39. Authorize impressing a carriage and horses from Messrs. Pemberton and Emlen, Jr., to remove General Roberdeau to Lancaster—no further restriction on salt—inhabitants permitted to sell as usual—books and treasury to be removed to Lancaster—wagon to be provided, 41. Wardens to appoint patrols—commitment, &c., of William Smith and J. Stansbury—militia ordered from Bucks county, 43. Seven members added by Assembly, 45. Employ Dunlap's printing materials—ask aid of citizens to General Putnam in throwing up works of defence, 46. Wagons—poor militia—powder from French creek—battalions to join General W., 49. Stores to be opened—prisoners sent to Baltimore under guards—sick soldiers—appointments, 51. Tolls on Schuylkill bridge—sick at hospital—wagoners, 53. Census of males fit to bear arms, 60. Pay for wagons, 60. Regulations for soldiers, 72. Send off expresses, 74. Rum sent to camp, 75. Appointments and orders for pay, 76–84. Cannon to be collected in Philadelphia, 84. Troops to be paraded, 85. Militia disgusted, return—under orders not given officially—Colonel Hubly, commissary, 86. Suspected persons—prisoners from Roebuck —from New York—provision for, 89. Thanks to officers, &c., at Lancaster, for remaining, 90. Colonel Hunter's battalion refuses to march to aid of General Washington, 95. Indian treaty at Easton, 96. Persons appointed to attend, 96. Secretary to Commissioners, 98. Officers of Major Williams' battalion, 98. Punishment of deserters from militia, 102–106. Officers prisoners with the enemy to retain their rank, 109. Resolution respecting business, 112. Against false reports, 114. Loan from Congress—letter to Hewes,

Tybout and Tuckness for supplies, 115. Order a regiment of artillery to be raised—officers and men—Colonel Proctor to be Colonel of it, 116. Justices to examine persons in jail suspected of stealing money from S. Lowry—Hessian and Waldecker prisoners to be delivered to Colonel Melchor—Major Williams resigns—Farmer and Murray appointed, 116. Ask loan of Assembly, 117. Order arrest of Joseph Atkinson for robbery, 123. Appointments—applications for regiments—gun-lock factory—fortifications at Billingsport—officers—cash brought from Baltimore, 125. Sends boat Delaware to defend salt-works in New Jersey from expected enemy—additions to Navy Board, 127. Offer bounty in navy, and fix pay of officers and men, 132. Regulations respecting sick, 133. Arrearages to Captain Brown's company—salt for beef, 135. Steward at Province Island—Committee to inquire about stores—Regiment to be raised to serve in any part of United States—bounty—appointments and pay, 137. Navy Board to take the Province shallop, 138. Sentence on Lieutenant John Dean referred to Navy Board, 138. Appoint Joseph Stiles superintendent of ordinance—necessary buildings, 143. George Ingles superintendent of gun-carriages—storing timber—state of troops in City—Ceneral Gates—officer to visit—also Barrack-Master and Town-major, 144. Smith's shop to be erected—pay of Jacob Howell, Secretary, 146. End of Council Minutes, 146. Memoranda of payment and occurrences, 149–176. Call for money on Supreme Executive Council, 176. James Read, Councilman, could not serve being in Assembly, 500. Also Mat. Smith, 502. Committee to settle accounts appointed, 645. Committee, Hambright & Lacey, to obtain minutes and papers of, relative to their proceedings and deposit them in Secy.'s office, xii., 242. Purchase by late, paid for, xiii., 28.

[Proclamation by the Council, showing that by the occupation of the City by the British, the Government by the Assembly became temporarily useless—they transferred their powers to a body composed of the Supreme Executive Council and other gentlemen therein named—which body they denominated "*A Council of Safety*, with all the powers for the time being of the Assembly. It only continued in existence for about one year, when the cause of their appointment being removed—the Council was by proclamation dissolved into the original Assembly and Supreme Executive Council, xi., 325–353.]

Colonel Galbraith to collect blankets for the sick, to be appraised by three individuals—seven persons authorized to collect in Chester Co., arms, blankets, &c., xi., 328; and others in Lancaster county—Ordain Commissioners in each County to seize and confiscate the property of individuals inimical to this country, 329. General Armstrong presents a statement relative to the militia—Provisions not to be procured at Hummelstown for gun factory—Joshua Elder to supply them even by force, 331. Order goods returned to J. Swanick—fix prices, 336. Removal of families from State Works—Ordinance against buying up and engrossing merchandize—number of commissioners to buy blankets increased, 337. Ordinance against distilling from grains, 338; or appoint persons to take blankets from certain persons—paying, &c., therefor, 339. Pay of Lieutenants on appeal days—wagons required, 341, 342. Appoint wagon-master—Indians—General Hand, 343. John Brown arrested and imprisoned—his examination, &c., 345, 347. Indian depredations—wagon for William Harris, 347. Additions to Commissioners to seize effects of tories—Remarks on John Brown's examination, 348. Wagons not to be impressed at Lancaster—militia

of this State complained of—Commissioners sent to camp to inquire into it, 350. Commissioners to collect arms, &c., may appoint assistants—Dr. Shannon to be arrested, 352. Proclamation of Supreme Executive Council dissolving and terminating the Council of Safety, 353.

[Here the minutes of Supreme Executive Council recommence. Though they appear to have kept separate minutes.]

Councillors, xi., 372, 595, 596; xii., 146, 147; xiv., 230, 232, 234, 236, 237; xv., 294, 296, 298, 300.

Council of War at Great Carrying Place, vi., 608. Articles adopted, 609.

Council of War by Governor Shirley at New York, vii., 23.

Counterfeits and counterfeiters, respecting, i., 72, 84, 87, 88, 89. Search-warrant for, 89; iii., 109, 110, 268. Arrested, &c., iv., 224. Demand on Massachusetts, 225, 241, 273, 274. Rob. Jenkins, 429; v., 119, 141, 268; x., 88, 97, 109, 172, 256. Proclamation against Richardson and Ford for, 99. J. M'Allister and Short, 256–258. Escape of and proclamation, 258. Deeds for land, 693; xi., 216, 234. Plates discovered, 234, 397, 663; xii., 87, 89, 199, 267, 268, 272, 375. Plates defaced, xiii., 385; xiv., 59, 347, 450, 454.

Counties, names of, i., 57. Names of Sheriffs, 57. Courts in, rules for proposed, 64. Seals for each ordered—their devices, 66. Court fined by Council, 76. Bounds of, 126, 129. Justices appointed, 129. To raise money, 131, 152, 162, 163, 298. Magistrates reminded of duty against debauchery, 201. A good understanding between upper and lower, to be preserved, 203. Confusion as to taxes and writs, 265. To elect members according to charter, 324. Clerks continued, 344. New negotiation respecting officers, 345. Clerks refuse to deliver records, 378. Probate of Wills for each, 461. Amount of revenue from first tax, 461, 466. Power to form, is in Proprietary, iii., 344. New, iv., 335, 755. To be formed, v., 398, 403, 404, 426, 428, 619.

County workhouses proposed, iii., 39. Justices, 28, 62, 175.

Courtney, Herculeus, First Lieutenant of Artillery company, x., 619. Made Captain Lt. of do., 775.

Court, Provincial to have five judges, to make two circuits yearly, i., 98, 107. And be a Court of Equity, 102. Records in a certain case to be burned, 106. Council to define jurisdiction of, 124. Special, 163, 164. Appeals from County Court—Judges commissioned, 169. Clerk of a, cannot act as attorney, 170. Ten days between a judgment and execution, 170, 171. Judges proposed, 187. Commissioned, 192. Necessity of a, 241, 247. Debate on, 248. Five judges decided on, 248. A decision in case Thomas Harris confirmed, 311. Expenses of summons, how paid, 311. Keeper of great seal may sit in County Courts, 321. Mercenary pleadings in, 327. Clerk appointed by Penn continues in office until convicted of crime charged against him, 327. John White, Clerk, case, 327, 329. Case of judgment under wrong name, 394. Proceedings in an urgent case, 395. Address Governor, 402. Judge appointed, 451. Place of holding, 453. Bills proposed respecting, 610. Bill for regulating, ii., 45, 184. Act for establishing, 155, 252, 253, 259, 337, 480–2. Magistrates obliged to hold their courts in ale-houses, 409. Revival of, 571. Justices appointed for the, 597. Act establishing, proposed, viii., 399, 400. Delayed by absence of great seal, 408. Opinion on, 543. Disallowed, 559, 573. To continue actions, &c., 673. A special, appointed for trial of Lt. R. Hamilton in Bedford county, x., 8. Justices to preside in, xii., 546. To be established by Congress for trial of piracies, 702.

Court of Admiralty, Judge F. Hopkinson re-appointed, xv., 191.

Court of Chancery, iv., 19, 21, 22. Report of James Logan on, 27. Violation of charter of privilege, 27. Petition of Phila. against, 35. Of Bucks, 36. Chester, 37. Assembly on, 40–46. Seal, 639. Contrary to Proprietary instructions, x., 20.

Court, City, xiii., 781.

Court of Common Pleas, A. Hamilton, Prothonotary, iii., 271. A. Hamilton, Clerk, applies for powers of a Justice — granted, but cannot sit as both at same time, iv., 153. M. Stedman, President, viii., 339. Justices superseded, 562. Prothonotaries to be Judges in their counties, xi., 221. P. Fleeson, President, to receive records of Mayor's office, xiii., 20. D. Pentecost appointed President, Washington, 732. E. Shippen, Justice, xiv., 103. H. Wynkoop, President, 150. F. Antes resigns, 169. Justices of, 180, 182. A. McAllister resigns—Henry Slagle appointed, 182. Justices, 224, 226, 242, 257. James Moore, resigns, 567. General Quarter Sessions and Jail delivery, and Orphans', J Maxwell, President, xv., 72, 124. Prothonotary, &c., 96, 97, 269, 271, 315. Dorsey Pentecost suspended on account of removal, 124. Edward Shippen resigns as President of Court of Quarter Sessions, 120, 128; xvi., 50, 119, 120.

Court, County, rules for proposed, i., 64. Fined by Council, 76. No circular, 147. Special, to be granted, 80, 515. County, ii., 254, 259, 571, 597; ix., 201, 237. Delaware county, xvi., 209, 212.

Court of Equity — Judge Guest complains that none have been held, ii., 114, 160, 184, 254. Rules for, 184; iii., 93, 105; iv., 19, 21, 22, 40.

Court, High, of Errors and Appeals, Judges appointed for, xii., 548. Judge resigns, 723. Judges appointed, xiii., 535, 545, 550. Judges to have access to library, 576. Opinion asked, 690; xiv., Samuel Miles, 306, 66. Judge, Edward Shippen, 207. H. Wynkoop, 229. T. Hopkinson, a Judge of, 310. Pay to Judge Wynkoop, xv., 645.

Court, Federal, to try private rights to lands in Wyoming, xiv., 31. At Hannas' Town, xiii., 699.

Court of Judicature, Act for establishing, ii., 222, 252, 434, 438, 440, 443, 454, 482, 485, 488, 489, 503, 518, 524, 540, 571-2, 578. Objections of Governor and Council, 263. Governor has power to establish, 296, 400. Chief Justice–A. Hamilton—died—Judge Mompesson, 239; iii., 171, 278, 398. Law of 1727 repealed, 418, 422. Message of Governor on continuation of actions, ix., 18, 361, 363, 369, 385, 390, 392, 581.

Court—Orphans—Clerk dies and another appointed, iv., 151. Clerk of, appointed, vii., 501. For city and county clerk—appointed William Nicolls, xiv., 667.

Court of Oyer and Terminer, ii., 18, 36, 86, 111, 254, 395. Commissions how to be issued, iii., 33–35. Repeal of laws respecting, 90, 156. Continued under Governor Gorden, 253; iv., 71, 244. Allen, Coleman, and Growden, viii., 336, 592. Judges, ix., 581; xvi., 17.

Court of Quarter Session—Justices oath, ii., 90. To administer certain oaths, 104. Trials, 396, 579. power of, over a road discussed, iii., 142; ix., 172, 237. Justices of, 393; xiii., 20.

Court of Philadelphia county—Justices commissioned, ii., 159, 254. Adjourned by Governor, 279.

Court, Supreme, iii., 254. Number of Judges equal as to Church of England and Quakers, 158. New commissions for, 253. Vacancies Hill and Lloyd, 398. C. J., being now President cannot act, iv., 71. Convictions by, 209. Prisoners for trial, 250. C. J. Langhorne dies—J. Kinsey succeeds, 640. Conviction of burglars, v., 155. 2nd Judge dead, vi., 135; viii., 335. Session of,—Judges Allen, Growden and Cole-

man, 481, 592. J. Evans dies, xiv., 41. Jacob Rush appointed, 43, 71, 483; xvi., 17.
Court, District, of Pennsylvania, to be held in Philadelphia, xvi., 433. Of United States, to be established, xvi., 100.
Court of Vice Admiralty—Andrew Hamilton appointed Judge, iv., 250.
Court-houses, i., 510; iii., 235, 241; xii., 181. In Philadelphia, to be built by a tax, ii., 406, 407, 409, 410.
Coutts James, Speaker of N. C. Assembly, ii., 425.
Cove—Great—destroyed, vi., 673-677. Inhabitants' letter to Justices of Cumberland County, v., 453. Election, 468.
Cove, Little—Inhabitants' letter to Justices of Cumberl'd Co., v., 452.
oventry Iron Works on French Creek, Chester county, iv., 152, 247.
Cowden, Captain, x., 699.
Cowperthwaite, Captain, x., 484, 757. Joseph conducts Continental powder mill, 757. Storekeeper of provisions at Reading, xi., 423. Justices, 619. Sheriff, xiv., 555; xv., 98.
Cowpland Caleb, 3rd Judge, dies-his place filled, viii., 77.
Cowpland, David, Burgess, xi., 729.
Cowpland, Captain Jonathan, xi., 678. Appointed Captain of a guard boat, x., 759.
Coxe, Colonel, letter, xii., 423.
Coxe, Dr., Iron works in Jersey, x., 575.
Cox, Isaac, paymaster of troops, x., 722. Resigns, 755.
Cox, Captain John, of ship Euryale from Barbadoes—letter of President to, v., 106. Complaints against, 108. Proclamation against, 109. Physicians to visit ship, 109.
Cox, John, taken by Indians, vii., 242. Feeble condition, 243. Complains of Thomas Forster of Lancaster county interrupting survey of land, ix., 335. Member of Council of Safety, x., 717. To purchase woodland in Jersey for salt works, xi., 294.
Cox, Captain Paul, appointed member of Navy Board, xi., 122. Commands a flag of truce, has permission to pass Mud Fort, xii., 557.
Coxe, Mrs. Sarah, too ill to travel, xii., 390.
Coxe, Tench, appointed commissioner, xv., 5. Commissioner to Commercial Convention, xv., 86, 135. To lay out a road, 425, 445. Paid as M. C., xvi., 10.
Cox, William, letter to, vii., 600.
Craig, Hugh, paymaster, xi., 32.
Craig, Captain Isaac, promoted to Major, xiii., 223, 233. Certificate of, xiv., 27. Memorial on lands in Westmoreland county, 291.
Craig, Colonel, commands a regiment, xii., 36.
Craig, Captain James, shot for, x., 598. A prisoner, xi., 292.
Craig, John, commander of privateer sloop Congress, x., 605. Resigns, xii., 88. Of dragoons, 275, 332. Resigns Council, elected to Assembly, xiii., 407. Collector of excise in Westmoreland, xv., 55. Lieutenant of Northampton county, 55. Revoked, 132, 621.
Craig, Captain Robert, paid, x., 686.
Craig, Thomas, commissioner of purchases, xii, 405, 409. Appointed Lieutenant, xiii., 617. Prothonotary of Montgomery county, xiv., 202, 204.
Craig, William, sheriff, v., 597. Appointed prothonotary of Northampton county, xv., 461. Justice, 579, 621.
Cramer, Philip, Sheriff, xi., 596.
Crapp, John, Surgeon, charged with ill-treatment of an insane patient and ordered to cure her, i., 512.
Cratho, John, authorized to trade and buy and hold lands, iii., 235.
Crawford, Captain, taken at St. John's, is on parole, x., 586.
Crawford, Colonel James, x., 687; xi., 104. Expedition, xvi., 42.
Crawford, Edward, Jr., prothonotary of Franklin County, xiv., 202, 204.
Crawford, Hugh, brings message from Twightwees, v., 437.
Crawford, James, Sheriff, xii., 137, 513; xiii., 92.

Crawford, Josiah, letter—Justice, xii., 486.
Crawford, William, Judge of Court in Westmoreland county, joins Virginia against Pennsylvania, x., 228.
Crawford, Colonel William, expedition against Indians, xiv., 310.
Credit, of the provinces assailed by Andrew Bradford, printer, for which he is summoned before Council, iii., 143.
Creigh, John, Clerk of Orphans' Court, xi., 200. Justice, resigns, xii., 3.
Cremshier, John Dutton, Notary, xiii., 15.
Cresap, Thomas, iii., 472. On west side of Susquehanna not disposed to return, iv., 57. On Maryland affairs, 68, 103. Arrested for murder of Knowles Dant, 109, 121, 122, 139. List of persons concerned in burning his house, 117, 130, 135. Character of, 111, 177. Petition of, 145, 256.
Cresap, Captain, alluded to, v., 218. Sends for Indians—their report, 439.
Cresson, Sam'l, collects excise, xv., 222.
"Crisis," payment to Thomas Paine for ten dozen, by the Council, xii., 503.
Crispin, William, provisions, xi., 142, 248, 257, 266, 267, 280, 405, 408, 440, 448, 465, 475, 528, 572, 576, 586, 640, 650; 689, 706, 717, 719, 728, 742, 750, 778. Commissary, xii., 10, 26, 44, 65, 86, 111, 204. To furnish rations and account, and be discharged, 226, 247, 450. Collector of excise, 554; xiv., 365.
Croasdell, William, Sheriff of Bucks, ii., 397.
Croghan, George, an Indian trader, informs of Indians formerly in French interest have changed to English, v., 72, 119, 211. Letter to, from R. Peters, 214. Narrative of his proceedings at Ohio, 287. Pay to, 294. His residence, 348, 349. Indian Conference at his house in Pennsboro, 431–436. Letters, 496, 515. Instructions respecting presents, 518. Private, say nothing about a fort, 522. Treaty with Twightwees, 523. His journal, 528, 530–540. Letter, 539. Bears a message from Shawnese to Governor—letter from, 569, His journal, 731. Letters to and from, vi., 21, 140, 160, 180, 181, 188, 218, 226, 373, 375, 398, 642, 699. Building fort at mouth of Monongahela, 21. At Auckwick, 150. Fort at Wills' Creek, 180. French at Ohio, 181. Commission for surveying roads, 318, 323. Letter from, and other Commissioners for laying out a road for Braddock, 368. Indian messages, 375. Indians return to Auckwick, 398. At Little Meadows, 460. French and Indians on Ohio, 642. Reported "cut off," 667. Act proposed for relief of, 743, 744. Account of interview with Indians, 781. Appointed by Sir Wm. Johnson agent of Indian affairs, vii., 354. Letters to and from, 355, 384, 385, 403, 465, 474, 475, 480, 481, 484, 503, 532, 608, 639, 644, 660, 681. Instructions of Johnson to, 355, 435. Gives opinion in Council, 382. Governor's letter to, on money, 384. Receives from J. Pemberton, &c., on part of friendly association, money for Indians, 391. Deputies from Indians, 485. Speech of chiefs at Lancaster, 485. Indians, 503. Minutes of his proceedings with Indians at Harris' and Lancaster, 506–517. Sent by W. Johnson, to Pennsylvania, 624. Letter to, from Gov., on a clerk, 658. Encloses a paper written by C. Thomson to Governor, 681. Teedyuscung's opinion of, 731. Indian agent for Sir. William Johnson, attends conference at Easton, viii., 175. Opinion of conference with Ohio Indians, 301. Act in favor of, and William Trent disallowed in England, 321. Holds conference with Indians at Pittsburg, 382–391, 429. Garrisons Fort Lyttleton, ix., 34. Letters to and from, 249, 321, 490. His journal of transactions with Indians, 250–264, 322. Goods for Indians, 302. Indian affairs, 433. Going to Fort

Pitt to condole with Indians, 490, 496. Conference at, 514–543. Speech to, 533.
Crohon, Dennis, petition of his wife, his case stated, and cannot appear in time, xii., 58, 65.
Croker, Joseph, (a mason) killed at Wyoming, viii., 134.
Croll, Michael, sub-Lieutenant, xii., 407. Justice, xiv., 629.
Crooks, Thomas, Justice, xiii., 122.
Crosby, John, Jr., Coroner, ix., 778; x., 56. Commissioner of purchases, xii., 393.
Crosier, Matthias, Coroner, vii., 267.
Croston, M., contractor, vii., 550.
Crown Point, intended expedition against, v., 199. French propose building a fort near, vi., 330. Supplies for, 616. Expedition—number of men to be raised in each State for, vii., 29.
Crows, George, forges deeds, x., 693, 695, 696, 698, 720.
Crozer, John, xi., 429.
Cruikshank, Alexander, sells negro, i., 556, 558.
Cryder, Michael, agent of estates, xiii., 115.
Cuba, Island of, enlistment of soldiers for, iv., 499.
Culbertson, Andrew, Justice, xi., 398.
Culbertson, Capt. Robert, x., 700. Wagon master, xii., 453.
Culbertson, Samuel, Commissioner to buy provisions Chester Co., xi., 424. Elected to Assembly—resigns as Justice, xii., 170.
Cumberland Co., formed, v., 428, 431. Justices appointed, 436. Early settlements, 440. Governor writes to Justices, 450. Sheriffs elected, 468, 551, 597, 662. Coroners elected, 468, 551, 597, 662. Petition from Great Cove in, 468. Boundary line between, and York co., 502, 514, 619. Workhouse and house of correction, 506, 512. Complaints against Indian traders, 528, 547. Andrew Montour applies to live in, 566. Has a commission and permitted to go there, 567. Act respecting Inspectors, 619. Petition for protection, vi., 130. Sheriffs elected, 144, 638. Coroners elected, 144, 638. Letter, Governor to Justices, respecting Col. Dunbar, 514. Company formed in Lurgan township for protection, ask for arms, 533. Difficulties with Maryland, 639. Indian murders, 645–662, 670. Destruction of Great Cove, 673–675. State of affairs in, 706. Orders of Governor Morris to Colonel Armstrong and others in, vii., 161. To commissaries of stores, 162. Petitions from, 241. Roads, 592. Justices decline serving, 595. New, commissioned, 637. Coroners appointed, viii., 223, 403, 506, 781. Sheriffs appointed, 223, 403, 506, 781. Inspectors, 400. Representation of proprietary tax in, 472. Tabular statements, 476. Sheriffs elected, ix., 57, 199, 286, 333, 398, 547, 624, 681, 691, 779. Coroners elected, 57, 199, 286, 333, 398, 547, 624, 673, 691, 732, 779. Justices, 293, 386, 470. A frontier county, 138. Letter, General Gage, and advertisement of Lieutenant Colonel Reid, complaining of insults to troops, 267. Letter to Justices, 272. Justice William Smith complained of for neglect of duty, 293. Removed, 293. Writ against James Smith as a ringleader of rioters near Fort Loudoun, 293, 297. Letter to magistrates respecting destruction of goods intended for Fort Pitt, 302, 304. Murders by F. Stump, 414–490. Ordered to Philadelphia, 441. From Sheriff Holmes, 463. From Justices, 486. Convictions, 513. H. Alrich resigns—T. Francis succeeds, 671. Convictions, ix., 548. Trial of negroes, 704. Division of, 719, 729. Bedford county taken from it, 730. Claims for carriages employed by Colonel Wilkins, x., 17. Sheriffs elected, 56, 101, 212, 271. Coroners elected, 56, 101, 212, 271. Justices elected, 56, 101, 212, 271. Division of, 32, 42. Convictions and executions, 50, 265. Associators ask for pattern guns, 300. Resolve of Committee of, for powder and lead, 398. Arms to be collected, 441.

A fifth battalion to be raised, 450. Officers appointed, 451. Removal of prisoners of war, 515. Aid to associators, 696. Colonel Joseph Armstrong, 700. Militia, xi., 77. Prothonotary, 178, 221, 244, 365. Lieutenant appointed, 187, 199, 205, 257. Clerk Orphans' Court, 200, 694. M. Agnew late Prothonotory refuses to deliver to W. Lyon the papers and records—proceeding, 244. Threatened destruction of public property at Carlisle, 307. To pay for arms, 358. Militia, 360. Col. Clarke, Paymaster, 361. Election, 366. Sheriffs, 366, 609. Coroner, 366, 609. Petition for defence from Indians in, 410. Pay for recruits, 444. Militia called out, 447. Justices, 453, 523, 621, 691, 781. Militia, 477, 740. Indians, 489, 491, 506, 520, 770. Justices, xii., 3. Lieutenants, 15. Wm. Lyon receives subscriptions to loan office, 47. Change in orders respecting Lieutenants, 76. Militia in Northumberland destitute, aid refused by Commissary, 100. Elections for Representatives, Councillor, Commissioners, Assessors, &c., 166, 518. Justices, 198, 376, 559, 667. Sheriffs, 166, 518. Coroners, 166, 518. Case of Robert Story, 179. He discloses a plot and is reprieved, 192. Taxes, 210. Petition to offer reward for apprehension certain persons, 248. Incendiaries in, proclamation for arrest, 294. Officers appointed, 322. Appointments, 554. Auditors, 646. Captain Carothers resigns, 721. Survey to Alexander Powers, 783. Elections, xiii., 133, 396, 726. Justices, 7, 266, 520, 647, 666. Sheriffs, 133, 396, 726. Coroners, 133, 396, 726. Militia called out, 53, 122. Colonel Brown's battalion and Colonel Purdy's, 222. Colonel Mitchell's to go to Northumberland, 223. Pay for troops, 269. Price of rations, 270. Prothonotary, 324. Call on for men, 349, 369. Taxes, 647. Censors, Representatives, 726. Agent of confiscated estates, xiv., 140. Justices, 157, 164, 180, 240, 307, 344, 357, 370, 465, 517. Elections, 236, 563. Representatives, 236. Sheriffs, 236, 567. Council, 236. Coroners, 236, 567. Commissioners, 236. Eighteen penny tax, 267. Militia, 400. Deputy Surveyors, 441, 442, 444, 445, 449. Lieutenant William Sterret, 482. Contested election, 485. Lieutenant John Wilkins, Jr., 551. President of Court C. P., &c., Samuel Laird appointed, 553. Road from Miller's spring to Pittsburg, xv., 13. John Wilkins resigns as Lieutenant, 87. George Gibbons appointed, 89. Collector of excise, 93. Election, 102, 300, 577. Sheriff, 102, 300, 577, 578. Coroner, 102, 300, 577, 578. Resignation of Justice Beale, 105. Justices, 90, 131, 154, 213, 570, 644. Militia, 178, 229. Election of town officers at Carlisle, 218. Execution ordered, 218. Collector of excise, 221, 222. Road from Miller's spring to Fort Pitt, 273, 274. Road by Burnt Cabins, 322, 371. Contested election, 325, 326. Western road to Bedford, 327, 330. Pension to Captain Walker Denny's widow, 345 William Elliott paid as a member of conference of committees, 353. Road between Clark's Gap and Burnt Cabins, 371, 393, 399, 486, 519. Riots, 415. Nol pros., 417. Pay to Colonel Gibson for printing, 457. Pension, 464. Election set aside, 520. Road to Pittsburg, 594. Sureties for officers, xvi., 32. Neglect charged on Commissioners, 39. Allen McGeechan, agent of confiscated estates in, 73. Road to Pittsburg, 73. Colonel George Gibson, Lieutenant, 73. Road through Black's Gap, 102. Militia returns, 149. Sheriffs, 193, 509. Coroners, 193, 509. Deputy Surveyer, 214. Militia, 319, 363, 445. Prothonotary, J, Agnew, deceased, 328. Pay and bounty for a detachment under command of Captain Samuel Holliday against the Indians, 363. Taxes received, &c., 380. Excise,

408. Pensions, 412. Militia, 22. Breakfasts for and price, 501. Militia, Captain George Hayes' company, 536, 542.
Cumberland Fort—flour not arrived at, for General Braddock, vi., 373, 445. Persons missing from, 4. Cannon for, 445, 465. Murders near, 475, 643. Colonel Dunbar with wounded arrives at, 502, 513. Cumberland or French Fort Beau Sejour, captured, 447. Communication cut off, vii., 133. Adam Stephen commander, letter from, 289, 381. Murders near, 381, 503. Respecting, 512. 600; viii., 224; ix., 35. Indians murdered near, 304.
Cunningham, Allen, coroner, xii., 513; xiii., 87.
Cunningham, Colonel, xi., 367.
Cunningham, James, examination of, respecting rescue of Stump, ix., 449, 450. Deposition respecting Peter Chartier, iv., 757; x. 683.
Cunningham, Peter, ensign, xii., 37.
Cuppaidge, Lieutenant George, prisoner of war removed, x., 574.
Curgill, Major Jno., to answer Council respecting obstructions at ferry, xi., 675.
Currency, Governor's views on, iii., 249, 250.
Curric, Dr. William, resigns as surgeon of Colonel Atlee's battalion, x., 734.
Curry, Robert, Coroner, takes a deserter, xi., 451.
Curtis, Jehu, 2nd Judge of Supreme Court dies, vi., 135.
Curtis, John, a justice of Kent accused of high treason, i., 158, 163, 164, 165, 196. Objected to as member of Council, 197, 268. News of robberies, v., 89. A Nanticoke Indian conference with, ix., 45.
Curwen, John, repaid for surveying Jones' lane, xvi., 11.
Cushietunk—Connecticut settlers at, J. Hyndshaw's deposition, viii., 612. Lands, &c., 646. Connecticut settlers at, ix., 27, 29.
Custologo, a Delaware Indian, and a leading man, v., 660.
Custom House fees, i., 67. Officers, 535, 537.
Customs, how raised, i, 99. Council refuse to take collector's oath but will receive his attestation, 148. Officers of, to be protected, iii., 64, 143.
Cuthbert, Anthony, claim for city lots, xv., 439. Claim to city lots, xvi., 119, 167, 170, 293, 299.
Cuthbert, Thomas, appointed agent for forfeited estates, xi., 758. Removed, 767.
Cutler, John, coroner of Bucks, iii., 56, 69.
Cuyler, Cornelius, bearer of letter from Governor of New York to Governor of Canada, v., 554.
Cypher, Michael, ensign leaves his colors, x., 694.

D.

Dagworthy, Cap., commands at fort Cumberland. Indian murders, vi., 643; vii., 601; letters, 602, 632, 633.
Dahauff, Cap. Abm., firelocks, x., 539.
Dale, Peter, his mill, ii., 10.
Dampier, Cap. (the navigator) ii., 99.
Darby Township, complaint respecting road from B. Chamber's ferry, ii., 33. Bridge at Cobbs' creek, iii., 426, 428, 431. Road to from Philadelphia, v., 121; laid but not cleared in 1706, 121, 202. Creek, banks, &c., to be made and repaired, viii., 575, 583, 683. Boats in x., 656, 682. Marsh, &c., Act to extend, ix., 12, 24. Rendezvous at, xi., 301. Road from to Schuylkill bridge, xii., 314, 70. Road between, and Lancaster, 592, 650, 667, 710. Report on, confirmed, 726.
Darlington, Abm., Coroner, iii., 370, 387.
Dartmouth, Earl of, letters to and from, x., 220, 221, 240, 248; non-importation; Congress; boundary line, 240. State Colonies, 248.
Darvall, William, Agent of Lord Baltimore, i., 113, 115, 116.
Dauphin county; Alexander Graydon, Prothonotary, xiv., 374. Register and Recorder, 376; other

offices added, 377; Justices, 396, 477. Lieutenant, 400. Sheriffs, 556. Coroners, 556; Represent, 556. Large petition from, in favor of Commissioners for not assessing for a Court-house at Harris's ferry, xv., 14. Elections, 100, 294. Justices, 41, 405. Sheriff, 100, 296, 570. Coroner, 100, 296, 570. Agent for sales at, 172, 223. Councillor, 296. Contested seat taken by Mr. Kucher, 309. Contested election of Justice, 405. Thomas Clark appointed, 405. Repair of arms, 421. Removal of prisoners, 469. Lieutenant of County, xvi., 40. Am'nt of tavern and marriage licenses, 61, 543. Colonel Hanna's battalion, gunner wounded, 121. Tavern and marriage licenses, 196. Sheriffs, 195, 498. Coroners, 195, 498, 499, 500. Deputy Surveyor, 214. Division into townships, 253. Justices, 204, 309, 352, 362, 387, 447, 537. Contested election, 274, 362. Excise, 408. J. Glonginger resigns as justice, elected to Senate, 537.

Dauphin of France—proceedings, xiii., 282, 284, 285. Cost of entertainment, 297.

Davenport, Josiah, appointed Commiss'r, with Col. Burd, to receive prisoners from Indians, viii., 776.

Davidson, Rev. James, assistant at salt works, xi., 403, 509.

Davidson, Joshua, Ensign, xii., 31.

Davidson, Captain Samuel, permitted to make a voyage for Congress, x., 415. Commands floating battery, 509. Boats resist his command, 606, 607, 608, 615, 624, 696. Appointed Commodore, x., 603, 701, 702. Censor, xiii., 729. Coroner, xiv., 567; xv., 139.

Davis, Lieutenant Abner, resigns x., 759.

Davis, Benjamin, Sheriff, iv., 469, 500, 601; v. 55, 120, 345; viii., 402, 506. To assist Captain Downey in a survey near the river, xi., 249; and from Salem downward, 250, 258. Notary, xv., 241. Measurer of, grain, xvi., 209.

Davis, Major Caleb, x., 697. Prothonotary, xi., 230, 235, 244. Justice, 274, 286. Complains of H. H. Graham, for detaining records of Chester Co.—authority to take them, 254. Complaint against, xiv., 204, 207.

Davis, Colonel, to provide horses for ammunition to Westmorèland county, xii., 386.

Davis Enoch, Justice, Philadelphia, ix., 237.

Davis, Henry, Coroner, ix., 199.

Davis, Doctor John, may buy instruments, x., 638.

Davis, John, Captain, xi., 18.

Davis, Llewellyn, ensign, xii., 10.

Davis, Merrick, Coroner of Philadelphia, iii., 140, 332, 370.

Davis, Samuel, Coroner of Sussex county, iii., 260, 289.

Davis, Ensign Septimus, appointed, x., 678.

Davis Thomas to build boats, &c., x. 283. Troops to Bord'n, 629.

Davis, William, a Justice of Chester County, left out of common, for indiscreetly marrying a couple, ii., 561.

Davison, John, an Indian trader was at Washington's defeat, vi., 195.

Davison, Commodore Samuel, complaint and trial, x. 701. Dismissed, 702.

Dawson, Captain Samuel, xi., 2.

Dawson, Captain, dies, xii., 435.

Dayagoughderesesh, alias Thomas King, an Oneida Indian, dies, ix., 775.

Dealer, Chas., storekeeper, xi., 437.

Dean, Lieutenant John, sentence of Court Martial referred to Navy Board, xi., 138.

Dean, Colonel Joseph, xi., 142. To rendezvous at Swedes ford, 301.

Dean, Joseph, Member of Council of Safety, xi., 45. Board of War, 201. Memorial. Purchases a forfeited estate in Philadelphia County, xii., 45. Appointed Auditor to settle accounts of troops, 589. Purchases, 639. Warden, xiii., 100. Deed to, 126. Bell's estate, 529, 570, 587. Sale of estate, 623, Appointed auctioneer for Philadelphia, xvi., 313, 316, 320, 460.

Dean, Samuel, Sheriff, xiii., 392, 720; xiv., 237. Councillor, 567. To superintend drawing donation land lottery, xv., 108.
Dean, Lieutenant Colonel, William x., 733.
Dean, William, Justice, xiii., 625.
Dean, William, Lieutenant, pay to, xvi., 267, 278. To examine rivers, 319.
Dearing, Wm., servants complained against, 149, 150, 152.
Death of King William III. announced, succeeded by Princess Ann of Denmark as Queen, ii., 69.
De Barras, Count, Commander of French fleet, applies for sailors deserted, xiii., 5, 54, 55.
Debts, priority of payment to inhabitants, ii., 363. Recovery of small, iii., 540, 541. Recovery of, iv., 38, 40, 41, 331, 332. Lands in execution for, ix., 147, 148, 160. Small, 204, 238, 243.
De Buc, Peter, his will, i., 443, 444.
De Canaveral, Commandant General of Carthagena, letter from, xvi., 381.
Decatur, Captain Stephen, petition that his wife Priscilla may come from New York, xii., 699.
Decker, Cobus, daughter captured by Indians, viii., 143.
Declaration, Pennsylvania against Lord Baltimore, i., 113, 115. Against Nicholas Moore, 134–137, 138. Of Governor and Council to continue the laws, 296. Of King William and Queen Mary, 304. Of allegiance signed by members, 322. Of Quakers, 526. Fidelity, form of, iii., 229. Representation from Quakers respecting, 234. Bill passed, 235. Form of change proposed, iv., 334. Of war between England and France, 690. Proclaiming King George III., viii., 517. Of war with Spain, 703. Of frontier inhabitants, &c., on murder of Indians, ix., 142, 146. Of war against the Delaware Indians, vii., 88. Adam Terrence, Indian murders, vi., 649.
De Cornay, Mons., letter, xii., 425.
Dedimus potestatem, to six persons to administer oath to the Governor, ii., 62. Discussion as to the keeper of it, ordered into hands of Master of Rolls, 63. Objections and difficulties, 63, 68. Legal opinions where to be kept, 68. Oath administered by Council, 69, 91. Commissioners objections to administer oaths and affirmations, and place of keeping it, 93–95. John Bewly, Collector, administers it, 96. Granted by Council, for Sussex and Kent, 97. To Robert Asheton, 98. Messenger to Chester with, paid, 111. To J. Yeates, &c., to administer oath to Governor Keith, iii., 13. To administer oaths at Bristol in absence of Secretary, v., 110. Issued to J. B. Smith, Jno. Morris, Jr., and George Campbell, for City and County of Philadelphia, xiv., 110. To Jno. Arndt and Rob. Levers, xv., 279.
Deeds, fraudulent, i., 207. From Indians to Wm. Penn, 1701, and agreements, iii., 600–603. From Six Nations to proprietaries for lands on Susquehannah at Albany, vi., 119–129. For lands between Pennsylvania and Indians, vii., 693, 698. For 1718, demanded by Teedyuscung, 731. For land, forged, x., 693. Issued for forfeited estates, xii., 45, 104, 157, 158, 185, 189, 196, 201, 202, 222, 238, 246, 256, 258, 265, 268, 276, 281, 283, 284, 299, 300, 317, 320, 323, 324, 326, 343–346, 348, 350, 352, 380, 381, 383, 413, 421, 430, 441, 445, 446, 448, 457, 458, 463, 468, 481, 552, 553, 560, 571, 575, 612, 614, 615, 617, 618, 619, 620, 621, 639, 661, 668, 671, 672, 673, 687, 709, 731, 733, 734, 737, 747, 751, 752, 755, 775, 781, 782. Diffanderfer, Michael, buys estates, xii., 275. Indian, or relating to Connecticut controversy, delivered to H. Osburne, xiii., 438, and returned per list, 462–471. xiii., 12, 20, 25, 26, 30, 33, 34, 35, 39, 40, 45, 46, 52, 54, 56, 57, 63, 64, 65, 66, 80, 81, 94, 97, 98, 108, 109, 117, 126, 127, 139, 142, 146, 159, 166, 170, 171, 172, 175, 176, 180, 181, 182, 183, 184,

193, 199, 204, 214, 217, 219, 235, 236, 246, 250, 251, 271, 273, 274, 277, 278, 279, 280, 305–308, 315, 316, 320, 325, 334, 335, 340, 344, 346, 366, 384, 389, 409, 432, 450, 505, 543, 548, 549, 552, 572, 576, 585, 587, 592, 599, 604, 617, 621, 623, 629, 631, 646, 686, 695, 701, 727, 735, 748, 759, 760, 767, 778. xiv., 34, 35, 54, 56, 65, 151, 176, 409, 453, 456, 459, 462, 486, 492, 495, 501, 583, 589, 591, 603, 607, 632, 639, 642, 649, 650, 653. xv., 4, 13, 14, 34, 37, 40, 43, 46, 50, 51, 72, 99, 124, 153, 173, 180, 181, 185, 230, 256, 434, 458, 468, 472, 538, 562. xvi., 283, 541.

Deedjoskon, Delaware Chief, vii., 431.

Deer and other wild beast not to be hunted on Indian lands, viii., 482–484.

De Ford, Vincent, xii., 86.

De Grafendriedt, Techarner, claim for lands, xv., 629.

De Haas, General. Petition of Robert Patton, for relief from ill treatment by, xi., 188.

De Haas, John Philip, appointed Justice, ix., 281. Deposition, his ill treatment by Connecticut men, 682. Dispute with Grubb of Lancaster, x., 346. His battalion, 514, 525, 529, 532. Has a negro pardoned, xvi., 107.

De Haas, Johannes, returned as Councillor for New Castle, i., 214, 222. Refuses to act as a magisistrate till he knows who is king, 302.

De Hart, Jacob, Lieutenant, xi., 751, 766.

De Hart, Colonel, letter respecting Ashur Levy, xii., 258.

De Haven, Peter, x., 467, 503, 527, 533, 650, 686. xi., 272, 273, 281, 314, 546, 663, 701, 754, 759. Agent for estates forfeited, 754. Resigns, 758. Health officer, 775. Agent to buy hay, xii., 543. Gun stocks, xvi., 460.

Dehuff, Henry, Chief Burgess, xi., 364.

De Kalb, Baron, Major General, killed at Camden—commissions as ensigns in Pennsylvania line granted to his sons, xiii., 52.

De Lafarge, Charles, letter to Gov. Keith on assuming the Governorship, iii., 73.

De la Grange, Arnoldus, claim against C. Taylor's estate, i. 201.

De la Luzerne, Chevalier, to be received publicly by Congress, xii., 170, 172. Visits President and Council, 180. Letter, 251, 433.

De Lancey, James, Governor of New York, v., 716, 717. Letters to and from, vi., 9, 13, 48, 511, 520, 554, 592. Answer to Commissioners, 92. Arrives in Philadelphia, 358. Examination of a French deserter, 416. On embargo, 511. On the defeat of General Braddock, 520. Intelligence from Admiral Boscawen, 592, 600. Letters to and from, vii., 560, 596, 606, 628, 716, 762; viii., 146, 165. Embargo —Sir Charles Hardy, 560, 606.

De Lancey, Captain, x., 560.

De Lancey, Dr., x., 689.

De Lancey, Mrs. Mary, pass to visit her father, Wm. Allen, and remain in Philadelphia, xi., 593.

De Lancey, Oliver, on parole, x., 40.

Delaney, Capt. Sharp, complains of insult, x., 753, 759. To attend Board, xiii., 294. Appointed by Assembly Collector of port Philadelphia, xiv., 52, 447. Urging collections, 405. Place of office, 406, 444, 450, 473. Sale of goods, 637. On collecting imposts, xv., 134. To render account of dues, 253. Reports, 254. Re-appointed Collector, 315. Office for, &c., 402, 440, 484. Commendation of, as Collector of Customs, xvi., 59, 217[2]. Paymaster of pensioners, 293. Accounts, 328.

De la Vega, letter from, respecting a prize, v., 199.

Delaware, armed boat, xi., 5, 10, 27, 47, 68, 74, 113. Thomas Philips, first Lieutenant, 47.

Delaware County, Prothonotary, xvi., 171. William R. Atlee appointed 172. Collector of Excise, Philip Sheaff—Lieutenant of, Luke Morris, Jr., 183. Opinion of Attorney General regarding Justices and Judges on division of county, 187. Justices, 190, 217, 218, 301, 402. Sheriff, 191, 493. Coroner,

191, 493, 498. Presidents of Courts, 209, 212. Elected, 214. Deputy Surveyor, 214. Justice Kean resigns, 352.

Delaware Indians, suspected of murder, ii., 70. No interpreter of their language but "Harry," Conference, with, 546. Conference with, and interpreter, iii., 19. Governor presents several papers relating to them and lands, iv., 481. Disturbance about lands, 575. Speech of Cannasatego to, 579. Petition of Capt. John Titame, a chief of, 624. Murders by—seizure by Shekalamy, 675. C. Weiser to be sent to, at Shamokin, to demand the murderers, 676, 678, 679. In Philadelphia, 742. Murderers arrested and in prison, 744. Speeches, 767. Olumpees, king of, dies, v., 212. Consultation about successor, 222; vi., 36. Under Shingas destroy Great Cove, 675. Scaroyady and Monteur sent to, 697. Cause of alienation, 724–728. Opposed to English, vii., 13. War urged—and scalps, 74. Declaration of war against, proclaimed, 88. Governor Morris blamed by Sir William Johnson for, 117. Temporary suspension of hostilities, 130, 134, 144, 171. Names of families at Bethlehem, 174. Message and wampum from Teedyuscung, 198. At war, 244, 297. Further suspension of hostilities, 390. Speech of Seneca chief to, 515. Hung in N. J.—described, 540. To be treated with at Col. Johnson's, 655. Fort and houses for, at Wyoming, vii., 730, 734. Arrive with skins—disappointed at not finding goods, 734. A family of settlers on Susquehanna coming from Tinogan, viii., 120. Message to, from Cherokees, 135. Copy of Sir William Johnson's speech to, on Ohio, 151. Opinion respecting, 194. Claims to lands, 202. Propose moving to Kuskusky, 305. Horses stolen by, 401. Chiefs propose holding a treaty, 676. Conference with relatives of Dr. John at Philadelphia, 709. Perfidy of, ix., 239. Treaty of peace with, by Sir Wm. Johnson, 277. Billy Champion complains of settlers on Susquehanna, 426. Message of Governor to Newsleeka, their chief, &c., respecting settlers on their lands, 428. Conference with, on Big Island, 620. Chief Newsleeka at Philadelphia, 656. Letter from Notawatways, a chief, 735. Conference in Philadelphia, x., 10, 61. Joseph Wipey murdered—reward offered, 199. And Shawnese separate from each other, 201. Message to, 204. At Conshocking declare war against Senecas, xii., 586.

Delaware, State of, Committee, to be written to, x., 571. Negotiation for inland navigation, xiv., 583, 669, 672. Inland navigation, xv., 71.

Delaware and New York, fees in, to be compared, i., 63.

Delaware River, buoys proposed, i., 82, 204, 205. Wharf at Chestnut street asked for, 267. Forts on, 109, 131, 370, 372. Watch to be stationed at Cape Henlopen, 479. Ferrymen to give bonds respecting strangers and pirates, ii., 13. A supposed privateer or pirate seized in, 99. Rendezvous for privateers, 468. New ferries, iii., 39, 43. At Falls, 43. Infested with pirates—Teach, a noted one, 54. Numerous shipwrecks in the bay—buoys required, 493. Pilots to have license, iv., 394. Lands in forks of, 576. Rules and regutations to be observed in cases of flags of truce—also how pilots are to act, v., 81. Spaniards commit robberies, 92. Privateers also, 110, 111, 245, 248. Intelligence boat commissioned, 266. Hector, man-of-war, captures a schooner off, 323. A French flag of truce, with prisoners captured by privateer Spry, viii., 139. Piers proposed, 574. Fish in, 583. Light house, buoys, &c., ix., 56, 57, 148, 197, 550. Embanking and draining marshes, 245, 247. Wardens appointed—bill to regulate pilots, 293, 593, 599, 676. Fisheries, 623. An accurate map of, 720, 721. Acts respecting light-house, buoys, x., 4. Pilot boat

loaded with goods seized by a revenue schooner in—proceedings, 9. Jurisdiction of Chester county does not extend into the river, 232. Ebenezer Robinson receives thanks for his plan for stopping the channel, 286. Committee to visit Red Bank and Mud Island—report—width—no boom can be placed there, 283. Chevaux-de-frise, 335. Rules for pilots, 356. Pilot boat to cruise in, 401. To be surveyed from Marcus Hook to Philadelphia, by persons named, 412. Coal to be taken out of, 421. Report on coal thrown into, 423. Jersey shore to be surveyed, 465. Report on, 474. Signals along, 489. Survey between Reedy Point and Pea Patch, 506, 507. Signals, 520. Piers at Fort Island, 524. Places for fortifications, 524. Logs for piers in, 530. Contract for piers, 530. McBean visits man-of-war fraudulently, 531. Vessels to cruise in—two more chevaux-de-frises, 534, 535. Man-of-war Roebuck aground—vessels sent to attack—boats return, 552, 553. Preparations for action—vessels in sight of Port Penn, 557. Stage boats, Captains Bush and Taylor, between Philadelphia and Wilmington, 563. Survey of, 567. Fortifications—chevaux-de-frise to be sunk, 600, 602. Engineers solicited from General Washington to erect fortifications at Billingsport, 604. Hog Island to be overflowed, 607. Defence endangered by dispute in naval department, 680. Piers, 718, 727. Chain-boom, 750. Eastern channel to be sounded near Fort Island, 761. Ferries not to be passed by persons with arms, xi., 27. Brig blown up at Cape May, 77. Stores moving across, 83. Vessels of war arrive in, 184. Survey near, 249. General Washington asks for a survey of—N. Sellers, Col. Lalor and Capt. J. Downey to make it, 250, 258. Barges to watch cruisers, 539. Sunken vessels, &c. to be secured, 555. Defence of, 556, 562, 570. To raise wrecks, 558. Light-house, 574, 620. Plan of, 587. Buoys, 715. Wrecks from fisheries to be removed, 720. Swept for anchors, 770, 773. Elegant plan of, by Du Portail, fortifications, 776. Col. Bull to execute, 777. James Hopkins allowed to search wrecks in, xii., 1. J. Knox reports articles found, 2, 14, 33. Pay to artillerists doing duty at Forts on, 10. W. Watkins petitions to sweep—rejected, 21. Wm. Watkins authorized, 33, 34. Petition to search for wrecks, 75, 76. Jehu Eyre, 263, 264. Deserters taken, 303. Commission to Abraham Bennett, pilot, for armed pilot boat, the Randolph, 326. A small boat, Capt. Buck occasions alarm, 331. Refugees taken to be exchanged, 413. Wrecks of vessels burned injure fisheries on Jersey shore, 611. Enemy about to leave New York for, 685. Conference on defence of—two companies to be raised, 686. Enemy expected, 707. Two companies to be raised for defence of, 719. Light-house in danger of being washed away, xiii., 100. A British vessel in, refusing to be examined by naval officers, to be taken by Captain Porter to Mud Island, 145. Defence of, 261. Proposals to buy ship General Monck for defence of, 270, 316. Hog Island, 11, 279, 280, 281. Preservation of fish in, 318. Boats to convey French army over the, 358. Vessel to be procured for defence, 384. Vessel for defence of—John Sneider commander, 445. Hyder Alley bought for State, 450. Vessel to be procured, with provisions for prisoners at New York, 457. Pay for flour, &c., 481. Sale of armed vessels authorized, 552. Chevaux-de-frises to be sold and pest houses repaired—boom at piers of, 590. Obstructions to be removed, 595. Wardens to have a survey made, to know which chevaux-de-frise to remove, 637, 671, 739. Agreement with Bassini and garrison for removal of obstructions, 744. Chevaux-de-frise, xiv., 58,

73, 75, 78, 79, 104, 105, 213, 636. Agreement with Donaldson and Hollingsworth—appropriation for improving, 105. Vessel purchased 119. Buoys removed from, and proclamation, 122. Expended by Wardens, 151. Paid Donaldson and Hollingsworth, 153, 200. Certificate to, 241. Improvements proposed by Wardens, 323, 325. Memorial of merchants respecting piers, 326. Commissioners to settle jurisdiction of islands in, 345–6. Erection of piers by Thomas Davis, 458. Land for piers at Marcus Hook, to be bought, 460, 464. Davis declines piers—new proposals, 468. Thos. Conarroe agrees to build piers at Marcus Hook, 479. Chevaux-de-frise, 500. Pay to Commissioners on Islands, 504. Damage to banks by uncommon freshet and high tides, 512. Buoys in river, 585. Report on jurisdiction of Islands in, with sketch of, 590, 599. Improvement of, 640. Engineer at Billingsport, xv., 24. Commissioners for dividing islands in—paid, 65. Support of Light-house, &c., in, 73. Newbold's Island, 184. Funds for improving, furnished Wardens, 197. Claim of Thos. Conarroe for building piers at Marcus Hook, 228. Report on, 233. May be made navigable to head waters, 659. Improvement of navigation of, xvi., 147. Commissioners to view, 178, 222[2]. John Lockhart petitions for preemption right of a small island between Hog and Tinicum, 230. Pay to Matlack Howell and Dean for maps of, and Lehigh, 278. Commissioners to examine, 319. Pay to R. Thorne for improving at Well's Falls and Howells, 322.

Delegates in Congress, xv., 19.

De Lignery, Monsieur, shot in thigh at Niagara, viii., 379. Formerly commanded at Pittsburg, 392.

Dellam, Richard, paymaster of flying camp, xi., 100, 140.

Delucena, Abraham, of New York, petition respecting goods seized, iii., 61.

De Marcellin, a young Frenchman recommended for 3rd brigade by Chev. Luzerne, xii., 116.

Dement, William, adjutant, x., 499.

Deniver, John, a highway robber taken, reward paid, xi., 20.

Denmark, Princess Ann, announced as Queen of England, ii., 70. Proclaimed, 70.

Dennis, Richard, appointed in place of Major Casdrop on Schuylkill, xi., 310.

Dennison, Col. Nat., councillor, xv., 162, 184, 191. Dispatched to Luzerne—his instructions, 293, 365, 384; xvi., 16, 20. Furnishes clothing to J. Franklin.

De Normandie, Abraham, sheriff of Bucks, iii., 69.

De Normandie, Anthony of Bristol, case of, xi., 480.

De Normandie, Dr. John Abraham, petitions to sell real estate, xi., 571.

Denny, David, Coroner, xii., 151.

Denny, William, Coroner, ix., 548, 624, 691.

Denny, William, Governor, presents his commission dated May 7, having taken the oath before his majesty in council, vii., 220. After the affixing of the seal, he issues an order for clearing out vessels after 22d August, 221. Proclamation is made for continuance of officers—and commission is published at court house, 221. Letters to and from Governor Hardy, 223. Proclamations of, 226. Address of Assembly, to 227. Order for £600. Governor's answer, 228. Speech to Assembly, 229. Messages to Assembly, 235, 238, 239, 248, 304, 306, 346, 350, 382, 387, 396, 409, 413, 417, 444, 562, 578, 582, 592, 605, 617, 718, 733, 736, 748, 751, 758, 763, 774, 779. Messages from Assembly, 233, 237, 238, 247, 307, 345, 384, 413, 418, 573, 579, 617, 721, 727, 730, 742, 751, 759, 781. Commission, &c., published at New Castle, 230. Asks advice of Council on intended message regarding exhibition of his instructions, 236, 237. Sends copies of instructions on money bills, 238, 344. Conference on money bill,

249, 251. Reasons of Committee on, 251-255. His reasons to be sent to his Majesty, 255. Visits frontiers, 265. Power to fill commissions, 265. Additional instructions, French war, 269. Letters to and from Lord Loudoun, 269, 380, 397. From Sir William Johnson, 278, 351, 434, 495. Speech to Assembly, 280, 622. Orders new writs of election to fill vacancies, 293. Meets Council at New Castle—message to, 295. Indian murders, 304. Address from Quakers on treaty, 311. His answer, 312. His opinion of Teedyuscung, 351. Letter to and instructions of George Crogham as Indian agent appointed by Sir William Johnson, 355. Sends minutes of Conference at Easton to Governor Belcher, 359. Issues warrant to sheriff to quarter troops in Philadelphia, 362. Various proceedings, 359-379. Writes to Mayor, 374. Answer, 376. Writes to Provincial Commissioners for money — they say there is none, 383. His letter to Croghan, 384. Assembly agree to pay expenses, 384-5. Embargo, 387, 388, 482, 606. Death warrant of Charles Jegler, 389. Further suspension of hostilities with Delawares proclaimed, 390. Warrant for respite of Jegler, 398. Remonstrance of Assembly on supply bill, 401. His answer, 403. Quartering troops, 409. On supply bill, 413, 417. Consults Lord Loudoun on supply bill—asks advice of Council, 441. Militia bill, 444. Short sketch of Province for Lord Loudoun, 444. Receives alarming intelligence from Fort Augusta—and agrees to pass money bill, 453, 454. And sends amendments to others, 455. Answer to petition for a watch at Bethlehem, 460. Meeting of Governors with E. Loudoun at Philadelphia, 470. Letter to Croghan—Sons of Teedyuscung at Fort Allen—small-pox at Lancaster, 474. To W, Parsons, 476. From George Croghan, 478, 480-481. To Earl Loudoun on shipping provisions, 482. Instructions to William Logan, 488. From Sir Charles Hardy, 496. To collector on allowing vessels to depart, 501. Speech to Indians, 519. Letter of Lord Loudoun on Indian support, 523. Writes to C. Armstrong to visit Cherokees, 527. Money all expended, 528. Proposes to invite Delawares to settle at Shamokin, 549. Message to Teedyuscung, 546. To Cherokees, 548. Letters to G. Croghan, 548. Passport and order to sheriff to guard Indians from Lancaster to Philadelphia, 549. Militia, Indians, Colonel Stanwix, &c., 563. Embargo, 569. Militia for South Carolina, 578. To Lord Loudoun, 581. Sir Charles Hardy, 581. Answer to Assembly, 582. Proclamation for a fast, 591. Roads, 592. To Croghan, 605, 634, 659, 679. Stanwix, 607. Long message on various matters, 609. Expected attack, 617. From Governor De Lancey, 628. Committee from Friendly Association, answer to, 637-648. Sends copy of remonstrance to Croghan, 658. Answer to, 661. Applies for list of goods for presents, 671, 672. Letter from provincial commissioners, 697. Authorized to send troops to New York, 721. Visit from Teedyuscung, 725. Certificate of having taken sacrament in Christ Church, 741. Long message between, and Assembly, 742, 751. Commissioners to Wyoming, 754. Interview with Teedyuscung at Philadelphia, 770. Estimate of expenses of the Government, 776, 779. William Moore's case, 741, 750, 764, 776, 781. Messages to Ass'bly, viii., 1, 12, 17, 29, 41, 61, 62, 66, 72, 78, 80, 111, 166, 169, 232, 237, 240, 275, 285, 291, 303, 317, 319, 326, 349, 369, 372, 382. Messages from Assembly, 4, 36, 39, 51, 53, 65, 71, 102-110, 112, 170. 229, 323, 324, 330, 331, 354, 356, 373, 396. On impeachment of William Moore, 1, 12-17. Letters to and from, 23, 26, 27, 37, 59, 69, 78, 116, 147, 155, 165, 167, 224, 232, 272, 274, 283, 289, 290, 292, 298, 316, 331, 341, 352,

373, 376, 391, 400, 403. Conferences with Indians, 9, 29, 30, 32, 86, 100, 114, 403. Speech to Teedyuscung, 42, 52. Letter to Colonel Washington, 56. Request for troops by General Forbes, 59, 65. Complains of provincial commissioners, 64. Various grievances, 72. Destitute Indians at Fort Loudoun, 78. Orders arms for General Forbes, 79. Complains of inactivity of Assembly, 80. A favor asked of him by Teedyuscung—his answer, 115. Speech to Indians, 117. Message to Indians at Wyoming, 129. Instructions to F. Post, 138. Lays embargo, 146. Visit, with Turner, Peters and Chew to Governor Bernard, 151. Writes to Spanish Governor respecting a Spanish vessel, 155. Declares William Moore innocent, 162. Admiral Boscawen asks men—Ass'bly decline—message to, 165, 166, 169. Letter from General Forbes, 169. Assembly on Boscawen and Indian affairs, 170. Speech to Indians at Easton, 183, 192. Answer to message of Ohio Indians, 206. Obliged to leave Ind'ns, bids farewell, 219. Speech to Assembly, 227. Respecting General Forbes, 229, 237. On tonnage duty, 231, 232. Letter, General Schuyler, 240. Address from Assembly–delivered by eight members—loss of wagons—quarters for soldiers—trial of William Moore, &c., 282, 441. To General Amherst on address of Assembly, 283. Resolve of Assembly respecting case of William Moore of Chester county, 286. Colonel Mercer succeeds General Forbes, 292. Bills credit—taxes, 303, 319, 323. Letters from W. Pitt and Lord Amherst on affairs at Du Quesne, 317. Distresses at Lancaster by quartering soldiers, 230. Supply bill, 331, 332. Grant by Assembly to, £1000, 333. Takes possession of great seal--is applied to the laws, 335. Visit from Teedyuscung, 344. Warrants and surveys, 349. Position of, 354. Bills of credit, 357. Insinuations against Council—and their reply—Mr. Chew protests, 357, 358. Refuses to sign bill, &c., on warrants, &c., 361. Signs several bills, 362. Receives £1000, 362. Sends letter from General Stanwix, 372, 373. Remarks on bill—Secretary and Surveyor General, 375. Signs bill—receives £1000, 376. On wagons, 376, 396. Speech to Teedyuscung, 405. Absence of great seal—call Assembly, 408. Superceded by James Hamilton, 409. Sends letter from General Stanwix, 426. Case of William Moore, 441.

Depositions, respecting dispute and riots between Maryland and Pennsylvania, iii., 472, 612. Francis Kip riots with Maryland, iv., 65. Henry Munday, 107. Elisha Gatchell, 229. Of Robert Savery on counterfeits, 274. Thomas McKee, skirmish with the Indians in Virginia, 630. James Hendricks, about Indians, 655. Of William Kelly, a pilot, v., 113. Of others relating to privateers, 115–119. Pyramus Green taken prisoner, 233. Captain George Porteus, 245. George Proctor, 248, 253. Roger Sheron, 249. Respecting privateers, 260–264. Captain T. Jenkins, 282. Morris Turner, 482. Ralph Kilgore, 482. Obstruction of surveys of land, 489. Respecting murder of Dudley Digges, 582–597. A. Montour and Jno. Patten, respecting distances, &c., on Ohio, 762. Stephen Coffin, vi., 9. Peter Frank on Indians, 54. Charles Courtenay, Francis C. Bouviere on arrival of French at Ohio, 224. Of Jean Silvester, 416. Matthew Laird, Michael Huber, Jacob Huber, Braddock's defeat, 482–484. By Henry Cole, Jno. M. Hute, J. McMichael on Indian hostilities in Northampton county, 758. George McSwaine, French and Indians vii., 395. M. Roup, 493. Of John Hogan, account of burning Fort Granville, 562. Arthur Henderson, 618. George Ebert, 620. James Hyndshaw, Connecticut settlers, viii., 612. Benjamin Kendal, Conestogo In-

dians, ix., 126. Wm. Blythe, murder of Indians by F. Stump, 414. Amos Ogden, Wyoming, 674. Of J. P. De Haas, ill treatment by several Connecticut men, 682. Aaron Van Campen and Peter Kachlein, 710. Respecting Wyoming, 751. Ashur Clayton, 767. Joseph Morris, 769. Henry Reed, respecting Dr. Conolly, x., 168. Samuel Whitesides, 227. John Carnahan, Sheriff, 235. Respecting robbery of ensign Vansant, xi., 513. Of Alexander Patterson, 528. Respecting Indians, 535. Respecting Wm. Moore Smith, for carrying letters for British prisoner, xii., 30. Of Wm. Geddis and Wm. Govett, respecting Arnold's conduct while in command of city, 225. Respecting, 307. Greenbury Hughes and Lawrence Maskill, respecting John Linch, 312. Drs. Bigham and Bevans against Captain Gardner, 316. John Seely, xiv., 32. John Armstrong, W, Brink, L. Meyers, Joseph Salmon, Wm. Jennings, 172. Of B. Chew, in case of Mrs. Allen's children, 463. Wm. Wilson, 498. Peter Audrain, robbery, 514. David Mead, 572. G. Smith, xv., 514.

Depreciation, scale to be published, xii., 612, 639, 648, 684, 703, 709, 716, 717, 747, 753; xiii., 74, 122, 140, 149. Certificate stopped, xv., 429.

Depreciation, lands, sales, xiv, 621. Plan of; ordered to be sold at Lancaster, xv., 18. Call for information, 46. Sales of, 58. Sale ordered, 138. Certificates, xvi., 148, 541. On pay, 230, 325. Survey, 418, 439, 454. Deputy Surveyor paid xvi., 303, 376, 422, 452, 514.

Depui, Moses, a Justice, v., 113.

Depui, Nicholas, letter to, on Indian invasions, xii., 312.

Depui, Benjamin, Justice, xiv., 198.

Depui, Captain Charles, petition to refit his vessel, v., 581. Survey on his vessel, 581. Report, 581.

Deputy Surveyors, xiv., 441, 443, 445, 449, 454, 456, 457, 458, 462, 653, 654; xv., 198; xvi., 214, 211[2]-252, 254, 256, 257, 278, 461, 463.

Derring, Christopher, Collector of excise, xiv., 652.

Deserters, xiii., 14, 22, 29, 96, 340.

Deshler, David, Commissioner of purchases, xii., 486; xiii. 109.

D'Estaing, Count, his squadron takes Wm. Straker prisoner, xi., 553. Arrives with French fleet, Act of Congress on, xii., 114. Permission asked for provisions to be sent to, 162.

Destitute, provision for the, i., 78.

Dewall, G., President of Court of Maryland, respecting H. Carberry, xiv., 106.

Dewees, Samuel, sub-Lieutenant, xi., 765.

Dewees, Colonel Thomas, Jailor of Philadelphia to take certain persons into custody, x., 359, 360 408. Order for removal of prisoners to new gaol, 429. Complaint, 567, 568. To purchase arms, 673.

Dewees, William, Sheriff, x., 100, 212, 270; xi., 201, 273. Complaint against, 210, 211. acquitted, 211.

Diahoga, Indians from, vii., 168. May be received at Bethlehem, 170. Indians from, intend an attack, 186, 187. Arrive at Philadelphia from, 198. At Easton, 206. New Castle, sent to, Indians remove to, 223. Arrival of Indians from Ohio, 281. Sketch of country from Easton to, 683.

Dick, John, letter respecting Wyoming, ix., 753.

Dickey, Robert Coroner, xv., 580; xvi., 215, 521.

Dickinson, gunboat, x., 335, 397. Steward discharged, 476, 488, 505; xi., 393.

Dickinson, proposed as the name of a new township in Washington county, xiv., 275.

Dickinson College, survey of lands for, xv., 139, 466. Order to, 4, 298, 616, 654.

Dickinson, James, a Deputy Surveyor removed, xiv., 653.

Dickinson, Jonathan, Mayor of Philadelphia, iii., 31. Speaker,

56. Governor's address to, 56. Visits Indians with Governor, 121.

Dickinson, Colonel John, to inspect ordnance and military stores, x., 283. Commands second battalion of associators, 314. to go to New York, 484, 487, 548. Colonel, x., 754; xi., 4. Writes to Brigadier General Philip Dickinson not to receive Continental money, 92. Councillor, xiii., 409. President, xiii., 413, 414, 736 Proclamation, 416, 737. Letter on Connecticut, &c., 479. Salary paid, 576. Letter to Council on their late measures respecting Wyoming, xiv., 218. Letter to Donalson & Hollingsworth on removal of Chevaux-de-frise, 241. Re-elected President, 249.

Dickinson, Brigadier General Philip, letter to, on Continental money, xi., 92.

Diemer, Jacob, appointed President C. C. B., Berks county, xvi., 125.

Diemer, Dr. James, appointed Justice in Berks county, xv., 462.

Dieskau, General, defeat of French under, at Lake George, vi., 637.

Digby, Admiral, grants passport for a flag vessel, with provisions for New York, xiii., 457, 459.

Digges, Dudley, murder of—correspondence and depositions respecting, v., 582.

Dill, Col. Matthew, x., 672; xi., 69, 113.

Dill, Matthew, Lieut., xi., 783.

Dillon, Amos, proclamation against, xiii., 616.

Dilworth, Charles, appointed Lieut. of Chester County, in place of R. Smith, xiv., 670. Sheriff, xvi., 192, 492.

Dingee, Charles, refuses to take oath of allegiance, is imprisoned, xi., 402.

Dinwiddie, ———, Surveyor Gen'l, v., 244.

Dinwiddie, Robert, Governor of Virginia, letters to and from, v., 632, 687, 698, 700, 712, 714, 755, 764, 767. Letter from French commander, 714. Proclamation to encourage enlistments, 766. Letters to and from, vi., 1, 3, 5, 7, 27, 31, 55, 136, 163, 177, 294, 295, 296, 297, 309, 419, 445, 455, 465, 602, 651; vii., 33, 133. Invasions of French and Indians, 1. Assembly of Pennsylvania will not aid, 27, 55. French operations—forts on Wills' creek, 136. Raising levies for Wills' creek, 177. Flour for Wills' creek, 297. Gen. Braddock complains of, 400. Attack on Niagara, 419. Sends men and cannon to Fort Cumberland, 445, 455. French and Indians—cannon for Fort Cumberland, 465. Proposes building a fort at Great Crossings—Dunbar's retreat, &c., 602. Examines at request of Lord Loudoun, the Indian trade bill, vii., 450. Meets Earl Loudoun and Governors at Philadelphia, 472.

Distances from Carlisle to Shanoppin's town, v., 750.

Distillery of liquors—Act to encourage by a bounty proposed—and objected to by inhabitants and traders, iii., 248. But favored prospectively, 249.

Divorces asked for, ix., 564, 566, 567, 568, 580; x., 27, 40, 53, 54, 103, 105.

Doan, Aaron, arrested, and bounty paid, xiv., 178. Case of, 384, 385, 386, 387. Pardoned, 387. Message to Assembly on, 388–392, 395. Pardoned on condition of leaving United States forever, xiv., 214.

Doan, Ab'm, proclamation against, xiii., 616, 631. Under sentence of death in Philadelphia—petition, xv., 497. Opinion of judges, 501. Captors rewarded, 502. Case, 504. Ordered to be executed, 505. Petition in favor of respite, 515. A free negro in jail afraid of—released, 516. Order for execution, 535. Respite negatived, 544.

Doan, Israel, xiii., 517.

Doan, Joseph, traitor, estate sold, xiii., 686. Taken, 741. Balance paid for his apprehension, to Joseph Wilson, xiv., 4.

Doan, Joseph, Jr., to Greer Ferguson, &c., for apprehending, xiv., 215.

Doan, Levi, reward for apprehending, xiii., 542, 630. Under sentence of death in jail in Philada., petition, xv., 497. Opinion of judges, 501. Captors rewarded, 502. Case, 504. Order for execution, 505. Petition in favor of respite, 515. A free negro afraid of—released, 516. Order for execution, 535. Respite negatived, 544.

Doan, Malin, proclamation against, xiii., 630.

Doan, Moses, proclamation against, xiii., 616, 630.

Dobbs, Governor Arthur, of Virg'a, meets Earl Loudoun at Philad., vii., 470.

Dobbs, Governor of North Carolina, daily expected, vi., 164. Letter on trade of Hudson's Bay, viii., 290.

Dobbs' Ferry—passes to be sent to, xiii., 419.

Dock creek landing, Philada., ii., 10, 12, 14, 19.

Dogs, Act against, x., 32, 42.

Dolby, Joseph, bell-ringer of Christ Church bells, xiii., 423, 563. Paid for ringing Christ Church bells on arrival of La Fayette, xiv,, 176. July 4th, 494. Paid for ringing the bells of Christ Church, xv., 60, 344, 363, 597; xvi., 224[2], 410.

Donaldson, Arthur, to launch chevaux-de-frises built at Gloucester, x., 513. To build piers at Fort Island, 525. To build two more chevaux-de-frises, 534, 535, 648, 651, 737. Builds floating battery, 725. To raise wrecks, &c., in Delaware, xi., 559, 692. Proposals for removing chevaux-de-frise, xiv., 75, 78. Agreement with, and pay, 104, 119. Entitled to third payment, 200, 213. Certificate to, from Wardens, and letter of President, 241. Letter, 500.

Donaldson, John, Member of Council, i., 492, 552. Tried and acquitted, 570.

Donation, lands, xiv., 454, 458, 653, 654. To officers of Penn'a line, xv., 17, 74, 102. Lottery for, 74, 97, 108, 128, 263. Explored by W. Irvine, 125. Patents for, 201, 220, 245. Fees, 358, 421. Battery, 580. Surveying of, xvi., 50.

Donegal, T., violent proceedings against house of John Scott, iii., 267.

Dongan, Governor of New York, his agency in purchase of land on Susquehanna, iii., 205. Receives pay from Proprietaries for lands on Susquehanna, vi., 124.

Donnaldson, John, resigns as Warden, xiv., 150. Register-General, his office, xvi., 45. May employ a clerk, 64. Pay to, 301. Expenses to Easton, 516.

Donnel, John. (See M'Daniels.)

Donnel, Nathaniel, Second Lieut. of Mattrosses, x., 524.

Dorothy, ship, a sickly vessel, arrives, iii., 292. Is released, 294.

Dorsey, Captain Thomas, paymaster, x., 436; xi., 266, 301, 406, 408, 424.

Dougherty, Bernard, x., 353, 531. To furnish rations, xiii., 375. Justice and President of Court, 446. Justice resigns, xiii., 101. On rations, 129, 595. Pay for rations, xiv., 181, 202. Accounts, 507.

Dougherty, Edward, Coroner, v., 120, 597.

Dougherty, Capt. Henry, appointed to command a boat, x., 287, 296, 419. Ordered from Liberty island, 427. To order boats to Philadelphia, 434. Seamen for public vessels, 442. Instruction, 617. To order guards at State House, 445. To command galley Delaware, 702. Captain of Artillery, xi., 223. Health officer, xii., 483.

Dougherty, John, Coroner, vi., 144, 662.

Dougherty, John, Jr., heads armed men from Wyoming, x., 86; to build a fort, 87.

Dougherty, ———, member of Assembly — letter from Bedford — road to Fort Pitt, xii., 73.

Douglass, Ephraim, Report on Indian agency, xiii., 681. Prothonotary, 702. Clerk of Courts, 704, 742. Member Council, 743. Letter, xiv., 525. Deputy Surveyor's

petition, xv., 122. Agency for Confiscated Estates in Fayette County, xvi., 26. For surveys of depreciation lands, 418, 422. Report on accounts, 446, 447.

Douglass, George, applies to go to Scotland—not granted, xi., 579.

Douglass, Captain John, xi., 2. Ensign, xii., 2.

Douglass, John, Captain of privateer—absconded, xii., 75.

Douglass, Captain Thomas, charges against, xiv., 621.

Dover, John, threatens life of a collector, xii., 402, 404. Commission refused, 407.

Dover, Kent Co., Canterbury Township, court house, &c., at, i., 556. Two good horses to be at, viii., 71. Act for sale of lots in, ix., 169. For improving marshes, x., 49. Prisoners sent from to New Cascastle for exchange, 564.

Dower, at common law forfeited by attainder of husband, &c., xii., 70.

Downar, Richard, and Randolph Mohr, case of, at Lancaster, iv., 256.

Downard William, and Maryland affairs, iv., 111.

Downey, Captain J., ordered to Billingsport. Benjamin Davis to assist him in a survey of ground near the river, xi., 248, 249. Of the river from Cooper's Ferry to Salem, 250.

Downingtown, militia sent to, from Philadelphia xi., 275. Provisions stored at, 423.

Doyle, Samuel, arrested for murder of Indians on Pine creek, xvi., 464. Reward paid for, 483, 484, 547.

Doyle, William, coroner, ix., 285, 333, 398.

Doz. Andrew, appointed Commissioner of Purchases, xii., 301, 375, 376, 392. Resigns, 397.

Drake, Oliver, Captain, xii., 70.

Draper, John, coroner, x. 106.

Draper, William, midshipman, prisoner, x., 596. Exchanged, 596.

Draper, Samuel, coroner, x. 271.

Driesback, Simon, censor, xiii., 723.

Drinker, Henry, to be seized, xi., 283. To lay out a road, xv., 425–445.

Drinker, John, refuses bills of credit, papers, &c., locked up, x., 486.

Dromgoole, Captain, Indian interpreter, xv., 238.

Drought, a long, vi., 422.

Drummond, Dr., applies to be enlarged on parole; granted on conditions, xi., 268.

Drummond, Lord, gives parol, x., 445.

Dryer, Jacob, irons to be taken off, the allowed time to leave the United States, xv., 348. Opinion of judges, 501. Case of, 611, 624, 627. Pardoned, 630. Doubts respecting opinion of judges; warrant for execution negatived, and he pardoned, 631.

Dry lands, in Northampton County, xvi., 217[2], 243.

Dublin, Second Township, petition for road to Philadelphia, i., 387. Opposed by First Township, 389.

Dublin, Lower Township, commissioners report respecting a road in, x., 51.

Dubrois, Captain John, i., 396, 435.

Duché, Anthony, xiii., 146.

Duché, Mrs. Elizabeth, asks to return from New York, xii., 17, 18. Allowed to return, being sick, 36, 309. (See below.)

Duché, Jacob, proposed as a clerk at Easton, vii., 669. Assistant to Mr. Croghan, signs minutes, 714.

Duché, Rev. Jacob, his wife applies for a pass to New York; granted on conditions, xi., 759, 762. Memorial of Francis Hopkinson respecting, 773.

Duché's house to be occupied by T. McKean, xii., 578.

Duché, T. S., letter from, xii., 18.

Duck Creek—petition for cutting a way through the marshes, i., 60. Draining, embanking, &c., ix., 313, 401. Church, trustees to sell lands, &c., x., 80–85.

Duckett, John, petition for pardon, referred to Supreme Court, iii., 276.

Ducking, a sentence for scolding, by xii., 235, 243.

Du Coudray, General, one of committee to examine works on river, xi., 231. Presents a plan for fort at Billingsport, 245, 246, to be

furnished a boat, 252. Ordinance in State House yard, xi., 252. Applies for a house at Fort Island, 265, 266.

Duff, Thomas, sheriff, ix., 57, 199, 286, 623, 688, 778.

Duffield, Dr., surgeon to boats, x., 362. Attends at pest house, 409, 545. And hospital, 549. Medicines, &c., 614.

Duffield, Dr. Benjamin, report on a prisoner, xvi., 211, 222.[2]

Duffield, Doctor John, Surgeon Mate Hospital United States, xiii., 157.

Duke, The, laws to be examined, i., 63. Address to, and king, proposed on forts, &c., 109; petition to, 116.

Duke of Normandie, birth of, xiv., 480.

Dulaney, Daniel, Attorney General of Maryland, iii., 614. Comes from Maryland with Edward Jennings as agent of Governor Ogle, iv., 115. Correspondence with President, 117, 131, 146.

Dun, Captain, imprisoned on charge of murder; how to be tried, ii., 86.

Dunbar, Colonel, sent with troops from England, vi., 201, 311.

Dunbar, Colonel, Thomas, retreat after defeat of Braddock, vi., 492, 494. Letter from and to, 494, 498, 515, 519, 521, 547, 593, 595. Arrives at fort Cumberland with wounded, 502, 513. Desires winter quarters in Philadelphia, 513, 514, 535. Directions of Governor to, 515. Not in the battle, 519. His account of the defeat from others, 519. Marches from Cumberland, 521. Field officers opinion, 547. General Shirley to, 549. Orders to, 558–561. Reasons for not going against Du Quesne, 593, 595. His retreat, 602, 604. Letters to and from, vii., 39.

Duncan, David, Commissioner of purchases, xii., 654, 656. Paid for supplies furnished troops in defence of frontiers, xvi., 400.

Duncan, James, Collector of Excise, resigns, xv., 126. Resigns, 222.

Duncan, Matthew, as Captain, x., 447.

Duncan, Stephen, resigns as Treasurer, xii., 527.

Dundas, James, pay at Billingsport, xi., 607. Paymaster at Billingsport, 756.

Dunlap & Claypoole, printers for Council, xv., 87, 113, 215, 360, 366. Their paper to be filed, 444. xvi., 21, 262. John D. loans money to recruit Pennsylvania Line, 489. Newspaper, 516, 539.

Dunlap, Doctor James, surgeon in Navy, x., 632. To have a mate, 634. Bandages, 638. Pay, xi., 68, 110, 111. Justice, xiv., 242.

Dunlap, Major James, made Lieutenant Colonel, x., 768.

Dunlap, John, printer, x., 136. printing press, &c., taken by Council of Safety, xi., 46. Decline to continue taking his paper, 521. Taken, 654. Newspapers order by Council, xii., 197. Deed for part of Tinicum, 256. Deed to, xii., 323, 331. Paid for printing votes of Assembly, xiii., 277. Laws, 447, 479. Buys City lots, xv., 13. Printer, 191.

Dunmore, Fort, Colonel Conolly's proclamation from, x., 228.

Dunmore, Lord, informs of a confession of murder in Philadelphia, x., 88. In connection with Doctor John Conolly, 141. Governor Penn's letter to, 149, 156. Letters to and from, 156, 158, 181, 191, 193, 236. Commissioners sent to 170, 173. Their instruction, 175. Report, 181. Correspondence with, 182–191. Goes on an expedition against Shawnese, 214. Two men desert from, 548.

Dunn, Abner, Lieutenant, xii., 10.

Dunn, James, a wounded militiaman aided, xi., 403.

Dunn, Thos., Sheriff, viii., 506, 781.

Dunning, Ezekiel, Sheriff, v., 551, 597, 662; viii., 781; ix., 51, 199. Coroner, vi., 638.

Dunning, James, charges against, v., 85.

Dunwick, Wm., time allowed, xi., 717.

Dunwoodie, James, Messenger, to collect election returns, xv., 634.

Duplessis, Peter Le Barbier, Notary and tab., public, xv., 221.

Duponceau, Peter S., applies to be Notary Public, xiii., 735. Appointed, 736. Paid for translations, xiv., 258.
Du Portail, General, Letter, xi., 732. Elegant plan of river Delaware, 776. Compliment to, for his plan of river, 776.
Dupui, Aaron, Commissioner to Indians, vi., 754, 764.
Du Quesne, Fort, capture of, vi., 141. Letters from Capt. Stobo, a hostage, 141, 161. List of deserters, 142. Dunbar's reasons for not going against, 593. Affairs at, 619. Commander killed, 614. Conduct of French commander with Indians, viii., 119–121. Burned and evacuated by French—General Forbes' letter on, 233. Respecting, 264, 265. To be restored, 315, 316. Expenses of expedition against, 322. Commissioners appointed to state account of, 322, 332. Site not fixed on, 392; vii., 153, 241, 502, 601, 602, 603, 631, 632, 716.
Durell, Adam, letters to Gov. from, asking men, &c., viii., 289, 318.
Durham, Iron Works, iii., 309, 329. Disturbances near, 329. Road through to Philad., v., 576. Road from Easton to, vi., 304. Claimed by George Taylor—difficulty between him and George Wall—agreement with Joseph Galloway—proceedings, xi., 537.
Durham tract, rule postponed, xii., 391.
Durkee, John, indicted for riot at Wyoming—imprisoned for debt, discharged, x., 52.
Dutch, grant of lands to Swedes, ii., 465. Vessels brought in, Gov'r embarassed by, viii., 155. Presbyterians—Act to sell land, x., 243.
Duties, retaliatory, laid on goods from New York, ii., 611; iii., 38, 163. On persons of convicts imported as servants, 163, 166. On foreigners, &c., not servants, 359. On convicts, iv., 304, 384, 386. Laid on persons convicted of heinous crimes — Act repealed at Court of St. James, v., 66, 499, 551. Proposed on tonnage, liquors, sugar, &c., viii., 30, 35, 40, 67, 100, 230. Reasons of merchants against, 231, 232, 334. On negroes and mulatto slaves, 576, 578, 580. Petition merchants against, 576. On, 601, 611; ix., 637, 641; x., 24, 25, 32, 34, 41, 72, 73. Act for laying, xvi., 112.
Duykinck, Colonel, to be imprisoned, xi., 365.
Dyer, Eliphalet, a Commissioner from Connecticut, arrives, x., 118.
Dyer, Thomas, Justice, xiv., 147.
Dyer, Major Wm., appointed Collector of Customs—also Surveyor-General of the Colonies—appoints a Deputy Waiter and Searcher, i., 148. Elected to Council, 197. Objected to, 197. Report of committee, 198, 210. Dismissed from Council, 211.

E.

"Eagle," armed boat, xi., 76.
Eaker, Dr. Joseph, paid to, for Captain Robinson's company, xix., 152.
Eakman, Captain John, x., 709.
Ealer, Peter, Sheriff, xiv., 248, 557. xv., 100.
Eastburn, Benjamin, run temporary line between Pennsylvania and Virginia, v., 760.
Eastburn, John, levy of Sheriff, ii., 182.
Eastburn, Robert, to collect linen from ladies, for bandages, x., 633. Sale of salt, 762, 781; xi., 51.
Easton, petition for road, v., 576. Commissioners return of, 610. To Reading — petitioner appointed, 611. Indians removed from Bethlehem to, there being troops, vii., 191. Governor's instructions to Mr. Parsons respecting them, 191. Proposed treaty at, 202. Gov'r holds treaty at, 204–220. No settling preliminaries, 206. Treaty at, 280. Teedyuscung at, 307. Letter from C. Weiser relating to Indians at, 308. Conference at, 309. Conference with Indians at, 313–338. Copy of minutes sent

to Gov. Belcher, 359. Answer, 385. Expenses of message to Indians to come to treaty at, 384. Messages to W. Parsons at, 477. Treaty at, 648. Minutes, 648–714. Charles Thomson appointed clerk to Teedyuscung, 665. Sketch of country from, to Diahoga, 683. Commissary of provisions at, 775. Treaty referred to, by Teedyuscung, viii., 33. By Assembly, 51, 63. Conference at, 165. Teedyuscung behaves badly at, 172. Conference with Indians at, 174–223, 228. Names of the several nations, 176. List of presents for Indians, 214. Treaty printed, 226. Report of Committee on claims made for lands by Indians at, 246–261. Meeting of Indians, &c., at, 630. Minutes of conferences at, 630–654a. Court-house at, ix., 23. Act passed for, 325. Ferry at, to be taken by committee, xi., 72. Indian treaty at, 96. Money and papers from loan office, to be removed to, 305, 306. Report of persons who read them, 307. Books to, 309. Petition of German Lutheran Reformed Ch. at, 422. Militia, 200. To be as guards for, 446. Myer Hart, of, complains of Sheriff not executing process against a tenant, xii., 75. Memorial from, respecting claims in Luzerne County, xv., 224. Resolutions at, declared seditious by Judges of Supreme Court, &c., and prosecution to be commenced against parties, 225. Continental troops sent to, for Luzerne, 502. Express to, 516.

Eckhart, John, Justice, xiv., 321.

Eckart, Valentine, Commissioner to purchase provisions, xi., 423. Letter on Indian murders in Berks County, xii., 466. Directed to order out militia in, 721. Letter on delinquent collectors, xiii., 570. Justice, xiv., 170. Dispatched to Berks, with call on militia, and instructions, xv., 295. Lieutenant of Berks County, xvi., 418.

Eckley, John, a Judge, i., 109. Register-General, 211. Refuses, 211. Lieut. Governor, 212. Election disputed, 268. Copy of writ of election, 280, 282. Proceedings, 293.

Eddy, John, appointed First Lieut. in Sixth Battalion Continental troops, x., 477.

Eden, Robert, Gov. of Maryland, letter to, on proceedings respecting boundary, x., 241, 247.

Edger, James, Censor, xiii., 740.

Edie, John, Sheriff, xv., 102, 297, 579.

Edie, Samuel, Sheriff, ix., 778; x., 56, 101; xv., 303.

Edmunds, William, letter relating to New Castle and other Indians, vii., 163, 165, 167, 172.

Education, first school established under E. Flower—terms, &c., i., 91. Of youth, its importance, xii., 98. Moral, recommended, xiii., 434.

Edwards, Fort, vii., 716. Attacked by Indians, viii., 60, 141.

Edwards, Chas., sentence remitted, owing to another's confession of guilt, xi., 624.

Edwards, Joshua, to be arrested, apprentice to Dr. Yedall, xii., 504, 505. To give security, 505, 506.

Edwards, Dr. Enoch, Justice, xiv., 629.

Edwards, Marshall, pay-master, xi., 266, 390, 448.

Edwards, Thomas, a Justice, iii., 359. Sheriff, xiii., 393, 723; xiv., 267, 268.

Edwin, John, letter, trouble with Teedyuscung's messengers, viii., 98.

Effingham, gunboat, launch of, x., 314. Captain Allen Moore, 328. Resigns, 442. H. Montgomery, Captain, 488, 505.

Egan, John, petition for removal to another vessel, xii., 82.

Egg Harbour, part of enemy's fleet arrives at, xi., 254. Wagons sent to, by Jesse Jordan, for goods, 672, 679, 684.

Egremont, Earl of, Secretary of State, letter, to raise men, viii., 677, 685, 703. Letters to and from, ix., 13, 15, 37.

Eichelberger, George, Sheriff, ix., 548, 624, 689. Examined on con-

tested election in York county, xi., 698. Guilty of misdemeanor, Sheriff sent for him, 700. Opinion of C. J. asked, 744.
Eichelberger, Lieutenant in Continental troops, resigns, x., 477.
Eichelberger, Jacob, Justice, xi., 443. Justice, letter, complaint, offers resignation, xii., 421. Not accepted, (see proceedings,) 422.
Eight per cent. per annum, x., 223, 226.
Ejectment, case, ii., 180.
Elaboratory, xi., 108. 113, 121, 125.
Elder, David, Justice, xi., 524.
Elder, Rev. John, on Indian murders, vi., 648, 652, 704. On French and Indians, intelligence from Monacatooha, 673. At Tulphehocken, 704.
Elder, John, petition, xv., 176.
Elder, Joshua, to find provisions for gun factory, xi., 330. Expenses of militia, 412. Sub-Lieutenant of Lancaster county, his accounts referred to Comptroller General, xv., 432. Petition, 441. Petitions for an audit, refused, xvi., 67. Deputy Surveyor's fees on purchases of lands, (depreciation,) not paid; memorial reported on, 374, 376.
Elder, Colonel, Sub-Lieutenant, xii., 3, 91. Wishes to resign, refused, 84.
Elder, Colonel Robert, battalion of Lancaster county militia, xiv., 380. Paid for services in 1777, 1778, 1779, xv., 291.
Election, no need of writs prior to, i., 240. Disputed, 267, 268, 270, 279, 281. Copy of a writ of, 281. Ballot box not used, 282. Except at Upland and Lower counties, 282. Tickets to be made distinct, iii., 166. Act respecting, 277. Gov.'s view of, 391. Acts, &c., respecting, x., 67, 68; xii., 129, 131, 133, 134, 136, 137, 145, 146, 147, 160, 506, 546; xiii., 132, 719, 723; xiv., 113, 158, 162, 196, 229, 230, 232, 238, 248, 282, 307, 312, 322, 382, 443, 462, 554, 556, 562, 567; xv., 62, 98, 100, 103, 113, 182, 270, 272, 294, 296, 298, 300, 301, 325, 326, 362, 398. Opinion of Judges of Supreme Court proposed on, 130; xvi., 36, 38, 44, 202, 209, 490, 492, 497, 499, 501, 509, 514, 518, 527, 542.
Election riot at Philadelphia, iv., 620.
Electors of President and Vice President of United States, xv., 658.
Elfrith, Henry's, house in Front street stopped, ii., 9. Taken by public for a landing, to be paid for, 10, 12. Proposal of S. Carpenter, 19. Considered, 54.
Elizabethtown, N. J., trunks of goods at, from New York, xii., 199, 206.
Ellicot, Andrew, gives parol to committee of safety, x., 445. Appointed Commissioner on northwest line and Ohio, xiv., 454. Accepts, 464. Commissioner to assist D. Rittenhouse to run northern boundary, 655. Commissioner to run west line, xv., 38, 114. Assisted by Colonel Andrew Porter on north, 175. Paid, 202. Jno. Adlum, 212, 340. Paid, 356, 458. Appointed to survey islands in Allegheny, xv., 615. Letter respecting survey referred, 631. Asks for loan of surveying instruments on triangle, xvi., 161 Asking to be furnished with copy of Indian deed given to Butler and Gibson, Commissioners, which is not on record, 375.
Ellicott, Joseph, Sheriff, ix., 547, 623, 689.
Elliott, Benjamin, Sheriff, xiv, 567; xv., 139, 300. Councillor, xvi., 220[1]. Commissioner to fix county lines of Huntingdon, 46.
Elliott, Mrs., and daughter, apply for pass from New York to recover property, her husband being attainted—declined, xi., 718.
Elliott, James, sent express to Wyoming with Act of Assembly and instructions, xiv., 636.
Ellis, John, Second Lieutenant, x., 457.
Ellis, Rowland, a Justice, ii., 159. A Justice, iii., 28.
Ellis, Thomas, appointed Register General, i., 211.
Ellison, Lieutenant, Colonel, to command regiment, vi., 294.

Elsenborough, Spanish privateer off, v., 248.
Elton, Captain Robert, x., 687.
Elwood, John, pilot, convicted of high treason, to be executed, xi., 624. Reprieved, 631, 653. Pardoned, xii., 48.
Ely, Isaac, Lieutenant, xi., 750. First Lieutenant, Franklin galley, xii., 139. Lieutenant, resigns, 489.
Embargo laid, 451. Removed, ii.. 467. On provisions, iv., 167, 479, 480, 506. On powder, 764. On provisions, v., 42, 269, 270. Removed, 273, 459. Warrant to Abm. Taylor, Collector, to lay, on provisions, vi., 319, 425, 439, 451, 463, 464-511, 592, 601. Permis'n to certain vessels, 451; vii., 94, 122, 129, 130, 135, 136, 142, 151, 169, 183, 184, 186, 195, 202, 221, 227, 270, 393, 417, 418, 429, 431. In lower counties, 195. Bond of vessels, 227, Order for, 386, 388, 409, 444, 455, 497, 500, 559, 560, 561, 567, 570, 593, 596, 606. Remonstrance of Assembly to Governor on, 571; viii., 26, 38, 59, 146, 713. Laid, 713. Proposed, xi., 192. On provisions, 545, 546, 569, 646, 682, 712, 761, 763, 777, 780, 783; provisions allowed to be exported, xii., 1, 2, 8, 10, 59, 61, 130, 191, 197, 398, 413. About to expire, opinion of Congress to be asked on its continuance, 70. Continued, 81, 99. Proclamation for, 171. President Congress, 362. Laid, 387. From Governor Lee, 400. Port open partially, 404. Enforced, 525; xiii., 41, 49.
Embezzlement of goods by master of a vessel complained of, i., 142
Emerson, Jonathan, a Justice, ix., 645.
Emlen, Caleb, to be seized, xi., 284.
Emlen, George, buys lot on Province Island, xv., 173.
Emlen, Samuel, Jr., to be seized, xi., 283.
Emmes, John, Lieutenant of fire-brig, x., 620, 627.
Empson, Cornelius, erects a mill, i., 301, 384.
Engineers, x., 457, 501.
England, proposed by Governor and decided that people in, should bear a portion of the public charge, i., 93. Order for transportation of a criminal to, for trial, 203. Goods not to be exported to other countries than, 232, 233, 240. Reported invasion by Prince of Orange brought by T. Whitpain, 246. Complains of French—prepares for war with, 302. Appealed to, in case against Society of Free Traders, 147. William and Mary King and Queen, 340. Who is King? 302. Discussion about William and Mary, 303. Declaration of King and Queen, 304. Discussion about, and defensive measures, 304-310. Declares war with France and Spain, ii., 70. Princess Ann of Denmark declared Queen, 70. Circumstances here may be very different from those in, 311. Expedition against Canada, 449. Taxes, how raised in, 463. Death of Queen—King George proclaimed, 575. King George I. dies—George II. proclaimed, iii., 282. Sugar Islands apply to Parliament to restrain trade of new colonies, 401. Informality in repeal of provincial laws, 534. Application of Lord Baltimore to King of, 594. Petition to, 597. Instructions, &c., iv., 422. Wishes to encourage importation of white servants rather than negroes, 437. Probable rupture with France, 670, 673. Declares war with France, 689, 690. Encourages ships of war and privateers, 693. Cessation of arms between, and France, &c., treaty signed at Aix la Chapelle, v., 330. Proclamation, 331. Third article of treaty and other papers, 359-362. Death of Prince of Wales, 527. Laws confirmed, 619. Report on claim to North America, vi., 100-105. Sends forces to North America under Sir Peter Halket and Colonel Dunbar, and will send Commander-in-chief, 202. Lieutenant-Colonels, Ellison and Mercer, 294. Church of, on marriage, ii., 26, 48. On alienation of lands, 222. Justices

of, appointed—decline on account of oaths, 531.

England, Philip, keeps ferry at Schuylkill, i., 126, 368. Swedes complain against, 373, 387. Complains against William Powell, 380, 381, 437.

England, Samuel, complaint against, by Governor Ogle, v., 382.

Engle, Lieutenant-Colonel Jacob, appointed sub-Colonel, xii., 298.

English, David, Justice. xii., 198, 376. Resigns, xiv., 597.

English Jack, authorized to be worn on intelligence boat, v., 267.

English, James, paid for securing.

English, Major, arrives from Maryland with armed men, i., 188.

Engraving, by H. D. Pursell and Robert Scott, xiv., 471.

Ennis, James, Ensign, xii., 10.

Ensigns recommended to Congress, x., 449. Appointed, 450, 643; xi., 32, 78, 89, 112, 557, 578; xii., 3, 7, 8, 9, 10, 31, 36, 53, 58, 65, 88, 89, 107, 338, 428, 480, 483, 662, 769; xiii., 16, 53, 215, 275.

Enyeart, Wm, Coroner, xvi., 527.

Episcopal Church complains against law about marriages, ii., 26, 48. In Stamford, Connecticut, wish a lottery to finish it, which they cannot have in Connecticut, vii., 113. Certificate of rector and assistant of Christ Church to Gov. Denny on taking sacrament, 741. Lottery for finishing the, in the city, viii., 340. Form of liturgy to be altered on death of King George II., 519. The bells of Christ Church rung, for peace between France and Spain, ix., 42. In compliment to Gov. John Penn, 72. Lottery for repairs and furnishing various, 243, 247. In behalf of Rev. Mr. Coombe, xi., 296, 300, 525. Obtains pass for Europe, 527. Rev. Mr. Thorne suspected, xii., 334. Wife of Rev. Thomas Coombe applies for a pass to New York for his son John, xiii., 123. Christ Church bells rung for capture of Cornwallis, 143. Joseph Dolby receives pay for ringing, 423. Letter from John Adams on American Bishop, xiv., 399. Christ Church ringing bells, 176, 494. Certificate from Council to, at request of deputies, that they may "keep up" a succession of religious teachers, 584. Ringing Christ Church bells, xv., 60, 344, 597. Views of Bishop White on marriage licenses, 614. Academy, lands for, xv., 585. Ringing of Christ Church bells paid for, xvi., 224[2], 410.

Epple, Andrew, xi., 124.

Equity, Courts, i., 102, 116, 127, 190; ii., 184; iii., 93, 105; iv., 21, 22, 27.

Erb, Ensign Lawrence appointed Lieutenant, xiii., 3, 6.

Erie, Lake, building vessels on, viii., 377. Reservation of a tract on, xv., 121. Description of the lands asked from Commissioners, 382. Terms of sale by Congress, 473. Authority to purchase triangle, 473. Proposal of delegates for purchase, 524. Transferred to Pennsylvania, 530, 531. Conference on subject of purchase, 532. Pay for map, &c., 561. Fund for purchase, 607. Survey by A. Ellicott refused, 631. Act of Congress relinquishing triangle, 530. Meeting of Indians at Muskingum favorable to, 531. Commissioners, Generals Butler and Gibson appointed—instructions to, 554. Permission asked to make observations in Canada, 650. Purchase of triangle from Indians—Commissioners appointed, xvi., 36. Reservations at, 47. Triangle on, survey, 161. Surveys of four reserve tracts by Jno. Adlum—surveys of, 161, 169.

Error, writs of, ii., 127.

Errors and Appeals—Court created, and James Smith, Judge, xii., 548. He resigns, 723. High Court of, William Moore and John Bayard appointed Judges, xiii., 535. Henry Wynkoop appointed Judge, 544. Samuel Miles appointed, 550. Judges to have access to Library, 576.

Erwin, Colonel Arthur, xi., 49. To rendezvous at Swedes' Fort, 301.

Erwin, Joseph, Sheriff, ix., 779. Coroner, x., 59.

Erwin, Matthew Captain, xi., 32, 305.
Erwin, Captain of Rangers, recommends Lieutenants, xii., 73.
Escheator General, xv., 285.
Escheats fee, xiii., 73. Message from Council to Assembly on, xiv., 269, 507.
Esler, Capt. Adam, complaint against election of, xiii., 619.
Espy, David, Register and Recorder of Bedford, xi., 629, 646, 718. Censor, xiii., 729; xiv., 196. Justice, xv., 51. Prothonotary, xvi., 517.
Estates, Intestate, how regulated, i., 103, 153. Practice respecting judgments, 157.
Estates, forfeited, proceeding respecting, xi., 479, 547, 556, 587, 599, 608, 714. Notice of sales, 745, 749. P. De Haven, agent, 754. Difficulty about deeds withheld, xii., 22. Agents have made no return in Reynold Keene's case, 23, 26, 80, 102. Traitors, 27, 49, Copies of papers asked for, 67. Case of Michael Witman, 69. Of Mrs. David Dawson, 70. In Bucks county, 72. Alexander McKee, Lancaster county, 76. Lawrence Growdens in Bucks county, 77. Jno. Rein, Reynold, Keen, H. Hopkinson, 81. Of James Rankins, 81, 218, 219. Isaac Melchior and estate of And'w Allen, 88, 152, 249. Sales of, 99. Resolutions of Assembly, sales postponed — of R. Keene's estate, 103. Deed for Joseph Galloway's estate, money received for house and lot of Arthur Thomas, 105. John Potts, 114, 115, 116. Sales in Bucks county of Gilbert Hicks' estate, and deed for—in Northampton county of John Young, 156, 157. James Rankin, David Sproat, 174. Samuel Shoemaker's property, deed for, 185, 265. Reservation by Assembly of, for benefit of University of Pennsylvania, rules and regulations for the future, Henry Jounkins sold, 189. J. Galloway's, 191. J. Custard, David Thompson, George Harding, 196, 238. Richard Swanwick, 199. Arthur Thomas, 200. Thomas Shoemaker, 202[2]. C. & A. Stedman, 204. David Thompson's, 222. M. Witman, 231, 276. Christopher Wilson, 246. Continental money declined as a tender for a ground rent, 249. J. Galloway's at Tinicum, 256. Thomas Mackiness, 259. John Tolley, 260. L. Fegan, 260. William McMullin appointed agent for, on dismission of Thomas Hale, 261, 264. Joseph Galloway in Bucks, 268. Interest in less than freehold to be sold, 272. C. Sawer in Germantown — Rules adopted for sale of, 281, 299. Deeds, 283, 284. On Boon's Island Joseph Galloway's estate, 284, 300. Petition of Jacob Morgan respecting mill late of C. Sawer, 303. Estate of Samuel Bell and Mrs. Parrock, 315. Of George Enser in city, 317. Of Peter Arthur, 320. In Northampton, 322. In Philadelphia Alex. Bartram, John Roberts, 323, 324, 374. Of Peter Campbell, 324. Christopher Sawer, Germantown, 326. Of George Rhine, decree against, 327. Joseph Galloway, 331. Jacob Hare, 340. Richard Swanwick, to be sold, 341. Sales to Hugh Horner, Jno. McNair, Jr., of Andrew Allen, 344, 345, 346. To Henry Shade, James Doak, 345, 346. Resolutions for sale of Commons, &c., in Philadelphia, 347. Of Jona. Jones, 350. Joseph Galloway at Tinicum to Kerline, 353. Petition of J. Roberts, estate rejected, also, Joseph Cornley's, 374. Edward Jones, Richard Swanwick, 381. Jno. Bartlett, 383. Sale of Durham tract postponed, and of Thomas West, 391. Sales of lots on Race street landing postponed, 401. S. Shoemaker's, 413, 430. Gid. Vernon, Peter Arthur, 421. Alexander Bartram, J. Galloway's, 441. C. Sauer, Jr., 445, 448. Of Joseph Comley, 447. Joseph Griswald, 450. John Parrock, 457. Geo. Harding, 458. David Dawson, 463. Joshua Thomas, 468. L. Fagan, 470. William Thomas, 481. W. Austins,

492. Agent resigns, 526. Goods, 536. Sales of, suspended, 539. Of John Parrock, 752, 755, 782. Agents to refrain from further sales, of Isaac Allen, 781. George Reine, 552. George Knapper, S. Shoemaker, Joseph Stansbury, 554. James Rankins, 560, 577. M. Roberts, 572. Jno. Potts, 577. Agents to make return of those unsold, 600. Agents appointed, 610. S. Shoemaker, 612, 615. Of Andrew Allen, 614. Joel Evans, Joseph Griswald, 617. Jno. Henderson, George Benner, 619. Jno. Wright, J. Butcher, 621. Hog Island, 630, 631. Account of all confiscated, sold or not, inquiry, 633, 634. Agents to make reports, Escheator general appointed, 634. Holton Jones, 639. John Parrocks, 661. Oswald Evans, Henry Welfling, 669. Daniel Williams, 671. Jno. Wright, Jno. Burke, 673. J. Rankins, 680. Hog Island to be divided, 679. Abram Carlisles, 687. Sales of, 693. C. Sauer, Isaac Allen, 709. Of William Rhodden, 731. Of Peter Purlie, 733. William Thomas, 734. Of Samuel Shoemaker, 737. Alexander Corbitts, Andrew Allen, 745, 746. Andrew Elliott, 747. B. Booth, J. Galloway, 751. Jno. Fox, 775. Of Abram Carlisle, xiii., 5. Of William Price, 9. Agents not to receive pay for sales at Hog Island, 11. Of Andrew Allen, 12, 57. J. Galloway, 12. Jno. Parrock, 20. Of Major Parr, 23. Of Benjamin Booth, 23. J. Duché, 25, 26. David Jones, 30. Jona. Adams, 34. Thomas Hughes, 38. Of Peter Campbell, 50. Stephen Anderson, John Jackson, George Sinclair, R. Swanwick, 56, 57. Ph. Marchington, Benedict Arnold, 80, 81. Of Jno. Meredith, 94. William Evans, 97. Of James Rankin, 98. Jno. Hannum, agent, resigning, William Will, discharged, H. Osburne appointed, agents to report estates unsold, 106. Of Nathan Roberts, 108. M. Cryder, agent, 115. Christopher Sauer, 126. John Rhine, 137. Agents appointed for Washington county, 139. Return of Robert Smith agent, estate of J. Parrock, Richard York, J. Adams and wife, 141. Of John Tolly, 146. J. Parrock, York, and Adams, 141, 164. Pay for searching records, 165. Mathias Aspden, John Parrock, 171. T. Forrest, 175. A. Bartrams, 175, 176. John Reid, Owen Roberts, 181, 182. William Armstrong, 182. Nicholas Houssecker, 199, 250. Evan Thomas, Jno. Overholz, Daniel Jeans, Jno. Reid, 204. C. Sauer, 207. Report on M. Aspden's, 209. Joshua Knight, 214. Of Andrew Allen, John Reid, 236, 273, 277. Jos. Paxson, 236, 266. Samuel Shoemaker, 246. William Maddock, 251. H. Steininger, 273. Of George P. Wertman, J. Galloway, 279. J. Galloway, 281. In Bedford county, H. Gordon, 301. Andrew Allen 303, 309. Agents, 302, 303. Of E. Milne, 309. Of Gilbert Hicks, 346. Of C. Werkieser remitted and divided among his children, 350. J. Dean, A. Bartram, and D. Burge, 361. J. Rankin, 384. Agents for, in Bucks county, 441. Of William Bell, 449. Galloway's, 450. Alleged fraud in sale of A. Bartram's estate tried and dismissed, 499. Of John Potts, 505. C. Saur, 509. Anthony Yeldall, 515, 519. W. Bell, 529, 587. Agent's accounts, 584. J. Romich, 592. Samuel Byles, 599. Estate of Joseph Dean, 623. A. Elliots, 646. Joseph Doan, 686. Estate of Charles Hook, John Hoster, A. Stedman, 695. Harvey Gordon, 701. Curtis Lewis, 735. Of Alex. Bartram, 748. Of A. Allen, reconveyed to State, 766. Agents in Westmoreland for, 774. Gideon Vernon, 778. Agents to report dates of sale, &c., xiv., 28. Of Dr. Andrew Ladlie, 34. Of William Thomas, 56. Execution against E. Milne stayed, estate of John Wilson, 140. Agents, 140. Aid of Attorney General directed on sales of lands, 175. In Westmoreland county, 287, 290. In Northumberland, A. Bartram's,

292. Letter to George Stewart agent for, 321. From, 385. Of A. Yorkes, 385. Accounts of George Smith, 395. Jona. Adams, 451. In York county, 462. Andrew Allen, 463, 589, 590, 592. J. Galloway, 494. In Westmoreland and Washington county, 607. William Thomas, 642. Of Samuel Shoemaker, 650. Sales ordered in Chester county, estate of M. Aspden, 663. C. P. Wertman, 666. Estate of Andrew Allen, xv., 2, 40, 43. J. Galloway's city lots, 6, 15. Sales of P. Bullas, postponed, 6. Also of F. & W. Armstrong's, 9. Evans Thomas, 14. Arthur Thomas, 51. Agent of, in Berks county, 62. M. Aspden, 72, 75. Walter Willitt, 99. Andrew Allen, 124. Title to a, to be defended, 127. A. Bartram, J. Meredith and Isaac Taylor, 153. A. Elliott and A. Bartram, 172, 185, 223. George Smith, agent, 170. Christian Huck, 180. Alexander Ross, 191. Agent for Montgomery county, 198. John Rhine, 205. Agent Dauphin county, James Clunie, 223. Andrew Allen, 237, 265. Agents in Philadelphia, 246. E. Perlee, Ab. Pastorius, 261. Ed- Stiles, 277. William Rankin, 425. Andrew Allen, 428. J. Rankin, 468. Of Anthony Yeldell, 606 B. Arnold, 640. Samuel Shoemaker, 657. Of Andrew Elliott, xvi., 23. Ephraim Douglass, agent, 26. Agents, 73. Of John Robinson, 136. A. Elliott, 216, 220. A. Bartram's, 283. F. & W. Armstrong, 299. Samuel Biles, 309, 390. William Austin, 387. Anthony Yeldall's, 422. S. Biles in Bucks, 507. Harry Gordon, 540.

Estimate of charge of equipment of a colony vessel, v., 272. Of pay to provincial forces, viii., 226, 287.

Etherington, Major George, of 2d Battalion, gives parol, x., 333.

Etting, Elijah, x., 729.

Eustace, Major, dies, xiii., 223.

Evans, Dr., Cadwalader, claim for city lots, xv., 379, in his favor, 387.

Evans, David, petition, i., 540, 549, 563, pirate, 578.

Evans, David, Judge of Supreme Court, iii., 269.

Evans, Edward, attend to vendues, xi., 766.

Evans, Evan, to take down spouts, xi., 279.

Evans, George, Surgeon, xi., 35.

Evans, Griffith, Assistant to Comptroller General, xiii,, 577, 646; xiv., 55, 160, 197. Deputy Surveyor, xiv., 654. Attends distribution of donation lands, xv., 128. Paid for filling patents for lands, 139. Clerk to Commissioner on New York line, paid, 356, 359.

Evans, Jabez, a Canada prisoner, given in exchange, v., 643.

Evans, John, arrives as Governor, ii., 115. Takes the oaths, 115, 116. Address to Council, 141. Long and angry message to the Assembly, proprietary views, &c., 187. Controversy with Assembly, 147, 157, 158, 163, 167, 169, 175, 188, 191 to 203, 419. His false alarm in 1706, 433. Proposes to visit the Conestoga Indians, 251. Visits the Susquehannah Indians, 385. Account of his journey, 386, 390, and expenses, 392, 394, 396. Message, 398, 401. Plantation near New Castle, meets Assembly, messages and answers, 424–426. Succeeded by Charles Gookin, as Deputy Governor, 427. Charges against, false alarm, &c., 433. Address to Council, on grievances, 436, 442. Misapplies funds, 464. Claim against Huston, 494. Saving clause in commission and instructions, submitted to Assembly, vi., 220, 529. Tax on proprietary estate, 524. Proceedings in his time, 721.

Evans, John, Justice, iv., 259.

Evans John, of Chester, appointed third judge of Supreme Court, xi., 270. Dies, xiv., 41. His successor, 42, 43. Pay, 47.

Evans, Lewis, map of Pennsylvania, materials for, sent to General St. Clair, vi., 301, 303. Certificate respecting Paschall's Steel Furnace in Philadelphia, ix., 633.

Evans Peter, Deputy Register for Probate of Wills, petition on, ii., 237, 391. Sheriff of Philadelphia, 397. Tax collector to give account, 473. Claims right to Register of probate under Wm. Penn; objections to, Register of Province at Philadelphia, 339. Withheld a portion from a relation of proprietary, 339. Register General for Probate of Wills, iv., 33. Commissioner to buy provisions, xi., 424.

Evans, Colonel William, to impress wagons in Chester connty, xi., 302. Justice, 542. Commissioner, xii., 370.

Eve, Oswald, Warden, ix., 293.

Everet, Edward, petition, i., 157.

Everly Michael, recommended by General Washington for promotion as Ensign, for "extraordinary exertions," &c., is promoted, xii., 352. And on recommendation by General Wayne, is promoted as Lieutenant, 483.

Ewer, Robert, declines being justice, i., 370.

Ewing, General, xi., 78, 691.

Ewing, James, a justice, x., 209. Councillor, xi., 623, 698.

Ewing, Hon. James, persons to be summoned before Council on contested election in York, xi., 676, 691.

Ewing, James, Vice-President, xiii., 413, 416, 417, 736.

Ewing, Jaspar, appointed Prothonotary of Court, xvi., 120, 122.

Ewing, Rev. Dr. John, apologizes for B. Chew, and asserts his willingness now to sign the parole, x., 267. Commissioner to run line between Virginia and Pennsylvania, xiii., 79. Buys a lot, 271, 685, 753. Paid, xiv., 317. Resigns, 443.

Ewing, Colonel John, xvi., 535.

Examinations of various persons at camp, at Armstrong's, (Fort Halifax) vii., 154. Of Daniel M'Mullen and Thomas Moffit, 283. Of Wm. Johnson, 341. On Indian murders, 357. Of Indian prisoners, 531.

Exchange of prisoners, x., 563, 564.

Excise, a bill of, i., 108, 109. Farming out, 111. Collection of, iv., 295, 686. Amount collected, vi., 241. On liquors, &c., vii., 58, 177, 181, 184. Bill, x., 24, 25, 34, 35, 41. Wm. Crispin, collector of, xii., 554. John Stokely appointed collector, xiii., 577, 597, 769. Coll'ors, &c., xiv., 396, 400, 445, 452, 486, 585, 590, 596, 652; xv., 315. Sale of W. Hays' estate postponed, xv., 2. Fine remitted, 44. John Craig, 54, 93. Resignation and appointment, 104, 127. Fine remitted, 127. Appointed, 132. Fines, 133. J. Duncan resigns—Richard Parker appointed, 222. Removed, and appointed in York County, 264, 266. Collectors of, 315. Resigns, 581. Collectors of, xvi., 83, 136, 194, 308, 311, 372, 374, 477. Deaths of, 383.

Execution—ten days allowed after judgment, i., 170, 171. Not to be levied on one property, if objected to, when there is enough to satisfy it elsewhere, 173. Nor to deprive family of all support, 174. Council prayed to revoke orders for, 203. In Kent County, 252.

Executions of criminals, iv., 47, 224, 253, 503; v., 125, 154, 157, 158, 269, 414, 488, 506, 567, 612, 699; vi., 136. Reprieves and pardons, vii., 172, 342, 398, 559; viii., 335, 336, 496, 506; ix., 5, 173, 192, 236, 238, 266, 334, 398, 402, 513, 545, 600, 601, 632, 666, 671, 678, 743; x., 44, 50, 64, 110, 172, 256; xi., 490, 616, 641, 753, 780; xii., 5, 178, 179, 181, 275, 329, 333, 335, 374, 387, 405, 535, 536, 667, 730, 750; xiii., 117, 137, 304, 382, 394, 505, 595, 704, 720, 725; xiv., 153, 203, 227, 240, 449, 567, 585, 586, 588, 591, 622, 624; xv., 2, 31, 203, 207, 311, 398, 400, 423, 427, 476, 483, 576, 578, 580, 583, 589, 633, 636; xvi., 9, 15, 27, 118, 485, 535.

Executors to give security, i., 553.

Expedition against Cape Breton, ii., 753, 754, 762, 763, 765.

Expenses of Government, including troops, vii., 778.

"Experiment," gun-boat, x., 289. Capt. Dougherty transferred from,

to the Washington, 296. Lieut. Allen Moore appointed to, 296, 328, 335, 505.

Exportation of goods, inquiry respecting, i., 232, 233, 240. Of flour and bread, iii., 536, 537, 538, 541.

Exports, 1773 to 1784, xiv., 336.

Extortion complained of, ii., 456.

Eyre, Major Benjamin, to value a boat, xi., 529, 670.

Eyre, Benjamin G., applies to search river for wrecks, xii., 76. To restore Schuylkill bridge, 205, 267, 293, 317. Warden, xiii., 100; xv., 12.

Eyre, Jehu, report of auditors on plank, &c., taken by enemy, xii., 263.

Eyre, John, has lumber taken by enemy, xi., 564. Claim for—committee on—"Genl. Greene," 756.

Eyre, Manuel, to build a boat, x., 283–285, 296. The "Bull Dog," 290. Committee at launch, 290. Failure to launch, and success, 290. "Congress." "Franklin." Appointed member of Navy Board, xi., 122. Resigns as Justice, xiv., 242.

Eyre, Richard, sent to salt works in command of "Delaware" boat, xi., 126, 191. Appointed to command Brig Convention, 543.

Eyre, Captain Robert, commands a boat, x., 339.

Eyres, Robert, claims pay for copies of laws, ii., 19, 20.

F.

Fabricius, Jacobus, petition to keep an ordinary—Refused, i., 143.

Fabricius, Rev. Jacob, minister of Swedes' Church, blind and in poverty, appeals to Council—Wardens summoned, i., 386.

Fair, a, asked, for New Castle, i., 180, 345. Also at Philadelphia, 218. "Contemptuous Paper" respecting, 224. Proceedings, 224. Another day for, appointed, 225. An addition at Philadelphia, 226, 555, 556.

Fairs, ii., 12. Objections to, 12. In Philadelphia—Act to suppress, x., 254. To be prevented, xiii., 753.

Fairfax, William, of Virginia, letter from respecting Indians, v., 657, 719.

Fairlamb, John, Sheriff, vi., 638. vii., 266; viii., 781; ix., 57. Provincial Commissioner, 237. Member of Assembly, dies, 301, 550. Ordered new election, 550.

Fairlamb, Nicholas, Sheriff of Chester, iii., 31, 56, 69, 108; xvi., 190, 494.

Fairman, Benj'n, Frankford bridge referred to him, iii., 247.

Fairman, Thomas, petition against Thomas Holme, i., 199. Complaint against, for forcible entry, 199, 201, 202, 320. Surveyor, to lay out a road, 499. About land in Bucks, ii., 434. And city lots, xiii., 322.

Falconer, Captain Joseph, paid for mounting guard at Magazine, Statehouse, &c., x., 709.

Falconer, Captain Nathaniel, order for lead, x., 437. On survey of River, 489. To fix signals at Cape Henlopen, 510. For arms, 535. For swivels, 554. A warden, xi., 538. Resigns as warden, xvi., 352. Health officer—Wharf at State Island, 493.

Falconer, Robert, ensign, xi., 78.

Falkner, Daniel, and Frankford Co. petition, ii., 431.

Falkner, John, Lieutenant, xii., 390.

False alarm, by Governor Evans, 1706, ii., 433, 453.

Families, registering of, i., 109.

Faries, Owen, buys a confiscated estate, xii., 189.

Farmer, Captain, x., 697.

Farmer, Edward, a Justice, ii., 159. Conference with Indians at, 546. A Justice, iii., 28.

Farmer, Jesper, Indians complain against his servants for making them drunk, i., 147–149.

Farmer, Lewis, Major, xi., 116, 129, 142, 651, 660, 710, 728, 743.

Farmer, Colonel Lewis, appointed Receiver General of Clothing, xi., 743. Commissary of the State—Appealed to in case of German Battalion, xii., 14. Money to, 16,

41, 62, 73, 106, 144, 212, 223. Stores to be delivered by Mr. Crispin to, 226, 247, 274, 381, 406, 429, 446, 506, 622, 662, 684, 701, 712. His pay, 717, 721, 782. To deliver shoes, xiii., 9, 47, 48, 143, 367. Stores in hand to be sold, 624. Appointed Register of German passengers, xiv., 447. Return of German passengers, xvi., 222.

Farmer, Michael, tobacconist, finding no sales here, petition for a pass to Boston—Granted, xii., 11.

Farmer, Thomas, Sheriff of Philadelphia county, ii., 25. Resigns, 98.

Farquhar, Rev. Colin M., asks pass to New York, xii., 106.

Fascines to be cut, x., 574.

Fast-day, proclamation for a, v., 169; vi., 422; vii., 110, 560. Appointed by Congress, xi., 175. Proclamation, 176, 438, 725, 751. Appointed, xii., 145, 183, 280, 282, 516, 671, 697; xiii., 101, 124, 267, 396, 400.

Fauquiere, Governor Francis, of Virginia, letter from Governor H. on Indian affairs, viii., 779. Letters to and from, ix., 305, 345, 349.

Fayette County, Prothonotary, E. Douglass, xiii., 702. Clerk, 704. Alex. McClean appointed Judge and President Court of Common Pleas, 732. Also Register of Wills, &c., 763. Lieutenants, xiv., 38. Justices, 54, 134, 322, 346, 362, 571. Contested election, 346. Elections, 563. Represent., xv., 109. Sheriffs, 109, 303. Coroner, 109, 303. Collector of Excise, Joseph Douglass, 132. Justices, 188, 294, 584. Ephraim Douglass, agent for estates confiscated in, xvi., 27. Sureties, 31. Edward Cook, President of Court of Common Pleas, 50. Justices, 138. Joseph Terrance, High-Sheriff, appointed Lieutenant in room of R. Bell, deceased, 148. Justices, 138, 231, 279, 407, 423, 536. Sheriff, 202, 518. Coroner, 202, 518. Councillor, 202. Irregular returns of militia officers, 376. Excise, 385. John Hoge resigns as Justice—Elected to Senate, 536.

Fayette, Marquis de la, recommends Chevalier de Lambert, xiii., 479.

Fayette, General de la, bells rung on his arrival in city, xiv., 176.

Feather, Peter, Junr., Coroner, xv., 294, 565; xvi., 491.

Feauss, Lieutenant Francis, of provincial ship, x., 521.

Febiger, Christian, auctioneer, N. L., xv., 52, 321. Memorial respecting Footman & Chaloner's vendue in Passyunk, 592. Of N. L., account, xvi., 10, 11. Resigns, 35. Certificate of fidelity, 67, 68. State Treasurer, 214[2], 237, 443. Trustee of Loan Office, 448. Letter, 466.

Federal City—proposals New York and Maryland for fixing, xiii., 600.

Federal constitution, order of procession in Philadelphia on ratification by Pennsylvania, xv., 350. Amendments proposed by North Carolina, xvi., 304.

Fees in New York and Delaware to be compared, i., 63. Custom House, 67. Certain vessels to be exempted, 68. For surveying, 69. In Philadelphia, 388. Respecting, 466. Officers, ii., 47, 54, 586. Do not pay expenses of Court, 102. Proposed. 219; iii., 245; v., 564, 578, 619.

Fegan, Elizabeth, wife of a traitor, order for her removal, xii., 243. Estate, 470.

Fegan, Lawrence, wife injured by Rioters, x., 701.

Felons—not to be brought to the country, i., 72.

Fell, Benjamin, Coroner, xi., 179, 219, 372, 378.

Fell, George, Coroner, x., 100, 211, 270.

Fell, Jesse, Sheriff, xvi., 196, 496, 499.

Feoffment—deeds, for Lower Counties to be recorded, ii., 39.

Ferguson, Charles, Commissioner, x., 702.

Ferguson, Mrs. Elizabeth, refused a pass to New York, xi., 629. Petition of George Meade, Thomas Franklin, and William White in

her behalf respecting sale of estate —referred to agents, xii., 352. Sale of Græme park deferred, and she to live rent free except taxes, 365. Message to Assembly respecting, 366. Prays to stay in country, 386.
Ferguson, Captain William, xii., 718.
Ferree, Joel, of Lancaster makes guns for Committee, x., 290.
Ferree, John, Sheriff, x., 101, 211, 270.
Ferree, Col. John, x., 686, 690, 699.
Ferree, Joseph of Germ'n, salt, x., 660, 665, 770. To collect leaden weights, 637.
Ferries, i., 126, 184, 368, 387, 461, 478, 498, 513, 514, 581; ii., 488, 525, 528; iii., 39, 43, 166, 171, 174, 233, 235, 360; iv., 22, 34, 40, 46. Not to be passed by persons with arms, xi., 27, 28, 31.
Ferris, Captain Owen, resigns, xii., 550.
Fetterman, George, x., 660.
Filbert, Peter, Sheriff, xiv., 232, 554; xv., 99.
Files, to be made by L. Bernie, x., 612.
Fincher, John and family murdered by Indians, ix., 44.
Fincher, Joshua, Coroner of Philadelphia, iii., 260.
Fine imposed on County Court of Philadelphia for giving judgment against law, i., 76.
Finley, James, Justice, xiii., 520; xiv., 54. Resigns as justice in Westmoreland, xv., 472.
Finley, Rev. James, undertakes a secret mission, xiii., 481. Pay to, 500.
Finley, William, Councillor, xvi., 216². Paid for team taken in 1778; xvi., 308.
Finney, David, Jr., naval officer at New Castle resigns, x., 109.
Finney, Captain Samuel, member of Council, ii., 37. A Justice, 159. Judge, 239.
Finney, Captain John, member of Council, ii., 68. Takes oath, 96. High Sheriff, 97. To take account of arms, 240. Resigns, 298. News of robberies by French and Spaniards, v., 89.
Finney, Captain Walter, memorial respecting land, xiii., 747.
Fire arms, spared to Virginia, x., 418. Not to be purchased to go out of Province, 498, 542.
Firelock, &c., to be purchased, x., 402, 420, 423, 443, 459, 501, 502, 503, 541, 545, 548, 560, 585, 588, 711.
Fire, buckets, in Philadelphia, petition for, and ladders, i., 478.
Fire rafts and sloops to be procured, x., 397, 543, 557, 560, 567, 597, 620, 699. Commanded by Captain John Hazelwood, 437. Captain W. Greenway, 525. Mr. Vernon's Brig, 536. Committee, 575. Guard for, i., 27, 247.
Fire ships, xi. 249, 255, 256.
Fire sloop to be manned, x., 585.
—— brig, 608.
Fish, preservation of, in the rivers, viii., 582. Act for preservation of, in western branches of Delaware, xiii., 318 Inspector of, xiv., 488.
Fishburn, Benjamin, appointed paymaster, x., 733.
Fishbourne, Ralph, proposed act to confirm to, the old Court house of Chester, ii., 218.
Fishburn, William, member of Council, iii., 226. Powder house referred to him, 242. Robbed, 389. Proceedings against, 395, 396. Disabled from holding office, 450. Acts in favor of 536, 537.
Fisher, Henry, appointed to furnish notice from Capes of the appearance of suspicious vessels, x., 337. His instructions, 339. Intelligence from, 526, 535. Pay to, 527, 559. Guard boat sent to, 593. Receipt for guard boat, &c., 620. Express to, respecting Hessians, 753. At Lewistown to give intelligence, xi., 9, 185. Light house, 574. To be written to respecting Dragon boat, xii., 120. Claim on for prize money, xv., 499.
Fisher, Jabez, Coroner, viii., 403.
Fisher, Joseph, arrested, i., 609.
Fisher & Roberts ask for remission of forfeiture on brandy, xiv., 76. Rent of stores, 570.
Fisher, Joshua, Coroner, iii., 465, 524, 575.

Fisher, Joshua & Sons, inquiry of Committee of Inspection as to property of, in their hands, x., 439. Decline lists, 449. Committee to procure invoice, 451. To be applied to, to sell, 453. They refuse to sell, 454. Order for sale by auction, 460. Refuse bills of credit—papers, &c., to be taken and sealed up, and stores locked up by Committee, 486. Refuse to deliver up their books, 488, 497. Sale of rigging by auction, 571.

Fisher, Joshua, to be seized, xi., 283, 290, 295, 308, 309.

Fisher, Miers, to be seized, xi., 283, 290, 295, 308, 309. Pleads claim for city lots, xv., 201. As attorney for Richard Howe and John Elliott—opinion of Attorney-Gen'l asked, 207. Claims for city lots, 399, 437, 481, 485. Claims a lot in Philadelphia for Widow Gaskill, of London, xvi., 55, 108, 130, 153. Southwark, &c., 238.

Fisher, Samuel, (son of Joshua,) to be seized, xi., 283, 290, 295, 308, 309. Ill in prison, released temporarily, xii., 221.

Fisher, Samuel R., intercepted letter, xi., 729, 735. In gaol two years, sick, discharged, xiii., 13.

Fisher, Capt. Thomas, x., 182.

Fisher, Thomas, (son of J.,) to be seized, xi., 283, 290, 295, 308, 309. Justice, xiv., 256.

Fisher's Island—sick passengers to be landed at, iv., 569.

Fisheries, preservation of, address from Assembly on, ix., 610, 707. Acts proposed, 719, 726, 729, 730; x., 73, 141, 226. Injured by wrecks of State, burned on Jersey shore, xii., 611.

Fitch, Thomas, Governor of Connecticut, letters to and from on dispute, v., 770, 773. Letters to and from on Connecticut claim, vi., 255, 261. Letter to on settlers in Northampton Co., viii., 598, 626.

Fitler, George, inquest on, xiv., 159.

Fitzpatrick, James, a noted robber, arrested, executed, and reward offered paid, xi., 616.

Fitzsimmons, Nicholas, Lieut., xi., 576. Appointed to new company, xii., 720.

Fitzsimons, Thomas, member of Council of Safety, xi., 45. Application with certificate of French Minister, respecting cargo of flour, 645.

Fitzsimons, Thomas, &c., petition respecting Mr. Levins, an absconding merchant, xiii., 370. Censor, 720; xiv., 230. Appointed commissioner, xv., 5; xvi., 2.

Fitzwater, Thomas, Coroner of Philadelphia County, i., 228.

Five Nations of Indians, lands purchased — presents to, iii., 273. Respecting, 330; iv., 434, 446.

Flag, purchased, to be raised on Gov. Thomas's arrival from Antigua—cost of, iv., 304.

"Flag, Union," v., 350.

Flag, altered, x., 694.

Flag, in exchange for Wampum, xi., 212. Letter from Board of War, respecting, 411. Pay at Chester for attending, 590.

Flags or standards for public use, with the arms of the State worked thereon, ordered, xii., 108.

Flag, State, xiii., 586. Mentioned, having been hoisted for two years, xiv., 518.

Flag of truce, with negroes, arrived from Hispaniola, v., 71, 74. With English prisoners, arrives from New Orleans, 77. Rules and regulations respecting, 80. Pilots, how to act in cases of arrival of flags of truce, 81, 98, 122. Sent with Negroes to Havana, 200. French prisoners sent to Hispaniola, 267. Mr. Burch applies to be released from contract—letter to M. De Chastenoy—pass for, 281. S. Phips, respecting, 419; xii., 10, 29, 30, 31, 502, 504, 506; xiii., 258.

Flag vessel expected with prisoners, xii., 521.

Fleeson Plunket paid for drums, x., 499; xi., 121. President of Court of Common Pleas and Quarter Sessions—to receive records, xiii., 20. President of City Court, 181. Justice, xiv., 135. Complaint against, 511. Resigns as President of Quarter Sessions, 548.

Fletcher, Benjamin, commission as Governor of New York and Pennsylvania, i., 345-364. Reasons for his commission to Penn'a, 355. His powers and duties, 356. Employ militia of New Jersey, 356. Appoints William Markham Lieutenant Governor, and several Councillors, 365. Going to frontiers—calls Assembly—asks advice of Council, 368. Visits New Castle, 368. Refuses by advice of Council, a letter from former Council, as inconsistent in the address, with his patent, 370. A man of arms, and not of Quaker principles, 373. Leaves for New York, 375. Letter, 383. Action upon it, 385. Request to Governors to send Commissioners to New York to settle quotas for defence, 393. Letter for support of the Government, 395. Address to Assembly on certain members refusing oaths, 398. Attends Council at New Castle, 398. Approves J. Growden as Speaker—address to, 399. To support New York against French and Indians, 400. Speaker's address to, 400, 402, 405. Discussions with Assembly, 406-433. Asks Assembly to answer Queen's letter, 446. Leaves for New York, 447. Adjourns courts, 453. Address to Assembly, 459, 463, 466, 468, 470. Opposes county levies, 471. Assembly wages, 471. Dissolves Assembly, 472. His authority as Gov. revoked, on restoration of Province to W. Penn, 474. Applies for troops for New York, 480, 484, 486, 490, 504. Speech to N. Y., 504. Report on Gov.'s letter, 520.

Fletcher, Thomas, Justice, iv., 259.

F leury, Francis, a Frenchman, impressed on the State ship—complaint of Consul, xii., 35. Report on his case, 37. Discharged and paid prize money, 86.

Flints for General Washington's army, x., 632; xi., 497.

Floating battery—Putnam—Nicho-l as Fitzsimons, Third Lieut., x., 531. To furnish men, 552. Com. Davison, 615, 725, 737; xi., 5, 17, 77, 85, 138.

Floating bridge at Schuylkill, xi., 55, 536. Guard at, 657.

Flour, inspections of, useful, iii., 390, 492. Exportation of, 536, 537, 538—and bread, bad, not to be exported, v., 33, 34, 459, 460. To be exported, x., 451. Inspector appointed in Philadelphia, Jacob Plankinhorn, xi., 201. Forestalled, 639, 640, 671, 766. Letters and papers respecting purchases of, xii., 16, 18, 47. To be purchased, 45, 46. Names of agents, 46. Scarcity of, 112, 117, 224. And salt exchanged, 136. Loaned to house of employment, 172. Forestalling, 224. For Mr. Holker, 275, 296. Inspectors, xiv., 444, 445, 487; xvi., 61, 63.

Flower, Enoch, appointed by Council first schoolmaster—His terms, &c., i., 91, 372.

Flowers, Colonel B., xi., 735. Died, xvi., 285.

Fly, the, an armed vessel, arrives with cannon for province sent by Congress, x., 632.

Flying-Camp, x., 664, 673, 679, 690, 703, 706, 708, 735; xi., 27, 29, 93, 119; xiv., 34, 604, 624, 634; xv., 10; xvi., 536

Fooks, Paul, xi., 48. Petition, 176. Notary Public, 200. Dies, xiii., 735.

Footman, Richard, petition, attorney of J. Warren, xi., 710; xvi., 36, 40, 196.

Forage, letters on, xi., 335.

Forbes, Brigadier-General John, appointed to command troops, viii., 27. Letters to and from, 59, 60, 79, 83, 100, 110, 167, 224, 232. Arms required, 79. Not received, 84. Suggestions of Sir William Johnson respecting Indians joining him, 97. Asks for a provincial treasurer and barrack-master, 100. Attends Council in Philadelphia with Major Halket and several Indians, 124. Council convened at request, on Indian affairs, 126. Message of Governor to Indians on Susquehannah, 131. Letter from Fort Loudoun — Every thing depends on the people of Pennsylvania, 167. Sends news of attack on Loyal

Hanning, 212. Letter from Raystown--Proposed operations--Forts to be garrisoned, &c., 224. Captures Fort Du Quesne—French burn and evacuate it, 233. Illness of, 262, 264, 283. Holds conference with Indians at Philadelphia, 264. Indian warriors who assisted him, 265. Leaves Colonel Mercer in command, 292. General Amherst appoints Brigadier-General Stanwix, 298, 317. His death alluded to, 298, 317. Did not pay for his wagons, 373.

Forbes, Lieutenant James, recruits, xi., 573.

Forbes, Hon. Mr., member Congress, dies—Invitation to funeral, xii., 293.

Forcible entry and detainer, i., 236, 253. Proceedings, 253, 258.

Ford, Philip, mortgage to, of province, ii., 455.

Ford, Philip, Sheriff, ix., 199, 285, 333. Writ for election of a new member of Assembly, 301. Coroner, viii., 781.

Ford, Samuel, sentenced to death, xi., 565. Warrant issued, 566.

Forest, Captain Thomas, commands troops sent to General Washington, xi., 25.

Forestalling in Philadelphia, petition against, xi., 639, 640, 671; xii., 190.

Forgery cases, ii., 108, 186.

Fornication, alteration in the law against proposed, i., 61. Charges for, i., 156, 176, 188.

Forrest, Captain Thomas, appointed of marines, x., 514. To recruit men, 517. Pay, &c., 518. Allowed a drummer and fifer, 521. Of artillery, 742. Committed to jail for assault on Mary Taylor, xi., 201. Claims two lots in Philadelphia, xiii., 136, 175, 331, 334, 500, 505, 507; xv., 3.

Forrest, Walter, his mill, i., 389.

Forster, John, Coroner, xii., 513.

Forster, Joseph, paid for removing exhibition frame from Market street to Statehouse, xiv., 157.

Forster, Thomas, Justice of Lancaster, complained of, for interrupting Sheriff in surveying land—He is removed from office, ix., 335.

Forsyth, John, Collector of Excise for York county, xiv., 585.

Forsyth, John, appointed Collector of Excise in York county, xv., 264.

Foster, David, released, x., 462.

Foster, John, Coroner, xii., 137, 138.

Fort Island, battery, &c., to be erected at, x., 383, 385, 432, 494. Captain Proctor to command artillery, 452. To have 6 guns made for, 494, 497. Committee to perfect fortifications, 498. Three armed boats to be sent down, 507. Armourer, 522. Piers to be built at, 525. John Reed appointed commissary and barrack master at, 553. Men and boats to be ready for action, 557. Committee to repair to, 559. Survey to Billingsport, 567. Furnace to heat shot, &c., 572. Barracks ready, 587. To desist from works at, 605. Pier cut loose, New London cannon for, 630. Piers at, 648, 718. Wood for, and stone, 699, 722, 734, 741, 755, 758. Council visit, 731. No persons to view, 758. Sounded, 761, 772. A fire to be created and nails to be manufactured at, 765. Artillery to parade at, xi., 1, 24, 28. Boom to be fixed to piers at, by Thomas Marle, 31. Takes men to, 33. Captain Jno. Read, barrack master, 51. Piers, 109, 114. Pay of armourer at, 115. Of John Read barrack master, 116. Under charge of Navy Board, 123. General Proctor's regiment, marches from, General Potter to furnish guard for stores, &c., 250. Removal of troops from Billingsport to, 269. The banks to be repaired, 285. Flood gate to be made at, 286. Lieutenant Colonel Samuel Smith in command, 397. Pickets taken up, 557. Cannon for, 572. Repairs at 725. Garrison relieved, 756. Workmen at, 767. Stores for, 771, 777.; xii., 10, 13, 26, 40, 65. Sickly state of garrison, 117. Times expiring, persons to be left in charge, 134. Workmen to be discharged when works are secured from weather, 146. Pay to Colonel Bull, 180. Wil-

liam Anderson's account of services, &c., at, 294. Cannon from, 312. Laborers to be employed at, 403. Major Armstrong, 402. William Earle, 427. Suspected vessels to unload at, 453. Quarantine at, 457. Fortifications, 468, 480. Captain Paul Cox in flag of truce to pass, 557. Pay to workmen, 588, 667. Under Captain Boys, 627. Pay to guard, 718, Troops for defence of, 719. Pirate hung in chains, 731. Pay for men at, xiii., 14. Supplies, men to be discharged, 16. Overseer wanted, 30. Supplies, 43. French General's views, 51. Under care of William Smith, 54. Pay to workmen, 91, 121. A British vessel to be stopped at, 145. Pay for, 149. Pay for repairing banks at, 296. Salary at, to cease, 429. Pay at, 444. Taxes, 449. Visit of Council to, 578. Lease of meadow to B. Brannon, 691. (See below.)

Forts—

Adjouquay, vii., 137, 159, 182, 184.

Allen, vii., 17, 189, 222, 429, 474, 723; viii., 98, 138, 150, 166, 234, 514, 515, 523; ix., 30, 42, 244, 246, 283, 441, 651; xv., 359.

Augusta at Shamoken, vi., 701; vii., 6, 54, 76, 79, 80, 90, 121, 157, 184, 281, 294, 302, 436, 503, 512, 543, 546, 550, 597, 603, 724, 736, 773; viii., 99, 128, 129, 406, 458, 499, 514, 522, 753; ix., 30, 42, 244, 246, 283, 284, 440, 651.

Bedford at Rayston, ix., 30, 304, 386.

Billingsport, x., 294, 474, 604, 626, 673, 678, 719; xii., 10, 13, 26; xiii., 14, 16, 43, 51, 121, 429, 449; xiv., 465, 581, 586, 617.

Boccalunce, v., 624.

Burd, xvi., 223[2].

Cadaraghqui, v., 549; vii., 10.

Carlisle, vi., 732; viii., 224.

Chambly and St. John, x., 410.

Christiana, i., 109, 131, 188, 370, 372; iii., 21. Reinforced from Maryland, i., 188.

Christiana—(Virginia,) murder of Indians at, iii., 21.

Forts—

Conococheague, vi., 641.

Cumberland, vi., 373, 513; vii., 289, 342, 502, 512, 565, 601, 632; viii., 224; ix., 35, 304.

Drumer, vi., 33.

Dunmore, x., 228.

Du Quesne, vi., 141; vii., 153, 341, 502, 601, 602, 632, 716; viii., 120, 147, 233, 315, 322, 427, 509.

Edward, (N. Y.) vii., 379, 714; viii., 60, 141.

Frederic, vii., 502, 529, 552, 553, 556; viii., 224.

Freeland, xii., 62; xvi., 170.

Fort Island, x., 525, 540, 566, 567, 568, 586, 605, 665, 722. (See above.)

—— Island, Mud Island, and Fort Mifflin, xii., 10, 13, 26, 40, 65.

Frontenac, vi., 20.

George, v., 640; vi., 59.

Granville, vii., 232, 233, 278, 561, 716.

Great Meadows, vi., 50, 158, 602.

Guadenhutten or Allen, vi., 772.

Halifax, vii., 154, 156, 724.

Hand, xi., 558.

Hannas Town, xvi., 341.

Harmar, xv., 605.

Harris, John—near, vii., 244.

Hunter, v., 470; vii., 502, 724, 773; ix., 30.

Jenkins, xi., 654.

Johnson, vii., 43, 74, 154, 159.

Juniata, viii., 224.

Lawrence, xi., 699.

Lebanon, vii., 35.

Le Bœuf, viii., 380, 513, 515; ix., 35; xv., 593; xvi., 47.

Liberty Island, x., 462.

Ligonier, ix., 35; xvi., 176.

Loudoun, vii., 395, 445, 555, 632; viii., 77, 78, 111, 167, 224, 776; ix., 88, 292.

Loyal Hanna, viii., 224.

Lyttleton, vii., 77, 553, 555, 632; viii., 224; ix., 34, 434, 490, 514, 684, 686, 718.

McCords, vii., 77.

McDowells, vii., 231, 233.

McIntosh, xiv., 373, 448; xvi., 340.

McKees, vii., 148.

Forts—
Mettols, vii., 399.
Mifflin, xi., 397, 654; xiv., 512, 586, 617. (See Mud.)
Montgom'y, x., 743, 756; xi., 4.
Morris, (Shippensb'g) vii., 599.
Mud Island, x., 283, 378, 382, 383, 385, 432, 452, 474, 494, 495, 498, 513, 520, 525, 540, 566, 567, 568, 586, 605, 665, 722; xi., 397, 654; xii., 10, 13, 26, 40, 65; xiii., 14, 16, 30, 43, 51, 449; xv., 175. (See Mifflin,)
Muncey, xiii., 214.
Necessity, vi., 50, 158, 602.
Niagara, viii., 147, 380, 400.
Norris, vii., 493.
On Ohio, v., 423, 447, 461, 482, 515, 608, 623, 659, 660, 687, 696, 712, 720, 761–763; vi., 4, 10, 31, 33, 140, 185, 223–226, 465, 642; vii., 133.
Oswego, vi, 13, 310.
Pitt, viii., 509, 582; ix., 32, 35, 42, 210, 239, 259, 264, 304, 321–323, 434, 490, 514, 684, 686, 718; x., 11, 17, 21, 68, 70, 71, 74, 176, 183, 200; xi., 699; xii., 716, 747; xiii., 79, 83, 162, 348, 408, 455; xiv., 476, 498, 517; xvi., 340. See Du Quesne.
Preservation, xv., 66; xvi., 170, 176.
Presque Isle, vi., 10; viii., 380, 513, 515; ix., 35, 193.
Rayston, viii., 224.
Red Bank, x., 283, 474, 617.
Redstone, vi., 137.
Rice, xiii., 117.
Shamokin, at, or Augusta, vi., 701; vii., 6, 54, 76, 79, 80, 90, 121, 157, 184, 281, 436, 503, 512, 543, 546, 550, 736, 773; viii., 99, 128, 129, 406, 458, 499, 514, 522, 753; ix., 30, 42, 244, 246, 283, 284, 440, 651.
Shippensburg, vi., 459, 732; viii., 224.
Shirley, vii., 232, 278.
Stanwix, ix., 545, 738; x., 257; xiv., 366.
Steele's, vi., 675.
Ticonderoga, viii., 380.
Venango, vii., 289, 341, 502; viii., 265, 380; ix., 35; xvi., 47.
Washington, L. I., xii., 34; xiv., 443; xvi., 535.

Forts—
Wiccacoa, vi., 770; viii., 39, 147.
William Henry, N. Y., vii., 515, 714; viii., 141.
Wills' Creek, vi., 137, 180.
Wyoming, vii., 730; ix., 377; x., 86.

Forts—Address proposed to King and Duke on building forts, &c., i., 109. At New Castle, 131, 370, 372. Suggested by Proprietaries, v., 515. Croghan, to say nothing about building, 522. Views of Assembly, 547. Necessity, at Great Meadows, defeat of Washington at, vi., 50, 137. Du Quesne taken, 141. Deserters and prisoners, 142. French taken by English—Murders, 643. Chain of forts recommended by Commissioners, vii., 153. A map of frontiers and forts alluded to, 228. Proposed near Wyoming, x., 86. In Virginia, 158.

Foulke, Judah, Sheriff, ix., 689, 777; x., 56. Clerk of market, and keeper of standard weights and measures, Philadelphia, 111.

Foulke, Stephen, conceals deserters, xi., 357.

Fowler, Captain, a British officer, now a settler here, xi., 658.

Fox, Edward, notary, xv., 89.

Fox, H., Sec'y of State, letter from —Appointm't of Earl of Loudoun, commander-in-chief, vi., 179, 180. Officers appointed to command troops about to embark, 180. Treatment of French prisoners, 269. Succeeded by Wm. Pitt, 412.

Fox, James, a Justice of Philadelphia county, i., 544. Treasurer, dies, 576.

Fox, John, to be seized, xi., 283.

Fox, Joseph, a Provincial Commissioner, viii., 499, 636, 657, 697. Elected Speaker of Assembly, ix., 236, 287, 591. Writ for a new election of a member, 301. Declines as Commissioner to Indian treaty at Fort Pitt, 491. Report respecting firelocks, x., 307, 357. Can't find workmen, 380, 381. Barrack-Master, 390, 408, 415, 427, 459. His apprentice enlisted

is discharged, 470. Fire-arms, 484, 486.

Foy, Miles, &c., petition, iv., 256.

Frame of government, i., 29, 42, 48. Debate respecting its having been printed in handbills, 278. Committee to prepare a new, 486, 507, 597.

Frampton, William, a councillor for Kent, i., 127. Petition for removal of caves from before his door, 167. Justice, 176. Register General pro tem., 185, 186. Death of, 195.

Frampton, Major General, to sail with troops for Louisburg, v., 37.

France, England declares war against, and Spain, ii., 70. Probable rupture with England, iv., 671, 673, 677. War declared, 689. In favor of Popish pretender, 677. Privateers capture vessels, 749. Commission to P. Chartier, 757. And Spain, peace declared, ix., 13, 37. And England, treaty of 1763, 80. Extract from treaty with, xi., 487. Consul of, Mr. St. John, letter, xiv., 2. Monsieur Marbois, consul, 43. Vessel of, detained by Court of Admiralty, 111. Consul General insulted, 115, 116. Two criminals pardoned on application of Marbois, Jr., 240. Conviction of L. Blanc, L. Collinet, 447, 449. Exequator to Vice-Consul, 491. Act of, for encouraging commerce with United States, xv., 463.

Francis, Tench is Attorney General, iv., 620. Replies to case stated respecting Connecticut claim, v., 775. Resigns as Attorney General, vi., 277. B. Chew appointed, 277. Capt., applied for rifle guns to Committee for his company, x., 288. Colonel, applies for powder, 598. To lay off lots at barracks, xiv., 76. Agent for proprietaries, demands first payment, 622. Warrants for city lots to issue in favor of, xv., 379, 383. Commissioner for Road, 425, 445.

Francis Turbut, letters to and from, ix., 587, 606. Respecting shooting Indian George, 603, 604. Indian conference at Shamokin, 610. Succeeds to sev'l offices, 671, 680.

Frankford Bridge, iii., 247, 263.

Frankford Company petition F. D. Pastorius, &c., ii., 430, 431. Quantity of land owned, 431. Plot against, 431, 432.

Frankford Creek, passage over, broken, to be repaired, ii., 52, 194. Through to Bristol, v., 59.

Franklin, Benjamin, Clerk of Assembly, iv., 424, 459. Commissioned to meet Indians at Carlisle, v., 658. Report, 665–684. Commissioner to Albany, vi., 25. His comm'n, 47. Appointed to make draught of a plan of union, 67, 100. Plan presented by, 105–109. Employed to procure waggons for General Braddock, 408. Holds office under general post-office—Complaint by Governor M., 600. As Committee of Assembly distributes arms, —. His course in Assembly represented by Governor M., 739. And Indians—Brief narrative of incursions, 1755, 766. Fort Allen, letters from, vii., 15. Expenses at, 17. Sent to build Fort Allen, 17. Expense of Companies—His proceedings, 19. Letter from, and other Commissioners, to Indians—They meet Council, 153. Has part charge of post office—Salary, &c., 447. Agent, delivers to proprietaries a paper entitled "Complaints unsigned," &c., from Assembly, at which they complain, viii., 276. Heads of complaint, 279. And answer by agents of proprietaries, 278. Answer to agents, 299. Appointed with R. Charles agent to England, 512, 547. Agent in England, ix., 10. Chosen Speaker of Assembly, 182. Agent for province in London—Salary, x., 53. A Commissioner at Albany, 177. President of Committee of Safety, 282. To thank Captain McPherson, 292. Makes a present of curious copper plates to Supreme Executive Council, xi., 233. Member of Congress, 385. Councillor, xiv., 555, 556. President of Supreme Council, 557, 565. President, xv., 110, 126. Receives pay for postage on his public letters while

President, xvi., 67. Dies—Powder for his funeral, 341. Testimonial of respect, 344. Bequeaths to Council a portrait of him by Martin in 1767, 358. Thanks of Council to executors, 359.

Franklin, boat, late commanded by Captain Biddle, now by Captain N. Boyce, x., 426. Captain Houston, 488, 506.

Franklin, galley, xi., 12, 706, 750. Lieutenant, xii., 139.

Franklin College, grant of land to, by Supreme Executive Council, survey of, xv., 367. Expense of surveying, 657.

Franklin Co., Prothonot'y, xiv., 202. Justices, 208, 345, 369, 567, 657, 669. Elections, 236, 486, 563. Representative, 236. Sheriff, 236, 563. Council, 236. Coroner, 236, 563. Lieutenant, 400. Representatives, 563. Election declared void, 487. Two election districts for Justices set off, 650. Justices, xv., 59, 108, 199, 269, 347, 537, 545, 588, 641. Sheriff, 120, 300, Coroner, 120, 301. Contested election, 129, 199. Collector of excise, Wm. Long, resigns, Councillor, 301. Lieut. of, resigns, 319. Jeremiah Talbot appointed, 343. Asks for a Justice of the Peace for Greencastle, 497. Division, 641. Order of Orphans' Court in favor of Wm. Dean's widow, xvi., 29. Sureties, 31. Amount of tavern and marriage licenses, 61. Lieut. paid, 63. Collector of excise resigns, 87. Justices, 167, 403, 478. Sheriff, 210, 495. Coroner, 210, 495. Militia fines, 279. Tavern and marriage licenses, 369. Taxes received, 462. Wm. Hobbert pardoned, 479. Edwd. Crawford Register and Recorder, 496. Receipts of tavern and marriage licenses, 522.

Franklin & Hall, printers, enjoined not to publish papers without approbation of Governor, vi., 327. Their answer to Governor, 327. Opinion of Council on, 328. Implicated in case of Wm. Moore and Dr. Smith, viii., 439.

Franklin, John, deed to, for city lot, xiv., 486. Letter to, xv., 35. Passport to, 67. Arrives—heard, 79. Member Assembly, 162, 408. Board paid, 427. Letter from Governor Huntingdon respecting his imprisonment, 575. Letters received from Governor Clinton, 578. Expense of removing from Northampton—Medical attendance, &c., 640. Arrested, 290. He to be closely confined and in irons, 291. To be furnished with a mattrass—Irons removed—On parole, 304. Memorial of his sickness, and irons to be removed, 385, 394. Expenses, 487. Conference respecting, 533. Sick, nurse for, 537. His letter asked for, 571. Expense of boarding as a State prisoner, xvi., 4. Conference on his case, 17. Clothing for, 21. Boarding paid, 50. Liquors for, 61, 82, 95. Removed from Philadelphia, 102.

Franklin, Gov. Wm., of New Jersey, letters to and from, ix., 113, 543. With Indians, 113. Robbery of treasury of New Jersey, 544.

Franks, David Solebury, present at riot at J. Wilson's, gives bail, xii., 141. Examined, 199. Claim for provisions, 296. To be arrested, 495, 496. To return to army, 496.

Franks, David, Brit. Commissary, xi., 679. Clerk, sent to N. York, 683. Petition for pass, xii., 141. To be arrested, 495. To depart the State, 498, 502, 505. Sick—Doctor to visit, 509, 546.

Franks, Isaac, Notary, and T. P., xvi., 1.

Franks, Peter, deposition against Indians, vi., 54.

Franks, Mr., x., 500.

Franks, Col., to receive tents for French emigrants, xvi., 513.

Frankstown road to Conemaugh, xvi., 252, 256, 434.

Fraud, meaning of, explained by Teedyuscung, vii., 325.

Frazer, John, petition for restoration of a vessel, iii., 76. Indian trader, store above the mouth of the Ohio, v., 659. Gives information respecting French and Indians,

and sites of several places, 659. Had a gun-smith shop at Weningo, 660. Sent with Indians from Fort Pitt to Redstone, ix., 539. Instructions to, 540.

Frazier, Persifer, appointed Comm'r of purchases, xii., 301. Declines, 334. Elected Brigadier General, xiii., 289. Recorder and Register, xv., 4. Justice, 38. Treasurer of Chester Co., 179.

Frederick, Fort, vii., 529, 552. Conference at, 552, 556; viii., 224.

Freeland, Fort, surrender of, xii., 62. Thanks and orders of Council, 63. Gun lost at, paid for, 1777, xvi., 170.

Freeman, Benjamin, wounded at Amboy—allowance to, xiii., 266.

Freeman, Moses, Sheriff, iii., 332.

Free Masonry, fatal effects from using in jest, iv., 277.

Free negro made prisoner by a Spanish vessel, asks a trial, ii., 112.

Free Society of Traders, stockholders in Virginia in trouble for want of their books and accounts —ordered to be sent — officers summoned—further sales of land forbidden, ii., 154. Officers, 154. E. Shippen to send full account of to England, 163. Act for sale of their lands for payment of debts, discussed by Governor and Council, iii., 138.

French from Maryland, rumored invasion by, i., 277, 299. War with England, 302. Fears in New York, 332. In Maryland, 334.

French and Indians conspire against England, i., 396.

French, fleet on coast, rumor of and alarm, i., 479. Arrive at and plunder Lewestown, 539. Traders with orders—fears of from Canada, ii., 19. Pirates, 21, 24. Squadron under M. De Coetlogon, 24. Prize, 99, 100, 101. Prisoners landed from privateer at Burlington, ordered by Lord Cornbury to be sent to Pennsylvania, 113. Men stopped by order of Governor, 182. Victory over, 215, Privateers on coast, 240, 241, 468. Traders arrested, 390. Complaint, 403, 534. Privateers, captures by, 411. Lands men at Whorekills, 448. The, incroach on New York by erecting fortifications near Albany, iii., 419. Arrives and blockades the British in New York, xi., 532. Minister is received by Congress, 548. Frigate Chimere, 618. Minister 645. Offers a reward for captures, 646. Fleet under Count D'Estaing arrives, xii., 114. Officers recommended by Chev. Luzerne, 116. Claims of their subjects here, 267. Opinion of Attorney-General and Councils on, 275. Minister and the State enter into an agreement, 368. Sailors desert, 370. Passport for Havana, 402. Desertion of sailors, 409. Exchange on, 419. Loan, 418, 420, 422. Fleet at Newport, 424, 430. Supplies for, enlistment of Hessians, 433. Get masts from Schuylkill, 488. Minister appoints William Young, Jr., as Botanist, 611. Sailors to be collected, 723. Want to ship flour to St. Domingo, 729, 730. Applied for by Count de Barras, resolution of Congress, xiii., 5. Generals visit forts, expenses paid, 51. Sieur Holker consul General, 59. State of subsidy to United States, 100. Minister has audience by Congress on birth of a Dauphin, 282. Costs of entertainment, 297. Army to be conveyed over the Delaware, 358. Deserters, 375, 473, 475. Memorial of Consul on powder, 619.

French, David, Attorney General of Lower Counties, iii., 253. Clerk of Peace and Court, 338.

French, John, Colonel, declines to administer oath to Governor Keith, iii., 13. Member of Council, 18. Keeper and Ranger, 37. Attends conference between Governor Hart of Maryland and Governor Keith, 60. Report on Indian visit, 77. Visits Indians with Governor, 121. designs against proprietary's interests, 138. Sent to investigate murder of Indians at Conestoga, 146. To survey Springetsbury manor, 185. Approves of Gover-

nor's course in directing the survey, 186. Agent respecting Chester and New Castle line, 235. Keeper of Great Seal, 253. Judge, 253. Dies, 338.

French, Captain John, Sheriff at New Castle, ii., 448. Sent to Indians, returns, 467. His account, 528.

French and Indians of Mississippi combining, v., 1, 2, 5, 27, 31. Flag of truce from W. I. arrives, with English prisoners and free negroes, 71. Flag of truce arrives, with prisoners, 77. Robberies on river by, and Spaniards, 89, 98. And Indians, 119. Cessation of arms between, and England--Proclamation, &c., 330, 331. Ship reported to be captured bound to Philadelphia, 347. Papers respecting peace, 359-362. A body of, moving to Ohio from Canada, 387, 423. And Indian affairs, 460. A trader captured, 461. Cause leaden plates to be buried in Ohio, 508, 510. Building a ship at Cadaraghque, 549. Ill-treatment by, 573. Letter from Governor Clinton on breach of treaty at Aix-la-Chapelle, 553. Answer of Governor of Canada to, 554. And Indians attack Twightwees town, 599. And Indians pass Fort Oswego on way to Ohio, 607. Affairs on Ohio, 624. Notice of Indians to commander near Weningo, 666. And his answer, 664-668. Have built two forts on Ohio, 687. On affairs on do., 708-710. Letter from Legardeur de St. Pierre, 715. Affairs with Indians, 732, 734. And Indian invasions, vi., 1-9. Report on claims to North America, 100-105. Influence on Indians, 129. Troops arrive at Ohio, 223-226, 233. Respecting, 309. Embargo on provisions, 319. Fit out a large fleet with troops for North America, 353. Notice from Governor to the, 411. Sent men to Ohio, 412, 427. Forts taken by English, 447. Fleet at Louisburg, 450, 459, 461. On Ohio, 602. At Lake George, 623. Defeat under General Dieskau, 637. And Indians pass Alleghanies, 651, 675. Neutrals, 711, 729, 751. Indians, vii., 43. Large body preparing for Fort Augusta, 453. Alarm from, 718. Neutrals, 14, 32, 45, 55, 58. Encroachments, 18. Petition, 239. Proposal to bind out, 390. Sufferings of, 393. Some arrested, 446. Expected at Fort Augusta, 512. Supposed at Little Meadows, 601. Prisoner taken, 604. Case of, 717, 720, 723. Will Sock takes colors from, viii., 132. Flag of truce with prisoners captured in Delaware Bay by privateer Spry, 139. Commander at Fort Niagara buys a white child from Indians, 147. And Indians attack Loyal Hanning, 212. Neutrals, 269, 718. Intelligence from, 377. Agreement for exchange of prisoners, 381. Arrest of Boyrie and Le Roy, 714.

French, Major Christian, a ministerial officer arrives and is ordered into custody, x., 302, 303. Gives his parole to proceed to General Washington's camp, 303. His baggage to be given up, 304. Applies for goods, is refused, going to camp under care of Willing and Wharton, 305. Goes security for two privates, 306.

French creek, Congress build powder mill on, magazine, x., 550. Powder mills on, xi., 49. Barracks at, guard for, 58. Le Bœuf at head of, to be reserved for commonwealth, 593.

French, Robert, enticing soldiers away, xi., 766. Arrest, 766, 770.

French emigrants bound to Sciota, to receive tents, xvi., 513.

Fretwell, Ralph, complains against Surveyor General for not issuing warrant to survey his lands, i., p. 124, 155. Pretends to a title for lands for friends in Barbadoes, v., 551.

Friendly Association contributes money for Indians, vii., 391.

Friendship, sloop, privateer, xi., 2.,

Frigates, four building by Congress, x., 115. Men at rope walk for, 707.

Frontier counties want troops, vi.. 601. Condition of, from Indians, vii., 130, 133, 228, 592; ix., 30,

58, 138. Condition and mode of defence, xii., 631. Inhabitants ask for defence, xiii., 206, 290.

Froom, Coarse, an Indian trader, iii., 329.

Fry, Colonel Joshua, a Virginia Commissioner and mathematician observes latitude of Shanoppins Town, &c., v., 751.

Fuller, Henry, Sheriff, x., 100, 270.

Fullerton, Major, arms, x., 672.

Fullerton, Ensign Richard, appointed lieutenant, xii., 550.

Fullerton, Humphrey, Justice, xiii., 266.

Fullerton, Dr. Humphrey, his widow (Ann McKnight) receives pension, xv., 413.

Fullerton, Mary, pension, xv., 185.

Fullerton, Lt. Richard, order to, xii., 717.

Funk, George, Coroner, xiii., 134.

Furby, Caleb, Coroner, x., 56, 101, 211.

Furman, Moore, teams discharged for want of money, xii., 435.

Furney, Adam, shot, but recovered, v., 377.

Furnaces, xi., 335. Oley, xv., 229.

G.

Gabriel, George, Indian murders in his neighborhood, vi., 645, 662, 668. His placed described, 669. Houses burned by Indians, vii., 154.

Gaddis, John, Justice, xiv., 54.

Gage, General Thomas, letters to and from, ix., 90, 110, 118, 119, 170, 238, 266, 267, 275, 292, 297, 318, 324, 403, 405, 663, 664, 686. On Paxton murders, 110. Order for troops, 118. Answer of Governor Colden respecting Indians, 119. Kind part taken by, 123. Places Indians under protection of Captain Schlosser, 124. Sends troops to Philadelphia, 129. Peace made by Colonel Bouquet, 238. Conference of Sir W. Johnson with Indians, 266. Insults to troops in Cumberland, 267. Rioters in, 299, 301, 303. Quarters for troops in Philadelphia, 318. Murders near Fort Pitt, 321. Settlers on Indian lands, 403, 405. Letters to and from, 422, 443, 581, 718. Murders by Stump, 441. Riots at Wyoming, 663. Answer to remonstrance of Assembly, 718. Letters to and from, x., 17, 19, 68. Carriages employed by Colonel Wilkins, 17. Acts in a hostile and cruel manner against American subjects, 302.

Galbraith, Bernard, Lieutenant, of Lancaster county, xiv., 478.

Galbreath, Colonel Bartram, arms, x., 674, 682, 690, 691, 692; xi., 83. to receive arms, 212. To send troops to Lancaster, 313, 496, 538, 574–5, 577, 776. To call out men, xii., 64. A commissioner to examine Susquehanna and Juniata rivers, xvi., 178. Instructions, 181, 208. Paid, 260, 308.

Galbraith, James, Sheriff, iv., 602, 669. A Justice, v. 600. Sends information about French and Indians at Ohio, 615. And others advise inhabitants to prepare against attacks of Indians, vi., 669. Appointed a Commissioner to Wyoming, vii., 754. Provincial Commissioner, ix., 237. Letter; finds a dead Indian, 487. Lieutenant of Cumberland, xi., 205. 208.

Galbraith, John, Sheriff, iii., 387, 416.

Galbraith, Robert, Prothonotary, xi., 187. Justice, 302, 303. Resigns, 646. Agent for confiscated estates, xiii., 774. Justice, xiv., 24. To measure between Susquehanna and Allegheny river, xv., 5. Runs above line, 85. President of Court petition against Prothonotary, 536. Contracts for road from Frankstown, 546. On road from Frankstown to Conemaugh, xvi., 252, 256, 257.

Galbraith, Thomas, on Indian murders, xiv., 476.

Gale, Levin, Commissioner, to run the line between Maryland and Pennsylvania, iv., 313.

Gallatin, Albert, of Fayette county, respecting confiscated lands purchased, xvi., 422.

Gallissoniere, Marquis, sends Celeron to Ohio—see letter in French, v., 425.

Gallespie, George, xi., 630.

Galleys, "Franklin," xi., 12, 572, 578, 706, 750, 765. To aid in searching wrecks, xii., 1, 14, 23, 192. Discharges from, 187, 190, 340. Pay, 223, 251, 263, 315. Reduced, 323, 376, 406, 477, 627, 657, 720. Memorial of officers of, xiii., 677.

Galloway, John, Captain, xii., 70. Of Bedford county, accounts, xiv., 637.

Galloway, Joseph, a provincial commissioner, vii., 499, 636, 657, 671, 697. Remarks on bill for recording warrants, &c., viii, 363–369. Elected Speaker of Assembly, ix., 335, 399, 551, 596, 625, 691. Commissioner to lay out money to Indians—his advice, 468. Sick and resigns, 590. re-elected, 625. Receives a threatening anonymous demand for money, signed "Chester County Man," and at his request Governor P. issues a proclamation for arrest of the unknown writer, x., 44. Chosen Speaker, 59, 105. His wife asks protection of council, xi., 196. Agreement with George Taylor for Durham furnace, 537. Deed signed to Richard Backhouse for his late estate in Bucks county, price, &c., xii., 104. Estate claim of widow Growden confirmed, paid, 191. Deed for Tinicum to several persons as part of his forfeited estate, 256. Sale of, in Bucks county to John Young, Jr., 268, 284. In Philadelphia, 300, 331, 353, 441, 751. Hog Island, 576, 631, 661. Sale of his confiscated estate, xiii., 280, 281, 325, 450. Estate in Bucks, sale of, xiv., 494. Notice of sale of his lots at Sixth and Market streets, xv., 6, 15, 37. Petitions by Thomas Clifford for a pardon—which he is allowed to withdraw, xvi., 363.

Galt, Captain, case of, xii., 266. Discharged, 340.

Gamble, James, letter from—reasons for not joining the militia, xii., 311. Ensign James to be Lieutenant, xiii., 492. Of artillery paid, xiv., 55.

Gamble, Wm., Captain of Ætna fire ship, x., 525. Resigns, 760.

Ganawese or Piscataway Indians, ask to settle here, ii., 191; iii., 19. Their residence, 501. Visit and speech at Philadelphia, 606. King, letter to, from Gov. Keith, 188.

Gaol, new in Philadelphia, x., 535. Persons complain of, 600.

Garcia Antonia, a mulatto prisoner, ii., 11, 18, 112, 120.

Gardner, Captain, complaint against, xii., 316, 449.

Gardner, D., member of Assembly, xi., 215.

Gardner, Hugh, flour inspector, xiv., 445.

Gardner, John, Sheriff, xii., 513; xiii., 87, 392, 617.

Gardner, Joseph, confirmed as Councillor from Chester Co., xii., 146. Appointed delegate to Congress, xiv., 261, 442, 549, 560.

Garland, George, Lieutenant of boat, x., 339. Of galley Hancock, xi., 578. Honorably discharged from gallies, xii., 315.

Garland, Silvester, and Indian, arrested for stealing silver cups, i., 376. Complained of, for selling rum to Indians, ii., 33, 45, 48.

Garrett, Capt. Morton, resigns, xi., 122.

Garrigues, Samuel, Notary Public, xv., 527.

Gaskill, Christina Gulielma, of London, by attorney Miers Fisher, claims city lots under Wm. Penn, xvi., 75, 108, 130, 144, 147. Negatived, 153.

Gatchill, Elisha, Justice of Chester county attacked at Nottingham by persons from Maryland, iv., 227, 242. Deposition of, 229, 252. Letter to Gov. Ogle on, 252.

Gateau, Nicholas, "the French cook" naturalized, ii., 131, 168. Petition, 170, 171, 180 182. Authorized to trade and buy and hold lands, iii., 235.

Gates, General Horatio, demands men, xi., 269.

Geddes, Captain, of privateer Holker, captures a vessel and crew

and liberates them, for which his bond is put in suit, xii., 49, 50.
Geddis, Wm., to make deposition respecting Arnold, xii., 225. Report unsatisfactory, 226.
Gee, Joshua, trustee of W. P., P. S. from, noticed, iii., 237.
Geiger, Col. Henry, xi., 89. Letter on Indians, xiii., 337.
Gennessee County Expedition, to pay to troops, xvi., 235.
Genoa, republic of, unites in treaty of peace, v., 360.
George, Fort, proceedings of Council at, v. 641.
George, a Seneca Indian, shot, ix., 603.
George I., King, dies—Prince proclaimed, iii., 280.
George II. proclaimed King, iii., 280. Addresses to, 291. Death of, viii., 514.
George III., King, ascends throne, viii., 515. Proclaimed, 516. Declaration proclaiming, 517.
Georges, John, Commissioner to Maryland — return — report, &c., iii., 545-563.
Georgia, loan asked for distressed inhabitants, xiii., 15.
Gerard, Sieur, French Minister, certificate respecting a cargo of flour, xi., 645. Offers a reward for capture of British vessels, 646. On subject of a supposed duel, 678. Letters to and from, xii., 66, 67. Approves of course of Council with Mr. Holker—papers, &c., to be sent to Congress, 71, 72. Letter and commission as Consul-General, 78. Address of Council to, on departure, 110.
German—battalion raised as part of State quota, xii., 14—Congregation ask for a brief, 90.
German—Luth'n Church, in Lancaster County—lottery for, ix., 390, 392, 567, 579—Philadelphia, mistake committed against them by land office in favor of Reformed, corrected, xvi., 149. Passengers, arrive in Philadelphia, 222. Property left to emigrants, 403. Reformed, surveys of lands, 422.
German, newspaper, petition for aid to — Council subscribe for five hundred, at Lancaster, xi., 409. Printed in Philadelphia by Melchior Steiner, ordered by Council, xv., 375.
German Reformed Church in York, lottery for, ix., 567, 579. Exchange of land warrants with, xvi., 297.
German regiment in Northumberland, xii., 461.
Germans apply to be naturalized, ii., 241, 480, 492, 493. Arrive in great numbers, required to take oath, iii., 29. Of Lancaster Co., ask to be naturalized, 374, 393. Proceed west of Susquehanna—discover error, and are willing to return, iv., 59. Difficulties with Maryland, 63-71. To be protected by Pennsylvania, 71, 189, 194. Diseased, 194. Apply for a pest house to be erected, 507, 509. Viewed with jealous eye, 508, 509. Number to be imported in a vessel, limited, v., 427. (See Palatines.) Allusion to by Assembly and Governor, vi., 621, 631. Act proposed to prevent importation of, in too great numbers, ix., 245, 246, 248. Riotous, at Wyoming, 663. Settle at the Glades on Stony creek, &c., in Bedford Co., x., 8. Battalion of, to be formed, 622. Captains appointed, 634. Officers recommended, 643, 685. Passengers—register of, xiv., 445. Lewis Farmer appointed, 447.
German — Township — road to, i., 387.
Germantown — Petition of F. D. Pastorius—want more room—exemption from County Court of Philadelphia, &c., ii., 10. Market-day, 28. Complaint about road from T. Leech's, 147. Sower's paper at, complained of, vii., 245. Records of, ancient, to be deposited with Recorder of Deeds, Philadelphia, ix., 578, 580. Salt sent to, x., 577. Iron, 575. Lt. Ball sent to, 578, 601. Storehouse to be engaged at, 596. Prisoners removed to York, 601, 622. Leaden weights to be collected by Dr. Charles Bensell, &c., 637. Salt from stores at, 660. Son of Joseph Blewer taken prisoner at battle of—pass for

his wife to New York, to visit him, xi., 571. Justices, 644. Inhabitants refuse to pay taxes, xii., 53. Proceedings of Council respecting, 54. C. & A. Stedman's estate at, 204. Sale of C. Sauer's estate in, 281. George Bay, type founder at, buys confiscated estate of C. Sauer, 326, 445. Case of John Dover, 402, 404, 407. Sale of Holton Jones' estate in, 639. Illegality of an election for Justice, xiv., 282, 363, 378, 382. Justice Howell resigned, 313, 315. John Nice, Justice, 315.

Gerrard, sloop, privateer, xi., 542.

Getshens, Captain, of privateer Impertinent, of New York, prays for exchange—declined, being a resident, xii., 147.

Gettig, Christopher, First Lieutenant, x., 752.

Gettigh, Christian, Justice, xii., 491.

Getting, Christopher, Coroner, xiii., 92.

Gibbons, Joseph, Coroner, ix., 547.

Gibbons, Joseph, Jr., Coroner, ix., 623, 688.

Gibbons, Lieut. Philip, xi., 470, 491.

Gibbons, Wm., xiii., 723. Sheriff, xiv., 238, 555.

Gibbons, Lieut., convicted of embezzling public money—Attorney-General to prosecute for damages, £6,000, xii., 139.

Gibbs, Edward, High Sheriff of New Castle Co., i., 331.

Gibbs, Richard, Sheriff, ix., 778; x., 56.

Gibbs, Mrs., imports firearms, &c., x., 399.

Gibbs, Sarah, authorized to sell property, i., 581.

Gibson, George, Lieut. of Cumberland Co., xv., 89. Pay to, xvi., 75.

Gibson, James, and M. Smith, &c., memorials respecting Indians on fron ier, ix., 138, 146.

Gibson, John, Auditor-General, xi., 202. Deed for city lots, for heirs of, xiii., 572. Coroner, xv., 125, 302.

Gibson, General John, Commiss'r on Erie triangle, xv., 554. Goods for Indians, 604, 618. Commissioner to purchase triangle at Lake Erie, from Indians, xvi., 36. Pay and expenses, 75, 95. Account, &c., xvi., 426.

Gibson, Captain Nathan, x., 686.

Gilbert, Francis, First Lieut., x., 404, 488.

Gilchrist, James, Ensign, xii., 36.

Gilfroy, John, tried for mutiny and desertion—convicted—pardoned, xi., 541.

Gill, John, Justice, xiv., 153; xv., 26.

Gill, Robert, Sheriff, iv., 748, 782.

Gillespie, George, refused a pass, xi., 478.

Gilliland, Wm., Justice, xiv., 247.

Gilpin, Thomas, to be seized, xi., 284. Sent to Virginia—dies, 472.

Girty, Simon, releases prisoners from Westmoreland jail, x., 227.

Glass, manufacture of, in Lancaster County, ix., 354.

Glass, Josiah, appointed Lieut. of Capt. Irwin's company, xii., 17.

Glatz, Captain Jacob, x., 734.

Glen, James, Gov. of S. Carolina, letters to and from, v., 303, 696, 699, 708; viii., 270. Sends bills to General Braddock, vi., 427.

Glazier, Cap. B., Braddock's defeat, vi., 480.

Glentworth, George, and R. Harris, petition, xiv., 617. Claims city lots, xv., 379. Warrants to issue in favor of, 382.

Gloninger, John, xiii., 732. Justice, xiv., 158. Lieut. of Dauphin County, 400.

Gloucester, chevaux-de-frise built at, x., 513.

Gnadenhutten, inhabitants flee to, from Mahoney, vi., 736. Address of Indians from Bethlehem, and answer, 747, 748. Destruction of, 772. Franklin's proceedings at, vii., 15.

Goad, Capt. Solomon, petitions to unload his vessel, &c., vii., 347. Referred to Peters & Mifflin, to report the facts, 349.

Goddard, William, printer of laws, ix., 395.

Godfrey, Lieutenant Rowley, of forty-eighth regiment of foot in

Grenada—a prisoner signs parole, x., 331.

Godfrey, Thomas, and T. Leach, case of a road, ii., 152.

Godin, Nicholas, an Indian trader, ii., 138, 141, 168. Lives among Indians—Gov. complains against, 385. Arrested—lawyers' opinions of, 390. Question as to his foreign allegiance, 385. Trial, 396.

Goforth, George, Coroner, v., 55.

Gold and Silver, value of, iv., 357, 363, 364. Bill for ascertaining fineness of, vii., 63, 72. Ware, Act to prevent frauds in, ix., 546, 650. Causes of scarcity, 652.

Golden, William, Sheriff, vii., 267.

Goldensher, William, Sheriff, vi., 638.

Goldney, Henry, named as agent for province in London, iii., 44. P. S. from, noticed, 237.

Gondolas, to be built, x., 599. Building, 627. To be sunk near Trenton—disposition of men—ammunition, &c., xi., 470, 471.

Gonne, Henry, Coroner, iii., 465, 521, 575, 615; iv., 470, 500.

Gooch, William, Governor of Virginia, administers oath to Governor Gordon and sends his certificate, iii., 530. Letter on Indian murders, 564. Answer to, 565. Correspondence with, iv., 203. Appointed to command of troops in North America, 431, 439. Letters, v., 55, 132. Letter to, on privateers, &c., 254. On man-of-war, 280. On privateers, 283, 301. Letter on Catawba Indians, 346, 347.

Good, Robert, sub-Lieutenant, xii., 395.

Good, Lieutenant, resigns, xii., 775.

Gooding, Abraham, Sheriff, iii., 387; iv., 470, 500.

Gooding, John, Sheriff of New Castle, iii., 260, 289, 416, 465, 615.

Goodson, John, appointed by Wm. Penn assistant to Governor Markham, i., 475. Declines, 498.

Goodson, Job, Frankford bridge referred to him, iii., 246.

Goodwin, Capt. George, xi., 30.

Goodwin, John, Second Lieutenant of artillery company in Philadelphia, vi., 770.

Gookin, Captain Charles, succeeds Evans as Governor—arrives, and is proclaimed at market place, ii., 427. His proclamation of continuance of laws and officers, 427–8. Takes the oath, 428. Visits New Castle to proclaim his commission, 428. Messages, 437, 461, 465. Visits New York, 449. Goes to Lewes, 468. Supply bill, 493. Invited to conference at Conestoga, 532. Account of his journey, &c., 533. Queen's order to attend at New York, 532. Hint respecting his pay, 541, 560. A great loser by coming here, 560. Superceded by Governor Keith, 631. Late Governor lays certain accusations before Governor Keith against individuals, iii.. 15. Which before Council he retracts, and attributes what he said to a disordered head from indisposition, 17.

Gordon, Adjutant, returned as belonging to Pennsylvania, xii., 235.

Gordon, Benj., Judge, Kent county, iii., 253.

Gordon, James, a British major, has goods seized at Lancaster, xiii., 453.

Gordon, Lewis, letter respecting New England settlers at Wyoming, ix., 572. Letters respecting Wyoming, 752, 756. To give up, to committee, ferry at Easton, xi., 72. Late Prothonotary to be imprisoned, 261.

Gordon, Major Patrick, Governor, arrives and produces commission from proprietaries—is introduced by Governor Keith, and published at Court House, iii., 251. Proclamation for continuing officers, 251. Speech to Assembly, 254. Receives letter from England on bills of credit—message to House, 262. Speech to Assembly on bills of credit—iron works, hemp, &c., receives £500, 280. Address to King George II., 292. Speech to Assembly, 292. From the eight withdrawing members of Assembly to, 300. Calls Assembly, 301. Visits Mahanatawny, 302. His report, 303. Proclamation respecting murder of Indians, 307.

Governor and Council visit Indians at Conestoga, 309–314. Speech to Assembly on rude treatment in Philadelphia, 341. Views on bills of credit, 347, 348–350. Proclamation on riots in Philadelphia, 351. On paper money, 352, 357, 360. Speech to Indians, 364. To Assemby, 373. On paper money, 377. Visits New York, 383. Speech, 390. Message on application of sugar islands, 401. Message to, and answer of Assembly, 406, 407. Proclamation on Indian trade, 411. Governor and Assembly, discussion about his message, &c., 427–8. Governor, Council, and a large escort go to Chester to wait on Thomas Penn, 433. Goes to Maryland relative to boundary, 464. Correspondence respecting riots, &c., and Maryland, 468, 470, 474, 481, 485, 487, 490, 495. Authority from Springett Penn—new commissions—Justices, 491. Speech to Assembly, 492. Doubts of his powers, 508. Seeks advice of Council, 508. Message to Assembly, 509. Commission from Thos. and Richard Penn, 525. Oath administered by Governor of Virginia, 527. Goes to Virginia to take it, 527. In a sloop, being largely escorted to it, 529. Returns, having received the oath from Governor Gooch, 529. Speech to Assembly, 531. On spirituous liquors, 534. On power of appointing officers, 537, 538. Message on, 539. On affairs with Maryland, 543. Commissioner on boundary, 544. Letter to Gov. Gooch of Virginia on Indian murders, 565. To Justices on Maryland affairs, 567. Speech to Assembly, 576. Death of Governor's lady, 571, 577. Letter, lords of trade giving an account of the products of the country, 584. Speech to Assembly on Lord Baltimore's claim to territories, 596. Speech to Indians, 605. Letter to Abraham Wendall, 609. Sick, 609. Assembly grant £400, 612. Speech to Assembly, 615. Sick—message, 616. Against wears and dams on rivers, iv., 18. Message to Assembly on wears, 23. On pounds, 26. Thanks Council for report on Courts of Chancery, 27. Obliged by ill-health to retire from active business of Council, 33. Message on Court of Chancery, 38. Receives £400—causes sentence to be executed on two men and reprieves one woman—attends Council, so far as the minutes show, for the last time—his death is announced by James Logan, who being oldest Councillor succeeds Governor Gooch as president, 47. Proclamation to be made and officers continued, 48. His death noticed by J. Logan in his speech to Assembly, and their answer, 50, 52. Indians notice his death, 54. Proceedings of Council in his time, vi., 723.

Gordon, Robert, Judge of Supreme Court, iii., 269. Register of Probate, 338.

Goshen Township, petition for road to Philadelphia, ii., 111, 189.

Gosner, Peter, second Lieutenant, x., 457.

Gotschuc, Capt., gives intelligence, xii., 19.

Gouger, Dunwick, and Kender, make fire arms, x., 484.

Governor—officers appointed by—not to continue for their lives, i., 69. But during his life, 69, 107. And afterwards to be chosen according to charter, 69. Expenses of his table to be paid, 99. Preservation of his person, 102, 107. Prisoner secreted in his house, 138. His absence accounted for and regretted, 199, 201. Instructions respecting caves to be pursued, 199. Commissions Lieutenant-Governor, 211. A member of Council to attend on, 231, 238. Authorizes Justices to hold courts, 231. Refuses great seal to commissions, but insists on the lesser, 232. Inquires about export of goods to other countries than England, 232, 238. Attendance of members of Council on, 239. Poverty plead in cause, 239. His powers, 244. Improper language to, 250. His remarks on it, 250.

Complains against Thos. Lloyd's election, 269. Samuel Richardson's, 270, 271. Speech, 286, 294. On proclaiming King William, 301.
Governor, of New York and Pennsylvania, Benjamin Fletcher's commissions, i., 345. Of Massachusetts—letter, 514.
Govett, Joseph, to build boats, &c., x., 283.
Govett, William, clerk of Committee of Safety, x., 282. To make deposition respecting Arnold's conduct while in command of city, xii., 225. Report unsatisfactory, 226; xiii., 721. Paid for services, xiv., 625.
Grace, Robert, compromise with, for a slave condemned to death, ii., 405.
Graeme, Dr. Thomas, member of council, iii., 247, 248. To visit sick vessels, 293. Third justice of Supreme Court, 400, Administers oath to commissioners, 544. Judge of Supreme Court, iv., 233. Sick, 244. Why don't he attend? 292, 295. Governor determines to call him, 295. Reports on sickly vessels, 306. Second justice, 348. Pay for his services asked for, 349. To attend on Henry Webb, sent from Minnisinks, wounded by an Indian, 413. Accounts, 469. Resolutions respecting, as health officer, 497–499. Report of Assembly respecting his appointment, 515. Controversy between Assembly and Council, 507–559. Visits vessels, 674. To visit a vessel arrived with passengers, v., 100. To visit ship from Barbadoes, 109, 112, 121. To visit vessel, 410. With Dr. Bond visits sickly ships, vi., 170. Their joint report, 171–173. Naval officer, 319.
Graeme, Mr. Thomas, collector at New Castle dies, is succeeded by William Till, v., 244.
Graeme, Park, sale to be deferred and Mrs. F. to live rent free, xii., 365.
Graff, George, Sheriff, xv., 297, 570; xvi., 192. Coroner, 193, 494, 499.
Graff, Rev. Mr., Indian hostilities, vi., 757.
Grafton, Richard, judge of Supreme Court, iii., 269.
Graham, Henry Hale, late prothonotary of Chester connty detains records, xi., 254.
Graham, William, collector of excise, xiv., 400.
Grant, Lieutenant Charles, commands at Fort Loudoun, ix., 268. Letter from Governor to, 273.
Grant, Captain George, xi., 273.
Grant, Captain John, xi., 423.
Grant, Thomas, sheriff, xiv., 558; xv., 118, 170.
Grantham, John vs. Thomas Woolaston, i., 236, 253, 258.
Granville, Fort, attack on, vii., 231, 232. Burned, 278. John Hogan, account of capture, 561. Street, ——, captured at, 716.
Gratz, ——, has blankets, x., 473.
Graves, Thomas, i., 435.
Gray, George, keeper of lower ferry complains of road to Cobb's creek, &c., v., 99. Member of Committee of Safety, to procure brushes and priming wires, x., 314. Committee on gaoler, 568. To sound channel. 761. Right of floating bridge on Schuylkill vested in, xii., 690. Objects to Darby road, 709. Arms from associators, 696. Batall., 696, 709.
Gray, John, Coroner, viii., 780; ix., 57, 286.
Gray, Thomas, Coroner, ix., 333.
Gray, William, to purchase provisions, xi., 423, 448.
Gray, William, a Captain, xi., 74.
Gray's ferry, to be guarded, xi., 302.
Graydon, Alexander, relates conversation of Israel Permberton, Jr., with him respecting Governor Thomas, iv,, 389. As Captain, x., 447. Prothonotary, xiv., 374. Register, Recorder, &c., 377. Expenses to Huntingdon, xvi., 169, Tavern and marriage licenses of Dauphin county, 176.
Great Britain, letters from Secretary Pitt, viii., 18, 26, 27, 272, 289, 315, 316, 449, 451, 590. Earl Loudoun succeeded by M. G. Abercromby, 26. B. G. Forbes appointed, 27. Bills of credit

ratified, 39. General Amherst appointed commander-in-chief in N. A., 236. Rear Admiral Saunders appointed commander-in-chief of Navy in N. A., 316. Death of Princess of Orange, 318. Report of Lords Committee of Council for plantation affairs on the case of Rev. Dr. William Smith, charged with libel, and other papers, 438–447. Money granted by parliament to Colonies, 400, 501, 546, 693. B. Franklin and R. Charles appointed agents to, 512. Death of King George II., succeeded by King George III., 515–520. Order of Council on report of Committee on Laws, 552, 558. Urges raising of troops, 588, 590, 677. Letters, Earl of Egremont, 678, 703. War with Spain declared, 703, 706–710. Letters from, ix., 13, 15, 47, 114, 298, 309, 310, 341, 342, 343, 545, 552, 629, 637, 706, 766. Peace between France and Spain, 13, 37. Grant by, to Colonies, 2, 4, 10, 47–51, 115, 125. Treaty of 1763 proclaimed, Canada obtained, 80. Relating to Stamp Act, 298, 309. Repeal of 309. Lord Colville, commissioner of the naval forces, 299. Address to King on repeal of Stamp Act, 315. Strength of a battalion of foot, 320. Instructions to Governor on settlers on western lands, 321. Order in Council, 341. Indian trade, 582. Approves of John Penn as Governor, 629. Scarcity of gold and silver owing to exports of them to, 652. Laws approved or annulled by, 760–766. Complains of Massachusetts circular, 545. Approval or annulling laws, x., 103. Letters from, 220, 221, 240, 248. Boundary with Maryland, 220, 240. Petitions from Colonies, 239, 248. Non-importation, 240. Resolutions of House of Commons, 250. Three ministerial officers arrive at Philadelphia from Cork, 302. Resolutions of Council respecting, and the power of Congress to make treaty with her, xiii., 286. Commission to Richard Oswald to treat, 459. Acknowledges independence, 545. Proclamation for peace with records from Congress, proclamation for, 749. A thanksgiving, 750. Proclamation on treaty with, xiv., 19–22. Complaints of British on infractions of treaty with, xv., 50. Phineas Bond consul, 215. Proclamation forbidding wheat from United States to be imported on account of Hessian fly, 524, 526.

Great Cove, destroyed by Indians, vi., 673–677. Murder at, vii., 599.

Great Crossings or Meadows, vi., 602, 623.

Great Meadows, Braddock at, vi., 466. Fort proposed by Governor Dinwiddie, 602.

Great Seal, viii., 335, 408.

Green, Rev. Ashbel, asks a respite for P. Waugh, xvi., 497, 519.

Green, Joseph, Commissioner to buy provisions, xi., 424.

Green, Pyramus, deposition relative to his capture by a privateer, v., 233.

Green, Thomas, Sheriff, iv., 748, 782.

Green, Colonel Timothy, battalion, x., 691.

Green, Timothy, Justice, xiv., 348, 394.

Green, William, a pilot, committed to prison, x., 405. Released on condition of entering continental service, 432.

Greene, Major-General N., representation respecting wagons, xi., 465, 467. Letter on want of money for forage, xii., 300. Account, 326. Letter, 428. Eulogium on, for his brave conduct in South Carolina, xiii., 107.

Greene, Ship General, to be fitted out, xi., 724. Captain Montgomery, 730. Valued, 739, 751. Pay for, 756, 758. Ordered to sea under Captain Montgomery, various officers appointed, xii., 4, 5. Return of seamen on board, 4. Takes a prize—Requires a mizzen-mast, 19. Takes a prize, 111. Cruise ended—She arrives and is to be sold, 150. Petition of officers, 158, 159. Sale of,

complained of, 159, 161. To be delivered, 175. Claim of H. W. Archer, 191.
Greene, William, Governor of Rhode Island, applies to export provisions—Declined, vii., 559. Asks release of a prisoner, x., 444.
Greenwalt's, Colonel, battalion to serve as guards at Lebanon, xi., 417.
Greeswahl, Joseph, traitor, xii., 83.
Greenwalt, Colonel Philip, xiii., 642.
Greenway, Joseph, ensign, x., 464. Master of provincial ship, 522. Resigns, 694.
Greenway, William, Captain of fire-raft, x., 525. Measurer of grain, &c., xi., 607. Measurer of salt—Price complained of, xiii., 593. Price fixed, 595.
Greer, Captain David, made Major, x., 768.
Greer, Joseph, deed to, xii., 350.
Gregg, Dr. Amos, Chief Burgess of Bristol, xv., 83. Councillor, 570. Committee on Indian fund, 607. xvi., 233.
Gregg, John, Sheriff, viii , 781; ix., 57, 199.
Gregg, Matthew, wagon-master, xi., 755. Resigns, xii., 453.
Gregory, James, Sub-Lieutenant, asks to resign—Not accepted, xii. 4. Accepted, 94.
Gressel, Colonel, at riot at James Wilson's, dismissed, xii., 145.
Grey, James, Coroner, v., 551.
Grey, John, of Donegal, messenger to Diahogo, vii., 549.
Grier, Major James, xiii., 592.
Griffin, John, Coroner, xi., 235.
Griffith, Daniel, Justice, xiv., 138.
Griffith, Gideon, Sheriff, iv., 55, 782.
Griffitts, Isaac, Sheriff, v., 464, 551. Removed, 561.
Griffitts, Thomas, member Council, iii., 529. Keeper of Seals, 530.
Griffitts, Thomas, 3d Justice, iv., 348. Resigns—William Till succeeds, 640.
Griffitts, William, case of, viii., 666, 667.
Grigg, Cap. John, resigns, xiii., 275.
Grist, John, a squatter on lands, in gaol, proceedings respecting, iii., 137, 138.
Griswald, Joseph, traitor, imprisoned, xii., 66.
Growden, Joseph, elected member of Council, i., 196. Called to account for having frame of government printed, 278. Proceedings, 293. Appointed Judge, 324, 331. Speaker of Assembly, 399. Address to Governor F., 400. His landing, 514. Member of new Council, 580. Speaker, 615. Appointed Speaker of Assembly, ii., 36, 204, 608. Speech to Governor and Council, 78. Claim against, 181. Judge, 239. Arrests J. Heaton, action of Trover, &c., 407.
Growden, Lawrence, appointed Justice, iv., 41. Commissioner to run the line between Maryland and Pennsylv'a, 313. Member of Council, v., 65. Complains against Sheriff at election—Not sustained, 345. Judge of Supreme Court, viii., 481, 592. Dies, ix., 663. His successor, 663. Estate forfeited in Bucks County—Claim of widow, xii., 77, 191. Paid, in lieu of annuity, 191.
Grono, Colonel G., election, xi., 39, 560, 773.
Gronow, Lewis — military officers elected in Chester county, xiii., 283.
Grubb, Adam, Flour Inspector of Chester county, xiv., 487.
Grubb, Adam, Justice, resigns, xvi., 218[4].
Grubb, Curtis, asks for divorce, ix., 564, 566, 567, 568, 580. To be prosecuted, xiii., 678.
Grubb, Colonel Peter, of Lancaster, dispute with De Haas, x., 346. Furnace for making salt pans, xi., 335. T. Edwards, manager, gone to the field—Hugh Lusk is employed, 350.
Grube, Rev. Bernard, Moravian missionary, pass to Pittsburg, &c., recommended to Colonel Brodhead, xii., 346.
Gruber, Edward, Justice, xv., 14.
Guard boats, x., 682.
Guards, pay of, x., 407, 599, 691, 709, 769.
Guest, John, member of Council, ii., 2. Takes the oath, 96.

Judge, complaining that no Equity Courts have been held, 114, 156. A Justice, 159. Respecting his salary as Chief Justice, 237.
Guildin, John, Justice, xii., 519.
Guion, Captain of Mermaid, respecting salt taken, xii., 143.
Gun barrels, art of boring and grinding—to be made public—by pay, to Tomlinson, x., 533, 602. Paid for, 648.
Gunckle, Michael, indulged in regard to barrack lots, xiv., 635.
Gun factory to be established at Hummelstown, for the present, xi., 314.
Gun locks, Committee to superintend manufacture, x., 506, 536, 636.
Gun lock manufactory, x., 606.
Gunpowder, petition of Philadelphia respecting, i., 478. Proposals for manufacture of, x., 482.
Guns, firing of, in Philadelphia to be stopped, as it frightens Indians and women and children, i., 586.
Gunsmiths, xii., 24.
Gunstockers, apply for higher wages, xi., 363, 364.
Gurney, Francis, member of Council of safety, x., 717, 726. To have pier finished, 718. To receive money for salt, 761; xi., 4, 33. Warden, xiii., 100. Commissioner for defence of Delaware, 316, 384. And George Westcoat, deeds for city lots, xiv., 453, 462, Arms belonging to his battalion to be delivered to John Nicholson, xv., 372.
Gurney, Captain Henry, not discharged, 23, 25.
Guthrie, James, Sheriff, xvi., 215, 521. Justice, xiii., 517.
Guthrie, John, Ensign, xii., 31.
Guyer, Casper, confined, xi., 565.

H.

Habeas Corpus, writ against Israel Pemberton, Jr., Governor, &c., objections to, iv., 392. Writ of, issues in favor of Israel Pemberton and others ordered to Virginia, xi., 308, 309.
Haberstick, Colonel Michael, guard, xi., 438.
Hack, Doctor, viii., 271.
Hadden, Samuel, fraud of a master of a vessel, i., 565.
Haffa, Henry, Sheriff, xi., 598; xii., 132, 508.
Hageman, Ulrich, liberty to trade and hold lands, iii., 248.
Hagner, Frederick, agent, xi., 667.
Hagner, Colonel, to superintend sale of salt works in New Jersey, xii., 160.
Haige, William, member of first Council, i., 57.
Haig, Captain of militia—a German murdered, v., 347.
Haines, Reuben, to furnish beer, x., 646. Warden, xi., 559. Petition to postpone sale of lands, xiii., 293.
Halderman, Colonel, asks for a hospital for the sick, viii., 63. Respecting ship King of Prussia, 64. And Sir J. St. Clair, complain of barracks, 71.
Haldiman, General, x., 140.
Haldyman, Colonel, at Carlisle, vii., 737.
Hale, John, to be imprisoned, x., 661, 694.
Hale, Thomas, agent for forfeited estates, and vendues, xi., 767; xii., 189; xiii., 584. Purchases a house and lot, late Arthur Thomas', xii., 104. Suspicions against, as agent, 256. Suspected of using money, 258. Dismissed as agent, 261. Dismissed, 261. To deliver up papers, 263. Letter from, on Indian lands, 265. Process against, for balance due, 268. Brought before Council, 324.
Haley, John, appointed Clerk of Orphans' Court of Philadelphia, xi., 240. J. Humphreys refuses to deliver papers, &c., 306.
Half-King, of the Six Nations, of very great note and esteem among them, v., 660. Speech of, 691.
Halifax, Fort, its disadvantages, vii., 724.
Halifax, Lord Dunk, his opinion on paper money, v., 605. Letters to and from, vi., 306, 333. By General Braddock, notice of his appointment as Commander-in-

Chief, 306. And other Lords of trade, on state of affairs in province, vii., 272, 278, 387, 738.
Halifax, Earl of, Secretary, letters to and from, ix., 113. Indian affairs, and Assembly, 113.
Halket, Major, attends Council in Philadelphia with several Indians and General Forbes, viii., 124.
Halkett, Sir Peter, sent with troops from England, vi., 200, 311. Killed in Braddock's engagement, 498.
Hall, Charles, agent forfeited estates, xi., 599.
Hall, David, Speaker of Assembly, at New Castle, x., 5. Justice, 108. Printer—case of William Moore and Dr. Smith, 468.
Hall, John, Sheriff of Bucks and Kent, iii., 31, 56, 108, 387, 416, 465, 520.
Hall, Peter, Sheriff, iv., 500, 602.
Hall & Sellers, newspaper, xi., 654; xv., 366. Papers ordered by Council, xii., 197.
Haller, Henry, Coroner, ix., 398; xii., 47, 250. Respecting Reading, 780.
Halliday, Wm., Sub-lieutenant, xi., 379.
Halliwell, Richard, a Commissioner under dedimus to administer oaths, ii., 62, 92.
Hambright, John, Lieutenant of marines, xi., 747. Member of Council, xii., 83, 286, 391. Account, 510.
Hamburg, Senate of, letter on ship Elve, Cath, xiii., 703.
Hamersley, Robert, Justice, xiv., 500.
Hamilton, ——, apprehended, xv., 300.
Hamilton, Colin, arrested—released, x., 468.
Hamilton, Dr., letter from John Franklin, xv., 575.
Hamilton, Alexander, Secretary of Treasury, xvi., 244.
Hamilton, Andrew, Governor of New Jersey, and Post Master General, memorial of, i., 469. For a road to Dunk's ferry, 498. Salary, 570. Asks for support of the post, 524. Petition respecting claim for salary, ii., 33. Suggested by Wm. Penn to Assembly, as his representative while absent, 48. Dedimus potestatem to six persons, to administer oath to, as Governor, 62, 92. Takes oath at hands of Council, 69. Communication from, 79. Dismisses them, 84. Dies, 87. His appointment approved by the Queen, 89, 98. Lord Cornbury to be addressed in consequence of death of, 91. Dedimus to Commis'rs to administer oaths—difficulty with Colonel Quarry, 92. Power of Legislation affected by his death, 114. Commission as Chief Justice arrives after his death, 239. Appointed by Penn Lt. Governor—dies vi., 720.
Hamilton, Andrew, prays confirmation of road to Wiccacoa, iii., 111. Attorney-General and member of Council, 113. Resigns as Attorney-General, 237. Appointed Prothonotary of Court of Common Pleas, 271. Recorder, 293. Visits Indians with Govr.—his remarks on Tulpehocken land, 326 Speaker, 371, 387, 417, 466, 576, 615. Commissioner on boundary line, 544. Return—report, &c,, 545-563; iv., 53, 95, 99, 249, 311. Signs petition to the King, 125. Appointed Judge of Vice Admiralty Court, 250. Why don't he attend? 293, 295. Agent for his Majesty—deceased, v., 106.
Hamilton & Georges, reference to their proceedings in 1734, iv., 137, 161, 168.
Hamilton, Hance, Sheriff, v., 411, 468, 550. Marches from Carlisle to Shippensburg, vi., 675. Letter, vii., 77, 230.
Hamilton, Henry, robbed and murdered near Philad., ix., 76.
Hamilton, James, Member of Council, v., 1. Arrives as Gov'r, and successor to Pres. Palmer, bearing a letter of thanks from proprietaries, 362. His commission read and proclaimed at court-house, 363. His proclamation to continue officers, 363. Appoints Richard Peters Secretary, 364. Messages and speeches to Assem-

bly, 365, 374, 395, 430, 454, 484, 491, 494, 502, 505, 524, 528, 578, 605, 608, 638, 639, 648, 652, 719, 729, 735, 747, 751, 759. Messages and speeches from Assembly to Governor, 367, 373, 414, 429, 484, 491, 494, 506, 510, 526, 545, 561, 606, 613, 648, 722. On bills of credit, 374. Presents to, 368, 376. Issues proclamation on treaty of peace between England and France, 380. Letters to Gov. Ogle on Maryland affairs, 383, 384. Message on Indian affairs, 395. To Duke of Bedford on paper currency, 416. Correspondence with Governor of Maryland, 421, 423. And Virginia, 423, 424. Letter from Captain Celeron, 425. Message to Twightwees, &c., 449, 450. Writes to Justices of Cumberland, 450. Letter from them, 452. Proclamation respecting iron, 459. From and to Governor Clinton, 463, 465, 480, 495, 575, 625, 639, 641. Controversy with Assembly on legality of meeting, 491–494. Letter from George Croghan to, on Indian affairs, 497. Message on lighting and watering, and raising money on city, 505, 506. Speeches to Indians, 533, 534. Geo. Croghan to, 539. From Mons. Joncaire, 541. Letter to and from Shawnese, 568–571. On fee bills, 576. Correspondence and deposition respecting murder of D. Digges, in Maryland, 582–596. Pardon for Hamilton Carson, 601. Warrant for execution of Danl. Horsley, 602. James Kelly and James Rice—and reprieve of Kelly to be a witness, 604. On paper money, 605. On French and Indians building forts at Ohio, 609. Present to, from Assembly, 618. Letters to and from Gov. Dinwiddie on Indian affairs, 628–634. Forts on Ohio, 629. Asks Govr. Dinwiddie of Virginia, for a copy of the descriptive deed (for Indian lands), executed at Lancaster, 634. Bills, credit and Indian affairs, 639, 648, 652. Letter from Wm. Fairfax, asking his presence at Carlisle, to meet Indians, 657. Appoints commis'rs to meet them, with presents, 658. Their commission, 658. Letter to British Consul at Teneriffe, in favor of Captain Nerie, 661. Answer to Indian speeches, 693. Letters to Gov. Glen, 696. To Dinwiddie, 696, 698. Sends Shawnese home with John Ketten, 704. Instructions to, 707. Letter to Gov. Glen of South Carolina, 708. To Lord Holdenesse, 709. Sickness, 711. Bills, credit, 729, 747. Reply to Assembly's violent address, 737–746. Boundary with Virginia, 759–767. To Gov'r of Connecticut, letters, &c., relative to dispute, 769–777. Letters to and from Governor Dinwiddie, vi., 1, 3, 27, 137. To and from Gov. De Lancey, 9, 13. Gov'r Shirley, 16. Messages to Assembly, 22, 23, 26, 31, 37, 41, 44, 133, 139. Messages from Assembly, 25, 45, 139. Sends C. Weiser to Shamokin, 24. Message to Indians, 25. Letters to and from G. Washington, 28. Speech of Half-King, 31. Gov. has half of legislative power, 41. Views on bills of credit bill, 41–44. Defeat of Virginia forces, also by French — protection of counties — treaty at Albany — death of Justices, &c., 133–136. He resigns—proprietaries accept his resignation, and appoint Robert Hunter Morris in his place, 143. Last appearance in Council, 143. To and from Geo. Croghan, 145, 160. Instructions to Conrad Weiser, 147. Letter to D. Clause, 182. Letters, Indian affairs in Northampton Co., 764. Report at Carlisle, 783. Appointed by Council on Committee to investigate proprietary purchases from Indians, vii., 354. Appointed by proprietary, Governor, to succeed Wm. Denny, viii., 409. Arrives — his commission, 409. His Majesty's certificate of approbation, 412. Proclamation to continue officers, 413. Goes to New Castle, 414. Conference with Teedyuscung, 415, 423. Speeches to Assembly, 422. Messages to

Assembly, 423, 426, 437, 446, 448, 449, 478, 480, 481, 495, 509, 512, 559, 563, 577, 578, 579, 581, 593, 603, 605, 666, 676, 681, 688, 690, 693, 695, 710. Messages from Assembly, 424, 425, 447, 510, 560, 572, 580, 692, 715. On Indian affairs, 426. Disbanding forces, 447. Letters to and from, 448, 449, 451, 452, 495, 568, 570, 578, 588, 590, 592, 600, 622, 626, 628, 678, 686, 687, 690, 776. Case of Dr. Wm. Smith, 446. Military affairs, 452. Proclamation respecting murder of Dr. John, at Carlisle, 456, 709, 712. Supply bill, 478. Passes supply bill by advice of Council, 480. Speech to Indians in conference, 490. Supply bill, 481, 494, 500, 603, 693, 695. Says Council is not a part of the Assembly, 503. Troops for Fort Pitt, 509. Objects to granting certificate to agents to England, 512. Instructions respecting Liturgy, 520. Letter of condolence to Assembly, on death of King George II., 521. Proclamation respecting laws disallowed, 559. King's death, 560. Bills of credit, taxes, &c., 562. Too unwell to attend Council, 563. Sends message and other papers, relating to settlers from Connecticut, in Northampton Co., 564, 572, 622, 626, 629. General demands three hundred men, 577, 581, 593, 602. Agents in England, 579. Assembly grants £1,000, 583. Proclamation offering bounty to soldiers, 587. Supply bill, 603. Asks for information on drafts on Treasurer, 605. On course of Assembly respecting bills of credit, &c., 606. To Gen. Amherst on Connecticut settlers, 622. From Gov. Fitch on Connecticut settlers, 626. Goes to Easton to meet Indians, 630. Proclamation against settlers on Indian lands, 662. Attorney-General's fees, 666. Proclamation against wounding women in streets of Philadelphia, 672. Treaty with Delawares, 676. From Earl of Egremont, for troops, 678, 685. Withholds consent for adjournment of Assembly, 684. They adjourn without it, 685. Letter to Beaver and Shingas, 690. Proclamation of war with Spain, 706, 710. Conferences with Indians at Philada., 707, 709, 712. Orders embargo, 713. Arrests Boyrie and Le Roy, 714. Report of Committee of Assembly on his messages, twenty-third and twenty-fifth, 716–719. Reply to Assembly, declining exhibition of minutes, 720. Conference with Western Indians at Lancaster, 720–774. Minutes of treaty sent to Assembly, 775. To Col. Burd and Mr. Davenport, Comm'rs to receive Indian prisoners, 776. Letter to King Beaver, 778. To Governors Sharpe and Fauquiere, 779. Message to Assembly, ix., 2, 10, 16, 18, 19, 21, 25, 31, 36, 42, 52, 53, 55, 58. Message from Assembly, 20. Letters to and from, 13, 15, 34, 38, 40, 43, 62, 74, 75. Receives £250, 5. Conference and speech to Teedyuscung, 7. Proclamation of peace between France and Spain, 14, 39. Courts, 18. Bills credit, &c., 19. Tavern licenses, 25. May enlist soldiers on frontiers, 36. Asks for his pay—Allowance, £500, 37. Engages 700 men, 42. Conferences with Indians, 44, 67. Bills of credit, 52. Indian murders, 58. Instructions from King, 60. To Colonel Burd, 61. Proclamation against highway robbery near Philadelphia, 70. John Penn arrives as Governor—Assembly of New Castle wait on Governor Hamilton, and take leave of him, 71. President of Council, 603. Succeeds John Penn on his going to England at death of Richard Penn, 733. Proclamation, 733. Holds conference with Indians, 737. Answers chief's letter, 739. Goes to New Castle—His proclamation, 743. Do. respecting laws, 766. Message on Wyoming, 772. Governor Richard Penn arrives, 780. Bounds to be named in parole, xi., 269. Pass and protection granted, 301. Parole delivered up, and he fully

discharged, 438. Asks for a pass for himself and retinue, 478. Register and Recorder of Westmoreland, xiv., 655. Justice, xv., 44.
Hamilton, Captain John, command boat "Congress," x., 296, 329, 335. Resigns, 665.
Hamilton, John, Commissioner, x., 702.
Hamilton, Lieut. Robert, charged with murder of Lieut. Tracy, x., 6. Special Court appointed for trial of, in Bedford county, 8. Ensign, xii., 3.
Hamilton, Thomas, Sheriff, vii., 267. Coroner, xv., 570.
Hamilton, William, Coroner, iv., 782. Traitor, to be arrested, xii., 495. To depart State, 499, 502. Asks further time, refused, 502; granted, and permitted to go to St. Eustatia, 503. May go to country-seat, 520. May retire to another State, 549. Petition for son, 632. May remain in the State, 681. Pass to New York, xiii., 559. Bonds cancelled, 698. Claim for ground rent at Lancaster, xv., 614, 618, 641. Paid, 645.
Hammon, Benjamin, murder of, and proclamation for arrest of murderers, xi., 446.
Hammond, James, Sheriff, xiv., 567; xv., 121.
Hampton Court, (E.,) proceedings respecting Articles of Agreement between Penn and Baltimore, iv., 254. Proceedings, 298–301.
"Hancock," gunboat, x., 351, 362, 488, 506.
"Hancock," privateer brig, x., 605.
"Hancock," galley, officers, xi., 576, 578, 706.
"Hancock," galley, xii., 23, 477.
Hancock, John, President of Congress, sends letter of General Washington, xi., 197. Elected President, xiv., 587.
Hand, Colonel, xi., 108, 342.
Hand, Daniel, special commission for, armed the "George" to capture vessels, xii., 364.
Hand, General Edward, letters to and from, asking for troops against Indians, xi., 261. Letters to and from, xii., 138, 284, 427. Brigadier-General, letter, xiv., 23. And report, 25, 159, 162, 180. Pay to, 200.
Hand, Fort, xi., 556.
Hand, Matthew, raises a company, x., 708.
Hanna, Colonel, battalion, xvi., 122.
Hanna, James, Register and Recorder, xv., 407, 441.
Hanna, Robert, at Westmoreland, to deliver ammunition, x., 597.
Hanna's Town, (Westmoreland,) xi., 477. For Courts, xiii., 699. Building fort at, 1776, xvi., 541.
Hannum, Colonel John, xi., 83, 507.
Hannum, Colonel John, escapes from enemy, xii., 114, 477. Resigns as Justice, xiii., 105; and as Agent, 106; Auditor, 264.
Hanover, Elector of, proclaimed George, King of England, ii., 575.
Hans, Captain of fire raft, x., 543.
Hanson, John, President, Congress, xiii., 105.
Hanson, Thomas, a justice, ix., 645. Quarter-Master, x., 479. Resigns, 499.
Hanssegar, Nicholas, recommended as Major, and appointed, x., 446.
Harbeson, Captain Benjamin, xi., 32.
Harbeson, Benjamin, to buy brass, x., 612.
Hardenbaugh, Abraham, New York Commissioner to run boundary line, xv., 340.
Hardie, Captain Robert, of fire rafts, x., 560.
Hardie, Captain Robert, receives arms for gun boats, x., 601. Not an officer, xi., 118. Prisoner with British, xiv., 637.
Harding, Rev. Robert, report on number of Roman Catholics, vii., 448. Claim for city lot, xvi., 522, 531.
Hardy, Sir Charles, Governor of New York, to and from, vii., 9, 10, 35, 101, 113, 122, 123, 142, 223, 307, 339, 494, 496, 581. On embargo, 197. On Teedyuscung, 223. Agent of newspapers, 307, 339, 447. Sails from N. Y., 560.
Hawley, Rev. Gideon, letters to and from, vii., 11.

Hardy, or Harding, George, case of, xi., 753, 754, 760–761, 764. Reprieved, xii., 149. Estate sold, 196, 458.
Hardy, Hon. Samuel, letter and act of Legislature of Connecticut, xiv., 162.
Hare, Captain, refuses continental money, x., 780.
Hare, Jacob, a tory, xii., 340.
Hare, Robert, paid for porter, xi., 137.
Hargiss, Abraham, Lieutenant, x., 708.
Harlin, Ezekiel, Indian interpreter, iii., 246.
Harman, Ephraim, has a patent from Lord Baltimore, i., 109.
Harmar, Fort, xv., 605.
Harmar, Captain Josiah, pay for muskets, x., 406, 418, 485. depreciation pay to, xii., 703. Case of, xiii., 671. Letter from, xiv., 185. For recruiting expenses, 216. Person to take charge of Fort McIntosh, 372. Returns, 473, 480, 517, 549, 559, 662. Register, xv., 6, 13, 340. Proposes a new arrangement of United States troops at Muskingum, 379, 393, 437. Surgeon, &c., elected, 498; xvi., 41. Letters and drafts on Treasury, 258, 263.
Harper, Dr. Andrew, applies for a pass to Scotland, rejected, xii., 302.
Harper, John, Quarter-Master, x., 480.
Harper, John, Coroner, xiii., 723; xiv., 238; xv., 99.
Harper, William, complains against Anthony Morris, Mayor, respecting an execution, ii., 151.
Harris, Captain David, prothonotary, xi., 301, 305. Prothonotary of Northumberland, letter, xii., 75.
Harris, James, commissioner on boundary lines of Huntingdon county, xvi., 46.
Harris (John?) builds a house on Choniata, (Juniata,) iii., 503. Road from the ferry on Susquehanna to Lancaster, 618. Road to Philadelphia, iv., 181, 279, 282, 284. Bring reports of French and Indians, at Logstown, v., 614. Letters to and from, vi., 184, 457, 645. Death of Monacatootha, 184. Goes with Indians to Will's creek, 226. Informs of murders at Will's creek, 458. Recommends block houses, 458. Murders at Penn's creek, 645, 646, 654, 655. Indian conference at, 780. Report of C. Weiser and Indians at his ferry, vii., 33. Plan to kill Indians at, 35. Fort Near, 245. Treaty at, 506–517.
Harris, Major John, xi., 86.
Harris, John, Captain, x., 752.
Harris' ferry, xi., 84. Resigns, 778. Transportation of ammunition to, xiii., 263. Military stores to be moved from, 698. Too inconvenient for a court house, xv., 14,
Harris, Dr. Robert, building a powder mill, x., 492. Saltpetre, 599, 644, 700. Respecting salt, xii., 144. Carries off clandestinely, 153.
Harris, Samuel, x., 270.
Harris, Thomas, case of, i., 327, 329.
Harrison, James, member of first Council, i., 57. Appointed Judge, 153, 156. A special commissioner to try a case, 164.
Harrison, Francis, a councillor, i.
Harrison, Governor, of Virginia, letter and act of Assembly, xiii., 637, 753. Resolution of House of Delegates, xiv., 38. Entries in land office, 200.
Harrison, Major James, attends conference between Governor Hart of Maryland and Governor Keith, iii., 60.
Harrison, Captain John, to command boat "Dickinson," xi., 393.
Harry, (an Indian and interpreter,) ii., 71. His brother arrives in Philadelphia, 155. Returns from Onondago, 204. At Philadelphia, 537.
Hart, James, house robbed by French and Spaniards, v., 89.
Hart, John, Sheriff, iv., 247, 309, 352, 500, 669, 748, 782. Coroner, 601; v., 345, 411. Sheriff of Bucks, certificate of furnaces and forges, ix., 635; x., 697. Survey of river from Salem downwards,

xi., 358. To receive subscriptions to loan office, xii., 47. Collector of excise, 554. To provide for recruits at Newtown, xiii., 8. Gratuities for soldiers, 22, 182. Treasurer of Bucks county robbed, 95.
Hart, Joseph, sheriff, v., 464, 550. xi., 122. Register, 187. Order for money, 213. Elected Councillor, 249. Pay, 359. Powder in hands of A. Wallace, 508. Delivers up key of Loan office chest to Assembly, xi., 395. Goes to Newtown, 399. Reports on Dr. Birkenhouts papers, 569. To examine gaol, 684; xii., 8, 11, 15, 93, 404, 721. Complaint against, 737, 762; xiii., 76, 82. Have ammunition, 94. Memorial on pay of troops, 523. Censor, 719. Accounts, xiv., 265. An intestate estate, 307; xvi., 490.
Hart, Myer, complains against sheriff of Northumberland xii., 75.
Hart, Colonel, Governor of Maryland, iii., 37. Meeting and conference with, and Governor Keith.
Hart, William, coroner, xi., 596.
Hartley, Colonel Thomas, recommended to Congress as Lieutenant Colonel, x., 444. Pay for firelocks, 487; xi., 34, 397, 452, 488. Petition, 530. Register, 531, 626, 628. Vote of thanks to, for gallant conduct, 640. His plan of defence adopted, 646. His plan for defence of frontiers adopted, and Colonel Hunter to supply at Potter's, 646. Claim on York township, xiii., 44. Censor, 723.
Hartshorne, Wm. of N. J. suspected, but sent to N. J., xi., 117.
Hartzell, John, Coroner, x., 211, 270.
Hartzell, John, Sheriff, xii., 134.
Hartzell, Jonas, Sheriff, xi., 597; xii., 506. Commissioner on jurisdiction of Islands in Delaware, xiv., 345. Councillor, xvi., 192. Applies for warrant, 237, 242. Sheriff, 491.
Harvey, Abm., complaints against, xii., 307.
Harvey, Joseph, of Bermuda, sells vessel and cargo, and becomes citizen, xii., 36.
Harwood, Susannah, case of, i., 578,
Hartman, Henry, murdered by Indians, vi., 668.
Hartman, Captain, x., 689.
Hartman, Thomas, xiv., 228, 559. Justice, petition for removal, xvi., 10.
Haslett, Colonel, of Delaware Regiment, xi., 125.
Hassel, Samuel, member Council, iii., 333.
Hassert, Asent, liberty to trade and hold lands, iii., 248.
Hastings, George, Captain, ship stranded at N. J., x., 391.
Hetaguantagechty, Indian chief, iii., 436, 511, 577, 608.
Hats, patent granted for weaving and working straw, &c., for, iii., 18.
Hatton, John, and J. Jr., arrest of, x., 665, 670, 694, 699.
Houghton, Geo., complaint against, xii., 287.
Haussign, Nicholas, Major to Colonel Wayne's battalion, x., 460.
Havanna, Spanish preparations at, iv., 167. Letter from Lieutenant Governor Penalosa, capture and ransom of English frigate, &c., v., 75. Negroes taken by Philadelphia privateers, sent to Havana on trial for their freedom, 79. Provisions allowed, xii., 398. Memorial of merchants of Philadel'a respecting flour shipped to, xv., 633. Conduct of officers at, xvi., 144.
Haverford, meeting-house, ii., 111.
Haverstick, Ensign, xi., 32.
Haverstick, Colonel Battalion, xv., 113.
Hawer, Jacob, Sheriff, xv., 565.
Hawker, Capt. James, stationed in Delaware river—stamp papers sent on board his ship, ix., 300.
Hawking and Peddling, a license granted for, xvi., 111.
Hay Creek, near Philadelphia, iii., 111.
Hay, John. Sheriff, viii., 781; ix., 57. Letter, 103.
Hay, William, complaint against, by Governor Ogle, v., 382. Collector of Excise, Lancaster, xiv., 106.

Hayes, Hon. Christopher, Sub-Lieutenant, xi., 445; xiii., 150, 584.
Hayes, Ensign, vii., 631.
Hayes, John, sent to Indians at Ohio, viii., 491. Sub-Lieutenant, xii., 384.
Hayes, Henry, Sheriff, x., 56, 100.
Hayes, Samuel, sub-Lieutenant, xi., 442.
Hayward, Henry, complaint, i., 578.
Hazard, Ebenezer, applies for use of documents, xiii., 122. And order in favor of, 354. Applied to, for papers respecting Connec'cut, 420.
Hazelwood, Capt. John, to command ten fire rafts, x., 437. And superintendent of all, 437. To value a brig, 536, 550. Survey river, 567, 603. To fit out guard boat, 592. Of fire rafts, &c., xi., 611. Combustibles, 661, 699. Commissioner of purchases in Philadelphia, xi., 155. Supplies J. Hopkins with a vessel for expedition down river, 237. Compliment to, 277. May seize provisions for fleet, 361. Rations, 471, 529. To offer pardon to all deserters who return, 541. To furnish men, 557. To receive prisoners, 566. And conduct to Chester—account of fleet, &c. to be made out, 577. Orders to stop vessel with flag, 595. Allowed to sail for West Indies, 643. Petition for a cannon, xii., 57. Appointed Commissioner of purchases, 397, 406, 423, 450, 456, 473, 474, 613. Commissioner to supply forts, xiii., 17, 44. Claim for expenditures in 1778, &c., xv., 455. Pay for services in navy and as Commissioner on purchases, xvi., 224.
Hazen, Colonel, regiment letter from officers, xii., 215. General Washington's opinion, 262. Regiment, 278. To guard prisoners, xiii., 165.
Hazlehurst, Isaac & Co., memorial respecting entry of brandy, xv., 366, 367.
Hazlet, Wm., Justice, xiii., 140.
Hazleton, Hamilton, x., 727.
Heads, lecture on, proposed and refused, xiii., 324.
Health Officer appointed, iii., 112, 293; iv., 496, 515, 674. Report of Assembly on, 515–523. Report in Council on, 524–540. Amendment to bill, vi., 345–352. P. De Haven appointed in Philadelphia, xi., 775. To examine vessels from Charleston, and stop them at Mud Island, xii., 457. H. Dougherty respecting vessel from South Carolina, 483. John Jones, 554. To attend to his duties, xiii., 578. Covers for sick, 695; xiv., 377, 467; xv., 317. Complaint against John Jones, xvi., 134, 142, 147, 151, 168, 170, 172. Displaced, 175. Extortion in fees, 402.
Heap, Geo., Coroner, v., 411, 464.
Heaton, James, petition against J. Growden, for arrest on action of trover, ii., 407, 508.
Hebrew Congregation of Philadelphia ask loan of lottery-wheels, xvi., 488.
Hector, man-of-war, captures a schooner, v., 323.
Heeston, Lieutenant-Colonel Edward, xii., 70.
Heidelberg, guard at, xi., 36.
Heinecken, Jan. Hendrick Christian, acknowledged as consul from United Netherlands, xiv., 451.
Heister, (See Hiester.)
"Hell-Cat," armed whale-boat, xii., 393.
Helm, John, Regulator of Weights and Measures, xiii., 633; xv., 322.
Hellstedt, Charles, Swedish Consul, letter from, xiv., 276. Complains of rude behaviour of constables, &c., xv., 348. On neutrality of Sweden, 433.
Hembel, William, proceedings in England respecting act to enable him, as a naturalized subject, to hold real estate, x., 103.
Hemp, raising, to be encouraged, iii., 166, 375. Governor's speech on, 264, 270, 392.
Hemplin, Captain Thomas, raises men in Northumberland, xii., 46.
Henderson, Lieutenant, appointed Captain, xii., 88.
Henderson, Ensign Andrew, declines, xiv., 237. Deputy Surveyor, xv., 407.
Henderson, Captain Alexander, com-

mander of gunboat Bull-Dog, x., 353.
Henderson, Rev. Jacob, letter to, from Henry Munday on Maryland affairs, iv., 103.
Henderson, Captain William, xi., 2.
Hendricks, Abraham, Justice, xiv., 256.
Hendricks, James, deposition respecting Indians, iv., 655. Lieutenant, xii., 9.
Hendricks, John, goes over to side of Maryland, iv., 150. House to be defended, 194.
Hendrick, (Peters,) Mohawk chief, v., 625; vi., 76, 97, 113, 117, 118, 124, 249, 251, 286–290. Influence with Indians respecting purchase of lands, 117, 118. Clause lives with him, 182. Arrives in Philadelphia, 243. Council in doubt what to say to him, 247, 249. Letter from Governor M., 252. In Philadelphia, 277. Speech about New York, 281.
Henricks, Tobias, Justice, iii., 358. Coroner, v., 551, 597.
Hendrickson, Yeshro, and Margaret Mattson tried for witches, i., 93, 95.
Henlopen, Cape, a watch to be stationed at, i., 479. Light-house, xiii., 100. Repairs paid for, 100, 293. Beacons, &c., ceded by Council to United States, xvi., 358.
Hennessey, Lieutenant John, floating-battery, x., 520, 530.
Henry, Captain, to survey river, x., 567.
Henry, George, to sell vessels, x., 641, 643. And tools, &c., 644, 649, 662, 669, 670, 718. Have guns valued, xii., 36.
Henry, John, magistrate, of Lancaster, dead, xi., 211.
Henry, John, applies to deliver a lecture on heads, refused, xiii., 324.
Henry, Patrick, Governor of Virginia, on road from Fort Cumberland, xiv., 467.
Henry, William, of Lancaster, a magistrate, x., 237, 252. To make rifles, x., 523. Receives powder at Lancaster, xi., 53. Justice, 252. Papers on land, estate of John Ruby, xiii., 19. Pay to, 90, 166, 195. Paid gratuities, 244. British goods seized, 329, 453. Justice and President of Court Common Pleas and General Quarter Sessions, xiv., 181. Delegate to Congress, 261, 442. Entitled to half proceeds of goods seized, 309. Deceased—His widow receives payment of several sums, xv., 546.
Henry, William M., Justice, xi., 379.
Henry, William, (member of Council,) to conduct John Brown to Lancaster, xi., 345. To employ men to make arms—Not to be enlisted, 380. Money, 569. Furnish arms, 631. Commissary of Naval Stores, xii., 56, 57, 148. Appointed Lieutenant of Philadelphia, 297, 487, 656. (City,) pay for guards, xiii., 336. To call out troops, 380. Countermanded, 380. Asks opinion as to his duty, 551. Guard for City and Liberties, xiv., 10. Militia fines and expenses, 77. Petition for share of sale of goods, 291. Pay for militia, 446. Expenses of militia, xv., 5, 76. Pay to, 95, 199, 265. Case of an election of officers referred to, 237. Justice in Northampton County, 367. To report on arms delivered, 373. To order election for captain, and to return arms, 381, 438, 489. To receive cartridges, 447. Paid for exercising militia, xvi., 68, 168. Resigns, 446.
Henry, Colonel William, to furnish account of state of city militia, xi., 218. Lieutenant of city, 218, 225, 228, 234, 242, 275. To send off militia, 275, 277, 318.
Herbert, Morgan, &c., convicted of murder of Indians, iii., 327. Applies for mercy, is referred to Justices, 327.
Herbert, Captain Thomas, x., 539.
Hersent, Samuel, appointed a subtreasurer for Philadelphia county, i., 111. To prosecute offenders, 167. High sheriff of Philadelphia, 170. Cannot act as attorney, 170. Petition, 199, 319.

Heslip, Thomas, commissioner for purchase of provisions in Chester county, xi., 424.

Hessians, embark at Staten Island for Pennsylvania, x., 753. Flags taken at Trenton, xi., 70. To be employed at Lancaster in making shoes, 85. Guard for, 94. Prisoners, 102, 116, 129. To be employed, 186. To Baltimore, 104, 129. Flags delivered to Board of war, xii., 245. Deserters, 433. Flags taken at Trenton, given to Pennsylvania, xiii., 559.

Hessian fly, supposed cause of prohibition against admission of wheat into England, correspondence with Agricultural Society respecting it, xv., 524, 526.

Hetherling, Captain Jacob, x., 686. Children, pension to, xvi., 125.

Hewes, Josiah, care of prisoners, xi., 89.

Hewson, John, calico printer in N. L., xvi., 85, 116, 196, 254.

Heydrick, Colonel Peter, x., 713.

Heysham, Captain William, xi., 538; xii., 83. Commissioner for salt complains of being insulted by L. Kuhn, 160, 161.

Hickard, John, justice, xii., 342.

Hicks, Gilbert, forfeited estate in Bucks county sold, xii., 156.

Hicks, Giles, applies to be prothonotary, xi., 178. Resigns his pay, xii., 643. Sub-Lieutenant resigns, 651.

Hicks, Isaac, a justice, x., 47. Of Bucks county, his house to be searched and all public books, &c., to be removed to building erected for them at Newtown, xi., 128.

Hicks, Captain Robert, murdered by Indians in Virginia, iii., 22. Also a negro, 22.

Hicks, William, succeeds Lawrence Growden in several offices, ix., 663. A member of council, x., 12.

Hicquoqueen, Indian King, i., 396.

Hides, to be sold in preference to tanners who are associators, xi., 58.

Hierback, John, justice, xiv., 162.

Hiester, Colonel of battalion to rendezvous at Swedes ford, xi., 301.

Hiester, Daniel, council, xiv., 230. Elected commissioner on Luzerne claim, in place of General Muhlenberg, resigned, xv., 217.

Hiester, Daniel, Jr., letter complains against Frederick Limback, xiii., 74. Elected Brigadier-General, 289.

Hiester, Gabriel, justice, xi., 471.

Highway, robbery, the first committed in the province, v., 414. About Philadelphia, proclamation against, ix., 70, 76, 316. Declared, 717, 720, 727.

Higginbotham, Charles, case of, with Maryland, iv., 101. Flees into Maryland, and is appointed Captain of militia and justice, 147, 150. Motions watched, 154, 155, 160, 189, 193. Claim from Maryland for land, temporary line, 187, 188. His statement, 190. Letter to and from council, 190. Govr.'s letter to Gov. Ogle respecting, 192. Appears before council, 218. Is examined, 220.

Hill, Colonel, x., 645.

Hill, Henry, a justice, x., 47. Councillor, xiv., 555, 556; xv., 30, 130. To receive two cannons from Billingsport, 192.

Hill, John, appointed High Sheriff of Sussex county, i., 165, 166, 213. Member of council, i., 268.

Hill, Richard, member of council, ii., 118. Goes to New Castle, 381. Speaker, 519, 541. Elected Mayor, gives a dinner, 575. A justice, iii., 28, 187. Visits Indians with Governor, 121. Goes to Albany with Governor, returns, 196. Site of powder house referred to him, 243. Judge, 257. Died, 381. Death of, 398. Petition with Dr. S. P. Moore respecting title of lands, vii., 728, 739, 740. Claims lots and liberty lands, xiii., 9. And city lots, 49, 321, 326, 503. Claims city lots, xiv., 359, 458, 464. Claim, xv., 481, 486.

Hill, Richard, Jr., dies, his executors petition to be able to make title deed for his lands, vii., 728, 739, 740.

Hill, Thomas, &c., process issued against, for illegal acts, iii., 234.

Hill, Captain William, keeper of powder house, iv., 765.
Hillegas, Michael, and George Clymer, Continental Treasurers—order of Congress on, x., 401, 415, 436, 438, 453, 457, 463. Appointed treasurer of Committee of Safety, 281. Orders on, 286. Orders on, 333, 344, 347, 348–361, 374, 379, 381, 382, 384, 395, 401, 402, 463, 485, 492, 502, 513, 599, 635. Member of Committee of Safety, 537. Treasurer United States, receipt of exchange, xii., 423. Letter, 444. To lay off lots at barracks, xiv., 76.
Hilliard, John, member of first Council, i., 57.
Hillman, Cornelius, inducing soldiers, xi., 766. To be arrested, 766. Dismissed, 769.
Hillsborough, Lord, letter complaining of Massachusetts' circular to colonies, ix., 546. Indian trade, 552, 706. Laws passed 1760, 636.
Hiltzseimer, Jacob, to have a guard over firelocks, x., 560.
Hines, Samuel, Coroner, xv., 294, 565.
Hislep, Capt. Thomas, company, x., 675.
Hitchcock, Mrs. Eleanor, paid for hoisting a pole and flag on it at Cape Henlopen in 1775, 1776, as signals, xv., 566.
Hobson, Captain, of forty-fourth regiment arrested, vii., 103.
Hockley, James, commissioner on Schuylkill, xvi., 240.
Hockley, Richard, resigns great seal to Governor, viii., 335. Receiver-General with R. Peters, secretary; represent a history of proprietary taxes in Cumberland county, 472. Receiver-General on proprietary estate, ix., 178.
Hockley, ———, Treasurer, refuses to supply Cherokees, viii., 77. Keeper of great seal, 408.
Hockley, ———, Receiver-General, refuses to lend Governor for use of province, vi., 681.
Hockley, Col. Thomas, proves muskets, x., 502. And repairs, 679, 682, 686, 696.
Hodgdon, Col. Samuel, letter respecting cannon taken at Yorktown, xiii., 614. Account between United States and Pennsylvania for stores, xiv., 551. Expenses of Indians, xv., 240, 277.
Hodge, Andrew, letter on General Howe's progress, xi., 39. Applies for broken cannon, 662.
Hodge, Andrew, Jr., pass, xiii., 543.
Hodge, Dr. Hugh, appointed surgeon to third battalion United Colony troops, x., 478.
Hodge, Hugh, Jr., surgeon's mate, xi., 24, 32.
Hodge, Miss Marg., pass for, from New York, xiii., 272.
Hodge, Wm., paid for a negro, xiii., 640.
Hodrick, Capt. Wm. Adolph, xi., 2.
Hoffman, Michael, Ensign, xii., 8.
Hoffnagle, Capt. Peter, x., 700.
Hogan, John, deposition and full account of capture of Fort Granville, vii., 560.
Hoge, David, Sheriff, ix., 548, 624, 691.
Hoge, John, Surveyor on west branch of Susquehanna, xv., 85.
Hog or Hogg Island, suitable for frames, x., 294. To be overflowed, 607. Taken forcible possession of by sundry persons, who give security to appear at Court, xii., 570. Sheriff of Chester to deliver possession to J. Mease, &c.—Abraham Kentzing to hold for the State as part of estate of Joseph Galloway, 591. Persons to attend survey of, 630. Retaining fee to J. D. Sergeant in case of—Committee of conference, 634. Claim to be prosecuted, 661. Partition line to be run between State and Messrs. Mease, C. & Co., 679. Agents not to receive money for sale at, xiii., 11. Sale of estate of Joseph Galloway, 279, 280, 281, 286, 299, 325, 508. Papers relating to purchase of part of, 675. Suit for recovery of a part sold Samuel Caldwell, xiv., 4. Suit between State and Thos. Proctor—counsel employed, xv., 116, 372. Papers necessary to trial to be loaned to Samuel Caldwell, 473. Suit respecting, xvi., 69. Island between, and Tinicum, 230.

Hogs, trial for killing, i., 150, 152. Not to run at large in Philadelphia and New Castle, 327.

Hohler, Peter, Justice, xii., 8.

Holder, George, a suspected person, applies for trial, xii., 11. Pardoned, 12.

Holdernesse, Earl of, sends despatches from England on movements of French and Indians, v., 689. Letter to, from Governor H., 709.

Holcpeeka, Packsinosa's son, vii., 187.

Holgate, applies for arms, xii., 61, 62.

Holgate, Col. Matthew, xv., 12, 17.

Holiday, Justice Thomas, complaint against, viii., 42.

Holker, ———, Adjutant General, shipment of provisions for French fleet, xi., 692. Letters from, 669, 714. Certificate, 779.

Holker, French Consul—exemption from militia fines to Frenchmen, xii., 30, 32. A Frenchman impressed on State ship, 35, 37. Complains of purchasers in Wilmington, 47. Complains of newspapers, 59, 60, 61. Ships for General Mercer, 191. And brig Trooper, 197. Respecting flour, 54, 56, 66, 68. Mons. Gerard approves of course taken by Council in regard to, 71. All papers, &c., to be sent to Congress, 72. His powers, 74. For flour, 85. Answer of Capt. Montgomery respecting Vincent de Ford and Francis Fleury, 86, 411. To exchange salt for flour, 90. Letters to and from, 100. Letter to, on flour, 108, 233. Fire at his house, 262. Requisition of Congress for flour, 275, 296. Conference with Council, 368, 413. Bills on French Governor, 419. Masts from Schuylkill, 488. Pay to, 634. Purchases lot on State Island, xiii., 8. French seamen, 54. Tax, 54. Recognized as Consul General, 59. Paid, 242. Agent, xiv., 405.

Holker, privateer brig, xi., 49. Capt. Geddes captures a vessel and liberates the captain and crew, for which bond is put in suit, xii., 50, 155.

Holland, extracts of treaty with, contrabands of war, &c., iv., 487.

Holland, Lieutenant Hitchen, letter on French and Indians, v., 622, 623, 641; vi., 411.

Holland, Nathaniel, appointed Indian agent at Shamokin, viii., 99, 128 129, 499. Letter on Indians, 499.

Holland, Thomas, resigns as first Lieutenant, x., 484, 515.

Hollander's Creek, near Philadelphia, iii., 111. Road and bridge leading to Greenwich Island, act proposed, ix., 360. Deed to Joseph Carson on, xiii., 52.

Holliday, John, Justice, xiv., 602.

Holliday, John, a Justice of Bedford county, vacated, xv., 26.

Holliday, William, paymaster, xi., 637.

Hollinback, John, paid for forage for Wyoming, xv., 221. Sale of Allen's estate, 237.

Hollenback, Matthias, proposals for rations, xv., 295. Paid, 519.

Hollingshead, Mr., master of ship General Greene, xi., 760. Elected to Assembly, xii., 129.

Hollingsworth, Levi, sent to New York for cannon arrived there, to bring them by land, x., 632. Petition respecting salt works at Turtle-Gut inlet, xi., 193. Sells flour to agent of Maryland, 767. Respecting flour in his hands, xii., 16. Papers delivered to Henry H., 18. Letter to, on supplies, 203. Proposals for removing cheveaux-de-frise, xiv., 75, 78. Agreement and pay, 104, 119, 200, 213. Certificate to, 241. Letter, 500. To distribute aid to the Chinese, 574, 616. Expenses paid for Chinese, xv., 106.

Holmes, Lieutenant James, appointed, x., 676. Resigns, xi., 68.

Holme, John, offers to take up arms against French, i., 334. Sheriff, ix., 286, 333, 398. Letter to Governor, 463. Ordered to take F. Stump and servant to Philadelphia, 441. In Philadelphia, 490.

Holme, Thomas, member of first Council, i., 67. Surveyor-General, 120. Reasons for not issu-

ing warrant to survey R. Fretwell's lands, 124. Order to survey them, 124, 154. Appointed Commis'r to treat with Indians for lands, 156. Complaints against Ashcome, 193, 201. F. Fairman, petition against, 199, 201, 202. Map of Pennsylvania, 264, 266.

Holmes, William, Coroner, xii., 166, 518.

Holt, Rives, Sheriff of Sussex, iii., 260, 289, 370. Letter from Governor to, on pilots not licensed, iv., 394.

Holt, Ryvers, Chief-Justice of Supreme Court, dies, ix., 203.

Holt, Samuel, to take account of arms, ii., 241.

Holton, Colonel Francis, battalion, x., 682.

Honeyman, Lieutenant to corps of invalids, xi., 647. Petition, 753. Petition for rations, xii., 14.

Honeyman, William, decree of Supreme Court favor of, xii., 114, 115.

Honoyoothack Indians, ii., 140.

Hooken, Henry, Sheriff, xvi., 490.

Hooper's trial at Morristown, xii., 250.

Hoops, Adam, commissioner, to cut road westward, vi., 318. Justice, ix., 583.

Hopkins, Commodore, takes cannon at Providence, x., 550. Resolution of Congress, 564.

Hopkins, General, (?) of the Alfred, obtains privilege of searching outward bound vessels for seamen, x., 435.

Hopkins, James, supplied with a vessel for an expedition down the river, xi., 237. Applies for eight men, 241, 242. Allowed to search wrecks in Delaware river, xii., 1.

Hopkins, John Estaugh, removal of wrecks from fishery—He to have them, xi., 720.

Hopkins, Captain William, sent by General Wentworth to enlist soldiers for Cuba, iv., 499.

Hopkinson, Francis, of Continental Navy Board, xi., 260. Memorial respecting claims of Rev. J. Duché, 773, 774. Applies for a pass for his sister, Mrs. Elizabeth Duché, from New York, xii., 17, 18. Appointed Judge of Admiralty, 49, 50, 307. To postpone sale of house, 81. Seal for admiralty, 102. Money for New Jersey, 197, 307. Impeachment of, as Judge of Admiralty, 567, 573, 578–583. Unanimously acquitted, 584. Complaint against, xiii., 183. Paid, 329, 451, 532. Judge Admiralty, paid, xiv., 142. Errors and appeals, 310, 314, 602. Accounts, xv., 133. Salary paid, 185. Reappointed as Judge of Admiralty Court, 191. Paid, 199, 282, 351. Call on Marshal for accounts of property, 397. Pay, 474. Complaint against British consul for a survey ordered, 517, 520, 626. Paid, xvi., 99. Repaid money lent for recruiting, 511.

Hopkinson, Thomas, appointed clerk of Orphans' Court, iv., 151. Member of Council, v., 65.

Horn, John, minister of Seventh-day Baptists, released from militia fine, xiv., 568.

Horses, importation and exportation of, i., 80, 81. Number to be kept, no stone horse to go at large, ii., 27. To draw double, 220, 222. Act to improve breed of, proposed, iii., 234. Passed, 235. Jockey-bill, v., 371, 372, 375. To be impressed for artillery, xi., 301. Purchased, 447, 449, 489, 491. Stolen, 608. A case not pardoned, 717. Stealing, xii., 86. To be seized, 450. Horrible sentence for, xiii., 195, 221. Lost, 521.

Horsefield, Timothy, letter—Attack on Gnadenhutten, vi., 736, 750, 757. Indians from Diahoga—Letter, vii., 169, 187, 189, 190, 192, 305, 461, 586, 622, 732, 736. States apprehended difficulty with, 191. Governor orders Indians to Easton, 192. Return of Indians, 587, 773. Letters to and from, viii., 84, 99, 353, 663. Conference with Indians, 84.

Horsham, a mill erected by Governor, who asks for a road to be laid out, iii., 158. Returns, 163, 177. Confirmed, 177.

Hoskins, John, Sheriff of Chester county, ii., 105, 150, 397.

Hoskins, Stephen, Coroner, iv., 247.
Hospital, establishment of, for sick poor and lunatics proposed, v., 513, 526.
Hospital, Pennsylvania, taken up for sick continentals, xi., 33, 52. Managers refuse continental bills, x., 779.
Hospital, Dr. Benjamin Rush, physician and surgeon to, x , 347, 548. Dr. Kuhn, 636.
Hospital, and pest house, x., 549, 636.
Hospital, sick soldiers at, xi., 52, 85.
Hospital, Navy report on, xi., 641.
Houber, Michael, deposition, Braddock's defeat, vi., 483.
Houghton, Rowland, merchant of Boston, charged as a counterfeiter. Governor of Massachusetts requested to have him arrested, and examination, iv., 225. Answer, 241.
His declaration, 241. Acquitted, 242.
House of Correction, iii., 39. In Bristol, v., 34.
House of Employment, sick at, xi., 56. Claim of Council against, for flour, &c., xv., 227.
Houston, Thomas, lieutenant of gun boat, x., 330. Commands Warren, 510. For recruits, 529. Recommended by navy board but not appointed, xi., 543. Command brig Convention, 555. Takes prizes, 592.
Houston, Lieutenant William, pension to his widow, xv., 430.
Howard, Joseph, coroner, v., 551.
Howe, General, invasion feared, x., 747. Intelligence from his army, 783. Advancing towards Princeton, xi., 39. Intentions, 199. John Brown's statement respecting his propositions through Mr. Willing, 345. Application for accommodation of troops, xiii., 619.
Howe, Lord, killed, viii., 147.
Howell, Isaac, justice, xiv., 116. Charge against, 136.
Howell, Jacob S., clerk of Board of war continued, xi., 262. Receives money, 264. Authorized to borrow money, if necessary, for the navy, 361, 366. Receiver General of clothing, 407, 424, 670. Resigns, 742.
Howell, John, justice, xii., 379. Justice resigns, xiv., 312.
Howell, Mordecai, complains of Colonel Quarry, ii., 517.
Howell, Reading, map of Pennsylvania, xvi., 275. Of Delaware and Lehigh rivers, 278, 319. Pay on account of maps, 337. Commissioner paid, 544.
Howell, Samuel, member of committee and to have floating battery built, x., 437. Chairman, 412. To buy copper, 612.
Howet, Captain, of a French flag of truce with prisoners captured in Del'are Bay, by privateer Spry—lands sugar—is tried by Admiralty Court, xiii., 139. Petition, 148.
Huber, Jacob, deposition, Braddock's defeat, vi., 483.
Huber, Colonel John, &c., petition for pay, xiii., 461.
Hubley, Adam Major, xi., 35. Lieutenant Colonel, 770. Succeeds Colonel Hartley, 778. Ensign, xii., 65. Letter, 85. Appointed lieutenant of Lancaster county, 628, 702, 769, 775. Letter on military guards for Lancaster, xiii., 141. Resigns as lieutenant, 732. Moneys received for State duty on auction sales in Southwark, xvi., 155, 303, 386.
Hubley, Bernard, as lieutenant, x., 685. Asks a staff appointment, xii., 659.
Hubley, George, a captain, x., 634.
Hubley, John, commissary of continental stores, xi., 86. Prothonotary, 187. Resigns council, is appointed prothonotary and clerk of Orphans' Court of Lancaster, 199. To search for records of Westmoreland, 252. Builds stores, 739. To deliver up key of magazine at Lancaster to order of Board of war, xii., 32. Purchase of Witman's estate, 231. Petition against, as prothonotary, xiii., 545; xvi., 216[2].
Hubley, Joseph, as captain, x., 447.
Hubley, Michael, Captain, barrack-master at Lancaster, xi., 92. Pay increased, 405. Justice, 252. Justice, xiv., 157. President of

Courts, xv., 499. Militia fines, rent of house in Lancaster for storing arms, &c., 412.

Hucksters, regulated, i., 582.

Hudson, William, complaint against for improper language, i., 371. Proceedings, 371. Acquitted, 371. Convicted for stealing a stick of fire wood, applies for a pardon, case referred to attorney-general, xvi., 387.

Huffnagle, Michael, charged with secreting records of Westmoreland in Lancaster, xi., 252. Ordered from camp of General Washington, 253. Order, 475. Asks for compensation for services under General McIntosh, xii., 73. Asks pay, 487. Petition to be prothonotary, 632. Agreement with, for supplies for militia, xiii., 157. Prothonotary of Westmoreland, 158. Accounts, 595. Justice, 700. Papers, &c., of A. Ross, 766, 754. Agent for estates, 774. On sale of confiscated estates in Westmoreland county, xiv., 289, 290. Property in ruins of Fort Pitt, 472. Confiscated estates in Washington and Westmoreland counties, 607.

Huffnagle, Philip, removed from Montgomery jail to Philadelphia, xv., 161. Complaint against, as prothonotary, xvi., 162, 163.

Hugg, Joseph, to have a boat of New Jersey, with man and pay, &c., x., 328.

Hughes, Captain of Washington county rangers, xiv., 215.

Hughes, John, commissioner of wagons, vi., 775. Provincial commissioner, vii., 657, 671, 697. Going to Wyoming to build fort, 730. Opposed by Governor and Council, 734. Commission and refusal, 754. Wants command, refused, 756. Stamp officer, Philadelphia, ix., 300. Resigns, 300. Of 7th Pennsylvania Regiment, xiii., 98. Justice resigns, xiv., 567.

Hughes, Joseph, report of houses built by him and Pawling at Wyoming, viii., 134.

Hulings, Captain John, xi., 32. Presents a model of a boat, and thanks, x., 296.

Hulings, Michael, Warden, ix., 293.

Hulings, Samuel, has pre-emption right to island in Alleghany river, xvi., 285.

Hulings, Thomas, a Commissioner to view rivers, xvi., 178. Instructions, 181, 208. Paid, 260, 308.

Hulk, an old, paid for, x., 647.

Hulscamp, Garret, pilot, x., 428.

Hume, Robert, Lieutenant of boat, x., 408, 488.

Hummelstown, (Derrytown,) gun-factory to be established at, xi., 314.

Humphreys, Assheton, applies to be notary public, xiii., 302. Notary, 445.

Humphreys, Colonel, succeeds to Colonel Nagle's command, xi., 457; xiii., 281.

Humphreys, Daniel, printer, paid, xv., 519, 642. Printer of Pennsylvania Mercury, xvi., 257.

Humphreys, James, appointed clerk of Orphans' Court in place of Mr. Price, vii., 561. A Justice, and Notary to take acknowledgment of deeds, ix., 678. A Justice, x., 46. Bounds to be fixed by parole, xi., 269. Refuses to deliver up the public papers, &c., 306, 525.

Humphreys, Whitehead, aided by Council in manufacture of steel, xv., 269.

Humpton, Colonel Richard, x., 754, 767. Commands regulars in continental service, xi., 2, 5, 6, 16, 32, 55, 108, 119, 270, 573. Letter—Clothing expenses, xii., 320, 718. Superintendent of recruiting service, xiii., 155. Money placed in his hands, 156. Pay to, 198, 205, 347. To enlist men from Pennsylvania line, 419. Letter of War Office sent to, 449. To produce soldiers for examination, 614, 711. Buys city lots, xiv., 605. Accounts, 644, 646. Accounts approved, xv., 356.

Hunt, John, to be seized, xi., 283. Sent to Virginia and dies, 472.

Hunt, Martha, pardoned, iii., 244.

Hunter, Alex'r, Paymaster, xi., 81.

Hunter, Alexander, Collector of Excise, leaves the country—his successor, xiv., 652.

Hunter, Col. Daniel, Paymaster, xi., 277.
Hunter, James, Paymaster, xi., 160.
Hunter, Col. James, xi., 491.
Hunter, John, Sheriff, v., 55. Consulted on law for bill of credit, viii., 342. Asks longer time, 342, 538, 694.
Hunter, Jonathan, imprisoned and enlarged, xi., 364.
Hunter, George, imprisoned and enlarged, xi., 364.
Hunter, Joseph, Coroner, ix., 57.
Hunter, Robert, an Indian marries Mrs. Montour, iii., 293. Paid for a gun, &c., when taken prisoner by the British in 1777, xvi., 311.
Hunter, Samuel, a Justice, ix., 680; x., 602; xi., 76, 110. Of Susquehanna county, paid for provisions, 394. Lieutenant-Colonel—arms, 491. Letters, 508. Troops, 510, 528. To supply men at Col. Potter's, 646. To be paid for recruits, 719; xii., 46. Asks for powder, 50. Letter, Indian incursions, 72, 230, 234. Lieutenant, 307, 743. For recruits, xiii., 132. Gun flints, 137, 150. Course approved, 292. Pay for recruiting, 312. To contract for supplies, 356. Horse lost, 520.
Hunter, William, Ensign, xii., 338.
Hunter, Fort, 471. Capt. Busse at, vii., 362. Described, 724, 772.
Hunter, Colonel, (Governor of New York) to meet at New York with Governor, ii., 534. Demands £2000 for Queen's use--decision of Council, 557. Respecting a counterfeiter, 567. Governor of New York, on Indian murder, iii., 21. Communication from, 59. 62. Going to England, 68. Has partly in charge the post office, vii., 447.
Huntingdon Co., divided from Bedford, xv., 278. Prothonotary appointed, Lazarus McLene, 279. Register and Recorder, A. Henderson, 283. Elections, 300. Councillor, 300, 327. Sheriffs, 300, 577. Coroners, 300, 577. Justices, 330, 368, 527. Disturbances in—proceedings of Councils respecting, 479. Justice Coyle resigns, 526. Complaint against Prothonotary of county, 536, 541, 542. His answer, 599. Further proceedings, 603. L. B. McLene, Prothonotary, removed—Andrew Henderson appointed, 622. Sureties, xvi., 32. Commissioners appointed to ascertain county lines, viz., Elliott Taylor and Harris 46. Disturbances, 94, 95, 97. Division of election districts, 111. List of tavern keepers, 123. Returns of militia officers, 171. Tavern licenses, 434. Sheriff, 210, 527. Captives in Ohio, 458. Coroners, 210, 527. Councillor, 221, 241. Road from Frankstown to Conemaugh, 252, 434. B. Elliott, treasurer, 284. Assemblyman, 539. Lieutenant, 454. Erected Sep. 20, 1787—stray horses, 315. Justices, 353.
Huntingdon, lottery for Episcopal church in, ix., 243.
Huntingdon, Hon. Samuel, elected Speaker of Congress, xii., 116.
Huntington, Gov. Samuel, letter to, respecting Jno. Franklin, xv., 386. Letters, 385, 386, 575.
Hurricane, destructive, in leeward islands, x., 57. Proclamation of Gov. Penn, 58.
Hurst, Baron & Co., *vs.* State—counsel employed, xiv., 52. Owned lot south of Lombard street, public burying ground, xv., 273.
Hurst, Charles, petition for a pass to England, xii., 72. To appear at Council, 258.
Hurst, Charles, and Timothy, claims, xv., 481.
Hustanecks, a great Indian captain, vii., 530.
Huston, Capt., recruits for Colonel Shirley's regiment—inquiry respecting, v., 105.
Huston, Lieut. W., wounded, allowed refreshments, xii., 308, 348.
Huston, John, Sheriff, xvi., 518.
Hutchins, Thomas, Commissioner on boundary with Virginia, xiii., 685. Paid as Commissioner to run line with Virginia, xiv., 236, 317. To run the new line, 402. To view roads, 442.
Hutchinson, Dr. James, with Dr. Rush, to advise health officer—

appointed surgeon of fleet, xi., 543. Report, &c., 641. State surgeon, case referred to, xii., 2, 267, 278. Pay, 323. Member of Assembly, 367. To deliver hospital stores, 506. To visit D. Franks, 509. Director-General of militia hospitals, 445. Deed to, xiii., 12, 57. Appointed director of hospitals, &c., 76. Certificate to, 247. To apply public funds to planting fruit trees in Pennsylvania hospital, xiv., 71. Paid as physician and surgeon to militia, 625. Asks for depreciation, 653, 655. Paid, xv., 356. For attendance, &c., on John Franklin, 640. Attendance, &c., on invalid guard, xvi., 82.

Hyatt, John, Sheriff, iv., 500, 601, 669.

Hyder Ally, sale of ship, xiii., 445. Bought for State, 450.

Hyndshaw, James, deposition respect'g Connecticut settlers, viii., 612.

Hynson, Col. Nathaniel, conference between Gov. Hart of Maryland, and Gov. Keith, at the house of, iii., 60.

I.

Ice, goods damaged by, permission asked to sell, xii., 210.

Ichelburg, F. and J., representation of Assembly respecting, xii., 280.

Ihrie, Conrad, Jr., Coroner, xiv., 557; xv., 100.

Imlay, Wm., to be seized, xi., 284. Released, 295.

Immel, Michael, to be closely confined, xi., 357.

Impeachment—Report of Committee to examine minutes, viii., 1, 12–17.

Impertinent—brig, prize to ship General Greene, xii., 19. Her condemnation to be obtained, 20.

Impressment of seamen, v., 326, 327.

Independence, declaration of, resolution of Congress to send copies to various bodies, x., 634. Letters written by Committee of Safety to counties to have it published, 635. Ordered to be read at State House July 8, every member of committee, &c., required to be present, 635.

Indian Corn, patent granted for curing, iii., 18.

Indians, agreement with, about rum, i., 98. To have rum on agreeing to be punished as white men are, 105. Selling rum to, 116. Kill hogs at the Falls, 139. Complain against Jesper Farmer's servants making them drunk, 147, 148, 149. Complaint against not selling powder and shot to them, 157, 158. Complaint against for rapine, &c., 162, 180. Sale of liquors to, 187. Injury to N. Skull, &c., 187. Letter, Governor and Council of New York, respecting Susquehanna and Schuylkill, 202. Rumored invasion by Senecas and French from Maryland, 277. And Papists, 299. Historical account of Mohawks in 1665, 300. Lassie Cock, proposed visit to; Council's instructions, 334. Proposed companions, 335. Visit Philadelphia, 340. Visit to the Governor, 372. His conference with them, 372, 373. Respecting drink, 373. Views of the Quakers, 373. Arrested for stealing silver cups, 376. French and, conspire—Mad. Le Tort, &c., 396. King Huquequeen, Shakuppoo, Kyenturrah, Olemeon, 396, 435. Called Shallnavooners, 397. Presents to, 435, 436. Captain Cock, Peter Reverdie, interpreters, 435. Petition against French traders with, 436. Arrive in Philadelphia, 447. Onteo, Menanges, Mohocksey, Tamance, Alemeon, &c., 447. Senecas, Onondagas, 447. Story of West Jersey, 449. And French, 453. Peace with, 454. Proposed to give part of one penny revenue to, 468. Money expended for, 519. Frightened by firing guns, 586. Trade bill proposed, 606.

Agreement between William Penn and the Susquehannah, Shawnee and others, ii., 15. Trade with, 18. False alarm

Indians—
from, 20. Indian trade regulations, 21. A joint stock proposed, 21. Not, but chiefs to buy rum, 21. License for selling to, necessary, 21. Various chiefs to be consulted, 26. Complaint on sale of rum, 33. Happy issue of conference between New York and, 35. Come to take leave of Governor, 44. To be permitted to give evidence, 46. Some Delaware and Conestoga, suspected of murder and robbery, 70. Attack families at Conestoga, 121, 122, 131. N. Godine, a trader, information respecting Carolina, and Potomacs, and Senecas and Conestoga, 138. Coming to Philadelphia to trade, Onondagoes, Honoyoothacks, 140, 141. Ortyiagh, chief of Conestogas, 141, 204. Complain of rum, 141. Conference on affairs, 143. Conspiracy against Shawnese, 145. Harry's brother arrives, 153. Kagundanoyagh, an Onondago chief arrives in Philadelphia, 159. Recommended by Governor to Assembly, 165. Arrive in Philadelphia, 183. From Conestoga, 186. Alarms, 187. Manangy, chief on Schuylkill, arrives in behalf of Ganawese or Piscataways, ask permission to settle here, 191. Violence to English families, 191. Indian Harry's brother returns with presents from Onondagoes, 204. To have advantage of our laws, 212. For improvement of trade with, 220, 224. Conestoga, Shawnese and Ganawese arrive in Philadelphia, 244. Conference with, 245. John Hans building a log trading house, 246. Nantikokes, 246. Large belt of wampum, its object, 246. Present skins in, when of friendship, 248. Cost of last treaty, 248. Governor Evans visits Conestoga, 251. Treaty with Conestogas, 299. To be secured in their allegiance and instructed in the Christian religion, 299. Assembly's address to Governor, 299. Governor Evans visits, 385. Account of his journey, 386–390.

Indians—
Nicole Godine, a French trader among, complained of by Governor, 385. Arrested, 390. Stranger, from Carolina at Shawnese town, 390. M. Chartiere sent to invite them to Philadelphia, 390. Expenses of treaties with, 392–3, 394, 461. Nantikokes, 394, 396, 397, 488. Message from, complaining of several French traders, 403. License to to trade with, 404. Five Nations to be engaged by New York in expedition to Canada, 450. Governor sends excuse for not meeting the Conestogas, 451. Message from Conestoga, 467. Presents for, 467, 473. Of several tribes arrive at, 469. Conference with, 468–475. Indian slave Mingo imported, 490. Peter Bizalion, a trader, arrested, 509. Suspicious belt of wampum—large meeting —Governor to attend, 509, 570. Report of conference with, at Conestoga, 511, 513, 516. Names of several Indian chiefs, 509, 511, 516. Queen of Conestogas, 516. Presents, 516. Expense of, 529, 546. Invite Governor to conference at Conestoga, 531, 532, 533. Presents to, 533. Come to Philadelphia on expedition to Canada, 537. Governor invited to conference with, at Manatanny, 545. At E. Farmer's, 546. Numerous belts and presents, 546–549. Arrive from Conestoga, names of several chiefs, 553. Refer to proprietary's promises, 553. Complain against traders, 554. Return from Five Nations, report, 557. Presents from several named tribes, 557. Death of Mechelokeety, 557. In Philadelphia, 561, 574. In Philadelphia, 599–602. Conestogas move off unexpectedly, 603. In Philadelphia, 603. Complain of rum being sold to them, 604. Arrive in Philadelphia, 606, 613.

Disturbance among, at Conestogoe, iii., 15, 17, 18. Several tribes meet at Conestoga, 19. Onechela's son killed, 20. Murder of Catawba, 21. Several

Indians—
murders by, in Virginia, 22. Traders plundered by, 22. Articles agreed to by, 24. Expenses of treaties with, 25, 58. Numerous chiefs arrive and hold conference, 45. Murders by Southern, and alarms from, on Susquehanna, 66. Report of Col. John French on visit to, 77–81. John Cartledge's account of expenses, 81. Propositions to Five Nations at Albany, 82. Of Pennsylvania—their conduct, 85. James Logan's report of his visit to Conestoga, 92. Inquiry as to right of Five Nations to lands on Susquehanna, 98. Letter—Governor of New York, on affairs of, 99–102. Conference at Philadelphia, 102. Presents to, 105. Expenses and presents, 107. Agreement between, of Virginia and Conestoga, 114. Deputies from Five Nations sent to Conestoga, 119. Governor, &c., visit them, 121. Conferences, 121–130. Murder of, near Conestoga, reported, and attributed to J. or. E. Cartledge, 146. Logan & French, sent to inquire about it—their report of the conference with, 148–156. Troubles on Susquehanna, 160. Arrive in Phila. from Conestoga — message from Five Nations, 163. Message from, by French & Logan, 165. Message from Gov. to Assembly respecting, 167. Conference with, 168–170. Lands on Susquehan'a, 178. Conference with at Conestoga, 181–185. Show Governor a parchment received from William Penn, containing many articles of friendship between him and the, 181. Declare his right to purchase (and their consent), lands on Susquehanna, 181. At Corray Town, 188. Governor's letter to Ganawese King, 188. The Five Nations in want of provisions, 189. Ask reprieve of John Cartledge, 189. Body to be examined, 191. Presents to, 191. Governor's visit to Albany, to meet Five Nations — heads of treaty, 193. Penn's treaty, or "leagues of friendship" with, at

Indians—
first settlement of province, 194, 197, 203. Presents for, to be purchased by Isaac Norris, in New York, 196. Governor's speech and presents at Albany, 197. Answer of—confirmation of "league of friendship," 200. Surrender of lands by, at Albany, 201. Governor's answer to, 202. Respecting, 204–207. Message to, from Council, 209. Answer to Governor's speech respecting Albany and Virginia, 215. Speech to Governor, 216. Address from Ocowellos, King of Shawnese, 219. Answer to, 219. Present of rum to, 219. Governor's answer to, 219–221. Complain of mill and dam on Brandywine creek, as hindering the fishing, 269. Conference in Philadelphia, 271. Purchase of lands on Susquehanna spoken of, and effected by Gov. Dongan, 278. "League of friendship" by Penn, alluded to, 273. Presents to chiefs of Five Nations, 273. Further conference with them, 274. Settlements along the Susquehanna objected to, 274. Governor's answer to, 275. Restricted in rum, 276. Expenses of, 280. Gov. to visit, 280. Kill Thomas Wright at Snaketown, 285. Munscoes on Susquehanna, 286. The first accident of the kind in the province, 286. Miamis and Tweechtwees threaten Mrs. Montour, Le Tort and Robert Hunter, 295. Examination of Indian reports of Mrs. Montour, &c., 295. Presents to, 297. Shawnese kill Conestoga, 302. Report of Gov. on visit to, at Mahanotawny, 303. Message and presents sent to, 305. Murder of, 306, 313. Proclamation respecting, 307. Presents to, 308. Flathead—propose making war against, 309. Council at Conestoga, 309–314. Messages from, 315. Meeting of several chiefs at Philada., 316. And an immense collection of inhabitants at the great meeting-house, 318. Complaints—James Logan, about Christians settling on their lands,

Indians—
which had never been paid for, 319. Deed for lands on Susquehanna, 321. Discussion between, and James Logan, relative to the intended lands, 322. Also of A. Hamilton, 324. And R. Hill, 324. Agreement with William Penn, &c., about sale of lands, 325. Interesting discussion about their lands, between Logan, Hamilton and Hill, 325. Minnissinks charged with murder at Snaketown, 326. Murder by Morgan Herbert, &c., in Chester County, 326. Disturbances near Durham Iron Works, 329, 330. Letters from, 333. In Philada., 333. And Council, 334. Presents to, 337. Expenses of, at Phila., 343. Conference at Phila., 361. Tawenna alludes to Penn's house in town, 363. Governor's speech to, 364. And presents, 365. Allowances to agents, 366. Of Brandywine creek, 382. Louisiana, 402. Treaty with Five Nations, 403. Conference at Philadelphia, 404. Treaty of trade, 406, 408, 409. Proclamation respecting, 409, 411. At Phila., 425. Conference with, at, 435. Proprietary addresses them, 435. And their answer, 437. Speech of chief, 438. Presents a mantle to Thomas Penn, 440. Strength of the Tweetwees, 440. Presents to 442. Respecting Shawnese, 443. Minutes, 446. Read to, 447. Present to, from proprietary and Council, 450. Conference with, 451. Attacked with small-pox—one dies in Phila., 463. Quassenungh recovers, 463. Treaties with, 493. Conference at Philad'a, 500–505. Speech of John Harris—building a house at Juniata, 503, 504. Presents to, 506. Shot dead by an officer, 513. Murder in Virginia, 564. At Phil'a, 571, 577. Arrive at Phil'a, 597. Conference with, 598. Deeds from, to Wm. Penn, for lands on Susquehanna, 600–603. Gov.'s speech to, 605. Answer of Ganawese chief respecting murders in Virginia, attended by Governor, asks him to take back a large belt of wampum, which he does, 606.

In Philadelphia, conference with, iv., 53. Notice Governor's death, 54. Speeches and answers, 54. Presents to, 55. Conference at Philadelphia, 79–85. An unusual number in Philadelphia—much disordered with liquor, 86. Order of Council against supplying them with liquor, 87. Release lands west of Susquehanna to proprietary, 88. Accidentally killed by Solomon Moffat, 88, 89. Recommend Shekellamy to special notice, 88. Proclamation for apprehending S. Moffat, 89. J. Logan's speech to, 90. Presents to, 90. Receive message and wampum from Governor of Maryland, 90. Request Governors of Maryland and Virginia to be written to respecting lands, 93. 203. Difference between, and white men in conducting business, 94. Expenses, 226. Treaty with Six Nations of, 233, 236. Shawnese on Alleghany, 234. Treaty with, 238. Message to, from proprietary, 245. Murders of Catawbas, 246. Commit outrage in Lancaster county, 280. At Philadelphia, 307. Presents to, 308. Special present from Governor to Allummappis, 310. Nutimus and other Indians arrive, 312, 337. Expenses, 319. Articles of agreement with, by William Penn, 1701, 338–340. Their time for business is "when the sun is rising and not declining," 341. Conference with, 336–346. New treaty with, 336. Conference—allude to the two deaths of their tribe, 341. Awannameak, of Mennesink, wounds Henry Webb, who is sent to Philadelphia and placed under care of Dr. Graeme, 413, 447. Letter from Governor to, 420, 573. Council with, at a Quaker meeting house, 432, 443. Presents to, 435. 446. Papers relating to the Delawares, 481. In Philadelphia, 500. Ask payment for land, 501. Presents to, 502. Letter from Shawnese and Mingoes, complain-

Indians—
ing of rum sent among them, 502. Expenses, 549. Deputies from Six Nations arrive—agree to quit claim to lands—receive presents, 559–583. Names of those present, 583–586. Presents to, 573, 575, 578. Expenses, 576, 583. Complain of deer getting scarce, hunting grounds less and trader's prices of goods higher, 581. Conspiracy with certain, and French, to cut off inhabitants of Pennsylvania and Maryland, 587. Nations, with whom the Six Nations are in alliance, 586. Letter to, from Gov. T., 588. Imprisoned in Maryland, 588. On Expenses, 600. Petition of Captain John Titami, 624. Respecting lands sold by Six Nations, 625. Skirmish with, in Virginia, 630. Governor's message respecting, 634. Letter of Governor to Conrad Weiser, 635. Message of Assembly on, 637. Letter from Governor of Virginia and report of C. Weiser on, 640. His second report, 646–650. Conference at Philadelphia, 651. Mediation of Governor Thomas with, in favor of Virginia, 653–655. James Hendrick's deposition respecting alarm from, in Lancaster county, 656. Letter from Conoy Indians, 657. Governor's message respecting, 658. Instructions to Conrad Weiser on journey to Onondago, 655. His report, 660. Murders by Delawares, 675, 678, 679. C. Weiser sent to Shamokin, 676. His report, 680–684. Treaty at Lancaster, 697–737. Prices of goods for, regulated, 747. Treaty, 739. Shawanese unfriendly with other tribes of, 741. Delawares in Philadelphia, 742. Trial of, by Supreme Court, 751, 752. Catawbas and Virginia dispute with, 755. From Shamokin arrive, 767. Negotiations at Onondago, 768. Presents to, 768. Affairs at Albany, 770. And French in Canada, 772, 773. Commissioners appointed to Albany, 772, 777. Journal and report of Conrad Weiser, 777.

Indians—
On Mississippi, threatening signs of joining French and attacking northern provinces—snow shoes, v., 1, 5 Treaty with, at Albany, 7. Report of Commissioners, 7–26. Six Nations, 36, 72. C. Weiser sent to Shamokin to inform of death of John Penn, 73. At Chamber's Mill—Scaientes from Cayuga nation, 83. Message, &c. by C. Weiser to Indians at Joseph Chambers, 84. Tistagechroanu, a nation of, N. of Lake Frontenac, 85. And French united against English, 97. On or near Lake Erie, 120. C. Weiser's visit to, at Shamokin, 136. Presents for, 139. Sent to John Harris's, 139. From Ohio arrive, 145. Conference with, 146–151. Presents to, 151. Letter from Conrad Weiser, 162. Arrive with him at Paxton, 164. Message from Assembly respecting Ohio, 184. Cost of presents ought to be divided among other colonies, 188. Letters to Govs. Gooch and Ogle, 189. Proclamation against rum, 193. Presents for, 197. Governor Ogle on affairs of, 209. Respecting Ohio, 210. Conrad Weiser and Shekalamy attend Council to consult about successor to Oluriny, deceased king of Delawares, 222. Onondago deputies expected, 222. Robbed by James Denny of horses, 229. Letter from Gov. Gooch respecting Ohio, 257. Account of moneys received and paid for to be prepared, 269. Maryland refuses to make allowance for Indians, 273. Message from Six Nations, 285. Letter to Governor Clinton respecting, 286. Instructions to Conrad Weiser, 290, 304. Letter from Governor Shirley, 295. Commissioners, 299, 305. Treaty at Lancaster—report, 306–319. Day and night means a year, 310. Calumet-pipe, explanation of ceremony with, 313. Dinner to, 315, Treaty signed, 316. Expenses of treaty at Lancaster, 327, 333. Message to Assembly respecting, 329. Gov-

Indians—
ernor of South Carolina complains against Catawbas, 346. Journal of Conrad Weiser to Ohio, 348–358. Distances to places, 348. Arrive in Philadelphia, 388. Conoys claim lands—discussion about—presents, 383. Proclamation against settlers on their lands, 394, 410. Consultations with Six Nations, 395. Proclamation, not to sell rum to, 397. Arrive, 398. Presents to, 403, 406, 517, 518. Injuries from, 404. Indians in Philadelphia, 405. In Ohio, 423, 431. Conference with Mr. Peters, &c., at Cumberland, 431. Views of Council, 436. Message from the Twightwees, 437. Lands unpurchased—report of R. Peters—proceedings against settlers on, 440–449. Indian traders killed by, 449. Governor's answer to message of Twightwees, 449. Col. Johnson on Indian affairs, 463. Assembly and Gov. of New York on do., 467. Cannasatego dies and is buried, 467. Also Soleon Wanaghly, 467. At head of affairs is a Roman Catholic, 467. Put out Council fire, 471. English traders taken prisoners, 481, 484. Letter from Governor Clinton to Governor H. on, 495. Letter from George Croghan, 496. Speech of a Cayuga Sachem to Colonel Johnson and his reply, 508–511. Affairs on Ohio, 513. Letter from C. Weiser, 517. Instructions to Croghan and Montour, 518. Private to Croghan—say nothing about a fort, 522. Information from G. C., 522. Treaty with Twightwees, 523, 524. Treaty with several tribes, 532. Speech of Governor H., 533. Nanticokes arrive from Wyomen, 543. Heavy expenses of their affairs, 546. Complaint against traders, 547. Expenses of treaty with, not to be borne by proprietaries, 544. Onondacks join French, 547. Message from Shawnese to Governor, and answer, 569–579. Moravian missionaries to, 576. Attack on Twightwees town by

Indians—
French and, 599. At Onondago invited by Governor of Virginia to a council at Winchester, 607. And French on way to build forts at Ohio, 607. Report of, on Ohio—Logstown, &c., 614. Presents, 617. Monocatootha, 615. Death of king of Twightwees, 619. On alliance between England and Six Nations, 617. Letters on, from Oswego, 622–628. On Virginia, 628–637. Woman's story, 643. Commissioners to meet at Carlisle, 658. Custologo, a Delaware, and leading man, 660. The "Half King" of the Six Nations of very great note and esteem, 660. Report of Commissioners to Carlisle to hold conference with, 665–684. Those present, 685. Various speeches, &c., 691. Proposal to release lands on Ohio, 695. Message from Governor H. to. 705. Sick in Philadelphia—sent home with John Patten, 707. And French, 707–722, 730. Croghan's journal, 731. Speeches, 733. Message, 749. Murder near Log's town, 753. Treaty at Carlisle, 754. Affairs, 763.

And French affairs, vi., 1–9. Commissioners to Albany, 23, 25. Message to, 25. Speech of Half King, 31. C. Weiser's report at Shamokin, &c., 35, 36. Proceedings of Congress at Albany, 57–129. Nations present, 75, 78. Murder of English fishermen at Canso, 87. Lands, 93. Speech of River, 94. Meetings of Commissioners of Pennsylvania at Albany with, for purchase of lands—deeds for, &c., 114–129. Influence of Lydius, Woodbridge and Hendrick, 117. Influence of French on, 129. Letter from Ononraguite—chief of Saulte taken prisoner by the French, 129. Governor H., &c. on Indian affairs, 145. Treaty at Auckquick, 147–169. Death of Kissakoquilla, 154. Present at treaty, 159. Notified by Governor Morris of his appointment, 169. Message to Delawares, 187. Proposals of

Indians—
French to, 188. Tanachrisson arrives, 193. Conference with, 192–200. Discourse between Twightwees and Owendats, Governor objects to mouth of Juniata as a place for, 218. Necessaries for—some gone to Wills' Creek, 226. Hendrick and other Mohocks arrive in Philadelphia, 243, 244, 247. Cherokee Indians, prisoners to French, arrive with a pass from Albany Commissioners, 276. Conference at Philadelphia, 277–286. Opinion of Lydius deed, 279. Letters respecting, 286, 287. Names of, present at Council, 291. Henry Brandt and Seth, 291. Scaroyady's account of proceedings, 340. Mohawks in Philadelphia, 341, 344, 352. Complain of being naked, 359. Conference in Philadelphia, 360–365. Names of, present, 360. Further proceedings, 370. Settlers on lands of, 420. Death of Kishycoquillas, a Shawnese chief, 421. C. Weiser and Shekallamy visit Ostreacky and confer with, from Canasoragy, 444, Persons missing from near Fort Cumberland, 455, 457. Murders near Shippensburg, 459. At Little Meadows, 460. Murders near Fort Cumberland, 461. Conference at Colonel Johnson's, 468–475. Jagrea on his return from Owendots, 495. Letter, C. Weiser, about women, 494. Women from Auckwick—understanding with their husbands, 494. In Philadelphia, 522. Col. Weiser's opinion of, 535. Anxious to hear from Government, 536. Scaroyady's son-in-law to return to Ohio, 536. Weiser's history of the Owendot, 551. Conference in Philadelphia, 566–568, 588. Council of war, 608. With, 612. Message of Scaroyady, 615. Message of Governor to, on defeat of French at Lake George, 637. Letters relating to, 640–643. Affairs at Jno. Penn's creek, 645–662. Murder of Henry Hartman, &c., 668, 669, 770. Advice of inhabitants to prepare against

Indians—
attacks of, 669. Great Cove destroyed by—Sherman's Valley, &c., 673–677, 680. Conference at Philadelphia, 680–689. Scaroyady and Montour sent under instructions to Delawares, 697. Braddock's defeat has occasioned war with, 700. Murders at Tulpehocken, 703–706. Cause of alienation, 710. Report on, 724–728. Attack and burn Mahoney and Gnadenhutten, 736, 738. Trade bill, 743. Invited to conference, 745. Address of Bethlehem Indian, 747, 750, Message from, at Wyomink, 751. Instructions to Commissioners to invite, to a conference at Harris's, 754. Hostilities in Northampton county, 756, 758–761. Council at New York on Indian affairs, 765. Brief narrative of incursions of French and, in province, 1755, 766–768. Conference at Carlisle, 773–784.

Conference at Carlisle, vii., 1–6. At Lancaster, 7. Conestogoes, 7. Names of those present, 1–7. Governor's speech to—hostilities, 1–7, 9. Presents to, 9, 58. Scalp and strings to be sent to Colonel Johnson, 10. Governor Hardy complains of, 10. Gideon Hawley says they are hostile, 12. And French affairs, 18, General Shirley's speech to Six Nations, 21. In Virginia, 31. Report of C. Weiser at Harris's ferry, 33. Plan to kill, at do., 34. Oneida's, Senecas, &c., 43. In Philadelphia, 46–55. Troubles in back counties, 55–58. Danger on the way from Conestogoes, 59. Prefer going to Pennsbury, 61. Conference at Philadelphia, 64. Of Auckwick before Braddock's defeat arrive in Philadelphia, 64. Entertained by Governor M., 64. Speech of Scaroyady, 65. Conference, 70–72. Number present at treaty at Mount Johnson, 72. Hostilities at McCord's fort, 77. Conference at Philadelphia, 78, 137, 144. Scalps—declaration of war recommended, 78. Bill for trade with, 93. At Philadelphia,

Indians—
90–94. Newcastle's child to be taken care of by Governor, 95. War with Delawares, 88–103, 144. Speech of New Castle, &c., to Governor, 145. Conversation of C. Weiser with, on the war, 106. Conference with, and speech of Governor, 107. Governor Hardie on, 113. Report of delegates from the Six Nations, 115. Conference with, 137–142. Memorandum of New Castle, &c., journey to, on Susquehanna, 137. At Phila., Delawares, Shawnese, &c., 137–142, 144. Suspension of hostilities with Delawares, 144. Address of Governor and people to, on Susquehanna, 145. Letters from Commissioners to Governor, they meet Council—examinations of persons, &c., 153–155. Burn houses at or near Shamokin, 154. Conference between Colonel Clapham and Ogaghraderisha, 156–160. Letters, Wm. Edmonds and Wm. Parsons—murder, &c., 165, 167. Scalping party to be recalled, 167. May be received at Bethlehem, 170. Messages to, at Diahoga, 170. At Bethlehem, speech to—and names, 174. Trade, 177. Conference with, 182. Intelligence of intended attack from Diahoga, 186. Nine nations in English interest, 188. Arrival at Bethlehem, 188. Difficulty feared, 190. At Philadelphia, 192. Declaration of war by New Jersey against, 194. At Philadelphia, 198. Message from Teedyuscung, 199. Address of New Castle, 199. Sunday not known to, 205. Treaty at Easton, 204–220. Murder on frontiers, 214. Wampum at treaty described, 216. Governor M. communicates several letters, &c. received by him on affairs of, 230–235. Indian captures at Kittanning, 242. Statement of cruelties to Richard Coxe, &c., 248. Colonel Armstrong's report, 257. At Wyoming on way to Easton, 267. Prisoners taken, 282–289. Letter, Wm. Parsons, respecting, 288. Fears of French and, at

Indians—
Fort Augusta, 294. Report of Cap. New Castle, 296. Conference at Fort Augusta, 299. Invade Berks county and murder, 302. At Fort Allen, 305. Right of proprietaries to make war with, on treaties, 305. Conference at Easton, 309. Governor complains of indulging their notions about treaty, 311. Treaty at Easton, 313–338. Teedyuscung explains "fraud," and alludes to the "Indian walk," 326, 351. Purchases from, by proprietaries—Committee of Council appointed to investigate, 354. George Croghan appointed by Sir Wm. Johnson agent, 355, 434. Murders in Berks and Northampton county, 357. Examination respecting, 357. Murdered near Muskingum, three, and a prisoner blown up, 381. Son of Captain Jacobs killed, 381. Various names—friendly association raise money for, 391. Deposition at Fort Loudoun, 395. Indian walk, 1737—N. Scull certificate respecting, 399. Memorandum at Fort Allen, 431. Cause of war, 431. In Philadelphia, 436. And French preparing for Fort Augusta, 453. At Bethlehem desire a watch, 459, 461. Arrive at Bethlehem from Diahoga, 461. At Harris's, 462, 465. New Jersey minute, 467. At Fort Allen, 474. On their way to Bethlehem to kill whites, 477. Shawnese and Delawares in Fort Allen—murder at Conegocheague, 379, 503. Provisions scarce at Wyoming, 479. Afraid of sickness in Philadelphia, 479. Conestoga, send deputies with letter to Governor D., 484. Speech of chiefs at Lancaster, 485. And Governor, 486. Wm. Logan sent to, with instructions, 488. Memorandum by C. Weisor, 489. At Lancaster, 497. Catawbas arrive at Fort Cumberland, 502. Murders, 379, 503. Croghan's minutes of his proceedings with, at Harris' and Lancaster, 506–517. Conference of Governor, &c. with, at Lancaster, 517–551.

Indians—
Names of representatives of Six Nations present, 507. Six Onondago warriors permitted to go to Fort Cumberland, 512. Speeches, 529. Two prisoners examined, 531. Murders at Swatara, 538. Hung in New Jersey for accidental homicide, 540. On lands at Wyoming and Juniata, 540. Propose Sir Wm. Johnson as a model, 542. Governor proposes to invite Delawares to settle at Shamokin, 543. Deaths by small-pox, 547. Governor's message to Teedyuscung, 546. Guard for, from Lancaster to Philadelphia, 549. Thomas McKee's instructions to conduct, to Shamokin, 550. Minutes of Conference with Cherokees, 552. Return of messengers to Bethlehem, 587. Minutes of, 588. Report of Thomas McKee, 597. Deaths from small-pox, 597. Murders at Great Cove, 599. Cherokees at Fort Cumberland, 601. The Swallow Warrior killed in Virginia and his son wounded—murders, 601, 603, 604. Murder of a sentry, 619. Proceedings at Fort Johnson, 622–624. In Virginia, 631. Murders near Fort Loudoun, 631. Letter from, 636. Lands purchased from, 636. Answer to Committee of Friendly association, 637. Address from, 638. Answer, 647. Treaty at Easton, 648–714. Presents for, at Easton—list of, 671, 672. Alarm from, and, 718. Alliance with, at Easton, 720, 733. Take off J. Keller's wife, &c., 735. Delawares disappointed at not finding goods, 735. Abuses in the trade with, 739, 742, 747, 759, 763, 768. Cherokees and Mohawks arrive in Philadelphia from Colonel Johnson, 753. Sent on to Winchester, 754. Murders in Northampton county, 757. Designs of, in New York, 762. Letter from chiefs of Onohaghguaga, 763. Council at Philadelphia with Conestogoes, 768. At Philadelphia, 770. Letter from Indian Commissioners, 772. Castirequa, a chief, 773. Report of

Indians—
Committee on complaints of, against proprietaries in, 756, 776.
Conference at Philadelphia, viii., 9, 29, 40, 51, 54, 86, 110, 114, 122, 149, 156, 403, 429–435, 466, 484–495, 698–702, 707, 709. Trade with, 19, 24, 29, 39, 51, 71, 76, 234, 241, 303, 332. Teedyuscung's insolent reply, 29. Insists on his clerk being present, 30, 31. Names of, in Philadelphia, 31. Residences of several nations, 35. Assembly in favor of distant, 39. Attack Fort Edward, 60. Cherokees at Fort Loudown, destitute, 77, 78, 111. Speech of Teedyuscung, &c., at Mr. Horsfield's, 84. Murders, 95. Letters from Jno. Edwin respecting, 98. Ravages in Berks Co., &c., 99. Catawbas at Fort Loudoun, 111. Cherokees, 112. Conestogas, 113. Speeches of Governor to, 117. "Caligh Wanorum," Custom of Northern with wampum, 119. "Fat Bear," meaning of, 119. Conduct of French Commander at Fort Duquesne towards, 119–121. Arrive from Winchester, Va., with passports from General St. Clair, 124. News brought by Benjamin, a Mahakin, living near Bethlehem, 126. On Susquehanna alarmed by arrival of Cherokees, 126. Messages to, proposed, 128. F. Campbell appointed agent to Fort Augusta, declines—N. Holland appointed, 99, 128, 129. Message of Governor to Teedyuscung and Indians at Wyoming, 129. Message of Governor and General Forbes to, on Susquehanna, 131. Charles Thomson and F. Post, messengers, hold conference with Teedyuscung, &c., at Nescopec, 132. Report of Hughes and Pauling on building houses at Wyoming—a mason killed by, 134. Message from two Cherokee chiefs to Delawares, 135. Barbarities in New Jersey complained of by Governor Bernard, 139, 140. Sent messengers to Ohio, 147. Girl delivered up, 148. Minnisinks and Senecas arrive, 149. Speech

Indians—
of Sir Wm. Johnson to Delawares, 151. Conference at Burlington, 156. Munseys are "women," 157. Mohawks and Cherokees with Scaroyady's wife and children arrive, one Cherokee sick, 162. Death of Annaly—they ask for guns and horses, 163. The port Mahon—Captain Wallace requires men—if three hundred are supplied, Admiral Boscawen promises to send the Echo of thirty-two guns, 163. Assemble at Easton, 165. Arrive at Fort Allen, 167. Assembly on Indian affairs, 170. Rum not to be sold to, 172. Report and conference with Pisquitom, 174. Conference at Easton, 174–223. Names of the several nations at, 176. Refer to being defrauded of land in Pennsylvania and New Jersey, 199. Teedyuscung's account of Waping Wapinger, or River Indians, and their peculiar wampum, 217. Settlement with, for lands by Messrs. Peters and Weiser, 218. Agents for Indian trade at Fort Allen, appointed, 234. Conference with General Forbes at Philadelphia, 263–269, 270. Thomas King, 270. R. Tuckness, Indian agent resigns, George Allen appointed, 286. Colonel Hugh Mercer's account of, 292. Minutes of conference with, at Pittsburgh, 293–297. F. Post, missionary to, 301. Ohio ought not to be invited to conference, 301. Delawares talk of moving to Kuskusky, 305. Conference with Colonel Mercer at Pittsburg, 306, 311. Messengers to, 341. News from Pittsburg, 377. Minutes of conference at, 382–391, 393, 395. Horse stolen by Delawares, 401. Conference, 415–421. Minutes of conference at Pittsburg, 429–435. With Teedyuscung, 435. Murder of Dr. John, &c., at Carlisle, 455, 709. Complaints, and conference with Conestoga Indians at Lancaster, 457. John Chickasalary at Fort Augusta sends for C. Weiser, 458. Conference in Philadelphia, 463–469. Instructions to F. Post on journey to conference on Ohio, 469, 491. Hunting forbidden on their lands, 482, 484. Conference at Philadelphia, names, &c., 484–495, 497–500. Letter from N. Holland, Indian agent at Shamokin, 500. Expected, 583. Conference with Jo Peepy, and message to Governor, 586. With Teedyuscung, &c., at Philadelphia, 594, 598. With Nanticoke, 614–620. English prisoners given up by, 628, 629. Arrive at Easton, and visit Governor, 629. Conferences at Easton, 630–654. At Philadelphia, 654–661. Letter of Governor H. to Beaver and Shingas, 690. Conferences with Western, at Lancaster, 721–774. Presents to, 774. Letter, Governor H. to King Beaver, &c., 778. To Governors of Maryland and Virginia respecting, 779.

Trade with, ix., 21, 24, 25, 552, 568, 582, 642, 656, 658, 660, 706. Complain of Connecticut settlers, 27. Agents sent to Wyoming, &c., 29. Hostilities by Western, 30, 74. Murders by, on frontiers, 31. Murder of John Fincher, &c., near Sinking Spring, 43, 69. Murders in Northampton county, 58. Conferences at Philadelphia, 44, 66, 76, 85–88, 328, 604, 610, 736, 773. Conestoga, address from, asking protection, 88. Murder by whites—E. Shippen's letter, 89, 94, 400. Troops called for by General Gage, 90. On Province island, greatly exposed, 100. List of Conestogas murdered, 103–113. Sent for William Johnson — Under protection of Captain Robinson—Reply of Governor of New York, 113–122. Memorial of Pompunagh and others in barracks, 135. Memorial, Smith, Gibson, &c., on frontiers, 138. Declaration of frontier inhabitants, 142, 146. To be removed from barracks, 170. Reward offered for scalps, 189. Approval by Sir Wm. Johnson, 189. David Owen lives with, 190. Treaty of peace concluded

Indians—
with, by Colonel Bradstreet, 192–197. Terms obtained by Colonel Bouquet, 208, 209, 238. Speech of Onondago and Oneidas, 209. Of Colonel Bouquet, 210–234. Peace with tribes on Ohio—Journal of conferences with Geo. Croghan and, 249–264. Names of tribes met at Fort Pitt, 256. Proclamation of Governor Penn at, 264. Trade with, 265. Conference with Sir Wm. Johnson, 266. Treaty between Sir Wm. Johnson and, 277–280. Murder near Fort Cumberland, 304. Conference at Fort Pitt—Murders, 321–323. Proclamation respecting settlers on lands of, 328, 403, 407, 408. Conference with Nanticokes, Conoys, Mohickons, &c., at Philadelphia—Presents, 329–332. Murder of an Indian regarded as meritorious on frontiers, 350. Of Bucks county complained of, 385. Causes of ill-temper of, 408. Assembly on Paxton murders, 408–412. Sir Wm. Johnson on difficulties with, 412. Murder of, by Frederick Stump, 414–490. Delawares complain of settlers on their lands, 426, 448. Message from Assembly, 465. Condolence with, 466. Money raised to pacify, 467. Presents for, 468. List of persons belonging to Pennsylvania murdered by, 469. Names of Indians killed by F. Stump, 470. Letter from, at Great Island, 480. Proclamation against settlers on lands of, 481. Are found dead in Susquehanna, 487. Commissioners to attend treaty at Fort Pitt, 491, 492, 493, 506. Sir William Johnson holds a conference with the Six Nations, 496, 568. From Susquehanna connected with murders arrive at general congress, 506. Reverend Mr. Steele's report of proceedings, 507. Names of Indians at Red Stone, also of inhabitants, 508. Conference with, at Fort Pitt, 514–543. Messages of Governor Penn to, 517, 519. Murders of English by, 521, Speech of commissioners to, 530.

Indians—
Presents, 536. Messengers refuse to go to Red Stone, 543. Seneca George shot, 603. Present of condolence with, 604. Minutes of conference at Shamokin, 610–620. Conference with, at Big Island, 620. Arrive from Diahoga in distress, 648. Munceys hold conference at Philadelphia, their chief, Meetham, 689, 694. Conference at German Flats, 708. Complaints against Pennsylvania satisfied, 709. Three thousand pounds given to, 709. Killbuck and others bring letter from Netotway, a Delaware chief, and hold conference at Philadelphia, 736–742. Peace between Six Nations and Southern, 776. A Shawnee, robbed, asks aid, 777.

Conferences at Phila., x., 10, 12, 61, 255. Trade with, &c., 21. Keyashuta, a Seneca chief, in Philadelphia, receives a present, 55. Garrison at Fort Pitt, 74. Lands, proclamation against settlers on, 95. War with, feared, 193. A Delaware, Joseph Wipey, murdered — proclamation, 199. Death of Sir William Johnson, 200. The Shawnese separate from the Delawares—threaten war with Virginia, 201. Message of Gov'r Penn to Shawnese, recommending peace with Virginia, 203. And to Delawares, 205. Disturbances in Virginia, 208. Arrive, 238, 255. Claim of lands by Conestoga, 255, 256. Shawnee John, a disabled, presented with powder, 435. To distribute prisoners, 500. At Fort Pitt, 754.

Treaty at Easton, xi., 97. Various articles provided for, 108, 142. Ask for a flag in exchange for Wampum, 212. Country to be penetrated, 261. Depredations in Westmoreland — Gen'l Hand, 342, 347. In Bedford co., 382. Murders in Northumberland co., 403. Alarm from, in Cumberland —militia to defend inhabitants from, 410. Murders by, 489, 506. Ravages at Wyoming, 528. Attack party going from Fort Pitt to Fort Lawrence, &c., 699. Murders

Indians—
at Bushy run, 718. Jesse Thompson scalped by, 747. Depredations near Sunbury, 765.

Invade Northampton co., xii., 57. In Northumberland co.—surrender of Fort Freeland, 62. Incursions in Maryland, 72. Fears from, in consequence of General Sullivan's removal from Northumberland, 138. In Northumberland, 230. Lands, 265. Premium offered for scalps in Northumberland, co., 311. Invasions, 312. Heavy rewards offered for prisoners and scalps, 328. Murders in Berks co., 466. Delawares at Conshocking declare war ag'st Senecas, 586. Scalp, reward to Capt. S. Brady, for one, 632. In Northampton co., 717.

Expedition against, proposed, xiii., 132. Invasions of, feared, 169. Scalp paid for, 201. Alarm from, 248. In Northampton co., 337. Invade Berks county, 350. Consultation with General W., on expedition against, 356, 368, 369, 371, 373, 406. Invade Northumberland co., 417. Deeds to be applied for, of John Penn, 419. Deeds delivered to Mr. Osborne, 438. Returned, 462. Pay for services against, 535. Scalps paid for, 536. Report of E. Douglass' agency, 681. Letter from Delegates in Congress, on affairs of, 699.

Commissioners for treaty with, xiv., 40, 47. Place of meeting, 51. Commissioners to have deeds, 54. Instructions, 72. Number of troops necessary for Comm'rs, 142. Assembly on, 185. Articles to be procured for Comm'rs, 186. Copies of deeds made for use at Trenton, 240. Letter from Commissioners, 261. Purchase from the Six Nations, 271. Pay to sundry persons for losses sustained in Crawford's expedition against, 310. Isaac Wilson, a prisoner, with, 344. Message informing of treaty at Fort Stanwix, with, 366. Representation from two sachems of Six Nation tribes, 374. Present of two guns

Indians—
to, 379, 400. Murders by—present to, 471, 507, 515. Murders, 476. Petitions to trade with, 521. Genl. Clark's expedition, 558. Execution of an, for murder, ordered, 585. William McClay distributes goods to, at Wyoming 604. Report of Wm. McClay relating to the Six Nations of, 658, 663.

Provisions for Scotosh, a Wyandot chief, &c., xv., 54, 58, 60. Robbery of, near Tioga—restored by Council, 91. Choctaws and Chickasaws, with John Woods, interpreter, in Philad'a—receive presents, 229. Horse purchased for Cherokee chief, 232. Change in resolution of Council, respecting chiefs, 233. Expenses of Cherokee chief and Capt. Dromgoole, interpreter, paid, 238. Presents—new suit of clothes for interpreter, John Woods, 239. Expenses, 240. Detained at Lancaster by sickness of interpreter, 250. Expenses paid to S. Hodgdon, 277. Pay for services in watching their movements on frontiers, 310. Murders in Washington co., 317. Depredations on frontiers, 323. Militia ordered out, 323. John Woods in service of the department respecting, 366. Troops called for by Congress, against, 515. Pacific, near Pittsburg, 531. Commissioners to, on Erie triangle, 553, 554. Generals Butler and Gibson send list of goods for, 604. Committee to inquire into fund for purchase of lands on Lake Erie, from, 607. Report of Committee on, and purchase of goods—Col. Johnston appointed, 609. Indian blankets at Pittsburg, 617. Goods purchased for, 618.

Purchase of triangle on Lake Erie from—Grant of land to Cornplanter, xvi., 38. goods for, 63. On their way to New York, ask for money, 135. Receive it, 136, 144. Act of Congress providing for expenses of treaties with, 141, 142. Payments to Generals Butler and Gibson, 178. A spy upon

Indians—
the, paid, 227. Depredations in Washington county, 264. Defence of frontiers against, 297. In Washington county, 306. Cornplanter and other chiefs petition, 353. Letter from Council to, in reply, 357. Joseph Nicholson, their interpreter, 362. Detachment of Cumberland militia under Captain Samuel Holliday against, 363. Colonel McGilivray and chiefs of Creeks on their way to New York—Arrive in Philadelphia, 395. Two friendly Indians (Senecas?) murdered by whites on Pine Creek—Proclamation, &c., against murderers, 396, 397, 398. Correspondence of Council with, and others on the subject of the murder, 398. Letter from Council to Colonel McGilivray, 404. Trade with, Act of Congress, and treaties, 415. Supposed murderers of, arrested in Portland, 422. Pine Creek murders, 437. Visit of Cornplanter, 438. Address and wampum from, by Oliver Phelps, 439. Council pay Indians for murders, 440. Robert King, messenger, paid, 442. In Berks and Bucks, 462. Doyle arrested, 464. Reward paid for, 483. Cornplanter and others in Philadelphia—Speeches to and from, 497. Their expenses paid, 498. Conference between Cornplanter and Council on, respecting treaty at Fort Stanwix for lands on Erie, 501-509. Letter to Cornplanter from Council—Payment to interpreter, 511. Chief Great-Tree wounded in his leg, under treatment by Dr. Jones, 512. Cornplanter and Half-Town asks to remain till arrival of President of United States, 513. Defence against, in Bedford and Northampton counties, 515.

Indigo, purchased by State, xi., 537.

Industry, brig, Captain Barton, privateer, xi., 21.

Ingelo, Richard, Clerk of Council, i., 47.

Ingels, George, Inspector of lumber, xv., 322.

Ingersoll, Jared, sent to Connecticut, xi., 291. Assists Attorney General in proprietary claims, 737. Delegate to Congress, xii., 371.

Inglis, John, named commissioner to settle accounts of Duquesne, viii., 323.

Inland navigation, correspondence with Maryland and Delaware respecting, xiv., 585, 669, 672. Commissioners meet, xv., 134, 135.

Innes, Colonel James, letters to and from—Defeat of Washington, vi., 50, 141. Going to Wills Creek, 141. Builds fort at Wills Creek, 180. Indian murders, 461. Braddock's defeat, 478 - 499. Noticed, 602.

Inn-keepers, to report strangers, ii., 13.

Inomoy Creek, running into Lake Erie, v., 97.

Inscription on leaden plates sunk by French in Ohio river, v., 510.

Insolvent Debtors, observations on, iii., 376.

Inspectors for Counties—Law for choosing, v., 566.

Inspectors, law respecting, vi., 623, 624. Of elections, ix., 17, 296. Of flour, xiv., 444, 445, 487. Of lumber, &c., 488. Of staves and heading, 488. Of fish, 488. Of salt provisions, xii., 486. General, xv., 77.

Instructions, Wm. Penn to Governor Keith, iii., 63. To Governor Burnett of New York about supplies for defence, 119. To Messrs. Preston and Kinsey on going to Maryland, iv., 206. From Proprietary on bills of credit, 318. Additional, to Governor Thomas, 471. To Commissioners to Albany, 775-777. To Captain Ballet, of the Otter, v., 241. Captain Taylor to John Sibbald, 284. To Croghan and Montour, respecting presents to Indians, 518. To John Patten, 707. To Conrad Weiser, vi., 147. Proprietary, discussion as to submitting to Assembly, 220-223. Long message of Assembly on, 226-236. Governor's answer, 236-243. To

Scarroyady and Montour, 697. To Commissioners to Indians, 754. To James Young, vii., 162. To Governor Denny (additional), war against France, 269. Sir Wm. Johnson to George Croghan as Indian agent, 355, 435. To Captain George Armstrong, 525. To Thomas McKee to conduct Indians to Shamokin, 550. From Governor D. to F. Post, with message to Teedyuscung, viii., 138. Proprietary, 324. To F. Post, 469. To James Burd and Thomas McKee, agents to Wyoming, ix., 29. To Governor H., 60. Colonel Burd, 61. From Proprietaries to Governor Penn, 117. To Captain Schlosser respecting Conestoga Indians, 126. To Governor Penn, on settlers on western lands, 321. To Reverend John Steele and other commissioners to Indian land settlers, 483. Of Commissioners for messengers from Fort Pitt to Redstone, 540. To Arthur St. Clair respecting Dr. Conolly, x., 145. To Andrew Allen and J. Tilghman as Commissioners to Virginia, 174. To Henry Fisher, at the Capes, 337. To John Read, at Fort Island, as barrack master and clerk, 568. To William Richards, ships husband, 576. To Captain Read for government of Navy, 587. To Captain Wm. Brown to exchange prisoners on board the Liverpool, 590. To Commodore Davidson, 608. To Captain Henry Dougherty, 616. To Captain John Rice, xi., 8. To commissioners for settling accounts in Berks county, 146. For arrest of disaffected persons, 285. To recruiting Lieutenants, 419, 420. To Commissioners under Act of Attainder, 479. To agents under, respecting attainder of factors, 504. Of General on celebration, 523. To James Searle, agent for loans, xii., 416. To Commissioners for running line with Virginia, 704. To Surveyor General respecting lands, xiii., 596. To Captains Robinson and Shrawder, 678. Major James Moore, 698. To R. Elliott—An express to Wyoming, xiv., 636. To delegates in Congress on form of cession by Connec'ut, xv., 20. For Commissioners on inland navigation to be drafted, 60. To Colonel N. Dennison, 293. Valentine Eckhart, 295. To Comptroller General, xvi., 80–81. To Evans Owen for a road, 85. To Commissioners to view rivers, 181, 208, 337. For sale of barracks at Lancaster, 350.

Interest or forbearance, i., 223, 226. On money, act proposed, ii., 214.

Interpreters, i., 435.

Intestate Estates, proposed act, ii., 224. Difficulties about, referred, iii., 234. Laws proposed or passed, 373, 375, 376, 429. Act respecting, ix., 153, 155, 156, 161, 339.

Intrenching tools, x., 599.

Inundation, at Wyoming, xiv., 61.

Invalids, corps of—transfer of Lieutenants Honeyman, Pugh and Wood to, xi., 647. Regiment—persons placed on, xii., 57. General Irwin complains that persons capable to do duty are placed in, 58, 64, 65, 95. General Potter and Colonel Cunningham appointed to decide cases of claims of discharge, 628; xiv., 39, 666. Proposed, 666; xv., 10, 17, 39, 63, 86, 144, 204, 212, 303, 365, 377, 380, 386, 446, 474, 500, 509, 556, 613, 633, 637, 651, 654; xvi., 7, 17, 37, 68, 75, 213², 388, 408.

Iredale, Abraham, a British prisoner, exchanged for John Knowles, xi., 564.

Irish, Nathaniel, presents model of a boat—thanks for, x., 241.

Irish Servants, duty on, iii., 359.

Iron chest purchased for Receiver General, xiv., 168.

Iron hill, near New Castle, i., 115.

Iron and steel furnaces and forges in Pennsylvania, 1750, 632–636.

Iron, pig and bar, importation of, into England from colonies encouraged, v., 457. Erecting mills for slitting or rolling—tilt hammers—making steel prohibited—proclamation of Governor, 457.

Iron manufactured, 1749–1756, in

province—inquiry of British government on, 738, 740.
Iron Works, rum not to be sold in neighborhood of, iii., 247, 248. Governor's speech on, 263. At Mahanatawny, 305. Durham, 309. To be encouraged, 392; iv., 47. Coventry, 152, 247. Dr. Coxe's in Jersey, x., 575. Masters may employ soldiers, 636.
Ironcutter, John, servant of Frederick Stump, confined in gaol at Carlisle, ix., 441.
Irons, Simon, appointed Ranger of Kent county, i., 165.
Irvine, Doctor, returned as belonging to Pennsylvania, xii., 235.
Irvine, Colonel James, Brigadier General, xi., 6. Pay to, 697. Councillor, xiii., 394. Paid, 599.
Irvine, Brigadier General James, reelected vice president, xiv., 249. Resigns, 552.
Irvine, John, Ensign, x., 464. Captain, xii., 374.
Irvine, Samuel, Justice, xiv., 344.
Irvine, Colonel William, battalion surgeon appointed, x., 458. Letter on desertion, xii., 330. Vacancies, 374, 760. Letter on recruiting, 569. Commands at Fort Pitt, Brig. General, xiii., 79. Call for militia, 83. Letters on emigration and killing of Indians at Muskingum, 297. On Indian expeditions, 406. A prisoner—his account approved, 447. Accounts, 491, 500, 583. Letter on laying out land in Ohio, 617. Letter, 686. Censor, 726. Survey land for, 776. Censor, xiv., 160. Allows improvements on reserved tract, xiv., 373. Appointed land agent, 386. Explores donation lands, xv., 125. M. C., 159. M. C. pay to, 577.
Irvine, Captain, of company of Rangers, xii., 17. Promoted, 92. Allow to company of, 173. Appointed Brigadier General, xi., 278. Recruits, 738.
Irwin, Matthew, appointed Quarter-Master, xi., 305. To procure loan, 741. Agent for navy, xii., 19. Collecting salt, 123. Warden, xiii., 100. Recorder and master of rolls–dedimus potestatem to, xiv., 567. Master of Rolls—accounts, xv., 165, 166. Recorder—Justice C. C. P., 192. Bankrupt, 621, 622. Master of Rolls, xvi., 106. Recorder and Register, 113. Paid for enrolling laws, 228. Provincial Commissioner, ix., 237.
Irwin, William, recommended to Congress as Lieutenant-Colonel, 444. Of sixth battalion, 487. Recommending an Ensign, xii., 58. Brigadier General, 368. Justice, xiv., 322.
Irwine, Lieutenant-Colonel James, made Colonel, x., 767.
Israel, Israel, expenses of Indians, xv., 240. Innkeeper, 623.

J.

Jack, James, Coroner, ix., 286, 333, 398. Justice, xiv., 65, 361.
Jack, Matthew, Sheriff, xii., 541; xiii., 158, 419. Justice, xiv., 180.
Jack (a negro), kills Wm. Rakestraw—trial, &c., ii., 11. Trial, 18.
Jacobs, Captain, vii., 232.
Jacobs, Benjamin (son of the Speaker), Prothonotary, xi., 188, 197.
Jackson, Dr. David, Paymaster, xi., 27. Appointed Quarter-Master of militia, xii., 146, 458, 497. To pay depreciation, 705. Late Quarter-Master, xiii., 71. Memorial, 597. Paid, 598.
Jackson, David, delegate to Congress, xiv., 442, 549.
Jackson, Joseph, Sheriff, iv., 469, 500, 600.
Jackson, Samuel, Coroner, ix., 688.
Jackson, Samuel, to be seized, xi., 284.
Jagren. arrives in Philad., vi., 522,
Jamaica, Governor of, letter respecting Stanwix privateer, viii., 171, Proclamation, i., 592. Resolutions of Assembly and House of Commons on, vii., 738, 740.
James, Abel, a Warden, ix., 293. To be seized, xi., 283.
James, James, Justice for Chester county, iii., 282.
James, John, to be seized, xi., 283, 342.

James, Richard, Coroner, iv., 470, 500.
James, Thomas, Sheriff, v., 550, 597, 662.
James II., King proclaimed, i., 132.
Jameson, Captain, vii., 294.
Jameeson, D., and J. Eichelberger, letter respecting J. McCallister's conduct, xii., 27.
Jameeson, John, Lieutenant of Rangers, xii., 73.
Janney, Abel, Coroner, ix., 285.
Janney, Robert, Rector of Christ's Church, administers sacrament to Governor Denny, vii., 741.
Janney, Thomas, appointed special Commissioner to try a case in Bucks, i., 164.
Janvier, Thomas, Provincial armorer—order for arms for General Forbes, viii., 79. Refuses to deliver by order, 84.
Jaquies, Jos., authorized to fit out an armed whale boat called "Hell Cat" to capture enemy, xii., 393.
Jawert, John, petition—member of Frankford Company, ii., 431.
Jay, John, sends commissions for privateers, xi., 699. Appointed by Congress Secretary of foreign affairs, xiv., 356, 363. On duties in French ports, 403. Secretary of foreign affairs, letter respecting a claim in Germany, xvi., 48.
Jefferson, Governor Thomas, letter on line between Virginia and Pennsylvania, xii., 444.
Jeffs, Robert, complaint against T. Fairman for forcible entry, i., 199. Answer of Council, 199, 201, 202, 318, 320.
Jegler, Charles, sentenced—warrant of execution, vii., 342, 389. Respited, 398. His character at Lancaster, 398.
Jenkins, Fort, Colonel Lindemoth stationed at, xi., 654.
Jenkins, Colonel David, of Lancaster county militia, 1777, &c., xvi., 154.
Jenkins, George, second Lieutenant, x., 457. Captain, 503.
Jenkins, John, letter to, xv., 35. Passport to, 67. Arrives—is heard, 79.
Jenkins, Robert, of Salem, New Jersey, counterfeits, in England, bills of credit of several counties, iv., 429. Arrested, 422, 429.
Jenkins, Captain Thomas, captured, v., 282. Deposition, 283.
Jennings, Edmund, comes from Maryland with D. Dulany as agent of Governor Ogle, iv., 115. Correspondence with President, 117, 131, 146.
Jennings, Edward, Coroner of Kent county, iii., 260.
Jennings, John, Sheriff, viii., 780; ix., 57, 398, 548, 623; xi., 364. Letter from, and C. Stewart, 573. 585. Instructions to, 608.
Jennings, Dr. Michael, resigns as surgeon, xi., 124.
Jennings, Samuel, refuses to serve as a Justice, i., 370. Assistant to Governor, 505.
Jennings, Solomon, deputy Sheriff, iv., 154.
Jervis, Charles, to be seized, xi., 284.
Jewell, Captain John, appointed Surveyor and Searcher of Customs, i., 538.
Jewell, Robert, Coroner, x., 270. Keeper of State Prison, 696; xi., 566. Coroner, 593.
Jews in Philadelphia, ask countenance and protection in erecting a synagogue, xiii., 367.
Job, Andrew, Sheriff of Chester county, ii., 22.
Jocelyn, Capt. Thomas, arrives at Philadelphia with troops sent by General Shirley, vi., 774. Governor's instructions to, 775.
Joel, Captain, a deserter from New Jersey imprisoned, xii., 495. Released, 498. Paid for secret services, 552.
John, Doctor (Indian), murder of, &c. at Carlisle, viii., 455. Conference with relatives of, at Philadelphia, 709, 712.
Johns, Capt. Reese, x., 696.
Johnson, Derrick, executed for murder, i., 378, 382. Complaint of wife, 442.
Johnson, Fort, vii., 43. Indian proceedings at, 622, 625.
Johnson, Governor of Maryland, letter, 647.
Johnson, Colonel Guy, letter announcing sudden death of Sir

William and his filling the station for the present, x., 200.

Johnson, Colonel J. M., letter to, on Lydius procuring a fraudulent deed for lands, vi., 249. From, 268, 269.

Johnson, Dr. Robert, appointed Surgeon to Colonel William Irvine's battalion, x., 458.

Johnson, Samuel, unwilling to take the oath, is permitted to sell his real estate and depart, xi., 498.

Johnson, William Samuel, a Commissioner from Connecticut, arrives, x., 119.

Johnson, William, examination on forts, &c., vii., 341.

Johnson, Colonel William, report at Onondoga, v., 463, 607, 641, 775. Letter to Richard Peters on Connecticut claim, vi., 269. Letter from Governor M., 286. To Governor Phips, 607. R. Peters, 287–290. Proposed for command of expedition against Nova Scotia, 313. Conference with Indians, 468–475. Holds Council of war with Indians, 610. Letter of Governor M. to, on Indian affairs after Braddock's defeat, 700. Gone to New York, vii., 41. Letters to and from, 97, 116, 117, 127, 193, 226, 278, 351, 622, 623, 624, 626, 753. Blames Governor Morris for issuing declaration of war, 117. Negotiates with Indians, 143. Message and wampum from, 171. Appointed sole superintendent of Six Nations of Indians, 193. Has made arrangements—letter to General Abercrombie, 192. New Castle sent to, 222–226, 305.

Johnson, Sir William, appoints George Croghan Indian agent, with instructions, vii., 355, 434. Letters to and from, 434, 488. Report of George Croghan's proceedings at Harris' and Lancaster, 506–517. Proposed by Indians as a model, 540. Speech of Indians to, 622, 624. Proprietary instructions to treat with Delawares, 655. Teedyuscung's opinion of, 731. To General Abercrombie, viii., 97. Speech to Delaware Indians, 151. Success at Niagara, 400. Letters to and from, 570. Letters to and from, ix., 105, 111, 137, 189, 306, 412, 468, 495. On Paxton riots, 111. On removal of Indians from barracks, 137. Approves of rewards for scalps, 190. Deputies sent to, with terms obtained by Colonel Bouquet of Indians on Ohio, 239. Murder of a Mohawk Indian, 306. On Indian affairs on frontier, 412. Murder of Indians—draws for money, Mr. Croghan, 496. Conference with Six Nations, 496–506. Dismisses officers of Indian trade, 582. Conference with Indians, 708. And other Indians, x., 11, 216. Letters to and from, 21, 192. Affairs on frontier of Virginia, 192. Sudden death of, 201.

Johnston, Alexander, Justice, xii., 15. Declines, 104.

Johnston, Andrew, Coroner, xv., 102, 297, 579; xvi., 194.

Johnston, Francis, recommended to Congress as Lieutenant-Colonel, x., 442, 444. Appointed, 445; xi., 48. Complains of Jacob Weaver as a suspected person, 190, 270. Sick—resigns, 407, 424. Petition, 710. Receiver General, xii., 689. To receive Physic's books, &c., 719. Call on, for settlement, 746. List of books, &c., received, 755. Commissioner to Indians, xiv., 40, 54, 508, 515. Letter respecting horses purchased, 360. Receiver General, 444, 447, 509. Receiver General's instructions respecting Erie land valuation, xv., 601. With J. Trimble to prepare conveyances for Alleghany lots and islands, 609. To accept proposals of Turnbull and O'Hara, 649. Receiver General of land office, xvi., 80. Re-appointed, 350. Fees, 377. Letter, 410. Accounts, 420.

Johnston, Lieut.-Colonel James, xi., 115.

Johnston, James, Sheriff, xi., 366, 609; xii., 166; xiv., 442.

Johnston, John, Sheriff, xv., 301, 589, 592; xvi., 210.

Johnston, Major, barns and houses

burned—reward and proclamation for apprehending three persons, xii., 261.
Johnston, Lt. Richard, xiii., 121.
Johnston, Robert, physician and surgeon in hospital, United States –depreciation, xiii., 136. Collector of Excise, xvi., 385.
Johnston, Samuel, president of North Carolina convention—transmitting declaration of rights and proposed amendments to federal constitution, xv., 524.
Johnston, Thomas, Justice, xiii., 266.
Johnstone, William, Justice, xiv., 634.
Johnston, William F., Governor's message recommending publication of Colonial Records, iv., 1.
Jolly, Charles, Justice, ix., 393. A Justice of Philadelphia complained of by Assembly, x., 30, 31.
Jones, Lieutenant Colonel Blathwaite, chief engineer at Billingsport, xi., 125. Paid as engineer, discharged, 486. Engineer at Billingsport, xv., 24.
Jones, Cadwalader, Governor of New Providence, i., 242.
Jones, David, appointed Chaplain to battalion of Shee and Wayne, x., 551. Justice, xiv., 495.
Jones, Reverend David, commutation of Pay, xv., 143. Asks further allowance as chaplain, 299.
Jones, Colonel, late Captain, appointed at Philadelphia, v., 257.
Jones, Dr. Evan, charged with murder, in diverting himself with ceremony of making free mason in jest, iv., 277. Sheriff, v., 597, 662.
Jones, Evan, Coroner, vi., 144.
Jones, Gibbs, appointed Captain, Lieutenant, x., 480. Resigns, xii., 286.
Jones, Griffith, Complaint against, i., 78. Testifies against J. Edmonson, 114. Council, 213. Member of Council, 452. Elected Mayor of Philadelphia, ii., 162. Qualified, 163.
Jones lane, or Lancaster road, commissioners to view—To be repaired with funds by lottery, xv., 449. Report on, 494.
Jones, John, Health officer, xii., 554; xiv., 375. Accounts, 467. Health officer, xv., 3, 321, 323. Justice, 323. Health officer, complaint against, xvi., 134, 142, 147, 151, 168, 170, 171, 172. He is displaced, 173. A Justice, ii., 159.
Jones, Captain, x., 436. Made Major, 76, 78, 697.
Jones, Joseph, trial of, ii., 396.
Jones, Sergeant Jonathan, Funeral expenses paid, xi., 106.
Jones, Owen, Jr., to be seized, xi., 284, 292. Pass, xiii., 571.
Jones, Robert, a justice, iii., 28.
Jones, R. Stuttle, Secretary of committee, x., 440.
Jones, Samuel, a justice, iii., 358; xiv., 307. Deputy surveyor, lays a plan of depreciation lands, xv., 18.
Jones, Thomas, &c., case of, stated, xii., 438.
Jonquiere, Mons. La, makes a speech to Indians, v., 528. French claims on this continent, 529. Letter to Governor Hamilton, 540. Letter to Governor Clinton, 554.
Jorachgnison, a Cayuga Indian, memorandum of news by him, viii., 118.
Jordan, Jesse, deputy wagon-master, sends a train to Egg Harbor for goods, improperly, xi., 672. To attend Council, 674. His examination, 680.
Jordan, John, wagon master, xi., 380. Justice, xiv., 164, 307.
Jordan, Thomas, pay master, xi., 618; xii., 83.
Josephson, Manuel, asks loan of lottery wheel for Hebrew congregation, xvi., 489.
Josiah, Captain James, resigns command to enter Continental service, x., 426. Sails for China, under sea letter from Supreme Executive Council, xvi., 224[2].
Jounkin, Henry, confiscated estate sold, xii., 189.
Journal of Conrad Weiser to Shamokin, iv., 640, 680. To Onondago, 660–669, 778. To Ohio, v., 348–

358. To Onondago, 470, 528. Of George Croghan at Ohio, 528. To Auckwick, vi., 150–160. Of New Castle, &c., to Indians on Susquehanna, vii., 137. Of Fred. Post to Wyoming, viii., 142. Of George Croghan and conference with Indians, ix., 249–264.

Joy, Daniel, on committee to survey Jersey shore, x., 474.

Judges, may be appointed by Governor during his life, i., 107, 121. Five to be appointed, 98, 108. Appointed, 119, 324. Their commission, 121, 190. Hire of a boat, 157. Continued, 199. One from lower counties, 204. Decree of, disobeyed, 218. Of P. Court — Commission postponed rather than the court, 226, 320. Appointed, 324, 331, 343. Two commissions to be drawn for, 344. Provincial, ii., 87. Required to take oaths, 89. Commission for, 123. Appointed, 239. Commissioned, iii., 254, 256, 257, 269; viii., 77. Of Courts of Common Pleas—Prothonotaries to be, xi., 221. Of Supreme Court, 254, 270 Oaths by dedimus, 271. Of Admiralty Court, appointed, 713. Of Errors and Appeals, xiv., 66. Of Supreme Court, 42, 43, 71, 117, 141, 175. Letter to, on Longschamp's case, 117.

Judicature, law of 1727, establishing courts of, repealed, iii., 418.

July 4, 1763, ix., 65. To be celebrated, how and why, xi., 522.

Juniata, mouth of, objected to as a settlement for Indians, vi., 218. Suffers, 674. John Harris builds at, iii., 503. Fort at, viii., 224. Frankstown branch road to Loyalhanna, xv., 346, 353–355.

Juniata river, commissioners to view, xvi., 178, 260, 319.

"Jupiter," privateer, x., 715.

Jurisdiction, of a county, does not extend into the river, x., 232.,

Justice, chief, of Supreme Court appointed, xi., 186, 195, 202, 254.

Justices, appointed, i., 120, 122, 127, 129, 152, 182, 211, 320, 343, 369, 375, 380, 544. Fines of, 134. A, accused of treason, 158. Refuse to serve, 370, 371, 382. Refuse to hold Court, 450. To lay out roads, 572. How considered by charter, ii., 67. Of County Court of Philadelphia commissioned, 159. Of county have concurrent power with those of city, 162. Complaint against, 180. Can they lawfully hold an inquest in absence of Coroner, 184? Appointed from Church of England, decline serving on account of oaths, opinion of Attorney General asked, 531, 546. For Bucks and Chester commissioned, 596, 597. Commission, iii., 28–50, 254, 256, 350, 491, 531. Of Lancaster county, letter to, on Maryland affairs, iv., 65. Appointed, iv., 141, 209, 312, 348, 482, 762. Of peace appointed, v., 106, 378, 387, 403, 436, 547, 572, 600. Appointed, vi., 136; vii., 417, 433, 437, 637, 769. Elected, viii., 18, 562, 573, 575. Commissioned, ix., 172, 201, 203, 205, 235, 237, 245, 266, 281, 308, 340, 374, 386, 393, 470, 601, 626, 645, 663, 672, 680, 730, 731, 732, 742, 746, 750. Death of two, 340. Commissioned, x., 8, 14, 27, 31, 41, 45, 46, 47, 81, 88, 155, 162, 173, 217, 263, 264. Chief of Supreme Court, x., 53, 108, 173, 213. Of peace, xi., 194, 195, 198, 211, 218, 220, 228, 229, 248, 251, 265, 274, 282, 300, 301, 302, 398, 405, 443, 553, 471–524, 527, 529, 541, 572, 599, 616, 619, 620, 621, 644, 666, 690, 708, 716, 741, 759, 779, 781. Appointed, xii., 3, 8, 15, 19, 46, 105, 112, 150, 170, 171, 198, 231, 285, 293, 336, 342, 353, 374, 378, 391, 393, 437, 455, 456, 459, 482, 486, 489, 490, 519, 524, 526, 556, 557, 595, 615, 635, 667, 752. To preside in Courts, 546; xiii., 7, 21, 38, 42, 98, 101, 118, 122, 140, 208, 219, 244, 263, 264, 266, 284, 290, 316, 367, 389, 400, 446, 517, 521, 542, 625, 633, 647, 666, 677, 683, 698, 700, 732, 748, 761, 765; xiv., 11, 24, 31, 45, 47, 54, 60, 65, 108, 116, 117, 118. 121, 134, 135, 138, 139, 147, 149, 151, 153, 158, 159, 162, 164, 167, 174, 175, 180, 196, 197, 198, 200, 201, 203, 205, 208, 211, 212, 216, 224, 226, 228, 229,

234, 237, 240, 255, 259, 260, 276, 280, 282, 289, 291, 307, 313, 321, 322, 344, 348, 357, 362, 368, 370, 373, 396, 442, 449, 454, 465, 477, 479, 485, 487, 495, 500, 504, 509, 517, 549, 563, 567, 584, 602, 605, 617, 627, 629, 635, 640, 653, 656, 657, 668, 670, 672; xv., 4, 8, 14, 17, 23, 24, 27, 30, 32, 35, 38, 39, 41, 51, 59, 60, 62, 65, 90, 92, 96, 104, 108, 124, 131, 139, 143, 149, 154, 160, 164, 171, 173, 182, 188, 192, 199, 202, 227, 233, 266, 269, 270, 271, 294, 302, 307, 323, 330, 347, 359, 369, 370, 376, 398, 405, 419, 420, 424, 437, 450, 462, 463, 475, 479, 480, 483, 497, 520, 522, 523, 526, 537, 545, 547, 551, 559, 570, 577, 579, 583, 589, 604, 605, 606, 619, 642, 647; xvi., 1, 4, 13, 14, 16, 20, 30, 37, 48, 49, 53, 80, 88, 94, 99, 126, 138, 154, 174, 190, 209, 217, 217^2, 218^2, 219^4, 226, 237, 239, 242, 253, 255, 259, 286, 301, 309, 319, 325, 341, 353, 377, 387. 395, 403, 407, 411, 423, 423, 428, 433, 446, 448, 450, 479, 536, 537, 539.

K.

Kachlein, Peter, sheriff, ix., 199, 285, 333, 688, 778; x., 56. Deposition, respecting Wyoming, 710. Militia to be called out, and premium for scalps in Northumberland county, xii., 312. Resigns as Lieutenant, 317.

Kagundanoyagh, chief of Onondagoe Indians arrives in Philadelphia, ii., 159.

Kakow-watchy, chief of Shawnese Indians, iii., 309. His son Quassenungh attacked with small-pox at Philadelphia and recovers, 463.

Kammerer, Henry, stationer, xv., 322, 648; xvi., 147, 464.

Kanuksusy, son of old, Allaguipas, vi., 589.

Kapp, Michael, Coroner, xv., 296.

Kargher, Ludwig, memorial, x., 638.

Karnaughan, John, justice of Chester, county, iii., 412. Left out, 533.

Karrod, Levi, justice, xiii., 264.

Katarioniecha, husband of Montour's daughter, iii., 501.

Kean, John, justice, xv., 41.

Keane, Patrick, Lieutenant of the Roman Catholic regiment of volunteers in British service to be watched, xii., 177.

Kearsley, Dr. David, x., 359.

Kearsley, Dr. John, x., writes sundry inflammatory papers, 358, 361. He is to be taken into custody, 361. His friends to be admitted, 371. Letter from Robert Shewell to, 372. Sent to York county, allowed a servant, &c., 373. Asks for a clerk, granted, 374. His oath, 374. Stephen Bayard, clerk, 374. Ordered to Yorktown jail, 378. Departs under escort for Lancaster, 380. Order for expenses. 381. Safe at Lancaster, and to be sent forward to York county, 385. Pay to guards of, 403, 408. Removed to Carlisle, 773.

Kearsley, Paul, x., 359.

Keating, Maurice, and others engaged in piracy, evidence from Jamaica to be published, xiv., 268.

Keble, Abraham, a justice, x., 8.

Keechline, Colonel Andrew, xi., 21, 36. Commissioned to buy provisions, 424, 506.

Keehmle, John, for medicines 1776, xv, 207.

Keekyuscung, (Indian) sent on message to Ohio, viii., 147.

Keely, Mathias, firelocks, x,, 501.

Keen, Reynold, act for relief of, xi., 630. His estate forfeited, xii., 23. Petition respecting, 26, 27, 80, 103.

Keene, Lawrence, appointed prothonotary of Northumberland county, xiii., 697. Justice, xiv., 11. To inquire into election in Penn township, 447. Prothonotary of Court of Common Pleas dies, xvi., 119.

Keesar, Sick, a Chinese, and thirty-five others arrive, xiv., 561. Letter to Assembly respecting, 569. Their wants to be supplied, 574, 616. Pay for, 659. Provisions for, xv., 28, 36, 52, 61, 78, 83, 84, 93, 99. To be sent to

Maryland, 75, 107, 160, 178, 386.
Keilin, John, Coroner, v., 597.
Keith, George, complains against Thomas Lloyd, i., 378.
Keith, Governor William, supersedes Governor Gookin, i., 631. Arrives as Governor, and is proclaimed at the Court-house, iii., 13. Oath administered under a dedimus by several persons, 13. Visits New Castle, 14. Lays before Council Governor Gookin's accusations, 15. At a subsequent meeting calls on Governor Gookin to substantiate them, who says he has none to make, 17. Goes to Conestoga--Proposes addition from Lower Counties, 17, 18. Proposes Colonel French, who is admitted, 18. Nominates Justices and Judges, 18. Attends a Council of Indians at Conestoga, 19. Expenses of journey to do., 25. Goes to Sussex, 25. His speeches, 25, 27. Goes to New York with Governor Spotswood, 30. Provision for his possible death, 30. His arguments against pardoning two murderers of Chester county, under sentence of death, 41. Speech about Teach and other pirates, 54. Announces to Assembly the death of William Penn, and pronounces an eulogium on, recommends a proclamation, &c., 58. Meets and comes to an amicable conclusion with Governor Hart of Maryland, 60. Style of commissions, 62. Continues the government after William Penn's death, 62. His speech to Assembly on supplies, 63. Instructions from William Penn, (Jr.,) 63. New commission, &c., laid before Council, 64. Speech to Assembly, 65. Sees probate of William Penn's will—Asks their advice, 66. Assembly's address to, 66. And advice to delay publication of commission, 67. Council give same advice, 68. Goes to New York to meet Governor Hunter before his sailing for England, 68. Speech to Assembly, and answer, 70. Speech to Council—Charges against Robert Assheton, 71, 77. Letter, Ch. Delafaye, to, approving his course, and allusion to agreement between Penn and Queen Anne for province, 73. Report of Lords Justices, 73. Opinion of Council on it, 74. Sends proposals of Commissioners on Indian affairs to Governors of Virginia and Maryland, 82. Writes letter to Governor of New York on Indian affairs, 99–102. Proposes a Court of Chancery or Equity, 105. Suggests examination of vessels from sickly ports, 113. Visits Virginia, 112, 113. And Maryland, 114. Returns, 115. Memorial to Governor of Virginia, 116. His answer, 117. Describes geographical position of Indians, 114–116. Visits with members of Council the Five Nations at Conestoga, 119. Returns and leaves James Logan, 130, 134. Opinion on law respecting Free Society of Traders, 138. Speech to Assembly, 141. His mill, 158. Visits Chester county on account of threatenings to Indians from Maryland, 160. Orders a survey of land on Susquehanna, 160. Lays before Board agreement between Maryland and Pennsylvania as to surveys on Susquehanna, 161. Message to Assembly respecting Conestoga Indians and the Cartledges, 167. Calls Robert and William Assheton to Council, 173. Vote of thanks and £500 to, 174. Road to Horsham returned and confirmed, 177. Orders survey of land on Susquehanna to Octorara for Indians, also a wagon load of provisions, 177. Writes to Governor of Maryland, 180. Refers to consent of Indians to William Penn's purchase of lands on Susquehanna, 181. His speech to, 181. Conference with, at Conestoga, 181–185. Warrant to survey Springetsbury Manor, 184. His settlement of Newbury, 185. His course approved by Colonel French, 186. Want of funds for expenses of government, 187. Letter to, and answer from, J. Mitchell on Council at Conoy town, 188. Letter to Ganawese king,

188. Purposes going to Albany, 190, 192. Speech to Indian messenger, 191. Speech to Five Nations at Albany, 197. Has Indians at his chamber—Surrender of land near Conestogoe by them, 201. His speech to Indians, 202. The papers to be published, 202. Going to Conestogoe with Governor Spotswood of Virginia to hold treaty with Indians, 202. Council object till they know Governor Spotswood's object, 202. Returns to Philadelphia, 203. Letter to Governor Burnet for leave to treat at Albany, 203. Minute of New York, agreeing to it—Governor Keith's speech, 204. Letter, Governor of Virginia to, 205. Answer to, 207. Consults Council about Maryland, 214. Letter to Lord Baltimore, 225. Letter to Governor of Maryland, with agreement of Lord Baltimore, 232. Receives and withholds instructions from William Penn's trustees, 237. Warrant to Sheriff for wrecked goods, 238. Produces a paper as a charge against J. Logan, who makes his defence, 243, 245. Attends Council for last time, 250. Governor Gordon succeeds him, 251. Member of Assembly from Philadelphia—Excused—Going to England, 298. Witnesses deed from Indians, 321. Petition of Palatines to, 322. (Former Governor,) submits instructions to Assembly, vi., 220, 235. Proceedings of Council in his time, 722. Allusion by Council to a bill passed in his time, viii., 359.

Keithian meeting-house and Christ church, petition respecting, iii., 394.

Kelcher, Anthony, Sheriff, xiv., 557; xv., 101, 296.

Keller, Joseph, affidavit of, Indians taking off his wife, &c., vii., 735.

Keller, Rudolph, Sheriff, xvi., 195.

Kelly, John, Justice, xiv., 509.

Kelly, William, pilot, deposition of, v., 113. Sheriff, xi., 222, 240, 606. Justice, xiii., 633.

Kelpius, Johannes, member of Frankford Company, petition, ii., 431.

Kembel, William, (see Hembell.)

Kendal, Benjamin, deposition respecting Conestogo Indians, ix., 127.

Kennedy, Daniel, Adjutant of 6th Pennsylvania regiment, prisoner on parole and in distress, relieved with clothing, xii., 249. Pay, xvi., 216[2], 243. Fees received, 380.

Kennedy, David, Justice, xi., 599. Petition respecting tract of land and wood, xii., 252. Secretary of Land Office, 689; xiv., 444; xvi., 82, 350. To apply to John Penn for deeds and papers, xiii., 418. Also to B. Chew and Joseph Turner, 435. Returned to him by H. Osburne, 462–471. Respecting a mistake, xvi., 149. Escheated estate, 174. Re-appointed Secretary, 350.

Kennedy, Dr. Samuel, appointed Surgeon of 4th battalion, x., 484.

Kennedy, William, estate of, xiv., 36. Estate paid for apprehending Moses Doan, 47.

Kent County—Sheriffs of, i., 58, 186. Seal for, ordered—its device, 66. Danger of revolt—Vessels not clearing at New Castle, 101. Members sent for, 103. Misdemeanors in, 103. Sub-Treasurer appointed, 111. Sheriff of, 127, 149. William Frampton, a Councillor, 127. John Curtis, a Justice, accused of high treason, 158, 161. Appointed, 159. Attorney General to prosecute John Curtis, 163, 196. Ranger appointed, 165. Clerk resigns, 170. Coroner, 187, 340. Justice appointed, 211, 286. W. Markham, member of Council, 212, 213. Ranger complained of, 226. Execution in, 252. Justices, 320, 339. Complaint against Court, 321. Man imprisoned for beating his wife, 337. John Barnes to be arrested, 439. Difficulty about holding a Court, 450, 452, 453. Amount of one penny tax, 462. Court-house, 510. Canterbury township formed, 556. R. Wilson, member of Assembly, dies, ii., 26. Dedimus to William Annand, 97. And William Rodeney, 97.

Names proposed for magistrates, iii., 15. William Rodeney, Sheriff, and Edward Jennings, Coroner, 260. M. Freeman, Sheriff, 332. Samuel Berry, Coroner, 332, 370. 575, William Rodney, Sheriff, 370, 575. Letters respecting dispute with Maryland, 474. B. Gordon and B. Shurmer, Judges, iv., 253. Thomas Skidmore, Sheriff, and Samuel Berry, Coroner, 289. Sheriffs, 416, 465, 524, 615. Coroners, 416, 465, 524, 615. Letter Governor to Justices, 490. Answer, 494. Sheriffs elected, 470, 500, 602, 748, 782. Coroners elected, 470, 500, 602, 748, 782. Sheriffs elected, v., 55, 411, 468, 551, 597, 662. Coroners elected, 55, 411, 468, 551, 597, 662. Officers elected by Associators, 248, 325. Justices dead—others appointed, vi., 136. Execution of J. Duffy, 136. Sheriffs elected, 145, 638. Coroners elected, 145, 638. Sheriffs elected, vii., 267. Coroners elected, 268. Coroners appointed, viii., 223, 403, 506, 781. Sheriffs appointed, 223, 403, 506, 781. Act for relief of poor, ix., 3, 4. Sheriffs elected, 57, 199, 286, 337, 398, 548, 624, 688, 778. Coroners elected, 57, 199, 286, 333, 398, 548, 624, 688, 778. Trustees of Loan Office for, 205. Justices, 266, 338. Execution, 600. Draining and embanking Pearman's Branch, 313, 400. Conviction in, 384, 601. Justices, 645. Special Court for trying negroes in, 655. Embanking, &c., 698. Justices appointed, x., 9, 217. Sheriffs elected, 56, 101, 211, 270. Coroners elected, 56, 101, 211, 270. Respecting Duck Creek Church, trustees to sell lands, &c., 80, 85.

Kentzing, Abraham, to hold possession of Hog island for the State, xii., 591.

Keppel, Commodore A., French supplied with provisions from Colonies, vi., 323.

Ker, Samuel, discharged, x., 772.

Kerlin, William, innkeeper, complaint against, xii., 536. License restored, 548.

Kermanvor, Monsieur, engineer at Billingsport, x., 631.

Kern, Jacob, Coroner, viii., 506.

Kern, Captain, account of Indian murders, ix., 43.

Kerr, John, appointed to collect clothing in Bucks county, xi., 411.

Kesselman, Frederick, traitor, xi., 767. Proclamation against, 768.

Keyashuta, a Seneca chief, in Philadelphia, present to, x., 55.

Keyser, Andrew, case of, xii., 261.

Kidd, Alexander, traitor, arrested, xii., 479, 481, 526, 551.

Kidd, John, Justice, ix., 393.

Kidd, Captain, privateer, visits Lewistown and sells goods to inhabitants, i., 579. The pirate, at Lewes, ii., 121.

Killbuck, bearer of letter from Delaware chief arrives in Philadelphia and holds conference with President Hamilton, ix., 736. His speech, 737. In Philadelphia, x., 10.

Kichline, Colonel, death of, xiii., 82.

Killburn, Joseph, paid for leaden spouts, xvi., 491.

Killer, Colonel, to rendezvous at Swedesford, xi., 301.

Kilner, James, complaint against and trial as master for abuses on board, i., 79, 80. A curious case.

Kimmel, Adam, xi., 381, 382, 385, 388.

Kimmel, Captain, applies for reward for arresting Thomas Taylor, a highwayman, xii., 275, 276.

Kindassowa, a chief of the Minnisink Indians, iii., 326.

King, Charles II., address to, proposed in building forts, i., 109. Petition to, 116.

King of England, address of Governor T. and Council to, v., 51.

King George, (Elector of Hanover,) proclaimed, ii., 575.

King, John, a convicted mariner applies for a pardon—Sustained by Judges—granted, v., 344.

King, Thomas, an Oneida Indian, dies in South Carolina, ix., 775. Quantity of wampum exhibited given by, 776.

King, Walter, his road, i., 387.
King William III., death of, ii., 70.
King, William, Coroner, xiii., 403, 506.
King's highway, i., 587.
Kingsley, N., Justice of Luzerne county, resigns, xvi., 269.
Kinkead, James, Coroner, x., 106, 212.
Kinsey, Abm. tenant of Hog Island, x., 607.
Kinney, Abraham, Ensign, xii., 3.
Kinsey, John, sent to Maryland, iv., 203. Instructions to, 206. Returns from Maryland and reports, 209. Speaker, 353, 470, 618, 669, 749. Appointed Chief Justice in place of Langhorne, 640. Commissioner to Albany 771. Speaker of Assembly, v., 4, 55, 123. Commissioner to Albany —Report, 26. Approbation of laws by Lords Justices, found among the papers of Assembly—Governor to Council, vi., 356.
Kirk, Ensign John, resigns, x., 673.
Kirk, Samuel, to be Sergeant at arms, v., 617. Appointed Sergeant at Arms of Assembly, vii., 313.
Kirkbride, Colonel Joseph, x., 711. Lieutenant of Bucks, xi., 206, 208, 217, 266, 275, 277, 396.
Kirkbride, Joseph, Jr., commissioner for building new court house and prison for Bucks county, iii., 241. Ferry, 363.
Kirkbride, Mahlon, provincial commissioner, ix., 237.
Kirkbridge, Colonel, to view fords above the Falls of Delaware, x., 783.
Kirkland, Colonel, escapes, x., 661. Order for arrest, 665, 694.
Kishycoquilla, a Shawnese chief, death of, vi., 154. Governor's letter to sons of, 421.
Kitchen, Stephen, pardoned, xi., 609.
Kittanning burned, vii., 294.
Kittanning, a town to be laid out in proprietary manor at, x., 201. Distances from Canoe place to, xv., 91.
Kitts, George, provisions, x., 651.
Kitzmiller, Jacob and Martin, correspondence and depositions respecting murder of D. Digges, v., 582--597.
Klotz, Colonel, xi., 89. Of Lancaster county—Case of Dr. B. Wilson referred to, xii., 101.
Knapsacks, ordered, x., 628, 636.
Kneeghnyaskoate (Indian Harry's brother), returns with presents from Onondagoes, ii., 204.
Knight, John, Coroner, x., 78, 100, 212.
Knight, Thomas, pardoned for horse stealing so far as relates to cutting off his ears, xiv., 243.
Knous, George, Coroner, xiv., 248.
Knowles, privateer schooner, Capt. Turner, captures Spanish vessels, viii., 225.
Knowles, Admiral Charles, letters from and to, v., 127, 133, 141, 207. For man-of-war, 207. Takes Port Louis—carries cannon to Jamaica, 228. Loan of some of them to be requested, 228. Inquiry on his account respecting impressment of seamen—Council's decision, 326,
Knowles, John, made prisoner—asks to be exchanged, xi., 564. Exchanged, 565. Resigns as Justice, xiv., 640.
Knox, Captain, x., 709.
Knox, Ensign George, xi., 620.
Knox, General Henry, letter on union of companies with Proctor's regiment, vi., 245. Wagons for General W., xii., 398. Secretary at War—letters to and from, xiv., 517, 560. For expenses Indians, xv., 240. Letter, 435.
Knox, John, sweeping river—reports articles found, xii., 2, 21. Called on to report, 33. Tonnage officer, xiv., 10.
Knox, Colonel Robert, xi., 556. To ask State shallop, 576, 592. Assembly, xii., 131.
Kollock, Jacob, letter from Governor to, respecting pilots not licensed, iv., 394. Chosen Speaker of Assembly of lower county, ix., 2, 71, 201. Resigns—son succeeds, 699.
Kollock, Jacob, Jr., Sheriff, v., 662; vi., 638.
Kollock, Philips, appointed to several offices in Sussex, ix., 699.

Captain of British vessel in Delaware, xiii., 145.
Kollock, Simon, Sheriff, iii., 387, 416, 465, 524.
Kreamer, Philip, Coroner, xi., 444. Sheriff, xiii., 88, 394, 617, 720; xvi., 491.
Krug, Jacob, receipts for taxes, 1787, 1788, xvi., 83.
Kucher, Christopher, xvi., 196. Letter, xii., 392.
Kuhn, Adam Simon, a Justice, v., 600. Appointed a Justice of Lancaster county, viii., 562. Estate of, at Lancaster confirmed, x., 32, 42.
Kuhn, Dr. Adam, recommends a surgeon, x., 458. Physician and Director General of hospital—plan, 636. M. D. to be seized, xi., 284. Arrives from St. Croix—is arrested and imprisoned, xii., 501. Vessel to be examined at his expense, 502. To depart for St. Croix with his family and give security not to return during the war, 504. To sail for St. Croix, not to return—memorial in his favor, 516, 517. Petition from his brothers for his return—granted, 650.
Kuhn, Dr. Frederick, xvi., 194.
Kuhn, Ludwig, insults Captain Heysham, xii., 160. Committed to gaol, 161.
Kuskuski on Beaver creek, viii., 265. Delawares propose moving to, 305, 393.

L.

Lacey, John, recommended as Captain, x., 447. Justice, xi., 372.
Lacey, General, to command militia between Schuylkill and Delaware, xi., 396. Appointed Brigadier General, 398. Troops for, 447. Sends suspected persons to prison, 472. (General,) on state of militia, 522. Commands on Susquehanna, 533. To grant furloughs, xiii., 74. Pay to, 252. Commissioner to Wyoming, xvi., 22. Berks county militia under General Lacey in Bucks county, 457.
Lacey, John, Jr., agent for estates, xi., 556. Councillor, xii., 136, 150. Account, 302. Examines Schuylkill bridge, 374. Pay, 420, 542, 600, 712. Account, &c., 682. Pay to, xiii., 52, 151, 358.
Lacey, General John, Jr., in command, 1777, 1778—Medicines furnished, xiv., 655.
Lack, Captain Jacob, company, x., 682.
Lackawaxen, exploration of, xv., 65.
Ladders and leather buckets in Philadelphia, i., 478.
Lahneman, Philip Thomas, Secretary of Governor, i., 47.
Laird, Hugh, Justice, xiv., 512. Resigns as Justice, xv., 212.
Laird, Mathew, deposition, Braddock's defeat, vi., 482.
Laird, Samuel, Coroner, ix., 779; x., 56, 101. Justice, xi., 691.
Lajonquiere, Governor of Canada, answer to Governor Clinton's letter to, v., 554.
Lake George, battle, &c., at, vi., 623. Defeat of French at, 637.
Lake, St. Sacrament, (see Lake George.)
Lambert, Chevalier De, recommended by Fayette, appointed Second Lieutenant, xiii., 479.
Lancaster County, formed from Chester county—Bounds, iii., 355, 358. Justices, Sheriff and Coroner appointed, 359, 370. Germans of, ask to be naturalized, 374. Loan, by province to build prison and court house, 379. Site of, and also for a town fixed on—Discussion as to title of the land, 381. Losses from Mingo Indians, 382. No roads laid out to Philadelphia, 394. To be, 395. Sheriffs, 416, 465, 520, 615. Coroners, 416, 465, 520, 615. Charged with riots in Maryland, 468. High road laid out and confirmed, and to be continued to Schuylkill ferry at Philadelphia, 521–524. Justices, 531. Wm. Rumsey of Maryland sent to, on trial, 593. High Sheriff attacked by persons from Maryland—Deposition of under Sheriff, 612. Petition for road from Susquehanna to—Commissioners to lay out, 618. Road to Schuylkill, 618.

Justices written to preserve order of settlers over Susquehanna, iv., 58. Complaints from Maryland against, 62, 63. Letter of President Logan to Justices relative to affairs with Maryland, 69, 71. Proclamation against men from Maryland, 73. Certificate from, 75. Sheriffs appointed, 86, 247, 309, 352, 470, 602, 669, 748, 782. Coroners elected, 86, 247, 309, 352, 470, 602, 669, 748, 782. And Maryland affairs, 101–151. Sheriff authorized to call out a force to protect the settlers, 151. And Justices to take depositions, 151. Justices needed, 152. Road to Coventry Iron Works, 152, 247, 266. Messrs. Lawrence and Ashton, members of Council, go to, to act with Justices, &c., in restoring peace, 153. Rewards offered by Maryland for magistrate of Lancaster county, 155, 165. Jail broken into by Marylanders, 251. Cases of Daniel Low and Rudolph Mohr, 255. Joseph Evans, a sufferer by Maryland and by fire, permitted to ask Charity, 259. Petition from, respecting road to Coventry Iron Works, 266. Roads, 278 282, 284, 365, 495. Outrages by Indians in, 280. Justices appointed, 312, 482. Praying for boundaries of a new county, 317. Map of Pennsylvania, 317. New county, petition, 335. Road from, to Philadelphia, 495. Return of, 503. Alarm from Indians, 656. Indian treaty at, 697–737. New county between, and Philadelphia proposed, 756. J. Hendricks' deposition, 655.

Circular letter of Governor to Captains of militia of, v., 2. Justices appointed, 3, 6. Petition for arms, &c., 26. Sheriffs elected, 55, 120, 411, 464, 551, 597, 662. Coroners elected, 55, 120, 411, 464, 551, 597, 662. Officers commissioned, 210, 247, 325. Commissioners to Lancaster, 306–319. Treaty at, signed, 316, 322. Expenses of treaty at, 327. Justices appointed, 378. Workhouse and house of correction, 506, 512. A Nanticoke Indian imprisoned for abusing a white girl, 543. Justices appointed for, 600. Robbery and pardon, 601. Law for erecting county out of, confirmed, 619. Act respecting inspectors, 619. Descriptive deed for lands executed by Indians at, 634.

Petitions for defence from Donegal, vi., 131. Pextang, Derry and Hanover, 132. Sheriffs elected, 144, 638, Coroners appointed, 144, 638. Inspectors, law for choosing, 623, 624. Danger from Indians, 670. Commissions to military officers in, 755.

Conference with Indians at, vii., 7. Large bodies from back counties to meet there and compel Assembly to pass certain laws, 87. Messrs. Chew, Stedman, West, Shippen, sent to meet the conspirators at, 93. They return and report. 96. Sheriffs elected, 266. Coroners elected, 266. Associated military companies formed, 294. New justices, 391. Mr. Handshue, Lutheran minister —Favorable character of C. Jegler, 398. Treaty at, 462, 485, 504–506–551. guard for Indians to Philadelphia, 549. Consultation on speech to Indians at, 517.

Justices commissioned, viii., 18, 562. Complaint against Justice Holliday, 42. Two good horses to be at, 71. Indian murders, 95. Coroners appointed, 223, 403, 506, 781. Sheriffs appointed, 223, 403, 506, 781. Distresses of, by quartering soldiers on the inhabitants, 330. Trials in, 336. Wagons furnished by, 376. Respecting choice of Inspectors, 400. Complaints of Conestoga Indians at—Conference with, 457. Courts —Supersedents — New justices commissioned, 562. Road to Galbraiths, 696. Carlisle, 676. Conferences with Indians at, 720–774.

Convictions, &c., ix., 5. House of correction, 22. Sheriffs elected, 57, 199, 285, 333, 398, 547, 623, 688, 778. Coroners elected, 57, 199, 285, 333, 398, 547, 623, 689,

778. Justices, 177, 281, 292, 386, 601. Murder of Conestoga Indians at, 89–113, 410, 460. Letter from Sheriff Hay of, 101, 103. Paxton boys forming a company to march to Philadelphia, 108–113. Sheriff and magistrates to give information, 124. Deposition of B. Kendal, 126. Troops ordered from Carlisle to, 127. Letter of Governor to magistrates of, 131. Intelligence from, 132. A frontier county, 138. Court of Quarter Session, 171. Justices, 172, 281, 292. Petition, quit rents, 179, 180. A pardon asked for and granted, 244. May raise money for nightly watch, 283–285, 292, 296, 549. E. Shippen, A. Stedman and J. Saunders, Justices of Court of Oyer and Terminer, &c., 292. Thomas Forster, a Justice, removed for interrupting sheriff in survey of land, 335. Manufacture of glass in, 354. Lottery for German Lutheran Church, 390, 392, 567, 576, 579. Letter of Governor to magistrates of, respecting murders by Frederick Stump, and other documents, 414–490. Sheriff to receive Stump and servant from sheriff of Cumberland and take to Chester county, 442. Convictions, 513, 601. James Webb declines as barrack master — James Ralph appointed, 556. Supplement to Act creating county, 556, 563, 579. Divorce case, 564, 580. Settlers from, go to Wyoming, 583. Lottery for bridge and paving streets, 621. Furnaces and forges, 1750, 632–636. New road to Philadelphia proposed, 657, 667, 681, 690. Justices, 673. Special court for trial of negroes, 680. Justice ill-treated by Connecticut men—To be arrested, 682. Orders for arrest, 683. Laz. Stewart taken and escapes, 683. Reward offered for, 685. Division of county, 707. Message of Governor respecting Laz. Stewart, 713. Conviction and reprieve, 745.

Claims for carriages employed by Colonel Wilkins, x., 17. Sheriffs elected, 56, 101, 211, 270. Coroners elected, 56, 101, 211, 270. Division of, 32, 42. Estate of Adam Simon Kuhn, 32, 42. Alleged errors in road from Philadelphia to, 65, 69. Special Court for trial of, 73. Estate of William Martin, 73. Executions or convictions, 110. Report of road from Philadelphia, 113. Regulation of buildings, &c., 149. Deputation of Conestoga Indians—murders — lands, &c., 255. Estate William Scott, 259. Joel Ferree makes guns for Committee of Safety, 290. Committee to settle dispute between Grubb and De Haas, 344. Arms to be collected in, 356, 441. Removal of prisoners from, 491, 514. Prisoners to be distributed, 502. Pay for arms, 520. Guns wanted from, 530. Matthias Slough appointed agent to buy clothing and accoutrements, 535. To permit General McKinley to contract for rifle guns, 598. Pay to M. Slough for firelocks, &c., 606. Troops to be ready, 627. Declaration of Independence to be published in, 635. Saltpetre manufactured at, 647. General McKinley may buy rifles in, 651. Money to families of associators — to be supplied with arms, 672. Colonel Crawford's battalion, 672. Colonel Porter's 682, 686. Orders respecting prisoners confined at, 687. To assist Captain M. Smith to procure rifles, 688. Prisoners from Carlisle, 688. Mr. Brooks, a prisoner, to have liberty, 699. Col. Ferree—various captains, 692. Powder for frontiers of, 702.

State prisoners sent to, xi., 4. Records removed to, 23. Books and treasury moved to, from Philadelphia, 41. Powder sent to, 64. Troops to march to Philadelphia, 78. Guard for barracks, &c., 78. Charles Wurtz, Town major, 78. Hessians to be employed in making shoes, 85. Thanks to officers who remained, 90. Colonel Timothy Green's battalion, 110.

12

Powder magazine to be built at, 115. Prothonotary, 187, 199. Coroners elected, 191. J. Hubley resigns in Council, 199. Case of Joseph Richardson inquired into, 202. Petition for magistrates and borough officers, 211. Death of John Henry, a magistrate—Mr. Schaffner elected, declines—Mr. Hubley and J. Hobson, Justices, 211. All arms in, to be delivered to Colonel Galbraith, 212. Wm. Kelly, Sheriff, 222, 606. Burgesses and other officers appointed, 223. Alarm from British prisoners—Town Major, 236. J. Hobson declines—William Henry appointed a magistrate, 237. Justices, 251. Records of Westmoreland secreted in, 252. J. Hubley to search for them, under warrant from Hubley and William Henry, Justices, 252, 265. Lieutenants, 257. William A. Atlee, Judge Supreme Court, 270. Powder house and magazine and expenses of militia at, 271. Destruction of public stores at, threatened, 307. Troops sent to, and guard for prisoners, 313. Supreme Executive Council meet at, 313. Order papers there, 314. C. Wurtz, sub-Lieutenant, 335. John Brown arrested and sent to, 345, 406. John Smith discharged, 347. Wagons bringing wood or provisions to, not to be impressed, 350. Militia, 360. Henry Dehuff, chief Burgess, 364. Coroner, 368. Wagon Master, 380. Barrack Master, 405. A German newspaper established and subscribed for, 409. Provisions stored at—Capt. William Will, Storekeeper, 423. Purchase of provisions in, 424. Orders to troops to proceed for camp—York militia to come to—order to remove powder, &c., over Susquehanna—cartridges to be filled and a guard to be furnished for, 442. Assembly inquire at whose expense public buildings are erected, 443. Pay of wagoners too low, 448. Prisoners from Virginia sent to, 462. May be discharged at, or Pottsgrove, 468. Horses to be delivered on General Washington's order, 476. Recruiting at, 477. President Wharton, Jr., dies and is buried at—order of funeral, 499. Barracks to be cleared and Hessians secured—guard at, 510. Making of clothing too expensive at, remove to Philadelphia, 521. Council intend to move to Philadelphia—declines taking Dunlap's paper, 521. Prisoners removed to Philadelphia, 573. Dedimus to administer oaths, &c., 585. Agent of forfeited estates, 599. Sheriff, 222, 606. Coroner, 606. Cost of storehouse at, built by John Hubley, 738. Case of Robert McNeill, 760. Executions, 780. Money for, 781.

Board of War ask for key of magazine at, xii., 32. William Barton receives subscriptions for loan office, 47. Case of Michael Witman's forfeited estate, 69. Change in orders respecting Lieutenants, 76. Case of Alexander McKee's forfeited estate—wheat to be purchased by Henry and Marshall, petition M. Reinhard for loss of horse, 85. Guards to be furnished from Philadelphia, 95. Complaints against Quarter Masters and other officers, 100. Claim of Christian Wurtz, Town Major—referred to Board of War—guard for prisoners to, 116. Election of Representative, 134, 508. Commissioners, 134. Sheriffs, 134, 508. Justices, 231, 556. Coroners, 134, 508. Assessors, 134, 508. Prices fixed for wheat and flour—purchase of, 142. William Henry's order for clothing, 148. Christian Wirtz pays for house and obtains deed, south-west corner Walnut and Front, Philadelphia, 174. Witman's estate, 231, 276. Execution of Thomas Taylor, a highwayman, 275. Simon Sneider, sub-Lieutenant, resigns, 279. Military officers appointed, 300. And Commissioner of purchases, 301. Militia fines, collector appointed, 386. To Northumberland county, 492. George Reine—estate sold, 552. Appointments, 554. Justice Cook

resigns, 556. Road between Darby and, 592. Colonel Hubley, Lieutenant, 628. Auditors, 646. Complaint against J. Bailey, Wagon Master, 647. Convention, troops to be removed to, 648. Road from Darby, 650. Repair of barracks, 659. Provisions for militia, 660. Troops called out, 695. Complaint against Wagon Master—repair of barracks, 697. Bayonets for, 702. Auditors to pay troops, 718, 722. Militia called out, 765, 767. Lieutenants appointed, 767.

Militia, xiii., 27. Called out, 53. About to march, 71. Troops discharged—cartouch boxes to be bought for militia, and arms, 82. Elections, 88, 393, 722. Sheriff, 88, 393, 722. Censors, 722. Coroner, 88, 393, 722. Representatives, 722. Councillor, 722. Execution, negro York, 137. Estate of John Rhine, 138. Military guard, 141. C. Wirtz commissioner, 154. Guard for prisoners to, 165. Estate of Nicholas Houssicker, 199, 251. Gratuities to soldiers, 244. Justices, 290. Clandestine traffic in British goods—William Henry to inquire into—arrest of persons, 317. Seizure of books, &c., 329. Men required, 365, 369. Militia fines, 383. Pardons, 453. Goods of Major James Gordon seized by William Henry, 453. Militia ask for pay, 457. British goods seized, 482. Justices, 542, 633. March, temper and intentions of troop stationed at, and conference with Committee of Congress on, 603. James Jacks, Recorder and Register, 681. Commissioner, 722. Adam Hubley resigns as Lieutenant of county—John Gloningher asks for it, 732. Colonel James Ross appointed Lieutenant, 746.

Justices, xiv., 45, 47, 65, 109, 157, 180, 181, 201, 208, 259, 276, 307, 479, 654, 656. John Shrieber appointed to care of barracks, 76. W. Hay, Collector of Excise, 106. Negro Cato pardoned, 109. Contested election for Justices, 196. Simon Schneider, sub-Lieutenant, 206. Storehouse and magazine at, 225. Disputed election, 232. Tax on writs, 236. Witnesses on election examined, 253, 254, 255, 258, 264, 266, 267. Decided by appointing Thomas Edwards, as Sheriff, and John Offner as Coroner, and J. Whitehill as Councillor, 267, 269. Sheriffs, 267, 556. Coroner, 267, 556. Parties engaged in election fraud to be prosecuted, 268. Election of Joseph Miller confirmed, 269, 270. William Henry entitled to half proceeds of goods seized, 309. Colonel Robert Elder's battalion of county militia, 380. Col. James Mercer and other militia officers, 396. County Lieutenants to give security, 400. Deputy Surveyor, 441, 443, 447, 453. Justices Kelly and Smith refusing to resign, are superseded, 454. Lieutenant B. Galbraith, 478. Adam Reigart—purchase of horses in, 519. Elections, 556. Justice Carpenter, representative, resigns as Justice, Contested election, 616, 617. Captain Michael Whitley paid for a gun and blanket, lost in action at Chestnut Hill, 637. Contested election decided for Justice Bailey, discharged from recognizance, 654.

Justices, xv., 4, 14, 38, 52, 149, 173, 515. Depreciation lands to be sold at, 18. Proceedings for taxes stayed, 22. J. Cornall pardoned so far as relates to "cutting off both ears," 25. Cases of criminals, 31. Petition of delinquent tax collector rejected, 49. Petition, J. Miller respecting excise, 81. William Hayes' estate, 90, 91. Elections, 98, 296. Sheriffs, 98, 296, 570. Coroner, 98, 296, 570. Representatives, 98. Councillor, 296. Colonel Haverstick's battalion and Captain Jacob Metzger, 113. Committee of inspection and observation, 1776 and '77, 167. Catharine Reinick, pension, 185. Sale of William Hayes' property referred to Comptroller, 244. Indians detained at, by sickness of interpreter Woods,

250. Pension to William Patterson's widow, 275. Rum seized from A. Moore, 282. Col. James Ross to deliver to M. Hollenback arms for Luzerne, 289. Captain John Graff, 363. Militia fines, house for storing arms, &c., 412. Jones' Lane to be improved, 448, 494. Sale of estate of William Hayes postponed, 461. Michael Hubley, president of Courts, 499. Henry Ream, Justice, 515. Wm. Henry's widow is paid—part sales of British merchandize seized—stores—expenses of Indian prisoner, &c., 546. Ground rent on lots due W. Hamilton, 614. Paid, 645.

Fines remitted, xvi., 12. Surveyor's district, 19. Sureties, 31. Remission of fines to Sheriff on several prisoners, 61. Tavern and marriage licenses, amount received, 62. Receipts for taxes, 1787, 1788—receipts for excise, 83. Taxes, 123. Repair of road, 124. Accounts of Collector of Excise—sale of J. Armor postponed, 136. Claim for military services under Colonel D. Jenkins, 1777, '78, '79, 154. J. Lutz, for services, 161. John Griffith, Collector of State taxes for, 180. Sheriff, 193, 493. Justices, 410. Coroner, 193, 493, 499. Taxes received by Jacob Krug, treasurer, 290. Excise collected, 311. Barracks at, to be sold—Commissioners, 325. Instructions, 350. Tavern and marriage licenses and tax on writs received by John Hubley, 355. Militia pay—on expedition to Northumberland county under John Slater, 363. And under Captain Caldwell, 364. Militia officers elected according to Colonel James Ross' certificate, 399. Pay for a servant enlisted, 408. Keeper of powder magazine, &c., 434. Doyle arrested for killing Indians, 464, 483. Excise received, 477. Pension to Sergeant N. Little's widow, 486. James Jack, Register and Recorder, 495. Forfeiture remitted, 495. Excise, 520.

Land, Samuel, appointed Sub-Treasurer for New Castle, i., 111. Sheriff of New Castle, 194.

Landis, Samuel, letter respecting visit of Colonel George Talbot to widow Ogle's house, i., 113. High Sheriff of New Castle, 121. Letter from, 194.

Land office, viii., 337. In Lower counties, not yet open, x., 208.

Land offices, Congress object to opening, xii., 160. John Lukens late Surveyor-General, to search for papers relating to Cox's neck, in New Castle county, 621. Officers appointed, 689. James Tilghman, Secretary under proprietaries—Books and papers, 690, 719, 749. Conference with Council on establishing a board of property, xiii., 132. David Kennedy, Secretary, 418. Late Secretaries James Tilghman and Edmund Physic, 420. Papers belonging to, to be demanded of J. Turner and B. Chew, 433. Title to city lot to Jacob Shallus confirmed, 631. Papers again referred to, 636. Report, 639. Conference on opening, xiv., 29. Commissioners to have Indian deeds and papers, 54. Iron chest for Receiver-General, 168. E. Blaine's letter referred to, 286. Papers respecting Virginia boundary, 288. On confiscated estates in Westmoreland, 290. On A. Power's claim, 292. Report, 343. Deputy surveyors in each county, 441, 442. Officers, 444. Lands to be surveyed, 452. Counterfeit certificates—Surveyors on donation lands, 454. To sell lands, 633. Dispute between Maclay and Edmiston about a line settled, xv., 6. Notice of sale of J. Galloway's city lots, 6. Lands for offices, 17. Depreciation lands to be sold, 18. Receiver, 27. To sell city lots, 58. Sale of depreciation, ordered, 138. To issue patent to John Hughes, 191. Parchment for patents, 201. Public notice of sale of reserved tracts opposite Pittsburg to be printed, 522. Report of committee on reserved lots opposite Pittsburg, xvi., 22. Advertising,

24. To furnish Attorney-General with necessary papers in case of Hog Island, 69. Fees received, 82. Receiver-General to sell certain city lots, 95. Depreciation certificates, 148. Mistake corrected, 149. Case of J. Hartzell, 237. Dry lands of Northampton county, 243. Exchange of warrants, 297. Fees received, 380. Form of conveyance for islands in Ohio and Allegheny rivers, 301. Fees received in, 311. Secretary and Receiver-General re-appointed, 350. Valuation—Error in survey of tract on Girtey's Run, opposite Pittsburg, 410. Fees received, 522.

Lands, to be taxed to meet charges, i., 70. Appeal from Sussex court for, on Prime Hook—Decision, 77. Issue of patents—Delay complained of, 86. Decision respecting Luke Watson, 89. Commissioners to dispose of, 144. Refusel to survey, 120, 124, 151, 153. Indians willing to sell lands between Upland and Apoquinimy —Commissioners appointed, 154. Fraud in a deed, 207. Regulations for enrolling proposed, 219. Estimated by distance from Philadelphia, 600. Quiet possession for seven years, 620. Purchased from Indians, ii., 17. Overplus —Near Pemmapeck, controversy respecting, 34. Deficiencies, 54. Free Society of Traders, not to make further sales of, 154. Seven years quiet possession, &c., 220, 221, 224. Belonging to Frankford Co., ii., 431. Swedes complain against proprietary and secretary for taking their Dutch lands, 465. Religious societies not to sell, 528. Aliens holding, 610. Have Indians right to those, on Susquehanna? iii., 98. John Grist settles on, 137, 138. Of Free Society of Traders to be sold for payment of debts, 138. On Susquehanna, consents to Wm. Penn's purchase of, 181. Surrendered to Governor Keith by Indians at Albany, 201. Palatines ask to purchase, 241. On Susquehanna purchased by Governor Dongan for Wm. Penn, 273. In execution for debts, 280. Complaint against Christians for settling on, for which Indians had not been paid—And Logan's reply to, 320. Indian deed for, on Susquehanna, 321. J. Logan's impressions about them, 322. Tulpehocken, Lechy, &c., petition of Palatines respecting, 322. Interesting discussion about, between Logan, Hamilton, Hill, &c., 325. Released by Indians west of Susquehanna, iv., 88, 92. Respecting, 336. Time granted to purchasers who have not paid, 343. From Delaware Indians, papers relating to, 481. Indians, Cayuga, ask payment for, 500. Quit claim to, on Susquehanna, 559–586. What raises their value, 571. Disturbance with the Delawares about, 575. Speech of Cannasatego to, 579. In Forks of Delaware, 576. Petition of Captain John Titami, a chief, 625. Reference to claims for, in 1736, 709. Claimed by Indians, v., 383. Proclamation of Governor H. against settlers on, 394, 410. Report of R. Peters —Proceedings against settlers on unpurchased, 440–449. Petitions of inhabitants, 454. Survey of, obstructed by Indians, 489. Abm. Taylor sets up a claim to, under early title, 551. Descriptive deed executed by Indians at Lancaster, 634. Deeds for, purchased from Indians, at Albany, by the Commissioners of Six Nations, vi., 119, 129. To George McCall, 235. Connecticut, claim to, 247–275. Bounty offered to officers and soldiers, 504. Were the Indians paid for, 710. Report, 724. Unpurchased, about Adjouquay—doubts respecting building fort there, vii., 182. Teedyuscung speaks of, 203. Fraud in, explained, 326, 327, 537, 540. And purchases, 327, 540. Committee appointed by council to investigate proprietary title to Indian purchases of, 354. Request to examine minutes respecting, 394. Memorandum at

Fort Allen, 431. Papers examined by committee, 464, 465. Partial report of committee, 465, 469. Purchased from Indians, 635, 636, 676. Deeds for, produced to Teedyuscung, 688, 693, 698. Lands in province and city —Petition of Richard Hill and S. P. Moore to make title to, 728. Teedyuscung demands deed of 1718, 731. Complaints of Indians about, viii., 199. Purchase at Albany from Susquehanna—from John Penn's creek to Ohio, 199, 203–205. Teedyuscung denies claims of Delawares, 202. Deeds produced, 205, 211. Conference at house of Nicholas Scull, at request of C. Weiser, 211. Settlement by Peters and Weiser with Indians for, 219. Proprietary release for, 222. On Teedyuscung's claims for, 242, 243. Report of committee of council on, 246–261. List of deeds, &c., produced, 259–261. Mr. Peters, in relation to papers in land office, &c., 335. Probity of officers, 337. Discussions by Governor, Council and Assembly, and remarks by Galloway on bill for recording warrants, &c., 361–372, 675. Views of Assembly on proprietary estates, 374, 530. Tax Act, 1759. Opinions on, 537, 538. Security of estates, 539. Claims of unnaturalized subjects, 545. Purchase of, 623. Indians not cheated for, 661. Conferences at Easton and Philadelphia, 630–661. Naturalized persons may hold, ix., 17, 24, 242, 325. In executions for debts, 146, 148, 160. Circular of Governor Penn on assessment of proprietary, 237. Answers to, 240. Instructions to Governor on settlers on western, 321, 403, 407, 408, 412. Proclamation of Governor respecting, 327, 353. Justice of Lancaster removed for interrupting survey of land, 335. Modes of granting, in province, 380. Mortgages unpaid, 395. Sir Wm. Johnson on settlers on Indian, 412. Settlers on, 421 426, 431, 448, 568, 578. Proceedings and resolutions of Susquehanna Company, 569. Roman Catholics may not hold, 596. Respecting settlers, 637, 641 Connecticut people settling on, x., 50. Proclamation against, 95. Near Pittsburg—Early survey of, 161. Deeds for, forged by George Crows, 693. Depreciation, xv., 42, 58, 426. Donation, 351, 580. Reservations, 593, 599, 601. Grant of eighteen tracts to Franklin College, 367. Reserved tract, 497, 509–512, 522, 649. Reserved, opposite Pittsburg, value of, xvi., 45, 340. Depreciation, 148, 303, 325, 376, 419, 439, 448, 452, 515. Fort McIntosh survey, 340.

Lane, Henry, traitor, to be arrested, xii., 338, 342. Enlarged, 346.

Lang, James, Ensign, appointed Lieutenant of battalion, x., 645. To raise volunteers, xi., 27. Clothing account, 645.

Langdon, John, Governor New Hampshire—letter and Act on navigation and commerce, xiv., 596.

Langdon, Woodbury, may export provisions, xii., 173.

Langhorn, Jeremiah, dedimus to, ii., 97. A Commissioner named for building a new Court House and prison for Bucks county, iii., 241. Appointed Judge, 258. Justice of Supreme Court, 400. Speaker, 528. Justice, iv., 244. C. J., 348. Dies, 640. Succeeded by John Kinsey, 640.

Lapackpitton, Indian chief, vi., 35.

Laquis, William, journey to Indians on Susquehanna, vii., 137, 182.

Lardner, Lynford, v., 600. Member of Council, vi., 414. Distribution of arms for Assembly—report on, 679. A Lieutenant, vii., 62. Provincial Commissioner, 671. Expenditures for provincial ship, viii., 81. Declines being a Commissioner, 86. Visits New Castle with Governor John Penn, &c., ix., 73.

Latcha, Major, xi., 110.

Latitude of Shanoppin's town, &c., v., 751–757.

Latta, Thomas, a Justice, x., 209.

Lattimore, Arthur, Coroner, viii., 780; ix., 57.
Lattimore, Robert, Coroner, ix., 548.
Laub, Conrad, Sheriff, xvi., 194, 492.
Laughlin, Alexander, Justice, xiv., 242.
Laughlin, Hugh, Justice, xiv., 362.
Laurens, Henry, president Congress, sends copy of confederation, xi., 379. Also commissions for privateers, 437.
Lawrence, Colonel Charles, Lieutenant-Governor and commander-in-chief of Nova Scotia—to concert with Governor Shirley measures against French, vi., 311. Letter, 451, 464, 554, 711. Sends French neutrals, 711. Captain of a fire raft, x., 536. Sent into guard boats to Lewes Town, 593.
Lawrence, John, elected Justice for Philadelphia, v., 106, 110. Justice of Supreme Court, ix., 393. Bounds to be fixed in parole, xi., 269, 525. Sentenced to death, 565. Reprieved, 566, 579. Pardoned, 624. Lieuten't, xii., 338.
Lawrence, John, Jr., at riot at Jas. Wilson's—bailed, xii., 152. Lieutenant-Colonel of Flying Camp, xiv., 634.
Lawrence, Joseph, Coroner, xiv., 558.
Lawrence, Staats, at riot at J. Wilson's—a minor—bond for, xii., 144.
Lawrence, Thomas, to receive wrecked goods from Cape May, iii., 238. Mayor of city, 293. Member of Council, 302. Goes to Lancaster at request of Council, iv., 153. Appointed to try a negro, 243. Commissioner to Albany, 771. Commissioner to treaty at Albany, v. 28. Committee on Indian affairs, 167. Lieutenant-Colonel of Associators, 175. Of Committee of merchants on currency, xii., 353.
Lawrie, Thomas, appointed secretary and clerk by Governor, iv., 289. Resigns, and P. Baird succeeds him, 429.
Law Cases, submitted by Assembly to Governor, ii., 627–629.
Law, practitioners of, draw up bill for Courts, ii., 252.
Law Suits, vexatious, to be avoided, i., 204.
Lawyers, to be sent for to New York, ii., 407.
Laws, agreed on in England, i., 37. Old, to be examined by Assembly, 67. Seal, &c., to be affixed to all, 72. Not to be printed, but copies to be sent to each county, 74. Proposed, 86. Marginal notes to be examined by a Committee, 97. Various motions respecting, 97. Can they be valid without consent of Assembly? 106. Passed, 110. Continuing the old, 133. To be according to charter, 134. And published, 171. New, confirmed, 171. Discussion between Assembly and Council about continuing, 183, 184. To be enforced, 197, 198, 199. Proposals from Assembly respecting, 205. Proposed, 216, 217, 219, 226, 274. What laws had been enrolled and sealed, 276. On parchment rolls, 276. To be published under Penn's seal, 276. Not to be depended upon, 277. Proceedings respecting, 294, 295. Declaration of Governor and Council to continue the, 296. Style of, to be as in 1685, 326. Proposed, 326, 335, 339. Sheriff to publish new laws in market place, Philadelphia, 376. List of, in force, 411. Objections to several, 429, 434, 455. Omissions, 462. To be renewed, 466. Proposed, 508, 521, 525, 552, 554, 571, 598, 600, 607, 610. Proposed, &c., ii., 12, 32, 45, 46, 48, 49, 54, 56, 154, 155, 156, 169, 184, 210–213, 218–222, 224, 231, 236, 251–253, 337, 363, 420, 444, 504, 518. Repealed, 251, 253. *Lower counties* object to confirm laws passed at New Castle, 49, 50. To be printed—copies to be sent to England, 64, 156. Separation, Assembly, 163. Members to be elected, 184. Meeting of Assembly at New Castle, 207. Change of members, 516, 528, 529, 550, 552, 563, 565, 571, 579–590, 609. Discussion about, between Governor and Assembly—respecting, iii., 27, 36, 39, 43, 71, 75, 138, 143, 165, 166, 171, 172, 174, 226,

233, 234, 235, 245, 247, 250, 277–280, 357, 359, 375, 379, 380, 394, 396, 400, 418, 422, 426, 435, 589. Proposed, passed or repealed, iv., 8, 14, 17, 18, 20, 22, 297, 304, 306, 331, 336, 384, 386, 398, 475, 483, 503, 549, 626, 628, 634, 638, 659, 687, 688, 752. Proposed, &c., v., 28, 29, 30, 32, 33, 67, 369, 370, 371, 375, 426, 427, 428, 499, 502, 511, 512, 514, 516, 559, 560, 576, 578, 619, 687. Historical view of certain Acts, 499. Confirmation of, 619. Proposed, &c., vi., 225, 344–357. Discovery of, among J. Kinsey's papers. 357, 673, 382, 441, 551, 702. Proposed, passed or repealed, vii., 63, 72, 87, 93, 181, 182, 184, 246, 275, 346, 390, 392, 396, 400, 416, 433, 436, 443, 580, 583, 593, 719, 722, 739, 761. Act for regulating officers and soldiers, 63. Proposed, amended, passed or repealed, viii., 19–27, 30, 40, 65, 69, 76, 80, 100, 101, 125, 170, 172, 173, 230, 318, 321, 332, 333, 335, 339, 342–351–356, 370, 376, 397, 400, 402, 407, 455, 478–480, 483, 524–557, 558, 573, 580, 582, 583, 610, 673, 683, 684, 715. Partially repealed in England owing to informality, 535, 542. Proposed, passed, repealed, &c., ix., 3, 4, 17, 22, 23, 25, 37, 55, 56, 57, 63, 64, 147, 148, 150, 151, 152, 168, 238, 242, 243, 245, 247, 283, 285, 294, 296, 313, 314, 325, 326, 337, 354, 356, 358, 360–366, 369, 389, 390, 392, 394, 401, 421, 439, 443, 446, 448, 461, 465, 470, 472, 549, 556, 561, 563, 564, 566, 576, 578, 580, 582, 599, 621, 622, 623, 626, 637, 640, 643, 649, 650, 652, 654, 658, 662, 681, 687, 698, 717, 719, 720, 722, 724, 729, 730, 760. Goddard, printer of the, 393. Proposed, enacted or repealed, x., 4, 18, 25, 26, 27, 32, 35, 41, 48, 70, 72, 74, 76, 79, 80, 98, 102, 104, 106, 109, 139, 144, 147, 197, 209, 218, 223, 224, 237, 239, 241, 243, 254, 261, 263, 274. Printing of, xiii., 90, 193, 275.

Lea, Isaac, Coroner, v., 55, 120, 345, 411, 464.

Leacock, John, Coroner, xiv., 555. Coroner, Philadelphia, xv., 98, 574; xvi., 208, 490.

Leacock, Joseph, Coroner, xv., 328. Inspector of pot and pearl ashes, xvi., 312.

Lead, only five hundred weight in Philadelphia, x., 300. To be imported, 301. Enquired for at Ticonderoga, 301. Order for, and flints, 305. Receiv'd, 328. Weights &c.—inhabitants called on for, 559, 649. Iron weights to be exchanged for, 561. To be delivered to secret Committee of Congress, 600. Required, 615. Weights to be collected—price, 637. Paid for, 648, 700. General Roberdeau asks pay for, xii., 162, 163.

Leaden plates buried in Ohio, one stolen from Jean Cœur, v., 508. Copy of inscription on it, 510, 634.

League of Friendship, William Penn and Indians, iii., 24. Heads of agreement, 311, 336.

League Island, dams, sluices, &c., ix., 390, 392.

Leaming, Thomas, fine remitted.

Leather, tanning and currying now proposed and discussed, iii., 139. Acts respecting, x., 22, 24, 41. Lebanon Co. Justice appointed, ix., 281; xiv., 159. Prisoners sent from Reading to, x., 547. Guards at, to be increased, xi., 417.

Lebanon, Fort, vii., 35.

Le Bœuf, fort burned, viii., 380, 513. Post at, cut off and massacred, ix., 35. To be reserved for Commonwealth, xv., 595. Reservation at, for State, xvi., 47.

Lechay Hills or mountains, described, iii., 322. (See Lehigh.)

Ledlie, Andrew, respecting Wyoming, ix., 756. Surgeon, xi., 94. With others send memorial and resolutions, which are declared seditious and ordered to be prosecuted by Attorney General, xv., 224, 225. Paid for medicines, &c., 344. Petition, 471.

Ledlie, William, Coroner, ix., 623, 688.

Lee, Captain ———, petition to have his company annexed to Colonel Proctor's regiment, xii., 210.

Lee, Lieutenant Joseph Brown, appointed, x., 678.
Lee, General ———, letter informing of Hessians embarking at Staten Island for Pennsylvania, x., 753.
Lee, Major ———, respecting supplies, xii., 210. Of light dragoons, 235.
Lee, Richard Henry, letter to, from Dr. Birkenhout, xi., 569. Elected president of Congress, xiv., 270.
Lee, Thomas, president of Virginia, letters to and from, v., 423, 424.
Lee, William, Coroner of Philadelphia, ii., 108.
Leech, Benjamin, claims a lot on Tenth street, as purchased by Tobias Leech from William Penn, xiii., 31.
Leech, Thomas, Committee of Assembly, vii., 637. Elected Speaker, 772. Chosen Speaker of Assembly, viii., 396. Succeeded by Norris, 407. To take care of sick soldiers, xi., 56.
Leech, Toby, ii., 540.
Leet, Edward, case of, with Maryland, iv., 101. Examination of, 104–106.
Legacy Act, vii., 416, 443.
Lehigh River, fisheries, ix., 623. Exploration of, xv., 65. Union saw mill on road to, 195, 229, 230. Survey of road between Susquehanna and Nescopec, xvi., 20, 83. Commissioners to examine, 319.
Lehigh Water Gap, road to Wyoming, xv., 22, 30.
Lehman, Christian, a Notary and Tabellion Public, x., 9.
Leib, Michael (Dr.), paid for medicines and attendances on a disabled militia man of Philadelphia, xvi., 61.
Leiper, Thomas, deed for part of Tinicum, xii., 256. Sheriff, xv., 102, 300, 578, 580.
Leisler, Jacob (of New York), letter to president Lloyd on defence against French, i., 332.
Le Marr, Captain, x., 503.
Lennot, William, to be seized, xi., 286.
Lenox, David, as Captain, x., 447. Arrested and confined, xi., 287.
Lenox, William, enlarged, x., 291, 292.
Leogane, flag of truce from, with prisoners, v., 122. Gets repairs, 122. Spanish prisoners to be sent back, 122. Spanish prisoners sent to, 130, 234.
Leonard, Ezekiel, Sheriff, xv., 97, 296, 566.
Le Roy, George, recommended by Chev. Luzerne, xii., 46.
Le Roy, Monsieur, and Boyne, two French subjects, arrested, viii., 714.
Lesher, John, Commissioner to purchase provisions, xi., 423.
Lesley, Robert, proposes alteration of hammer of State House clock, xv., 380, 387. Care of State House clock, xvi., 220, 488.
Le Tort, Captain Jacques (and wife Ann), asks permission to go to England, i., 340. Madame and Indians, conspiracy, 396, 435, 436. Indian trader returns from Canada—testimony in his favor—gives security, ii., 100. Letter from Madame on attacks of Indians, 121. And Indians, 138, 140, 155. Petition from jail, 163. Petition, 170, 171. Complaint against, 403, 471, 554. Gives recognizance, 539. Asks to trade with Indians, 562. At Council at Conay T. with J. Mitchell, iii., 187. Noticed by Indians, 274. Arrives from Chenasty, reports Indian threatenings, 294. Presents a claim for services, iv., 237. Letter from, 574.
Letters of Marque, proclamation for commissions to, against Spain, iv., 451, 486; xi., 23, 24.
Letters—
Abercrombie, General James, vii., 193; viii., 37, 69, 78, 141.
Adams, John, xiii., 702; xv., 50.
Adams, Robert, vii., 43.
Agents of Parliamentary grant, ix., 49.
Allen, Ira, xii., 233.
Alexander, James, vi., 267, 270, 273.
Alexander, William, vi., 248, 262.
Allinson, William, vi., 434.

Letters—
Amherst, General Jeff., viii., 236, 261, 262, 274, 285, 298, 322, 331, 380, 381, 437, 448, 452, 454, 503, 504, 578, 590, 602, 628, 679, 687; ix., 34, 62, 74.
Archer, Henry William, xv., 51.
Armand, General, xix, 12.
Armstrong, George, vii., 557.
Armstrong, Colonel John, vi., 378, 400, 403; vii., 231, 257, 503, 552, 599; ix., 444, 448, 462, 484; xii., 322.
Arndt, Jacob, xii., 317.
Arnold, General Benedict, xi., 228.
Arnold, Thomas, xvi., 307.
Assembly, xiii., 352.
Assembly of Maryland, i., 334.
Atlee, Colonel, xii., 330, 437, 480.
Atlee, Judge, xii., 220.
Atlee, Samuel J., xiii., 697; xiv., 310.
Atlee, William Aug., xiv., 314.
Attorney-General, xiv., 619;
Auditor-General, xii., 177.
xv., 647; xvi., 210^{2}–433, 452.
Bache, Benj. Franklin, xiv., 409.
Baker, Hilary, xiii., 549.
Ballet, Captain, v , 256.
Baltimore, Lord, iii., 468, 479, 486.
Barton, Reverend Thomas, vi., 675.
Bayard, John, xi., 39.
Bayard, Jno., and C. Pettit, xiv., 618.
Beatty, Colonel, xii., 101.
Beckley, John, xvi., 439.
Bedford, Duke of, v., 360, 379, 411.
Belcher, J., Governor, v., 5; 266; vii., 384.
Bernard, Governor Francis, viii., 139.
Biddle, Edward, vi., 704.
Biddle, Colonel Clement, xii., 393; xiii., 330.
Birkenhout, Dr., xi., 569.
Blaine, Ephraim, xii., 111, 522; xiv., 283, 286.
Blair, W., ix., 342.
Blakeney, Colonel, iv., 430.
Blanchard, Col. Joseph, vi., 623.

Letters—
Blaithwaite, Secretary, i., 526.
Blunston, Samuel, iii., 470 iv., 147, 155, 158.
Blythe, Colonel Benjamin, xi., 564; xiii., 522.
Board of Admiralty, xii., 393, 707.
Board of Treasury, xii., 55, 198, 324; xiv, 604; xv., 82, 106, 123.
Board of War, xi., 468, 509, 626, 637, 758; xii., 16, 32, 90, 92, 198, 210, 215, 221, 262, 312, 433, 454, 702, 743; xiii., 97, 128, 449, 551.
Boggs, John, xiv., 140.
Bond, Phineas, xv., 408, 416.
Boscawen, Admiral, vi., 451.
Boscawen, Admiral E., viii., 164.
Bouchet, Cheval., iv., 173.
Bouquet, Colonel Henry, ix., 35, 207.
Bowen and Beatty, xiv., 178; 401.
Boyd, Samuel, &c., xvi., 209^{2}.
Braddock, General E., vi., 307, 331, 332, 371, 398, 399, 401, 426, 430, 445, 475.
Bradford, William, Jr., Attorney General, xii., 583, xiv., 134; xv., 446.
Bradstreet, Colonel Jno., vi., 413; ix., 193.
Brearly, Adam, xiii., 3.
Brearly, David, C. J., xiii., 74.
Brodhead, Daniel, xii., 25, 80, 84, 173, 215, 245, 287, 377, 435, 445, 498, 586, 743; xvi., 171, 216, 224, 211^{2}, 212^{4}, 253, 256, 261, 288, 292, 317, 384, 461.
Broughton, Thomas, iv., 165.
Bryan, George, C. J., xii., 423.
Buchannan, William, vi., 435.
Bull, William, Governor of South Carolina, ix., 775.
Burd, James, &c., vi., 377, 403, 435, 436, 466. 484, 485, 499, 555, vii., 436, 453, 618, 734.
Burd, John, xi., 773.
Butler, Colonel, xi., 690.
Butler, Colonel Richard, xii., 36, 428; xiii., 503, 603; xvi., 45, 422, 537.
Butler, Walter, v., 624.

Letters—
Butler, Zebulon, xv., 505; xvi., 317.
Buyers, Hon. Jno., xiii., 686.
Cadenhead, John, xiii, 764.
Callender, Robert, ix., 302.
Callender, William, and J. Pemberton, vii., 394.
Calvert, Charles, iii., 222, 224.
Campbell, Francis, vi., 699.
Campbell, George, xvi., 462.
Campbell, Captain James, viii., 290.
Campbell, John, vi., 481.
Cannon, John, xiii., 584.
Cariljas, Don Francisco, viii., 171.
Carmarthen, Lord, xv., 50.
Carmichael, ———, xvi., 144.
Carothers, John, xii., 4, 93., 100, 398, 721.
Carson, John, vii., 773; xii., 8.
Caswell, Governor of North Carolina, xv., 159.
Celeron, a French Captain, v.,
Cellender, Robert, v., 600.
425.
Chambers, Benjamin, vi., 675.
Chambers, John, xii., 391.
Chastenoy, Mons., to, v., 131.
Christ, Henry, xii., 780.
Chrystie, Captain James, xiv., 32.
Clapham, Colonel William, vii., 156.
Clark, Brigadier-General, xiv., 162.
Clarkson, Major Mathew, xi., 676, 677.
Clarkson, Mathew, xii., 482; xiii., 182.
Claus, Daniel, vi., 182, 249, 292, 468; vii., 155.
Clinton, Governor of New York, iv., 772. From and to, v., 30, 56, 133, 187, 215, 265, 286, 305, 431, 462, 480, 495, 508, 517, 524, 553, 573, 625, 639, 642; xii., 64, 306; xiii., 350; xiv., 457.
Cluggage, Captain, xii., 147.
Coates, Colonel Wm., xiii., 641.
Colden, Cadwalader, ix., 120, 656,
Commercial Committee of Congress, xii., 130.
Commercial convention, xv., 107.

Letters—
Commissioners of Berks county, xii., 275; xv., 428.
Commissioners of Connecticut, x.. 121, 126, 133.
Commissioners to Indians, vii., 153, 498, 772.
Commissioners of Lancaster, xvi., 123.
Commissioners to Luzerne, xv., 276.
Commissioners on defence of Delaware, xii., 361, 487.
Commissioners to view Rivers, xvi., 209[2], 222[2].
Commissioners of Taxes, Philadelphia, xiii., 453, 647, 573; xiv., 151.
Commissioners of Trade and plantations, ix., 343.
Commissioners on Boundary, xiv., 69.
Commissioners of Virginia and Maryland, xiv., 398.
Committee of Assembly on purchase of lands, vii., 635, 636.
Committee of Safety, x., 497.
Comptroller General, xiv., 457; xv., 69, 413, 429; xvi., 94, 293, 317, 318, 332, 348, 359.
Congress, x., 564, 565, 660; xi., 197, 379, 437, 487, 619, 636, 752, 759, 767; xii., 2, 25, 49, 65, 66, 75, 80, 84, 108, 116, 147, 160, 176, 197, 200, 201, 227, 230, 234, 250, 263, 275, 279, 287, 331, 334, 370, 387, 392, 398, 400, 403, 410, 423, 424, 427, 459, 484, 517, 529, 569, 597, 599, 615, 671, 675, 683, 685, 702, 718, 733, 735, 736, 740, 742, 750, 758, 778, 783; xiii., 16, 41, 101, 105, 123, 137, 148, 170, 173, 185, 311, 502, 512, 574, 576, 600, 618, 635, 637, 681, 682, 697, 699, 730, 744; xiv., 12, 43, 51, 52, 72, 78, 143, 270, 343, 347, 372, 384, 443, 473, 480, 509, 516, 561, 587, 618, 643, 652; xv., 102, 106, 215, 286, 455, 474, 480, 515; xvi., 438.
Connecticut, Governor of, xiv., 317; xv., 575.
Connor, John, xiii., 148.
Contrecœur, Captain, vi., 39.
Conway, Rt. Hon. H. C., ix., 298, 309, 310.
Cook, Jacob ———, xii., 556.

Letters—
Cookson, Thomas, v., 377.
Cookson, William, iv., 657, 675.
Cornbury, Lord, ii., 136.
Cornplanter, Indian, xvi., 499, 510.
Council, v., 320; xiii., 680; xiv., 56, 262, 276, 282, 286, 317, 321, 356, 359, 381, 405, 447, 509, 571, 572, 585; xv., 20, 26, 35, 106, 170, 180, 276, 301, 362, 381, 396, 401, 442, 443, 472, 493, 505, 524, 571, 618, 641; xvi., 26, 39, 126, 149, 181, 266, 357, 358, 361, 399, 404, 511.
Council of Safety, x., 654, 657, 667, 669, 681, 743; xi., 115, 123, 335.
Coxe, Colonel ———, xii., 423.
Coxe, Tench, xv., 86.
Coyle, James, xv., 527.
Craig, John, xiii., 407.
Crawford, Josiah, xii., 486.
Crawford, William, x., 165.
Crispin, William, xi., 440.
Croghan, George, v., 72, 119, 496, 539, 569; vi., 21, 145, 160, 180, 181, 188, 226, 398, 642, 699; vii., 355, 403, 465, 478, 479, 480, 482, 484, 503, 525, 600, 630, 660; ix., 249, 323.
Cumberland Co., Justices, ix., 486.
Dagworthy, John, vii., 603, 632, 633.
Dartmouth, Earl of, x., 220, 240, 248.
Davis, Caleb, xv., 406.
Deane, Joseph, xii., 607.
De Canaveral, Exc'y, J., xvi., 381.
De Cornay, Monsieur, xiv., 425.
De Hart, Colonel ———, xii., 258.
De Lancey, Governor James, v., 717; vi., 9, 32, 511, 554, 592; vii., 560, 596, 628, 716, 762; viii., 146, 165.
Delany, Sharp, xv., 599.
De la Vega, v., 199, 200.
Delegates in Congress, xiv., 3, 12, 105, 119, 357, 379, 521, 549; xv., 19, 37, 300, 472, 502, 514; xvi., 100, 119, 409.
De Marcellin and Le Roy, xiv., 30.
Denny, Governor William, vii., 223,

Letters—
359, 377, 382, 384, 385, 388, 467 473, 475, 476, 482, 501, 543, 549, 571, 580, 581, 605, 606, 607, 608, 634, 637, 647, 657, 658, 661, 672, 679, 738, 773; viii., 56, 283.
Deshler, David, xii., 596.
Dewalt, G., president of General Court of Maryland, xiv., 106.
Dick, John, ix., 753.
Dickinson, John (intercepted), xi., 92. President, xiii., 478. To C., xiv., 219, 243.
Digges, Dudley, xii., 522.
Dinwiddie, Governor Robert, of Virginia, v., 632, 687, 712, 765, 767; vi., 5, 7, 27, 31, 55, 163, 177, 294, 296, 297, 308, 419, 445, 451, 602; vii., 31.
Dobbs, Governor Arthur, viii., 290.
Dongan, Governor, N. Y., relating to French and Indians, i., 217.
Dougherty, ———, xii., 72.
Dougherty, Bernard, xiii., 101, 310.
Douglass, Ephraim, xiv., 525.
Duché, T. S., xii., 18.
Duffey, Capt. ———, xii., 67.
Dunbar, Col. Thomas, vi., 498, 547, 593, 595.
Dunmore, Lord, x., 156, 183, 188.
Du Portail, General, xi., 732, 779.
Durell, Admiral Phil., viii., 289.
Dyson, J., ix., 49.
Eckart, Col. Valentine, xii., 466; xiii., 570.
Edmonds, Wm., vii., 163, 773.
Edwin, John, viii., 99.
Egremont, Earl of, viii., 678, 686; ix., 13, 15, 37.
Eichelberger Jacob, xii., 421.
Elder, Rev. John, vi., 652, 704.
Elder, Col. ———, xii., 71.
Ellicott, Andrew, xiv., 464; xv., 631.
Espy, David, xvi., 517.
Espy, Mr. ———, xiii., 284.
Ewing, James, xi., 676; xiv., 443.
Fairfax, William, v., 657.
Falconer, Nathaniel, xv., 331.
Farmer, Lewis, xvi., 222.
Fayette, Marquis de la, xiii., 479.

Letters—
Febiger, Christian, xvi., 35, 466.
Ferris, Capt. Owen, xii., 556.
Field officers of Pennsylvania line, xi., 731.
Findley, Wm., xvi., 434.
Finley, Rev. James, xiii., 617.
Fishbourne, Benj. A. D. C., xi., 468.
Fisher, Samuel R., xi., 729.
Fitch, Thomas, Governor of Connecticut, v., 773; vi., 261; viii., 627.
Fitzsimons, Thomas, xiii., 555: xvi., 2.
Fleeson, Plunket, xiv., 548.
Fletcher, Gov. Benjamin, i., 383, 384.
Flint, Royal Commissary, xii., 227.
Forbes, General John, viii., 59, 60, 79, 100, 110, 167, 224, 232.
Forsyth, Robert, xii., 522.
Fox, H., Secretary, vii., 179, 180, 268.
France, Minister of, xii., 723; xii., 723, 487, 647, 672, 682.
Francis, Tench, v., 775; xv., 153.
Franklin, Benjamin, vii., 16; xiv., 165. Executors of, xvi., 358.
Franklin, John, and John Jennings, xv., 79.
Franks, David, xii., 547.
Fraser, John. v., 659.
French Minister, xii., 723.
Furman, Moore, xii., 435.
Gage, General Thomas, ix., 90, 118, 119, 170, 238, 264, 267, 281, 292, 300, 302, 318, 321, 403, 581, 665, 718; x., 17, 19.
Galbraith, Colonel Bartram, xi., 776.
Galbraith, James, and John Hoge, ix., 487.
Galbraith, Robert, xvi., 252, 256.
Galbraith, Thomas, xiv., 476.
Gamble, James, xii., 311.
Ganawese, King, from Governor, iii., 188.
Gardner, Joseph, xiv., 549.
Gerard, Sieur, xi., 679; xii., 60, 66, 78.
Glasier, B., vi., 480.

Letters—
Glen, Governor James, of South Carolina, v., 699.
Glonsinger, John, xiii., 424.
Gooch, William, Governor of Virginia, iii., 564; iv., 655, 755; v., 56, 189, 221, 257, 280, 301, 346.
Gordon, James, xiii., 453.
Gordon, Lewis, ix., 572, 744, 752, 756.
Gordon, Patrick, Governor of Pennsylvania, iii., 469, 475, 481, 483, 487, 489, 495, 565, 567, 583.
Governor of Connecticut, xii., 287.
Governor of Maryland, xii., 400, xv., 463.
Governor of Massachusetts, xii., 400; xiv., 516, 643; xv., 53, 170, 183, 435.
Governor of North Carolina, xii., 314; xvi., 309.
Governor of New Jersey, xv., 493.
Governor of New York, i., 202; xii., 301; xiv., 380; xv., 497; xvi., 103.
Governor Green of Rhode Island, xii., 444.
Governor of Virginia, iv., 655, 755; vii., 570; xiv., 467, 643, 651.
Graff, Reverend Mr., vi., 757.
Greene, General Nathaniel, xii., 300, 305, 428.
Green, Wm., Gov. R. I., xii., 444.
Gregg, Mathew, xii., 455.
Gregory, James, Sub-Lieutenant, xii., 4, 93.
Griffin, ——, xii., 250.
Gronow, Lewis, xii., 600; xiii., 283.
Gurney, Francis, xv., 340.
Hale, Thomas, xii., 265.
Halifax, Earl of, ix., 113.
Hall, Charles, xii., 76; xiii., 128.
Haller, Mr. Henry, xi., 771; xii., 12, 48, 436, 780.
Hamilton, A., and John Georges, iii., 554, 558, 559, 560.
Hamilton, Hance, vii., 77.
Hamilton, Governor James, v., 383, 384, 463, 570, 582, 586, 596, 628, 632, 661, 693, 696, 698, 700,

Letters—
708, 709, 753, 768; vi., 1, 3, 27, 31, 145, 148, 181, 182, 763; viii., 568, 570, 622, 691, 776, 778, 779; ix., 777.
Hamilton, Captain John, x., 665.
Hammond, William, Sheriff of Baltimore, iv., 66, 69.
Hancock, John, Governor of Massachusetts, xv., 435.
Hand, General Edward, xi., 261; xii., 138, 284, 427; xiv., 23, 25, 72, 159, 162, 165, 173, 180.
Hannums, John, xiii., 105, 508.
Hardy, Governor, Sir Charles, vii., 9, 35, 41, 113, 122, 123, 142, 307, 339.
Hardy, Samuel, xiv., 162.
Harmar, Colonel Josiah, xiv., 185, 311, 356, 373, 447, 470, 473, 480, 516; xv., 379; xvi., 258, 262.
Harris, John, vi., 184, 226, 457, 645, 654, 655, 661.
Harrison, Governor Benjamin, of Virginia, xiii., 753; xiv., 38.
Hart, Colonel Joseph, xiii., 82; xiv., 307.
Hartley, David, xiv., 165.
Hartley, Colonel Thomas, xi., 452, 626.
Hawley, Rev. Gideon, vi., 11.
Hay, John, Sheriff, ix., 103; xii., 108.
Hazard, Ebenezer, xiii., 122.
Helsted, Charles, Swedish Consul, xiv., 276.
Henry, George, xi., 765.
Henry, John, xiii., 324.
Henry, Governor Patrick, of Virginia, xii., 16.
Henry, Colonel William, xi., 779; xii., 570; xiii., 603, 641; xv., 241.
Hewitt, Thomas, xii., 490.
Hiester, Daniel, Jr., xiii., 74.
Hill, Thomas, Secretary, v., 686.
Hillegas, Michael, xii., 423, 444.
Hillsborough, Lord, ix., 546, 552, 637, 706, 760.
Hodgdon, Colonel Samuel, xiii., 614; xv., 9.
Holdernesse, Earl of, v., 689.
Holker, Mons., French Consul,

Letters—
xi., 699, 749; xii., 30, 54, 59, 61, 65, 90, 94, 233, 296, 402, 419.
Holland, Hitchen, v., 622, 623; vi., 53, 411.
Holland, Nathaniel, viii., 501.
Holmes, John, Sheriff, ix., 463.
Hopkinson, Judge Francis, xii., 267, 574; xiv., 144; xv., 398.
Hopson, P., v., 228.
Horsefield, Timothy, vi., 736, 756, 757; vii., 169, 187, 190, 305, 461, 587, 732; viii., 84, 99, 353, 663.
Hubley, Lieutenant Adam, xi., 770; xii., 732.
Hubley, Colonel John, xii., 53, 84, 231; xiii., 71, 140.
Huffnagle, Michael, xiii., 731, 754, 766, 774; xiv., 471, 472, 607; xv., 179.
Humpton, Colonel Richard, letter, xi., 761; xii., 320.
Hunter, Colonel Samuel, xii., 23, 72, 229, 308, 461, 490, 743, 744; xiii., 521.
Huntington, Governor Samuel, xv., 575.
Innes, Colonel James, vi., 51, 478.
Irvine, Brigadier-General, Jas., xi., 569, 696.
Irvine, Colonel William, xi., 569.
Irvin, Brigadier-General, xii., 58, 227; xiii., 297, 406, 430, 491, 616, 617, 677, 686.
Jacks, James, xiv., 331.
Jackson, David, xiv., 549.
Jamaica, Governor of, viii,, 171.
Jameison, D., &c., xii., 27.
Jay, John, xiv., 165, 405, 451, 560.
Jefferson, Thomas, Secretary, xvi., 314, 374, 415, 428, 433, 456.
Jennings, Edm., and D. Dubarry, iv., 108, 130, 141.
Jennings, John, ix., 585.
Jocelyn, Thomas, vi., 774, 778.
Johnson, Colonel, v., 431, 480, 549; vi., 269, 359, 509, 607.
Johnson, Colonel Francis, xi., 190, 407; xiv., 311; xv., 426.
Johnson, Governor of Maryland, xi., 647.

Letters—
Johnson, Colonel Guy, x., 200.
Johnson, Sir William, vii., 117, 193, 279, 434, 622, 626, 723; viii., 97, 507; ix., 21, 63, 129, 189, 412, 495; x., 21.
Jones, Cadwalader, Governor of New Providence, i., 342.
Judges Supreme Court, xi., 753; xiv., 141; xv., 452; xvi., 14.
Justices of Berks county, vi., 503.
Justices of Cumberland, v., 452.
Justices of Philadelp'a, xii., 80.
Justices of Lancaster county, iv., 66, 109.
Justices of Lewistown respecting piratical vessels, i., 539.
Kachlein, Peter, xii., 317.
Keene, Lawrence, xiii., 697.
Keith, Wm., Governor, iii., 223.
Kellogg, Martin, v., 573.
Knowles, Governor or Admiral Charles, v., 127, 133.
Knox, General Henry, xii., 245, 398, 400; xiv., 517.
Kucher, Christopher, xii., 393.
Laird, Hugh, xv., 213.
La Jonquiere, v., 554.
Langdon, John, Governor of New Hampshire, xiv., 596.
Lawrens, Henry, xi., 437, 487.
Lawrence, T., Governor, vi., 249, 451, 464, 554, 711.
Lawrence, Thomas, letters of, v., 92, 133.
Ledlie, Andrew, ix., 756.
Lee, Arthur, and R. Butler, xiv., 165.
Lee, General, x., 753.
Lee, Major ———, xii., 210.
Lee, Thomas, President of Virginia, v., 423.
Leisler, J., Governor of New York, defence against French, i., 332.
Lenox, David, xiv., 454.
Levan, Daniel, xiii., 750.
Levers, Robert, xi., 528; xiii., 74.
Lewis, William, xvi., 456.
Lieutenants of Philadelphia, xii., 338.
Limback, F., and P. Burnholder, xiii., 91.

Letters—
Lincoln, Benjamin, xiii., 254.
Livingston, Robert R., minister for Foreign Affairs, xiii., 211, 282, 459, 487, 543, 555.
Livingston, Gov. Wm., of New Jersey, xi., 185; xii., 87, 89, 386, 495, 685.
Lloyd, P. Zachary, xvi., 458.
Lochrey, D. Arch'd., xi., 773.
Lochrey, Arch'd., xii., 72, 245.
Logan, James, president, iv., 64, 70, 75, 112, 121, 137, 140, 146, 159, 190, 198, 206, 252, 288, 311.
Long, Andrew, xii., 537.
Long, Thomas, xiii., 98.
Long, William, xv., 266.
Lords of Trade, iv., 356, 503, 567; vii., 272, 278, 386, 738; ix., 40, 79.
Lords, Justices, iv., 671, 675.
Louisiana, Governor of, viii., 124.
Loudoun, Lord, vii., 234, 269, 340, 342, 379, 429, 453, 495, 523, 525, 596, 597, 732, 737, 756; viii., 23.
Lovell, James, Del. Mass., xii., 51.
Lukens, John, Surv'r General, xv., 49.
Luzerne, Chev. de la, xii., 251, 433.
Lynch, Jno. Patrick, xii., 353.
Lyttle, Andrew, xii., 334; xiii., 508.
McAllister, Richard, xiv., 182; xv., 126.
McCleery, Wm., xiii., 698.
McClenachan and Irwine, xi., 766.
McDowell, John Rev., xiii., 481.
McFarlane, Andrew, x., 169.
McGauhey, ———, xiii., 647, 672.
McGinty, Alexander, v., 627.
Mackay, Æneas, x., 140, 169.
McKean, C. J. Thomas, xii., 75, 112.
McKee, Thomas, vii., 597, 619, 734.
McKinley, John, x., 669.
McIntosh, Gen'l, xi., 699, 773.
McLean, Alexander, xiii., 334, 510, 516, 531.
McLean, Mr., xii., 93.
McMichael, John, vi., 254.

Letters—
Maclay, Wm., xiv., 374, 604.
Magistrates of Huntingdon, xv., 479. Of Westmoreland, x., 323.
Maisterson, Captain Samuel, v., 323.
Managers of State Lottery, xiv., 275, 286; xv., 36, 159.
Marbois, Mons., xiii., 486, 596, 600, 645, 672, xiv., 111, 135, 140, 173, 282, 290, 405.
Marine Committee, xi., 646.
Marshall, Lt. James, xiv., 165; xv., 107.
Marsteller, Philip, xii., 67, 116, 392.
Maryland, Gov. of, xii., 433.
Massachusetts, Gov. of, xi., 629, 682.
Maseracre, Col., xii., 52.
Maxwell, William, vi., 434.
Mead, David, insurrection in Northumberland, xiv., 358, 398, 497.
Mercer, Lieut.-Colonel Hugh, viii., 292, 305, 391, 394.
Merchants of Philadelphia, xiv., 54.
Melcher, Col. Isaac, xv., 597.
Miles, Hon. Samuel, xiv., 66.
Militia Officers, xii., 215.
Miller, Rev. Peter, xiii., 510.
Milligan James, xiv., 586.
Mills, Lieutenant, v., 573.
Minister of France, xiv., 115, 121, 136, 144, 173.
Minister, United Netherlands, xiv., 135.
Mitchell, James, to Governor, iii., 187.
Mitchell, John D., Quarter-Master-General, xii., 18.
Mitchell, Col. John, xii., 321.
Monakatootha, v., 635.
Monckton, General Robert, viii., 495, 509.
Montgomery, Capt., xii., 19, 86.
Montgomery, Daniel, xiii., 697.
Montgomery, Joseph, xv., 221.
Montgomery, Capt. James, x., 665.
Montgomery, Wm., xvi., 538.
Montour, Andrew, vi., 46, 130.
Moody, Robert, x., 86.
Moore, Ann, xiii., 105.
Moore, Sir Henry, Governor, ix., 569, 642.

Letters—
Moore, Major James, xii., 92; xiv., 29, 31, 32.
Moore, Col. James, xiv., 144.
Morales, Francis, xiv., 484.
Morgan, Capt. Jacob, vii., 35; xi., 531; xii., 53, 117, 743.
Morris, Cadwalader, xiv., 29.
Morris, Governor of New York, v., 1.
Morris, Gov. Robert H., vi., 187, 249, 252, 254, 255, 286, 295, 296, 297, 299, 301, 303, 327, 334, 335, 338, 372, 406, 408, 410, 412, 415, 419, 420, 421, 452, 453, 455, 461, 462, 463, 476, 495, 496, 511, 519, 563, 565, 595, 599, 604, 639, 652, 660, 662, 666, 700, 744, 771, 772, 774, 776; vii., 10, 97, 109, 120, 136, 151, 170, 189, 191; xi., 690.
Morris, Robert, x., 784; xii., 2. Sup. fin., xii., 783; xiii., 19, 100, 128, 173, 195, 211, 282, 374, 404, 406, 408, 425, 487, 551, xiv., 182, 468.
Muhlenberg, Fred. Aug., xii., 263, 568. Speaker, xii., 568, 584.
Munday, Henry, iv., 102.
Murray, Gov. James, ix., 290.
Nathaniel, Mr., vi., 756.
Navy Board, xii., 398.
Nesbitt, Mr., xii., 283.
Netotways (Indian chief), ix., 735.
New Castle, Capt. vii., 189.
New Castle, Duke of, iv., 422, 428, 430, 490, 689, 766; v., 37, 127.
New York, Governor and Council of, respecting D. Plessie, i., 202.
Nice, John, xv., 432.
Nicholson, Francis, Governor of Maryland, i., 515.
Nicholson, John, Comptroller-General, xiii., 417; xvi., 332.
Nicola, Colonel, xii., 400, 450, 730.
Norris, Isaac, Speaker, vii., 149.
North Carolina, xv., 524.
Ogden, Aaron, xi., 752.
Ogle, Samuel, Governor of Maryland, iii., 480, 557, 559; iv., 60, 116, 156, 167, 175, 187, 195, 206, 219, 223, 242, 311; v., 187, 192, 202, 209, 273, 376, 382, 422.

Letters—
Ononraguite (Indian chief), vi., 130.
Orndt, Capt. Jacob, vii., 305, 429, 475, 723.
Orndt, Major, viii., 167, 401, 406.
Orth, Adam, xiii., 485.
Osborne, Henry, xiii., 350.
Owen, Evan, xvi., 259.
Palmer, Anthony, President, v., 76, 131, 143, 145, 165, 186, 189, 190, 201, 215, 223, 225, 254, 286.
Paris, Capt. Richard, vii., 529, 557.
Parker, Robert, xvi., 87.
Parsons, William, vi., 668, 737, 761; vii., 163, 284–289, 305, 475, 620.
Patterson, Alexander, xiii., 731, 760, 763; xiv., 32, 47, 162.
Patterson, James, ix., 453.
Payne, Sir Ralph, Governor, &c., x., 57.
Pearson, James, xiv., 285, 406.
Pemberton, James, xvi., 210[2].
Pendleton, Edmund, xv., 498.
Penn, Gov. John, ix., 92, 104, 110, 111, 112, 113, 127, 135, 268, 277, 297, 299, 303, 306, 344, 351, 353, 377, 405, 416, 422, 424, 440, 442, 446, 468, 483, 564, 573, 585, 586, 600, 664; x., 119, 121, 123, 130, 149, 152, 158, 164, 171, 176, 192, 193, 194, 202, 221, 236, 242, 247.
Penn, Richard, Governor, x., 68, 86.
Penn, Thomas, v., 228, 239, 240, 499.
Penn, William, i., 527, 528.
Pepperell, Sir William, vii., 570.
Perie, Nicholas, v., 219.
Perry, Samuel, v., 135.
Peters, Richard, v., 213, 214, 376, 403, 462, 760; vi., 287. Secretary, vii., 149, 151, 397; x., 177; xv., 493.
Peters, William, vii., 167.
Pettit, Charles, xi., 117, 490; xii., 2, 326, 328, 330; xvi., 411.
Phelps, Oliver, xvi., 439.
Philadelphia Library Company, xii., 318.

Letters—
Phile, Frederick, xiii., 563; xvi., 58.
Phips, S., v., 418.
Phips, Gov. S. of Massachusetts, vi., 451, 605, 606; vii., 135, 169, 186.
Phipp, Paul, Gov. of Jamaica, xiv., 269.
Pickering, Timothy, xii., 451; xv., 212, 465, 502, 505, 514, 546.
Pierce, John, xv., 5, 87.
Pierce, Joseph, xiv., 582.
Pinalosa, Gov. of Havana, v., 75.
Pitkin, Gov. William, of Connecticut, ix., 602.
Pitt, William, Secretary, vii., 413, 564; viii., 18, 26, 27, 272, 288, 315, 316, 449, 451, 588.
Plunkett, William, x., 86.
Pomroy, Ralph, xi., 749, 752.
Popple, Sir Alfred, iii., 262.
Porter, Col. Andrew, xiv., 285.
Porter, Stephen, xv., 108.
Potter, General, xii., 490, 492.
Potter, John, Sheriff, vi., 673.
Potts, Dr., xii., 101.
Powell, Jeremiah, Gov. of Massachusetts, xi., 690, 728.
Pownall, John, Secretary of Trade, vii., 738; viii., 515.
Pownal, Thomas, vi., 267.
Pownall, Gov. Thomas, vii., 717; viii., 483.
President United States, xvi., 93, 119, 123, 141, 154, 169, 289, 306.
Proctor, Col. Thomas, xi., 781; xii., 9.
Proprietary from Maryland, i., 230, 298; ii., 136; v., 216, 362, 515; vi., 485.
Prothonotary of Huntingdon, xvi., 123.
Provincial Commissioners, vii., 694.
Provincial Council, ix., 757, 779.
Purdy, R., A. C., xii., 131.
Putnam, General Israel, xi., 203.
Quincey, Josiah, vi., 339.
Randolph, Edmund, xiv., 651.
Randolph, Gov. of Virg'a, xv., 159, 416, 465.

Letters—
Rea, Samuel, xii., 336, 374, 485.
Receiver-General, Land Office, xiv., 454; xvi., 95, 410.
Redick, David, xv., 493.
Reed, Justice Adam, vii., 303.
Reed, James R., xv., 505.
Reed, Joseph, President, xiii., 70.
Register General, xvi., 63.
Reid, Lieutenant-Colonel, ix., 268, 269.
Rendon, Don Franc., xii., 398.
Rhea, Samuel, xiii., 736.
Riffetts, Philip, xv., 483,
Rittenhouse, David, xiii., 519, 522.
Robbins, Ezekiel, xiii., 459.
Roberdeau, General, xi., 677.
Robeson, Capt. Thomas, xiii., 565.
Robinson, Lieut. Andrew, xiii., 698.
Robinson, Capt. Thomas, xiii., 503-699.
Robinson, Sir Thomas, vi., 176, 200, 302, 373, 395, 451, 644.
Ross, James, xvi., 464.
Rush, Dr. Benjamin, xv., 616.
Ruston, Dr. Thomas, xvi., 201.
Rutherford, John, vi., 303.
Ryerson, Thomas, xvi., 297.
St. Clair, Arthur, x., 140; xi., 762, 770; xii., 36, 52, 139, 240, 421; xiii., 505; xv., 183, 194, 518; xvi., 422.
St. Clair, Sir John, vi., 298, 300; viii., 70.
St. John, Mons. xiv., 2.
St. Pierre, Legardeur, v., 716.
Sanders, Robert, v., 626.
Sargent, Aufrere and B., ix., 47.
Schrawder, Captain, xiii., 645, 731.
Schuyler, Col. Peter, viii., 240.
Scott, Hon. Thomas, xi., 773; xii., 235; xiii., 403, 672.
Scott, William, xiii., 318.
Secretary of foreign affairs, xv., 51, 465; xvi., 48. Of land office, 237. Of treasury, 189, 244. Of war, xiv., 465; xv., 435; xvi., 189, 200.
Seely, Jonas, ix., 43, 44.
Senate of Hamburgh, xiii., 703.

Letters—
Sharp, Lieutenant Geo., xii., 15.
Sharpe, Gov., Horatio, vi., 178, 410, 420, 456, 477, 643; vii., 32, 341, 570, 716; ix., 377,
Shawana, Ben., (Indian,) ix., 480.
Shawnese, v., 289.
Shee, John, xiii., 744.
Shelburne, Earl of, ix., 341, 342, 343, 378, 379.
Sheriff of York County, xii., 82.
Shippen, Edward, v., 659; vi., 431, 459; vii., 294; viii., 113; ix., 89, 100, 108; xv., 120.
Shippen, Joseph, Jr., xii., 327.
Shirley, Gov., iv., 753; v., 30, 56, 72, 127, 141, 152, 170, 295, 297, 305 718; vi., 16, 52, 309, 310, 404, 410, 439, 450, 558, 561; vii., 19, 39, 45, 111, 112, 127.
Shirley, Will'm, Secretary, vi., 404.
Shoemaker, Colonel Jacob, xii., 103.
Shrewsbury, Secretary of England, war with French, i., 302.
Smallwood, W., Gov., of Maryland, xiv., 589.
Smith, Col. vi., 20; xii., 210.
Smith, Devereux, x., 169; xii., 287.
Smith, Jon. B., xv., 595.
Smith, Matthew, xi., 461, 751.
Smith, Samuel, Sheriff of Lancaster, iii., 615; iv., 67.
Smith, Samuel, Jr., iii., 615.
Smith, Thomas, xii., 551; xiv., 450.
Smith, Wm. Moore, xv., 428.
Spangenberg, Rev. Mr., vi., 358; vii., 118, 173; viii., 304.
Sprogell, Ludowick, xi., 655, 779; xii., 44.
Spry, Captain, vii., 127, 128.
Spycker, Peter, vi., 703.
Stanwix, Col. John, vii., 598, 599, 600, 602, 629; viii., 146, 341, 343, 352, 373, 376, 377, 378.
Steele, Rev. John, ix., 486, 506, 509.
Stephen, Adam, vii., 289, 381, 502.
Stephenson, George, xii., 201, 296.
Stevens, Arent, v., 625.

Letters—
Stevenson, James, vi., 248.
Stewart, Charles, ix., 583, 756, x., 50.
Stewart, Col., xi., 782; xii., 116.
Stewart, George, xiv., 385.
Stewart, Chas., and John Jennings, ix., 573.
Stiles, Joseph, xiv., 29.
Stoddert, Benjamin, v., 550.
Stobo, Captain Robert, vi., 141, 161.
Stone, Andrew, Secretary, iv., 671, 675.
Stout, Captain Hermann, xii., 89.
Street Commission's, xiii., 596.
Strettell, Robert, vi., 773, 777; vii., 167.
Stroud, Col., x., 717.
Sullivan, Major, xii., 9, 107.
Sullivan, David, xiii., 172.
Supreme Executive Council, xi., 215, 394, 401, 425, 759; xii., 46, 48, 54, 109, 117, 198, 203, 210, 230, 234, 245, 256, 312, 399.
Superintend't of Finance, xiii., 619, 731.
Surveyor General, xiv., 454, 639; xv., 427, 452; xvi., 171, 216, 211[2], 212[2], 219[2], 223[2], 224, 231.
Sutherland, Captain Nicholas x., 16.
Swaine, Charles, vi., 643.
Swaine, Francis, xii., 61, 284.
Tanner, Michael, &c., iv., 69.
Tasker, Benjamin, President of Maryland, v., 582, 583, 589.
Teedyuscung, viii., 96.
Thomas, Gov. Geo., iv., 635, 653; v., 2.
Thomson, Charles, vii., 724; xiv., 23, 31, 72, 143, 643.
Thompson, James, xii., 75.
Thompson, Captain Wm., viii., 111; xiii., 221.
Tilghman, J. & A. Allen, x., 182, 186, 191.
Till, William, (Pres.,) vii., 267.
Tinker, Gov. John, of R. I., vii., 151.
Torbert, John, xvi., 174.
Townsend, Admiral, vii., 571.
Trade, Lords of, v., 711, 718; vi., 59.

Letters—
Traill, Robert, xv., 461.
Trelawney, Gov., of Jamaica, v. 326.
Trent, William, v., 462, 616; vi., 481, 641; vii., 601.
Troup, Robert, Sec. Treasury, xii., 198.
Trumbull, Gov. Jonathan, x., 3, 119, 157, 163; xiv. 2, 12.
Trustees of Westmoreland, xiii., 698.
Tucker, Henry, x., 321.
Turnbull, Mr., xii., 334.
Turnbull, Marmie, & Co., xiv., 517; xv., 617.
Turnbull, William, xv., 445.
Udree, Capt. Daniel, xii., 675.
Ulm, city of, xiv., 356.
Van Campen, John, xii., 570, 585; xiv., 443.
Van Sice, John, vii., 43.
Vernon, Admiral, iv., 478.
Virginia, Delegates, xi., 690.
Wall, Col. George, Jr., xi., 636; xii., 101, 250.
War, Secretary of, xiii., 425; xv., 250, 641.
Wardens of Philadelphia, xiv., 78, 122, 212, 578; xv., 233.
Warren, Admiral, v., 6.
Washington, Col. George, vii., 603, 604.
Washington, General George, xi., 197, 228, 428, 436, 490, 626, 650, 654; xii., 8, 32, 90, 92, 123, 203, 227, 262, 313, 335, 376, 392, 474, 517, 545, 574, 591, 706, 742, 761, 778; xiii., 41, 184, 211, 321, 362, 457, 487, 502, 603.
Wayne, General Anthony, xi., 619; xii., 437.
Wharton, Joseph, xv., 499.
Weiser, Conrad, iv., 768; v., 121, 133, 166, 467, 517; vi., 147, 148, 248, 291, 443, 467, 495, 503, 613, 640, 647, 649, 650, 652, 656, 659, 681, 760, 762; vii., 302, 308.
Weiss, Lewis, xiii., 9.
West, Justice, viii., 455.
West, William, v., 761.
Weitzel, Colonel, xii., 57.
Wikoff, Wm., and L. Clark, xiii., 486.
Wilkins, John, xv., 86.
Wilkinson,——Clothier-General, xii., 87.

Letters—
Williams, Lieut.-Colonel Wm., xii., 88; xiv., 641.
Willing, Thomas, president B. N. A., xiii., 200.
Wilmot, Henry, ix., 749.
Wilson, James, and Wm. Lewis, xii., 324.
Wilson, James, xiv., 317.
Wilson, Col. Wm., xvi., 464, 483.
Wiltner, Col. ———, xii., 215, 297, 309.
Wink, Jacob, xv. 331.
Wolcott. Roger, Gov. of Connecticut, v., 771.
Woods, George, xiii., 509; xvi., 361.
Wraxall, Peter, vii., 195.
Wright, James, viii., 116.
Wright, John, iii., 470.
Wynkoop, Henry, xii., 490; xiii., 95, 357, 601, 616, 768; xvi., 104.
Wyoming, Commiss'rs, xiv., 215.
Zeigler, Capt., xii., 220, 334.

[The foregoing list is intended merely to show the persons from whom letters were received. Very generally, the letters themselves are not given (having probably been lost), though in some cases they are; and others not found here, will (if printed) be found under the same head in the index to the Archives.]

Levan, Daniel, Jr., Sheriff, xi., 187, 358. Prothonotary and Justice, 542.
Levan, Isaac, Jr., Coroner, ix., 778; x., 56.
Levan, Colonel Sebastian, xi., 35.
Levers, Robert, Prothonotary, xi., 187. Clerk of Orphans' Court, 191, 228.
Levers, Robert, a Justice, ix., 245. Paymaster, xi., 2. Prothonotary, 187. Clerk of Orphans' Court, 191, 228. Sends goods to Boston for sale, &c., 401. Letters, 528; xii., 47, 316. Lieutenant, of Northampton, 767. Letter of non-acceptance of Thos. Anderson, xiii., 21, 44, 74. Complaint against, 91. To contract for supplies, 402. Resigns, 617. Account, xiv., 23. Taxes, 67. Justice, 231. Prothonotary of Northumberland, dies, xv., 460.
Levis, Thomas, Justice, xiv., 212. Appeals, xv., 392.
Levis, William, printing, xiii., 136.
Levy, Aaron, supplies troops, xvi., 316.
Levy, Ashur, appears as supposed spy, xii., 258.
Levy, Hyman, has goods of enemy in hand after evacuation of Philadelphia, xi., 525.
Levys County, iii., 38, 244, 246.
Lewis, a French Canadian prisoner, i., 435.
Lewis, Colonel, battalion, x., 651, 682.
Lewis, Colonel Robert, battalion, xi., 35.
Lewis, Major, &c., petition to ship tobacco—granted, xii., 747.
Lewis, Wrixam, Coroner, vii., 267.
Lewis, William, sister and servants, pass to, xiii, 621. Attorney, xiv., 463. Letter, xvi., 456, 459.
Lewes County, i., 127. Councillor for port of Whorekills—Duties on goods at New Castle, 205. William Massey, collector at, 537.
Lewestown, arrival, and plunder by, French vessels at, i., 539. Captain Kidd's privateer visits—Complaint against inhabitants for purchasing goods from him, 579. To be tried by Admiralty Court, 580. Watch against pirates, ii., 23, 24. H. Brooke, collector, 99. Complaint against sheriff, 101. Prize, 101. Samuel Louman, collector, 121. French privateer at, 448, 468. Address from, against J. Bailey, justice, 465. Governor at—Message from—Pilot asks for pay, 506.
Lewes, Henry Brooke, collector of customs at—A member of council, iii., 143. Robberies by French and Spaniards, v., 88. Express from, respecting captures by privateers in sight of, 110. Express sent to, 257. Commission to Abraham Wiltbank to com-

mand intelligence boat, 266. Embargo, vii., 388. To be supplied with ammunition, x., 353. Man-of-war and tender arrive, 526. Rifle Company at, 615.

Lexington, brig fitted out by Congress, x., 524. Commanded by Captain Barry, 526. Ammunition for, 528.

Libertines, to be discountenanced, iii., 64.

Liberty, charter of, to be kept by Master of Rolls, i., 111. Religious, declared, ii., 57.

Liberty Island, order respecting, x., 419. Three boats to be always at, 426. Lieutenant Symonds to command artillery company at, 437. Committee to lay out works at, 492.

Library, State, funds for inclosing, xii., 588. Books to be returned to State, 699. Judges of Appeals to have access to, xiii., 576. Keys for, xvi., 72.

License, for publishing, to be given by council, i., 165. For selling liquors, 165; ii., 159, 160, 455. New form, v., 69, 71. Marriage fees, xi., 760. To travel through the State granted to Alexander Cathcart and James Shirly, xiv., 592. To John Sheriden to travel through the State and sell goods, xv., 243. Tavern and marriage, in several counties, xvi., 61, 62, 83, 176, 522.

Lieutenants of boats, &c., x., 339, 505, 643. Recommended as, and appointed, 448–473, 645. Second do., 449, 453, 505, 572. Appointed, xi., 23, 31, 32, 37, 47, 56, 61, 199, 202, 205, 229 257, 303, 310, 318, 333, 358, 370, 378, 437, 448, 453, 455, 557. And subs chosen, xii., 2, 9, 10, 14, 70, 73, 88, 89, 132, 139, 297, 298, 307, 317, 322, 338, 372, 374, 384, 390, 437, 477, 483, 489, 490, 595, 603, 632, 662, 681, 720, 733, 777; xiii., 82, 83, 158, 160, 167, 168, 240, 262, 275, 316, 731; xiv., 38, 180, 205, 217, 478, 482; xvi., 42.

Ligonier, express dispatched to St. Clair from, x., 201.

Lightbourne, Captain, asks for provisions for a circuitous voyage, xi., 636.

Lightfoot, Benjamin, Sheriff, v., 597, 662; vi., 144.

Lightfoot, Samuel, a Justice, v., 547.

Lightfoot, Thomas, arrest ordered by Congress, but declined, he not being a resident, xi., 269. Claims lots in city, xiii., 18.

Lighthouse at mouth of Delaware Bay, ix., 56, 57, 148, 296, 550. Supported by tonnage tax, xi., 620.

Lighthouse on Cape Henlopen in danger of being washed away, xiii., 100.

Lighthouses, beacons, &c., xvi., 132.

Limbach, Frederick, Justice, xiv., 185, 261.

Linch, or Lynch, to be arrested, xii., 312. Is imprisoned; letter from James Wilson and William Lewis respecting, ordered before board; sent back, &c., 324, 326, 350, 353. Considered a prisoner of war and removed to new gaol, under charge of Mr. Bradford, 353.

Lindenmuth, Michael, Justice, xi., 479. Colonel, at Fort Jenkins, 654.

Lindemuth, Colonel, not to be paid money, xii., 567.

Lindley, Thomas, road near, iii., 227, 230.

Lincoln, Major General, minister of war department—guards for prisoners, xiii., 165. Failure of expedition against Sandusky, 323. Artillery commissions, 460.

Lincoln, Hon. Benjamin, letter and resolution of Congress, xiii., 254.

Lindt, Michael, paid for repair of Court house for Assembly and Council, xi., 362.

Linen, cloth manufacture to be encouraged, i., 93. To have a price set on it, 98. Premium claimed, 194. Manufacture of, in Philadelphia, ix., 354. Old, for bandages and lint, x., 471, 633.

Linington, John, applies to be measurer of salt, wheat, &c., xi., 590. Inspector of staves, heading, &c., Philadelphia, xiv., 488.

Linn, Rev. William, appointed chaplain to Pennsylvania troops, x., 487.

Liston, Edmund, robbed by French and Spaniards, v., 89.

Lite, Daniel, appointed sub-Lieutenant of Washington county, xii., 681.

Literary Property, letter of Congress on, xiii., 574.

Little, John, purchaser of provisions, xi., 423, 448.

Little, John, Justice, xiv., 667.

Little Meadows, affairs at, vi., 460. French at, vii., 601.

Littleton, Fort, viii., 224.

Liturgy, to be altered on death of King George II., viii., 518. Instructions to Governor Hamilton respecting, 520.

Livergood, Captain Jacob, of rifle company appointed, xiii., 71, 177.

Liverpool, man-of-war and prisoners, x., 596. Exchange, 606.

Lievzey, Thomas, provincial Commissioner, ix., 237.

Livingston, Philip, secretary for Indian affairs, New York, iii., 201.

Livingston, R. R., list of his negroes, xiii., 154. Commission from King for R. Oswald to treat, 459.

Livingston, Gov. William, of New Jersey, on prisoners, xi., 185. Applied to, for a robber, 512. Prisoner sent to, xii., 38. Letter 87. Receives trunks from New York, 224, 386. Capt. Joel, 495. Letters to and from, xiii., 680. Letter respecting captors of Col. Pickering, xv., 493.

Llewellyn, Daniel, claims a city lot, xiii., 119.

Llewellyn, David, Surveyor of roads, iii., 231.

Lloyd, David, Commissioned by Governor as Attorney General, i., 188. Proposed as clerk of county Court, 190. Appointed, 192. Accused, 244, 247. Refuses to deliver up papers to J. Claypoole, 256. Proceedings, 256, 257, 258, 269, 279. Petition against, 383, 386. Complaint against, for adjourning Assembly, 445. Speaker, 454. Proposal to give him £200, 468. Lots in Chester town, 557. Charges against, by Colonel Quarry, 602, 603. Illegally arrested, 607. To produce papers relating to Blue Anchor, ii., 10. Draws, and obtains Governor's signature to, a charter of privileges, 62. Speaker, 106, 398. Proceedings respecting a forged remonstrance signed by, 186, 192. Charged with bribery, 432. Speaker, 506. Chief Justice, iii., 257. Speaker, 260, 289. Sickness renders him incapable, 398.

Lloyd, Thomas, appointed first master of rolls, i., 91. Commissioner to New York, 103, 104. President of C., 119. Has great seal, 119. Deputy Lieutenant, 211. Called on for blanks sent by proprietary, 230. Asks advice about going to N. Y. and leaving the great seal, 234, 235. His letter to Council, 236. Letter from, respecting papers received, 238. Complaint and proceeding against, 245, 250, 261, 265, 270–274, 275. His answer, 275. Proceedings, 279, 293. Elected president, 317, 323. Refuses to be Lieutenant Deputy Governor under Fletcher, 364. Has records of New Castle, 389. Dead, 522.

Lloyd, Peter Zachary, Captain of a company of Philadelphia battalion of militia, resigns, xvi., 336. In charge of books and papers of Assembly, 446, 449.

Lloyd, Captain, vii., 294; x., 560.

Loan office, Trustees, removal of, iii., 383. Robbery of W. Fishbourne, 389, 536, 537. Trustees, removal of, &c., iv., 297, 658, 673, 676, 688. Bill for new trustees, v., 369, 375. Of, authorized to draw for appropriation by parliament, viii., 666; ix., 205, 394; x., 27, 29, 31, 37, 68. Money in, xi., 211. Order on, 213, 448, 475. Money, books, &c., to be removed under guard to Easton, 305, 306, 307. To be placed in hands of Robert Levers, 307. Committee of Assembly demand the key of loan office chest, which Colonel Hart, by consent of council, delivers to

them, 395. Certificates to be paid Joseph Carson for goods, 397. Persons in each county to receive subscriptions, xii., 47. Certificates, amount, value, &c., 360. Bills exchange, 422. Letter, Thomas Smith, Commissioner, 551, 556. Continental, Thomas Smith, xiii., 6. Thomas Smith, Commissioner, 585. Claim for interest on certificates of, xiv., 169, 338. Counterfeit certificates, 450. Draft on, 457, 504, 589. Paper for certificates, xv., 10. Thomas Smith, loan officer, and Corn. Barnes, and Jona. Smith, Jr., clerks, 11. Printing new certificates, 30. Certificates to Pennsylvania line, 87. T. Smith asks protection of council from Comptroller-General, 218. Certificates printed, xvi., 88. To be removed, 99. To remove to accommodate convention, 214[2].

Loan, for invalid soldiers, xvi., 213[2].

Lock, manufac'y, provincial, x., 651.

Lockrey, Lieutenant Colonel Archibald, of Westmoreland county, xi., 110. Receives rifles and guns and money, 186. Prothonotary, 187. Clerk of Orphans' Court, 190, 436. Money to, 477. Letter, 773. Prothonotary of Orphans' Court, 430. Recommends lieutenants, xii., 73. Lieutenant, 372. To have arms repaired, 641. Supposed death or captivity of, his commission annulled, xiii., 155. Successor appointed, 167.

Lockart, John, petition for small Island between Tinicum and Hogg Island, xvi., 230.

Lockerman, Nicholas, Coroner, iii., 416, 465, 524, 575.

Lodge Jonathan, Sheriff, xi., 367, 638, 639. Sheriff of Northumberland county, suspended by Justices of which he complains, xii., 43. Complaints against, 65. Trial, referred to Chief Justice, 105. Case referred to Supreme Court after opinion of Chief Justice, 108.

Lofland, Dorman, Sheriff, x., 211, 274.

Logan, James, appointed a commissioner of property, ii., 61. Secretary and member of council, 68. Receiver General, 112, 237. Member of council, 117. Complains against collectors of tax, 122. Asks recompense for past services, 213. Charges against, by Assembly, ask his removal from council, 278–9. Articles of impeachment by Assembly against, 344–347. His reply to, 353–356. Various discussions respecting, 365–385. Petition to Governor respecting impeachment, ii., 376. Goes to Virginia, 397. Petition for salary, 412. Charge against, by Swedes, 465. His answer, 466, 482. Remonstrance against, 495–502. His justification, 500–502, 504. Assembly order committal to jail, 507. Governor interferes, 508. Returns from England, 567 A Justice, iii., 28. Visits and holds conference with Indians at Conestoga, 92–98. To inquire into right of Five Nations to lands on Susquehanna, 98. Visits Indians with Governor, 121. Sent to Conestoga to inquire about murder of Indians, 146. Report, 148–156. Succeeds Patrick Robinson in 1700 as Secretary, 163. Returns with letters from H. Penn, and two trustees, 237. To receive wrecked goods, 238. Complains of injurious aspersions on his character in a printed paper, and asks to be heard in defence—a day fixed for it, 242. Governor produces a paper, 243. Decision, 245. Receives as Secretary, possession of lesser seal, 252. His remarks as to the manner in which it had been removed by Governor Keith, 252. he delivers it to Governor, 252. Sends message to Conestoga Indians, 305. Indians charge Christians settling on their lands which had never been paid for, 319. His reply, 320. His impression respecting lands conveyed by Indians, 322, 324. Repudiates stories about sale of lands by Indians, 325. Chief Justice in place of J. Norris, 412. Commis-

sioner on boundary line, 544. Draws up a long and full report on Court of Chancery, iv., 27. Becomes President of council and Governor on death of Patrick Gordon, 47. Issues proclamation to continue officers, &c., 48. Is to sign all public instruments, 49. Returns from New Castle prepares a speech for the Assembly sitting, referring to late Governor's death, and the consequent change of Governors, which he delivers, 50. And receives their reply, 53. Which he answers in name of Council, 53. Letters on Maryland affairs, 65, 70, 75, 76–79. Receives Indians at his house, 79. Issues order against selling liquor to Indians in Philadelphia, 87. Proclamation for apprehending Moffat, 89. Concluding speech to Indians, 90. Documents respecting Maryland affairs, 101–151. Calls Assembly, 114. Answer to Jennings and Dulaney, 121. Signs petition to the King, 125. Correspondence with Jennings and Delaney, 121, 137, 140. Vindicates himself from charges made by commissioners to Governor Ogle, 145, 146, 159. Proclamation against Spanish preparations at Havana, 166. Correspondence with Governor Ogle, 167, 175, 190, 195, 198, 205, 228, 252, 253, 257, 265. Message to Assembly on Maryland affairs, 201. Instructions to Preston and Kinsey, 208. Asks for salary, 237, 240, 241. A house of his burned by a negro, 244. Message to Indians, 246. Proclamation on order in council, 263. Speaks of resigning as C. J., 306. Visit of Indians to, 580. Succeeded by J. Langhorne, 348. Renounces all claim to seat in board, v., 67. Succeeded as Secretary by R. Peters, 68. To examine negroes of flag of truce, 74, 75. Indian references to, 147. Committee on Indian affairs, 167.

Logan, William, made member of council, v., 68. Dissents to declaration of war against Indians, vii., 70. In New Jersey, soliciting aid of Indians, 145. Goes to Easton with Governor, 204. One of committee to investigate proprietary Indian purchases, 359, 462. Instructions to, 488. At Harris' ferry, 513. Appointed to confer with Teedyuscung, viii., 31, 40. Takes care of a child delivered up by Indians, 147.

Loggstown, where situated, v., 289, 634, 645. C. Weiser at, 349. Indians and French about, 614. Fort at Boccalunce, one hundred and twenty miles from, 634, 659, 660. Forts built by French, 675, 690. Distances, 730. Distances and longitude, 753. Latitude of, 763. Extent of province, W. of, 759, 763.

Lohra, P., notary public, xv., 527.

Lollor, Col. Robert, to survey river Delaware from Christiana downward, xi., 250, 318. Paymaster, 448, 475, 759; xii., 463. Register, xvi., 446.

Long, Capt. Peter, ship's husband, x., 361. Instructions, 364.

Long, William, Collector of Excise, xiv., 573. Resigns as Collector of Excise, xv., 266.

Long Island, memorial of prisoners on, xii., 480, 481.

Longschamp, Charles Julian de, insults Mons. Marbois, Consul-General of France, xiv., 115, 116, 117, 120, 121, 123, 135, 136, 137, 140, 144, 149, 162, 163, 171, 184, 262, 395, 466. Memorial, 572. Petition, 589, 592. Has leave of absence, 638. To be kept closely confined, xv., 59.

Longville, Chevalier, despatch respecting building a house at Cadaraghqui, v., 549.

Lords of Trade to Justices, on Wm. Keith's occupying government, and alluding to agreement between Queen Anne and William Penn for province, iii., 74. Letter from Sir Alfred Popple, Secretary of, on issues of bills of credit, 262. Letter from—rates of gold and silver coin—bills of credit, iv., 357, 474. Letters of marque, &c., 486.

Lords Commissioners of Trade, letter from, ix., 79.

Lord's Justices, letters from, iv., 671, 675. Approbation of laws, vi., 356.

Lords of privy Council, letter to proprietaries on death of King George II. ; viii., 516.

Lorentz, Joseph, Coroner, xvi., 194, 494, 499, 530.

Lorne, Caleb, cuts, in metal, State arms, xi., 552.

Lotteries, forbidden in Connecticut, permitted in Pennsylvania, vii., 113. One asked for, to finish an Episcopal church in Connecticut, 113. And plays, Act for suppressing proposed, viii., 339. Their continuance vindicated and instances of useful application, 340. Their prohibition unreasonable, 340, 355, 356. Considered as very different, 542, 676, 684. For various purposes in Philadelphia, ix., 56, 57, 148, 243, 247, 540, 580, 638, 639. Passed, 247. For bridge over Skippack, 284, 285. Time prolonged, 296. Act passed, 325, 326, 360, 389, 392, 459, 472, 549, 567, 576, 579, 622. For first and third Presbyterian church, 580. For Lancaster, 621. King objects to, 621, 622, 636, 638. In Bucks county, x., 26. Parsonage at Newtown, 41. In New Castle, 48. United States—tickets in received—and sent to Board of Treasury, xi. 576. Managers of State, xiv., 286, 451, 471, 652. State, xv., 36, 93, 97, 125, 159, 180. Donation land, 74, 97, 108, 128, 179, 316, 351, 356, 580. For improving roads, 448. Money to be collected for Lancaster road and improvement of Schuylkill, xvi., 98, 140. Conference on, 143. For Hebrew congregation, 488.

Louden, Hugh, violent proceedings against Speaker and Secretary, ii., 627.

Loudoun, Fort, deposition of prisoners at, vii., 395. Mentioned, 503, 504, 602. Cherokees at, destitute, viii., 77, 78, 224. Indian goods lying at, 776. Losses at, from Indians, ix., 190. Capt. Grant commands at, 268. Riots near, 269, 292, 301.

Loudoun, Lord, appointed to command in Virginia, vii., 134, 179, 180. Letters to and from, 234, 270, 305, 340, 342, 376, 379, 380, 429, 453, 482, 495, 571, 581, 596, 732, 737. Fears respecting Oswego, 234. Advises various measures, 271. Remarks on his letters in Council, 305. Military affairs, 340. Requires quarters for military in Philadelphia, 369–379 In New York, 379. Proposes embargo, 429, 444. Requests of Governor, account of province, 444. Also arrest of five neutrals, 446. Meeting of–inquiry respecting Constitution, &c., reply of R. Peters, vii., 448. Advises Governor to pass money bill, 453. Meeting at Philadelphia with Governors of North Carolina, &c.—minutes, 470. Quotas of each State, &c., 471. From Gov. D. on shipping provisions, 482. Going with the fleet—appoints General Webb at Albany, Col. S. Stanwix of Philadelphia, and Lt.-Col. Bouquet to South Carolina, &c., 525. Conference with southern Governors, 552. Embargo, 591, 593, 596. Absence of, 718. Respecting barracks and roads, 756. Letters to and from, viii., 23. Asks aid to carry on war, 28. Returning to England is succeeded by M. G. Abercrombie, 26.

Loudon, Richard and wife, keeper of jail at Lancaster, attack on them, iv., 251.

Loughead, James, Paymaster, xi., 233, 260. Paymaster at Billingsport, xii., 86. Paymaster, 451, 453, 454, 486. Paymaster to militia, xiv., 159. Justice, 344. Complaint against, by Swedish Consul for rude behavior of constables—ordered to send apology, xv., 348.

Louisburg, reduction of, iv., 765. 766, 773; v., 32. Troops sent from England under General St, Clair and Major General Frampton, 37. French fleet arrives, vi., 451.

Louisiana, map of, 1721, referred to respecting Sugar Islands, iii., 402. Susquehanna laid down as

a boundary of Pennsylvania, 402. Governor of, letter from with prisoners in a flag of truce from New Orleans, viii., 124, 150. Demand for a free negro held in bondage there, xvi., 33.

Love, Alexander., Coroner, v., 597, 662.

Lovell, James, delegate for Massachusetts—letter—resolve of Council, xii., 51.

Lovering, Joseph, a child of fourteen or fifteen, enlisted, to be discharged, xii., 686.

Low, Joshua, Coroner of Lancaster county, iii., 370, 387, 416, 465, 520, 575; iv., 86, 309, 352, 469, 500.

Lowe's Ferry, changed to B. Galbraith's, viii. 676.

Lower Counties—Shall their expenses be a public charge? i., 117. Practice in, respecting judgments on estates of deceased persons, 157. Good understanding between upper and, to be preserved, by having one judge from, 204. Can't agree about bill for support of government, 623. Address proprietary on defence of New York, ii., 31. Object to confirmation, and threaten to separate. Governor's address to 50. Object to act of union and other difficulties, 51. Difficulties about charter of privileges, 52. May have a separate Assembly—if they will not unite with the Province, 60. Difficulties with Province in regard to charter, separation, &c., discussed, 70–74. Conference with Governor, 75. Questions proposed by Governor and Council, 82. Answers, 82. Members of Council from, 117. Division of, from Province, 119, Conference, 120–124. Governor advised not to meet at New Castle, 136. New writs issued, 136. Col. French, a member of Council, iii., 18. Judges and Justices named, 18. Interested in the government, 64. Member of Council, 143. Attempt of Lord Baltimore and Lord Sunderland to obtain, 252. David French Attorney General for, 253. Justices, 254.

Lower Dublin Township, Roads in, ii., 530. Petition respecting road to Philadelphia, ix., 628.

Lowman, Samuel, Collector of Lewes—Witness in Kidd's case, ii., 121. Judge of Supreme Court of Lower Counties, iii., 253.

Lownes, Caleb, cuts a seal for Court of Admiralty, xii., 102.

Lowry, James, examination, vii., 155.

Lowry, Lazarus, examination, vii., 155.

Lowry, Stephen, Commissary, robbed, xi., 116.

Lowther, G., Attorney General, ii., 224, 254.

Loxley, Benjamin, 1st Lieutenant of Artillery Company in Philadelphia, vi., 770. Orders on for guns and stores, x., 285, 407. Proposals for brass cannon, 626. Air furnaces, erecting a boring mill, 641, 656, 688. To examine furnace, 622. Called on for his accounts, xi., 76.

Loxley. Benjamin, Jr., to be arrested for inducing soldiers away, xi., 760, 770.

Loyal Hanning, attacked by French and Indians, viii., 212. Fort, 224. Block-house and saw-mill proposed by General Forbes near, 234. Letter James Burd from—account of capture of Du Quesne, 234.

Loyd, Colonel Hugh, x., 697–698, 708.

Loyd, Thomas, council take copies of proceedings and debates in Assembly, published by him, xv., 345. Paid for, 504, 627.

Ludgar, Peter, arrested, i., 244–5. Case confirmed, 245.

Ludwick, Christopher, powder, x., 421; xi., 32, 303.

Ludwig, John, Justice, xiv., 170.

Lukens, Charles, Sheriff, x., 212, 270. Sheriff elect of York declines, xi., 219.

Lukens, John, applies to be Surveyor-General, xii., 233. To hunt for papers, 621. A Commissioner to extend Mason and Dixon's line, 635, 703. Instructions, 704. Late Surveyor-General called on for copies of papers relating to

forfeited estates, 67, 252. Has gout–Surveyor-General appointed. 689. Commissioner, pay, 714. Pay, xiii., 50. Report on a city lot, 123. Paid for plans of city lots, 148. Report, 321. Committee on Virginia, 685. Reappointed Surveyor-General, xiv., 444, 447. Appoints deputies, 451. And of donation lands, 454. Recommend a deputy, xv., 49. Recommends Andrew Elliott as Surveyor of Alleghany, 615. Accounts, xvi., 137. Death of, 199, 208.

Lumber, Inspectors of, xiv., 488.

Lumsden, Robert, wharfinger and weighmaster of hay at draw bridge, xi., 545.

Lunatics, bill proposed respecting, v., 512. Expense of a soldier, xii., 280.

Lurgan, Township Cumberland Co., a military company formed for mutual protection—ask for arms, &c., vi., 533.

Lusk, Hugh, appointed manager at Grubb's furnace, xi., 350.

Luther, John, Justice, xv., 4.

Lutheran Church of Albany, asks for a brief to collect, xv., 14.

Lutheran Reformed German congregation of Easton, petition to be allowed to ask aid in completing their church—granted, xi., 422.

Lutheran Congregation of Philadelphia, tender and pay money for lot in city, xiii., 36.

Lutterlish, Col., applies for a number of wagons, xi., 409.

Luzerne, Chevalier de la, recommends two young men for Second Regiment, xii., 116. French Minister on Birth of Dauphin, audience by Congress, xiii., 282. Address to, 284. Answer, 285. Letter on insult to Mons. Marbois, xiv., 115, 116, 121, 137. Address of Council to, on his approaching departure, 145. His answer, 147.

Luzerne County, Timothy Pickering elected Prothonotary and Clerk of Courts, &c., xv., 96, 97. Register and Recorder, 134. Election, 162, 300. Representatives, 160. Sheriff, 192, 300, 577. Coroner, 192, 300, 577. Justices, 212, 366. 605, 606. Claims in, Commissioners to adjust; General Muhlenberg resigns; Joseph Montgomery resigns; Stephen Balliet chosen, 221. Memorial from Easton, respecting claims in, 224, 225, 235. Commissioners paid—sale of Andrew Allen's estate—Mr. Hollinback to superintend, 237. Daniel Hiester resigns as Commissioner, 245. Z. Butler, Lieutenant—Conference of Judges with Council, &c., fresh disturbances in, 265. Proclamation against John Franklin, John Jenkins, &c., for opposition to government, 280. Arms for, 289. John Franklin arrested—to be closely confined—news from, sent to Governor of New York by Dr. Redick, 291. Militia of Berks county called out to quell riots in, 292. Colonel Dennison despatched to—his instructions, 293. Message to Assembly on, 304. Enforcement of laws in, recommended to Assembly, 314. Commissioner paid, 355. Griffith Evans, clerk to Commissioners paid, 356. Intelligence from, 361. Illegal military election, 362. Supplies for troops, 380. J. Franklin's irons to be removed, 385. Roads, 425, 445. Complaint against Justices of—quantity and quality of land claimed by Pennsylvania owners in, also drafts of land held by them by Surveyor General, 450, 452, 454. Commissioners appointed to proceed there, viz.: Stephen Balliet and Maj. William Armstrong, 455. Pay of Commissioners, 470–471. Letter of Instructions to Commissioners—spirited proceedings on arrest of Col. T. Pickering, 484. Proclamation against captors of T. Pickering, 487, 489. Expense of T. Wigton, in going and returning from, on public business—Request to Congress for Continental troops to expel rioters from, 493. Letters, Governor of New York, 497. Troops for, to proceed to Easton, 502. Release of T. Pickering—Opinion asked respecting troops for Tioga—Let-

ters from Z. Butler, 505. Despatches to, 506. Opinion of Judges respecting, 507. Troops not necessary, 505. Intelligence from Colonel Pickering—Express paid, 514. Return of field and company officers by Z. Butler, rejected, 525. Conference respecting John Franklin, 533. Sword presented by Council to Captain William Ross, for opposing the late rioters, 543. Rewards to Captain Ross—Roswell Franklin, for capturing Benjamin Earl and Thomas Kinney, 547. Letter, Colonel Pickering on rioters, 606. Petition for removal of fines from captors of Colonel Pickering, 610. Expense of removing John Franklin, &c., 640. Military officers in first battalion of, xvi., 1–2. Rewards for arresting rioters in, 11. Justices, 4, 12, 126, 219, 395, 407, 539. Contested election in, 15, 121. Sheriffs, 17, 196, 204, 496. Coroners, 196, 204, 496. Officers of 8th Company, 1st battalion, militia, elected, 195. Councillor, 204. Justice Kingsley resigns, 269. Collector of Excise—Arnold Colt, 308. Division of 2d batallion, and appointment of officers, 317. Mr. Spalding carries presents to Indians, 440. Militia officers elected, 464. Justice Montgomery resigns, 539.

Lycons, Andrew, place, vii., 155.

Lydia, ship, arrives from London—Committee to inquire about arms, vi., 679.

Lyons, William, examined, respecting Stump, ix., 510–511. Member of Council of Safety from Cumberland, x., 756. Prothonotary, xi., 178, 221, 244, 697; xii., 47.

Lyons, Samuel, sentenced to death, xi., 564, 566; xiii., 311.

Lyttle, Andrew, commissary, complains to Council, xii., 334, 437. Memorial complaining of being displaced as deputy Surveyor—Referred to General Brodhead, &c., xv., 383. Report in his favor—May be re-appointed, 459.

Lykin, Neils, a Swede, ii., 480.

Lynch, John, about absconding, xi., 214.

Lyttlèton, Fort, murder of G. Pendegrast's daughter, vii., 632. Garrison attacked, ix., 34.

Lydius, John, has influence with Indians, respecting purchase of lands, vi., 117. His conduct, 248, 249, 251. Indian opinion of his deed, 277. Invalidation of deed, 284. Respecting, 288. Sells shares, 293.

M.

McAffee, Captain, robbed of goods, xi., 563, 564. Is paid reward for arrest, 616.

McAulay, Cornelius, Coroner, xiii., 730; xiv., 245.

McBean, Angus, obtains fraudulently a pilot-boat to visit man-of-war, x., 531. To be brought back, 531. Proceeding of Committee respecting, 532.

McCall, Archibald, sends ship "Brothers" to China, xvi., 224.[2]

McCall, George, Act for vesting certain lands in, iii., 597. Conveys to Cape Breton Governor's request for cannon, v., 204. Vesting lands in, vi., 235.

McCall, Samuel, elected Major of Associators, v., 175.

McCalla, Rev. Daniel, appointed Chaplain to Colonel Bull's battalion, x., 458.

McCallister, John, Commissary, complaints against, xii., 27. Prosecuted, 41. His account objected to, 198.

McCallister, Colonel Richard, of York county, battalion, x., 682; xi., 444. Censor, xiii., 723. Resigns as President of Courts, xiv., 182. Councillor, 234, 239. As Councillor resigns, xv., 126.

McCalmont, James, memorial respecting his seizure by Captain John Barry and others, against whom a prosecution is ordered, xv., 286.

McCalmont, John, paid, per decision of Supreme Court, xvi., 46.

McCandless, Captain James, x., 697. Superseded, xi., 448.

McCartney, Dr. John, to be arrested as an incendiary, xii., 294.
McCay, William, Justice, xiv., 242.
McClance, Lieutenant John, xi., 576.
McClare, Michael, Coroner, iv., 247.
McClay, Samuel, to examine rivers, xvi., 319.
McClay, William, Coroner, ix., 547. A Justice, x., 43, 47. Prothonotary, xi., 187. Commissioner to Indians, xiv., 40, 54, 518. To examine Susquehannah River, 182. Justice, 322. Respecting Six Nations of Indians, 374. Goods to Indians, 604. Report, 658, 662. Deputy Surveyor, xvi., 243, 254.
McClean, Alexander, Sub-Lieutenant, xiii., 168. To run Virginia line, 252, 253, 335, 510–519. Prothonotary, 254. Appointed Judge and President Court Common Pleas of Fayette county, xiii., 732. Register of Wills, &c., 763. Deputy Surveyor, xvi., 257. Report on road to Pittsburg, 466.
McClean, Archibald, draft to, xii., 683. Justice, xiv., 164. Death of, xv., 15, 17. Account of survey referred, 635.
McClean, James, Member Congress, xii., 172, 371.
McCleery, William, letter and memorial, xiii., 698.
McClellan, John, appointed Collector of Excise, xiv., 590. Collector of Excise, removed, xv., 264. Lieutenant of Pennsylvania troops—His daughter receives a pension, 312.
McClellan, Captain Joseph, Lieutenant of battalion, appointed Captain, x., 645. To recruit, xi., 555.
McClenachan, Blair, Owns brig Convention, xi., 714. To fit out ship General Greene, 730, 735. Complaint against, by the Marshal, xii., 155. Passport to New York, xiii., 558; xvi., 316.
McClenachan & Irwin, xi., 743. Report case of F. Fleury, xii., 37. Letter to, on supplies, 280.
McClenachan & Moore, memorial respecting loss of goods on Brig Philadelphia, and person to inspect, xiii., 768. Report, 769.
McClester, Francis, builds chevaux de frise, xi., 752.
McClure, John, Coroner, vi., 144; vii., 267.
McClure, David, Justice, xiv., 180.
McComb, William, Coroner, xiv., 244, 597; xv., 121.
McConaghy, David, Sheriff, ix., 286, 333, 398.
McConneaughy, James, to be confined, x., 677. Discharged, 693.
McConnel, Captain James, of flying camp, x., 679. At riot at J. Wilson's, gives bail, xii., 139. Buys land, xiii., 273.
McCord's Fort, vii., 77.
McCoskrey, William, Coroner, ix., 199.
McCoy, Colonel Æneas, commands regiment, xi., 2.
McCracken, Henry, pension to widow, xv., 341.
McCulloch, Lieutenant James, recruits, xi., 542, 573.
McCullogh, Captain John, pay for artillerists at forts on Delaware, xii., 10.
McCune, James, Justice, xiv., 180.
McCaskey, William, a Justice, x., 209.
McCutcheon, David, a tory, arrested and imprisoned, x., 616.
McDade, Philip, dies intestate, xii., 204. State claim, 331.
McDaniel, James, not to proceed to New Jersey, x., 660.
McDaniel (alias Donnel), John, accomplice of L. Stewart, to be arrested, ix., 717.
McDermont, Terence, an English cadet, arrives from Cork, and is ordered into custody, x., 302, 303.
McDonald, Captain Allen, released from gaol, x., 647. Expenses paid by Congress, 648.
McDonald, General Alexander, in gaol—room mate, Allen Cameron, x., 595. To be released by order of Congress, 639, 647, 648.
McDonald, Francis, a soldier, bounty paid to, xiv., 138.
McDonald, Captain James, x., 697.
McDonald, John, proclamation ag't for murder of wife and son of L. Kraymer, Jr., of Bucks—and arson, xiv., 489.

McDowell, Alexander, deputy surveyor, report of line run on new purchase, xiv., 604.
McDowell, Col. James, xi., 208.
McDowell, John, Censor, xiii., 741; xiv., 170.
McDowell, Nath'l, Ensign, xiv., 237.
McDowell's Mill—Colonel Dunbar's troops to be placed near, vi., 514.
McElhatton, William, First Lieutenant, x., 756. (See McIlh'n.)
McFarlane, Andrew, respecting Dr. Conolly, x., 169.
McFarlane, John, to be arrested, xii., 521. Imprisoned, 523.
McFarlan, William, Coroner, xiii., 135, 443, 740.
McFatridge, John, Second Lieut. of Floating Battery, x., 536.
McFerran, ——, paymaster, xii., 767.
McGaughey, Arthur, Collector of Excise, xiii., 597. Declines, 647, 672. Sheriff, xv., 298, 600; xvi., 212.
McGaughey, Thomas, Sheriff, xv., 600; xvi., 498.
McGee's Fort. (See McKee's.)
McGilivray, Colonel, and Chiefs of Creek Indians, on their way to New York, visit Philadelphia, xvi., 395, 524, 525.
McGinley, Captain, asking for pay, xii., 80. Claim for work, 83.
McGinty, Alexander, &c., letter on Indian and French affairs, v., 627. Indian trader, petitions for aid, and deposition recommended to Assembly, 663.
McGowan, John, appointed Lieutenant, x., 698. Captain, 766. Pay, xii., 321.
McGowan, Major, loses a certificate, xvi., 409.
McGraw, Colonel Robert, to discharge hands, x., 600.
McGrew, Archibald, Coroner, vi., 144.
McHenry, Lieut. Charles, xi., 593.
McHenry, William, appointed sub-Lieutenant, xiii., 82.
McIlhadden, John, appointed Captain, xi., 740.
McIlhatton, Captain, xii., 279.
McIlhatton, Lt. William, disabled, put on invalid list, xii., 51, 279, 338, 421.
McIlwaine, Colonel, to rendezvous in city, xi., 301.
McIlwaine, Captain, troops to Bordentown, x., 620; xi., 32.
McIlwaine, Ferguson, appointed wagon-master, xi., 342.
McIlwaine, Joseph, Inspector of flour in Bucks county, xiv., 488.
McIlwaine, Robert, Coroner, v., 468.
McIlwaine, William, Justice, xiv., 200, 203.
McIntosh, General, letter on attack of Indians, xi., 526, 679, 699, 773.
McIntosh, Fort, General Harmar asks for a person to take charge of, xiv., 373, 448. Lands at, surveyed, xvi., 340.
McKay, Abigail, released, but confined to fixed limits, xi., 236.
McKean, Joseph Borden, pays expenses of Judges, &c., on circuit, xv., 34, 239.
McKean, Thomas, Trustee of general loan office, ix., 205. Speaker of New Castle Assembly, x., 83. Colonel, 548. Receives articles, 638. Paid for muskets, 648. Appointed Chief Justice, xi., 254. Oath to be administered by dedimus, 271. Takes oath, 304. Report to Judges, 563, 564. Charges against Brigadier General William Thompson—proceedings, 653. Denies — General T. called before Council—declines, 660. Opinion on prisoners taken, xii., 74. Also in new gaol, 110, 112. May occupy J. Duche's house, 578. Speaker of Congress, 782. Deed for Duche's lot, xiii., 25. President of Congress, 41. Answer of Supreme Court, 219. Opinion, case of Wm. Hanks, 543. Re-appointed Chief Justice, xiv., 167. Case of A. Bare, 318. Pay, 603, 669. Paid, xv., 360, 636; xvi., 312.
McKee, Alexander, forfeited estate, petition of James, respecting, xii., 76.
McKee's Fort, vii., 148. His house burned, 154.
McKee, Captain Robert, x., 692.
McKee, Thomas, deposition respecting skirmish with Indians in Virginia, iv., 630, 634, 635. Upper place in danger from Indians, vi.,

669; viii., 513, 622. Instructions to, to conduct Indians to Shamokin, 550. Report of his expedition to Indians, 597. Letter from, respecting Delawares, 735, 736. And Conestogo Indians, viii., 113, 121. Sent with Colonel Burd, under instructions, to Wyoming, ix., 29, 534.
McKinzie, Samuel, surgeon, x., 530.
McKinly, John, sheriff, viii , 403.
McKinley, Brigadier General, x., 651. Of Wilmington, letter to from Council of Safety, 743.
McKinney, David, Justice, xi., 528.
McKinney, Mordecai, Justice, xi., 398.
McKissack, Captain William, xi., 2.
McLane, Samuel, buys one of the old jail lots, xiv., 583.
McLaughlin, Captain, vi., 764.
McLean, Alex.r, Justice, xiv., 54.
McLean, Archibald, Prothonotary, xi., 187, 191, 274, 388; xii., 47, 93. A commissioner to extend Mason and Dixon's Line, 635. Instructions, 704.
McLean, Captain, ix., 190.
McLean, Captain James, unable to attend to command of Invalid Corps, is displaced by Colonel L. Nicola, xv., 633.
McLean, Mr., a prisoner, x., 603.
McLean, William, a Justice, x., 209.
McLene, Alexander, assistant to Colonel Andrew Porter, xv., 19.
McLene, James, member of Assembly, xii., 424. Commissioner to Congress at Yorktown, 435. Of Council, 618.
McLene, James, Censor, xiii., 726. Council, xiv., 34.
McLene, Lazarus, Prothonotary and Clerk of Orphans' Court of Huntingdon, xv., 279.
McLene, Lazarus Brown, complaint against, xv., 588. Answer to charges made against him, 599. Further proceedings, 603, 620, 621. Removed from office, 622.
McLochrey, Archibald, Prothonotary, xi., 187.
McMichael, John, letter to R. Peters on Conn. claim, vi., 254.
McMullen, Daniel, examination of, who escaped from Indians at Conestoga, vii., 282.
McMullen, Captain, x., 710.
McMullen, James, Coroner, v., 55.
McMullin, Wm., agent of confiscated estates, xii., 261. Takes oath, 264, 330. Complaint, 695.
McMurdy, Rev. Robert, to receive a suit of black, xii., 464.
McNair, Robert, agent of forfeited estates, xi., 749.
McNair, W., Justice, xiv., 200, 362.
McNeal, John, declines to be appointed engineer, x., 457. To survey Jersey shore, x., 474.
McNemera, Thomas (a lawyer), complained against, ii., 457.
McPherson, Robert, sheriff, viii., 781. Sheriff, ix., 57, 199. Colonel of battalion, x., 687, 710.
McPherson, Captain John, offers plan for defence—thanks to, x., 292. Asks cannon—may purchase, xii., 36, 39.
McPherson, Lieutenant William, recommended to Congress, xi., 655.
McPherson, Major John, killed before walls of Quebec, xi., 655.
McPherson, Captain William, a resigned British officer, appears before Council, having escaped from New York, xi., 657.
McPherson, Colonel, xi., 121.
McPherson, Major, Aid to General St. Clair, leaves British service—draws clothing, xii., 241.
McVeaugh, Colonel—battalion to rendezvous at Falls of Schuylkill and Darby, xi., 301.
McWilliam, Richard, Justice, ix., 203. Trustee of General Loan office, 205, 206. Second Judge of Supreme Court, 581. Judge of Oyer and Terminer, 581. Chief Justice of Supreme Court of Lower Counties, x., 108.
Mack, Rev. Martin, pass for to the Indians, as Moravian missionary, v., 576.
Mackay, Æneas, letter respecting Dr. Conolly's advertisement, &c., x., 140, 169.
Mackay, Hon. John, pay to, xi., 592; xii., 66.
Mackey, David, Justice, xii., 105. Sheriff, 150. Justice, xiii., 219.
Mackey, Robert, brings off a boat, xi., 529. Appraises schooner Viper, 679.

Mackay, Captain William, wounded at Battle of Brandywine, xi., 667. Receives clothing, 667.
Mackiness, Thomas, a traitor, xii., 106.
Maclay, ———, charged with suffering a traitor to escape, xi., 566.
Maclay, William, Deputy Surveyor, dispute about a line, xv., 8. Paid for surveying; accounts, xiii., 420, 494, 567. To remove stores from Harris's, 690.
Madagascar, trade with, i., 592.
Maffat, Solomon, accidentally kills an Indian, iv., 88. Proclamation for apprehending, 89.
Magaw, Col., recommended to Congress as a Colonel, x., 442. Elected, 443, 464. To have use of pest-house, 490.
Magaw, Colonel Robert, xi., 124, 436.
Magazine for stores, x., 778.
Magistrates, iii., 259.
Mahanatawny, Governor visits, iii., 302. His report, 303. Iron-works at, 305.
Mahanoy, also John Penn's Creek (which see), vi., 645, 646.
Mahanoy, settlements at, burned, vii., 493.
Mahonoy attacked and burned by Indians, vi., 737.
Mahoning, township, divided, xv., 41.
Mail, Robbery of Southern, xiii., 312.
Maisterson, Captain Samuel, in the Hector, captures a Schooner off the Delaware, v., 323. Letter of President to, 324.
Maitland, Richard, D. A. G., orders for troops to aid Provinces, ix., 307.
Majors, persons recommended to Congress as, x., 444. Appointed, 446; xi., 35, 116, 214.
Makin, Thomas, notified not to keep the Free Schools without license, i., 383.
Maloney, Colonel William, petition respecting horses taken by him from traitors, xii., 115.
Mamachtaguin, an Indian, ordered to be executed for murder, xiv., 585.
Manlon, Luke, complaint against for stealing a heifer, i., 579.
Manlove, Boaz, Sheriff, ix., 548, 624, 688.
Manlove, Matthew, Coroner, ix., 199.
Manatanny, Assemblage of Indian kings at, ii., 545, 546.
Manaukyhickon, an Indian, iii., 295, 304, 315.
Manor of Springetsbury, warrant for survey of, iii., 785.
Manufacture of linen cloth to be to be encouraged, i., 93. Steel, xv., 269; to be encouraged, iii., 392. Of Pennsylvania, Governor, called on for an account of, since 1734, ix., 343. Letter of Governor Penn on, 353. Number of stated, 354. And Useful Arts Society, for encouragement, receives aid from Council, Christopher Marshall, Jr., Treasurer, xvi,, 51. Meeting, 313. Factory burned by design—Proclamation against incendiary, 326.
Map of Pennsylvania, by T. Holme, acknowledged, i., 264, 266. Mentioned, iv., 317. Of distances, by Patten, v., 747. Of Frontiers and Forts presented by Governor Morris, vii., 228. By John Reed, payments for, x., 260, 267.
Maqua, or Mohock Indians, v., 11. On Susquehanna, viii., 128.
Marache, Solomon, City lots, xiii., 587.
Marbois, Monsieur, with Luzerne, visit President and Council, xii., 180. Letter respecting duties, xiii., 597, 598, 600. Memorial, 618. On Consular powers, 619, 645, 671.
Marbois, Sieur de Francis, Exequator as French Consul, xiv., 43. On a French ship detained by Court of Admiralty, 111. Insulted by Longschamps, 115, 116, 117, 120, 121, 135, 137, 140, 143, 144. On his privileges, 282. On ship Venus, 291. On going to New York, 404. Case of Lieutenant Colonel, 447.
Marbois, Sieur Pierre Francis, Barbe de, Jr., applies for a pardon of two French criminals—granted, xiv., 240. Exequator as Vice-Consul, 491. Consul of France, to receive

Monsieur de Brassini and send him to France, xv., 215, 236.
March, the first month in the year, i., 58.
March, Joseph, Member of Council of Safety, xi., 45.
Marcus Hook, land to be purchased at, for piers, xiv., 460. Plan of, 464. Agreement between Council and Landholders at, for site of piers, 475. Piers at, xv., 228.
Marginal notes, Committee appointed to inspect, on laws, i., 97.
Marine Committee of Congress, x., 648. Informs of a reward offered by French Minister for capture of British vessels laden with spars, inward bound, xi., 646.
Mariners, petition for wages, i., 63, 64. Not to be trusted, ii., 212. Decision in their favor, 73. Pay of, x., 650.
Maris, Jesse, Sheriff, ix., 623, 688, 777.
Markets in Philadelphia, notices and regulations of, i., 92, 110, 145, 190, 376, 377, 382, 388, 391, 442, 443, 444, 461, 515, 580, 582; ii., 26, 28. Callowhill street, proposed act for, ix., 650; xi., 195. To be repaired, 523, 524, 526, 640. Forestalling, 639, 640. Repairs to, 659. xii., 41, 80, 110, 190; xiii., 3. License to buy and sell dismissed, xiii., 86.
Markham, Wm. Governor, papers on frame of Government, 1696, i., 48, at first Council, 57, appointed Secretary of the Province, &c., 142. To proclaim King James at New Castle, 142. Appointed to treat with Indians for lands, 156. Appointed Ranger for Philadelphia County, 166. Commission to, 206. Member of Council, 212. On defensive measures, 306. Respecting a bill drawn on John Moll, 233. Letter, Thomas Lloyd to, on affixing seal, 250. And others offer to take up arms, 335. Refuses to deliver Seals and Records, 342, 343. Appointed Lieutenant Governor by Fletcher, 365, 366. Takes oath, 367. Goes to New Castle—his reception and confirmation, 369. Indorses a commission to Justices to hold a Court in an urgent case, 395. Discussions with Council and Assembly, 418. Addresses Assembly, 459. £200 to be given to, 468. Informs Council of restoration of Province to William Penn—His Commission as Governor, &c., 472–475. Takes oath, 472, Address to Assembly, 480, 484, 488. A new frame, 507–8. Proclamation against Pirates, &c., 529. Charters a School for poor children, 532. Asks advice of Council respecting goods seized, 543–4. Receives a new Commission from Proprietary as Deputy Governor, 546. Published at Market-place, 546. Addresses to Assembly, 548. Takes oath of fidelity, 553. Letter to, as late Governor respecting old Charters, 573. Appointed by Proprietary Register-general, ii., 96, 97. May use his own seal, the official one being withheld, 113. J. Moore refuses to deliver Records, &c., 121. His death noticed, 151.
Markland, John, Lieutenant, xii., 10.
Markoe, Abm., buys a lot, xii., 271.
Markoe, Captain, escorts Dr. Kearsley and H. Brooke to Lancaster, x., 381. His report, 385.
Marle, Thomas Stationed at Fort Island and to fix boom, xi., 31, 33.
Marple, Richard, murdered, xiv., 57.
Marriage, Law proposed for young men at a certain age, i., 93. Laws respecting, ii., 12. Complaint against, 26, 48. Illegal, 114. With, first cousins, &c., fine proposed, 219. Licenses objected to—Case of Israel Taylor's daughter, 455. Clandestine, Act to prevent, iii., 379. And other licenses to be changed in form, v., 69, 71. Fees changed, xi., 760. Licenses—Views of Bishop White on, xv., 614.
Marsh, Colonel, of Second Battalion, xiii., 98.
Marsh Creek, vi., 675.
Marsh, Joseph, to build boats, &c., x., 283. The "Warren," 328; xv., 12.
Marshal of Court of Admiralty appointed, x., 538. Of Admiralty

bound to obey Judge of Admiralty, xi., 657. M. Clarkson appointed, 576, 657, 760. Complaints against, xii., 520, 531, 533. Clement Biddle appointed, 537.
Marshall, Captain Abraham, resigns, x., 645.
Marshall, Benj., Ensign, xi., 754.
Marshall, Christopher, to take care of sick, xi., 34. Of Lancaster to purchase wheat, xii. 85.
Marshall, Christopher, Jr., Secretary of Society for encouraging manufactures and arts, xvi., 51.
Marshall, Edw'd, on the "Walkers" to run line, 1837, vii., 400.
Marshall, James, Register of Wills, xii., 582. Sheriff, xiv., 245, 597. Sheriff, xv., 121.
Marshall, John wishes to establish manufactory of thread—Declined, xii., 81.
Marshall, Cap. John, xi., 428, 508.
Marshall, William, inserted by mistake in proclamation, respecting forfeited estates, obtains a certificate from Council, xi., 615.
Marsteller, Philip, paymaster, xi., 272, 388, 412.
Marsteller, Major Phillip, xi., 35, 448, 493. Paymaster, 368; xii., 25. Letter, purchase flour, 57. On flour, 117, 203. Paymaster, 361. Letter, 392.
Martial Law—Council authorized to declare, in the State, xii., 374. Proclamation of, 383.
Martin, Alexander, x., 696. Gov'r of North Carolina, xvi. 305.
Martin, Henry, brings back sailors from Baltimore, xi. 782.
Martin, Dr. Hugh,—Surgeon, iii., 270. Justice, xiv., 257.
Martin, Jas., Sub. Lieut., xi., 303.
Martin, John, Sheriff, xi., 366. Justice, xiii., 583.
Martin, Joseph, Coroner, xvi., 491.
Martin, Robert, Paymaster, xi., 34. Ensign, xii., 53.
Maryland,—a long journey from Pennsylvania, i., 79. Land sued for in, 101. Patents from Lord Baltimore, 109. Reinforce fort at Christiana, and otherwise complained of, 188. Major English arrives from, with armed men,
Maryland—
188. Rumored invasion from, by Senecas, 277. Letter received from, occasions council to be convened, 298. Alarm from, by Indians, French and Papists, 299. Letter from Assembly of, 334. Transportation ot tobacco from, to Lower counties, to be stopped, 465, 468. Extraordinary letter of Gov. Francis Nicholson, on his reported conduct in Sussex Co., 515. Commission to Gov. Nicholson to appoint certain officers for Pennsylvania, 533, 534. Against piracy, 562. Indians of Conestoga alarmed by threats from, ii., 191. Violence to English families in, 191. Gov. Seymour informs of French privateers on coast, 240. Justices of New Castle complain of encroachments by, 353. Address from, to Queen, on boundary lines between, and Pennsylvania, 362. Sheriff seizes property, and is arrested by Sheriff of New Castle, 393. Militia of Cecil Co. ordered out to execute writ of ejectment, 395. Governor Seymour, 417, 421. Conference with Indians at Conestoga, 513. Indian settlements in, iii., 20. Trespassers from, on lands, 37. Col. Hart, governor, 39. Gov. Keith meets Gov. Hart at Colonel Hynson's—conference—amicable conclusion, 60. On Indian affairs, 82. Interference with Indian lands on Susquehanna, 160. Expense of messenger to, 175. Philip Syng, of Philadelphia, committed to Sheriff, for survey under Maryland title, 176. Difficulties on Susquehanna, 178. Advice of Council of Pennsylvania—on survey to Octorara, 180. Governor writes to Governor Calvert, 180. Intrusions on lands on Susquehanna, 181. Condition of affairs between, and Pennsylvania. Surveyor and others made prisoners, 212, 216. Decision of Council on, 216. Letter from Governor of Maryland, 222. Answer of Governor Keith, 223. Descriptions by patent, 223. Boundaries, 224. Original agreement between Lord

Maryland—
Baltimore and Hannah Penn, 232, 234. Letter Governor Keith to Governor of, 232. Governor Gordon speaks of Lord Baltimore's attempts to obtain counties in Delaware, 252. Governor of, complains of new county line—Governor Gordon to point out his error, 347. Agreement on division line, 461, 463, 464, 497. Commissioners under agreement with—Governor goes to, 464. Correspondence respecting riots, 468. Precept against rioters, 468. Letters of Governor Ogle, 480, 543. Commissioners on boundary, 544. Return—report, &c., 545, 563. Outrage by William Rumsey, a surveyor of, 591. Claims the territories of Pennsylvania, 594. Robert Buchanan, High Sheriff of Lancaster County, attacked by persons from, 612. Daniel Dulaney, Attorney-General of, 612. Germans go west of Susquehanna by interference from, but finding their error, propose returning to Pennsylvania, iv., 57. Letter from Lieutenant-Governor Ogle, against certain settlers on lands on Susquehanna, 61. Statement of the parties, 61. Deposition of Francis Kip, 62. Letter, Governor Ogle, 66. Proclamation against soldiers from, 73. Letter to Governor Ogle, 76, 79. Governor of, sends message and wampum to Indians, assuring them of his protection, by order of King of England, 92. Difficulties with from an association in Chester County, 100. Case of Henry Munday, 101, and Edward Leet, &c., 101. Various documents respecting these disputes, 101–151. Certificate of Governor Ogle to 49 persons for 200 acres, 102. Statement by Jennings and Dulany, 117. Correspondence with, and Governor, 116, 117, 121, 130, 137, 141, 142, 146. Higginbotham flees into, and receives an appointment, 147, 154. Letters from Governor Ogle and S. Blunston, 155. Rewards for magistrates of Lancaster County, 155.

aryland—
Letters to and from Governor Ogle, 156, 159, 167. 252, 253, Reference to patent, 162. Hamilton and Georges, 168. Letters to and from Governor Ogle, 175. Intention of rioters, 190. Letter to and from Governor Ogle, 190, 195, 198, 228, 242, 257. Respecting German settlers, 194, 197, 201. Messrs. Preston and Kinsey sent to, 204. Their report, 210. Instructions to them, 206. Various documents with report, 215–223. Case of Elisha Gatchell, 227. Deposition of, 229. Governor goes to Virginia—express leaves dispatches for him, 232. Affair at Lancaster County gaol, 250, 254. Governor sends order in Council—and to have proclamations printed in Philadelphia, 254. Proceedings at Hampton Court, on petitions from, respecting articles of agreement, 255. Case of Daniel Lowe, 254. Rudolph, Mohr, and R. Downer, 256. Governor Ogle to President Logan, on views of order in Council, 260. Proclamation of Pennsylvania, on order of Council, 263, 265. Correspondence between Governor Ogle and Governor Thomas, 294. Proceedings at Hampton Court for quieting, and Pennsylvania, 298—301. Commissioners appointed to run the line, 313. Correspondence with, 329. Notice of commissioner being appointed in England by Court of Chancery, and to meet in Annapolis, 394. Complaints against settlers on Susquehanna, 572, 573. Letter to Governor, with extract of Indian treaty, 576. Letter from Governor—account of conspiracy between French and Indians, 587. Letter to Governor Ogle, 576. From Governor, 601. Letter of Governor Ogle, respecting Higginbotham, v., 187, 218, 222. Temporary line, 187. Relative dispute with Pennsylvania, 187–192, 202, 209, 221, 222, 224, 225. On Indian affairs, 209. Case of Higginbotham and Price, 218. Examination of Colonel White, as

Maryland—
surveyor, 221. Refuses to make allowance for Indians, 273. Case of Samuel England, 376. Case of Adam Furney, 377. Governor Ogle complains against Samuel England and William Hay, 382, 383, 384. Correspondence with Governor H., 421, 582–597. Temporary line, 421. Proceedings in Great and Little Cove, 553. Correspondence and depositions respecting murder of Dudley Digges, 582–597. Bryan Doran arrested in, 604. Proposes building magazine, &c., at Will's Creek, vi., 137. Letters to and from Governor Sharpe, 178. Informs of safe arrival of troops in Virginia for General Braddock, 331. Petition of Wat. Sipple, 417. Letter to Gov. Sharp, respecting, 418, 419. Resolution to provide means for paying men and expenses, 457. Difficulties on Conolloway's creek, 639. Letters to and from Governor Sharpe, vii., 32, 570. No embargo on provisions, 183. Complaints from borders of, 241. Fort Frederick, 529, 552, 553, 556, 558. Vessels to depart, 570. Letter from C. J. Holt, respecting murder of, under Sheriff of Worcester County, viii., 286. He is convicted and punished, 372. Letter to Governor Sharp, 372, 779. Letters to and from Governors of, ix., 305, 375, 564. Governor Sharpe of, administers oath to Governor Penn, 348. Complaint of John Redick, deprived of his land, 375, 376. Boundary question between, and Pennsylvania, 375, 379, 564. Complaint against. Letter of Governor Penn to Gov. Sharpe, 564. Laws respecting fisheries, 623. Agreement of 1732, between Pennsylvania and. Proclamation respecting boundary line, x., 206, 216. Jurisdiction of Pennsylvania to be not extended at present, owing to incapacity of heir of Lord Baltimore, 220. Governor Penn's proclamation, 220. Letters, Earl of Dartmouth and William Penn, respecting, 220,

Maryland—
221. Boundary, 240. Proclamation to be recalled, 241, 243, 245. Letter to Governor Eden, 242. Act for establishing and fixing lines, 263, 272. Committee of Safety offer to instruct in art of making Saltpetre, 478. Money to be changed for Soldiers, 682. Flying camp to cross at Delaware Ferry, xi., 28. Capt. Hindman's Company, 109. British army landed in, 283. A prisoner handed over to battalion, 364. John White Swift sent to Penna., 407. Act against whiskey, 647. Embargo, 712. Sailors taken to, and brought back, 782. Letter from Gov. Lee on Embargo, xii., 400. Wants copy of embargo law, 433. Remark on confederation, and remonstrance, 491. Convention, German and English troops, to be removed from, 648. Letter from G. Dewall, President of General Court, respecting Henry Carberry, xiv., 106. On opening Potomac, 398. To, on Inland Navigation,5 83, 584, 669. Letter, Governor Smallwood, 589. From Governor, 651. Commissioners to be appointed, 669. Inland Navigation, xv., 70. Chinese to be sent to, 75. Governor of, demands a Criminal, 463. For a Burglar, 499.

Maseraere, Joshua, letter, xi., 52.

Mason & Dixon's line, extension of, xii., 635. Pay to Commissioners for extending, 661. Instructions, 704. Pay, 714.

Masons' Lodge, prisoners in, xi., 292, 293, 294. To be removed to Virginia, 296. Habeas Corpus, 308, 309, 525.

Mason, Rich., petition road, ii., 527.

Mason, Thomas, claim for land and lots, xiii., 140.

Mason, Captain Thomas, may ship flour to Bermuda, xiii., 50.

Massachusetts, Governor, Stoughton applies for provisions for his Majesty's Army and Navy against New Foundland, i., 515. Gov. Belcher of, applied to, to examine Rowland Houghton, arrested as a counterfeiter, iv., 225. Expedition against Cape Breton, 753.

Letter from Governor, asking for aid, 773. Represented at treaty at Albany, v., 7. Letters to and from Governor, 31, 341. Governor Shirley recommends a meeting of Commissioners at New York, to consider and digest plans for united co-operation against French and Indians, 83. Governor Shirley respecting Indians and French, 97. Governor Shirley and Indians, 101, 141. Discharge of Pennsylvania forces, 141. Cannon requested from, 173. Answer of Gov. Shirley, 198. Letter to, 206. Charge for transporting prisoners, 420, 427. To and from Governor of, vi., 16. Union of Colonies, 18. Resolutions cutting off supplies from French, 309. Sends Commissioners to Pennsylvania, 314. Message of Governor to Assembly, 314. Resolutions of, 317. Embargo ordered, 439. Vote of Assembly to ask a supply of provisions, 614. Message to Governor. Vote of Assembly respecting share of arms, vii., 111. Applies to export provisions, 135, 136, 168, 186, 570. Governor Pownall, 717. Gov'r Pownall asks aid for sufferers by great fire at Boston, viii., 483. Assembly grants £1000, 483. Sends circular to colonies, ix., 546. Lord Hillsboro' complains of it, 546. Letter from respecting Tories, xi., 629. To be allowed to export flour, 682, 690, 728, 729. Resolution respecting exchange of prisoners, xii., 51. From Governor respecting a captured traitor, 400. Acts for regulation of trade, xiv., 517. Letter Governor on operation of Navigation Act, xv., 53. Letter of Governor and reward for Daniel Shay, &c., 171. Repeal, 435, 442.

Massey, Samuel, Member of Navy Board, xi., 127.

Master at Arms, x., 512.

Master of Rolls, Thomas Lloyd, appointed first, i., 91. To keep Charter of Liberty, 111. His answer respecting laws enrolled, 276. To keep the dedimus to administer oaths to the Governor, ii., 62. Objections to, and difficulty about it, 63. To print Laws at his own charge, 64. Thomas Story to have a Seal—described, 233. petition for Salary, 412; ix., 397; xiv., 378. John Morris dies. Matthew Irwin, appointed, 379.

Masters, authorized to chastise their servants, and punish persons who inveigle them, i., 79. To give security for their servants, 93.

Masters, Thomas, Provincial Judge, ii., 87. Obtains patents for curing &c. Indian corn, and also for working and weaving straw, &c., for hats. Council grant and authorize publication, iii., 18. Mem. of Council, 113. Dies, 232.

Masters, William, a Provincial Commissioner, vii., 498, 636, 657, 671, 697. Paymaster, xi., 34.

Matlack, Colonel Timothy, asks for Haversacks, x., 600. To have Rifles, 634, 683, 690. To keep register of all attainted persons, xi., 503. To provide stores for clothing, &c., xi., 1. Register of Forfeited Estates, 745. Secretary, xii., 189, 405. Delegate to Congress, 371, 464. Accounts of Tavern and marriage Licenses reported on, xiii., 537, 538. Requested to resign, 539. John Armstrong, Jr., in his place, 540. Counsel in his case—paid, 591. Comptrollers report on accounts, 625. Case of, xiv., 282, 284. His accounts, 604. Keeper of the Seal, Secretary of Council, Commissioner for forming flying Camp, Colonel of a Rifle Battalion of Militia and prosecutor of General Arnold, 604. Appeal, xv., 220. Pay for services on Delaware and Lehigh, xvi., 278. To examine Rivers, 319, Wife paid in his absence, 349, 366, 384, 407, 429, 462, 512.

Matrimony, Banns of, required to be published, x., 31.

Matson—A Shawnese Town, iii., 350.

Mattson, Margaret, and Yeshro Hendrickson, trial as witches, i., 93, 95, 96.

Mattrosses, Company of, to be raised

for service of United Colonies, x., 477. Captain Lieutenant for — Gibbs Jones, appointed, 180. Matth. Whitlow, first Lieutenant, 483. N. Donnell, second Lieutenant, 524.

Maule, John, Commissioned to command Intelligence Boat, and authorized to wear an English Jack, v., 267.

Maul, Nehemiah, Pilot, x., 376.

Maurice, Alexander, imprisoned, x., 668.

Mavericke, S., On bounds of Conn., 1664, vi., 263.

Maxwell, General, letter respecting Miss Levy, xi., 675.

Maxwell, James, Justice, xii., 667.

Maxwell, William, On condition of Braddock's Road, vi., 434.

May, Cape, Wrecked goods arrive from—Proceedings, iii., 238.

May, Daniel, Justice, xiv., 234.

Mayors of Philadelphia, iii., 31. iv., 752; xvi., 52.

Meade, David, letter, 399, 497. Justice, xiii., 683. Insurrection in Northumberland, xiv., 359.

Mead, Eli, Justice, xv., 51.

Means, William, Second Lieutenant, xi., 32.

Mease, Ann, sentenced as a scold to be ducked, pardoned, xii., 235, 243.

Mease, James, Clothier General, to be prosecuted as well as his deputy, xii., 599. Petition, xiv., 393. Paid, 477.

Mease, John of Light-horse, asks for wagons to remove his goods from Trenton to Lancaster, xi., Deed for part of Tinicum, xii., 256. Deed to, xiii., 236. Appointed Auctioneer for Southwark, xiv., 38; xv., 50, 153, 186.

Mease and Caldwell, order to, for use of battalion, x., 401, 405, 415, 418, 426, 436, 445, 462, 479. To provide beds, &c., for battalion in Barracks, 419.

Meason, John, Justice, xiv., 134.

Measures, proposed act to regulate sale of Beer and Ale by, ii., 218, 221. Sealer of, v., 280.

Mechelokeety, an Indian Chief, dies, i., 557.

Medicines for Hospital, ordered, x., 292, 305, 339, 489.

Meetings, Religious, right to sell, &c., ii., 221, 222, 228. Bill respecting, 553.

Melcher, Isaac appointed Captain, x., 497. Declines, 526. Major, xi., 31, 305, 408. Barrack Master General, 51. To receive Hessian and Waldecker prisoners, 116. And forfeited estate of Andrew Allen, xii., 88. Asks renewal of Patents defaced by fire, xv., 560. Letter and Maps, 597, 612, 626. Barrack Master General, certificate to, 1776–1778, xvi., 301.

Memorials, American Philosophical and Historical Society, respecting Publication of C. R., i., 9. Report on, 12. Act respecting, 15, 16. Of William Markham, in behalf of William Penn, 328. Of Captain Christopher Smith on Murder of Catawba Indians, iii., 21. Of Governor Keith to Governor of Virginia, and answer, 118. For Hon. Thomas Penn, why certain bills were not presented to his Majesty, &c., v., 499. See Jno. St. Clair, on roads, vii., 592. Of Pompunagh and other Indians in Philadelphia Barracks, ix., 135. Of M. Smith, James Gibson, &c., respecting Indians on Frontiers, 138. From City, &c., to Committee of Safety, x., 297. From Committee to Assembly, 348. Of Captains and Lieutenants of Boats, against Thomas Austin, 472. To Congress for cannon, 550. To Congress, 572. To Assembly, on Roebuck, 582. To Congress, Fortifications on Delaware, 601. Of Captains of Boats resisting command of Commodore S. Davison, 616. L. Kargher, 638. To Assembly, on refusal of Continental Currency, xi., 2. Of officers to Assembly, 15. Of Officers of State Regiment against Colonel Bull, 210. Major N. McCurry against Captain Morrow, 210. From prisoners in Virginia, 395. Of Mrs. Ferguson, 322. Of Francis Hopkinson, respecting claims on Estate of Rev. J. Duché, 773, 774. Matthew Clarkson, Marshal,

xii., 105. Of James Bell, respecting property, 315. Prisoners on Long Island, 480, 481. Of merchants, 480, 482. Dr. Kuhn, 517. Judge of Admiralty, respecting desertion of French Sailors, 409. Owners of brig Fame, 507. Officers of Proctor's Artillery officers, 729. From Land Office, 749. Samuel Preston Moore, Henry Hill and R. Wells, claim for lots, xiii., 9, 503. Of Citizens of Philadelphia, on an unfair Election, 119, 120. Report of Surveyor General, 321. Colonel Joseph Hart, 523. Jacob Shallus, for a lot in City, 548, 549. Of Officers Pennsylvania Line and Galleys, 677, 682. Officers of State Navy, 683. W. McCleery, 699. Of Quakers, 741. Jno. Mitchell, W. Finney, 747, 760. William Pollard, 748. J. Cadenhead, D. Drais, two Frenchmen, 764. McClenachan and Moore, 718. A. Yarrington, xiv., 32. Of Philada., 140. John Reynolds, 164. Isaac Craig, 291. A. Power and report of Surveyor General, 292. E. Blaine, 468. Of thirty-six natives of Bengal and China, 561. Longschamps, inhabitants of Philadelphia, 572. Officers of Pennsylvania Line, xv., 17. Of Proprietaries, 63. From Luzerne County, 234, 235. Charles Simms, 250. James McCalmont, 286. Isaac Hazlehurst & Co., 367. T. Wade, John Franklin, merchants of Philadelphia, 385. Turnbull, Marmie & Co., 444. C. Febiger, 592. Merchants, Philadelphia, 633. J. Fisher, 635. Of Committee of Society, for abolition of Slavery, respecting a free Negro held in bondage in Louisiana, xvi., 33. Public creditors, 107. Joshua Elder, 374. Of Mayor, &c., of Philadelphia, 387. Mich. Morg. O'Brien, City lots, 393.

Mendenhall, John, Coroner of Chester County, iii., 260, 289.

Menonists released from taking oath, iii., 29.

Mentges, Francis, made Major, x., 768. Inspector of Militia, xv., 14. Appointed Inspector General, 77. His pay considered, 135. Applies for tents, 483. Inspector of Militia, xvi., 92.

Mercer, Colonel James, xiv., 396.

Mercer, Lieutenant Colonel, commissioned to a regiment, vi., 294.

Mercer, Colonel Hugh, vi., 604; vii., 230. At Frederick, 553, 772. Cannon sent to, for flying camp, x., 660, 712. To send guard to salt works in New Jersey, 777. Letters to and from, viii., 292, 305, 309, 391, 394. Left in Command by General Forbes, 292. Is succeeded by General Stanwix, 298. Conference with Indians—their intentions, &c., 305. Conference with Indians at Pittsburg, 306–309. On Indian affairs, 309–313, 382–391, 394.

Mercer, Ship, General, provisions shipped by Mr. Holker on, xii., 194.

"Mercer," Privateer, General, captures Codfish, xii., 161.

Merchants of Philadelphia, in England, petition against bills of credit, iv., 750. Petition against tonnage duty, viii., 230, 232. Petition against duty on rum under proof, x., 247.

Meinzies, James, of Boston, petition, i., 560.

Mercier, Mon. Le, bearer of summons from Contracœur, vi., 30.

Mercury, the Weekly, printed by Andrew Bradford—Arraigned before Council, iii., 145.

Mercury Packet, to be attended by armed boats, xii., 392.

Meredith, Major, Samuel, x., 464, 503, 533. Appointed Fourth Brigadier-General, xi., 199. M. C. xv., 184. Sale of land postponed, 265, 341.

Marion Ford,—Road, i., 396.

Marion, Upper, T. petition for a Ferry on Schuylkill, ii., 276.

Meshonekek Creek, viii., 143.

Messages of Governor, ii., 451, 461, 465; xi., 685, 711.

Metschir, John Gotlieb—Suspected, imprisoned, xi., 409. To be discharged on taking oath, 413.

Meyers, George, Lieutenant, xi., 576. Resigns, xii., 477.

Michael, Everhart, Agent of forfeited Estates, dies, xi., 599.

Middletown, Guard at, xi., 512.
Miercken, Peter, Sugar Refiner, authorized to hold land, ix., 727.
Meirs, Jacob, to receive beer, x., 646.
Miers, (or Mears,) John, of Berks County, to pay for saltpetre, x., 481, 490.
Mifflin County. Prothonotary &c., Samuel Edmondson, xvi., 166. Justices, 166, 168, 199, 217,[2] 407. Lieutenants, Samuel Bryson, 183. Sheriff, 198, 542. Coroner, 198, 542. President of Courts, 224. Collector of Excise, William Purdy, 294. Register and Recorder, 444, 537.
Mifflin, Fort, [See Mud Fort]. Lt. Colonel Samuel Smith, commands at, xi., 397.
Mifflin, Brigadier General, privateer, x., 702.
Mifflin, John, Member of Council, vi., 666. To inquire about arms by ship Lydia, from London, 679. Commissioner, of wagons, 775. Goes to Easton with Gov., vii., 204. A Provincial Commissioner, 499, 636, 671.
Mifflin, Jona., Deputy Quartermaster-General, applies for Wagons, xi., 294.
Mifflin, Captain Samuel, asks to Export Provisions, vii., 571. Commands at Fort Wiccacoa, viii., 39. Appointed Commodore and Commander-in-chief of all the Naval Armaments of the State, 708, 712, 718. Declines, 724. Sent for, x. 784. To deliver cannon to Chester County, xi., 220. A Warden, xi., 538.
Mifflin, Major, delivers powder to Towers, x., 312, 500. To inquire what stores are wanted, x., 612.
Mifflin, General Thomas, orders Wagons, xi,, 222, 223. Message from, General Sullivan's order for Militia, 225. One of Committee to examine works on river, 231. M. C. pay to, xiii., 587. (Delagate in Congress,) sends papers, xiv., 3. Asks for powder to celebrate the Fourth of July, xv., 235. President, 584. President, xvi., 219. Paid for leaden spouts, 479.
Mifflin, Warner, a Justice, ix., 645. Signs address from Quakers, xi., 427.
Mileage, paid Councillors, xi., 205.
Miles, Colonel Samuel, x., 330. To purchase Rifles, 530, 601, 683. Ordered to Billingsport—And ordered back, 626, 694, 697. Rifle Regiment, 708; xi., 47. Brigadier General, 61. At Marcus Hook, 119, 215. Deputy Quartermaster General, xii., 450, 498, 512, 543. Deputy Quartermaster General, xiii., 41. Petition to postpone sale of lands, 293. Elected Judge of High Court of Errors and Appeals, 550, 551. Censor, xiii., 720. Resigns as Judge, xiv., 66. Pay, 229. Of Battalion Rifles, accounts, xv., 137. Enters appeal 302. Committee on Indian funds, 607. Appeal from Comptroller General, xvi., 4. On bench of Mayor's Court, 240, 242.
Miley, Abram, Sheriff, xiii., 400, 730; xiv., 294.
Military Stores, Inspectors of, appointed, x., 283. Ordered, 285. Books to be purchased, 500.
Militia, necessity of, in province, ii., 79. Those who enlist to be exempt from watching, &c., in Philadelphia, 151, 161, 204, 205. Law passed, 424. Law suggested by William Penn, Jr. Quakers not to be oppressed by it, iii., 64. Circular to Captains, v., 2, 6. Bill, vi., 534, 588, 597, 601, 724, 735, 741. Officers, 766, 769, 773. County Officers and regulations, vii., 36, 40, 62, 70, 76, 92, 152, 390. Association in Philadelphia, 62. Officers' names, 62. John Nixon, in room of Thomas Willing, Lieutenant, irregular, 76. Of York County, 76. Powder and ammunition wanted, 76. Returns of Comp. from several Counties, 82, 120. Notice of, 274. Remonstrance of Quakers against, 404. Quartering Soldiers, 406, 407. Bill, 463, 464, 572, 575, 593, 618, 718, 722, 729, 734, 737, 744, 757, 758; ix., 128, 133, 150, 151. Called out, xi., 17, 39. To be formed into brigades—John Cadwalader appointed Brigadier General, and

S. Miles, Brigadier General of regular forces, 62. Regulations, 72. Disgusted with unofficial orders, return, xi., 86. Deserters, 102, 106. To be called out by Congress, 198. Ordered from counties, 222. General Arnold appointed by Congress to command, 225. Congress call for 4000, 254. To be paid for lost blankets, &c., 291. Called out, 293. Drawn by lot, 313. Troops to be placed, 446, 477, 478, 581, 636. Ordinances respecting, xi., 332. Called out, 359. Expenses referred to County Paymasters, 413. Sent to Susquehanna, 532. Ammunition for, 538. Time of, expiring, 574. Complained of, at camp, Commissioners sent to enquire about it, 350. In Cumberland County, 410. Short, 580. Called out, 581, 733. Return of, by Jno. Carothers, 772. Officers chosen, xii., 2, 15, Term of service expired, 42. Call of, of county in seed time, and other evil effects of time expiring at Billingsport, 71. To be practised—Steuben's work on discipline, 73. Change in orders, 76. Destitute, 100. Refuse to pay fines, 103. Called out, 123. Of Chester county, 142. Called out by General W., equipment of, 144. Dr. D. Jackson, Quarter Master, 146. Counties, 200, 202. Law, 299. Proclamation respecting, 320. Desertion of, 322. Changes in—arrangement of, 373. Resolution for greater care of, in certain counties, 373, 375. To be in readiness — enemy approaching, 386. Collection of fines, 388. Inspector, 388, 389. Arms to be collected, &c., 389. Duty, 454. Paymasters, 463. Muster Masters, 462. Doubts on law, 469. To Northumberland, 492. Judge Advocate appointed, 504. Pay off Berks county, 567. Auditors appointed, 589. Fines, &c., 611. Discharged, 638. Pay, 650. Called out, 695. Exemption from, pay of, xiii., 21. Gratuities, trial for desertion, 22. Order 3000 men out in several counties, 53. At Lancaster discharged, 82. Ordered out, 98. Bedford, 121. Westmoreland, 157. Called out, 169, 203, 269. Stores to be provided for, 296. Petition, 298. Call of, 330, 349, 368. Fines, 382. Pay to, 421, 423. Three regiments to be completed, 445. Want pay, 461. Recruits, 494. Discharged, 592. Election in York irregular, 695; xiv., 3, 23, 77, 159, 167, 168, 177, 380, 513, 549, 584, 624, 634; xv., 5, 13, 14, 30, 40, 98, 105, 107, 109, 199, 209, 234, 237, 283, 301, 328, 357, 358, 371, 391, 432, 473, 590, 603. Officers appointed by Council, 437. Laws and pensions, 590. Fines, 603, 604; xvi., 1, 2, 8, 18, 38, 66, 149, 166, 168, 195, 216[2], 227, 251, 317, 337, 340, 348, 382, 445, 535.

Mill and Mill Race, Cornelius Empson, i., 301. Walter Forrest's, 389. Peter Dales, ii., 10. Proprietary's, 64, 65.

Miller, Abm., Justice, xii., 19.

Miller, Captain, x., 689.

Miller, George, a delinquent Collector, xiii., 641.

Miller, Henry, Sheriff, xii., 513; xiii., 93, 397. Prothonotary of York, xv., 17.

Miller, Jacob, to build boats, &c., x., 283. Has lumber taken by enemy, xi., 564.

Miller, John, Coroner, viii., 403. Examined respecting Stump, ix., 510, 511. Commissioner of purchases, Lancaster, xii., 660. Justice, 150; xiii., 677. Sheriff, xiv., 557; xv., 79, 296.

Miller, Joseph, Justice, xiv., 158.

Miller, Miss, pass for, to New York, xi., 577.

Miller, Peter, a Justice, x., 15, 46. Printer, x., 420. Traitor bailed out, xii., 145, 149. Coroner, xiv, 557.

Miller, Rev. Peter, intercedes for Henry Martin, xiii., 510.

Mills, Alexander, to be arrested for discouraging enlistments, xii., 378. Taken and dismissed, 379.

Mills, Griffith, ii., 541.

Milsheimer, Rev., a chaplain in a German regiment, taken at Sara-

toga—to be sent to New York, per order of Board of War, xii., 262.
Mingo or Conestoga Indians, iii., 19.
Mingo, an Indian slave, imported, ii., 489, 509.
Minnisink Indians, charged with murders at Snaketown, their residence — Kindassowa, their chief, iii., 326. Wounds Henry Webb, iv., 413, 420. Governors letter to, 420. Murders by, invited to Burlington. Messengers Moses Tetamy and J. Still, viii., 141. Arrive on way to Burlington, 149. Opinions respecting, 194.
Minor, John, Justice, xiii., 264.
Minshall, Joshua, his house broke open by Higginbotham, iv., 156.
Mint of the United States, Act of Congress passed for establishing a, xv., 104.
Mintges, Adjutant, Francis, appointed Lieutenant, x., 678.
Minutes of a Council, at New York, held by Governor Shirley, vii., 23–31. Of New York Council, 497. Of Croghan with Indians, 506–517.
Miralles, Don Juan de, asks to export flour for his private use, xii., 314.
Miranda, George, an Indian trader, letter from, detailing account of accidental killing of an Indian, iv., 88.
Mirchell, Richard, appointed Sub-Treasurer, for Kent, i., 111.
Mitchell, Alexander, Justice, xii., 336.
Mitchell, James, to survey Springetsbury Manor, iii., 185. Letter to Governor—Council at Conaytown, 187. Expenses, 382. Sheriff, iv., 500.
Mitchell, First Lieutenant, x., 488.
Mitchell, John, Muster Master of army and navy—gratis, x., 504. Commissary of provisions for artillery, 510. Master of provincial ship, 522. Storekeeper, xi., 423. Proceedings against, for Arnold's wagons, 707, 708, 709. Deputy Quarter Master General asks for two hundred wagons, xii., 18. Has charge of Schuylkill bridge, 269. Pays rent on, 340, 385. Letter, 321. Battalion to protect Northumberland, xiii., 223. Memorial, xiii., 717. Contractor for State navy, 1776, 77. Appeal respecting his accounts, xv., 432. Assigns of, for an arrest, 617. Deputy Quarter Master General, United States, xvi., 456.
Mitchell, Ann, wife of John, under sentence of death, pardoned, iii., 240.
Mitchell, (a Swiss) Indian trader, ii., 403, 405. In search of mines, 403.
Mitchell, Wm., elected Justice, xii., 19. Resigns, 526.
Moffit, Thos., escapes from Indians, vii., 282.
Mohawks, Indians, historical accounts of, in 1665, alluded to, i., 300; v., 10, 624–628. In Philadelphia, vi., 341. Murdered near Fort Cumberland, ix., 304.
Molan, John, a lawyer, viii., 339, 342, 344, 361. Member of Council, 360.
Moland, John, proposed new bill on warrants, &c., viii., 369.
Moland, Wm., made prisoner, asks to be exchanged, xi., 564. Disabused of treason under great seal, xv., 382.
Molatton, an Indian town, iii., 315.
Molesworth, James, examination, executed as a spy, xi., 197. A spy, executed in 1777, bond to, xiii., 385.
Moll, John, member of first Council, i., 57. Has patent from Lord Baltimore, 109. Refuses to provide for a bill in favor of proprietor, 233. Member of New Council, 580. Damage to his estate alleged, ii., 109.
Molleston, Alexander, complains against the official conduct of Wm. Hill, a magistrate of Sussex county, iii., 259.
Molliston, John, Coroner, v., 55.
Mompesson, Roger, Judge of Admiralty, Counsellor at Law, appointed member of Council, ii., 117, 134. Chief Justice, 239.
Monakatootha, letter apprizing of arrival of large body of French at Ohio, v., 635. Half-king

of great note, 660. Speech of, 691. Or Half-king, dies at John Harris's, vi., 184. Indian and French, 673.

Monck, ship General, proposals to buy for defence of the Delaware, xiii., 270. Name changed to Gen'l Washington, and allowed to make a voyage, 283.

Monckton, Brig. Gen'l Robert, letters to and from, viii., 495. Asks for troops, 495, 506, 509. Goes to Phila., 592.

Money, bill proposed, i., 72. Arrest of counterfeiters proposed, 84. Case of Charles Pickering, 84. Edmund Lassell, 380. Raised, 558. Act proposed for paying and receiving, for contracts, at certain rates, ii., 220, 223, 224. Queen's proclamation respecting, 435. No price to be set on English, or gold—commodities to be lowered, 444, 445. Act published in market place, 447. And dollars, discussion on raising value of, iii., 173. Coiners, convicted, vii., 725.

Monroe, George, Sheriff, v., 551, 597, 662.

Montgomery County, Prothonotary, xiv., 202. Dr. Abel Morgan appointed Lieutenant of county, 205. Register of Wills and Recorder of Deeds, 210. Justices, 215, 279, 504, 629. Sheriffs, 230, 555. Representatives, 230, 555. Coroners, 230, 555. Commissioners, 230, 555. Justices, 244, 282. Memorial respecting payment for a purchase of land out of sale of old prison, Phila., 282. No jail at, 313. Public buildings, 456. Laid off from Philad., 457. Deed for land, 492. Elections, xv., 100. Sheriff, 100, 294, 564. Coroner, 100, 294, 564. Representative, 100. Militia, 107. Justices, 124, 164, 279, 323, 537, 605, 609, 644, 647. Sales of estates, Alex. Bartram, John Meredith and Isaac Taylor — George Smith, agent, 153. Fine on Commissioners for not furnishing return of assessments, remitted, —Captain R. Coleman to be put in possession of tract of land purchased as part of estate of A. Bartram, 192. Agent for sale of confiscated estates, 198. Change of districts in, 233. Execution of John Brown, ordered and postponed, 423, 432. Asks for a new election district for Justices, 483. Case of J. Eckley, Collector of Taxes, 534. New election district for justices, 551. Councillor, 546. Express to, 572. Norristown to have three Justices, 609. Complaint against Lieutenant of Philadelphia for moneys detained, 636. Gunpowder furnished, paid for, 642. F. A. Muhlenberg resigns as Justice, 644. Justices, xvi., 1, 138, 189. Militia, 29. Contested election, 30, 43, 48, 49, 55. Election confirmed, 59. Amount of tavern and marriage licenses, 61. Collector of excise, Jacob Auld, owes a balance, 64. Returns of field officers, 71. Estate of John Robinson, 136. Robert Loller, Register and Recorder, 156. Militia fines, 166. Sheriffs, 191, 490. Coroners, 191, 490. Fines against overseers of poor, remitted, 288. Tax collected, 311. Militia officers elected, 362. Taxes received, 384. Register, 446. Fines received, 460. Error corrected, 463. Contested elections, 501.

Montgomery, Fort, x., 743, 756. New York, xi., 4.

Montgomery, Lt. Hugh, of gunboat, x., 329. To command gunboat Warren, 437. Captain of Effingham, 488; xi., 225, 531. Applies for wagons, 520, 530; xii., 44.

Montgomery, Capt. James, to have command of boats, x., 328. Called to answer — his command changed, 586. Resigns, 665. Commands privateer, 706. Of ship Genl. Greene, xi., 730, 747. Ordered to sea, xii., 4. Takes a prize and wants a mast, 19. Letter to Holker, 86. Takes a prize, 111. Complaint against, 155.

Montgomery, Hon. Joseph, xii., 778. Recorder and Register for Dauphin, xiv., 376. Justice, 378; xv., 41. Resigns as Commis'r, 221.

Montgomery, Col. Wm., to purchase lead for Associators, x., 592. Delegate to Congress, xiv., 261. Justice, 596. President of Common Pleas and Quarter Sessions, 400. Letter on disturbances at Wyoming, xv., 27. Runs line between Susquehanna and Allegheny, 85. Pay as member of Council of Censors, and Commissioner to Wyoming, 539. Justice, resigns—elected to Assembly, xvi., 539.

"Montgomery," The Provincial ship to be called, x., 525. Sent to attack man-of-war Roebuck, aground, 552. Captain Read resigns, 595. Pilot for, 679. Greenway resigns, 694. W. Whitpain resigns, 712, 741. Fitted out for a voyage, 745. Sails for, xi., 6, 75, 86, 128. Paid for a silver call, xiv., 600.

"Montgomery," privateer brig, x., 701.

Montour, Andrew, sent by Governor of Virginia to Indians at Onondago, iv., 607, 634. To be examined on distances, 730, 762. v., 290, 349, 497. Instructions to, respecting presents, 518. Applies to live in Cumberland Co., 566. Has a commission, 567. To interpret for Virginia, 568. Letters to and from, affairs on Ohio, vi., 47, 130. Near Shamokin, 669, 673. Arrives, 681. Instructions to, on visit to Delawares, 697. Arrives with Scaroyady at Onohquoge, vii., 12. At Philadelphia, 64. Report, 65. viii., 270, 429.

Montour, Mrs., wife of Carondowana, (an Indian,) iii., 295. Makes a long report of the intentions of the Delawares and other Indians, 296. Presents for, 337. Her daughter marries Indian, 501.

Montour, Lewis, vii., 506.

Montreal, General Amherst's success at, and Isle Royal, viii., 503. Great fire at, relief asked, ix., 390.

Moody, Robert, Letter from, on Wyoming, x., 87.

Moore, Lieut. and Captain, Allen, appointed to command boat "Experiment, x., 296. Of gun-boat "Effingham," 328. Resigns from the "Effingham," 442.

Moore, Charles, Clerk of Assembly, viii., 512.

Moore, Colonel, battalion, x., 687. Battalion to rendezvous at Falls of Schuylkill and Darby, xi., 301.

Moore, Doctor, (see Nicholas M.)

Morris, Governeur, pass to N. York, xiii., 586.

Moore, Henry, Gov. of New York, letter and papers respecting New England settlers at Wyoming, ix., 569. Indian trade, 642, 645.

Moore, Jacob, appointed Attorney-Gen'l of Lower counties, x., 216.

Moore, Col. James, x., 659, 665, 686. Resigns as Justice, xiii., 118. Major, of Pennsylvania line, 9. His instructions to, 698, 703. Detachment, xiv., 23. Letter, 29. Accounts, 37, 110. Troops at Wyoming, 110. Colonel, 118, 159, 229. Petition, 621. Fine for a riot, remitted, 622. Resigns as Justice, xiv., 567.

Moore, John, appears before Gov'r in relation to complaints against Col. Quarry, i., 545. A lawyer, 551. Deputy of Colonel Quarry, Judge of Admiralty, 580, 603. Attorney-General, 11. Comm'r to administer oaths, 62, 92, 390. Register-Gen'l, 97. Succeeded by Markham, 97. Refuses to deliver papers and seal, 113, 121. Gives oath to Gov. Evans, 116. Collector, 240. Seizes a Boston vessel from Salem, 240. Reasons for withholding records, &c., from Markham, ii., 122. Proposed as successor to Colonel Wm. Markham, who dies, 151. Collector of customs, 240. Sheriff, viii., 403, 506. Provincial Commissioner, ix., 237. Justice, 750. Captain of gun-boat Hanoock, x., 362. Commissioner to buy provisions in Philadelphia county, xi., 424. Sale of estates, 538. Major, letter, xii., 93. Frivolous complaint against, dismissed, 26. Justice, xiv., 180. President of Court of Common Pleas and Quarter Sessions, 559 ; xv., 109.

Moore, Mordecai, Chief Burgess of Chester, vii., 417.
Moore, Nicholas, (President of Free Traders,) complained against—his rebuke and apology, i. 59. Speaker, 105. Asks for an alteration in law respecting fornication, 61. Appointed, by Governor, Secretary of Council, 73. A Judge, 119. Declaration against, 134, 137, 138, 139, 141. To desist from exercising authority, 142. In a languishing condition, not expected to recover, 153. Judicial act complained of, 145, 151, 152, 153. Judgment against, 189, 190. A large purchase of land from Penn, xiii., 321.
Moore, Robert, murderer, escapes from goal in New York, iii., 108. Proclamation for, 108.
Moore, Dr. Samuel Preston, with Richard Hill, petition to make title deed for R. Hill, Jr's. land in city, &c., vii., 728, 739, 740. Claims lots and liberty lands, xiii., 9. For city lots, 49, 321, 326.
Moore, Thomas, Mill road, near, iii., 142, 227. Collec'r of customs proposes alteration of law, 278.
Moore, William, Justice of Chester County. Address of Assembly to Governor, complaining of, vii., 741. Proceedings, 750, 764, 776, 781. Address to Governor, 764. Letter from, in prison, 776. Case of, viii., 1, 11–17, 162, 287, 442. Governor Denny's message on, 1. Answer of Assembly, 4. Proceedings in Council, 161. Declared innocent of all charges, 162. Resolve of Assembly respecting his case, 287. Member of Council of Safety, xi., 45. Chosen Vice-President, xii., 163, 541, xiii., 50. Councillor, 133. Pres't, 112. Appointed Judge of High Court of Errors and Appeals, 535.
Morales, Francis, asks discharge of Spanish sailor from prison, xiv., 484.
Moravian—Missionaries to Indians, petition for a pass, v., 576. C. Weiser to be consulted—but the design is abandoned, 375. At Bethlehem, authorized to receive Indians from Diahoga, vii., 170. Number of, in Bethlehem, 353. Settlements burned, 494. Send F. Post miss'ary to Indians, viii., 301. Ask exemption from Taxes, 304. Indians viewed suspiciously, ix., 140. Sisterhood at Bethlehem present rags—thanks for, x., 553. Missionaries have pass for Pittsburg, &c., xii., 346. John Bull and John Mygant—missionaries—pass to Albany and the Lakes, xiii., 570.
More, Capt. Francis, James, x., 766.
Morey, Jacob, Justice, xiv., 584.
Morgan, Dr. Abel, Surgeon, xi., 124. resigns, xiii., 262. Lieutenant of Montgomery county, xiv., 205.
Morgan, Enoch, Paymaster, xi., 125.
Morgan, Evan, one of Committee of Assembly to distribute arms, vi., 679. Com'r of wagons, 775.
Morgan, Col. George, asks for a pass for his wife to go into the city for her child, xi., 486. Patent for city lots, xvi., 499.
Morgan, Capt. Jacob, letter from, vii. 35.
Morgan, Col. Jacob, appointed Colonel, xi., 31. Lieutenant, 194. resigns, 203. Pay, 208. Applies for arms, 218. Berks, 423. Resigns seat in Council, 457, 466. Letter, 531. Purchase of flour, xii., 53. Money to, 65. Decree of Supreme Court against John Potts' estate, 114. On flour, 117. Mill, 299. To pay militia, 567, 595, 686, 705, 743, 778. See also
Morgan, Jacob, Jr., buys paper mills, &c., in Roxboro—estate of C. Sawer, xii., 299, 303. Deed for part of Tinicum, 256. Superintendent of Commissioners of purchases, payment to, xiii., 7, 43, 74, 142, 219, 220, 262.
Morgan, Morgan, Coroner of New Castle, iii., 260, 289, 332, 370.
Morgan, Thos., Coroner, iv., 669, 747. 782.
Morocco, treaty of peace with, sent to Assembly, xv., 268.
Morris, Abel, resigns as Ensign, x., 501.
Morris, Anthony, appointed Judge, i., 451. Appointed Justice of Philadelphia county, 370. Grants

replevin in case of seized goods, 544. Complaint against, offers to resign, 566. Col. Quarry's speech respecting, 575. Elected Mayor of Philadelphia, ii., 104. Case of Wm. Harper, 151. Address of Philadelphia to Governor, 161. To have key of the large house at Barracks for soldiers, x., 415. Made Lieutenant-Colonel, 767.

Morris, Hon. Cadwallader, xiv., 29. Delegate to Congress, 261.

Morris, Fort, vii., 599.

Morris, Jacob, Inspector, xii , 487. Appointed Auditor to settle accounts of troops, 589. Resigns, 614.

Morris, James, Justice, xiv., 215. And president of Courts, 504. President of Courts, xvi., 138.

Morris, John, Coroner, iv., 669. Appointed Quarter-Master, with title of Lieutenant-Colonel, xi., 25. Authorized to appear in City Court and prosecute for State, 246, 276, 285.

Morris, John, Jr., Master of Rolls, xi., 187. To Courts as Attorney for State, 258, 294, 357. Recorder of Deeds to send charter of Academy, xii., 38. Master of Rolls, deceased, xiv., 378.

Morris, Dr. John, Cor'r, xvi., 492.

Morris, Joshua, resigns as member of Assembly, vii., 148.

Morris, Luke, a Warden, xi., 538. xiii., 100.

Morris, Morris, a Justice, iii., 28.

Morris, Robert, Warden, ix., 293. Member of Committee of Safety, to procure powder and saltpetre, x., 282. To apply for guns, 288. To order medicines, 292. May export produce for powder, 469. Cargoes, 579. Statement of John Brown of interview with, xi., 345. Member of Congress, 385. Imports arms for State, 653, 771. Letters to and from, xii., 2. Superintendent of finance—letter on requisitions, 782. Superintendent of finance, presents order for money under Act of Assembly, xiii., 7. Pay to, for Congress, 73, 110. Paid for supplies, 83. Letter, 96. On French subsidy, 10?. Barracks, 128. Letter, Massachusetts, &c., on revenue on impost, 174. For supplies, 193. Long circular from, 195. Capt. Van Heer's corps, 211. On supplies, 374. Papers from Congress, 541. Letters, xiv., 119, 182. Report on accounts, 464, 466, 473, 481, 482, 488. Appeal to Supreme Court, 488, 495, 497. Suit against, 555. Appointed Commissioner, xv., 5. Deeds to, for property corner Sixth and Market streets, 151. Petition for city lots of S. Shoemaker's estate, 657. A city lot lately owned by, xvi., 540.

Morris, Gov. New York, letter respecting Indians and French, v., 1.

Morris, Robert Hunter, appointed Governor by Proprietary, vi., 143. Late Chief Justice of New Jersey, 143. Appears in Council, 144. Is received at Bush Hill by Gov. and Council—his commissions, &c., exhibited, and then published at the Court House, 144. Notifies Indians at Auckwick of his appointment, 169. Speech to Assembly, 184. On French affairs, 185. Message to Delaware Indians, 187. Messages to Assembly, 221, 243, 244, 247, 320, 322, 330, 332, 413, 415, 432, 440, 443, 504, 525, 536, 546. Messages from do., 220, 226–236, 243, 244, 325, 359, 437, 441, 525, 546, 550, 554, 555, 565, 569–586. Objects to Act limiting number of passengers arriving, 225. Long message from Assembly on instructions, 226–236. His answer to, 236–243. Message on emigrant bill, 243. Amount of Excise collected, 211. Messages to and from Assembly, 244–247. On Connecticut claim, 249, 252, 254, 255, 261, 262, 267, 268–274. Council's advice to, 275. Letters, 286, 295, 299, 301, 380, 382, 418, 421, 424, 452, 453, 455, 511–519, 563, 565, 639, 739, 742, 744, 760, 771, 773, 774, 776. Conduct of Assembly, 295, 302, 322. Asks for Assembly's minutes, 305, 322. Correspondence with General Braddock, 307, 331, 332, 335, 377, 380, 394, 398, 399, 400, 406, 415, 431, 461.

Morris, Robert Hunter—
Against Assembly publishing letters, &c., 322, 616. Injunction to Franklin and Hall not to publish, 327. Mr. Franklin's answer to, 327. Letter from Josiah Quincey, 329. Sends Secretary to make copy of Assembly's minutes, 331, 339, 392. Genl. B. desires a meeting of Governors at Annapolis, 333. Complains of Assembly, 335. Letters to and from, 373. Sir Thos. Robinson on General Braddock's affairs, 394, 407, 408, 414, 494, 496, 536, 566, 644. "Quaking Assembly," 409. From Col. Bradstreet, 412. General Braddock has begun his march, 413. Letters to and from Gov. Sharp, 410, 418, 420. Writes to Shekallamy respecting settlers on Indian lands north of Albany, 420. On death of Kishycoquillas, 421. Appoints a fast, 422. Demand of Assembly for a letter from General Braddock, 424–5, 433. From Gov. Shirley, 439. Power to call Assembly, 441. Printing papers, 442. Address of Assembly to King on proprietary restrictions, 448. Recommends an embargo on account of arrival of French fleet at Louisburg, 450. To Commissioners on Braddock's road, 452. To Gov. Sharp, French and Indians in Cumberland county, &c., 454. To Gov. Dinwiddie respectiug cannon for General, 455. Receives various accounts of Braddock's defeat and death, 480–485, 486, 495, 496, 511, 519, 599, 604. Speech to Assembly, 486. Letters on Dunbar's retreat, 494. To General Shirley, 496. On Catholics, 504, 533. To Colonel Dunbar, 515. His answer, 519. Tax on proprietary estate, 525–532, 536–546. Answer on providing quarters by Mayor, &c., 516, 532. Militia bill, 534, 588. Indians, 536, 554. Letters to and from General Shirley, 563, 594, 595. To Colonel Dunbar, 565. Tax on proprietary estate, 569–587, 617, 627, &c. Messages to Assembly, 597, 617, 670, 675,

Morris, Robert Hunter—
684, 689, 706, 724, 728, 729, 733, 745. Do. from do., 597, 598, 616, 677, 691, 692, 707, 746, 747. Militia bill, 598, 724. To Sir Thos. Robinson, 592. Disposition of forces—conduct of Assembly, 599, 600. To Gov. Dinwiddie respecting Dunbar, 604. Supplies for Crown Point, 617. Answer to long message of Assembly—supply bills—proprietary estates—taxes—Germans, &c., &c., 617–623. Their answer to him, 624–637. Defeat of French at Lake George under Gen. Dieskau, message to Indians, 637. Maryland temporary line, 639. Letters to, on Indian murders, 649–662. Complains of distribution of arms, &c. by Assembly, 663. Informs Mayor, &c., of French in city, 663. Indian murders, 670, 677. Advised to visit frontiers, 679. Proposes associations in counties, 680. Proposes to borrow from Receiver-General for province, 681. Bill for taxing proprietary estates, 682, 684. Going to frontiers, 688. Speech to Indians on, 688. Stays by advice of Indians, 689. Explains his situation to Indians, 692. Instructions to Scaroyady and Montour, 697. Effect of Braddock's defeat in producing Indian wars, 700. Proposes a plan respecting tax on proprietary estate, 703, 705. Asks for money, &c. by advice of Council, 706. Calls on Philadelphia for help against Indians, 710. Letter from proprietaries, 733. Letter to Thomas Penn—views of Franklin—Quakers and their addresses–French neutrals—militia bill, &c., 737–742. Receives £5000 from T. Penn, 742. Gov. Shirley requests him to meet at New York, 745. Invites Indians to Conference at Harris' Ferry, 745. Answer to address of Bethlehem Indians, 750. Message from Indians at Wyomick, 751. Answer, 753. At Reading, 760. Attends council of war at New York, 765. Conference at Harris'

Morris, Robert Hunter—
Ferry, 770, 778. At Carlisle, 773, 776, 778, 780. Directs disposition of troops from New York, 772–775. Instructions to Captain Jocelyn respecting, 775. Letters from, vii., 3, 97. Conference with Indians at Carlisle, 1–6. At Lancaster, 7. Speech on hostilities, 2. Message to Assembly, 18, 19, 39, 44, 55, 87, 91, 120, 130, 131, 142, 143, 178, 195, 202. Messages from Assembly, 37, 45, 91, 92, 93, 125, 143, 183, 196, 203. Attends Council of war at New York, 23. Correspondence with Governor Dinwiddie, 31, 133. Do. with Gov. Sharp, 32, 132. Enlisting servants, 37. Entertains Indians, 64. Informs Council, &c., of a conspiracy to compel passage of certain laws, 87. Proclaims war against Delaware Indians, 88, 92. Correspondence with Sir William Johnson, 97. With Sir Charles Hardy, 9, 10, 35, 100, 113. Speech to Indians, 107. Letters to and from Gen. Shirley, 109. Asks for arms for colony, 109. Don't trouble himself about church building, 113. Blamed by Sir William Johnson for declaring war against Delaware Indians, 117. Prospects on frontiers, 120. Letters to and from Gov. Phipps, 135, 136. On support of government, 143. Address to Susquehanna Indians, 145. Discusses election of members to fill places of several resigned, 148. Answer to speech of Ogagroderisha, 158. Orders to Lieutenant-Colonel Armstrong, &c. in Cumberland county, 161. Authorizes Moravians to receive Indians, 170. Letters to and from H. Fox, Secretary of State, 179, 180. To and from Horsefield, 169, 187, 190. Receives Indians from Diahoga, 199, 200. Receives money from Assembly—gives Indians a part, and taking four members with him proceeds to Easton, 204. Proceedings there, 204–220. Attends Council for the last time, William Denny producing at this meeting his

Morris, Robert Hunter—
commission as Governor—before signing warrant Gov. M. invites attention of Council to orders previously given for continuing the embargo, which is now discontinued after a certain day, 221. Gov. M., by request, attended Council, 222. Renders to Assembly a particular account of the condition of the province, and a map of the frontiers and forts, 228. His resignation alluded to, 229. Meets Council at New Castle—publishes Denny's commission and declaration of war, 231. Communicates to Council at Philadelphia several letters, &c. addressed to him before change of Gov. was generally known, 231.

Morris, Governeur, letter to and from, respecting flour, xii., 16.

Morris, Samuel (Senior), and oththers, petition for a pardon of four prisoners, xi., 565.

Morris, Samuel (Jr.)? Appointed Sheriff of Philadelphia county, in room of Isaac Griffiths removed, v., 561. Elected, 597, 662; vi., 144; viii., 402, 505. Member of Committee of Safety, to procure patterns of muskets, &c., x. 282. To survey Jersey Shore, 474. Pay of, 650. Letter to, 753. Appointed Register of Philadelphia county, xi., 186. To remove records if necessary, 258. May export codfish captured by privateer Gen. Mercer, xii., 161.

Morris, Samuel C., member Council of Safety, x., 718, 726, 729. To fit out an armed boat, xi., 2. Has charge of prisoners of war, 5. Applies for shot, &c. for brig Achilles, 747.

Morris, Capt. Staats, supplies money, vi., 292.

Morris, William W., New York Commissioner to run boundary line, xv., 340.

Morris, Lieutenant-Colonel, on soldiers' quarters at Philadelphia, viii., 262.

Morrison, James, Ensign, xii., 31. Sheriff, xvi., 204.

Morrison, Robert, Coroner, v., 662; vi., 638; vii., 266.

Morrison, Sergeant, x., 480.
Morrow, Captain, complaint against, xi., 210.
Morrow, Abraham, Gunsmith, xi., 358. Repairs arms, xv., 406.
Morton, John, seat vacant in Assembly, ix., 374. Sheriff, 398, 548. To receive Stump and servant from Lancaster, 442. Appointed fourth Justice of Supreme Court, x., 173. Speaker, 241, 272.
Morton, Sketchly, to supply boats in Darby creek, x., 656.
Mortonson, Morton, a Swede, ii., 480.
Moses, Isaac, may sell teas at auction, xii., 427.
Moshowatshong River, viii., 143.
Motto, for a seal for Committee of Safety, x., 328.
Moulder, Capt. John, commands a boat, x., 339. To gunboat—resigns, 362.
Moulder, Capt. Joseph, x., 407, 632.
Moulder, Wm., appointed 2d Lieut. of fourth battalion, x., 484, 541.
Mountfort, Count, horse for his being lame, xi., 486.
Mount Johnson, treaty at, vii , 70.
Mount Providence, Justice, xii , 482.
Moyamensing, road from, to Philadelphia complained of, i , 189. Regulation of, xvi., 41, 228, 234, 238. Report, 245–251. Draft of, 493.
Moyes, John, attends on signal gun at Billingsport, xi., 573.
Moylan, Colonel, certificate to, as officer in eleventh Pennsylvania regiment, xii., 609.
Moylan, Jasper, petition respecting a perishable cargo—rejected, xiii., 656.
Moylan, Col. Stephen, makes return of fourth regiment of dragoons, xii., 333, 740, 759.
Mud Island, (see Fort Island.)
Mud Island (or Fort), committee to visit — report — width — a boom cannot be placed there, x., 283. Chevaux-de-frise to be sunk opposite, 334. Boards for, 378. Battery to be erected, 383, 385. Captain Proctor to command artillery at, 453. On defence of, 474. Rooms at, 494, 495. Fortifications, 499. Hire of mud scow in repairing banks at, xiv., 170. Damage to banks by freshets, 512. Stone for, 586. Report to be made, xv., 175, 204. Repairs of banks, 225, 236, 365; xvi., 32, 86, 95, 97, 99, 100, 101, 110, 121, 131, 140, 147, 160, 174, 301, 365. To be kept up at expense of State, 100. Piers at, 147. Proposals for repairs, 160.
Muhlenberg, Fred. Augustus, member Congress, xii., 172. Letter respecting Rev. Mr. Melsheimer, 262. Draws salary, 263. Delegate to Congress, 371. Speaker of Assembly, xiii., 352. Censor, 723. President of Council of Censors—receives his pay, xiv., 2. Justice in Philadelphia county, 54. Register of Wills—Recorder of Deeds, 210. Dedimus to, 229. Resigns as Justice of Montgomery county, xv., 644. Speaker H. R., xvi., 438.
Muhlenberg, Henry A., chairman of committee of Senate, reports in favor of publishing Colonial Records, iv., 1.
Muhlenberg, Michael, Expenses of prisoners to Virginia, xi., 437. Account objected to, 481.
Muhlenberg, Peter, superintends drawing of lottery of donation lands, xv., 97. Pay to, 126, 236, 252. Vice President, 308. Resigns, 563.
Muhlenberg, General, resigns as Commissioner on claims in Luzerne, xv., 214.
Mullinax, Nathaniel, ferryman at Schuylkill, i., 438.
Muncey, Fort, Captain Robeson's head quarters to be at, repairs to be made by order Col. Hunter, xiii., 214.
Muncey Indians, are women and cannot hold treaties by themselves, viii., 156. Conference with, at Philadelphia, ix., 689. Meetham, chief, 689, 694.
Muncey, troops to rendezvous at, xiii., 368, 374.
Munday, Henry, case of, with Maryland, iv., 101. Address of thirty-one persons to, 101, 102. Letter to Rev. Jacob Henderson respecting settlers near Susquehan-

nah, 103. His examination, 107–109.
Murders, ii., 513. In Chester Co., petitions of, iii., 40. In New York, 108.
Murdoch, Samuel, to be seized, xi., 284. Enlarged, 296. Not discharged, 525.
Murphy, Commissioners of Lord Baltimore, conduct complained of, i., 104. Sheriff denied a warrant to arrest, 106.
Murphey, Capt. Daniel, reinstated, xi., 119.
Murran, William, Ensign, xi., 783.
Murray, Rev. Alexander, missionary, &c., permitted to sell his real estate, and to depart and travel into several counties., xi, 502, 503, 565. Made prisoner, his petition, 564, 565. Pass for self and wife, 578.
Murray, Alexander, Sr., Justice, xiv., 487, 517.
Murray, Capt. Francis, second major, xi., 116. Applies to be appointed Lieutenant of Bucks, xiii., 745. Appointed, 746.
Murray, General James, Governor of Quebec applies for aid for loss by fire in Montreal, ix., 290, 534.
Murray, Jas,, Coroner, x., 101, 212.
Murray, Jas., Cap., x., 701; xii., 42.
Murray, Major, ix., 322.
Murray, Mrs., message respecting, xii., 366.
Murray, Capt. William, commanding troops at Carlisle—General Gage's order for troops at, ix., 118. Letter from Gov. Penn to, to move with troops to Lancaster, 127.
Murthwait, Richard, an invalid soldier, fined for selling liquors—remitted, xii., 374. Sergeant, convicted by Court Martial of embezzling money entrusted to him for recruiting, xiii., 149.
Mushett, Capt. Thomas, of a custom house schooner, captures a pilot boat loaded with goods in Delaware river—proceedings, x., 9. Proclamation of Governor, 12.
Muskets, &c., patterns for, to be procured—description of, x., 282, 542. Sizes of, 588. Price of, 711.
Muskingum, murder of Indians at, xiii., 297.
Muster, Masters, x., 493, 500.
Mutiny, laws against, vii., 347.
Myers, Lieutenant George, appointed, xi., 202.
Myers, Henry, case of, xi., 655.
Myers, Jacob, appointed armorer to boats, &c., x., 490. Pay, 520.

N.

Nagle, George, Sheriff, ix., 778; x., 56, 100. Recommended to Congress, as Major, 446. Made Lieutenant Col., x., 767; xi., 6, 49, 110, 456.
Nagle, Sergeant of third regiment, to be arrested as concerned in riot, xiii., 617.
Nagle, Henry, Justice, xi., 619.
Nagel, Peter, Coroner, xii., 508; xiii., 88, 394, 720; xiv., 232, 554.
Nails, screws and gimblets, machine by Sam'l Brigs, for making, xvi., 88.
Nancarrow, John's, air furnace, he objects to have it taken possession of, (being a Quaker) for making shot and shells, xii., 435.
Nancy, Brig, arms from, x., 633. Lost on return, and paid for, 642. Blown up, at Cape May, 745.
Nanticoke Indians, iii., 188. Conference with, in Philadelphia, viii., 614; ix., 44, 63.
Nantucket applies to be allowed to ship provisions, refused, xii., 525.
Nash, Brigadier General, wagons for, xi., 277.
Nathan, Simon, seizes goods from Virginia—proceedings, xiii., 2.
Nathaniel, Mr., letter on Indian hostilities, vi., 756.
Naturalizations, i., 538; ii., 184, 241, 493. Of high and low Germans. Bill proposed, 480; iii., 241, 248, 282, 284, 287, 288, 290, 326, 331, 367, 368, 374, 385, 392, 410, 413–417, 429, 431, 465, 467, 515–520, 525, 587, 593, 597, 607; iv., 59, 60, 72, 99, 331, 627, 638; ix., 17, 245; x., 103. Foreign Protestants, 629.
Nautilus, Gun-boat, x., 314.

Naval affairs, Committee on, may enlist from the boats, 200 seamen, x., 432. Russia sheeting, 438.

Naval Officer of Philadelphia appointed, xi., 198. Office, xiv., 406. Elected, xv., 315. Seizes a suspected vessel, 377.

Naval Stores, x., 522.

Navigation of Rivers, acts for improving, ix., 719, 728.

Navigation Act, operation of, xv., 53. Instruction for Commissioners, on inland, 60, 70, 135.

Navy, boats to be built, x., 765. Bounty to and pay of officers and men, xi., 132. Proposed disbanding of, 552. Ship General Greene, ordered to sea, seamen on board, officers appointed, xii., 4, 5. Discharges from State service, 187. Officers to be discharged on account of expense. 316. Fisheries injured by wrecks of burned State vessels, 611.

Navy Board appointed, to have superintendence of all naval affairs as well as fortifications, xi., 122. Additions to, 127. To take Province sloop. Sentence of court-martial referred to, 138. Appointed, names and duties, 182. Object to oath, 182, 183. State of affairs, 191. Action, 193. To be increased. State of old jail, 194. List of officers recommended to command various boats and vessels, 199, 202. List of vessels, 199, 202. Paymaster's pay, 202. Apply for money, 217, 221. Visits Billingsport, 243. Money paid to, 246. To furnish General Potter with boats, 248. To furnish Du Coudray with a boat, 252. To purchase twelve fire ships, 255, To furnish continental ships with pilots, 260. Request assistance to be sent to Captain Alexander, 275. Money sent to, at Red Bank, 361. Payment to, 365. Wm. Bradford, paymaster, 366. Allowance instead of spirituous liquors in, 408. Pay to officers, 521. Boats afloat. Convention brig to be fitted out, 529. First deserter tried—pardoned, 541. Proclamation for pardon to all deserters who return, 541. Recommended an officer as Commander of brig Convention, belonging to State. Councils appoint Captain Eyre, 543. Dismissed and Captain Blewer ordered to send out brig Convention, 552. Enemy's vessels in Delaware river, 557. Sales of public vessels. Report on hospital medicine chest, 641. Limit on prices of vessels, and on guns, 643. Distribution of prize money, 659. Surgeon, 691. Account sales, 718. Cutter Revenge as Guarda Costa, 720. Order for money, 728. Of Pennsylvania repayment to New Jersey of money advanced by Treasurer to, xii., 197. Sale of negroes, 398. Continental for pig iron, 483.

Navy of Pennsylvania, gun-boats, x., 283, 284, 287, 289, 290, 291, 296, 305, 314, 328, 351, 353, 355, 357, 383, 489, 490, 505, 506, 533, 575, 581. Commodore Thomas Read, 379. A ship of war to be built, 395, 401. May purchase one, 401. Andrew Caldwell, Commander, 457. Nauticus' plan for a fire ship, 366. Hands for, 462. Ship to be finished with expedition, 486, 518. William Brown, Captain of marines on board, 488. Character of Lieutenants inquired into, 488. Muster Master, 495. Rations, 500. Pay and bounty, 513, 518. Vessel for, 536, 559, 560. Ships husband, 576. Commodore Caldwell resigns, 581. Captains, 583, Officers appointed, 584. Vessels to be equipped—pay. Fire sloop to be manned, 584. Two shallops to be bought for officers of guard boats, 586. Captain Montgomery, 586. Instructions to Captain Read, 587. Galleys altered, 593. Pay, 759. Hulks to be purchased, 593, Appointment of a Commodore considered, 593. Gondolas ordered —pay—victualling—Captain Read resigns, 595. Exchange of prisoners, 594. Samuel Davidson, Commodore, 603. The Fly, 632, Officers pay, 534, 650. Resigna. tion—colors altered, 694, 697-

702. Galley building, 702. Sam'l Mifflin, Commodore, &c., 708. To be considered, 716. Guards for, 720. Muster roll to be formed for, 726. Pay, 727. Mifflin declines, 724. T. Seymour appointed, 731. Memorial of, xiii., 683. Pay to T. Morarity, xvi., 198. Pay to John Hazelwood, 224. W. Bradford, 527. William Webb, Paymaster, 539.

Nawgle, Anthony, Coroner, xv., 298.

Neagley, Jno., asks to be naturalized, iii., 375.

Neall, James, Justice, xiv., 346.

Neall, William, charged with counterfeiting, but acquitted, iv., 226.

Necessity, Fort, at Great Meadows, vi., 50. Articles of capitulation, 52, 137.

Nees, Adam, Justice, xiv., 479.

Negro boy taken on the lines—case discussed, xii., 335. Sale of a, 361.

Negroes, in Philadelphia, presented for riotous conduct, i., 380. Jack kills J. Rakestraw, ii., 12. Trial of, 11, 18, 112, 160, 211, 275. A, from Jersey arrested, 275. Duties on, iii., 165, 247, 248, 250. Prisoners to be tried, 254. Sets fire to a house in Bristol—new commission for trial of, iv., 243. Confessed his crime—reprieved for three months, 244. Insolence of, in Philadelphia, 243. To be transported, 259. White servants preferred to, 437. Free, arrive in a French flag of truce from West Indies, v., 71, 74. Sent to Havana, 79. Rules and regulations for flags of truce, 80. Duties on, viii., 575, 576, 578, 583, 601. Trial and conviction of, in Philadelphia, ix., 6, 542. Duties on, 446, 472, 637, 641. For rape, 648. In Kent, 655. In Lancaster, 680. Pardoned in Philadelphia, 699. In Cumberland, 704. Trial in Chester county, 705. New Castle, 707. Duties on, x., 72. Special Courts for trial of, 73, 276. Enlisting, 427. Duties on, xiv., 264, 506. Of Philadelphia, apply to make a fence around burying ground, 637.

Nehffield, ———, dedimus to, ii., 97.

Nelson, Colonel, x., 737.

Nelson, John, Captain, vi., 34.

Nelson, William, Coroner, xiv., 555.

Neri, Capt. Philippe, petition to repair vessel, v., 620, 654, 656, 661.

Nesbitt, Rev. Dr. Charles, petition for interest to Dickinson College, xv., 298.

Nesbitt, John Maxwell, Paymaster to the boats, x., 385. Warrant and instructions, 356; 408. Paymaster, 498. Treasurer to Council, 657. Treasurer of Board of War, xi., 202. Applies for a pass for Mrs. Elliott—declined for reasons, 718; xii., 285. Committee of merchants on currency, 353. In Front street, 746; xiii., 294. Pass to New York, 551. Buys land, 646. Paymaster of naval and land forces, &c., xv., 144. Late Treasurer of Council of Safety—report on account, 219.

Nescopec, conference of C. Thomson and F. Post with Indians at, viii., 132. Road from Susquehannah to Lehigh, xvi., 83, 213[2], 259, 284.

Neshamekacton, creek about three miles from Fort Allen, vii., 317.

Neshaminy Creek, ferry at, i., 514. Ferry over, iii, 233. Passed, 235.

Netherlands—United—Minister calls on Presid't and Council to thank them for asserting the law of nations in Longschamp's case, xiv., 121. Letter from minister, threatening to leave, 135. J. H. C. Heinecken—Consul received, 451.

Netotways alias King New Comer, a Delaware chief, letter from, ix., 736. Answer to his letter by president of Council, 739.

Neutrals, French, sent to Philadelphia by Gov. Lawrence of Nova Scotia, vi., 711, 729. Land at Province Island, 751. Their number, 751. Arrive, vii., 15, 32. To be dispersed among counties, 45, 55, 58. Petition, 239. Not to be treated as prisoners of war, 241. Proposal to bind out children of, 390, Passed, 392. Sufferings of, 393. Five arrested at request of Lord Loudoun, 446.

Case of, 717, 720, 723, 739. At Philadelphia in distress, viii., 269, 718.
Neville, Gen., to place a person in charge of Fort McIntosh, xiv., 448.
Neville, Hon. John, xiv., 631.
Neville, Presley, Surveyor complains of being deprived of his district in Washington county—referred to Surveyor-General, xv., 218.
Nevill, Thomas, repairs of State House, xii., 702, 703, 712, 720, 783. To estimate leaden spouts in Philadelphia, xiii., 268.
Newaleka, a Delaware chief, arrives in Philadelphia, ix., 656.
Newbold, island in Delaware, pork taken from, xv., 184.
Newbury, Keith's settlement of, iii., 185.
New Castle Co., Assembly to sit at, i., 96, 97, 100. Complaints for not entering and clearing vessels at, 101. Iron hill near, 115. Justices to visit a ship and demand wages, 131. Proceedings in case of a sailor suspended by Council, 132. A fair asked for, 180. Sheriffs of, 58, 126. Seal for, ordered—its device, 66. Watchmen to be paid out of Treasury, 118. Surveyor-General, 120. Register, 121. High Sheriff, 121, 174, 197, 213. Ranger—Justices appointed, 127. Fort, 130. Collector in, 130. King James to be proclaimed by Justices at, 142. Judicial act complained of, 145. Justices, 152. Surveyor and Register, 157, 164. Coroner, 174. Duties on goods at Whorekills, 205. Appeal from Collector, 205. Court complained of, 207, 220. Councillor, 214. Forcible entry and detainer, 236, 253. Causes transferred to Philadelphia, 252. Violent proceedings, 252–258, 261. Fort at, 109, 130, 337, 370. Taxes collected for Chester county, 265. Alarm of invasion from Maryland, also dissatisfied that King William had not been proclaimed there, 299. Taxes, question between, and Chester county, 311. Justices, 320, 340, 369. Assembly to meet at, 324. Court complained of, 325. Complaint of clerk of

New Castle Co.—
Court, 327, 329. Decision, 327. Hogs not to run at large, 327. Thomas Harris, 329. Complaint against High Sheriff, Edward Gibbs, 331. Jno. White asks for the papers and records, 333, 339, 341, 387. Complaint against King's collector, 335, 336, 337. Capt. Peter Alrichs appointed by Penn Lieutenant and Commander-in-chief of town and fort, 337, 370. Sheriffs, 339, 370, Coroners, 340, 370. Fair to be held twice a year, 345. Number of Representatives, 366. Fletcher visits, 368. And Lieut.-Gov., their reception, 369. His Majesty's letters patent published, 369. Gov. seeks place for a fort, 370. Petition to divide from Chester county, 379, 388. Case of widow Wynne respecting judgment against her husband under wrong name, 394 Council meets at, 401. Address to Governor, 402. Amount of 1*d*. tax, 462. Petition to take children to New York, 479. Petitions for roads, 499. Thomas Pierson, Surveyor, 499. Act to prevent fires, 508. Matthew Birch, Collector of Cu. oms at, 534. Goods at, seized by order of Judge of Admiralty, 541. Complaint against Collector, 559, 560. Pirates at, 563. Case of Collins and Sheriff, 576. Boats sent to, for intelligence respecting pirates, ii., 21. Privileges asked for of proprietary, 39. Division lines between, and Chester, 39. Privileges asked for and granted, 39, 42. Objections to laws passed at, and desire of lower counties to withdraw, 49. Reply of Governor, 50. Magistrates, 137. Wm. Tonge, clerk and naval officer, 97. Meeting of Assembly at, 209. Petition from Justices on encroachments by Maryland, 353. Abuses from the fort complained of by merchants of Philadelphia, 379–383, 433. Sheriff of, arrests Sheriff of Maryland, 393. Militia of Maryland ordered out to execute writ of ejectment, 395. Governor's plantation near. 423.

New Castle Co.—
Message to Assembly of, 424. Answer—Governor's reply, 425. Gov. Gookin visits, 428. Firing on subjects, 433. Privateer at Whorekills — action of Council on, 448. John French, High Sheriff, 448. Advises Philadelphia to protect against privateers, 451. Governor Keith visits, iii., 14. Complaints against, for encroachments on Chester county, 234. Division line, 234. Magistrates to state their objections, 235. Commission of Governor Gookin proclaimed at, 252. Jno. Gooding, Sheriff, and Morgan Morgan, Coroner, 260, 289, 382. Complaint of Indians against mill and dam on Brandywine Creek, 269. Justices appointed, 270. King George II., proclaimed, 282. W. Read, Sheriff, 332. Mr. French, the clerk, dies, 338. Successors to, 338. David French, Attorney-General—Evans, Peter, claims office of Register—objections to, 339. Sheriffs, 416, 465, 520, 615. Coroners, 416, 465, 520, 615. Meeting of Commissioners on boundary, 497. Lord P timore claims New Castle, Kent and Sussex, 594. Duke of, letters, iv., 422, 428, 430, 490. Declaration of war with France, 689. James Logan goes to, on death of Gov. Gordon, 50. Assembly at, 356. Sheriff elected, 470, 500, 602, 748, 782. Coroners elected, 470, 500, 602, 748, 782. Assembly at, 619. Sheriffs elected, v., 55, 411, 468, 551, 597, 662. Coroners elected, 55, 411, 468, 551, 597, 662. Express with news of robberies by French and Spaniards, 89. Road from Philadelphia to, orders respecting, 107, 121, 130. 202. Officers elected by Associators, 194, 248. Commissioned, 210. Till, Collector, in room of Thomas Græme, deceased, 244. Letter from, respecting Spanish privateers, 252. Defenceless state of, 258. Cannon procured for, 270, 301. Road to Philadelphia, 301. Officers appointed, 326, 327. Sheriffs elected,

New Castle Co.—
vi., 145, 638. Coroners elected, 145, 638. Indian chief and others journal to Indians on Susquehannah, vii., 137. Three Indians from New Jersey go with him to Diahoga, 152, 165. Messages to Indians, 170. Speech to at Bethlehem, 175. Letter to Captain of Fort Allen, 189. Arrives at Philadelphia with message and wampum from Teedyuscung, 198. Address, 199. Asks protection for prisoners, 200. Sent with letters to Gov. Hardie and Sir Wm. Johnson, 222. Sheriff elected, 267. Coroner elected, 267. Indian chief, returns from Six Nations and reports, 296. Visits C. Weiser and arrives with him, 307. Dies of small pox at Philadelphia, 337, 338. News of embargo sent to, 129. Assembly at, meet, choose Benjamin Chew, Speaker, 295, 296. Message to, 295. Embargo, 388. Supreme Judges, 558. Complaint of Quakers against D. Bush, 559. Embargo at, viii., 39. Two good horses to be at, 71. Coroners appointed, 223, 403, 506, 781. Sheriffs oppointed, 223, 403, 506, 781. Assembly meets, choose E. Kollock, Speaker, ix., 2, 71. Estate of A. and A. Thomas vested in trustees, 3, 4. Marsh, &c., to be embanked, 3, 4. Reviving actions in Supreme Court of, 3. Roads, 4, 5, 314. Sheriffs elected, 57, 199, 286, 333, 398, 547, 623, 688, 778. Coroners elected, 57, 199, 286, 333, 398, 547, 623, 688, 778. Gov. John Penn, Gov. visits with Earl of Stirling, &c., 73. Is proclaimed, 73. Assembly take leave of Governor H., 71. Assembly at—their proceedings and laws, 165-169, 405, 625. Justices, 203, 626. Justices—trustees of general loan office, 204, 266. Roads—streets and other laws, 314. Present to, 314, 400, Laws, 337, 401. Conviction in, 384. Judges—deaths and appointments, 581. Laws for various embankments, 600, 662. Executions, 671. Pardons, 699. Trial of ne-

New Castle Co.—
groes, 707. Governor H. goes to, 742. His proclamation at, 743. Assembly meet, and Governor proclaimed at, x., 5. Meet at Misses Clay's house, 6. Acts relating to, 48, 49, 79, 80, 244, 265, 272, 274. State House at, 48. Sheriffs elected, 56, 100, 211, 270. Coroners elected, 56, 100, 211, 270. Convictions, &c., 61. Presbyterian church, &c. vested in trustees, 79, 85. Justices, 81, 217. Gov. John Penn proclaimed at, 93. Naval officers at, 109. Geo. Read resigns as Attorney-General, and Jacob Moore appointed, 216. Boundary lines, 273. Justices, 275. Special Court for trial of negroes, 276. Applies for powder, 531. Surveyor G. Lukens to search for papers relative to "Cox's Neck" in, xii., 620.

New Castle, Duke of—letters, v., 37, 127, 129. Respecting troops, &c. raised, 129.

New-Comer, a Delaware Indian chief, x., 64.

New Counties, iv., 317, 335, 755. formed west of Susquehannah, v., 398, 403, 404, 426, 428, 559, 565.

New Hampshire, Act of Legislature on commerce and navigation, xiv., 596.

New Jersey, letter sent from West Indies to England complained of as injurious to this province—satisfaction asked, i., 75. (See Archives, vol. 1, 58–63.) Commissioners appointed, 75, 76. Agreement between, and Pennsylvania respecting criminals, 101. Demand from Governor Olive for seaman's wages, 131. Hue and cry from East Jersey endorsed, 147. Voters said to have come from, 279. Number of militia, 356. Indians of West Indies, 448. Road to New York through, 514. Complaint that carries off our coin to pay for cattle—remedy, ii., 27. J. Spicer's negro from, arrested, 275. Col. Hunter, Governor of, iii., 60, 62. Going to England, 68. Letter of Gov. Burnett on Indian affairs, 135. Robert Jenkins of Salem, counter-

New Jersey—
feits bills in England, iv., 429. President and Conucil of, to be applied to, to prevent danger from flags of truce, v., 81. Demands a fugitive, 94. Gov. Belcher in Philadelphia—applied to respecting privateers in bay, 111, 112. Pilots petition, 226. Governor on privateers, 266. Col. Schuyler with five hundred men raised in, to go with Shirley, 398, 410. Minute of Council respecting Connecticut, 555–558. Embargo, 592. Wm. Logan in, asking aid of Indians, vii., 145. Prevails on two to undertake the journey to Diahoga, 152. A scalping party from, 163. Letters to and from Gov. Belcher, 165. Scalping party to be recalled, 167. On embargo, 196. Memorandum of 1755—claim of Indians to pine land in, 325, 337. Copy of minutes of treaty at Easton sent to Gov. Belcher, 359. Answer, 385. Council minutes, 467. Indian hung for accidental homicide, 540. Governor sends law for march of troops into New York or Pennsylvania, 566, Complaint against people opposite Easton, 634. Gov. Bernard arrives and takes possession, viii., 139. Complains of Indian barbarities, 139. Indians arrive on way to Burlington, 149. Opposition of people to pacific measures—Governor D., &c. pay visit to Gov. Bernard, 151. Indian conference at Burlington, 156. Complaints by Indians about lands, 199, 209. River Indians near Esopus, 217. An old bill of the currency refused by Indian, replaced by Governor H., 489, Letter to Gov. Franklin asking protection for Indians on their way to Col. Johnson, ix., 113. Treasury robbed — letter Gov. Franklin, 543. Proclamation of Gov. Penn, 544. Laws respecting fisheries, 623. Inhabitants applied to in defence of river—will furnish logs, &c., x., 287. Account of logs furnished, 289. Associators may buy lead and have powder, 313. Proposals

New Jersey—
to, for a boat, 328. Ship with men and arms stranded in, 378. 383, 384, 391. Orders of Congress respecting, 385–387, 409. Shore from Billingsport to be surveyed to Newtown creek, 465. Report, 474. Shore to be defended, 571. Dr. Coxe's iron works, 575. Salt works in, 614. Troops sent to, 628. Supplies for troops in, 635. Boxes of cartridges sent to, 644. Escort of prisoners from Burlington to Yorktown by order of Congress, 645. Troops for camp, 675. Ferry open for troops on Delaware, xi., 31. Salt works, 114. Salt works defended, 127. Letters to and from Governor, 185. Prisoner sent to, xii., 38. Payment to, of money advanced by Joseph Borden, Treasurer, to late Navy Board of Pennsylvania, 197. Enemy leaves, 404. Captain Joel, 495. Traitors arrested, 553, 557. Prisoners in gaol, 585. Traitors to be arrested from, 663. Troops called out by Congress, xiii., 59. Jurisdiction of islands in Delaware river—Commissioners appointed by Pennsylvania and, xiv., 345, 460. Protection of buoys in Delaware river, 585, 591. Report on islands, 591. Governor of, demands Andrew Allen, a forger, xvi., 15.

Newman, Wingate, commander of privateer brig Hancock, x., 605.

New Orleans, flag of truce with prisoners from, arrives at Philadelphia, viii., 124.

Newport, R. I., French fleet arrive at, xii., 424.

New Providence, letter from Gov. of, and proclamation encouraging return of landholders, i., 342.

ewspapers, complained of, vii., 245, 307, 339, 447. German, established, xi., 409. Dunlap's declined, 529. Taken, 647. Subscribed for, 654. Publications complained against, xii., 59, 60, 61. Ten copies of each ordered for Council, 197. Taken by Supreme Executive Council, xv., 366, 375. What are to be filed, 444. Paid for, 639, 642, 652. Pittsburg Gazette, xvi., 89, 126, 222[2], 257, 262.

Newton, Henry, Sheriff, iii., 520, 575.

Newtown, Bucks county, lottery for repair of meeting house and residence of Presbyterian minister at, x., 41. Magazine to be removed and public books, &c., to be deposited there, 128.

New York, complaint to, against Lord Baltimore's agents, i., 103, 104. To render their account, 105. Letter from Governor and Council of, respecting Du Plessie, 202. And Susquehannah and Schuylkill Indians, 202. Keeper of the great seal—proposes to visit, 234. Letter from J. Leisler to president Lloyd for defence against French, 332. Commiss'rs meet to fix on quotas of each colony for defence, 393, 401. Two Councilmen from, in town, 401. Governor of, asks for defence, 449, 459, 460, 462, 463, 466, 468, 471, 484, 486, 504, 506, 520. Laws of, in England, 460. Governor applies for troops, 480. Road to, through Jersey, 514. King's soldiers desert from fort at, ii., 20. Proclamation ordered, 20. Application for assistance, 31, 35. Happy issue of conference with Indians and, 35. Atwood, Chief Justice, 68. Defence of, 114. Lord Cornbury applies for means, 136, 138, 142, 144. Gov. Gookin visits, 449. Expedition against Canada, 449. Governors to meet at, on expedition against French, 532. Governor Hunter's letter from, 532, 534, 557. A counterfeiter in, 566. Duties laid on goods from Pennsylvania, 611. Gov. Hunter obtains confession of murder of Catawba Indians, iii., 21. Gov. Spotswood of Virginia on do., 30. Gov. Keith visits, 30. Governor Hunter communicates certain letters patent—proceedings on, 59, 61. Gov. Hunter going to England, 68. Indian affairs at Albany, 82–89. Complaint to, against Five Nations, 98. Letter of Gov. Keith to, 99. Murderer

New York—
escapes from gaol at, 108. Letter from Gov. Burnet of, and instructions, 119. Contributions towards defence required, 119. Council's answer respecting contributions to fortifications, 134. Road, 177. Philip Livingston, secretary for Indian affairs, 200. Letter to Gov. Burnet for permission to treat with Indians at Albany, 203. Minute of Governor and Council in answer, 204. Aludes to Penn's purchases on Susquehannah through Governor Dongan, 205. Lands on Susquehannah purchased by Gov. Dongan for William Penn, 273. Palatines leave for Pennsylvania, 323. Gov. Gordon visits, 381. Encroachments of French—fortifications, 418, 635. Governor of, sends account of Indian affairs at Albany, iv., 770. Letter Governor Clinton, 772. Letter from Gov. Morris—suspicious appearances of Indians and French, v., 1, 5. Message from Governor of, 8. Treaty at Albany, 7–26. Attack by French and Indians on "Great Meadow fort," 19. Letters to and from Governor of, 31. Embargo, 42. Proposed meeting of Commissioners at, to consider plans for united exertions against French and Indians, 83. Cannon requested from, 173. Letter from Gov. Clinton, 175. To do., respecting cannon, 189. Messengers sent to, for, 205. Furnishes cannon, 215, 216. On privateers, 265. Commissioners at, 296, 305. From Governor, on Indian affairs and letter from Col. Johnson, 431. Message of Governor C. to Assembly, and address of Assembly to Governor C. on Indian affairs, 465. From Governor, to Governor H. on do., 495, 508. Leaden plate from Jean Cœur, 508. Letter of Governor C. to Governor of Canada — also to Governor H., 553. Answer to, 554. On Indian and French affairs from Oswego, &c., 622–628. Council at Fort George, 640. Weiser's journal, 642. Letters from Gov. Delancey

New York—
on French and Indian affairs, 717. Letters to and from Governor, vi., 9, 13, 33, 48, 520. Ohio affairs, 13, 33. Treaty at Albany, 25. Commissioners, 47–129. Resolution of Assembly—Indian alliance, 33. Proceedings of Congress at Albany, 57–129. Proceedings at Luttridge's, 61. Remonstrance from Oswego traders, 63. Col. Dongan's agency in lands on Susquehannah, 124. Hendrick's speech about, 281, 285. Letter to Governor, 411, 416. Embargo, 511. Battle, &c. at Lake George, 623. Congress of Governors at, 749, 751, 765. Soldiers arrive from, 772. Disposition of, 775. Letters to and from Gov. Sir Charles Hardy, vii., 9, 35, 41, 113, 122, 123. Neutrals at, 14. Minutes of a Council of war held by Governor Shirley at, 23. Raising of men for Crown Point, 35, Resolves of Assembly, 36. Indians, 41, 120–123. Embargo, 130, 196, 560, 596. Stage boat, and wagon between Philadelphia and, 222. Fears respecting Oswego, 234. Troops find quarters in, 379. Minutes of Council, 497. Sir Charles Hardy sails from, 560. Fort Edward—Fort William Henry invested, 714, 716. Relief for, 715, 719, 721, 723. Letters to and from Governor, viii., 146. Embargo laid, 146. Letter to Governor with Conestoga Indians asking protection on their way to Sir. Wm. Johnson, ix., 112. Unfavorable answer, 119, 120. Proceedings of Council on, 121. Refuse passage through to Conestoga Indians, 119, 120, 121. Effects of Stamp Act in, 300, 301. Governor to administer oath to Governor John Penn, 347. Letter, &c., Gov. Moore respecting New England settlers, 569. Indian trade, 642. Appoints Commissioners on Indian trade, 656. Provincial Congress ask for loan of powder, x., 312, 315, 328. Recruiting at, 520. Sends Wm. Sutton to be confined, 677. Let-

New York—
ter respecting, written, 681. Transports arrive at, xi., 3. Fort Montgomery, 4. British fleet blockaded by French at, 532. Movement of enemy at, passes to, restricted, 757. Large reinforcement of enemy expected at, xii., 75. Passes to, to be denied, 172. Foreign merchandize from, 199. Gov. Clinton respecting provisions, 305. Act of, on confederation, 492. Enemy about to leave for the Delaware, 683. No danger of invasion of Pennsylvania—troops discharged, xiii., 82. Prisoners on British ships at, 431. Vessel sent to, with provisions for prisoners, 459. Letter to Governor on northern boundary line, xiv., 363. Bill before Legislature relative to partition line, 372. Respecting, 380, 385, 399, 443, 457, 460, 464, 507. From Governor Clinton, 457. Demand on, for a thief, xv., 125. Governor's letter to, on riots at Tioga, 276. Boundary line completed, 340–356. Commissioners Abraham Hardenburgh and Wm. W. Morris, 340. Ratifies Federal Constitution, 506. Proposes amendment of Constitution of United States, xvi., 103.

Niagara, Fort, French at, buy an English child, viii., 147. Taken, 379, 393, 400.

Nice, John, Justice, resigns, xiv., 672. Major of 2d battalion Philadelphia militia, resigns, xv., 432.

Nicodemus, (Indian) on Indian murders, vii., 357.

Nicola, Lewis, makes a plan for a calavat—thanks to, x., 284. To ask for key of old gaol, 491. Barrack master, order on for arms, 517, 748. Appointed town major, xi., 27, 33, 48, 222, 266, 306, 528, 538, 637, 647, 741. To find guard for floating bridge, 56. Town Major, xii., 10, 37, 38, 62, 66, 68, 92, 177, 250, 279, 338, 400, 448, 450, 455, 464, 492, 550, 555, 588, 599, 622, 633, 639, 649, 693, 723, 781. Dismissed, with thanks as Town Major, xiii., 185. Appointed to command of invalid corps, in place of Capt. James McLean, unable, xv., 633. Pay for invalids, xvi., 17. To deliver all arms, &c., to Joseph Stiles, 70, 75. Pay to, 37

Nicholason, Joseph, interpreter to to the Indian chiefs, xvi., 362, 534.

Nichols, Major Francis, present at riot at J. Wilson's—gives bail, xii., 137.

Nicholls, Richard, on bounds of Connecticut, 1664, vi., 263.

Nicholls, William, 1st Lieutenant, xii., 70.

Nicolls, Col. F., xiv., 634.

Nichols, William, Clerk of Orphans' Court of Philadelphia, xiv , 668. Notary Public, xv., 45. Reappointed Clerk of City and Orphans' Courts, 315, 367.

Nicholson, Gov. Francis, of Maryland, extraordinary letter from, i., 515. Commission to, to appoint certain officers in Pennsylvania, 533. Volunteers in expedition to Canada, ii., 450. Proclamation of, and Col. Vetch, 451. To meet at New York, 532, 534.

Nicholson, John, xiii., 72. Reports as Comptroller-General, 420, 421. Takes oath as Comptroller-General, xiv., 456. Deed to, for a city lot, xv., 230. Escheator-General, 285. To lay out a road, 425, 445, 623. Comptroller-General—sureties, xvi., 31. Pay to, 54. Escheator-General report, 179. Report of public debt, 264. Books relative to certificates, 272. Censured for pension report, 329. Resolutions and votes respecting his accounts — letter and statement from, 330–336. Proceedings to be published, 337, 339. Reasons of those who voted for his dismission, 344. Resolutions and inquiries of Council, 357.

Nishewatshowall, viii., 143.

Nitzillius, Mathias, a Swede, ii., 480.

Nixon, Benjamin, Captain of a company of foot, ix., 204. Justice, 626.

Nixon, John, a Warden, 293. Chairman of Comm. of Safety, x., 406. To superintend boats, 480; xi., 117. Rank, 650. Explains letter to Andrew Elliott, xii., 353.

Patent to, for lands in Northumberland county, 781.

Noble, Richard, Sheriff of Bucks county, i., 58. Petition, 75. Case decided, 76. Marries unlawfully, 144.

Non-Associators, x., 643, 691, 696, 697.

Non-Conformist, oath taken by Wm. Clark as privy Councillor, i., 369.

Non-importation in colonies—Earl Dartmouth on, x., 240.

Norbury, Captain, captures privateers, v., 301.

Normandy, Abraham de, Sheriff of Bucks, iii., 69.

Normandie, Duke of, birth, xiv., 480.

Norris, Fort, vii., 493.

Norris, Isaac, Member of Council, ii., 429. A Justice, iii., 28. Accompanies Governor to Albany to purchase presents at New York, 196. Site of powder house referred to, 242. Chief Justice of Supreme Court, 400. Declines, 412. Commis'rs on boundary, 544. Commissioner to Albany, iv., 771. Speaker, v., 484, 558, 599, 662. Commissioner to Carlisle, to meet Indians, 658. Report, 665. Commissioner to Albany, vi., 25. His commission, 47. Speaker of Assembly, 167, 639. Indians arrive at his house, 276. Speaker, vii., 268. Sick—resigns, 770. Chosen Speaker, viii., 227. Sick and resigns, 396, 407, 506, 671. Speaker of Assembly, ix., 1, 58, 200. Resigns as Speaker on account of ill health, 181, 236. A Commissioner at Albany, x., 177.

Norris, Lieutenant James, applies for clothing, xii., 247.

North, Caleb, recommended as Captain, x., 447; xi., 620; xiii., 743.

North, Captain George, of artillery company in Philadelphia, vi., 770.

North America, bank of—money from, xiii., 176. Copy of its rules and regulations sent to Council, xv., 192.

Northampton county, mentioned, v., 564, 565. Justices appointed, 573. Petition for road, 576. Sheriffs elected, 597, 662. Coroners elected, 597, 662. Return of road, 610. Act respecting Inspectors, 619. Symptoms of disturbance from Connecticut between, 41° and 42°, of North latitude, on account pretended claim, 735. Letter from D. Brodhead, 757. Various letters and papers respecting Connecticut dispute, 767–777. Purchase of lands at Albany, vi., 111–129. Sheriffs elected, 144, 638. Coroners do., 144, 638. Indian hostilities in, 756–764, 771. Various depositions respecting, 758. New York soldiers sent to, 775. Sheriffs elected, vii., 266. Coroners elected, 266. Indian murders, 357, 757. Justices, 769. Coroners appointed, viii., 223, 403, 506, 781. Sheriffs appointed, 223, 403, 506, 781. Inspectors, 400. Connecticut settlers in, 564, 599. Report of Sheriffs and Justices to Governor on, 564. Governor's proclamation, 566. Letters from, to Governor of Connecticut and Sir Wm. Johnson, 563–572. And other papers, 612, 621, 628, 662. Proclamation against settlers, 663. Court house at Easton, ix., 23. Sheriffs elected, 57, 199, 286, 333, 398, 548, 623, 688, 778. Coroners elected, 57, 199, 286, 333, 398, 548, 623, 688, 778. Indian murders in, 58. A frontier county, 138. Petition on quit rents, &c., 179, 180. Justices appointed, 205, 245, 308, 575, 660, 746. Instructions to Sheriff of, 608. To elect two members of Assembly, 650. For road, 703. Road to Wyoming, 731. Connecticut people on their way, armed, to Wyoming, 747. Report of Tilghman and Shippen, 750. Division of, x., 32. Sheriffs elected, 56, 100. Coroners elected, 56, 100. Justices, 155. Executions, &c., 129. Z. Butler distributes advertisements in, 154. Road to Wyoming, 219. Governor's letter to magistrates, 275. Associators ask for pattern guns, 300. Petition for powder, 363, 366. Commissioners receive money, 404. Re-

Northampton Co.—
solutions sent to, for powder, 439. To collect arms, 441. Person to learn to make saltpetre, 498. Fire locks from, 585. Declaration of Independence to be published in, 635. Troops to be called out, xi., 55. Disaffected persons taken in, 109. Col. Jost Trisbach's battalion, 126. Prothonotary, 187. Register and Recorder of Deeds, 190. Clerk of Orphans' Court, 191. Justices, 211. Militia ordered, 222, 360. Lieutenants, 257. Justices decline to take oath—others appointed, 260, 760. Lewis Gordon to be imprisoned, 261. Militia to march to Lancaster, 275, 302. Election, 364. Militia called out, 308. Books in library belonging to State, to be sent to Easton, 309. Storekeeper, 437. Guards at, 446, Agent to distribute provisions collected in, 422, 512. Ammunition for, 538. Recommendation of criminals to mercy, 586. Sheriffs elected, 597. Coroners, 597. Militia complain against Col. John Weitzell, 705. Wagons, xii., 2. Pay for purchase of provisions in, 44. Robert Levers receives subscriptions to loan office, 47. Money for, through Philip Bœhm, Paymaster, 55. Indians invade, 57, 64. Approval of government, 72. Militia refuse to pay fines, 103. Elections, 134. Representatives, 134, 506. Sheriffs, 134, 506. Coroner, 134, 506. Petition of Captain Jacob Buss and others of 5th battalion and resolutions of Council in the case, 141. To furnish wagons to remove baggage from west, 143. Estate of John Young sold, 157. Militia fines, 243. Military officers appointed, 298. Premium for scalps—militia called out, 312. Express paid from, 313. Resignation and appointment of Lieutenants, 317. Pay for estates, 322. Needs ammunition, 374. Militia for, 483. Ammunition for, 488. Petition of officers of miltia against Col. S. Rea, 607. Auditors, 646. Petition for defence,

Northampton Co.—
677. Incursions of Indians, 717. Robert Levers, Lieut., J. McFerran, Paymaster, 767. Sheriff to return of property of George Bachman, xiii., 47, 89, 395, 723. Censor, 723. Sheriff, 47, 89, 395, 723. Representatives, 723. Troops called out, 53. Complaint against Col. Robert Levers, 91. Justices, 122. Relief of, 127. Bounty paid to Rangers, 132, 137. Petitions on militia fines and taxes, 236. Pay for militia, 270. Petition of militia of, 298. Troops raised in, 316. Number to be called out, 317. Indian depredations, 337. Contract for rations, 362. Supplies, 376, 402. Elections, 89, 395. Pay to troops, 425. Pay for provisions, 441. Estimate of damages by enemy, 528. Claim of Elizabeth Kurtz for land in, 548. Col. Thomas Craig appointed Lieutenant of county, 617. Justice, 775. Sale of estate of Wm. Thomas, xiv., 56. Contested election, 158. Troops to be kept in readiness for Wyoming, 166, 167, 168. A Justice of Court appointed, 174, 226. Justices, 174, 185, 198, 200, 228, 261, 362, 442, 559, 584, 642, 649. Contested election, 232, 248, 443. Sheriffs, 248, 556. Coroners, 248, 556. Eighteen penny tax, 267. Collector of Excise, 445. Deputy Surveyors, 458. Militia, 586. Deed A. Allen's estate, 587, 590. Collector of Excise, Geo. Graff—resigns—and George Schriver appointed, 620. Separation of two townships — petition respecting taxes, 627. Collector of Excise, 628. Pay for provisions furnished, 658, 659. Claim for estate of G. P. Wertman, 666. Justices, 666. Provisions for, 668. Deed for lands, xv., 4. Road from Lehigh Water Gap to Wyoming, 22. Justices, 35, 43, 92, 143, 178, 247, 367, 480, 579, 589, 619, 642. Deeds, 43, 124. Lieut. Archer resigns, 51. Lieutenant, 55. Northern part to be made into a new county, 91. Election, 100, 297. Sheriff, 100, 297, 570, 640.

Northampton Co.—
Coroner, 100, 297, 570. Representatives, 100. Councillor, 100, 103, 297. Thos. Hartman removed from, 141. Sub-Lieutenant paid, 168. Claims in Luzerne county—memorial, 224. Seditious resolutions at Easton—prosecution to be commenced, 225. Contested election—John McNair agent for confiscated estates, 248. Lieut. of county accounts, 249. Proprietaries claim "Indian land" in—petition against, 265. Contested election, 298, Roads, 425, 445. Estate of A. Allen, 428. Robert Levers, Prothonotary, dies, 460. Wm. Craig elected, 461. Contested election, 480. Fines, 537. Excise from P. Pettigrew, 562. George Sinclair, 572. Collector of Excise resigns, 581. Jno. Craig, Collector of Excise, 582, 621. Complaint against Commissioners and Treasurer for withholding information, 614, 618. Expense of removing John Franklin to Philadelphia, 640. Petition for removal of a Justice—sureties for Prothonotary, xvi., 20, 32. Petition against Commissioner of Taxes and Treasurer, 45. Proceedings of Council respecting, 48. Order favor of John Chambers, late sub-Lieutenant, 65. John Franklin removed to, 102. Sheriffs, 192, 490. Coroners, 192, 490. Councillor, 192. Militia, 195, 382. Petition of removal of George Sinclair to Philadelphia, 208. Contested election, 209. Nescopec road, 213[2], 215[2], 284. Settlers on dry lands refuse to pay, 217[2]. Justices, 282, 286, 325, 450. Deputy Surveyor, 288. John Dorr, Lieutenant, and John Dillinger, Ensign of 7th company of 1st battalion, 295. Captain L. Stacker, paid, 311. Capt. Greenmyer's company battalion commanded by Col. S. Baillot, 364. Col. Philip Bœhm's battalion, 382. Capt. Paul Knaus's company, for men in service against Indians, 383. Excise, 408. Tax on writs—tavern licenses received, 411. Militia and Indians in, 487.

Northampton Co.—
Taxes received, 478. Suit between Commonwealth and late Commissioners of, 493. Militia, 515.

North Carolina, strange Indians from, arrive at Shawnois town, ii., 391. Gov. Dobbes daily expected, vi., 164. Powder belonging to, x., 416. Prisoners from, committed to Philadelphia gaol, 581, 584. Disposal of, 591, 638, 648. Letter Governor Caswell on refugee, xii., 314. Act of Legislature ceding lands to United States, xiv., 162. Letter Gov. C. delegates to convention, xv., 159. Declaration of rights, and desired amendment in Federal Constitution, 524. Acts of Congress respecting, xvi., 289. Resolution amendment of Constitution, 304. Relinquishes a part western territory, 329. Act of Congress for pay due from United States, 384.

Northumberland County, formed, x., 42. Justices commissioned, 43, 47, 262. Sheriffs elected, 59, 101, 217, 271. Wm. Maclay appointed to several offices, 43. Wm. Plunket, president of Court at, 87. Petition of inhabitants against Connecticut people, 111. Message to Assembly respecting, 117, 143. Z. Butler distributes advertisements in, 154. Money to build Court house and prison, 198. Governor's letter to magistrates, 275, 366. Powder for, 662. Officers commissioned for battalion of Associators in, 746. Col. Hunter of, xi., 110. Prothonotary, 187, 301. Register and Recorder, 194. Justices, 218, 398, 405, 528. Militia called out, 302, 360. Elections, 367. Sheriffs, 367, 638. Coroner, 367, 639. Paymaster, 372. Joseph Green paid for provisions for Lieutenant Hunter for Susquehanna county, 393. Indian murders in—militia called out, 403. Provisions purchased in, 423. Militia, 478, 508. Indians in, 508, 509, 510. Petition from, 541. Fort Jenkins in, 654. Improper election, 730. Case of John Taylor, 779. Wa-

Northumberland Co.—
gons, xii., 2. Complaints against Justices of—John Lodge, Sheriff, 43. Sheriffs, 43, 75, 137, 513. Coroners, 137, 513. Justices, 46, 437, 490. Prothonotary, 42, 75, 243. He must reside in the county, 42. Troops raised in, 46. Powder for Col. Hunter, 50. Complaint against John Lodge, Sheriff, 75. Militia destitute, 100, 105, 108. Against Justices Weiser and Atkinson, 112. Volunteers turn out in a case of invasion—claim of Col. Smith for, 114. Defence of frontiers, 120. Elections—Representatives—Commissioners—Assessors, 137. Fears of Indians, owing to General Sullivan's removal, 138. Indians in, 230. Letters respecting situation of, 308. Lieutenants and subs, 308, 384. Officers of the ranging company chosen—premium offered in, for prisoners and Indian scalps, 311. Justices, 342. Provision for troops in, 365. Justices superceded, 376. Defenceless state of, 459, 461, 492. General J. Potter, Councilman, 543. Appointments, 554. Volunteers in, 678. Ensign, 769. Patent for lands in Turbutt township to John Nixon, 781. Rangers to be raised in—Alexander Smith appointed Surgeon, xiii., 10. Complaint against Matthew Smith, Prothonotary, 29, 446, Estate of Thomas Hughes, 38. Election, 92, 398. Sheriff, 92, 398. Coroner, 92, 398. Protection for, 117. Pay for recruits, 132. Ammunition for, 150. Rations, 186. Militia, 204. Cumberland battalion sent to, 223. Pay to seven month's men, 268. Lieutenant Samuel McGrady and volunteers raised by Capt. Robinson approved—petition of R. Haines and S. Miles to postpone sales of land—rejected, 293. Contract for provisions, 356. Suit, Henry Gross against D. Deshler for purchase of horses, 367. Rendezvous at Muncy, 368, 374. Indians in, 417, 421. Agreement with John Weitzell for rations, 428. Prothonotary,

Northumberland Co.—
493. Troops for Wyoming, 519. Col. Harmer's case, 671. Justices, 683. Matthew Smith, Prothonotary, dismissed, and Lawrence Keene appointed, 696. Irregular returns, 726. Election, 746, 750, 751. Justices, xiv., 11, 32, 158, 322. Disturbance among soldiery at Wyoming—letter to Sheriff, 116, 120. Letter on disturbances at Wyoming, 165. Justice Antes resigns—resolution of Council in reference to Wyoming, 167, 168, 184. Repair of arms, 238. Elections, 256, 558. Sheriff, 256, 558. Representatives, 256, 558. Coroners, 256, 558. Justice dismissed by Assembly, 288. Confiscated estates, 292. Collection of fines against Col. James Moore, &c.—insurrection in, 358, 359. Justices, 369, 396, 493, 509. Troops, pay for, 382. President of Courts of Common Pleas and Quarter Session, 400. Deputy Surveyors, 441, 445, 457. Collector of Excise, 445, 653. List of militia officers, 453. Andrew Allen's estate, 464. Justices, 627. Division of Mahoning township, xv., 41. Justices, 51, 60, 92, 271, 307. Estate of Thomas Mackiness, 82. Election, 101, 103. Sheriffs, 118, 171, 310, 570. Coroner, 118, 310, 570. Councillor, 103. Sales of estate Thomas Mackiness, 153. Of A. Bartram, 185. Road from Berks to, by saw mill of Conrad Minnick, 252, 254. Cattawissa, a separate district for electing Justices, also Lycoming—latter rejected, 271. Division of townships, xvi., 6. Justices, 15, 99, 107. Pay to widow of Baltzer K. Smith, ordered by Orphans' Court, 16. Pay for provisions furnished by Evan Owen, 38. Return of militia officers, 66. Lawrence Keene, Prothonotary, dies—Jasper Ewing elected, 120. Sheriffs, 195, 494. Coroner, 195, 494. Councillor, 195. Return of male white inhabitants made, 201. Riot in, 223[2], 225. Lieut. Breading resigns, 231. Deputy Sur-

Northumberland Co.—
veyor, 254. A. Bartram's estate sale, 283. John Brady wounded at Brandywine, 289. Supplies for Wyoming, 364. Preemption right to two islands in Susquehannah—asked for by J. Byers and F. McPherson, &c., 395, 399. Murder of two Indians on Pine creek, 396, 398. Excise collected, 460. John Simpson, Register and Recorder, 495. Taxes received, 516. Execution of J. E. Jones ordered, 535. W. Montgomery resigns as Justice—elected to Assembly, 539.

Notary and Tabellion Public, x., 9; xi., 200, 201, 685; xiii., 13, 15, 20, 36, 302, 445; xiv., 287, 362, 568, 571. Appointed, xv., 45, 89, 222, 241, 255, 295, 358, 527; xvi., 16, 163, 586.

Nottingham, Maryland, settlement of, iii., 60, 212.

Nova Scotia, expedition against, vi., 321. Col. Wm. Johnson proposed for command, 313. French neutrals from, 711. Act for binding out persons imported from—neutrals, vii., 739, 740.

Nunes, Daniel, Coroner, iii., 615.

Nunes, Daniel, Jr., Sheriff, viii., 781; ix., 57, 199.

Nutimus and other Indians arrive at Philadelphia, iv., 312.

O.

Oath, Council refuse to take a collector's, but will his attestation, 148. Refusal to take, 398. Administered to Gov. Hamilton by Council, ii., 68. To be taken by Judges and other officers, 89. Difficulties of administering it, 90–96. Collector does administer it, 96. To be administered by Court Quarter Sessions, 104. Administerod to Gov. Evans, 115, 116. Affirmation instead of, 169. Rejected, 170, 215, 227. Man fined for not taking, 180. Address to Queen on, 219. Remonstrance of Assembly on, 455. Lawyer complained of, 457. Difficulties, 615, 616. Administered to Gov.

Oath—
Keith under dedimus, iii., 13. Not required of Menonists, &c., 29. Difficulties on account of, iv., 482, 629. Act to relieve from taking, x., 32, 42. Or affirmation, objected to by Navy Board, xi., 183, 195. Act of Congress respecting, xvi., 94, 96. Taken by President, &c., 96.

O'Brien, James, under sentence of death, reprieved, xi., 653.

Octorara, survey to, advice of Council on, iii., 180. To consult Gov. Calvert, 180, 212.

Odell, Rev. John, letter to Mrs. Bullock, x., 359. Handed over to New Jersey committee, 361.

Officers, on Governor's power to appoint, iii., 537, 538. Commission in each county, v., 209. And soldiers, bill to regulate, viii,, 482. Of Governors and their salaries, x., 260, 266, 634. Form of commission for Associators, 295, 314. Recommendations as to rank, 315–321. Commissions, 322. Of artillery, ask for alterations in field pieces, 327. Pay of men and, of boats, 329. And allowance, 329. Disputes about rank, 334. Pay and rations, &c., 5[illegible], 521. Of provincial ship, 522. Pay of, 586. Names of several, 697, 700, 704, 708, 711, 712, 715, 717, 720, 722, 738, 741, 756, 766, 768. Of Maj. Thos. Proctor's companies, 742. Of battalion in Northumberland, 746. Promotions, 767, 668. Order to, 769. Pay of, armed boats, xi., 8. Memorial to Assembly on calling out militia, 15. Appointed, 23, 36, 54, 56, 61, 62, 111, 116, 272. Rank of, 54, 109, 272. To be nominated in different counties, 24. Of Maj. Williams' regiment, 98. Of the twelve battalions, 179. And of twelve regiments in continental service, 181. Of 10th regiment remonstrate, 184. Proceedings, 185. Answer, 190. List of, named by Navy Board, and Brigadier Generals appointed, 190. Memorial of, against Col. Bull and Capt. Morrow, 210. An artillery company and, commissioned, 223. Pay of, 232, 272.

Officers—
Recruiting, 419, 464, 468, 469, 578. Of State fleet allowed their expenses to Lancaster, &c., 521. Circular of Council to, on defence, 531. Of galleys appointed, 576, 578. For recruiting, 578. Capt. R. Hardie not an, having been broke, 718. Resolutions of Congress and Assembly respecting, 727. Letter from field, of Pennsylvania line, 731. Of marines on ship General Greene—of rangers, 740. Pay of, 757. Court of inquiry on, charged with misbehavior, 775. Militia chosen for several counties, xii., 2, 7, 8, 9, 10, 70. Of ship General Greene, 4, 5. Commissioned, 70. Roll on western frontiers, 74. Promotions in army of Captains, Lieutenants, Ensigns, &c., by name of, 88, 89. List of, who have violated patrol, 91. Petition of, of ship General Greene and action of Council, 158, 159. Application for bounties, 200. Of Col. Hazen's regiment returned in war office as belonging to Pennsylvania, 235. Mistakes in commissions, 240. Union of certain companies with Col. Proctor's regiment, 245. Of Col. Hazen's regiment to receive supplies, &c., 278. Memorial on promotions—rank, 286. Lieutenants and subs., &c. appointed for Philadelphia and other counties, 298. Of ranging company of Northumberland co., 311. Complain of desertions—referred to General W., 316. Desertions in army—appointed in Cumberland county, 322. And men of 4th regiment of dragoons, 332. By what—oaths to be taken, 341. Vacancies in Penn's division and names, entitled to fill them in camp, 355–357, 368. Vacancies, 374, 379. Prisoners on Long Island ask for preservation of their rank, 387. Militia Inspectors with rank of Lieut.-Colonel, 389. Independent corps, petition for, 383. Objected to, 389. James Searle, Lieutenant-Colonel, 418. Surgeons, 437. Resolutions of Congress respecting, 471. For promotion, 545 Capt. Owen Ferris resigns, 550. Promotions, 550, 572. To draw stores, 574. Quarters for, in Philadelphia, 586, 605. Recruiting stations, 606. Petition of, 606, 607. Officers in 11th Pennsylvania regiment, 609. For new companies, 622. Resignation, 650. Gratuities, &c., 655. Orders to, for defence of frontiers, 659. Appointments, 662. Accounts received, 676. Promotions, 684, 687. Depreciation accounts, 702, 705, 716. Pay to, by name, 705. Pay to, under General Wayne at south, of two companies to be raised, 719. And terms, 720. Election ordered, 720. Memorial of Proctor's artillery, 727. Pay of Pennsylvania line, 732, 747, 754. Transfers of, 761. Rank, xiii., 25. Appointed, 71, 167, 168. Depreciation, 144. Vacancies and promotions in Pennsylvania regiments, 202, 223. Resignations and appointments, 275. Election in Chester county, 282. Officers elected by Council, 289. Memorial of Maj. A. Porter and, of regiment of artillery, late Proctors, for promotion, 367. To make monthly returns, 448. List of promotions, 457, Commissions to be issued, 460. Want pay, 461. Rank of Capt. Oberton, 543. Appointments, 581. Lands to be sold to pay off depreciation certificates to, 596. Half pay and commutation of, 603. Anonymous paper from soldiers to Governor, &c., respecting—Council's action on, 605. Conference respecting complaints of insult to Congress, 606, 607, 609. Henry Carberry, James Sullivan, and Lieutenant Nagle to be arrested, 617. Memorial of, of State navy, 683. List of, entitled to benefits of resolution of Assembly, Sept. 22, 1783, 712–718. Dates of commissions, 731. Appointed for protection of frontiers, xiv., 177. Commissioned with dates, 181. Act for benefit of, 185. Letters of administration for estates of,

Officers—
200. J. Armstrong appointed Adjutant General, in place of James Wilkinson, removed from State, 217, 219. Declined, 337. Of Capt. Stokely's rangers paid, 367. Of Captain Guthrie's regiment, 376. Col. Samuel J. Atlee paid, 378. Capt. Thomas Houston's claims, 381. Comptroller-General reports in favor of, 406–440. List of, entitled to lands, 451–452. List of, in Northumberland, 453. Comptroller's reports on accounts of, 465, 518. Appointed of Fed. militia, 559. Report of Comptroller-General on accounts of—soldiers and invalids, 613–615. Of Pennsylvania line—memorial for land in Beaver county—donation lands, xv., 16. Claim of Capt. James O'Hara for depreciation, 142. Petition of city, 205. Complain of an election, 237. Lieut. Joseph Ashton made Captain, in room of Captain F. R. Thompson, Ensign—question of rank between Capt. Ferguson and Capt. Ziegler, 381, 394. Letter Secretary of War on appointment of commissioned officers, 435. Capt. Wm. Paulus removes from State, 436. Appointed artillery of infantry and rank, 437. Of artillery present thanks to Council, 438. Richard Allison elected Surgeon and John F. Carmichael Surgeon's mate of troops under Col. J. Harmar, 498. Returns to be made of, put in, appointed by Council, 599. Of first battalion—Luzerne, xvi., 1. Rank—E. Denny, Lieutenant, 41. Return of, in Northumberland county, 66. Do. of Montgomery, of civil, 71. Inquiry into conduct of, 72. Annuities to widows, &c. of, 140, 142. Returns of election in Cumberland, 149. Returns of Berks and Huntingdon, 171. York, 173. Luzerne county militia elected, 195. Depreciation pay, 229. Lieutenant-Colonel B. Flowers dies—account for depreciation, 278. Lieutenant and Ensign of 1st battalion of Northampton county, 295. Appoint-

Officers—
ments in Luzerne county, 317. Elected in 3d battalion of Berks county, also of 1st of Montgomery county, 362. Elected in Lancaster county, 399. In Berks county, 418. Chester county, 419. In Luzerne county, 464.

Offley, Daniel, asks for money to search for coal mine in Bucks co., x., 428. Makes anchors for frigates, 717. Iron work for battery Putnam, &c., xi., 10. Pay for anchor, &c., 118.

Offner, John, Coroner, xiii., 88, 393, 723. Sheriff, xiv., 267, 557; xv., 99, 296.

Ogaghradarisha, see Agag.

Ogden, Amos, appointed Justice in Northampton county, ix., 575. Letter to, 607. Deposition of, 674. Arrives at Philadelphia from Wyoming, 743.

Ogden, David, a suspicious character, arrested—sent to New Jersey, xii., 37.

Ogden, Nathan, deposition respecting Wyoming, ix., 674. He is treacherously murdered, 714, 749.

Ogle, Samuel, Governor of Maryland, correspondence relative to disputes and riots with Maryland, iii., 480, 483, 557, 559. Letters to and from, on Maryland affairs, iv., 66, 76, 116, 155, 156, 167, 175, 187, 190, 195, 198, 205, 219, 223, 228, 242, 252, 253, 257, 260, 265. Gone to Virginia, 232. Sends Jennings and Dulany with letter, &c., 116. Long time after date of letter, 158. Correspondence with Governor Thomas, 302, 311. Letters to and from, v., 187, 202, 209, 273, 376, 382, 421, 422.

Ogle, widow's house visited by Col. Talbot, i., 113, 120.

O'Hara, James, applies for money to buy provisions for troops in western country, xv., 367, 430, 442, 475, 575.

Oglethorp, General, account of transactions in Georgia on Spanish invasion, iv., 619.

Ohio, Virginia going to build forts against French on, v., 423, 461. Leaden plates sunk by, in, 508,

Ohio—
510. Fort suggested by proprietary, 515. View taken of it by Assembly, 547. French building forts on—Indian affairs, 622–637. Captain Trent views ground for a fort to be built, 660. French have built two forts on, 687. Various papers relating to lands and Indians on, 690–710. Distances, 730, 731. Distances on, 753. French and Indian affairs on, vi., 1–9, 31, 46, 57–129, 605, 642. Forts on, 32, 33, 141, 185, 223. French troops arrive, 223–226. On their way from Canada, 427. Indians, Governor Denny's answer to message of, viii., 206. Settlers on, xiii., 425, 426, 431. State lands on, 754. Proposals to be received for sale of island in, xv., 513. Islands in, surveyed by D. Redick, xvi., 97. Act for Government of territory north-west of, 133, 375. Form of conveyance for islands in, 301.
Okely, John, Commissioner to Wyoming, xiv., 202. On islands in Delaware river, 345.
Old, James, list of shot to be cast by, xi., 129, 131. Justice, xv., 52.
Oley, furnace in Berks co., xv., 229.
Oliver, Andrew, Commissioner from Massachusetts to Pennsylvania for aid, vi., 314.
Olomipas, King of Delawares, dies, v., 212, 533. His successor, 222.
Onantio, or Onontio, name given by Indians to Governor of Canada, iv., 733.
Onas, Indian name given to Penn, explained, iii., 199.
Oneida Indian dies, ix., 775.
Onichkaryagoes Indians, iii., 513.
Onigh, an Indian, speaks, viii., 120.
Onohaghguaga, chiefs of, letter from, vii., 763.
Onondago Indians, i., 447; ii., 140. Instructions to Conrad Weiser on journey to, iv., 655. His report, 660. Negotiations at, 768. Message from Indians at, to Gov. H., v., 637.
Onontio, Indian chief, viii., 121.
Opakethwa, and another Indian chief, dies at Philadelphia with small pox, iii., 463.
Opdengrafe, Abraham, claims premium for finest piece of linen cloth, i., 194.
Opekasset, an Indian chief, iii., 304, 315, 333.
Opinion of C. Pratt, Attorney-General, on Connecticut trespassers, viii., 620. Of Chief Justice on prisoners of war and traitors, xii., 75. Of Attorney-General on property of French subjects being paid into Consul's hands as a depository of monies, having no legal representatives here, 275. On French deserters, 423. Of Supreme Court on section of Constitution, xiii., 218–221. On Philadelphia election, 222–231. Case of Wm. Hanks and election of Justices, 543. Of Judges of Supreme Court in case of J. and A. Melchior, xiv., 553. On election case asked of Judges of Supreme Court, xv., 130. On pay to proprietaries for interest asked, 202, 205. Of Judges Supreme Court for payment to proprietaries, 210. Of Attorney-General on power of Council to pardon in certain cases, 329. On militia fines in Chester county, 371. Of Attorney-General on right of a non-resident to vote in a county where he holds estate, 376. Of judges' case of Doans and Dryer, 501, 631. Of judges on imports—authority and powers of Collector and naval officer, xvi., 128. Of Attorney-General with regard to Justices on division of Delaware and Chester counties, 187.
Orange, Prince of, invasion of England by, reported, i., 247.
Orange, death of Princess of, viii., 318.
Ord, Captain George, arrives with detachment from Nova Scotia, vi., 417. Applies for wagon and chaise for, 417. Brings powder from Bermuda, x., 321.
Ord, John, Notary Public, xi., 201, 206. Sick—substitute appointed, xiii., 13.
Orders in British Council, iv., 254, 262, 266, 298, 483, 487, 766. Of Council favor of Rev. Dr. William Smith on Assembly, viii., 438.

To Capt. Montgomery x., 586. Capt. Valentine Opp's company to march for Jersey, 690.

Ordnance and military stores, inspectors of, appointed, x., 283 Field pieces to be altered, 327.

Ordinance for seizing and selling estates, xi., 329. Respecting militia, 332. Increasing number of Sub-Lieutenants, 333. Against buying up and engrossing merchandize, 337. Against distilling from grains, 338.

Ordinary, keepers to have three months to sell off liquors, &c., after license taken away, i., 167.

Orme, Captain Robert, letter from Governor to, with presents for General Braddock, vi., 414. Letter from, wounded, 487. Account of action, 488.

Ormsby, Mr. John, has a ferry on Alleghany river, xii., 309. Patent for, 317.

Orndt, Captain Jacob, letter advising of Teedyuscung, &c., being at Wyoming, vii., 267, 305. Letter, Teedyuscung coming to treaty at Easton, 429. Letters to and from, 474, 723. Marching with Teedyuscung, 723. Letter from, 128; Indians arrive at Fort Allen, viii., 117. Horses stolen, 401, 406.

Orndt, John, Register and Recorder of Deeds, xi., 191.

Orphan daughter of John McClellan receives a pension, xv., 312.

Orphans' Court, ii., 565. Charles Read, clerk, dies; Thomas Hopkinson appointed, iv., 151 Clerk of, appointed, vii., 501.

Orr, Robert, Sheriff, xiii., 730. Coroner, xiv., 289. Sheriff, 656.

Orr, Thos., alien duty, xv., 408, 415.

Osborne, Henry, appointed Judge Advocate of militia, xii., 504. Appointed Escheator General, 634. Notary, xiii., 15. Agent of estates, 106. Searching records, 165. Solicitor on Connecticut claim, 266, 310, 328, 332, 361, 411. Indian deeds, 438. Returns them per list, 462, 547. To deliver paper to secretary, 472. Asks loan of papers, 476. Discharged; all papers to be given up, 596. Escheator-General, xv., 425.

Oster, Monsieur, Vice-Consul of France, on deserted sailors, xii., 370. Certificate, 551.

Oswald, Eleazer, printer, xv., 108, 367, 381. Petitions respecting, 494. Proceedings of Council respecting fine and imprisonment, 495, 501, 502, 503. Adverse decision of Council and Dr. Redick's reasons for a vote in his favor, 506. Fine remitted, 514. Paid for newspaper, 652.

Oswald, Richard, commissioned by King of Great Britain to treat, xiii., 459.

Oswego, Fort—French and Indians pass, on way to Ohio to build forts there, v., 607. Letters from Lieutenant Holland, 623. From Gov. De Lancey on French and Indian affairs, 716. Intelligence, vi., 33. Troops pass, 428.

Oswego, treaty to be held at, vii., 156. Fears respecting, 234. List of Philadelphia shipwrights taken at, 717, 737. Gen. Amherst embarks at, for Isle Royal and Montreal—his success, viii., 503, 504.

Otstuacky, an Indian town on Susquehanna, vi., 443.

Ottendorff's Company, xii., 297.

Otter, man-of-war, Commander Ballot, arrives, v., 239. Capture of French prizes, 324. Remarks of Assembly respecting, 334.

Otto, Dr. Bodo, xiii., 115.

Otto, Dr. Frederick, x., 695.

Otto, John, Justice, xiv., 442.

Otto, Monsieur, Chargé of France, applies for delivery of Monsieur de Brassines, xv., 215.

Otway, Gen'l—regiment to strengthen Fort at Wiccacoa, viii., 39. Soldiers ask for relief, 164.

Outen, William, Sub-Sheriff of Worcester, Md., shot by John Willey, who is convicted and punished, viii., 372.

Owendat Indians—history by Conrad Weiser, vi., 551.

Owechela (Indian chief), his son killed, iii., 20.

Owens, David, a corporal in Captain McKean's company, kills his wife, &c., ix., 190. Committed to jail for enlisting negroes, x., 427. Discharged, 439.

Owen, Evan, member of Council, iii., 247, 248, 269. To survey route for road between Susquehanna and Lehigh, xv., 195. Return and survey, 230. Paid to, 234. Survey of road between Nescopec and Lehigh, xvi., 20, 83, 85, 259.

Owen, Griffith, member of new Council, i., 580. Appointed a commissioner of property, ii., 61. Takes affirmation, 96. Sent to Assembly, 155, 167. Keeper of State-House clock, discharged, xiv., 55. Repairs State House clock, xv., 414.

Owen, John, Sheriff, iii., 370, 387, 416, 615; iv., 86, 247, 669, 748, 782; v., 411, 464, 550. Sheriff of Chester county, certificate respecting furnaces, &c., ix., 635.

Owen Owen, Sheriff of Philadelphia, iii., 260, 289, 312. Coroner, 370, 387, 416, 464, 520, 575, 614. Coroner, iv., 85, 247, 309, 352, 469.

Owen, Robert, has a boat seized at Schuylkill ferry, i., 441.

Oxford, Church—Act proposed for sale and purchase of lands, viii., 574, 583.

Oxford Township, petition for road, i., 389, 502. To assist in repair of water passage at Frankford, ii., 52.

Oyer and Terminer Court, commission of, issued, ii., 18. For gaol delivery, called, 86; iii., 398.

Oysters, out of season, Act respecting, ix., 549, 707, 729.

P.

Paca, William, respecting court martial on General Arnold, xi., 702.

Packsinosa, his son, Holepeeka, Indians, vii., 187. Shawnee chief, 726.

Paine, Thomas, appointed Secretary to Commissioners at Easton, ix., 98. Paid by Council for ten dozen of Crisis, xii., 503. Paid for services as clerk of General Assembly, 594. Message from Council to Assembly respecting the services and merits of, xiv., 275. Payment to, 402.

Palatines—lists of those imported to be prepared, iii., 29. Ask to purchase land, 241, 284. Arrive—some fears from their numbers, required to take oath, &c., 283. One hundred and nine naturalized, 283, 287, 288, 290, 328, 330, 331. Petition to Governor Keith respecting Tulpehocken lands, 322. Leave New York and settle at Tulpehocken, 323, 367, 368. Naturalized, 374, 385, 386, 389, 413–415, 417, 429, 431, 452–459, 465, 467, 515–520, 524, 569, 570, 587, 593–597, 607. Naturalized, iv., 59, 72, 99, 331, 332. Commended by Governor, 315. Arrive, v., 112. Arrive sickly, Doctors to visit ships, vi., 169. Reports of Doctors Bond and Græme, 171–175. Number buried, 175. Act limiting numbers, 225, 243. Amendments to bill, 345–352, 354–356.

Paleske, Charles, duties on tea, xv., 371, 372.

Palmer, Anthony, member of Council, ii., 429. A Justice, iii., 28. Neglects Council, 384. Becomes, as eldest Councillor, President, and succeeds Governor Thomas, v., 68. Issues proclamation for continuing offices, 70. Letters, 76. For pilots and flags of truce, 83. Orders Captain Cox, of ship Euryale, from Barbadoes, below, 106. Proclamation against, 109. Messages, 124, 154. Letter, Mons. Chastenoy with prisoners, 131. Letter to Governor Shirley, 143. To Governor Clinton, 145. Speech to Indians, 149. Message to Assembly, 157. Letters to Governors Shirley and Clinton, 165, 215. Issues a proclamation for a fast day, 169. Mortal sickness, Letter to Governor Clinton respecting cannon, 189. Letters to Governor Ogle, 189, 192, 222, 224, 225. To Governor Gooch, 189. To Higginbotham, 192. Proclamation against selling rum to Indians, 195. Letter to De la Vega, 201. Signs a pardon for William Ward, 210. Letters to and from Governor Clinton, on cannon, 217,

218. Writes to Governors Gooch and Ogle, 223. Proclamation about pilots, 227. Message to Assembly, 230, 234, 270. Writes to Governor of Virginia respecting privateers, 254; also to Governor Clinton, 256, 265. To and from Governor Belcher on privateers, 266. Commission to Abm. Wiltbank to command intelligence boat, 266. Message from Assembly on money for defence, 275. Pass for flag of truce, 281. Letter to Governor Clinton, 286. Instructions to C. Weiser, 292, 304. Message to Assembly, 329. Assembly's message disapproving his course, 333–338. Message to Assembly in reply, 339. To Governor Gooch, respecting Catawba Indians, 346. Is informed by letter from the Proprietaries of Governor James Hamilton's appointment and tendering their thanks for his past services, 3C2.

Palmer, George, Coroner, xiii., 89, 396, 724.

Palmer, John, undertakes masonwork on Fort Island, x., 371.

Palmer, Thomas, makes rifles, x., 633. To deliver rifles, 653.

Paper money, Message of Governor, &c., on, iii., 377, 393, 396. Report of committee of Assembly on, v., 415, 416. Advantages of, 605. In circulation, xiii., 422.

Paper for cartridges wanted, x., 701.

Papists, alarm from, to Protestants, council called, i., 299.

Pardons, i., 379. Complained of, ii., 455; iii., 240, 244, 370, 372, 390, 429, 591; iv., 24, 47, 209, 224, 252, 253, 278, 330. Reprieves, &c., v., 75, 141, 162, 210, 268, 344, 506, 601, 612. Releases, &c., viii., 78, 336, 667. And respites of criminals, ix., 173, 244, 334, 384, 387, 399, 510, 513, 549, 601, 626, 666, 699, 734, 743, 778. Reprieves, &c., x., 44, 50, 60, 89, 92, 172, 228, 258; xi., 250, 384, 462, 470, 503, 539, 566, 579, 583, 609, 637, 642, 650, 655, 695, 703, 719, 747, 748, 753, 760, 763, 765; xii., 13, 21, 33, 48, 61, 69, 77, 86, 93, 101, 102, 113, 116, 134, 159, 178, 190, 192, 197, 200, 201, 205, 222, 223, 243, 260, 261, 271, 309, 336, 337, 338, 339, 361, 364, 374, 388, 390, 400, 409, 419, 427, 430, 433, 436, 447, 450, 455, 462, 484, 494, 514, 519, 522, 524, 526, 536, 542, 563, 568, 571, 575, 592, 598, 602, 607, 611, 618, 651, 654, 657, 662, 674, 684, 694, 718, 722, 729, 730, 735, 746, 747, 759, 767, 778, 779; xiii., 17, 18, 50, 53, 72, 87, 94, 100, 117, 120, 121, 127, 135, 143, 163, 185, 196, 221, 240, 247, 253, 271, 277, 280, 285, 294, 299, 303, 308, 314, 346, 360, 368, 373, 383, 395, 407, 432, 442, 449, 450, 452, 453, 454, 455, 457, 470, 480, 481, 494, 496, 499, 501, 503, 507, 508, 511, 513, 524, 527, 529, 531, 535, 542, 545, 551, 553, 566, 571, 572, 575, 578, 584, 588, 595, 597, 603, 605, 614, 619, 620, 634, 639, 642, 666, 671, 673, 681, 691, 725, 727, 741, 744, 745, 747, 753, 763, 768; xiv., 3, 9, 11, 30, 31, 33, 36, 43, 50, 59, 66, 76, 77, 104, 108, 116, 121, 138, 140, 142, 143, 144, 146, 151, 153, 160, 171, 173, 175, 182, 184, 198, 226, 234, 235, 239, 242, 248, 254, 262, 263, 265, 266, 277, 279, 284, 307, 309, 322, 327, 357, 362, 370, 378, 383, 384, 387, 404, 441, 449, 452, 453, 454, 459, 461, 465, 466, 470, 473, 477, 481, 486, 492, 501, 503, 504, 508, 510, 511, 520, 553, 554, 555, 558, 563, 568, 570, 571, 575, 579, 580, 585, 586, 589, 590, 591, 606, 607, 616, 622, 624, 628, 629, 631, 632, 633, 635, 636, 639, 642, 646, 647, 650, 652, 653, 654, 655, 657, 659, 671; xv., 3, 4, 5, 7, 11, 13, 16, 17, 22, 23, 25, 27, 31, 32, 33, 35, 38, 40, 43, 44, 47, 55, 57, 59, 62, 65, 68, 71, 73, 74, 81, 82, 90, 92, 93, 101, 105, 109, 110, 112, 118, 123, 125, 129, 131, 139, 141, 142, 143, 148, 149, 151, 163, 164, 165, 166, 168, 171, 183, 195, 196, 203, 205, 209, 213, 215, 217, 219, 224, 227, 229, 230, 239, 240, 242, 252, 255, 258, 259, 263, 267, 279, 283, 286, 288, 290, 298, 302, 305, 309, 310, 322, 325, 326, 327, 328, 330, 341, 345, 347, 348, 350, 357, 360, 362, 363, 365, 366, 371, 373, 379, 381, 386, 390, 401, 403, 407, 412, 414, 417, 420, 422, 423, 425,

Pardons—
427, 431, 434, 442, 445, 449, 451, 452, 463, 464, 466, 469, 471, 475, 476, 483, 486, 488, 497, 499, 503, 509, 514, 516, 519, 521, 523, 525, 528, 531, 535, 541, 549, 552, 557, 560, 565, 580, 583, 586, 606, 611, 613, 617, 618, 619, 630, 645, 652; xvi., 3, 5, 6, 8, 18, 28, 40, 43, 45, 54, 55, 61, 62, 69, 76, 79, 85, 87, 89, 91, 93, 99, 101, 103, 104, 107, 109, 111, 112, 115, 116, 119, 131, 132, 134, 135, 141, 144, 154, 157, 162, 165, 169, 171, 176, 190, 193, 197, 199, 204, 209, 211, 213, 215, 211[2], 213[2], 215[2], 219[2], 223[2], 225, 232, 241, 254, 259, 260, 268, 270, 273, 277, 281, 283, 284, 288, 290, 292, 295, 297, 299, 301, 303, 305, 306, 308, 310, 313, 318, 328, 329, 349, 365, 366, 367, 371, 374, 377, 379, 380, 383, 388, 391, 393, 394, 397, 399, 401, 403, 405, 411, 413, 415, 417, 419, 427, 441, 451, 452, 463, 479, 480, 482, 488, 495, 497, 512, 519, 520, 522, 538, 540, 542, 547.

Pardoning power by Council, opinion of Attorney-General, xv., 329.

Paris, Ferdinand John, agent in England, iii., 401, 535, 539. Agent in England, papers respecting Maryland sent to, iv., 129. New orders asked for, 302. Discovers counterfeit bills, 429. Sends papers, 476. Agent of Proprietaries, answer to B. Franklin's complaints, viii., 279. B. Franklin's answer to it, 300.

Paris, Isaac, Ensign, xii., 8.

Paris, Captain Richard, a trader, vii., 503. Letter to Gov., 538.

Park, Col. Joseph, xi., 85.

Park, Robert, Coroner, iii., 332.

Parke, Thomas, Coroner, iv., 748, 782. Sheriff, v., 411, 468, 551.

Parke, Dr. Thomas, to attend soldiers sick in barracks, x., 653.

Parker, Alexander, Lieutenant, xi., 740.

Parker, Eli, Coroner, ix., 779.

Parker, Joseph, member Committee of Safety, x., 537.

Parker, Richard, Collector of Excise, xv., 222.

Parker, Robert, resigns as Collector of Excise, xvi., 87.

Parker, Thomas, Sheriff, viii., 403.

Parker, William, Sheriff, vii., 267. Coroner, x., 398. Justice, xiii., 240.

Parlee, Peter, xiii., 74.

Parliament, grant from — portion received, ix., 2, 4, 10, 47, 115. Agreement between agents respecting, 47–51.

Parliamentary, grant to colonies to be shared, viii., 401, 501, 512, 546, 606, 610, 665, 667, 693.

Parole, taken, x., 553. Prisoners' orders respecting, 553.

Parr, Mr., asks permission to sell claret at vendue—refused, xii., 3.

Parr, James, Coroner, x., 59. Aid-de-camp to Major General Potter, xiv., 165.

Parr, William, Sheriff, ix., 286, 323. Writ for new election for Assembly, 288. Master of Rolls, 397. Recorder to remove records, &c. to Lancaster, xi., 23. Rent of office, 384.

Parrock, wife of John, claims rent on property left by father escheated illegally—referred to Attorney-General, xi., 668.

Parrock, John's, Estate, xii., 315, 457, 661, 752, 755, 782; xiii., 170, 309.

Parry, John, Sheriff, iii., 464, 520, 574; iv., 309, 352.

Parry, Thomas, a Justice, xi., 300.

Parsons, William, Surveyor-General, resigns on account of ill health—N. Scull succeeds him, v., 274. Letter from, to Governor on Connecticut claimants, 736. Letters, vi., 668, 737, 781. Letters to and from, vii., 163, 164, 191, 267, 284, 305, 376, 475. Indian murders, &c., 165. Instructions to, respecting Indians, 191, 476, 620.

Parvin, Francis, resigns as member Assembly, vii., 148.

Paschall, Benjamin, sick soldiers, xi., 52. Justice, 667.

Paschal, Col. Jonathan—of city battalion, x., 677, 659, 694, 698.

Paschall, Stephen, account of his steel furnace in Walnut street Philadelphia and certificates of others, ix., 633, 634. To make a pike, x., 284.

Paschal, Wm., road to Swede's ford, iii., 225, 230, 231.
Passengers, proposed Act limiting number—objections to, vi., 225, 243. Amendments to bill, 345-352, 354-356, 382.
Passes, strangers required to have, ii., 13; Granted, xi., 599, 641, 642, 645, 648, 657, 673, 695, 703, 718, 756, 757, 761, 762, 766, 770, 772, 783; xii., 1, 2, 11, 21, 23, 24, 29, 32, 33, 36, 44, 50, 67, 68, 73, 78, 79, 85, 86, 101, 149, 156, 159, 163, 172, 177, 180, 243, 250, 251, 256 257, 259, 260, 271, 300, 314, 337, 342, 346, 347, 365, 391, 479, 489, 494, 504, 505, 514, 518, 522, 524, 563, 573, 589, 591, 594, 657, 662, 674, 684, 686, 690, 741, 749, 781, 782; xiii., 21, 28, 30, 38, 39, 50, 63, 66, 128, 131, 157, 161, 163, 175, 179, 180, 181, 184, 186, 187, 202, 208, 241, 247, 248, 253, 254, 255, 271, 272, 277, 279, 281, 282, 283, 284, 286, 294, 300, 302, 304, 313, 314, 324, 325, 329, 330, 336, 340, 341, 346, 353, 356, 358, 369, 370, 381, 383, 386, 389, 391, 395, 403, 404, 418, 422, 424, 429, 431, 432, 439, 441, 443, 444, 447, 448, 450, 454, 457, 471, 474, 486, 499, 501, 503, 505, 507, 509, 511, 513, 515, 517, 521, 524, 527, 529, 531, 533, 535, 538, 543, 545, 547, 548, 549, 551, 552, 554, 561, 563, 565, 567, 571, 575, 577, 579, 585, 595, 607. 620, 632, 642, 687, 696; xiv., 50, 66, 76, 107, 120, 204, 216, 562.
Passport for Indians, from Lancaster to Philadelphia, vii., 549.
Pastorius, Francis Daniel, a Justice and takes the oath, i., 371. Petition in behalf of Germantown, exemption from County Court of Philadelphia, ii., 13. Petition against J. H. Sprogel, 430.
Pastorius, Daniel, and city lots, xiii., 322.
Pastorius, Henry, a Justice, iii., 531.
Passyunk, roads in, ix., 719, 720, 729. Regulation of, xvi., 228, 236, 238. Report, 245-251, 262. Draft of, 493.
Patents, complaints that they have not been issued--reason for, i., 86. To Wm. Penn on restoration, 473. 483. Office proposed, ii., 38. Granted to Thos. Master for weaving straw for hats and curing Indian corn, iii., 18. Fees for, v., 578. To John Ormsby for ferry over Alleghany and Monongahela rivers, xii., 317. For lands to Jacob Clement, xvi., 220². To M. Biles, 309. To Col. George Morgan, 499.
Pateraroes Brass, to be procured, x., 328.
Patrols, for city, x., 630.
Patterson, Alexander, Justice, xiii., 683. Letters on commitment of Z. Butler, 760, 762. Letter to, from Major Moore, xiv., 31, 32. Resigns as Justice, 117. Letter, 162.
Patterson, James, appointed Commissioner on Virginia line, xiii., 205.
Patterson, John, Collector, x., 213.
Patterson, Thomas, prisoner from Virginia, to be discharged, xi., 474.
Patterson, William, letter on capture of Stump and servant, ix., 453. Talk with Indians at Great Island, 453. Made Justice on account of capture, 470. Letter to, from Indian chief, 480. Justice, xv., 58.
Patterson's Creek, murders at, vi., 641.
Patton, James, wagon master, xi., 438.
Patten, John, sent with Indians, v., 705. Instructions to, 707. Arrives—examined as to distances, 730. His journal, 731. Map of distances, 747, 758, 762. Sheriff, xi., 48; xv., 577; xvi., 210, 527.
Patton, John, his declaration, vi., 20. Made Major, x., 768. Commissioner for defence of the Delaware, xiii,, 316. Auctioneer, xv., 322. Suitable lot for powder magazine, xvi., 328, 532.
Patton, Robert, petition against General De Haas, xi., 188. Station at Long Island, asks to be restored to his former rank in 11th Pennsylvania regiment, xii., 609.
Paul, John, Justice, xiv., 200.

Pauling, Mr., vii., 772. Report of Joseph Hughes on return from building houses at Wyoming, viii., 134.

Pauling, P., claim for lands, x., 35.

Paxinosa and son, Indian chief, talks of removal from Susquehannah—alarmed by news from Cherokees, viii., 126.

Paxton, Capt. John, x., 683, 687.

Paxton, Joseph, in prison—sick may be released on giving bonds, xii., 546.

Paxton, Phineas, tory, prohibited from keeping public house, xii., 401, 403.

Paxton Boys, (see Conestoga Indians.)

Paymasters, xi., 2, 23, 32, 79, 124, 233, 260, 266, 272, 277, 279, 297, 304, 368, 372, 406, 444, 637, 718; xii., 463, 489, 629.

Payne, Sir Ralph, Gov. of leeward islands—letter—account of destructive hurricane—asking assistance, x., 57. Proclamation of Gov. Penn, 58. Letter sent to Assembly, 60. Answer, 60.

Pea Patch, x., 506.

Peace, preliminaries of a general, xiii., 543. Proclamat'n for thanksgiving, 749. Ratification by Congress received, 750. Public demonstration for, 752, 761.

Peace Makers, i., 90.

Peale, Chas. Wilson, 1st Lieut., xi., 32. To take portrait of Gen. Washington for Council, 671. Elected to Assembly, xii., 129. Sells property, 174. Deed for lots in city forfeited by John Smith, &c., 247, 441. Late agent for confiscated estates, xiv., 264.

Pearis, Capt. Richard, letters to and from, vii., 529, 531, 557. Interpreter, 553.

Pearson, George, repairs of State House, xv., 115.

Pearson, Isaac, Sheriff, v., 597, 662; vi., 144, 638. Declines as Commissioner to Fort Pitt, ix., 491, 596. A supersedeas, xii., 287.

Pearson, James, improvement of State House lot, xiv., 406. Repairs of State House—agrees to cover with copper, 596. Repairs of State House—accounts referred, xv., 10, 90, 204. Builds barracks for invalids, 204. Claims city lots, 482.

Pearson, Capt. John, xi., 577, 653. Justice, xii., 286. Of Pennsylvania regiments, xiv., 655.

Pechoquealin, near Durham Iron works, iii., 309, 329.

Peebles, Col. Robert, x., 700.

Peepe, Joseph, vii., 506. Indian, viii., 151. Conference with Governor, 586. Speech about Thos. Penn and lands, 661; ix., 738. A Delaware Indian in Philadelphia, x., 61.

Pemberton, Israel, Jr., Governor complains of, iv., 389. Warrant issued for his arrest, 391. Answer of Sheriff Robinson, 391. Governor objects to form of writ, 392. Conduct of, under it—declaration of Sheriff, 393. On behalf of Quakers intercedes for Delaware Indians, vii., 103. Breach of confidence charged to, 362. And others pay over money from friendly association, 391. Asks to examine minutes, 394, 397. Delivers address, 638, 647. Receives at Philadelphia a message by Lowe from Cherokees to Delawares, viii., 135. At conference at N. Scull's, 214. To be seized, xi., 283. Returned from Virginia, 472.

Pemberton, James, resigns as member of Assembly, vii., 148. Signs address of Quakers as clerk, 405. Introduces a French merchant—agrees to pay a ransom of a vessel taken by a Spanish privateer—difficulty, viii., 151. Clerk of meeting of sufferings, 239. Chosen by tie vote member of Assembly, new election ordered, ix., 288. Advice of, commission to lay out money for Indians, 468. John and Israel and S. Emlen, carriage and horses to be impressed from, to remove Gen. Roberdeau to Lancaster, xi., 41. To be seized, 283. Habeas corpus, 308, 309. Returned, 472. Asks protection for wagons going to Winchester, 457. See, 473.

Pemberton, John, to be seized, xi., 284.

Pemberton, Phineas, member of Council, to keep debates in secret, i., 125. Complains against Indians for killing hogs, 134. Road to New York, 514. Speaker, 548.

Pemepecca, mills and road, i., 587. Overplus land near—controversy respecting, ii., 34.

Penalties, remitted, ii., 103, 108.

Pendleton, Edmund, letter with ratification by Virginia of the Federal Constitution, xv., 499.

Pendergrasse Gerard, murder of his daughter, vii., 632.

Penet, Mons., proposes to supply State with arms—Council agree with him, xii., 104,

Pennington, Edward, to be seized, xi., 284.

Penington, Ephraim, Coroner, xiv., 234, 557, 558.

Pennington, Isaac, Sheriff Bucks county, iii., 416, 465.

Penn, Hannah, widow of William, and others, agreement with Lord Baltimore, iii., 231, 236. Letter from, noticed, 235.

Penn, John, Eldest proprietary, arrives, iii., 569. Received by Mayor, &c., and addressed, 570. Meets Indians and Council, 571–574. Born in America, 599. Going to England, is waited on and addressed by Assembly, 611. Answer, 611. One of the proprietaries, dies, v., 62, 73. Eldest son of Richard, arrives—is admitted as member of Council and assigned rank of eldest councilman, 606. Is present at Council, 618. Commissioner to Albany, vi., 25. His commission, 47. Report of proceedings at Albany, 111–129. Appointed Governor by Thomas and Richard Penn, ix., 71, 72, 347, 629. Arrives, 71. Issues proclamation—joyful reception at Philadelphia, 72. Visits New Castle with Earl of Stirling and L. Lardner, 73. Letters to and from, 74, 89, 92, 100, 102, 104, 108, 110, 111, 112, 113, 114, 118, 119, 120, 122, 127, 129, 131, 137, 239, 240, 266, 267, 273–277, 281, 290, 292, 297, 300, 301. Proclamation on highway robbery and murder of

Penn, John—
Henry Hamilton, 76. Conferences with Indians, 77. Proclaims treaty of 1763 with France, 80. Conferences with, 77, 85–88. Address to, from Conestoga Indians, 89. Murders of, 89, 352. Letter to Assembly on, 92, 94. Proclamation respecting, 95. Speech to Assembly respecting troops, 91. Messages to Assembly, 94, 108, 115, 116, 122, 133, 149, 153, 155, 158, 177, 179, 181, 183, 241, 283, 291, 311, 312, 323, 363, 394, 396, 398, 407. Messages from Assembly, 109, 116, 122, 123, 125, 134, 152, 154, 156, 161, 180, 182, 284, 324, 361, 369. Proclamation respecting murder of Indians, 95, 107. Address from Assembly, 97. Answer to, 99. Proposes admission of his brother, Richard, to Council, 101. Paxton boys at Lancaster, 109. Proprietary, instructions to, 117. Conestoga Indians, 118. Proposes militia law, 133. Asks advice of Sir Wm. Johnson, on removal of Indians from barracks, 137. Answer to committee of Assembly on remonstrance of Smith & Gibson, 147. Supply bill, 149, 158, 161. Militia bill objected to, 151. Objects to Assembly naming officers in bills, as infringing his prerogative, 152. Proprietary estate tax, 153, 155, 156, 158, 161. Meets Assembly at New Castle—speech to, 166–168. From, 167. Ill-treatment of self and proprietary by Assembly, supply bill, &c., 175, 179, 180. Passes it, 184. Circular to Provincial Commissioners on assessment of proprietary lands, 237. Answer to, 240. Proclamation of peace with Indians on Ohio, 234. Rioters of Cumberland, 273. Evacuation of Fort Augusta, 283, 284. Writ to sheriff for a new election of Assembly, 288. Fire at Montreal, 290. Present to, 296. Riots in Cumberland county, 297. To H. J. Conway on effects of Stamp Act, 299. Repeal of, 311, 312, 315. Letters to and from, 303, 305, 306, 307, 320, 321, 344, 349, 351, 375, 377, 379, 403, 405, 412,

Penn, John—
422, 424, 440–442, 443, 444, 446, 448, 462, 463. To magistrates in Cumberland respecting goods, 303. Instructions to, respecting settlers on Western lands, 321. Proclamation respecting, 327. Convictions for highway robbery, burglary—executions, 334, 396. Order to prepare an account of manufactures since 1734, 343. Letter to Governor of Virginia on settlers on Western lands, 344. Receives from Thomas and Richard a new commission as Governor till December 1, 1769, 345. Commission, 346. Oath of office to be administered by Governor of New York or other Governor, 347. Goes to Maryland, and takes oath, &c., 348. Letter from Governor of Virginia, 349. To Earl Shelburne—massacre of Indians, settlers on Indian lands, 352. To Commissioners of Trade, &c., on manufactures, 353. To Governor Sharpe on J. Redick's land, 377. Grants of land, quit rents, expense of Province, 379–382. Right to nominate printer of laws, 395. Messages to Assembly, 407, 427, 430, 434, 459, 466, 545, 554, 582, 595, 645, 656, 660, 682, 686, 713, 720. Messages from Assembly, 407, 408, 432, 447, 454, 458, 465, 473–480, 568, 594, 656, 685, 692, 708, 714, 721. Settlers on Indian lands, 407, 408, 427, 432, 434, 481, 483, 573, 692, 709. Murders of Indians by Frederick Stump in Cumberland—various documents relating to, 414–490, (see F. Stump.) Message to Newoleeka, chief of the Delawares, 428. To Wyalusing, 436. To sheriffs, respecting Stump, 442. His reply to Colonel Armstrong, 446. Instructions to, 451. Assembly reflect on Governor's course in cases of Indian murders, 454–458. Message in reply, 459, 473. Raising money, 460. Receives £500, 472. Message from, Ass'bly on charges, 473–480. Proclamation for removal of settlers from Indian lands—commissioners appointed, 481. Letters to and from, 484,

Penn, John—
486, 487, 495, 506, 508, 572, 573, 582, 585, 586, 606, 642, 664, 706, 718, 736. Second proclamation for arrest of Stump and his servant, 488. Messages to Six Nations, 517, 519. Proclamation on robbery of Treasury of New Jersey, 544. Attends a treaty at Fort Stanwix respecting Indian boundary, 545. Letter from Lord Hillsboro' on letter to Colonies from Massachusetts, 546. Indian boundary described, 554, 568. Indian trade, 555. Letter to Gov. Sharpe on complaints against Maryland, 564. Letter to Governor of Connecticut on New England settlers, 573. Proclamation on, 588. Letter to Colonel Francis, Stewart and Ogden, 607. Instruct'ns to J. Jennings, Shff., 608. Address from Assembly on fisheries, 610, 623. Makes present to Indians, 614. Proclamation on fisheries, 623. Receives new commission from Thomas and Richard Penn as Governor, 346, 628. Proclamation continuing officers, 644. Indian trade, 645. For arrest of Joseph Billings, 647. Indian trade, 656. Arrival of Newaleka, 656. To General Gage on riots at Wyoming, 654. Proclamation against Connecticut settlers, 679. Arrest of Connecticut settlers, 682. Roads from Philadelphia, 686. Remonstrance of Assembly, 684, 686. Proclamation against L. Stewart, 687, 716. Grant to, 687. Money for Indians, 692. Message respecting Laz. Stewart, 713; and murder of N. Ogden, 714. Improvement of rivers, 720, 721. Goes to England on account of death of Richard—is succeeded by James Hamilton as President, being oldest member of Council, 733. John, by will, becomes proprietary, 742. With Thomas Penn, having revoked Governor Richard's commission, is appointed, with King's approbation, Governor a second time—arrives and is present in Council, who fix his "state and title," x., 90, 91. Continues Joseph Shippen, Jr., as

Penn, John—
Provincial Secretary, 91. Is proclaimed at court-house, 92. Issues a proclamation continuing officers, 92. Is proclaimed at New Castle, 93. Against settlers on lands, 95. Address from Assembly, 96. Answer, 97. Receives a present from Assembly, 97. Against counterfeiters, 99. Proclamation respecting laws void, 104. Address from Assembly at New Castle, 107. Answer, 108. Messages to Assembly, 117, 146, 196, 208, 214, 216, 224, 237, 243, 251, 260. Messages from Assembly, 142, 215, 225, 237, 252. Letters to and from, 119, 121, 123, 130, 145, 149, 151, 152, 156, 164, 171, 176, 192, 193, 194, 202, 220, 221, 236, 240, 242, 247. Receives commissioners and papers from Connecticut, 119. Letters, &c., 121–139. Connecticut affairs, 142. Dr. Conolly, 140, 165, 171. Fortifications in Philadelphia, 146. Proclamation against Connecticut settlers, 153. Commission and instructions to A. Allen and J. Tilghman, commissioners to Virginia, 174. Letter to Lord Dunmore, 176. A commissioner at treaty at Albany, 177. Declines calling Assembly on account of Boston port bill, 181. To Arthur St. Clair on affairs in Westmoreland, 194, 197. Proclamation for murderer of a Delaware Indian, 199. Message to chiefs, &c., of Shawnese, 203; and to Delawares, 204. Indians and Virginia, 208. Proclamation for recovery of goods, 214. Expedition from Virginia against Shawnese, 214. Boundary line with Maryland, 216. Barracks out of order—guns not to be fired, 224, 225. Letter to Governor Eden of North Carolina, on proclamation respecting boundary, 242. Recalled by proclamation, 245. With resolutions of House of Commons, 251, 252. Proclamation for arrest of a murderer, 269. Late Governor, a prisoner, to be removed by Congress, xi., 264. Escort for, 265, 266. Receives the public papers from Jos.

Penn, John—
Shippen, Jr., and is required by Council to hand them to Secretary, xii., 326. To be applied to for Indian deeds and papers respecting Connecticut claim, xiii., 418. Delivered to Council, 437. Passport for self and family to New York, 561. Payments to, xvi., 4, 33, 300, 305. Proprietaries (John Penn and John, Jr.,)—claim and title to province stated and referred to Supreme Court, xiv., 502. Tench Francis, agent for, demands first payment, 622, 624. Paid, 625. Proprietaries, xv., 63, 153. City lots, 430. Petition and claim, 440, 478. Claim for Springettsbury Manor, 541, 542, 554. Instalment due, 634, 651, 663. Payment to, xv., 235.

Penn, John, Jr., payments to, xvi., 4, 33, 300, 305.

Penn, Lætitia's Manor, iii., 144.

Penn, Richard, joins in commission to Governor Gordon, iii., 525. (Brother of John) visits New Castle with Governor John, &c., ix., 73. Admitted as a member of Council, 101. Subscribes oaths, and takes his seat, 116. Appointed to compare bills, 246. Appointed Governor, arrives, 780. Meets Council, 782. His proclamation, 783. (Brother of John), Governor—address to from Assembly, x., 1. His answer, 2. His former residence here, 2. Receives £600 from Assembly—affair of Laz. Stewart—barracks, 3. Proclaimed at New Castle, 5. Address from and to Assembly, 6. Conferences with Indians, 10, 12. Proclamation respecting pilot-boat taken, 12. Message to Assembly, 2, 16, 28, 30, 68, 71, 84. Message from Assembly, 1, 17, 28, 29, 70, 74, 81. Respecting carriages impressed by Colonel Wilkins for Fort Pitt, 17. Complaint of Assembly against Justice, 30, 31. Loan Office bill, 30, 31, 37, 68. Proclamation respecting hurricane in West Indies, 58. Conference with Indians, 61. Evacuation of Fort Pitt, 68, 70, 71, 74.

Penn, Richard—
Letters to and from, 3, 16, 17, 19, 21, 50, 57, 68, 86. Message from Lower Counties, 82. Answer to, 84. Wyoming, 86. Letter to Dr. William Plunket, 87. Proclamation against counterfeiters of bills of credit, 88. Goes to New Jersey—James Hamilton acts as President, 90. Commission to Richard Penn revoked by Thomas and John—John succeeds Richard as Governor again, 91.

Penn, Springett, his manor to be surveyed, iii., 185.

Penn, Thomas, arrives at Chester, iii., 433. First presence in Council, 433. Indians present him with a fine painted mantle of otter skins, 440. Speaks to Indians, 445. Presents guns to Indians, 450. Conference with Indians at Philadelphia, 500. Commission to Governor Gordon, 525. Present in Council, iv., 53. And confers with Indians, 54. Obtains release of lands from Indians, 88. Letter from on the peace with France, v., 342. Memorial to, relating to certain bills, 499. To build forts with Governor of Virginia, vi., 4. Letter to, from Governor, on Braddock's defeat, 517, 733. Letter from Governor on various subjects, 737–742. Sends £5000, 742. And Richard, proprietaries, message to Assembly complaining of a paper delivered by B. Franklin, agent for province, viii., 276. Answer by F. J. Paris, their agent, 276–280. Jo. Peepy's statement about, 661.

Penn, Thomas and Richard, [father of Governor John,] appoint (as Proprietaries) John Penn as Governor, ix., 71–73. Instructions to Governor, 117. Send new commission to John Penn as Governor, 346, 628. Richard dies, 733. Leaves, by will, his son John his share as proprietary, 736. Change of seal, 736.

Penn, William, charter to, i., 17. Conditions and concessions, 26. Frames of government, 29, 42, 48. Laws agreed on in England,

Penn, William—
37. Present at first Council, 57. May secure himself, 60. Complains of letters written from Jersey to England, 75. Allegiance to, promised, 81. Charge against, for not entering and clearing vessels at New Castle, 101. Appoints Wm. Markham Secretary of province, 142. His absence accounted for and regretted, 199, 201. Supplies, 199, 200. Blanks sent by him for patents and commissions, 230, 231. Despatches from, 252. His seal to be attached to published laws, 276. Letter from on proclaiming King William, 301. Hopes to visit the province, 313. Authorizes Governor Blackwell to resign, and sends two commissions for the successor to be filled by Council, 315. Letter from, to Council, 316. Instructions to Council, 318. Asks Council to pay £600 and build a house and stock a plantation for each child, 317, 328. Declaration of allegiance to, signed by members of Council, 321. Markham refers Council to his requests, 328. Ordered to proclaim William and Mary, 340. His example followed in case of Judges, 344. The government placed in hands of Benjamin Fletcher, 345–364. His right to Schuylkill Ferry, 445, 461. He is restored to the government of the province—Authority to Governor Fletcher revoked—Patent for the restoration—Commissions William Markham as Governor, and John Goodson and Samuel Carpenter as assistants, 472–475, 483. Defence of province, 503. His charter, 506. His letter to Council on abuses reported to him, 527. Answer to, 528. New commission to William Markham, 546. Complains of advance on money, 559. Appears in Council, 565. Orders proclamation against pirates, 565. Suspicions of England on pirates, 565. Old and new charters, 573, 574. Letter to, from Lords Justices, on trade and navigation and piracy—Calls Assembly, 574. Charter

Penn, William—
given up—He forms a new Council, 580. Commissions Thomas Story Keeper of Great Seal, 581. His advice to Assembly, 596, 613. Poll tax proposed, 599. Reference to his agreements with Indians, iii., 24, 310, 313. Death of, announced by Governor Keith, 58. His kind treatment of Indians, 94. Speech of Governor respecting, 122. Consent of Indians to his purchase of lands on Susquehannah, 181. "Leagues of friendship" with Indians at first settlement alluded to, 194, 197. Often referred to by Indians, 216. His arrangement with Indians about lands, 325. Indians allude to his speeches to them, 363. Love for Indians, 600. Seen by the Indians then present, 600. Deeds to, 1701, 607. His treaty with Indians in 1701 alluded to, iv., 337. Articles of agreement with Indians in 1701, 338–340. His provisions for liberty of conscience—Views of Assembly and Governor, 368–371. His speeches to Indians remembered, vii., 317. Purchase of lands, 327. Reservation of commons, &c., in Philadelphia, xii., 347. Claims under old rights from, xiv., 323, 359, 361. First payment to devisees and legatees of, &c., for vesting their rights in State, 397. Claims to city lots—Reports on, xv., 379, 383, 399, 413, 429, 437, 440, 442, 478, 481, 485, 627. Lots in city claimed under grant from, xvi., 55, 108, 299, 300, 457, 522, 531, 532.

Penn, William, Jr., invited to be present at Council, ii., 117. In trouble, 160. Instructions to Governor Keith, iii., 63. Member of Church of England, 64.

Pennell, Joseph, Commissioner for settling public accounts in marine department, xiv., 139.

Pennock, Joseph, petition respecting land purchased from William Penn, xiv., 26.

Pennsboro' Township, Cumberland Co., v., 431.

Pennsbury, Penn's wish to have three plantations near, settled for his children, i., 328. Preferred as a residence by Indians to Conestoga, vii., 61.

Penn, John's, creek, murders on, vi., 645, (Alias Mahonoy.) Petition of inhabitants, 647. Letters, 649, 662, 669. Murders by F. Stump of ten Indians near, ix., 414–490.

Penn, Port, vessels of war in sight, express from, x., 557.

Penn's Valley, petition from, respecting militia, xii., 104.

Pennsylvania—Charter, i., 17. Conditions and concessions, 26. Frame of government, 29. Laws agreed on in England, 37. Second frame of government, 1683, 42. Frame passed by W. Markham, 1696, 48. First meeting of Council, 57. Alterations in charter proposed, 58, 61. Difficulty with Jersey about letters sent to England, 75, 76. Provision to be made for the sustenance of the people, 78. Provisions scarce, 78. Arrangement with West Jersey respecting criminals, 101. Commissioners sent to New York to complain against agents of Lord Baltimore, 103, 104. Council to act for Governor, 119. Death of Charles II., and proclamation of King James II., 132, 133. William Markham Secretary of province, 142. Collector of Customs and Surveyor General appointed, 148. Governor appoints Lieutenant-Governor, 211. Captain John Blackwell, Governor, arrives, 228. Takes his seat at Council, 229. Thanksgiving-day on account of birth of a prince, 229. Inquiry for blank parchments left by proprietary for patents and commissions, 230. Produced, 231. And cancelled, 231. Use of greater and lesser seal, 232. Goods to be exported only to England, 232, 233. Decision respecting keeper of great seal's right to absent himself, 234. Map of Thomas Holme acknowledged, 264. Boundary of Philadelphia and Chester counties, 263, 265, 266. Discussion about proclaiming King William and Queen Mary, 301, 303,

Pennsylvania—
304, 341. And defensive measures, 306–310. Governor Blackwell resigns — Penn sends two commissions for successor to be appointed by Council, 316. Thos. Lloyd elected President, and the other commission destroyed, 317. Instructions of Penn, 318. Proposal of Markham, &c., to take up arms against the French, 334. Benjamin Chambers appointed Water-Bailiff, 342. Commission to Benjamin Fletcher as Governor of New York and, 345–364. Neglect and mismanagement in the government assigned as reasons for his appointment, and taking out of the hands of proprietary, 355. A Lieutenant-Governor to be appointed—Also Councillors, 356. Arrival of Governor Fletcher, 364. Thos. Lloyd refuses to be Deputy Gov'r, 364. Wm. Markham appointed Lieutenant Governor — Also Councillors, 365. Who take the oaths, &c., 365, 367. Number of representatives changed, 366. Difficulty about a letter addressed by former Council to Governor, 370. Letter from Governor Fletcher, and reply to it by Council, 384. Sends Commissioners to New York to meet those of other provinces—Their report, 393. Means for support of Government, 397. List of laws in force, 411. Amount of revenue in each county from one penny tax, 462. Transportation of tobacco from Maryland to Lower Counties to be stopped, 465, 468. The province restored to William Penn, and the authority of Governor Fletcher revoked, 472. Patent to William Penn, 472, 473. His commission to William Markham as Governor, 474. And to John Goodson and Samuel Carpenter as his assistants, 475. Committee appointed to consider a new frame of government, 486. Edward Shippen, Speaker, 490. Defence of province, 503. Tax of one penny, 520. An Association proposed by Secretary Blathwaite, 526. Proclamation against

Pennsylvania—
pirates, &c., 529. Commission to Governor Nicholson of Maryland to appoint certain officers in, 533. Commission to Matthew Birch as Collector of customs at New Castle, 534. And as Surveyor and Searcher of customs in Pennsylvania, 535. To John Bewley, Collector at Philadelphia, 535. To William Massey at Lewes, Collector, 537. Discussion about piracies, 539, 547. Tobacco shipped from, to Scotland, 551. William Penn appears in Council, 565. James Fox, Treasurer, dies—Samuel Carpenter appointed, 576. New Charter, Act of Settlement, &c., 597.

Claims on government for small arms in Markham's time ordered to be paid, ii., 19. Weak and defenceless condition of, 31. Bill before Parliament to annex to the Crown the proprietary governments, 32. Patrick Robinson, late Secretary, 33. Joseph Growden, Speaker, 36. Charter of privileges, 56–60. Commissioners of property appointed—Their commission, 61. Andrew Hamilton, Governor, oath, how to be administered to, 62. Difficulty with Lower Counties discussed in regard to separation, 71–74. Exposed situation of, 78, 79. Disputes with Lower Counties continued--Address of representatives of Philadelphia, Bucks and Chester to Governor on position of affairs, 85. Andrew Hamilton, Lieutenant Governor, dies—Succeeded by Edward Shippen, &c., President of Council under Commission of Proprietary, 88. Wm. Markham appointed by proprietary Register General, 96, 97. Representatives debate on extra numbers of members owing to Governor Hamilton's death, 105. Decision, 106. David Lloyd chosen Speaker, 106. French prisoners ordered from Burlington to, 113. John Evans, Governor, arrives, 115. Commission to Council read, 115. On division of the territories, 119, 123, 124, 126. Speech of Governor, 126. Address of territories, 128. Difficulties

Pennsylvania—
towards union continue, 130. Separation of territories in Legislature, 133, 134. Judge Mompesson's opinion as to the Governor's meeting the representatives of the three Lower Counties at New Castle, 136. Affairs of "Pennsylv'a Company" to be inquired into, 136. Death of Wm. Markham, 151. Bill for securing and confirming rights and properties, 154. Expenses of government provided for, 159. Separation of territories—Assembly summoned, 165. Various documents, &c., received from England, 179. Rates of foreign coins, 179. Long message from Governor to Assembly giving proprietary's views on various matters, 187. Joseph Growden, Speaker, 206. Defenceless state, 241. Address from Maryland to Queen on running boundary lines, 362. Case of William Clark, 362. Proprietary rights, 416. Extent of province on Delaware river, 421. Gov. Charles Gookin succeeds Evans as Governor, 427. Required to raise troops for Canada expedition, 449. Mortgage to Philip Ford, 455. Remonstrance of Assembly, 513. S. Carpenter, Treasurer--finances, 530. Not yet surrendered to the Crown, 568. Governor Gookin superseded by Governor Keith, 631.

William Keith appointed by proprietary as Governor—Arrives and is proclaimed at Court House, Philadelphia, iii., 13. Agreements with Indians at Conestoga, 24. £2000 for Queen's use, 32. Interference from Maryland, 37. Agent for the province in London to be appointed—Henry Goldney named, 44. Governor Keith and Governor Hart meet, and come to an amicable conclusion, 60. Governor Keith announces death of William Penn, 58. Continues the Governor, 62. Instructions from William Penn, Jr., to Governor Keith, 63. State of affairs in consequence of death of proprietary, 66, 73. Sale to Queen Anne

Pennsylvania—
and payment of money for it alluded to in letter and report to Governor Keith, 73. Governor Keith describes the position of various tribes of Indians, 114–116. Andrew Bradford publishes reflections on the credit of the province, for which he is summoned before Council, 143. Difficulties from Maryland with Indians on Susquehanna, 160. Commission to Joseph Pidgeon relating to stipulations with Maryland on surveys and settlements, 161. Act proposed for trial of felonies out of bounds of counties, 171. State of finances, 187. Allusion to first settlement by Penn--"his leagues of friendship with them," 194, 197. Conference with Five Nations at Albany, 197. The Five Nations at Albany surrender lands to, by Governor Keith, 201, 202. Papers to be printed, 202. Respecting Albany Conference, 202, 207. State of things with Maryland—Surveyors and others taken prisoners, 212. Original agreement between Lord Baltimore and Hannah Penn, &c., about boundaries, Feb. 17, 1723, 231. Letter to Governor of Maryland with, 232. Proclamation to be prepared, 232, 233. Prepared and ordered to be published, 236. J. Logan returns with proprietary's instructions, which Governor withholds for reasons stated, 236. Governor Keith's administration closes—Major Patrick Gordon produces his commission from Springet Penn, with Hannah Penn's assent and his Majesty's approbation, and is published as Governor at Court House, Philadelphia, 251. Lesser seal placed in hands of James Logan, as Secretary, 252. Re-delivers it to Governor, 252. Attempts of Maryland and Lord Sunderland on Lower Counties, 252. Great seal to be kept by Colonel John French, 253. Proclamation published in all province and counties, 253. Letter of Sir Alfred Popple on issues of bills of credit, 262. Issue of paper money or

Pennsylvania—
bills of credit, 347, 348, 396. Alleged robbery of treasury, 386, 305, 306. Trade with Sugar Islands, Governor's message on, 401, 418. Map of Louisiana, 1721 —Boundaries of Pennsylvania, &c., 402. Address of Assembly, Governor and Council to King on Sugar Islands, 423. Thomas Penn, proprietary, arrives, 433. Division line with Maryland, agreement, &c., 461, 463, 464. Correspondence respecting riots in Maryland, 468, 469, 474–491. New commission to Governor Gordon, 526. Jeremiah Langhorn, Speaker, 528. New greater and lesser seals given by proprietaries, 530. New commissions granted throughout, 531. Troubles with Maryland, 542, 591. Commissioners and report on boundary, 549. Speaker of Assembly on Maryland difficulties, 566. Death of Governor's lady, 571. John Penn arrives, 569. Maryland claims the territories, 594. Assembly called, 594. Indian deeds to William Penn, 1701, 600. Difficulties with Maryland, 614.

State House, &c., vested in trustees, iv., 46, 483. Governor Gordon dies, and is succeeded by James Logan as president, 47. Proclamation to be made, 48. Notices also to be given by virtue of Act of Queen Anne in Great Britain, 49. Germans go over to Maryland, 57. Complaints against settlers on Susquehannah, 61, 63, 64, 66, 71. Release of lands west of Susquehannah by Indians to proprietary, 88. Dispute between Maryland and, 101, 151, 190–199, 203, 227, 232. Preston and Kinsey sent to Maryland, 204. Instructions to, 206. Their report, 210. Various documents with it, 215–223. New Governor mentioned as appointed, 233. Papers received from proprietary, 234. George Thomas recommended as Governor, 249. Lord Baltimore's petition against, 249. Proceedings at Hampton Court respecting petitions from Maryland on articles of agreement between Penn and Lord Baltimore, 1732, 254. Proclamation on order in Council respecting Maryland, 262, 265. Gov. George Thomas arrives and enters on his duties, 288. Thomas Lawrie appointed by Governor, Secretary and Clerk of Council, 289. Proceedings at Hampton Court for quieting, and Maryland, 298–301. Proclamation to be made, 301. Justices appointed, 312. Commissioners appointed to run the line, 313. A map of, mentioned, 317. Correspondence with, 329. Articles of agreement 1701, between Wm. Penn and Indians, for lands in Susquehannah, 338–340. New treaty with Indians, 347. Various papers on value of coin and on bills of credit from Lords of Trade, as also reports on, from Assembly and Governor, 356–366. On state of province, 367–371. Notice of Commissioners appointed in England on Maryland affairs, 394. Samuel Preston is Provincial Treasurer, 412. Defence of, 422. Counterfeit bills discovered in England, 429. Gen. Wentworth to enlist soldiers for Cuba, 499. Controversy between Assembly and Council on pest house, health officer, powers of Governor, &c., 507–559. Indians quit claims to lands on Susquehannah, 559. Value of lands—settlers on Juniata, &c., 571, 572. Richard Peters appointed Secretary on resignation of P. Baird, 639. Treaty with Indians at Lancaster, 697–737, 739.

Troops to be raised for Louisburg, v., 38, 39. John Penn, one of the proprietaries, dies, 62, 73. Gov. Thomas sails for England and president Anthony Palmer succeeds him, 68. Richard Peters, Secretary, 68. Proper notices to be sent to England and other colonies, 68. Also proclamation, 68, 70. Reported capture of an English frigate bound from Havana, 75. Returns of men belonging to, by Samuel Perry, 135, Forces

Pennsylvania—
discharged by Gov. Shirley and Admiral Knowles, 141. State of the province, 158. Expedition to Canada, 130, 132, 134, 140–145, 148, 152, 159, 168, 170. Amount of pay due four companies from, 176. Wm. Parsons resigns as Surveyor-General, Nicholas Scull succeeds, 274. Various documents respecting treaty at Aix la Chapelle, 330, 331, 359–362. James Hamilton succeeds President Palmer, 362. Richard Peters appointed Secretary of province and Clerk of Council, 364. Words punched out of the seals, 382. Respecting dispute with Maryland, 383, 386, 421, 582–597. French from Canada on way to Ohio, 387. Temporary line with Maryland, 423. Early settlements along Susquehannah, &c., 440–449. French claims, speech of Mr. Joncaire, 528. Correspondence with Virginia and New York on Indian affairs, 622–637. Western boundary of, and Virginia, 758. Calculations of latitude and longitude, &c., 759–767.

Commissioners to Albany, vi., 25. And Virginia affairs, 83. Report of proceedings, 111–129. Meeting of Commissioners with Six Nations at J. Stevenson's relative to purchase of lands, 114–119. Deeds for lands at Albany, 119–129. Gov. Hamilton resigns, and Robert Hunter Morris, late Chief Justice of New Jersey, appointed and is proclaimed at Court House, 144. Various papers relating to Connecticut claim, 247–275. Loans, 555–558. Map, 300, 302. Commissioners from Massachusetts, 314. Embargo, 319. Disputes with Maryland, 417, 639. Fast Day—long drought, 422. Embargo, 511. Braddock's defeat, &c., 415, 424, 426, 428, 429, 430, 445, 461, 475, 476. Temporary line between Maryland, 639. Brief narrative of incursions of French and Indians, 1755, 766–768.

Number of men to be raised and measures to be taken in, for

Pennsylvania—
Crown Point expedition, vii., 29. War declared against Delaware Indians, 88. Conspiracy against Assembly in back counties, 91. A share of arms requested from General Shirley, 109, 111. Wm. Denny succeeds Governor Morris, 221. Account of condition of province, with a map, 228. Various documents from Dunk Halifax, &c., on defenceless state of the province, 272–278. Proprietary purchases from Indians — Committee of Council appointed to investigate, 354. Affirmation of N. Scull respecting, 399. Account of, by Gov. Denny at request of Lord Loudoun, 445. Roman Catholics, 448. Constitution, &c., in reply to Lord Loudoun, 448. Brockden, Recorder of Deeds, 465. Fast appointed, 560. Government growing worse, 633. Proprietaries to come over, 633. Committee of Assembly ask to inspect minutes of purchase of lands from Indians, 635, 636. Deeds for lands produced to Teedyuscung, 688, 693, 698. Alarming condition of, from French and Indians, 719. Troops for New York, 721. Enquiry by British government respecting manufacture of iron, 738, 740. Estimate of expenses of government, 778.

Connecticut settlers, ix., 7, 27, 602. Sum granted to colonies by, 2, 4, 10, 47, 115. Quota of each colony, 48–52. Paxton riots, 88–113. Act for payment to colonies, 160. Stamp Act in, 298, 299. Address to King on repeal, 315. An account of manufactures since 1734 ordered, 343. John Penn receives new commission as Governor from Thomas and Richard, and takes oath before Gov. Sharpe of Maryland, 345–349. Number of manufacturing establishments in, 354. Boundary question between Maryland and, 377. Quit rents—cost or expenses of province—grants of lands, &c., in reply to Earl Shelburne, 379–384. Modes of granting land, 380. Funds in, 382. Settlers on Indian

Pennsylvania—
lands, 404, 405, 407, 412, 480. Boundary line, 413, 545. Treaty at Fort Stanwix with Indians respecting boundary, 545. Described, 554, 568. Proceedings and resolutions of Susquehannah comp'y, 569–572. Respecting purchasers, 602. Laws respecting fisheries, 623. New commission to Gov. Penn—oath administered by Gov. Colden, 629. Slitting mills, plating forges, and steel furnaces in 1750, 632–636. Richard Penn, one of the proprietaries and father of Gov. John, dies, 736. Gov. John goes to England and James Hamilton as President of Council succeeds him, 736. By will of Richard, his son, John becomes proprietary, 742. Alteration of the seal to John's name, 742. Richard Penn appointed Governor, arrives, 780. His proclamation, 783.

Richard Penn, Governor, x., 1. Relating to difficulties with Connecticut, 50. List of public debts, 53. Public officers, their salaries, 53. His commission is revoked, and John Penn appointed Governor, 91. Joseph Shippen, Jr., secretary, 91. Respecting Connecticut claim, 117–139, 143, 151. Dr. Conolly, 140, 145, 149, 175, 176. Boundary line with Virginia, 149, 158, 175, 176, 181–194. Connecticut claim, 177, 275. Boundary with Maryland, 206, 216, 220, 240, 245. Jurisdiction not to be extended at present, 220. Proclamation respecting, 220. Letter to Earl Dartmouth, 221. Proclamation to be recalled, 241. Letter to Governor Eden on, 242, 243. Proclamation recalling former on boundary, 245. Reed's map—payments for, 260. Expenses of Government, 266. Taxes to be laid, 282.

Master of Rolls, xi., 187. Four Brigadier-Generals appointed, 199. Dissatisfaction with present frame of government, purpose taking sense of the people, 220. Boundary between, and Virginia, 238. Joseph Reed appointed chief justice, 186, 195, 202. Declines, 249. Thomas McKean appointed, 254. Jonathan Dickinson Serjeant, appointed Attorney General, 254. Congress call for four thousand militia, 254. Death and funeral of Thomas Wharton, Jr., President of the State, at Lancaster, 499, 500. Joseph Reed, President, George Bryan, Vice President, 632.

Boundary line with Virginia, xii., 16, 476, 700. Messages between President and Assembly, 96. Arms of the State ordered to be worked on standards for public use, 108. Joseph Reed, elected President, and William Moore, Vice President, 113, 541. Letter, Auditor General on accounts, boundaries between, and Virginia and Connecticut, 176, 177. Great seal of late province to be secured, 178. Dispute between Virginia and, 211, 287. Proclamation on Virginia and, 212–214. Dispute with Connecticut, 287. D. Rittenhouse, State Treasurer, 554. Extension of Mason and Dixon's line, 635. Dispute with Connecticut, 657. Line between Virginia and, 700. Instructions, 704. Pay, 714.

Resolution and petition respecting Connecticut claim, xiii., 10. Troops called out by Congress, 53. Proceedings respecting Virginia, 79, 192, 209, 253, 269, 334, 510, 519, 541, 685, 753. And Connecticut, 79, 123, 128, 203, 205, 266, 310, 313, 334, 417, 418, 420, 421, 430, 434, 437, 462. William Moore, President, and James Potter, Vice President, 112, 114. Counsel appointed on Connecticut claim, 128. Congress asks a return of number of white inhabitants of, 148. Paid F. Bailey for printing laws, 193. Council, &c., decide Virginia line is not to be run by astronomical observations, 209. Congress advice, 150. Men to be sent to Fort Pitt, 348. John Dickinson, President, and James Ewing, Vice President, 413. Duplicate of charter, 437. Indian deeds and papers retur'd by H. Osborne,

Pennsylvania—
462–471. Decree against Connecticut, 473. Proclamation confirming boundary between Pennsylvania and Virginia, 541. Proclamation of peace, Mr. Stille appointed to settle accounts with United States—bells to be rung, 559. Messages to Assembly on state of Province, 647–666. John Dickinson, President, and James Ewing, Vice President, 737. Boundary Commissioners, 753.

Corps of infantry, xiv., 5. Boundary with Virginia, 56, 59, 69, 74, 114, 119, 200, 211, 286, 288, 361, 388, 394, 399, 518, 651. Connecticut claim, 2, 51, 141, 159. T. McKean re-appointed Chief Justice, resolutions respecting Wyoming, 167. Arrangement of militia for protection of western frontiers, 177. John Armstrong, Adjutant General with rank of Brigadier General, in place of James Wilkinson, 219. John Dickinson elected President, and James Irvine, Vice President, 249, 250. Purchase, by the Commissioners of lands, from the Six Nations of Indians, 271. Population, taxables, 1760, 1770. Exports, 1773, 1784—336. Message containing a general view of affairs, 328–342. New York boundary, 363, 380, 385, 399, 443, 445, 460, 464, 507, 586. Treaty at Fort Stanwix for lands, 366. Interfering claims on Virginia, 368. First payment to devisees and legatees of William Penn, &c., and copy of notice in the papers, for vesting their rights in the State, 397. Requisition for Federal troops, 465. State of the claims and title of Messrs. Penn to the Province read and referred to Supreme Court, 502. Fort Pitt to be taken possession of, 517. "State Flag" mentioned, 518. State road from Miller's Spring to be marked out, 574. Report of Alexander McDowell of survey of new purchase, 604. Proprietary paid, 625.

Boundary lines, xv., 12, 15, 16, 19, 31, 33, 39, 107, 108, 212, 340, 356. Cession of lands by commissioners, accepted by Congress, 28. Lands opposite to Pittsburg, 42. Accounts between United States and this State, 83. Benjamin Franklin elected President, and Charles Biddle, Vice President, 110. Proclamation on Virginia agreement, 289. Connecticut claimants, 279, 280. Great seal, 299. Benjamin Franklin, President, and P. Muhlenburg, Vice President, 308. Boundary with New York completed, 340. Order of procession in Philadelphia on ratification of Federal constitution by, 350, Commissioners to run line paid, 356. A description of Erie lands asked of commissioners, 382. Asks for copies of Acts of Virginia respecting lands in, 451. Terms of sale of triangle at Erie, 472. Troops against Indians on frontiers called for in Congress, 515. Triangle on Erie, 524. Erie, 530, 531, 532, 554. Thomas Mifflin, President, George Ross, Vice President, 584. Maps, 597.

Triangle at Lake Erie to be purchased, xvi., 36. Master of rolls, M. Irwin, 106. Call of a convention by Assembly to amend constitution, proceedings of Council on, 41, 159. John Lukens, Surveyor General, dies, Daniel Brodhead elected, 208. Thomas Mifflin, President, George Ross, Vice President, 219. Suit for depreciation and counsel fees, 226. Public debt of, 264. Instalments paid proprietaries, 306. Howell's map of, 275, 337. Cedes to United States light-house at Cape Henlopen, beacons, piers, &c., 358.

Pennsylvania arms mentioned to be engraved on presents to Indians in Philadelphia, xv., 229.

Pennsylvania artillery captured, xiii., 253.

Pennsylvania battalion, x., 415, 419, 420. Colonel Bull, 420. Captain Williams of, 420, 435. Captain Willet, 434. Supplies ordered by Congress for, 439, 440, 441. Resolution of Congress to supply, 454.

Rev. William Linn, chaplain, 487. Surgeon Samuel McKenzie, 530. Colonel Miles of, 549. Of Germans, 622. Captains appointed, 634, 678. New arrangement for continental service, 742.

Pennsylvania brigade 3d, promotion of officers in, xii., 88, 89, 107.

Pennsylvania company, affairs to be inquired into, ii., 137, 160.

Pennsylvania hospital proposed, v., 513, 516, 526. Taken for sick soldiers, xi., 34, 85. John Storer, steward, 85, 130. Illegality of election of managers, 776; xii., 280, 688. Paid for board of disabled men, xiii., 252, 457, Fruit trees to be planted at with public funds, xiv., 71; xv., 155, 187. Pensions paid to, 640. For board of David Grady, a pensioner, xvi., 413.

Pennsylvania land company, ii., 160.

Pennsylvania line, Lieutenants placed on invalid list, xi., 647. Provisions for, xii., 106. Purchases for, 112. Case of Larry Burns, alleged theft, his excuse, 275. Released, 276. Supplies for, 409. Recruits—bounties, 431. Pay, 578. Mutiny, 593. Quarters for officers, &c., 605. Recruiting stations, petition, 606. Inquiry into causes of discontent in, committee to inquire, 632. Enlistment in, complained of, committee on causes of late discontent, 633. Account of monies advanced to, 661. Means for expediting march of, 693. Pay to, 701. Again formed, and on march under General Wayne, 739. Pay to, 747. Recruiting, 750. Pay, 752, 782. Pay to, xiii., 1. Clothing for, 23, 48, 67. Pay, 24, 71, 72, 149. Recruits, 151. Place for recruiting, Colonel Humpton appointed superintendent, 155, 156. No British deserter or soldier to be enlisted, 156. Pay, 187, 198, 205, 266, 272, 285. Major Porter to command 4th regiment of artillery, 223. Captain Francis Proctor, his claim, 244. Bounties, 258. Recruiting, 330. Pay, 395, 407. Recruiting from, 418, 443, 500, 562, 571, 597. Arrests, 617. Affidavits of James Bennett on mutiny, 618. Memorial of officers, 682. Field officers appointed, 697. Colonel Humpton's report, 711. Council on, 733. General Armand, 763. Auditor of depreciation, xiv., 139, 150, 160, 178, 206. Act for benefit of officers and soldiers, 184. Letters of administration granted on estates of officers and soldiers in, 200. Memorial of officers for land, xv., 16, 17. Payment in certificates for arrears to, 86. Claims for services, 260. Donation, land lottery, time extended, 263. Accounts of William Turnbull, as purchaser for, 299. Distressed soldiers of, provision for, xvi., 220. Recruits for, 492, 533, 535.

Pennsylvania Regiments, Paymaster, x., 2. Fourth, xii., 321, 572. Sixth, 209. Tenth, 320. Eleventh, promotions, 586, 684. Colonel Robert Patton asks to be restored to rank as before being taken prisoner, 600. Certificate respecting other officers, 609. At Fort Pitt, 716. Third, recruits at New town, xiii., 1, 8. Arrest of Lieut. Nagle, 617. Eighth, 25. Seventh, 98. Vacancies and promotions, 202.

Pennsylvania University, see University of Pennsylvania.

Pennypot Landing, confirmed, ii., 39.

Penrose, Joseph, recommended to Congress Lieutenant-Colonel, x., 444. Appointed, 445. R. Seward appointed a Lieutenant in his battalion. 472. Made Colonel, 767. Battalion, xi., 17, 20, 47, 83.

Penrose, Jonathan, Justice, xiv., 197; xv., 256.

Penrose, Thomas, to fix piers near Fort Island, x., 648.

Pensions, xv., 185, 186, 190, 286, 312, 322, 327, 341, 343, 345, 357, 358, 401, 403, 413, 430, 457, 464, 465, 472, 481, 485, 513, 545, 590, 634, 640; xvi., 125, 148, 163, 200, 213², 217, 223, 224, 224², 286, 328, 361, 370, 407, 408, 412, 413,

420, 434, 481, 486, 489, 538. List of persons entitled to ask for, 200, 320.

Pentecost, Dorset, presents accounts by Lieut. James Marshall of Washington county, xiii., 144, 150, 152, 253, 541. Resigns as member of Council, 703. Appointed Judge and President of Court Common Pleas, 732. Late Judge of Court Common Pleas and President, suspended on account of removal from Washington co., xv., 124.

Pepperell, Sir William, orders to, vi., 201. Raising troops, 298, 311.

Pequea, petition from, on roads, iii., 263.

Per diem, pay objected to by Gen. Amherst, viii., 323.

Perie, Nicholas, letter from, in case of C. Higginbotham, v., 218. Deemed offensive by Council—apology—had a grant for his land from Thomas Penn, 1736—form of it, 219. Arrested and carried to Maryland, 220. Examination of Col. White in his case, 221. His own defence, 218.

Perkins, Attorney, petition for pardon, v., 75.

Perkiomen, copper mine, x., 23, 41. Vested in trustees, 41.

Perry, James, as a favor, Teedyuscung asks his appointment by Governor as Captain, viii., 115.

Perry, John, Commissioner of purchase, xii., 465. Enquiry respecting, 648. Report, 653. Superceded, 654.

Perry, Micajah, agent on subject of paper money, iii., 377.

Perry, Samuel, letter from—return of men belonging to Pennsylvania, v., 135.

Perry, Wm., Sheriff, xi., 373, 377, 638; xv., 125, 302, 580; xvi., 72.

Pest House, petition of Germans for, iv., 507. Assembly and Governor on, 508, 509, 510, 511, 515–526, 549, 629. Bad condition of, v., 410. Sick attended by Drs. Rush and Duffield, x., 409. Sick to be sent to, 412. Soldiers to be put into, if barracks are too small, 485. To cease to T. Smith, xiii., 429. To be repaired, 590. Nicholas Fitzsimons appointed Steward, 631. Officers' lands, 753. On State or Province Island—repairs to, xiv., 6, 655.

Peters, Capt. John, resigns, xii., 613.

Peters, Richard, Commissioner to run line between Maryland and Pennsylvania, iv., 313. Appointed Secretary on resignation of P. Baird, 639. Appointed Secretary and Clerk of Council, v., 68. Letter to C Weiser, 211. Made member at request of proprietary, 382. In Cumberland county, 431. Report of proceedings against settlers on Indian lands, 440. To meet Indians at Carlisle, 658. Report, 664. Information respecting west bounds, 760. Commissioner to Albany, vi., 25. Thanks to, for his sermon, 66. Report of proceedings at Albany, 111–129. Letters on Connecticut claim, 253, 254, 287. On Indian affairs, 287, 673. Letter to and from Commissioners on road, 376, 377. Report on Braddock's road—Indians at camp—and arrest of two persons charged with correspondence with the French—committee on distribution of arms by Assembly—report, 679. Goes to Easton with Governor, vii., 204. Letters to and from, 394, 397. On money bills, 441, 442. Answers inquiries of Lord Loudoun on Constitution, &c., 448. Answer to Committee of Assembly for minutes, 636. Secretary goes to New York, viii., 19. Receives at Philadelphia by Lowe, a message from Cherokees to Delawares, 135. Sent to Easton to quell Indians, 172. Settles with Indians for lands, 219. Letters to and from, 305, 309. Respecting papers, 337. Resigns as Secretary, 671. Claims protection of Governor, 361. Representation with R. Hockley on proprietary taxes in Cumberland county, 472. Secretary, letter to Henry Wilmot London, giving history of Indian deed to Susquehannah county, x., 177. Capt.

461, 503, 533. Of militia, 649. Rank, 650. Secretary of War, 741. Petition respecting lots in Philadelphia granted to late R. Peters by Wm. Penn, xii., 779. Of Board of War—barracks, xiii., 128. Witness at Trenton, 442. Pay to, 580. Member of Congress, xiv., 5. Claim for liberty land, xv., 433. Warrant, issues to, 436. Claim, 481, 485. Under Mason, 485. On Jones' Lane, 494. Claims two city lots—sale postponed, xvi., 50. Referred to Supreme Court, 492. Repaid for survey of Jones' Lane, 11. Claim to city lot, 523, 526, 529, 532, 534, 539. Referred to Judge Shippen, 520.

Peters, Wm., resigns as member Assembly, vii., 148. Clerk to Committee on lands, 464. Letters to and from, 167. Secretary of Council petition, viii., 19.

Petersburgh, mediation of, xii., 742.

Peter's Township, Washington co., proposed division of, xiv., 275.

Petitions, of Duck Creek, for a way through the marshes, i., 60. Of mariners for wages, 63, 64. Of Charles Pickering, 67, 73. Richard Noble, 75. Nicholas Bartlett, 75, 77. Against master of a ship and trial, 79. Respecting patents, 86. Of Samuel Hersant for furnishing the prison, 101. Edward Everett for money, for "waiting on the provincial judges with his boat in the going their circuit, 157. Wm. Frampton removal of caves, 167. For a fair at New Castle, 181. Benj. Chambers, 189. C. Empson, 199. Robert Jeffs, against forcible entry into his house, 199. Respecting exportation, 213. For a fair at centre of Philadelphia, 218. Of R. Turner, S. Carpenter and others, for a bank, 236. To extend Chester county, 263. To build a wharf at Chestnut street, 267. Of Brandywine on obstructions, 292. Roads from Philadelphia, 298. John White, clerk of Court, 327, 329. Samuel Carpenter—hogs not to run at large in towns, 327. Of Benjamin Chambers and F.

Petitions—

Rawle for a bridge over Arch and Front streets, 330. Of Markham and others, to take up arms against the French, 334. Justice Edmond Lassell on counterfeiting, 380. Against D. Lloyd, 383. Southampton township, 389. Respecting roads, 386, 388, 389. Radnor township, 396. Against French traders, 436. Various, 478. For roads, 499. For bridges, 522. Nich. Scull, &c., for a road, 536.

For roads, ii., 10, 33, 111, 527. For fairs, 12. F. D. Pastorius in behalf of Germantown, 13. For repairs of High street wharf, 23. A. Hamilton, Post Master General, 33. Patrick Robinson for claims, 33. Of Philadelphia, 37. And Chester township, 40. From Philadelphia, 52. Wm. Markham, 121. James le Tort from jail, 163, 170. N. Gateau, 170. John Tatham for land, 179. Philadelphia on money, 221. Jacob Spicer on negro slave arrested in Philadelphia, 275. From Welsh tract for a ferry, 276. Of John Powell against it, 277. James Logan, 376. Of Philadelphia against New Castle, 379. Peter Evans, 391. James Heaton, 407. Philadelphia, 410. Story and Logan, 412. Bucks county, 488. Pastorius, Jawert, Kelpius and Falkner, 431. Thos. Fairman, 434. Robert Clay for release of goods, 513. R. Mason, road, 527. P. Bizalion, 545. Chester township, 546. Bristol, &c., respecting road, 547. Philadelphia road, 561. J. Le Tort, 562. Wm. Dilort to sell goods, 576. Wm. Eburn—rum seized, 605.

Hugh Pugh and Lazarus Thomas under sentence of death, iii., 41. Road from Conestoga to Brandywine, 43. Abraham Delucena—goods seized, 61. John Frazer for a vessel, 77. John Burrowes for release, 81. Inhabitants of Delaware—road from Philadelphia to Wiccacoa, 106, 107. From Schuylkill respecting taxes, 111. For roads in Chester county, &c.,

etitions—
142. J. and E. Cartledge, 186. Mary Woolvin, 187. Against powder house, 242, 244. Alexander Molliston against Wm. Till, 259. Roads—Frankford and Pequea, 263. Of John Duckett for a pardon, referred to Supreme Court, 276. Palatines to Gov. Keith respecting lands, 322. For new road to Wiccacoa, 547. Road from Philadelphia—stone bridge, &c., 573, 618. Respecting Courts of Chancery—its history, 617.

Respecting wears on Schuylkill river, iv., 17, 18, 20. Of Philadelphia against Courts of Chancery, 35. Of Bucks county against it, 36. From Germans on Susquehannah, 64. For road in Chester county, 152, 266, 278. Durst Thome, &c., 171. N. Tainy, &c., on condemned goods, 173. Jacob Chamberlin — fine, 224. Roads, 247, 495. Thomas Cresap, Miles Foy, &c., on Maryland affairs, 256. For roads, 278. Of criminals, 329. For new county out of Lancaster, 335. Mayor, &c., of Philadelphia to Governor to raise money, 379, 384, 385. Seven companies of soldiers, 466. Chester county — weights and measures, 507. Of Germans for pest house, 508, 509. Of Capt. John Titami, 625. Merchants against bills of credit, 750. For division of Philadelphia and Lancaster county, 756.

Against road to Bristol by N. Craft, &c., v., 61. Uty Perkins for pardon, 75. George Gray, &c., road to Cobb's creek, 99. Hugh Bruslam for pardon, 105. From criminals, 157, 158. Pilots of Sussex county, 226. Of John King, 343. Of Chester county, 378. Of Hans Hamilton as Sheriff, 468. Of trespassers in Great Cove, 468. Moravian missionaries, 576. Roads, 577. Charles Bellamy to refit vessel, 597. Capt. Nery, 620, 654, 656. Alexander McGinty for aid, 662.

Inhabitants of Cumberland co., &c., asking for protection, vi., 130. Watt. Sipple, Maryland dispute, 417. Lurgan T. C. Co. for arms, 533. Of frontiers for protection, 550. Inhabitants near Penn's creek, 647. From several counties for defence, 670, 680.

Inhabitants of York—alarmed by successes of Indians, vii., 234. Of French neutrals support, 239. Cumberland county—Rev. John Steele, 241. Inhabitants of Lurgan township, 241. Capt. Solomon Goad, 347. Of merchants to ship provisions, 393, 459. Philip Bader, 399. From Bethlehem for a watch against Indians, 459. Samson Mifflin on embargo, 571. Inhabitants of Pextang about forts Hunter and Halifax, 724. Of two convicted coiners, 725. R. Hill and S. P. Moore title to lands, 728. Of Philadelphia shipwrights taken at Oswego, 737. Of Lehigh township on Indians, 757.

Berks county on Indian ravaages, viii., 99. Capt. Huet, 148. Of Philadelphia merchants against tonnage duty, 230. Of French neutrals, 269. F. Post to be sent as missionary to Indians, 301. Of merchants of Philadelphia against sale of Provincial ship, piers, &c., 574. For roads, 676.

Captain Armaolia of Spanish ship in distress, ix., 26. R. Hockley and E. Physick on proprietary estate, 178. From several counties on proprietary quit rents, 179. Of Wardens of Phila'a, 366. Of merchants of Philadelphia, lumber, staves, &c., 366, 367. John Reddick, land in Maryland, 375, 376. Road from Reading to Fort Augusta, 440. Philadelphia road, 623, 627. Lower Dublin township road, 628. For road from Fort Augusta, 651. Of Chester against road from Philadelphia, 692, 703.

Respecting road from Philadelphia to Lancaster, x., 65, 69. Inhabitants of Northumberland county against Connecticut people, 111. To call Assembly on account of Boston port bill, 180. From colonies, 239. Of Captain Du Casse, 262. From Bermuda

Petitions—
for provisions, 413. Boats in Darby creek, 656.
Matthew Clarkson, &c., xi., 177. Robert Patton, 188. Levi Hollingsworth, 193. Of Lancaster for magistrates, &c., 211. Of Walter Hall against a debtor, 214. Of Bristol, 254. Of negro Harry, a slave, 263. Of Henry Funk and George Kreibel, 269. Of Captain Joseph Brady's company on drawing lots, 313. Jno. Swanwick for goods, 359. On calling out whole force, 394. Of Lutheran Reformed German Church at Easton, 422. Of soldiers, 458. Of Fannet township for arms, 524. Chester co. battalion, 524. Eve Jeder and Esther Blackman, 579. Of prisoners to be exchanged—verbal of Samuel Morris and others for a pardon of four prisoners, 564. Rev. S. Barton and A. Murray—negro Ralph for remission of punishment of death, 565. From Fort Pitt, for pass for a boat with furs, for New Orleans, 568. Favor of Roberts and Carlisle, 606, 607. Of their wives, 613. Of Captain Lightbourne, 636. L. Nicola—Wm. Low, 637. Against forestalling in Philadelphia, 638, 640. Wm. Streaker, 641. Of Henry Sherer and others, 647. Thos. Fell, &c., Peregrine Jones, H. Meyers, 650. Of Matthew Clarkson in case of sloop Active, 657. Of sundry persons for broken cannon, 662. Of Lts. David Brown and Edward Randolph, 665. Of disabled soldiers, and for stores—of Purviance, Dean and Henderson for stores—Christopher Getting, 667. Of Lieut. Sproat, 675. Of George Allen, Jona. Cowpland, John Wilson, David Franks, 679. Of Dr. Valentine Standley, 691. For rum for boats, 694. Peter De Haven, 702. For pay—passes and pardon and against privateers, 703. For passes, clothing, &c., 704. Col. Johnston, R. Footman and Mag. Devine, porter brewery, 710. Of E. L. Treckel, claim on a house, 714. Thos. Hazelwood,

Petitions—
&c., Lewis Nicola, 741. R. McNeill, C. Crawford, sub-Lieuts. Northumberland, 749. Jno. Reynolds, Isaac Ely, Ann Tatnall, 750. Lieut. Honeyman, James Dundas, Matthew Gregg—wagon master for payment, 755. Arms to be brought to, 757. Mr. Hunter, A. Kleir, 759. Jacob Deisher for records, 764. Various, for passes, 770. Of military men, 766. Merchants of Philadelphia, 783.
For rations instead of money, xii., 2. Thos. Crouch, 3. Geo. Holder, Ann Calvert, Abigail Ault, Michael Farmer, Captain Newton Cannon, to sell cargo, 11. John Tully, Philip Nagle, Boudes Burke, and Wm. Phillips, 13. Capt. Watkins, Margaret Chalmers, Lieutenant Honeyman and Pugh, 14. Of Philadelphia co., 15. Francis Hopkinson, 17. Thos. Hanson for pardon, and for a pass—Rev. W. Rogers for rations—to sweep Delaware for pay, 20, 21. For passes, 22, 23, 24. Reynold Keen respecting his estate, 26. John Hayes, flag of truce, 31. Lucy Thompson, Joseph Musgenung, Nathaniel Sackett, 32, 33. Abraham Chapman, 32. Timothy Hooker, 34. Elizabeth Young, Rachael Shubert—L. Nicola for reward, 37. Capt. Jno. McPherson, 38, 39. Joseph Dean, 45. Fred. Sneider, doorkeeper, 48, 49. Mrs. Mary Matlack, 50. Commodore Hazelwood—W. Johnston and John Lewis bail for two men who join British army in Philadelphia, 57. John Swanwick, Margaret Crohan, Catharine Malone, Ann Williams, 58, 59. Invalid corps, 64. John Young, Elizabeth Condor, 67. Charles Hurst, Augustus Willett, Daniel Gomez, 72, 73. To search river for wrecks—of Michael Huffnagle, of Susannah Simmons, Mary Cressons, not granted—Myer Hart, 75. Andrew Sponseller, James McKee, John Donnelly, Ellen Kirchenschlaeger, (bastard)—of Sarah Growden, 76, 77. Andrew Right, Catharine Ebert, Michael Teter,

'etitions—
Susannah Simons, Elizabeth Stewart, 78, 79. Of John Rein, Reynolds Keen, Captain McGinley, Mary Cussans, Mary Gunnerson, Ernst Ludwick Baish, John Marshall, 80, 81. Joseph Greeswald, 83. Edward Fitzrandolph, James Pannel, 86. Wm. Call of Germantown and Matthias Stimmell, 92. Inhabitants of Penn's valley respecting militia duty, 104. For passes, 106, 112. In favor of Ralph, a negro, an imposition, 113. Jed. Snowden, 116. Chas. Willing, &c., 120. Abraham Ristean for negro slave, 134. Inhabitants of Northumberland, 138. Major S. Bush, Capt. Jacob Buss, &c., David Franks, 141. Jeremiah Simmons, Thomas Guion, 142, 143. Mary Flood, George Harding, 149. Catherine Fritz, Francis Nelson, 150. For passes, not granted, 157. Of officers of ship General Greene, Ann Winters, Ann Nicholson, 158, 159. Capt. Williams to take provisions to French fleet, 162. Elizabeth Rapp, 163. Mary Miller, Henry Wauher, 190, 191. Jane Smith, 197. B. Soden, 200. Mary Jones, Samuel Kenny, &c., 201, 202. Wm. Mackey, 202. Daniel Wingate, 205. John Paul Schott, Eleanor Quinn, Francis Lally, 216, 217. Wm. Cassidy, Peter Swope, 257. Isaac Kauffman, Frederick Koble, Wm. Keyser, 223. Margaret Brown, 225. President's house, 236, 244. Of John Reine—wife of Casper Guyer, 237. John Wright, Dr. Adams, 238. Mary Harding, Elizabeth Voght, and Owen Ryan, 242. Joseph Walker, James Norris, 247. Of Cumberland, 248. Isaac Melchior, &c., to receive continental money—prisoner for clothing, 248. Dr. Kennedy, C. Mifflin, S. McGinnis, 253. Wm. Barton and Paul Zantzinger, Cornelius Lery, Mary Machbanks, Ann Riche, Peter Schwoope, 256, 257. Rebecca Paul, Jane Evans, Magdalen Divine, 258. John Ensmenger, 267. Jacob Taney, 271.

Petitions—
John Clarke—officers of Colonel Hazen's regiment, 278. Ann Riche, 284. Capt. Gibbs Jones, 286. Of inhabitants of State on Schuylkill bridge and road to Darby--Charles Cook, 293. York county for defence, 296. Various, 309. Elizabeth Rinedollas, Capt. Daniel Topham, 311. George Montgomery, 317. Mary Murray, 322. John Dunlap and James Budden, &c., 331. Robert McKnight, 332. Capt. Turnbull, 333. Edward Grisel, Capt. Wren and Lieut. Fick, 334. F. Merchant, David Coleman, 336, 337. Isabella Grant, George Montgomery, Capt. Manifold, P. Zantzinger and W. Barton, 338, 339. 357. George Brett—a number rejected — Robert Dunlap, Mary Roher and Mary Bird, 343. Elizabeth Rhinedoller, Ann Dunkin, Margaret McKewn, Jno. and Mary Whittinham, 347. In favor of Mrs. Ferguson, 351. Capt. Wm. Barber, 354. Pennsylvania division, vacancies in, 354, 368. Christopher Schulz, 357. Judith Doyle, Mary Sharp, 361. A. Darkness, M. O'Harra, Joseph Myers, Mary Murray, 365. Richard Murthwait, Jehu Roberts, 374. For independent corps, 383. Objected to, 389. B. Rue, Daniel Zieber, Wm. Richardson, 390, 391. M. Johnson, 400. Jane Kerr, 410. Elizabeth Powers, 420. Meade & Co., Jno. Nesbitt, 428. Geo. Brett, 436. George Hunton, 447. Moses Lamb, 455. Chester county, 456. Northumberland, 459. Edward West, Joseph Burns, 469. E. L. Friechell—Merchants of Philadelphia, 478. J. & S. Holt, J. McGuire, Mary Meyer, 479. Henry Matthews, 483. J. De Rey, 483. Abm. Surgert, A. Miller and Kilion Dewinger, 484. J. Connolly, M. Huffnagle, &c., 487. M. Gomez, 489. Jno. Eve, Nathan Mitchell, W. Austin, 493. Respecting negroes, 501, 502. W. Constable, S. Jeffries, T. Mendenhall, D. Franks, 504, 505. L.

Petitions—
Prahl, J. Clay, O. Stevens, 514. H. Moore, C. Pattison, 523. M. Eshler, 531. J. Swanwick, H. Dunahow, Wm. Montgomery, Jacob Sponseller, J. McCarty, 536, 537. J. Boyd, 542. D. Dawson, M. Lapp, 553. J. Davis, E. Ruell, M. Copple, T. Wade, H. Smith, and W. Wood, 563. Opposers of collections of taxes in Berks co., G. Palmer, H. Bidstein, J. Stansbury, W. Hammil, A. Darens, A. Harvey, 568. W. Erskine, M. Wilson, 577. E. Haines, J. Stansbury, 579. M. Dyer, Cavenaugh, 586. M. Bryan, C. Holmes, 590. Taxes in Berks, 601, 608. Of officers of Pennsylvania line—of Northampton—C. Stewart, 607. Tax payers in Berks, 608. J. Becker, 618. Mary Scanlan, 619. E. Pettit, J. Davis, 629. G. Aertes, 631. M. Hamilton, M. Hufnagle, 632. Brothers of Dr. Kuhn, 650. Jno. Millis, Jr., 654. Jasper Moylan, E. Davis, I. and J. Baker, M. Martin, J. Rogers, J. Fitzgerald, 657. J. Reine, Mary Emmes, 674. Northampton for defence, 678. Several, 684. Berks county—S. Carson, 687. J. Hicks, D. Sullivan, S. and D. Potts, 694. Of Captain Stephen Decatur, 699. Major Hamilton, C. Archibald, 708. H. Shrupp, 728. E. Fox, 729. J. Philip's wife, a soldier for clothing—supplied, 735. Capt. Hart, 737. C. Koon, Mary Harding, 740. John Deans, 743. Mich'l Parker, Andw. Allen, 745. Not granted, 746. Eliz. Stoops, Maj. Lewis, 747. W. Williamson, S. Collins, A. Humphreys, 762. J. Conner, F. Oberlin, 755. J. Patton and B. Davis, Jr., 759. Of Capt. Hart against Col. H., 762. Mons. Massonnare, S. Rooks, 767. S. York, E. Overholtz, P. Iserlo, M. Brown, Jno. Miller, M. Winstanley, 773. T. Murphy, J. Parr and W. Gray, 777.
N. Miller, J. Green, Jr., G. A. Baker, xiii., 4, 5. E. Wade, Wm. Angelo, 17. E. Mooney, B. Sonmans, James Packer, for Thos.

Petitions—
Lightfoot, 18, 19. J. Howard, 18. Wm. Barton, C. Philips, 21. L. Fohrer, 23. David Mead, 29. S. Simpson, B. Leech, J. Parr and W. Gray, 30, 31. H. Pauling, M. Maguire, 32. E. O'Flaherty, 38. S. Preston Moore, Hill & Wells, for City lots, 49. Cap. Thomas Mason, M. Martin, Negro George, 50. Several, 53. B. Duncan, 59. M. Burns, A. Beam and J. Barkman, 72. S. Leshincksy and John Hasse, &c., 82. E. Burgess, J. Auckley, 87. R. Wetherill, for two deserters. Richard for D. Rundle. Thomas Forrest, 96, 97. J. J. Rice, 100. J. Swanwick, 104. Ph. Schreiner, 111. Doctors Bond, Wilson, Beatty, and Otto, 115. John Shirgold, &c., 115. D. Llwellyn, 119. J. J. Gilmore, J. Green, Mary Hall, M. Lukens, 120, 121. J. Cannon, Samuel Sterrett, 123. M. Robbins, 125. M. Hall, J. Jones, 127. R. & R. Rundle, 132. Thomas Forrest, R. Johnston, 137. F. Hogan, J. Cowell, T. Mason. J. R. B. Rodgers, M. Turner, Surgeon, Alex. Stewart, 145. R. Murthwaite, William Semple, 149. J. Stille, 150. Thomas Prudden, &c., in Hospital, U. S., 153. N. Miller, C. Worts, 155. B. Young, Doctor Duffield, 157. M. Maus, 159. Mrs. S. Trickett, 161. W. Peeland, George Clift, 162. Asheton Humphreys, J. Wallace, Sarah Kennedy, 166. G. Wilson, 169. D. Sullivan, 172. M. Jenkins, J. Elderston, 175. M. McCausland, 178, 179. D. Reeder, J. Hill, W. Benezet, 181. J. Egg, Negro Violet, 185. P. Fritz, H. Barnhold, S. Thompson, M. Conrad, 187. J. Heiner, 195. W. Smith, G. Pancake, 196. J. Stevenson and N. Nicholson, R. White, 202. S. Whitebread, E. Sower, 209. John Bollen, 213. H. Wolfe, P. McConnell, 214. G. Haines, 218. J. McCullough, 221. P. Frick, W. Hoofman, A. Gibson, 223. Northampton Taxes and Militia fines, C. Dorsey, B.

etitions—
Shoemaker, M. Knight, W. Green, 245. J. Hale, 243. Cap. J. Wilson, M. Young, 248. H. Spering, F. Sneider, L. Kale, M. Nichols, 253. A. McClean, Sol. Moses Cohen, Israel Campbell, John Hood, 254. B. Robinson, Dr. Edmiston, 263. S. Lindley, S. Ingliss, 271. M. Beck, R. McCawley, 273. J. Hildeburn, T. Allison, 277. Gideon Walker, 280. From Philadelphia, relating to Sugar seized, 282, 283. Of R. Haines, and S. Miles, 293. Jane Bartram, J. Taylor, S. P. Moore. M. Jenkins, N. Young, 294, 295. Fifth Battalion, 298. C. McAfee, S. Walsh, R. Hartshorne, M. Mann, 300. Colors taken from Hessians, 301. Geo. Thomson, A. Humphreys, 302. H. Geiger, M. C. Hartman, 310. L. Bailey, 314. C. Werkeiser, A. Carpenter, 319. G. Gensil, 324. J. Mitchel, 330. M. Pickles, T. Periam, William Ford, &c., M. McKonky, C. Musselman, 337. E. Stevenson, and M. Shannon, 338. Captain John Gensill, 356. E. Tracey, N. Boyling, J. Downing, G. Wall, Jr., C. Campbell, 360. T. Haney, Various persons, J. Britain, 368. Merchants of Philadelphia on absconding Merchants, 370. A. Martin, Lancaster, P. Godshall, George Weidell, 383. J. Jeffries, 411. F. Mourer and P. Klein, John Fishel, F. Hutchinson, P. Newcomer, 432. D. Hoge, J. Annan, F. McCawley and E. Briddle, J. Shaw, J. Harkins, J. Fell, and J. Johnston, 439. A. Humphreys, 444. Ed. Stiles, J. Johnston, G. Grover, Captain J. Lees, Thomas Stites, 449. Widow Hartman, William Tanner and Wife, 451. J. Thompson, N. Cline, G. Bough, 453. C. Stoever, 454. S. Bonsal, J. Heater, F. Stokely and John Boyd, Colonel John Huber, &c., M. Miller, 461. L. Barnett, 474. N. Sharkey, 476. J. A. De Normandy, A. Shinnard, 479. N. Forsyth, Sieur Fermier, 481. H. Wynkoop, 486. A. Holmes, 497. J. Jeanes,

Petitions—
H. Baker, A. Castner, 499. B Knouse, A. Helme, J. Bowman, R. Hamer, G. Davis, M. Iseet, 501. J. Boyd, M. Urner, S. Longacre, G. Levering, Colonel Coates, J. Loder, R. Wells, 503. M. Stackhouse, J. Wood, 505. M. Hartsbock, 508. Joseph Roberts, J. Tyson, E. Dyer, 511. H. Martin, C. Weaver, J. and B. S. Judah, A. Allen, J. Livergood, Jr., S. and J. McCulloh, 513. M. Eddy, Christopher Painter, N. Low, D. Norman, Israel Doan, W. Moland, C. Bittenhousen, D. Adams, L. Spring, J. Moyes, 517. F. Buzzard, T. Christwell, J. Moyer, T. Barnes, Jr., W. Nugent, T. Canby, Alexander Power, 521. J. Cuyler, S. Massey, Several persons, J. Merckley, 523. T. McCloud, 525. P. Helick, J. Evans, J. Dorset, L. Subzey, M. Freeman, H. Ritchie, 527. E. Forman, J. Dorset, J. Prescot, J. Fisher, M. York, 529. Negro Took, R. Skinner, E. Botner, 531. Benjamin Poultney, William Bennet and Wife, H. McGaskey, Thomas Clayton, H. Dickson and J. Leary, Jr., B. Bowman, J. Peck, J. Meyers, M. Meyers, A. Meyers, Joseph Roberts, 535. S. Porter, H. McCahan, Ann Hart, J. Vanderen, &c., 539. C. Van Phul, C. Waltz, S. Porter, A. Hodge, Jr., A. and W. Chapman, &c., 543. M. Irvin, J. Carson, Thos. Irvine, G. Dalley, Captain D. Brodhead, Jr., D. Norman, R. Shoemaker, &c., J. Mather, J. Riddle, D. Pastorius, &c., 545. M. Urner, T. Cheney, 546. B. Norris, F. Lewis, Jr., and M. M. O'Brian, J. Leary and M. York, 549. J. Richardson, &c., 551. A. McGreggor, W. Frizby and Wm. Potts, H. Driver, E. Coxwell, 553. A. Barr, 559. W. Layland, 556. M. Hillegas, 571. Ward Spooner, 572. F. Wade, J. Durant, 572. J. Snyder, 584. T. Hill, J. Keane, 589. J. Briggs, A. Mideoff, 590. Of Merchants, &c., on price of Salt, 593. T. Ward, William Green, Samuel

Petitions—
Burrows, 595. Luenze and Mullet, David Jackson, 597. Thomas Norton, J. Harvey, Inhabitants of Southwark, 626. J. O'Neal, 634. Geo. Binckes, 639. G. Wrightman, 642. Thomas Duval, 666. D. Hillyer and J. Johnston, 669. E. Allen, J. Wedburn, Thomas Green, W. Nugent, 673. David Welgar, 675. J. Jacks, C. Nell, 681. J. P. De Haas, 727. M. Brattelli, 735. D. Clymer, J. Foster and J. Kelly, 735. N. Lloyd, 741. C. Wilstack, B. Fuller, M. Brattelli, 743. J. Caldwell, John Butler, Colonel F. Murray, 745. Godfrey Diffendoffer, &c., 747. A. Fund, 753. Officers Pennsylvania Line, 753. Of J. Bœhm, J. Patton, D. Lenox, 755. J. Adair, 762. Pennsylvania Line, Memorial from De Marcelin and Le Roy, two Frenchmen in service, 764. J. Thompson, 771. W. Pilmer, J. White, 773.

Wm. Nugent, A. Ruff, xiv., 9. C. Wilstack, 11. J. Keitby, J. Pennock, J. Thompson, 27. R. Anderson, 29. W. McMeen, T. Charles, 31. M. Slough, 33. D. Pettet, 36. William Perkins, 41. A. French, 43. J. Dorvil, Andrew Carson, 49. William Trickett, George Davis, W. Conner, M. Stein, 50. H. Schitz, S. Clindell, 59. E. Milnes C. Darragh, William Pollard, A. Carson, 69. Inhabitants of Philadelphia co., 75. Peter Schneider, 76. Negro Thomas, Fisher and Roberts, 77. J. Shrieve, 104. T. Murphy and Jno. Chandler, M. Curral, Thomas Green, J. Bailey, negro Cato, 109. Henry Bailey, George McGuire, 119. S. Kerrigan from Westmoreland, 137. J. Kelly, W. Whitebread, J. Langay, 141. C. and C. Marshall, 149. M. McGuire, 151. A. Jack, 153. A. Ruff, 156. Lieut.-Colonel James Moore, 159. T. Smith, M. McNally, Jno. Spalding, 160. Massachusetts Bay, 162. P. Weis, J. Kean, 165. B. O'Neal, M. Barnard, T. Pentlin, E. Milne,

Petitions—
171. N. Bulrick, A. McIlwaine, 173. James Stewart, 175. T. McCulloms, Robert Hannah, Andrew Jack, M. Ryan, 179. T. Wall and A. Carson, 183. J. Lesher, 184. J. Bottomly 198. B. Norris, 201. Ephraim Pennington, Jno. Griffey, 203. J. Jacobs, A. Characher, 205. Edward Cunnard, Daniel Williams, 208. N. Loomis, 225. Luke Keating, Jno. Carrel, 227. E. Morgan, 229. M. Lukens, H. Horn—Washington county, 235. R. Colton, 239. S. Kerrigan, J. Benson, James Brown and B. Gregory, T. Knight, 243. From Lancaster, 255. G. Davis, Wm. Conner, 262. J. Glauss, J. Hammersley, 263. A. Le Blanc, J. Monk, J. Kane, 265. T. A. Mount, M. Moore, 267. Washington county, 275. M. Standley, J. Morgan, P. Fowler, 277. J. Vanderslice, H. McDowell, Ann Foster, 279. From Montgomery co., from Germantown, William Cavenaugh, 283, 287. J. Egolf, 284. William Henry (Philadelphia), 291, 309. J. Chandler, 307. R. Hackett, 314. Mary Monroe, &c., 316. M. Barnet, 323. Peter Hosterman, 325. W. Stringer, H. Doran, 327. Robert Kennedy, 348. S. Burroughs, 357. J. Van Vleck, F. Banseman, H. McDowell, A. Carlisle, 363. Wm. Crispin, J. Gregg, J. Snodgrass, 364. R. Rodgers, M. Sharp, 270. Of George Elder, 375, E. McKenzie, Jane Barker, 378. J. Rakestraw, 380. Captain J. Lang, 382. M. Barker, 383. J. Mease, 393. J. Livergood, J. Bestor, 405. Lewis Weiss, Lewis Farmer, 441. C. Champaign, 455. City lots, 456. James Moore, 462. B. Grest, C. J. De Longschamp, J. Neagle, 467. T. Moore, 470. Captain Robinson, L. Lenox, of Fisher and Roberts, 492. J. McDowell, M. Dawson, 500. J. Pleini, &c., E. Burgess, 509. W. Stringer, R. Moore, 511. B. Brannan, Thomas Wall, 513, 522. George Deeks, 517. J. Hatchcook, T.

Petitions—
Marmee & Co., 521. J. Manley, 525. W. and E. Huggins, J. Melchior, J. Maddox, &c., L. Hollingsworth, 550. E. and M. Wilson, 554. W. Jack, D. Clayton, 563. G. McCrea, 567. M. Spence, 573. B. Kreemer, 577. Favor Matthias Aspden, 578. J. Simson, 579. J. Potts, 580. J. Smith, M. McKenzie and Hugh Jones, 581. Of clerical and lay deputies of Episcopal church on succession,—William Parsons, 585. L. Keating, 586. Longschamp, 589. J. McClelland, R. Patterson, Elizabeth Wilson, 591. G. Schlosser, L. Ross, 591. W. Pollard, 601. G. Glentworth and R. Harris, Charles and H. Read, 617. Philadelphia — Chester county, 619. Eliz. Elliott, 620. Thomas Douglass, 621. J. Pettigrew, 622. M. Aspden, 625. P. Kenney, E. Burd, T. Wilkinson, Jane Gardner, 629. Charles Smith, M. Joiner, E. Wright, 631. J. Durant, F. Wade, 633. J. Lang, Colonel T. Nichols, 635. W. Callahan—negroes of Philadelphia for a fence, 637. Deed J. Sanse, Dr. J. Hutchinson, 653. G. Garnick, 654. R. Ellis, J. Barnes, W. Swartz, 657. Wm. Rice, 665, 666. William Pollard, Gotlieb Moise, 669.

M. Aspden, xv., 4. J. Taylor, 6. Robert Biggs, J. Kinkaldy, Thomas Smith, 5. W. Bond, F. Welt, 7. Dauphin county court house, 14. B. Edgsworth, 16. J. Cornall, 24. Jno. Potts, 25, 26. Bedford county, J. Levering, 26. J. Kelly, Alexander Carlisle, 33. William Baker, 34. Hudson Springer, 36. Malcolm McDonald for Jeremiah Taylor, 38. E. A. Smith, 41. Jno. Funk, R. How, Jno. Elliott, 44. M. Conner, 49, 51. Geo. Sturmfels, 51. E. McVicar, J. Talbot, 56. H. Hubbs, R. Young, 60. Wm. Barton, 66. Of B. Davies, Jno. Penn, &c., 63, 68. T. Cuthbert, &c., H. Revers, 69. E. Armstrong, I. and J. Vernon, 71. D. Lenox, E. Kenan, &c., 74. Late settlers at

Petitions—
Wyoming, 79. J. Miller, 81 George Davis, 82. Earl of Shelburne, E. Fox, Abraham Shoemaker, 88. Eph. Douglass, 122. Edward Milne, 123. Of Joseph Thomas, 127. P. Dowsett, 131. J. Bond and son, 135. J. Robinson and C. Hurst, T. Rogan, 136, J. Lindsay, W. Henderson, &c., inhabitants of Bethlehem, 141. M. Bennett, 143. B. Davis, 160. T. Hutchins, 168. C. Howell, 168. Hugh Neely, 175. Thos. Gordon, 177. J. McGee, B. Smith, A. Greble, John Elder, R. Stephenson, 178. Chester county election, 182. J. Duffey, J. Steen, 183. D. Neiss, J. Hughes, 191. Capt. R. Coleman, Charles Syng, Commissioners of Montgomery county, 193. F. Wade, P. Smith, H. Higgins, J. Patton, J. Bayard, 195. Wm. Rees, R. Fawcett, J. McGee, 202. Officers of Philadelphia, 205. J. Rheiner, Geo. W. Steinhauer, R. Fawcett and J. McGee, 209. A. Andaully, Mary Landell, R. Wells, John Clifford, 215. B. Edgeworth, Jonas Phillips, 216, 217. J. Dryerrig. J. Knight, W. Pettit, 221. Peter Le Barbier Duplessis, 222. P. Le Barbier Duplessis not published, 222. R. Newton, Thomas Connarroe, J. Woods, Indian interpreter, 228, 229. Daniel Hoffman, Jr. and Jacob H., R. Newton, 230. T. McCrum, Jno. Lewis, T. Wigley, John Edgeworth, Jno. Collins, 246. M. Slough, 250. Thomas Wright, J. Anderson, Jno. Lewis, C. Young, 255. R. Somers, 259. M. Ahanger, A. Hoak, Godfrey King, Edward Pickering, B. Pittfield, 261. J. Edgeworth, T. Gardner, A. Hoki, G. King, 263. Of Northampton county, 265. Militia, 265. J. McCammon, J. Bell, 267. Sol. Hayes, 274. A. Moore, John Mears, 282. Alien duty not taken—paid, 283. R. Adams, M. Phœnix, T. Lee, 285. Jno. Logan, B. Edgeworth, 290, 299. David Jones, 299. J. Jones, 302. D. Hunter, 305. H. Martin, J. Har-

Petitions—
grave, 307. J. Skinner, Christ. Schreffler, 323, 324. H. Aughlerbaugh, J. Witherspoon, Cumberland county, 325. Thomas Gordon, Chester county and Cumberland county, 327. J. Irvin, 329. C. Eddy, 330. Court room repairs, J. Wink, N. Falconer, 337. N. Chalfant, 337. J. Mines, 342. William Alexander, 343. R. Wells and Clifford, J. Hatfield, C. Hall, T. Lloyd, 344. T. Reynolds and R. Skinner, D. Richey, George McLaughlin, John Brannon, 347. John Rinn, 350. J. Taylor, G. Watts, P. Cook, J. Sunkles, Joseph Perkins, 357. M. Owen, J. Morris, Lieut. Bulkly for William Beatty, 365. E. Ross, M. Owens, 367. C. Paleske, 371. J. Conrad Matsch, J. Letts, James Jackson, 373. Merchants of Philadelphia, 375. From Berks county, 376. William Eckhart, M. Moyer, T. Tate, Eleanor Armstrong, 378. J. Moore, 381, 382. William Moland, Andrew Lytle, 382. A. Bety, 384. S. Coutty and S. Lehman, gunsmiths, 384. J. B. Knox, Cato Forster, R. Dowdle, R. Smither, 386. J. Muntzger, Cad. Evans, J. Humphreys, J. Rock, W. White, T. Wardell, W. Courtney, 390. J. Match, J. Egg, M. Fisher, T. Hurst, Charles Hurst, E. Blaine, Jona. Thompson, William Harris, L. Harris, &c., heirs, &c., N. Young, 399. D. Shutz, Bedford and Neville, 401. J. Thompson, F. Fast, M. Baker, L. McNeal, 403. James Cunningham and T. Stokely for pay, 405. J. Knight, S. Steward, J. Chapman, M. Polly, W. Smith, Berks county, C. Eyler, 407. J. Elliott, P. Forsythe, P. Savakee, 409. H. Burney, P. Ely, William Roberts, &c., 413. T. Gordon, T. Williams, Berks county militia, J. Rheiner, 415, 423. Quakers of Chester county, P. Kitchen, 418. J. Manderfeldt, J. McAlpine, P. Douglass, J. Reynolds, T. Armor, N. Liberties, F. Fultz, J. Price and B. Humphreys, 425. H. McCutcheon, G. Cooper, 426. J.

Petitions—
Boyd, E. Elliott, T. Matlack, &c., 429, 430. R. Peters, H. R. Taylor, &c., claims, 430. J. Lawson, 431. J. Elder, J. Logan, 432, 433. M. Fisher, &c., G. Fellker, A. Cuthbert, M. Jenkins, 439. J. Penn and J. P., jr., J. Egg, 441. P. Thompson, J. Reynolds, 442. Turnbull, M. & Co., M. Conner, 445. J. Armor, 445. H. Fisch, 447. W. Cole, 449. J. Chesnut, 451. George Eversew, E. Allen, M. O'Brien, R. Heney, 453. John Hazlewood, 453. D. Fogg, J. O'Bryan, R. Crossley, J. Donahue, 463. T. Carmichael, T. Bagley, 464. Removal of J. Reynolds, jailor, 469. Dr. Andrew Ladlie, 471. T. Jennings, M. Shoemaker, J. Dugan, 475. P. Nagle, 475, 476. D. Brunner, 481. J. Berriman, &c., 482. A. Goldsmith, 484. J. Bowman, J. McLaughlin, T. Wigley, E. Emery, 486. J. Garden from several persons respecting Colonel Oswald, 494. Abraham and Levi Doan, J. Baird, 497. John Douglass, H. Winkler, &c., 499. Joseph Banks, M. Dukey, 503. E. Emery, A. Elmor, J. Hyde, Jno. Weikart, 509. Lancaster, Philadelphia, 515. Berks county, A. Shaw, H. Dickey, R. Riffitts, 523. N. L., Philadelphia, 532. J. Eckley, T. Kennedy, P. Juner, 535. Huntingdon, 536. J. Slough, J. Livergood, 539. W. McHenry, A. Barr, J. Hoover, 541. Wm. Barton, Jno. Redman, T. Fowler, 543. Ann Atkinson, Yorktown, J. Match, 549. Montgomery co., 551. J. Glen, Berks county, 558. H. Grim, 561. Hugh Patton, 562. William Hill, 567. T. Shaffer, 581. O. Paul, R. Gibbs, Amos Watson, 587. N. Field, J. Quigley, 606. S. Hulings, W. Alexander, &c., 609. Lancaster co., N. Seitzinger, S. Jenkins, &c., A. Fox, 611. John Hudson, various prisoners in jail referred, Northampton county, 613. R. Gibbs, 614. J. Fureman, Thos. Keys, D. McFarlane, M. Sharp, 617. F. Hudson, 618, 619. L.

Petitions—
Gloss, E. Withington, 641, 643. J. Stackhouse, J. Pursell, 645. S. Jones, &c., 652. William Hay, 654.

Isaac Franks, xvi., 1. E. Glass, 2. J. Jenkins, 5. Jacob Hugely, 6. Brown and Shortall, T. McCormick and T. Jones, W. A. Patterson, 9. Colonel C. Febiger, 10. B. Williams, N. Yanett, 12. William Jones and John Tate, William Price, M. Blair, H. Ream, 19. J. Doran, B. Jacobs, 23. D. Yoder, &c., 30. Wm. Sutherland, 34. G. Everson, Mary Nees, 45. J. McPherson, G. Ingram, 55. J. Miller, 61. Matthias Hollapeter, 62. Joshua Elder, 67. M. Lukens, 69. P. Quinn, 71. F. Renkhart, 73. E. Mooney, 75. G. Burford, B. Morgan, Enoch Supplee, 76. S. Garrigues and E. Pole, Elisha Mills, B. Smith, Pat. Queen, J. McGill, Joseph Rogers, C. Kalkerson, J. Countryman, 79. G. Ingram and wife, J. Schulz, P. Bell, 85. J. Brigs, Ann Woodby, P. Jack and J. Henry, 91. B. Jacobs, J. Stark, University, J. Logue, P. Cleare, 93. Captains McCurdy and Ferguson, 95. T. Kelly, B. Oldwine, 99. J. Ryan, &c., W. Holton, &c., H. Wall, J. Hunous, 104. L. Lesher, A. Cagle, J. P. De Haas, R. Cunard, 107. W. Lloyd, T. Gregory, H. Wells, 111. J. Coburne, A. French, 112, 120. J. Thompson, 116. T. McCarty, Crousillat and Oliver, E. Bayona, G. Benedict, 121. Washington county, 124. P. Shaw, J. Mullen, 132. Judge of Quarter Sessions, 133. J. Whitehill, S. Pauboul, J. Burnside, S. Shannon, 137. Bedford, 143. John Irwin, J. Armstrong, 144. D. Leet, G. Burford, 147. Mary Adams, J. Campbell, 155. G. Ebert, E. Baker, 157. J. Dewberry, Ch. Jones, D. Fennel, 162. Thomas Campbell, 176. R. Wall, S. Burk, 165. A. Keebner, C. Miller, S. Goodman, 167. R. Lollar, 169. W. Long, 170. W. Coats, J. Potts, 179. E. Anthony, H. McDowell, T. Combes, D. Sullivan, 191. T. Wright, 193. B. Vanheer, 195. W. Kintzler, 196. J. Archibald, 200. J. McPherson, A. French, Thomas McCartney, J. Simpson, 211. D. English, 214. Repairs of State House, 215. J. Logan, B. Miller, 211[2]. B. Miller, George Harple, J. Lovely, 213[2]. A. Neilly, F. Wing, Northampton county, 215[2]. Settlers on dry land, 217[2]. S. Shannon, 221[2]. Arthur French, T. McCartney, 211[2]. J. McCoy, Thomas Robinson, J. Faulkner, J. Hamilton, 223[2]. J. Smith, J. Wilson, R. Campbell, M. Jefferies, 225. J. Lockhart, A. Foulke, 231. J. Bowling, S. Shewell, J. Logan, C. Kunius, M. Williams, 233. W. Goggan, D. Morrison, 237. F. Clow, 241. A. Cusick, 254. James Brown, E. Robinson, 259. J. Williams, L. Billew, 260. W. Davis, Thomas McCalvey, 267. P. Emery, W. Nichols, 269. J. Smith, 270. A. Thomas, 273. From Dauphin county, 274. J. Lowry, 277. J. Cesna, 280. C. Tantlinger, J. Plowman, 282. J. Hagey, 284. Clement Biddle, 287. John Wright, J. Moore, E. Williams, Walter Hood, 291. R. Thompson, W. Purdy, 294. John Rankin, 297. M. Reib, J. Bryce, G. Logan, 299. J. Hunter, 301. John McGarvey, M. Stanup, 303. J. Simpson, 305. H. Hoover, A. Moore, 306. William Butler, B. Carr, A. Premier, 309. H. Groom, Sarah Brown and B. Ferguson, 310. Thomas Morgan, J. Thorn, 312. M. Biles, B. Peters, 322. John Weitzle from Carlisle, 328. P. Forepaugh, 329. Favor Mrs. C. Thompson, 341. T. Black, E. Brown, 348. Of Cornplanter and other Indian chiefs, 353. D. Dean, J. Galoway for a pardon (not granted), 363. Samuel Henry, J. Shaw, 365. M. Morgan O'Brien, 367, 393. E. Gorrecht, 367. T. Green, 369. C. Rowand, 371. J. Bowers, 374. J. Robinson, J. Johnson, 379. J. Maxwell, 380. J. Barent, 383. W.

Petitious—
Hudson, J. Austin, 387. J. Smith, Edward Taylor, H. Hewes, 388. R. Paisley, 391. J. Middleton, E. Mullery, 393. Laur. Penington, William Nelson, 395. Chr. Fox, 397. George Isler, 399. Leonard Lesher, M. Bough, 401. J. Dugan, William Henderson, J. McLaughlin, 403. R. and H. Crosser, J. Cloyd, 405. H. Wiley, P. Meyer, J. Shireberger, 411. J. Rudolph, 413. Herpst and Lex, 415. E. Byron, Mary Cunningham, 417. A. Sheridan, P. Roberts, 419. R. Breek, 423. J. Bridges, J. Winnamore, 425. J. Haga, J. Gorgas and P. Martin, E. Eastburn, 427. William Kinsler, 428. J. Berry, J. Ubell, 432. D. Leet, 439. S. Roney, 441. D. Leet, M. Herrin, 448. A. Cunningham, J. Rumble, Wm. Beatty, J. Willisby, 451. B. Kentzler, J. Osburne, 452. T. Thrope, 455. Captain A. Miller, 455. F. Deimling, 457. C. Brandel, 463. T. Gregory, G. D. Molk, William Hobbert, E. Mooney, 479. E. Eyre, S. Finley, D. Dougherty, Thomas Shockney, J. Ryan, 481. J. Burket, D. Bickley, B. Miller, 483. Jas. Thomas, J. Cinle, 489. Robert Campbell, 495. A. Brodie, P. Waugh, 497. T. Wigton, W. Dean, 501. W. Alexander, 510. Jesse Wilson, 512. J. Greenwalt, J. Rock, J. B. Knox, G. Row, D. McCulloch, 519. P. Waugh, 497, 519. Thos. Paul, 522, 530. S. Coates, 522. W. Rosell, R. Peters' claim allowed, 529. J. E. Jones, 534. J. Carmichael, 538. W. Fulton, M. Boggs, 539. Dr. A. Ledlie, 542. P. Woods, 543. J. Brown, &c., 547.

Pettigrew, James, collector of excise, resigns, xv., 581.

Pettit, Charles, letter respecting W. Hartshorne, xi., 117. A. Q. M. General, 709. A. Q. M. General, letter from, with draft, xii., 326, 328, 330. Q. M. G., letter for wagons and clothing order, 246. Delegate Congress, xiv., 549. Sent to New York in relation to accounts with United States, xvi., 387, 411. Letter from, 540. Resolutions in favor of, 545.

Petty, John, from Shamokin, iii., 333, 344.

Pextang, proposed by Indians as a limit of settlement, iii., 274. Indians live near, 501. Petition of inhabitants about Fort Hunter, vii., 724.

Pharaoh, ship, a sickly vessel arrives, iii., 294.

Phelps, Oliver, Address from Indians and Wampum, xvi., 439.

Philadelphia City and County, Sheriffs of, i., 58, 170, 190, 195, 211, 368. Seal for, ordered—its device, 66. Court fined by Council for deciding a case belonging to Bucks county, 76. Bill to double number of members in Council, 98. Prison in, 101. Sub-Treasurers appointed for, 111. Charter for, 117. Division line between Bucks, 126, 130. And Chester county, 126. King James II. proclaimed, 133. A watch to be kept, 144, City lots, 154. Notice to be "set up at the gate," 157. A deputy Coroner appointed, 159. Cage ordered to be built, 92. A man whipped at the market place, 92. Families living in caves to appear before Council, 160, 163, 199, 201. Justices, 162, 176, 182, 320. Ranger appointed, 165, 166. William Frampton petitions to remove caves before his door, 167. Sheriff cannot act as attorney, 170. Council adjourns to Quaker meeting-house, 178, 224, 226. Badness of road from Moyamensing complained of, 189. Paper against amagis trate, 191. Road from, to Falls Delaware, 195. To Plymouth township, 200. Buoys to be erected, 204, 205. Roads in, 205. James Claypoole dies—new member for, 208. Road from Radnor to ferry at—also from Darby to—and shortest from centre of, to the Falls, 209, 251. Claypoole, John, appointed Sheriff, 211. Samuel Richardson member of Council for, 213. Fair at centre of, petitioned for, 218. "Sub-

hiladelphia—scribers of a contemptuous paper" relative to fair at Centre, summoned, 224. Proceedings, 224. Day altered, because it interferes with business of Council, 225. An additional Fair, 226. Coroners, 228. A Bank proposed to be set up by R. Turner and others, 236. Boundary between, and Chester, 263, 265, 266, 267. Wharf at Chestnut street, asked for, 267. Disputed election, account of Welsh votes from Chester county, 268. Road from, to Bucks county, 298. Penn's advice to Council respecting, 316. Asks Council to build him a house in the city upon his lot, 317, 328. Hogs not to run at large, 327. Bridge prayed for, to be built over, and a wharf made against Mulberry street, 330. Indians visit, 340. William Markham refuses to deliver up Seal and Records, 342, 343. Watch to be strengthened, 342. Justices, 343, 371. President to provide a seal for, 344. Governor Fletcher arrives, and is proclaimed, 364. Number of Representatives for, 366. Ferry at Schuylkill, 368. Indians visit to Governor, and conference, 372–3. New laws to be published in market place, 376. Place for a market to be determined, 377, 388. Regulations of markets, 377, 382. After New York custom, 377. Road from Cheltenham to, 379, 384, 387. William Powel interferes with Schuylkill ferry, 380, 381. Presentment by Grand Jury against conduct of negroes in, 380. Want of a water-way between Walnut and Chestnut, along Front, presented by Grand Jury, 381, 382. Appeal of J. Fabricius, pastor of Swedish Church to Council, on account of poverty, 386. Roads to, 396, 389. Place of market fixed—regulations, 391–2. Petition against French traders, 436. Clerk of market complained of, 442, 443, 444. John White, sheriff, dead—rent of jail to be

Philadelphia—paid, 445. Schuylkill ferry belongs to Proprietary, 445. Petition to have Water street thirty feet wide—to be surveyed and cleared, and called King street, 446. Governor signs proclamation for encouraging Proprietor's ferry on Schuylkill, 445, 461. Arrival of Indians, 447. Removal of clerk of market, 461. Amount of revenue from one penny tax, 462. Petition for securing gunpowder, and providing ladders and leather buckets, 478. Against disorders—and tanned leather, 478. A watch to be stationed at Cape Henlopen—alarm of French fleet, 479. Road from Dunk's by Kings' road to, 498. From Benjamin Chambers, or lower ferry on Schuylkill to, 498. Petitions for various roads to, 498, 502. Act for preventing fires, 508. Sale of Richard Keys house authorized, 511. Case of John Crapp, a surgeon, 512. Petition of merchants on fees of Naval Officer, 513. Thomas Curtis appointed clerk of market and corder of wood, 515. Growth of vice in, 528. Ordinaries too numerous, 528. Proclamation against, 530. Petitions of William Southbee and others, 531. New meeting-house on High street. Petition of Quakers for a school for poor children, 531. Charter for, 532. John Bewley appointed Collector of Customs, 534. Matthew Birch, Surveyor and Searcher, 535. Road from lime kiln, 536. Justices of County Court, answer about seized goods, 543. New commission to Governor Markham published at "Market place," 546. Bill for regulating water-courses, 552. Office of Probate of Wills only at, 555. Fair at Centre a nuisance, 555. Levelling streets, 351. Complaints against bakers for size of bread—assize, 576. Tobacco cutters regulated, 576. Person appointed to "go round the town with a small bell in the night time, to give notice of the time

Philadelphia—
of night and weather, &c.," 581. Keepers of Schuylkill ferry not to transport passengers "after day light is shut in," 581. Markets regulated, 582. William Southbee, clerk, 582. Jail to be removed to Third street—how money is to be raised, 583. Property of John Sanders, deceased, to be sold, 584. Firing of guns frightens Indians and women, and children—to be stopped, 586. Roads from, to be cleared of trees, &c., to Falls of Delaware, 587. Road to Pennepac Mills, 587. Griffith Jones' bank lots over against Blue Anchor, 588. Lands estimated by distance from, 600. More tobacco than could be shipped, 610.

Overseers of the poor out of pocket, ii., 9, 10. Complaint about bank lot in Front street "before the Blue Anchor—Henry Elfreth's house stopped, 9, 10, 19, 54. Public landing at Blue Anchor, 54. The reason for settling the city here, 10, D. Lloyd to produce the papers respecting Blue Anchor, 10. Young man killed by negro Jack, 11. Blue Anchor, 12, 14. Strangers to have passes, and to be reported by inn-keepers, 13. S. Carpenter's proposal to settle claims for Blue Anchor landing, 19, 39. Case of witchcraft, 20. Wharf at end of High street broken down and complained of, 23. Commissioners appointed to regulate water courses, 23. Report, 24. Tax for, 25. Sheriffs, 21, 25. Taxes, payment of, refused, 25. Assembly to meet in Whitpain's great front room, 26. Claim of W. Clayton for building cage in, 26. A "Say Master" proposed to attend to packing tobacco, 26. Proposed regulations to prevent coin going to E. Jersey for cattle, 27. Markets, 27. Slaughter houses in city to be forbidden, 27. Petition to Assembly, 37, 39. Privileges asked for, of the proprietary, 38, 39. Pennypot landing confirmed, 39.

Philadelphia—
Governor claims a fourth part of, 42. Shawnese Indians come to take leave of Governor, 16. Petition to remove Burdens of Trade, 53. Charter for, submitted and read, 53. Signed, 61. "Road and broken bridge leading out of the north end of the town," 63, 64, 65. Commissioners appointed, 65. Governor Mill, 64, 65. Taxes not collected—Thomas Farmer and William Tongue collectors, 66. Version of the charter as applied to Justices, 67. Princess Ann of Denmark proclaimed Queen of England, 70. Provincial Court Judges ask how "benefit of clergy" is to be administered, 87. Call of a special Court of General Gaol delivery, 86. Provincial Court—Attorney-General absent—Judges may administer "benefit of clergy," 87. John Bewly, Collector of Customs, 95, 96. Thomas Farmer, High Sheriff, resigns—Jno. Finney appointed, 97. Dedimus to Robert Asheton, 97. Prisoners to be discharged from gaol, 102. Pentecost Teague, Coroner—expenses of a drowned man not paid, 102. Court fees do not pay expenses, 102. Survey on goods, 103. Man to be whipped at the "bell of the city," remitted, 103. Anthony Morris elected Mayor of, and makes promise of fidelity to Queen, 104. Wm. Lee, Coroner, 108. Governor John Evans arrives—proclaimed at "market place," 115. Commission to Council read, 115. "Bull's Head," 134. Indians visit, to trade, 140, 141. Militia duty exempts from watching, &c., 151. Bills to confirm charter proposed, 153. Indian Harry's brother arrives, 155. An Indian chief arrives at, 159. Justices of County Court commissioned, 159. Tax Collector—remonstrance against enlistments, licenses, &c., 161. Answer, 161. Griffith Jones elected Mayor, 162, 163. Great disorders in—proclamation, 162. Coroner, 163. A great fray in the city,

Philadelphia—
Mayor, &c. charged with being concerned in it, 171. Not guilty, 171. Governor and Assembly—difference as to people's right to choose Sheriff, 178. Two candidates, Wright and Budd, nominated, 177. Proclamation of rates of foreign coins, 179. Address of Mayor, complaining that county Justices interfere, 180. Indians arrive, 183. Indian chief Manangy, on Schuylkill, arrives, 191. Tax Collectors, 197. Road to Goshen, 111, 189. Proceedings on act of Mayor, &c., respecting night watches — considered as clashing with Governor's proclamation on militia and exempts, 159, 161, 204, 205. Disputed election of Sheriff, 205. Christ Church vestry to be informed of proposed bill to alienate lands, 222. Petition for rates of money, 222, 223, 224. Sheriff to collect tax, 233. Benj. Wright declines, 233. John Moore, Collector, seizes a Boston vessel for want of certificate, 240. Citizens to give account of what arms they have to Committee appointed by Council, 241. French privateers, 241. Defensive measures proposed, 241. Arrival of Indian chiefs, Conestogoes, Shawnese and Ganawese, 244. Cost of treaty with Conestogoes at, 248. False alarm in, 250. Fortifications spoken of as too costly, and postponed, 250. Powers of magistrates not abridged, 254. Opinions of lawyers on Courts for, 254. A negro slave from Jersey arrested, on suspicion of arson, 275. Right to elect a double number for Sheriff—Jno. Budd and Henry Flower elected, 296, 307. Records to be demanded from Pat. Robinson's widow, 297. John Fenny, Sheriff, 297. Resigns, 298. Elections asked by military, 358. Petition of merchants of, against abuses at New Castle by a fort, 379. Assembly's action on, 380–383. Indians sent for by M. Chartiere, 390. Unseated lots and taxes, 391–2. Peter Evans,

Philadelphia—
Tax Collector, 391. Sheriff, 397, 406. Severe and singular punishment of slaves by way of compromise, 406. Complaint against Sheriff, 406. Petition of Mayor, &c., on tax of 1d. to build bridges and a Court house, 406. Case of action of trover and conversion, 407. Mayor and Recorder appear before Council, relative to levy of taxes for bridges and a court house—city claim right to assess for their own purposes, 407. Petition of Mayor, &c., respecting raising funds for Court house, &c., 410. Address of merchants to Lord Cornbury on French privateers, 411. Captain Charles Gookin arrives as Governor, 427. Mayor to publish proclamation of Colonels Vetch and Nicholson on Canada expedition, 451. General embargo to be laid, 451. Advised to protect against privateers, 451. Inhabitants not to serve on inquests, complain, 455. Complaint against holding several offices at same time, 456. Complaint against T. McMara, a lawyer, 457. Embargo removed, 467. Taxes, 468, 478. Various tribes of Indians at, 469. Swedish minister attacks B. Chambers, 477, 478. James Logan to be committed to jail, 507. Governor's order to Sheriff to protect him, 508. Indians at, 516. Act for regulating property in, 528. Acts, various, relating to, passed and published at the Court house, 529. Indians arrive on way to Canada, 537. Road from opposite Jno. Reading's landing to, record of, 542, 549, 561. Laws, 550. N. Pool's road, 561, 562. Indians in, 565. A suspicious vessel to be seized and examined, 566. Given up, 567. Reputation of flour injured, 568. Corporation to attend Council at publication of laws, 571. Indians arrive, 574. King George proclaimed at market place, 575. Mayor Hill gives a dinner, 575. Justices for the several Courts appointed, 597. Indians arrive, 599, 603, 606, 613.

Philadelphia—
Wm. Keith arrives and is proclaimed at Court house Governor of province, iii., 13. Justices commissioned, 28. Mayor and Recorder commissioned by Governor, 28. Governor Spotswood of Virginia in, 30. Owen Roberts, Sheriff—Enoch Story, Sheriff, 30, 69, 140. Jonathan Dickinson, Mayor, 31. Richard Walker, Coroner, 31, 56, 169. Indian chiefs arrive at, and have a conference, 45. Justices, 50. Petition from inhabitants of Northern Liberties respecting land between, and Whitsahickon mills, there being no road, 50. Suspected pirates cognizable in Mayor's Court, 63. Complaints against vendue master for selling small quantities of shop goods, 91, 102. Indians at, 102. Court of Chancery to be held at, 106. Road to Wiccacoa, 106. Petition of B. Vining respecting, 107. Deferred, 108. Prisoners under sentence of death at, 109. Road to Wiccacoa described and confirmed, 110. Hollander's creek—Hay creek, 111. A convenient road cannot be built between, and Chester, on account of "rocks and mountains," 111. Division from Chester county, 111. Vessels from sickly ports to be examined by Patrick Baird, Surgeon, 112. Sheriffs and Coroners, 108, 140. Registers of, vessels, 115. Difficulty about taxes for want of dividing line between Chester county and—decision of Council about, 144-5, 158. A mill erected at Horsham—road asked for, 158. Indians arrive at, 163. Conference with, 163. Ferry at end of High street, postponed, already sufficient, 166. Wm. Asheton, Recorder, 172. Road to Swede's ford, 225. Wrecked goods arrive from Cape May—proceedings respecting, 238, 239, 240. Ann Mitchell, under sentence of death, pardoned, 240. Petition against location of powder house, referred to four members of Council, 242, 244. Peti-

Philadelphia—
tion of merchants against duty on rum, under proof, 247. Gov. Gordon arrives and is published at Court house, 251. Justices, 257. Robert Asheton invited to this country by proprietary—his long service as Clerk, Prothonotary, Recorder, &c.—his duties and powers as Recorder, 258. Riots and disorderly practices complained of by Governor—pillory and stocks burned down in the "open" market place—proclamation, &c., 260, 261. Owen Owen, Sheriff, and Joshua Fincher, Coroner, 260, 289. Assembly ask Governor to protect them from the "rude people of the city," 260. Indians at, 273. Ferry to Wm. Cooper's and Gloucester—Governor objects to an Act, the power being proprietary, 277. Number of Inspectors of election, 278. King George II. proclaimed, 282. Palatines arrive from Holland, 282. Samuel Preston resigns as Justice, 282. Sickly vessels arrive—health regulations and physicians, 292, 294. Sir Wm. Keith, a member of Assembly from, goes to England, 298. Governor and some of Council leave for Conestogoe, 309. Large meeting of Indians and inhabitants at the great meeting house, 318. Owen Owen, Sheriff, 332. Mench Davis, Coroner, 332. Indians at, 333. Council, 334. Rude treatment to Assembly complained of, 340. Recommendation of Council on, 340. Governor's speech to Assembly on, 342. Proclamation on riots in, 351. Indian conference at, 361. Sheriffs and Coroners, 370. Examination of servants and passengers to be before Mayor of, 375. Wm. Fishburn reported to be robbed, as Treasurer, 387. No roads to Lancaster, 395. To be, 395. Petition of wardens of Christ Church and Keithian meeting house, 394. Act against fire in, 396, 400. Trade with Sugar Islands, 401. Indian conference in, 404. Sheriffs, 416, 464, 520, 574. Coroners, 416, 464, 520, 574. In-

Philadelphia—
dians at, 425. Bridge over Cobb's creek, 426, 428, 431. Small-pox prevails, 426, 428. Thomas Penn arrives and is congratulated, 433. Conference with Indians at, 435. Indians attacked with small-pox die at, though no person beside was known to have it, 463. Justices commissioned, 491. Buoys, 493. Indians arrive at, 500. Road from Lancaster laid out, 521. Justices, 531. Evil effects and number of tippling places in, 534. Road from Bucks county, 542. Proprietor complains of Romish chapel or mass-house erected in Walnut street, and declares that religion contrary to the laws of England, 546, 563. Petition for a new road to Wiccacoa, 547. John Penn, eldest proprietary, arrives, 569. Death of Governor's lady mentioned, 574, 577. Conference with Indians at, 571. Road in Northern Liberties to be reviewed, stone bridge, &c., 573. Alms-house and provision for the poor, 589, 590. Road to Macousie, 591. Address from Mayor to Council on claim of Maryland to the territories, 594. Conestoga and Susquehanna Indians arrive at, 598, 608; and conference, 608. Sheriffs, 614. Coroner, 614. Return of road from Maquenusic to, 617. Petition respecting Court of Chancery, history of, &c., 617.

Act proposed for providing for safe-keeping of public records in, iv., 11, 17, 21, 35, 483. Evans, Register Gen'l of Probate of Wills, 33. State House vested in trustees, 46, 483. Petition against Court of Chancery, 35. Execution of two men, 47. Indian conference in Philadelphia, 53. Trial of criminals in jail, 71. Indian conference at, 79–85. Sheriffs elected, 85, 247, 309, 352, 469, 500, 600, 669, 748, 782. Coroners elected, 85, 247, 309, 352, 469, 500, 601, 669, 782. Unusual number of Indians in, much disordered with liquor—public order against supplying it, 86, 87. Treaty and purchase of lands from Indians, and

Philadelphia—
speeches, 65–95. Charles Read, clerk of Orphans' Court, dies—Thomas Hopkinson is appointed, 151. Insolence of negroes in, 244. Road from Lancaster to, 247, 495, 503. Proclamations ordered to be printed in, for Maryland, 254. Road from John Harris's to, 278. Governor Thomas arrives and enters on his duties, 288. Proclamation to be made, 289. Cost of flag to be raised on Governor's arrival from Antigua, 304. Reports of Dr. Græme on sickly vessels, 306. Indians at, 307, 312, 337. Petition from Mayor, &c., to Governor to raise money on citizens, 376–379. Edward Roberts is Mayor, 379. Bill for raising money, 384, 385. Governor's message on, 385. Objects to it, 386. Pilots to be restrained from taking vessels up without license, 394. Proclamation against Spain read at Town-house, rejoicings, &c., 396. Assembly's reasons on bill for raising money from, 408. Governor's answer to, 409. A man wounded by an Indian, sent to and placed under care of Dr. Græme, 413. Messages to and from Governor and Assembly on money bill, 414–420. Council with Indians in Quaker meeting-house, 432, 443–447. Justices, 482. Acts for vesting State House in trustees confirmed, 483. Petition for roads, 495, 503. Resolution respecting Drs. Græme and Zachary as health officers, 496. Dispute between Assembly and Council as to appointment, 497-8. Cayuga Indians arrive, 500. Pest house — discussion about, and health office, &c., 507–559. Indians of Six Nations arrive and hold conference about lands, &c., 559–583. Names of Indians present, 583–586. Famine and great distress among Senecas, 564. Sick passengers arrive and are landed at, 568. Council at, 569–586. Election riots in, 620–624. Indians at, 742. French privateers capture vessels, 749. Indians to be tried by Supreme Court at, 751,

Philadelphia—
752. Division of County with Lancaster proposed, 756. Robert Strettell, Mayor, 762. Indians from Shamokin arrive, 767.

Poor-house and overseers, v., 30, 32. Sheriffs elected, 55, 120, 411, 464, 561, 597, 662. Coroners elected, 55, 120, 411, 464, 597, 662. Road from Bristol laid out and confirmed, 59, 60, 61. Petition of N. Craft against, rejected, 61. Council Chamber to be in State House, 69. A French flag of truce arrives with prisoners and free negroes, 71, 74. Another flag of truce arrives, 77. Proclamation respecting flags of truce and pilots to be read at Court House, 82. Spaniards design stealing a boat in harbor, 92. Road to New Castle, 105, 121, 130. Captain Huston recruits for Colonel Shirley's regiment, 105. Vessel from Barbadoes, with yellow fever, arrives —ordered below, 104. Justices elected, 106, 110. Orders of President to Captain Cox to remove his vessel from, 106. Road to New Castle, order respecting, 107. Complaint against Captain Cox's ship, 107. Proclamation against, 109. Drs. Græme and Bond to visit her, 109. Arrival of palatines, 113. Spanish prisoners suffering in jail, 121. Pieces of eight counterfeited by Jones and Barnes, 119, 141. Indians from Ohio arrive, 145. Conference with, 146–151. Petition from merchants to Assembly to put the city, &c., in a state of defence—a man-of-war, &c.—association formed, &c., 158. Letter to proprietaries on defenceless state of, 160. Batteries formed, 161. Declaration of Council to, 168. Alarming state of affairs, from sickness, war, &c., 168. Proclamation for a fast day, 169. Attack from enemies expected, 169. Loan of cannon requested from Governors Clinton and Shirley, till those from England should arrive, 173; and cruizers off capes, 174. Associators form companies and elect officers, 174. A list of them, 193.

Philadelphia—
Answers of Governors Clinton and Shirley, 189, 198. Commander of Cape Breton written to for cannon, 203. Governor Clinton, 205. Governor Shirley, 206. Ad. Knowles, 207. For men-of-war, 207. Officers commissioned, 209, 247. Governor Clinton furnishes cannon, 215, 216. Prisoners require provisions, 232. Their arrival not approved of, 237. Prisoners to keep house after sunset, 238. Otter, man-of-war, John Ballet, commander, arrives, 239. T. Penn promises cannon when batteries are erected and militia law passed, 240. Captain Ballet meets Council, 241. Entertained at Roberts' coffee-house, 243. T. Penn on sickness about the dock, 244. Capture of Captain Geo. Porteus, 245, Council sits every morning at City Court-house, 246. Committee to consult with Captain Ballet, 246. Batteries erected—Colonel Taylor commands, 249. Disappointment in procuring Trembleur privateer, resolutions adopted by Council, 250. Commission to Colonel Taylor, 251. Alarms from privateers —embargo, &c., 245–260. Captain Jones elected Colonel, 256. Express sent to Lewes T., 257. Proceedings to fit out a privateer at, 258, 260. Fears of Captain Randolph's ship at New Castle, 260. Various depositions, 260–264. Captain Randolph's ship ordered up by Captain Ballet—protest, &c., 264. Intelligence-boat commissioned, 266. Captain Sibbald to command batteries, 267. Artillery company formed, 267. Powder house—order respecting watch, &c., 268. Block-house at battery, 269. Recruits to be raised, 269. Embargo removed, 274. Road to New Castle, 303. Letter to proprietaries respecting, 320. Officers appointed, 325. Proclamation of treaty at Aix la Chapelle, &c., published at Court-house, 362. Gov. James Hamilton arrives, and commission published, 362. Proclamation of peace published, 381. Justices

Philadelphia—
appointed, 388. Indians arrive and have conference, 388. Proclamation against selling rum to Indians in the city, 397. Indians arrive, 398. Bills for regulating nightly watch, lighting streets, and raising money, 502, 505, 506, 512, 514, 619; and accidents by fire, 505, 514, 619. Hospital for sick poor and lunatics proposed, 513, 516, 526, 619. A French vessel puts in, in distress, and is allowed to refit, 528. Nanticoke Indians arrive from Wyomen, 543. Justices appointed, 572. John Penn, eldest son of Richard, arrives and becomes member of Council, 606. Law respecting fires, 619. New county out of, 619. Two Shawnese sick in, 704. Distances, &c., from, to Ohio, 759.

Governor Hamilton resigns, and Robert Hunter Morris' commission is read at Court-house, vi., 144. Sheriffs elected, 144, 638. Coroners elected, 144, 638. Sickness prevails from palatine ships —Mr. Bourne, health officer—Council doubt their power to visit ships, 169. Full reports of Drs. Bond and Græme, 171–173; and also on contagious fevers in city, 173–175. Report of palatines buried, 175. History of contagious fevers in, 173–190. Indian conferences at, 193–199, 204–206, 243, 244, 277–286. An open road from, to mouth of Conogochege, 302. General Shirley's son recruiting in Philadelphia, 303. General Shirley and Governor De Lancey arrive, on way to Annapolis, 358. Indian conferences at, 360–365, 370. Embargo, 451. Permission to certain vessels to sail, 451. Colonel Dunbar desires winter quarters for his troops after Braddock's defeat, 513. Governor to Mayor, &c., on winter quarters for Col. Dunbar's troops, 516, 521, 533. Indians arrive and have conference, 522–524. Governor informs Mayor, &c., of French being secreted in city, 663. Account of arms taken, 665. Indian conference at, 682–689.

Philadelphia—
Letter of Governor calling for help against Indians, 710. French neutrals, 711. Proceedings respecting, 713, 729. Large delegations from Chester and Berks coming to compel passage of certain laws, 729. Remonstrance of Mayor, &c., to Assembly, on militia bill and means of defence, 734, 766. Artillery company, and officers in, 770. Soldiers arrive from New York, 773–775.

Companies formed and officers elected, vii., 36, 40. French neutrals, 15, 32, 44, 55, 58, 390. Indian conference, 46–55, 64, 137, 144. Battery company, 62. Company officers, their names, 62. Magistrates appointed, 62. Nightly watch, 63, 72, 90, 177, 184, 246, 390, 392. Address of Quakers to Governor on declaration of war with Delaware Indians, 84. War proclaimed at Court-house, 88. Suspension of, 144. M. Bell applies to export provisions, 168. William Denny proclaimed Governor at Court-house, 221. Stageboat and wagon between, and New York, 222. Fines diverted from corporation, 257. Small-pox at, 309, 358. Address of Quakers to, and answer, 312. Number of public houses—quarters required for military, 349, 352, 356, 359, 400, 406, 407, 430, 443. Colonel Bouquet, Earl Loudoun, Col. Stanwix, through Captain Tulliken, demand quarters for soldiers—proceedings of Mayor Shute and others respecting them, 359, 367, 406, 443. Various proceedings respecting, 360–374. Mayor and aldermen remonstrate against Assembly, 366. Merchants petition to ship provisions—rejected, 393. Justices, 433. Indians arrive, 436. Number of Roman Catholics in, 448. Minutes of meeting of Governors at, with Earl of Loudoun, 470. Clerks of Orphans' Court, 501. Passport for Indians from Lancaster to, 549. Complaint of treaty made by Quakers at, 634. Chas. Thomson, keeper of Quaker

Philadelphia—
school, 665. List of Philadelphia shipwrights taken at Oswego, 717, 737. Proposal to send troops from, to New York, 719. Names of chiefs at, 726. Petition of Richard Hill and S. Preston Moore to make title to certain lands in, 728, 739, 740. Petition of shipwrights from Oswego, 737. Governor produces certificate of Robert Jenny, Rector of Christ Church, of having taken sacrament, 741. Justices of peace, 769.

Conference with Indians at, viii., 9, 29, 40, 51, 54, 86, 101, 114, 149, 265, 484–494, 667, 698, 707, 709, 712. Tonnage duty objected to, as injurious to business of, 31, 41. Names of Indians in, 31. Conference with, 32, 86. Embargo at, 38. Abraham Taylor, collector, 39. Fort at Wiccacoa to prevent passage of vessels, 39. Guards to be reinforced from General Otway's regiment, 39. Two good horses to be at, 71. Tax on unimproved lots in, 80. Teedyuscung in, 86. Flag of truce arrives with prisoners from New Orleans, 124. Indians arrive from Virginia, 124. Message received by Peters and Pemberton from Cherokees to Delawares, 135. A French flag of truce captured by privateer Spry in Delaware Bay, 139. Embargo, 146. Fort at Wiccacoa to be guarded, and cannon charged, to prevent evasion of embargo, 147. Barracks at, 147. Spanish vessel arrives with goods wrecked on an English vessel near Cuba, 155. Embarrassm't about Dutch vessels and registers, 155. Arrival of Cherokees, Mohawks, Scarroyda's wife and children ask for guns and horses, 163. Coroners appointed, 223, 403, 506, 781. Sheriffs appointed, 223, 403, 506, 781. Petition of merchants against duty on tonnage, 230, 232. Thanksgiving day appointed, 235. Difficulty about soldiers' quarters at, 262. Indian conference with General Forbes at, 263–269, 270. French neutrals at, in distress, 268, 719. General Amherst in, 324. Barracks of, described, 331. College, Academy and Charity School, condition and statistics of, 339. Act for suppressing lotteries and plays proposed, and instances in which they have been useful, 340. Lottery for fortification of, 340; and for finishing the Episcopal church, 340. Order to James Coultas, sheriff, to imprison Rev. Dr. Wm. Smith, 443. Act passed for keeping banks, dams, &c., at Point-no-Point, in order, 480; and at Greenwich Island, 482, 484. Conference with Indians at, 489–494, 497–500. Execution of Jas. Bruleman, 506. Proceedings on death of King George II., 515–520. Sale and purchase of lands for Oxford Church, 574. For keeping banks, &c., in order—merchants' memorial against, 574. Piers in Delaware, 574. Banks at Darby creek to be made, &c., 575. Justices commissioned, 575. Old ones superseded, 575. Petition of merchants against duty on negroes, 576. Vaughan's regiment to be moved from New York to Philadelphia, 578. Conference at, 594, 614–620, 654–661, 667. Women attacked and wounded in streets of, 671. Proclamation against, 672. Act proposed for vesting State House in trustees, 676, 715. Act proposed erecting District of Southwark, 695, 698. Roads and highways, 694, 695. War with Spain proclaimed, 698, 703, 706. Embargo laid, 713. Arrest of Messrs. Boyrie and Le Roy, 714. Trustees of State House to purchase rest of the square, 715.

Record of Court for trial of negroes in, ix., 5. Indian conferences at, 6–9, 44, 77, 328, 604, 689, 737. Proclamation of peace between France and Spain, 15, 39, 41. Nuisances to be removed—highways, &c., to be regulated, and wagoners, &c., 22, 24. Marsh and meadows, 24. Tavern licenses, 24. Petition, Spanish ship in distress at; J. Gibson appointed factor, 26. Thanksgiving

Philadelphia—
day, 41. Christ Church bells rung and cannons fired for peace between France and Spain, 41. Watching and lighting, 54, 243, 247, 543, 723. Lighthouse, buoys, lottery for paving streets, &c., 56, 580. Sheriffs elected, 57, 199, 286, 333, 398, 547, 623, 688, 777. Coroners elected, 57, 199, 286, 333, 398, 547, 688, 777. Governor's proclamation against highway robbery about, 70, 76, 316. Governor John Penn proclaimed, bells rung and battery guns fired, &c., 72. Proclamation of Governor Penn for highway robbery and murder of Henry Hamilton, 76. Paxton boys preparing to march to, 108. Highlanders, under Captain Robinson, in, 110. Troops from Genl. Gage, 129. Attack on barracks expected, meeting called at State House, 132. Memorial of Indians in barracks at, 135. On their removal, 137. An interior county, 138. Indians to be removed from barracks, 170. Or retained at public expense, 171. Justices, 205, 237. Provincial Commissioners, 237. Letter from, 240. Lotteries for various purposes, 56, 57, 148, 243, 579. Embanking and draining a lot in Kinsessing, 245, 247. New election ordered for member of Assembly, on account of tie vote, 287. Seven Wardens appointed, for bill regulating pilots, their names, 293, 294. Lighting, watching, pilotage, &c., 294, 366, 549, 723. Poor, 295, 296, 549, 561. Relating to Stamp Act, 298, 299, 300, 301, 315. Arrival of stamped papers, 300. John Hughes, Captain James Hawker, General Gage, 301. Quakers, peaceable conduct of, 301. Address to King, 315. Highway robbery near—Governor's proclamation, 316, 396. General Gage asks quarters for troops—Highland regiment, returns of, 318. Message to Assembly respecting, 323. Manufacture of sail-cloth, ticking and linens in, 354. Regulation of streets, &c., 361. Memorial of Wardens on pilotage, &c., 366, 388. Names of Wardens, 366, 367, 549. Of merchants, 366. Moyamensing meadows, 367, 368, 376. John Allen, Justice, 374. Conviction and reprieve, 387, 399. Executions, 398. Poor Indians arrive from Wyalusing, 426, 436. Complaint of Billy Champion, 426. Philadelphia Contribution apply for a charter, 440, 447. Lottery asked for by Northern Liberties to buy a public landing, 440, 447, 472, 638. Building middle house, W, of barracks, 461, 472, 688. Division of county, 556, 563, 579, 707, 729. Act passed for sale of a church in, 566, 579. Ship-masters' Society incorporated, 566. Recorder to receive Germantown records, 575. Lottery for First and Third Presbyterian church, 580. Petition respecting road and steep hills between, and Chester, 623, 627. Lower Dublin, road, 628. Forges and furnaces in 1750, 632, 636. Stephen Paschall's account of his steel furnace in Walnut street, 633. Certificates respecting, 634. Act for erection of Callowhill street market, 650. Newalika, Indian chief, arrives, 656. Road from Lancaster to, 657, 667, 681, 686, 693. Executions and pardon, 666, 697, 734. Justices, 671. Notary Public to take acknowledgment of deeds, 678. Road in Passyunk, 686. Return of road to Lancaster, 700. Road on dividing line, 703. In Passyunk—regulators for Northern Liberties, 719. Wardens and pilots, 723. Defence of, 729. Lighting and watching, 730. Road on line between, and Bucks, 745, 750, 760. Justices, 750, 760. Conference with several Indian tribes at, 773–775. Conviction and reprieve, 778. Richard Penn, Governor, arrives, 780. Road through widow Master's land, 781. Governor proclaimed at Court house, 782. His proclamation for continuing officers, 783.
John Swift, Collector of Port,

Philadelphia—
x., 8. Notaries and Tabellion Public, 9, 15. Sheriffs elected, 56, 100, 212, 270. Coroners elected, 56, 78, 100, 212, 270. Justices commissioned, 15, 30, 31, 45, 46, 156. Indian conferences at, 10, 12, 55, 61, 255. Barracks, condition of, complaint of Captain Sutherland, 16, 21, 415. Chimney sweepers, 23, 41. Perkiomen copper mine, 23. Damage from dogs, 33. Estate of J. Pauling, 35. Convictions and executions, 50, 60, 89, 92, 172, 256. Alleged errors in road from, to Lancaster, and petition, 65, 69, 70, 113. Wardens, 70, 72, 259, 261, 263. Vendues, 72, 74. Roads, 73, 87. New jail, 73. Old road laid out sixty years through Master's land, 87. A murder confessed, 88. Governor John Penn proclaimed, 92. A French vessel arrives in distress, 92, 102. Judah Foulke, clerk of market and keeper of weights and measures, 111. Report on road to Lancaster, 113. Act to prevent infectious diseases, 139. A grant and authority to Governor John Penn to build fortifications, 146. Meeting of Committee of all the counties—delegates to General Congress, 200. Complaint against Sheriff for not aiding in seizing a quantity of sugars in Jeremiah Warder's store, 210. John Patterson, Collector of Port, 213. Goods stolen from vessel—proclamation of, 213. Against murderer of Edward Carey, 228. Sheriff, &c. of Chester refuse to aid in seizure of a vessel in river, 230. Work house, &c., 237, 243. Act to suppress fairs in, 254. Indians arrive, 255. Counterfeiter escapes, 257. Proclamation for his arrest, 258. Reed's map, 260, 267. Petition of Captain Dominique Du Casse, of schooner Mary, in distress, 262. Guards for military stores &c. at State House, 287. Guard at new jail on account of powder, 296. Memorial to Committee of Safety, 297. Only five hundred weight of lead in city, 300. Three ministerial officers arrive from Cork—Captain Bradford to conduct them to Smith's tavern, 302. Committee to inspect goods from Cork, 313. Watch at the Capes, 359. Barracks to be repaired, 389. Defence of city, 390. Committee to procure logs for third tier of chevaux-de-frize, 390. Captain Thomas Proctor's company admitted to barracks, 390, Committee furnish powder, 407. Survey of river from Marcus Hook to, 412. Coal to be taken out of river, 421. Racks for arms in State House, 422. Coal thrown into, 423. Inquiry as to quantity of coal in city, 423. Return of, 425. Part of new gaol ready to receive prisoners—they are removed from old, 429. Or work-house, 429. The armed boats ordered up to, 434. Continental troops in, 438. Resolutions respecting, 440. D. Connolly, Allen Cameron and servants committed, send resolutions of Congress, 444. Guards at State house, 445. Parole of N. Ellicott and Lord Drummond, 445. Soldiers to be placed in pest-house and gaol, if barracks will not contain them, 485. Called on for blankets, 498, 508. Riot in gaol—military called out to quell it—guards for powder house, State House, and fire rafts, 512. City battalions, 521. Six rooms in new gaol with iron doors, 534. Fitting out two privateers, 536. Saltpetre made at Provincial works, 543. Notices to be put up at coffee house, to inhabitants to furnish leaden window weights, &c., 558. Iron clock weights to be cast and exchanged for leaden, 561. Stage boats, Captains Bush and Taylor, between, and Wilmington, 563. Conduct of gaoler—survey of river from Billingsport to Fort Island, 567. Company of volunteers for defence of river, 569, 570. Lead, shot—list of necessaries—complain against Committee of Assembly, 573. Survey of river, 575. Gaol to be strength-

Philadelphia—
ened by bars, &c.—prisoners from North Carolina committed—guard for, 581. Colonel Atlee to order his battalion from Chester, 605. Firelocks purchased in Dock Ward, 606. George Bryan, naval officer, pilots for chevaux-de-frize, distribution of powder to boats by Committee—report of Committee of Assembly on conduct of this Committee to be published in newspapers—appointment of J. Hazelwood as Captain of fire vessels, &c.—flying camp, 611. Troops to be ready, 627. Guard removed from old powder house to new magazine, 627. Gondola building, 627. Troops ordered to and from Billingsport, 627. Col. Miles to order most speedy march of battalions to, also Col. Atlee, 628. Awnings and coarse linens to be bought up for tents—officers memorial for a patrol for safety of city—resolutions respecting, 630. Ladies appealed to for old linen for bandages, &c.—Robert Eastburn employed to collect it, 633. Awnings for tents, 633, 641. Declaration of Independence to be read at State house under direction of Sheriff, 635. Prisoners discharged, 639. Prisoners sent to York—boring mill near, 641. British officers—prisoners to leave city—provision for families of poor associators, 646. Leaden weights required, 649. Guard ordered, 649. Stage at State House for guard—Council of Safety sit, 653. Committee on complaints of families of associators, 671. Troops to be quartered in places of worship—elders to have notice, 672. Marching of associators inconvenient to public service, 673. William Sutton and James McConnaughy confined as tories—soldeirs quartered in private houses—families of poor associators provided for—battalion of Colonel Paschall to be passed by Muster Master, though short of officers, 677. Sash weights, 681. Orders respecting guards for city, 691. Barracks, 698. Commissary's quarters, Fifth near Market, 698. Riots in, L. Fagan stabbed, 701. Reward, 701. Urgent order for troops in city to depart for Amboy, 706. Guard at State House, 709, 710. House for an hospital to be taken—Dr. Gerardus Clarkson, physician, 719. Fortifications at Billingsport—blankets, purchase of, 719. Guards over frigates, 720. George Bryan, naval officer, 728. Militia to be employed at Billingsport—Dr. Currie resigns as Surgeon, 734. L. Nicola, barrack master, 736. Guard for city, 747, 750. Invasion of General Howe feared, 747. Arms to be distributed—Hessians from Long Island expected—complaint of Captain Sharp Delaney, 753.

Fleet to rendezvous at, xi., 1. Alarm from transports expected, 3. Cannon hauled from State house to commons to be proved, 5. Sick soldiers placed in bettering house, 13. Not to receive share of salt having been before supplied, 16. Blankets and stockings collected from, 18, 20. Poor women &c. of army, to be cared for, 20. Public stores to be moved, 21. Salt for, 22. No vessel suffered to leave port or through chevaux-de-frize—money for families of Associators—guard for salt vessels, 23. Records, &c., to be removed to Lancaster, 23. Colonel Jno. Bayard commands battalion of militia of—Redman and Hodge, Surgeons, 24. Field pieces from State house yard for assistance to General Washington, 24. Barracks repaired, 24. Troops sent in shallops, with oars, to Trenton, 24. Vessels already cleared may pass, 25. No person to pass ferries with arms—L. Nicola, Town Major—his duty—citizens unfit to march to form a guard—volunteers to be raised—shops and schools to be shut up—Associates to form a brigade under Colonel John Cadwalader, 27. Ferryman on Delaware to bring over Maryland flying camp, 29. Council offer to reward those who

Philadelphia—
form a troop of horse—John Schaffer, Paymaster—commendation of shopkeepers, 20. Watchmen not to be enlisted—records sent to Reading, 31. To detain printers of continental money—names—Colonels appointed—old ferry, 31. Medicines stored in college hall, 35. Provision for sick soldiers, 35. River craft allowed to pass, 36. Opening of the port, 36. Schools opened, 38. To impress carriage and horses from Messrs. Pemberton and Emlen—stores open—books and treasury removed to Lancaster, 41. Carpenters' work at State house—Wardens to employ patrols—horses impressed—six men to inquire into causes of commitment of William Smith and Joseph Stanbury, &c., 43. Continental stores to be removed, 44. Dunlap's printing press taken into service of Council of Safety—General Washington asks for aid to General Putnam in throwing up works of defence, 46, Stores opened, 51. Men compelled to join militia—guard for floating bridge at Schuylkill, 56. Men to apply to General Putnam for orders, 58. Census of persons fit to bear arms taken, 60. Old arms to be collected and repaired, 61. Wood for poor to be cut on commons and in lanes, 70. Cannon to be collected, 83. Troops to be paraded before the lodge—regulations, 85. Barracks, 86. Public smith's shops to be erected at corner of Chestnut and Fifth, 145. Small pox hospital in Vine street and in Pine street, 154. Hospital opposite to sign of "Noah's Ark," 158. Samuel Morris appointed Register, 186. Master of Rolls for State, 187. George Campbell, Prothonotary, 190. Justices—dedimus to James Young, 194. State of old jail, 194. Lieutenant, 194. Clerk of market, 195. Prothonotary, 197. Fred. Phile, naval officer, 198. Jacob Plankinhorn appointed flour inspector, 201. Wm. Dewees resigns as Sheriff, 201. Gaol to be

Philadelphia—
repaired, 205. Sheriff elect declines—James Claypoole applies for the office, 217. Plan for removing citizens—state of militia required, 218. Wm. Henry appointed Lieutenant and E. Bonham and W. Semple sub-Lieutenants—dedimus, 218. Militia to be arranged and in readiness, 219. Judges of City Court appointed, 220. Neither wagons nor drums to be permitted to enter the State house yard, as they disturb Council, Congress, and Assembly, 229. July 4 celebrated—measures to prevent a riot, 237. Application by James Hopkins by order from General Washington, for a vessel to go down the river on an expedition—supplied at General Arnold's request, 237. Wm. Sykes arrested for moving goods contrary to order, 234, 237, 238. Advertisement for election of Justices, 238. Committee for driving off cattle ask to be increased—names, 244. Justices, 251. Ordnance in State House yard, 252. General Wayne and General Nash present situation of the army approaching city, 253. To furnish men for guards, 256. Public papers to be removed when in danger, 258. Committee to drive off cattle increased, 266. Wood for barracks 269. Colonel Henry, Lieutenant, to complete and send off, militia to Chester and Downingstown, 275. J. B. Smith, Prothonotary of county, to bring papers to city, 276. Col. Henry to deliver spare arms to General Armstrong, 277. Officers object to removal of troops, 278. Leaden spouts to be taken down—houses searched for arms—disaffected persons to be arrested, 279, 283, 284. Persons appointed to make arrests—Col. Nicola to furnish guards—arrests and committal to prison, 287. Free Mason's lodge, 290. Prisoners to be sent to Virginia, 290. Mason's lodge, remonstrance from, 292. Boats and other water crafts, except shallops, to be detained, 297.

Philadelphia—
Great number of prisoners in new gaol, 298. Guard at Schuylkill bridge to remove it when ordered, 298. None to pass without pass properly signed—light horse to proceed to camp—proclamation on approach of enemy—militia called out—horses not to be procured to guard prisoners, 299. Shops and stores to be shut—armies now engaged, 301. Cols. Toomb and McElwaine to rendezvous in, 301. Bucks county troops in barracks to send guards to protect artillery at Gray's ferry, &c., 302. Col. Charles Stewart to seize all the hard bread he can find in, 303. Bells to be removed from—John Haley, Clerk of Orphans' Court, complains of not being able to receive the papers from James Humphreys, late clerk, 306. Militia called out, 359. Repair of Court House for use of Assembly and Council, 362. Paymaster, 390. Resolution of Congress on proposed attack on, 404. And act for supply of armies, 404. Col. John Moore and Peter Evans commissioned to buy provisions in, 424. Provisions brought from Chester county, 445. Sheriffs elected, 502, 512, 595. Coroners, 502, 595. Commissioners, 502. Enemy preparing to leave, 507. News of evacuation of, reaches Gen. Washington, 520. Making up of clothing removed from Lancaster, 521. First meeting at, after evacuation, 522. Celebration of 4th July—inquiry of Gen. Arnold, why he has ordered the shops to be shut, 522. His answer and papers—warrant against all traitors in, 523. Markets to be repaired after destruction by enemy–butchers, &c., to be agreed with—Act for regulating prices of goods suspended—discharge of persons from parole—enemy's goods found in the city—enemy's goods found in, after evacuation, in hands of Heyman Levy, 525. Markets placed by Assembly in charge of Council—Joseph Redman, clerk, to have them well

Philadelphia—
cleansed, &c., 526. Necessity of opening Courts of Justice—J. B. Smith appointed Prothonotary and Justice of Common Pleas—galley from Trenton to be repaired, Rev. Thomas Coombe, Jr., refuses to take oath—pass for him to leave State, 527. Petition respecting enemy's property found after evacuation—armed boats afloat—brig to be fitted out, 529. Records brought from Reading—Court room in State House to be repaired—trees on lines near the city to be cut down and given to the poor—Council room ready except chairs—ordered, 535. Bridge at Schuylkill to be restorad to its place by Major Casdrop—Commissioners of Taxes and Levies, 536. Wardens of, appointed—rations of Town Major, value of—guard boats to watch cruisers in Delaware bay—resolutions of Congress in case of evacuation, 539. Health officer and advisers, 543. Wharfinger and weighmaster of hay at drawbridge appointed—vessel sunk in Delaware, embargo on provisions, 545. Measurer of wheat and other corn and salt appointed—Clerk of Court Quarter Sessions, 546, 547. Wardens in want of money to pay city debts–reception of French minister, 548–9. Repairs to State house, 564. Lumber taken by enemy, 566. Edward Burd, Prothonotary Supreme Court, 566. Robert Jewell, keeper of United States prison in, 566. Militia called out, 568, 581. Guard for prisoners from Lancaster to, 573. Old work house to be used for casting ball and room in State House for magazine of small arms, 590. Pass for Mrs. Margaret De Lancey to visit and remain with her father, William Allen, 593. Joseph Reed, Councillor, 595. General Armstrong ordered to, and take commands of militia—militia of counties to be ready, 597. Justices, 599, 619, 644, 656, 658. Measurer of grain, Bedford, removed, Capt. W. Greenway ap-

Philadelphia—
pointed, 697. Militia as guards, 617. Lime—State House, 620. Militia ordered out, 636. Wood for L. Nicola, 637. Forestallers, petition against, 639. Inquiry, 640. Execution, 641. Newspapers subscribed for by State, 654. Repairs of State House—guard at middle ferry-against keeping gunpowder in, 657. Work at market house, 659. Pay for guard—salt seized—petition of Matthew Irwin, Andrew Hodge and John Bayard, for broken cannon from frigate Augusta, 661. Rent of ferry on Schuylkill—riot of sailors, Justices to aid in quelling—Maj.-General Arnold to furnish troops—election—ferry not rented to Ogden—notice to be given that proposals will be received, 665. Bridge over middle ferry, 666. Court of Quarter Sessions before trial of persons for treason—committee of merchants ask for a vessel to protect bay and river Delaware from British vessels, 683. State of prison and prisoners to be inquired into, 684. Hilary Baker, Jr., appointed Notary and Tabellion Public—General Arnold leaves while inquiry is going on respecting wagons to Egg Harbor, 684, 685. Schuylkill upper bridge partly carried away-middle bridge secured—severe season, 686. Gallies disposed of—officers discharged—forestallers, 687. Forestalling, 690. Report on prison, 695. Merchants against privateers, 702. Charge against United States for use of public buildings, except State House, 705. Major-General Armstrong in, 707. T. Hare's porter brewery—Schuylkill bridge expensive, 711. Timber taken from redoubts to make buoys, 715. Arnold resigns command of—Colonel Bull to repair Fort Island, cable and bridge, 725. Plumstead's wharf, 748. Acts on sale by vendues, openly violated, to be published, 751. Prisoners discharged, 753. Execution of George Hardy, 754. P. De Haven agent for forfeited estates, 754. Books missing from State Library, 755. Two brass field pieces and writing paper from Lancaster, 754. Plank and timber stolen by enemy at redoubts near, 756. Embargo for fifteen days, 761. Wm. Rush, Justice—seamen disappear—river to be swept for anchors—arms arrive from West Indies, 771. P. De Haven appointed health officer, 775. Prisoners shipped. 781. Merchants petition Congress respecting a Court of Appeals, 783.

Stores transported from, to frontiers, xii., 2. L. Nicola, town major, 10. A tobacconist finding no asles here applies to go to Boston, 11. Petition to remove wagon duty, 15. Agent for prisoners sent to, 23. Charter of Academy and College to be sent Council by John Morris, Recorder of Deeds—James Claypoole, Sheriff—costs in cases of Roberts and Carlisle and Geo. Hardy, 36. Willing Morris's wharf, 38. Sheriffs, 38, 131, 507. Coroners, 131, 507. Justices, 150, 379. Settees for Court room made by John Pinkerton, 40. Irregularities and rules of markets in, 41. Markets in, 41. Commencement at college deferred till constitutional difficulties are removed, 43. Door-keepers of Council and Congress have same pay and privilege of State House yard, 49. Boards for Court room, 56. Two men join British army in, 57. Plan of citizens for restoring public credit, 65. Approved by Councils, 67. Sheets of paper money distributed—militia to be practiced and receive ammunition, 72. Letter from Justices relative to nuisances in markets, 80. Scarcity of salt, to be distributed, 87. German congregation for a brief, 92. Resolutions of Council respecting militia, guards, &c., 95. House and lot of Arthur Thomas, money for, 104, 149. President's house, 106. Marshal hindered by merchants, 105. Joseph Redman, clerk of market, dies—Robert Smith, hatter, appointed in his

Philadelphia—
place—prisoners in new gaol, 110, 112. Boards for Court room, 112. Riot at Hon. James Wilson's 121. Proclamation respecting, 122. Bounty for wood offered—it and flour scarce, 125. Embargo laid, proclamation, 126. Militia called out—Wm. Moore elected to Council and George Bryan, Charles W. Peale, Michael Shubert, William Hollingshead and Jacob Schreiner to Assembly, 129. Joseph Reed elected Councillor—Ass'bly, 131. Persons present at riot at James Wilson's house, 128, 130, 137, 138, 139, 141, 144, 145. Artillery called out, 143. Declaration of President and Vice President, J. Reed and Wm. Moore, 164. Order of procession to proclaim, 165. Read at Court house—salt, 166. A charitable society ask to cut wood from land on Lancaster road for the poor and to pay to treasurer, 170. Managers of House of Employment, loan of flour granted to, 172. Deed for house and price at south-west corner Front and Walnut, 174. Abuses in wood on wharves, 175, 190. Military store in Race street, 177. Vendue master (Wm. Brown) elected—deed for Shoemaker's property, 185. Auctioneer gives bond, 186. Francis Bailey, printer, 186. Wardens of, order respecting wood—forestalling in markets—taxes, 190, 191. Commissioners and Assessors meet Council—amount of tax, 193. Broken cannon to be sold—Schuylkill bridge, condition—tolls—to be valued—David Thompson's estate, deed for, 195, 196. Newspapers ordered by Council to be called for, 197. House of Robert White and wife to be searched for counterfeit money, merchandise, &c.—sale of Richard Swanwick's property, 199. Sub-Lieutenants apply for bounties, 200. Deeds for confiscated estates in, 201, 202. Schuylkill bridge and ferry, boats and ropes for, till season proper for replacing bridge, 202. Letters to W. Turnbull, P. McClenachan,

Philadelphia—
L. Hollingsworth and Capt. Allibone, on probability of procuring supplies in, 203. Answers to, complaints against irregularities, &c. at the barracks—escheated property of P. McDade near China factory, &c., 204. Schuylkill bridge replaced, 205. Barracks, Committee to inquire about, 206. Wood west of Schuylkill to be cut down for poor, 207. Abuses of—state of barracks reported by Committee—persons employed there, 208, 209, 211. Wood taken, Schuylkill ferry, 212. Fines collected by clerk of Sessions and Sheriff, 215. Committee to fix salaries of officers retained—return of galley men—express expense—militia, special pay—quarters for troops in public houses—Schott and Armand's corps, 217. Peter Swope, turnkey of gaol, allows prisoners to escape, 222. President's house, 236, 238. A scold sentenced to be ducked—pardoned, 235, 243. Deed to C. W. Peale, for lots late of John Smith forfeited, 247. Continental money refused in payment of ground rent on forfeited estate, 249. Deeds for forfeited estates, 259, 260, 553. Insecure state of gaol—guard ordered to, from Court house, 259. President's house in danger from fire at Mr. Holker's—taxes difficult to be collected, arising from misconstruction of an Act, 260, 261. Memorial of Commissioner of taxes, 263. Referred to Assembly, 264. Deed S. Shoemaker's estate, 265. Schuylkill bridge carried away by ice, to be restored by B. Eyre, 266. Schuylkill bridge, under Quarter Master-General—continental teams to pass free—rates of toll, 269. Damages to houses of Edward Barrett in Southwark, by Flying camp, 271. Scarcity of powder, 279. Deeds for confiscated estate in, 283, 284. Against enclosing lands heretofore open, or commons, 286. Petition respecting Schuylkill bridge and road to Darby, 293. Ex-

Philadelphia—
penses of and support—death of Mr. Forbes, M. C.—sales of broken cannon, 296. Wm. Henry appointed Lieutenant and Ephraim Bonham and Frederick Hagner subs., and various other officers, 297, 298. Edward Evan's claim for city lots rejected—deed to Jacob Morgan, Jr., in Northern Liberties, 298, 299. Joseph Galloway's property sold—Andrew Doz elected Commissioner of purchases for, 299. And Col. Jno. Bull for county—Captain Topham applies for the brick yard in Northern Liberties, 311. Property of Samuel Bell and Mrs. Parrock to be restored—rent of middle ferry paid, 315. Deed for George Enser's estate, 317. Expense of replacing middle ferry bridge, 317, 321. A seditious paper posted at corners, proclamation against, 319. Deed for Peter Arthur's estate, 320. Library company not permitted to receive books from New York, 318. Estate of Alexander Bartram and John Roberts, 323. Peter Campbell's, 324. Wm. Young, apprentice of Benjamin Town, arrested for seditious paper, 325. Arms to Col. Henry, 330. Alarm from a small boat, Captain Buck, 331. Two wards neglect to elect Lieutenants, Council appoint, 338. Pay to militia to Trenton—resolutions for sale of forfeited estates, reference to W. Penn's reservation of commons, now vested in State—fences to be removed, 347. R. Wells and lot on Arch street, 353. Committee of merchants appointed to confer with Council relative to difficulties in currency, 353. Expense of examining and valuing Schuylkill bridge, 374. Alexander Mills arrested and discharged, on charge of discouraging enlistments, 378, 379. Taxes in Dock Ward, 382. Sale of estate John Bartlett, 383. Rent of bridge, 385. Inspector of militia, 388, 389. Expense of bridge, 391. Sheriff to arrest Jemima Forrester or Biles, wife of

Philadelphia—
a refugee, 397. Lots near Race street wharf required for public landing—sales postponed, 402. Life of a collector of militia fine threatened, 402. Port opened for clearing vessels—case of John Dover, 402, 404, 407. Taxes—Sheriff to arrest Mrs. Bartram, Mrs. Stark, Mrs. Volans and Mrs. Preston, wives of traitors, 425. Deed S. Shoemaker's estate to P. and J. Wikoff and G. Hutchinson, 430. Recruits for Pennsylvania line—bounties—deserters from—subscription for recruits, 431. Arrears to militia—John Nancarrow's air furnace—Lieutenant Brady recommended for promotion, 435. Alexander Bartram's estate, J. Galloway's, 441. Deed, 457, 458. Memorial James Mease, &c., to purchase a vessel in Bermuda, not granted, 465. Petition of merchants against Marshal—President's house—auction sale, 479. Of merchants against Marshal, 480, 482. Inspector of salt provisions, 487. Shingling old workhouse, 520. Complaints against Lieutenants, 523. Three auctioneers appointed, John Bayard, Alexander Boyd and Wm. Brown, 525. Joseph Reed proclaimed at Court house president, and Wm. Moore, vice president, 541. Order of procession, 542. S. Shoemaker's estate—George Knapper's estate sold, 553. Wm. Crispin, Collector of Excise, 554. John Jones, health officer, inspector of staves, &c., 554. Col. Miles to have wood on Lancaster road cut, 559. Suspicious vessel at Warder's wharf, 562. Petition of Capt. John Davis, committee on, 563. Fine of a constable remitted, 563. Petition of H. Smith and W. Wood, respecting fencing "Mark's" liberty land—pay of militia, 564. Auctioneer, 569. Estate of Wm. Austin assigned to University, 584. Vessels may clear, 602. Merchants, &c., complain of ill-treatment to sailors at New York, 603. Quarters for officers of Pennsylvania line, 605.

Philadelphia—
Naval officer, 608. Scale of depreciation published—repairs to barracks—sale of S. Shoemaker's estate—militia called out, 612, 613. S. Shoemaker's, 615. John Henderson's estate, George Benners, 619. Pay of soldiers, 620. Bounty on recruits, 622. Repairs of barracks, 632. Discharge of militia—barracks to be preserved, Petition Catherine Graff for brick yard, 639. Prohibition against occupying vacant lands in—pay to Philadelphia troop, 641. Repair of barracks, 649. Pay of militia—public stores on Race street wharf—road from Darby to, 650. Jno. Parrock's estate sold, 661. Estate of Henry Welfling, 669. State house steeple to be taken down and repaired, 682. Lt. Poht resigns, 684. Repairs of barracks, 685. Abraham Carlisle's estate sold to Robert Bethell, 687. Property of floating bridge on Schuylkill to be vested in George Gray, on his paying a certain sum to the State, 690. Thos. Neville to purchase materials for repairs of State house steeple and blocks, tackles, &c., 702, 703, 712, 720. Lower rooms of State house fitted for land office, 712. Two companies for defence of forts to be raised, 719. Sales of lots in—road to Darby confirmed and opened, 726. Petition of H. Shrupp, to be paid for a horse—of naval officer, vessel without papers, 728. Executions of criminals—Thos. Wilkinson, a pirate, ordered to be hung on Windmill Isl'd, and his body in chains at Mud Island — deed estate William Rhodden, 730, 731. Pirate respited for twenty-one days, 732. Taxes, 735. Deed estate Samuel Shoemaker, 737. Andrew Elliott's estate sold, 746. Estate of Joseph Galloway, next to Presbyterian meeting house, north by alley formerly called Appletree Alley, between Third and Fourth, 751. Estate of John Parrock, 752, 755. Lot of Thomas Seny, 759. Sales of city lots, 772. Es-

Philadelphia—
tate of Jno. Fox, 775. Excess of militia offering—estate of Richard Wall, 776. Claim by Richard Peters for lots in, 779. Sale of lots at coffee house, 780. Deed for estate of Isaac Allen, 781. Of John Parrock, 782. Repairs of State house, 783.

Inhabitants of Charleston arrive in distress, and are provided for, xiii., 1. Sales of Episcopal and Presbyterian Church lots postponed, 3. Importation of British base half pence, proclamation respecting, 4. Estate of Abraham Carlisle sold to R. Bethel—City lot claimed by Evans and Linnington as part of W. Salway, 6. Claims of Moore, Hill and Wells, for lots and Liberty lands, 9. Deeds, 12, 20, 25, 26, 30. Condition of prisoners in gaol, health, of S. R. Fisher, discharged, 13. Repairs of State house, 16. Claim of Thomas Lightfoot for lots, 18. Papers in hands of Samuel Powell, Mayor, to be delivered in, 19. City lots, 23. Deed for Duché's lot to Thomas McKean, 25. Deeds to B. Leech, 30, 31. To be located for James Parr, William Gray, 31. Lots for Pyke Land Co., 33. City lots for redemption of bills of credit, 35. Lutheran congregation purchase lots of Mr. Penn, 1777, he refused receiving the money then, 36. Militia to be called out, 37. City lots, 39, 40. Appraisement of leaden spouts, 42. Sales of liquor by vendue to, made up, 42. Hospital for wounded applied for by Rochambeau, 42. Deeds for city lots, 45, 46, 47, 49. Petition of Moore, Hill, and Wells for city lots—embargo raised—repairs of State House steeple, 49. Militia called out, 53. Deeds for city lots, 63, 65. Clothing from Yorktown, 77. Sale of city lots, 80, 81. General election in, 85, 391, 393, 721. Sheriffs, 85, 391, 721. Wardens, 721. Coroners, 85, 391, 721. Censors, 721. Colonel Tilghman, aid of General Washington, ar-

Philadelphia—
rives with news of surrender of Lord Cornwallis at Yorktown, orders of Council for rejoicings, 94, 96. Estate of Wm. Evans sold, 97. Pay to militia guards, 98. State House steeple, 98. Militia called into service, 98. Light house in danger — New Board of Wardens chosen, 100. Thos. Coombe, late collector, to deliver books and papers to wardens, 104. Claim of John Shergold, &c., for a lot, 115. Deeds for lots, 118, 119. Unfair election, 118, 120, 127. Report of Surveyor General on city lot claimed by Joseph Egg, 123. Deeds for city lots—Barracks, 128. Lot of Samul Fox, 130. Sheriff to permit certain persons to embark for France, 135. Tho's Forrest claims two lots, 136. Plan of city lots, sale postponed, 139. Lot of Samuel Allen and Thomas Sison, 140. John Parrock, Richard York, &c., S. Farlan, 141. Christ Church bells rung for capture of Cornwallis, 143. John Lukens, Surveyor General, paid for plans of city lots—deed to Patrick Robertson, 146, 148. Difficulty on election of a councilman, 148, 154, 160, 161. Deeds for city lots, 159. Auctioneer, 163. John Connelly, a British officer, to be arrested and examined — violates parol, and is imprisoned, 161. Reported value of lots, 164. Deeds for city lots—pay to militia, 166. Claim of James Wallace for a city lot, 167. Committee to view house and lot late of M. Aspden—deeds for several lots, 171, 172. Claim for city lot — deed for land, 175. Guard house near Magazine wants repairs, 178. President and Judge of City Court —deed, 180, 181. L. Nicola dismissed with thanks as Town Major—deed for lots, 185. Report on election of Councillor for, 188—192, 193, 194, 195, 197, 198, 200, 201, 206, 210, 211, 212, 216, 217, 220, 220, 223, 232. Deeds, 193. Estate of Daniel Jeanes,

Philadelphia—
204. Report on value of M. Aspden's lot, 209. Deeds for City lots, 217. Deed for City lots to Wardens 218. To J. Mease, 235, 236. City lots, 240, 246. Estate Samuel Shoemaker, 246. Pay to J. Loughead, paymaster, 248. City lots, 250. George Campbell appointed Register of Wills, 253. Committee to estimate leaden spouts taken, 268. Deeds, 271, 274. Claim N. Young, for City lots purchased from William Penn, 275. Expense of erecting fence between President's house and Mr. Morris', 279. Seizure of sugars on a Sloop of L. Hollingsworth, 282, 283. Ship General Washington, (late Monk,) hired for a voyage, 283. Interest on purchase money for City lots, when not paid duly, 285. Pay for an entertainment, 289. Guard for prisoners—Repairs of light-house at Cape Henlopen, 293. Report of Surveyor General for City lots, 295. State of accounts of individuals called before Council—Cost of entertainment on birth of Dauphin, 288, 297. Deeds for City lots, 305, 306, 307, 308, 315, 316, 317, 321, 322. Report of Surveyor General on claim of Moore, Hill and Wells, Daniel Pastorius and Thomas Fairman, 322. T. Forrest, B. Davis, 323. Deed, 325, 326. Proceedings on claims to lots, 326, 328, 330, 331. Deeds, 334. Deeds for City lots, 340. Deed for City lots, 344, 346. Men called out, 364. Deeds for City lots—Jews ask for countenance and protection in erecting Synagogue, 367. General Potter to command troops on Indian expedition—National Bank of North America—Absconding Merchant, 371. Execution, 382. Complaint on calling out Militia on election day—Commissioners for defence ask for a vessel of small draft—Papers of James Molesworth, 385. Surveyor General paid for plans of lots—Deeds, 389. James Irvine, Councillor—

Philadelphia—
other elections---Deeds-- Pardon, 395. Deeds, 409. Expense of fitting Comptroller General's office, 417. President and Vice-President proclaimed at Court-house—procession, &c., 413, 417. Joseph Dolby receives pay for ringing Christ Church bells, 423. Deeds for City lots, 432. Repairs of government house, 441. Commissioners on taxes, 453. Becoming a place of much resort--Police, 489. Goods per Amazon—Arrears of payments for city lots, 491. Claim to city lots, 495, 497, 500, 503, 505, 507. Pay to seven months' men, 503. Deeds for city lots, 505, 506, 507, 543, 552, 572, 578, 587, 604, 617, 623, 629. Claims of heirs of John Whitpain, 506. Moore and Wells, 509. Robberies, 515. Paid G. Owen, for winding up State-house clock, 536. Memorial Jacob Shallus for a lot, 548, 549. William Henry asks opinion respecting certain duties, 541. Merchants ask advice respecting importation of British goods, 553. Proclamation of peace—Christ Church bells to be rung, 559, 563. British prisoners allowed to pass through, 572. Repairs of State-house pumps, 575. Deeds—Health officer, 578. Deed, 585. Thomas Turner, keeper of State Flag, 586. Prisoners to new gaol, 589. William Greenway, Measurer of Salt—Price, 593. Price of Salt fixed—Wardens to have obstructions removed, 595. Paving Fifth Street, between Walnut and Chestnut Streets, 602. Congress complain of being insulted at, 606, 607, 609. Field officers convened by Council, 609. Conference with officers—Attack on Bank meditated—Arms to be delivered to Militia, 611, 612. Arrests ordered, 613. Examination of soldiers to be made—Cannon taken at Yorktown to be delivered, 614. Proclamation against M. and A. Doan, A. Dillon, &c.—Complaints to be heard against Captain Esler's appointment, 617. Report to

Philadelphia—
Congress on disturbances, &c., 618. Justice, 625. Complaint of Southwark of danger to health from Brig Congress—Vessel to be removed, and sick to pest-house, 627. Murder in, 629. City lot confirmed to J. Shallus, 631. Again referred to Land office, 636. Congress propose to return to—Wardens to have surveys of the Delaware made, 637. Report of Land office, 639. Deed, 646. State-house to be laid out by Act of Assembly as a public green and walk forever, 692. Bed-covers for sick at State Island, 695. Execution, 704, 720. Election—Censors—Representatives, Wardens, 721. Sheriffs—Coroners—Commissioners, 722. Joseph Cowperthwaite contests election of Sheriff, 720. William Brann murdered at Centre Square—Inquest and proclamation and description—Deeds for lots, 728. President and Vice-President proclaimed, 738. Thanksgiving-demonstration on account of peace, 752. Petitions D. Lennox, &c., to be auctioneers, 753. List of deeds, &c., of late corporation, transmitted by order of Assembly to Council, 759, 760. Vendues, 761. Deeds, 767.

Taxes, xiv., 4. Regulations of wagons, &c., 17. Deeds for City lots, 34, 35, 65. A. St. Clair, John Mease, appointed Vendue Masters, 38. Inspectors of goods Justices, 47, 54. Report on goods to be sold by auction, 48. Sharp Delany appointed Collector of Port—Names of purchasers of City lots to be furnished, 52. F. A. Muhlenburg, Justice—letter from Merchants—Accounts of John Hazelwood—Commissioners of purchases in—Griffith Owen, keeper of State-house clock, discharged, 55. Murder of Richard Marple, 57. Chevaux de frize—City lots sold,—Report on,—Virginia boundary, 59. H. Schitz resigns as justice, 60. Inspectors of goods, 61, 67, 68. Sales of goods by auction, 70.

Philadelphia—
Fruit trees to be planted with Health office funds, at discretion of Dr. James Hutchinson—Goods per Ship Minerva to be inspected, 71. Proposals for removing Chevaux de frize, 73, 75, 78. Complaint against Constables, 75. Hillegas and Francis to lay out lots at Barracks—Inspection of goods—Remission of forfeitures on Brandy—Militia fines and expenses, 77. Chevaux de frize, agreement with Donaldson & Hollingsworth. —— Appropriation for River Delaware, 105. Memorial of Merchants for inspection of goods, 106. Justices—Irregular elections, 108. Dedimus potestatem, issues for City and County of, 110. Triumphal arch, the carpenters' work valued by a committee of persons—Sales of goods by Wardens, 111. Robbery in Southwark, and arrest of persons—Proclamation, 112. Inspection of goods, 114, 115. Insult to Monsieur Marbois, Consul General of France, by Longschamps, 115, 116, 117, 120, 121, 135, 137. Justices, 116, 121, 135, 149, 151, 159, 197. Buoys removed from Delaware—Proclamation, 122. Claim of John Balderston for a lot, 138. Memorial against a bridge on Germantown Road, 140. J. B. Smith, prothonotary, 143. Deeds for lots —Wardens expenditures on River —J. Donaldson resigns—Joseph Bullock appointed, 151. Expense of removing exhibition frame from Market to State House, 157. Persons in gaol—Return of arms, &c.—Inquest on George Fitler, 159. Payment to Wardens, 162. Leaden spouts taken in 1777, paid for, 174. Deed for lots—Bells rung on LaFayette's arrival in, 176. Commissioners ask for sale of old iron from jail—Council refuse, 179. Jonathan Penrose, justice, 197. Repairs to State Mansion-house, 206. Deed, 209. Removal of Chevaux-de-frize, 212. Repairs of State House, 235. Elections,

Philadelphia—
229, 555. Representatives, 229, 555. Sheriff's, 230, 555. Coroner's, 230, 555. Warden's, 230, 555. Declaration of election of President and Vice-President, 249. Procession, 250. Proclaimed at Court House, 251, 252. Repairs in Secretary's office, 268. Box to be delivered to Marbois free of duty, 283. Sale of old jail—Purchase of part of Statehouse lot, corners of Fifth St. and Sixth Street, for public buildings, 284, 285. Repairs of Statehouse, 285. Improvement of State house lot, 286. Ground rent paid by Council on lot corner Sixth and Market to Wm. Altmore, 289. Contested election of Justice, 291, 307 323, 325, 344. Cl'k of city, Lieut., 314, 640. Claims for city lots under old rights from Wm. Penn, 323, 326, 327, 343. State lottery drawing, 324. Memorial of merchants on piers in the Del're, 326. Population 1760 and 1770—exports 1773, 1784, 336. James Loughead, Justice, 344. Report on city lot in favor of John Lownes, 347. Memorial of merchants on piers, &c., 356. Old jail and workhouse to be pulled down—city lots for Richard Wells and Henry Hill, devisees of Richard Bacon–Patrick Haley arrested and reward to be paid, 359. Right of Pennocks to city lot, 361. Right to city lot referred to Surveyor-General, 362. All military and other stores to be removed to a place of safety, on account of destruction of old jail, 366. Wm. Whitebread offers to pay his bond and mortgage given to late Mayor, &c., 368. Improvement of State house lot—letter to merchants and traders, 369. Contested election of Justice for New Market Ward, 370. 377, 380, 381. Justices, 370. Old jail, 409. Repairs of State house, 375. Matthew Irwin, Recorder of Deeds, 378, 379. Gen. St. Clair, Auctioneer, 394. Repairs of State house and clock, 395. House to cover cannon, 401.

Philadelphia—
Thos. Paine paid—Dr. Ewing and Thos. Hutchins to run N. W. line, 402. Offices of Collector, Naval Officer and Wardens—improvement of State house lot, 406, 444. Report of Comptroller-General on sums due military officers, 406-440. Deputy-Surveyors in each county—a tent for Captain Porter, 441. Deputy-Surveyor, 441, 443. James Read appointed flour inspector, 444, 445. Register of German passengers, 445, 447. Improvement of State House lot, 446. L. Farmer appointed Register of Germans, 447. Election in Penn Township, 447. City lots to Francis Gurney and G. Westcoat, 453. Montgomery county formed from, 456. Claim Thos. Mason—Wells, Hill and Young, referred to Mr. Story, 458. Money to Wardens, to enable Thomas Davis to erect piers—order for erecting an arsenal first on 8th and Locust &c., ordered on "corner of public square, between Thirteenth and Juniper Alley"—deeds, 457, 459, 460, 461. Wardens to contract for land at Marcus Hook for piers—navigation above city—jurisdiction of islands, 460. Edward Bartholomew, Collector of Excise, 461. City lots — deeds, 462. Richard Hill's devisees—plan of piers, 464. New proposals for piers-improvements of State house lot—E. Blaine claims a lot, 469. China factory, 479. Agreement with Thomas Conarroe for building piers at Marcus Hook, 479. Call on Commissioners to report, improvement of State house lot, 483. A Spanish frigate at, 484. Deed for city lot to John Franklin, 486. Inspectors of lumber, salt provisions—Robert Morris appeals to Supreme Court from Comptroller-General's decision respecting his accounts—deed for barrack lots, 489. Mons. Marbois, vice French Consul at—proceedings relative to old gaols and buildings in Montgomery county, 491. Rent of store on Market street

Philadelphia—
wharf, 492. Repairing State house and building arsenal, 495. Deed, 501. Edward Shippen appointed Justice for Dock Ward—Plunket Fleeson resigns as president of Court—Edward Shippen appointed in his place—improvement of State house lot, 549. Three stone steps for State house paid for, 550. B. Franklin, Councillor, 554. Geo. Gray, Commissioner, 555. Arrival of Sick Keesar and thirty-five others from Bengal and China to seek a passage home, 561. John Biddle, measurer of grain, 568. Clement Biddle, Notary—Mercantile Committee, 571. Memor'l of Longschamps—of inhabitants against test law—debate and resolution on the law, 573, 574. Aid to the Chinese, 574. Petition in favor of M. Aspden—Purchase of a lot at Cape May by Wardens, 578. Repairs of State house, 581. Deeds for old jail and adjoining lots—consideration and names of purchasers—grant of room in State house to Surveyor-General for an office, 583. Improvement of State house yard, execution of Elizabeth Wilson ordered, 586, 588. Petition of Longschamps, 587. Arsenal, 588. Agreement with James Pearson to cover State house with copper, 597. Petition Wm. Smith to construct a wharf—jurisdiction of Delaware river, 598, 599. Deed for barrack lots—State house lot, 601. Deed city lots, 605. Leaden spouts, 618. Respecting M. Aspden—instructions respecting barrack lots, 625. State house lot, 626. Edward Burd, Prothonotary of Supreme Court, petition for Justice, 629. Justices, 629. Deeds barrack lots, 632. Delinquents for barrack lots, 634. Negroes ask to enclose their burying ground, referred to Surveyor-General, 637. Deeds for barrack lots, 638. Abuse of public property in Southwark by militia—appropriation for improving river Delaware, 641. Schuylkill bridge by Davis and Casdrop—abuse of

Philadelphia—
public property in Southwark, 643. Deeds city lots, 649. Barracks and city lots, 650. Thos. Davis, wharf builder-deed city lot, 653. John Baynton, Collector of tonnage—State house clock, 654. Wm. Craig, Justice of High street Ward, 660. State house improvement—Clerk of Orphans' Courts, W. Nicolls, 667. Justice Nice resigns, 672.

Health officer, xv., 3. City lots, 3. Improvement of State house, 4. Notice of the public sale of Joseph Galloway's property, Sixth and Market streets, 6, 15, 37. Repairs of State house, 10. Justices, 8, 17, 23, 26, 160, 256. 367, 422, 452, 520, 522, 541, 606. Deeds for city lots, 13, 35, 37, 46. Barrack lots to be sold, 18, 20. City lots to be sold, 23. Plan be furnished by Surveyor-General, 28. State house improvement, 30. John Cowan, execution not now issued, 31. J. Kelly's ears not be cut off, 33 City lots, 46. Auctioneers-deed for barrack lots, 50. C. Febiger, auctioneer for Northern Liberties, 53. State house, 57. City lots between Fifth and Seventh, in Market, to be sold (from Schuylkill, 58. Pay for ringing Christ Church bells, 60. Claim of proprietaries for city lots, 63, 68. Leaden spouts, pay for, 66. Pay to agent on sale of barrack lots, 69. Report of Attorney-General on claim to city lot, 71. Support of light house, &c., 73. Sale of city lots, Chinese to be sent to Maryland, 75. Materials for houses at barracks, 76. Improvement of State house lot, 77. Sales of lot postponed, 85. City lots to be sold, 87. Repairs of State house—Earl of Shelburne claims city lots, Notaries Public appointed, 87. State house, 90, 103. Elections, 98. Wardens, 98, 559, 562. Representatives, 98. Councillors, 567. Street Commissioners, 98. Sheriffs, 98, 328, 567, 579. Coroners, 98, 328, 567, 574. Commissioners, 98. State house repairs, 99,

Philadelphia—
115. Militia, 109. Proclamation and procession on election of President and Vice President, 111. Bells rung, 121. Demand on New York for a horse thief, 125 Claims for city lots to be considered, 134. Favor of J. Robinson, claim of R. Peters & C. Hurst, 136. Deed to Robert Morris, corner Sixth and Market, and price—city lots ordered to be sold, 151. Alexander Todd, Justice—sale of lot postponed, 160. Jno. Mease, auctioneer, Matthew Irwin, Master of Rolls, 166. Convicts to be punished with eight inch sheds, 169. R. McKnight, Justice of Dock Ward, 171. State house, 172. Clock, 174. Sundry lots to be sold—flour inspector, 172. Plan for Court house adopted, 174. Deeds barrack lots, 180. 181. Auctioneer's accounts of St. Clair, 183. J. Mease, auctioneer, 186. Notices distributed respecting city lots, 188. Sheriff to postpone sale of flour, 191. Peter Wikoff, auctioneer, in place of General St. Clair—Wardens to improve Delaware river, 197. Claim for city lots by R. Howe and J. Elliott, 201. Execution of a criminal postponed—claim for taking care of State lot by Wm. Rees rejected, 202. Barracks for invalids--officers of light infantry, fines suspended, &c.—removal of stores from, 1777, 265. Claim by Miers Fisher, attorney for city lots, &c., 207. Militia, 209. Mons. De Brassines delivered up to Mons. Marbois, French Consul, 215. Jonas Philips charged with usury, dismissed, 217. State house yard, 220. Sale of merchandize for duties, 225. Piers at Marcus Hook—presents to Choctaw and Chickasaw Indians in, 229. Deeds to John Nicholson for city lot, 230. Gunpowder delivered to Col. Mifflin to celebrate 4th July, 235. And to Wm. Will—officers of militia complain of an election, referred to Wm. Henry—appeal of executors of Caleb Newbold, 237. Claim for

Philadelphia—
city lot—report of contested election for Mayor—another election, 241, 242. Agents of forfeited estates, 246. Indians detained at Lancaster by sickness of interpreter, 251. Plan of forty-two city lots on Lombard street reported by Comptroller, to be sold, 255. Deed for barrack lot, 256. Robert McKnight, Justice, 272. Lot on Lombard street, between Tenth and Twelfth, appropriated, on request of Wardens, as a burying ground for strangers—"Act April 8, 1786," for directing sale of such city lots as remain the property of the State and for disposing of the house and lots in High street, late the property of Joseph Galloway and forfeited, 273. Minutes of convention met in, transmitted by Congress, 286. Report of plan of city lots south side Market and west side of Tenth for sale, 301. New members—elections—invalid guard, 303. Procession President and Vice President Franklin and Muhlenberg, 308. Execution of Jacob Dryer ordered, 311. Collector, Naval Officer and Clerk of Court appointed, 315. Murder of a Spaniard in, Coroner's inquisition and proclamation to arrest rioters—Dr. Rush, &c. called on conduct of Mr. Jones, health officer, 317. Proclamation against rioters at house of Maj. Alexander Boyd, also against murderer of a Spaniard at house of Margaret Bailey, 319. John Jones elected health officer—plan of forty city lots to be sold—Jacob Dryer pardoned, 320. New order of Council, conduct of officers, 321. Election of officers, John Baynton, Collector of Tonnage, Abm. Hubley, Auctioneer, Christian Febiger, Auctioneer, and other officers, 322. Wardens appointed—C. Biddle, Marshal—M. Sadler has use of old sashes, 323. Jona. B. Smith, Prothonotary of Court C. Pleas, 325. Council attend speaking in Zion church, 340. Duties refunded on package received by mistake—all the public

Philadelphia—
arms to be collected and repaired, 343. Swedish Consul complains of rude behavior of two constables, &c., 348. Plan of city lots to be sold—State house, 349. Order of procession on adopting Federal Constitution, 350. Joseph Perkins to repair arms, 357. E. Pole, Notary, 358. Guard at State house, 365. Newspapers published in, taken by Council, expense of, to be curtailed, 366. Invalid corps on duty at State house, 367. Sheriff ordered to set up Francis Wade's house at a limit for the Commonwealth—city Lieutenant to deliver to Jno. Nicholson arms belonging to Col. F. Gurney's battalion—petition of merchants respecting goods sold to, and insolvent in, Delaware, asking not be charged duties on their return—German newspaper by Melchior Steiner in, ordered by Council, 375. Suspected vessel seized by naval officer—soldiers granted him to enforce laws—powder purchased for celebration of ratification of Constitution, 377. Notices for enclosing city lots—reports of Board of property on sundry claims under Wm. Penn — conference asked with Judges, 379, 383. Robert Leslie proposes an alteration in the hammer of State house clock, granted, 380, 387. Report on certain claims to city lots—warrants to issue in favor of Tench Francis and George Glentworth, 383. Sale of Wade's house referred to Attorney-General—arms for repair placed in hands of Samuel Coutty and Samuel Lehman, gunsmiths—John Franklin's irons to be removed — merchants ask a postponement of suits on bonds, 385, 387. Title of Joseph Egg for city lot, 391. Numerous claims for city lots by grant from W. Penn, 399. Sharp Delaney to contract for house for public offices, 402. Claims of sundry persons for city lots, 413. State house clock, 414. J. Baynton dies—Samuel Caldwell appointed

Philadelphia—
Collector of tonnage duties, 417. Repair of arms, 421, 422. Papers relating to claim of Chas. Cecil, in hands of Mord. Lewis, called for, 423, 424. Jacob Weaver, Justice--claim for lots, 424, 425, 429. Major John Nice of 2d battalion of militia resigns--Collector to furnish account of moneys due on imposts—magazine for powder so full as not to receive a quantity arrived, it is placed in "guard house" adjoining, 433, 434. Deed for barrack lot—Collector, 434. Warrant to R. Peters for liberty land—Capt. William Paulus removes, vacancy to be supplied by election, 436. Capt. Ziegler to have room in house of employment for soldiers, 437, 438. Claims for city lots, 438, 439. Thanks of artillery officers, 438. Claims for city lots, 440, 441. Sundry claims for, 442. Militia, 443. Lieutenant asks for powder and cartridges, order for--opinion asked of Judges respecting storage of more powder, 447. Expenses for State house yard for 1787, 449. Disputed military election, 454. Carriages for artillery cannon, 455, 457. Deeds for city lots—claim of Charles Cecil, 459. Repairs of arms, 465, 468. Deed barrack lot, 472. Claims for city lots, 477, 478, 479, 480, 481, 485, 520, 524. Federal ship Union placed in State house yard, 487. Care to be taken to prevent escape of John Franklin, 490. Petitions of Abraham and Levi Doan, now in jail under sentence of death, 497, 501. Execution ordered, 505. Petition favor of Doans—respite, 515. A free negro afraid of Doans, released, 515. Complaints against British Consul, 517, 520. Repairs of artillery, 517. Caveat of Davis Bevan set aside and patent to issue to Mary Meredith for city lots—D. Humphreys for printing—repairs of arms—Wardens for rent of offices, 518, 519. Hessian fly, answer of Agricultural Society to—Notaries

Philadelphia—
appointed—report on Jones' lane, 527. Petition Northern Liberties for certain city lots, 532, 533. Militia expenses—John Franklin, conference respecting, 533. Powder for militia—J. Franklin ill in prison—expense of nurse allowed, city lots corner Green and Third to Wm. Sheaff, and price, 537, 538. Report on roads and streets laid out in Southwark, &c., 539, 547, 554. Board of Wardens established and members appointed —Samuel Caldwell, Collector, 559. Deed for city lot to W. Sheaff—entry of teas, 562. Contested election for Sheriff, between Wm. Will and James Ash, 567, 568, 569, 570, 571, 572, 573, 575, 576, 577, 578, 579. Triumphal arch made by Gunning Bedford—John Leacock, Coroner, 574. James Ash declared Sheriff, 579. Election frauds complained of and enquired into—State house roof, &c., to be examined–lottery—gunpowder to celebrate election of President and Vice President, 580. Procession — President, Thomas Mifflin, George Ross, Vice President—survey of lands for Episcopal Academy, 585. Infested with robbers—disorderly and wicked persons—resolutions against—report against vice and immorality, 589. Christ Church bells rung—pilots, 597. Powder magazine, 599. Inquiry into manner of conducting jail, 602. Contested election, 612. Robert Lesley's memorial respecting G. Owen and State house clock–election fraud, report on, 619. Regulation of Southwark—health officer, 627, 628. Postpone choice of health officer, petitioners may withdraw, 629. Memorial of merchants relative to flour shipped to Havana – Capt. McLean unable to command the corps of invalids, Col. L. Nicola is appointed in his place, 633. Returns of members of Congress, 636. Hearing of landholders in Southwark on report of Commissioners, 648.

Notaries, xvi., 1. Paid to Capt. John Morrell for powder to cele-

hiladelphia—
brate Washington's birthday, 4. Regulation of Moyamensing and Passyunk, 4. Southwark, 4. Orders for executions, 9. Repairs of arms, 14. Andrew Allen to be given up to Governor of New Jersey, 14. Arrangements for reception of General Washington—an address by President--Escort; no illumination—estimate of expenses, 25. Letter to Assembly on, execution ordered, 26. Sales of J. Kenzey's city lots ordered—State house clock, 29. C. Febiger, auctioneer, 35. R. Footman and Wm. Shannon appointed—invalids, 36. Sheriff to read to prisoners in jail act on penal laws, 43. Register-General's office in Receiver-General's, 45. Two city lots claimed by Richard Peters—sale postponed--society for encouragement of manufactures, &c., paid, 51. Mayor and aldermen under Act of incorporation, 53. Relative to title of State to lot between Cedar and Lombard, claimed by Miers Fisher, &c., for widow Gaskill of London, under a grant from Wm. Penn, 55. M. Leib paid for medicines and attendance on a militia man, 61. James Read re-appointed inspector of flour—Matthew Irwin paid for enrolling laws, 63. Lot on Vine between Schuylkill Front and Second appropriated as a stranger's burial ground, 69. Stores for president's celebration--road, 85. Lamps placed in State house yard, &c., 86. Samuel Brigs presents machine for making nails, screws and gimblets, 88, 346. Payment to Rakestraw and Colliday for repairs of State house, 90. City lots by J. Nicholson—by Dr. D. Christie and J. Mercer to be sold—expenses of fireworks, &c., on arrival of President of United States, 94. John Franklin removed from jail in, to Northampton, 102. Claim of Chr. Gula. Gaskill for city lots, 108, 109. Wm. Shannon auctioneer Northern Liberties, 109. Execution of Wm. Cole ordered, 118.

Philadelphia—
Claim of Ay. Cuthbert for city lots, 119. Procession for commencement, 121. Powder for 4th July — Samuel Powell, Mayor, takes oath in Council, 123. Watch houses, lamps, &c., in State house yard, 127. Enoch Edwards, Pres't. of General Court Quarter Sessions, in place of Edward Shippen, 133. Indians on their way to New York ask for money, 134. Repair of gun carriages, 136. Export of potashes from, 140. Lots in Southwark, 140. State house, care of—mistake committed by issuing land warrants for the Reformed congregation instead of German Lutheran, corrected, 148. C. G. Gaskill's claim negatived, 153. State duty on auction sales in Southwark, 155. Tavern licenses received, 157. Loan of drafts of Southwark and leveling instruments by Council to—Notary, 164. Claim of A. Cuthbert and N. Young, 167, 170. Nathaniel Falconer appointed health officer, 174. Repairs of public arms, 178. State house clock put under care of Robert Lesley, in place of G. Owen, 180. Account G. Owen for care of State house clock, 197. Report on accounts of J. Perkins and A. Morton for repair of arms, 198. Powder, &c. for celebrating election of President and Vice President—repairs of arms belonging to, 201. John Biddle, measurer of grain, dies, 204. James Ash, Sheriff—J. Leacock, Coroner, 208. Benjamin Davis, measurer of grain, 209. State house, 219. Clock, 220. Tax on writs received, 220. German passengers arrived, 222. Committee of Safety, 1776, take salt from a store which is now paid for—address from Abolition society, 210². Tavern licenses, 217². Regulation of Southwark, &c., 220². Pay for lamps, watch house in State house yard and watchmen for public offices, 220². Dr. Duffield reports sick prisoners to be removed from jail—Deputy

Philadelphia—
Surveyor, 223[2]. Sea letter granted by Council to Capt. James Josiah, of ship Brothers, bound to China—Christ Church bells rung—regulation of Southwark, 225, 228, 238. Jno. Patton, auctioneer, A. Hubley, auctioneer, Southwark. Report of Commissioners to regulate streets, lanes and alleys in Southwark, Passyunk and Moyamensing, 245-251, 262. Wm. Shannon, auctioneer's account of duty on sales in Northern Liberties, 253. Two city lots for sale, 271. W. Ferguson, Joseph Snowden and Christian Carberry released from jail, 281. Lighting lamps, watchmen about State house, 291. Anthony Cuthbert claims city lot, 293, 299. Exchange of warrants for land with German Reformed congregation, 297. Duty on sales at auction in Southwark, 303. Tavern licenses — House of Employment paid for J. McManus, injured while in public service—Excise collected—duty on sales at auction by R. Footman, 311. Joseph Leacock, inspector of pot and pearl ashes—subscribers to manufacturing fund meet at the college—additional auctioneers appointed, Joseph Dean and John Chaloner for Northern Liberties, 315. Manufacturing building burned by design, proclamation against incendiaries, 326. Powder magazine—Lot of Col. John Patton on Walnut street near Schuylkill proposed to be purchased, 328. Value of, 337. Capt. P. Z. Lloyd resigns, 337. Jonas Philips applies to be auctioneer for Moyamensing—not vacant, 340. Powder for celebrating birthday of President United States, 365. M. O'Bryan for city lots—plan and dimensions of powder magazine, 367. Charles Biddle, paid for State house yard, &c., improvements—W. Shannon, duties on sales at auction, 369, 386. Repairs of State house yard, 370. Stephen Prosser, Notary, 386. Attack of Castner Jones of Delaware on two

Philadelphia—
constables of—pardoned—conviction for stealing a stick of fire wood—referred to Attorney-General, 387. W. Austin's estate sold, 387. Money for building cells and walls in jail yard, 388. Conference with Mayor, Assembly and Common Council on the subject of their representation respecting gunpowder magazine now erecting, 387, 390. Powder for 4th of July, 391. Mistake in sale of city lots to M. M. O'Brien rectified, 393. Repairs of State house—attention requested for Colonel McGilivray and principal chiefs of Creek Indians on their way to New York—invitation to commencement in German Reformed church in Race street, 395, 396. Deputy of health officer extorts fees, 402. Benj. F. Bache establishes "The Daily Advertizer," 409. City Hall being erected—a building pulled down—ringing of Christ Church bells 4th July, 410. Survey of land for German Reformed congregation, 423. Circuit Court United States to be held in, 433. Powder for celebrating arrival of General Washington, 436. Lieutenant Wm. Henry resigns, 447. Nicholas Miller paid for billeting soldiers, 447. Thomas Proctor appointed Lieutenant of, 449, 485. P. Thompson claims city lot, 457. Duties on sales at auction, 460. Tonnage duty and fines collected, 461. R. Peters claims city lots, 462. Expenses of President's reception, &c., 465. Fees received by Master of Rolls—Gov. Mifflin receives pay for leaden spouts taken from him in 1777—report on conduct of several prisoners, 479. Militia, 481. Execution of Pat. Waugh ordered, 485. Thos. Willing paid for leaden spouts taken in 1777–arrangements for accommodation of Congress in west wing of State house and sundry offices in Carpenter's Hall, 486. Paid R. Lesley for taking care of State house clock—M. Josephson, for Hebrew congregation, asks

Philadelphia—
loan of lottery wheels, 489. Jas. Ash, Sheriff, John Leacock, Coroner, 490. Samuel Powell and Joseph Kilburn paid for leaden spouts, 490. R. Peters' claim for city lot referred to Supreme Court, 492. Nathaniel Falconer, health officer—Brown's Federal Gazette—repairs at State Island—draft of Southwark, Moyamensing and Passyunk, 493. A "necessary" to be sunk in State house yard, 496. P. Waugh respited—Cornplanter and other Indians in, 497. Their expenses paid, 498. Patent to Col. George Morgan for city lots, 499. Duty on sales at auction received, 500. Indian chief "Great Tree" wounded in leg—attended by Dr. Jones—Cornplanter and Half Town permitted to remain till arrival of President United States—French emigrants furnished with tents, 513. W Gosline repairs east wing of State house for Register-General's office, 515. Public officers called on for information, 517. A city lot—gunpowder for arrival of President United States, 522. Claim of Richard Peters for city lots, 523, 526, 529, 532, 534. C. Biddle, account of expenditures on State House, &c., 522, 523. Printing for convention–pay to Commissioners to explore rivers, 525. Claim of Thomas Harding confirmed, 522, 531. Lot for powder magazine, cost, &c., by Jno. Patton, 532. Wm. Semple, sub-Lieutenant of—lecture by Judge Wilson, 533. R. Peters' claim rejected, 539. Sale of city lots ordered, 540. Receipts from auction — table covers for Senate chamber, 541. Deed John Patton and wife for lot for powder magazine, 541. Repairs at State house, 542. Materials for powder magazine—expenses of offices, 544. Cornplanter's expenses paid, Charles Cecil's claim dismissed, 547.

Philadelphia Contributionship for insuring houses ask for a charter, ix., 440, 447, 472, 637, 641.

Philadelphia Library Company, not permitted to receive books from New York, xii., 318.

Phile, Dr. Frederick, appointed Naval Officer of Philadelphia, xi., 198, 513, 520. Certificate respecting health of S. Fisher, xii , 221. Naval Officer, 608. Letter, xiii., 563. Draft on, 700. Appointed Naval officer, xv., 315, 621. Certificate of his fidelity as Naval Officer, xvi., 59.

Philips, Jonas, charged with usury, but dismissed, xv., 216.

Philips, Thomas, Lieutenant of boat, xi., 47. Lieutenant, 557.

Phipps, S., letter on charge of transporting English prisoners, v., 418.

Phips, Gov. P., sends letter from Gov. Lawrence on French fleet, vi., 451, 555. To Governor M., 606. To General Johnson, 607.

Phipps, Gov. S., Massachusetts applies for export of provisions vii., 135, 136, 169, 186.

Phœnix, privateer, captures a Portuguese vessel illegally, xii., 63.

Physick, Edmund, Receiver-General, petition respecting proprietary estate, ix., 178. Called on for books, papers, &c., xii., 256, 280, 316, 332, 357, 359, 362, 409. Delivered to Secretary and Col. Johnston, 719. Secretary of land office, xiii., 420. To examine papers for quit rents due proprietaries, xiv., 71. Paid for services as keeper of great seal, xv., 299.

Pickering, Charles, petition, i., 67, 68. Decision in favor of, 73. Testimony, 101. Charged with counterfeiting money, 84. Jury summoned, 86. Names of jury, 87. Sentence, 88, 91, 92. Testimony, 135. Pleads for servants, 150.

Pickering Timothy, order from Board of War, xi., 497. Letters, xii., 451, 693. Quarter-Master-General United States, xiii., 48. Elected Prothonotary, &c. of Luzerne county, xv., 96, 97, 99. Register and Recorder, 134. Elections in Luzerne, 212. Letter to, 362. From, 465. Arrested by mob, 484, 493. Released, 502. Letter to, asking his opinion on

sending troops to Tioga, 505. Intelligence from, 514. Letter on reward to captors, 547. Paid as Commissioner on Connecticut claims, 573. Proclamation respecting captors of, annulled, 605. Letter from, referred, 606. Petition of captors, 611. Report respecting captors, 627. Reward, 627. Register and Recorder of Luzerne county, xvi., 444, 446.

Pidgeon, Joseph, interested in Free Society Trade, ii., 154. A Justice, 159. Member of Council, 168. Commission to, stipulations between Maryland and Pennsylvania respecting surveys, iii., 161.

Pieces-of-Eight, bill proposed, i., 72. Not to pass by weight, 72. Counterfeited by C. Pickering and S. Buckley, 85. Proclamation to put down, 89. Respecting, 91, 92. In Robert Turner's hands, 209. Counterfeited by Jones and Barnes, v., 119, 141. Stamps defaced, 145.

Pierce, George, Justice, xiv., 138.

Pierce, John, Paymaster-General, xii., 712. Paymaster-General United States, xiii., 7.

Piercy, Lieutenant Henry, recruits, xi., 567.

Piers, to be fixed, x., 648, 682. To be erected in Delaware river, xiv., 458. And land purchased at Marcus Hook for, 460, 464, 468. Agreement with Thomas Conarroe to build, 479. At Marcus Hook, xv., 228, 233.

Pike, Thomas (dancing master), to be seized, xi., 284.

Pike—Dr. Franklin to procure a pattern for a, x., 283, 284. S. Paschall to make, 284. To be procured, 328. Pay Owen Biddle for, 482.

Pilots, not licensed, restrained from going on board vessels bound up the river, iv., 394. Directions to, in cases of flags of truce, v., 81. Each to have printed copy of proclamation, 82. Interference of Jersey asked, 111. Examination of, 111, 112. Of Sussex county, petition, 226. Proclamation not to board vessels inward bound, 227. For Delaware bay and river, Act regulating, ix., 293, 295, 296, 671, 729. Rules for, x., 337, 344, 357. Petition, 354, 405, 543. Special grant to, 340, 341, 344, 357, 416, 428, 520, 555, 678. Special, for chevaux de frize, 363. Rules and regulations for, 396. Boat to cruise in bay, 401. A, restricted to Chester, 402, 535. Pay increased, 430, 520. To cruise in bay, 535. For privateers, 542. Pay of, 555. Raised, 745; xi., 574.

Pine Creek, two friendly Indians murdered by whites, xvi., 396. Proclamation against murderers, 397. Depositions sent Attorney-General, 418, 437. Doyle arrested—reward paid, 483, 484, 508.

Pine Street Church, lots enclosed with, not to be sold now, xiii., 3.

Pipe, the—Captain of Shawnese, vii., 382.

Piper, James, Sheriff, x., 101, 212, 270.

Piper, Col. John, xi., 83, 240. Censured for enlisting men in Bedford, 411. Lieutenant, 187, 708. Lieutenant authorized to call out militia of Bedford county in case of invasion, xii., 10. Officers named, 70. Ammunition sent to, 104. Lieutenant, 372. Resigns as Lieutenant, 549. To receive clothing for Captain Boyd at Bedford, xiii., 145, 152.

Piper, John, Justice Court Common Pleas, xiv., 208.

Piracy, execution for, xii., 537. Evidence from Jamaica against Maurice Keating, &c., xiv., 268.

Pirates, vessels arrive at and plunder Lewestown, i., 539, 549, 554, 555. Proclamation against, 555, 559, 562, 563, 566, 572, 574. Proclamation against, 565. Question about sending, for trial, 577. James Brown, 580. Law against, 590. Alarm from, ii., 21, 22, 24, 25, 100, 148, 566, 567. Proclamation against, iii., 32, 38, 50, 58, 63. Sailors taken by, arrive, 51, 55. Governor's speech on, 54. Teach, a noted, 54. In gaol ask for clothing, &c., 430. To be executed on Wind-

mill Island and in chains at Mud Island, xii., 731. Sentenced, xv., 397.

Piscataway Indians ask to settle here, ii., 191.

Pisqutomen (Indian), sent on message to Ohio, viii., 147. Returns and reports, 174.

Pitcher, James, appointed Commissary, vi., 303.

Pitkin, William, Governor of Connecticut, letter of Governor P. to, on New England settlers, ix., 573. Answer, 602.

Pitt, Captain, may hire prisoners from gaol, x., 542.

Pitt, Fort, General Monckton asks for four hundred troops, viii., 509—ix., 34, 42, 269. Conference and speeches at, 219. Indian prisoners to be sent to, 239. Indian conferences at, 249-264. Lieutenant-Colonel Reid commands at, 269. Goods for, in danger, 303. Murders near, 321–323. Lands, 434. Croghan going to, to condole with Indians, 490. Commissioners appointed to attend treaty, decline, 491. Messrs. Allen and Shippen appointed, 491. Commission and instructions, 492, 493. Indians from, 496. Conference at, 514–543. Messengers with Indians from, to Redstone, 539. Indian councils at, referred to, x., 11. Evacuation of, 68, 71, 74. Petition of Labatte and Angle, xi., 568. Party attacked by Indians, 699. Rawlin's regiment about to march for, 758. Brigadier-General Wm. Irvine commands, xiii., 79, 83, 150, 162. Men to be sent to, 348. G. Blakeney offers to raise men, 454. Sale of ruins, xiv., 498. To be taken possession of for Committee, 517.

Pittsburg, minutes of conference with Indians at, viii., 293–297. Brigadier-General Stanwix succeeds Forbes and Mercer at, 298. Conference at, 306. Returns of the garrison at, 314. News from, 379. Captain Gordon, engineer, arrived, spot for fort not fixed on, 392. De Lignery shot at Niagara, 393. News from, 392. Stanwix's letter on progress of works at, 427. Conference at, 429–435. Three hundred men to be raised for, 582. Early survey of lands near, x., 161. Geographical situation of Fort Pitt, 175. Proceedings against Samuel Sample, a supposed accomplice of Dr. Conolly, 533. Patent to John Ormsby for ferry at junction of Alleghany and Monongahela rivers, xii., 317. Captain Craig ordered to, by General Washington, 330. Pass to, for Moravians, 346. Justices, xiii., 698. Petition of M. Boggs respecting improvements in reserved tract opposite to, xiv., 373. State road to, 574. Road from Miller's Spring to, xv., 13. Privileges to Wm. Butler on account of land opposite to, being overflowed—ferry, 42. Draughts of depreciation lands to be put up at, 43. Favor of James Robinson, 73. Sale of lands proposed, 118. Road to, from Miller's Spring, 121. Road through Western Counties to, 273. Members of Assembly confer on, 274. David Reddick to lay common and lots in lands opposite to, 289. Scull and Hall, printers, 390. Reserved tract opposite, 497, 501. To be arranged for sale, 504. Plan reported, 509–512. Lots to be sold in Philadelphia, 522. Indians pacific near, 531. Road to, from Bedford, 599. Lots opposite, not to be sacrificed, 600. Valuation, 601. Lots on reserved tract opposite to, xvi., 22. Road between Bedford and, 27, 51, 466, 550. Value of reserved lands opposite, 45. Road from Cumberland county to, 73. Reserved tract opposite, surveyed, 97, 340. David Duncan of, furnishes troops on frontiers with supplies, 400. Error in survey of a tract opposite to, 411.

Pitt, Wm., appointed one of the principal secretaries, vii., 412. Letters to and from, 564; viii., 18, 26, 272, 288, 315, 316, 449, 451, 590. Complaints against America by Spain, 18. Lord Loudoun's successor, 26. To raise troops under

General Forbes, 27. Restoration of Fort Du Quesne, 315.
Plague, master of vessel imprisoned on account of, iv., 674.
Plankinhorn, Jacob, appointed flour inspector Philadelphia, xi., 201.
Plate, leaden, taken from Jean Cœur, made by French on Ohio, v., 508. Copy of inscription on it, 510.
Plates, for counterfeiting, defaced by Council, xiii., 385.
Plays and Lotteries, Act against, proposed, viii., 339. Vindicated, 340, 355, 356. Considered in a very different light, 542.
Pleasants, Samuel, to be seized, xi., 283.
Plumsted, Clement, a Justice, iii., 28. Member Council, 269.
Plumsted, William, to draw for money granted by Parliament, ix., 3, 4.
Plumstead's wharf, xi., 748.
Plunket, Dr. William, letter from, on Wyoming, x., 86. Governor's answer to, 87. President of Court at Northumberland, 87.
Plymouth, township, asks for a cart road, i., 200, 218.
Poetquessing Creek, road, ferry and bridge, i., 514.
Poht, Lieutenant, resigns, xii., 685.
Pole, Edward, to attend vendues, xi., 767; xiv., 495. Petition to be Notary—is appointed, xv., 358.
Pollard, Jeffrey, Coroner for Bucks, iii., 108.
Pollard, William, x., 699. Member of Navy Board, xi., 127. Indebted for purchase of a traitor's estate, xiii., 3, 9. Memorial respecting money of W. Price, 748. Justice —new trial to, xiv., 669.
Pollock, James, Coroner, x., 212, 270. Superceded because no taking oath, by Geo. Reading, xi., 455.
Pollock, Capt. Wm., x., 701.
Pomroy, Robert, Lieutenant of gun boat, x., 327, 353.
Pomroy, Ralph, xi., 749.
Pompunagh and other Indians in Philadelphia barracks—memorial, ix., 135.
Pools, Nathaniel, former road from, to Wm. Coat's corner, ii., 561, 562. Record, 562.
Poor, relief of the, iii., 43, 588, 590. And almshouse Philadelphia, 598, 590. And impotent persons not to be imported, iv., 304. Laws, proposed or passed, v., 371, 372, 396, 403. Bill laying duties on, 499. Relief of, ix., 3, 4, 243, 294, 394, 396, 434, 446, 470, 472, 593, 599, 637, 640, 719, 721, 724, 729. Relief of, 243, 294, 396, 470. Poor wood from commons, xi., 70. Overseers of, ask a pass for pauper, xiii., 28.
Pope, John, a Justice, ix., 543.
Popple, Sir Alfred, Secretary of Lords of Trade—on bills of credit, iii., 262.
Population, of city and each county, 1760, 1770, xiv., 336.
"Porcupine," guard boat, xi., 750.
Porter Brewery in Philadelphia, xi., 710.
Porter, Col., battalion, x., 683, 686, 708, 710.
Porter, Captain Andrew, to stop and examine a British vessel at Mud Island, xiii., 145. Promoted to major, 223, 233. Memorandum of officers on promotion, 367, 491. Error in commission, 617.
Porter, David, pay to, as wagon master, xii., 703.
Porter, Capt. ———, asks that his company may be annexed to Col. Proctor's regiment, xii., 210, 266.
Porter, Stephen, Commissary, xiv., 403, 643. Receives a tent, 441. Pay for necessaries for Commissioners to run line, 442, 445. Commissary to Commissioners on west boundary, xv., 108, 120; xvi., 209[2].
Porter, Col. Andrew, error in commission, xiii., 617. Pay for provisions for Virginia Commissioners, xiv., 104, 114, 119, 134. Commissary to Commissioners to sell public horses, 286. Reversed, 308. On north line, 399, 586. Resigns as Commissary, 400. To run western boundary, xv., 19, 106. And assist A. Ellicott on northern line, 195, 220. Paid, 356. Asked for description of Erie lands, 382. Claim for a horse, 642, 644.
Porteus, Captain George, captured

off the capes by a French privateer—deposition of, v., 245.
Portrait of Benjamin Franklin, bequeathed by him to Council, xvi., 358. Thanks for it, to executors, 359.
Posackaselt (an Indian), suspected of murder, ii., 71.
Post, aid for the, asked for, i., 524. Office, petition of Post Master-General for salary, ii., 33. Law for settling Post Office, 33. Gen. Braddock recommends a, between Philadelphia and Winchester, vi., 321. Office, western, mentioned, vii., 120. Managed by Franklin and Hunter—extent, salaries, privileges, &c., in reply to Sir C. Hardy, 447. Riders paid, xiv., 548.
Post, Frederick (a German), appointed with Charles Thomson messengers to Indians, holds conference with, at Niscopec, viii., 132. Sent with message from Cherokees to Teedyuscung, 137. Instructions from Governor, 138. Journal to Wyoming, 142. Sent with Indians, 147, 148. Arrives with news from General Forbes. 212, 223. Authorized to go as a Moravian missionary to Indians, 301. Sent to Indians by Governor, 341. News sent to, of murder of Dr. John at Carlisle, 455. Instructions for journey to Indians on Ohio, 469. Not allowed to pass through Seneca country, 491. Letter from Delaware chiefs, 676.
Postlethwaite, Samuel, Sheriff, xiv., 236, 567.
Pot-ashes, export of, from Philadelphia, xvi., 140. Inspector of, 312.
Potomac River, Indian name for, Cohongoruton, iv., 719.
Potter, Captain, vii., 230.
Potter, Capt. James, a Commissioner to remove settlers from Indian lands, ix., 481. Appointed third Brigadier-General, xi., 199. Asks for boats to convey troops from Chester to Billingsp't—he attends Council, 248. To send guard to Fort Island, 250. Letter, 266; xii., 70. Expenses paid, 365, 593. Marches against tories, &c., 490. Requesting militia for Northumberland, 492. Councilman, 543. Vice President, xiii., 112. Elected Major-Gen'l., 289. Course approved, 292. Censor, xiv., 212, 442. Command on Susquehannah, 485, 655. Death of Deputy Surveyor, xvi., 257. His son James appointed in his place, 261, 264.
Potter, John, Sheriff, v., 468; vi., 144, 638. Letter from, Great Cove destroyed, 673. State of affairs in Cumberland, 706.
Pottinger, James, leaves his mistress, joins enemy and deserts to Washington, xii., 219.
Potts, Major James, of musket battalion, has leave to resign, x., 643.
Potts, John, a Magistrate, vii., 62.
Potts, John, estate of, xii., 114, 116, 117.
Potts, John, Jr., at riot at J. Wilson's, xii., 137.
Potts, Doctor Jona., censured, xii., 100, 101. At riot at J. Wilson's, 139, 577.
Potts, Capt. Joseph, xi., 379.
Potts, Nathaniel, at riot at J. Wilson's, gives bail, xii., 138.
Potts, Samuel, to cast heavy cannon, x., 412, 530.
Potts, Col. Thomas, battalion, x., 701, 710; xi., 47.
Potts, Zebulon, Sheriff, xiv., 230, 555; xv., 101.
Pottsgrove, stores of provisions at, Mitchell, storekeeper, xi., 423. Virginia prisoners, 468, 472, 473.
Poultney, x., 528.
Poultney, Benj., xi., 74, 137. Pass to New York, xiii., 534.
Poultney, Thomas, buys an old jail lot, xiv., 583.
Pounds, to be erected in each township, iii., 345, 356. Erection of, iv., 19, 21, 40.
Povey, John, confirms proceedings at Kensington respecting bounds of Connecticut, vi., 267.
Powder, money to be paid at New Castle complained of by Philadelphia merchants, ii., 379, 382, 433. And powder house, petition against, and bill proposed, iii., 242. Referred to Richard Hill, &c., 242, 244. Embargo to be

laid on, iv., 765. House at Philadelphia, order respecting watch, &c. at, v., 269. Scarcity of, vi., 666. And saltpetre, committee to procure, x., 282. Robt. Tower appointed Commissary of maga zine, 301. Sent to General Schuyler to be proved – made by Lush and Eve, 301. To be removed from jail, 308, 312. Receipts, &c. of, 312, 314. Provincial Congress of New York apply for loan of, 312, 315, 327, 328. Associators of New Jersey to have, 313. Bounty on importation, 330. General Washington asks for, 330. Account Congress and Pennsylvania for, produced, 340. Lent to Congress, 361. For Northampton county, 363. To be purchased in Reading, 395. Loan of, to Congress, 395. From Cumberland county, 398. On hand, 399. Belonging to North Carolina, 416. Guards for magazine, 420. Bought of J. Pringle, 420. To be paid for saltpetre, 430, 431. To Congress, 432, 440. Places for magazines to be selected, 455. Bounty to persons erecting powder mills, 459, 479. To be employed, 467. To be made in Bucks co., 472. Proposals for manufacture of, 482. Mills to be erected, 488. Clement Biddle to look out for a site and contract for it, 488, 494, 495. Site for mill, 497, 498. Used by Dr. Bond at gaol—to friendly Indians, 512. For Chester county, 527. For Bucks, &c., 537. Various committees to import, 543. Mill building by order of Congress, 549. At French creek a magazine, 550. Money to Thomas Heinberger for mill, 561. Vessel for magazine, 567. From Congress, 578. Weight of, to ball in cartridges, 587. Sizes of muskets, 588. House, 599. To be manufactured at Continental mill, 600, 626. For boats, 610. For Associators, 622. Cartridges with buck shot, 626. Furnished Associators, 636. For frontiers of Lancaster county, 703. For General Washington, 703. For camp at Amboy, 703. All to be delivered to R. Towers, 744. To be removed from mills on French creek and Norrington towards Lancaster, xi., 49. Magazine to be built at Lancaster, 115. Mill at French creek burned, evidence of, 184. In hands of William Wallace of Bucks, 508. Asked for a privateer, 543. For privateer "Addition," 630. Against keeping in Philadelphia, &c., 637. Scarce, xii., 298. Magazine full—a quantity placed in "guard house," xv., 433. Committee on, 599. Lot for, proposed to be purchased, xvi., 328. Lot valued, 337. Plan and dimensions of, 367. Proceedings suspended, 387. Erecting, 390. Cost of, &c., 532.

Powell, Jeremiah, President of Maschusetts—letters, xi., 690, 728.

Powell, John, &c., petition against another ferry on Schuylkill, ii., 277. Ferry not granted, 289. Under Sheriff of Lancaster county, deposition, attack on High Sheriff Buchanan by persons from Maryland, iii., 612.

Powell, Samuel, a Justice, x., 47. Mayor of Philadelphia, xvi., 53, 123. Paid for leaden spouts in 1777, 490.

Powell, Wm., interferes with P. England on Schuylkill ferry, i., 380, 381, 437. Welsh petition for a ferry at, 478. Regulations, 581.

Powers, Alexander, survey to, for land in Cumberland county, xii., 782. Memorial on land in Northumberland county—Report of Surveyor-General, xiv., 292.

Powers, Captain, united to Colonel Proctor's regiment, xii., 210, 266.

Power, Lieutenant John, appointed, xii., 2.

Powle, John, charges against, v., 87.

Pownall, John, secretary Lords Trade, letter on iron works, vii., 738. Death of King George, II., viii., 514, 520.

Pownal, Thomas, letter to Governor M. on Connecticut claim, vi., 267. Commissioner to Pennsylvania for aid, 314.

Pownal, Gov. Thomas, of Massachusetts, sends list of Philadelphia shipwrights captured at Oswego, vii., 717. Letter on great fire at Boston, asks aid, viii., 483.
Poyntell, Wm., Station'r, xvi., 221[2].
Pratt, C., Attorney-General, opinion on Connecticut trespassers, viii., 620.
Pratt, Henry, Coroner, iv., 500, 601, 669, 748, 782, v., 55, 120, 345.
Praul, John, Justice, xv., 256.
Presbyterians, in Chester county—magistrates embittered, v., 378. Of a New Engl'd missionary, vii., 11. Church, lottery for 1st, 2d and 3d, ix., 580. Church, &c. at Newtown, Bucks county, lottery for, x., 41. At New Castle vested in trustees, 79, 85. In Market street, 471. Church, sale of lots of Pine street postponed, xiii., 3.
Presentment of Grand Jury against negroes, i., 380.
"Preservation" Fort, built, xv., 66; xvi., 170.
President's House, belonging to the State, repairs, xii., 106, 236, 238, 244, 262.
President United States, mode of administering oaths and transmitting acts of government, xvi., 94. Celebration of his arrival in Philadelphia, 95. Letters, 93, 119, 123, 141, 144, 169, 189, 289, 306. Proclamation for Thanksgiving, 188. Indian outrages in Washington county, 306. Birthday celebrated, 365.
Presqu' isle, fort described, vi., 10. Fort burned, viii., 311, 380, 514. Post at, cut off and massacred, ix., 35. Treaty with Indians at, concluded by Colonel Bradstreet, 193–197. Reservation at, for State, xvi., 47.
Press, publication by, to be licensed by Council, i., 165. Liberty of the, vii., 339.
Preston, Samuel, appointed Sheriff of New Castle county, i., 340. Collector of Sussex, ii., 183. Member of Council, 429. Resigns as Justice of Philadelphia, iii., 282. Provincial Treasurer, 446. Commissioner on boundary, 544. Sent to Maryland, iv., 203. Instructions, 205. Report, 210. Is Provincial Treasurer, 413. Justice, xvi , 325.
Pretender, Popish, abjuration oath administered to Governor, iii., 13. Sustained by French power, iv., 677. Rebellion in Scotland in favor of, v., 6. Success over, thanksgiving, 50.
Price, Henry Yelverton, tory speeches, committed, x., 503. Released, 524.
Prichett, Thomas, Inspector of beef and pork, shad and herring, Philadelphia, xiv., 488. Inspector of salted provisions, xv.,
Pride, Chetmall, in prison for murder of apprentice, ii., 513.
Pride, the Indian chief, vii., 382. Dies in Carolina, 540.
Prime-hook, Luke Watson's title to, i., 118.
Prince, birth of a, Thanksgiving day, i., 229.
Princeton College, pay for damage to, by militia, xiii., 44. Congress adjourn from, to Annapolis, 746.
Pringle, John, may ship produce, x., 425.
Printing, debate on D. Growden's printing the frame of government, i., 278. Proprietor's objections to use of the press, 278. A. Bradford ordered before Council—not to be done but by permission of Governor, iii., 143–145.
Printers of Continental money, excused from militia, xi., 31.
Prison, in Philadelphia, i., 101, 445, 582, 583; iii., 235, 241. Heads of, regulation for, by Council, xiv., 353–356. Sales of lots of old jail, &c., 583.
Prisoners, on flag of truce, charges to be paid by respecting, v., 417. Charge of, to each government, 420. Of war, a list of them to be sent, x., 776. Exchange of, xi., 564. Removed from Lancaster to Philadelphia, 573. Convention, 637. Taken at sea, Chief Justice to inquire as to their character and circumstances as traitors or pirates, xii., 71. Opinion of Chief Justice, 74. Exchange of, 6, 23, 29, 51, 59, 147, 241, 494, 574.

Privateers, ii., 148, 187, 240, 411, 413, 448, 468. Encouraged by England, iv., 693. French capture four vessels, 749. Spanish and French, in Delaware, v., 93, 111. Depositions respecting, 112, 115—119, 124, 159, 233, 245, 248, 254, 257, 258, 260-264, 265. 268, 280, 282, 284, 300, 301, 320. Complaints of Spain against American, viii., 18, 235. Difficulty about Dutch vessels brought in by, 105. Convoy of, 156. Officers of Stanwix to be arrested, 171. Spry, Captain Spring, captures a French flag of truce in Delaware bay, 139. Complaint of Gov. of Monte Cristo against, 235. Also Knowles, Captain Turner, 235. Fitting out at Philadelphia, apply for shot, x., 536, 591. Resolution of Congress, 590, 605. Commissioned, 626, 642, 702. Owners and Commissioners, 702, 706, 713, 715, 741, 743, 773; xi., 2, 4, 21, 282, 541. Comm'ns from Cong'ss, 437, 630, 661, 697, 703, 714; xii., 63, 326.

Privileges, asked for, by Assembly, ii., 37. Governor's answer to, 41. And property, distinction between, 40. Charter read, 44. Delivered to Speaker by Governor, 48. Charter signed—copy of it, 56-60.

Prize Money, how to be shared, x., 476. How to be distributed, xi., 658, 740.

Prize Guard, Capt. Thomas may export to Antigua, xiii., 254. Breaks health law, 258. J. Seely, 407.

Process, bill for continuing, proposed, ii., 336.

Procession in Phila., on ratification of Federal Constitution, xv., 350.

Proclamation to be issued, that no person shall deal with servants for goods or money, i., 74. Constables to visit public houses—people not to stay longer than an hour, 76. Masters allowed to chastise servants, 79. To put down counterfeit money, 89. Against Lord Baltimore's agents, 104. Of James II. as King, 132. Against selling rum to Indians, 154. For thanksgiving on birth of a prince, 229. Of King William and Queen Mary,

Proclamations—

341. For encouraging proprietor's ferry on Schuylkill, 446. Of Governor against reputed piracies, &c., 529, 535. Proroguing Assembly, ii., 12, 69. Respecting strangers, 13. Deserters from King's soldiers at New York, 20. Of Ann of Denmark as Queen of England, 70. Relative to change of Governor by death of Andrew Hamilton—registers of vessels, &c., 86. To continue officers, 116. Against disorders in Philadelphia, 162. Respecting rates of foreign coins, 178. For thanksgiving day, 215, 217. Respecting French privateers and arms, 241. Of Council, 336. Of Gov. Gookin, 427. Peace with Spain, 571. For continuing officers, iii., 14. Against pirates, 32. Occasioned by death of Wm. Penn, 59. Of letters patent from New York, 62. For Court of Chancery, 106, 107. For Robert Moore's arrest, 108. Respecting agreement between Lord Baltimore and Hannah Penn, 232, 234. Prepared to be published respecting Hannah Penn and Lord Baltimore's agreement, 236. Of Governor Gordon, 252. Riots in the city, 260, 261. Respecting murder of Indians, 307. Riots in Philadelphia, 351. Respecting Indian trade, 409, 411. Of Governor Gordon's death and continuance of officers, iv., 48. Against Marylanders, 73. For apprehending Sol. Moffat, 89. Against Spaniards, 166. Of Gov. Ogle, 254. On order of Council on dispute with Maryland, 263. Of proceedings at Hampton Court, 301. Against Spain, 351, 396. To enlist soldiers for Cuba, 499. Of war between England and France, 688. Against selling rum to Indians, 759. Troops for Louisburg, v., 40. Thanksgiving day, 50. For continuance of officers, 68, 69, 70. Respecting flags of truce, 82. For a fast, 169. Against rum, 194. To pilots not to board vessels coming in, 227. Treaty at Aix la Chapelle, 360. Of peace, 379. By Governor, 379. Against

Proclamations—
rum, 397. Relative to iron and steel, 457. For fast, vi., 422. War against Delaware Indians, vii., 88. For a fast, 110. For suspension of hostilities with Delawares, 134, 144, 192, 247, 390. Of Governor Denny, 221, 226. For fast day, 591. Against sale of rum to Indians, viii., 172. Thanksgiving day, 235. Of Gov. Hamilton to officers, 413. Murder Dr. John, 456. Of King George III., 517, 518. Of laws disallowed, 558. Respecting Connecticut settlers, 566. Bounty to soldiers, 587. Against settlers on Indian lands, 662. Of war with Spain, 706. Peace between France and Spain, ix., 13, 37, 39. Against Connecticut settlers, 27. Thanksgiving day, 41. Against highway robbery near Philadelphia, 70, 76, 316, 398. Of Gov. John Penn for continuance of officers, 72. On murder of Conestogoes, 94, 107. Governor Penn for scalps, 190. Of Bouquet's treaty with Indians, 206, 234. Peace with Indians on Ohio, 264. Respecting settlers on western lands, 327, 481. Reward for arrest of Stump and his servant, 488. Governor Penn on robbery of Treasury of New Jersey, 544. Respecting New England settlers, 588, Fisheries, 623. Continuing officers, 644. Arrest of Joseph Billings, 647. Against Wyoming New England settlers, 679. Against Lazarus Stewart, 687. Of Governor Hamilton, 733. At New Castle, 743. Against Connecticut settlers, 747. Respecting laws, 766. Of Gov. Richard Penn, 783. Apprehension of persons engaged in taking revenue schooner and pilot boat, x., 12. For arrest of "Chester County Man," demanding money from J. Galloway, 44. Respecting hurricane in West Indies, 58. Against counterfeiters, 88. John Penn continuance of officers, 92. Against settlers on Indian lands, 95. Against counterfeiters, 99. Declaring laws void, 104. Against Connecticut

Proclamations—
settlers, 153. For murderer of Delaware Indian, 199. On boundary line, 206. Against persons rescuing goods not entered, 214. Respecting boundary with Maryland, 220. Against murderer of Edward Carey, 228. Recalled, 241, 245. For a murderer, 269. For a fast day, xi., 176. On approach of enemy towards city, 299. Respecting error in printing bills of credit, 362. Thanksgiving day, 369. Respecting stock cattle, 429. For a fast, 438. For arrest of murders, 446. Against certain traitors, 483, 493, 513–518. Of General Arnold, 523. Embargo on provisions, 545. For traitors to take trial of estates, 610–612. Arrest of a noted robber under a, claim and payment of reward, 616. For thanksgiving day, 627. Partial suspension of embargo, 646, 763. Against forestalling, 671. Against British course, 733. For a fast, 751. Embargo, 777. Taking off, 784. Against suspicious persons, xii., 27. Favor Dennis Crohon, 65. Respecting riot at Hon. James Wilson's, 122. Embargo, 171. Fast, 183. Respecting dispute with Virginia, 212–214. For apprehension of three persons suspected of burning property of Maj. Johnston, 261. J. Richardson, 294. For fast, 282. For arrest of incendiaries in Cumberland co., 294. Against a seditious paper, 319, (see 325.) For arrest of Jno. and Robert Smith for murder, 349. Of martial law, 283. Suspending purchases, 408. Against traitors, 496. Fast day, 517, 537. On bills of credit, 589. Against traitors, 665. Fast day, 697. For arrest of Wm. Rankin, 710. To receive continental money, 724. On importation of British half pence, xiii., 4. Embargo, 41, 49. For a fast, 124, 267. On robbery of mail, 312. Robberies in Chester and Bucks, 338, 533. French deserters, 375. Of Congress for thanksgiving, 396, 400. Against vice and im-

Proclamations—morality, 433. On French sailors, 473. Decree against Connecticut, 475. Confirming boundary line between Pennsylvania and Virginia, 541. Of Congress on cessation of hostilities, 555. Against Doans, &c., 616. For a murderer, 629. Against the Doans for robbery, 631, 687. Counterfeit coin, 643. Fraudulent sales of land, 644. Robbers, 687. For murderer, 728. Thanksgiving for peace, 748. On treaty with Great Britain, xiv., 19–22. For a murderer, 57. For robbers in Philadelphia, 112. Removal of buoys, 122. Against conspirators in Westmoreland, 151. Respecting Wyoming, 220–224. Of Congress on counterfeiting certificates, 347. Against Jno. McDonald for murder, 489. Against robbers, 514. Against James Burn, xv., 79. President and Vice President, 111. For apprehension of Daniel Shay, 176, 435, 442. Against rioters in Luzerne county, 278. Respecting agreement with Virginia, 279. For arrest of rioters and murderer of a Spaniard, 317, 319. Against captors of Col. T. Pickering, 488, 603. Against conspiracy against the laws, 489, 497. Members of Congress, 638. Electors, President and Vice President United States, 655. For arrest of incendiaries, xvi., 327. For arrest of murderers on Pine creek, 397.

Proctor, Francis, Lieutenant of artillery, x., 416. Discharged from service on complaint of Captain Williams, &c., 423, 424. Lieut. fire worker, 620. Second Lieutenant, 742. Claim, xiii., 244.

Proctor, George, deposition respecting Spanish privat'r, v., 248, 253.

Proctor, John, Jr., Sheriff, ix., 779; x., 59, 106.

Proctor, Colonel John, xi., 118, 477, 531, 576; xii., 123.

Proctor, Thomas, appointed Captain of artillery at Fort Island, x., 382. His company to be received into the barracks, 390. To be furnished with firelocks, &c., 394. To receive cannon, 402. Order for firearms, 403. Gunners, &c., to be allowed accoutrements 405. To provide drum and fife, 405. Straw for bedding, 406. Discharged on complaint of Captain Williams, 422, 424. Restored, 438. To enlist volunteers, 467. Form of enlistments, 468. To use rooms in pest house, 494. Called on to quell riot in gaol, 512. Express sent to, 526. Troops increased—brevet Major, 685, To enlist men, 722. Officers of companies, 742. To be ready to march for Fort Montgomery, 757, 769. To parade artillery at Fort Island, xi., 1. To send men to General Washington, 25. To be Colonel of regiment, 116, 215. Marches from Fort Island, 250. Part of quota, 568. Letter, 781. Letters to and from, xii., 9. Artillery, 622, 727. Sheriff, xiii., 722. Sheriff has committed Longschamps, xiv., 120. Sheriff, 230. Suit with State for Hogg Island, xv., 116. Elected Lieutenant of Philadelphia county in place of Wm. Henry, xvi., 449, 485. Applies for powder for arrival President U. S., 522.

Proctor, William, Justice, xiii., 389.

Promotions, army and navy, xii., 88, 92; xiii., 223, 367, 441, 456; xv., 337.

Property, charter of, ii., 37, 44, 48, 54. Comm'rs of, appointed, 61.

Proprietary, promise on proroguing Assembly, ii., 12. Articles of agreement between, and the Susquehannah and other Indians, 15. Commission to regulators of water courses, 23. King's letter, 28, 30. Assembly to, on King's letter respecting defence of New York, 30. Address from lower counties to, on do., 31. Communicates to Assembly a bill before Parliament to annex proprietary governments to the crown, 32. Decides respecting overplus land near Pennepack, 34. Speech to Assembly—compelled to go to England, 35. Conferences with Assembly, 37. Address of Assembly to, on privileges, 37. Re-

Proprietary—
ply to each request, 41–43. Indians come to take leave of, 46. Wishes Indians to be permitted to give evidence—asks Assembly to think of some person to represent him in his absence—suggests A. Hamilton, 48. Delivers the charter of privileges to Speaker, 48. Bill prepared to grant £2000 to, and carried to Assembly, 51. Charter of privileges delivered by Speaker to Governor, 51. Goes to Pennsbury, 52. Warns Assembly of the short time he has to stay, 52. Answer to petition from Philadelphia on removal of burdens of trade, 53. Charter for, submitted and read, 53. Inquiry, who he intends to leave in his place, 53. Answer to Assembly respecting charter of property, 54, 55. Messages to Assembly, 54. From Assembly, 55. Signs charter of privileges, 54. A copy of it, 55. Commission to Commissioners of property, 61. Signs a charter of property to be sealed in six months, if he does not direct otherwise, 62. Authorizes Governor and Council to open letters in his absence—one arrives, 64. His mill, 64, 65. Tax of £2000 for, 70, 71, 135, 185, 213, 363. Sends papers from England, 71. Governor Hamilton dies and is succeeded by Council under commission of the, 86. Appoints William Markham, Register-General, 96. Road to Goshen, 111. Commissions John Evans as Governor, 115. Commission to Council read, 115. His son William, Jr., invited to Council, 117. Urges Governor and Council to inquire into affairs of "Pennsylvania Company," (Free Traders?) 137. Expenses of Government to be paid by the country, 143. Opinion of Assembly and Council on saving clause of commissions, 146. W. Markham dies, 151. Letter from, approving of Governor's refusal to confirm bills, 186. Remonstrance signed by D. Lloyd for the House—prosecution

Proprietary—
for forgery, &c., 186. Governor communicates the proprietor's views on various matters, 187. Original rights, 416. Governor Evans on quit rents, 419. Revenues, 423. Mortgages the province to Philip Ford in 1690, 455. Swedes complain against, 465, 480. Letter from, 494. Right to ferries, 526. Position at first, 617.

Appoints William Keith Governor of province, iii., 13. Gives dedimus to J. Yeates, &c., to administer oath to Governor, 13. Scheme concerning quit rents, 32. To nominate an agent for the province, Henry Goldney designated by Governor and Council, 44. Death of William Penn announced to Council by Governor Keith—his eulogium, 58. Instructions from W. Penn, Jr., 63. Line between Chester and Philadelphia county, 144. Instructions received by Governor but not communicated for reasons stated, 235. Interests opposed by Colonel John French, 268. Thomas Penn arrives, 433. Respect to, 433, Thos. and Richard Penn grant new commission to Governor Gordon, 526. Gives new greater and lesser seals bearing their names—receives the old one and gives the new in charge of T. Griffiths, 530. Address Indians, 573. Presents to, 574. Meet Indians at Philadelphia, 579. Speech, 579. Address of Assembly and answer, 582. Sick at Pennsbury, 598. To Abraham Wendall, 609. Obtains from Indians release of lands between Susquehannah and Kittoctinny hills, iv., 88. Sends with Council message to Indians, 245. Proceedings of Hampton Court, 254. Instructions respecting bills of credit, 318. Demand for quit rents becomes oppressive, 330. Applies to Assembly respecting lands, 348. Sails for England,

John Penn dies, v., 62, 73. Letter to, from Council on robberies of French and Spanish, 92. Letter to, on defenceless state of city and province—and

Proprietary—
asking cannons, &c., 161. Letter from—alteration in the family, &c., 216. Letter from Thomas Penn—for man-of-war, 228. By her, 239, 246. Promises cannon, 240. Letter alluding to sickly state of city, especially about the dock, 244. Letter to, from Council, 319. Inform President Palmer of Governor Hamilton's appointment and thank him for his services, 362. Recommends building a fort or block house on Ohio, 515, 547. View of it by Assembly, 547. Decline bearing part in expenses of treaties with Indians, 546. Order Abraham Taylor's name to be struck from Council, 551. Letter respecting title set up by Ralph Fretwell and A. Taylor for friends in Barbadoes, 551. On paper money, 605.

Deeds to, from Indians for lands purchased by Commissioners at Albany from Six Nations, vi., 119–129. Instructions—is the Governor required to exhibit them to Assembly? 220–223. Long messages from Assembly to Governor, 226–236. And answer of Governor, 236–243. Present address of Assembly to King, 448. Letter, 485. Answer to address, 504–510. Tax on their estate, 525, 619, 680, 682, 689, 692, 702, 715–720, 738. Opinion of Council on saving clause of W. P.'s commission to Colonel Evans, 529. Discussion, on, 525–532, 569–587. Philadelphia proposes to pay, 568. Assembly ask, was not withholding payment for land the cause of Indian alienation, 710. Report, 724. On Braddock's defeat, 730. Tax on estate of, vii., 203, 396, 409, 463. Instructions on money bills, 247, 396. Charter, &c., 273. Right to make treaties on war with Indians, 305. Charged by Indians with injustice, 352. Committee of Council appointed to investigate the state of their Indian purchases, 354, 431, 536. Instructions, 441, 442. Taxes and quit rents, 469. To come

Proprietary—
over, 633. Complaint of treaty by Quakers at Philadelphia, 634. Report on complaints against, 776.

Estate tax on, viii., 67, 74, 82, 105, 278, 299, 301, 302, 319, 324, 326, 350, 456, 460. Approve of supply bill, 125. Message from Thomas and Richard Penn on receipt of a paper by Dr. Franklin from Assembly without address, &c., at which, they complain, 276. As well as of its detention by lawyers for a year, 276. B. Franklin's to agent of, 299. Compensation for loss of quit rent omitted in bill, 350. Discussion in Council about, 357. Protest of Council, quit rents, &c., 358, 361. Galloway's remarks on bill, 363–369. Their position with regard to propriety, 374. Appoint James Hamilton Governor, 409. Report of agents on assessment of, 456. Objections to tax, 460. Representation of R. Peters and R. Hockley on tax in Cumberland county, 472. Right to complain, 524. Tax on estates, 530, 540, 584, 606. Wish of, respecting lands, officers, &c., 675. Proceedings of privy Council to be secret, 720.

Instructions to Governor H. on report of Committee-bills of credit, taxes--grant by Parliam't--agents, &c., ix., 11, 21, 47, 51, 53. Ill treatment by Assembly, 174. Impossibility to render account of, by Receiver-General, 178. Quit rents, 180, 379–382. Let. to, from Council respecting Wyoming, 757, 779.

Thomas and John Penn revoked Richard's commission as Governor, and Thomas, with King's approbation, appoints John Governor, who arrives and is present in Council, xi., 91. Abuses practiced on their lands under color of old rights, xii., 264. And message of Council to Assembly on it, 264. Late Sec'y. James Tilghman called on for books, &c., 690. Arrears of ground rent on confiscated estate, claim for, xv., 51. Claims to city lots, 63, 68. Patent asked for Springettbury Manor

lands, 153. Question raised in Council on payments to, 202. Answer of Judges Supreme Court, 210. Payment of interest, 211.
Proprietary Estates, tax on, &c., ix., 153, 155, 157, 158, 161, 179, 180, 185, 237, 240.
Proprietary Lands, settling on, by Connecticut people, x., 50. Town to be laid out at the manor at Kittanning, 201.
Proprietary Claims, Jared Ingersoll employed to assist Attorney-General—allowance, xi., 737.
Prosser, Stephen, Notary Public, xvi., 286.
Protest, of Council against Governor for assenting to a bill for reemission of a bill of credit, quit rents, &c., viii., 358. Of Supreme Executive Council against Congress laying an embargo on provisions in Pennsylvania as an infringement of the power and authority of Council, xi., 546.
Prothonotaries appointed, xi., 178, 187, 221, 230, 240, 244, 301, 365, 566, 694. Circular to 188. To be judges of Common Pleas, 221; xii., 243, 681; xiii., 158, 324, 702; xiv., 202, 204, 376; xv., 17, 97, 269, 271, 461; xvi., 35, 122, 164, 166, 168, 172.
Providence, Rhode Island. cannon taken at, by Com. Hopkins, x., 550. Res. of Congress, 564.
Province Island, act introduced for vesting in trustees, iv., 629, 635. Passed 638. Indians on, much exposed, ix., 100. To be guarded for safety, 101. Paxton Boys at Lancaster, forming company to march to Philadelphia, and kill Indians at, 108. Pest house on, x., 409, 412. Hospital, xi., 21. Fergus Purden, steward, 136. Or State Island to be sold in lots to redeem bills of credit, xii., 671. By Mr. Holker, purchase of lots, xiii., 8. Sale of lots, 26, 28, 34, 54, 56, 65, 66, 76, 241, 242, 307, 505. Commission on sales, 313, 543. Deed to John Wilcocks, 549, Trustees of, 578. Bed covers for sick at, 695. Deed, 727. Pest house, xiv., 6, B. Brannon and use of pump, 72, removal of military stores, 72. Repairs of Marine Hospital, 373. Rent of, 383, 387. Surveyor-General to survey and mark ground for Hospital, 655. Land remaining to be sold, xv., 146, 148. Sale of lot. Repairs, xvi., 353. Sick in Hospital, 437. Trustees appointed, 448. Wharf at, 493.
Provincial Commissioners, complained of, viii., 64, 66. Commissioners to attend treaty with Indians, 586. Circular of Governor Penn to, respecting proprietary lands and assessments, ix., 237. Names of, Commissioners, 237. Answer to circular, 240.
Provincial Court, Judges, and queries on certain points, ii., 87.
Provincial—ship of War proposed, viii., 30, 36, 81, 334, 573, 574, 583. Condition province, 83. Settlement with Indians for lands, by Peters and Weiser, at Easton, 219. Report of committee appointed by Councils to investigate the claims made by Indians at Easton, respecting lands, also a list of deeds, &c., produced, 246, 261. Correspondence between Assembly and proprietaries about Tax on estates, &c., 276, 279. Lottery for defence of Province, 340. Agent to be appointed to receive share of money granted by Parliament to colonies, 400, 501, 512, 546. Gov. James Hamilton, succeeds Denny, 409. Assembly agrees to raise 2700 men, Estimated expense of, 458. Representation of R. Hockley proprietary Receiver-General, and R. Peters, Secretary, on proprietary taxes in Cumberland County, 472. With tabular statements, 476. Benjamin Franklin and Robert Charles appointed agents to England, 512, 693. Relating to Connecticut settlers, 563–572, 612, 621–628; x., 401, 495, 521, 522, Ship to be called Montgomery, 525. Surgeon for, 541. Committee on, 543. Sent to Roebuck, 552. Pay of Pilot, 555. Memorial to Congress, 575, 694. Montgomery pilot for, appointed, 679
Provisions to be furnished Massa-

chusetts, i., 515. Embargo on, iv., 479, 480. Exportation of 491–495, 506. Embargo on, vi., 319, 351. Law passed, 356. Applications to export, vii., 135, 136, 151, 168, 186. Embargo on, 183, 184. (See Embargo.) Exported from Maryland, 183. Message to Lower Counties on, 195, 202. Embargo taken off, 221. Order, 387. petitions to ship read and rejected, 393, 459. Scarce at Wyoming, 479. On shipping, to sundry places, 482, 497. Report of vessels loaded with, 500, 561. Rhode Island applies, 509, 560. Massachusetts applies, 570. Exported, 606. Stored at different places, —. Commissioners for purchasing, xi., 423, 424, 425. Embargo on, 545. Suspension in favor of, 646. Distribution among troops, 710. For Massachusetts, 729. Allowed to be exported, xii., 1, 2, 8, 10, 59, 130, 173, 191, 197.

Public houses, regulations, i., 74, 75, 76.

Pugh, Capt. xi., 215. Lieut., placed on invalid list, 647. Asks for rations, xii., 14.

Pugh, Hugh, of Chester County.—A murderer under sentence of death, petitions for pardon, arguments for and against; iii., 40,

Pugh, Joseph, Sheriff, vi., 638; vii., 266.

Pulaski's, Count, Corps, xii., 76.

Pumpshire, John, Indian agrees to go to Diahoga, vii., 152, 307, 431. Interpreter at Easton, 672.

Punishment for telling truth, i., 88. modes of, 92. Number of stripes to be inflicted; 97. Severe and singular, on slaves in Philadelphia, 406. Severe, xiii., 314.

Purchases, Commissioners of, appointed, xii., 300, 301, 302, 305. Orders to, 309. Asks more pay, 362, 370, 371, 405, 406, 409, 410, Returns of, 411, 412, 420, 449, 453, 456, 464, 465, 488, 493, 514, 559, 584, 595, 612, 615, 648, 653, 654, 658, 660, 678, 700, 705, 722, 779; xiii., 7, 17, 44, 58, 59, 67, 92, 142, 155, 201, 208, 218, 222, 223 263, 269, 294, 295 298, 300, 311, 315, 356, 367, 384, 420, 421, 441, 444, 509, 514, 519, 525, 542, 603, 604, 646, 684, 698, 741, 752; xiv., 54.

Purden, Fergus, Steward at Province Island Hospital, xi., 136.

Purdey's, Colonel Battalion to relieve Colonel Brown's, xiii., 222.

Pursell, Henry D., engraves borders for paper money, xiv., 470.

Purviance, John, to examine British Goods, xiii., 491.

Purviance, Sam'l Andrew, resigns, xii., 487.

Pusey, Caleb, member of new Council, i., 580. Member of Council, takes affirmation, ii., 96.

Pusey, Joshua, a Justice, v., 547.

Putnam, Brig General, Privateer, x., 702.

"Putnam" Floating Battery—hand cuffs for, xi., 5, 18, 79.

"Putnam" Galley, xi., 176. Petitions of officers.

Putnam, Gen. Israel, Aid asked for in throwing up works of defence around Philadelphia, xi., 46. All able bodied men to apply to him, 56, 176, Letter on enemy's movements, 202.

Pykeland, County, Claim for city lots, xiii., 33, 60.

Q.

Quahanoquesie Indians, live over Allegheny, viii., 96.

Quaker Assembly meet at meeting-house, i., 178. Gov. Fletcher a man of arms and not of Quaker principles, 373. Opinion of the Indians respecting, 372. Declaration of, on loyalty to King, 526.
Answer to, on war, ii., 242. Account of arms to be taken, 241. Defensive measures proposed, 242. Objections, 243. Complaint about oath, 457. Object to defensive measures, 460. And affirm'n, 617.
Address to King respecting, iii., 26. Not to be oppressed by militia duties, 64. Assembly's views on, 66. Numbers of, and Church of England equal in Council, 143. And on Supreme Court bench, 158. Object to style of address to King, 226. Another to be chosen

member of Council, 232. Representation from, respecting forms of declaration of fidelity, 235.

And liberty of conscience, Assembly's and Governor's views of, iv., 367–371, 380–384. Assembly decline defence on account of their principles, 425, 435. Council with Indians in their meeting-house, 432, 443. Oaths, 628.

Form bulk of Assembly, v., 207. Reflected on by Council, 278. Defence of, by Assembly, 336.

"Political Engines," vi., 600. Conduct of, represented by Gov. Morris, their address, 739.

Address against war with Indians, vii., 83, 84. Intercede in behalf of Delaware Indians through Israel Pemberton, 103, 105. Gen. Shirley on, 112. At Treaty at Easton take leave of Tedyuscung, 215. Requested by ministers to resign seats in Assembly, to be filled by other denominations, 292. Address Governor on treaty at Easton, 311. His answer, 312. Referred to, 332. With Sheriff, carry Governor's order for quartering troops to Assembly, considered a breach of confidence, 362. Money raised by Friendly Association for Indians, 391. Address to Governor on Militia bill—liberty of conscience, 404. Threats against, 502. Address of, meeting of sufferings against David Bush, 559. Law proposed in favor of religious scruples, 593. Treaty made at Philadelphia by, complained of by proprietaries, 634. Their offers to be refused, 635. Committee of Friendly Association answer to, 637. Address from, 638. Answer, 647. Urge Tedyuscung to ask for a clerk, 659. Charles Thomson master of school, 665.

Attend Indian Conference at Easton, viii., 175, 211. Address from, meetings of sufferings on Indian complaints, 239, 241. Another, 243. Governor's answer, 242. Remarks of Logan and Shoemaker in Council on, 245. Report of committee appointed by Council to inquire into Indian claims to lands, 246, 261. Attend Conference in Philadelphia, 490.

Peaceable efforts of, ix., 301.

Suspected—confined in Mason's Lodge and removed to Virginia—proceedings, xi., 283, 284, 286, 288, 290, 292, 293, 295, 296, 299, 300, 303. Obtain writs of habeas corpus, 308. Proceeding of Supreme Executive Council, 309. Conduct in Virginia—various papers, 382. Expenses paid to Reading, 394. Memorial from prisoners in Virginia—they belong to United States, 395. Address to Council—verbal answer, 426. Another address—conference with and proceedings of Council, 427. Conference respecting prisoners in Virginia, 435. Expenses paid to M. Muhlenburg, 437. Mrs. Pemberton asks protection for wagons, 457, 458. To be sent from Staunton to Shippensburg and discharged—they to pay their expenses, 461. To Lancaster, 462. Or may be discharged at Pottsgrove, 468, 472. Arrived at Lancaster, &c., 472, 473. Pass given to, 473. Also to several of their wives to return to Philadelphia from head-quarters, with consent of Gen. Washington, 473. Account of expenses, 481. Roberts and Carlisle, proceedings against, 606. Expenses to Virginia, 682. S. R. Fisher, 729, 734.

Paper purporting to be from a meeting in Warrington, respecting negro Ralph, considered an imposition, xii., 113. Paper on militia fines and taxes, 245. John Nancarrow objects to having shot and shells cast in his air furnace, 435.

S. R. Fisher two years in gaol sick—discharged, xiii., 13. Address to Council on the rejoicings for victory, &c., 131. Pass to Owen Jones, Jr., Ann Howell, &c., 249. Memorial of, against theatres, &c., 741.

Of Chester county petition respecting militia fines—order of Council on it, xv 418. Expense

of prisoners sent to Virginia via Reading, 1777, 641.

Quakers--Society of Free, memorial for a lot of ground, xiii., 775.

Quality, Joseph, Lieut., xi., 576.

Quarier, Alex., Capt., xii., 338.

Quarry, Col. Robert—Judge of Admiralty seizes goods at New Castle, i., 541, 544, 545, 546, 548, 561, 562, 565, 566, 575, 580. Judge, &c., and Jno. Moore, exhibit charges against David Lloyd, 602, 603. Reply, ii., 71, 89. Communicates to Council, sundry papers from the government, 89, 90. Remarks to Council about dedimus, 92. And difficulties about oaths, 93, 94, 96, 115, 116. Complaints against, 517.

Quartermasters appointed, x., 479, 480. xi., 25, 84, 279, 305. Pay, 371. Certificates as pay, 496. Elected, xii., 146. Complaints against, at Reamstown, 158.

Quassenungh, son of the old King of the Shawnese, Kakewatchy, attacked with small-pox in Philadelphia, and recovers, while his attendant dies with it, iii., 463.

Quebec, walls of—Major John McPherson killed before, xi., 655. Edw. Agnew a prisoner at—in distress—relieved by Council, 658.

Queen Anne ascends the throne, ii., 60. Order from—approves of A. Hamilton as Governor, 89. Issues new Commissions, 104. Address to, on oaths, 209. Proclamation about money, 435. Letter on expedition against, 449. Instructions for Col. Veitch, 449. Meets part of Assembly, 459. Order to Governor to meet at New York on Canada expedition, 532. Objections of Council, 532, 534. Repeals laws, 571, 572. Death of, 574, 575. King George proclaimed, 574. £2000 for her use, iii., 32.

Quick, Jacobus, prisoner from Virginia, sent under parole to Governor of New Jersey, to answer charges, xi., 474.

Quigley, Henry, Coroner, xvi., 194, 509.

Quincey, Josiah, appointed Commissioner to Pennsylvania for aid, vi., 314. Letter to Governor, 329. Arrives, 330.

Quisagechroanu, an Indian, speaks, vii., 120.

Quit Rents, Act to collect, proposed, ii., 221. Governor Evans's view of, 419. Concerning, iii., 32. Being payable in specie oppressive, iv., 330, 331, 333, 334. May be taxed, viii., 301, 450, 530, 537. Complaint of omission in a bill for compensation to Proprietaries for loss of, 350. Protest of Council against Governor on, 358. Governor Penn on—Manner of imposing, &c., ix., 379, 382. Due Proprietaries, search for, xiv., 71.

R.

Radine, Colonel, La, Assistant engineer to General De Portland—compliment to, xi., 776.

Radmore, T. Petition for Road, i., 396.

Rags for lint and bandages advertized for, x., 471.

Rahm, Michael, Coroner, xv., 570. Coroner, xvi., 195, 498, 500.

Rains, Heavy, prevent the meeting of Assembly, iii., 267. Long absence of, vi., 422.

Rakestraw, Joseph, killed by negro Jack, ii., 11. Trial, 18. Joseph, petition, xiv., 380.

Ralph, (Negro), petition, xi., 565. Referred to Assembly, 570. Result, 571. A negro formerly property of John Rankin, a traitor—imposition practised in a paper purporting to be from a Quaker meeting, -- Referred to York County, xii. 113.

Ralston, Captain, x., 689.

Ralston, John, Justice, xiv., 216.

Ralston, Robert, to muster militia, to guard prisoners, xiii., 293.

Rambo, John, accused of fornication, i., 156.

Randolph, Lieut. Edward, Surveyor General, commissions Matthew Birch to be surveyor and searcher of customs in Pennsylvania, i., 534, 551. Paid for enlisting men,

xi., 487. Stationed on frontiers—complains of want of clothing—is supplied, 665.
Randolph, Edmund, on Commercial Condition of States, xiv., 651.
Randolph, Governor, of Virginia, Letter, xv., 159.
Randolph, Isham—Captain of ship Rachel from London—his protest on being ordered up from New Castle, v., 264.
"Randolph," armed Pilot boat under commission to Abraham Bennett, pilot, xii., 326.
Rangers, appointed, i., 165, 166, 206, 226. Regulated by law, iii., 235.
"Ranger," Gunboat x. 488, 505.
Rank of Officers. Rules for settling in North America, vii., 472, 473. Disputes, about, x., 334; xi., 54, 272; xiii., 543; xv., 381.
Rankin, James, confiscated estate, xii., 82, 113, 174, 218, 219, 577.
Rankin, John, petition, xii., 82, 113, 174, 218, 219. Justice, 342.
Rankin, William, escapes from jail, Proclamation against, xii., 710.
Ranniston, John, Sergeant and Ensign, xii., 58.
Rape, cases of, i., 588, ii., 11. To be punished by death, 211. Special Court for trial of a negro for, ix., 648.
Rations, x., 415, 500, 515; xi., 379, 471, 538, 710, 750; xii., 21, 406, 492; xiii., 71, 129, 162, 359, 375, 448, 534, 743; xv., 17, 295, 349, 493, 494, 519, 613.
Rawle, Francis, petition for bridge at Arch and Front streets, i., 330. Interested in society of Free Traders, ii., 154, 163. Elected Member of Council, iii., 232.
Rawlings' Regiment marches for Fort Pitt, xi., 758.
Razers, Bernard, of Lancaster, asks to be naturalized, iii., 374.
Rea, John, Coroner, xiii., 726.
Rea, Samuel, Coroner, x., 100. Lieutenant of Northampton Co. xii., 317, 336, 374, 485. Complainants against, 607. Resigns, 739.
Read, Adam, a Justice, v., 600. Letter to, Indian murders, vi., 668.
Read, Justice Adam, Letters, condition of frontiers, murders, &c., vii., 303.
Read, Charles, Sheriff, Philadelphia, iii., 370, 387, 416. Member of Council, 529. Clerk of Orphans' Court, dies, iv., 151, 243. Commissioner for Indian affairs for New Jersey, at Easton, viii., 175.
Read, George, resigns as Attorney-General of Lower Counties, x. 216.
Read, James, Letters to and from, on Indian affairs, xi., 650, 651.
Read, James, appointed Councilman, xi., 500, 525, 596; xii., 155. Resigns, 744. Appointed Register of Admiralty Court, 745, 748. Commissioner to Wyoming, xiv., 202. Flour Inspector, 445; xv., 172; xvi., 62, 63. Councilman, xv., 294, 295.
Read, John, Barrack Master, &c., instructions to, x., 568. Commands fleet, 387. Barrack Master at Fort Island, xi., 51.
Read, Joseph, elected to Assembly from York County—resigns as a Justice, xv., 364.
Read, Moses, Justice, xii., 93.
Read, Peter, arrested on suspicion of shooting Indian George, ix., 603.
Read, Captain Thomas, sent to General Washington, xi., 24.
Read, William, Sheriff, iii., 332, 370. Clerk of Court, 338, 387.
Reading, petition for road from, to Easton, v., 610. Commissary of Provisions at, vi., 775. Ravages of Indians at, viii., 100, 102. Letters for Episcopal Church in, ix., 243. Road from, returns of, 556. Powder purchased from, x., 420. Prisoners removed from, 546, 679. Prisoners taken to, 648. Guard for, 714. Records removed to, xi., 30. Prisoners sent under guard to, 302. Expenses of paid to, 394. Provisions stored at, 423. Two hundred militia to be at, 446. Disturbances between prisoners and inhabitants, xii., 12. Deposition respecting William Moore Smith, 30. Letter Christ and Haller claim for town plot, 780. Election for Burgess, xiv., 462.

Prisoners sent to Virginia, via, 1777, xv., 641.
Reading, Lieut. George, xi., 455.
Reading, John, landing, ii., 539. Record of Road opposite, 541, 549, 561. President of New Jersey, demands a fugitive, v., 94.
Reamstown, complaints against Dep. Quarter-mast., at, xii., 158.
"Rebecca," privateer, xi., 642.
Receiver General, ii., 112, 122; xiv., 444, 447.
Receiver General of Land Office, xv., 27. To give notice of sale, 522. Orders to sell City Lots, xvi., 95, 271. Reappointed, 350.
Receiver of Provisions appointed, xii., 585.
Recorders, iii., 173.
Recorders of Deeds, xiv., 584.
Recorders and Registers, xv., 5, 134.
Records, safe keeping of, iv., 17, 21, 33, 35. Sent to Lancaster, xi., 23. To Reading, 31. To Easton, 306.
Recruits, x., 519, 520; xiii., 168.
Red Bank, committee to visit—Report—Width of river, x., 283. Report of committee on defence of, 474. Money sent to, for Navy Board, xi., 360. Work done at, 399.
Reddick, John, petition respecting his land in Maryland, taken from him, ix., 375.
Redick, David, appointed to lay out common and town lots in reserved lands opposite to Pittsburg, xv., 289. Sent to New Jersey and New York, with news from Wyoming, 490. Returns, 495. Expenses paid, 498. Vice-president, 565. To arrange lots opposite Pittsburg for sale, 504. Reasons for his vote, favor E. Oswald, 506. Reports plan for reserved tract with Mr Cannon, 509-512. To receive proposals for lots, and for islands in Ohio and Allegheny rivers, 513. Surveys islands in Ohio and Alleghany rivers, xvi., 97.
Redman, John, Jr., appointed paymaster, x., 756.
Redman, Dr. John, asks for a pass for self, daughter, Sarah Coxe and children, to New York, xiii., 551.
Redman, Joseph, sheriff, viii., 781 ix., 57, 398, 547, 623. Clerk of Market, xi., 195. Dies, xii., 110.
Redman, Joseph, Jr., appointed surgeon, xi., 24, 32. Secretary of convention, xvi., 524.
Red Stone creek, location, vi., 29. Fort, 137. Proceedings of commissioners to Indians at, ix., 506. Names of inhabitants and Indians, 508. Indians proceed to, 539. Indian messengers refuse to go, 542.
Redwood, John, taken by pirates, i., 539.
Reed Collinson, xvi., 130.
Reed, Henry, deposition concerning Dr. Conolly, x., 168.
Reed, Col. Jacob, xv., 109.
Reed, James, Prothonotary, xi., 197. Lieutenant of City, 203, 206. Censor, xiii., 720.
Reed, James R., xv., 341. Delegate to Congress, xv., 449.
Reed, John, payments to, for his map, x., 260, 267.
Reed, Joseph, x., 330. Appointed Chief Justice of Supreme Court, xi., 186. Requested to come and qualify, 195. Reasons for not deciding to take it, 202. Declines being Chief Justice, 249. T. McKean appointed, 254. Member of Congress, 385. Attends conference with Council, 456. Elected member of Council—Apology of business in Congress, 535. To assist Attorney-General, 558. Resigns seat in Congress, 594. Elected Councillor, 595, 625. Elected President, 632, 634. Sick, 723. Proclamation, 646, 671, 733, 763, 777, 784. President, Letters to and from—Proclamations, xii., 27, 122. Messages to Assembly, 96—99. Messages from Assembly, 96, 99. Riot at Hon. J. Wilsons, 121, 122. Councillor, 131. President, 131, 163, 541. Takes oath, 169. Salary, 182. Loses a hanger at J. Wilson's—Paid for, 341. To take command of troops, 452. At Trenton—Specie sent to, 596. Appointed to see Pennsylvania Line mutineers, 593. Counsel on

Connecticut controversy, xiii., 128. Retaining fee, 136. Appointed in case of Big Spring tract, 236, 280, 296, 310. Assists Attorney-General in Bucks Co. case, 381. Delegate to Congress, xiv., 261.
Reed, Major of Hazens' regiment, xii., 262.
Reed, Samuel, Ensign, xii., 65.
Reed, Captain Thomas, named for Commodore of fleet, x., 379. Survey of river, 489. To fix signals, 510. Captain of armed ship building, 516. Sent to Roebuck, man-of-war, 552. Resigns, 595.
Reedy Point, x., 506.
Rees, Daniel, dies from ether used by Dr. Jones in making a free Mason in jest, iv., 277.
Reeve, Peter, Warden, ix., 293.
Reformed Congregation Philadelphia [See German Lutheran.]
Regiments, officers of the 12th Pennsylvania, in Continental Service, xi., 179.
Registered vessels, ii., 96, 112.
Register of Admiralty Court appointed, xii., 14, 745.
Registers appointed, i., 121, 185, 195, 211. Register General dies —Commissioners appointed till Governor does, 185, 186; xi., 186.
Register General appointed, ii., 96, 97, 113, 121, 151, 569. Respecting, 551. John Donaldson, xvi., 45. May employ a clerk, 64. Office expenses, 215. As Comptroller, 241, 272. Pay to, 301. Report respecting, 314. Clerk paid, 416. Resolutions respecting, 531.
Register of German passengers, xiv., 445. L. Farmer, appointed, 447, 586.
Register General of Probate of Wills, iv., 33, 40
Register of Wills and Deeds, xiii., 763 &c., appointed xvi., 443, 444, 495, 515.
Registration bill of freemen and servants proposed, i., 98. Of families, 110.
Reichel, John Frederick, Moravian missionary, has permission to return to Saxony with his wife, &c., xii., 782.
Reid, Lieutenant Colonel, letters to and from, ix, 268, 269. Insults of troops, 268, 271.
Reigart, A., Sh'ff, ix, 623. Purchases horses for troops, xi., 446, 489.
Rein, John, traitor, xii., 80.
Reinick, Dr. Richard, dies, payments to his daughters, xv., 249.
Religious Societies. Worship restricted to the Christian religion, ii., 222. Power of, to sell lands, &c., objected to, ii., 528. To purchase lands for burying grounds, &c., iii., 394, 400.
Remington, John, a lawyer, in trouble for performing ceremony of Free Masonry in jest, iv., 277.
Remonstrance sent by Robert Barber, signed D. Lloyd as from Assembly to Proprietary—forgery, ii., 187. Of Assembly against various matters, 455. Of inhabitants of Philadelphia on oaths, 457. Of Assembly, 513. Of Mayor, &c., of Philadelphia to Assembly, on quartering troops, vii., 366. Of Assembly against Governor's message on supply bill, 401. Of Assembly on embargo, 571. Of Commissioners at Easton, 657, 658. Of Smith & Gibson, on Indian affairs and frontiers, ix., 138–146. Of Assembly against impressment of carriages, by Col. Wilkins, 684, 686. Answer of Genl. Gage to, 718. From Masons' Lodge, xi., 292, 294. Of Maryland, xii., on confederation. Of Virginia against Vandalia or Indiana Companies, 491.
Rent, sale of goods distrained for, x., 41.
Repeal of laws, ii., 251.
Replevin, writ of, granted by A. Morris against seized goods, i., 544, 566. Presenter of a petition for, "reprehended for his insolence," ii., 109.
Reports, on publishing Colonial Records, i., 12. Of Wm. Salway and other Commissioners to New York, 393.
Of Commissioners to regulate water courses, Philad'a, ii., 25.
Of Hamilton & Georges, on return from Maryland, iii., 547.
On Chancery Court, iv., 27.

Reports—
On Maryland affairs, 154. Of Assembly, on value of gold and silver coins, and of bills of credit issued, 361–364. Do. by Council, 364. Of Lords of Trade on various laws, 475. Conrad Weiser on Indian skirmish in Virginia, 640. Of Conrad Weiser on journey to Onondago, 660–668. On journey to Shamokin, 680–684. Journey to Onondago, 778, 782. T. Lawrence and J. Kinsey, of treaty at Albany, v , 7–26. Of treaty at Lancaster, 306–309. Of committee on paper currency, 415. Also of Lower Counties, 417. Of Richard Peters of proceedings against settlers on unpurchased lands, 440, 449. Of Com'rs to Carlisle to hold conference with Indians, 665.

On respective claims of French and English to North America, vi., 100, 105. On what forts are necessary, 109. Of John Penn and Richard Peters to Gov. H., of their proceedings at Albany, iii., 129. John Armstrong, of mission to Connecticut, 259, 261. Of Road from Easton to Durham furnace, 304. Of Committee of Council on distribution of arms, &c., by Ass'bly, 679. Of Com'ee to inquire into cause of Indian alienation on acc't of lands, 724, 728. On Shawnese claims, 724.

Of Conrad Weiser at Harris's ferry, vii., 33. Of Montour and Scarroyady, 65. Of delegates from six Indian nations, 115. Of Col. John Armstrong on Indian affairs, 257, 263. Of Capt. Newcastle, 296. Of Committee of Ass'bly on supply bill, 421. Thos. McKee, 597. Of Committee on complaints against propri'ry, 776.

Of Committee on Impeachment, viii., 1, 4. Of Hughes and Pawling on return from building houses at Wyoming, 134. Of Committee of Council to inquire into claims of Indians at Easton respecting lands, 246, 261. On law respecting warrants and surveys, 345. Of Lords of Committee of Council for plantation affairs in case of Dr. Wm. Smith, Provost, and Wm. Moore, 438. Of Committee of Privy Council on laws submitted, 524, 552. Order of Council on, 552, 557. Of sheriff and justices of Northampton County, on settlers in, from Connecticut, 564. Tax on proprietary estates, 584. Of Committee of Assembly on Governor's messages, 716, 719. Of Rev. John Steele, of proceedings with Indians, ix., 506. Of Tilghman and Shippen, respecting Wyoming, 750.

Of Comm'rs Allen and Tilghman, x., 181. Of Committee to procure copies of petitions, &c., to the throne since 1760, 461. On survey of Jersey shore, 474. On cartridges and muskets, 588. Of Assembly on conduct of Committee of Safety, 611. Of joint Committee of Assembly and Council on various matters, xi., 735.

Of Committee on barracks, xii., 208, 209. Of auditors on case of JehuEyre, 263.

Of Comm. of grievances, xiii., 694; John Lukens, Surveyor Gen., respecting a city lot, 123, 175. On election of councillor in Phila. 184, 188. Of Surveyor General, 295. On city lots, 321. Of Comptroller Genl., 420, 421. Of decree against Connecticut, 474. Of Commissioners for running line between Pennsylvania and Virginia, 510, 531. Of Comptroller General, 509, 511, 517, 532, 534, 536, 546, 552, 553, 557, 561, 563, 566, 570. Of Commissioners on C. H., Washington, County, 531. Of Committee on Congress on late disturbances, 619. On Gov. Harrison's let'r, 685.

Of Commissioners of taxes, xiv., 9. General Hand, 25. Of W. Bradford, Jr., and James Wilson, counsel on Connecticut claim, 159. Of Pennsylvania Commissioners on Virginia boundary, 286. On Wyoming, 462. Managers of State Lottery, 471. Of Genl. William Irvine, 522. Of Commissioners on jurisdiction of islands in Delaware, 590. Of Alexander McDowell, deputy surveyor, respecting the new purchase, 604,

Reports—
On case of George Schlosser, 660. Of Comptroller on payment to Deputy Surveyors of fees for donation land.—Lottery tickets remaining in the wheel, xv., 351. Of Commissioners on land near Erie, 382, 522. On election in Berks, 482. On do in Cumberland, 520. Of Commissioners to lay out streets, &c., 539. Against theatrical exhibitons, 590. Rules and regulations, 591. Names for streets, &c., in Alleghany, 610. Election frauds, 619. L. B. McLean, 620.
On purchase of triangle at Erie, xvi., 37. Respecting city lots, 60. In by John Nicholson, 94. On case of Turnbull, M. & Co., 158. On memorial in behalf of child of R. Wilson, 183. On public debts, 221. Of Commissioners on streets, &c., Southwark, Passyunk and Moyamensing, 245, 251, 262, Of Committee on accounts with United States, 253. On case of John Bryce, 298. Committee on controversy between Comptroller and Register General, 314, 349. On Memorial of Joshua Elder, 374. On Genl. R. Butler's letter, and Genl. St. Clair, respecting requisition, 424. Of Committee on case of Genl. Thompson's widow, 465 Of Committee on certificates in Comptroller's office, 485.
Representation of Quakers, xi., 427. Of Supreme Executive Council to Assembly, 431.
Representatives elected, xii., 134, 136, 145 ; xiii., 391, 393, 395, 397, 419, 443, 719, 723, 726, 729 ; xiv., 229, 230, 234, 236, 237, 244, 256, 554, 556, 558. Elected, xv., 98, 100.
Reprieve of William Ward, form of, v. 162, 211. Of Alexander Urie, 269, 293. Thomas Kelly, 604. Of Catharine Reynolds, 612.
Resolutions—Of Massachusetts, cutting off supplies of provisions from French, vi. 309. Of Assembly of Connecticut respecting claims to lands in province, x., 119. Of Congress, 292, 316, 357. Of Convention, 655. Of Committee of Safety, 337. Congress,
Resolutions—
410, 412, 418, 432, 433, 439, 453, 455, 458, 463, 484, 485, 502, 510, 522, 523, 529, 541, 546, 563, 567, 590, 592, 620, 629, 631, 634, 638, 639, 647, 654, 681. On Independence, 634. Of Congress, xi., 31, 194, 203, 212, 224, 226, 248, 254, 295, 344, 369, 404, 415, 446, 461, 507, 523, 539, 596, 627, 636, 663, 669, 677, 704, 727, 776, 782. Of Assembly, 213, 215, 217, 220, 227, 228, 230, 568, 644, 739. Of Congress, xii., 6, 26, 31, 36, 74, 76, 114, 147, 170, 176, 183, 210, 214, 227, 228, 230, 234, 242, 280, 360, 378, 396, 398, 433, 471–473, 484, 500, 517, 521, 522, 562, 571, 593, 615, 648, 653, 657, 692, 719, 758, 759. Of Massachusetts, 51. Of Councils, 141, 142, 151, 155, 238, 347, 367, 377, 697. Against vendues, 151. Of Assembly 258, 261, 371, 537, 545, 554, 561, 570, 636, 645, 653, 655, 661, 690, 740, 769, 770. Of Congress, xiii., 5, 42, 53, 61, 79, 83, 123, 146, 154, 254, 348, 404, 407, 605, 606, 609, 636, 744. Assembly, 61, 123, 132, 236, 420, 422, 436, 514, 525, 685, 712, 761. Of Council, 291. Of Censors, 751. Congress, xiv., 25, 31, 38, 145, 280, 286, 347, 384, 443, 509, 562, 647. Assembly, 202, 285, 286, 363, 369, 476, 666. Council, 167. Congress, xv., 315, 502, 515. General Assembly, 594, 596. Of Assembly, xvi., 73, 74, 315. Of Congress, 154, 375, 423. Of Council, 459, 545.
Respite, of punishment on account of pregnancy, xii., 110. Of a pirate on account of doubt as to legality of sentence, 732.
Revenge, cutter to be appraised for guard a costa, xi., 720.
Rex, Abraham, buys confiscated estate, xii., 445.
Reynell, John, prisoner, xi., 292.
Reynolds, James, frames portrait of Washington, &c., xiv., 265.
Reynolds, John, Justice, iv., 348. Discharged, x., 465. Lieutenant, xi., 750. Late Lieutenant John of Franklin galley—Dr. Hutchinson presents case of widow and

sick children—rations granted, xii., 106; xiv., 242.
Rhea, John, Coroner, xiv., 237.
Rhine, Michael, decree of Supreme Court against estate of George Rhine, xii., 327.
Rhoads, Capt. ——, officers elected, xii., 9.
Rhoads, Henry, Justice of Bedford county, resigns, xi., 616.
Rhoads, Peter, member of Council of Safety, x., 762. President of Court Common Pleas and Quarter Sessions, xiv., 226.
Rhode Island, Gov. Hopkins says Assembly will raise men, vi., 606. Gov. Tinker applies for provisions, vii., 151. Gov. Greene applies—declined, 559, 560. Letter from Gov., xii., 446. And Providence Plantation, Act of Congress respecting, xvi., 384, 393, 402.
Rhodes, Wm., Sh'ff, viii., 506, 781.
Rice, Benjamin, Ensign, x., 464. Capt. to assist with chevaux-de-frise, 514. Captain sells clothing, xii., 297.
Rice, Evan, trustee of General Loan office, ix., 205.
Rice, Fort, guard at—supplies for, xiii., 117.
Rice, Capt. John, pardoned and handed over to Maryland battalion, xi., 364.
Rice Capt. John, appointed to command of boat, x., 287, 702. Builds gun boat "Dickinson," 335. Chevaux-de-frise, 535. To command "Convention," 702. To raise men, 725. Commands armed "Convention," xi., 2. Ordered to Cape May—instructions, 9.
Rice, Lewis, repairs banks at Mud Island, xv., 204, 225, 236.
Rice, Patrick, clerk of Dr. Franks, allowed to go to New York to settle accounts—required to give bond and take oath, xi., 683.
Rice, Ensign Robert, xi., 573.
Richards, John and Ann, charged with witchcraft, ii., 20.
Richards, Peter, sub-Lieutenant, xii., 131.
Richards, Capt. William, on survey of river, x., 481, 488. To purchase articles, 598, 660. To fix signals at Cape Henlopen, 510. Appointed ship's husband, 560, 576. To send troops in shallops to Trenton, xi., 24. Examined as to frauds in Quarter-Master's department—dismissed, xii., 387.
Richardson, John, member of first Council, i., 57. Member of Council, removed for absence, 210. Attainder taken off, 619.
Richardson, Joseph, charged with counterfeiting, xi., 216. Enlarged on bail, 226. A traitor and counterfeiter, apprehended and imprisoned, xii., 270, 272. Brought before Council and remanded, 273. Discharged, 339.
Richardson, Samuel, member of Council for Philadelphia, i., 213. Complaint against, 244, 270, 292. Justice of Peace, 544, ii., 159.
Richardson, Thomas, sent to New York for cannon, x., 635.
Ried, J. R., applies to command troops, xiv., 157.
Riflemen, a body of, proposed, x., 491.
Rifles, x., 522.
Righton, William, compromised, with, for a slave condemned to death, ii., 405.
Rinker, John, Sheriff, vii., 266
Riots iii., 260, 267, 468–491. Election, in Philadelphia, iv., 620, 623. Bill for preventing tumults and riotous assemblies—passed, ix., 717, 720, 729. Acts respecting, x., 4, 52. In gaol, 512. In Philadelphia, 701; xi., 307, 665.
Rippey, Wm., Sheriff, xi., 609. Coroner, xiii., 134, 396.
Ritchie, Capt. Craig, xiv., 216.
Ritchie, Robert, appointed member of Navy Board, xi., 122.
Rittenhouse, Benjamin, gun-lock factory, x., 481. Proposals accepted—ordered to city, 495. Superintendent of the gun-lock factory, xi., 458. Appointed a Commissioner to view river Schuylkill, xvi., 194.
Rittenhouse, David, appointed Engineer to Committee of Safety, x., 382. Member of Committee, 537. Vice President of Council of Safety, 673. Appointed on Committee to survey Jersey Shore,

474. Engineer to prove cannon, 501. To purchase, 538. On Fort Island, Committee, 546. Receives a compliment as member of Council, xi., 52. Treasurer, 670, 754. Member of Board War, 201. Treasurer, 242, 257. Appointed State Treasurer, xii., 554, 657. Draft on York, 684, 688. Commissioner to run line between Virginia and Pennsylvania, xiii., 70, 685. Commissioner on northern boundary, xiv., 319 To view roads, 442. Assisted by Andrew Ellicott on northern boundary, 655. Commissioner to run western line, xv., 33. To recover moneys due, 253. Pay to, 614.

River Indians, Wapers or Wapingers, singular wampum described by Teedyuscung, viii., 217.

Roach, Isaac, pilot, x., 344. Second Lieutenant of boats, 383, 488; xi., 562, 578.

Roades, John, Coroner, iii., 371.

Roads and Highways, i., 184, 189, 195, 199, 200, 205, 209, 218, 251, 298, 379, 384, 387, 389, 396, 498, 499–502, 510, 514, 536, 572, 587. Walter King's, 387. The King's, 389; ii., 10, 33, 64, 65, 111, 147, 152, 203, 236, 238, 485, 520, 526, 536, 539, 541, 549, 561, 562; iii., 43, 50, 106, 107, 108, 138, 142, 158, 163, 177, 219, 225, 227, 230, 231, 263, 521, 524, 542, 547, 573, 585–7, 590, 617, 618. Confirmed, 231; iv., 21, 46, 152, 181, 186, 247, 266, 276, 279, 282, 285, 365, 495, 503; v., 59, 61, 99, 100, 105, 107, 120, 202, 376, 577, 610, 611; vi., 300, 302, 304, 317, 318, 369, 376, 377, 378, 409, 433, 476, 607, 629. Braddock's, 395–403, 430, 434, 446, 460, 466, 476, 485, 493, 497, 521, 555, 617; vii., 592; viii., 677, 694; ix., 4, 22, 23, 169, 248, 361, 440, 556, 623, 627, 651, 657, 667, 681, 686, 693, 699, 719, 720, 729, 732, 745, 750, 781; x., 23, 39, 41, 51, 65, 69, 73, 113, 219; xi., 481, 492. And highways, xii., 154, 314, 592, 656, 667, 726. Commissioners for viewing, paid, xiv., 442; xv., 13, 22, 30, 95, 121, 191, 195, 229, 230, 252, 273, 274, 322, 326, 330. Western, 326, 330–337, 346, 351, 355, 358, 359, 370, 399, 425, 431, 445, 448, 519, 546, 594, 599, 635; xvi., 19, 27, 51, 73, 83, 102, 252, 256, 259, 292, 434, 466, 484, 530. Rations, 68.

Robb, Andrew, Justice, xiv., 323.

Robb, Robert, Coroner, viii., 506, 781.

Robberies in Bucks and Chester counties, xiii., 338, 339, 515, 532. Proclamation respecting, 339, 533.

Robbins, Ezekiel, appointed to distribute provisions at New York, xiii., 459, 533. D. Sproat demands moneys, without authority of Council, 553.

Roberdeau, Captain, company, vii., 76.

Roberdeau, Col. Daniel, a member of Committee of Safety, to inspect ordnance and military stores, x., 283. Guards at State House, 287. To procure pikes, 328. To apply to Congress for powder, 505. To have iron doors made for gaol, 535, 548. To receive provincial arms, 640. Removed to Lancaster, xi., 41. Member of Congress, 385. Troops to work at Billingsport, 242. Attends Council, 548. Asks pay for lead, xii., 162, 163. Letter and resolution of Congress, 669. Letter from, 677. Trial at Carlisle with State, xiii., 319.

Roberts, Algernon, Commander, xii., 410, 420.

Roberts, Capt. Charles, of schooner Thetis, to be secured with his papers, x., 765.

Roberts, George, to be seized, xi., 283.

Roberts, Hugh, to be seized, xi., 283.

Roberts, Jane, draws money for self and children, xiii., 671.

Roberts, John, transcript of the record of Court of Oyer and Terminer, xi., 600. Order for execution, 606. Petitions for suspension of execution till after meeting of Assembly, 607. Petitions in favor of, 606, 613. Of his wife, children, &c.—notes of Chief Justice, 613. Condemned, 614. His

estate to be sold, xii., 323. Petition for suspension—rejected, 374. Costs in case of, 38. Estate sold, 571. Payment to Jane Roberts out of his estate, xiv., 174. Payment to his widow, xv., 467. His widow receives a payment out of his estate under decree of Supreme Court, xvi., 65, 350.
Roberts, John, Cor'r, xvi., 191, 490.
Roberts, Jona., Commissioner for erecting public buildings in Montgomery county, xiv., 456.
Roberts, Joseph, petition for remission of fine, xiii., 511. Fine remitted, 535.
Roberts, Owen, Sheriff of Philadelphia, iii., 31, 56, 140. Traitor, xiii., 180.
Roberts, Col. William, to rendezvous at Swede's Ford, xi., 301. Powder, 508. Resigns his commission, xii., 548. Sheriff of Montgomery county, xiv., 555; xv., 97, 296.
Robertson, Daniel, Sheriff, ix., 57.
Robertson, Robert, Coroner of New Castle, i., 174; iii., 416.
Robeson, Andrew, Register of Admiralty, xii., 316. Dies, 745.
Robeson, Captain Thomas, letter on stores for Wyoming, xiii., 565. Sent to, 567.
Robin Hood, ford on Schuylkill to be guarded, xi.. 302.
Robbins, Samuel, sent express to Virginia—his expenses, iii., 162. Builds a boat, "Ranger," x., 335.
Robinson, Andrew, a Councillor, i., 365. To enquire respecting W. Hudson, 371. Warrant for taxes to, 447. Commands Highlanders, ix., 110. Appointed Register of Admiralty Court, xii., 14. Rangers to go to Lancaster, xiii., 117. To have his head quarters at Fort Muncey, 215. Sent to Wyoming, 509. Instructions to, 678. Letter, 698. Of Rangers, xiv., 152.
Robinson, Ebenezer, plan for stopping channel—thanks to, for it, x., 286.
Robinson, Pat., complaint against, i., 136. Proposed to be displaced, 141. Can't be removed till convicted, 142. To deliver up papers, 158, 181, 191, 192. Removed, 192. Committee sent to, for the Records, 102, 103. Councillor, 365. Warrant for taxes to, 447. Petition for claims due him as Secretary, ii., 33. Dies—records to be demanded of his widow, 297. Secretary's papers in his widow's hands, iii., 159. Order for, 160. Succeed as Secretary by James Logan in 1700, 163.
Robinson, Peter, Coroner, viii., 402, 506, 781. Sheriff, ix., 779; x., 56.
Robinson, Samuel, Sheriff, iv., 470, 500, 602.
Robinson, Septimus, Sheriff, iii., 464, 520, 574; iv., 309, 352, 469. Answer to warrant against J. Pemberton, Jr., 391.
Robinson, Thomas, (Merchant) vessel arrives from sickly ports, iv., 674. Sheriff, x., 106; xi., 639.
Robinson, Sir Thomas, letter to act vigorously in defence of government, vi., 177. Union of colonies—French, &c , 177. Troops sent to Virginia, 200. Appointment of James Pitcher as Commissary, 303. Letters, 373, 395, 511, 599, 639. On Braddock's defeat, 511, 599.
Rochambeau, Count de, asks for a hospital in city—house of employment proposed, xiii., 42.
Rochambeau, General, commands French army, xiii., 358.
Roche, Capt. George, member of Council, ii., 140. Justice, 159.
Rodan, John, from Virginia, sent to gaol, xi., 473. (See William.)
Rodan, Wm., sent under parole to Chester to be discharged, xi., 474. (See John.)
Rodgers, Col., xv., 24.
Rodman, Wm., declines appointment as Commissioner to attend Indian treaty at Fort Pitt, ix., 491.
Rodney, Cæsar, Sheriff, vi., 638; vii., 266. Trustee of General Loan Office, ix., 204. Third Judge of Supreme Court, 581. And Judge of Oyer and Terminer, 581. Speaker of Assembly, 625. Speaker of lower Assembly, x., 105,

216, 272. Justice of Supreme Court, 108.
Rodney, Daniel, Sheriff, iii., 524, 575.
Rodney, John, Coroner, v., 551, 597. Sheriff, vii., 267.
Rodney, Thomas, a Justice, ix., 645.
Rodney, Wm., member of Council, ii., 117.
Rodeney, William, dedimus to, ii., 97. Sheriff of Kent county, iii., 260.
Roebuck, man-of-war aground in Delaware bay, x., 554. Lieutenant Ball of, to be exchanged, 563. Sent to Germantown, 580. Engagement with, 582. Man-of-war, prisoners from, xi., 89.
Rogers, Major, an English captain, made prisoner—arrest referred to in Congress, x., 343. On parole, 344, 354.
Rogers, Major John, xi., 87.
Rogers, Maurice, clerk of Committee of Accounts, x., 652.
Rogers, Nicholas, one of a committee to examine works on river (he speaks French), xi.,
Rogers, Thomas, convicted of refusing Continental bills, x., 497. Major R., reward offered for his apprehension, 640.
Rogers, Rev. Dr. William, chaplain, applies for clothing, xi., 727, 728, 740. Petition for half ration to be drawn in city—rejected, xii., 21.
Rolfe, Josiah, a Justice, iii., 28. Member of Council, 227.
Rolls office, ii., 579.
Rolls, Master of, first appointed, i., 91. To keep Charter of Liberty, 111; xiv., 378, 379.
Rotton, John, an English ensign, arrives and is taken into custody, x., 302, 303.
Roman Catholics—proprietor complains of a house built in Walnut street, in which mass is said by Romish priest, and declares it contrary to the laws of England, iii., 546, 563. An Indian, v., 467. In Berks county—Justice's letter to Governor respecting, vi., 503, 533. Complaints against, vii., 344. Inquiry as to number in Province—Mr. Harding, the priest, applied to, 447. His report, 448. John Cottringer and Joseph Cauffman, refused right to hold lands, ix., 596. Regiment of volunteers in British service—Lieutenant Patrick Keane to be closely watched, xii., 176.
Romand, Mr., engineer—materials for experiments, xi., 13.
Romans, Bernard, appointed Captain of a company of Mattrosses, x., 479.
Rongfong, Fred., resigns as Captain, xiii., 15.
Rope-walk of Stacey Hepburn, x., 778. Jas Wharton's, 707.
Rosborough, Rev. John, chaplain of Militia, dies—pension to widow, xv., 234, 442, 485, 643. Pension paid to widow of, xvi., 407.
Rose, John, secretary of Council of Censors, xiii., 770.
Rose, Polycarpus, gives intelligence respecting Indian and French conspiracy, i., 396, 435.
Rosencrange, Jacob, Justice, xv., 35.
Ross, Rev. Æneas, at New Castle, ix., 100.
Ross, Colonel, to draw rules for boats, x., 327.
Ross, Colonel George, member of Continental Congress, receives his pay, x., 287. To inspect ordnance, 283. Order for rifles, 644. Appointed Ensign, 501, 700. Complains against wagon owners, xi., 349. Appointed Judge of Admiralty, 713, 755. Judge of Admiralty Court, dies, xii., 46.
Ross, George, Councillor, xv., 296. President, 584. Vice-President, xvi., 219.
Ross, John, viii., 113, 342. A lawyer, 339. Report, 345. Commissioner to attend Indian treaty at Fort Pitt, declines, ix., 491. Appointed Muster-master of boats, x., 338. Warrant and instructions, 355, 427. Number of men on boats, 430.
Ross, James, applies to be Lieutenant of Lancaster county, xiii., 735. Appointed, 409, 570, 746. Lieutenant of Lancaster county, return of militia officers elected, xvi., 399. Sheriff, 193, 494.

Ross, Captain Joseph, x., 686.

Ross, Captain William, is presented by Council with a sword, for meritorious conduct in Luzerne county, xv., 543. Report in his favor, 547. Paid, 548. Sword presented, 551.

Ross, William, bail refused, x., 729.

Rothrock, Jacob, Coroner, xii., 513; xiii., 93.

Rough, Michael, Coroner, xii., 540.

Rowan, James, deed to, xii., 320. Inspector, 487.

Rowan, William, sheriff, xi., 371, 375, 599. Of York, 229, 599. Sheriff, xii., 161, 162.

Rowing-wheel, an invention by M. Bigland, x., 295.

Rowland, Samuel, Jr., viii., 781.

Roxborough, paper mills, &c., of C. Sauer sold in, xii., 299.

Royer, Samuel, Justice, xiv., 669.

Ruddisell, Jacob, Coroner, xiii., 397.

Ruddisel, Jacob, Coroner, xiii., 723.

Rudman, Andrew, case with Benjamin Chambers, ii., 137, 147.

Rue, Benjamin, asks to form an independent company of artillery, xii., 391.

Rue, Benjamin, sheriff, xiii., 392.

Rugh, Michael, Coroner, xiii., 158, 419.

Rules and Regulations respecting flags of Truce, v., 80. Of Continental army ordered to be printed, by John Dunlap, for use of Associators, x., 636.

Rules and regulations of Council, xv., 341, 586, 590. Report of Committee, 591.

Rum, proposed changes of duty on, ii., 27. Sent from New Castle to Conestoga, 140, 141. Seized by collector, 605. And Indian trade in, iii., 409. Proclamation against sale of, to Indians, viii., 172.

Rumsey, William, a surveyor of Maryland, outrage by, iii., 591. Proceedings against, 592.

Rund, Gottfried, pass for, with Moravian missionaries to the Indians at Onondago, v., 576.

Rundle, Richard, petition for Daniel R., xiii., 96, 132. Daniel and George, 132.

Rush, Dr. Benjamin, appointed physician and surgeon to hospital, x., 347. Attends sick, 409. To receive medicines from Dr. Bass, 489. And Dr. Duffield, 545, 549. Surgical instruments, 604, 614. And Dr. Hutchinson to advise health officer, xi., 543. Director-General of hospitals, xiv., 634. Applies to Council for interest due Dickinson College, xv., 616, 654.

Rush, Jacob, appointed to assist Attorney-General in case of Ship Albion, sunk in Delaware and claimed by Beveridge and others, xi., 544. On Philadelphia election, xiii., 200. Judge of Supreme Court, xiv., 42, 43. Takes oath, 70. Pay to, 481, 602, 666. Judge Supreme Court pay, xv., 135, 358. Paid, xvi., 305.

Rush, Joseph, to value ship General Greene, xi., 720, 739; Coroner, xii., 507; xiii., 85, 391, 723; xiv., 230.

Rush, Dr. Richard, to examine surgeons, x., 452.

Rush, William, purchases firelocks, x., 478, 544. Procure bars, &c., for gaol, 580. Order to, 720. Paid, xi., 697. Elected Justice of Philadelphia, 770. Judge of City Court, xiii., 181, 581. Justice of N. Mulbery ward, and of Court of Common Pleas, xv., 26.

Russell, William, lost a leg at battle of Brandywine, asks aid, xii., 107.

Ruston, Justice, complaints against, v., 78, 95, 99.

Ruston, Dr. Thomas, claiming his seat in Council from Chester, xvi., 201, 202.

Rutherford, John, letter announcing arrival of General Braddock, vi., 303.

Rutter, Thomas, Sr., at meeting of Indians at Philadelphia, iii., 319. Casts cannon, x., 530.

Ryan, John, confined as dangerous, x., 574.

Ryan, Michael, appointed Adjutant of 4th battalion, x., 515.

Ryan, Michael, may be employed by Lieutenant of city as inspector of the militia, with rank of Lieu-

tenant-colonel, xii., 388, 389, 393, 571. Arrested, xiii., 670.
Ryder, D., opinion on law without suspending clause, vi., 209.
Ryland, Nicholas, v., 410.

S.

Sabbath, law respecting, ii., 210, 212.
"Sachem," Privateer, takes prisoners of war, x., 713.
Sackett, Nathaniel, petition, xii., 33.
Sacrament, certificate of Rector and Assistant Rector of Christ Church of administering, to Gov. Denny, vii., 741.
Sail Cloth, manufacture of in Philadelphia, ix., 354. Loaned to Virginia, x., 422, 549.
Sailors engage in a riot at an election in Philadelphia, iv., 621.
St. Clair, Arthur, appointed Prothonotary, &c., of Bedford county, ix., 731. Appointed on special Court in Bedford county, x., 8. Prothonotary of Westmoreland, 77. Letters, 140. Instructions to, respecting Conolly, 144. Letters to and from, 194, 201, 202. Fire-locks, 417. Recommended as a Colonel to Congress, 442. Elected, 443. Major appointed to battalion, 460. xi., 770–7. Recommends Ensigns, xii., 3. Letters to and from, 36, 52, 420. Supplying troops in other States with provisions, 52. On Lieut. Gibbon's case, 139. Recommends Captains, ——. Letter mistakes in dates of commissions, 240. Recruits, 421. Promotions, 545. Asks for money for troops, 613. To court-martial Lieut. Bigham, 675, 685, 686. Returns of recruits to be made, xiii., 39, 47. Message, 408. List of promotions, 441. On Light Dragoons, 504. Buys land, 505. Delivers message from Soldiers, 605, Censor, 721. Appointed Auctioneer of City, xiv., 38, 163, 374. Sale of ruins at Fort Pitt, 498. Paid as member of Congress, xv., 18, 28. Accounts, 153, 183, 194. Appointed to Congress—ceases as Auctioneer—resolutions respecting, 197. Pay to, 218. Letter, 518. Debt due from him as late Auctioneer, and Gov. of Western Territory, xvi., 176, 423. Fees on auctions, 460.
St. Clair, Lieut. Genl., appointed to command troops for Louisburg, v., 37. Letters, to and from, vi., 298, 380. Appointed Deputy Quarter Master, 298, 320. Gov. M. sends maps, 298. Proposes opening roads to Ohio, proposes floats for crossing creeks, &c., 301.
St. Clair, Sir John, Dep. Quart. Gen. on opening Roads—memorial, vii., 592. Letters to and from, viii., 71. Proposes establishing two good horses at several places to keep up quick communication, 71. Grants pass-ports to Indians from Virginia, 124. Commissioner on accounts of Du Quesne, 322.
St. Croix, arrivals from, xii., 20, 29.
St. Domingo, provisions to be shipped to, xii., 59.
St. Eustatia, equipments imported from, x., 708. Vessel allowed to take provisions to, xii., 130.
St. Georges' Creek to be stopped, ix., 600.
St. John, Monsr., French Consul, letters from, xiv., 2.
St. Sacrament, see Lake George, vi., 637.
Salaries of Deputy Treasurer, &c., i., 111.
Salaway, William, a Councillor, i., 365. Also, a Justice, 370, Commissioner to New York, report, 393.
Salem, New Jersey, a Boston vessel from, seized at Philadelphia, ii., 240. Col. Kirkland to be arrested, x., 665.
Salt to Germantown, x., 577, 699. Monopoly of, 748. Sent to Trenton, 759. Arrives, 779. Purchased, 780, 782. xi., 7. To be divided among counties, 13. Terms, 14, 16. Commissioners to distribute, 17. To militia in actual service, 20. Cargo sold at $10, 249. In Prichard's

Store, xi., 654, 661, 670. Great scarcity of, xii., 87. Commissioners for collection and distribution, 123. Exchanged for flour, 136. Pay for, 141, 144, 151. Price of, 133. Distribution, 262, 263. Commissioners for procuring, 161. Complain of it and Flour being smuggled, 152. Per Brig Active, 159. Commissioner insulted by L. Kuhn, 160, 161. From Jeremiah Warder, 191. Price complained of, xiii., 595.

Saltpetre, to be procured, x., 282, 700; Purchased from, J. Sims, 314, 315. A person from York arrives and engages to show how to make, 384. To be paid in part with powder, 430. Instruction to inhabitants to make, 443, 456. Maryland to be instructed, 479, 480, 481. Received from Congress, 484. Made by Mears in Berks, 490. Persons instructed to make, 498. Made in Philadelphia, 543. Works, 604. In Lancaster, 647.

Salt Provisions, Inspectors of, xiv., 488.

Salt Works in New Jersey, under Mr. Savage, Commissioner on, x., 678, 701–6. Guard sent to, 776, 777. At Turtle Gut inlet for sale, xi., 193. Troops sent to, 114. Boat "Delaware" Capt. Eyre, sent to defend, 127, 191. Woodland for, 294. Salt pans, 335. James Davidson, appointed assistant, 403. Account of expenditure, 509. Deeds for land, xii., 84. Manager dead, works to be sold, 160. Sold, price and Deed for, to Jno. Thompson, 186, 190.

Sample, Samuel, a supposed accomplice of Dr. John Conolly at Pittsburg, proceedings against, x., 533.

Sample, Robert, Sheriff, x., 212, 270.

Sandall, Andrew, Minister of Swedish Church, attacks Benjamin Chambers at Schuylkill, ii., 147, 477, 478. His answer in writing, and action of Council, 485. Case of Schuylkill Ferry, iii., 147, 149, 150.

Sandeland, Jonas, Coronor of Chester, iii., 56, 69, 108.

Sanders, Charles, member of Council, i., 440.

Sanders, John, estate sold, i., 564.

Sanders, Robert, letter on French and Indian affairs, v., 626.

Sandusky, failure of expedition against, xiii., 323. Expedition against, 373; xvi., 233, 234, 283. Claim for a horse lost on, 445.

Saratoga, German Regiment, and Chaplain taken at, xiii., 262.

Saristagoa, Indian Interpreter, iii., 571.

Sassoonan or Alummappees, iii., 318. King of Delaware Indians, &c., deed from, 322, 333. Speech, 334. Grief of, 404. In Philadelphia, 404; iv., 53. An old man 54. Presents a belt of wampum of ten rows, 54. Arrives, 307, 443, 446.

Satacaroupes, Indian,—journey to Indians on Susquehannah, vii., 137.

Satcheechoe, Indian messenger, iii., 191.

Saunders, John, a pilot, restricted to Chester, x., 402. Committed to jail, 402. Released—oath, 416.

Saunders, Rear Admiral, appointed Commander-in-Chief of English Navy in North America, viii., 316.

Saunderson, Robert, to be discharged, x., 618.

Sauer, Christopher, Sr., his estate sold in Germantown, xii., 281, 299, 303, 326, 348, 445, 448, 709. See Sower.

Savadge, Thomas, to make salt in Jersey, x., 614, 650, 678. Makes salt in New Jersey, x., 679, 701. At salt works New Jersey, expects enemy, xi., 126, 279, 462. salt works, xii., 84.

Scaientes, a man of note of Cayuga Nation of Indians, v., 83, 84.

Scalps, proposed, vii., 74. Premiums offered, 76, 78, 89. Opinions of C. Weiser and Teedyuscung on, 735. Reward offered for, ix., 189. Sir William Johnson approves of it, 190. Gov.

Penn's Proclamation for, 191. Premium offered in Northumberland county for Indian, xii., 311. And Northampton county, 312. Reward to Capt. Samuel Brady for, 632. Indian paid for, xiii., 201.
Scarborough, man-of-war, about to sail from New York for England, to take copies of papers from Council, v., 104.
Scaroyady, v., 167, 674. Message to, 705. Half King, vi., 140. Speech to by Gov. on Connecticut people, 216. Respecting, 287, 202, 331, 340, 344, 352. Account of his proceedings, 340. Death of son, 523. Message from, 612. Arrives, 681. Presented to Governor Shirley and De Lancey, 358. Complains of the Indians being naked, 359. Message to Gov. Morris, 615. Advises English, vii., 12; 64. Speech, 65. Drunk for several days, 87. Promises to build Fort at Shamokin, 90 Wife and children arrive, viii., 163.
Schaffer, David, Jr., Warden, xiii., 721
Schaffer, Henry, Justice, xiv., 307.
Schaffer, John, Pay Master, xi., 29.
Scheline, Lambertus, counterfeiter, confined—pardoned and discharged, blind, xi., 397.
Schitz, Henry, Justice—contested, xiv., 47, 50, 59. Resigns, 60.
Schlosser, Capt., J., of Royal American Regiment protects Indians, ix., 124. Instructions to, 127, 132.
Schlosser, George, report in favor of, xiv., 661.
Schmick, Rev., John Jacob, Missionary to Indians, presents their memorial from Philadelphia barracks, ix., 135.
Schnider, Capt. Jacob.
Schneider, Lieut. Godfrey, sells clothing, xii., 297.
Schonover, Nicholas, an Indian trader, iii., 309, 320.
School, petition of Quakers for a, in Philadelphia, i., 532.
School of Arts and Sciences proposed, i., 93.
School-master, the first appointed, his terms, &c., i., 91. Convicted and fined for keeping school not having taken oath of allegiance, xi., 653.
Schott, Capt. John P., now commands Armand's corps—petition, xii., 217, 218, 221, 297. An express from Wyoming to Philadelphia, xiv., 176.
Schrawder, Philip, recommended to Congress as 2d Lieutenant, x., 679. Recommended for command of a company, xii., 297; xiii., 136, 574.
Schrawder, Simon, sub-Lieutenant of Lancaster county, xiv., 206.
Schreiner, Jacob, elected to Assembly, xii., 129.
Schreyver, George, Coroner, xv., 297, 570.
Schuyler, Colonel, to go with Shirley, vi., 398. General, asks pay for prisoners in Canada, viii., 240. Applies for gunpowder, x., 301. May loan it to Provincial Congress of New York, 312. Powder received, 327. Lead from Ticonderoga, 330.
Schuylkill, ferry at, established, let to Philip England, i., 126, 184, 368, 387. Swedes complain against keeper, 373. Against William Powell, 380, 381, 437. A boat seized, 441. Belongs to proprietary, 445. Proclamation respecting, 446. More ferries proposed—referred to proprietary as his right, 461. Passengers not to be ferried over after night, 581. B. Chambers complains of another boat being about to be set up by two Swedes, ministers, ii., 137. Council forbid it, 137. Case of Rudman and Sandal, 147, 149, 150. Indian chief Manangy arrives, 191. Benjamin Chambers invents a boat for, 258. Objects to other ferries, 258. Petition from Welsh tract for another ferry on, 276. Opposed by Wm. Powell, 277. Ferry not granted, 289. B. Chambers at, attacked by Swedes, 477, 478. Ferries and roads belong to public, 485, 525. Ferry, proposed law, 528. Petition from inhabitants on taxes, iii., 91. On road, 225. Fishing dams to be

Schuylkill—
removed, 233. Act against dams, &c., 383. Road from Lancaster to, laid out, 523, 618. Wears on, act against, 566. River, petition respecting wears on, iv., 17, 2[illegible], 23, 284. Road from Lancaster to, 503. History of early action, 18. Riot respecting wears, 284. To be made navigable, viii., 582. Act to keep banks, &c., in order, 667. Ferry, Act for protecting, ix., 296, 549. Fisheries, 610, 620, 707. Navigation and fisheries, x., 73. Not to be passed by persons with arms, xi., 27. Toll bridge at, 53. Floating bridge, guard at, 55, 56. Bridge nearly ready to be passed with wagons, 210. To Christiana, 250. Bridge, guard for—no one to pass, 299. Falls, troops to rendezvous at, 301. Guard, 202 Bridge to be removed and taken to the Delaware —boats to be removed, 81, 305. Major Casdrop there, 298, 305. Called into service—Richard Dennis supplies his place, 310. Bridge to be repaired and brought again to its place, 536. Guard for middle bridge, 657. Rent of, 664, 667. Toll from United States, 675. Partly carried away, 686. Expensive, 711. Cable, &c., 724. Bridge to be examined—tolls charged, xii., 195. Committee appointed to employ person to take care of, and procure boats and ropes for ferry, till season for replacing bridge, 202. Benj. G. Eyre paid for replacing, 205. Wood on tract west of, to be cut down for the poor, 207. Abuses of, 208. Wood taken—terms of continental teams, 212. Carried away by ice—to be restored by B. Eyres, 266. Under charge Quarter-Master-General's department, J. Mitchell to keep in repair—continental teams, &c., to pass free—rates of tolls, 269. And road to Darby—petition, 292. Road from, 314. Rent paid, 315. Expense of replacing, 317, 318, 321. Rent paid, 340, 385. Expense of examining, 374. Expenses, 391. Rent, 458. Road to, from Darby, 650, 667, 727. French get masts from, 488 Floating bridge vested in George Gray, 690. River, examination of, xvi., 122. Commissioners to view, 178. J. Hockley paid, 240. Commissioners to examine, 319.

Sherman, Conrad, xiv., 486.

Scofield, Nath., Cor., xvi., 192, 492.

Scold, a common, sentenced to be ducked, but pardoned, xii., 235, 243.

Scotland, rebellion in favor of Popish Pretender, v., 6. Success in, 50.

Scott, Alex., Proth'aryy, xvi., 41.

Scott, James, a traitor, imprisoned, xii., 329.

Scott, John, violent proceedings against his house in Donegal township, iii., 266. Coroner, xiii., 751; xiv., 256; xv., 118. Justice, 59.

Scott, Josiah, a Justice, x., 209.

Scott, Philip, Justice, xiv., 321.

Scott, Robert, resigns as Justice, xiii., 748. Engraver, xiv., 471.

Scott, Thomas, Commissioners to Congress at Yorktown, xi., 435. Letter, 773. Sales of land in this province by Virginia, xii., 234. Appointed Prothonotary of Washington county, 681. Election in Washington county, xiii., 403. Acccounts, 586. Resigns as member Congress—referred to Assembly, xv., 656. Requested to continue as member Congress, xvi., 7. Member Congress, resigns from Council, 40.

Scott, Capt. Wm., x., 687. Paymaster, xi., 308, 390, 406, 493, 509; xii., 461; xiii., 27.

Scruneyattha, Indian half king—speech to Governors, vi., 31.

Scull, Edward, obstructed by Indians in survey of lands, v., 489.

Scull and Hall, printers, Pittsburg, xv., 390.

Scull, Jasper, Sheriff, v., 662. Coroner, vi., 144. Sheriff, ix., 285, 333, 398.

Scull, John, presents for Indians, iii., 297. Sent with message to Indians, 305. Interprets, 313. Expenses, 344, 425.

Scull, Nicholas, &c., petition for

road from lime kilns to Philadelphia, i., 536. Sent to Indians, iii., 305. Expenses, 344. Interprets, iv., 742. Sheriff, 748, 782; v., 55, 662. Appointed Surveyor-General, 274. Sheriff, vi., 144, 638. Surveyor-General's certificate respecting Indian walk, vii., 399. Indian conference at his house, at which Commissioners, Quakers, &c., were present, respecting lands, &c., viii., 212.

Scull, Nicholas, Ensign, x., 464.

Scull, William, Sheriff, x., 270.

Sea letters, Act of Congress for granting, xv., 392.

Seagrove, James, to be arrested, xii. 495. Released, 498.

Seals for each County ordered—their devices, i., 65. Use of great and lesser, 232. Keeper of great, proposes to visit New York—doubts of his right to do so solved, 234. Difficulty about, 235. Greater, when applied, 243. Refused to a paper, 250. To be delivered to keeper, 319. Keeper may sit in Co'ty Courts, 321. For Philadelphia county, 343. Keeper refuses to affix it, 345. Keeper, 581. County, law changed, ii., 210. For Master of Rolls' office described, 233. Greater and lesser, new ones given by Proprietaries, iii., 530. Delivered to Secretary, iv., 639. Words punched out, v., 382. Great, the, viii., 335, 408. Difficulty in absence of keeper, 408. And motto for Committee of Safety, x., 328. For Court of Admiralty, cut and paid for, xii., 102. The Great, of late Province, to be secured, 178. The Great, of late Province, Mr. Physic, keeper, delivers it—directions respecting it, 205. Assembly apply for, part delivered, 237. The Great, xv., 299.

Sealer of weights and measures, i., 128.

Seamen may be searched for on board of vessels, x., 435.

Search warrant granted, i., 151.

Searle, James, xi , 715. Member of Congress—change of flour to ship-bread for shipment, xii., 77–82, 172. Asks to be Aid-de-Camp of President, 138. Sloop Active, 144. Attends Council, 210. Paid, 274, 314. Member of Congress, 371. Pay as Member of Congress, xii., 409, 410. Appointed agent to Europe to solicit loans, 414. Commission, 415. Instructions, 416. List of goods to be purchased, 417. Made Lieutenant-Colonel by brevet, 418. Compensation, 418. Interest, 422. Report on his recall, 694. Return from Europe requested, xiii., 11. To be written to, 242. Arrives from France and waits on Council, 310. Respecting his pay as agent, 751. Before Council, 752. Committee on accounts of, xiv., 373.

Secret Committee (of Congress) to furnish saltpetre, x., 484.

Seddon, Thomas, paper-maker, xv., 462.

Seditious papers, persons spreading, to be secured, xi., 396.

Seely, John, Ensign, xi., 112. Justice, xiii., 683. Deposition of, xiv., 32.

Seely, Jonas, letter from, in relation to Indian murders, ix., 43. Provincial Commissioner, 237.

Seidel, Nathan, a Moravian, sent to consult with Governor M., vii., 190.

Seigler, Charles, (see Jegler.)

Seip, Peter, Coroner, ix., 778; x., 56.

Selin, Captain, rank, xii., 297.

Sell, Ludwig, Coroner, xv., 577 xvi., 210.

Sellers, John, a commissioner to view river Schuylkill, resigns, xvi., 194.

Sellers, Nathan, appointed to make a survey of river Delaware from Schuylkill to Christiana creek, xi., 251. Commissioner to view roads, xiv , 442.

Semple, Captain, xi., 33.

Semple, Cunningham, Justice, xiii., 666.

Semple, William, Sub-Lieutenant, resigns—thanks for services, xii., 210.

Seneca Indians, rumored invasion by, from Maryland, i., 277, 447. Confess to murder of Catawba Indians, iii., 21. Famine and great

distress among, iv., 564; vii., 40, 43. Chief's speech to Delawares, 515. Their chief town, viii., 118, 149. A chief dies at Easton, 213. Seneca George, shot, ix., 603, 604; Speech of Shoanaszowa, 604. War declared by Delawares against, xii., 586.

Senseman, Gotlieb, and wife, Moravians—pass to Pittsburg, &c., with letters to Colonel Brodhead, xii., 346.

Sergeant, Jona. Dickinson, appointed Attorney-General, xi., 254. Case of Mrs. Parrock, 667. Attorney-General, paid salary, xii., 102, 155, 493. Resigns as Attorney-General, 550. To assist in a prosecution, 600. Retaining fee, case of Hog Island, 634. Resigns as Attorney-General, thanks to, 548, 550. Appointed a counsel on Connecticut claim, xiii., 215, 299, 310. Buys city lots, 335. Employed in case of children of Andrew Allen and State, xiv., 448, 459. Attorney-General, paid to, 623. To aid Attorney-General, xv., 127.

Sermon, Joseph, convicted of refusing Continental bills, x., 497.

Serrill, Isaac, Commissioner, xii., 420.

Servants, law to prevent sale of, into other Provinces proposed, i., 61. Sale of a, 63. Proclamation against dealing with, 74. Masters authorized to chastise, 78. To serve five for every day's absence, 80. Punished for telling truth, 88. Rules respecting, 117, 129. Complaint against, 146, 149, 150. Master of a vessel threatens to carry, to Virginia, 161, 162. Trial for sale of a, 185, 223. Duty on convicts imported as, iii., 163, 166. On Irish, 359. Enlisting of, iv., 437, 466, 468. England wishes white servants, rather than negroes, 437, 438, 449, 468. Indentured, clamor against enlisting, vi., 777. Letter to General Shirley respecting, 777. Address of Assembly to Governor on enlistment of, vii., 37. And apprentices, enlistment of, ix., 17, 23, 24. Regulation of, 729. Not to be enlisted, x., 724. And apprentices, not to be enlisted, xi., 242.

Settlement—bill of, passed, i., 62, 63. Act of, does it vacate the charter? 597.

Sewaise, or Sohaise, chief of Conestoga Indians, viii., 115. Speech to Governor, 118.

Seward, Richard, appointed Lieutenant in Colonel Penrose's battalion, x., 473.

Sewell, Richard, Sheriff, v., 120, 345, 411. Sheriff of Philadelphia, returns furnaces and forges in 1750, ix., 633.

Seyfert, Conrad, Lieutenant, xii., 338.

Seymour, Col., Governor of Maryland, expresses from, relative to French privateers, ii., 240. Is he Vice Admiral of the Province? 417, 421.

Seymour, Thomas, appointed Commodore, &c., instructions to, x., 731. Council visit, at Fort Island, 732. To man fleet, 754. Not to allow persons to examine works, 758. Men of boats improperly detained, 777. To inspect vessels, 779. To weigh chevaux-de-frise, 781. Not to allow vessel to pass, 781. To man fleet and rendezvous at Philadelphia, xi., 1. To station guard-boats, 4. Ordered with boats to Trenton, 39. Orders to issue through Com. Hazelwood, 74, 131, 242, 257.

Shade, Captain Henry, of Rifle company, x., 605.

Shaffer, David, "a good Whig"—pass, xi., 593.

Shaffner, George, Ensign, x., 704.

Shakuppo, Indian King, i., 435.

Shakatawlins, Indian Chief, death of—grief of Sassoonan, iii., 404.

Shallnarooners Indians, i., 397.

Shallop, the State, to be sold, as she lies half full of water, xi., 576.

Shallus, Jacob, memorial and brief of title to land, referred to Land Office, xiii., 548, 549. Title to city lot confirmed, 632, 633. Again referred to Land Office, 636. Report, 637. Notary, xv., 295.

Shambough, Valentine, recovers from R. Swanwick's estate, xii., 199.

Shamokin, (see Fort Augusta,) journal of C. Weiser to, iv., 640, 646, 680. Conrad Weiser sent to demand of Delaware Indians the murderers of John Armstrong, 676, 678, 679. His report, 680, 684. Removal of Indians from, 747, 758. Indians from, arrive, 767. Message, &c., delivered by Conrad Weiser to Indians at Joseph Chamber's, v., 84. Called in Indian Zenachson, 84. Visit of C. Weiser to, vi., 35. Lands purchased, Indians, 119, 129. Murders at J. Penn's Creek, 645, 662. Described by Governor, 665. Murders by Indians, 668, 669. Governor intends building a fort at, 701. Governor promises to erect a fort at, vii., 6. Fort at, 6, 54, 76, 79, 80, 90, 96, 121, 159, 163, 184, 281, 294. Houses burned, 154. Indian Conference at, 299. Governor proposes to invite Delawares to settle at, 543, 546. Instructions to Thomas McKee to conduct Indians to, 556. Indian Agents at, viii., 99, 128, 501. Conference between Col. Francis, &c., and Indians at, ix., 610–620; xi., 84.

Shankland, David, Coroner, viii., 506.

Shankland, John, Sheriff, iii., 615.

Shankland, Joseph, viii., 403, 506.

Shankland, Rhoads, Sheriff, ix., 286, 333, 398.

Shankland, William, Sheriff, iv., 748, 782. Sheriff, v., 55, 551, 597. Coroner, 411, 468.

Shannon, Dr., to be arrested, xi., 332, 386.

Shannon, William, auctioneer, Northern Liberties, xvi., 36, 40. Duty on sales, 253.

Shanoppin, Town W., of Carlisle, v., 707. Distance and latitude, 751–762.

Sharpe, Gov. Hor., of Maryland, vi., 178. Number of enemy at Wenango, 179. Letters to and from, 418, 453, 477, 639; vii., 14, 132, 341, 570, 716. Meets E. Loudoun at Philadelphia, 470. Letter to, on Indian affairs, from Governor, viii., 779. Letters to and from, ix., 306, 375. Administers oath to Governor Penn, 348. Petition of John Redick, 375.

Sharp, Lt. George, offers resignation—declined, xii., 15.

Sharp, William—proceeding of Hampton Court respecting Maryland and Pennsylvania, iv., 254. Certificate of confirmation of acts by Court at Kensington, viii., 40.

Sharpless, Daniel, to make fire arms, x., 338.

Shaver, George, Ensign, xii., 70.

Shaw Anthony, Coroner, iii., 465, 520.

Shaw, William, Attorney-General, iii., 338. Commissioner of purchases, xii., 584. Letters on disturbances at Wyoming, xv., 27.

Shawannah Indians, articles of agreement with, ii., 15. Conspiracy against, 145.

Shawnese Indians, iii., 19, 45. Virginia slaves among, 215. Message from their chief, 309. Louisiana, 402. Respecting, 443. Second conference with, at Philadelphia, iii., 459–463. Unfriendly, with other tribes, iv., 739, 741. Ask Delawares to remove from Shamokin to Ohio, 747, 757; v., 292. Message from, 569, 571. Imprisoned in South Carolina, 696. Sick in Philadelphia, 704. Death of Kishocoquilla, a chief, vi., 154, 178, 421. Report on claims of, 724. Chief, the Pride, dies in Carolina, vii., 540. Tribes, perfidy of—terms of peace obtained by Colonel Bouquet, ix., 239. Hostages escape, 239. Separate from Delawares and move to Scioto, x., 201. Message of Governor Penn to, 203. Expedition against, from Virginia, 214.

Shawana, Ben, Indian Chief, at Great Island—letter to W. Patterson, ix., 480.

Shawana, John, a Shawnese Indian, asks aid of Council, ix., 776.

Shawnois Town, strange Indians from North Carolina arrive at, ii , 390.

Shay, Daniel, rewards offered for him by Council and Governor of

Massachusetts, xv., 171. Repeal by Massachusetts, 435, 442.
Sheaff, Philip, Collector of Excise, xvi., 194.
Sheaff, William, complains of short measure in city lots purchased, xv., 537, 562.
Shee, Colonel John, recommended as a colonel to Congress, x., 442. Elected, 443. Officers, 497. Capt. Alles resigns, 497. Firelocks lent to, 501. D. Jones, chaplain, 551. Asks for arms, 600. Auditor of Accounts, xii., 486, 717; xvi., 543.
Shee, Walter, appointed Tonnage Officer, &c., xi., 191, 197, 200. Member of Board of War, 200, 272. (Deceased,) Collector of Tonnage and Duty on Negroes, xiv., 264.
Sheik, Sede, a Christian nobleman from Syria—bill presented by Governor for his entertainment—requests it may be paid, iv., 296.
Sheep, ten, to be kept by every owner of forty acres, ii., 27.
Sheep stealing, conviction for, xii., 261.
Sheeting, Russia, x., 439, 441.
Shekillamy, Indian Chief, iii., 337. To be sent as messenger to Indians, 409. Returns with Indians, 425. Reward to, 447. At Philadelphia, 500, 608. To be specially noticed by request of Indians, iv., 88. Attends conference, 434, 447. His cousin killed, 641. Orders Delaware murderers arrested, 675. They are in prison, 746. On Shamokin Indians, 747, 757. Complains of rum, 758; v., 83, 84, 212, 213, 222, 284.
Shekallamy, John's, lame son, James Logan, vi., 35. Complains of strangers from New York, 216. Informs of settlers north of Albany, 420. Letter of Governor to, 420. Goes with C. Wiser up Susquehanna, 444.
Shekallamy, John—his statement in reply to D. Zeisberger, vii., 245.
Shelburne, Earl of, letters to and from, ix., 341, 342, 378, 379. On Indian murders, &c., 342. Charge of Provincial establishment, 378. Modes of granting land—quit rents, &c., 379, 382. Claims city lots, xv., 88, 235, 481, 485.
Sholby, Captain, vii., 531.
Shemekenwhoa, a Shawnee Chief, complains of sale of rum, ii., 33.
Sherard's ferry, xi., 636.
Sheriffs of counties, i., 58,126, 165, 166, 170, 186, 195, 197, 206, 211, 213, 267, 269, 332, 339, 368. Fined for not doing duty, 125. Cannot act as attorneys, 170. Complained of, 301. Continued for a season, Claypoole excepted, 321. To receive Governor's rents, &c., 343; ii., 20, 22, 25, 101, 105, 177, 178, 205, 233, 397, 298, 448; iii., 30, 56, 69, 108, 139, 260, 289, 332, 359, 370, 387, 464, 465, 520, 574, 614. Elected, iv., 85, 247, 309, 352, 469, 500, 669, 748, 782. Elected, v., 55, 120, 345, 464, 551, 561, 597, 662. Elected, vi., 144, 638; vii., 753; viii. 223, 403, 781; ix., 57, 199, 285, 398, 547, 548, 623, 624, 688, 691, 697, 777, 778, 779; x., 56, 100, 106, 211, 212, 270; xi., 178, 186, 217, 222, 229, 234, 240, 363, 365, 371, 372, 373, 375, 377, 378, 503. 512, 525, 595, 606, 609, 623, 638; xii., 38, 43, 131, 134, 136, 145, 147, 161, 162, 166, 182, 506, 507, 508. Fines, 215, 510, 513, 518, 540. Elected, xiii., 85, 87, 88, 89, 90, 92, 133, 158, 391, 393, 397, 419, 443, 719, 726, 730, 740, 751; xiv., 230, 232, 234, 236, 237, 244, 245, 248, 256, 267, 269, 554, 557, 558, 567, 597. Elected, xv., 98, 100, 102, 109, 116, 118, 120, 125, 195, 294, 296, 297, 301, 302, 325, 565, 570, 578, 584, 600, 646; xvi., 17, 72, 191, 192, 194, 210, 212, 215, 490, 492, 494, 495, 496, 498, 509, 514, 521, 527, 542.
Sherman's Valley, suffers from Indians, vi., 674. Creek, navigation of, x., 70.
Shewell, Robert, claim on, xi., 669. And Isaac Wikoff, 670. Case of, resolution of committee on States, xiv., 162.
Shick, Calamy, youngest son, alias John Petit, viii., 263.
Shingas, Delaware King, destroys great cove, vi., 675.

Ship Montgomery, pays wharfage and storage, xii., 35.

Ship, provincial, of war to be built, x., 395. Progress, 401, 495. Officers, 521, 522. To be called Montgomery, 525.

Shippen, Edward, appointed speaker of Assembly, i., 490. Gone to England, 545. Member of Council, 547. Member of new Council, 580. Appointed Commissioner of property, ii., 61. Provincial judge, 87. President of Council of Governors, 86. Takes affirmation, 96. To send accounts of Free Society of Traders to England, 163. A commissioner of property, iv., 31. Letter, describing several places and persons, v., 660. Letter informing of French on Ohio, vi., 431. Murders near Shippensburg, 459, 655. Letters to and from, vii., 294. Appointed commissioner to Wyoming, 754. Letters to and from, viii., 113. Judge of admiralty, 171. Justice of Lancaster, 562; ix., 89. Letter respecting murder of Conestoga Indians, 89. Second account, 100. Sent to for intelligence, 100. Informs Governor of designs of Paxton Boys to march to Philadelphia and kill Indians at Province Island, 108. Justice, &c., 292. Appointed Justice and President of Court of Common Pleas, xiv., 103. Judge of errors and appeals, 207, 210. Justice of Dock ward, 548. President of Quarter Sessions, 549. Resigns as President of Court General Quarter Sessions, and Justice, xv., 120. Accepted, 128. Claim on estate of B. Arnold, 640. Resigns as President of Court of General Quarter Session, xvi,, 133. Judge claims of R. Peters, 562. Judge of Court of Errors, &c., 534.

Shippen, Edward, Jr., Commissioner to Lancaster, vii., 93, 96. Member of Council, ix., 704. Bounds to be fixed by parole, xi., 269.

Shippen, Joseph, occupies Whitpains front room, ii., 26. Assembly to meet in his "great chamber," 129. Sent to Easton on Wyoming affairs, ix., 749. Report, 750. Justice, &c., xv., 38.

Shippen, Joseph, Jr., elected Secretary of Council in place of R. Peters, viii., 671. Continued Secretary and Clerk of Council, ix., 72, 782. Appointed Commissioner to Indian treaty at Fort Pitt, 491. Report, 514. Continued provincial Secretary, x., 91. Letters to and from, 140. Bounds to be fixed by parole, xi., 269. Discharged, 490. Applied to for records, 764. Late Secretary to deliver papers, &c., to Timothy Matlack, xii., 293. To John Penn who is called on for them, 327.

Shippen, William, member of Congress, xii., 172. Recommends surgeon, 271.

Shippen, Dr. William, Jr., to examine surgeons, x., 452, 458.

Shippen, Captain William, guardian of children of, receives pension, xv., 267, 327, 330, 337. Pension paid, 343, 361. Papers referred, 434, 441, 520, 524, 560, 562, 627, 635. Pay for lumber furnished guardians of his children, xvi., 8.

Shippensburg, road from, through Raystown, Wells creek to Du Quesne, vi., 317. Commission to George Croghan, J. Armstrong, &c., 318. Murder near Fort at, provisions, &c., 460. Fort at, 493, 732; vii., 599, 603; viii., 224. Provisions from Virginia to be discharged at, xi., 461. Sent to Lancaster, 462.

Shipmaster's Society incorporated, ix., 566, 578, 650.

Ships, "unfree" proceeded against, i., 90.

Shirley, Fort, vii., 230. Evacuated, 278.

Shirley, Captain Morris, recruiting for his father's regiment in Philadelphia, vi., 295, 303. In west, 335, 337.

Shirley, Governor William, expedition against Cape Breton, iv., 753, 762. Embargo on powder, 764. On reduction of Lewisburg, 764. Letters, &c., v., 31, 55, 63, 73, 74, 76, 83, 97, 105, 127, 133, 141,

Shirley, Gov. William—152, 165, 171, 296, 303. Asks for rolls of soldiers, &c., 127. Letters to and from, vi., 16, 57, 439, 463, 496, 511, 655. To be consulted, 200. Message to Assembly, 314. Proposes building a fort near Crown Point, 330. To take Colonel Schuyler and men, 398. Embargo, 439. Successes at Louisburg, 463. Letter from Governor M. on Braddock's defeat, death of his son, &c., 496. Command devolves on him, 497. Braddock's defeat, arrival of Colonel Dunbar at Cumberland, 513. Governor M. informs him, of Indian murders, &c., near Shamokin, 665. Of Massachusett, his son recruiting in Philadelphia, 296, 298. Proposes stopping supplies from French, 309. Letters to and from, 309, 310, 334. Arrives at Philadelphia, 358. 548, 549, 558, 593, 595, 777. Plans of French, provision in England against fort proposed, Commissioners appointed, &c., 310, 313. Message to Assembly, 314. Arrival of French fleet at Louisburg, 450. Opinion of Colonel Dunbar's retreat and orders to him, 548. Letter to Dunbar, 549. On French neutrals, 730. Invites Governor M. to meet at New York, 745. Council at New York, 765. Sends soldiers to Philadelphia, 774. Respecting indented servants, 777. Request appointment of Commissioners to settle General Braddock's wagoner's accounts, vii., 10. Letters to and from, 19, 39, 109, 111, 127. To General Johnson, 19. Appointed Commander-in-chief, 19. Instructions to General Johnson, 19. Speech to Six Nations, 21. Holds council of war at New York, 23. Measures to be taken and number of men to be raised for Crown Point, 29–31. Enlisting servants, 37, 39. Called on for a share of arms, 109. Sent, 110, 111. On decl'n of war, 112.

Shirley, William, Secretary to General Braddock to Governor Morris, state of the camp, &c., vi., 405. Killed, 489, 496.

Shoanaszowa, Seneca Indian's speech at Philadelphia, ix., 604.

Shirts for soldiers, xi., 471.

Shoemaker, Abraham, notary public, xv., 89.

Shoemaker, Anthony, for pass, xii., 252.

Shoemaker, Benjamin, commissioner to Indians, vi., 754. Appointed on Committee to investigate proprietary purchases from Indians, vii., 354. Pass to Shrewsbury, xii., 782.

Shoemaker, Lieutenant-Colonel, letter—militia refuse to pay fines, xii., 103.

Shoemaker, Henry, Justice, xiv., 33.

Shoemaker, Jacob, Sheriff, ix., 547, 623, 688. Certificate respecting steel furnace, 633.

Shoemaker, Jonathan, Justice, xv., 279.

Shoemaker, Samuel, to be seized, xi., 284. Confiscated estate in Arch, between Front and Second, north side, sold, and deed executed, xii., 185, 265, 271, 413, 553, 613, 737. Intercepted journal—his wife, 271. Her pass to New York, 352. Estate sold, xv., 657.

Shoemaker, Thomas, certificate respecting steel furnace in Philadelphia, ix., 634. Confiscated estate sold, xii., 202.

Shoes for soldiers, xi., 56.

Shops and schools to be shut up; xi., 27. Opened, 50.

Shot to be made, x., 561, 575, 578.

Shreiber, John, to have care of barracks, stores, and magazine at Lancaster, xiv., 76.

Shreuer, Colonel, Miss Levy, xi., 676.

Shrewer, George, Coroner, xvi., 192.

Shrewsbury, Secretary of State, England, letter respecting invasions of French, and preparation for war, i., 302.

Shrewsbury, Duke of, letter on pirates, i., 555.

Shubart, Michael, elected to Assembly, xii., 129.

Shubel, Theodore, memorial, xi., 755.

Shugart, Peter, Sheriff, viii., 403.

Shugart, Zechariah, Sheriff, viii., 506. Pass for his wife, xi., 567.
Shurlock, Simon, to finish with expedition the ship he is building for the province, x., 486, 495.
Shumann, John Ludwig, children called on to pursue a claim in Germany, xvi., 49. Heirs of property in Germany, 126.
Shurmer, Benjamin, Judge of Supreme Court for Kent, iii., 253, 269.
Sibbald, Captain John, appointed to command the batteries, v., 267. Col. Taylor's instructions to, 284.
Sigfriedt, John, Sheriff, xi., 525; xiii., 47, 48.
Signals, x., 515, 521.
Silk to be encouraged, iii., 392.
Silsby, Samuel, Coroner, v., 411, 468.
Simcock, John, member of first Council, i., 57. Appointed to treat with Indians for lands, 156. Councillor, 169. To act as Lieutenant-Governor, 212. Declines to attend Council, 234. Speaker, 503.
Simmons, Jeremiah, Lieutenant of a boat, x., 339. Appointed Captain of artillery company, 584. Respecting salt taken, xii., 142.
Simmons, Captain Leeson, signals, x., 521.
Simms, Charles, claim to land on Ohio, xv., 242. Memorial, 250.
Simple, Wm., Sub-Lieut., xi., 218.
Simpson, James, appointed master of provision vessels, x., 584. Lieutenant, xi., 557.
Simpson, John, accomplice of L. Stewart, to be arrested, ix., 717. Paymaster, xi., 2. Register and Recorder of Deeds, 195.
Sims, Captain, complained of as insulting inhabitants of Bristol, xi., 254.
Sims, Joseph, sells saltpetre, x. 314.
Sims, Woodrop, buys a lot, xiii., 395.
Sipple, Jonathan, Coroner, ix., 624; x., 270.
Sipple, Waltham, petition against Maryland's proceedings, vi., 417.
Six Nations of Indians, arrival of some of their chiefs at Philadelphia, iii., 608. Message from, v., 284. Deeds for lands purchased from, by Commissioners at Albany, vi., 119–129. Settlers on their lands, 420. Scaroyady and Montour sent to, in reference to Delawares, 697. General Shirley's speech to, vii., 21, 59. Captain Newcastle sent to, 222. Croghan's proceedings with, at Harris's, 506–517.
Skidmore, Thomas, Sheriff of Kent County, iii., 289.
Skinner, John, paid on account of contract with State, xv., 227, 431, 486, 519, 543, 635.
Skins, presented by Indians on renewal of treaties, iv., 571.
Skippack creek, bridge over, lottery for, ix., 284, 285, 719, 729.
Skull, Nicholas, complained of, i., 187. Injury from Indians, 187. (See N. Scull.)
Slagle, Colonel Henry, x., 735.
Slater, Thomas, and mate of brig Betsey, from Virginia, imprisoned for going with Roebuck, x., 563.
Slaughter, Colonel George, allowed to purchase powder for a new settlement in Virginia or Kentucky, x., 332.
Slave, "and Slavery," negro Harry, case of, xi., 263. Act to prohibit importation proposed, ii., 213. Condemned to death — Owners compromised with, 405. Singular punishment, 406. Gradual abolition proposed, 688. Memorial of Committee of the Society for the Abolition of, relative to a free negro held in bondage in Louisiana, xvi., 33.
Sleeping Place, or Black Log, v., 348.
Sloan, Lieutenant David, appointed, x., 678.
Slough, Matthias, Coroner, vi., 638; vii., 266; viii., 402, 506, 781; ix., 57, 199, 285, 333, 398, 547. Colonel, x., 503. Agent to buy clothing, 538. Saltpetre, 540. Pay for troops, 554. Delivers certain articles, 726.
Small, Major, x., 500.
Smallman, Lieutenant Thomas, at Frederick, vii., 553.
Small-pox prevails—Assembly adjourns in consequence, iii., 426,

428. Indian dies at Philadelphia, 463. Prevails in Virginia, v., 221. At Philadelphia, vii., 309, 358, 517. At Lancaster, 474. Deaths by, 546, 597.

Smallwood, General, xii., 549.

Smallwood, John, fined, imprisoned, and reprieved, xi., 663.

Smallwood, W., Governor of Maryland, resolution of Legislature, xiv., 589, 651. Demands a criminal, xv., 463.

Smith, Captain Lieutenant, xii., 718.

Smith, Colonel, xi., 553; xii., 89, 114

Smith, Mr., a custom-house officer, arms taken from, x., 524.

Smith, Abraham, Lieutenant, xii., 322. Resigns, 487. Paid for provisions, xiii., 247. County Lieut., xiv., 400. Councillor, xv., 302, 358; xvi., 409.

Smith, Alexander, Surgeon, xiii., 10.

Smith, Baltzer Cline, pension to widow of, xv., 545.

Smith, Capt. Christopher, commissioned by Governor Spotswood to go to Albany respecting murder of Catawba Indians, iii., 21.

Smith, Devereux, letter respecting D. Conolly, x., 169. Letter, xii., 286.

Smith, Ezekiel, Sheriff, viii., 506.

Smith, Garrett, deposition respecting Col. Pickering, xv., 514.

Smith, George, agent for sale of estates, xi., 538, 608. Agent of confiscated estates, xii., 189.

Smith, Jahbel, captured in flag of truce by a privateer under E. Skellinger—bond put in suit, xiii., 49.

Smith, James (Yorktown), member of Congress, xi., 385. Of York, appointed Judge of Court of Errors and Appeals, xii., 548. Resigns, 723. Controversy with S. Lyons. xiii., 222, 311.

Smith, John, an Indian trader, iii., 309.

Smith, Dr. John, arrested and imprisoned as a tory, x., 460. Convicted and remanded to gaol, 469. A suspected person discharged from prison, xi., 347.

Smith, John and Robert, murder Wm. Boyd in Chester county—proclamation against, xii., 349. Reward paid, 362. To be executed, 405.

Smith, Jona., Jr., clerk in Loan Office, xv., 11.

Smith, Jona. Bayard, member of Council of Safety, xi., 45. Prothonotary, 197. To bring papers to Philadelphia, 275. Member of Congress, 385. To furnish copies of papers, 425. Appointed Prothonotary and Justice of Philadelphia county, 527. Applies to have records of Prothonotary's office brought from Reading, 534. Appointed Auditor to adjust accounts of troops, xii., 589. Resigns, 614. Prothonotary of Philadelphia, xiv., 143. Prothonotary of Court of Common Pleas of Philadelphia, xv., 329, 330, 331. Resigns, 595.

Smith, Matthew, and James Gibson, &c., memorial respecting Indians on frontiers, ix., 138–142, 146. To buy arms at Lancaster, x., 688. Member of Council, xi., 503, 618. Letter, 751; xii., 3, 20, 72, 114. Elected Vice President of Council, 127. Resigns, 221, 222, 493. Prothonotary, 243. Complaints against, xiii., 29, 446, 493. Dismissed, 696.

Smith, Robert, at works at Fort Island, x., 605. Paid for building chevaux-de-frise, 645, 700. Builder, at Billingsport, xi., 6. Lieutenant, 230, 370. Sheriff, 624. Hatter, appointed clerk of market, xii., 110. Lieutenant of county of Chester, proceedings respecting, xiv., 650, 658, 660, 661, 664, 665, 666. Paid for newspapers, &c., xv., 239, 366, 370, 373.

Smith, Samuel, Sheriff of Lancaster county on Maryland affairs, iv., 68.

Smith, Lieut.-Colonel Samuel, commanding at Fort Mifflin, gives his receipt for sundry articles, xi., 397. Committee to Gen. Arnold, 523.

Smith, Samuel, Sheriff, iii., 615; iv., 86, 247. Censor, xiii., 719. Justice, xiv., 313.

Smith, Samuel, Jr., Escheat, xiv., 405.
Smith, Col. Thomas, attends conference between Governor Hart of Maryland and Governor Keith, iii., 60. Sheriff, 332. Sheriff, v., 597, 662. Sheriff, vi., 144. Of Bedford, x., 672; xi., 108. Late Prothonotary refuses to deliver papers—arrested, 373; xii., 8, 15, 70. Respecting militia, 210. Commissioner of Loan Office, letter from, 551. 556. Continental Loan officer, payment to, xiii., 6, 585. Loan officer, xv., 11.
Smith, Timothy, Sheriff, iii., 362, 370, 574, 615. Sheriff, iv., 86.
Smith, William, committed, enquiry why? xi., 43. To be seized, 284.
Smith, William, Lieutenant, xii., 776.
Smith, Wm., Coroner, v., 411, 464, 551. Sheriff, viii., 402, 506. (New Castle), Coroner, 403. Justice, ix., 272. Complained of for neglect of duty, 293. Removed, 293; x., 687. Battalion, 688. Justice, xiii., 653. Has care of pest house and Mud Island and Billingsport, 429. Builds a wharf, xiv., 598, 599.
Smith, Wm. Drewitt, to be seized, xi., 284.
Smith, William Rev. Provost, case of, viii., 11, 17. Charged with libel against Assembly, &c., 11, 17. Serves Assembly with an order of Council, 438. Found guilty of libel and imprisoned, 438–442. Order of committal to the Sheriff of Philadelphia county, 442. At Indian conference at Shamokin, ix., 611. Holds divine service, which Indians attend, 612. To be seized, xi., 284, 525.
Smith, Wm. Hooker, claims, xiv., 395, 396. Letter to, xv., 35.
Smith, Wm. Moore, deposition respecting at Reading for carrying letters for British prisoners, xii., 30.
Smither, John, Coroner, ix., 689, 778.
Smout, Edward, Justice, iii., 531.
Smuggling, i., 285.

Smyther, Capt. ———, of militia, x., 649.
Snake Town, Thomas Wright killed by Indians at, iii., 285, 313, 326.
Sneider, Fred., doorkeeper, xi., 606. Doorkeeper, donation to, xiii., 258. Pay on business of election, 276.
Sneider, Simon, sub-Lieutenant, resigns, xiii., 279. Justice, xiv., 322. Petition against, 325, 493.
Snow Shoes, preparing by Indians, v., 1.
Snowden, Christopher, appointed searcher and waiter of customs, i., 148.
Snowden, Isaac, slave, convicted, x., 93. Commissioner for taxes and levies, xi., 536. Collector of public taxes not to pay militia fines, xii., 636. Buys city lots, xiii., 334, 340. Accounts, 380. Treasurer of City and County of Philadelphia, xv., 89.
Snowden, Jedediah, to send stores to Lancaster, xi., 58. For negro run off to enemy, xii., 116. And Sarah, pass granted to, xiii., 369.
Snowden, Leonard, to be arrested, x., 359. Friends may visit, 397, 409. To be released on parole, 455. His expenses paid, 457, 467.
Snyder, Conrad, Coroner, xv., 120, 301.
Snyder, Ensign Philip, xi., 557.
Society of Free Traders (see Pennsylvania Company), execution against, i., 146, 189.
Society for Propagating the Gospel in Foreign Parts—Rev. Alexander Murray, missionary, x., 503.
Sock, William and Betty, viii., 113, 115, 116, 134. News by him, 118. Takes colors from French, 131.
Soldiers petition Governor and Council, iv., 666. In want of clothing, v., 56. Purchased, 65.
Solebury Township, road, ii., 520, 539. Bucks county, ferry at, iii., 171, 174.
Soleonwanaghty, an Indian chief, dies, v., 467.
Sotcher, John, keeper of ferry from Bristol to Burlington, ii., 488.

Southampton Township, about road, i., 389.
Southbee, William, sells land for Dover Court House, i., 556. Clerk of market, assize of bread, 582.
South Carolina, Governor of, letter to Governor of Virginia—Spanish troops and armament preparing at Havana, iv., 165. Counterfeiter, 276. Governor Glen sends bells to General Braddock, vi., 427. An Indian chief dies in, vii., 540. Militia for, 575, 578. Letter from Governor Bull respecting peace with Indians and death of an Oneida, ix., 775. Troops from, may be employed at Billingsport, xi., 236, 242. Military stores lent to, 691. Loan asked by Congress for distressed inhabitants, xiii., 15. "South Carolina," ship, Commodore Gilliam, 368. Act of Legislature, xiv., 165.
Southersby, William, commissioned as Register-General, pro tem., i., 183, 186. Resigns, 195.
Southwark, District of, Philadelphia, Act for erecting, viii., 694, 698. Regulation of, xvi., 4, 155, 220[2], 225, 234, 238. Report, 245–251, Draft of, 493.
Sowers' Christ'r, Newspaper, complaints against, vii., 245, 339. Forfeited estate, xiii., 207, 508.
Spain and France—war with England proclaimed, ii., 70. Warrant and proclamation for Letters of Marque against, iv., 350, 396. Report of peace with, 427. Relative to, 491–495. Unites in treaty at Aix-la-Chapelle, v., 359, 360. Complains against American privateers, viii., 18. War with, declared by Great Britain, and proclaimed at Philadelphia, 703, 706, 710. Peace with France, ix., 13, 37.
Spangenberg, Rev. Augustus, petitions for a pass for Messrs. Mack, Zeisberger and Rund, to go as missionaries from the Moravians to the Indians, v., 576. Letter informing Governor of Indians on their way from Wyoming, vi., 358. Attends, at request of Indians, a conference with Governor, vii., 107. Letters to and from, 118, 173. On Indian affairs, 118. Goes to Lancaster county, 165. Jo. Pepy and Nicodemus to be sent away, 173. Number of Moravians in Bethlehem, 353. Asks exemption from taxes for Moravians, viii., 304.
Spangler, George, for expenses of Captain Campbell's men—to conduct prisoners to Yorktown, x., 640.
Spaniards, trade with, in West Indies to be opened, ii., 179. Commit robberies on Delaware, v., 92. 111, 119.
Spanish preparations at Havana, iv., 165. Prisoners in jail, in a suffering condition, v., 121. Sent to Leogane, 131. Captain De Cheverie to be arrested, 168. Privateer off Elsenborough, 248. Depositions respecting, 248, 253. Letter from New Castle, 252.
Sparhawk, John, appeal, xv., 234, 235.
Speakers of Assembly, i., 105, 399, 490, 518, 548, 568, 615; ii., 36, 206, 398, 503, 560, 575, 608. Elected, iii., 69, 140, 261, 289, 337, 371, 576; v., 486; ix., 1, 2, 58, 71, 181, 200, 236, 287, 289, 335, 399, 551, 591, 625, 691, 742; x., 2, 5, 59, 81, 105, 213, 216, 241, 270, 271, 273.
Speech of Half-King Seruneyattha sent to Governors of Virginia and Pennsylvania, vi., 31.
Speedwell, ship, letter-of-marque, xi., 2.
Speedwell, sloop, pay for, xi., 706. Belonging to State, work on, xii., 385.
Spees, Henry, Second Lieutenant on Franklin galley, xii., 139. Lieutenant, resigns, 305.
Spence, Lieutenant Douglass, appointed, xi., 202.
Spencer, John, Coroner, v., 662.
Spencer, Colonel, xii., 53.
Spicer, Jacob, Petition respecting a negro slave arrested in Philadelphia, ii., 275. New Jersey Commissioner for Indian affairs, at Easton, viii., 175.
Spicker, Henry, paymaster, xi., 572.
Spirituous liquors, man fined for being disordered by, i., 60, 68. Or-

der to be preserved in public houses, 74. Decision respecting estate of a person who killed himself with drink, 94, 98. Agreement with Indians about, 98. Bargains made with persons under effects of, not valid, 98. Tax on, 99, 100. Adulteration of, 101. To be furnished Indians, if they will agree to be punished as white men are, 105. Sale to Indians, 117, 187. License to sell, 165, 166, 167; ii., 21, 26, 33, 45, 159; iii., 247, 249, 534. And Indians, iv., 758, 760. Not to be sold to Indians, v., 397. Excise on, x., 35. For soldiers, xi., 508. Fine for selling, not remitted, 719. Sale of, without license, punished, xiii., 449.

Spotswood, Alex., Governor of Virginia—commission to Captain C. Smith, to go to Albany, iii., 21. In Philadelphia, in respect to Northern Colonies, 30. Letter to Governor on Indian affairs, 82-89. Conference with Governor Keith, 116. Answer to memorial, 117. Describes position of Indians, 114-116. Letter to Governor Keith—conference with Indians at Albany, 206; and answer, 207. Letter from, to Governor Keith, complaining of Council in relation to Indians, 208. Obliged to return to Virginia, and not attend treaty with Indians, 209.

Spotswood, William, paid for newspapers, xv., 366. And printing, 372. Printer, paid for newspapers, xvi., 189.

Spouts taken down, xi., 291.

Springetsbury, manor of—warrant for survey of, iii., 184. Return of survey, 185. Manor claimed by J. Penn, Jr., and J. Penn, xv., 541.

Sproat, David, property at S. W. corner Front and Walnut Streets sold, xii., 174; xvi., 217².

Sproat, Rev. Dr. James, pay to, as Chaplain to General Hospital, xiii., 561.

Sproegel, Jno. Henry and L. C., naturalized, ii., 184. Petition of F. D. Pastorius against, for an ejectment, 430.

Sprogel, Ludwick, Muster-master, pay, x., 771, 772. Muster-roll, xi., 655, 779. Muster-master General, asks for rum, xii., 44. Discharged, 192.

Spry, Privateer, captures a French flag of truce with prisoners in Delaware bay, viii., 139. At Monte Christo, 234.

Spry, Captain R., vii., 128. Wants seamen, having buried 170, x., 129.

Spur, Lieut., paid as a spy, xi., 117.

Spyker, Henry, Paymaster, xi., 277, 493.

Spyker, Peter, to C. Weiser on Indian murders, vi., 703.

Stacker, Lewis, Justice, xiv., 584.

Staddle, Christian, Second Lieut., x., 457.

Stagle, Henry, appointed President of Courts of Common Pleas and General Quarter Sessions, xiv., 182. Justice, 234.

Stake, George, Justice, xiii., 422.

Stamp Act—letter of H. S. Conway to Governor respecting effects of, in Pennsylvania, ix., 298. Answer of Governor Penn to, 299. Papers arrive at Philadelphia—John Hughes resigns—stamps sent on board vessels of war, 300. Effects of, in New York, 301. Letter Secretary Conway, 309, 310. Bill proposed in Parliament for repeal, 309. Passed, 309, 310. Address of Governor and Council on repeal of, 315.

Standiford, George, Ensign, xii., 70.

Standing Stone, Colonel Brodhead's regiment ordered to, xi., 531. Ammunition removed to Cumberland county, 538.

Standley, Joseph, Ensign, x., 460.

Standley, Dr. Valentine, xi., 691.

Stansbury, Jos. committed—inquiry why, xi., 43, 75. Estate sold, xii., 554. Pass to enemy's line rejected, 568, 573. Pass for his wife, 594.

Stansbury, Nath., a Justice, ii., 159; iii. 28.

Stanwix, Fort, Governor goes to attend a treaty at, respecting boundary, with Indians, ix., 545. Treaty of Sir Wm. Johnson, 553. Boundries described, 554. Treaty

at, x., 257. Treaty with Indians for lands at, xiv., 366. Treaty at, for lands with Indians—terms of sale and purchase, xvi., 501, 506.

Stanwix, Colonel John, at treaty at Lancaster, vii., 533, 563, 597, 600, 602, 603, 607, 629. At Carlisle, 629, 716, 772. Brigadier-General, letters to and from, viii., 146, 341, 343, 352, 373, 376, 377, 378, 400, 427. Death of Lord Howe, 147. Appointed by Gen. Amherst to succeed Gen. Forbes, 298. To appoint Commissioner to settle account of Du Quesne, 323. Consulted in case of a soldier under sentence of death, 336, Letter from Indians, 341, 343. Recommends raising troops of horse, 352. Successes at Niagara, 400. Progress at Pittsburg, 427. Indian Conference at Pittsburg, 429–435.

Stanwix, Journal of the Congress at Fort, xiii., 440. Treaty to be returned, 442.

Stanwix, privateer, warrant against officers of, on complaint of Governor of Jamaica, viii., 171. Proceedings against, 172.

State House, Philadelphia, Act passed for vesting in trustees for use of Province, iv., 46, 483. Keeping of records in, 17, 21, 33, 40, 85. Vested in trustees, viii., 684. Trustees to purchase rest of, 715. Lot a public green forever, xiii., 692. (See Philadelphia.)

State or Province Island to be sold in lots to redeem bills of credit, xii., 667, 671.

Staten Island, enemy at, xiii., 73.

State Lottery. See Lottery.

States, New, out of lands ceded to the United States, xii., 517, 518.

Staves and Heading, regulations on export, viii., 333, 548. Board, plank and timber, xiv., 488.

Stayner, Roger, Second Lieut., x., 457.

Stealing provisions, lad of 13 convicted—pardoned, xii., 69.

Stedifort, Garret, Quartermaster, x., 480. Captain, xii., 215.

Steddicorn Simon, paper maker, xv., 462.

Stedman, Alex., Commissioner to Lancaster, vii., 93, 96. Commissioner on accounts of Du Quesne, viii., 322. President of Court of Common Pleas, 339. Warrants referred to, 342. To be seized, xi., 284.

Stedman, Charles, to be seized, xi., 284.

Stedman, Charles and Alex., forfeited estate at Germantown, xii., 204.

Stedman, Joseph, Coroner, x., 56, 211, 270.

Steel, James, orders to, make survey beyond Susquehanna, iii., 161. Commissioner on boundary, 544.

Steel, Lieut. John, recruits, xi., 444.

Steel, making of, prohibited, v., 437.

Steel furnaces in Philadelphia, &c., 1750, ix., 632–636.

Steel, manufacturing of, by Whitehead Humphreys, aided by Council, xv., 269.

Steele, Rev. Mr. Jno., meeting house, fort at, vi., 675. Captain, &c., affairs on borders of Maryland, vii., 241. Appointed Commissioner for removal of settlers on Indian lands, ix., 481. Instructions, 483. Letters to and from, 486. Letter on report of proceedings, 506, 509. Lottery for his church at Carlisle, 622.

Steele, John, printer, xiv., 494.

Steelman, Hans, of Maryland, sells goods to Indians without license, ii., 21.

Steiner & Cist, printers, xi., 200.

Steiner, Melchior, Council order two copies of German newspapers printed by him in Philadelphia, xv., 375. Prints a German newspaper, xvi., 126, 375.

Steinmetz, John, City lots, xiii., 576.

Stenton, James Logan's residence—Indians entertained at, iv., 82.

Stephen, Adam, vii., 289. Commands at Fort Cumberland, 289, 381, 502.

Stephens, (or Stevens,) General, x., 755, 757.

Stephenson, George, agent of forfeited estates, dead, xii., 64. Rev. Mr. Batwell's land, 296.

Sterling, Captain James, paid for expenses of escort of prisoners to York Town—allowed horses, x., 645. Order to, 647.
Sternfield, John, deed to, xii., 201.
Sterrat, James, Sheriff, v., 55, 120.
Sterratt, John, Sheriff, iv., 748, 782.
Sterrett, Samuel, muster-master, xii., 462. Applies for pay, xiii., 123. Asking copy of Act respecting university lands, 454.
Sterrett, William, Lieutenant, xiv., 483.
Steuben, Baron, on military discipline, subscribed for, xii., 72. To occupy Arnold's country-seat, 519.
Stevens, Arent, letter on French and Indian affairs, v., 625.
Stevenson, George, Commissioner on accounts of Du Quesne, viii., 322. Ensign, xii., 8.
Stevenson, James, letters to and from, vi., 248. Deed to Lydius, 248. Auditor of depreciation of Pennsylvania Line, xiv. 139.
Steward—of Penns'a Hospital, (Dr. Story,) paid for stores, &c., xi., 85, 130.
Stewart, Charles, and Jennings, on New England settlers in Wyoming, ix., 573. Appointed a justice, 575. Letters to and from, 583, 586, 607. Letter respecting Wyoming, 756. Letter from, respecting Connecticut settlers, x., 50. Says army is in want of bread, xi., 303.
Stewart, George, Sub-Lieutenant, xi., 378. Summoned to appear on charge of misbehaviour as agent for sale of forfeited estates — Notices to be put up near Ephrata, calling for evidence, 547, 570. Letter to — agent of confiscated estates, xiv., 3.
Stewart, James, accomplice of Laz., to be arrested, ix., 717. A counterfeiter, arrested, xi., 234.
Stewart, John, paid for a mare, xiii., 636.
Stewart, Lazarus, order for arrest of, for ill treating Justice De Haas, ix., 682. Capture and escape, 682. Reward offered for, 685. Proclamation against, 687. Deposition respecting capture, 710. Message of Governor to Assembly respecting, 713. Murder of N. Ogden, 714, 749. Proclamation against him and his accomplices named, 717. Joins Connecticut people against Wyoming, 749. Notice of his conduct by Governor R. Penn, x., 3.
Stewart, Robert, Cor., v., 411, 464.
Stewart, Walter, as Captain, x., 447. Order to, xi., 421. To take Colonel Becker's command, 456. Money, 526. Colonel, xii., 368.
Stewart, William, accomplice of Lazarus, to be arrested, ix., 717.
Stewart, William, Coroner, ix., 57, 199.
Stiles, Captain, and his mate, murdered, viii., 436.
Stiles, Captain, ordnance, xi., 252. To furnish arms and men to Captain McAffee, 564. Repairs, 590, 606, 662.
Stiles, Edward, may export provisions to Bermuda, x., 414 Negro sold as part of his confiscated estate, xv., 277.
Stiles, Captain Joseph, Commissary Military Stores. Superintendent of laboratory for providing stores for galleys, &c., xi., 47, 125. Superintendent of ordnance, 142, 242. Takes charge shallops with ammunition, 310. To have shirts made, 470. A warden, 538—orders to, xii., 3, 20, 72, 111, 139, 145. Price of storage on powder raised, 172. Repair of arms, 266. Pay for men, 287. Orders to, 313, 405, 428, 456, 614, 641, 662, 702, 712, 774. To deliver ammunition, xiii., 1. To have arms ready, 19, 20, 28, 48, 70, 82, 137, 149, 178, 213, 239, 247, 263, 310, 311, 329, 335, 341, 345, 508, 567, 603, 670. To deliver over cannon taken at Yorktown, 614. Letters, &c., xiv., 29, 72, 159, 183, 185, 199, 206, 231, 366. To remove stores from old jail, 366. To erect a frame arsenal, 401, 469, 477, 588, 655. Commissary of Military Stores, xv., 12, 15, 33, 46, 82, 110, 204, 235, 277. His pay, 61. Tents to Colonel Armstrong, 204. Powder for Fourth of July, 235, 236, 307.

Complains of powder magazine being full, 433, 434, 447, 453. Commissary, xvi., 154, 408. Commissary, &c., 270, 513.

Still, Isaac, Indian interpreter, viii., 30. Messenger to Minnisinks, 140. Sent to Indians, 341.

Stille, Benjamin, appointed to settle accounts between United States and Pennsylvania, xiii., 558, 597.

Stillwell, John, Coroner, x., 270.

Stinton, ——, murder of, by Indians, ix., 140.

Stirling, Earl of, visits New Castle with Governor John Penn, &c., ix., 73.

Stites, Henry, Quarter-Master, xi., 54, 112.

Stobo, Captain Robert, hostage at Fort Du Quesne, letters from, vi., 141, 161.

Stocker, Anthony, executors indemnified, xvi., 4.

Stocker, Clement, pass to, with books of accounts of Thomas Wharton, late Pres't, xii., 594.

Stockton, Major, taken, and a boy, xi., 200. Sick in prison—his wife attends on him, 216.

Stocker and Wharton, claim against executors of estate of xv., 647. Proposals accepted, xvi., 223.

Stokely, Nehemiah, Justice, xiii., 244.

Stokely, Paynter, Coroner, vi., 638.

Stokely, Thomas, Register and Recorder, xiv., 260. Of Rangers, payment of officers and privates, 366.

Stone, Andrew, Secretary of Lords Regents, letter from, iv., 671, 675.

Stone, Frederick, Sheriff, ix., 689, 778; x., 56.

Stoneburner, Leonard, to collect leaden weights at Germantown, x., 637.

Stony Point, victory at, by General Anthony Wayne, votes of thanks to, xii., 124, 135.

Storekeepers of provisions appointed, xi., 423, 437.

Story, Enoch, indicted for entertaining Wm. Bevan's servants, ii., 160. Claim for entertaining County Justices, 180. Estate sold, xii., 283.

Story, James, Commissioner on United States accounts, xiv., 386.

Story, John, to settle accounts, xiv., 405, 451.

Story, Dr. John, Steward of Penn'a Hospital, paid, xi , 85, 130.

Story, Samuel, Lieutenant, xi., 776.

Story, Thomas, appointed Keeper of Great Seal, i., 580. Appointed Commissioner of property, ii., 61. To have a seal, described—as Master of Rolls, 233. Petition for salary, 412. To appear before Council, xii., 259.

Stotesbury, Lieutenant John, xi., 92. Appointed, xiii., 25.

Stoughton, William, Governor of Massachusetts, applies for provisions, i., 515.

Stout, Captain Harman, recruits, xi., 573. Lieutenant, pay, 596. Letter, xii., 89.

Stoy, Capt., xi., 424.

Stoy, Lieut. J., to recruit, xi., 572.

Straker, William, made prisoner by Count D'Estaing's squad'n, order of Congress respecting, &c., referred to French Minister, xi., 553. Decided to be a citizen of this State, 554. Going to West Indies, 641, 684.

Strangers, required to have passes, ii., 12. To be protected, iii., 64.

Straw, &c., weaving and working, patent granted for, iii., 18.

Strawbridge, Thomas, x., 738.

Strawbridge, Col. Thomas, superceded as sub-Lieutenant, xi., 437; xii., 514.

Streaker, Wm., pass for, xi., 641.

Street, ———, captured at Fort Granville, vii., 716.

Streeter, James, petition about apprentice, i., 583, 584.

Streets, bill for regulating, i., 552.

Stretcher, Henry, a member of Assembly from Sussex, complaint against, i., 185.

Strettell, Robert, member Council, iv., 506. President of Council, letters from, vi., 773, 777.

Strickland, Amos, Sh'ff, v., 55, 120, 345. Complained against—acquitted, 345.

Stringer, Wm., applies for a pass, xi., 569.

Strohbogh, Captain, sent for, xi., 4.

Strohbogh, John Mertin, Lieutenant of 3d artillery company, x., 567. Second Lieutenant, 619.
Strong, Jedediah, a Commissioner from Connecticut, arrives, x., 118.
Strong, Matthew, proposes to sweep river for anchors, xi., 770.
Stroud, Col., xi., 717.
Stroud, Col. Jacob, his conduct disapproved of, xii., 64, 65. Censured, but mitigated, 100, 101. Letter to, on Indian invasions, &c., 312. Memorial and deposition respecting, xiv., 32.
Stuart, Alexander, depreciation, xiii., 154.
Stump, Frederick, murders ten Indians—deposition of Wm. Blythe, &c., ix., 414-490. Letter from Gov., &c., to magistrates of Cumberland, 416. Do. of Lancaster, 418. And Berks, 419. Proclamation of Governor, 420. Capture of, 438. He and his servant John Iron Cutter, ordered from Carlisle gaol to Philadelphia, to be examined, 441. Letters from Governor to Sheriffs, 440, 442. From General Gage respecting, 443. Letter from Colonel John Armstrong to Governor respecting the murder, and his arrest, 444. Governor's answer, 446. Message from Assembly, 447. Rescue of, 448. Examination of James Cunningham, 449, 450. Proceedings of Council, 451. Instructions to Colonel Armstrong to regain him, 451. Letter from William Patterson, his captor, 453, 470. Message of Assembly, reflecting on Governor, 454. Governor's message, 460. Letter General Armstrong means used to regain, 462. From Sheriff of Cumberland respecting, 463. Letter to Sir William Johnson, 468. Names of Indians killed by, 470. Letter from Colonel Armstrong in his vindication, 484. An Indian found dead in Susquehannah by James Thompson, 487. Second proclamation for their arrest, 488. Description of, and Iron Cutter, 489. General Armstrong and Sheriff Holmes in Philadelphia to be examined, 490. Funds allotted for taking, 494. Sir Wm. Johnson's account of, 501, 506. Examination of Armstrong, Miller and Lyons respecting, 510. Admonished and dismissed, 512. Governor Penn to Indians—message of condolence, 521.
Stump, George and wife, case of, xii., 723.
Sturgeon, William, assistant rector of Christ Church, vii., 741.
Sturmfels, George, claims for ground rent due proprietary on a confiscated estate, xv., 51.
Sugar Islands, apply to Parliament to restrain trade of northern colonies, iii., 401. Answer of Assembly to Governor on, 406, 418.
Sugars, Zecharias, Coroner, vi., 638. Coroner, vii., 266.
Suicide, case of, ii., 181.
Sullivan, General, orders militia to Jersey, xi., 225. Quota for, xii., 26. Men to be urged on to, 43. His army to be supported, 72. Militia to be placed at Sunbury to protect stores, &c., for, 74, 92. Letter from, 107. Removal from Northumberland, 138. Wagons to be obtained, 143.
Sullivan's Bridge, xi., 709.
Sullivan, Lieut. James, of dragoons, to be arrested, xiii., 617.
Sulphur Ore, discovery of, x., 314. Refining, 519, 593, 608.
Summons of Contrecœur to surrender, vi., 29.
Sunbury, Congress request militia placed at, xii., 73. To be removed from Wyoming, 138. Military stores at, xiv., 165.
Sunday, unknown to Indians, vii., 205.
Sunderland, Lord, on expedition against Canada, ii., 449. Attempts to obtain lower counties, iii., 252.
Superintendent of Finance—reports, &c., xiii., 566, 619, 637.
Supply Bill, viii., 478, 481, 693, 695, 717; ix., 158, 161, 180, 183. Passed, 184.
Supreme Court, ii., 524, 526. Justices commissioned, 596. Reasons for delaying trials, 615. New commission for Judges named, iii., 253, 269. Judges commis-

Supreme Court—iii.
sioned, 269. M. Hill dies, 381, 396. Two vacancies, 398. Isaac Norris, Chief Justice—Jeremiah Langhorne and D. Græme, 400. Convictions by, iv., 209. Chief Justice Langhorne dies and is succeeded by J. Kinsey—Thomas Griffitts resigns as Third Judge, Wm. Till succeeds, 640. To try Indians, 751, 752. Convictions of burglars, v., 155. Of murder, 269. Report in case of A. Ure, 277. Jehu Curtis, Second Judge, dies—W. Till proposed, vi., 135; viii., 66, 335; ix., 3, 4, 169, 203, 205, 272, 393, 581. Act proposed to enable, to take evidence in foreign countries, x., 18, 21. Judges, salaries, 53. Of lower counties—John Vining dies, 108. J. McWilliams, Chief Justice, 108. Wm. Allen resigns—Benjamin Chew appointed Chief Justice, 173. John Morton, Fourth Judge, 173. John Lawrence and Thomas Willing, second and third, 173, 265. Joseph Reed appointed Chief Justice, xi., 186, 195, 202, 249. Judges appointed, 254, 270. Decrees respecting purchase of forfeited estates, xii., 48, 49. Judges of, 69. Decrees favor J. Morgan and Wm. Honeyman, 114. Decrees on estates, 174, 175, 191, 199, 249. George Bryant, Judge, 303, 305. Decree, 327, 702. Power of Assembly over, 721. Asked opinion on 20th section of Constitution, xiii., 218. Answer, 219–221 Opinions on Philadelphia election, 229–231. Powers of Council to appoint Judges, 259. Judges recommend Jessie and S. Vicars and Jno. Shebell to mercy, 373. Conference requested with Council, 607, 619. Jacob Rush, Judge, xiv., 42, 43, 71. Longschamp's case, 117. W. A. Atlee resigns and is re-appointed, 175. Robert Morris appeals to, respecting accounts, 488. Claim and title of Messrs. Penn to province referred to the, 502. Opinion, 553. Expenses, 554. Prothonotary, 628. E. Burd, 629. Expenses of Judges paid, while

Supreme Court—
traveling from Carlisle to Philadelphia, xv., 34. Deed—Justices—division of Mahoning township, 41. Accounts with United States—sale of city lot postponed, 85. Balance paid Isaac Snowden as Treasurer—fines not to be paid, for laying off a part of west branch of Susquehannah, 85. Opinion asked of, in an election case, 131. George Bryan re-appointed, 189. Opinion asked relative to allowing interest to proprietaries, 202. Expenses paid, 204. Answer of Judges, 210. Judges to confer with Council respecting resolutions at Easton, 224. Account of conference and result, 225. Expenses paid, 226. 264, 328, 379. Conference asked, 261–265. Letter on magazine—opinion on J. Rheiner's case, 452. Expenses of judges and servants, 495. Case of E. Oswald, 494, 495. Opinion, 501. Expenses, 623. Pay, 636. Pay to Judges, xvi., 39. Decision favor of Jno. McCalmont, 46. Paper referred to Judges, 97. Pay to, 349.

Supreme Executive Council — Assembly and Council jointly elect President, Thomas Wharton, Jr., and Vice-Presid't, George Bryan, xi., 173. The election proclaimed at Court House by the proper title, 174. Oaths administered—Timothy Matlack, secretary of Council and of Commonwealth, 174. Licenses for public-house keepers, 175. Day of fasting and humiliation appointed by Congress, 175. Proclamation, 176. Council of Safety call for money—law books to be purchased, 177. Letter from George Washington, 178. Establish a Board of War—their names and duties, 181; and a Navy Board, 182. Officers object to oath, 183. Explosion of powder mill—letter from Henry Fisher, arrival of vessels of war, 184. Proceedings on remonstrance of officers, 185. Letter, Governor Livingston, of New Jersey, relative to prisoners, 185. Hessians may be employed—appoint-

Supreme Executive Council—xi. ments, 186, 187, 188, 189, 191, 194, 195, 196, 197. Petition of Robert Patton, 189. Official arrangements of 10th battalion, 190. Navy Board's state of affairs, 191–193. Petition of L. Hollingworth, 194. Mrs. Galloway to be protected, 196. Money returned to Hyde & Co., 197. Congress asked to call out militia of Pennsylvania—conference with Representatives in Congress on Genl. Howe's intention—Board of War want more money—officers in navy recommended—appoint four Brigadier-Generals, 199. Also officers for navy—appointments, 200. Dr. Conolly enlarged—appoint Board of War, 201. Money from Congress—appointments—movements of enemy, 202. Conference—resolution of Congress, 203. Address to the people on taking active measures against the approaching enemy, 204. Lieutenants to be written to, 209. Assembly ask respecting quota required from the State on Continental service—Board of War to give a return, 210. Complaints against officers, 210. Pecuniary affairs of Board of War complained of, 211. Referred to Assembly—blankets to be collected, 211. Order of Assembly for money, 213. Orders for money, 214. Walter Hall petitions to have an absconding debtor detained, 214. Plan for turning over certain troops—Justices—letter to Assembly respecting provincial forces, 215. Money for Navy Board, 217. Minute of Assembly, ask conference on state of affairs, 217. Plan for removing citizens, 218. Appointments—Justices—orders for arms—conference with Assembly, 219. Representation to Assembly on dissatisfaction with present frame of government-propose taking sense of people on a convention, 220. Prothonotaries to be judges in their counties, 221. James Claypoole, sheriff, 222. Circular to counties to send militia, 222; and wagons—order from Congress for

Supreme Executive Council—arms, 223. Artillery company, and officers commissioned, 223. Resolution of Congress appointing General Arnold commander of militia—ask for money—John Kidd declines being a member, 224. Col. Walter Stewart—Col. Bull promoted—militia ordered by Gen'l Sullivan to Coryell's ferry, 225. Resolution of Congress respecting rank, &c., in army, 226. Of Assembly—probable attack of enemy, 227. Loan from Congress—Justices, &c., 229. Committee to view works on river, report—Colonel Stewart on change of orders—orders for militia, 231. A present of fourteen copper-plates from Dr. Franklin to Council, 232. Pay of Commodore fixed, &c.—movements of enemy—Orders, 232. Paymaster, complaint by Board of War—pilots—William Sykes contemptuously removes goods from, 234, 235, 236. Advertisement for election of Justices, 238. Boundary between Virginia and Pennsylvania—Markoe family sent to St. Croix, 240. Servants not to be enlisted—proclamation—visit Billingsport, 243. Du Coudray's plan—ask for money from Congress, 245, 246. Order for boats to convey militia from Chester to Billingsport, to General Potter—General Armstrong and General Potter attend—Justices of Little Britain—resolutions of Congress on Billingsport, Capt. Downey ordered there, 248. A cargo of salt arrives at Tom's river—for sale at ten dollars per bushel—ordered to be bought—Joseph Hart elected a member—survey of Delaware river by Davis and Downey—Joseph Reed declines being Chief Justice, 249. Order surveys of river, and appoint persons to do it—order guard for Fort Island, 250. And money—committee of Board of War attend and consult on best mode of procuring intelligence—persons appointed to proceed to Capes—Justices, 251. Proceedings respecting Westmoreland

Supreme Executive Council—xi. records—increase committee of Bucks county for driving off cattle—arrival of part of enemy's fleet at Egg Harbor--Genls. Wayne and Nash attend, and present situation of army approaching city, 253. Appoint Chief Justice and Attorney-General — call of Congress for 4,000 militia - detention of records, 254. Change in committee on cattle---Congress authorize purchase of twelve fire-ships, 255, 256. Ask for money, 256. Money sent to County Lieutenants, 257. Papers and records in Philadelphia to be removed in case of danger—attorney for certain Courts, 258. Discontinue Board of War—Justices—suspected persons delivered up, 261. L. Gordon imprisoned--Letter from General Hand, asking for troops for Indian country, 261. Wagons —accounts of Board of War to be settled—person enlarged on parole, 263. Proceedings respecting a slave—pilot discharged—Benj. Chew and John Penn made prisoners, refuse parole—Congress to order them removed, 264. Arrest of several persons for riot in York county—Rev. Dr. Ewing apologizes for Mr. Chew, offers his parole, 267. Parole of Doctor Drummond--Navy Board to assist in removal of troops from Billingsport to Fort Island—knapsacks—examination of three more rioters, and discharge of two—petition in case of not taking test of allegiance—Thomas Lightfoot ordered to be arrested by Congress, but is not a resident—demand of Genl. Gates for men—bounds prescribed in parole—wood for barracks—declined, 269. Judges of Supreme Court appointed — removal of troops from Billingsport—storehouses and magazine at Lancaster—Clerk of Court, 271. Congress to be consulted about discharge of militia—appointments, &c., 273. Orders to Col Henry —aid for Captain Alexander, 275, 276. Books and papers ordered to Philadelphia—compliment to

Supreme Executive Council—Commodore Hazelwood—appointments, 277. Application of Genl. Knox for cannons—call on P. De Haven for arms, for stores—Leaden spouts to be taken down—search houses for arms—disaffected persons to be arrested—wagons and horses–appointments, 279. Com'tee to drive off cattle—company raised by J. Williams —arms from French creek, 280 —privateer commissioned—list of disaffected persons, to be arrested, 282. Raising troops—resolutions for arrest of disaffected persons named, 283, 284. Instructions—blankets, 284. Persons appointed to make arrests, report of arrests, 287, 289. Refuse to hear the parties—order Jared Ingersoll to Connecticut—wagons from counties — guards for prisoners—liberty granted to Thomas Asheton - lost blankets, &c., to be paid for—William Lenox enlarged, 291. Remonstrance from Masons' lodge —to be sent to Congress—answer —enlarged, 292. Militia called out—Hazelwood, Commodore of fleet in Delaware—prisoners, 293. Prisoners in Masons' lodge to remove to Virginia—enlargements --paymaster—purchase of guns —water craft to be detained, 297. Light horse to proceed to camp—guard for bridge—proclamation—approach of enemy—militia to be ready—horses scarce, 299. "The two armies being now engaged, and the event doubtful," stores and shops ordered to be shut, and all except those making or repairing arms to repair to Captains' quarters at two o'clock—battalions to rendezvous at Swedesford and Falls of Schuylkill—provisions to be supplied there and at Darby--army engaged with Gen. Washington—troops from Bucks to turn out, with or without arms, bringing axes, shovels, &c.—appointments — horses to be impressed, 301. And wagons—guards—bakers not to be enlisted --boats to be collected, 303. Call out militia of Bucks and

Supreme Executive Council—xi. Philadelphia, order loan office books and money to Easton under guard, bridge over Schuylkill to be removed and brought to the Delaware, Quarter-master appointed, money asked of Congress, 305. Boats on Schuylkill to be hauled on land—bells to be taken down and removed to places of safety—order for public records detained - report to, on loan office books and papers—threatened destruction of public property, 307. Proceedings on writ of habeas corpus issued against persons arrested—riots in Carlisle -guard for stores-books in library to go to Easton, 308, 309 Appoint R. Dennis in place of Major Casdrop — place shallops and ammunition under care of J. Stiles — proceedings respecting driving cattle, pay for pasture— B. Vancampen Sub-Lieutenant— various orders for money, 311. Decide on petition of Captain Joseph Brady's co. on Lots— orders—meet at Lancaster, 313. Gun factory at Hummelstown— establish expresses between Council and Camp, 314. Two prisoners escape on way to Virginia—jailer examined and implicated—several arrests connected with the escape, 315, 316. Ask for money—Treasurer can't comply—wagons sent for goods to Trenton or Bristol —Assembly ask a conference on state of affairs—granted—Colonel Hart takes his seat, 317. Militia to defend inhabitants of Chester, 318. Blankets—a private escapes —pay for Colonel Piper's family, 319.

Here begin minutes of "Council of Safety," 323. [Which see.]

Proclamation dissolving the Council of Safety, 353. John Morris, Jr., to attend Court in York and Cumberland—M. Immel to be closely confined—complaint against Wm. Lees, 357. Appointments, 358. Pay for arms—petition of John Swanwick--militia called out, 359. New members, 366. Appointments, 367. Thomas Wharton,

Supreme Executive Council— President, and George Bryan, Vice-President—new member, 375, 378. Receive from Congress copy of the confederation, 379. Congress recommends calling in the old bills of credit issued by G. B.—also to abolish substitutes, 382. Receive various papers relative to Quakers sent to Virginia, 383. Delegates to Congress, payment of wagoners, 385. Conference with Assembly on state of Continental army—remonstrance against its going into cantonments, —Dr. Shannon, 389. Representation to Assembly respecting impressing wagoners, &c., 390. Conference on calling out whole force against enemy on petition, 394. Referred to Congress, 394. Deliver up key of loan office chest—orders respecting militia—prisoners of Virginia belong to United States, 395. Block tin and lead at Carlisle—Colonel Lacey to command militia—Colonel Kirkbride to send out light horse, 396. Complaint of Colonel Hartley for impressing wagons—clothing for Fort Mifflin-- pardon and discharge of Lombartus Schelline—pay Joseph Carson for goods, 397. Appoint Justices— wagon masters—Brig.-General— pay Col. Bull for work at Red Bank and Billingsport, 399. And as Col. commandant--services of Adjut't-General unnecessary—dispense with Colonel Bull—apologize to him, 400. Capt. Woelper's claim, R. Levers and goods sent to Boston for sale—write to General Washington about recruiting officers, 401. Case of C. Dingee— of W. Montgomery—appoint J. Davidson assistant at salt works —murders by Indians—aid a wounded militiaman, 403, 404. Resolution of Congress on proposal to regain city—Act for supply of arms—provision in Berks county for fleet—pay of M. Hubley increased, 405. John Brown enlarged—letter from R. McCallister —J. White Swift—Col. Johnston resigns—J. S. Howell appointed Receiver-General, 407. Offers a

Supreme Executive Council—xi. price in lieu of rations of liquors —subscribe for 500 copies of German newspaper in Lancaster, also of Dunlap's—wagons to be furnished from each county—to Colonel Lutterlish—arrest of J. G. Metscher as suspected, 409. Indians in Cumberland County—Colonel Piper censured for enlisting men in Bedford — General Lacey's place as clothier supplied —letter from board of war respecting flag, 411. J. G. Metscher to be discharged on taking oath—county paymasters to examine militia accounts of expenses, 413. Prisoners under guard on their way to Yorktown—Captain Long and company continued in service, 414. Resolutions of Congress respecting oaths to be taken by officers, 415. Order commissions for persons recommended by General Washington to recruit—clothing delivered by J. G. Howell, 418, 424. Colonel Coates a prisoner with enemy—Colonel Thompson to act in his behalf—orders for recruiting, 419. Payment to Commissioners to purchase provisions, 422. Allow congregation at Easton to ask aid in finishing their church—granted—agent to distribute provisions—arms for Bedford—money to buy provisions in Lancaster—storekeepers of provisions at several places, 423. Store committee from Assembly, 424, 425. Interference of board of war in buying provisions—copies of papers to be furnished by J. B. Smith, 425. Address from Quakers, 426, 427. Answer and representation and conference with, 427. Wagonmaster appointed — address of General Washington to inhabitants — proclamation respecting stock cattle—address of General Washington from Valley Forge, 429. Representation to Assembly, 431. Conference on magazines, 434. Resolution of Congress on prisoners and troops—horses—Commissioners to Congress at Yorktown—prisoners in

Supreme Executive Council—Virginia, 435. Money—Wagonmaster—proclamation for a fast, 438. Wages of, 441. Various orders, for cartridges, guard, &c., for Lancaster, 442. Old powder-mill ground to be let—Assembly inquire into expense of the public buildings in Lancaster—Justice for York, 443. Provisions introduced from Chester — appointments, &c., 445. Resolution of Congress requesting five hundred militia at various points in the State, and order thereon—reward offered by proclamation for arrest of murderers of W. Hammond—horses and stables, &c., 446, 447. John Bailey resigns—Money from Congress for provisions—various orders for money, 449. Resolves of Assembly for quota — Order taken—Sub-Lieutenant appointed —Resolve of Assembly—conference respecting battalions and reduction of certain regiments—exemption of persons engaged in making bayonets—Jacob Morgan resigns his seat—letter from General, in favor of Mrs. Pemberton, 457, 458. B. Rittenhouse's pay—petition of soldiers from Antrim and Peters Township, 458. John Brown discharged — Resolve of Congress respecting accoutrements —Virginia prisoners to go to Shippensburg, and be discharged, 460. Expenses to be paid by prisoners—money from Congress to buy horses—prisoners sent to Lancaster — to be delivered to Francis & Long—horses bought, 461. J. Carson paid for goods seized in Bucks county—salt-works, 463. Orders to various recruiting officers named, 464. Wagons—old spirits seized, paid for, 465. Money from Congress—various orders for money, 466. Representation of General Greene respecting wagons, 467. Recruits—prisoners from Virginia, 468, 469, 472, 473, 474. James Hamilton discharged, 469. Direction respecting men, &c., of gondolas ordered to be sunk at Trenton, 470, 471. Rations of

Supreme Executive Council---xi. Commodore H.—Justices of Berks, 471. Suspected persons seized by General Lacey—orders, 473. Recruits for continental army—recruits horses—orders, 474, 475, 476. United States lottery tickets received and disposed of—recruiting money and for buying horses—militia for defence of frontiers, 477, 478. Grants a pass on request of James Hamilton, 478. Appointment of commissioners on Attainder Act—their instructions, 479. Case of Anthony De Normandie, 480. Roads—object to Michael Muhlenbergh's account of expenses of prisoners to Virginia, 481. Pass for Mrs. Col. Morgan—Col. Jones paid and discharged—Lieut. Edward Randolph paid for enlisting men—letters and papers received from Congress to be read in churches — horse for Count Mountfort, his being lame, 487. J. Tilghman discharged—Indian murders—recruiting—situation of frontiers—orders, 489. J. Bone to be executed—Joseph Shippen, Jr., discharged—arms for Northumberland—General Wayne, &c. —Indians, 491. Proclamation printed--horses--recruiting-Board of War, 493. Rank of Captain Biles, 498. Treason in Chester county—Samuel Johnson may sell his real estate and depart—guard at Lebanon increased — Thomas Wharton, Jr., President, dies at Lancaster—order of funeral, 499. Purchases of clothing to cease—order for rifles and muskets for defence of frontiers—guard for collecting militia fines — enemy preparing to leave Philadelphia—ravages committed by, in Chester county—expenses in transporting prisoners, 507. Powder—spirits —salt-works—troops for defence, 509. Proclamation against persons who joined the enemy—Reward against robbers in Bucks county—clothing for troops marching west, 519. Guard for Lancaster—troops for defence—clothing for field officers—reward for criminals, 511. Clapyoole, Sheriff — robbery in Bucks county —Proclamation against traitors, 512, 518. Reward for robbers —clothing for troops, 519. Evacuation of Philadelphia — Election for Councillor—wagons for Capt. Montgomery—clothing to be made in Phil'a—intend removing from Lancaster, discontinue to take Dunlap's paper—officers of State fleet—paid expenses from Trenton to Lancas'r, 521. Arms in Genl. Lacey's hands to be sent to city—memorial of Mrs. Ferguson —celebration of Fourth of July—Genl. Arnold to be inquired of, why he had ordered shops to be shut—his reasons for so doing—also, with regard to clothing—a warrant for bringing up traitors—invites Council to dinner, 523. Justices—markets to be repaired—early call of Assembly —arms - resolve of Congress, suspension of Act of Assembly regulating prices of goods, marriage and tavern licenses--Sheriff- sundry persons discharged from parol —new member—goods found in City after evacuation belonging to enemy—exceptions to discharge, 525. Courts for Philadelphia county—J. B. Smith appointed Prothonotary and Justice—Revd. Thomas Combes, Jr., receives a pass to leave the State, 527. Petition from Hale & Weaver on property of enemy in city after evacuation—Col. Nicola asks for rations—Indian depredations at Wyoming— Justices— recruiting, 528. Traitor's property—armed boats afloat—brig to be fitted out, 529. Apply to Board of War for ammunition — petition of Col. Hartley—aid to wives of Privates in fleet, 530. Insulting application of Charles Thomson to Vice President about a house—circular to officers on defence—disposition of troops—representation to Congress on frontiers, 531. Order troops to Susquehanna and distribute at various places—money from Congress—Genl. Lacey commands—drugs—money to Col.

Supreme Executive Council—xi. Hartley, 533. Money from Congress—recruiting—records of Prothonotary's office brought from Reading—articles left by enemy to be secured and State House repaired—trees in city to be removed and given to the poor—Indians—Joseph Reed a member—apology, 536. Appoint committee to meet one from Congress on resolutions—sales of, by permission of Genl. Arnold—a deserter, the first from the fleet—pardoned—all who return to be pardoned—petition from Northumberland, 541. Appointments—privateer—advisers to Health officer—appoint commander of Brig "Convention" over one recommended by Navy Board—claim for a vessel sunk in Delaware, 543. Appoint Jacob Rush to assist Attorney General in case of ship Albion—Wharfinger and Weigh Master at drawbridge - cartridges to Henry Bunner — proclamation for embargo on provisions, 545. Protest against Congress laying an embargo in this State—return to be made of men in State fleet—appoint measurer of Wheat, &c., 546. Clerk of Court—charge against agent for sale of forfeited estates—notice to be put up, 547. Attend public reception of French Minister by Congress—Wardens ask for money—heavy bill for spirits—brig "Convention" nearly ready—prop'd to send on a cruise, 549 Disposition of arms from West Indies—propose discharge of certain officers of Navy—disarming galleys—orders of Congress respecting Wm. Straker, 553. Resolutions of Assembly respecting discharge of Navy, &c., 554. Armed Galleys to be at Cape May—armed brig Convention fitting out—traitors—galleys to be sent down Delaware — Indigo—men—Lieutenants, 557. Frederick Verner—Joseph Reed employed as counsel — a pass —raising wrecks in Delaware, 561. Conference on defence of

Supreme Executive Council—Delaware, 562. Commissions for private ships of war—enquiry for goods, 563. Petitions for pardons —exchange of prisoners — appointments — passes, 565. Appoint Prothonotary of Supreme Court—warrants of death and reprieves—arrest of a British Doctor —pass to Mrs. Shugart—orders for money, 566. Pass for Labatu and Anglo—Resolution of Assembly, embargo—militia of City called out—recruits— treasonable letter to R. H. Lee—embargo—militia called out, 569. Letter to R. H. Lee—petition of negro Ralph referred to Assembly—visit Bilingsport—case of Col. Geo. Stewart—pass for Mrs. Blewer, whose son was taken prisoner at Germantown—permission to Dr. De Normandie to sell real estate, 570, 571. Cannon for Bilingsport and Mud Island—Justices appointed—recruiting officers — guard from Lancaster to Philadelphia of prisoners—signal gun at Billingsport 573. Summons of Justices to take oath of allegiance—Quarter Master General, certificates in pay for services—purchase of linens by late President in Maryland. Col. Bull to be employed at Billingsport and Mud Island, his pay—Pay Master and Steward there—to use articles taken from enemy, 574, 575. Time of Militia expiring, 574. Old draft to Moses Ward—supplies for forts—officers for galleys —State shallop to be sold—prisoners to Chester—account of State fleet to be made—Marshal—recruits—passes, 577. Officers appointed—passes granted—others refused—galleys in service—recruits—tools, &c., belonging to State — reprieve, 579. Money from Congress—militia of Philadelphia called out, 581. Appoint commissioners to try Henry Bunthant a murderer—passes—recruits—execution, 582. Pardon —Indigo—purchase of clothing, 583. Prisoner in Chester gaol endeavoring to escape is ordered

Supreme Executive Council—xi. to the new gaol in Philadelphia—a dissenting minister in England applauded for his kindness to prisoners—passes, 584. Order to Commodore Hazelwood for cannon for Congress—Assembly ask for copies of Laws &c.,—wood for galleys, &c., 585. Pass—pardon—Board of War ask for plan of river Delaware for General Washington—sales of forfeited estates, 587. Surprise at requisition for wagons referred to Congress, 589, Order respecting old work house and State House—clothing—pass for Mrs. De Lancey—clothing, 593. British propose to send a flag—orders to Commander to stop the vessel at Delaware—pass to Mrs. Yard, &c., 595. Appointments—seditious papers and persons to be secured, 596—troops to repair to City to be ready, 597. Appointments — orders— pardons sentence for murder, 609. Proclamations for traitors to take their trials, 610, 612. Execution suspended, 612. Proceedings in case of Roberts and Carlisle, 606-614. Pay reward for arrest of a noted robber—Assembly met—payments to Jno. Hambright and Cap., Stokely—militia of Philadelphia called out as guards, 617. French Frigate, convoy of—new members—message to Assembly—Justices—Sloop Active, 619. Tonnage tax for Light House-disputed election in Chester county—discharge of militia—march of troops, 621, 623. Embargo, 622. New member, 623. Choice of President—joint committee—arms for militia—Genl. Washington asks for a guard for convention prisoners going South—militia of Bucks called out for purpose—as well as of Philadelphia — proclamation for a Thanksgiving day, 626, 627. Conduct of Col. Hartley approved—letter from Massachusetts to prevent return of tories—pass for Mrs. Ferguson to New York refused—permit provisions for Bermuda—galleys, 628, 629. Galleys

Supreme Executive Council—629. Choosing President, and Vice President—dinner— Joseph Reed and George Bryan elected, 633. Militia ordered out—men guarding cannon at Billingsport—Capt. Lightbourne's circuitous voyage—Wm. Low—paymaster of Bedford—letters from Board of War—convention prisoners, 637. Appointments—sale of public vessels by auction—pay to tavern keepers for militia on march—forestalling, 638, 639, 640. Pass—forestalling inquiry—vote of thanks for brave conduct to Col. Thomas Hartley—sales of public vessels—gun factory—report on Navy Hospital—permit to William Streaker—execution ordered, 640, 641. Pardons—powder for privateers—marching orders countermanded—sales of vessels—limits and guns—pay at Billingsport, 641, 643, 644. Justices—passes—sale of tools, &c.,—accounts of late Committee and Council of safety to be settled—reprieve—certificate of French Minister respecting a cargo of flour, 644, 645. British property, 645. Suspension of embargo—Prothonotary, &c.,—Col. Hartley's plan of defence adopted—French Minister offers a reward for captures — invalid corps—their clothing—Attorney General to confer respecting case of Sloop Active—Act of Maryland against distillers of Whiskey—militia to be mustered, 647. Passports—commiss'ns —oaths—commissary circular to delegates, 649. Clothing, 651. Account of Jacob Arndt as councillor paid—a school-master convicted for keeping a school without having taken oath of allegiance and fined—remitted—Robert Morris receives arms from West Indies—charges against Thomas McKean, member of Congress—reprieve of Elwood, 653. Caution against purchase of traitor's estates—subscribe for newspapers — salt in possession of Wilcocks—letter from Lieut. Col. Hunter—Washington—Sprogell. Major John McPherson dies

Supreme Executive Council—xi.
—his brother recommended, 654. Justices for Philadelphia—Joseph Hart paid—guard at Middle ferry ---Sloop Active—Capt. Wm. McPherson, British Officer, against keeping gun powder in Philadelphia, 657. Case of Gens Thomson and McKean, 659, 660. Pay of guard—salt seized, 661. Committee of Congress confer with, on bills of credit, 664. Justices required to aid in suppressing riots, and General Arnold to furnish military aid—want of clothing in 4th Pennsylvania regiment complained of by Lieutenants, and clothes to be given, 665. Pass, applications to be in writing—Bridge over Schuylkill —Justices—money from Congress —clothing to a disabled soldier, 667. Money from Congress—letter from Delegates of Virginia inclosing resolves on boundary line, 669. Salt in Prichard's store—valuation boat "Viper"—proclamation against forestalling—request General Washington to sit for his portrait, 671. Complaint of wagons improperly sent for merchandise to Egg Harbor by Jesse Jordan--provisions for Pennsylvania forces—opinion of Gen. Washington asked as to Colonel Atlee's claim to be Brigadier-General—letter Governor Morris and Wm. Whipples—respecting trials of persons for treason—value of "Viper,"—a pass to New York, 673. Contested election—Miss Levy's pass from Arnold—Letter from Matthew Clarkson, A. D. C., respec'g, 677. Petitions—prisoner with British—supposed duel with a French citizen disproved--passes —David Franks British Commissary—militia law—proclamation for attainder--wagons for Egg Harbor, 679. Massachusetts asks to export flour, 682. Pass for clerk of D. Franks for New York, 683. Committee of merchants ask for protection to Bay and River Delaware, 683. Inquiry respecting General Arnold and wagons to Egg Harbor—state of gaol and

Supreme Executive Council—
prisoners--militia fines—pass for Mr. & Mrs. Straker for St. Eustatia—Notary and Tabellion public —provisions and stores—address to Ass'y, 685—bills of credit—war —ship of war—forestallers, 687—plan for gradual abol. of slavery—Western frontiers—clandestine marriages—Proprietary estates, 689. Dr. Stanley's pay, &c., 691. Mr. Holker and brig Industry--resolves respecting Arnold to be published, and of Congress—signals to vessels--pay to Arthur Donaldson—resolves of Virginia —Joseph Jeffries and wagons—money from Congress, 693. Conference with Assembly on 20th section of Constitution, 695, 699. Message respecting Mr. Holker to Assembly, 699. Repudiate claim to propose bills on house—may advise Delegates in absence of Assembly—pay to invalid on a galley, 701. Merchants meet on a letter from Baltimore complaining of small privateers on coast, 702. Petitions from militia of Northumberland---passes—pardon, 703. Rules for entering enemy's lines, 704. Complaint against Colonel John Weitzell, 705. Orders for money for galleys—charge against United States for use of public buildings except State House—Arnold's wagons—proceedings against Jno. Mitchell, 707. Petitions—Col. Johnston—distribution of articles provided for troops—rules for and prices—message to Assembly, 711, 714. New member—timber for buoys—privateers, 715. Expenses—money from Congress—committee of Assembly—Justices—sloop Active—Wm. Dunwick--horse stealing not pardoned—boats for Col. Bull—militia, 715. Murders at Bushy Run—pass declined—Capt. Hazel an officer—sales of vessels —Col. Hunter—D. Morgan not pardoned, 719. Defence of frontiers, 719. Committee to value cutter Revenge, as a guarda costa —removal of wrecks from fishery —expenses—exchange of prison-

Supreme Executive Council—xi.
ers—proceedings in case of Arnold to be printed and sent to Congress, 721. Conference with Delegates—bridge and cables—fast—ship General Greene to be fitted out—conference with Assembly—Arnold resigns command of Philadelphia, 725—conference with committee of Congress and Assembly respecting Arnold, &c., 726, 727. Resolution that State military officers shall be entitled to same benefits as those of United States—Rev. Dr. Rogers applies for clothing—list of officers to be made out by Captain Boys, 727. Conference with Congress and Assembly, 730. Captain of Gen. Greene—outfit—election—conference Congress and Assembly—thanks of officers, &c.—Captains—letter from field officers, 731. Letter General Washington—Du Portail—petitions—proclamation—militia law, 733. Message to Assembly on provisions seized—military stores—S. R. Fisher to be confined—report of Joint Committee, 735. Exchange of Bills of Credit—pay of members, and of delegates, 736. Resolution of Assembly—repair of rifles—persons to value ship Gen. Greene, 739. Officers on ditto—distribution of articles—prize money—loan to State, 740, 741. Resolutions of Assembly—officers McClenachan and Irwin to obtain loan—bills of credit to be taken—resolutions of Congress—Major John Browne, receiver of clothing, resigns—Lieut. Col. Farmer receiver, 742, 743. Ask opinion in case of Eichelberger—petitions—notice to be given of sale of forfeited estates, 745. Rules to be required in future for pardons, 747. Pardons—sale of cannons—orders—Justice for Northumberland—forfeited estates, 749. Resolution respecting wagon masters, 755. Resolution appointing auditors to settle claims of Jno. Eyre, &c., for timber and plank stolen by enemy, employed in building redoubts and bridge near

Supreme Executive Council—
city—garrison relieved at Mud Island and Billingsport—petitions—ship General Greene—arms—Billingsport—passes to New York limited—pay of officers of Ship Gen. Greene, 756, 757. Is this State a separate department from that of commander-in-chief—appointments—Arnold's case—Justices—pass for Mrs. Duché on conditions, 758, 759, 762. Elect M. Clarkson Marshal—elections in Chester county—fees on marriage licenses—Justices—passes—pay for wagons—difficulty to man ship General Greene—embargo—George Harding, 761, 764. Accounts of General St. Clair—Justices informed that the Court has not power to discharge soldiers—pass for vessels with provision—pass for Mrs. Duché—proclamation for embargo, 762, 763. Record of a road in Bucks inquired for—permits for vessels—Indians—medicines—orders for money—appointments—exchange of bills—petitions, 765. Permit to a vessel to depart not granted—resolve of Congress asking militia to occupy forts in room of Colonel Proctor's men—seamen induced away—persons to be arrested for it—Dr. Jennings asks for clothing—agent for forfeited estates—vendues—William Armstrong paymaster — agent of Maryland purchases flour—order respecting, 766, 767, 770, 771. Justices—passes—seamen disappear—Captain Martin sent to Baltimore for them—stores for Mud Island—R. Morris's letter respecting arms from West Indies, 770, 771, 772—passes—provisions allowed to be exported in several vessels for Bermuda, 772. Elections in Chester county—Delaware to be swept for cannons and anchors, 773. Petition of Col. Eyre's battalion—Colonel Bull to execute plan of fortifications—his pay and rations—embargo continued—proclamation, 777. Money to several counties—Commissions, 779. Executions—

Supreme Executive Council—ix. shipment of convicts—Justice restricted to one in certain counties, 781. Expenses of sailors divided Congress advise export of some provisions—Court of Appeals—embargo off, 783. Proclamation—arms, 784.

Resignations of officers offered and not accepted—Captain Montgomery ordered to sea—Return of seamen—Various officers appointed to ship General Greene—Militia of Philadelphia, pay for—Pardons not granted, xii., 4, 5. Agents of forfeited estates to make returns, 6. Flag of truce arrives—family on board allowed to land, 7. Unruly characters taken on public ships—Ensign appointed, 7. Justices—Military officers—Suspicious characters, orders respecting, 8, 9. Permit Captain Cannon to sell cargo—Pardon to George Holder—Disturbances at Reading with prisoners—a defaulting Sub-Lieutenant—Petitions—Soldiers pardoned, 12, 13. Sweeping Delaware—German battalion—Petitions—Register of Admiralty Court appointed—Justices—Wagon duty referred—Decline a sub-Lieutenant's resignation, 15. Wagons—Purchases by John Carson—Letter, P. Henry on boundary with Virginia—Stores for troops—Lieutenants appointed—Pass for Mrs. Duché asked for—Flour in hands of Levi Hollingsworth, 17, 18. Wagons required—Conference with delegates in Congress—Prize to Lieutenant Carson—Mast for ship General Greene—Captain Gotschue—Justices, 18, 19. Prize brig to be condemned—M. Smith's pay—Petitions for pardons, pass—Rations, to sweep Delaware rejected, 20, 21. Warrants for wagons in different counties—Forfeited estates, deeds withheld—Bounty for recruiting—Order to Colonel Nicola—Discharge from a galley—Thomas Bradford agent for marine prisoners, 22, 23. Claim for purchases, referred to Congress—Guns to be repaired—Indian

Supreme Executive Council—xii. affairs—Wagon service, by Congress, 25, 26. Conduct of J. McAllister, 31. Proclamation against traitors, 27. Flags of truce and prisoners—Pass, 29. Wm. Moore Smith—French Consul on exempts from militia duty and fines—Flag of truce—Ensigns, 30, 31. Sweeping Delaware—Pardons—Lieutenant N. Sackett, 33. Mrs. Duché—passes—Case of David Ogden, 36. Prisoners to New Jersey—Sales of cannon—Charter of Academy—Costs Carlisle, Roberts and Handy—Fleury, 38, 39. Markets—J. McCallister to be prosecuted, 41. Terms of militia expired—Complaint against Justices of Northumberland—Resolves of Congress—Letters General Washington—Minute of Trustees of College, 43. Order purchase of flour through William Turnbull, agent, 45, 46. Death of Judge Ross—Complaint of Holker respecting purchases of flour in Wilmington, 47. Agents to receive subscriptions to Loan Office, 47. John Elwood pardoned—Letter to delegate in Congress—transcripts from courts—Francis Hopkinson appointed Judge of Admiralty—List of traitors—Privateer Holker, 48, 49, 50. Passes—Exchange of prisoners—Disabled men on invalid list, 51. Military affairs—Ensigns—Col. Spencer and Captain Wilkie—Purchase of flour at Reading, 52, 53. Monsieur Holker—Remonstrance from Germantown, a guard asked for, 56, 57. Ensigns—Affairs of Academy and College—Shipment of provisions—Holker complains of newspapers, 59. Preservation of public buildings erected by Congress—Resolves of Congress and various papers from—Letters from Holker and Gerard on flour—Swaine's securities and his duties—Pardons—Pass—Congress ask to export provisions—Petition for arms, 60, 61. Surrender of Fort Freeland—Thanks and orders—Capture of a Portuguese ship, 62, 63. Incursions of Indians—Let-

Supreme Executive Council—xii. ter, Gov. Clinton—Forfeited estates—Case of Colonel Stroud—Jonathan Lodge—Invalid corps—Plan from Philadelphia for restoration of credit—Ensign, 64, 65. Mons. Holker and flour—L. Nicola—Hospital at Valley Forge—Pardon for a challenge—Plan for restoring credit--Forfeited estates, 66, 67. Passes—Congress and Mons. Holker respecting flour at Wilmington—Pardon of a youth of thirteen for stealing provisions—Forfeited estate of Michael Witman, 68, 69. Militia officers, 70. Forfeited estates—Embargo—Militia, times expiring, others to be called out—Prisoners taken at sea in arms against United States—Mons. Gerard and Holker, 70, 71. Approval of their government—Letters relating to forfeited estates—pass—road in Bedford Co. to Fort Pitt--sheets of paper money—practicing of the militia—Steuben's treatise to be printed—Lieutenant appointed, 72, 73. Muster rolls—opinion Chief Justice on prisoners—enemy expected at New York—distressed state of Westmoreland Co., 75 Change of orders to militia–forfeited estates—search for wrecks—purchases of flour, 76, 77. Course to be pursued by Michael Teter, a disabled soldier—passes, 78, 79. Mons. Gerard's powers—confiscated estates—state of frontiers—papers, &c., in hands of Francis Hopkinson—manufacture of thread, 81. Embargo—estates—fines in York county—petition and passes, 83. Wheat to be purchased at mills by Henry and Marshall—letters from Col. Brodhead—Col. Hubley—Salt Works—provision to be made for officers, &c.—prisoners, pardon on condition of serving United States—Mons. Holker applies for flour, 84, 85. Horse stealing—counterfeiting—distribution of salt—inspection of clothing, 87. Promotions of officers, 89. Counterfeiters, 89. Brief to solicit money for a church--flour for salt—guards

Supreme Executive Council—for prisoners—army deficiency—rations for soldiers' wives—list of officers violating parole, 90, 91. Clothing—provisions for General Sullivan at Wyoming—promotions—militia, 92, 93. Mr. Holker—resignations—answer of Attorney-General to queries—clothing—guards, loan of arms—address to Assembly, 94, 95. Resolutions respecting militia--guard—invalid regiment, Board of War, &c., 95. Message to Assembly—successes—addition of another power--Proprietary estates--army and navy—government education of youth—college—embargo—roads—provision for officers of government—sale of confiscated estates, 96–99. Colonel Stroud, D. Potts, Holker, &c., 100, 101. Seal for Admiralty Court—R. Keene's estate—militia, resolutions respecting not paying fines, 102. Deeds for confiscated property—agree with Mons. Penet for arms—lot—petition from Penn's valley and answer—Justices—Jona. Lodge, trial—memorial Matthew Clarkson Marshall, 105. Shot for confederacy frigate—Wm. Russell loses leg at Brandywine, 107. Guards for gaol at York—Congress on public credit—embargo, &c.—arms of State to be worked on public standards—case of Jona. Lodge referred to Supreme Court—decline furnishing flour to M. Holker on account of scarcity—Assembly propose address to Sieur Gerard, 109. Address of Council to him—an execution respited on account of pregnancy—prisoners in new gaol—Clerk of market appointed—prisoner with enemy—prize taken by the Genl. Greene, 110, 111, 112. Case of negro Ralph—imposition practiced, 113. Decree of Supreme Court favor Jacob Morgan—Col. Hannum's escape from enemy—voluntary turn out of militia in Northumberland county—order to William Honeyman—arrival of Count D'-Estaing—aid asked on petition of Col. Maloney respecting horses

Supreme Executive Council—xii. taken by him, 114, 115. Pardons, petitions, claims—resolutions of Assembly respecting supply of flour and salt—sickly state of garrisons at the forts, 116, 117. Resolutions of Assembly on flour and salt, distribution, 119. Defence of frontiers—pass for Chas. Willing—order to Henry Fisher, 120. Riot at Judge Wilson's—proclamation—letter from General Washington, 122, 123. Messages to Assembly, 96, 124, 125, 167, 175, 176, 474, 530–533, 555, 575, 630, 667, 675, 738, 753, 758, 759, 763. Thanks to General Wayne proposed, 124. Distribution of flour, &c., to poor of city—also wood—offering a bounty, 125. Proclamation for embargo, 126. Vice-President Bryan resigns—Matthew Smith elected Vice-President, 127. Daniel Clymer at Wilson's—surrenders and gives bail—militia of city and some counties called out—execution of D. Dunn ordered—election of Wm. Moore for Council and five others for Assembly, 128, 129, 131. Wm. Bell at riot—passes for Germany—Joseph Reed elected Councillor and President—prices for wagons, 130, 131, 132.—Of salt, 133. Joseph Gardner elected member—against persons going at large charged with high treason, 133. Soldiers' times expire at Billingsport and Mud Island—persons to be left in charge—negro slave pardoned—elections—vote of thanks to General Wayne for services at Stony Point, 134, 135. Resolutions respecting salt and flour exchanged—Major Francis Nicols at riot at J. Wilson's, with others named, to give bail, 136, 137. Jno. Lacey, Jr., a member, 137. Case and proceeding of Major Sol. Buss—Captain Jacob Buss and other captains of Northampton—and resolutions—David Franks refused a pass—pay for salt claimed—D. Solebury Franks at riot at J. Wilson's—bailed, 140, 141. Militia of Chester county—prices of flour and wheat in Lancaster county—case of Jeremiah Simmons—Captain Guion, salt—flour and wagons on frontier—artillery called out, 142, 143. Staats Lawrence at riot—flour and salt—sloop Active—Robert Harris, salt for Trenton objected to—equipment of militia called out by General Washington—Peter Miller bailed out—fast appointed by Congress—elections, 144, 145. Additional Commissioners appointed to procure salt—election of Joseph Gardner, from Chester, confirmed — elections — case of Captain Getshens—resolutions of Congress, 146, 147. Impressment of seamen of State on frigate Confederacy—Matthew Smith resigns—complaint from Bedford against Lieutenant—order of Congress favor James Wilkinson, Clothier-General—additional Commissioners to procure salt—pay to workmen at President's house—Geo. Harding reprieved, 148, 149. Sale of ship General Greene ordered—vendues condemned—resolutions respecting—Solomon Bush referred to Board of War, 151. Sustain Commissioners for procuring salt—riot at Wilson's—Dr. Harris threatened for carrying off salt, 152, 153. Roads and highways—the Marshal complains of Blair McClenachan—complaints against sale of General Greene, 154, 155. Conference with Committee of Assembly—on bounty to militia—salt returned to Colonel Smith—Justices resigned being elected to Assembly—payment for land by Isaac Hicks—deed for—two other receipts for land, 156, 157. Complaint against Deputy Quartermasters at Reamstown—owners of brig Active—brass kettles in hands of Joseph Fox—petition of officers of ship General Greene—are they officers of Navy?—salt—pay for—sales of General Greene complained of, 158, 159. Election of President and Vice-President

Supreme Executive Council—xii. —complaint of Captain Heysham against L. Kuhn—House of Employment ask for flour—letter of Congress against opening Land Offices—manager of salt works in New Jersey dead—they ordered to be sold—money for salt—codfish captured by the Gen. Mercer may be exported—Sheriff and Coroner of York county, 160, 161. Election of President and Vice-President—Joseph Reed and Wm. Moore, 163. Message to Assembly—general condition of affairs, 167. President and Vice-President elected—audience of Chev. De La Luzerne,—embargo continued 170, 172. Members of Congress elect—loan flour for poor —passes to New York to be referred—sale of ship Gen. Greene —allowance to Captain Irwine's company—Colonel Brodhead, 172, 173. Resolution, &c., sent to Assembly, 176. Case of Pat. Keane, Lieutenant of the Roman Catholic Regiment of Volunteers in British service—to be closely watched—Resolutions on bounds sent to Virginia and Connecticut—returns of gallies to be made out—pass for child eight years old, 177. Various orders for executions—cargo for account of United States cleared, 178. Visit from Chev. De La Luzerne and Mons. Marbois—discharges from gallies —execution — passes — election, 180, 181. Pay of wagons—question about seat between Thomas Uric and John Piper—Mr. Holker sends ship General Greene to Martinico — proclamation for a fast, 183. Auctioneer elected, William Browne—firewood—deed for property in Philadelphia, late of Samuel Shoemaker, 185, 186. Sale of salt works in New Jersey —discharges from State service, 186, 187, 190. Confiscated estates for University, &c., 189. Wood —markets forestalling, 190. Galloway's estate—petitions—Holker exports provisions—salt—taxes, 190, 191, 192. Discharges—pardon, 193. Prisoners of war in

Supreme Executive Council— New Jersey—boundary with Connecticut—broken cannon to be sold—state of and tolls on Schuylkill bridge—to be valued—petition of David Franks for a pass—deeds executed, 194, 195, 196. Pardons—money repaid to New Jersey—to Mrs. Sarah Chesnut per decree of Supreme Court—Mr. Holker ships—newspapers to be called for—Congress on supplies for army, 196, 197, 198. Monthly receipts to be sent to Treasury of Congress—Justices—two trunks of goods at Elizabethtown from New York—Captain Clunn to be arrested—David Franks examined —illegal practices—counterfeiting —Robert White's wife—house to be searched—confiscated estate—R. Swanwick, 198, 199. Bounties —provisions — pardons — embargoes — deeds for confiscated estates, 200, 201. Conference with Committee of Congress on supplies—public credit, &c.—meeting of Merchants on supplies —Schuylkill bridge, &c.—Gen. Washington on alarming scarcity of provisions, 202, 203. And to others on procuring supplies, 203, 204. David Franks' petition refused—suspicion against—alleged suspicious intimacy between Elizabethtown and the enemy at New York—persons named, 206. Scarcity of wood—to be cut for poor, 207, 208. Difficulty with a portion of militia—amount in Treasury subject to order of Congress — W. Semple, Sub-Lieut. resigns—thanks for his services—annexation of two companies to Colonel Proctor's Regiment—taxes —goods damaged by ice—survey to be had— disputes between Pennsylvania and Virginia—recommendation of Congress—proclamation respecting—barracks—account of late Vice-Pres't, 210, 211. New Members—wood taken —Schuylkill ferry and Continental teams—proclamation respecting dispute with Virginia, 212, 214. Rates of pay to Soldiers—tavern-keepers—pay to Almoner

Supreme Executive Council—xii. for absent militia — quarters to be provided for more in public houses — passes — Captain J. P. Schott has Armand's corps, 217, 218, 221. Door-keepers' pay—pardons—auditors do not attend on account of bad weather—abuse of weight in flour—James Pottingers' petition, 218, 219. Express to Gov. Livingston—militia to be mustered and paid—Mr. Atlee's account of Connestoga manor—cash in treasury —Samuel Fisher ill in prison, to be removed—Col. Smith resigns, 220, 221. Pay to President—to witnesses in case of Arnold—objections to certificate of Geddis and Govett in case of, 225, 226. Pay to James Read, commissary, unnecessary—W. Crispin to furnish rations and account, and be discharged, 226. W. C. Bradford to render account—wishes of Congress to be ascertained, 227. Sale of salt ordered—letter to Congress on supplies—money from Congress—return of clothing —coopers' work for galleys, 229. Indians in Northumberland—names of officers, &c., held as prisoners of war—elections, 230, 231. Messages to Assembly, 96, 124, 125, 167, 175, 233, 246, 264, 285, 358, 564, 567, 624, 626, 637, 641, 667, 676, 733, 748, 749. Ceasing of issues of Continental bills —taxes—property of aliens and sundry papers before Assembly, 233. Sales of lands by Virginia—Indians—Taxes—petitions—resolution of Congress—clothing—order of Congress, 234, 235. Officers returned as belonging to State—a scold pardoned, 235, 243. Order from Congress for moneys—case of Capt. Papley, 236. Conference on supplies—application for Great Seal—delivered in part to Assembly, 237. Orders of Congress, 238. Order for Beef—pardon for regrating pork—mistake in date of commission—Salt, price of—Major T. McPherson received—exchange of prisoners—door-keeper, 241. Petitions—trophies

Supreme Executive Council—of war—minutes of Council of Safety to be placed in Secretary's office, 242. Militia fines—pardon a scold, 243. Paper from Quakers on militia fines, 244. Trophies, colours taken from Hessians delivered to Board of War, 245. On supplies—Deed to C. W. Peale—clothing, 247. Conference with Assembly on defence of frontiers—money—decision respecting continental money being received in discharge of ground rent on forfeited estates—aid of clothing to a prisoner, 249. Conference with Assembly on case of Col. Haller, wagon master—troops to be raised —returns of troops—affairs with Virginia—laws of State sent to Congress—passes to be applied for within ten days—pay to galleys, 251. Petition D. Kennedy —Surveyor Genl. has gout—accounts of Bucks county for purchases—pay to commissary of prisoners — against partial provision for regiment — salt, 253. Speedy collection of debts—message to Assembly on number of troops—views of French Minister, 255. Pass for Wm. Barton and Paul Zantzinger to Elizabeth Town—suspicions of speculation against an agent for forfeited estates — deed for marsh land at Tinicum, part of Jos. Galloway's estate—call on Edmd. Physic, late Receiver General of Pennsylvania, for books, papers, &c.,—sundry petitions, 256, 257, 258. Resolution of Assembly to raise four companies—several persons to appear, 258. Deeds for estates forfeited, 259, 260. Proclamation and reward, $3000 offered to arrest four persons—return of clothing—dismissal of Thos. Hale as agent—Wm. McMullin appointed, 261. President's house in danger from fire at Mr. Holker's—salt distributed—Col. Hazen's men and officers—Revd. M. Milsheimer, a chaplain, taken at Saratoga—dispute with Virginia—Mr. Hale to deliver up

Supreme Executive Council—xii. papers—auditors in case of Jehu Eyre—supplies—taxes, 262, 263. Letter of Mr. Hale on Indian lands, 265. Deed to Thomas Britton, late S. Shoemaker's estate, 265. Decison against Capt. Galt, 266. John Ensmenger's case referred to Dr. Hutchinson—right of France as depositories of moneys of her citizens who have no claimants here, referred to Attorney General —accounts of Wm. Turnbull for purchases of flour—reward for apprehension of Thos. Burney. a notorious counterfeiter, 267. Deed for J. Galloway's property—Schuylkill Bridge tolls, &c., 268, 269. Jos. Richardson arrested--Dr. Martine app'd Surgeon--passes for Soldiers' wives to New York limited to 15th April—intercepted Journal—Mrs. Shoemaker—valuation of damages by flying camp to Edw. Barrett in Southwark—petition of Jacob Taney for recognizance forfeited, 270, 271. Dr. Wm. Cooper to be arrested—Jos. Richardson—Henry Carter —marriage interests less than freehold in confiscated estates to be sold, 272, 273. Scarcity in camp—opinion of Attorney General on moneys of French subjects to be paid to Consuls —Mr. Holker, requisition for flour —Berks county commissioners—Thos. Taylor apprehended and executed—case of Larry Burns a soldier, 274, 275. Deeds, 276. Grants to Col. Hazen's Regiment—petitions—powder--cannon sold—fast day by Congress — Simon Sneider resigns as sub-Lieutenant, 279. Books, papers, seals, &c., from Edmd. Physic—fast day —resolution of Assembly against F. and J. Ichelbury—expense of a lunatic—deed for estate of Christopher Sawer—neglect to comply with terms of sale—rules, 280, 281. Proclamation for a fast, 282. Names collected who joined British Army in 1777. State of frontiers, and dispute with Virginia, 287, 289—account of clothing—resolutions for Congress

Supreme Executive Council—respecting frontiers–letter to, 289-292. Petition of inhabitants respecting bridge and road to Darby —letter of Genl. Washington and returns of Col. Moylan's corps—Major Eyre has charge of Bridge —resolve of Congress relative to officers—Joseph Shippen, Jr., late Secretary, to deliver papers, &c., to T. Matlack—funeral of Mr. Forbes, Member of Congress—election–petition of Charles Cook, 293. Doubtful election in Manallen and Tyrone Township—account of Wm. Anderson--burning of houses in Cumberland and proclamation for arrest of incendaries, 294. Land of Revd. Mr. Batwell—petition from York for defence—broken cannon sold—Major D. Frank's claim—Mr. Holker for flour—officers of Ottendorf's Company--for rank–militia laws--appointments of Lieutenants and Subs, 296, 297, 298. Paper money moulds--deeds for sales of confiscated estates, 297, 300. Commissioners of purchases for each county--George Bryant appointed Judge of Supreme Court--conduct of Virginia Commissioners--petition of Jacob Morgan respecting mill, &c., purchased by him—deserters received from vessels in river, 302, 303. Officers of Ranging Company--premium for prisoners and scalps, 311, 312. John Lynch's case--letters to Northampton on Indian invasions and resolutions —Gen. Washington names posts for supplies—powder, 312, 313. Road from Darby--forage at Tinicum--flour to be exported by Don Juan de Miralles--refugee in North Carolina--discharge of Navy Officers on account of expense--rent of Middle ferry paid —property of Saml. Bell, 315. Admiralty — Physick's papers—desertions of army—deed--patent to Jno. Ormsby for ferry--resignation, 317. Refuse to allow Philadelphia Library Company to import books from New York—Lieut. W. Huston a wounded

Supreme Executive Council—xii. officer—seditious paper pasted up —Proclamation against, 319. Deed—clothing—Schuylkil Bridge —disposition of supplies, 320, 321. Desertions—forfeited estates in Northampton, pay for—appointments—change in number and pay of Surgeons in galleys—deeds, 322, 323, 324. Case of John Lynch—Thomas Hale, agent —pay for gallies—taxes—Wm. Young and Benj. Town suspected of printing seditious paper "Slow and Sure," imprisoned, 324, 325. Deed to Jacob Bay, type founder, at Germantown—Treasurer always to have £30,000 in hand—commission to Abm. Bennett for armed Pilot boat Randolph—draft of Congress—Jos. Shippen, Jr., delivers papers, &c., to John Penn who is called on to deliver to Secretary—decree against estate of Michael Reine—order to, 326, 327. Rewards for Indian prisoners and scalps—seditious papers—Wm. Young released—draft of Congress—executions ordered—clothing, 328, 329. Purchasers of Tinicum to be put in possession—alarm from a boat—letters—appointments, 331. Sale of clothing by vendue—claim of a prize—Physic's books and papers—return of officers and men in fourth regiment of dragoons, 332. Clothing—execution, 333. Pay for estates—discharge of Mr. Galt—all confiscated estates to be sold—oaths to be taken by officers, 341. Resolutions respecting sales of commons, &c., in Philadelphia—missionaries pass to Pittsburg—pay of militia, 347. Cases of Captain Carberry and Lieut. Houston—deeds—great distress for meat in camp—murder of William Boyd—proclamation for arrest of John and Robert Smith, 348, 349. Conference with Congress and Assembly on scarcity at camp—case of Mrs. Ferguson, 351. Deeds—M. Everly promoted—new gaol—Justices—John Nixon explains letter —Merchants on currency, 352,

Supreme Executive Council—353. Expenses of boats—vacancies in army, 354–356. Pass refused—suit of black for Rev. Samuel Blair—Physick's books, 358. Order of Congress, 359. Conference on loan office certificates—value —supplies, &c., 360. Sale of negro Aaron of P'r Campbell's estate—paymaster—Physick's books —resolutions of Congress—petitions, 360, 361. Pay to commissioners of purchases—embargo—orders, 362. Expenses of express from frontiers—supplies for army —sale of Græme park, and Mrs. Ferguson to live rent free, she paying taxes—allowance to Gen. Potter for travelling expenses—provision for troops in Northumberland county, 364, 365. Message to Assembly respecting Mrs. Murray and Mrs. Ferguson—Jas. Hutchinson elected to Assembly, 367. Sailor taken—several not to be exchanged—Expenses of store at Walnut and Sixth—agreement and memorandum between French minister and the State, 368. Debts from quartermasters, 369. French sailors desert—supplies—orders for purchases—commissioner appointed—delegates in Congress chosen, 370, 371. Appoint persons to execute act for procuring supplies—appointments —change in company of rangers —arrangement of militia in several counties, 372, 373. Value of bridge—petition respecting John Roberts' estate—rejected report from Assembly—on claims of Erie, &c.—complaints of malpractice—authority to declare martial law—justices superceded —resolution for greater ease of militia in certain counties—executions ordered, 374, 375 Resolutions respecting supplies and other measures of support and security—regulation of passes, &c.—resolution of approbation of Congress, 376, 377. Supplies—taxes—new mills—wrong election of lieutenants—wagons, 378, 379. Committee of Congress at camp—wants of army—petition, John

Supreme Executive Council—xii. Swanwick--deeds--estate R. Swanwick and Edward Jones, 381. Drafts from Congress—deed—petition for independent corps—proclamation for martial law, &c., 383. Enemy approaching—troops to be in readiness—rank to officers—fraud in transportation to Trenton—passes, Mrs. Ferguson, Mrs. Allen—critical state of army, 386, 387. Embargo, 387. Mititia fines—Mr. Ryan, militia inspector—arms to be collected and none left with disaffected—object to independent corps, 388, 389. Arms for Colonel Rea—artillery company—Durham tract, 390, 391. allowance to volunteers for arms—light horse for General W.—armed boats to attend Mercury packet—special commission for an armed whaleboat—appointments, 392, 393. Orders for wagons—for money, 395, 396. Desertion of French sailors—order for arrest of wife of a refugee—A. Doz, resigns, and Captain Hazelwood appointed commissioner, 397. Congress inquire what action under various resolves—sale of negroes at request of navy board—provisions allowed for Havana—enlistment fines remitted--circular on taxes—resolutions of Congress, 398, 399. A traitor prohibited from keeping public house.—Traitor captured and carried into mountains—embargo—Cap. Burd resigns—recruits and teams, 400, 401. Lot for public landing on Race street—sale postponed—pass for Havana--labors at Mud island--Letters and resolutions from Congress, 402, 403. Enemy leaves New Jersey--port partially opened—printing—John Dover's case, 402, 404, 407. Execution ordered of R. and J. Smith—purchases, 405. Decision on taxes—payments—appointments, 407. Proclamation suspending purchases, 408. Desertion of French sailors, 409. Returns of purchases, 411. Congress and bills of exchange—pardons—spy executed—opinion on capture of French subjects by

Supreme Executive Council—British—deed—confiscated estate—shipment to Cape Francois, 413. Application of James Searle for a loan, 414. His commission, 415. Instructions, 416. Compensation, &c., 418. Cases of E. Grizzle and J. Wilson, traitors—French bills of exchange, 419, 422. Purchases—deeds—recruits for St. Clair—clothes for General Armstrong and son—J. Eichelberger, 421. Interest on loan—exchange on Dr. Franklin—opinion, George Bryant on French deserters--forage on Hudson river—purchases, &c., 423. Sales of teas, 423, 427. March of troops—arrival of French fleet at Rhode Island—sheriff to arrest four females, wives of tories—letters to and from De Corney, 425. Suspicious trade from Bermuda—Mud island—pardons—appointments, 426, 427. Recruits for Pennsylvania line—bounties—deserters, 431. Supplies for French fleet--Hessian enlistments—wagons—pay of, 432, 433. Nancarrow's air furnace—death of Captain Dawson—Lieutenant Brady promoted 435. General Wayne on expedition against Bergen—surgeons appointed, 437. Statement of case of Thomas Jones, &c., of Captain Coren's artillery artificers, 438. Orders for money--frame for Thos. Wharton's picture—deeds to C. W. Peale—Thos. Lawrence, &c., reserved for University, 441. Pledge for money to be borrowed—sale of damaged provisions at auction—orders for money, 442, 443, 444. Congress—Warrants—Confirmation of line with Virginia—resolution of Rhode Island—deed to A. Rex—Dr. Hutchinson Director General of military hospitals—horses to be collected, 444, 445, 446. Deed—orders—pardons, 447. Deed, 448. Conduct of Rufus Gardner—paymaster orders, 449. Appointments, 451. Advise President to take command of troops—two boats to be fitted out to seize provisions, 452. Scanty of provisions and

Supreme Executive Council—xii. hands in New Jersey—deserters—provisions shipped, 454. Petition, Chester county—debts—justices died—yellow fever at Charleston—quarantine at Mud island, 457. Deed, 458. Orders countermanding march of militia—paymaster—defenceless state of Northumberland in case of withdrawal of German regiment, 461. Drafts of Congress—deed, 463. Resignation of Lieutenant Currie—suit of clothes for Reverend R. McMurdy—commissioner of purchases, 465. Murders by Indians in Berks—troops sent, 467. Fortifications at Mud island—deed—doubts on militia law, 469, 470. Mr. Holker ships—provisions scarce at fort Pitt—confiscated estate—letters and resolutions of Congress respecting pay and lands to officers, 471–473. Capture of provisions—order respecting—militia fines—message to Assembly on taxes—militia—letters, General W., 475. Decision of Virginia on boundary—scarcity in the army—contracts for captured provisions—resignation of Lieutenant Myers—privateers, 477. Merchants of Philadelphia against Marshal, 478. Ensigns—apprehension of suspected persons—B. Galbraith refuses to deliver up papers—deed—conference on prisoners on Long Island—sales by auction, 480, 481. Conference on finances, 481. Answer, M. Clarkson—justices—appointments—yellow fever, 483. Orders—resolution of Congress—supplies—pardons—militia for Northampton—account, T. Scott, 485. Conference respecting Virginia—petitions—Westmoreland co., 487. Arnold's joining enemy—search for his papers—various letters—justices appointed—confederation—Vandalia or Indiana county, 491. Confederation in New York—militia to Northumberland—W. Austin's estate—orders for pay—Colonel M. Smith, resigns—shipments of provisions for Bermuda refused, 493. Traitors' papers—

Supreme Executive Council—passes—pardon—purchase of cattle—warrants to arrest certain traitors Captain Joel, 405, 406. Proclamation against certain traitors, 496. Distresses of army—pay of teams—release, &c., of traitors—pay of militia, 499. Flour for army—resolutions of Congress—arrival and arrest of Dr. Adam Kuhn—negroes, 501, 502. Pardon of negroes—refuse further time to depart to D. Franks and W. Hamilton—pay J. Arndt—passes, 502, 503. Vessel in which Dr. Kuhn arrives examined at his expense—Thomas Paine paid for ten dozen of the "Crisis." W. Hamilton allowed to go to St. Eustatia, 503. W. Constable to give bond—Dr. Kuhn and family to depart for St. Croix, and to give security not to return—Joshua Edwards to be arrested—judge advocate of militia—pass to D. Franks, &c., 504, 505. New members-elections-pardons, &c., 506, 507. Election—pass to Miss Arnold—D. Franks sick, 509. Elections, 513. Passes—mulatto slave—Pennsylvania Hospital—Dr. Kuhn, 515. Proclamation for fast, 516. Dr. Kuhn—unappropriated lands ceded to Congress—General Washington against temporary enlistments, 517. Baron Steuben to occupy Arnold's country seat, 519. W. Hamilton to go to his country seat—Arnold's wife to depart from the State—shingling old work house—militia company augmented by resolution of Congress—John McFarlane to be arrested, 521. Resolution of Congress—various papers—consideration of complaints against Marshal, &c., 522. Resignation of Justices, &c.—Traitors allowed to embark for West Indies—refuse allowing provisions to go to Nantucket—three auctioneers for Philadelphia, 524, 525. Justices and Treasurer resign–inquiry into Marshal's conduct—new member, 526, 527. Message to Assembly, on army—Virginia boundary, &c., 528–531. Marshal exonerated, but

Supreme Executive Council—xii. superceded, 533. Promotions—Wm. Hamilton—executions—reprieves, 535. Orders for executions, &c.-appoint Clement Biddle Marshal—proclamation for fast, 538. Suspend sales of estates, 539. Elect President and Vice-President, 541. To prevent frauds of using American prize papers, by British vessels—purchase of pay—General Potter, a member, 543. Jno. Piper, a member—State money—clothing for army and quarters—message to Assembly—expenses of Governor—promotions, 545. Appoint Justices to preside over Courts, 546. J. D. Sergeant resigns as Attorney-General—W. Roberts as Lieutenant-Colonel—license restored—Colonel J. Piper Lieutenant—new member—Wm. Hamilton may go to country seat, 549. W. Bradford, Attorney-General—promotions—Mons. Oster, certificate---money for Congress, 551. Deeds—Traitors from Jersey, 553. Appointments by Assembly—Joseph Stansbury's estate—message to Assembly, finances, 555. Loan office—Captain Coxe on a flag of truce--New Jersey traitor--Justice resigned, 557. Wm. West, Jr.—Colonel Miles authorized to cut wood from land near city—Justice resigns—corn to be purchased for Federal army, 559. Deed---conference—Captain Moore's volunteers paid and discharged—purchase of corn rescinded, 561. Suspicious vessel, at Warder's wharf—Congress ask names of Commissioner for supply of southern army--Messrs. Bache and Smith to indorse bills emitted by State—petitions, 563. Message respecting powers of council—Supreme Court, &c., to apprehend suspected persons, &c., 564. Suspected persons—Col. Morgan to pay off Berks county militia—no money to Col. Lindemuth-impeachment of Francis Hopkinson-payments--message to Assembly—who decline to pay Commissioners of purchases in continental

Supreme Executive Council—money, 567. Petitions Joseph Stansbury, &c.—Resolution of Congress—Wyoming garrison--of Assembly, finances—pay for York county—auctioneer, 569. Forcible possession taken of Hog Island—pay for Mud Island—pardon in Bucks county--loan under resolution of Assembly—deed, 571, 572. Defence of suits for militia fines—pardon—pay General Potter—new charge against Francis Hopkinson—J. Stansbury, 573. Stolen property—F. Hopkinson—deposits of provisions—message to Assembly—arms taken, 575. Suits for arms taken—troops entitled to draw stores—deeds—petitions, 577. Case of F. Hopkinson—tried, 578, 579, 580, 581, 582, 583. Unanimously acquit him, 581. Assembly on Commissioners and Quarter-Master certificates—Commissioner of purchases—estate of Wm. Austin, assigned to University—Receiver of provisions—New Jersey prisoners--proceedings of Connecticut convention--Wyoming--alarm for supplies, 584, 585. War between Delaware and Seneca Indians—Mud Island—repairs to public magazine—purchase of cannons declined—promotions, 587. Tonnage duty—pedlar refused a licence—Auditors to settle accounts of troops—inclosure of Library, 588. Bills of credit, proclamation, 589. Relief of Wyoming—Hog Island held for State, 591, 592. Mutiny of Pennsylvania line—President and General Potter sent to, 593. Loan on Treasurer's note—appointment--Justices—pass for Joseph Stansbury's wife—Thomas Wharton's estate—Thomas Paine paid as Clerk of Assembly—orders for money 595. Specie to be sent to President—ill-treatment of prisoners--money raised for by each State, 597. Money required by Congress—clearance of vessels—ill-treatment of prisoners at New York, 603. Opinion in answer to Treasurer to pay pension to Lieu-

Supreme Executive Council—xii. tenant Bush--suit against Mease and West, 604. Quarters for officers of Pennsylvania Line term of service, 605. Officers and recruitng stations--claims of officers in Pennsylvania Line—complaints against Colonel Rea, 607. Petition of Tax-payers in Berks county, 608. Officers of Pennsylvania Line, 609. Agents appointed for confiscated estates—Money to each county for enlisting—burnt vessels injure fisheries on Jersey shore—persons authorized to remove them, 611. Exchange between State and continental money—to be published monthly in newspaper—to fix the rate--repairs to barracks—money to make purchases—resignation of John Peters,jr.-deed for S.Shoemaker's estate—militia called out—depreciation accounts—where to be settled—pay to wife of Robert McCabe, killed—General St. Clair wants money for troops, 613. Conference with committee of Congress on money—Auditors for settling depreciation on officers' accounts resign--deeds--Congress ask 100 rank and file—Justice appointed, 615. Officers to go to their regiments, 616. Deeds, 617, 618, 619, 620, 621. Suryeyor-General to search for papers, 621. Bounty on recruits—clothing—officers for new companies—value of a cargo, 623. Message to Assembly on state of affairs—soldiers' Taxes—new counties in the west, 624, 626. Soldiers discharged-Captain Boys has charge of forts and gallies, 727. Orders—A. Hubley Lieutenant—cases of claims for discharge from invalid corps-stations for recruits, 629. Expenses of Governor, 630. Hog Island survey—Committee on part--Jo. Galloway's property—petitions--state of frontiers, 631. Lieutenants appointed—reward to Captain S. Brady, for an Indian scalp—causes of discontent in Pennsylvania line—account from agents for confiscated estates--resignation of

Supreme Executive Council—Sub-Lieutenant Agnew, 633. Escheator-General appointed—Hog Island case—extension of Mason & Dixon's line—Commissioners—Jacob Weaver, a Justice, removed for adultery, 635. Taxes and fines—pay at Billingsport—pay to seven months men, 637. Discharge of militia—depreciation pay—account of provisions purchased—deed-—barracks—brick-yard, 639. Vacant lots in city—arms to be repaired—attesting recruits—Colonel Hart's accounts—message to Assembly on protection of inhabitants—plan for, 641. Returns of taxable property—pay of volunteers—composition of southern army—wagons, 643. Message on tender of a portion of flour exported--depreciation--confinement of soldiers inquired into—increase of auditors—appropriation by Assembly for raising infantry, 645. Auditors appointed in each county—complaint against J. Martin and J. Bailey, 647. Depreciation—convention—troops to be removed—conference on calling in continental money—articles of confederation ratified by all the States—Auditors ready—repair of barracks, 649. Grant permission to Dr. Kuhn to return—pay of militia—Darby road—resignation, 651. Resolution of Assembly on pay of militia, pay of Auditor—report on case of John Perry, 653. Dismissed—D. Duncan appointed—resolution on gratuities, &c., to officers, 655, 656. Orders—dispute with Connecticut, 657. Orders for defence of frontiers to officers of several counties—barracks at Lancaster, 659. Call of militia—conference on convention prisoners—C. Wirtz removed and J. Miller appointed—deed to Jonas Philips—account of pay to Pennsylvania line ordered—claim on Hog Island to be prosecuted—pay for extending Mason and Dixon's line, 661. Officers of volunteer company appointed—respite—

Supreme Executive Council—xii. traitor from New Jersey to be arrested, 663. Number of recruits for federal army—cannon—flag of truce granted only by Congress—return of clothing to be made—proclamation for attainder of traitors, 665. Darby road—Justice—execution ordered — message—State Island to be sold in lots, 667. Deeds—city lots laid off and sold—Congress ask march of the line in detachments, 669. Report on taxes—enlistments—State or Province Island to be sold in lots—proceeds to be applied to sinking bills of credit—day of fasting fixed by Congress—deed, 671. Accounts of Lieutenant's deeds, 673. Money called for by Congress—Court Martial on Lieut. Bigham—account for newspapers—Col. Udree resigns as sub-Lieut.—message on Acts of Assembly towards traitors, 675. Message on Lieutenants and Lieutenant's accounts—defence of frontiers, 677. Conference with Assembly—division line of Hog Island—enlistments in Northumberland and Bedford, 679. Assembly ask conference on recall of agent to Europe on loans—J. Rankin's estate—nolle prosequi—W. Hamilton may remain in the State—Washington county formed out of Westmoreland—Prothonotary appointed, 681. State House steeple to be taken down and repaired—Probate of Wills, &c., appointed—account J. Lacey, Jr.—capture, &c., of prizes—prosecution of Lieutenant Bigham, 683. Money to York—clothing—depreciation—enemy about to leave New York for Delaware, 685. Order a soldier of fourteen or fifteen years to be discharged—defenceless state of Berks county and defence of Delaware—two companies to be raised—delinquent Commissioners liable to fine—promotions—case of Samuel Carson—arrest of an offender—deed, 687. Appoint officers of Land Office—confiscated estate, expenses—partial pardon, 689.

Supreme Executive Council—Jas. Tilghman, late Surveyor of Land Office, called on for books, &c.—property of Schuylkill floating bridge vested in Geo. Gray, 690. Resolutions of Assembly—pay of militia—supplies of federal army—recruiting—calling in continental and State money, 691. Purchases—bounty—new levies—conference on means of expediting march of Penna. line—sale of confiscated estates, 692. Doorkeeper not to pay militia fines, 696. State Library, books to be returned, 699. Guard for Commissioners on boundary — Wagon Masters—Darby road—purchases—epaulets—pay to Joseph Gardner, 701. Muskets from Board of War—bayonets for Lancaster—materials purchased for repair of State House steeple—establishment of Courts for trial of piracies, &c,, by Congress—Commissioners to pay depreciation certificates—none but officers of the line entitled to it—pay to Commissioners for running the line, 702, 703. Instructions to Commissioners, 704. List of officers to be paid depreciation certificates, 705. Conference on supplies—enemy about leaving New York for Delaware—defence—depreciation pay, 707. Renewal of a lost certificate — various orders for money—gaol fees—deeds, 708, 709. Proclamation for arrest of W. Rankin, 710. State House for Land Office—frigate Trumbull, purchase of powder—depreciation to be made good to Colonel Hazen's regiment, 713. Orders for money—Commissioners on line—defence of frontiers—Pennsylvania line — prize money—printing—depreciation, 714. Depreciation, 716, 718. Taxes—call of Assembly, 717. Pay of troops—Col. Humpton—guard at forts—depreciation — officers for south under General Wayne—Physick's books and papers to Col. Johnston—two companies for defence of forts, 719. Terms and officers—repairs of State House—military

Supreme Executive Council—xii. election—disputed powers of Assembly in Executive affairs—case of Isaac Austin—Capt. Carothers resigns—pay of State Clothier—militia in Berks ordered out, 720, 721. Militia—George Stump—Judge Smith resigns—French sailors—orders, 722, 723. Proclamation to receive continental money—sales of land in Philadelphia, 724, 725. Darby road—petition of D. A. Henning referred to Supreme Court—memorial officers of Proctor's regiment, 727. H. Shrupp paid for a horse—memorandum of Naval Officer, vessel without papers—Act respecting bills of credit—French marine desires to ship flour to St. Domingo, 729. Executions—pirate hung in chains—deed, 730, 731, 733. Pirate respited, 732. A. Boyd resigns—circular of Congress asking that master and chief may sign in presence of Naval Officer, 732, 733. Deed—reprieves—Commissioners of taxes, Philadelphia—quota of troops—clothing a soldier's wife, 735. Convention troops—liquidation of United States' debts—expenses of campaign — deed — accounts of Lieutenants—complaint of Capt. John against Col. Joseph Hart, 736, 737. Message to Assembly—Pennsylvania line—formed and on march under General Wayne—militia—prisoners, &c.—Lieut. S. Rea resigns, 739. Resolution of Assembly, and conference, 740, 741. Message to Assembly, demands of Congress, &c.—call of Gen. Wayne for men—mediation of Vienna and Petersburg—Congress ask for men—distresses in Northumberland county—report on taxes from Bedford—letters from Board of War—Col. Brodhead, Col. Morgan—purchases—Baron De Arentz—referred to Congress, 742, 743. James Read resigns—no more bills of credit to be issued—a claim to A. Corbitt's estate—message to Assembly, bills of credit—Register of Court of Admiralty in room of Andrew

Supreme Executive Council—Robinson, deceased—James Read elected—Andrew Allen's estate, 745. Deed—Colonel Johnston—Col. Brodhead—tobacco to be shipped—pay officers at Fort Pitt, 747. Message to Assembly, finances—Auditors of accounts-amendment of land office laws, 749. Stamping bills paid—barracks of Lancaster—estate of Benj. Booth—deed, 751. Message — militia—price of labor—Pennsylvania line, 753. Estate Alexander Corbitt—defence of frontiers—brig Elizabeth—books, &c., delivered to Receiver-General — deed, 755. Message, requisition of cavalry, 758, 759. Volunteers, 763. Petition Captain Hart against Col. H., who is cleared—message to Assembly on state of affairs, 763. Recruits of federal army—militia called out, 765. Mons. Massonnare forfeits goods, 767. Militia called out—Paymaster of York, Ensign Samuel Quinn, 769. Resolutions of Assembly, 770. Militia ordered out—sale of city lots under G. Bryan and Geo. Schlosser—petitions, 773. Receivers of recruits—orders—deed—Jno. Sigfriedt—moneys—resignation of R. Good, 775. Excess of militia offering, 777. Riflemen for General W.—returns to be made up by R. Morris — lots in Philadelphia claimed by R. Peters—pardons of prisoners in gaol, 779. Accounts of sappers and miners at camp—claim of H. Christ and H. Haller for land in Reading—leave of absence to Col. Nicola—sale of lots in Philadelphia—deed and patent, 781. Jno. F. Reichell returns to Saxony—B. Shoemaker to New Jersey—deed—survey of land in Cumberland county—Thos. McKean elected President of Congress—Robert Morris to be furnished with account of requisitions of money, 784.

Ammunition—provide for prisoners from Charlestown, xiii., 1. Resolutions respecting goods from Virginia under seizure to be given up, and Simon Nathan, plaintiff,

Supreme Executive Council—xiii. called up and discharged, 2. Riflemen—pay for traitor funds —robber arrested in Trenton—sales of lots inclosed with Episcopal and Presbyterian Churches to be suspended—clerk of market at York appointed, 3. Proclamation respecting British halfpence, 4. French sailors—A. Carlisle's estate, 5. City lots—payment to R. Morris—Justices—order of Congress for money, 7. Recruits at Newtown—sale of lots on State Island to Mr. Holker—deeds in all cases to be made to purchasers at public sale—shoes to be delivered to Captain Zeigler —case of Wm. Pollard, 8, 9. Settlement between Connecticut and Pennsylvania—resolutions of Assembly and petition to Congress —against receiving money for sale of Hogg Island—return of Mr. Searle, 10, 11. Deeds—S. R. Fisher discharged—notary appointed, 13. No pay for sales at Hogg Island—deserters—loan for South Carolina and Georgia, 15. Connecticut claim—State House —ensign removed—supplies to forts—men there to be discharged —pardons, 16, 17. Papers of Mayor—militia of Northampton, 19. Courts—deeds—notary public—gunpowder—exemption from militia by Justices—pay of militia, 20, 21. Deserter—escheator to take estates—claim of Major Parr —of Benj. Booth given up—clothing for Pennsylvania line—two pipes wine seized, 22, 23. Wagon hire in New Jersey, 24. Deeds, 26, 30, 31, 32. Claims of H. Paulding for lands at Wyalusing, sale stopped--sundry persons to be delivered up by Sheriff, 32. Claim of Pikeland county for city lots—deed—James Cunningham's account, 33. Sale on Province Island, 34. City lots, 35. Notary public, 36. Claim for Lutheran Church, 36. Call on militia, 37. Justices in Chester county, 38. Sale postponed, 39. Recruits—city lots, 39, 40. Embargo, 41. Appraisement of leaden spouts,

Supreme Executive Council—43. Pay for damage of Princeton College by militia, 44. Lands claimed by Yorktown, 44. City lots, 45, 46, 47. Estate of George Backman—clothing for Pennsylvania line—Mud Fort and Billingsport—T. Pickering, Quartermaster-General—capture of a flag of truce—city lots—embargo proclamation revoked — repairs of steeple, 48, 49. Appoint the sons of Baron De Kalb ensigns, 51. Deed to Joseph Carson—appointment of Clement Biddle Quartermaster-General, and W. Cooper ensign—order out 3000 men—French seamen, 53, 54. Petition respecting tax—agreement with Wm. Smith for care of Forts and Pest-house—deeds, 55, 56, 57. Messages to Assembly, 58, 66, 107, 128, 248, 258–262, 348, 363, 408, 425, 439, 483, 517, 537, 538, 682, 733, 761. Various orders for purchases, &c.—recognition of Sieur Holker as Consul-General, 59. Conference on finances, 60. Pikeland case—conference on defence, 61, 62. Call on Commodore Hazelwood for men —deed for city lots, 63, 64. Wagons, 65, 66. Deed—purchases — message to Assembly, 67. Quarters for troops, 68. March of enemy—militia called out and orders—Captain J. Livergood appointed—Dr. Jackson, 70, 71. Rations, 71. Money to Congress through R. Morris—retaining fee in Bucks—enemy at Staten Island—militia delayed, 73. Militia detained—Peter Parlee—Frederick Limback—Thos. Anderson resigns, 74. Justices to revise their rules, 74, 75. Sale at Province Island vacated, 75. Director of Hospitals, 76. Attainted persons—resolutions — boundary with Virginia—commissioners to run line—Connecticut claim—march of troops, 79. Deeds, 80, 81. Discharge of troops—taxes—death of Colonel Kichline—another elected—election in Bucks—supplies paid Congress—Col. Irvine to be obeyed at Fort Pitt, 82, 83.

Supreme Executive Council—xiii. Movements of enemy—discharge of militia—religious visit to Ireland how viewed by Council—election—Philadelphia, 84, 85. Elections—boxes for public papers, 87. Elections, 88, 89. News of surrender of Lord Cornwallis arrives—orders for rejoicings—Treasurer of Bucks county robbed—proclamation respecting, 95. Suit against Jno. Vanderen for breach of contract—case of Benj. Ford, a prisoner—enlargement—deed—nolle pros. in case of mother of Thomas Forrest, 97. Light House—new wardens chosen—fast day—Justice resigns, 100, 101. Wardens—John Hanson, President of Congress—Justice resigns, 105. Agents resigned or appointed—to report estates unsold, 107. Eulogium on Gen. Greene—taxes—frontiers—muster of militia—deeds, 108, 109. President and Vice-President—damaged arms to be sold, 110, 111. Wm. Moore, President, and James Potter, Vice-President—Declaration signed—read at Court House—order of procession, 112, 113. Executions ordered—certain troops to proceed to Lancaster from Fort Rice, 117. Deeds for city lots, 118, 119. Unfair election in Philadelphia, 119, 120. Petitions for pardon—orders for money, 121. Use of documents granted to Ebenezer Hazard—Justices—Dr. Barnabas Binney applies for depreciation pay—pass to New York for son of Rev. Thomas Coombe, 122. Mode of assessing taxes- Samuel Sterret—report of Surveyor-General on claim, John Egg for city lots—resolutions of Congress on Connecticut controversy—and of General Assembly, 123. Pay of militia of Philadelphia—proclamation for a fast day—supplies to United States, 125. Sales of Province Island—election deeds—frontiers, 126, 127. Appoint Reed, Bradford, and Wilson counsel on Connecticut claim—state of Barracks—frontiers—

Supreme Executive Council—rations and prices—robbery of collectors in Chester County—message, 128, 129. Lot of Samuel Fox—address to General Washington on capture of Cornwallis—and his answer—representation on bahalf of the Quakers, 130, 131. Resolutions and conference on expedition against Indians—establishment of—board of property—election, 133. Persons to embark for France—elections—reprieves—change in bounty, 135. Claim for City lots—retaining fees to counsel in Connecticut case—depreciation to Physician—execution, 137. Deed—City lots—plan—postponed sale—depositions on robbery on collectors in Bucks and Chester—agents of estates appointed, 139. Lots and lands—persons to view, 140. Deeds for city lots—Christ Church bells, pay for ringing—clothing, 143. Accounts of J. Marshall—Mons. Holker—depreciation—taxes to be collected—British vessel in Delaware, refuses to be examined—to be stopped by Capt. A. Porter at Mud Island—clothing for Bedford, 145. John Lukens, Surveyor General for plan of City lots—deeds, 146. Election of a Councillor for Philadelphia—plans of City lots paid for—Lieutenant resigns, 149. Ammunition for various places—Captain Boyds discharged from service with compliments to his merit, 151. Sailors for French frigate, 153. What captures are lawful—servants of R. R. Livingston—depreciation case of A. Stuart to be settled—purchases commission—plan for recruiting Pennsylvania line—places of rendezvous—Col. Richard Hampton appointed superintendent, 154, 165. Agreement for supplies of militia—Dr. Duffield's depreciation, — election — Westmoreland, 157, 158. Arrest and imprisonment of John Connolly—election in Philadelphia, 161, 163; Supplies—rations, Connolly's servant, 163. Report

Supreme Executive Council—xiii. on value of estates—guard for prisoners—orders for money, 165. Deeds for City lots—pay to militia of city; Claim of James Wallace for a lot—Edward Cooke, appointed sub-Lieutenant, 167, 168. Recruits—depreciation—rations for State Fleet, paid for defences of frontiers, 169. British goods to be seized, Committee to value lot of M. Aspden—deeds, 170, 171, 172. What captures are lawful—pay for Riflemen—pay for watching the British fleet, 173. On revenue from imports, claim for a lot in city, report of surveyor-general on T. Forrest's claim for city lots, and also by B. Davis—Deeds, 175, 176. Capt. Livergood's pay—Moses Scott's, &c. Colonel Stephen Balliott, 177. Guard house to be repaired, 178. Deeds—places of rendezvous. President and Judge of City Courts, 181. Deeds—complaint against F. Hopkinson, 182. Gen. Washington on supplies—Deeds—Report on election of Councillor, 184, 188. Speedy modes of justice between French and American subjects—Colonel Nicola dismissed with thanks as Town Major, 185. Report and discussion on election of Councillor, 184, 188, 192, 194, 195, 196, 197, 200, 203, 206, 210, 212, 216, 217, 221, 223. Money borrowed of Congress to be repaid——supplies—horrible sentence of a Criminal—remitted—pay to militia, 195. Submit various papers to Assembly—deeds, 199. Bank of North America, 201. Vacancies and promotions in Regiments—Line with Virginia—militia called out, 203, 206. Deeds—James Paterson appointed Commissioner on line in Virginia, 205. Defence of Frontiers—Taxes—money due C. Sower, to be paid—State—recruiting, 207. Conference with Assembly on Virginia line—not to be by astronomical observation—fear of revolt at Fort Pitt—report on M. Aspden's estate, 209. Vansteer's corps, 211. Various or-

Supreme Executive Council—ders for money, 213. Deed—Fort Muncey,—Ensign—appointed J. Dickinson Sergeant—additional counsel on Connecticut Claim, 215. Deeds—inquiry about Connecticut troops, 217. Ask opinion of Supreme Court—20th Section of Constitution—deed—supplies—Justices—answer of Supreme Court, 219, 220 Election—extension of authority in case of siege—horse thief, 221. Controversy between S. Lyons and Major J. Smith, respecting cattle—defence of frontiers—Captain Porter promoted, also Captain Craig—election of Councillor, 222, 232, 233. Conference on defence of frontiers—accounts, 235. J. Reed appointed counsel in case of Big Spring tract—deeds, 236. Petitions referred by Assembly—land in Bucks to be valued—arms to be delivered to Petit & Fitzsimons, 236, 237. Sheriff to return—sales of merchandise from St. Thomas—case of Baron, Hurst & Co.—purchasers of City lots to be put in possession—on Province Island to pay, 241. Committee to draw up message to Assembly—settlement with Mr. Holker, 242. Remonstrance of Captain F. Proctor—rations for Colonel S. Balliott—election in Washington County, 245. Deeds for city lots, Dr. Hutchinson's pay, 247. Message on defence of frontiers, 249. Deeds, 250, 251. A. McLean to run Virginia line—to have militia from Washington County—Worsley Emes as Capt.—George Campbell, Register of Wills, 253. Permit exports to Antigua—reward for prisoners, 254. Class men—Rangers of Bedford County, 257. Grant to P. Snyder—Captain Prizgard breaks health laws—may draw on State Treasury—message,—various grievances—interference, with powers of, 258 262. Appoint justices—on failure to elect in certain counties 264. Proclamation for fast day—solicitor on

Supreme Executive Council—xiii. Connecticut claim, 267. Estimate of leaden spouts—provisions for persons engaged in running Virginia line, 269. Approve of buying ship General Monk to defend the Delaware—deeds, 271. Paper for laws—resignation—appointments of officers, 275. Seven months men—deed—pay to Congress—fees to counsel—J. Galloway's estate and J. Reid's sold, 281. Adjourn to attend reception of news of birth of Dauphin of France—delivery of a deserter from—Pennsylvania line, 281. Petition for goods seized on L. Hollingsworth's shallop—statement from Robert Morris on old Continental money—officers elected in Chester county militia—Dauphin of France—address to French Minister—ship General Washington hired to superintendent of finance for a voyage—commissions issued to Captain Joshua Barney, &c., 282, 283. Address to French Minister and reply—interest to be charged on delinquent city lot purchasers, 285. Surplus purchases not needed, to be sold at auction—resolutions as to powers of Congress alone to make treaties with Great Britain, 286, 288. Order pay for an entertainment, 288. Military generals elected—dates of commissions, 289. Military in counties to be in readiness--conference with Congress on pursuing war with vigor, &c., 291. Approve of military proceedings in Northumberland County—election of Justice—state of frontiers—petition to defer sales of land in Northumberland County,—military officers elected—repairs of lighthouse—guard for prisoners, 293. Certain persons summoned before Council—to State indebtedness, 294, 297. Reports of Surveyor-General on claims to City lots—also call for demands for horses and cattle purchased, 295. Board of property, members appointed—stores to be furnished militia—letters from General Ir-

Supreme Executive Council—vine proposing emigration and killing of Indians at Muskingum—cost of entertainment in Dauphin, 288, 297. Counsellors—fees—banks at Mud Island, 297. Reprieve—orders for money. J. D. Sergeant, in case of Hog Island, 299. Deeds, city lots, 305. Public creditors, 307. Deeds, 304. Sale of articles ordered, 311. James Searle arrives—ammunition ordered—counsellors appointed on Connecticut claims—case of Smith & Lyons—robbery of Southern mail—reward offered, 311. Proclamation, 312, 313. Severe sentence—Connecticut claim—militia called out—trade with enemy—city lots, 315, 317, 320. Report of Surveyor-General on lots claimed by Moore, Hill & Wells, 321. Refuse to allow John Henry to lecture on heads—claims to city lots—fencing lands at Billingsport--Hog I'ld, 325. Seizure of British goods, 329. H. Osburne to have books and papers — deserters—proclamation against traitors, 332. Deeds — Virginia line — arms brought from Billingsport, 335. Proclamation for robbers—prize money—pay of deserters forfeited, 339. Deed—clothing—lead to be delivered, 341. British deserters to report themselves — Jesse Vickers to be executed, but if he make discoveries to be pardoned—conference on Connecticut claim—General Greene proposed as seventh Judge—pay to Van Etten's Company — meeting of Board of property—Jesse Vickers partially confesses, 343. Execution deferred, he and others to be removed to Philadelphia gaol, and militia discharged—Caleb Paul to be demanded of Governor of New Jersey—ammunition to Chester county—deed for city lots, 344—loans—British goods—robberies—taxes--moneys due militia — execution of J. Vickers further postponed, 349. Indians in Berks county—C Werkeiser's estate divided among

Supreme Executive Council—xiii. his children—resolutions of New York—loan—election of Justice rejected, 351. Supplies required —an answer to assembly—defence of the Delaware—permission to sell ship Genl. Washington—pay for taking prisoners of war, 353, 354. Permit to Ebenezer Hazard to examine public documents—conference with Assembly on present critical situation of affairs, 355. Committee to confer with Gen. Washington on Indian expedition—Col. Hunter to contract for provisions—action for a dead horse—militia of Berks called out, 357. Boats to transport Rochambeau's army across Delaware—meeting of Board of property—price of rations for Bedford county, 359. Papers relative to Connecticut claim to be examined—sale of ship Gen. Washington—opposition to militia law, 361. Rations—Indian expedition —authority to draw on Assembly and object—damage by enemy, 363. Men required by Board of War—called out, 365. Assembly inquire amount of expenses of suit against Connecticut—deeds—action of H. Gross against Dishler for purchases—shoes disposed of—officers in Proctor's artillery regiment ask for promotion—invitation to attend consecration of Jews' Synagogue, asking protection, 367. Various petitions and pardons—call on militia of certain counties—damage by enemy estimated, 369. General Potter to command troops on Indian expedition—money to be drawn from National Bank of North America—appointments for purchases—marshal of admiralty to pay moneys to Treasurer, 371. Loan of arms from State—expense of Sandusky expedition, 373. Rations for militia—troops under General Potter at Muncey—French seamen—proclamation, 375. Troops called out from city—General W. against Indian expedition-troops recalled-passes—J. Reed assistant counsel to Attorney-General in case of

Supreme Executive Council— robberies in Bucks county, 381. Defence of frontiers—deeds—purchase vessel for defence of Delaware—plates for counterfeiting, 385. Articles furnished General Potter—passes, &c., 386. Surveyor-General paid for plans of city lots, 389. Elections, 391, 393, 395, 397, 398. Proclamation of Congress for thanksgiving, 396, 400. Letter to General W. on abandonment of Wyoming, 399. Col. Levers to contract for supplies—H. Welflang—Justices in Washington county—election in do., 403. Estimates—quotas of States, 405. Supplies — Indian expedition from Fort Pitt—J. Craig resigns, 407. John Dickinson elected—cattle in bad order—time for electing President and Vice President—expense of trial with Connecticut, 411. Programme of election of President and Vice President, 412. Conference with Connecticut—election—John Dickinson and James Ewing, 413. Conference with counsel and Solicitor on evidence respecting Connecticut claim—Indians in Northumberland—expenses of fitting up Comptroller's office, 417. Order respecting Indian deeds and other papers respecting Connecticut—John Penn to be applied to—enlistment of eighteen months' men—election—Dobb's ferry for receipt of flags, 419. Funds for defence—deeds respecting Connecticut—destitute Indian prisoners—report of Comptroller-General on accounts for rations—Ebenezer Hazard to be applied to for papers on Connecticut—state of ranging companies—expenses of Connecticut controversy—report on accounts of Wm. Maclay, 420, 421. Paper money now in circulation—Indian expeditions countermanded—various orders for money, 423. Robert Morris, Colonel Butler—National Bank—settlements on Ohio, 425, 426. Disposal of money for defence, 426. Contracts for supplies in Northumberland—for pest

Supreme Executive Council—xiii. houses to cease and salary at Mud Island and Billingsport, 429. Court on Connecticut meets at Trenton—General Irvine on settlers on Ohio—prisoners in prison ships at New York—reward for apprehending John Tomlinson of Bucks, 431. Deeds—proclamation against vice and immorality—case of John Fishel, a prisoner by General Burgoyne, 432. Papers from J. Turner and B. Chew belonging to Land Office to be demanded, 435. Papers delivered up by Jno. Penn—quantity of supplies to be credited—various orders for money, 437. Indian deeds to be delivered to Mr. Osburn—message to Assembly—powers of counties to levy money—evils of debts to the State—pay to militia—Court House for Washington county—reward for apprehending Levi Dean, 439. Journal at Fort Stanwix connected with Connecticut claim—commission to counsel and Solicitor in do.—agent for forfeited estates in Bucks—pay for provisions—call on Gen. St. Clair for promotions—repairs to government mansion house, 441. Connecticut papers returned, 442. Election, 443. Copies of laws purchased—complaints against Prothonotary of Northumberland—Journal at Fort Stanwix returned—counsel fees in Connecticut case—accounts of Brigadier-General Irvine while prisoner, approved, 447. Officers to make monthly returns—rations—claim for negroes taken—estate of Wm. Bell—letter—war office—E. Tyson, 449. Discharge of a soldier by substitute—Hyder Ally bought for State—report on excise—deed, 451. Pay on account of Connecticut suit—taxes—Major Gordon on goods seized at Lancaster, 453. Act respecting University requested—proposal of Gabriel Blakency to raise men at Fort Pitt declined—promotions, 455. Promotions—passport for flag for New York—vessel to be sent with provisions—account of Pennsylvania Hospital—militia want pay, 457. Pass from Admiral Digby for vessel with provisions Ezekiel Robbins to distribute them among prisoners, 459. Commissioners for officers, 461. H. Osburne returns deeds per list and they are handed to D. Kennedy—accounts and payments, 462–470. Letter—John Dickinson on state of affairs—eighteen months men—H. Osburne directed to place extracts in hands of Secretary—proclamation—desertions of French sailors, 473. Prisoners return from among Indians, pay and clothes—vessels in Delaware river to be searched for French sailors—pay to rangers—decree in favor Pennsylvania against Connecticut—proclamation respecting, 475. Loan of papers to H. Osburne—rent of room at Marcus Hook—copies of Act adverse to erecting an independent State within Pennsylvania, 477. Fee to counsel—President on business to be attended to—LaFayette recommends Chevalier de Lambert—copies of printed minutes—orders for money, 479. Pay for flour—mission of Rev. Jas. Finley, 481. Paid Council—British goods, 483, 484, 485. Return of military stores—report of agents respecting Connecticut—militia fines, 485. Mons. Marbois to receive powder into magazine—pass down Ohio—recovery of Charlestown—end of Connecticut suit—various letters—negotiations at Paris, 487. Pennsylvania line—revenue—taxes—prisoners at New York—new State—police for city—militia laws, 489, 490. Wyoming lands, 497. Alleged frauds in sale of Alexander Bartram's estate tried and dismissed, 499. Pay to Rev. James Finley—to General Irvine on account of captivity—Pennsylvania line—estate of C. Saur, 500. Indian incursions stopped—treaty with United Netherlands ratified—memorial Cols. Coates and Loller on payment to men in State money—city lots—deserters, 503. Executions ordered—various pa-

Supreme Executive Council—xiii. pers read—deeds, 505. City lots, 507. Claims for estate C. Saur—complaint against C. Cesna—British goods seized—lands at Wyoming, 509. Rev. Peter Miller intercedes for H. Martin—Commissioners on line between Pennsylvania and Virginia—Joseph Roberts, petition, 511. Case of H. Martin, Pentecost and Cannon—of C. Cesna, 513. Account of Wm. Henry of L. for arms—papers relating to C. Cesna—of Colonel J. Morgan, Jr.—Acts and orders of Congress—accounts of Adam Hubley, &c.—robberies in Philadelphia and Bucks—depreciation to Pennsylvania line—account for writing paper, 515. Confiscated estate—Israel Doan—accounts of Commissioners for defence of Delaware—John Potts, 517. Report of Commissioners Pennsylvania and Virginia—exchange of certificate—lands of A. Yeldal—companies for Wyoming, 519. Horse lost—Justices, 521. Exchange of certificates — soldiers to march for Wyoming—pay for soldiers in Bucks county, 523. Flag of truce from Bermuda — memorial, A. Young for purchases—extracts and resolution of Assembly on accounts, &c., 525. Pay to W. A. Atlee—account N. Stokely, 527. E. Bryson Smith to report himself—damages from enemy to Northampton county—estate of Wm. Bell, 529. Expenses in running line between Pennsylvania and Virginia, 531. Report of purchase of land for Court House in Washington county—militia ordered out, 531. Robberies in Bucks and Chester, 533. Judges of High Court of Errors, &c., appointed—Wm. Moore and John Bayard—rations, &c., 535. Reports on accounts—State House clock—Bell's estate—ask conference Committee on Comptroller's report on T. Matlack's accounts for tavern and marriage licenses—reward for scalps, 537. Message on Secretary's accounts—proclamation offering reward for Indian

Supreme Executive Council—scalps annulled, 538. Clothing for British soldiers—part of goods seized in Chester county—embezzled—Sheriff ordered to appear—Capt. John Hughes discharged—T. Matlack requested to resign—another Sec'y. to be appointed—the body of Luz. Subzey to be delivered to D. Brodhead, Jr., 539. John Armstrong, Jr., appointed sec'y—papers from Congress — proclamation confirming boundary line between Pennsylvania and Virginia, 541. Reward for apprehending Levi Doan—against John Hubley as Prothonotary—purchases—rank—deeds—preliminary articles for a general peace—opinion of Supreme Court, 543. Henry Wynkoop, Judge of Court of Errors and Appeals, 545. Pay to H. Osburne, 547. Deeds for city lots—claim of Eliz. Kurtz for land—receipts and expenditures of public moneys by Superintendent of Finances—H. Baker asks opinion respecting a law of Assembly—Province Island—additional clerk allowed, 549. Sale of armed vessels—deed—demand on Ezekiel Robbins by David Sproat for moneys, 553. Proclamation of Congress on cessation of hostilities, 555. Benj. Still's appointed Commissioner to settle accounts between Penn. and United States—bells of Christ Church to be rung—proclamation of peace—Hessian flags taken at Trenton to be demanded, 559. Passport to John Penn and family, 561. Return of stores at Wyoming—answers of Judges respecting entry of British goods, 565. Superintendent of Finance circular, ammunition for Wyoming—not to be delivered on receipt of officers, 567. British prisoners pass through city-stores for Wyoming, 572. On literary property, 574. On finance—deeds—Collector of Excise—Appraiser of goods, 577. Health officer to discharge his duty—meeting of trustees of State Island—visit forts, 579. Prisoners removed to new gaol, 589.

Supreme Executive Council—xiii. Chevaux-de-frise to be sold—pest house repaired boom—at piers—counsel in case of T. Matlack paid, 591. Deed—price of salt complained of—discharge of certain military companies, 592. Taxes—papers delivered up—execution—Wardens to remove obstructions—price of salt fixed, 595. M. Marbois, duties on a part of a cargo—instructions to Surveyor-General — H. Osburne discharged—papers to be given up--accounts with United States--Street Commissioners—new Collector of Excise, 597. Request of Marbois not granted — pay to Dougherty and Huffnagle—pay to Quarter-Master—deed, 599. Duties on French vessel—Federal city—Berks militia—instructions to loan officer—memorial from Berks county—apprehension of banditti, 601. Paving in city — half pay and Commutation — troops at Lancaster — and conference with committee of Congress on, 603. Deeds—anonymous letter of officers for appointment of officers to Governor and Council, 605. Resolutions of Congress on and conference respecting—requested with Judges, 607. Resolutions of Congress and further action — field officers of city convened, 609. Answer from Col. Shee in name of officers—conference—letter from Captain Christie — attack on the Bank meditated—Capt. Stiles to deliver arms to militia, 611. Three papers from Jas. Bennett presented, refusal to consider them—a large guard of militia called out--arms--H. Carberry and J. Sullivan to be arrested—Robert Patton's commission, 613. Examination of soldiers—cannon taken at Yorktown to be delivered Col. Hodgdon, 614. Deposition and proclamation respecting robbery in Bucks county—omission in Col. Porter's commission — Captain Carberry, Captain of Pennsylvania line, to be arrested, also Lieut. James Sullivan and Sergeant Nagle—

Supreme Executive Council—complaints against appointment of Capt. Esler to be heard—letters Rev. J. Finley and Gen. Irvine—deed, 617. Memorial of Consul of France-conference with Judges, &c. — affidavit of J. Bennett—resolution of Congress—report on late disturbances—Capt. Esler's appointment — conference with Judges, &c., on consular powers—application of Major-General Howe for stores, 618, 619. New members of Board, property—deeds, 621. Proclamation against murderer of J. Molineaux—deed, 629. Title confirmed to J. Shallus, which had before been confirmed by land office to William Sallaway—the right is inquired into — Justices — regulator of weights and measures, 633. Return of Congress to city proposed and welcomed by—Act of Virginia Assembly—survey of the Delaware respecting Chevaux-de-frise, 637. Report of Land Office—send copy of Gov. Harrison's letter to Prothonotary of Washington co., 639. Proclamation against base coins, 643. Fraudulent settlement on lands—Mons. Marbois on a cargo—letter from Capt Schrawder on Wyoming, 645. Messages to Assembly on various subjects, 647–666. Governors — Commissioner—health—land for officers--Courts—discharge of debts—auctions—a Chamber of Commerce—chevaux-de-frise — canals—boundaries — religion — old prison—measures—French seamen—disturbances among soldiers, officers-Congress at Princeton—Captain Carberry, 666. Money for lots — Major Ryan seized for debt for another—cause of Col. Harmer's disappointment — memorial of French merchants—chevaux-de-frise, 671. Col. Harmer's memorial, 671. Case of Ephraim Allen referred to Judges of Supreme Court, 671. Various papers sent to Assembly — conference with Committee of Assembly on Act for sale of certain lands, 673. Hog Island, decision—patent for

Supreme Executive Council—xiii. E. Blaine—case decided—B. Shoemaker to receive papers from his father, 675. Memorial of Pennsylvania line—letter Comptroller-General, 683. Charles Cesna to be sued for perjury and forgery—Virginia boundary—Commissioners—report of committee on Gov. Harrison's letter—resolution of Assembly, 685, 686. Deed—proclamation against robbers in Bucks county, 687. Laying out State House grounds as a public green forever, 692. Matthew Smith dismissed—Hamilton's bonds cancelled—Hanna's-town for Courts, 699. New members, 719, 724, 730. Proclamation for a murderer, 728. Dates of commissions, 731. Appointments and resignations, 732. Message to Assembly—sundry letters—elections—barracks in Lancaster—eulogium on Pennsylvania line, 733. New member—time for choosing President and Vice President, 733. President and Vice President chosen—Dickinson and Ewing—Duponceau, Notary, &c., 737. S. Rhea and accounts—Col. Craig—proposal to raise chevaux-de-frise by De Brattine and Garrison—order to Wardens for money for, 739. New member—memorial from Quakers, 741. New members-pay for apprehending Joseph Doan, 742. New members—applicant as a navy officer—rations for Northumberland, 743. President council of Censors—barracks—removal of obstruction in Delaware river, 744. Committee on contested election in Northumberland—Col. Ross, Lieutenant of Lancaster—memorial Captain F. Finney for land—correspondence with Congress, 747. Resignation of Justices—deed—money of a traitor—propriety of public demonstration on account of peace—proclamation for public thanksgiving, 749. Ratification by Congress received, 750. Resolution of Council of Censors—division of Berks into election districts—new member and elections in Northumberland—James Searle, pay as agent, 751. Public demonstration for peace—J. Searle, before—Act against vice and immorality—Comm'rs appointed by Virginia on boundary—letter from Governor H.—against fairs—Pennsylvania line and land in Bucks, 753. Survey on a ship and cargo, 755. List of deeds, mortgages, bonds, &c., transmitted by order of Assembly to, 759, 760. Inventory of goods by John Cadenhead—papers from Major James Moore—demonstrations on account of peace—vendue laws, 761. Conference with Assembly—General Armand and his corps—Z. Butler's commitment, 760, 763. Address to General Washington, 765. Papers of A. Ross to be received from Mrs. McCoy—answer of G. Washington—deeds, 667. Brig Philadelphia, loss of goods, and inspection, 768, 769, 770. Council of Censors, 770. Ship "Two Friends," 771. Globes, maps, &c., purchased, 775. Secretary to record correspondence, 774. Deed, 778.

Order sent against Hogg Island, xiv., 4. Draft on Treasurer for interest due on certificate for money loaned United States, 7. Various orders for money, 7–9, 10. Messages to Assembly, 11, 15, 30, 39, 44, 45, 61, 163, 183, 185, 246, 269, 271, 275, 276, 281, 284, 328–342, 343, 366, 380, 381, 522. Messages from Assembly, 289. Settlers on lands of State—agreement with New Jersey on trials—prisoners—regulation of carts, &c., in Philadelphia, 17. Proclamation on treaty with Great Britain, 19–22. Conference with Committee of Assembly—letter Brig.-General Hand and report, 25. Gratuity to soldiers, 27. Conference with Assembly on opening Land Office, 29. Claims of J. Campbell on Virginia land—memorial of De Marcellin and Le Roy—President of Congress on Federal Court to try private rights to Wyoming lands—letter Major

Supreme Executive Council—xiv. Moore, 31. Drafts of letters to delegates, &c.—report on tea, to be sold—Wm. Kennedy's estate, 36. Election of Justices, 39. Pay to Commissioners for treaty with Indians—Commissioners appointed, 40, 45. Jacob Rush appointed third Judge of Supreme Court—States unrepresented in Congress—Mons. Marbois, French Consul, 43. Messages to Assembly—debts due by State—confiscated estates—Commissioners to Indians, 45. Contested election for Justice, 47, 51. Congress on Wyoming, place of meeting of Indian Commissioners—donation to encourage agriculture and commerce, 51. Pay to counsel in case Baron Hurst & Co. vs. State—names of purchasers of city lots to be prepared—pay to Judge of Admiralty—conference on withdrawing troops from Wyoming—Sharp Delany, Collector, 53. Indian Commissioners to have deeds, &c. — letter from merchants of Philadelphia—Jnstices—discharge of State House clock keeper, 55. Commissioners on Virginia boundary line to meet—deed—proclamation for a murderer, 57. Chevaux-de-frise—report on sales of city lots—boundary with Virginia, 58. Inundation at Wyoming, 61. Judge of Errors and Appeals resigns—Ferguson's lectures and a scale—inspection of goods, 67, 71. Sold at auction—oaths to Judge Rush—fruit trees to be planted in Pennsylvania Hospital - Ed. Physic to examine papers for quit rents due Proprietaries, 71. Province Island, military stores, removal—copies of letters to be made—inspection of goods—removal of chevaux-de-frise, 73. Commissioners on boundary with Virginia to meet—proposals for moving chevaux-de-frise—complaint against Constables, 75. Barracks to be laid off into lots—forfeiture on brandy—militia fines and expenses, 77. L'Orient a free port—chevaux-de-frise, 79. E. Shippen, President Justice of

Supreme Executive Council—

Court of Common Pleas, 103. Pay to Col. A. Porter for provisions to Virginia Commissioners and Donaldson and Hollingsworth for chevaux-de-frise—Wardens, 105, 109. Dedimus issues for Philadelphia–triumphal arch–pay to troops at Wyoming—Mons. Marbois on a detained French ship, 111, 113. Proclamation to arrest robbers in Southwark, Philadelphia–election for no vacancy, 113. Insult to French Consul by Longschamps, 115, 116, 117, 121, 123. [See also vols. X., XI., P. A.] A. Patterson resigns as Justice, 117. Ministers of France and United Netherlands call on President, 121. Removal of buoys from Delaware, proclamation respecting—writ of Habeas Corpus, case of Longschamps, 123. Letter to Judges of Supreme Court, of Minister of Netherlands and Mons. Marbois—James Wilson to assist as counsel, 135. Person concerned with Longschamps, and proclamation concerning, 137. Recorders to take bonds and Prothonotaries to see that oaths are taken, 138. Oath to Joseph Pennell, Commissioner to settle public accounts in marine department, and J. Stevenson, Auditor of depreciation of Pennsylvania Line—Justices appointed, 139. Escape of Longschamps—bridge—claim of J. Wilson's estate—Connecticut claim—Judges Supreme Court—case of Longschamps, 142. Rations for Northampton county—return of threatening letters to Marbois—seven hundred men for western posts and number of troops for Commissioners to Indians, 143. Call of Assembly, requesting delivery of Longschamp—address to Luzerne on his departure, 145. Distress of frontiers—answer of Luzerne, 147. President of Court of Common Pleas—resignation of a Warden and another appointed—deeds—expended for improvements in the Delaware—conspiracy against taxes in Westmoreland county—proclamation, 151. Illegal elec-

Supreme Executive Council—xiv. tion in Northumberland county—persons in gaol in Philadelphia—reports of counsel in case of Connecticut—return of arms, &c., in city—inquest on George Fitler, 159. Act of Legislature of Massachusetts, &c., cession of lands to the United States, 163. Military arrangements and resolutions respecting Wyoming—C. J. McKean reappointed, 166, 167. Resignations of Antes and Ashman accepted, 169. Conference respecting Wyoming and Longschamp—case of E. Milne account of stores, &c., of United States taken by the enemy, 171. Salaries to Judges of Supreme Court—instructions to Lieutenants of Northumberland—depositions—message to Assembly—various matters, 173. Payment to Jane Roberts out of estate John Roberts—proceedings against F. Lembach—accounts of President for leaden spouts taken for public use in 1777—resignation of Justice Atlee—reappointed—recovery of debts, 175. Refuse to sell old iron from jail—military officers appointed for frontiers—bounty to Ogden and McClellan, captors of Aaron Doan, 177. Officers, Commissioners, Justices, 181. Expenses of troops—appointments—examination of Susquehannah river--Wyoming—A. Carson, 183. Pennsylvania Line—list of officers who have taken oath of allegiance—Wyoming, 185. Goods for Commissioners to treat with Indians and warrants for, 187. Minutes of, delivered to Council of Censors—transfers of certificates by officers to other persons—Jona. Penrose, Justice, 197. Spies on frontiers paid, 199. List of entries of land in Virginia—inquiry about letters of administration taken out by officers of Pennsylvania Line, 200. Justices appointed, 200. Commissioners to Wyoming—execution, 203. Appointments of Justices, Prothonotaries pay to Commissioners to Indians, 205, Ed. Shippen

Supreme Executive Council—appointed Judge of Court of Errors and Appeals—Contested elections, 207, 208. Deed—Complaint against Prothonotary of Chester county, 209. Appointments of Register and Recorder—Provisions for Westmoreland—Commissioner on Virginia boundary, 211. Removal of Chevaux de frize—Pay to censors—and State clothiers, 213. Various orders for money—Bounty to captors of Jos. Doane, Jr., 215. Lieutenant for Northampton county — Jno. Armstrong, Jr., Adjutant-General in place of James Wilkinson—left the State, 217. To have charge of troops sent from Bucks and Berks to Wyoming, 217, 218. Order to him for expenses—His rank — Letter from President Dickinson on propriety of call on militia to be reconsidered—Fort to be levelled — Colonel Armstrong's appointment objected to —he objects generally to their measures, 219, 220. Proclamation respecting Wyoming, 220–224. Pay for provisions furnished flying camp in 1776--For framing, varnishing and gilding pictures in council chamber—and various other orders for money, 225. Order for execution, 228. Disputed election, 232, Inspection of goods, 232. Repair of State House, 235. Complaint of Washington county against Commissioners of taxes, 235. Pay for copies of Indian deeds—execution ordered—criminals pardoned on application of Mons. Marbois, Jr.,—Certificate of removal of Chevaux de frise to Donaldson & Hollingsworth—and letter of President, 241. Message to Assembly—Obstructions in Delaware—Virginia boundary—irregular elections, 247. Conference on election for President and Vice President—John Dickinson and J. Irvine re-elected—contested election, 249. Proclamation at C. H. and procession, 251. Resignation of James Wilkinson as Adjutant and Brigadier-General

Supreme Executive Council—xiv. —Contested election in Lancaster, 253, 254, 255, 258, 264, 266, 267, 268, 269. Conference on Wyoming, 258, 259, 260. Six trustees for Lancaster appointed, 259. Contested election in Chester—Delegates to Congress appointed by Assembly, 261. Picture frames —Portrait of Washington, 265. Lancaster election decided and councellor, sheriff and coroner appointed, 267. Prosecution of persons engaged in fraud at Lancaster election—Repairs in Secretary's office—Message on escheats —Election of William Miller in Lancaster confirmed, 268, 269. Evidence in a contested election in Bucks county—R. H. Lee, President of Congress — Purchase from Six Nations—Public debt and payment—Proposed plans discussed in a message to Assembly, 270-274. Thomas Paine's services and reward, 275. Division of Peter's township proposed and named, 275. Swedish Consul —March of troops to Wyoming, 277. Jurisdiction of islands in Delaware—Petition for Justices, 279. Claims against United States — Conference — letter to Governor of New Jersey-Accounts of Timothy Matlack, 281. Illegal election at Germantown—Letter of Marbois on his privileges as consul—Identity of Amos Williams—Public accounts—Box to be delivered to Marbois free of duty—Bounty for capture of A. Williams—Memorial from Montgomery county-Respecting money for C. H., 282, 283. T. Matlack —Money for C. H. at Montgomery —Sale of prison—Purchase of part of State House lot—Repairs of State House, 285. And for improving the Square—T. Matlack —Boundary line—Sale of public horses—Notary Public—C. H. in Westmoreland—Sale of Confiscated estates, 287. Papers from Commissioners on Virginia boundary—Justice dismissed—Election message from Assembly—Ground rent for lot at Sixth and Market,

Supreme Executive Council—289. Intestate estate in Bucks county-Justices, 307. Pay Attorney-General—Wardens' accounts —Hon. William Henry entitled to half sales of goods seized—Order for sale of horses reversed, 308, 309. Payments to persons on Crawford's expedition—To F. H. Judge of Errors and Appeals—Colonel James Moore and others —Letters—Atlee — Johnson — D. Harmer, 311. Complainants from Wyoming attend and receive money, 315. Letters on Connecticut claim, &c., 317. List of papers, &c., relating to Wyoming controversy, 318-320. Elections, 321. Claim to city lots under Penn, 323. Drawing of State lottery—Appointment of S. Sneider as justice objected to, 325. Memorial of merchants on piers—Message to Assembly—City lots, 327. Long message to Assembly —Containing a general view of the condition of the province, 328-342. Act of Congress—New members, 342. Commissioners on jurisdiction of island, 345. Contested election in Fayette county, 346. Counterfeit certificates—Proclamation of Congress respecting, 347. Claims of Captain Thomas Houston, 348. Message to Assembly—Revenue—Taxes—Prisons—Foreigners, &c., 349-355. Insurrection in Northumberland—Old jail and workhouse to be pulled down—City lots—Patrick Haley arrested and reward paid, 359. Boundary line between Virginia—Sale of horses —Merchants on Barbary savages —Right of Pennock to city lot, 361. Notary—Marbois—Governor of New York—Germantown election, 363. Reward for apprehending Sol. Vickars claimed—Report of Commissioners to Indians, 365. Removal of military stores, &c., from old jail—Treaty at Fort Stanwix with Indians, 366-7. Payment of William Whitebread's bond, &c., to city—Interfering claims for cession of Virginia—Copy of agreement to

Supreme Executive Council—xiv. be obtained—Merchants of Philadelphia—Justices, 368. Improvement of State House lot, 369. Division of a township in Westmoreland proposed — Commissioners for liquidating and settling accounts with United States—List of deputies to issue certificates—Bill of New York respecting partition line—Martha Boggs' petition for improvements on reserved tract near Pittsburg—Committee of Conference on accounts of James Searle — Person to take charge of Fort McIntosh, 373. Boundary line with New York—Election in New Market ward—Captain Houston's demands, 381. Rent of Province island—Wyoming — Committee on rumor against Jno. Armstrong, Jr., 383. Case of Aaron Doane—Resolution of Congress to be published—Ground rent on estate of Andrew Yorkes—Conference on New York line—Mortgage on confiscated estate—Adjourn for Good Friday, 385. General William Irvine appointed land agent—John Story additional commissioner to settle United States accounts—Case of Aaron Doane, 386, 387. Pardoned, 387. Message to Assembly—With reasons for proceedings in case of Aaron Doane, 388, 393. Papers relating to Virginia to be handed over to J. Lukens by D. Kennedy—Warning to Sheriff to prevent escape of Doane and Longschamps—Repairs of State House and clock—Petition of William Hooker Smith and Dr. Smith, 394, 395, 396. Payment ordered to the devisees and legatees, &c., of William Penn for their estates in Pennsylvania according to a law passed for vesting them in the province, 397, 398. Outrages at Wyoming—Letter from Commissioners on opening Potomac—Jn. Adams on American Bishop—minister of Netherlands—Andrew Porter appointed Commissioner for running northern line with D. Rittenhouse, 399. Boundary with Virginia, 402. Dr. John

Supreme Executive Council—Ewing and Thos. Hutchins, commissioners on, 402. Debate on powers of Council, 403. Duties in French ports—An escheat—Mons. Marbois goes to New York -leaves Mr. Holker-French sailor —Petition from Bucks county, 405. Troops to be raised—Deputy surveyors, 441. Commissioners for viewing roads—Delegates to Congress-Rev. Dr. Ewing resigns as Commissioner — Fort Washington—Irregular elections, 443. Duties on imports—Public offices—Deputy surveyors—Flour inspectors—Collectors of excise—Register of German passengers, 445. State House lot—Case of Lewis Collinet—Conference with Mons. Marbois respecting—Election in Penn's Township—securities, 447. Case between children of Andrew Allen and State—counsel employed—Execution ordered of Le Blanc and Preston—L. Collinet pardoned, 449. Counterfeit loan office certificates, 450. Mons. Heinecken consul—State lottery —List of officers and soldiers entitled to land—Estate of Jno. Adams relinquished—J. H. C. Heinecken, consul from N. Netherlands, 451. Survey of lands reported by Comptroller—J. Story to enter on his duties early—city lots—Militia officers, 453. Resolution respecting northern and northwestern boundaries-appoint Andrew Ellicott—Deputy surveyors of donation lands—Complaint against Plunket Fleeson—Counterfeit land office certificates, 454. Draft on loan office—Boundary with New York—Montgomery County public building, 457. Piers to be erected in Delaware river — arsenal in Philadelphia, 458. Purchase of land at Marcus Hook for piers—jurisdiction of islands—western boundary—pay to a prisoner out of eighteen pence tax—pay for apprehending Sol. Vickars, 461. Confiscated estates in York county—Burgess of Reading—deeds for city lots—for lands in Northampton county—

Supreme Executive Council—xiv. report on Wyoming—deposition respecting Mrs. Allen's children, 463. Richard Hill's devisees claim—plan for piers—Andrew Ellicott accepts—report on officers' accounts—federal troops, 465. Order for new issue of bills—petition of Longschamps rejected—road from Fort Cumberland—report on Warden's account and Health Officers—sale of Crispin's estate deferred, 467. Davis declines an agreement for piers—new proposals-city lots--improvement of State House lot, 469. Engraving borders for new emission paid to D. H. Pursell—western territory—Indian murders—State lottery—Robert Scott, engraver, 471. Acts of Congress—property in ruins of Fort Pitt—Col. Harmer and his men—duties, 473. Agreement with property holders at Marcus Hook, 474. Emission of bills of credit—Indian murders—depreciation pay—public arsenal—back pay to Council of Safety, 477. Agree with Thos. Conarroe to build piers at Marcus Hook—purchase of books, 479. Grant two licenses to travel through the Commonwealth-birth of Duke of Normandy—State lottery, 481. Appeal in case of Robert Wilson allowed—Robert Morris' accounts—public buildings of Montgomery county—call on Commissioners of Philadelphia to report—quota for interest—State House lot, 483. Commissioners on improvement of Susquehannah appointed—illegal election in Cumberland—release of a Spanish prisoner from gaol, 485. Deed, 486. Appoint Inspectors of lumber, &c.—Robert Morris appeals to Supreme Court respecting his accounts—deed for barrack lots—inquest and proclamation of a murder and arson by Jno. McDonald, 489. Decide not to sell old jail now—to pay for public buildings in Montgomery out of proceeds of jail—exequator to Mons. Marbois as Vice Consul of France at Philadelphia, 490.

Supreme Executive Council—Deed for land--report on election--duties, 493. Deed—prosecuting for taxes—ringing bells, 495. Postage—R. Morris' accounts—Wyoming—State House, 497. Rent, Pickering and Hodgdon, 501. Claim and title of Miss Penn to province stated and referred to Supreme Court, 502. List of Commissioners elected between 1781 and 1785 to be made out—order for payment of interest of United States—pay to Commissioners on islands in Delaware river, 505. Urging Commissioners on western boundary—presents to Indians, 507. Conference with C. J. on Wyoming and member of Assembly, 508. Repairs of banks at Mud Island—copy of charter returned to B. Chew—militia in service of Congress, 513. Proclamation against robber of P. Audrain—list of goods for Indians—lots to be surveyed, 515. Congress, delegates to attend—Acts of Massachusetts for regulation of trade—letters to General Knox, &c., 517. Petitions to trade with Indians—improvement of State House lot—report on complaints of Thomas Shields and Spanish captain, 521. Message, numerous resolutions and letters--raising of troops—militia laws—defects of confederation—trade with Indians—invalids—correspondence with Governor of Massachusetts—resolutions respecting Mayor, &c., 525. Ed. Shippen appointed Justice for Dock Ward-P. Fleeson resigns as President of Quarter Session, &c., and E. Shippen appointed—State House lot—post rider paid, 549. Fees to counsel in case of Robert Morris and R. Wilson—claim for lands, 551. Opinion of Judges in case of J. and A. Melchior and extinguishment of ground rent—General J. Irvine resigns as Vice President of Council and Charles Biddle elected, 553. Expenses of Judges of Supreme Court paid—elections, 554. Henry Hill, Councillor, 555. Elections—B. Frank-

Supreme Executive Council—xiv. lin, President, 557. Appoint officers for federal militia, 559. Inform General Knox—Algiers declares war against United States—P. Muhlenberg a member—memorial of Sick Keesar, &c., from Bengal and China, 561. Pass to Indians to Ohio, 562. Message with sundry papers, 564. B. Franklin elected President and Charles Biddle, Vice President—proclamation and procession, 565. Release a Seventh Day Baptist minister from militia fine—Jno. Biddle, measurer of grain—Jno. Vanderen, Jr., Notary Public—execution—letter to Assembly on the Chinese lately arrived, 569. Clement Biddle, Notary Public, 571. Disturbances in Wyoming—memorial from Longschamps, from inhabitants of Philadelphia on test law and resolution, 572-574. Message to Assembly on taxes, revenue and test laws, 575. Pay for arrest of McDowell—sale of lots—delegates to Congress appointed, 577. Conference with Committee of House on disturbances at Wyoming, 578, 579. Negotiation with Maryland and Delaware on inland navigation—deeds for old jail and adjoining lots and names of purchasers—grant to Surveyor-General, for an office, a room in State House, 583. Grant to Episcopal Church a certificate in favor of "keeping up a regular succession"—letter to Governor of Maryland on inland navigation and to Governor of New Jersey respecting buoys in Delaware—order for execution of an Indian for murder, 585. And of E. Wilson, purchase Jacobs' Law Dictionary, 587. Arsenal—petition—Longschamps—letter--Gov. Smallwood—deed of lands, 589. Report of Committee on Islands in Delaware--deed for land—respite, 691. Collector of excise appointed—licenses to travel through the State, granted — Longschamps—deed for land, 593. Act of New Hampshire on Commerce and Navigation—agreement with Jas.

Supreme Executive Council—Pearson for copper roof to State-house, 597. Wm. Smith builds a wharf—jurisdiction of Delaware—report of wardens on suit between Thomas Davis and Commonwealth, 599. Paid for silver call furnished ship Montgomery—State house lot—for horses, sale of depreciated lands, 601. Report of Alex. M'Dowell, surveyor on the new purchase—accounts of T. Matlack, Commissioner, &c—medicines for a soldier wounded at Wyoming—deed for city lots—distribution of goods to Indians at Tioga, 605. Confiscated estates—deed for lands at Braddock's upper crossings, 607. Controller General's reports on account of officers, soldiers and invalids, 607—615. Contested election at Lancaster, 617. Lots not paid for to be resold—Collector of excise resigns, and another elected, 620. Tench Francis demands first payment—Stephen Porter asks pay to be raised—rejected, 623. British goods seized, 621. R. Wilson respited—demand of proprietaries—paid, 625. Opinion asked of Judges as to interest, 626. Stay of suits for taxes in Northampton, 627. Collector of excise—Edward Burd, Prothonotary of Supreme Court, 629. Case of R. Elliott—deeds—sales of land valued—F. Wade's petition rejected, 633. R. Elliott pardoned, 635. Send express to Wyoming with act of Assembly and instructions, 636. Leave of absence to Longschamps—deeds—case of John Buchanan, surveyor, 639. F. Wade to be prosecuted as a defaulter — appropriation for improvement of Delaware River—abuse of public property in Southwark by militia, 641. Deed—bridge over Schuylkill, 643. Message to Assembly—representation in Congress—Indians—disorders in Northumberland—John Franklin — inland navigation—western frontier and Virginia—foreigners, &c., 645. Abuses and irregularities in Chester county—

Supreme Executive Council—xiv. letter to Assembly, 646. Deeds, 649. Separation in Franklin co. —managers of State lottery—deeds—Justice in Chester removed—letter from Governor of Maryland on inland navigation—Gov. of Virginia on disputes on Territory—Edmund Randolph on Convention of States, 651. State of representation in Congress—State lottery, 2d class, to draw—collector of excise—deed—division of Washington county—donation lands—removal of a deputy surveyor, 653. Conference on Wyoming—persons from Maryland discharged from a recognizance—Attorney General to defend a suit for land in Bucks county—R. Smith re-appointed in Chester county, 657. Further proceedings, 658, 660, 661, 663, 664, 665. Supplies to Chinese, 659, 666, 670. Report of committee respecting Geo. Schlosser, in his favor, 661. Letter to Assembly respecting case of John R. Shaw—sale of estates in Chester county, division of Westmoreland into districts, 663. Claim for lands in Northampton—an invalid corps to be formed — reward to Alexander Carlisle for apprehending persons —Receiver to sell district of A. M'Clean—Clerk of Court appointed, 667. New trial granted in case of Pollard—Commissioners with Maryland and Delaware on inland navigation to be appointed —repairs of iron chest, 669.—Lieut. of Chester county, 670. Commissioners on inland navigation postponed, 672.

Order sale of estates confiscated, xv., 2--elect Commissioners, 2, 3. Execution ordered — suspended sale—claim of T. Forest to city lots, 3. Of Joseph Galloway's, 6. Dispute between Maclay and Edmonston-Deputy Surveyors decided-arms of U. S. on Susquehanna, claimed by Commissary, ordered to be delivered-sale of estate of Wiliam Armstrong postponed, 9. Deeds for city lots, 13.--For lands, 14. Brief to Lutherans of Albany--petition of Dauphin on Court house at Harris's ferry, 14. Memorial of officers for land Prothonotary of York—C. Biddles' proposal for rations, 17. Order sales of depreciation lands and barrack lots — exact account of military stores to be obtained—Commissioners of N. W. boundary paid--A. M'Lene to assist And. Porter in running line--pay to Commissioner to examine river Delaware--form of deed of cession by Connecticut, 19. Sale of goods for duties--instructions to delegates on cession--sale of barrack lots, 21. Stop proceedings in a case of taxes—W. Armstrong, Commissary, &c.--sale of city lots ordered, 23. Disturbances at Wyoming--deleg'es, St Clair and Wilson announce acceptance by Congress of cession of lands by Connecticut — Surveyor General to furnish plan of unsold city lots —provisions for Chinese, 28, 34. Deed for city lots—letters to Wyoming, 35. Expenses of W. H. Smith to and from Wyoming paid —disturbances there—deeds for lots—claim for a frame building taken by British at Billingsport—State lottery, 37. Petition respecting duties—western line—D. Rittenhouse and And'w Ellicott to run western line, 38, 39. Plans of depreciation lands—deeds—division of Mahoning township, 40. Privileges to Wm. Butler on depreciation lands, 42. Salaries to Judges — Notary Public appointed, 45. Deeds—State house, 47. Petition of tax collector rejected — survey of depreciation lands ordered—surveyor recommended, 49. Letters J. Jay, Sec., on infractions of treaty with Great Britain — auctioneers — claim for arrears of ground rent on A. Thomas's estate — resignation of Lt. Archer, 51. Controversy between Comptroller and State Treasurer, 55. Expenses of High Court of Errors and Appeals—State house, 57. Expense of Wyandot Chief—sales of land and

Supreme Executive Council—xv. city lots—Longschamps to be kept confined, 59. Ringing of bells for 4th of July—inland navigation—pay of Commissary of military stores, 61. Memorial of proprietaries for city lots, 63, 68. Pay to Commissioners for dividing island in Delaware river, 65. Pay for building Fort "Preservation" —petition of Wm. Barton for stay of execution—passport to John Franklin and J. Jenkins, &c., 67. Memorial B. Davis, J. Penn, &c., for city lots, referred to Attorney General—claim of Ed. Williams for half pay—allowance to agent for sale of barrack lots, 69. Messages to Assembly, 70, 77, 116, 167, 268, 276, 304, 393, 400, 401, 408, 419, 532, 536, 541, 547, 582, 592, 594, 605, 659.—requisition of Congress for quota of Federal supply—papers relating to Wyoming—report of attorney general on claim to City lot, 71. Claim of J. Robinson for land opposite Pittsburg—deed—Wm. Barton, 73. Lottery for donation lands—relief of D. Lenox—Chinese to be removed to Maryland—sale of City lots, 75. Counterfeit gold—division of Smith, T.—militia—appoints Colonel F. Mentges inspector-general—arms, 78, Arrival of J. Franklin and J. Jenkins—petition from settlers at W.—proclamation respecting a kidnapped negro—letter to Assembly, 79. Sales of land in Northumberland —accounts with United States—Burgess of Bristol elected, 83. Sales and fines postponed—lines run on West Branch of Susquehannah—and between old and new purchase, 85. Commercial convention—sales of City lots ordered—Lieutenant of Cumberland resigns—issue of certificates to Pennsylvania line for arrears—division of Pitt Township, 87. Robbery of Indians near Tioga—division of Northumberland Co. —estate of Wm. Hay—distances from Susquehannah to Allegheny river, 91. Drawing of lottery, 93. Reward for Brinkhurst a fraudulent person—highway from Lehigh Water Gap to Wyoming—pay to Wm. Henry while waiting for papers, 59. Officers of Luzerne County—lottery of donation lands, 96, 97. Deed, 98. Elections, 99, 100. Send various papers to Assembly—mint United States—increase of Federal troops, 105, 106. Order sales of property in hands of Commissioners on West line, 109. B. Franklin elected President, and Charles Biddle vice president, 110. Contested election in Bedford County, 112. Express from Washington to Cantwell's bridge. Do. to Wyoming, 115. Western boundary, Lake Erie--Indian purchase, 116. Reservation on road between Clark's Gap and Burnt Cabins—and from Miller's Spring to Fort Pitt, 121. Dorsey Pentecost, late Judge, suspended on account of removal to another county—deed for land, 124. Ask opinion of Judges of Supreme Court on an election question—report on election in Chester County, 131. Bedford election—excise taxes, 133. Order purchase of latest edition, 4to, of the Bible—and transactions of A. P. Society—proceedings stayed—survey of land for Dickinson College—Pennsylvania Herald—for filling patents for donation lands, 139. Appeals by executor of Thomas Wharton and Anthony Stocker, 141. Case Jno. Bond & Son for seizure of goods, 140. Disturbances in York County—list of purchases of depreciation lands, 147. Sales of land-disturbances in York County, 148. New Member—deeds to Robert Morris—Sixth and Market and price—City lots to be sold, 151. Deeds for lands and City lots—accounts of Gen. St. Clair—patents for Proprietary lands — Springetberry Manor, 153. Report of Committee on various accounts—discharge of delinquents—pay for signing bills of credit, 155. Election in Luzerne—T. Pickering—arrearages

Supreme Executive Council—xv. on lands—reduction of price—Bedford and Neville—contingencies, 167. Resolutions respecting delinquents—commissioners to be furnished with eight inch shells to be used on convicts, 169. Rewards for Daniel Shay, &c , 171. J. Clunie, agent in Dauphin, 173. Letter M. Huffnagle on a purchase—Col. And. Porter to assist A. Ellicott in running northern Line—report on Mud Island—provisions and buildings to be made, 175. Resolutions on Bedford election—proclamation for Daniel Shay, &c.—sale of goods seized, 177. Deeds, 180, 181. Letters—Governor of New York on line—State lottery, 180, 182. Contested election in Chester County—letter to Governor Massachusetts on arrest of criminals—St. Clair's accounts as auctioneer, 183. Order newspaper—George Bryan reappointed Judge of Supreme Court, 189, 190. F. Hopkinson reappointed—sale of flour postponed—patent to John Hughes for land in Westmoreland—Commissioners appointed to lay out road between Juniata and Conemaugh, 191. Copy of By-Laws, &c., of Bank of N. America presented—two cannons from Billingsport to Henry Hill—land in Montgomery County delivered up—claim to land to be insisted on, 193. Resolution offered respecting appointments of officers by Council—petition respecting collections of money due the State—Secretary J. Armstrong, Jr., appointed—Member of Congress asks leave of absence—Evan Owen appointed to survey better route for road between falls of Nescopee and Lehigh, 195. Codorus T.—York County divided—Gen. St. Clair promoted by Congress—removed as auctioneer—Peter Wikoff appointed—improvement of the Delaware, 197. Deputy surveyors ousted to be replaced—lease of Mud Island relinquished, to be released by Comptroller general on conditions

Supreme Executive Council——election in Franklin confirmed, 199. Miers Fisher, claim for city lots—resolutions respecting sale of flour rescinded, 201. Northern Boundary—questions proposed respecting payments to proprietaries—reprieve, 203. Repairs of Mud Island—questions adopted—Lieutenants of City, 205. Reward for apprehending Philip Jones—opinion asked of attorney general respecting city lots and lands—execution ordered, 207. Answer of Judges of Supreme Court—order for an arrest, 211. J. Adlum surveyor on North Line—Justices of Luzerne, 212. Pardon of Aaron Doane on condition of never returning to the United States, 212. Resignation of Genl. Muhlenberg as Commissioner on claims in Luzerne—seizure of Ship Anne—Phineas Bond, British Consul—Mons. de Brassines to be delivered up to Consul of France, 215. Appoint Danl. Hiester in place of Genl. Muhlenberg as Commissioner on Luzerne claims—election at Carlisle, 217. Claim of Presley Neville—Thos. Smith Loan Officer, 219. Conference with Judges, &c., on resolutions at Easton—prosecution against persons as seditious, 225. Expenses of Judges, &c., paid E. Burd—account against House of Employment, and against Treasurer of Chester County for taxes and supplies, 227. Wardens to examine claim of Thos. Conarroe for piers at Marcus Hook—presents to Choctaw and Chickasaw Indians in Philadelphia—road to Lehigh—transportation of military stores from Oley furnace—registering patents, 229. Road from Susquehannah to Lehigh—deeds, 230. Horse for Indian Chief—change of resolution respecting the Choctaw and Chickasaw Indian Chiefs—payment to John Penn — compensation to Thos. Conarroe—change of districts in Montgomery County, 233. Pension,---appeal of John Sparhawk—claim of Earl of Shelburne

Supreme Executive Council—xv. to City lots--claims in Luzerne and Northampton, 235. State house, &c.,—powder for 4th of July, 235. Brassines debts discharged—he to be delivered over to French Consul—pay to Commissioners on Luzerne claims—appeal on case of Caleb Newbold — officers of militia complain of an election—sales of land in Luzerne ordered, 237. John White appointed by Treasury to settle accounts between Pennsylvania, Delaware and Maryland and United States—J. Nicholson's advances for Indians, &c.—expenses of Judges, &c., 239. Treasurer not to draw for revenue at present, 245. Resolutions of Genl. Muhlenberg respecting Jno. Rheiner estate lost--plan of City lots—for sale, 246. Conference with Judge Bryan on case of Jno. Rheiner agent in Northampton for confiscated estates — Wm. Montgomery commissioner on Luzerne claims, 249. Indians at Lancaster detained by sickness of Interpreter, require more money, 250. D. Rittenhouse to recover moneys loaned--account of moneys due for customs to be rendered, 253. Conference with Judges on petition of rioters in York, and for land in Bucks county, 260. Decide case of duties between two States, 261. Time for applicants for donation land lottery extended, 263. Collectors of excise in York county —petition of Northampton county against claim of proprietaries for the Indian land in—referred to Attorney General — conference with Judges on fresh disturbances in Luzerne county, 265. Pension to children of Wm. Shippen—negro pardoned, 267. Message to Assembly with various papers—lend money to Whitehead Humphreys to enable him to manufacture steel, 269. Division of Northumberland — districts for electing Justices, 271. Wardens apply for strangers burying ground — acts for sale of forfeited city lots and J. Galloway's

Supreme Executive Council—house---Burgesses of Bristol—road to Pittsburg, 273. Members of Assembly from western counties confer on it—a travelling license to Geo. Kinnear being altered in date—put into suit—pension to Widow Patterson, 275. Pension to Widow of Christian Reinick—Commissioners report on line between Luzerne and Northumberland, 276. Expenses of Indians paid—claim of Col. Bull for a negro bought of Edward Stiles, 277. Armed banditti at Tioga—letter to Governor of New York and delegates in Congress, 279. Proclamation against rioters in Luzerne county—and also on Virginia agreement—inquiry by Assembly relative to operation of law respecting Connecticut claimants, 281. Case of A. Moore—Register of Wills, 283. Jno. Nicholson appointed Escheator General—alien duty not paid—expenses of a man wounded by a tree falling while in service of Commissioners not taken, 285. Suit against Captain Jno. Barry, &c., for seizing James McCalmont —a protest against decision, 287. D. Redick to lay out lots opposite Pittsburg, 289. To go to New York to communicate to the Governor intelligence respecting Luzerne—Col. Robert Elder paid for his services, 1777-78-79. paid for arrest of John Franklin, he to be closely confined and in irons, 291. Thanks to Charles Biddle, Vice President—riots in Luzerne--militia of Berks called out—pay to H. McCormick for information respecting — Colonel Dennison dispatched to Luzerne--his instructions—and to Tioga—President advances specie for expenses of Colonel Dennison, 293. Stationery for--elections--notary—instructions to Valentine Eckhart —proposals for rations by M. Hollenback, 295. Elections, 296, 298. E. Physick as keeper of Great Seal—Dd. Jones, chaplain asks allowance, 299. Hamilton apprehended-elections-city lots--

Supreme Executive Council—xv. Genl. Armstrong resigns as Secretary and Charles Biddle chosen—clothing for troops on Ohio, 301. New member—John Franklin's irons to be removed on his parole—message — Wyoming and Luzerne—currency fees—price of lands—taxes—lands for officers, 305. Conference on Wyoming—powder on election of President and Vice President — Colonel Pickering and riots at Tioga—ask permission of Congress to raise troops—patents, 307. B. Franklin, President, and P. Muhlenberg Vice President — procession—McKucher takes his seat, 309. Delinquent fines—order respecting—pay for services in watching movements of Indians on frontiers—order for execution, 311. Appoint Committee to amend resolutions of Assembly on annual appointment of officers—message to Assembly — recommending enforcement of Laws in Luzerne county — expulsion of Commissioners from Wyoming—Colonel Mentges—taxes, 314. Proclamation against rioters in Philadelphia—Indian murders in and arms sent to Washington county, 317. Election of auctioneers in city and other officers—Clement Biddle—marshal, 323. Contract for specie to be complied with—excise—Prothonotary Common Pleas, Philadelphia — contested election, 325. Attend commencement — expenses of Judges paid—report of Attorney General on case of Jno. McCannon—also on power to pardon in certain cases, 329. Wardens appointed, 339, 341. Prothonotary to hold office where his court is—account of public arms delivered—pension — resignation of Lieutenants — delegates of Congress—Wardens, 341. Mr. Redick to have island in Ohio surveyed—Drs. Rush and Hutchinson to examine vessels—commissioners report line between New York and Pennsylvania finished in 42° — attend speaking in Zion Church-Lieutenant for

Supreme Executive Council—Bedford appointed — rules and regulations for Council, 341. Duties received by mistake refunded—Lieutenant of Franklin chosen—pension paid to children of Captain Wm. Shippen—public arms to be collected and repaired—fees from Deputy Surveyors, 343. Pensions, 345. Complaint of Swedish Consul for rude behaviour of Constables and Attorney—orders respecting—plan of city lots and sale ordered, 349. Order of procession in Philadelphia on ratifying Federal Constitution—report on Deputy Surveyor's fees—on Donation Land Lottery tickets remaining in wheel, 351. Road from Frankstown Branch of Juniata to Loyal Hanna confirmed and ordered, 353, 355. Payment to Porter and Ellicott for boundary line, 356. Petition of Bedford respecting width of road—order on—decision respecting case of R. Wells, 359. Pension to Captain Shippen's children, 361. John Woods Member of Congress applies for money—taken sick while engaged in business of Indian department, 362. Ringing Christ Church bells, 363. Repairs of houses at Mud Island — N. Dennison's expenses to and from Wyoming, 365. Expenses of newspapers in city to be reduced—resolutions respecting invalid corps—money to James O'Hara to buy provisions for troops in western country—grant of land to Franklin College, 367, 368. Resolution respecting public arms to be republished—donation lands—memorial of J. Hazlehurst & Co. —brandy—public arms when repaired to be exhibited, 369. Road by "burnt cabins"—militia fines reduced—duties and bonds, 371. R. Elliott from Lancaster to Philadelphia by order of Supreme Court—pay in certificates for horses furnished—counsel in suit for Hog Island—W. Bradford, Sergeant and E. Tilghman—report on arms called for, 373.

Supreme Executive Council—xv. Sheriff ordered to set up F. Wade's house at a limit for—arms of Col. Gurney's battalion to be delivered to J. Nicholson—arms to be repaired by Abraham Morrow—petition of merchants respecting duties—stove and repairs for chamber—subscribe for German newspapers by M. Steiner—opinion asked by Comptroller respecting certificates and order, 375. Contested election in Berks county—Attorney-General gives opinion that holding freehold estate by a non-resident entitles to a vote—powder purchased for celebrating ratification of Constitution—naval officer seizes a vessel suspected of wishing to escape duties—asks for a military company--granted, 377. Alteration of State House clock—supply of troops in Luzerne—wood for invalids—conveyance of public despatches—pension to widow of Lieut. John McClellan—rank of Capt. Ferguson, 381. Commissioners of western boundary asked for a description of the lands—memorial of Wm. Moland, showing that he is not a traitor—confirmed by pardon under great seal—report on certain claims to city lots — warrants to issue in favor of Tench Francis and Geo. Glentworth—memorial of Andrew Lytle, Deputy-Surveyor-referred-suit against John Moore dismissed, 383. Papers respecting sale of F. Wade's house referred to Attorney-General — certain gunsmiths to be employed—road from Juniata, pay for laying out—memorial of John Franklin, to be released from irons, being in bad health—memorial of merchants asking to postpone suits on bonds-pay for newspapers, 385. Favor of Dr. Evans' claim, line between Edmunson and Maclay—message to Assembly—ratification of Constitution—description of western purchase—bonds for duties—land warrants—pensions--depreciation-land titles, Wardens — Luzerne county—Col. Pickering—map of northern boundary, 393. Large

Supreme Executive Council—table—rank, 394. Conference on depreciation of paper money—Marshal called on for accounts—petitions, claims for city lots—road to Pittsburg, 399. Execution of pirates, &c., ordered, 400. Letter Governor Massachusetts—Bedford and Neville, 401. Respite of pirates—Collector to contract for offices, 403. Complaints against Richard Davis, 404, 405. Report of Board of Treasury on bills of credit—contested election in Dauphin county, 405. Contested election in Berks, 407. Representation in Congress, 409. Money drawn without appropriation, 407. Representation in Congress—British Consul, suggestions on laws, 408, 410. Claims of J. Mitchell for city lots, 409, 410, 413. Difficulties between Treasurer and Comptroller, 410. Pensions, 413. Federal gazette subscribed for—riots in Cumberland, 415, 416. Gov. Randolph respecting a negro—P. Bond on rights, &c., of British subjects—Samuel Caldwell, Collector of tonnage duties, 417. Refer P. Bond's letter to Assembly—pay to Judges Supreme Court—order on petition of Quakers of Chester county, 419. Contested election in York county, 420. Commissioners to lay out roads in Northampton and Luzerne, 425. Depreciation lands, John Brown's case, 426, 427. Estate of M. Conner—Jno. Franklin, deputy's fees, 427. Appeal of John Mitchell—Joshua Elder's account—Maj. Jno. Nice resigns—execution of John Brown and difficulties—case of John Logan, 432, 433, 434. Neutrality of Sweden—duties outstanding—powder magazine full, 433. Pay to Judges—deed for barrack lot—children of Capt. William Shippen—commissioned officers to be appointed—regiment of artillery—repeal of proceeding in case of Daniel Shay, 435. Warrant to R. Peters—C. Cecil—troops to have room in bettering house—quota of troops--officers appointed—claim for land

Supreme Executive Council—xv. through Miers Fisher, 437. Claims for city lots—thanks of artillery officers contested election- claim Anthony Cuthbert, 439. Letter to Justices of Northampton respecting Mrs. Roseborough--repeal of proclamation in case D. Shay, 445. Memorial on depreciation—what newspapers are to be filed—pay to Commissioners for opening certain roads in Northampton and Luzerne, 445. Case of J. Rheiner submitted to Judges, 446. Also respecting storage of powder, 447. Lottery for improving roads--Jones' lane, Commissioners to view—expenses of State House yard for 1787, 449. Asks for Acts of Virginia respecting lands—order Surveyor-General to furnish drafts of lands, also quantity and quality of lands claimed by Pennsylvania in Luzerne county, 451. Opinion of Judges on powder magazine and on Jno. Rheiner's case—instructions to Capt. Stiles respecting powder, 453. Expenses of State Navy in 1778, &c.—report from Lieut. Henry on contested military election—repairs to cannon carriages — Commissioners appointed to proceed to Luzerne county, 455. Their pay--pensions--pay for printing to Col. Gibson, 457. Resolution on Surveyors having but one district rescinded--opinion of Miers Fisher respecting claim of Charles Cecil, 459. Death of R. Levers—resignation of R. Truitt not accepted--Wm. Craig appointed—Sheriff to postpone sale of W. Hay's estate, 461. Commerce of France and United States—Governor of Maryland demands a criminal, 463, 464. Pensions—a Swedish ship runs away—T. Pickering on conduct of J. Jenkins, 465. Deed to Dr. Harris—paid Jno. Duffield—removal of sailors—removal of prisoners, 469. Terms of sale of triangle on Erie—letters of instructions of Commissioners to Luzerne, 472. James Finley resigns--authority to buy triangle--papers necessary for trial on Hogg

Supreme Executive Council—
Island, to be loaned, 473. Election of Justice in York settled and another contested—accounts between United States—pay for supplies to troops in western country, 475. Executions ordered — city lots—pension, 477. Discussions relative to city lots, 478, 479, 481. Disturbances in Huntingdon co., 479. City lots—further time allowed on accounts, 481, 485. Colonel Timothy Pickering made prisoner, 484. Proceedings respecting, 484, 487. Proclamation for arrest of captors, 487. Mr. Redick to go to New Jersey and New York on subject of capture of Col. Pickering and other outrages—his instructions, 490. Expenses of messenger to and from Luzerne—request to Congress for troops to expel rioters from Luzerne—letter to Col. Zeb. Butler approving of his conduct towards rioters—news from D. Redick and Gov. Livingston, 493. Jones' lane road, report, &c.--case of E. Oswald, 494, 495. Expenses of Judges of Supreme Court and their servants paid--proceedings in case of Eleazer Oswald--Mr. Redick returns from New York, 495. Proclamation and warrant of Governor Clinton--troops asked from Congress--disposal of lands in western country — a Justice asked for Franklin county--letter, &c., Gov. Clinton, New York--petition Abraham and Levi Doan referred to Judges—sale of reserved tract opposite Pittsburg to be considered, 497, 501. Claim for prize money at Lewistown--referred to Attorney-General, 499. Reward claimed for capture of A. and L. Doan—answer of Judges to reference respecting, 501. Col. Pickering released-Congress send troops to Luzerne county--reward to captors of Doans—case of E. Oswald--provision for the support of troops at Easton, 503. Reserved tract to be arranged for sale--T. Pickering asked opinion respecting troops for Tioga--letters and depositions respecting Lu-

Supreme Executive Council—xv. zerne county—execution of A. and L. Doan ordered, 505. Case of E. Oswald decided adversely—D. Redick's reasons for his vote—letter Governor of New York, with ratification of Federal Constitution—opinion of Judges respecting measures in Luzerne—division of Washington county, 507. Arranged plan for reserved tract, 509-512. Fine against E. Oswald remitted—news from Col. Pickering—petitions favor of Doans—respite—call of Congress for troops against Indians on frontiers, 515. Release a free negro from jail in danger of his life from the Doan's—pay express to and from Easton—complaint of Admiralty Court against British Consul for a survey ordered on a vessel, referred to Judges—Washington county militia—city artillery, 517. Submit letters and papers respecting call of troops to Assembly—Davis Bevan's caveat for city lots set aside and patent to Mary Meredith—pay Carlisle Gazette for advertising, also D. Humphreys—repairs of arms—J Skinner for road—rations—expense of recruiting—Wardens of Philadelphia, 519. Justice in Carlisle—sundry claims for city lots—election set aside—British Consul—requisition of Congress, 521. Wheat prohibited in England on account of Hessian fly—proposals in Congress on triangle on Erie—declaration of rights by North Carolina and amendment of Constitution—claims for lots, &c., postponed—return and election of Luzerne county, 525. Amicable suit with Captain Christie—Notaries public—Report on Jones' Lane—Proposals for roads—Acts relative to election of Justices, 527. Message, 528, 529. Act of Congress relinquishing to the State, Lake Erie tract, 530. Large meeting of Indians at Muskingum — Commissioners to be appointed to attend, 531. Conference with Assembly on purchase of triangle—Taxes in Montgomery county—City lots in N. L.—John Franklin, 533. Case of J. Eckley—Powder magazine—Act of Congress putting in operation the constitution adopted by eleven States — Order for executing A. & L. Doane, 535. City lots fall short in quantity, 537, 538. Forage commissioners report on street roads, &c., laid out—Council of censors—Wyoming, 539. Permit to C. Wyerman to travel—Memorial of D. Linton for reward for apprehending a villain—Captain Schott to receive stores—Claim for a shallop burned in 1777—Claim of J. Penn and J. Penn, Jr., for Springetsbury manor, 541, 542. Complaint against Prothonotary of Huntingdon–Importation of malefactors to be prevented—William Barton — W. Lawrence — Road in Bedford county completed—Compliment to Captain William Ross of a sword for his conduct in Luzerne county, 543, 544. Respite of A. & L. Doane negatived—Pensions, 545. Road from Frankstown—Sundry payments to William Henry's widow of Lancaster—Rewards of captors in Luzerne, 547. Prayer to Congress for extension of time on accounts—Appointments for Alleghany county—Sword to Captain William Ross and his thanks—New district in Montgomery county, 551. Justices, &c.—Washington county—J. Hubley for conducting recruits to Lancaster—Commissioners Generals Butler and Gibson appointed to negotiate, &c,, for the Erie triangle, 553. Instructions—Patents under seal—Claims of Penns postponed, 555. Clothing for invalid corps, 556 Renewal of patents injured by fire—Pay to A. Ellicott for running line, and B. Ellicott for making a map of triangle on Erie, 561. Warden Craig resigns, and L. Simmons is elected-Entry of Teas—W. Shippen's children—Deed for city lot—Letter to Peter Muhlenburg requesting resignation as

Supreme Executive Council—xv. Vice President—Received, 563. D. Redick, Vice President — Z. Potts, councillor—Elections, 565. Elections — In Philadelphia for Sheriff — Proceedings, 567, 568, 569, 570, 571, 573, 575, 576. Governor Clinton written to for letters between John Franklin and Dr. Hamilton, 571. Triumphal arch in Philadelphia, 574. Franklin's letters received-J. Ash decided to be Sheriff, 579. State House—Lottery, 581, Message to Assembly, 582. Boundaries —Donation lands, 583. Election of Thomas Mifflin, President, and George Ross, Vice President, 584. Lands for Episcopal academy, 585. Act against vice and immorality, 587. Against vice and immorality and wickedness in Philadelphia — Resolutions, 589. Report on rules and regulations—Theatrical exhibitions, 591, 592. Auctions—Charles Biddle reappointed Secretary—J. Trimble, Assist. Secr'y—Message—Federal constit'n compromised—New government influence—Sheriffs—Reservations for the Commonwealth —Road from Cumberland to Pittsburgh—Boundary lines to be engraved—Congress ask for copies of laws—Auction duties—Laws against vice, &c., to be published and enforced-J. B. Smith resigns as prothonotary — James Biddle elected-Committee for inquiry, report, 590-595. Vote to reconsider message - Conference respecting returns of Lieutenants—Account for office rents—Map of part of State presented — Wardens respecting pilots — Ringing Christ church bells, 597. Furniture—Proposals for purchase of reserved lots opposite Pittsburgh—Island in Alleghany river — Complaint against prothonotary of Huntingdon—Road from Bedford to Fort Pitt — Public officers appointed by council—Powder magazine, 599. Lots opposite Pittsburgh not to be sacrificed—Act respecting elections of Justices—Third Justice—Powers of Comptroller-

Supreme Executive Council—General — Valuation of lots at Alleghany by Council, 601, 602. Committee to inquire respecting the jail — Proclamation against captors of Colonel Pickering annulled—Further proceedings in case of prothonotary of Huntingdon—Collector of military fines, 603, 604. Committee to name streets, &c., in Alleghany—Restrictions on removed—Goods to Indians—Justices, 607. Lots and Island in Alleghany—Petitions and decisions, 608. Report on Indian fund and goods—Colonel Johnson to purchase—Sale of lots in Alleghany to J. Robinson, 609. Petition of rioters in Luzerne—Lancaster county on Justices—Board of Jno. Franklin—Names of streets, &c., in Alleghany—Case of Jacob Dryer—and S. Hulings, 611. Committee on election in Philadelphia—Returns of Islands in Alleghany, 612. Bishop White on marriage licenses—Arrears due W. Hamilton for ground rent in Lancaster, 614. A. Ellicott appointed Surveyor of Islands in Alleghany, 615. Report on resolution of Assembly, November 14, 1787, embracing many charges, 621. Removal and appointment of prothonotary of Huntingdon—Comptroller-General—Public officers objected to as sureties—Committee to name streets, &c., in Alleghany, 623. Officers to render accounts or be removed—Dedimus pot.—Names of streets — Rioters pardoned—other cases, 625. Debate on claim of De Graffendriedt, 628. Case of J. Dryer discussed—Opinion of Judges and Attorney-General—Is pardoned—Claim of De Graffendriedt decided against him—A. Ellicott on survey of triangle referred, 631. Memorial of merchants of Philadelphia to be sent to Spain, on flour shiped to Havana — Colonel L. Nicola appointed to command of invalid corps—Captain McLean unable—Messengers to be sent to certain counties for returns of election for

Supreme Executive Council—xv. President and Vice President of United States—Pension to widow of Peter Nees, 633, 634. Instalment due J. and J. Penn, Jr.—Children of Captain Shippen—Account of A. McClean for surveying, &c., of reservation lands—Referred — Road in Bedford county, 635. Returns of election of members of Congress in each county except Fayette — Provisions paid for continental army, 637. Fayette returned—Proclamation of members of Congress—Newspapers paid for, 639. Expenses of John Franklin—Pensions paid Pennsylvania Hospital—Edward Shippen's claim for purchase of B. Arnolds estate—Division of election district in Franklin county — Account of William Hamilton calling out militia on frontiers — Report of members elected to Congress—Expenses of prisoners to Virginia 1777, via Reading, 641. Claim of A. Porter—Resolution to refer claim of Eve Withington to Judges of Supreme Court—Payment to widow of Rev. J. Roseborough, chaplain of militia, balance of half pay awarded by Assembly, 1780, 643. Arrears to W. Hamilton paid—A. Porter paid for horse, 645. N. Little's widow paid—Suit with Stocker & Wharton — Counsel employed, 647. Hearing of landholders in Southwark, &c., on report of Commissioners—Expenses—Express paid for bringing returns of election—Defect in laying off an election district of Huntingdon County—Proposals for land in reserved tract—Colonel Johnston to accept them, 649. Payment to John Mitchell according to decision—Inquiry as to permission of Canada to surveyors to make observations with reference to Erie—Assignment of a bond by J. Redman, Jr.—Accounts of William Turnbull, clothier — Claims of Penns, 651. Adoption of reports of Committee on message, 652. Dickinson College paid—Invalid

Supreme Executive Council—guards — Returns of President and Vice President of United States—Proclamation respecting, 655. Interference asked respecting city lots sold as estate of S. Shoemaker, 657. Message to Assembly on Members of Congress—electors—Road, canals, &c., 660.

Committee of Conference on pensions, xvi., 2. On letter from Gen. Knox and on Mr Scott's resignation, 3. instalments to be paid proprietaries, 5. Thomas Scott resigns as M. C.—requested to continue, 7. Credentials to members of Congress not advisable, 13. Case of John Franklin, 17. Commissioners on quantity and quality of land at Wyoming, 22. Complaints against Prothonotaries of Westmoreland county, 23. Appoint Committee to report mode of receiving Gen. Washington—report and resolutions, 25. Letter to assembly on expenses of escort—E. Douglass, agent of estates in Fayette county—persons appointed to mark out a road between Bedford and Pittsburgh—execution ordered, 27. Sureties on different officers—respecting a third justice, 31. Demand on Gov. of Louisiana for a free negro in bondage there—payments to Messrs. Penn, 33. Appeal respecting account of Robert Wilson—resignation of C. Febiger as auctioneer — sale of R. Robertson postponed, 35. Purchase of triangle on lake Erie, 37. Alteration in Constitution of State proposed, 41. Reward paid for apprehending a deserter, 43. Reserved lands opposite Pittsburg valued—office of Register General—claim on General Brodhead, 45. Reservations for State according to resolutions of Assembly, to be located and surveyed—Commissioners to run lines of Huntingdon county, 47. Order prosecution against Commissioners of taxes in Northampton county—call on heirs of John Ludwig Shaurman to present their claim

Supreme Executive Council—xvi. in Germany—election in Montgomery contested, 49. Subscribe to society for encouraging manufactures and useful arts—city lots —road from Bedford to Pittsburg, 51. Repair of Jones's lane—Aldermen of Philadelphia and Mayor—case of R. Wells, 53, 55, 57. Title of lot in city, 55.—Address to President General U. S., Washington, congratulatory, 57. Commendatory certificate to F. Philo as naval officer, 58. Of Sharp Delaney as collector—answer of President Washington—election in Montgomery confirmed, 59, 60. Receiver General to employ a clerk—Secretary to provide for safety of records—application from Mrs. Physic for certificate of donation lands surveyed—John Roberts' widow paid out of his estate, 65. J. Adlum, surveyor of reserved lands, refused pay—W. C. Bradford, late paymaster of State navy, owes a balance—militia officers of Northumberland--pay for leaden spouts taken in 1777—Benjamin Franklin is paid postage on public letters received during his Presidency—printing—Joshua Elder applies for an audit—refused—certificate to C. Febiger, late auctioneer, 67. Rations to invalid guard—expenses of Judge of Supreme Court paid — contested election in Chester county—land office to furnish papers to Attorney General in case of Hogg Island—a lot appropriated to burial of strangers—William Turnbull's accounts, 69. Inquiry into conduct of officers—agent appointed for Cumberland—road to Pittsburgh—act of Assembly on board of appeals—and collection of fines and taxes to be printed, 73. Duties between States—Dickinson College per Dr. Rush, 77. Instructions to Comptroller General, 80. Licenses—excise—road, 83. Instructions to E. Owen—Calico printing encouraged—instructions to Evan Owen—resolution to rescind resolution Nov. 14, 1787—as

Supreme Executive Council—to choice of Secretary, 85. R. Parker resigns as collector of excise, 87. S. Briggs' model of nail machine, 89. Additional instructions to Comptroller proposed—repairs of State house, 91. Mode of communication with Congress —University ask temporary use of State house bell, 93. Certain lots in city bought in by Comptroller—disturbances in Huntingdon county — expense of fire works on arrival of President U. S.—repairs at Mud Island—board of John Franklin—city lots to be sold--recruiting, 95. Oath administered--D. Redick is paid for islands in Ohio and Allegheny, rivers surveyed by him, &c,--papers respecting Huntingdon referred to Judges, 97. Lottery money--loan office to be removed --Mud Island repairs, 99. Establishment of United States Courts --Eve Withington paid for board of prisoners to Virginia--licenses for sale of spirituous liquors, 101. Road through Black's gap—expense of removing John Franklin --division of election districts in Washington county—cannon to be repaired—amendments proposed by New York, 103. Memorial of public creditors—taxes, 107. Claim of C. G. Gaskill, 108, 109. Auctioneer of N. Liberties, 109. Division of Huntingdon—license to peddle, 111. Certificate to Samuel Caldwell, Collector of tonnage--oaths by Judges, &c., 114. Proclamation requiring oaths to be taken by officers--second payment to encourage calico printing, 116. German letter delivered — execution ordered--claim of A. Cuthbert—duty on tonnage--certificates, 119. Invitation to commencement, 121. State duty on goods imported--reward for capture of George Sinclair--President Judge, Berks co --Capt. J. Hetherlings' children —pension, 125. German newspaper--property bequeathed in Germany--watch house--lamps, &c., in State house yard--duties

Supreme Executive Council—xvi. on imports--exchange of certificates—answers to Col. Delaney's questions, 127. Answer of Judges to questions on imposts, &c., proposed by Judges, 128. President to Collector--complaint in Bucks against election of justices, 129. C. G. Gaskill, 130. Purchase of triangle—resolution of New York to amend the Constitution, 139. Messages from Council, 139, 140, 148, 206, 275, 277, 317, 429—431, 437, 440. Powder magazine — lottery money — annuities to widows, &c., of officers — Mud Island — potashes from Philadelphia--donation lands —lots, 140. Expense of Indian treaties, 141. Expense of Indian treaties provided for, 142. Complaint against military officers—C. G. Gaskill's claim, 143, 147. Complaint against officers at Havana—expense of Indian chiefs refunded, 143. Children of Robert Wilson, 144. Survey ordered by Congress, 146. D. Leet, &c., surveyors of depreciation lands —mistake of land office corrected —division of districts in Allegheny, 149. Confirmed, 150. Case of health officer Jones postponed, 151. Mr. Watt has authority to withdraw a representation to Grand Jury of Cumberland - petition rejected as too indecent—C. G. Gaskill's claim to city lots registered—fees to counsel for defense of title in Bucks county, 153. Acts of Congress received —fees in land office—forfeited recognizances — tavern licenses, 157. Case of Turnbull M. & co. —Assembly propose calling a convention to amend State constitution—council oppose—postponed —Assembly in mean time resolve on it, 159. Loan of instruments —A. Ellicott, 161. Notary—returns of militia, 163. Release of ground rent to John Dunlap, 164. Loan of drafts of Southwark and leveling instruments--murder of J. M'Farland, 165. Acts of Congress—A. Cuthbert's and N. Young's claim, 167. Deputy surveyor—Prothonotary Delaware—J. Jones removed, 172 Nathaniel Falconer appointed — escheated property—Acts of Congress, 174. Temporary post office—safe keeping of United States prisoners, 175. Debt of Gov. St. Clair, 177. Commissioners appointed to view rivers—Indian affairs—testimony from South Carolina—Escheator General's report, 179. Instructions to Commissioners to view rivers, 181. Pensions—articles for Commissioners on rivers-report on memorial of child of R. Wilson, 183. Articles required by Commissioners to view River Delaware—opinion of Attorney-general asked respecting justices, in case of a County division—execution ordered—answer of Attorney-general about justices, 187. Acts of Congress—general Thanksgiving —letter from Secretary of Treasury respecting public debts — and Secretary of War empowering him to call out militia—newspapers, 189. Journals Senate United States received, and Acts of Congress — elections and appointments, 191, 193, 199. J. Lukens Surveyor-General dies, 199. Contested election expenses—payments to poor lists of pensioners —powder for celebration—repairs of arms, 201. Dr. Ruston defeated by Col. Willing—proclamation for Thanksgiving, 203. Appointments, 205. Message to Assembly—Acts of Congress—amendments to Constitution—call of militia—bills of credit—health office—pensions—sureties, 207. Surveyor-general elected—instructions to commissioners to view Rivers—petition for removal of George Sinclair from Northampton to Philadelphia—justices, 209. Elections, 210, 212. Claims on United States list of pensions —election of President and Vice President, order of procession, 212. Deputy Surveyors in counties—suit at issue between judges of Supreme Court and Commonwealth—Jared Ingersoll to assist Attorney-

Supreme Executive Council—xvi. general—repairs of State House, 215. Expenses Deputy Surveyor—sale of land in Cumberland—a pension to W. Whitman, 217^2. Election T. Mifflin, president, and George Ross, Vice President—procession, 219. Case of George Woods—public debt, 221. Report on account of James Searle, agent, 222. Proposal of Stocker and Wharton for Exchange accepted, 223. Jury in suit of judges against State differ—report of commissioners on rivers—Indian interpreter, 209^2. A non-suit, 210^2. Deputy Surveyors appointed—Dr. John Wilkins councillor, 211^2. Deputy Surveyors—loan for disabled soldiers made and accepted--Nescopec road--list of pensioners, 213^2. Request removal of loan office to accommodate the Convention—Nescopec road report—C. Febiger treasurer, 215^2. Dry lands in Northampton County, 219^2. Title to Islands in Delaware river, 218^2. Councillor, 219^2. District of Southwark, 221^2. Commissioners to view rivers—letters—newspapers—removal from jail of diseased prisoners—supension of taxes for the year, 223^2, 224^2. Rioters in Northumberland County pardoned—Deputy Surveyors, 223^2. Grant sea letter to ship Brothers for China—list of pensioners, 224^2. Deputy Surveyors — District of Southwark, 225. Suspension of taxes not agreed to, 224, 225. Fees to counsel, 227. Dep. Survey's, 229. John Lockhart applies for preemption rights to island in Delaware bet. Hogg and Tinicum—refused, 230. Memorial respecting Southwark, &c., 232. Comptrollers accounts 236. Advice to C. Febiger, Treasurer, respecting revenue--case of Jonas Hartzell, 237. Fees of Secretary's office — report of committee on Southwark, Moyamensing, and Passyunk—laying out and naming streets and Wharves, &c., 245–251. Road from Frankstown, 254, 257. Accounts with United States—

Supreme Executive Council

Comptroller to employ clerks—division of Townships in Dauphin County—auctioneer's account in Northern Liberties for duty on sales, 253. Deputy Surveyors—Calico printing, 254. Deputy Surveyors, 257, 258. Nescopec road—Townships in Washington County—Death of General Potter, 259. His son appointed Deputy Surveyor, 261. Newspapers—report respecting Southwark, &c., to be recorded—letter of Col. J. Harmar respecting drafts on Treasury, 263. Depredations in Washington County by Indians—public debt of Pennsylvania, 264. Message-commissioners, on rivers report—public records—Howell's map—bills of credit, 275. John Bayard trustee for Province Island deceased—and Robert Knox removed to New Jersey—commissioners on rivers—message, 277. James Searle balance due, 278. Deeds, 283. Pay for Chartier's Island in the Ohio — Nescopec road—Sam Hulings' preemption right to island in Alleghany river—time extended, 285. Clement Biddle allowed time to pay his debt, 287. Deputy Surveyor—Island in Alleghany granted to Wm. Todd, 289. Exchange of warrants for land, with German Reformed congregation of Philadelphia—letters of Thomas Ryerson on defence of frontiers against Indians—Deputy Surveyor, 297. Report on claim of John Bryce for land — deed — claim of Anthony Cuthbert postponed, 299. J. and J. Penn, jr., ask for Sixth instalment—Excise officers to pay—list of, required, 300. Form of conveyance of islands in Ohio and Alleghany rivers, 301. Controversy between Comptroller and Register General, 304, 307. Resolution of North Carolina—amendments to Federal Constitution, 305. Indian difficulties in Washington County — claim for an estate, 307. Auctioneers appointed, 313, 314; and Inspector of Pot and Pearl ashes — Treasurer

Supreme Executiue Council—xvi., to attend meeting of subscribers to manufacturing fund at the College, 313. Report of committee on controversy between comptroller and register, 314. Property claimed for a German—commissioners to examine certain rivers to be appointed—to settle accounts of Treasurer of Bedford, 315. Paid R. Martin for services, 1775. —Against Connecticut settlers—Deputy surveyors—Case of Francis Wade—Conference with Assembly—Division—Militia of Luzerne county, 317. Debts due by United States, 324. Barracks at Lancaster to be sold, 325. Fire of manufactory—Proclamation of incendiary, 327. Gunpowder magazine–Suitable lot on Walnut street, 328. Censure Comptroller for misstatement of pensions—North Carolina cedes part of western territory—Powder magazine-Persons to appraise value of the lot, 329. Resolutions condemning and dismissing John Nicholson, Comptroller-General — Postponed —Votes on various motions, 331. Letter and statement from Comptroller-General, 332, 336. Proceedings to be published, 337, 339. Order in favor of Reading Howell on account of his map of Pennsylvania — Instructions to Commissioners on western waters, 337. Order to, 339, Survey of lands opposite Pittsburgh and at Fort McIntosh—Militia for frontier—Comptroller to furnish list of certificates — Gunpowder for Dr. B. Franklin's funeral—Certificate to Brigadier-General Thompson's widow, 341. Reasons for voting for John Nicholson's dismission, 342-344. Surveying fees of undrawn donation lots—Testimonial of respect to Dr. Franklin—Two negatives—Order to Captain Christie—Order to G. Delaney late collector to return a deposit by Reed & Forde —Account of powder, flannel, &c., supplied for Dr. Benjamin Franklin's funeral, 345, 346. Model for nail machine delivered

Supreme Executive Council— to Samuel Briggs—Instructions to Commissioners to view Delaware, &c., Rivers—Acts of Congress to promote useful arts—and collect duties—Order to Commissioners on rivers, 347, 348. Commission to, 350. Pay to John Robert's widow out of his estate–Re-appointment of secretary—and Receiver-General of land office—Instruction to Commissioners for sale of barracks at Lancaster, 351. Resignation of Warden—Justice —Inquiry respecting certificates issued by Comptroller—Reward to captor of George Sinclair—Claims of States against United States, 353. Call on Comptroller for accounts—Pay John Weitzell for provisions for Wyoming, 354. Captain Stiles to make returns of all stores in his charge—Fees received and tax on writs, 355. Resolutions calling on Comptroller for accounts with United States, &c.—Indians complain of being plundered of their property —Letter to, 357. Cede Cape Henlopen lighthouse beacon, &c., to United States—Dr. Franklin bequeaths his portrait to Council —Accounts received from Comptroller—Letter to delegates respecting, 359. Letter to executors of Dr. Franklin for his portrait—Acts of Congress—Crimes against United States and military establishments—Pay for branding irons for pot and pearl ash casks, 361. Joseph Galloway applies for a pardon—not granted–Banks at Mud Island—Proposals for repairs of, 363. Pay to militia against Wyoming, 365. City lots–Mud Island—Officers of militia of Westmoreland county—Plan and dimensions of powder magazine, 367, 387. Provisions, &c., furnished, 372, 374. Acts of Congress, 372. Report of Committee on Joshua Elder's memorial on fees and depreciation lands, 374, 376. Proposals of Dr. Gregg to pardon generally persons attainted of high treason, 378, 379. Acts of Congress received–Encour-

Supreme Executive Council—xvi. agement of learning--Claims of Steuben-Courts in North Carolina —Letter commandant General of Carthagena respecting citizens now returned, 381. Acts of Congress, 384. Accounts with United States--Grant to William Owen Island in Alleghany river--Collector of excise, 385. Reform of penal system—Appropriation for building cells and walls in jail yard of Philadelphia, 388. Powder magazine, 390. Proceedings against Robt. Paisley-Suspended, 391, 392. Act of Congress respecting Courts in Rhode Island, 392. Mistake of Land Office in case of W. M. O'Brien corrected, 393. Secretary at War asks attention to Colonel McGillavry—and Chiefs of Creek nation on their Way to New York—Invitation to commencement, 395, 396. Preemption right to two islands in West Branch of Susquehanna asked for by J. Byers and F. McPherson, 395. Murder of two Indians on Pine Creek—and proclamation for murderers, 396, 397, 398. Letters to Indians and others respecting it, 398. Election of military officers of Lancaster county—Preemption right to island in Susquehanna river, 399. Letter to Colonel McGilivray, 404, 405. Payment on account of surveys of rivers, 407. Delegates in Congress on removal of seat of government, 408. Supposed murderers of Indians on Pine Creek, arrested in Portland, 422. Land purchased on Dunlap's creek--Patent to issue for, 422. Report on General Butler and St. Clair's letters for requisition of men, 424. Powder magazine—Message to Assembly-Mud Island —Claims against United States--Reciprocity with nations of Europe —Aliens holding land--Murder on Pine creek, 436. Return of messenger to Indians respecting Pine creek murder, 440. Procession at proclamation of Council —Committee of convention invite —Pay to Indians for murders,

p reme Executive Council—441. Report on R. Galbraith and Frankstown road, 442. Powers of Legislature expire--Reappointment of various officers, 443, 444. William Henry Lieut. of Philadelphia resigns, 447. Officers re-appointod, 448. Drawing of donation lands, 452. Claim S. McCoskry, 454. Breaches of Treaty with Great Britain--Inquired for, 457, 459. Payments for pensions to invalids — City lot, 457. P. Lloyd Zachery, clerk of Assembly asks to insert in Journals, address of fifty-six members —Letters from Ohio captives by savages, 458. Resolutions respecting treaty with Great Britain, 459. Report on case of General Thompson's widow, 465. Report and specification of road, Bedford to Pittsburg, 466-477. Report of Committee to examine certificates in Comptroller's office--Execution ordered, 485. Cornplanter and other Indians in Philadelphia--Speeches to and from, 497. Their expenses paid, 498. Conference with Cornplanter at Philadelphia —Terms of sale and purchase of lands on Lake Erie at Fort Stanwix, 501-509. Depreciation lots --Letter to Cornplanter—Asking money--Declined payment to interpreter for expenses-Recruiting Pennsylvania line, 511. Certificate of Dr. Jones respecting Indian chief Great Tree--Cornplanter and Half Town request to stay in city--French emigrants to receive tents, 513. Recruits of Pennsylvania line—Books for—Various payments, 515. Public officers called upon for accounts and information, 517. Powder to celebrate arrival of President of United States, 522. Proposals for a general pardon to traitors, 528. Confirm claim of Thomas Harding to city lot, 531. Resolutions respecting Comptroller--Register-General, &c., for information and statements--Claim of R. Peters for lot--Invitation to a lecture by Judge Wilson--Powder magazine, 533. Execution of J.

Supreme Executive Council—
E. Jones ordered — Repairs to Senate Chamber, 535. Resignations of Justices—Election to Assembly, 537. Claim of R. Peters rejected, 539. Sale of city lots ordered, 540. Various accounts approved—Receipts from several sources—Building fort at Hannastown, 541. Powder magazine—Commissioners to view rivers—Sundry payments — Resolutions favoring appointment of C. Pettit, 545.

Surgeons, to be examined by Drs. Cadwalader, Bond, Rush and Shippen, x., 452, 458; xii., 215, 307, 437, 622; xiii., 11, 115, 157, 158.

Surgical Instruments, x., 614.

Survey of Jersey Shore, x., 465.

Surveyor-General of Customs, i., 337, 538.

Surveyor-General of Land Office, i., 120, 124, 148, 151, 161; v., 274. Complaint against, 330. Reports, xiii., 175. Instructions to, respecting lands, 596. Claim for land referred to, xiv., 26. Report on A. Power's claim, 292. To deliver to D. Kennedy papers on Virginia claims, 394. Deputies, 441, 443, 445, 449, 456, 462. Jno. Lukens appointed, 444. Office in State House, 583. Reports, xiv., 343. Appoints deputies for each county, 441, 442. Caveat against J. Buchanan, 639. Removal of a deputy, 653, 654. Lots to be surveyed, 515. Report of survey of new purchase by Alex. McDowell, 604. To survey and mark ground for hospital at Province or State Island, 655. Difficulty about a line settled, xv., 8. Lands for officers, 17. To furnish plan of lots in Philadelphia unsold, 28. To make plans of depreciation lands, 43, 74. Call on, for surveys, 46. Recommend Major Wm. Alexander as deputy, 49. To settle Presley Neville's claim, 218. Fees from Deputy Surveyors, 343. Deputies not to hold two districts at same time, 344. Lottery fees to Deputy-Surveyor,

Surveyor General of Land office,— 351, 358. To furnish drafts of land held by Pennsylvania claimants in Luzerne county, 451, 452. Resolution respecting Surveyors having but one district rescinded, 459. Recommends Andrew Ellicott to survey islands in Alleghany river, 615. Complaint of Mr. Woods against, xvi., 11. Has power to appoint deputies, 28. To have located certain reservations according to resolution of Assembly, 47. Of donation lands, 50. Appoints James Harris deputy, 171. John Lukens dies, Daniel Brodhead elected, 208. Appoints his deputies for counties, 214, 216, 224, 211², 219², 229, 254, 257, 261, 280, 288, 292, 317, 384, 390, 461. Must appoint, not recommend deputies, 258. Appoints General Potter's son, 261. Of depreciation lands, deputy paid—Act for, 303. Fees received, 311. Of lands opposite Fort Pitt and at Fort McIntosh, 340. Depreciation lands, survey of, 439. Fees, 541.

Surveyor's fees, i., 69, 499.

Susquehannah Company, proceedings and resolutions of, ix., 569–572. Letters respecting, 572, 573. 602. Gov. Trumbull's view of, x., 4. Secretary Peter's letter to Henry Wilmot at London respecting Indian deed to, 177.

Susquehannah Indians, articles of agreement with, ii., 15. Towns on, vi., 35. Deeds for purchase of lands at Albany, 119-129. Col. Dongan's agency in, 125. Lands, 289. Complain of settlers, ix., 426. 428. Connected with murders arrive at General Congress, 506. Conference with Delawares at Big Island, 620.

Susquehannah River, Indian tribes on or near, iii., 19. Lands to be surveyed on, for Indians, 178. Indians consent to W. Penn's purchase of lands on, 183. Munsoe Indians on, 286. Minnisinks live at forks of, 326. Laid down as a boundary of Pennsylvania in map of Lousiana, 1721, 402. Lands applied for west of, 546. Deeds

Susquehanna River, to Wm. Penn 1701, for lands on, 600-603. Road from John Harris's to Lancaster, 618. Germans move over, iv., 57. Complaints from Maryland, 61. Lands west of, released by Indians to Proprietary, 88. Road from, to Chester, return of, 181, 284. Justices, 348. Indians quit claims to lands on, 559. New county to be formed west of, v., 398, 403, 404, 426, 428. History of settlements, 440-449. A family of Delaware Indians coming from Tinigou, settles between Wyoming and Fort Augusta, viii., 120. Indians there alarmed by news from Cherokees, 126. Indians in motion above Wyoming, 127. Message of Governor and Gen. Forbes to Indians on, 131. Fisheries, ix., 623, 719. A highway, 717. Gen. Lacey to command militia sent to, xi., 533. Pay to Commissioners to examination of, xiv., 182. New appointment, 485. Expenses of laying off a part of west branch of, and also of running and marking the line between the old and new purchase between Alleghany and, xv., 85. Distances from Canoe place to Kittanning, 91. Road from, to Lehigh, 229, 230. Commissioners to view, xvi., 178, 208, 260, 319, 462. Obstructions in, 208. Preemption to two Islands to J. Byers and F. McPherson, 395.

Sussex County, Sheriff of, i., 58, 165. Seal for, ordered—its device, 66. Decision of Court appealed from, 77. Sub-Treasurer appointed, 111. Ranger appointed, 165, 166. Complaint against Assemblyman, 185. Justices, 188. A Justice accused of ill fame, 186. Major Dyer elected and objected to as member of Council, 197. Sheriff and Ranger, 206, 368. Members dismissed, 211. Justices, 211, 320, 369. Complaint against Sheriff for not returning a member, 213. Complaint by H. Bowman, 228. Sheriff asks aid, 247. New Sheriff, 249, 340. Report from, of invasion by Senecas and French from Maryland, 277. Member from, objected to on account of debauchery, but admitted to sit, 323. Sheriff goes to England—Samuel Preston appointed, 340. And a member also, 344. Three Representatives for, 366. Clerk appointed, 371. Amount of one penny tax, 462. Ask for defence, 522. Watch at Cape Henlopen, 524. Arrival and acts of French, enemy's vessels at, 539. Complaint against inhabitants for purchasing goods from Captain Kidd, 579. Watch against pirates, ii., 23, 24, 25. Dedimus to Nehfield, 97. Jona. Bailey, Sheriff, 101. Luke Watson, Sheriff, 101. Sam'l Preston, Collector of Levies, 183. Wm. Clark, complaint of actions arising out of boundary lines between Maryland, 362. French privateer lands men at Whorekills, 448, 468. Complaints against Wm. Till, a magistrate—he is superceded, iii., 259. Rives Holt, Sheriff and Samuel Davis, Coroner, 260, 289. Justices appointed, 270. Rives Holt, Sheriff, 332. Jno. Jacobs, Coroner, 333. Sheriffs, 416, 465, 524, 575, 615. Coroners, 416, 465, 524, 575, 615. Sheriffs elected, iv., 470, 602, 748, 782. Coroners, 470, 602, 748, 782. Sheriffs elected, v., 55, 411, 468, 551, 597, 662. Coroners do., 55, 411, 468, 597, 662. Petition of pilots of, 226. Sheriffs, vi., 145, 638. Coroners elected, 145, 638. Coroners appointed, vii., 266; viii., 223, 403, 506, 781. Sheriffs appointed, vii., 266; viii., 223, 403, 506, 781. Sheriffs elected, ix., 57, 199, 286, 333, 398, 548, 624, 688, 778. Coroners elected, 57, 199, 286, 333, 398, 548, 624, 688, 778. Justices, 266, 278, 374. Clerks of Courts appointed, 699. Sheriffs elected, x., 56, 106, 211, 270. Coroners elected, 56, 106, 211, 270. Justices, 81, 217, 264. Acts respecting, 49. Ammunition sent to, 352.

Sutherland, Capt. Nicholas, of King's

troops, complains of the barracks in Philadelphia, x., 16.
Sutter, James, Superintendent of transportation, arrested, xii., 387.
Sutton, William, in prison, x., 681. From New York, committed as a tory, 676.
Swaine, Charles, in charge of provisions, vi., 460, 473 Letter from Geo. Croghan on French and Indian affairs, 642. To Gov. M., 643.
Swaine, Francis, clothier, xii., 56. 61. Sheriff, xv., 56, 294.
Swaine, Captain Jonathan, complains of seizure of his vessel by Collector—asks for freight of goods, &c., iii., 240.
Swaine, Major, State Clothier, xii., 247. Return of clothing, deficiencies, 261, 266, 285.
Swanson, Swan, offers to take up arms against French, i., 334.
Swanwick, John, goods of his father seized to be returned, xi., 336. Petition, 359. Petition respecting his father's property—Referred to Supreme Court, xii., 58, 199. Petition, 536.
Swatara settlement, murders by Indians, vii., 538.
Swatara creek, murders on, by Indians, viii., 95.
Swatara river, Commissioners to examine, xvi., 319.
Swearing, profane, Act to prevent, v., 33, 34.
Swearingen, Van, Sheriff, xiii., 740.
Swede, a young, raises a false alarm respecting Indians, ii., 20. Swedes ministers propose setting up another boat on Schuylkill—Council forbid it, 137.
Sweden maintains neutrality during war with Russia and the Ottoman Porte, xv., 433.
Swedes complain of P. England, keeper of ferry at Schuylkill, not taking them to meeting over the river, i., 373. Complain of their Dutch grants of land being taken by Proprietary and Secretary, ii., 465. Secretary Logan's answer to, 466. Attack B. Chambers at Schuylkill, 477, 478. Answer to petition requested by Council of Governor—his answer, 480-481-2. Answer of A. Sandal, 483.
Swedes-ford, road to, iii., 225, 230, 231. Troops to rendezvous at, xi., 301; xii., 71.
Swedish Church minister (Rev'd Jacob Fabricius) blind and reduced to poverty, i., 386. Wardens to appear, 386.
Swedish Consul, letter, xiv., 277. Complains of rude behavior from constables sent by attorney—order of Council, xv., 348.
Swift, John, a Justice, iii., 28. Collector of Port, x., 8. Complains of pilot boat captured, 9. Asks reward to be offered, 10, 12. A Justice, 88.
Swift, John White, from Maryland, xi., 407.
Swoop, Major, x., 658.
Swoope, Michael, Coroner, viii., 781. Provincial Commissioner, ix., 237; x., 735. Justice, xiii., 422.
Sykes, William, complaint against, xi., 234, 237.
Symes, Lieutenant James Smyth, an English officer, on a ship stranded in New Jersey, x., 387. Released on parole, 410. Money for, 418.
Symonds, Lieutenant, late of the Warren, to command artillery company at Liberty Island, x., 437.
Syng, Philip, silversmith, of Philadelphia, committed for a survey on Susquehannah, under a Maryland title, iii., 176. Provincial Commissioner for Philadelphia, ix., 237.
Syper, Anthony, counterfeits deeds for land, x., 694.
Syria, a nobleman from, arrives, and is entertained at public expense, iv., 296.

T.

Tackawheetap, (an Indian) suspected of murder, ii., 71.
Tashnichtorous, Indian chief, iii., 500.
Taghneghdorrus, an Indian, v., 84.
Tagotolessa, or Cap. Civility, and

several chiefs at Philadelphia conference, iii., 45–49.

Tail, estates, v., 426.

Tainey, Nicholas, &c., petition respecting condemned goods, iv., 173.

Talbot, Colonel, agent of Lord Baltimore, conduct complained of, i., 103, 104, 120. Proposal to arrest him, 104. Visits widow Ogle, 113. Joseph Bowles, 115.

Talbot, Jeremiah, Sheriff, xiv., 237; xv., 120.

Tamanee, arrives in Philadelphia, his speech, i., 447,

Tanacharisson, or Half king, vi., 85. Death of, noticed, vii., 5.

Tanners who are associators to have preference in hides, xi., 58.

Taquehsekachkawad, viii., 143.

Tarachawagon, name given by Indians to Conrad Weiser, iv., 733.

Tasker, Benjamin, President of Maryland, correspondence and depositions respecting murder of Dudley Digges, v., 582–597.

Tate, Dr, James, pass to, xiii., 537.

Tatham, John, vs. Jos. Growden, a claim for land, ii., 179.

Tatnall, Robert, captain of a guard boat, x., 580.

Taverns, ii., 159. Licenses, &c., ix., 24, 25.

Tawenna, Indian chief, iii., 313, 363.

Tax, to be laid on land, to pay public charges, i., 70. Import and export, 99. High, complained of, 101. His son asks to administer, 185. Of one penny, 520. Collectors summoned, 521. Amount, 522. Refusal or failure to pay, ii., 25, 70, 71, 122, 127, 150, 159, 391, 456, 463, 468, 542. Not raised here as in England, 463; iii., 91, 144. Difficulty between Chester and Philadelphia counties, 144, 158; viii., 301, 302, 304, 324, 326. Proprietary, 472–477; x., 420. Remonstrance of inhabitants of Germantown against, xii., 53, 54. Collection of, 191, 193, 233. On Philadelphia county, 233. Misconstruction of law on, 379. In Dock ward, 382. Circular on, 399. Opposition in Berks, 601. In Philadelphia county, 735, 743. And levies, Commissioners of, xi., 536; xiv., 151, 235, 267. Eighteen penny tax, 287, 461. Suspension of, for the year proposed, xvi., 223[2]. Not agreed to, 224[2]. Received, 478.

Taxables, in each county, 1760, 1770, xiv., 336.

Taylor, Abraham, member of council, iv., 506. Elected Colonel by associators, v., 175. Commissioned to command batteries, 251. Instructs Captain Sibbald, 284, Name struck out by order of proprietary, 551. Sets up a claim for lands under title, for which he is removed from council, 551. Collector of customs, vi., 319. (Collector,) order to, of Governor to ship provisions to Governor Tinker of R. I., vii., 152. Order for embargo, 388. To allow vessels to depart, 501. Collector of Philadelphia, viii., 39.

Taylor, Christopher, member of first council, i., 57. A justice, 182. Death of, commissioner to take charge of his papers as Register General, 185. Administrators appointed, 186, 187, 191, 193, 195, 201, 210, 332, 380.

Taylor, George, claims Durham furnace, xi., 537.

Taylor, Isaac, son of Christopher, i., 185. Administers on his estate, 185, 187. Repecting father's will, 195. Joseph, 331. Daughter, case of, ii., 455. Surveyor, made prisoner by Maryland, iii., 212, 214. Appointed regulator of weights and measures for Chester county, iv., 507.

Taylor, James, coroner, xvi., 199.

Taylor, John, sheriff of Chester county, iii., 140, 260, 289. Order on, for a cannon, x., 598.

Taylor, Matthew, commissioner on boundary line of Huntingdon county, xvi., 46.

Taylor, Thomas, Register and recorder of deeds, xi., 190. To be written to, respecting papers, 216. A highwayman executed, xii., 275.

Tea, Richard, resigns council, xi., 201.

Tea, inspection board appointed on, imported from Amsterdam, xiv., 33.

Teach, a noted pirate, iii., 54.

Teague, Wm., Coroner of Philadelphia, resigns, ii., 108, 163.

Teedyuscung, Delaware king, sends Governor a message and string of wampum, vii , 198. At Easton treaty objects to Pumpshire as interpreter, having one of his own, 205. Benjamin, his character, 205. Agrees to open, 206. His speech, 207. Explains "Whish Shickoy," 209. Answers Governor, 213. Explains the belt, the square means "Lands of Indians," 213. Dines with Governor, 213. Reply to news of Indian murders, 214. Philadelphia Quakers take leave of him, 215. His speech, 215. Strange conduct of, 217. New belt given, 218. Answers Governor, 218. Presents to, 219. Continues at Fort Allen, he and his party perpetually drunk, 222. Proceedings respecting, 222–225. At Wyoming on way to Easton with Indian prisoners, 267, 287, 305, 309. Fears for his death, 317. Explains what he understands by fraud, 325. Charged by Charles Brodhead with Indian murders, 326. How received by Governor Denny, 351. Committee appointed by council to investigate proprietary purchases from Indians, 354. Message to, 384. Coming to treaty at Easton, 429. Memorandum of his remarks about lands, 431. His sons at Fort Allen, 474, 476. Two messages from, to W. Parsons, 477. News from, 478, 488, 510–517. At Lancaster, 517. Respecting, 517–551. Message of Governor to, 546. John Grey, messenger to, 548. Rehearsal of messages to, 551. Minutes of messengers to, 589. Respecting, 605, 607. At Fort Allen, 622. At treaty at Easton, 649. Demands a clerk, 656, 659. Appoints Chas. Thomson clerk, 665. Respecting lands, 676, 677, 679, Deeds for lands produced to, 688, 693. Interview respecting, 694, 698. His conduct, 699. And Captain Orndt, 723. Visits Governor, 725. His son Amos, 726. Demands deed of 1718, his opinion of Croghan and Johnson, 731. Opinion on building, and scalps, 735. Commissioners to Wyoming appointed, 754. Arrives in Philadelphia respecting belt and scalps, 756. At Philadelphia on his return from Wyoming, 770. Mr. Edmonds sent to, 773. Conference with, at Philadelphia, viii., 9, 29, 100. Sends insolent reply to Governor, 30. Insists on his clerk being present, 30, 31. Holds conference and smokes pipe with Governor, 32. Speech, 32. Refers to treaty at Easton, 33, 39, W. Logan confers with, 31, 40. Governor's speech to, 42, 54. Letter of Governor to Colonel Washington, by, 56. Speech, &c., at Mr. Horsfield's, 84. In Philadelphia, 86. Letter by his sons, named to three nations on Allegheny, 96. His demands, 114. Ask as a favor of Governor to appoint James Perry as a captain, 115. Message of Governor to, 129. Conference with, at Nescopec, 133. Asks for colors taken by Will. Sock from French, 134. Message sent by F. Post from Cherokees, 135. Behaves badly at Easton, 172. Inquiry as to the cause of his alleged greatness, 190. Speaks on claims to lands, 202. Describes River Indians living near Esopus, 217. Quakers' views of his complaints for lands, 243. Report of committee appointed by council on, 246–261. Visits Governor, 344, 403, 414, 463. Delivers prisoners, 414. Conference with Governor H., 435, 500. To be informed of murder of Dr. John, 455. Goes to Ohio with F. Post, 469. Conference at Philadelphia, 484. Stopped, 491. Conference at Philadelphia about N. E. settlers at Wyoming, 500. Letter to, from Sir William Johnson, 507. Sends message about Connecticut settlers, 570. Conference

at Philadelphia, 600, 622, 707. Assertions about lands, related by Isaac Stille at conference, 454, 661, 667. Conferences with, ix., 6.

Telfair, Rev. Dr., and wife, deed to, xii., 259.

Temple, John, seized and imprisoned, xi., 362. Enlarged, 371.

Tents to be made of awnings, x., 630, 633. To be procured for troops at Chester, x., 540, 640.

Terrans, James, Justice, xii., 391.

Terrence, Adam, dec'n Indian murders, vi., 648.

Territories, difficulties between, and Province, ii., 124–129, 130. Address to Governor, 128. Make proposals, 130. Separation in legislation, 133. Meeting of Representatives of, 134. To meet at New Castle, 134. Separated from Provinces—Assembly to be called, 163. Governor has not met them, 423. Meeting, messages and answers, 424-426.

Test Law, memorial of Philadelphia, xiv., 573. Referred to Assembly, 574.

Tetamy, Moses, bears insolent message from Tedyuscung to Governor, viii., 30, 31. Sent on message to Minnisink Indians, 140, 149. At Easton, 175. Sent to Ohio, 491.

Teter, Michael, a disabled soldier, case of, and course to be pursued, xii., 78.

Thanksgiving days—for birth of a Prince, i., 229. For victory over French, ii., 215. Appointed, v., 50. viii., 235; ix., 41; xi., 627; xii., 369. Appointed by United States, xvi., 189. Proclamation of Council for, 232.

Theatres, &c., memorial of Quakers against, xiii., 741.

Theatrical exhibitions, against, xv., 590, 595.

Thomas, Arthur, and sons, to have their papers secured, x., 661. Money received for house and lot of Arthur Thomas, xii., 104.

Thomas, Lieut.-Colonel David, battalion, x., 686, 695.

Thomas, Evan, Justice, iii., 531.

Thomas, George, recommended by Proprietary as Governor — Lord Baltimore petitions against him, iv., 249. Arrives, presents commission, takes oath, and is proclaimed Governor at Court House, 288. Appoints Thos. Lawrie secretary, 289. Message to Assembly, 290. Receives opposition from Lord Baltimore, 290. Address from Assembly, 292. Correspondence with Governor Ogle, 302. Message to Assembly on bills of credit, 303. Flag to be raised on his arrival from Antigua, 304. Messages to Assembly, 290, 305. Rule for passing laws, 306. Makes a special present to Allummappes, 310. Messages, 314, 319, 322, 331-333, 335, 348, 352, 355, 359. Answers of Assembly, 316, 321, 330, 333, 348, 355, 360, 365. On bills of credit, 319, 335. Correspondence with Commissioners on Maryland line, 329. On elections, 335. On Spanish affairs, 354. Meets Assembly at New Castle, 356. Calls Assembly at Philadelphia, submits papers from England on coin and bills of credit, 359. Messages to Assembly, 368, 380, 398, 405, 407, 409, 413. 419. Do., and answers from do., 367, 371, 387, 402-405, 414, 435. On liberty of conscience, 368-371, 381. Orders petitioners of Philadelphia for raising money to appear before Council, 379. Bill, Governor's message on, 384. Complains of Israel Pemberton, 389. Letter to pilots, not licensed, 394. Proclamation on war with Spain, 396. Message to Assembly reviewing various proceedings, 398, 401. On defence of Province, 401. Answer to Assembly on bill to raise money on Philadelphia, 409-413. Orders a man wounded by an Indian under care of Dr. Græme, 413. Answers to Assembly on Philadelphia money bill, 419. Letter to Indians respecting wounded man, 420. Speech to Assembly on defence, 422. On communicating to Assembly originals received from England, 425, 426. On peace with Spain, 427. On draft on Treasury, 461.

Messages to Assembly, 438-443, 449, 461-466, 473, 491-495, 507, 510. Do. from, 435, 438, 448, 450, 476, 491-495, 509. On enlisting servants, 438, 443. Additional instructions on bills of credit, 471-473. Proclamation for enlisting soldiers for Cuba, 500. On pest-house, 507, 508, 510. Messages, 510, 540, 590-600, 601, 602, 621, 626, 627, 634, 658, 672, 677, 678, 679, 737, 749, 750, 754, 756, 757. Letter to Indians, 588, 602, 763, 772. Messages from Assembly, 549, 602, 603-618, 637, 659, 673, 678, 679, 687, 730, 754, 763, 773. Seal at arms, 639. On election riots in Philadelphia, 623. On naturalizing Protestants, 627. On Indian skirmish in Virginia, 634. Receives money from Assembly, 639. Mediates with Indians on behalf of Virginia, 653. Letter to Governor Gooch, and answer, 653-655. Indian affairs, 658. Dispatches from England on probable rupture with France, 670. Speech to Assembly on, 671, 672. Trustees of Loan Office, bills of credit, 673. Rupture with France, 677. Murder by Delawares, 678, 687. Going to Virginia and Maryland, 689. Proclamation of war between England and France, 696 Treaty with Indians at Lancaster, 697–737. War with France — privateers — treaty with Indians, &c., 737. On capture of vessels by French privateers, 749. Expedition against Cape Breton, 754, 763. New county, 756. Catawbas and Virginia, 757, 758. Proclamation against selling rum to Indians, 759. Letter to Wm. Hill, keeper of powder-house, 764. Answer to Assembly on grant of provisions for King's use, 768. Importance of gaining over the Indians from the French, 792. Commission and instructions to Commissioners to Albany, 773-777.

Proposes new members of Council, v., 1. Circular to Captains of militia, 2, 6. Messages to Assembly, 4, 26, 36, 44, 45, 46, 56, 57, 62. Messages from Assembly, 26, 36, 44, 46, 48, 54, 58, 63. Men to be raised, 42. Bills of credit, 44, 45, 46. Reduction of Canada, 49. Proclamation for Thanksgiving Day, 50. Address to King, 51. Money and clothing for troops, 56, 57. Proposes going to England for his health, 61. Announces in a message his intention, 62; also, death of John Penn, 62. Short review of Governor's administration, 62. Nominates members of Council, 64, 68. Has sailed for Great Britain - succeeded by Anthony Palmer, 68, 76.

Additional instructions to, vi., 192. Message of Assembly on, 226-236. Proceedings of Council in his time, 723.

Thomas, Joshua, sale of estate, xii., 468.

Thomas, Lazarus, a murderer, under sentence of death, petitions for a pardon — arguments for and against, iii., 40.

Thomas, Colonel Richard, receives accoutrements, x., 673, 733. Stationed at French Creek powder works, xi., 48, 130.

Thomas, William, sale of estate, xii., 481.

Thome, Durst, petition respecting condemned goods, iv., 171, 227.

Thome, John, Justice, xiv., 180.

Thompson, Alex., member of Assembly, dies, xii., 188.

Thompson, Andrew, Justice, xiv., 247.

Thompson, Capt. Archibald, x., 692. Sub-Lieutenant of Philadelphia, to act in Col. Coates' place, he being a prisoner with the enemy, xi., 419.

Thompson, Benjamin, Lieutenant of boat "Experiment," x., 335.

Thompson, Isaac, Lieutenant, xi., 640. Coroner, xiv., 555.

Thompson, James, Councillor, xi., 699. Purchases flour, xii., 75, 77, 143. Account as member, 304.

Thompson, Jesse, wounded and scalped by Indians on Susquehanna, clothing for, xi., 747.

Thompson, John, Coroner, v., 552, 662. Sheriff, ix., 333, 398, 547. Sent with Indians from Fort Pitt

to Redstone, 539. Instructions to, 540. Sheriff, x., 56, 100, 211, 372; xi., 179, 378, 596. Paymaster, 751. Commissary of musters—sends rolls and names of officers, xii., 73, 78.

Thompson, Joseph, Coroner, vii., 266.

Thompson, Joshua, Coroner, vi., 638; viii., 402, 506.

Thompson, Peter, claim, xv., 481.

Thompson, Robert, Coroner, iv., 748.

Thompson, Lieutenant Robert, xii., 2.

Thompson, Samuel, Captain, xii., 70. Resigns as Justice, xiii, 748. Coroner, xv., 300.

Thompson, Colonel William, Letter respecting Indians, viii., 111; xi., 556, 567, 573.

Thompson, Brigadier-General William, makes charges against Thomas McKean, xi., 653. Denial, 659. Called before Council—Declines, 660. Dies—Pension to widow, xv., 234, 286, 345, 413, 472. Certificate to his widow, xvi., 341.

Thompson, Schooner General, privateer, x., 743.

Thomson, Charles, master of Quaker school, appointed by Teedyuscung his clerk, vii., 665. Asks for copies of letters, &c., 724, 725. Attends with Teedyuscung at a conference in Philadelphia, viii., 114. Appointed with Frederick Post messenger to Indians, 132, 147. Conference with, at Nescopec, 132. (Secretary) makes an "indecent and affronting application" to the Vice-President respecting a house, xi., 531. Secretary of Congress, xii., 187. Paid for kettles taken for public service, xiii., 319. Letter, xiv., 23, 143.

Thorne, Rev. Mr., Episcopal clergyman complained of and suspicious, xii., 334.

Thornton, Joseph, Sheriff, viii., 402, 506.

Thread, manufacture of, proposed by John Marshall, xii., 81.

Tiadaughton creek, ix., 554.

Tiaogon, great number of Indians at, vii., 137.

Tickings, manufacture of, in Philadelphia, ix., 354.

Tilghman, Colonel, aid of General Washington, arrives with news of surrender of Lord Cornwallis, xiii., 94.

Tilghman, Edward, employed as counsel in suit, Thomas Proctor for Hogg Island, xv., 372.

Tilghman, James, elected member of Council in room of William Till, deceased, ix., 354. Sent to Easton on Wyoming affairs, 749. Report, 750. Sent to Williamsburg as a Commisssioner to Lord Dunmore, x., 173. Instructions, 175. Report, 181. Allowed to visit his family, xi., 285. Parole returned, and he discharged, 489, 492. Late Secretary of the Land Office under Proprietaries—called on for the books, papers, &c., xii., 690. Secretary of Land Office, xiii., 420.

Till, William, a magistrate of Sussex county, is complained against for indecent expressions against proprietary's family, and arbitrary acts against Alexander Molliston—he is superseded, iii., 259. Confesses his error, and is re-instated, 269, 270. Member Council, iv., 506. Mayor of Philadelphia, 623. 3d Judge of Supreme Court, 640. Appointed Collector of Customs at New Castle in room of Thomas Græme, deceased, v., 244. (President Council,) to William Parsons, vii., 267. A Supreme Judge, vii., 558. Collector of New Castle, viii., 39. Justice of Supreme Court—infirm, is displaced, ix., 203. Member of Council, dies, 354.

Timber wheels for General Armstrong, xi., 757.

Tin to be purchased, x., 640.

Tinicum, part of Joseph Galloway's forfeited estate, deed for, xii., 256, 331, 352. (Bucks county,) deed to E. Carson, xiii., 236. To Colonel F. Murrry, 277.

Tinker, Governor John, of Rhode Island, applies for permission to obtain provisions, vii., 151.

Tinogon, Delaware Indians move from, to Susquehanna, viii., 120.

Tioga, riots at—Letter to Governor of New York and delegation in Congress on, xv., 278. Intelligence from, 307. N. Dennison sent to, receives pay, 312. Goods distributed to Indians at, xiv., 604. Report of Maclay, 658, 662.
Tissue, William, Captain, xii., 70.
Titami, Captain John, a Delaware chief, petition, iv., 624.
Tittemy, Joseph, vii., 431.
Tittermary, John, pass for, xi., 578.
Tobacco, seized by Governor, asked to be restored, i., 343. Casks regulated, i., 465. Transportation from Maryland to be stopped, 465, 468. More at Philadelphia than can be shipped, 610, 611. A "Say Master" proposed to prevent packing unmerchantable, ii., 26.
Todd, Alexander, Justice for Dock Ward, xv., 160.
Todd, Andrew, Surgeon, General Greene, xi., 765. Justice, xii., 753.
Tolbert, Captain, xi., 423.
Tolbert, Major Jeremiah, xii., 678.
Tomlinson, John, art of boring and grinding gun barrels to be purchased from, x., 533, 648.
Tonge, William, applies to have papers delivered to him as Clerk of New Castle county—as naval officer—requirement of Council, ii., 97.
Tonnage, duty on, proposed—objected to, viii., 30, 31, 35, 67, 100. Petition of merchants against, 230, 232, 334. Duty, how and at what rate to be estimated, xii., 588.
Toombs, Colonel, to rendezvous at Swedesford, xi., 301.
Tootelaes, alias Chaponick, iii., 511.
Topham, Captain Daniel, applies for the brick-yard in Northern Liberties, xii., 311.
Tories, proceedings, persons and papers, x., 358, 360, 460, 503, 616, 677. Committed — their names, xi., 58, 89, 190, 472, 478, 479, 481. Suspected persons to be arrested, 283. Proceedings against, 283. Remonstrance of, 292. Arrests, 308. Act against, 481.
Torrance, Joseph, Sheriff, xv., 303, 584; xvi., 202, 208.
Tortnor, Robert, Ensign, xii., 10.
Tost, John, Sheriff of Philadelphia county, i., 58.
Touche, Chevalier de la, authorized to collect French sailors, xii., 723.
Toutasariaga, Indian chief, iii., 500.
Towers, John, may deliver lanterns and knapsacks to Colonel Miles, v., 636. Various orders to, 640, 648, 649, 651, 657, 658, 662, 664, 672, 677, 688.
Towers, Robert, appointed Commissary of powder magazine, x., 301. Powder at Germantown, &c., 304, 306, 307, 308, 313. Reports, 328, 331, 333, 339, 340, 352, 375, 378, 382, 398, 404, 417, 421, 426, 428, 430, 435, 436, 440, 510, 527, 555. To keep key of magazine, 341. To prove and stamp muskets, 383. Commissary, to deliver cannon, 402. To deliver powder to Congress, 415, 416. To receive and examine arms, &c., 422. Fix racks for arms in State-house, 422. Quantity of shot in store, 431. To furnish Congress with powder, &c., 435. And shot, 443. Reports, 447, 456, 458, 463, 496. Powder to Virginia, 458, 468. Lives next but one door to Presbyterian Church, Market street, 471. To furnish brass, 483. Pay increased, 497. Reports, 503, 566. To procure formers, &c., 589. Orders on, for ammunition, &c., 613. Orders for delivery of stores, &c., xi., 4.
Town, Benjamin, gunsmith, x., 422. Printer, suspected of printing seditious paper, "Slow and Sure," and William Young, his apprentice, committed, xii., 325. (See 319.)
Townsend, Admiral, applies for export of provisions for fleet, vii., 571.
Townsend, Lyttleton, Coroner, x., 211.
Townships, ii., 520, 530. Pounds to be erected in each, iii., 345; iv., 278.
Tracey, Lieutenant, murdered by Lieutenant Hamilton, x., 8.
Trade, Act in favor of certain per-

sons to, proposed, iii., 234. Of Northern colonies restrained, 401, 408. Indian, bill to regulate, vi., 743. With Indians, vii., 177, 433, 455, 463; viii., 19, 24, 29, 39, 51, 71, 76, 234, 332; ix., 53, 264, 552, 642, 656, 706. English government take it into their hands, 581.

Trade and Navigation, to be encouraged, i., 574.

Trade, Lords of, letter from, on defence of New York, ii., 114. With Spaniards in West Indies to be opened, 179. Appoint new Commissioners of, 403. On coin, and bills of credit, iv., 356-360, 500. On presents to Indians, v., 711. Letter on Indian affairs, and proceedings at Fort George, vi., 59. Additional instructions to Governor Thomas, 192. Letters to and from, vii., 272, 278, 386, 738, 740. Order embargo, 387. Ask account of iron manufactures, 1749-1756, 738. And plantations, Commissioners' proceedings respecting regulations, ix., 341, 343. Order Governor Penn to send an account of manufactures in Pennsylvania since 1734, 343, 354. With Indians, 552.

Traders--see Free Society of.

Traill, Robert, appointed to receive and distribute provisions collected in Northampton county, xi., 422. Store keeper declines, 437. Councillor, xv., 100.

Traill, Thomas, Sheriff, xiii., 89, 395, 724.

Train, David, Coroner, x., 56.

Traitors, Act for attainder of, xi., 481, proclamation against certain, 483, 493, 496. Secretary to keep register of attainted persons, 503, 504. Instructions to agents, 504. Proclamation against, 513, 518, 523. Estates, 529, 535, 538, 539, 556, 587. Letter from Massachusetts respecting, 629. Caution against purchasing estates of, on account of frauds, 654. Sales of estates, 745. Suspicious persons, xii., 8, 11, 12, 49, 80, 83, 106, 113, 114, 133, 145, 177, 199, 206, 222, 223, 237, 243. Proclamation against, 27, 287, 312. Estates, 80, 114, 116, 117, 174, 185, 204, 222, 246, 247, 259, 260, 265, 268, 299, 300, 309. Not to go at large, 133, 323, 331. Traitors, 268, 270, 271, 272, 277, 293, 334, 336, 339, 340, 390, 401, 416, 419, 425, 470, 478, 481, 495, 496, 501, 515, 521, 524, 536, 553, 557, 558, 566, 577, 610, 612, 615, 617, 619, 651, 663, 665, 674, 675, 709, 710, 722, 729, 730, 733, 734, 737, 742, 745, 747, 751, 752, 775, 778, 781, 782. xiii., 5, 9, 11, 12, 20, 23, 26, 30, 31, 32, 35, 38, 52, 56, 57, 78, 80, 94, 97, 98, 101, 108, 140, 146, 163, 170, 171, 175, 180, 182, 199, 204, 207, 209, 236, 246, 251, 252, 273, 277, 281, 296, 297, 301, 303, 333, 346, 361, 385, 403, 430, 448, 450, 498, 505, 516, 519, 529, 590, 592, 599, 623, 646, 695, 701, 735, 748, 766, 776. xiv., 34, 47, 56, 140, 290, 292, 359, 385, 451, 463, 495, 498, 578, 589, 590, 642, 651, 663. xv., 4, 6, 8, 9, 14, 26, 40, 43, 51, 73, 74, 82, 99, 124, 126, 149, 153, 172, 180, 185, 187, 191, 192, 220, 223, 237, 260, 261, 265, 277, 382, 406, 413, 425, 427, 428, 468, 471, 606, 640, 657. xvi., 23, 107, 136, 155, 179, 217, 273, 283, 309, 350, 363, 387, 422, 507, 540.

Transports arrive at New York and sail southward, xi., 3.

Trapnall, Jno. Coroner, ix., 333, 398.

Treason—prisoners under sentence of death for, iii., 110. Treasonable plans discovered and persons arrested at Carlisle, xi., 307.

Treasurer and deputy, salary, i., 111. Appointed, 111. ii., 122. Provincial, Security, ix, 578, 580 State appointed, xi., 257., xii., 554.—Treasury of New Jersey robbed, ix., 543, 544. Treasury department United States, act of Congress establishing, xvi., 164.

Treaties with Indians, ii., 15, 299. To be made with five nations, iii., 403. Penn and Indians, 338.—With Holland on contrabands of war, iv., 487, at Lancaster, 697. With Six Nations at Albany, reports, v., 7, 26. At Easton, vii., 204, 220. Preliminaries, 206. Opening, 207. Persons present,

207. Governor's speech, 210. Particular description of wampum used, 216. Strange conduct of Teedyuscung, 217. Strange speech of New Castle, 218. Speech of Governor on giving belt, 218. Meeting breaks up, 219. Names of Indians present at, 220. At Harris's and Lancaster, 506, 551. Of 1763, between France and England, proclaimed, ix., 80. With Indians at Fort Stanwix, boundaries described, 554. Of peace with Morocco, xv., 268.

Trees, penalty for cutting, marked on boundary, i., 128.

Trego, Benjamin and Joseph, arrested and enlarged, xi. 308,

Trelawney, Governor of Jamaica, to be asked for loan of cannon, v., 228. Ask to levy forces, 233. Letter respecting impressing seamen, 326. Decision of Council, 327.

Trembleur, privateer, at Philadelphia, v., 249. Her French prisoners ordered to Newtown jail, 264.

Trent, William, Member of Council, ii., 118. Judge, 239. Speaker, iii., 69. Claim for bearing present to Indians at Ohio, v., 490. Account from Ohio, 616. At the forks, 660. Views ground for Fort, 660. Ensign Ward of his company, surrenders Fort at Monongahela, vi., 28. Braddock's defeat, 481. Affairs at Patterson's creek, 641. Aid proposed for his relief, 743, 744. Proposed as Secretary at treaty, vii., 516. Letters, 601, 669.

Trenton Ferry—two good horses to be established at, viii., 71. Troops sent to, in shallops, xi., 25. Boats and Commodore sent to, 39. Six colors taken from Hessians, 40. Prisoners from, 76. Gondolas to be sunk near, 470, 471. Officers of State fleet—leave for Lancaster, 521. Court on Connecticut claim meets at, xiii., 430. Witnesses, 442.

Trevis, Capt. John, sub-Lieutenant, xi., 448.

Triesback, Colonel Jost, battalion, xi., 126.

Trindle, John, sub-Lieutenant, xii., 322.

Trimble, James, xii, 718. Summoned as a witness, xiii., 296. xiv., 466. Paid for filling patents for land, xv., 139, 229. Assistant Secretary, 592. To draw conveyances with Colonel Johnston, 609.

Trophies of war — resolution of Congress, 1778, request of board of war for, xii., 242.

Troops to be raised from different counties, x., 757.

Trover and Conversion—action for, ii., 407.

Trueby, Christopher, Justice, xiv., 180.

Trumbull, Jonathan, Governor of Connecticut. Letter from President Hamilton, ix., 777. Letters to and from on Susquehanna county, x., 4, 119, 151, 152, 163, 164. Resolutions of Council and Assembly, 119. Letter from, xiv., 2.

Trumbull, Continental frigate, xii., 712, 722, 760, 778.

Trump, Capt., vi., 764.

Tsanandowa—lands at, iii., 273. Letter from Abraham Wendall at, to Governor of Virginia, 609.

Tuck, Peter, of Bucks county, complains of Indians, ix., 385.

Tucker, Henry, chairman of department of Bermuda—letter with powder, x., 321.

Tucking, Robert, care of prisoners, xi., 89.

Tuckness, Robert, appointed agent for Indian trade at Fort Allen, viii, 234. Resigns, 286.

Tudor, Henry, appointed to ship Montgomery as pilot, x., 679.

Tulleken, Captain, demands quarters for troops, vii., 359.

Tulpehocken—lands, J. Logan and Indians, respecting, iii., 322. The farthest inhabited part of the province assigned to Palatines from New York, 323. Indian murders near, vi., 704, 738.—Horses stolen by, viii., 401.

Turbett, Captain Thomas, x., 686, 692.

Tulbert, Henry, Sheriff, x., 211.

Turbutt, Samuel, collector of excise, xvi., 83.

Turnbull, Marmee & Co. Paid, 324. Claim land on which Fort Pitt was erected, xiv., 124. Petition to trade with Indians, 520. Report on their case, xvi., 158.

Turnbull, William, agent for purchase of flour, xii., 45, 76, 107, 112, 142, 144, 202, 203, 252.—Accounts, 252, 267, 380, 385, 595, 634. Orders to, for money, xiii., 43. To appraise goods, 577. Accounts, xv ; 302, 345, 651.

Turner, Joseph, member of Council, v., 65. To examine negroes of flag of truce, 74, 75. Committee on Indian land claims, viii., 259. Papers belonging to land office to be demanded of, xiii., 434.

Turner, Robert, a judge, i., 119. A justice, 120, 176. Register, pro. tem., 185. Resigns, 195. Has pieces of eight, petition respecting, 209. Scandalous report about, is justified by Council, 210. Lieut. of Governor, 211. Petition for road to Bucks, 298. Councillor, 365. Treasurer, 436, 443. Member of New Council, 580. Arrested, 608.

Turner, Thomas, keeper of State flag, xiii., 586.

Tuscorora suffers from Indians, vi., 674.

Twightwees, described, iii., 440. town attacked by French and Indians, v., 599.—Message from, 600. Death of King, 617. Present of condolence, 617. Discourse with Owendats, vi., 199.

Tybout, Andrew, care of prisoners, xi., 89.

Tyler, John, armorer, xi., 408. Petition, xi., 655.

Tyng, Charles, to distribute salt and flour, xii., 119.

Tyoninhogaroa, Indian chief, iii., 440.

Type founder, Jacob Bay, at Germantown, xii., 326.

U.

Udrie, Colonel Daniel, resigns as sub-Lieutenant, xii., 675.

Ullaloes, a chief of Ganawese Indians, xiii., 605, 606.

Ulm, city of, burgomasters and magistrates of, answer to letters from, xiv., 356.

Underwood, John, Sheriff, xv., 296, 566.

Unfree Ships, proceeded against, i., 90, 121, 122. Condemnation, 122. Difficulty with purchaser, 124.

Union, act of, i., 619. Flag, v., 350. Of colonies, vi., 16, 38, 71, 72, 78, 87, 89, 93, 96, 100. Plan of, 105, 109.

Union saw-mill, on the Lehigh, xv., 194, 229, 230 ; xvi., 83.

Union, Federal ship, placed by permission of Council, in State-house yard, after procession, xv., 487.

United States, lottery tickets received and sent to Board of Treasury, xi., 477. Independence acknowledged, xiii., 543. Proclamation of Congress on cessation of hostilities, 555. Benj. Stille approved to settle accounts with, 558. Proclamation of Pennsylvania on peace—Hessian flags given to Pennsylvania, 559. State of expenditures under head of contingencies, xiv., 652. Returns of electors of President and Vice-president, and proclamation, xv., 655. President's letter on mode of transmitting acts of Congress, &c., xvi., 93. Thanksgiving appointed by, 189. Claims of the several States against, 353. Temporary and permanent seat of Government, 408. Accounts with 429. Pay for loss while in service of, 536. Claims on, 540.

University of Pennsylvania, (see Academy and College.) Confiscated estates reserved for, xii., 189, 441. Estate of William Austin, in Philadelphia, assigned to, 585. Proceeds of estates, xiii., 209, 255, 280, 310. James Patterson, teacher in, 205. Copy of act called for, 454. Lands appropriated to, xiv., 26, 488. Incomes of land accruing to, xv., 40. Council attend commencement, 328. Ask for use of bell of State-house, while the University is in Philosophical Hall, 93, 170. Invitation to commencement, 121, 301, 403.

Updegraff, Derick, justice, iii., 531.
Upland, goods left at, to be brought to Philadelphia, i., 64. Indians willing to sell lands, 156.
Urie, Alexander, convicted of murder, v., 269, 274. Report of Supreme Court, 277. Action of Council, 280. Reprieve for, 293.
Urie, Thomas, Sheriff, xi., 234. Sub-Lieutenant, 303. To receive sulphur, &c., at Yellow Springs, 389.
Urie, Thomas, Junior, Sub-Lieutenant, xi., 379. Rifles for Bedford, 423. Respecting election, 774; xii., 93. Counsellor, 147. Difficulty with, and John Piper, about seats, 182. Resigns as a member, 334.
Urquehart, Eneas, traitor, arrested, xii., 479, 480, 494, 524.
Usher, Thomas, Sheriff of Chester Co., i., 58, 174. Appointed sub-treasurer for Chester, 111. Complaint against, 200. His answer, 201.
Usury, bill against to be renewed, i., 466, 468.
Uttendorf, Monsieur, appointed adjutant, x., 773.

V.

Valentine, Robert, intends a religious visit to Ireland—views of Council on, xiii., 85.
Valley Forge, Hospital at, attended by Captain Duffey, xii., 67.
Vanbebber, Jacob, Justice of Supreme Court, ix., 203, 206. Dies, 581.
Van Campen, Aaron, deposition respecting Wyoming, ix., 710.
Van Campen, Benjamin, appointed Sub-Lieutenant, xi., 310. Justice, xiv., 661. Complaint against and his defence,—dismissed, xv., 439.
Van Campen, John, appointed justice, ix., 660. Letter to, on Indian invasions, xii., 312. Councillor, 506. Letter on alarm, for supplies to Wyoming, 585. Account, 658, 715; xiii, 428. Letter, xiv., 443 To refund, xvi., 324.
Vanderen, John, jr., notary and tabellion public, xiv., 568. Purchases —Depreciation lands, xvi., 374.
Vanderslice, Henry, Sheriff, x., 270.
Vanderslice, Lieutenant Jacob, recruiting instructions, xi., 577.
Vandike, Henry, Berks Co., complains of damage to farm, by roads, ii., 238.
Vandyke, John, Sheriff, v., 411, 464.
Vance, John, apprehends a notorious counterfeiter, and receives reward, xii., 268, 272.
Van Etten, John, Coroner, viii, 506.
Van Hier, Captain B., petition for certain articles for his troop of horse, xi., 737. Recruits, xiii., 188, 202, 211.
Vanhorn, Isaac, coroner, xv., 99, 296, 566; xvi., 192.
Vanikin, Rebecca, pretended marriage with John Martin, x., 40, 53, 54.
Vankemp, John, letter respecting Indians in Northampton Co., xii., 326. Councillor,
Van Leer, Gerhard, to hold lands, &c., 111.
Van Leer, Lieut. Wm., recruits, xi., 492.
Van Lenkensdorf, Lewis, recommended to Congress, First Lieut., x., 679. Appointed Adjutant, another nominated as Lieutenant, 685.
Vansant, Ensign Garrett, robbed in Bucks County, xi., 512.
Van Sice, John, letter, vii., 44.
Van Swearingen, Captain of company of foot in Westmoreland County, xi., 46; Sheriff xiii., 135, 443.
Van Vlieck, Isaac, applies to be notary, xiv., 362; appointed, 363.
Vastine, Jeremiah, coroner, xiv., 555.
Vaudrevil, Gov. of Canada, Major Gen'l Abercrombie's letter to, on capitulation of Fort Wm. Henry, viii., 141; letter from, 504.
Vega, Don. F. C. De la, Governor of Havana, letters respecting negroes, v. 200.
Vetch, Col., instructions to, respecting expedition to Canada, ii., 448.
Venango, see Weningo, v., 659, 660. Number of enemy at, vi., 179; fort

described, vii., 341; fort, viii., 265; burned, 380; French at, in great confusion, 392, 396; post at, cut off, massacred, ix., 35; reservation at, for State, xvi., 47.

Vendue Masters, complaints against, in Philadelphia, iii., 91, 102.

Vendues, x., 72, 74; act to prohibit sales by, xi., 751; expressly prohibited by law, except in particular cases, xii., 4; resolutions of Supreme Executive Council against, 151; auctioneer for Philadelphia elected, 185, 525; sales of clothing by, 354; act amended, 325; laws, new, &c., xiii., 761; sale of tea, xiv., 36; Masters appointed, 38; memorial of C. Febiger, on Footman and Chaloner's, in Passyunk, xv., 592.

"Venus," privateer to receive certain articles, x., 642.

Verner, Frederick, pardoned, and to be tried, xi., 559.

Vernon, Admiral to Gov., on Spanish Squadron, in West Indies, iv., 479.

Vernon, Secretary, letters to Gov. from, respecting pirates, and a French squadron, ii., 24.

Vernon, James, signs proceedings at Hampton Court, iv., 298, 301.

Vernon, Nat., sheriff, x., 270, 742.

Vernon, Jon'n, cor'r, xv., 191, 230.

Vessels, complaints against masters of, i., 175, 343, 344; master lost overboard, 376, 379; complaint of sailors put on shore from a, 439; seized, to be tried in Chester Co., 475; registers of, ii., 90, 96, 97, 112; sickly, orders respecting, iv., 307, 314, 317, 496; not to be piloted up river, except by persons having license, 394; resolutions, &c., respecting visits of health officers, 496; arrive and land passengers, 568; to be landed at Fisher's Island, 569; Dr. Græme and Board visit, 587, 674; with passengers arrive, to be visited by Dr.s Bond and Græme, v., 100; sickly vessel, ship Euryale arrives with yellow fever, ordered below, 106, 107; to be visited by Drs. Græme and Bond, 109; certificates of physicians, 112; put in, in distress for repairs, 597, 620, 654, 656, 661; puts in, in distress, and asks to unload, vii., 347.

Vice, suppression of, instrument to be drawn for, by proprietary instructions, i., 321; and immorality, proclamation against, xiii., 434; act against, 753; defects in laws for, xiv., 352; act to prevent, xv., 587, 589, 595.

Vickers, Jesse and Solomon, recommended to mercy, robbers in Bucks county, xii., 338, 339, 343, 373.

Vickers, Solomon, claim for reward for arresting, xiv., 364, 393, 398, 459, 461.

Vickry, Thomas, coroner, xvi., 212, 498.

Victory, over French, thanksgiving for, ii., 215.

Vienna, mediation of, xii., 742.

Vallepanche, assistant engineer in plan of River, compliment to, xi., 776.

Villier, Mon. Coulon de, Fort Necessity capitulates with, vi., 52.

Vines, John, Sheriff of Sussex co., i., 58, 174.

Vining, Benjamin, a Justice, iii., 28. Petition respecting road from Philadelphia to Wiccacoa, 107.

Vining, Henry, Coroner, ix., 623, 688, 778.

Vining, John, Supreme Judge, vii., 558. Chief Justice of Supreme Court, ix., 203. Trustee of General Loan Office, 204, 206. Chosen Speaker of Assembly, 336, 400, 697. Judge of Oyer and Terminer, 581. Dies, 743; x., 108. Chief Justice of Supreme Court for lower counties dies, x., 108.

Virginia, acts of piracy, i., 562. Indian settlements in, iii., 20. Gov. Spotswood commissions Capt. Christopher Smith to confer with Indians at Albany on murder of Catawba Indians at Fort Christiana, 21. Various murders by Indians in, 22, Gov. Spotswood in Philadelphia, 30. Gov. Spotswood on Indian affairs at Albany, 82-84. Gov. Keith visits Virginia on Indian affairs, 112, 113. Agreement between Indians of, and

Virginia—
Conestogoes, 114. Samuel Robbins sent express to—his expenses, 162. Gov. Spotswood's letter to Gov. Keith—conference with Indians, 206. Letter complaining of Council on Indian conference, 209. Runaway negroes, 209-211. Indian robberies in, 210. Runaway negroes among Indians, 215. Reported war with Indians, 500. Governor to administer oath to Gov. Gordon under new commission, 526. Letter Gov. Gooch on Indian murders, 564. Speech of Gov. Gordon to Indians, and answer of their chief on the murders, 606. Indians request Council to write to Governor of, about lands, iv., 93, 94. Correspondence with Governor, 203. Demands a murderer, 245. Indian news, 245. Skirmish with Indians in, 630. Deposition of Thos. McKee, 631, 634, 635. Letter from Governor and report of C. Weiser on, 640. Col. Gooch accepts Gov. Thomas' mediation with Indians, 646. Thanks of Governor for his success, 654. Treat with Indians for lands, 655, 658. Aid in settling peace with Catawba Indians, 755, 757, 758. Letter from Governor Gooch on presents to Indians—prevalence of small-pox, v., 221. Letter to, on privateers, 254. From, on Ohio Indians and presents to, 257. Governor on man-of-war, 280. And Catawba Indians, wampum returned, 402. Correspondence with, 421. President Lee, after retirement of Gov. Gooch, 423, 424. On erection of forts against French, 423. A. Montour to interpret for, 568. Sends him to Indians at Onondago to invite them to conference at, 607. Letters to and from Gov. Dinwiddie on French and Indian affairs, 629, 630-635, 687, 712, 714, 754. Letter to Governor from Monakatootah—large number of French at Ohio, 635. Letter from W. Fairfax, 657. Commissioners to meet Indians at Carlisle, 658. Report, 664. French build two forts, 687. Man-of-war from

Virginia—
England arrives, 689. Sends men to build forts on Ohio, 712. Documents and calculations respecting boundary of Pennsylvania and, 758-767. Grant of money to encourage enlistments, 765. French and Indian affairs, vi., 1-9, 643. Correspondence with Governor, 1, 3, 5, 7, 27, 31, 55, 136, 163, 177, 294, 296, 297, 308. Forts on Ohio, 4. Speech of Half King, 31. Large force of French before fort on Ohio, 37. Forces, 138. Forts Will's creek and Redstone, 137. Assembly disappoints Governor, 165. Raise funds, 177. Troops driven from Ohio, 184. Troops from England, 200. Arrive in, 331. Correspondence with Gov Dinwiddie, vii., 31. Neutrals arrive from Nova Scotia, 32. Indian affairs in, 31. Lord Loudoun appointed to command in, 133. Letter Gov. and Council to customs on embargo, 570. Troops at Winchester—Col. Washington, 601. Indian murders, 601. Post to be continued through, viii., 71. Indians arrive at Philadelphia from Winchester, 124. Letter to Gov. Fauquier, 779. Letters to and from Governor of, ix., 305, 344. Settlers on western lands, 321-325, 344. Answer to Gov. Penn's letter, 349. Difficult to bring murderers of Indians to justice, 350. Frontier, complaints against, 460. Respecting Dr. Connolly, x., 140, 146, 148. Letters to and from Lord Dunmore, 149, 156, 158. Boundary between, and Pennsylvania, 149, 156, 158. Forts on Ohio, 158. Commissioners sent to, 170, 173. Instructions, 174. And letter to Lord D., 176. Murders on frontiers, 180. Complaints against Dr. C., 181. Report of Tilghman and Allen, Commissioners, 181. Correspondence, 182-191. Indians threaten war with, 201. Gov. Penn's message to Indians recommending peace, 204. And to Delawares, 204. Disposed for war with Indians, 208. Expedition against Shawnese, 214. Judge

Virginia—
Crawford joins, 228. James Innes to purchase second hand arms, 418, 518. Borrow sail cloth from Pennsylvania, 422. Powder to, 458. Arms to, 546. Coal brought from, 707. Boundary between, and Pennsylvania, xi., 240. Troops to work at Billingsport, 242. Disaffected persons sent to, 290, 295, 296. Habeas Corpus issues, 308, 309. Various papers respecting, 383, 394, 395, 427. Conference respecting, 435, 437, 460, 462, 468, 472, 473, 481, 483. To be discharged at Pottsgrove, 472. Letter, Delegates in Congress—resolutions, boundary line, 669. Letter of Delegates on ditto. 690. Letters to and from Gov. P. Henry, xii., 16, 263, 444. Relating to boundary line, 16, 177. Congress on dispute between Pennsylvania and, — recommendation not to sell at present, 211. Proclamation respecting dispute with, 214. Letters and various papers to Governor Jefferson, 224. Sales of land in this province by, 234. Affairs of, and Westmoreland, 250. Letter from Governor of, respecting dispute, 263. Boundaries with Pennsylvania, 287. Commiss'rs complained of, 303. Line with, 444. Decision on boundary, 476. Conference respecting, 486. Remonstrance against Vandalia or Indiana county, 491. Extension of Mason and Dixon's line, 635. Convention, British and German troops to be removed, 648. Guard for Commissioners and provisions, 700. Instructions to, 706. Pay, 714. Proceedings respecting goods seized, xiii., 2. Commissioners to run line between, and Pennsylvania, 79, 192, 203, 205, 209-253, 269, 334. Congress recommend, 150. Men to be sent to Fort Pitt, 348. Expenses of State prisoners from—report of Commissioners for running line, 510, 518. Proclamation confirming line run, 541. Letter Gov. Harrison with act of, 637. Boundary—resolutions of Assembly—report on Gov. Harrison's letter—Commissioners appointed, 685. Letter from Governor Harrison on boundary, 753. Resolution of, xiv., 38, 60, 69, 74, 114, 119. Boundary with, 56, 59, 104, 174, 211, 286, 317, 361, 518. Act of Legislature of, respecting cession of lands to the United States, 165. Governor sends entries made in their land office within Pennsylvania, 200. Repayment of loan to R. Andrews, 236. T. Hutchins, Commissioner, paid, 238. Report of Pennsylvania Commissioners, 288. Interfering claims for lands ceded by—copy of agreement to be obtained, 368. Papers to be delivered John Lukens by D. Kennedy, 394. Commissioners appointed, 399. Opening Potomac, 399. Proposes road from Fort Cumberland, 467. Letter from Governor relative to disputes from Edmund Randolph on commercial convention, 651. Letter Governor Randolph, memorial of C. S., xv., 159. Proclamation on agreement, with, 279. Letter Governor Randolph respecting a negro, 416. Copies of all Acts of Legislature of Virginia relating to lands in this State asked for by Council, 451. Ratification of Constitution received through Edmund Pendleton, 498. Call of Congress for troops against Indians on frontiers, 515. Expenses of prisoners sent via Reading, 1777, 641. Act of Congress—arrears of pay from United States, xvi., 384.

Viviat, Captain, arrives in a flag of truce with prisoners from New Orleans, viii., 124. Receives his papers, 151, 155. Sails under convoy of Captain Atkins, 156.

Voght, Christian, sale of house, &c., xiii., 79.

Vroessen, Andrew, an original purchaser from Wm. Penn, xvi., 523, 526, 529, 532, 534. Rejected claim, 539. A first purchaser from Wm. Penn—claim of Richard Peters under him, xv., 481, 485.

"Vulture," armed Boat, xi., 107.

W.

Waddie, Henry, plantation, i., 389.
Waddle, Francis, Coroner, x., 273.
Waddell, William, Coroner, xi., 373, 638. Coroner, xii., 182; xiv., 289.
Wade, Captain of State Shallop, xi., 576. To precede French Frigate, 619.
Wade, Francis, obtains contract for supplying boats, x., 423. Furnishes provisions, 485, 640.—Complaint against, for not returning paper money, xiv., 631. Petition rejected, 633. To be prosecuted as a defaulter, 640. His house to be sold at the suit of the State—title disputed—ordered to be set up at a bid fixed for the commonwealth, xv., 374. Considered, 482, 483, 520, 524.
Wade, Captain Joseph, resigns, xi., 682.
Wade, Robert, complains of authorities of Chester, for taking his property for public use, i., 440, 477.
Wadsworth, Jeremiah, Commissary General, xii., 91.
Wager, Philip, and Geo. Habucker, deed to, on Province Island, xiii., 28.
Wages not to be discounted from from rates, ii., 457.
Waggoner, Christopher, Justice, ix., 245.
Wagons, Commissioners of, vi., 775. General Stanwix, circular letter to managers of, viii., 377. Order for, xi,, 222, 588. To be provided, 291, 302, 341, 343, 349. Representation, 390, 589. Not to be impressed at Lancaster, 350. Master, pay of, 371. Change of, 589. Seized, rescued by five persons who are to be arrested, 381, 382, 385, 389. Duty, xii., 15, 25; 2, 16, 18, 22, 26, 132, 394, 433, 436. From each county, 132, 143. Pay, 182. Wanted, 227; xiv., 66, 71, 725.
Wagoners, xi., 28. Regulations, 55, 63, 64. Pay too low, 448.
Wagon Masters, xi., 398, 438, 448; xii., 2, 16, 22, 26, 379, 390, 393, 394, 432, 436, 453, 697, 700; xii., 2, 16, 22, 26, 379, 390, 393, 394, 432, 436, 453, 697, 700; xiii., 28, 66, 71.
Walbron, Major Ensign, x., 464.
Waldecker, prisoners to be delivered to Colonel Melchor, xi , 116.
Wales, death of the Prince of, address of Governor and Council to King, on, v., 527.
Walk, Indian, Teedyuscung's views of, vii., 326. Committee of Councils appointed to investigate charges, &c., 354. N. Scull's certificate, 399.
Walker, George, Coroner, ix., 548.
Walker, Jacob, Lieutenant, xii., 9.
Walker, James, Coroner, viii., 506, 781; ix., 286, 333, 398.
Walker, John, Coroner, xv., 300, 578.
Walker, Rachel, claims reward under proclamation for arrest of James Fitzpatrick, a noted robber—her examination—is paid by Council, xi., 616.
Walker, Richard, Coroner of Philadelphia, iii., 56, 108.
Wall, George, Lieutenant, xi., 453, 473. Agent for estates, 556. Troops from Bucks county, 636. Agent for forfeited estates in Bucks county, xii., 73, 78. Letter, 101. Hooper's trial, 250. Commissioners on Islands in Delaware river, xiv., 345, 460. Accounts as agent of confiscated estates, xvi., 509.
Wall, George, Jr., Sheriff, xii., 136, 510, xiii., 86, paid 295, 361, 481.
Wallace, George, Justice, xiv., 118.
Wallace, James, Coroner, ix., 547, 623, 688, 778; x., 56. Justice, deceased xi., 372.
Wallace, Michael, memorial respecting seizure of his brother as a soldier, xi., 381.
Wallace, Robert, Coroner, v., 55.
Wallace, Solomon, Coroner, ix., 333, 398, 548.
Wallace, William, Sheriff, xvi., 514, 537.
Williams, James, King's Collector for bay and river Delaware, i., 194, 285. Complaint against, 335, 336, 338. Appointed Surveyor General of Customs, 336.

Wallis, Samuel, a prisoner, act for relief of, ix., 151, 161.
Walton, Benjamin, of Bucks, confined, xi., 565.
Wampum, large belt presented by Indians, ii., 246. Its object, 247. Belts of, iii., 188, 199, 205, 209, 314, 425, 440, 443, 445, 446, 449, 572, 577, 606, 608. Belts and strings, iv., 54, 99, 307, 308, 340, 433, 434, 563, 567, 568, 569, 570, 573, 576, 579, 580, 588, 590, 642, 646-650, 665, 700-737, 747, 772. v., 9, 11, 14, 72, 84, 119, 146-151, 288, 308, 315, 348-358, 388-392, 399, 402, 405, 432-436, 450, 470, 480, 508, 530-540, 543, 599, 600, 624-634, 637, 644, 657, 665-684, 691, 731. Belts and strings returned, 402. Belts and strings, vi., 31, 36, 55, 78-129, 145-160, 180, 187, 276-287, 343, 360-365, 446, 468-475, 522, 524, 551, 566, 615, 645-646, 669, 682, 685, 751, 763, 778-784; vii., 1-7, 10, 13, 42, 56, 64-69, 80, 95, 107, 115, 137-142, 145-148, 157, 170, 189, 198, 201, 204-220, 205, 206, 224, 281, 296, 309-485,-506-551, 622, 634, 648-714, 735, 768, 770. Particular description of, used at treaty at Easton, 216; viii., 10, 40, 42, 84, 86, 100, 117, 119, 127, 128-132, 148, 150, 156, 175-223, 293-297, 306-309, 343, 382, 391, 403, 415-421, 508. Indian custom with, 119. A particular kind described, 217; viii., 429-435, 466, 484-494, 500, 586, 594, 615, 653, 670, 698, 702-707, 709,720-774; ix., 6-9, 44, 47, 77, 85, 210-234, 249-264, 328-332, 428-430, 480, 497-498, 514-543, 605, 689, 694, 736, 773, 776. Large quantity exhibited by Indian from South Carolina; x., 10, 61, 257. Analogous with writing, 9; xi., 212; xvi., 439.
Wapping or Wappinger Indians, alias River Indians, speech of Teedyuscung, respecting, viii., 217.
War, declared between England and France, iv., 689. Proclamation of Governor Thomas, 696.
War, Board of, x., 696, 777. For the land service, established — their names—their duties and powers, xi., 181. To apply to Congress for money, 182. Additions made to, 188, 194, 198, 200. New appointed, 201. Treasurer appointed, 202. Want money, 211, 218. Applies for, 221. Send resolves of Congress, 226. To make estimate of expenses of militia, 227. Money paid—two ships asked for by Navy Board, 247. Fort Island, 250. Discharged as no further necessary, with thanks, 260. Clerk continued, 261. Continental to deliver powder for Westmoreland, 394. Resolution Congress, Flag, 411. Orders respecting provisions, 425. Orders on, 497. Letter from, raising a Company in Northumberland, 508, 509. Order for sundry articles, 556. Plan of river Delaware, 587. Of loan of arms asked of, xii., 95. Letter to, commission for two young men recommended by Chevalier de Luzerne, 116, 117. Claim of C. Wurtz, Town Major of Lancaster referred to. Guards for prisoners, 116. Letter, 215. To rectify dates of Commissions, 241. Ask for trophies of War, 242. Letter respecting Chaplain Milsheimer, 263. Cannon from Fort Island, 312. Respecting Captain Joel, 495. To receive arms, 509. Muskets distributed to States, 702. Supplies, 707. On Wyoming papers, 741. Requisition, 759. Case of B. Ford, xiii., 96. Barracks 128. Letter, 449, 459.
War, Council of, at New York, vii., 23, 31. Quaker address against, 83.
War, departm't, establ'd, xvi., 133.
Ward, Capt., vii., 230.
Ward, ensign, surrenders fort on Forks of Monongahela, vi., 29.
Ward, John, ensign, xii., 31.
Ward, Moses, xi., 576.
Wardens of Philadelphia, petition on pilotage, &c., ix., 366, 367, 388. Act respecting, 550, 593, 597, 729. Respecting, x., 70, 72, 76, 239, 243, 259, 261, 295, 297. Committee of safety, ask to borrow money from, 295, 296. Pilots,

358; to employ patrols, xi., 42. Appointed, 538, 549, 557. Order respecting wood, xii., 190. To order watch for gaol, 259; to sell lots, 726. To sell lands, xvi., 6. George Honey, clerk, 205. New chosen, xiii., 98. Light house in danger of being washed away, 500. Order on Peter Reeve, late treasurer, for books and papers, 102;—buy city lots, 218. To have obstructions removed, 595, 671. Elected, 721. Paid, 739. To meet council respecting chevaux-de-frise, xiv., 58, 73. To inspect goods on ship Clementine, 77. And ship Fortune, 79. Letter to Council and conference on chevaux-de-frise, 79. Appropriation for improving Delaware river, 105. Inspection of goods, 109. reports of sales of goods, 110, 114, 115. To deliver vessels purchased to Hollingsworth and Donaldson, 119. Council agrees to indemnify them for expenses on Delaware, 120. Removal of buoys—and proclamation, 122. Expended on Delaware river improvements—J. Donaldson, resigns, and Joseph Bullock, appointed, 151 Payment to, 162. Certificate to Donaldson and Hollingsworth, 199. Pay for removing chevaux-de-frise, 212. elected, 230. Certificates to Donaldson and Hollingsworth, 241. Accounts, 309. Hearing before council, 323. Conference on improvement of Delaware, 325, 356. their office, 444. paid towards erecting piers by Thomas Davis, 458. To purchase land at Marcus Hook, for piers, 460. Plan of piers, 464. Accounts, 467. Their office in Front st. New proposals for piers, 468, 474. Thomas Conarroe, to build piers, 479. To and from Hollingsworth and Donaldson, 500. Elected, 555. Purchase of a wharf at Cape May, for a beacon, 578. Report on Wm. Smith's wharf, 599. Accounts, 632. Appropriation for improving river Delaware, 640. Pay for support of lighthouse, &c., in Delaware Bay, xv., 73. Elected, Phillip Wager and Andrew Bunner, 98. Funds for improving the Delaware, 197. To examine and report on claims of Thomas Conarroe, for building piers at Marcus Hook, 228. Report on T. Conarroe, 233. Wardens ask for a burying ground for strangers, 273. Appointed, 322. N. Falconer resigns--James Montgomery appointed, 337. F. Gurney, resigns—Wm. Allibone, appointed, 341. Office for, 402. Office rent paid, 519. Board established—appointed viz., Nesbit, Craig, Allibone, Falconer, Paisely, Gurney, and Benezet, 559. J. Craig, resigns — Capt. Leeson Simmons chosen, 582. Respecting pilots, 597. Public lots in Southwark, xvi., 140. N. Falconer, resigns, 352.

Warder, Jeremiah, sells salt, xii., 191. To be seized, xi., 284.

Warner, Col. ————, to rendezvous at Darby, xi., 301.

Warrant to sheriff to quarter troops in Philadelphia, vii., 362.

Warrants and Surveys, record of, viii., 337, 338, 345, 349, 369. Referred to Judges and Lawyers, 339, 342. Report on, 345, 361. New bill, 370. Passed, 374. Opinion, 539, 541. New Bill, 674.

Warren, Admiral, letter, v., 6.

Warren, Commodore, on expedition to Cape Breton, iv., 762, 763.

"Warren," gun boat, x., 328. Lt. Symonds, now Lt. Hugh Montgomery, x., 437, 501, 506, 511.

Warren, John, coroner, viii., 402.

Warrans Geo., meeting of Indians near, ii., 509.

Washington County, formed out of Westmoreland — Thomas Scott, appointed prothonotary — James Marshall, Lieutenant, and John Cannon and Daniel Lite, sub-lieutenants, xii., 681--James Marshall, Register of Wills, Recorder deeds, and lieut., 683. Guard for Commissioners to run line between Virginia and Pennsylvania, 700. Justices, xiii., 38, 122, 248, 263, 264. Courts, 38. Sheriffs, 134, 443, 740. Elections, 443, 740, Coroners, 134, 443, 740. Censors, 740. Agents for confiscated

Washington County—xiii. estates, appointed, 139. Accounts of Lt. James Marshall, 144. Lt. Connor resigns, 149. Ammunition for, 150. Lieutenants, 158, 168, 240. Other officers, 168. Military officers, 160, 168. Supplies, 165. A company of rangers for defence, 168. Taxes, 206. Irregular military elections, 245. Militia to guard in running Virginia line, 253. Failure to elect justices, 264. Pay for supplies, 265. Pay to, 302. Bounties, 308. Trials by special commission, 337. Election, 403. Court house, 439. Land purchased for, 531. Militia ordered out at call of General Irvine, 531. Pay to lieutenant, 533, 534. Capt. John Hughes, discharged from, xiii., 539. Extract of letter from Gov. Harrison of Virginia, 639. Election, 740. Complaints on magistracy, 799. James Marshall lieutenant, letter, xiv., 165. Execution in order, 203. Company of rangers, Capt. Hughes, paid, 215. Militia, Capt. Craig Ritchie, 216. Justices of the Court of Common Pleas, 224, 367. Complaint against Commissioners of Taxes, 235, 597. Elections, 244, 563, 597. Represen's., 244. Sheriff 244, 597. Justices, 689. J. Marshall resigns as register and recorder, 245. Thomas Stokely appointed, 260. Eighteen penny tax, 267. Division of Peter's Township proposed—to be named Dickinson, 275. Capt. Hughes' company of rangers, 322, 323. Freight paid, 456. Confiscated estates in, 607. Justice, 164. Town of Washington into a separate election district, 634, 653 provisions for Militia on frontiers of, xv., 8. Division of Smithtownship 76. Elections, 103, 119. Councillor, 103. Sheriff, 103, 121, 646. Coroner, 103, 121, 646. Report of Mr. Dale and letter of James Marshall, 107. Justices, 120, 266, 279, 450, 483, 552, 589, 591. Division of Peters Township, 126. Dorsey Pentecost, suspended as Judge on account of removal, 124. Collector of excise, John Dodd, 132. Murders by Indians in—arms, &c., sent to, 317. Expense of transporting arms and amunition from Philadelphia to, 382. Division of Cumberland and Morgan Townships, 450. Allowed a third justice, 483. Division of Townships, 507. Repair of public arms, and militia services, 517. A portion taken to Alleghany County, 552. Contested election, 589. Justices, xvi., 50, 227, 237, 255, 319, 411, 536, 428, 536. Sureties, 32. Prothonotary, 35, 41, Militia, 39, 42. Election of Justices illegal and set aside, 44. Division of districts, 103. Petition against register, provisions for military, 147. Sheriff, 212, 514, 537. Coroner, 212, 514, 537. Division of Townships for election of Justices, 226, 228, 259. Gen. Washington's land in—militia, 227. Payments for various services on frontiers of, 228. Payments to militia, &c., for, 234. Depredations by Indians in, 264. Militia, pay for defence, 283. Indian outrages, 306. Lieutenant authorized to call out militia, for frontiers, 340. Call for militia returns, 425. Fees for tavern licenses, 460. Militia, 460. Thos. Stockly, register and recorder, 515. John Hoge, elected to Senate, resigns as justice, 536.

Washington Fort, L. I., Margaret Corbin rewarded for her bravery, whose husband was killed at her side, xii., 34. Pay for arms, &c., lost at, xiv., 443; xvi., 535.

"Washington," Galley, xi., 701.

Washington, General George, letters to and from, vi., 29, 37. Surrender of fort in the forks by Mr. Ward, 28. Arrives with a detachment, 29. Progress-makes roads, 29. Large force of French at Ohio, 37. Defeated at Great Meadows—detailed by Col. Innes, 50, 138. Defeat, 177. Davison's account of, 195. Raising militia in Virginia, vii., 601. Letters, 603, 604. Letter from Gov. Denny to, viii., 56. British Officers sent to his camp, x., 306. Asks

Gen. Washington—
for powder for camp at Cambridge, 330. Letter to, from committee, asking for engineers to erect fortifications, 604. Flints for his army, 632. In Jersey—cannon from State House yard sent to, xi., 24. Officers sent to, 24, 25. Orders troops from Bucks Co., 43. To call out troops from Bucks and Northampton, 54. Letter from to council of safety, 177. Letters from, 197, 228, 436, 457, 490, 650, 730. On fortifying the Delaware, 228. Inteligence from, 232. Asks for a survey of the river—persons appointed to make it, 250. Requested to send Michael Huffnagle to Lancaster, 263. Engages the enemy, 301. Written to about recruiting officers, 401. Recommends persons to recruit, 419. Address to inhabitants New Jersey, Pennsylvania, &c., 428. Respecting cattle, 429. Protection for Mrs. Pemberton's wagons, 457. Order for horses at Lancaster, 476. Arms needed, 491. Receives account of evacuation of Philadelphia, 520. Instructions on 4th July, 523. Requires troops to be sent from Philadelphia to the main army, 568. Draft of Delaware, 587. Clothing sent to, 607. Asks for a guard for prisoners, 626. On supplying spirits, 654. Consul asks for his portrait to be taken by Peale, 671. Taking vigorous measure to protect frontiers, 724. Letters to and from, xii., 8. Wagons to transport provisions, 26. Letters to and from, 8, 32, 43, 89, 90, 92, 203, 204, 227, 262, 313, 321, 352, 370, 387. Return of Pennsylvania troops, 32. Men to be urged on to Major General Sullivan, 43. List of officers—depositions of Col. Hannum's escape from enemy, sent to, 114. Calls out militia, 123, 129, 144. Opinion in regard to officers and men in Col. Hazen's regiment, 262. Names posts for supplies, 313. Desertions in army referred to 316. Disposition of

Gen. Washington—
supplies, 321. Orders Captain Craig to Pittsburg, 330. On supplies from State, 335. Recommends promotion of Michael Everly from Serjeant to Ensign for services, 352. Address to soldiery from enemy, his situation and difficulties, 370. Pressing for recruits — critical state of army, 387. Letters, 392, 394, 398, 404, 498, 545, 574, 591. Light horse, 392. Wagons, 394, 398. Enemy has left New Jersey, 407. Ensigns to be appointed, 428. Demand for horses, 446. Countermands march of troops, 460. Want of provisions, capture of, in a prize, 474, 476, 498. Recommends Ensigns, 482, 483. Against temporary enlistments, 517. Clothing for army, 545. Deposit of provisions, 574. Relief of Wyoming, 591. Want of provisions, enemy about to leave New York for Delaware, 706. On memorial of Proctor's officers, 727. Calls for men, 742. For four battalions of infantry, 754. Transfer of officers, 761. Wants, 300 riflemen, 778; Going to move troops, requires vessels to transport, xiii. 41. Col. Tilghman—his aid brings news of surrender of Yorktown by Lord Cornwallis, 94. Address from Supreme Executive Council to, on capture of Lord Cornwallis, and answer, 130, 131. On supplies, 184. Recruits for Van Heer's troop, 188, 202, 211, 221. Election of Justices, 264. Consulted about expedition against Indians, 356, 362. Against it, 380. Letters to, on abandonment of post at Wyoming, 399. Indian expedition, 408. Letter respecting passes to be sent to Dobb's Ferry, 419. Gen. Washington asked to procure a passport for flag vessel for New York with provisions for our prisoners, 446. Sends a passport from Admiral Digby, 457. Incursions of savages stopped, 502. Half pay and commutation by Congress to officers, 603. A returned captive, 603. Address of council to, on

Gen. Washington—
peace, &c., 765. His answer, 767. Agents for sale of confiscated estates in, 774. Portrait of, xiv. 265. Celebration of birth day, xvi., 4. Arrangements for his reception, 25. Congratulatory address of Council to, 57, 58. His answer, 59. His land in Washington Co., 227. Powder for celebrating his arrival in Philadelphia, 465.

"Washington," gun boat, launch of, x., 314, 407, 488, 505.

"Washington, ship General," formerly General Monck — allowed to make a voyage for Superintendent of finance. Commission to Captain Joshua Barney, &c., xiii., 283, 352, 354, 361.

Wasp, continental Schooner, Capt. Alexander, takes Brig Betsey from Virginia, x., 563, 777.

Watch to be set at Cape Henlopen for pirates, ii., 23.

Watching in Philadelphia, soldiers to be exempt from, ii., 204.

Watkins, Major, lead and tin for buttons, xi., 440.

Watkins, Wm., Captain of a guard boat, x., 583.

Watkins, Wm., applies to sweep Delaware River rejected, xii., 21. Authorized, 32, 34.

Watson, David, Commissioner to buy provisions, xi., 423. Justice, xii., 231. Depositions respecting, 307.

Watson, James, Coroner, xvi., 204.

Watson, Lieut. Colonel, x., 686.

Watson, Luke, charges against, i., 179, 180, 213. Takes his seat in Council, 222. His hogs killed, 224, 226. Sheriff of Sussex county, ii., 101.

Watson, Thos., of Bucks, iii., 233. A Commissioner for building a new Court house and prison for Bucks county, 241.

Wattom, John, Coroner, ix., 57.

Watts, Colonel Fred., payment to, x. 688, xi., 88. Elected to Assembly, resigns as Justice, xii., 170. Sub-Lieutenant, 322. Paid, xiv., 348. Storage on arms, xv., 565. As Councilman, xv., 300, 653, xvi., 294.

Waugh, Patrick, convicted of murder, xvi., 497, 519. Respited, 520, 536, 542.

Waughhaughy, Cherokee Chief, speech of vii., 520, 553.

Wayne, Anthony, recommended to Congress as Colonel of a battalion, x., 442. Elected, 443. Major to, appointed, 460. Applies for money for battalion, 518. D. Jones, Chaplain to, 551. Attends Council, and presents situation of army approaching city, xi., 253. Recommends by name recruiting officers, 464, 477. Arms for, 490, 557. Conference of Assembly and Council, on a vote of thanks to, and Pennsylvania line for their important services at Stony Point, xii., 124, 135. Letter, 437. Recommends Ensign Everly as Lieutenant, 483. Others for promotion, 550, 586. On meeting of Pennsylvania line, 593. To furnish names of officers going South, 719, 739. Decides rank of an officer, xiii., 25. Regiment, 671. Pay as Council of Censors, xiv., 167.

Wears, &c., against erecting on rivers, iv., 18. Views of Assembly on, 20, 23, 284.

Weatherby, Benjamin, paid for land bought by Congress for fortifications at Billingsport, x., 645.

Weaver, Jacob, sheriff, viii., 402; ix., 57, 199. A justice of Berks county removed, xii., 635.

Webb, Brigadier-General, vii., 714.

Webb, Henry, wounded by an Indian, iv., 413, 420, 447. (William,) 573.

Webb, James, Jr., sheriff, ix., 398, 547, 623. To receive Stump and servant from Carlisle, and send to Chester county, 442.

Webb, Lieutenant John, of Boat Bull Dog, discharged, suspended, and restored, x., 643.

Webb, Robert, Marshal of Admiralty Court seizes goods, i., 539.

Webb, William, appointed notary public, xiii., 13.

Weber, Christian, justice, xv., 124.

Webster, Pelatiah, receives pay for salt, xii., 316.

Weed, Captain Elijah, storekeeper of provisions, xi., 423.

Weickart, Geo., justice, xiv., 271.

Weights and measures, bill for proposed, i., 66, 128, 466. Seal for John White, sealer, 514. Regulation of, iii., 372. Standard purchased by Chester county. Regulator of, appointed by Governor, iv. 507. Regulated, xiii. 632.

Weiser, Benjamin, a Captain, x., 634. Justice, xi., 405.

Weiser, Conrad, comes with Indians to Philadelphia, iii., 425. Interprets at Philadelphia, 435, 438, 500. Reward to, 447, 598, 607. Interpreter for the province with the Indians, iv., 56. Pay to, 86, 96. Indian presents to, 88, 245, 576. In Philadelphia, 500, 560. Letter of Governor to, respecting Indian skirmish in Virginia, 635. Report on, 640–646. Second report, 646–650. Instructions for, on embassy to Onondago, 655. Report of journey there, 660–669. Sent to Delaware Indians at Shamokin to demand murderers, 676, 678, 679. His report, 680–684. Attends treaty at Lancaster—his Indian name, 733. To invite Indians to Governor's house, 747. And Virginia, 757. Letter from Onondago, 768. Report and journal to, 778–779. To employ scouts to watch Indians, v., 2. Sent to inform Indians at Shamokin of death of John Penn, 73 Letters from—meets Indians at Chamber's mill, 83. Report of his message, &c., to Indians at Shamokin, 84. To be consulted, 119, 120. Letter in reply, 121. Letter giving account of his visit to Indians, 136. To be advised of presents sent to John Harris, 139. Coming to Philadelphia, 140. Arrives, 145. Statement respecting Indians from Ohio, 148. Letter from, on Indian affairs, 162. Arrives with Indians at Paxton, 166. Letter from, 166. Presents for Indians, 197. Letter from Tulpehochen, 212. Respecting Ohio Indians, 212. Answer to, by R. Peters, 211. Attends with Shekalemy, 222. Writes of robbery by James Denny, of horses from Indians, 228. Presents a message from the Six Nations, 284. At Philadelphia, 290. Instructions to, 290, 304. At Lancaster, 306. Journal to Ohio, 348–358. In Philadelphia, 388. In Cumberland county, 431. To Secretary, 467. Journal to Onondago, 470–480, 528, 541. Letter, 517. Speaks of his son "Sammy," 543. To be consulted about missionaries to Indians, 576. Governor Clinton to, 642. His journal to the Mohawks, 642–648. At Carlisle, 670. Distances, 730. Consulted on Connecticut dispute—his opinion, 775. Sent to Shamokin, vi., 24. Takes message to Indians, 25. Letter to Governor H.,—report of visit to Shamokin, &c., 35, 36. Speech to Indians, 82. At treaty at Albany, renders important service, 117. Instructions to, on journey to Auckquick, 147. Letter from, to Governor H., 148. Journal to, 150–160. Letters respecting Connecticut, 215, 249, 291. Sent for, 331. In Philadelphia, 340. Returns homeward from Ostuacky, purchases provisions, &c., for Indians, 446. Respecting Indians, &c., 469. Letter about Indian women from Auckwich, 494. On catholics, 503, 533. On Indians, 535. History of Owandot Indians, 550–553. Conference with and presents, 553. Letter to Governor from, 615. Letters to and from, 640, 647, 649, 650, 652, 656, 729, 760, 762. Indian murders, 649–662. Intelligence from, and others, respecting their sad condition, 667. Arrives with Indians, 681. On Indian affairs in Northampton county, 760, 762. Letters to and from, vii., 35, 302, 308, 619, 735. Report of proceedings with Indians at Harris' ferry, 33, 106. At Philadelphia, 137, 182. Consulted about fort at Adjouquay, the land not having been purchased, 182–184. At treaty at Easton, 206. Express to be sent to, 222. Complains of Sowers' newspaper, 245. Sick, sends son Sammy to interpret, 302. And New Castle arrive,

Weiser, Conrad—
307. Memorand'm of conversation with Tittamy of Teedyuscung's remarks about lands, 431. Memorandum on Indian affairs made by, 489. At treaty at Lancaster, 517. Croghan, answers Indians, 542. At Easton, opinion of Teedyuscung, 658. To take management of building fort and houses for Delawares at Wyoming, 734. His opinion about offering a price for scalps, 735. Sick, objects to building, 735. Trading house at Fort Augusta, Rum, &c., 735. Excused, 736. In Philadelphia, viii., 113. Sends a memorandum of news, &c., from Indians, 118. Advised with on messages to Indians, 128. R. complains of Teedyuscung's conduct at Easton, 172. And Peters settle for lands with Indians, 219. Being sick sends son to Fort Augusta to confer with John Chickasalary, 457. His son makes a speech to Indians at Shamokin, ix., 619; x., 177.

Weiser, Samuel, coroner, ix., 57, 199, 285.

Weiss, Colonel, xi., 452.

Weiss, Dr. Daniel, dies intestate, escheated, xv., 482.

Weiss, Jacob, paid, xiv., 348.

Weiss, Lewis, sale to Mr. Holker, xiii., 9. Justice, xv., 23, 26.

Weiss, Philip, forestaller, xi., 650. Assists Longschamp to escape, xiv., 184.

Weitzel, John, to make purchases, x., 733; xi., 207, 278, 538. Complaint against, 704. Northumberland county, letter from, xii., 57. To, about Indians, 64. Militia fines, 243. Agreement for rations for Northumberland, xiii., 428, 519–536, 743. For provisions for Wyoming, xvi., 354.

Welawanung or Big Horn, ix, 638.

Welch, William, sent as commissioner to New York to complain against Lord Baltimore and his agents, i., 103, 104. To give in his account, 105. Appointed commissioner to receive public aid, 111. Justice of peace, 112. A judge, 119. Dead, 119.

Wells, James, sheriff, ix., 398, 548. Justice, xv., 24.

Wells, John, justice, iii., 531.

Wells, Richard, pilot boat, x., 567.

Wells, Richard, asks for lot on Arch street notwithstanding action of Congress, rejected, xii., 353. Claims lots and liberty lands, xiii., 9, 49, 321, 326. Claims city lot, xiv., 359, 458, 464; xv., 344, 347, 349, 351. Decision, 359, 482, 487, 500, 524, 622. Memorial relative to Comptroller, &c., xvi., 27, 28, 34, 40, 47. Death of mother, and postponement, 49. Case continued, 52, 53, 55, 57.

Wells, William, coroner, viii., 403.

Welner, Colonel, complaint against, xii., 305.

Welsh, interfere in Philadelphia election, i., 268. Petition for a ferry at William Powells, 478.

Welsh, Francis, letter relating circumstances attending rescue of a vessel seized by Custom-house officers, x., 231.

Welsh Tract, inhabitants complain against Indians, i., 162, 202. And Chester county, 263, 265. Not in Philadelphia county, 265. A barony, 265, 266, 267. Inhabitants petition for road from Goshen to Philadelphia—Commissioners appointed, ii., 111. Petition for a ferry, 276. Opposed, 277, 289. Settlers seized by Sheriff of Maryland, 393.

Wendall, Abraham, letter from Tsanandowas' country to Governor, and his answer, iii., 609.

Weningo, Indian town, location of, v., 659, 660. John Frazer, gunsmith's shop at, 660. Casewago, twenty miles above, 660. Fort near, 698. Course and distance from Ohio, &c., 753, 763.

Wentworth, Brigadier-General, in Cuba, appoints Captain William Hopkins to levy soldiers in Pennsylvania—proclamation allowing, iv., 499.

West, Martin, appointed master of ammunition vessel, x., 584.

West, Justice, of Carlisle, sends ac-

count of murder of Dr. John, (Indian,) viii., 455.

West, William, gives information respecting distances and latitudes, &c., of various places near Ohio, v., 761. Commissioner to Lancaster, vii., 97. Member of Assembly, 636. Made Major, x., 768.

West, William, Jr., proclamation against, xii., 496. To give security, 558. Deputy Clothier General, to be prosecuted, 599.

Western Road, xv., 273, 274, 327, 330, 353-355. Report of survey to Bedford, 330.

Western Territory, Congress propose to lay off into States, xiv., 471.

West Jersey—(see New Jersey.)

Weston, Anthony, his case and punishment, i., 92.

West Point, letter from Col. Wm. Williams of Third Pennsylvania Battalion—list of promotions of officers in consequence of Captain Lt. Henderson being made Captain, xii., 88, 89.

Westmoreland County formed out of Bedford, x., 77. Arthur St. Clair appointed Prothonotary, &c., 77. Justices of, 78, 142. Sheriffs elected, 106, 212, 273. Coroners elected, 106, 212, 273.—Condition of things—Dr. Conolly's address to magistrates of, 167. Answer to, 167. Deposition of Henry Read, 168. Letter, W. Crawford, respecting disturbances in, from Virginia, 165. Letters, Æneas Mackay, D. Smith, Andrew McFarlane, 169. Letter, Gov. Penn to magistrates, 171. Commissioners sent to Lord Dunmore, 173, 174, 176. Murders committed in—condition of County, 180. Require ammunition, 181. Correspondence between Commissioners and Governor Dunmore on boundary, 181-195. Money to build court-house and garrison, 198. Affairs in—town to be built at Kittaning, 201. Forcible release of prisoners by Christy, Girty and Dr. Conolly, 227. Dr. Conolly's proclamation against tax collectors, &c., 227.

Westmoreland Co.
Judge Crawford joins Virginia against Pennsylvania, 228. Deposition of Samuel Whitesides, jailor, 228. Letters from magistrates, 234. Deposition of John Carnahan, Sheriff, 235. Letter to Earl of Dartmouth, 236. Powder sent to, 346. To be written to by Committee respecting arms, 411, 417. Petition to have powder remain, 449. Ask for ammunition, 525, 597. Two Companies raised for defence of frontiers considered as militia in actual service, 655. Pay of troops in, 711. Members of Convention to purchase arms, 724, 726. Company of foot—Captain Van Swearingen to defend, xi., 46. Col. Proctor's battalion of, 110. Powder and lead for, 114. Prothonotary, 187, 430. Justices, 220, 773, 774. Sheriffs, 373, 377, 638. Coroner, 235, 373, 638. Records taken to and secreted at Lancaster—supposed by late Prothonotary, Michael Huffnagle, 252. Col. Proctor, paymaster, 304. Complain of Indian depredations, 342, 347, 382. Money due militia, 392. To be paid Colonel Archibald Lockrey, 392. Powder for, 394. Money sent to, 477, 511. Hanna's Town, 477. Money to Colonel John Proctor, 576. Military stores for, 716. Letter, Thomas Scott, General McIntosh and A. Lockrey, relating to frontiers, 773. Money for—Justice appointed—limited to one, 781. Lieutenants recommended by A. Lockrey, and appointed, xii., 73. Distressed state of, 75. Elections, 182, 336, 540. Sheriff, 182, 540. Coroner, 182, 540. Colonel John Proctor, paymaster. 182. Sales of land in, by Virginia, 234. Petition for defence, 246. And Virginia, 250. Conduct of Virginia Commissioners complained of, 303. Justices, 336. Commissioners of purchases, 371. Lieutenants change in Rangers, 373. Ammunition for, 385. Justices, 391, 482. Commiss'rs of purchases, 465. Accounts, 487. Ap-

Westmoreland Co. pointments, 554. Inquiry respecting J. Perry, Commissioner, &c., 648. Report on, 653. Removed —D. Duncan appointed, 654. Purchases, 659. Officers of volunteer company appointed, 662. Washington formed out of it, 681. Ensigns appointed, xiii., 53. Ammunition for, 150. A. Lockery's commission annulled, 155. Agreement for supplies for, 157. Election, 157, 158, 244, 419, 730. Censors, 730. Sheriffs, 158, 419, 730. Coroners, 158, 419, 730. Prothonotary, 158. Edw. Cooke appointed Lieutenant, 167. And Alexander McClean Sub-Lieutenant — Recruits, 168. Clothing, 179. Taxes, 206. Justice, 244, 517. Guard to run Virginia line, 253. Rating paid for, 288. Call of militia, 313. Trials by special Commissioners, 337. Lieutenant Campbell, 361. Pay to militia, 423. Estate of Anthony Yeldal, 516. Militia ordered out at call of General Irwine, 531. Purchases in, 542. Justice, 677, 700. Letter, trustees of, 698. Justices, xiv., 118, 180, 227, 257, 262, 561, 567. Provisions for, 197, 211. Captain Stokely paid for Rangers, 245. Eighteen-penny tax, 267. Lot for court-house near Hanna's town, 287. Sheriffs, 289, 656. Coroners, 289, 656 Confiscated estates in, 289, 290, 291. Memorial, Isaac Craig, 291. Reports on militia accounts, 312. Lieutenant Thomas Mason, 314. A division proposed, 372. Collector of excise, 400. Flour inspector, 445. Proceedings in Court in a case of hog stealing suspended, 452. Election, 563. John Hughes resigns as Justice, 567. Militia fines—Edward Cook Lieutenant of County, 587. Execution of Joseph Ross ordered, 588. Confiscated estates in, 607. Pardons, 633. Register and Recorder, Jas. Hamilton, 655. Divided—pay to troops, 663. Collector of excise, xv., 54, 132. Fort Preservation built, 66. Division of Pitt township, 88. Sheriff, 109, 125, 302, 580. Coroner, 109, 125, 302, 580. Representatives, 119. Justices, 44, 125, 271, 473, 552. Collector of excise, 173. Lieutenant of County, 173. Wm. Courtney's estate, 175. Patent to J. Hughes for estate of Alexander Ross, 191. Road from Bedford to Loyal Hanna, 346, 353, 355, 546. Fees of Collector of excise returned, 461. Justice Finley resigns, 473. Sheriffs, xvi., 92, 215, 521. Coroners, 215, 521. Collector of excise, John Giffin, 162. Complaint against M. Huffnagle, prothonotary, 162, 163, 466. Division of townships, 167. Councillor, 216. Justices, 226. Memorial from, on excise, 300. Taxes, 460. Chas. Campbell, Lieutenant, 462. R. Butler, elected to Assembly, resigns as Justice, 537. Militia, 538. Colonel Archibald Lockrey Lieutenant in 1777, 538.

Wetherspoon, D., sends news of robbery by French and Spaniards, v., 89.

Wharf, to be built on Delaware at Chestnut street, i., 267.

Wharton, Capt. ———, of militia, x., 649.

Wharton, Carpenter, Commissary of provisions, x., 408.

Wharton, James, Rope-walk, x., 706.

Wharton, John, Coroner, iii., 387, 416, 575, 615; iv., 86. To build boats, &c., x., 283 By model, 284. To be called "Experiment," 289. "Washington," 296. Launched, 314. To accompany, with instructions, Major French to camp, 305, 306.

Wharton, Joseph, petition for negro, xii., 501.

Wharton, Samuel, witness at Trenton, xiii., 442. Justice, xiv., 108.

Wharton, Thomas, Sr., to be seized, xi., 283.

Wharton, Thomas, Jr., member of Committee of Safety, to procure powder and saltpetre, x., 282. President of Council of Safety, 673. President of Supreme Executive Council, xi., 373, 375. Proclamations, 176, 299, 362, 369,

429, 438, 446, 483. Dies at Lancaster—order of funeral, &c., 499. To be published, 500. Frame for picture of, xii., 441. Late President, his account books, 594. Pay to executors, xiii., 707. Claim against executors, xv., 141. Executors of, indemnification, xvi., 4.
Whealon, Capt. ———, x., 689.
Wheat, exports of, iv., 491-495.
Wheat, John Clayton, invents a machine for threshing, ix., 698.
Wheat, from United States, prohibited in England on account of Hessian fly, xv., 524.
Wheeler & Wiley, piers, xi., 109.
Wheeler, Gilbert, i., 588.
Wheeler, Samuel, works at chevaux-de-frise, xi., 5.
Whiskey, ordinance against distilling from grains, xi., 338. Act of Maryland against, 647.
White, Capt. ———, Committee to prepare rules for boats, x., 327.
White, George, Coroner of Bucks county, i., 228.
White, John, Speaker of Assembly, imprisoned, i., 292. Clerk of Court N. C., petition, 327, 387. Decision, 327. And recommendation, 329. Asks for county seal and records, 333. To be reinstated as clerk, 339. Sheriff dead—rent of jail to be paid, 445. Sealer of measures, 514. Appointed by Treasurer to settle accounts between Pennsylvania, Delaware, Maryland and United States, xv., 238.
White, Mr. ———, Paymaster, xi., 266.
White, Robert, member of Committee of Safety, to procure powder and saltpetre, x., 282. To have boats built, 283. Concerned in illegal practices—his house to be searched, xii., 199.
White, William, Bishop of Pennsylvania, letter on marriage licenses, xv., 614.
Whitebread, Wm., pay bonds, &c., to city, xiv., 368.
Whitehead, James, keeper of work house—order for removal of prisoners to new gaol, x., 429. Account, 437. Ensign, 704. Coroner, xi., 596.
Whitehead, James, Jr., Coroner, ix., 547, 623.
Whitehill, John, Censor, xiii., 722. Council, xiv., 267.
Whitehill, R., Commissioner to Congress at Yorktown, xi., 435.
Whitesides, Abraham, Justice, xiv., 656.
Whitesides, Peter, allowed to sell damaged goods by auction, xii., 404.
Whitesides, Samuel, jailor, deposition respecting attack, x., 228.
Whitlow, Matthew, 1st Lieutenant of Matrosses, x., 483.
Whitman, Adam, Coroner, viii., 781.
Whitman, Michael, estate sold, xii., 277.
Whitman, Wm., memorial for a pension as a prisoner of war from battle of Germantown, xvi., 217, 218.
Whitpaine, John, Assembly to meet in his "great front room, ii., 26. Occupied by Joseph Shippen—Assembly to meet in his "great chamber," 129.
Whitpaine, John, heirs of, claim city lots, xiii., 507.
Whitpain, William, midshipman on ship Montgomery, resigns, x., 712.
Whitpain, Zach., brings report from England of invasion, i., 246.
Whitsaken Mill, no road to, iii., 50.
Whitwell, Francis, member of first Council, i., 57.
Whiwhinjac, King of Gannawese Indians, his speech, iii., 216.
Whorekills, ancient port of, at Lewes, to be settled in regard to duties, i., 205. French privateer lands men at, ii., 448.
Whyte, Robert, member of committee and to have floating battery built, x., 437. Chevaux-de-frise, 648.
Wiatt, Thomas, Ensign, xii., 31.
Wiccacoa, road from, to Philadelphia, Commissioners to lay out, iii., 106. Petition to lay out a new one—Commissioners to lay out, 547. Vessel not to pass, viii., 39. Samuel Mifflin commands, 39. Guards to be reinforced from Otway's regiment, 39. Fort at Philadelphia to be guarded and cannons to be loaded

to avoid evasions of embargo, viii., 147. Meadow banks to be kept in order, 677, 683, 684. Battery guns fire royal salute for peace between France and Spain, ix., 42. Also in compliment to Gov. John Penn, 72. Embankments of meadows, Moyamensing, 577, 580.

Wickes, Capt. Benj., xii., 354, 385.

Wigfall, Samuel, advance to, for making gun locks, x., 417. Contract with, 421.

Wigton, Lieut. John, xii., 718.

Wikoff, Isaac, case between, and Robert Shewell, xi., 670.

Wikoff, Peter, auctioneer of Philadelphia, xv., 197.

Wilcocks, Alexander, a Justice, x., 155. Member of Committee of Safety, 493. Commonwealth *vs.*, xiv., 33.

Wilcocks, Capt. ———, x., 503.

Wilcocks, John, x., 533. To load produce to buy powder, x., 413. Applies for pass for vessel with provisions, xi., 762, 764. Deed for lot on Province Island, xiii., 549,

Wilcocks & McMurtrie, hold British property, xi., 645. Salt in Prichard's store, 654. Letter, 661, 670.

Wilcox, Mark, for paper, xiii., 515. Paper seized and used by Council in 1777, 536. Furnishes paper for new loan certificates, xv., 10. To lay out a road, 425, 445.

Wilcox, Dr. Robert, xi., 230.

Wiler, Capt. Jacob Lawson, xi., 122.

Wilkie, Capt. ———, xii., 53.

Wilkins, Colonel ———, impresses wagons—remonstrance of Assembly against, ix., 684. Carriages impressed, x., 17, 69.

Wilkins, Dr. John, Councillor, xvi., 210[2].

Wilkinson, Amos, 2d Lieutenant, x., 457. To distribute certain articles, xi., 739, 740.

Wilkinson, Gen. ———, xiii., 266. Buys J. Galloway's land in Bedford, 450.

Wilkinson, James, Adjutant-General, leaves State—J. Armstrong, Jr., appointed in his place, with rank of Brigadier-General, xiv., 217. His resignation, 252.

Wilkinson, James, Clothier-general, xii., 87, 238, 462.

Wilkinson, Thomas, a pirate, convicted by Admiralty Court to be executed on Windmill Island—his body in chains on Mud Island, xii., 730. Respited in consequence of a doubt of the legality of his sentence, the Chief Justice being a member of Congress, 732.

Wilkson, Thomas, cost of a gibbet for, xiii., 76.

Will, Col. Wm., storekeeper of provisions at Lancaster, xi., 423, 436. Sheriff, xii., 507; xiii., 85, 391. Discharged as agent of estates, 106, 581; xv., 12, 236. Battalion for celebrating 4th July, 386. Contest with James Ash as Sheriff of Philadelphia, 567, 568, 569, 570, 571, 572, 573, 575, 576, 577, 578. James Ash elected, 579

Willett, Augustine, claim on forfeited estate of G. Hicks, xii., 73. Commissioner, 394, 494.

Willey, John, shoots sub-Sheriff of Maryland and is burned in the hand, viii., 372.

William III., King of England, dies, ii., 70.

William, King, and Queen Mary, complaint that they had not been proclaimed at New Castle, i., 299, 301, 303, 304. Declaration of, 301. Discussions, 304-310. Order to proclaim, 340.

William Henry, fort, vii., 515, 716. Capitulates—order of Gen. Abercrombie respecting, viii., 141. And letter to Governor of Canada respecting, 141.

Williams, Capt., ———., of Pennsylvania battalion, x., 420. Complains of Captain and Lieutenant Proctor, 423, 438.

Williams, Charles, house burned by Indians, vii., 154. Convicted, xi., 625.

Williams, Lieutenant-Colonel Wm., proceedings of Board of Officers at West Point—list of promotions in consequence of Captain Lieut. Henderson's promotion, xii., 88.

Williams Dunk, roads, i., 503.

Williams, Edward, claim for ser-

vices as clerk in military hospital, xvi., 290, 291, 294.
Williams, Capt. Ennion, firelocks for, x., 519.
Williams, Isaac, Commiss'er, made prisoner, xi., 536.
Williams, John, commits suicide—question, whether an inquest made by a Justice in absence of Coroner is valid? ii., 184.
Williams, Joshua, to be Captain, xi., 280, 282, 357, 358.
Williams, Major ———, xi., 21, 84. Resigns, 116.
Williams, Richard, Justice, xiv. 605.
Williams, Captain Samuel, appointed Lieutenant to Gen. Washington, xi., 24.
Williams, William, Adjutant of Southwark militia, complains of abuse of public property, xiv., 641.
Williamson, Daniel, a member of Assembly, dies, iii., 298.
Williamson, David, Sheriff, xv., 646; xvi., 212.
Williamson, Dr. Hugh, xiv., 317.
Williamson, Samuel, late chaplain regiment of dragoons, pass for Europe, xii., 81.
Willing, Captain Richard, to accompany Major French to camp, x., 305, 306, 481.
Willing, Col. Richard, Councillor, xv., 566, 614, 632. Board property, 637; xvi., 16, 194, 545. Decision in his favor as councilman over Dr. Ruston, 202.
Willing, Thomas, owner of ship Dorothea, iii., 294. Justice of Supreme Court, ix., 393. A Judge of Supreme Court, salary, x., 53, 173, 265. Statement of John Brown of interview with, xi., 345. President B. N. A., letter respecting, xiii., 200, 201.
Willing, Morris & Co., loading vessel with produce for account of Committee, x., 426.
Willis, Captain, paid, xi. 428.
Willis, John, gunsmith, x., 422.
Wilmington, Del., Act respecting wharves, walls, &c., x., 49. Banks, drains, &c., of Christiana to be kept in repair, 80. Mr. Holker, and flour purchased at, xii., 47, 55, 56, 66, 68.
Wilmot, Henry, letter from, ix., 749. Letter to, (London,) from R. Peters, Secretary, giving history of Indian deed to Susquehannah County, x., 177.
Wills, Probate for each County, i., 461; iv., 33, 40; v., 457, 502, 504, 511, 512.
Will's Creek—proposed fortifications at, vi., 137. Col. Innes going to, 141. Levies for, 177. Builds fort at, 180. Camp at, 197. Indians go with John Harris to, 226. Best mode of sending provisions to, 296, 477.
Wilson, Christ., complaint against, vii., 463.
Wilson, Geo., Sheriff, xvi., 198, 542.
Wilson, Dr. Goodwin, Physician and Surgeon, xiii., 115.
Wilson, Hon. James, member of Continental Congress, receives his pay, x, 286. Colonel's battalion, 686, 692, 710, Riot at his house, xii., 121. Proclamation respecting, 122. Daniel Clymer, present, surrenders and gives bail, 128. Wm. Bell to give security, 130. Persons present, 137, 138, 139, 141, 144, 145. 152. Letter from, 324. President loses a hanger at, 341 Counsel on Connecticut claim, xiii., 128. Retaining fee, 136. Elected Brigadier General, 289. Counsel, 310. Appointed agent to try private rights at Wyoming, xiv., 35. To act as counsel in case Longschamps, 135. 149. Fees on Connecticut claim, 141. Report, 159, 162. Letter, 373. Lecture by, xvi., 533.
Wilson, James, a deserter, xiii., 22.
Wilson, John, Justice, xi., 741. Sentenced to death, 565. Reprieved, 566, 579. Pardon, 624.
Wilson, Lieut. Phillip, xi., 624.
Wilson, Richard, Member of Assembly, dies, ii., 26.
Wilson, Robert, mate of ship Cambridge, petition—loss of Captain—asks advice of counsel, iv., 96. Placed under care of merchants, 97. Appointed Sub-Lieutenant of Chester County, xi., 437. Children of, claim a division of land in Northumberland Co., xvi., 146, 183, 185.

Wilson, Thomas, Coroner, v., 597. Justice, xiv., 666.
Wilson, Captain Wm., of Northumberland, xi., 423. Asks for time to pay for island in Allegheny river, xvi., 85. Councillor, xvi., 195, 197. Paid for services in case of Walkers and Doyle, &c., 547.
Wilt, John, Coroner, xii., 544; xiii., 400.
Wiltbank, Abraham, (pilot,) commission to command intelligence boat, v., 266. Reports, 273.
Wiltbank, Cornelius, Coroner, iii., 387, 575. Sheriff, iv., 47[illegible].
Wiltner, Col., letter, xii., 215.
Winchester, Va., post to be continued at, viii., 71. Indians arrive from, 124.
Wines and other liquors—duties on, ii., 234.
Winjack, Indian Ganawese King, iii., 188.
Wipey, Joseph, a Delaware Indian, murdered--reward offered for murderer, x., 199.
Wirtz, Christian, Sub-Lieutenant and Major, x., 335, 575. Of Lancaster, pays for house south-west corner Walnut and Front streets, and obtains deed, xii., 174. Superceded as Commissioner of purchases, 660. Commissioner of purchases. Commissions raised, xiii., 154. Exempted from operation of law respecting barracks, xiv., 634.
Wissahickon Hill, now Vanderin's Mill, x., 778. Deed for lands with Snuff Mill, &c., xiii., 33.
Wistar, Caspar, authorized to trade, and buy and hold lands, iii., 235.
Wistar, John, of Lancaster, asks to be naturalized, iii., 374.
Wistar, Richard, deed for city lot, xiv., 456.
Witchcraft, alleged case of, ii., 20.
Witches, trials of persons as, i., 93, 95, 96.
Withers, Ralph, member of first Council, i., 57.
Withers, Captain John, x., 701.
Witherspoon, Dr John, asks for release of suspicious persons, xi., 261. Hon. John, Member of Congress, xiii., 43.
Withington, Cap., x., 737.
Wittington, Eve, petition for payment of expenses of prisoners to Virginia, xv., 641. Report of Compt. General on resolution of Council, to refer it to Judges, 643. Paid for boarding prisoners on their way to Virginia, xvi., 101.
Withington, Martin, Sheriff, xv., 570; xvi., 195, 494.
Witman, Christopher, Coroner, ix., 333.
Witman, Michael, forfeited estate in Lancaster Co., case of, xii., 69.
Wivall, Wm., messenger to Indians at Manatanny—report of, ii., 546.
Wood, Lt. Ab'm, disabled—on invalid list, xii., 51.
Wood, frauds in, xii., 175, 190.
Wood, Joseph, recommended to Congress as Lt. Major, x., 444. Appointed, 446. Major to Col. St. Clair's battalion, 460. Battalion, xi., 32, 54.
Wood, Sacherville, appointed doorkeeper of Council of Safety, x., 653.
Wood, Wm., a Judge, i., 119.
Woodbridge, Mr., supposed influence with Indians in purchase of lands, vi., 117.
Woods, John, interpreter to Choctaw and Chickasaw Indians in Philadelphia, xv., 229.
Woelper, Capt. John David, of German battalion, xi., 401. Disabled and put on invalid list, xii., 51, 279.
Wolcott, Roger, Gov. of Connecticut —letters to and from on dispute, v., 768, 771.
Wolf, Peter, Justice, xiv., 255.
Wolfe, Reese, Coroner, ix., 689.
Woolsey, John, a Canadian prisoner from Reading, at Philadelphia by permission, x., 679.
Woolston, Jona'n, Coroner of Bucks County, iii., 260, 289, 332, 370, 387, 416; iv., 85.
Woolaston, Thos., and Jno. Grantham proceedings, i., 236, 253, 258, 261.
Work, Andrew, Sheriff, v., 464. Of Lancaster—certificate of furnaces and forges, ix., 636.
Work, Henry, Sheriff, xvi., 495.

Work, Joseph, Sheriff, xii., 134, 508; xiii., 88.
Work-houses and prisons, i., 582; iii., 39. To be erected in counties, v., 506, 512.
Workmen in employ of Province not to be enlisted, x., 636.
Worley, Francis, to survey Springetsbury manor, iii., 185.
Worrick, Andrew, Sheriff, v., 411.
Worrell, Jas., to take down spouts, xi., 279.
Worrall, Peter, resigns as member of Assembly, vii., 148.
Wraxall, Peter, Secretary of Indian affairs, vii., 195.
Wrecked goods arrive from Cape May—delivered to J. Logan and Thomas Lawrence—proceedings, iii., 238, 239, 240, 241.
Wright, Abijah, to be executed, xi., 631.
Wright, Alex., Justice, xiii., 263.
Wright, Benj., Sheriff of Phila., declines collecting, is fined and removed, ii., 233.
Wright, Enoch, Adjutant, xi., 110.
Wright, Major Geo., xv., 109.
Wright, James, takes a place for the Indians at Lancaster, vii., 510. To obtain information respecting Conestogas, viii., 115. His letter to Gov., giving it, 116.
Wright, John, relative to dispute with Maryl'd, iii., 472. Speaker, iv., 782.
Wright, Thomas, killed by Indians at Snaketown, iii., 285. Assault on Joseph Thomas, of Bucks—petition and pardon, xv., 255, 256.
Wright's ferry, xi., 637.
Writs of Error, ii., 127.
Wurts, Charles, Town-major of Lancaster, xi., 78.
Wurtz, Christian, Town-major of Lancaster, applies for pay and rations, xii., 116. (See Wirts.)
Wyalusing, Indians at, to be provided for, ix., 97, 137, 139. Poor Indians arrive from, at Philadelphia, 425, 435. Message to, 436.
Wyalusing creek, claim to land on, xiii., 33.
Wygant, John, a Moravian missionary—pass to, xiii., 570.
Wynkoop, Henry, member of Council of Safety, x., 675. Quota of wheat, xii., 490. Of Bucks, appointed Judge of High Court of Errors and Appeals, 548. Letter on robbery of Treasury of Bucks county, xiii., 95. Judge of Court of Errors and Appeals, 544, 550. Depositions respecting robbery, 616. Justice, xiv., 139. President of Court Common Pleas, 150. Paid as Judge High Court of Errors and Appeals, 229. Pay as a Judge of High Court of Errors and Appeals, xv., 645. Resigns as Judge and Justice in Bucks, xvi., 105, 133.
Wynkoop, John, Coroner, iv., 470, 500.
Wynne, Thomas, his widow applies to Council in case of a Judgment under a wrong name, i., 394.
Wynne, Major Joshua, murdered by Indians in Virginia, iii., 22.
Wyoming — Six Nations propose meeting at, on way to Philadelphia, iv., 500. Four Indians arrive from, v., 543.—Symptoms of disturbance in Northampton county, from Connecticut claimants, 735. Letter from William Parsons, 736. Letter from D. Brodhead, 757. Connecticut movements, 757, 758. Dispute, 767-777. Paxinosa—Indian Chief, vi., 35. Influence of Lydius, &c. with Indians respecting lands, 117, 247-275. Indians from, on their way to Philadelphia, 358. Message from Indians at, 751. Answer, 753. Indian hostilities, 756.
Indians at, vii., 108. New Castle, &c., arrive at, on journey to Indians on Susquehannah, vii., 137. Fort proposed at Adjouquay, fourteen miles above, 159. Indians now belong to Diahoga, 188. Remove back to Diahoga, 222. Teedyuscung, &c. at, 267, 284, 328. Indian murders, 357. Provisions scarce at, 479. Indians on lands at, 540, 676, 677, 723. Indians intending to settle at, 726. Mr. Hughes, Commissioner, going to build fort and Indian houses at, 730, 735. Opposed by Council, 734. C. Weiser to be employed, 734. His opinion on

Wyoming—
building, 735. Messrs. Hughes, Shippen and Galbraith, to go, 736. Commission to—Mr. Hughes refuses — Charles Beatty added, 754, Teedyuscung visits Governor Denny on his return from, 770.

Houses for Teedyscung at, viii., 112. Indians above, in motion, 127. Message of Gov. to Teedyuscung and Indians at, 129. Conference with C. Thomson and F. Post and Indians at Nescopec, 132. Report of Hughes and Pawling, of houses built at, 134. Mason killed by Indians, 134. Journal of Fred. Post to, 142. Building houses at, 129. Indians at, to be informed of murder of Dr. John, at Carlisle, 455. N. E. people about to settle on lands at, 500. Indians hold conference at Philadelphia, 594, 600. Connecticut settlers, 563-572, 612, 621-628. Indians at, on way to Easton, 630, 646. Proclamation, 663.

Settlers from Connecticut, ix., 7, 27, 602. Indians complain, 27. James Burd and Thomas McKee sent to under instructions, 29. James Burd appointed Commissioner to, 59. Instructions to Governor H., 60. To Colonel Burd, 61. Indian mine at, 329. Proceedings and resolutions of Susquehanna Company, 569-572. Letters Lewis Gorden, C. Stewart and J. Jennings, respecting New England settlers, 572, 573, 584. Letter to Governor of Connecticut, 573. Charles Stewart and Amos Ogden appointed Justices, 573. Settlers from Lancaster county, 583. Governor to John Jennings, 585. To Charles Stewart, 586. Colonel Francis, 587. Governor's proclamation, 588. Letters sent by Governor P. to sundry persons, 606. Instructions to Sheriff of Northamption, 608. Justices appointed, 660. Germans and New England men behave riotously, 663. Deposition of Amos Ogden, 674. Terms on delivery of the fort at, between A. Ogden

Wyoming—
and Zeb. Butler, 677. Proclamation of Governor against Connecticut settlers, 679. Warrant to arrest several persons for ill treatment of a Justice, 682, 687. Depositions, 710, 711. Message of Governor to Assembly, respecting, 713. Murder of Nathan Ogden at the fort, 714. Proclamation for capture of Stewart and his accomplices there named, 717. Road from Blue Mountain, asked for, 731. Commissioners appointed, 732. Connecticut people armed on their way to—proclamation against, 747. Captain Amos Ogden arrives at Philadelphia with news from, 748. Proceedings of Council, 749. Report of Tilghman and Shippen, 750. Depositions of Neal Arnott and Scott, skirmish at block house, 751. Letter of Lewis Gordon, 752, 754. John Dick, 753. Council order one hundred men to be raised, 753. Several letters, 756. From Council to Proprietaries, 757. Deposition of Ashur Clayton, 767. Joseph Morris, 769. Articles of capitulation at block house, 771. Message of Governor to Assembly, 773. Letter from President Hamilton to Governor Trumbull, Governor of Connecticut, 777.

Case of Laz. Stewart, x., 3. Governor Trumbull on Susquehannah Company, 4. Connecticut people settling on proprietary lands, 50. John Durkee — indicted for riot at—imprisoned—discharged, 52. Fort proposed at J. Dougherty's, 86. Letters from R. Moodie—Wm. Plunkett and Governor Penn, 87. John Dougherty, Jr. heads armed men, 86. Petition of Northumberland against Connecticut people, 111. Message to Assembly on, 117. Messrs. Dyer, Johnson and Strong, sent by Governor Trumbull, arrive at Philadelphia, 118. Letter from Governor Trumbull with resolutions of Assembly of Connecticut, 119 - 139, 151. Proclamation against settlers and Z. Butler for

Wyoming—
circulating advertisements, 154. Governor Trumbull's account of, 164. History of Indian deed, 177. Road from Blue Mountain, 219. Refuse to submit to laws of Pennsylvania, 275. Governor's letter to Magistrates, 275.

Ravages of Indians at, xi., 528. troops for, 531.

Troops to be sent to, for Genl. Sullivan, xii., 92. Troops to be ordered from, to Sunbury, at request of Genl. Hand, out of garrison left there, 138. Relief of garrison, 569. Alarm about supplies, 585. Commandant Mitchell sends papers, referred to Board of War, 741.

On abandonment of post at, xiii., 399. Conference respecting lands at, 509. Capt. Robeson's and Capt. Shrawder's companies for, 519. Stores, &c., asked for, 565, 567, 572. Letters from, 645. Justices, 683. Armed force to be stationed at, 693. Major Jas. Moore, with troops, ordered to, 721. Provisions for, 725, 741. Zeb. Butler committed, 760, 763. Petition of A. Yarrington—referred to A. Patterson, 765.

Expenses of a soldier paid to, xiv., 5. Federal Court to try private right of soil to the lands at, 31. Memorial of A. Yarrington and deposition of John Seely respecting Col. Jacob Stroud, 32. James Wilson and Wm. Bradford, Jr., agents to conduct trial of private rights at, 35. Petition to Congress of settlers, 51. Conference on withdrawing troops from, 53. Distress from inundation, 61. Pay for troops at, 110. Disturbances among soldiery at—A. Patterson resigns as Justice, 116, 117. Letter from Z. Butler in behalf of Connecticut people, 120. Petition in favor of Wm. Shrader, 137. Conspiracy against taxes—proclamation, 151. Report of Counsel on controversy with Conn., 159, 163. Return of stores at, 164. Disturbance at, 165. Troops to be in readiness in Northampton county for, 166.

Wyoming—
Various papers and depositions relating to disturbances at—resolutions respecting preparations for, 167. Provisions for, 168. Conference respecting, 171. Depositions—narrative of Benaiah Mundy, 172. Conference with Council and Ass'y, 183, 184, 188. Relating to Connecticut settlers driven off in May last, 186. Messrs. Boyd, Armstrong, Read and Okely, commissioners to proceed to, on claims, 207. Ammunition sent to, 207. Commissioners, letter from, 215. Fifty men to be drawn from Bucks and Berks counties, to proceed to, to quell disturbances, 217. President Dickinson's letter to Council, object to their late measures respecting, 219, 220. Proclamation respecting, 220-224. Expenses of commissioners, 235. Repair of arms, 238. Provisions, 238. Express to, with dispatches, paid, 254. Conference between Assembly and Council on, 258, 259, 260. Complainants attend Council and receive money, 315. Deposition taken, 317. List or collection of all the acts of governors, and other papers relating to, 318-320. Rations for militia, 343. Insurrection at—letter of David Mead, 359. Some of Berks county troops refuse to do duty, 374. Northumberland troops, 382. Outrages at, 398. Pay to commissioners, 446. Rations for, 457. Report of committee of Assembly at, 463. Letter, D. Mead, 495. Conference with Chief Justice, 508. Disturbances at, 572, 578, 579. Capt. Sawyer's subsistence account, 581. Medicines for a soldier wounded at, 605. Express to, for distributing Act of Assembly—instructions to J. Elliott, 636. General John Armstrong paid as commissioner to, 637. Committee of Assembly meets Council, 656. Paid Dr. Schetta for healing a man wounded at, 671.

Road to, from Water Gap, xv., 22, 30, 93. Letters to William Montgomery and Wm. Shaw, on

Wyoming—
disturbances at, 27. Cession of lands by Connecticut, accepted by Congress, 28. Letter to J. Franklin, W. H. Smith and J. Jenkins, 35. W. H. Smith's expenses to and from, paid by Council, 36. Disturbances, 37. Eli Mead, Justice, 51. Wounded soldier, 64. Protection to John Franklin, John Jenkins, &c., 67. John Franklin and J. Jennings arrived, examined — petition from "late settlers," 79. Express to, 115. John Franklin, member of Assembly—N. Dennizen, Councillor, 162. Forage for troops, 221. Mission with despatches in 1786, respecting disturbances, paid to Col. John Bull, 276. Proclamation against John Franklin, &c., 280. Message to Assembly respecting disturbances, 305. Conference respecting—affairs at Tioga—troops to be raised, 307. Fines on delinquents of Northampton county, arising from a tour of duty to, 310. Expulsion of commissioners from, 314. Dr. Andrew Ledie paid for medicines, &c., 344. Commissioners paid, 355. Col. T. Pickering is made prisoner — conduct of Luzerne county—proceedings of Council —letters to Governors of New York and New Jersey, 484. Mr. Redick sent to New Jersey and New York by Council—proclamations respecting captors of Col. Pickering, &c., 489, 490. Pay to W. Montgomery as commissioner to, 539. Letters between John Franklin and D. Hamilton requested from Governor Clinton, 571. Letters received, 578. Expenses of commissioners to, 594.
Arrest of rioters in, xvi., 11, 12. Expenses, 15, 16. Commissioners for ascertaining claims, 16. Case of John Franklin, a state prisoner, 16. Sheriff, 17. Expenses of taking John Franklin to Easton, 17. Committee to ascertain quantity and quality of land at and near, 22. Boarding of John Franklin paid for, 50. Provisions for, 230. Enforcing of

Wyoming—
laws against Connecticut settlers in 1775, 317, 322, 352. Provisions furnished by John Weitzell, 354; and by Wm. Sawers—militia sent to, paid, 364. Supplies, 389.

Y.

Yard, John, fined for not taking oath, ii., 180. Remitted, 181.
Yardley, Thos., ferry at, iii. 166, 174.
Yardley, William, appointed a special Commissioner to try a case, i., 164. Member of Council for Bucks, 213. Proceedings, 293. Sheriff, v., 597, 662.
Yarrington, Abel, Coroner, xvi., 196, 496.
Yates, Ab'm, Chairman of Com'ee of Albany, receives powder, x. 327.
Yaughtanno, Cherokee Ch'f, speech, vii., 529, 553. Answer to Gov.'s message at Fort Frederick, 556.
Year, commences in March, i., 58. An Indian's, v., 310.
Yeates, James, one who ran the line, 1737, or Indian walk, vii., 400.
Yeates, Jasper, a Commissioner under dedimus, to administer oaths, ii., 62, 92, 116. Member of Council, 119. Judge, 239. Administers oath to Gov. Keith, iii., 13. Member of Council dies, 143.
Yeates, John, Coroner, v., 551, 597.
Yeldell, Dr. Anthony, traitor—his apprentice arrested, xii., 504. Wife and children to depart the State, 509. Case of, referred to Committee, xv., 606, 614.
Yellow Fever brought to Phila., by ship from Barbadoes, v., 105, 106, 107, 109. At Charleston, quarantine, xii., 457, 483.
Yellow Springs, sulphur, &c., at, xi., 389.
Yocum, Mounce, i., 435.
Yocum, Peter, i., 397.
York, Edward, Lieut. of Provincial ship, x., 521.
York, Thomas, may ship produce, x., 425.
York County formed, v., 398, 403, 404, 551, 662. Sheriff elected, 411, 468, 551, 597, 662. Coroners elected, 411, 597. Another coun-

York County—
ty west of, proposed to be formed, 426. Early settlements, 440. Boundary between and Cumberland, 502, 514, 619. Work-house and house of correction, 506, 512. Act respecting Inspectors, 619. Sheriffs elected, vi., 144, 638. Coroners elected, 144, 638. Danger from Indians, 670. Return of seven companies of militia, vii., 76. Petition on Indian successes, 233. Associated companies formed, 294. Two good horses to be at, viii., 71. Coroners appointed, 223, 403, 506, 781. Sh'ffs appointed, 223, 403, 506, 781. Trials in, 336. Choice of Inspectors, 400. Sheriffs elected, ix., 57, 199, 286, 333, 398, 548, 624, 688, 778. Coroners elected, 57, 199, 286, 333, 398, 548, 624, 689, 778. A frontier county, 138. Petition—quit-rents, 179, 180. Justices, 235, 543, 731. Lottery for Episcopal Church in, 243. Convictions, 282, 549. Special court to try negroes, 543. Lottery for German Reformed and German Lutheran Churches, 567, 579. Regulation of fisheries in Codorus and Conewago, 719. Sheriffs elected, x., 56, 101, 212, 271. Coroners elected, 56, 101, 212, 271. Justices, 162, 209. Relief of prisoners, 42. Convictions and executions, 50. Associators ask for pattern guns, 300. Purchase powder and lead, 344. Powder for Westmoreland, 346. Dr. Kearsley sent to, 373, 380. And J. Brooks also, 380. Arrived, 385. To collect arms, 441. Prisoners of war, 515. Prisoners removed from Germantown to, 601, 622, 626. Firelocks bought in, 615. Prisoners, 639, 640. Escort of prisoners to, paid for, 645. Col. Matthew Dill, 672. Arms, &c., 681. Col. Richard M'Allister, 683. Capt. William Smith, 687. Colonel, 693. Col. Matthew Dill, xi., 113. Col. McPherson's battalion, 121, A. McLean, Prothonotary, 187. Chas Lukens declines being Sheriff, 219, 229. Justices, 219, 443.

York County—
Counterfeiter in jail, 234. Lieutenants, 257. Abuses by, complained of, and orders for arrest, 266. Riot in, several persons charged and arrested, and warrant issued in Philada., County, 267, 268. Archibald M'Lean, Cl'k of Orphans' Court, 274. Militia called out, 302, 360. Threats against public stores at, 307. John Brown, 344, 406. Stephen Foulke conceals deserters, 357. Elections, 371, 656, 695, 697, 698. Sheriff, 371, 375, 599. Coroner, 371, 599. Prothonotary, 388. Case of Wm. Montgomery, 402. Paymaster, 406. Joseph Boone convicted, 490. Indians, 535. Wm. Low, 637. Escort of prisoners, 637, 643. Election, 676. Wagons, 693. Councillor, 715. Councillor elected—contested election—George Eichelburger examined — decision, 698. His conduct condemned, and Sheriff sent for him, 750. Opinion asked—contested election, 744. Justices, xii., 19. Archibald McLean receives subscription to loan office, 47. Forfeited estates—Mr. Stephenson, agent, dead, 64. Wm. Mitchell appointed, 65. Estate of James Rankin, 82, 113, 174, 218. Sheriff sends money, 83. Guard at gaol, 108. Case of Negro Ralph referred to, 113. Militia called out, 129. Rep's, Comm'rs, Assessors, 145, 513. Sheriffs, 145, 146, 161, 513. Coroners, 145, 146, 161, 513. Case of Thos. Readly, 178. Petition for protection, 297. Military officers app'd, 298. Justices, 342, 353, 595. Wagon masters, 390. Appointments, 554. J. Rankin's estate, 560, 681. Expenses of county, 569. Auditors, 647. Convention, troops to be removed to, 648. Military guard for convention—prisoners—Committee of Conference on, 660. Draft to A. McLean, 684. Sales of estates in, 688. Col. W. Rankin escapes from gaol—proclamation for arrest, 710. Clerk of Market app'd, xiii., 3. Pay for horses, 28.

York County—
Claims for land in York town, 44. Troops called out, 53. Estate of James Rankin, 98. Horrible sentence for horse stealing, 195. Militia called out, 203. Justices, 208, 422, 666. Call on for men, 348, 365. Sheriff, 397, 723. Coroner, 397, 723. Execution of W. Bibb and T. Hiler for murder, 595. Irregular military election, 695, 723. Censors, 723. Representatives., 723. Justices, xiv., 162, 164, 182, 201, 208, 211, 212, 224, 229, 234, 247, 255, 256, 449, 486. Illegal election, 162. Wm. Scott, Lieut. of County, complained of, 203. Irregular election, 208, 256, 557. General election, 234, 557. Sheriffs, 234, 557. Coroners, 234, 557. Representati's, 234, 557. Deputy Surveyor, 441, 459. Confiscated estates, 462. Register and Recorder, 584. Collector of Excise, 585, 590, 591. Militia, 590. Archibald M'Lean, Prothonotary, death of, xv., 15. Henry Miller, his successor, 17. Col. Andrews' battalion, 43. Justices, 65, 227, 302, 474, 615. Confiscated estates in, 73. Election, 102, 296. Sheriffs, 102, 297, 579. Coroners, 102, 297, 579. Richard McAllister resigns as Councillor, 126. Appeal of Wm. Scott, paymaster, 144. Disturbances, in, 148. Councillor, 149. Militia of, 152. Division of Codorus district, 196. Militia, 243. Paymaster of, 249. Petition of Hoak & King for a riot, referred to Judges, 260. John McClellan, Collector of Excise, removed, and John Forsyth appointed, 264. Appeal of Wm. Young, agent, 282. Representatives, 302. Contested election, 420, 474. Claim for title to estate of Wm. Rankin, 425. Contested election—a former election reported on and confirmed, and Elihu Underwood declared Justice, 474. Execution of negro Jack Durham ordered, 475, 476. And Philip Nagle, 476. Postponed, 483. Pardon, 549. Election irregular—commission to Justice M'Ilhenny revoked, 615. Road between

York County—
Chambersburg, through Black's Gap, xvi., 103. Justices, 13, 154. Sheriff, 193, 492. Coroner, 193, 492. Paid John Harris for a gun and blanket, taken in 1776, on way to Amboy—also to M. Peterman, Conrad Giessey, Jacob Lefevre, 160. Reward to Abr'm Moser, 162. Returns of officers, 173. Tax on writs—executions received by Henry Miller, Prothonotary, 356. Troops for Wyoming, 364. Col. Albright's battalion—Capt. Dodd's co., 427. Capt. Trett's co., 536. Tax on writs, 541.

Yorke, Thos., Committee of Assembly, vii., 636.

Yorktown, Congress of Commissioners at, xi., 435. Lord Cornwallis surrenders at, xiii., 94. Bedford Rangers ordered to, 121. Cannon taken at, the property of the State, 614.

Young, ———, letter to, from John Fraser, v., 659.

Young, Charles, Notary Public, xv., 255. Claim City lot, 481.

Young, James, appointed Comm'ry General of muster—orders and instructions of Gov. to, vii., 162, Commissary to pay troops, 476. Paymaster—estimate of pay to Provincial forces, viii., 224, 287. Justice, ix., 393. Captain, x., 697. Justice, xi., 228. Requisition for wagons, 588, 589.

Young, Capt. John, confined for giving a challenge, xii., 62, 67. Estate in Northampton Co., sold, 157, 158. Deed to for gr'd rt., 283.

Young, Lazarus, order for his arrest, ix., 682.

Young, Moses, appointed Assistant Secretary, xi., 78.

Young, Nathan, Coroner, ix., 286.

Young, Dr. Thomas, to assist Dr. Potts, xi., 50, 52.

Young, Wm., to be arrested as accomplice of Stewart, ix., 717. As apprentice of Ben. Town, printer, arrested on suspicion of being concerned in seditious paper, "Slow and Sure," xii., 325. Discharged, 328.

Young, William, Jr., appointed by

Minister of France to collect plants, xii., 610.
Youth, to be provided with learning—school of arts and sciences, i., 93. Reprieved under gallows on account of, iv., 224. A person acquitted of crime on account of, xii., 202.

Z.

Zachary, Dr. Lloyd, to visit sick vessels, iii., 293. As health officer, to visit vessels, 496–498. Report of Assembly on, 517. Report in Council, 524.
Zadousky, Anthony, sent as messenger to Indians, iii., 305. Expenses, 345.
Zane, Isaac, at Indian conference at Nicholas Scull's house, viii., 211.
Zantzinger, Adam, x., 481, 647, 689
Zantzinger, Catherine, pension to, xvi., 148.
Zantzinger, Paul, pass for, to New York, xii., 256. Rejected, 314. Granted, 317. Asks for pass for Rev. Thos. Barton and wife from New York--rejected, 339, 357. Public papers in his hands relating to estate of J. Ruby, xiii., 19.
Zeigler, Capt., Daniel, to distribute to troops articles left, xi., 710, 750. Account of expenses, xii., 64. Letter, 220. To furnish companies with refreshments, 266, 278. Account as distributor of stores, 297. Letter, 334, 335. To distribute articles, 547. Letter for books and accounts, 628. Pay, 635. Clothing for troops, 684. Shoes delivered to, xiii., 9. Order to, 76, 91, 164.
Zeigler, Capt. David, question of rank with Captain Ferguson, xv., 381, 395. Appointed Captain, 437, 438, 439, 473.
Zeisberger, Rev. David, pass for, as missionary to Indians, v., 576. Examines John Shekallamy, vii., 245. Arrives at Bethlehem with accounts from Guadenhutten, vi., 736.
Zigrea, "drunken," an Indian, arrives at Philadelphia, vi., 681.
Zimmerman, Matthew, ii., 541.
Zistagechroanu, a nation of Indians north of Lake Frontenac, v., 85, 212.
Zinachson, Indian name for Shamokin, v., 84.

INDEX

TO

PENNSYLVANIA ARCHIVES.

VOLUMES I. TO XII., INCLUSIVE.

INDEX TO PENNSYLVANIA ARCHIVES.

A.

Abercrombie, Major General, appointed Colonel, ii., 647; iii., 321, 364, 366, 371, 376, 380, 392, 552. Going to England, 518.

Abolition of Slavery proposed to Assembly, vii., 79.

Abraham's plains, action at, xi., 435, 436.

Academy, of Philadelphia, address from Students to Governor Morris, ii., 193. At Newark, Delaware, seeks aid, iv., 468. Washington, lands for, xi., 215.

Acadian, French Spy, captured, iv., 206. Or French neutrals, their history, iii., 565–568.

Accounts, reports on, xii., 6, 9.

Achilles, Brig, owners ask for shot, vii., 308.

Ackowanothro, speech of, iii., 548.

Active, Sloop, capture and case of, vii., 170, 172, 468. Agents of sloop, prize money, viii., 209. Sloop, Arnold, &c., charged with concern in, ix., 10, 33. Brig, (1780,) x., 161. (See vol. viii.)

Acts of Assembly, opinion of attorney on, ii., 100 For forming and regulating the militia, iii., 110, 115, 117, 120. For issuing bills of credit, 99. Various notices, 114, 117. To remove settlers from Indian lands, iv., 283. Of New York on Indian trade, 361. Of Virginia, 372. Of Virginia respecting clothing, vi., 125. Of Congress, vii., 102, 152, 159. For vesting proprietary estates in the State, viii., 113. To prevent and stay suits against Wyoming, x., 5. Of 1705, for bailing prisoners, 407. Of New York on boundary, 422. Restoring lands at Wyoming, 658. Complained of by British merchants, 747. Of North Carolina, appointing deputies to convention in Philadelphia for revising Constitution, xi., 117. For purchase of Erie, xii., 89.

Adams, John, and B. Franklin, letter from Paris, vi., 521. Minister to France, introduction of Mr. Searle, viii., 399, 563. Minister to Holland, ix., 589. Advises of acknowledgment of independence by Holland, 633. On public debt to France, x., 384, 386. Relating to American Bishops, 432. On British grievances, 745.

Adams, Samuel, on expected seditious papers, vii., 14. On representation, 763.

Addresses from churches, &c., to Governor Morris, ii., 183, 184, 185, 192, 200. From Germans, 217, 225. To Governor Denny, 760, 762, 763. Of Indians at Bethlehem, 636. Of Representatives of New Jersey to Governor Belcher, 1757, iii., 170. Of Assembly of Lower counties to Governor, 309, 721. Of Commissioners for Indian affairs, 555. Of Council of Safety, v., 642. Of officers to Assembly, 724. Of Congress to inhabitants, vi., 488. Of Colonel Hartley to Congress, vii., 5. A serious, to inhabitants of Wyoming, by W. Hooker Smith, xi., 105. Governor Mifflin to Assembly, xii., 34, 46. Senate to Gov. Mifflin, 44. House of Representatives to Governor Mifflin, 45.

Adlum, John, on surveys, xi., 576. Report on, 577. Letter from J.

Hart, 593. Recommendation, 620, 629.
Administration of government, Act securing, in case of death, &c., i., 155.
Admirality, orders, i., 194, 206, 207, 234, 242, 243, 306. Opposition to judge of Vice adm., 205. Orders respecting shipwrecked seamen, 234. On impressments, 638, 640, 641. Court, complaint against Judge of, 205. Orders from, iv., 243, 331, 622. Court, Judge of, George Ross appointed, vii., 212. Business delayed for want of a Register, 451. Judge Ross dies, 554. F. Hopkinson succeeds him, 554, 558. Letter from, respecting seal, 694. Board of, to fit out vessels of war, viii., 273. Privateers, 340. Court grant warrant for sale of ship Albion's cargo, 491. Letter on cutting masts on Schuylkill for French fleet, 542. Board of, ix., 95, 101, 106. Court fees received, 555, 567, 630, 672; x., 58. Letter of Judge H., on a vessel escaping under writ of, 356 Cases, xi., 53–55. Fees, 125, 126, 375, 381, 383.
African Trade, Board of Trade make inquiries about it, i., 153. Duties on negroes, 159, 160.
Agents, of confiscated estates, viii., 735, 760.
Agnew, John, ix., 135.
Agreement, between Lord Baltimore and Thomas and Richard Penn, to have line run in 1760, (Mason and Dixon's,) iv., 1–36. Entered into with Wyoming rioters, 350–352. Between Pennsylvania and Virginia about boundary, viii., 352, 488, 516, 570. With Six Nations, xi., 529–533.
Agricultural Society, Philadelphia, grant by Assembly to encourage, x., 204. On Hessian fly, xi., 384, 385, 527.
Air Furnaces, by Mr. Nancarrow, viii., 456.
Aix la Chapelle, preliminary of peace, signed at, ii., 3.
Albany, minutes of commissioners at, &c., letter to Governor Van Dam, i., 296, 297. Representation of Captains at, on condition of
Albany—
soldiers, 724, 736. Secretary Peters to, Captains at, 738. Indian treaty at, commissioners to, ii., 137–143, 181.
Albion, ship, captured and condemned, viii., 491.
Alexander, Charles, v., 626, 637.
Alexander, Captain, of seventh regiment, promotions, viii., 248.
Alexander, Major, ix., 109.
Alexander, James, ii., 462.
Alexander, William, letter introducing an extraordinary writing master, ii., 170. Letters to and from, 170, 315, 348, 375.
Algiers and United States, war between, xi., 522.
Alison, Francis, Jr., on surrender of Fort Freeland, vii., 592.
Allegheny, Indians, letter from, i., 550, 552. Mountains, notice to inhabitants, iv., 252. River, land bad near, x., 509. County, formed, xi., 640. River, island in, applied for, 623, 645.
Allegiance, Assembly pass act repecting oath of, vi., 433.
Alleminga, Fort, above, [See Fort.] Murders by Indians, iii., 77.
Allen, Andrew, case of Big Spring tract at Reading, x., 712. A counterfeiter, demanded by New Jersey, xi., 550.
Allen, Ethan, at Wyoming, x., 765, 766. Respecting, xi., 68, 108
Allen, Fort, [See Fort]; iii., 5, 68, 81, 119, 152, 194, 218, 420, 424, 504, 521; iv., 139; viii., 286; Captain Shrawder leaving, ix., 649; xii., 70.
Allen, Ira, viii., 88.
Allen, James, statements respecting, vi., 407.
Allen, Mrs., asks pay for lead taken, vii., 452.
Allen, William, letters to and from, ii., 362. Chief Justice, iii., 64, 304.
Allentown, arms, &c., at, vi., 51, 135, 473, 655.
Allface, a Seneca chief, xii., 300.
Allibone, Wm., a warden, xii., 314.
Allomappis, (Indian,) answer to Governor, i., 224. Letter to, 266. Reported death of, 772.
Alricks, Hermanus, letters, ii., 383.

Alricks, Wessel, letter, W. P. to, i., 131,
Amazon, ship, seizure of British goods on, ix., 742, 756.
Amberson, William, viii., 289, 487.
America, North, Indian tribes in, list of, iv., 188.
American Bishops, x., 434. (See Bishop.)
American Philosophical Society, invitation to council to annual oration, viii., 136. Grant to, by Assembly, x., 204.
American regiment at Schuylkill heights, x., 323. Deserters from, 388.
Amherst, Major General Jeffrie, appointed to succeed General Abercrombie, iii., 518, Letters, 634, 694, 701, 706, 710, 712, 715, 718, 726, 734. Letters to and from, iv., 37, 39, 45, 46, 48, 50, 64, 68, 71, 73, 74, 76, 79, 87.
Ammunition, waste of, v., 27.
Anderson's Fort, xii., 461.
Anderson, Patrick, letter on state of the army, v., 27.
Anderson, Thomas, return of provisions to third Pennsylvania regiment, ix., 175.
Andover Iron Works, N. J., vi., 178.
Andrea Doria, brig, &c., destroyed by fire for safety, vi., 28.
Andrews, Robert, a Virginia commissioner, to run line between Virginia and Pennsylvania, viii., 353. Reverend, appointed by Virginia, to run line, ix., 78. Appointed by Virginia commissioner on boundary, x., 146, 171, (1783.)
Anonymous remarks on J. Brown's examination, vi., 36.
Anstey, John, applies for certified list of traitors, xi., 148.
Anstruthers, Lieut. Philip, British officer, prisoner of war, v., 77.
Antes, Colonel Fred., viii., 206, 219.
Antes, Henry, Sheriff of Northumberland county, to arrest insurgents at Wyoming, x., 344. Complaints against, 482.
Antes, Lieutenant Colonel, vi., 176.
Antes, William, vi., 456; ix., 381, 758.
Antil, Colonel, ix., 476.
Antrobus, Joseph, auctioneers petition for an act against purchasers, i., 167.
Apoquinimy, Reverend Mr. Campbell, appointed minister of, i., 191. To be removed, 236.
Appeal, instructions respecting, i., 196. From Courts, instructions to T and R. Penn, on, ii., 107. Court of, recommended by Council, vii., 78. Advice asked by delegates, 192. In cases of captures at sea, Congress resolves respecting, 265, 436.
Appointment, viii., 335. Of officers, ix., 27.
Apportionment of $636,000 among the States, x., 238.
Apprentices, and indented servants, General Shirley's letter on enlisting, ii., 417.
Apty, Thomas, letter, stopped by New York while conducting Indians, iv., 157.
Arbuthnot, Admiral, viii., 339.
Arbuthnot, Captain Alexander, merchandize seized, ix., 574.
Archives, Pennsylvania, messages of Governor respecting, i., 3, 16. Report of committees on, 3, 10. Law for publishing, 14, 22. Person to superintend, 15. Report of S. Hazard to Governor, on, 17–21. Preface, xii., iii. Report of editor, v. Supplementary act, April 12, 1855. MSS. to be bound and placed in State library. Certain documents to be framed, xii., 10.
Armand's corps, complaints against, vii., 377 General, Legion, and mutiny of soldiers, x., 62. Petition against, 133.
Armory, state of, v., 731, 733.
Armour, Lieutenant, vi., 451.
Arms, bond given to King for, ii., 300. Sent to Bucks county, 393.
Arms and ammunition, account of purchases, iii., 25. Great scarcity of, iv., 694. Agreement to import by H. B. & Co., 708. Commissioners of York county respecting, 708. In Lancaster county, 717. To be collected, vi., 47, 51, 52, 58, 86, 193, 244, 375, 395, 452, 456, 463, 480, 482, 486, 488, 495, 504, 505, 522, 547, 549,

558, 562, 576, 639, 654, 745. Received from France, 108; vii., 12, 125, 146, 190, 202, 238, 239, 290, 294, 296, 308, 338, 375, 376, 386, 417, 437, 562, 579, 711, 748; viii., 139, 238, 242, 305, 360, 453, 505, 572, 580; ix., 26, 31, 94, 192, 200, 350, 391, 393, 416, 465. &c., to be taken care of by the States, x., 154. At Carlisle, xi., 379, 458.

Armstrong, Edward, report on archives, i., 10.

Armstrong's, Fort at, [See Fort Halifax,]

Armstrong, Fort, (Kittanning,) viii., 38. Evacuated, 106. Named, xii., 134, 135, 139, 147, 156, 170, 220, 327–329. To be evacuated, 193, 194. Men sent to, 215, 234

Armstrong, John, &c., murder of, by Indians, i., 643, 646, 759.

Armstrong, Captain John, at Abraham's plains, xi., 437.

Armstrong, Captain, commander at Pittsburg, xii., 300.

Armstrong, Colonel John, letters, ii., 451, 457, 719, 767. Account of expedition and attack on Kittanning, 767–775. List of killed and wounded, 774; iii., 40, 48, 51, 54, 78, 83, 146, 173, 187, 191, 196, 201, 212, 239, 282, 289, 296, 303, 365, 446, 447, 448, 482, 551, 621, 627, 688. To provide horses, 163. Indicted, 621. Letters to and from, iv., 108, 135, 136, 146, 152, 175, 203, 205. Recruiting instructions to, 116. Murder of Conestoga Indians, 152. Asks for a battalion, 693; v., 164, 229, 324, 558, 560, 563, 568, 572, 581, 587, 598, 636, 641, 645, 653, 672, 684. On rum in army, 561. Complains of militia, vi., 100. Letters to and from, 30, 43, 53, 60, 70, 85, 90, 100, 122, 148, 149, 230, 238, 293, 412, 489, 516, 612, 613, 635, 657, 661, 669, 680, 715, 717, 744. His position, 91, 153. Lead mine, 412. Account of operations at Chestnut Hill, &c., 70. Letters to and from, viii., 31, 152, 243, 636. Letter of council respecting Wyoming, x., 307. Appointed to command under Colonel Harmer, 315. Complains of his rank, 316. Wheat to be secured, 317. Appointed commissioner to Wyoming, 327, 330. Ordered to return to Philadelphia, 360. Deposition, 623. Letters, 427, 653, 658, 675, 677, 685, 686. To inhabitants of Wyoming, 685. To President Dickinson, 686. Letters to and from, xii., 109, 285. Time of settling Sherman's valley, 285.

Armstrong, John, Jr., asks to be Secretary of council, ix., 650. Appointed to Congress, continues secretary, xi., 137. Letter, 407.

Armstrong, Joseph, letters to and from, ii., 247, 248.

Armstrong, Cap. William, wagoners stopped with British clothing, x., 12.

Armstrong, Major William, viii., 34, 311, 599. Hands employed on N. boundary, xi., 215. Describes Erie country, 242. Appointed commissioner to view lands in Luzerne county, 304, 460. Dispatches from Wyoming, (1784,) 447.

Army, proposals for raising an, iv., 654. American, v., 63, 79, 8[illegible], 84, 87, 103, 104, 105, 106, 107, 108, 112, 114, 115, 117, 119, 120, 127, 129, 132, 135, 136, 141, 142, 143, 144, 157, 158, 160, 162, 163, 168, 171, 175, 176, 178, 180, 186, 192, 196, 215, 230, 234, 236, 248, 249, 253, 300, 304, 306, 325, 370, 451, 452, 455, 485, 505, 584, 586, 598, 615, 617, 624, 636, 645, 655, 669, 672, 676, 679, 681, 683, 685, 691, 694, 697, 701, 712, 724, 731, 732, 739. Movements of, vi., 31, 43, 70, 83, 90, 97, 100, 104, 108, 144, 150, 151, 152, 155, 169, 189, 190, 230, 238, 241, 263, 265, 296, 301, 350, 369, 374, 461, 471, 556, 568, 586, 592, 659, 673, 734-736, 755; vii., 102, 103, 142, 167, 181, 237, 244, 263, 268, 300, 339, 377, 387, 392, 412, 442, 482, 494, 567, 581, 583, 607, 716, 736, 748, 752, 760, 771. Rank of officers in, 162, 607. Cost of provisions and clothing, 181. Pay and half pay of, 263; viii., 70, 72, 74, 75, 76, 85, 100, 103, 141, 168, 214, 267, 287, 295, 314, 317, 326, 333,

345, 351, 355, 389, 394, 417, 480, 603, 731, 747. Great want of provisions, 122. Success at the South, 731; ix., 71, 73, 77, 84, 120, 129, 136, 139, 151, 301, 387, 393, 430, 513, 514, 586. For the South, 109. Pay of soldiers and officers, x., 113.

Army, British, movements of, v., 43, 49, 67, 79, 80, 81, 82, 84, 96, 105, 108, 136, 141, 148, 157, 158, 161, 163, 168, 169, 171, 173, 178, 186, 194, 215, 216, 217, 230, 236, 244, 249, 289, 290, 300, 306, 351, 367, 380, 438, 450, 452, 556, 567, 606, 615, 617, 645; vi., 23, 31, 32, 43, 70, 83, 90, 97, 100, 101, 226, 263. 265, 285, 299, 366, 387, 399, 470, 500, 503, 568, 604, 622, 673, 706, 734-736, 749. Barbarity of, 470, 500-502, 503; vii., 387, 393, 412, 452, 460, 479, 484, 486, 489, 492, 509, 519, 523, 526, 561, 562, 576, 608, 635, 646, 647, 648, 663, 674, 697, 736, 775; viii., 95, 100, 293, 308, 312, 314, 333, 336, 361, 415, 539, 708; ix., 71, 102, 210, 301, 345, 347, 393, 422, 430, 436, 437.

Army, of Pennsylvania, number of men in, condition of, v., 27, 29, 33, 34, 37, 51, 52, 58.

Arndt, John, v., 421; vi., 336. Letter, ix., 53, 109, 135, 175.

Arnold, Benedict, Gen'l, appointed to command of militia at Bristol and east of Philadelphia, v., 366, 376. Wounded, 657, 675. Commands in Philadelphia, vi., 568. Proclamation on evacuation of Philadelphia, 606. Letters, 687, 704, 708, 748. Sends wagons to Egg Harbor, on private account, vii., 160, 175, 179, 181, 183, 194. Yeas and nays to be required by delegates in Congress in his case, 174. About to leave the State, 183. General Washington, respecting, 188. Votes in Congress respecting M. Clarkson, aid to, 204. Statement of John Mitchell respecting wagons used by, 207, 209, 213, 220. Letter to Wm. Shippen respecting M. Clarkson, 209. Letter to Mitchell, 216. Secretary Matlack to, respecting a name, 223. His answer, 224. Letter from John Brown, on impeachment of, 226. Board of War declines calling out militia while he commands, 230. To Board of War, resigning his command in Philadelphia, 256. Deposition of John Gardener, wagoner, 241. Passport signed by, 262, 264. Letter to John Brown, 270. Share of the Charming Nancy, 275. Court martial on, 327, 337, 351, 406. Letters to and from, 370. Letters from President Reed respecting, 325, 327, 337, 347, 351, 380. Purchase of goods in Philadelphia, his aid, David S. Franks, 370. Money borrowed, 449. And Mr. Seagrove, 450. Letter of J. D. Sergeant, on death of Jesse Jordan, abating trial, 743. Trial of, viii., 12, 35, 73. President Reed requests Congress to dispense with part of sentence of court martial in respect for his previous good services, 99. Charge against, 639. A suspected messenger to, from New York, ix., 20, 24. Mons. Holker charged with connection with, 10, 33, 178. Letter, 308. Burns New London, 404.

Arrests of Tories, v., 478, 479, 480.

Arrest of Prothonotary of Bedford county, vi., 12.

Artificers, regiment of, under Colonel Baldwin, memorial of ix., 105. Captain Wylies' return of, 665.

Artillery, Regiment of, established under Col. Thos. Proctor, v., 234. Officers, letter to Council, vii., 154. Battalion, 121, 135, 294, 339, 393. Colonel of, viii., 111. Returns of, under Gen. A. Wayne, 647, 726, 747. Returns of those paid, ix., 30, 55, 74, 123, 141, 207. Pennsylvania regiment of officers petition—confederation, 168. Col. Carrington, 207. Artificers, under Captains Wylie and Jordan, gratuity to men, x., 94. Stores in Philadelphia, xi., 257.

Ash, James, elected sheriff of Philadelphia, xi., 410.

Ashman, George, respecting attacks and murders by Indians, ix., 152, 202.

Asheton Robert, letter W. P. to,

i., 134. Draft of a law respecting courts, 165.

Assembly, writ for calling, i., 504. Remarks on the, ii., 181. Censured for not paying hands on road, 393. Print letters against Governor's wishes, 274. Remarks on by Gov. Dobbs, 280. Governor asks for minutes, 284, 286 Issues money without Governor's consent, 285. Letter to, from Gov. Morris, 356. Demand from Philadelphia, of means of defence, 485. Address of Quakers to, giving their views, 487. Committee of, letters between Governor and, 316, 318. Letters not to be submitted to, 367. Thomas Penn, letters respecting the, 367. Pass militia law, 515, 531. Character of, 226, 529. Address to Governor, iv., 77. Governor's message to, 290. Petition of, to his Majesty, 311. Message to President and Council, 436. Answer, 436. Powder offered, 679. At New Castle, message, 72, 585. Message from, 72, 248, 474. Minutes, 466, 474, 548, 665 ; v., 179, 264, 482, 491, 513, 681. Address of officers to, 724. Respecting prisoners, 513. Resolutions, 617. Laws recommended by Council to, vi., 685. Resolutions, 64, 73, 84, 155, 396, 694, 733. Ask for papers, 272. Assembly and Council to Congress, 104, 109, 111, 333. Letters to, 124, 152, 369, 518, 709. Laws to be proclaimed, 396. Laws recommended by Council, 518, 685. Letters to and from, vii., 77, 94, 100, 191, 194, 195, 202, 712, 720, 738. Statement of cost of provisions and clothing for State troops, 181. Resolutions, &c., 187, 195, 237, 244, 269, 278, 284, 294, 295, 718, 740, 741. Letters to County members of, 472. Order flour to be distributed to poor, 740. General Committee of, viii., 694, 737. Grant money for raising troops, 752. Letters to and from, 21, 262, 609, 625, 656, 685, 687, 692. Memorials to, 27, 39. Resolutions of, 8, 14, 21, 276, 280, 569, 570, 646, 657, 663, 685, 728, 729, 732,

Assembly—

734, 736, 738, 739, 751, 752, 757, 761. Letters to and from, ix., 5, 16, 51, 61, 188, 197, 209, 221, 232, 241, 248, 412, 425, 447, 459, 461, 463, 467, 501, 509, 510, 513, 620, 664. Resolutions, 4, 5, 11, 22, 52, 66, 68, 69, 506, 666, 754, 762. Committee of, 14, 22, 62, 415, 515. Recommends settlement of Connecticut question, 4. Letter to, on convention prisoners, 5, 11, 197. President's statement of affairs, 219. On State of militia, 221, 232. On money matters, 241, 248. Loans, 248. Collection of fines, 415. Infractions of laws of nations, 462, 464. Troops for federal army, 467. Boundary line, 506. Connecticut claim, 510. Operations of army, 513. Fees, 515. Supplies, 620. To employ person to collect information respecting frontiers, 666. Letters to and from, x., 8, 126, 195, 198, 407, 427, 429. Resolutions of, 8, 9, 111, 129, 130, 149, 166, 177, 178, 179, 184, 195, 196, 203, 204, 209, 233, 315, 316, 332, 334, 335, 336, 365, 367, 412, 420, 531, 538, 542, 557-561, 611, 695, 710, 711, 749. Boundary with Virginia, 8, 95. Purchase of lands from Indians, 111. Message from, 379. Reports, 224, 316, (1784,) 551, 552, 749. Of Connecticut, resolutions of, 116. Proceedings on internal Commerce, 128, 130. Rejoicings for peace, 151. Repairs to Government mansion, (1783,) 166, 332. Removal of obstructions in Delaware river, (1783,) 177. Death of Major Kennedy, 178. Officers of Pennsylvania line, 179, (1783.) Allotment of estates for University, 195. Wyoming and Connecticut, intentions of Pennsylvania, 196 Papers asked for by council, 198. Grant to American Philosophical Society, 204. Elect Auctioneers for Philadelphia, 206, 209. Wyoming, 224. Pay to W. Maclay, 315. Indian affairs, 316. Order to R. Andrews, Commissioner on boundary with Virginia, 336, 412. T. Matlack, 367. Sale of lands, 379-384. Respecting

Assembly—
James Searle, 420. Chinese strangers from Pallas, Indiaman, 532. Election of Delegates to Congress, 534. Treasurer, 534. Report on inland navigation, 538, 541. State House, 542. Wyoming, (1784,) 551, 552, 557-561. Jurisdiction of Islands in Delaware, 611, 710. Act restoring lands in Wyoming, 657. Removal of Henry Shoemaker as a justice, 695. Petition from Wyoming, 699-704. Boundary line N. Y.—Jurisdiction, &c., of Islands, 710. Custom house bonds, 711. Report on Wyoming recommitted, 749. Election of J. Hamilton in Westmoreland County, 750. Election of Persifer Frazer in Chester Co., as Register, &c., 756. Resolutions, xi., 84, 87, 103, 207, 211, 393, 395, 398, 402, 406, 523, 545, 547, 635, 665, 669, 675, 677, 682. T. Pickering elected register, &c., 84. Respecting pay to Col. Mentges, 103. For men for Luzerne Co., 207. Address of, 728. Letters to, 187, 206, 390, 348, 528. Respecting Erie Lands, 211. Thos. Lloyd proposes to publish the debates of, 212. Bill respecting Wyoming, 260. Powder magazine, 392. Purchase of Erie, 395. Respite of the Doans, 398. Accounts, 406. To Gov. Mifflin, xiii., 44.

Assembly of Three Lower counties address to Gov., on the rights assumed by that part of the province, iii., 309. Speech to, 377, 721. Message from, 380, 723. Messages to and from, 19, 380, 384. Urged by Secretary Pitt to raise troops, 95. Insult Gov. Denny, 112. Print report of Conference, 112. On road to Augusta, 561.

Assembly of Delaware, on Internal navigation, xi., 25.

Assembly of Massachusetts, resolutions of, i., 666.

Assembly of Virginia, resolutions, viii., 352.

Asswikales, Indians, number of, iv., 302.

Association Battery, Phil., xii., 437.

Associators of York County, rules for, iv., 657.

Atkins, Edmund, appointed Superintendent, of Indian affairs, iii., 155. Letters, 175, 183, 197, 268, 288. On Scalps, 185, 199.

Atlee, Judge, criminals at York, vii., 773.

Atlee, Col. Samuel J., letters to and from, state of army, v., 6, 10. On rank of, vii., 188. Return to the line opposed, 582. To purchase Flour, 674; viii., 216, 242, 250, 305, 311, 333, 335, 351, 423, 437, 438, 469, 484, 580, 673. Commissioner to treat with Indians, x., 265. Letters from, on election—deed of Six nations, 360.

Atlee, William, v., 248, 301, 327, 365, 376; vi., 212. (Judge) respecting State lands, viii., 56. Tories, 125; ix., 8. Falls from his horse, 170. Prisoners and troops, 203, 335, 347. Guards, 212. Robbery, 596. Muster rolls of Lancaster Co., x., 394.

Attainder, legal evidence of, ix., 656.

Attorney's fees, report on, xi., 647.

Attorney General to be more liberally provided for, vi., 686. Commission to J. D. Sergeant as, viii., 613. He resigns it, 612. William Bradford, Jr., appointed, 613, 621. Letters to and from, xii., 99.

Auction duties, xi., 127. Auctioneers appointed, 128, 565, 680. Reports, 748, 755, 761.

Auctioneer, complaint of an, i., 167. For Philadelphia, elected by Assembly, x., 206, 209.

Auditor General, U. S., state of finances U. S., vi., 591.

Auditors of accounts of troops to be appointed, viii., 751. Queries by, 762. And answers to, 764. Letters to and from, ix., 11, 12, 13, 17, 18, 29, 36, 47, 67, 104.

Augusta Fort, ii., [See Forts.] Respecting, iii., 4, 9, 12, 13, 14, 17, 41, 43, 47, 64, 79, 88, 98, 100, 119, 161, 249, 279, 283, 287, 326, 327, 347, 349, 374, 388, 403, 406, 408, 431, 478, 480, 502, 513, 515, 521, 550, 568, 570, 574, 621, 686, 696,

721, 727. Regiment officers in Province, pay and date of commissions, 88. Forces refuse to do duty for want of pay, 98 ; iv., 38, 82, 88, 112, 122, 123, 128, 140, 165, 195, 207, 214, 463 ; v., 377, 414, 611, 763. Letters from, respecting Indians, vi., 57, 175, 191, 393, 478, 499, 537, 552, 564, 570, 571, 573, 599, 615, 624, 631, 637, 711 ; vii., 574. At Sunbury, xii., 329-339.

Augusta, sixty-four blown up, v., 696, 703, 721, 698, 699.

Augustus, (an Indian) intelligence received by, ii., 729.

Augwick, speech of Governor Morris to Indians at, ii., 193. Indians near, viii., 278.

Avery, John, Jr., letter from, vii., 477.

B.

Bache, Richard, v., 409. Appointed to superintend magazines of flour, vi., 235. Appointed by Congress to sign bills, viii., 635, 639 ; ix., 185.

Bache, Benjamin F., establishes his Daily Advertiser, xi., 713.

Backhouse, Rev. Mr., appointed Missionary at Chester, i., 226.

Bail, by whom to be taken, vi., 595.

Bailey, Francis, and Captain Lang, vi., 404.

Baily, James, vi., 766 ; viii., 390. Wagons, ix., 160. Prisoners, 204, 210, 212, 231.

Bailey, John, v., 405, 413.

Bailey, William, v., 349.

Baird, Richard, capture, iii., 391. Deposition, 396.

Baker, Hilary on Tavern Licenses, xi., 604.

Baker, Hilary, Jr., asks explanation of late act abolishing slavery, viii., 720. Forfeited estates, ix., 195.

Bald Eagle Creek—Indian murders on, vi., 515, 552.

Baldwin, Col., commands regiment of artificers, memorial, ix., 105.

Ballet, Captain of His Majesty's ship Otter, pipe of wine, &c., presented by city, ii., 5. Letter from, 7. Long action with a large ship, 7.

Balliett, Col. Stephen, viii., 565. Supplies, ix., 649, 744. Observations on Lehigh river and roads, vi., 131. Remarks on, 135. Council to, respecting Wyoming, 179. Appointed commissioner to view lands in Luzerne Co., 304. Instructions, 461.

Ballot, voting by, Censors inquire of Council respecting, x., 302. Answer of Council, 306.

Balme, Col. De la, viii., 766, 767.

Baltimore, letter to Magistrates of, on sailors, vii., 399. Commissioners on boundary with Virginia, meet and agree at, x., 96.

Baltimore, Lord, Letter from Gov. Markham, to, i., 39. His commissioners waiting for Gov. Markham, 46. Letter to, from Gov. Dongan, 86. Sends Geo. Talbot, his proceedings, 87. W. Penn's declaration against, 88. Notice to, of meeting of commissioners, 623. Letters from, 393, 395.

Bamper, Mr., suspicions against him as a messenger to Arnold, ix. 20, 24.

Bancroft, Daniel, v., 231, 246. In prison, 231, 246.

Bank of North America, resolutions of Congress respecting establishment, ix., 173, 471, 477, 496. Charter, 471.

Bankrupt laws, do they affect proceedings on Collector's bonds? xi., 250.

Baptist Church, Philadelphia, (See Keithian B. C.,) i., 285.

Barbary Powers, memorial from merchants on Capture by, x., 410, 411, 705.

Barclay, John, Hog Island, xi., 89.

Barclay, Thomas, on Dutch Loans, ix., 563. Free ports of France, x., 267.

Bard, Peter, letter, ii., 764; iii., 432, 499. Letter, iv., 210.

Barge and Tyng respecting salt, vii., 728.

Barney, Capt. Joshua, captures in the Delaware, ship General Monk, in the Hyder Ally, after a brilliant action, ix., 531, 532.

Barnsley, Cap. Thos., iv., 209, 212.

Barracks, in Philadelphia, building, iii., 279; iv., 170. Lancaster, 179. Expense of converting old

jail into, 715. At Fort, defective, 729. At Fort Island nearly finished, 786; v., 7, 48, 71, 75, 78, 148, 179, 184, 224. Used by U. S., out of repair, viii., 61, 161. Near Basley's Mill, 41; ix., 326, 426. At Lancaster, x., 233, 237, 307. At Philadelphia, 239, 241, 261, 268, 276, 737. Lots, sale of, Philadelphia, xi., 506.

Barrack master's report of filthy houses left by soldiers, v. 265.

Barras, Mons. de, commander of French squadron at Newport, ix., 273, 353, 354.

Barry, John, (Capt.), recommends the Lexington sent down, iv., 750; vi., 243.

Bartholomew, Edward, appointed Collector of Excise, x., 442.

Barton, Job, collector, Bucks Co., robbed, ix., 459.

Barton, Rev. Thomas, letters to and from, ii., 568, 755, 756; iii., 245, 377, 447, 450, 452. Complains as Chaplain, 451. Letter from Gen. Forbes, 451; iv., 132; v., 634. Accepts Chaplaincy in British Reg't at N. Y., vii., 226. Gone over to enemy, viii., 30.

Battalions, Letter to Colonels of, viii., 111.

Battery, at Newcastle, order to pay workmen at, iii., 317.

Batwell, Rev. Mr., v., 770; vi., 95, 144. Daniel, (Episcopal missionary from England,) grant of land to—a tory, viii., 107. Imprisoned —goes to N. Y., 107.

Bautcher, Samuel, ix., 127, 153.

Baxter, Lt. Col. Wm., Letter, v., 31.

Bayard, Maj. John, proposes to import arms, &c., for Committee, iv., 707, 708. Agreement with Congress, 708. Memorial on confusion of troops in city, v., 17. Letter, few troops joining Gen. W., 107, 148; vi., 61, 75; vii., 136, 189, 194, 311; viii., 111. A pass to Charleston, viii., 247. Commands at Fort Pitt, (1783,) x., 167. Delegate to Congress, 534. Letter as Delegate, xi., 456.

Bayard, Col. Stephen, xii., 113, 116, 127, 131, 133, 134, 139, 181.

Baynton & Wharton, goods destroyed, iv., 226.

Baynton, John, Collector of Tonnage, statement respecting, x., 511.

Beahm, Philip, vii., 13.

Beall, Capt. Thomas, detachment arrives at Pittsburg, xii., 120. Letters, 225, 230. Trial, 256.

Beaton, John, vi., 494.

Beatty, Rev. Charles, Chaplain, iii, 297.

Beatty, Capt., xii., 300.

Beatty, Ercurius, and F. Bowen, Agents, to distribute certificates to Pennsylvania Line—Report, x., 437, 506. Resignation, (1784,) 604. Resumed, 605.

Beatty, John, ix., 125.

Beaver Creek, number of houses, iii., 563.

Beck, Ensign, xii., 142, 276.

Becker, Lieut. Col., v., 485.

Bedford, Raystown, iii., 293, 482, 489, 510. Alarm from Indians, iv., 111. Highway roberry near, 458. Road to Pittsburg, xi., 560, 643. Provisions arrive at, xii., 112, 114. Boat-builders tools at, 114.

Bedford County, Commissioners of, letter, on firelocks, iv., 712. Only one gunsmith in County, 712. Troops required to march to Gen. Washington, (v.) 149. Riflemen behave bravely at Lawrence's Is'd under Col. Neilson, 230. Demand of records, Court held at, 730. Election, 730. Alarming condition from Indians, vi., 38. Prothonotary, arrest of, 12. Records, 12. Alarms of Indians, 194. Militia, 229. Records, Court, &c., 238, 511. Alarms from Indians and Tories, 438, 458, 459, 460, 469, 478, 505, 524, 682. Arms in, 506. Supplies for, 539. Freeholders of 577. Prisoners, 569. Justices, 577. Destitute of arms, &c., 619. Tory trials at, 750, 764, 769. R. Galbraith resigns office in, vii., 99. Case of Culbertson, 186. United States arms to Militia of, 202. Captain Cluggage appointed to a Command in, 296. Letter, B. Dougherty, on trial at, 297. Magazine for provisions at, 305. Lieut. Piper, 578. Troops for, 341, 370. Affairs in, 446, 515, 534, 696. Murders by Indians, 534. Election of Justices, viii.,

101. Troops sent to, alarm from Indians, 408. Capt. Phillips, &c., killed by Indians, 488. Plan of defence, 740. Military division of, ix., 149. Murders by Indians, 152, 192, 202. Distresses of, 234, 236. Militia, 410, 514, 539. Position, 467. Distress from Indians, 619, 628. M. Doane in jail at, x., 112. Prisoners to be sent to Lancaster, 119. Census of white males under 53, 512.

Bedford, Gunning, commissioner of Taxes, ix., 140.

Bedwell, Thomas, letter, respecting refining of sulphur, iv., 719, 752. ix., 601.

Beelor, Col., boundary with Virginia, viii., 583. Provisions, xii., 238, 253, 278.

Belcher, Gov., letters to and from, ii., 172, 242, 243, 261, 269, 471, 478, 489, 501, 513, 527, 530, 699. Orders to Col. Andrew Johnston, 480. Petition to, respecting Indians, 488. Letters, iii., 54, 151. Speech, 98. Address of Representatives to, (1757,) 170.

Bell, John, letters, ii., 692; iii., 282. Capt'n, xii., 123.

Bell, Major, reasons for not building a house for him, viii., 287.

Belten, Joseph, invents a submarine mode of defence, iv., 650, 654.

Benezet, James, v., 469.

Bens, Peter, taken prisoner by Indians, viii., 171.

Bensell, C., letter, respecting fugitives from Germantown, v., 10.

Benton, Caleb, letter to Col. John Franklin, respecting, towns in Tioga, xi., 175.

Bergen, Gen. Wayne's attack on, viii., 450.

Berkenhaut, Dr., arrest of, vii., 742.

Berks county, petition for road, ii., 98. Number of Roman Catholics in, iii., 144. Petition from, 361. Petition of Lutheran Church in, iv., 279. Petition for improving Schuylkill, 360. Minutes of Committee of, 649. Resolutions respecting conscientiously scrupulous, 649, 653. Powder for sale, 679. Petition from, complain of Indians as a burden and expense, iv., 273. Committee respecting powder and arms, 697. Resolution to purchase arms, 725. Fears from negroes, 792. Proceedings of Committee respecting prisoners of War, v., 19. Powder, 111. Fire-arms, 112. Troops desert, 196. Officers of counties, 341. Number of inhabitants between eighteen and fifty-three years, 322. Commissions for Justices, 323. For Prothonotary, 323. Court in, 464. Militia, 466, 523, 530, 756. Militia, vi., 47, 119. Justices, letter from, 138, 722. Wagons, 212. Courts, 234. No attorney who practices in Courts, 245, 496. Commissioner for purchasing provisions, 327, 347. Tories, 342, 344, 346, 362. Commissioner of, 395, 520. Militia, 418. Census of, 418. Tax assessed, 520. Justices of, insulted by Lieut. Col. Moy, 722. Purchases of wheat ordered in, vii., 559. Taxes, viii., 124, 132, 136, 138. N. Lutz appointed commissioner of purchases, 201. Militia, 273, 742. Drunken officers, 742. James Read, Register of Court of Admiralty—appointed—death of Andrew Robinson, Register, 191. Proprietary land, 231, 237. Prisoners, 234. Shot and shells from, 432. List of officers of the militia in, x., 190, 331. Troops to march to Wyoming, 345. Irregularity of election to be inquired into, xi., 287, 310.

Bermuda, request from, for provisions, ii., 661.

Bermudians, distress of, apply for flour, &c., vii., 412. Recommendation of Congress, 413.

Bernard, Gov. Fra., Letter, iii., 453.

Berry, Cap., a Virginia officer, xii., 274.

Berwick, Philadelphia Society, for manufacture, &c., propose a road, xi., 428.

Bethlehem, dreadful state of neighborhood, ii., 523, 549, 565, 636, 714, 715. Indian refugees at, 384. Address, 636. Articles sent from, 658. Indians there, iii., 52. List of Moravians at, 69–76, 242. Hospitals, v., 768. A suspicious

box direc'd to, vi., 5-7. Deposi'ns respecting, 7. Flour to be sent to, 177. Gen. Gates at, 197. Troops ordered by Congress to, 374. Guards at to be dismissed, 541. Orders for wafers sent to, from Philadelphia, vii., 295.

Biddle, Charles, elected V. P, x., 527. Letter respecting Chinese, &c., x., 527. Appointed Secretary of Council, xi., 2)7.

Biddle, Col. Clement, letters, v., 141, 145, 170, 197, 721, 739, 744, 756. Clothier General, vi., 76, 92, 104, 123, 139, 187, 299, 321, 540, 738; ix., 129. Marshal, bonds, xi., 236. On exchange of loans, 573. Tents for French emigrants, 743. Letter, xii., 314.

Biddle, James, opinion on making returns of property for Taxes, viii., 136.

Biddle, John, vi., 242.

Biddle, Owen, letters to and from, v., 3, 10, 80, 105, 117, 148, 158, 182, 192, 249, 267, 301, 315. Letter to Gen. Greene on forage, viii., 151, 223. Horses, 169.

Big Bone Lick, viii., 152.

Biggs, Cap. Benjamin, xii., 195, 235.

Bigham, Fort, xii., 341.

Bigham, Lieutenant, viii., 316, 748; ix., 148, 207, 256, 285.

Billet, Crooked, surprise and action at, on General Lacey, vi., 470. Barbarity of British soldiers, 471, 500. Depositions respecting, 500.

Billiard Tables, taxes on, Philadelphia, x., 222, 224.

Billingsport, works at, iv., 784. Fortifications at, v., 8, 9, 11, 37, 46, 66, 118, 167, 230, 238, 305, 306, 359, 361, 377, 409, 411, 418, 423, 431, 437, 438, 449, 451, 461. Return of troops at, 423. In need of officers, 437. Of blankets, 462. Expenses at, 471. Respecting, 511, 558, 563, 568, 572, 590, 591, 626, 644, 663, 721. Captured by enemy, 649. Action near, 663, 697. Lord Cornwallis gone to, vi., 23, 3). Battery to be erected by Colonel Bull, 746. Claims against, vii., 140. Visits of President, &c. to., 199, 200, 393. Troops for, 270. Cannon for, 290, 298. Troops, &c., for, 339, 365, 366, 369, 393, 425, 507, 673. To officers at, respecting embargo aids, 409, 424. Officers relieved, 502. Orders about vessels, 538. Col. McCulloh relieves Col. Proctor's Artillery at, 371. Stores wanted at, 539. Orders to vessels, 537. Return of cannon at, 562. William Hamell in charge of, ix., 330. William Smith stationed at, 544. Returns of military stores at, x., 284. Lease of, xi., 139. Fort at, xii., 341-346.

Bills of Credit, Board of Trade, orders on, i., 187. Letters on, 197, 206. Counterfeit, 579, 580, 589. History of, ii., 102. Instructions to Governor Thomas respecting, 104. Board of Trade on New Jersey, 128. Letters respecting, 221, 223; iii., 99, 113, 115, 117, 195. Counterfeit, 365. Resolutions of House of Commons on, iv., 173. Counterfeited, 461, 466. Of States to be received by United States Loan Office, v., 183. At Loan Office, vi., 184. Depreciation, 212. Issued, 270. Struck by British called in, 59. Inquiry respecting, 538, 548. (under the Crown) Resolutions of Congress respecting, vii., 154. Signing, x., 456; xii., 34.

Bingham, William, Delegate in Congress, xi., 308.

Birch, M., collector, W. P. to, i., 131. Inquiry respecting, 138.

Bird, Colonel Mark, pay of soldiers, v., 9.

Birthday of King of France, celebrated at Philadelphia, vii., 648.

Bishop, Rev. Nathaniel, Moravian preacher at Bethlehem, on murders at Muskingum, ix., 523.

Bishop of London, commissions Rev. Mr. Cummings to exercise jurisdiction over the Clergy of Pennsylvania, removal of Mr. Campbell, i., 236. Ministers licensed by, not allowed to preach in Christ Church, 628.

Bishop, an American, letters relating to consecration of in Denmark and England, x., 433-435. Consecration of Bishops White and Provoost, x., 434.

Black Logg, xii., 461.

Blackiston, Governor, Letter, W. P., to, i., 135.

Blackwell, John, appointed Governor, arrives at Boston, i., 106. And at Philadelphia, 106. Letter from, 107.

Blackwood, John, letter iii., 402, 403.

Bladen, Governor Thomas, letters to and from, i., 645, 686, 692, 726.

Blaine, Ephraim, commands at Ligonier, iv. 108. Letter, on dry lands near Carlisle, iv., 591. Declines a commission as Sub-Lieutenant, v., 299. Letter, 677. D. C. G., vi., 252. Commissioner of purchases, vii., 17. Scarcity of flour, names of assistants, 707. Letters, viii., 13, 92, 260, 304, 479, 480, 494, 565, 577, 602, 630, 646, 705. Appointed Commissary General, 151, 625; ix., 54, 73, 98, 121, 143. Payment of interest on city lots, x., 609; xii., 278.

Blair, Rev. James, memorial from Christ Church, against, i., 150.

Blair, James, letter respecting men of galleys to work at rope walk, v., 24. Powder, 50.

Blair, Rev. Samuel, Chaplain in army, asks for his own servant, ix., 111.

Blakiston, Presley, commissioner of Taxes, ix., 140.

Bland, Colonel Theodore, K., vii., 99, 107.

Blankets, account of, sent west of Susquehanna, iii., 95, &c., scarcity of, v., 376, 572; 630, 632, 751, 762; vi., 93, 253.

Blewer, Captain Joseph, vi., 671.

Block-house, built by Col. Lochry, ix., 80.

Blue Bell, skirmish at between Potter's and Cornwallis's men, vi., 32.

Blunston, Samuel, letters to and from, i., 216, 295, 316, 353, 363, 410, 436, 437, 530, 547. Instructions to, 229. Letters to and from, ii., 66.

Blythe, Col. Benjamin, vii., 496. Letter, viii., 97.

Board of Admiralty, ix., 95, 100.

Board of Trade, report on laws, i., 721. Letters to and from Gov. Hamilton, describing the boundaries of the State, &c., ii., 60, 65. Letters, 377, 418, 467, 527, 778. On New Jersey paper money, 128.

Board of War, Continental, v., 306, 371, 382, 399, 430, 434, 439, 450, 502, 512, 535, 570, 583, 585, 675, 685, 686, 751, 756. Order to Col. Mackay to march to Kittanning, 93; vi., 35, 42, 52, 63, 74, 79, 84, 86, 93, 118, 127, 175, 185, 188, 192, 195, 205, 208, 214, 216, 233, 268, 281, 339, 351, 360, 370, 392, 403, 429, 444, 454, 492, 515, 526, 529, 533, 540, 546, 549, 556, 558, 576, 581, 586, 593, 605, 608, 643, 644, 646, 648, 649, 654, 655, 667, 668, 676, 684, 688, 727, 745, 749, 758, 768. Resolutions of, 74. Inquiries respecting provisions, &c., 185. Order of, 199. Letter to Congress from, 315. Plan for support of frontiers, 526; vii., 89, 90, 98, 99, 101, 107, 201, 202, 227, 229, 230, 232, 233, 256, 282, 284, 286, 287, 289, 292, 305, 308, 312, 329, 332, 339, 340, 375, 385, 387, 397, 404, 418, 420, 421, 424, 437, 442, 450, 454, 456, 459, 460, 469, 480, 495, 496, 508, 538, 627, 640, 649, 681, 691, 696, 709, 713, 719, 727, 730, 731. Resolution of, 256; viii., 5, 8, 38, 43, 57, 62, 74, 96, 98, 110, 119, 122, 132, 141, 153, 159, 161, 165, 171, 175, 181, 218, 224, 248, 308, 343, 425, 432, 434, 435, 436, 442, 453, 456, 471, 478, 485, 498, 505, 508, 509, 515, 549, 552, 554, 573, 575, 579, 580, 600, 601, 611, 633, 689, 722, 727, 728, 739, 747; ix., 3, 7. 14, 19, 23, 24, 26, 31, 53, 57, 58, 95, 96, 103, 111, 124, 150, 167, 186, 187, 198, 206, 290, 291, 391, 526. Committees of conference, 23; xi., 208, 240, 268, 281, 291, 300, 534, 555, 621, 624, 645, 685, 686, 707, 716, 728.

Board of War, State, appointed, v., 252. Discontinued, 253. Letters to and from, 264, 268, 281, 282, 283, 292, 295, 306, 314, 319, 320, 325, 328, 342, 345, 346, 348, 350, 355, 358, 364, 376, 382, 396, 398, 401, 409, 418, 427, 428, 434, 451,

683. Resignation of Wm. Moore, 264.
Boat, model of, for defence of Delaware, by N. Irish, iv., 638.
Boats, armed, in Delaware river, pay of men, v. 30. Destroyed or lost, xii., 217.
Boehm, Lieut. Col., v., 253.
Boger, Richard, Letter, v., 31.
Boggs, Maj., sent with prisoners to Philadelphia, v., 233.
Boggs, Martha, reserved lands opposite Fort Pitt, x., 699.
Bond, Col., of New Jersey, attacks a party of tories at Delaware Water Gap, viii., 259.
Bond, Phineas, respecting parole, v., 578; vi., 655. Acknowledged as British Consul, in Middle States, xi., 145. Suggestions as to laws affecting interest of Great Britain, 255. Letter on complaint of Judges of Admiralty, 381. Opinion of Judges on, 383.
Bond, Dr. Thomas, iii., 673, 676. Report on sickly vessels, iv., 59, 374. Preparations for his family's removal, v., 79. Removes sick to Philadelphia, 79. Advice respecting, 89. On military hospitals, 89. Letter, 383.
Bondfield, John, vi., 172, 330.
Bonumtown, skirmish at, v., 211.
Books wanted by Congressmen, v., 754, 757, 772.
Boone, Capt., vii., 57. Killed, at Fort Freeland, 590, 610. List of his party, 610.
Boone, George, to Gov. on Indian affairs, i., 217. Dams on Schuylkill, 315.
Boone, Thomas, letter respecting Indians, iv., 67.
Borden, Joseph, finds sulphur at Bordentown, iv., 753.
Bornie, Laurence, file cutter, petition, iv., 777.
Boscawen, Vice-Admiral, appointed to command of fleet for North America, ii., 291, 322, 421. Off Newfoundland with his fleet, 373. Takes two men of war, 375. Letters to and from, 323, 421. Letter, on surrender of Louisburg, vessels taken, &c., iii., 498.
Bosley's Mills, viii., 171.
Boston, Select men of, ask for provisions, ii., 708. Great fire in, aid solicited, iii., 714. Granted by Assembly, 715. Commissioners of customs at, appointed, iv., 289. Letters from, 289, 305, 310, Arrival of British men-of-war, 685. British prisoners escape from, vii., 698, 717.
Botetourt, Lord, Gov. of Virginia, iv., 364, 368, 371.
Boudinot, Elias, on discovery of sulphur, iv., 720, 727; v., 313, 443. Commissary Genl. of prisoners, 313, 502; vi., 89, 127, 162, Letter, x., 74.
Boundary line between Maryland and Pennsylvania, correspondence between Gov. G. and O., i., 336, 342, 343, 347. Commissioners Letters, 556, 557, 558, 568, 574, 613. Various proceedings of commissioners and surveyors, 595–615. Commissioners of Pennsylvania, 599. Do. of Maryland, 603. Meeting of commissioners at Philadelphia, 623. See Maryland. Agreement to run the line between Lord Baltimore and Thomas and Richard Penn, in 1760, iv., 1–36. Commissioners appointed by Pennsylvania, Delaware, and Maryland, to retrace the line between these States, report, &c., 37. Between New York and New Jersey, 337, 339, 340. Western, of Pennsylvania, 346, 424.
Boundary between Pennsylvania and Virginia, vii., 309, 310, 441, ix., 28, 78, 189. Commissioners of Virginia, 78, 160, 233, 234, 301, 303, 315, 375, 402, 439, 506, 518, 533, 549, 562, 566, 585, 607, 772. Report to, and resolution of Assembly, x., 8, 56, 72, 95, 96. Col. Cox, &c., 96, 125, 131. Gov. Harrison on, 56, 72, 77, 95, 96, 145, 171. Commissioners appointed by Virginia, 146, 336; by Pennsylvania, 223, 230, 233, 236, 269, 372, 373, 412, 413, 428, 438, 439, 489, 506, 573, 602, 608.
Boundary—the Western, described, x., 439. Commissioners, 443, 452, 760. With New York, x., 412, 413, 414, 422, 435, 444, 450,

454, 710. Commissioners on, 422, 450.
Boundary with Indians, x., 418.
Boundary line, Western, xi., 26, 52, 69, 71. With Virginia, 497, 499, 501, 507. Northern, 134, 141, 156, 178, 187, 203, 214, 215, 216, 241, 243, 313. Complete, 214. New York and Pennsylvania, 523, 526.
Boundary lines between Virginia and Pennsylvania, xii., 178, 182.
Bounties, vii., 355; viii., 26, 52, 206; and gratuities to soldiers, &c., ix., 18, 69, 75, 80, 114, 118, 174.
Bouquet, Col. Henry, letters, iii., 82, 85. On quarters for soldiers, 111. Respecting, 145, 265, 547, 571, 670. Conference with Indians at Pittsburg, 571. Letters to and from, iv., 166, 199, 205, 206, 208. Express to, 173. Memorandum for equipment of troops, 179, 194, 206, 210.
Bowdoin, Gov. James, of Massachusetts, letters to Congress on insulting correspondence of Captain Henry Stanhope, x., 499-506.
Bowen, Capt. J. B., letter, v., 114.
Bowen, Major, and Cap. Beatty, xi., 504.
Bowman, Col., xii., 243, 244.
Boyd, Capt. Alex., instructions, v., 43. Letter, 49. Ranging Company, ix., 543. Elected Auctioneer for Philadelphia, x., 206, 209.
Boyd, Col. Andrew, v., 712, 748; vi., 355, 432, 483, 582, 646; vii., 97, 471. Taken prisoner at Fort Washington, 384. Death of Jesse Jordan, viii., 12. Teams, 322.
Boyd, L't, massacred by Indians, vii., 723.
Boyd, Col. J., vi., 596. Letter of Council to, respecting Wyoming, x., 307. Appointed Commiss'r to, 330. Letter, 627.
Boyd, Mr., murder of, by the Smiths, vii., 410. Murderers of, to be arrested, viii., 244.
Boyle, Alexander, instructions with prisoners from, iv., 51. Instructions, with prisoners from St. Johns, &c., 688.
Boyrie, Mons., supposed plot, iv., 79.
Boys, Capt. Nathan, orders to prepare for President's visit to fortifications, vii., 200. To get gallies ready, 240, 248, 566. At Mud Island Fort, viii., 728. Orders for Capt. Roach to return, ix., 175. Ordnance, 416.
Braddock, Gen. E., instructions to, ii., 203, 261. Arrival, 277. Letters to and from, 258, 261, 263, 269, 285, 288, 290, 299, 372. Letters respecting, 284, 286, 363, 365, 366, 369, 377, 379, 382, 383, 419, 462, 525. His movements, 277. Franklin undertakes to procure wagons for, 292. His advertisement for them, 294. Wm. Shirley, Secretary to, 307. Respecting his road, 313, 321, 329, 345, 347, 359, 363, 373, 569. Gives passes to soldiers' wives, 348. Letter from Governor Morris to committee of Assembly for wagons for, 357, 377. Asks aid for Mr. Leslie in purchases, 316, 356. Captain Orde commands train, 346, 356, 358. Letter Charles Swaine respecting provisions for, 360, 362, 364, 372. Dispatches for, 377. His defeat, 379, 381, 382, 383, 394. [See Colon. Rec., VI.] Col. Dunbar turns towards Philadelphia—destroys provisions, &c., 383, 419, 422, 446. Effect of defeat on Indians, 394. Captain Orne, 399, 400. Col. Burton, 400. Orders recruits, 401. Complaint of, cattle purchased for, 410. And for not being paid for wagons, 576. Commissioners appointed to settle accounts, 583, 598, 638. Award of Commissioners, 639. Croghan a Captain of Indians under, 689; iii., 549.
Bradford, Thomas, escort of prisoners, vii., 560. Provision for prisoners, 731. List of officers and prisoners of war, viii., 93. Prisoners, 97. To prevent intercourse between officers and disaffected, 502; ix., 338, 380.
Bradford, Wm., president of convention at Hartford, viii., 616.
Bradford, Col. William, v., 401, 430, 557, 575, 582, 615, 644, 648, 663, 668, 707, 740, 745; vi., 11, 24, 27, 80, 204, 332; viii., 111.
Bradford, Wm. C., paymaster to

fleet, v., 746; vi., 451. P. M., vii., 556.
Bradford, Wm., Jr., appointed Attorney-General, viii., 613, 621. Statement of facts respecting his official acts, 666. Lieut. Bigham, 725. Hog Island and Colonel Proctor, 730, 760. Letters, ix., 199, 266, 272, 407, 408, 515, 553, 656, 659, 676, 731. Opinions on prize flour, 407, 408, 690. Fees, 515. City lots, 553. On Molesworth's estate, 659. On Connecticut trial, 576, 695. Opinion on British goods seized in Chester county, 731. Wilcock's salt and city lots, 750. Case of T. Matlack, x., 202, 635. Case of Big Spring tract, 712. Fees in Montgomery county, 743. List of Commissioners, taxes, &c., 494. Militia fines, 748. Opinion case J. O'Hara, xi., 58. Col. Thomas Hartly to, on trial of York rioters, 115. Opinion on militia appeals, 122. On case of Charles Sims' claim to lands, 162. His fees and duties as Attorney-General, 232. Opinion of Judges on, 233. And of Council, 234. Permission to publish, 234. On effect of bankrupt laws, 250. On citizenship, 260. Case Neiss and Rheiner, 273. Election in Berks co., 310. Papers from New York, 415. 419. To committee of States on Wyoming (1784), 446. Case of Longschamps, 467. Health office fees, 618. On weights and measures, 734. On demand of a fugitive to Connecticut, 737.
Bradford & Hall, author of "Detector," ix., 266.
Bradshaw, Thomas, letter, iv., 297. Demand of murderer in New York, 297.
Bradstreet, Col., death of, ii., 702, 734. Success at Cadaraqui, iii., 517, 518. Grants a peace with Indians of Erie and Ohio, iv., 207.
Brady, son of Captain, mortally wounded, vi., 688. Particulars, 689.
Brady, Capt. John, number of men iv., 108.
Brady, Capt., vii., 505; viii., 378, 565. Expedition against Indians, ix., 39. Returned from Sandusky and takes prisoners, good conduct, &c., xii., 130, 131, 132, 139, 186, 210, 243, 244. Letters to, 213, 276.
Brady's fort, viii., 157.
Brandywine Creek, Indians complain of encroachments at, i., 239.
Brandywine, killed and wounded, &c. at battle of, v., 666, 672, 714. Battle of, vi., 58, 214, 286. Wounded at, vii., 608. Indian purchase of, xii., 281.
Brant, Indians does mischief at Pennipack, vii., 63, 623.
Brant, Captain, x., 88.
Brearly, David, C. J. of N. J., demand of fugitives—the practice, xi., 548.
Breckenridge, Hugh M., deposition, ix., 572. Answer to, 661. Delivers an eulogium on those who fell in the revolution (1779), 162,
Breckenridge, H., on Cornplanter, Indian Chief, xi., 732.
Brewer, Colonel, (Secretary to General Sullivan,) vii., 724.
Bridge at Cobb's creek, site for, i., 329.
Bridges and roads, i., 767. Guard, orders to, v., 121, 124. On Burlington road to be destroyed, 95. Governor of New Jersey, respecting, 238. Over Schuylkill, vi., 685, 768. On Schuylkill, Sullivan's, vii., 152, 196.
Bridgeton, New Jersey, salt scarce, pork plenty, v., 86.
Brigade Majors, not furnished with commissions, vi., 240.
Brigadier-Generals needed, vi., 149, 151.
Bright, Doct., ix., 575.
Brigs, Captain, at McIntosh, xii., 277.
Brison, James, justice at Pittsburg, xi., 422. Licenses, 624.
Bristol, sulphur discovered, iv., 723. Sick and wounded at, v., 175. Arms and ammunition at, 181. Camp near, 321, 342, 352, 368, 414.
British Soldiers to be escorted to Newtown, 96. Vessels trade with tories in Delaware, 504. Captain Murphey, action with, 504, 510. Vessels of war, 118, 126, 132,

216, 217, 263, 305, 315, 351, 352, 410, 435, 439, 450, 452, 453, 454, 457, 462, 465, 467, 468, 470, 472, 480, 488, 504, 532, 591, 604, 648, 668, 680, 721, 746. Flag and escort at Lancaster, affair between, and officers, vi., 268. Vessels of war, 706. Fleet off Rhode Island, 733–736. Charged with using papers of vessels taken, ix., 151 ; plot of prisoners to escape discovered, 155 ; goods per ship Amazon seized, 742, 756 ; damages sustained in Northampton county, from the, 765. British goods seized in Chester county, 731 — and opinion respecting, 731 ; in ship Amazon, 742, 756 ; seizure of, 475, 476, 479, 742, 756, 757. Prison ships described, 757, 763 ; prisoners of war, 515. [See Prisoners.] And German clothing deficient, x., 7. Commercial arrangements, remedy for evils of, 155. Merchants complain of grievances from America, 745. Capture of negroes by, xi., 75. Consul, Phineas Bond, acknowledged as, 145. Interferes with rights of States, 375.

Brocden, Charles, Master of Rolls, iii., 703.

Brodhead, Daniel, letter on state of troops after battle of Long Island, v., 21. And account of, 22. Sickness, 40. Letters, 21, 29, 158, 283, 345 ; vi., 462, 492, 650, 660, 662, 687, 772. Letters respecting state of frontiers, vii., 465, 495. Account of affairs with Indians, 505. Letters to, respecting frontiers, 516, 521, 525, 541, 564, 569, 664, 702, 710, 771. Letters, &c., viii., 21, 22, 36, 38, 50, 65, 66, 68, 69, 78, 79, 106, 109, 119, 120, 140, 149, 152, 158, 197, 210, 246, 249, 283, 300, 378, 478, 487, 488, 513, 536, 558, 565, 583, 584, 588, 595, 596, 640, 641, 707, 743, 766, 770. Places soldiers in private houses, (Ward and Smallman's) at Pittsburg, 22, 119, 120, 149. Proposes purchase of proprietary manors, offers to interest others in it, 121. Answer to, 150. Attacks of savages, 140. Congress resolve to sustain, 195, 250. Explains his course, 197. Suit against in Virginia, 202. Militia, 210. State of frontiers, 246, 249 283. Scalps, 301. Misunderstanding with officers at Fort Pitt, 405. Apprehends to use force to obtain provisions, 471. Respecting frontiers, 478. Danger of evacuating his post, 487, 488. Murder by Wyandots, 513. Short of provisions, 515, 518. Murder by Indians, 536. Scarce of provisions, 558. Instructions to Captain Samuel Brady, 566. Base attempt to destroy Indians near Hanna's town, 596. War between Delaware and Seneca Indians, murder on French creek, 640. His force, 708. Frontiers, 743. Boundary, 744. Letters to and from, ix., 39, 51, 57, 75, 98, 143, 307, 365, 379, 405. On campaign, against Delaware Indians, &c., 97, 161. Successes, 161. (1779,) x., 161. (See Vol. VII.) Applies as surveyor in room of I. Lukens, and is appointed, xi., 630. Renewal of Commissioners necessary by change of counties, 640. Death of General Potter, 660. His son appointed Deputy Surveyor, 662, 663. Report Surveyor General, 758. Letters from his letter book, 1779–1780, xii., 105–279. Expedition against Indians, 137, 139, 140, 147. Proposes building a fort at Kittanning, 124. Names it, 134, 135, 139, 147. Expedition, 149, 150, 153, 154. Burns Seneca towns, 156, 159. Proposes expedition to Detroit, 160, 164, 166, 169, 183, 184, 186, 221, 238, 260, 277. Calls for troops, 223, 260. Wants provisions, 254, 257, 259, 263, 266, 273, 274, 277. Issues his last meat, 274. Counter orders, 275.

Brodhead, Mr. applies, for Lieutenancy, vii., 606. Reasons for decision of officers in his case, 660.

Brook, John, viii., 81. Comm'r of Taxes, ix., 140.

Brooks, Wm., Town Major of York, vii., 459.

Brown, Andrew, against E. Oswald

for a libel, xi., 349. Asks patronage for Federal Gazette, 412.

Brown, Col. Alex., letter to, on non-compliance with orders, vii., 515.

Brown, John, mittimus, &c. for, vi., 25, 30, 45. Anonymous remarks on his examination, 36.

Brown, Col. John, on impeachment of Arnold, vii., 226, 271.

Brown, John, Collector, Chester Co., robbed, ix., 459.

Brown, John, his case by the Judges, xi., 264. Petition, 265. Respecting execution, 269, 276, 277, 279.

Brown, Richard, deposition respecting murder of Indians by his servant, iv., 430.

Brown, William, letters, v., 37, 106, 135. Of Cumberland Co., Petition respecting Indians, ix., 522, 529. Letter to, 641.

Brown's Fort, ii., 738; xii., 316.

Brunswick, New, army at, v., 159. British leave, 161. Increased at, 244. Lord Sterling's brigade on way to, 67. Army at, 79. Sick sent to Philadelphia, 79. Gen. Howe in possession of, 84, 381.

Bryan, George, elected Vice President of State, v., 252. Letters, 352, 463, 490, 514, 529, 530, 543, 575. V. P., vi., 10, 108, 109, 128, 144. Resigns as V. P., vii., 745. A Pennsylvania commissioner to run line between Virginia, viii., 353. Counterfeit coin, ix., 279, 288, 299, 305, 309, 384. Error in a law, 422. Pardon, 634. Answer to questions of Council on Justices of the Peace, x., 16–19. Commissioners on boundary, (1783,) 171. On trial of Indian for murder, 473. On case of Doane, 609. Opinion on depreciation of pay, xi., 120. On Brown's case, 264. State Island, 286.

Buchanan, Arthur, vi., 485, 487, 603. Indian murders, ix., 192. His Battalion of Cumberland Co., (1779,) x., 161. (See Vol. VII.)

Buchannan, Capt. Thomas, viii., 31.

Buchannan, Wm., v., 552, 667, 677, 690,711, 742; vi., 34.

Buchloons, an Indian Town on French Creek, xii., 157.

Bucks County, Courts, business of, i., 279. Iron furnaces in, (1750,) ii., 53. Soldiers at Newtown, 596. Associated military company of, iii., 19. Number of Roman Catholics in, 144. Justices of, 182. Troops don't intend to march, v., 18. Tory election in, 31, 32. Troops to join Washington, 115. Records, 237. Militia, 322, 331, 342, 368, 463, 464, 511, 523, 549, 567, 591. Account of flour taken, 421. Blankets from, 469. Driving off cattle, 546. Records to be removed, vi., 88. Militia, 96. Clothing found, 92, 107, 146, 180, 187. Alarms in, 280. Insolence of Tories in, 291. Captures by enemy in, 261, 263, 361. Exposure to enemies, 595. Letter to Colonels of militia, vii., 104. Militia, 98, 103, 104, 108. Forage Master, 620. Agents for Confiscated estates, viii., 178. Taxes, 481. Auditors, ix., 11, 13, 17, 29, 36, 47. Sales of forfeited estates in, 105. Commissioner, ill treated, 199. Troops at Newtown, 278. Troops, 338, 376, 378, 433. Robberies, 459, 501, 507, 529, 608, 609, 610, 611, 617, 635. Sheriff of, on arrest of Sergeant Nagle, x., 67. Death of Major Kennedy by robbers, (1783,) 178. Orders to Troops to march to Wyoming, 345. Case of Solomon Vickers, 432. Banditti from, on frontiers, 583. Aaron Doane, 597. Robber of Treasury in jail, 698. Robbery of Tax Collectors, xii., 298, 302.

Budden, James, v., 599.

Buffalo Creek, prisoners taken by Indians on, (1783,) x., 167.

Buffalo, Fort, iii., 13.

Buffalo Valley, Indians attack, viii., 249.

Bulkley, John, iii., 349, 351.

Bull, Col. John, letters, v., 59, 102, 201, 203, 208, 255, 304, 306, 709. Meets Indians at Easton, 201, 203, 208; vi., 128, 133, 150, 190, 746. To erect Battery at Billingsport, 746. Marches brigade to enemy's lines, 133. Complains of removal, 190. To repair banks at Mud Island, vii., 240, 544. Asks to be employed against

Indians, 544. Raising chevaux de frize, 544, 566, 587, 635. Instructions to viii., 164. Appointed commissioner of purchases for Philadelphia co., 164.
Bull, Capt. Thomas, iii., 423.
Bullets from Batsto ——, iv., 761, 762.
Bullitt, Thomas, letter, iii., 370.
Bunting, Joshua, a prisoner, viii., 648.
Burd, Capt., viii., 297.
Burd, Col. James, complains against Assembly for not paying hands on roads, ii., 393. Letters to and from, 393, 454, 566, 631, 705. Fort, 609. Account against Teedyuscung, iii., 293. Proposal for means of protection, 99. Letters, 333, 334, 367. Journal, 352. Letters iv., 88, 105, 111, 125, 128, 140, 165.
Burd, Edward, appointed prothonotary vi., 695.
Burgen, Mrs., receives provisions by order of General Washington, viii., 60.
Burgoyne, Gen., affairs at Ticonderoga, v., 437, 541. Captured by Gen. Gates, details, 657, 674, 676, 680, 684, 695. Letters from G. Gates, 687. Prisoners from, 726, 729. Articles of Capitulation, 726-728. Stores taken from, 729, Conduct in Convention, General Gates' answer respecting, vi., 108. Report to, and resolution of Congress, on breach of Convention, 162-166, 176.
Burial ground reserved for strangers in Philadelphia, xi., 570, 571.
Burk, Lawrance, letter, iii., 478.
Burke, Thomas, vii., 170, 172.
Burnet, Silas, deposition, vi., 7.
Bush, David, ferry at Christiana, i., 674. Erects battery at Wilmington, Delaware, ii., 6. Collector of militia fines at Wilmington, complaints against, iii., 154, 165-170 ; ix., 174.
Bush Island, works on, v., 591.
Busse, Capt., fort, ii., 159.
Busse, Christian, letter, iii., 279. Sick, 293, 362, 425.
Butcher, Zacariah, his letters on affairs at Marsh Creek, i., 625, 635.
Butler, Anthony, v., 553, 557.
Butler, Col., money sent to, ix., 80, 105, 113.
Butler, Richard, account of the rise of the Indian War, iv., 568-570.
Butler, Col. Richard, vi., 252, 386, 404, 420, 663 ; vii., 3, 65, 482, 514. Recommendation for appointments, viii., 607. Partial issues, 741. Recruits, 748. Respecting prisoners of war, ix., 561. Soldiers' times expiring, 664 ; x., 69, 88, 294. Conference with him and A. Lee, on Indian treaties, 295. And Lee to Council, on officers, 332. Letter to, respecting Indians, xi., 206. Commissioner to purchase Erie, 405. Purchase of Erie, 427. Proposes present of lands to Cornplanter, 562, 660. Report on accounts, 588. Letter on Erie, 591. Indians, 716. Quota of Militia demanded by Governor of Western Territory, 715, 716. Indian captures, 723. Resigns as justice, xii., 5.
Butler, Col. Wm., vi., 529, 537. Letter, recruiting, provisions, inactivity of officers, &c., viii., 747. Proposes printing office at Pittsburg, x., 421.
Butler, Capt. Zebulon, iv., 364. Letter to, from Delegates in Congress, 643. To Ellis Hughes, 647, 648.
Butler, Lieut. Col. Zebulon, at Sunbury, vi., 690 ; vii., 283, 289 ; viii., 162, 600, 601, 602, 633. At Wyoming, rations to troops at, ix., 166. Petition, x., 559, 580, 613. Appointed Lieutenant of Luzerne County, xi., 179. Disturbances at, 192. Respecting Wyoming, 351, 381. Arrest of Rioters, Dudley is wounded, 356. Militia, 414. Arms, (1787,) 459. Deposition, 553. On difficulties of meeting of Militia in Luzerne Co., 676.
Buyers, John, letter respecting Fort Freeland, vii., 591. Affairs at Wyoming, xi., 439, 440.
Byers, James, casts brass cannon, v., 369.
Byers, Capt. John, vi., 235.
Byles, Daniel, chosen Major of regiment of Philad'a county, ii., 608.

Byng, Ad. Robert, instructions to Gov. Gordon, i., 194, 206, 207, 306.

C.

Cable, Abm., resigns as Justice, xii., 5.
Cadaraqui, Colonel Bradstreet's success at, iii., 517, 518.
Cade, Zebulon, conviction, xi., 421.
Cadwalader, Colonel John, officers of armed boats, reflect on Committee of Safety, iv., 704, 757. Orders to destroy bridges on Burlington road, v., 95. Letters, 95, 136, 160, 161, 178, 180, 186.
Cadwalader, Colonel Lambert, commission for, v., 53. Expected attack at Bristol, 136; vi., 655.
Caldwell, Andrew, v., 261.
Caldwell, Charles, demand of him for money paid for his apprehension, vi., 502.
Caldwell, Commissioner Sir James, vi., 32.
Caldwell, Commodore Samuel, letter, iv., 717. Suggestions respecting pay, gallies, &c., 720. Letter from Captains, complaining, 706. From committee on, 724, 738. Reason of his return, 738. Obtains possession of Hog Island, ix., 252, 520. Respecting Hog Island, x., 185. Hog Island, xi., 89. On tonnage duties, 594.
Calendar, Act for, change from old to new style, ii., 68.
Callender, Robert, letter, iv., 411.
Calvert, Benedict Leond., Governor, letter from Governor Gordon to, i., 289. Answer, 292.
Calvert, Charles, conference with Penn, i., 74.
Calvins, Stephen, recommended by Reverend William Tennent as interpreter, iii., 514.
Cambray, Colonel, ix., 324.
Camden, S. C., General Greene's affair at, ix., 154.
Cameron, A., examination and history of, iv., 682. Taken prisoner, v., 382. Letter, 383.
Campbell, George, v., 269.
Campbell, John, agent from Virginia at Pittsburg, vii., 79. Taken prisoner, xii., 190.
Campbell, Captain Thomas, appointed to a company of Rangers, vii., 300. Rank, 446; viii., 37, 70, 109. To be arrested, 68, 71. Letters, xii., 160, 171, 172, 179, 187, 194, 202, 203. Recruits at Newtown, ix., 79, 435.
Campbell, Lieutenant Colonel, letter to, xii., 135, 141, 154, 200, 211, 232, 237.
Campbell, Rev. Mr., appointed minister of Apoquinimy, i., 191. To be removed, 236.
Canada, union with, anticipated by Colonel Hazen, viii., 105. Expedition, ix., 308.
Canan, Colonel John, Justice of peace, xi., 588.
Canasatego, &c., deed from, for lands between Delaware and Susquehanna, August 22, 1749, ii., 33, 36.
Canhawa, fort at, xii., 126. Attacked, 126.
Cannisters for cartridges, described, vi., 393.
Cannon, casting of, by J. Old, iv., 721. Has cast a 24lb., 721. Asked for from Congress, 735. Letter to Captain Joy, 738. Number cast at Reading and Warwick furnaces, v., 36. Proved, 62. Carriages, 64. At Hibernia furnace, 72. Proved, &c., 121, 170. Cast, 203, 369, 535. Copper wanted for, 535.
Cannon, Mrs., seditious conduct, ix., 193.
Canoes, hired for Fort Augusta, iv., 112.
Canterbury, Archbishop of, refuses to consecrate American Bishops, x., 434.
Cape Breton, expedition, ii., 339, 388.
Cape May, wardens purchase ground for Beacon at, xi., 93; xii., 101. Lot purchased by wardens, 295.
Capitulation, articles of, Fort Freeland, vii., 611.
Carberry, Mr., skirmish with Indians, vii., 8, 10. Henry and Sullivan, affair of, x., 61, 74 Correspondence, &c., with Mary

land, respecting, 290-293. Delegates on, 575, 576. Depositions, &c., 576-580. Letter, Governor of Maryland, 320. Instructions to sheriff, 323. Governor Paca, respecting, 324. And John Sullivan, respecting mutiny, xi., 27. List of papers, 29.

Carleton, Guy, Governor of Quebec, iv., 364. Grants a passport at request of General Washington, ix., 674. Letter relating to preliminaries of peace and termination of hostilities, x., 13. Robber, in New York, 101, 131.

Carlton, Joseph, letter to, xii., 267.

Carlisle, state of things at and near, iii., 79, 192, 196, 448, 450, 483, 484, 489, 627, 691. Muster of effective men at, iv., 196. Respecting dry lands near, 590. Committee, letter respecting saltpetre manufacture, 706. Commissioners letter to Committee of Safety, 713. Prisoners of war at, v., 77. Militia at, 164, 324. But one lawyer practising under Constitution, vi., 228. Magistrates, 228. Court held at, 238, 511, 661. Replevins issued, excuses, case of Wm. Montgomery, a traitor, 239. Lands near grant of, viii., 107. All artificers ordered by Congress to—magazine required, 630, 632. Proprietary lots, 636. State of things, 747. Continental works near, ix , 460. Provisions, xii., 117. Magazine at, 119. Fort Lowther at, 348.

Carlisle, Abraham, memorials in favor of his pardon, vii., 21-24, 52-59. Notes of C. J. McKean, on trial of, 44-52.

Carmathen, (British Secretary,) to Mr. Adams, complaining of grievances to British creditors, x., 746.

Carnahan, Captain James, xii., 10, 193, 254.

Carothers, John, v., 634, 639. Lieut. vi., 436, 438, 447, 467, 487, 491, 539, 559, 609, 619, 700. Resigns, vii., 405, 618; viii., 696.

Caruthers, Robert, taken prisoner by Indians, ix., 657.

Carrington, Colonel, proceedings against, v., 328. E. J., vacancy, ix., 487.

Carson, John, vii., 401, 437, 470, 637, 659, 679.

Carson, Joseph, account for cloths seized in Bucks county, vi., 146.

Carson, Samuel, Lieutenant of Ship General Greene, vii., 310, 706.

Cartledge, Edmund, memorial on Indian trade, i., 261, 304, 327. Letter to Governor, 304, 327. His examination, 305.

Cartouch boxes, ordered, vii., 358.

Casdorp, Thomas, letter, invents a swivel skid for guns, v., 200.

Caswell, Richard, Governor of North Carolina, viii., 191. Deputies to convention—Act of Assembly, xi., 116.

Cataragues, Indian town, xii., 301.

Cavalry, recommended by Committee of Congress in letter to President Wharton, vi., 316. Resolutions of Congress to respectable young men to join, 323, 339. General Lacey on, 391.

Cavet, James, letter, iv., 623.

Censors, Council of, resolutions, &c., of, x., 149, 153, 302, 327, 329, 333, 336, 363, 596, 604, 605, 656. On voting by ballot, 302. Answer, 316.

Census of Bedford county, x., 512. United States, xi., 709, 718.

Certificate of Indian Isaac, respecting Sergeant Falconer being at battle at Sideling Hill, iii., 315. Of John Penn's appointment as Governor, iv., 119. Of Governor's election, xii., 28.

Cessation of Indian hostilities, ix., 641.

Cessna, Captain Charles, distress from Indians in Bedford county, ix., 236, 467.

Chains to be placed across Chestnut street, vi., 741.

Chaloner, John, vi., 320, 321. Appointed auctioneer, xi., 680. Report, 762.

Chaloner & White, vi., 761, 762. Fat cattle, viii., 248.

Chamberlain, Samuel, commissioner of Maryland on, boundary line, i., 603.

Chambers, Benjamin, deposition on Maryland affairs, i., 519. Has a private fort and cannon, iii., 12, 79. Refuses to deliver cannon,

order for arrest, 165, 192. Letter, iv., 535. Letter from, xii., 281.
Chambers, Colonel James, v., 364. Men applauded, vi., 97.
Chambers, Colonel, xii., 122, 130.
Chambers, Colonel John, viii., 32, 320, 374.
Chambers, John, Sub-Lieutenant, vi., 504, 629.
Chambers, Lieutenant, viii., 286.
Chambers, Colonel Maxwell, ix., 292.
Chambers, Wm., killed by Indians, ii., 612.
Chambers, Fort, xii., 349.
Chancery, Court established, i., 171. Proceedings, i., 440, 442, 456.
Charles, Robert, letters to and from, i., 215, 295. Appointed assistant agent in England to Benjamin Franklin, iii., 759.
Charleston, fallen, viii., 312, 316, 326, 470. Flags of truce from, ix., 338.
Chartier's Creek, Indians near, xii., 234, 243.
Charts, variation, xi., 718.
Chastenoy, Mons., Letter to, respecting captured negroes, i., 755.
Chastisement in the Navy, iv., 770.
Chauvignerie, Michael la, (a French prisoner,) examination of, 294, 305, letter to parents, iii., 329.
Cheat river, child killed by Indians, xii., 163, 164, 256.
Chelsea Forge for iron, vi., 627.
Chemung, expedition proposed against, vii., 3, 86.
Cheney, Colonel, v,, 732,
Cherokee Indians, passport for, iii., 405. Names and signification, 428; xii., 131, 147.
Cherokee Indian women address President Franklin, xi., 181. Letter to President Mifflin, 584. Arrive in Virginia, 600.
Chesapeake, General Howe approaches, v., 544. Movements of enemy in, ix., 315, 351.
Chesapeake and Delaware, connection proposed, x., 540. Communication between proposed, xi., 25, 27.
Chesney, William, vii., 599.
Chesnut Hill, precipitate retreat of enemy, vi., 100.
Chester, first council at, i., 37. Court at, 51. Rev. Mr. Backhouse appointed missionary at, 226. Troops ordered to, v., 352, 353, 529, 532, 536, 563. In possession of enemy, 616.
Chester county, election return for Assembly, i., 86. Council, 115. Business of Courts in, 279. Returns of iron furnaces in, 1750, ii., 56. Petition from, for defence, 656. Number of Roman Catholics in, iii., 144. 'Mordecai Thompson, Wagon Master, 398. Committee, letter, iv., 718. Return of Members of Assembly, 740. Estimate of fire arms fit for use, in, 776. Lieutenants of, v., 475. Flour in, 421. Militia, 324, 426. Records 462. Persons to take account of grain, &c., in, 476, 477. Memorial, 476. Complaints about substitutes, 487. Letters to Lieutenants of, 582. Militia, 581, 582. Enemy supplied from, 686. Blankets, &c., to be impressed, 691. Light horse militia, 732. Letters, vi., 4, 98, 258, 731, Head Quarters in, 98, 101. Militia, 494. Arms in, 496. Commissioner's Taxes, 561. Illegal election, vii., 97. List of Justices since Revolution, 444. Bad conduct of East Marlbro, 470. Murder of Jesse Jordan in, 743. Mr. Boyd of, murdered by the Smiths, viii., 244. Backward in furnishing volunteers, 456. Accounts of sales of forfeited estates in, ix., 105. Militia, 421, 434. Collectors robbed, 459, 501, 507. Seizure of British goods in, and opinion of Attorney General respecting, 731. Wagons stopped in, with British clothing, x., 12. Wagoners' names, 13. Execution of David Dawson of, 609. Persifer Frazer appointed Register of Wills and Recorder of Deeds in, 756. Militia fines, xi., 258. Contest for seat in Council, 632.
Chevaux de frize, regulations about vessels passing in, &c., iv., 717, 774, 775; v., 37, 39, 45, 66, 67, 83, 238, 426, 431, 626, 649, 681, 699, 721, 747; vi., 20. Colonel Bull engaged in raising, vii., 544, 566, 587. Removal of, x., 93,

144-146, 177, 210, 212, 219, 221, 349, 350, 565, 585, Number and situation, (1784) 590. To be raised, xii., 290, 292.

Chew, Benjamin, iii., 397. Letter, iv., 44. Arrested, to be escorted to Virginia, v., 478, 512. Request in favor of, vi., 61. Removal of, 85. Release, 364, 367, 378, 380, 389, 507, 523.

Chicochinican, Indian chief, letter from, i., 239.

Chignecto, French forts at, ii., 376.

Chilesquake, murder of J. Martin and wife by Indians, ix., 659.

Chillaway, Job, an Indian chief, iii., 582.

Chillicoffi, Shawnese Indian town, destroyed by Colonel Clarke, xii., 258.

Chilohock's Town, xii., 177.

Chinese, sick from an Indiaman, and thirty-four others, and crew of the Pallas, seek and obtain aid, x., 527, 528. Resolution of Assembly, 531. Levi Hollingsworth respecting, 546, 548 Sent to Maryland, xi., 56.

Chippewa Indians, x., 16; xii., 131, 147.

Christ Church, Philadelphia, Rev. Dr. Evans arrives, i., 134. Memorial from, in favor of Gov. Nicholson, 150. Claim on Baptist Church, 284. Address to Gov. Denny, ii., 762. Petition in favor Rev. Thomas Coombe, prisoner, v., 600, 603.

Christ, Henry, v., 605, 734; ix., 80, 133, 196, 237, 347. Proprietary lands in Reading, 237.

Christina, Fort, curious relics found and battery erected, ii., 6.

Christie Captain Jacob, abuses on officers at Easton, &c., ix., 385.

Chrystie, Captain James, arrives at Easton with a detachment, x., 135. At Fort Dickinson, 209.

Christy, James, deposition respecting counterfeits found in wagons, vi., 233.

Church, Major, viii., 515.

Churchman, John, charts, xi., 718.

Cincinnati Society invites Executive Council, xi., 726.

Circular of Massachusetts Assembly, iv., 286.

Circulars of Council, vi., 65, 88, 179, 193, 294, 452, 638, 650; vii., 104, 105, 183, 304, 747. Of Congress, viii., 277, 414, 441, 454, 476; ix., 226, 251, 252, 387, 407, 548. To Prothonotaries, x., 268. Of Council to Lieutenants and Commissioners, xi., 379, 498, 746.

Cisney, John, murdered by Indians in his field, list of killed, iii., 219.

City Guard, orders to, v., 121, 122-124.

Civility, Captain, (Indian) letters to and from, i., 229, 233, 238, 271. Reminds Blunston of promise to the Conestogas, 295.

Claims of Pennsylvania against United States, xi., 234, 655.

Clapham, Colonel William, letters to and from, ii., 596, 612, 615, 663, 665, 669, 671, 672, 674, 687, 705, 739, 744, 751, 766, 779. Orders to Captain Miles, 687. Instructions, 666. Letters to and from, iii., 9, 10, 38, 41, 42, 58, 64.

Clarke, Abraham, vi., 367, 389.

Clarke, John, Jr., vi., 23. And H. Miller, vii., 609.

Clarke, Governor of New York, letters from, i., 619, 620.

Clarke, Captain John, viii., 65, 66, 68, 79, xii., 173, 174, 279. Sent after trespassers on Indian lands, 177.

Clarke, General, viii., 767, 769.

Clarke, Brigad'r General G., answer to President Reed respecting expedition, ix., 331, 353, 354, 367, 369, 375, 405, 458. Meeting at Westmoreland, 560. Capture and death of Colonel Lochry, &c., 458, 468. Memorial of prisoners on, 574. Irvine expects co-operation of, 649. Proposes expedition to, 23, 137, 141, 201, 235, 239, 247, 306, 307, 315, 325, 343, 352. To officers of Westmoreland county, 189. Injurious to Pennsylvania, 325.

Clarke, Col., destroys two Shawnese towns, viii., 537, 580, 743. At Richmond, 768.

Clark, Col. Geo. R., expedition, xii., 111. Takes Hamilton at Detroit, 116, 120. Takes prisoners, 120,

125. Deserters to, 142. Making peace, 157. Has Virg. troops, 177, 223. Goes against Detroit with Virginia troops, 177. Destroys town at Chillicoffi, 258, 263. Letters to, 216, 238.
Clark, James, scalped by Indians, viii., 23, 29.
Clark, John, v., 699.
Clark, Mich., v., 712. Serg xii., 230.
Clark, Walter, ix., 381.
Clark, William, letter to W. P., i., 77.
Clarkson, Dr. Gerardus, letter respecting sick soldiers, v., 165.
Clarkson, J. L., ix., 226, 229.
Clarkson, Matthew, (Marshal) announces death of Judge Ross, vii., 554. Letter of Pres. on sale of salt, viii., 498. F. Hopkinson to, on ditto, 500. Forbids sale, 500. Letter respecting F. Hopkinson's charges, xii., 250.
Clarkson, Matthew, (aid to General Arnold) action of Congress against, vii., 204, 270.
Claypoole, Capt. A. G., ix., 278, 376, 378.
Claypoole, James, vi., 624. Sheriff of Philadelphia, to replace whipping post and pillory, vii., 252. Instructions respecting S. R. Fisher, 291. G. Harding, 360. Captain Sutter, 632. Peter Miller, 765. guard for prison, viii., 117, 321.
Claus, Daniel, letters from, ii., 116, 174, 645. Interpreter, iv., 41.
Clayton, Ashur, letters, iv., 137, 142, 174. Orders to, 194.
Clergy to be furnished with copies of address of Congress to inhabitants, vi., 489.
Clingham, William, vii., 158.
Clinton, Gov. George, of N. Y., Letters, i., 654, 661, 678, 687, 712, 736, 766. Letters from, ii., 16, 26, 29, 30, 32, 65, 99; v., 244. Genl. takes a spy, 639. Account of Ticonderoga Battle, 676. Letter of inquiry respecting act of Congress, viii., 132, 179; ix., 122. On boundary, x., 422, 435, 458, 513. On Wyoming affairs, xi., 96. Partition line, 125. Pres. Franklin to, respecting line, &c., 187. Wyoming, 196, 335, 341, 412. Arms at Fishkiln, 456; xii. 33.
Clinton, Gen. (British) vi., 27, 32. His expedition to Connecticut, vii., 561.
Clinton, Brig. Gen., ix., 125.
Clinton, Gen., arrives at Fort Sullivan, x., 719.
Clinton, Sir Henry, viii., 312; ix., 71, 102, 404.
Clinton, James, appointed commissioner on boundary with N. Y., x., 450.
Clothiers, each State to pay its own, vii., 293, 304, 312. Guard for store, 689; viii., 52, 53, 67, 707.
Clothing, vi., 9, 12, 22, 27, 33, 38, 42, 52, 61, 75, 85, 87, 92. 107, 125, 134, 142, 146, 179, 181, 186, 189, 198, 251, 253, 275, 291, 343, 387, 404, 412, 419, 426, 428, 559, 566, 643, 660; vii., 129, 135, 181, 221, 273, 293, 304, 312, 336, 359, 637, 405, 411, 423, 440, 470, 570, 590, 659, 666, 670, 679, 685, 696, 714, 740, 744. Prices of, for Army, 182; 17, 26, 34, 36, 53, 56, 67, 76, 96, 105, 109, 116, 117, 140, 161, 162, 185, 199. Officer sells, 161, 162, 165; ix., 16, 19, 31, 237, 405, 406; x., 6, 7, 12, 13; xii., 106, 113, 149, 151, 158, 180, 198, 225, 226, 250, 267.
Clover seed, John Penn sends for, vi., 10.
Cluggage, Major Robert, viii., 278, 297.
Cluggage, Capt. Thomas, appointed to an independent company in Bedford, vii., 296. Letters to, 512, 624, 659, 697, 742.
Clymer, Dan'l, vi., 105.
Clymer, George, Commissioner on Commercial regulations, xi., 522. On call of a State Convention, 562.
Coasting trade, xi., 607.
Coats, Col. Wm., letter respecting battle at Princeton, v., 159. Army, 162, 528, 767; vi., 376, 377, 763, 764. Asks to be exchanged as prisoner, 377, 477. Letters to and from, viii., 43, 378. Troops for, 508. Sends troops to Flower Town, ix., 250. Light horse, 273. Lieut. Col., 325, 358, 377. Reviews militia, 535; x., 759. Asks for arms for Seventh battalion, xi., 273. Officers, 274.

Cobb's Creek, Bridge and Road over, i., 768.
Cock, Peter, Island in Del., granted, to, i., 20.
Coins, Foreign, remarks of Attorney-General on several acts respecting value of, ii., 102.
Coins, regulation of, xii., 36.
Cold weather, severe, at Muskingum and Pittsburg, xi., 244.
Colden, Alexander, letter, iii., 444. 479.
Colden, Governor Cadwalader, letters to and from, iv., 167, 364, 562, 578. Asks reason for Penn's pushing his request for Indians to pass through New York, 166.
Colebrookdale, petition against Indians, i., 213.
Coleman, Robert, letter, v., 39.
Coleman, Ensign, xii., 138. Order to evacuate Fort Crawford, 141.
Collectors, appointed, i., 385, 389. Of clothing, vii., 33. Of Bucks and Chester Cos., robbed, ix., 459.
College of Philadelphia, address to Council, interrupted by soldiers, v., 199.
Collins, Luke, letter on Western boundaries, iv., 455.
Collins, Thomas W., accomplice of Molesworth, v., 281, 315.
Colonels of battalions, circulars to, viii., 111. Of city battalions, 309.
Colonial Records, to be published, i., 14, 22, 23.
Colonies, to have management of Indian affairs, iv., 182. Circular of Massachusetts Assembly, 286. The, complained of, 311.
Commerce, resolution of Congress on regulation of, x., 507-8. Internal, proceedings of Assembly respecting, 128. Commissioners appointed, 730. Report to Congress on, xi., 75, 79. Treaty with France, 220-228.
Commercial Convention, commissioners on, xi., 27, 60, 61, 522. Regulations, 521, 523-526. Treaty with France, 220-228, 287.
Commissaries, department, complaints against, vi., 135, 295, 425, 431. To be regulated, vii., 84, 557. Conduct in, 490, 542, 550, 551, 552. Of purchases and issues, letter to, 304, 567, 579; viii., 69, 92, 151. Of supplies—scarcity of provisions, 287. General, of purchases, 92, 150, 240.
Commission, W. P. to W. Welch, &c., to Jersey, i., 85. To Governor A. Hamilton, respecting the seal, 148. For Searcher of Customs, 117. To Hamilton and Georges, 428. To Gov. Thomas from Thomas Penn, 625. To R. Peters as Secretary of Land Office, 545. For Captain John Shannon, 688. To Samuel Kirk, ii., 100. To commissioners to Indian treaty at Albany, from Massachusetts, 137. New York, 138. Maryland, 139. Connecticut, 140. Rhode Island, 141. Pennsylvania, 142. New Hampshire, 138. Diary of Pennsylvania commissioners, 145. Of officers in Pennsylvania regiment, and their date, iii., 88. Letter to Governor on provisions for soldiers, 93. To affix seal, 238. Of Captain John Sibbald of Pennsylvania frigate, 190. To Thomas McKee, 219. General Forbes, 398. To appraisers of transports, iv., 53. To physicians to examine sickly vessels, 59. To Dr. Thomas Coombe, 70. John Gibson, 105. To mayor of Philadelphia to impress wagons, 108. Colonel Turbut Francis, 176. For Judges of New Castle Courts, &c., 339. Bernard Ratzer, surveyor of boundary between New York and New Jersey, 339. Do. of Anthony Dennis, 340. To Colonel Lambert Cadwalader, v., 53. F. Phyle as Naval Officer at Philadelphia, 298 Not to be antedated, 371. Not necessary for Brigade Major, vi., 255. For privateers, granted, 329. For privateers, vii., 127, 536, 608. viii., 613.
Commissioners, appointed to treat with New Jersey, i., 58. Their instructions, 58. Of customs on Navigation Act, 119. For distributing prize money, 654. On boundary line, letters from, 556, 557, 558, 568, 574, 601, 605, 613. Minutes of, 571-574. Reports of, 575, 595-615. Notice of meeting

Commissioners—
at Philadelphia, 623. To borrow money, order of, ii., 252. From colonies, meeting proposed, 460. To settle accounts for wagons for General Braddock, appointed, 598. Letter of Hugh Mercer to, iii., 27. To Governor on quality of provisions, 93. Letters to and from Provincial, 93, 141, 161, 214, 235, 258, 281, 287, 398, 440, 454, 476, 498, 675. Accounts, report on, 452. Their right to pay out money disputed, 157. Authorize Colonel Armstrong to provide horses, 163. Of Customs, 547. For Indian affairs, 555. Of Lower Counties—letter to Gov. Denny for drums, colors, &c., 401. Of Bedford Co., on providing fire-locks, iv., 712. Of Carlisle, letter on fire-locks, 713. Lords of Trade, plan for the management of Indian trade, 182. For defence, minutes of, 195. Of customs, letter, 253, 254. Of customs, Boston, 289. On Indian trade at N. York, 361, 364. Of Connecticut, 471. Of York Co., respecting fire-arms to be made, 708. Of clothing to be appointed, vii, 221. For forfeited estates, 243. For purchase of flour, 753. Of purchases—appointed, viii., 154, 164, 219, 277, 441, 720. For procuring salt—scarcity feared, 4, 24, 28. Of Phila. Co., 80. For procuring flour, 84. Of Virginia, 91, 353. Of Taxes, 125. Of Berks Co., taxes, 124, 132. On boundary between Virga., and Penna., 353. On Connecticut claim, ix., 526, 624, 676, 693. Of Cumberland Co., 736. For defence of the Delaware, 586, 618, 621, 625 647, 672. Propose sale of Hyder Ally, 672. Of Northumberland Co., 440. Of purchases, 17, 417, Of taxes Philadelphia Co., 116, 139, 328, 478. To run line with Virginia, 20, 78, 519. On boundary, x., 230, 233, 236, 372, 373, 438, 489, 506. Anxious to be correct, 236. Report, 506. On northern boundary, ask for a transit instrument, 416. Of Bucks, 75. For de-

Commissioners—
fence of Delaware., 26. Of Cumberland, 79. Of land office, 541, 545. To treat with Indians appointed, 265 ; letter from, 266, 332 ; instructions, 320 ; from Pres., respecting prisoners, 325 ; arrive at Fort Stanwix, 346 ; treaty with Six Nations, 357, 395, 410, 489, 496, 610 ; obligation to deliver goods, &c., to Indians, 610. Lancaster Co., 82. Appointed to examine Roads and Rivers for internal commerce, 129, 130, 312, 533, 710. Northampton Co., 92. Of Philada., object to appropriating site of Jail for an Exchange, 104 ; old iron, 307. To take possession of Pittsburg when relinquished by United States, 477, 498. On navigation of Susquehanna River, 755. Of Taxes for Phila., Co., 51, 222, 224, 238. On trade of United States appointed by Virginia, 738. Of Washington Co., 584, 587. Of Westmoreland on supplies, 98. On Wyoming, correspondence with, 30—37 ; to magistrate as to safety, 662 ; answer, 663 ; to Pres. Dickinson, 664 ; advertisement, 669 ; letter from inhabitants to, 671 ; to Pres. Dickinson, 677. On Western Boundary Line, xi., 26, 52, 69, 178, 499. To Commercial Convention, 27. On subject of Canal Navigation, 27. For improving Inland Navigation, 77. On Connecticut claims, 159, 160. Northern Boundary, 203. To purchase Erie from Indians, 405, 507, 509, 691. On Boundary with Virginia Commissioners, appointed, 501. Of Maryland and Virginia, Internal Navigation, 511. To Maryland and Virginia On Commercial Regulations, 521. To run lines of Huntingdon Co., 571. To view rivers, 681, 683, 690. Of Taxes, 498. To Indians, 503, 506, 507, 508, 509, 510. On Commerce, 522. Of Washington Co., xii., 288.

Committe on Indian affairs, minutes of meeting, iii., 382 ; letter to Gov., 734. On Naval affairs, letter, iv., 692. Of Berks Co.,—

Committee on Indian affairs—Proceedings respecting prisoners v., 19. For driving off Cattle, 315, 456, 461, 473, 512, 545, 565 600. Of Cumberland Co.,—letter 12. Of inspection in, letter respecting prisoners, 77, Of fifty, 384, 473. Of Lancaster Co., 251, 266, 349, 365, 571. Of Trenton receive salt from Council, 69. Of New York Letter, 40. Of York T., Troops marched in, 151. Of Congress, vi., 316, 362, 389, Letters on Cavalry, 317, 365, 367, 384, 677, 753. Of city, letters to dealers in flour and importers, vii. 461-465. Of Congress, 83, 84, 85, 88. Of Congress at camp, viii., 266, 267, 293, 312, 314, 315, 337, 355, 404, 412. Complained of, by Pres., Reed, 419. Of Congress, ix., 281. Of Assembly, 14, 62, 415. Of Ways and Means—pensions, xi., 545.

Committee of Safety, how and when formed, iv., 637. Letters to and from, 635, 638, 642, 643, 644, 646, 647, 650, 653, 654, 656, 664, 666, 668, 680, 686, 690, 692, 696, 697, 702, 703, 706, 707, 708, 711, 712, 713, 714, 717, 718, 720, 721, 722, 723, 724, 725, 726, 729, 730, 731, 733, 734, 736, 737, 738, 740, 742, 743, 745, 746, 747, 760, 762, 764, 765, 768, 769, 775, 776, 777, 778, 779, 780, 784, 785, 786, 787, 788. Address of Rangers armed boat for provisions, 704. Complaint of ill treatment, 705. Changed to Council of S., (which see) v., 26. Their expense account for dinners, &c., 213. Resolutions, 317. Letters to and from, Col. Samuel J. Atlee, 6, 10. Committee of Berks Co, 111. Elmer, Jona'n., 7. Miles, Col. Samuel, 5. Proctor, Maj. Thomas, 11. Read, John, 12. Richards, Wm., 13. Rittenhouse, David, 10, Smith, Robert, 8, 9.

Compass, sign of Lt. Hammond killed, vi., 258, 275, 291, 326.

Complaint against Captain Harding, vii., 761.

Comptroller Gen., Memorial on City Lots, xi., 571. On accounts, 578-582, 586, 591, 659. Acc'ts, xii., 3. Letters, 90, 97, 99.

Conedogwinet Creek, petition, iv., 392.

Conemach, Road from Frankstown, xi., 186, 656, 725.

Conestogoe, Indians on Susquehannah, i., 295. List of, ii., 242. Manor, Indians sent to, under John Ross, ii., 595. Coroner's Inquest on murder of, iv., 147. Letter John Elder, 148, 153. Beatty and Miller 151. Armstrong, 152. J. Shippen on 154. Sir William Johnson, 162. Manor purchased by J. Musser of Delaware, viii., 30, 54, 56.

Conestoga manor, title of Indians to, ix., 49.

Conewago, Petition from, i., 681, 682, 724.

Conewago Falls, improvement of, xi., 608; xii., 155, 156, 157.

Confederacy, frigate, vii., 533, 695. Capt. Harding of, ship complained of, for impressing seamen, viii., 643.

Confederacy completed, ix., 4.

Confederation of States, act for, vi., 19, Agreed to by Pennsylvania Council, 455. Consented to by Virginia, 144, 232. Articles of, signed by Maryland, thus completing the whole thirteen States, viii., 749.

Conferences with Indians, iv., 63. At Onandago, x., 63; for purchase of lands from, 105.

Confession of Jesse and Solomon Vickars, ix., 609, to 617.

Confiscated Estates, instructions for sale of, viii., 345. Letter to agents of, 760. Agents to report, x., 154; Hog Island, 185.

Congress, Committee of Secrecy agree for powder, iv., 696. Letters to and from, 681. Resolutions, 692. Delegates in, letter to, from officers in York county, 641. To Zeb. Butler, 643. President to B. Franklin, 643, 644, 646. Agreement with Hodge, Bayard & Co. to import arms, 708. Intelligence from, 729. Invites Committee to hear Oration on General Montgomery, 714. Leaves appointments with the States, v., 25. Confers with Councils on defence of Del., 62. Pay of Officers, 124. Continental

Congress—
money, 126. Removal of, from Phila., 132. Punishment on refusal of Continental money, 137, 147. To Assembly, 179. Letters to and from, 129, 179, 219, 244, 289, 290, 351, 366, 411, 435, 439, 471, 491, 526, 536, 544, 574, 586, 593, 599, 626, 630, 681, 687, 738. Proceedings against Quakers, 554. Resolutions, 25, 62, 124, 137, 183, 268, 283, 290, 304, 309, 310, 319, 325, 328, 366, 418, 461, 469, 470, 492, 513, 525, 527, 528, 539, 551, 552, 554, 575, 580, 583, 589, 596, 604, 606, 616, 623, 627, 647, 669, 675, 678, 736. Confer with Committee of Pennsylvania, 311. Proceedings against Capt. Nicholson for contempt of Gov'r Johnson, 328, Books wanted by members, 754, 757, 771. Letters to and from, vi., 4, 9, 12, 30, 41, 115, 136, 152, 153, 158, 161, 162, 176, 207, 208, 210, 242, 249, 284, 298, 316, 318, 327, 333, 340, 341, 350, 351, 358, 364, 378, 394, 403, 448, 460, 485, 488, 493, 507, 523, 524, 589, 592, 607, 613, 657, 670, 671, 672, 708, 710, 712, 713, 724, 726, 729, 737, 742, 754, 771. Resolutions, 9, 59, 79, 82, 111, 145, 150, 163, 177, 184, 215, 257, 273, 286, 299, 300, 323, 341, 356, 364, 365, 374, 375, 377, 382, 388, 399, 422, 433, 442, 458, 461, 507, 508, 557, 578, 585, 586, 602, 659, 672, 702, 705, 732, 753, 758. In relation to Genl. Burgoyne, 163. In relation to respectable young men forming troops of Cavalry, 323, Remonstrance of Council and Assembly against cantonment of army, 104, 109, 111, 333. Memorial from prisoners at Winchester, 111. Printing of Journals, 191, 237. At least three members necessary from each State, 358. Inattentive to support of frontiers, 535. Letters from Lord Howe and Gen. Clinton under consideration, 584, Resolve on embargo, 585. Invite Councils to reception of Mons. Gerard, 677. Objects to expense of fortifications, 705. Letters to and from, vii., 5, 13, 14, 75, 81, 89, 102, 106, 127, 152, 224, 243, 246,

Congress—
261, 265, 270, 274, 304, 312, 313, 324, 347, 369, 374, 396, 417, 490, 513, 522, 532, 536, 550, 552, 631, 647, 662, 664, 695, 716, 738, 757, 761, 765. Resolutions of, 15, 20, 75, 76, 83, 87, 101, 128, 154-158, 173, 204, 221, 249, 250, 251, 263, 287, 293, 315, 316, 365, 413, 436, 439, 500, 520, 542, 641, 732, 734. Complimentary to Pennsa., vii., 312. Marine Committee of, 12, 76, 120, 187, 235, 241, 587, 657. Committee of, 83, 84, 85, 88, 170, 172. Commercial Committee of, 579, 605. Appoint Thanksgiving Day, 89. Delegates in, 134, 137, 140, 141, 158, 160, 162, 174, 181, 184, 189, 192, 422, 478, 551, 556, 639. Case of C. J. McKean and Gen. Thomson, 137. Do. of Gen. Maxwell, 138. Delegates to require yeas and nays in case of Arnold, &c., 174. Proclamation for a fast, 257. Supply of Troops, 244. Resolutions in favor of Pennsa., 288, 313. Delegates in, from Virginia, 73, 184. Resolutions respecting clothiers, 293, 304. For five Companies of Rangers, 300. Letter from Washington, to, 479. Resolutions respecting Gen. Trumbull, 374. On Right of Petition, 439. Plan for recruiting, 442. Journals distributed, 472. Reformation of Qr. Mr. and Commissary Departments, 557. Men and provisions to be supplied, 716. Quotas of States, 733. Proclamation for thanksgiving, 757. Letters to and from, viii., 20, 75, 85, 87, 98, 99, 135, 142, 177, 199, 202, 203, 229, 251, 263, 277, 299, 325, 340, 343, 348, 375, 395, 419, 429, 458, 517, 529, 534, 535, 560, 583, 591, 606, 609, 635, 636, 639, 657, 685, 686, 694, 702, 705, 719, 722, 723, 751. Resolutions of, 86, 142, 173, 175, 185, 195, 255, 256, 261, 272, 285, 332, 346, 352, 375, 391, 448, 519, 520, 553, 603, 629, 649, 687, 699, 700, 724, 737, 749, 753. Marine Committee of, 231. Delegates in, 9, 46, 61, 161, 191, 351, 392, 494, 643, 703, 711, 722, 745. Do. from Connecticut, 111, 112, 239. Cir-

Congress—
culars of, 20, 203, 251, 277. Journals printed, 98. Order military trophies to be collected, 98. Pres. Reed requests a part of sentence of General Arnold to be dispensed with in view of his previous good services, 99. Draw for money, 104, 121, 195, 252, 255, 342. Proclamation for a fast, 131, 135. Appointment of officers to be suspended, 142. Minute respecting John Holker's flour, 147. Respecting commissions to privateers, 173. Horses, 175. Clothing to officers of Medical Staff, 185. Col. Brodhead to be sustained, 195. Want of money, supplies, &c., 203, 375. French fleet, 251. Quotas of States of ten millions, 255. Committee of co-operation at camp, 266, 267, 293, 312, 314, 315, 337, 355, 356, 404, 412. Direct Admiralty to fit out vessels of war, 273, 277. Conference of Committee, 281. Commissions for Privateers, 340. Ask to be informed of measures taken, 343. Respecting furnishing to French allies, 25,000 men, 346, 348. Furnish exchange on Minister to France, 391. Money asked for by Pennsylvania, 392, 395. Pres. Reed's statement of State proceedings, 458–468. Resolutions on emission of bills, 520. Appoint fast day, 590. Commissions for private armed vessels, 606. Appoint signers of bills for Pennsylvania, 634, 639. Non payment of interest, 711. Letters to and from, ix., 21, 43, 54, 76, 81, 83, 84, 94, 102, 108, 110, 112, 151, 162, 163, 172, 194, 210, 242, 273, 309, 369, 383, 395, 400, 417, 423, 433, 441, 446, 447, 448, 450, 463, 476, 479, 518, 523, 540, 561, 757. Committee of, 281. Resolutions, 73, 77, 109, 134, 152, 164, 168, 185, 188, 209, 243, 273, 300, 309, 366, 391, 394, 411, 417, 464, 476, 483, 484, 509, 548, 560, 582, 609, 645, 741, 756. Circulars, 194, 252, 463, 548. Delegates in, 103, 163, 306, 307, 420, 434. Delegates of Virginia in, 260, 266, 271, 274. Appoint a fast, 21.

Congress—
Committees of Conference, 22. Convention prisoners, 26. Ordinance on capture and condemnation of prizes, 43. Report of committee on public debt, 85-93. Courts for trial of Piracies and Felonies, 94. Provisions, 134. Wants of the army, 151. On false papers of vessels, 151. Exporters of flour, 133, 162. Approving of National Bank, 172. Signers of bills of credit appointed, 185. Bills of credit, 188, 195. Requisition of Infantry, 195. Of three hundred riflemen, 242, 243. Supplies of money, &c., 252. President Huntington resigns—Thomas McKean, elected, 267. Subscription to loan for citizens of South Carolina in Philadelphia, 309. Connecticut claim, 306. Value of leaden spouts to be taken, 366. Holker, Consul General of France, 383, 394, 400. Form of Exequator for, 390. Raise troops, 394-5. Letter of Governor New Jersey, 411. Consular power, 416, 417. Instructions to Gen. Irvine, 419. Respecting general officers, 423. Proclaim thanksgiving—victory over Cornwallis, 441, 443, 518, 650. John Hanson elected President of, 444. Connecticut and Pennsylvania, 444, 448. In favor of Ebenezer Hazard, for materials of History, 450. Infraction of laws of nations, 463, 464. Charters Bank of North America, 471. Impost on goods, 474. Seizure of British manufactures, 475, 476, 479. Rendezvous for recruits, 485. Report on letter of Robert Morris, 499. Massacre at Muskingum, 523. Honors to French Minister in consequence of the birth of a Dauphin of France, 542-547. Illegal intercourse between private armed ships and enemy, 548. Loss of mails—orders for recovery, 560. Proceedings on Connecticut claim, 568, 582. [See Connecticut.] Not to enter into treaty of peace without consent of allies, 645. Abuse of passes, 741, 750. Seizure of British goods, 741, 756. Letters

Congress—
to and from, x., 7, 27, 61, 62, 98, 135, 151, 193, 206, 231, 234, 263, 358, 371, 397, 441, 442, 457, 461, 472, 488, 490, 507, 514, 532, 535, 539, 543, 544, 549, 736, 745, 754. Resolutions of, 7, 27, 46, 90, 105, 136, 139, 168, (1783) 179, 194, 239, 242, 369, 507, 520, 524, 528, 536, 543, 544, 549, 550, 561, 562, (1784) 566, 590, 716. Delegates to, 7, 25, 38, 45, 48, 52, 53, 73, 101, 126, 151, 154, 155, 156, 184, 204, 209, 243, 358, 369, 405, 410, 440, 457, 477, 488, 511, 534, 549, 556, 563, 575, 581, 593, 601, 697, 705, 713, 759, 768. To arrange for claims in treaty, 7. Treaty with Indians on peace, 45, 46. Finances, 233. Delivery of New prison, 52. Maintaining garrison at Fort Pitt, 53. Attack expected at Philadelphia, 61. Public documents taken, to be restored to England, 90. Indian affairs, 101. On purchase of lands by Pennsylvania from Indians, 105. Report on Indian affairs, 119-125. Proclamation for thanksgiving for peace, 134. Removal of seat of Government, 136-139. On full representation, 139, 153, 156. Care of arms, artillery, &c., 154. Gratuity to Washington, 155, 185. Debate whether seven States can ratify treaty of peace, 156, 184, 193. Loan office, (1783,) 169. Financial plan, (1780,) rejected by Va., 173. Commutations in lieu of half pay to officers, 179. Washington, renounces his commission, 183, (1783). Treaty of peace ratified by nine States, 193. Court for determining right of soil at Wyoming, 194, 204, 210, 216, 231. Representation not full, 206. Members attending, 207. States represented in, 220. Importance of full representation from each State, 239. Arrears of interest on National debt, 242–256, 263. Delegates to, elected, 354. Proceedings in case of Longschamps, 358. Richard Henry Lee, elected President of, 359. Delays in settling French accounts, 369. Accounts, 371. John Jay elected

Congress—
secretary of Foreign affairs, 401, 557. Claims of Penna,. 405, 424. Captures by Barbary powers, 410, 411. Delegates elected to, 437. May appoint Commissioners on boundary, 440. Respecting troops for defence of frontiers, 440. Laying off States in western territory, 457. Soldiers' certificates, 461. Relief of disabled soldiers and seamen, 472. Asks for copies of Journal, 488. Sends Journal to States, 493. Papers relating to Governor of Massachusetts and Captain Stanhope, 499 Commerce—States to vest, with power to regulate for fifteen years, &c., 508, 738. Proportion of officers and privates to be furnished by Penna., 511. Report on National debt, 514–520. Resolution on loan office, 520-523. Issue of certificates to Continental army, 524. Military claims, 528, 535. State of representation, 532. Certificates for soldiers, 536. Short representation, 537. John Hancock elected President, 539. Copies of Journals, 543. Ratification of definitive Treaty, 549. Temple, Consul General from Great Britain, 544. Treaty with Indians, 549. Wyoming, (1784,) 550, 563, 716. Appointment of Delegates, 562. Removal of seat of Government, 136–139, 566–574, (1784,) 575. Committee of States to act in recess, 566. Indemnification to Washington, 575. Temporary form of Government for western territory, 575. Captain Carberry, 575, 576. Petition of Z. Butler, 581, 716. Collection of debts, 590. Removal of papers from Annapolis, 601. Propose places for the public buildings and seat of Government. 697. On Barbary powers, 705. Longschamps—Wyoming, 706. Complaint of Thomas Shields, 715. Report on Revenue system, 732–735. Acknowledgment of Sieur de la Forrest as vice consul of France, 735. Provision for disabled soldiers and seamen, 745; xi., 3, 4, 50, 51, 56, 70, 71, 79, 121, 122, 132, 143, 145, 168, 171,

Congress—
173, 175, 180, 190, 191, 214, 239, 285, 292, 311, 314, 323, 339, 353, 375, 387, 433, 472, 476, 483, 562, 585, 601. Resolutions, 38, 50, 64, 73, 74, 75, 128, 129, 141, 142, 190, 282, 292, 316, 352, 387, 407, 555, 582, 586, 612, 616. Delegates to, 4, 27, 37, 40, 83, 106, 188, 189, 207, 237, 251, 252, 308, 342, 350, 352, 364, 373, 382, 383, 408, 433, 451, 453, 456, 457, 460, 504, 505, 537, 543, 590, 595, 684. Reports to, 15, 79-83, 107. Committee of the States, 483. Treaty with Prussia, 4. Treasury Board Reports and letters, 15, 41. Domestic debt, 37, 50. Requisitions, 38, 65, 198. Circulars, 50, 71. Foreign debt, 38, 65. Indents for interest, 51. Representation, 51, 56. Finances, 64, Liquidation of accounts, 71. Hostile intention of Indians, 72. Negroes captured by English, 75. Report on uniform system of Commerce, 75, 79. On claim of Pennsylvania, 80-83, 106. Delegates elected, 83. Cession by Connecticut of lands west of Pennsylvania, proposed, 107. State of representation, 122, 132, 168, 175, 180, 192, 263, 275, 298, 311. Rights of States to interpret treaties, 128. Revenues, salaries of officers of Government, 129. John Armstrong, Jr., appointed to, 137. Sale of Townships in western territory, 141. On coining copper, 142. Franking privilege to members of Convention, 142. Phineas Bond, British Consul, 145. On claims unsettled, 170. Boundary of New York and Pennsylvania, 188. Report of Convention at Philadelphia, 190. Privileges of Consuls, 191. Application for men for Luzerne, 206. The new Constitution, 214. Prospects, 204. Require full representations, 214. Sea letters, 239. Purchase of Erie, 247. Quantity of land in Erie tract, 251, 308. Bills of credit against State, 252. Committee of Ways and Means on finances, 258. Settlement of accounts, 282, 285, 292, 316. Pay

Congress—
of invalids, 314. Report on letter of Commissioner of accounts of Virginia, 317. Further time for presenting accounts, 323. Act respecting western territory, 332, 339. Wyoming, 342. Troops for do., 350, 352, 373. T. Pickering's release, 364. Erie, 382, 383. Transfer of Erie, 387. Commissioner of accounts, 406, 408. Constitution to be submitted to Convention, 407. On Wyoming, (1784,) 434, 451, 453, 456, 461. Marbois and Longschamps, 483. Appointment Bowen and Beatty, 504. Erie, 540. Recruiting, 555. On imposts, 582, 583. Copies of Papers to be sent to each State, 586. Judicial Courts, 590. Loan certificates, 595. Indian Chiefs in Virginia, 600. Accounts, 602. Public credit, 612. Amendments of Constitution, 616. Defence of frontiers, 622. Useful arts, 685, 689. Duties, 689. Copyrights, 705. Intercourse with foreign nations, 708. Census, 709, 718. Letter to, from Council on infractions of treaty with Great Britain, xii., 76.

Connecticut correspondence with, ii., 120, 122, 125, 126, 190, 208, 255. Settlers on Penn'a lands, 120-127, 197, 225, 240. Commissioners to Albany, 140. Indian deeds for lands to Susquehanna Company, (supposed Lydias) 147, Lydias, John, 171, 174, 176, 190, 323. Petition of officers of Northumberland county, against, 240, Thomas Penn's letter respecting, 370. Letter from Thos. Penn, 255, 370. From Governor De Lancey on, 273. Men to be raised for Crown Point, 326. Assembly grants Western lands to S. Hazard, 301. Action on petition of Susquehanna county, for lands, 303.

Connecticut settlers from, at Cushitunck, iii., 754, 756, 757, 760.

Connecticut, land purchase and settlers, iv., 41, 51, 56, 70, 83, 88, 103, 105, 127, 129, 343. Letters between Gov. J. Trumbull and E. Dyer, 394, 401. Proclamation of Gov. R. Penn against intruders,

453. Commissioners letter to Gov. Penn, 470. W. S. Johnson to Rev. Dr. Smith, 475. Delegates in Congress to Butler, &c., 643. W. Maclay respecting, 660. Memorial Northumberland and Northampton counties, showing a history of the dispute, 670, 678. Obligation of settlers, 687. Resolution of Congress, respecting, 692, (See Wyoming.)

Connecticut, settlers suffering from Indians, vi., 686.

Connecticut Troops, viii., 421. Letter to Delegates of, on Wyoming lands, 111. Gov. Trumbull, of, 111.

Connecticut, claim to be settled, ix., 4. Letter to delegates on, 306, 307. Resolution, &c., of Congress respecting claim on, 416, 510, 526, 563, 567, 622, 624, 629, 639, 643, 652, 653, 654, 677, 679–692. Proceedings in Congress, list of names for Judges, 679. Minutes of Commissioners, 679, 680, 681, 684, 689. Commission of Commissioners, 680. Letters H. Osborne, Solicitor, 681, 682, 685, 688, 689, 690. Letters of Connecticut Agents to, 682. Selection of Judges, 684. Conference, Council and Agents report on Judges to Congress—and with respect to pay, 686. Report of Committee of Congress, 686. Letter of Pennsylvania agents to Council respecting funds, 688. Letters W. Bradford and J. Reed on impediments thrown in their way to progress, 690, 691. Testimony of Lord Stirling important—he is sick, 692. Time of settlement above Walpeck, 693. Notice of deeds for purchase by Dongan, release of Duke of York, &c., 694. Commission to examine Lord Sterling, 694, Letters W. Bradford respecting trial, 695. Various papers and proceedings at Trenton, 679–724. Copies of Records of State obtained, 730. Proclamation respecting decree at Trenton, 732. Accounts of Sergeant and Reed in case, 738.

Connecticut and Wyoming—[See Wyoming]; resolutions of Assembly of, x., 116, 117; proclamation of Governor Trumbull, 146; letters to and from Gov., 147, 148, 213; resolution of Assembly of Penna., 204; complained of, 204; claims, 398; claimants disposed to violence to Benj. Luce to depart, 679; memorial of John Franklin to Assembly of, 681; resolutions of Assembly on ditto, 683; cession proposed by, 760. Proceedings in Congress respecting, and Wyoming, xi., 5, 106. Act to comply with requisitions, 17, 22. Cession proposed of lands west of Pennsylvania, report on, 107. Claims, 159. Letters to and from Governor, 239, 409, 414, 447, 451, 735. Holders of land ask for division in Luzerne Co., 386. Claimants in arms at Abraham's plains, 437. Letter from Dr. Hugh Williamson, 449. Rights of Settlers, (1784) 447, 451. Agreement with E. Dyer, 533. Absconding debtor claimed, 735.

Connor, Col. Morgan, letter, v., 315; vii., 336.

Connor, Col., viii., 537.

Conolly, Dr. John, taken by order of A. St. Clair, iv., 477. His advertisement, 477. Commission from Dunmore, letters, &c., respecting, 476, 478, 481, 484, 487, 489, 493, 495, 502, 514, 525, 530, 539, 541, 545, 551, 574, 577, 586, 603, 605, 607, 612, 618, 624, 627, 630. Arrested, 476, 484, 637. Released by sheriff, 484. In possession of Fort, 485. Proceedings at Court-house, 485. Depositions respecting, 492, 564–568, 571, 582. Advertisement of, 521. Fort at Wheeling proposed, 522. Petition from Pittsburg against, 526. Remarks on proceedings of, 528. Letter to A. St. Clair, 548. Duty on skins to Virginia, 539. Letter Dr. C. to A. St. Clair, 548, 551. St. Clair's answer, 549. Account of his arrest, 637. Letter committee of Maryland, with one of Conolly to Capt. McKee, 695. Letter of, to committee of Safety, 703. Examination of, and history, 682. Letter to John Gibson, 683. Plans escape from jail, 728, 729. Letter to Committee on his

confinement, 770. Mrs., asks for company for Dr. C. as he is ill, 778. (See Westmoreland,) v., 101, 130, 242, 245, 297, 298. Obliga-tions, 247, 298. In prison, asks return of a favorite pair of pistols, &c., viii., 104.
Conolly, Col. taken prisoner, ix., 102, 473.
Conolly, Mrs. Susanna, letter from, x., 778.
Conoquieson, (Indian,) speech to Sir Wm. Johnson, iv., 373.
Conscience, liberty of, explained i., 634. Rights of, protected in mili-tia bill, iii., 128.
Constitution of United States, amendments proposed by North Carolina, xi., 617, 674.
Constitution of 1776, xii., 52, 68.
——— 1790, xii. 12, 27.
——— U. S., ratification by state, xii., 82.
Consuls, British, xi., 145. Privi-leges of, 191. Phineas Bond ap-pointed, 145. Suggestions, 255. Supposed infringement of rights of State, 375. Letter from on, 381. Opinion of Judges on, 383.
Consul General of France, form of exequator recommended by Con-gress, ix., 390.
Contempt of Court, legal opinions on, xii., 83.
Continental money, v., 126, 327, 396, 602. Signers wanted, 602. Operations of Owen Jones, jr., in, vi., 53–56. Counterfeits, 111, 365. On wagoners, 200, 206, 215, 233. On a coachma-ker, 359,; vii., 156–158, 186, 192; viii., 141, 277, 302, 304, 383, 385, 416, 517, 534, 757. Signers appointed, 635. Called in by Council, ix., 38, 77, 117, 119, 129, 130, 134, 141, 145, 171, 188. Signers of, 184. Regiment, estimate of a, v., 43. Money value, 125. Refusal of, 136, 147. Vessels, 501. Troops and militia don't agree, vi., 291.
Conway, S. H. Secretary, letter, iv., 244.
Conway, B. G. T., v., 522, 530. Com-plains of sending off, Militia, 531.
Convention of the State will visit fortifications, iv., 791.
Convention Troops to be escorted, vii., 89, 95, 99, 101, 104, 106, 107, 108, 110, 129.
Convention at Hartford, proceedings sent Pres., viii., 617.
Convention prisoners, ix., 5, 6, 7, 12, 24, 225, 227, 230, 232, 234, 235, 319. Troops, 14, 277. Dis-posal of, 25, 37. Congress on, 167, at Reading, 225.
Convention in Philadelphia to revise Federal Constitution, xi., 119, 122, 214. Members letters to be free, 142.
Convention, resolutions in Assem-bly to call, on the Constitution, 565.
Conyngham, Capt., G. respecting purchase of his vessel, vii.. 228, 235, 289, 319. His conduct, 318. His explanation, 319, 322.
Coochocking, ix., 39; xii., 120, 135, 158, 219, 220. Block houses not built, 177. Council at, 219, 220, 228, 231.
Cook, Colonel, ix., 51, 79, 595. Col., Edward, Sub lieutenant, 246. Distress of Hanna's Town, 629. Colonel, John—Letter of General Sullivan to, vii., 593.
Cooke, Colonel Wm., ordered to Brunswick, condition of Army forbids, v., 84.
Cook, Wm., proposal for suplies at Sunbury, ix., 411.
Cooke, Wm., respecting lands, xii. 286.
Cookson, Thomas, letters to and from, i., 637, 646. 657, 680, 682, 684, 727, 730. Thomas, letters from, ii., 9, 42.
Coombe, Thomas, health officer of Philadelphia, iv., 59, 70.
Coombe, Rev. Thomas, of Episcopal, Church, arrested, v., 575. Petition of Episcopal Churhes in his behalf 600, 603. Rev. Thomas, Jr., vi., 627. Pass for, 626.
Cooper, Ensign, viii., 65. Ensign William, state of troops, ix., 750, 750. Ensign, xii., 254. Leonard, damages to the barracks at Phila, ix., 424.
Copper, coinage of, Resolution of Congress respecting, xi., 142. Substitute for, as sheathing, ix., 430. Mine, at Gap, in Lancaster

Co., ii., 311. Penn's interest in, 369.
Copy Rights, act passed by Congress, xi., 705.
Coran, Captain, of Artillery, refuses obedience to Colonel Flower, viii., 469.
Corin, Captain Isaac, raises a Company, and is received into State service, viii., 294.
Cornplanter, (Indian Chief,) land proposed to be given, xi., 562. Comes to Phila., 733, 739, 740, 741. Indian Chief, xii., 32. Message of Gov., Mifflin in favor of, for lands, 85. Ensign Jeffers' letter respecting, 86, 300. On his way, 321, 322.
Cornwallis, Lord, gone to Billingsport, going to Red Bank, vi., 23, 30, 43, vii., 663. Report of junction with Gen. Phillips in Virginia, xi., 173. Retreat of, 283, 301. Movements of, 337, 358, 375, 430. Rejoicing at Philadelphia, 440. Proclamation for thanksgiving by Congress, 442. Prisoners at Lancaster, 674. Lord, operations at south, x., (1780,) 173.
Coroners, iv., 460. Inquest on Conestoga Indians, 147.
Coroner, of Franklin Co., xi., 765. [See the Counties.]
Correy, Jonathan, letter to, from Colonel John Franklin, xi., 161.
Coshicton, destroyed by Indians, vi., 651; vii., 63.
Cotes, Admiral Thos., iii., 187, 298.
Coudray, [see Du Coudray.]
Coughenawage, burned, vii., 387.
Coultas, James, chosen Lieutenant Colonel of regiment of Phila., county, ii., 608. Sheriff of Philadelphia, iii., 64.
Council, first, at Upland, obligations of members to keep secrets, &c., i., 37. Penn's difficulty to find members of, 132. With Delaware Indians at Philadelphia, 539. Letters to Governor, iii., 8; at Newcastle, minutes of, 631. Letters, [see Sup., Exec., C.,] Resolutions, vi., 64. Circulars, 65, 88, 179, 193, 240, 294. Complaint to Congress, 279. Resolution of, viii., 608. Accounts of members, xii., 9. At Coochocking xii., 528. Of Censors, resolutions of, x., 149, 153, 302, 306, 326, 327, 333, 336, 363, 546. At Fort George, iv., 167.
Council of Safety appointed, iv., 636, 792; v., 26. Circulars, 76. To clergy, 82. Resolutions, 81, 82, 84, 115. To Congress, 129, 131. Circular to Inhabitants, 134. Resolutions, 134, 147. Address of, to Citizens on Hessian prisoners, 146. Discontinued, 252. Recommend embargo, 319. Can't form a quorum, 349. Address to citizens, 642. Letters to and from. Anderson, Patrick, 27, Armstrong, General John, 164, 229, 324. Assembly, 264. Atlee, Wm., 248. Bancroft, Daniel, 231, 246. Baxter, Lieutenant Colonel William, 31. Bayard, Colonel John, 107. Berks Committee, 111, 112. Biddle, Clement, 140, 145, 197, 744. Bird, Col. Mark, 9. Blair, James, 24, 50. Bond, Dr. Thomas, 89. Bowen, Capt. J. B. 114. Boyd, Alexander, 49, 748. Bradford, Col. William, 745. Brodhead, Daniel, 21, 29, 158. Brown, Wm., 37, 135. Buchanan, William, 744. Bull, John, 58, 102, 201, 203, 208. Cadwallader, Gen. John, 95, 136, 160, 161, 178. Caldwell, Andrew, 261. Casdorp, Thomas, 200. Circular, 45, 81, 82, 84, 99, 119. Coats, Col. Wm., 159, 528. Coleman, Robert, 39. College of Philadelphia, 198. Commissioners of Berks Co., 112. Commissioners of Lancaster, 762. Committee of Berks Co., 111, 112. Committee of Cumberland, 12. Committee of Lancaster, 250, 266. Committee of New York, 40. Committee at Trenton, 69. Committee of Yorktown, 151. Congress, 129, 137, 179, 218, 244, 681. Connolly, John, 101, 130, 242, 245. Cook, Colonel William, 84. Crispin, William, 114, 681, 748. De Haven, Peter, 155. De Normandie, Dr. J. A. C., 176. Dewees, Thomas, 266. Dickinson, Brigadier Gen., 116, 117, 233, 244.

Council of Safety—
Elder, Robert, 753. Evans, John, 246, 529. Ewing, James, 146. Farmer, Captain Lewis, 51. Fisher, Henry, 42, 47, 53, 61, 70, 99, 100, 108, 152, 263. Flower, Colonel Benjamin, 27, 138, 184. Gibson, John, 65. Hale, Thos., 203. Haller, Colonel Henry, 144, 250. Hancock, John, President, 137, 179, 219, 244. Hannigan, Thomas, 253. Harris, John, 753, 758. Hart, Joseph, 18, 97, 236. Hazlewood, Commodore John, 205, 747. Heard, Gen. Nathaniel, 262. Hubly, John, 128. Huff, Joseph, 72, Hunter, Lieutenant Samuel, 133, 762. Irvine, Gen. Wm., 172. Irwine, Col. Wm., 162. Johnston, Col. Francis, 172. Joy, Daniel, 62, 121, 179. Knight, Peter, 239. Kuhn, Ludgwig, 39. Lacey, Captain John, Jr., 154. Lancaster Commissioners, 762. Livingston, Gov. Wm., 238, 243, 251. Lochry, W., 135. Mackay, Æneas, 59. McKinley, Brigadier General John, 34. Meade, George & Co., 61. Mease, James, 193. Mease & Caldwell, 104, 120. Melchor, Col. Isaac, 178, 206. Mercer, Brigadier General, 41, 67, 71. Mifflin, Jonathan, 86. Miles, Colonel, S. 5. Mitchell, John, 62. Montgomery, Hugh, 57, 120. Moore, John, 135. Morgan, Col. J., 761. Morris, John, Jr., 161, 749. Morris, Robert, 28, 31, 126, 132, 138, 189, 255, 758, 769. Morris, Samuel, C., 109. Navy Board, 746. Nelson, Thomas, 167. Nesbit, Mr., 240. Nevell, Thomas, 64. Nicola, Lewis, 7, 29, 71, 75, 78, 90, 92, 121, 200. Parke, Lt. Col. John, 181. Patton, Maj. John, 41. Pennell, Jos., 143, 197. Peters, Richard, 15. Pintard, Lewis, 196. Piper, John, 148. Potter, David, 86, 218. Potter, Gen. Jas., 752, 755. Proctor, John, 202, Proctor, Major Thos., 11, 23, 45, 50, 52, 97, 118, 130, 134, 189, 192, 207, 234, 236, 249. Putnam, General Israel, 163, 168, 170, 177, 196, 208, 215, 230. Read, James, 20, 138, 258. Read, John, 23, 24,

Council of Safety—
26, 47, 60, 69, 91, 92. Reed, Joseph, A. G., 109, 151 Richards, William, 13, 46, 63, 169, 242. Richardson, Joseph, 254. Rittenhouse, David, 62. Roberdeau Daniel, 757. Ross, George, 758. Rush, Dr. Benjamin, 38, 58. Savadge, Thomas, 55, 195, 216, 217, 229. Seymour, Commodore Thomas, 67, 104. Smith, Robert, 37. Sprogell, Lodick, 230. Stansbury, Joseph, 94, 98. Stirling, Lord, 157, 166, 173, 195. Stevenson, George, 68. Tallman, Peter, 64. Taylor, George, 49. Thorne, William, 143. Tilghman, James, 156, 174. Trenton, Committee, 69. Virginians, 14. Walters, John, 182, 244. Washington, General George, 253. Wayne, Colonel Anthony, 88. Weedon, Colonel G., 241. Weitzill, John, 85. Wells, Richard, 189. Williams, Major Ennion, 34, 35, 39, 51, 52, 80, 103, 105, 107, 112, 115, 117, 127, 204, 212. Wirtz, Christian, 202, 208. Wood, Colonel Joseph, 87. Wynkoop, Henry, 32. Letters, vi., 3, 4. Ordinances of the, considered, confirmed or repealed by the Assembly, 73. Dissolution of, 64. Order of, 92. And Assembly, to Congress, 333.

Council of Safety of Kent County, Delaware, apply for salt, v., 79, 80.

Council, Sup. Executive, Resolutions, v., 691. [See Supreme Executive Council.]

Council of War, at Oswego, minutes of, ii., 413, 427. On the fleet, vi., 20.

Counterfeit, bills of credit, made in England, i., 578. Capture of Jenkens, 619, 620. Depositions respecting, 621, 623. Described, 589. Counterfeit bills of credit, iii., 365; iv., 460, 461, 462, 466; v., 239, 240, 248, 258, 327, 525. Continental bills found on wagoners, &c., vi., 200, 206, 215, 233, 555. Half pence, ix., 279. Loan office certificates in circulation, x., 447.

Counterfeiters in prison, vii., 694,
County Lieutenants—circular, to Battalion districts, x., 419.
Court, Provincial, proceedings, i., 98. Of Judicature, establishing of, Act respecting, 157. Draught of a law for better establishing 165. Of Chancery, proclamation establishing it, 171. Report of business in Philadelphia, Bucks, and Chester County, 279.
Court, Worcester, County, Md., proceedings, iii., 586.
Courts, vi., 228, 234, 245, 294, 661, 685. Court of Admiralty necessary, 685.
Courts, no State attorney in Northumberland, vii., 73. Long suspension of Justice renders people licentious, 73. Of appeal from Courts of law recommended, 78. At York, 773.
Courts, viii., 326, 622. Of Common Pleas, 622.
Courts, judicial, Delegates on, xi., 590.
Court, District U. S., to sit in Philadelphia, xi., 723.
Court martial proceedings, vi., 581, 697, 704. Appeal from, by Capt. R. Hardie, vii., 91, 327; viii., 70. Francis Swaine, 397, 429, 433; ix., 207; xii., 192, 256, 263.
Cove, Great, Indian murders at, vi., 138.
Cowell, Ebenezer, vi., 51.
Cowperthwaite, Col., viii., 111.
Cox, Lieutenant Col. Gabriel, suits against, arising from boundary with Va, x., 81, 96, 125, 131. Letter to Michael Huffnagle, 125.
Coxe, Col., Iron furnace, v., 56.
Coxe, John, to transport all the shot he has made, iv., 757.
Cox, John, letter, vi., 16, 29.
Coxe, Col. John, wagons, vii., 749.
Cox, Col. John, viii., 359, 406.
Coxe, Tench, Commissioner to Commercial Convention, to Maryland Commissioners, xi., 61. To Council, 60. Appointed on Commerce, 522. His views of purchase of Erie lands, Gorham & Co.'s claim, 539. Application to Governor of Canada suggested, 542, 543.
Coxe's Town, stores at, vii., 508.
Coysgarne, Joseph, Letter W. P. to, i., 136.
Craig, Captain J., viii., 76, 254, 303, 397, 717; ix., 39, 114.
Craig, Capt. Isaac, memorial and History, ix., 497.
Craig, Isaac, letter from Pittsburg, xii., 300.
Craig, Colonel John, instructions to, to take Franklin, xi., 188, 196. Pay for troops, 236. Militia fines of John Youngman, 304.
Craig, Robert, vi., 41.
Craig, Col. Thos vi., 412. Deserters, ix., 18, 563.
Craig, Thomas, Lieutenant of Northampton Co.—letters of Council to, respecting Wyoming, x., 296, 303, 305.
Craig, Thomas, respecting Brown's execution, xi., 276.
Crawford, Col., commands expedition to Sandusky—he missing, ix., 556, 576; xii., 202.
Crawford, Edward, Jr., licenses, xi., 690.
Crawford, Fort, viii., 77, 106. Evacuated, ix., 89; xii., 129, 134, 139. Order to Ensign Coleman to evacuate, 141. To be evacuated, 195. Men to, 160, 215, 261. Captain Stokely to take his station at, 255. Described, 350-352.
Crawford, James, vii., 760.
Credit, public, resolutions of Congress on, xi., 612.
Cresap, Michael, iv., 502, 512, 539, 561.
Cresap, Thos. Deposition of, i., 311, 352. Respecting, 313, 320, 321, 326, 336, 338, 352, 398, 410, 412, 415, 417, 419, 462, 464, 476, 489, 501, 556. Warrant to arrest, 489. Depositions respecting, 504-528.
Cress, Peter, deposition, vii., 259.
Creveceur, Mons., letter to, from Pres. Dickinson, x., 195, (1784) 550.
Crispin Wm., letter, v., 114, 681, 706, 748; vi, 151, 175, 203, 208, 440. Orders to prepare for Prest's visit to fortifications, vii., 200. Asks for money, 314. Soldiers demand liquor of, ix., 437.
Croghan's Fort, xii., 352.

Croghan, George, Letter, i., 247, 770; ii., 689, 694. And Indians, 9, 115. Letters to and from, 10, 31, 118, 119, 132, 144, 173, 203, 209, 212, 218, 219, 483. Gov. Morris's account of him, 689. Fort, 571, 623. Orders to, 536. Captain of Indians under Braddock, 689. Letters to and from, iii., 175, 247, 248, 319, 428, 544, 671, 733; iv., 42, 44, 483, 507. Speech of Indians to, 497.

Crosswicks, v., 181.

Crown Point expedition against, ii., 20, 21, 29, 257, 326, 330, 332, 341, 345, 350, 365, 374, 442, 579, 585, 589, 631.

Crows' Town, xii., 201.

Culbertson, Col. Robert, vi., 448.

Culpepper, Thos. Letter to W. Penn, i., 51.

Cumberland county, letter D. Magard, on proper site for County town, ii., 39. From T. Cookson, 42. Letter Gov. Hamilton to Justices, 49. Petitions for defence, 239, 749, 755, 756, 757, 760. Indian Massacres, 571, 575, 611, 613. Orders to Captains of, 602. Want of Arms, 636. Number of Roman Catholics in, iii., 144; recruits in, 406; Gov'r's orders to sheriff of, 108; troops, 448; fort, 196. Indian murders, iv., 117. Military at, 131. Claims, 168, 170, 219. People from, moving up Susquehannah, 218. Passes given by justices, 218. Battalion to be raised, 693. N. J., petition of, for powder from City, v., 30. Committee letter, 12. Petition, (N. J.) 30. Condition of affairs in, 299, 334. Opposition to Government, 324. Resolutions of, 340. Books and Records, 416. Militia, 501, 752. Tories, 624. Tory Estate seized, vi., 94. Militia, 169, 379, 426, 605. Horse thieves in, 381. Taxes, 550. List of Justices, vii., 144. High price of wheat—Justices, &c., 399. Ought to guard frontiers, 419. Resolve to defend themselves, 437. Martial spirit in, 623. Lieutenants, viii., 152. Taxes not demanded by collectors, 61. Indians, 243. Wagons in, 447. Officers of, 522.

Cumberland county—Indians, 558. Troops, ix., 15, 71, 400. Col. Abm. Smith, of militia, 203. Lands in, 409. Provisions, 459. Prisoners of war, 575. Indians, 522. New township, Green, 647. Taxes, 736. Case of Peter Dill, 736. Commissioners on taxes, x., 79; Indians in (1779) 159; —(See Vol. XII.)—return of sheriffs, 1777 to 1783, 285; officers of militia in, 599, 600. State road, xi., 158. Returns of militia, 605.

Cumberland Fort [See Forts.] ii.; xii., 353.

Cummings, Lieut., orders to, ix., 28.

Cummings, Lieut., John, Indian murders &c., x., 23.

Cummins, Major J. R. ix., 20, 24.

Cunningham, Mr., ix., 606.

Cunningham, Hon. James, Taxes, ix., 495.

Cunningham, James, report of surveys of depreciation land xi., 263,

Currency, state and improvements of, vii., 416, 448, 481, 543, 572, 643, 721, 738. Plan for improving—Town meeting in Phil., 621. Emissions stopped, viii., 58.

Curry, Col., viii., 52.

Curtis and Finney, Letters, i., 759.

Curwin, Jno., on Turnpike, xi., 572.

Cushing, Thomas, vii., 250.

Cushitunck, settlers from Connecticut on lands at, iii., 754, 756, 757, 760. Settlement at, iv., 70, 83, 88. Proclamation, at, 70.

Cushcushking, iii., 523.

Cuscushing, xii., 156.

Cuskusky, prisoners at, xii., 243.

Customs, Searcher of, i., 116. Commissioners of, on Navigation Act to Governor, 119. Letters of W. P., on complaints of merchants respecting duties on Tobacco, 149, Commissioners of, Letter, of W. P., i., 138. Letters from, 185, 238. Officers to reside in their Districts, 185. Collectors, &c., appointed, 195, 196, 199, 238, 395. Transports not liable to, iii., 137, 138; commissioners of, letter, 546; collectors, 546. Officers appointed, iv., 253, 254, 255, 305,

Customs—
449, 451. Meet with obstructions in America, 299. Officer killed, 297, 302. Life of Searcher at Philada. threatened, 310. Table of fees asked for, 380.
Cut-cheek, an Indian, xii., 301,

D.

Dale, Samuel, instructions as agent to Wyoming, xi., 66.
Dallas, Alex. J., appointed Sec'y of State, xii., 46. Letters to and from, 99.
Dalley, Gifford—quarters for citizens from South Carolina, ix., 274.
Dana, Francis, vi., 318, 384.
Darby Creek, works on, v., 591.
Darby, skirmish near, with Genl. Potter's men, vi , 141.
Darnall, Henry, attorney general of Maryland, to Judges of Court, at York, ii., 93.
Dartmouth, Earl of, appointed Secr'y of State, iv., 456. Letters, 456, 464, 480, 482, 538, 577, 579, 585, 588, 613, 614, 621, 625.
Dauphin of France born, honors by Congress in consequence, ix., 542, 544, 545, 547.
Davenport, Jonah, an Indian trader's examination, i., 299.
Davidson, Mr. Jas., instructions, &c., to, vi., 16, 160, 181, 186,
Davis, Alban, deposition respectting a smuggler, iv., 445.
Davis, Benj'n, jr., Report, xi., 766.
Davis, Col. Caleb, v., 292.
Davis, Caleb, list of Justices in Chester Co., vii., 444.
Davis, Col., vii., 565.
Davis, David, commissioner of purchases, viii., 382, 458.
Davis, Issachar, instructions to, respecting accommodations, at Easton, iii., 209.
Davis, John, vi., 562.
Davis, Col. John, letter to, xii., 117, 152, 175.
Davis, Doct. John, taken prisoner--exchanged, v., 204.
Davis, Capt. Peter, to be arrested, xii., 166. Trial, 256. Escapes, 266.
Davis, Thomas, contractor for building piers in River Delaware x., 456, 713.
Davis, Mr., xii., 205.
Davis' Fort, xii., 354.
Davison, Com. Samuel, appointed commander of the fleet, iv., 759. Replies of different officers, 759; v., 378.
Davison, Hugh, resigns as Lt., vi, 504.
Dawson, David, of Chester Co., executed, x., 609.
Dawson, Captain Samuel, xii., 107. Troops required, 143. Letter to, 151.
Deane frigate, vii., 198, 521, 533.
Deane, James, vii., 11.
Dean, Joseph, Petition respecting land, and forfeited estate, vii., 540; viii., 81, 712.
Death of King George II., iv., 37. Of Conrad Weiser, iv., 41. Of Queen of Denmark, sister of his Majesty, 625.
De Barras, Mons., ix., 353, 372. [See Barras]
De Brussine & Garrison propose to remove Chevaux-de-frize, x., 144 -145.
Debts, Priority, of, act respecting, i., 159.
Debt, Public, of Pennsylvania, certificates granted for, iv., 257, 333, 345. Report of Committee to Congress on the public, ix., 85–93. Public—States called on for statements of, xi., 613, 639, 640.
Decker, Cox & Co., invaded Indian lands, xii., 176.
Debtors not to leave the State, v., 356.
Declaration, W. Penn against L. Baltimore, i., 88. Of War, England and France, ii., 635, 735.
De Corney, Monsieur, viii., 383, 396, 406, 416.
Dedimus, Potestatem, i., 289, 393. To James Hamilton, ii., 461. To Wm. and Richard Peters, iv., 40. J. Shippen, jr., 101, 104.
Deeds to sundry persons on Del. by Gov. Nicolls, i., 27, 28. To Peter Cock by Gov. Lovelace, 29. For lands in West Jersey, 29, 31. From Indians, to Cantwell and De Haes, 32. To Fopp Outhout,

Deeds—
33, 34. To Henderson 34. To Peterson 35. To J. P. Jacquett, 36. Indian To William Penn: July 15, 1682, 47; June 23, 1683, 62, 63, 64; June 25, 1683, 62, 63, 64; June 25, 1683, 65; July 14, 1683, 65, 66; Sep. 10, 1683, 67; Oct. 18, 1683, 67; June 3, 1684, 88, June 7, 1684, 92; July 30, 1685, 93; Oct. 2, 1685, 95. June 15, 1692, 116; Gov. Dongan to W. P. 121, 122; July 5, 1697, 125; Sep. 13, 1700, 133, 146; Lands on Schuylkill, Sept, 7, 1732, 344. John Newton, abstract of, 374. For settlement at Tulpehocken, 404. For lands on Susquehanna, Oct. 11, 1736, 494. For lands on Delaware, Aug. 25, 1737, 541. Indian, for lands in New Jersey, Feb. 21, 1743, 641. Of feoffment, Duke of Y. for N. Castle, Aug. 24, 1682, 52. Acknowledgment and recording act respecting, 155, 158. Indian, for lands between Delaware and Susquehanna, ii., 33. Indian, to "Susquehanna Company," for lands, 147—158, 175. Questions proposed respecting, iii., 262, Memorandum Richard Peters respecting that of 1718, 262. For land, defective, viii., 49. Petition on acknowledgment of, xi., 136. From Indians, for Erie, xii., 100.

De Grasse, Count, present of cannon for, x., 59.

De Haas, Major, iv., 206.

De Haas, Gen. J. P., vi., 646, 648, 649, 674. Proposes to raise volunteers, 646. Difficulty respecting command, 670, 684, 729. Respecting seizure of flour, vii., 330—332. Letter to, 332.

De Hart, Jacob, Lieutenant of ship General Greene, vii., 310, 364.

De Haven, Hugh, iv., 569; vi., 58.

De Haven, Peter, letter respecting gun factory, v., 155. Explosion of Powder Mill, 255, 256, 261, 606, 607; vi., 52, 453, 475, 632; at Gun factory, vii., 12, 133, 175, 194. Applies to be Wagon Master, 175; viii., 360.

De la Balme, Col. and party—fate of, viii. 766, 767.

De la Fayette, Marquis, ix., 283, 359, 430, 627.

De la Luzerne, Chevalier, viii., 383.

De Lambert, Chevalier, introduced by Marquis Fayette, ix., 627, 734, 735. General St. Clair, respecting, 735.

De Lancey, James, Governor of New York, letters to and from, ii., 168, 179, 220, 233, 243, 261, 264, 267, 270, 273, 278, 279, 280, 326, 331, 338, 345, 346, 359, 384, 391, 396, 398. Controversy with General Shirley about cannons, 349; iii., 434, 691.

De Lancey, ——, surprises and kills Colonel Green, at White Plains, ix., 155.

De Laney, Col. viii., 111.

Delaney, John, petition from, wounded at Germantown, vii., 94.

Delany, Sharp, (Collector,) on Memorial of Captain vii., 762; Darie, x., 97. Heavy demand, 441, 715 Report Mr. Orr's duty as an alien, xi., 259. Attorney General's opinion as to Citizenship, 260. Queries, respecting duties, 397. Answer of Judges to, 601, 602.

Delapt, Richard, &c., vii., 702

De La Vega, F. C., Governor of Havana, letter, to, iii., 508.

Delaware County, Justice of peace, xi., 638.

Delaware Indians, number of, i., 301. Letter of Governor to, 303. Declaration of war against, views of council on, ii., 654. Suspension of hostilities, 669. Conference with, at Pittsburg, by Colonel Bouquet, 571—574. Murders, iv., 503; v., 314; viii., 120, 152. Towns destroyed by Colonel Clarke, of Virginia, 515. Indians, base attempt by whites to destroy, near Hanna's Town, 596; ix., 39, 97, 247; x., 85, 86. Behave well at Muskingum, xii., 237. Councils, 239, 246. Towns, 256, 270. —— 111, 147, 153, 155, 156, 166, 211, 228, 231, 233, 235. Council, 219, 267, 269, 305.

Delaware River, grant of lands on, by Governor Richard Nicolls, i., 27. Grant of island to Peter Cock, 29. Commissioners to treat with New Jersey, respecting, 58, 59, 60, 61. Letter, William Penn, on, 60. Deed for lands on, 541. Spanish privateers in, 759, 763, 765, 766. Deed for lands between, and Susquehanna, ii., 33, 36. Defence of, 477, 509. Description of cannons required, 511. Joshua Fisher about to publish a map of, is stopped by Governor, letters respecting, 492, 593. Memorial of Pilots, iv., 263. Proclamation respecting Fish, 347. Lord Dunmore's designs on Islands in, 637. British vessels appear in, 724, 725, 732, 736, 737, 740, 743, 747, 748, 753, 762, 769. Complaint of officers of armed boats, 705. Engagement with Roebuck and Liverpool, 748. River and Bay pilots, v., 28. Pay of men in the armed vessels on, 30. Chevaux-de-frize, respecting, 37, 39, 45, 66, 67, 83, 238, 426, 431, 591, 626, 648, 649, 680, 696, 699, 721. Fortifications and defence of, 8, 9, 11, 37, 39, 45, 57, 62, 130, 138, 166, 242, 346, 359, 376, 425, 431, 434, 501, 526, 542, 565, 620, 626. Dispatches from H. Fisher respecting vessels of war, 42, 47, 53, 61, 70, 99, 100, 108, 153, 263, 402, 465, 504. No person to pass without a permit, 82. River craft to be removed from Jersey side, 84. Attempt to bribe pilots to bring fleet from New York by James Molesworth, (who was executed) 270-282, 315, 336, 337. Actions on, 453, 504, 648, 696, 697, 701, 702, 703, 706, 707, 709. British vessels in or near the, 99, 118, 126, 132, 216, 217, 263, 305, 315, 402, 453, 457, 462, 465, 467, 468, 472, 488, 538, 591, 668, 699, 721. Augusta and Merlin blown up, 698, 699, 706, 707, 719, 720, 721. All the lumber used for fire rafts, —fords on the, 375, 441. Trade carried on with enemy, 403, 504. Capture of traders by Captain Murphy, 504, 510. Guns for Cape May, 346. Du Coudray's

Delaware River—
reports on defences of the, 359-363, 430, 431, 526, 565. Shore, survey of, instructions for, 441. Twelve fireships ordered by Congress, 464. Dispatches from John Hunn respecting vessels of war in, 451, 453, 462, 467, 468, 474, 475. Dispatch from Leeson Simmons, respecting vessels, 538. Defects in the defences of, 626 Capture of Billingsport, 648. State vessels in, 648. Operations on the, 648, 649, 663, 718. French Frigate Chimere arrives—pilot for requested, 665. Forts attacked by land and water, 667. A chevaux-de-frize removed, 668. Commodore Hazlewood's account of action between the fleets, 721. Fort Mifflin, 723. Ship Montgomery and other vessels burned near Burlington for safety, 740. [See also Billingsport, Fort Mifflin, Mud Fort and Red Bank.] Naval and military operations on, vi., 11, 19, 20, 21, 23, 24, 27, 28, 44, 47, 50, 110, 121, 130, 133, 204. Fort Mifflin, 11, 19, 24, 27, 246. British vessels in, 11, 27. Red Bank, 11, 28, 80, 246. Billingsport, 23, 27, Lord Cornwallis, 23, 31. General Clinton with troops arrives, 27. Vessels burned for safety, 28, 80. Proposal to salt fish from, for the army, 380. Sunken vessel of enemy to be raised, 652. British vessels in, 706. Council of War, Chevaux-de-frize, 20. Fort Mercer, Red Bank, 21. Fortifying, 710. Map of, 758, 768. Defence of, vii., 19, 180, 191, 197, 199, 200, 270, 282, 290, 298, 329, 410. Letter to Governor, on defence of, 180. Visit of Governor, &c., to fortifications of, 199, 200, 203. Map of, 233. Survey of, by Gen. Du Portail, 201, 227, 229, 232, 272, 279, 280, 366, 399, 403, 409. Banks at Mud Island, to be repaired, 240. Troops sent to the Forts on, 270, and cannon, 290, 298. Billingsport, 290, 298. 339, 365, 366, 369, 371, 409, 502, 507, 562, 673, 720, 745. Mud Island, 270, 290, 339, 369, 385,

Delaware River—
397, 410, 502, 562 652, 673, 720, 745, 764. Timber wheels required, 345. Treatment of vessels bound up and down, 372, 456, 537. A piece of heavy cannon from Princeton, 375. Waste of powder in bringing vessels to, 398, 404. Letters to and from Henry Fisher, 396, 410. Sweeping for lost articles, 433, 541. Chevaux-de-frize, 544, 566, 587, 635. Raising sunken vessels, 644. Mrs. Hitchcock's claim for giving notice, 705. Henry Fisher's letters, 390, 410, 705, 730. Officers ordered up from forts, 720. Armed boats in, viii., 216, 231, 254, 274, 339, 437. Claim for Hog Island, ix., 5, 42, 252, 520. Defence of, 60. British fleet expected—Isaac Roach sent to Capes to watch, 80, 112. Orders to, 96. Danger from enemy, 105. Ship ashore and lost, 113. Capt. Roach to return, 175. Chart of, near Mud Island mentioned, 255. Flags of truce from S. C. ordered down river, 338. Frigate Trumbull in, 338. British ship of war Gen. Monk captured in, by Hyder Ally, Capt. Barney, 529. Purchased for defence of, 530. Ask for a vessel of easy draught, 647. Comm'rs for defence of, 586, 618, 621, 625, 647, 672. Sale of Hyder Ally proposed, 672. Armed Schooner equipped for defence of, and commanded by John Snyder, 672. Equipping armament to defend, x., 26. Removal of Chevaux-de-frize, 95, 144. Commissioners appointed to examine, 130. Inquiry respecting islands above Falls, 130. Falls of, as seat of Government, 137. Proposals of De Brussine & Garrrison to remove Chevaux-de-frize, 93, 144-146, 349, 359, 565. Resolutions of Assembly on removing, (1783) 177, 210. Amount expended for improvement. 240. Military stores at Fort Island and Billingsport, 284, (1784.) Removal of chevaux-de-frizes, 340, 350. Jurisdiction of Islands, 130, 366, 696. Federal buildings on the Delaware, 693. Piers to be erected, 407. Contract for, 456. Proposals, 471, 713. Improvements contemplated by the Wardens, (1784) 571. Buoys taken away, 580. Beacon on Cross Ledge, 588. Chevaux-de-frizes, 589, 606, 607, Jurisdiction of Islands, 611. And navigation of, 710. Inquiry as to ownership of Islands in the River, 739. Navigable communication between Chesapeake and, Proceedings, xi., 25, 27. Sloop and negro Jim brought into, 53. Beacon at Cape May, 93. Spanish Frigate at Marcus Hook, 99–102. Examination of rivers, 677. Comm'rs to examine, 622. Soundings in, 1776, opposite Billingsport, xii. 68. Jurisdiction of Islands in, 75. Report on claims to islands in, 87. Report on jurisdiction of Islands, 289. On improving, 292, 294. Of Wardens, on light house, capes, beacons, buoys, winter harbors, &c., 310.

Delaware, State of, comm'r appointed on boundary line. George Read Riddle appointed 1849, (note) iv., 37. Troops want clothing, v., 34. Prisoners in Phila., jail, sureties for, 309. vii., 152. Letter to Governor on exportation of provisions, from, viii 10. Allows export of provisions, 229, 609. Insecurity of public stores in, ix., 95, 100, 105. Removal of, ordered, 101. Inland navigation, x , 538, 540. Act of, to comply with requisitions, xi., 16, 22. Proceedings on internal navigation, 25, 27, 77. Letter from Governor, 33.

Delegates in Congress, v., 536. Letters, vi., 4, 116, 136, 207, 231, 268, 279, 298, 359, 380, 455, 535, 577; vii., 134, 140, 160, 162, 174, 181, 184, 189, 192, 422, 476, 551, 557, 639. To require yeas and nays in certain cases, 174. From Virginia, 73, 184. Letters to and from, viii., 9, 61, 161, 191, 351, 392, 494, 643, 711, 722, 745. From Connecticut, letter to, on Wyoming Lands, 111, 112. Of State, in Congress, ix., 103, 163, 306, 307, 420, 434,

Delegates in Congress—
763. Query on legality of trial by a judge, who is a, 163. Prison ships, 762. Of Virginia, in Congress, 260, 266, 271, 274, In Congress, letter to, x., 25, 27. 45, 48, 52, 69, 72, 101, 126, 151, 154, 155, 156, 184, 204, 210, 223, 358, 369, 397, 405, 410, 440, 457, 476, 534, 549, 564, 592, 681, 697, 705, 713, 759, 768. On gratuity to General Washington, 151. Election of, 354, 437, 534. No. of, 564. Letters, xi., 4, 27, 37, 40, 87, 106, (see Vol., x., 759,) 188, 189, 207, 237, 251, 308, 342, 350, 352, 364, 373, 382, 383, 408. 433, 451, 453, 456, 457, 461, 504, 505, 537, 543, 590, 684. Elected, 83.

Deluge in Luzerne County, xi., 85,

Denmark, Queen of, death, iv., 625. Willing to consecrate American Bishops. Letters from Mr. De St. Saphorin, &c., x., 434.

Denison, Colonel, vii., 16. Nathan, instructions with arms for Wyoming, xi., 212. A Scotch Emissary, 213. Letter on insurgents, 327.

Dennis, Anthony, commission as surveyor of boundary between N. York and N. Jersey, iv., 340.

Denny, William, Governor, arrives and succeeds Morris, ii., 760. Address of Unitas Fratrum to him, 760. Of Ministers, Vestry, &c., of Christ Church, 762. Of Regim't of Philada. Co., 763. His reply, 763. Letters to and from, 779; iii., 5, 8, 13, 18, 29, 35, 36, 38, 39, 40, 48, 50 53, 54, 58, 64, 69, 76, 78, 83, 93, 95, 96, 106, 137, 138, 141, 145, 146, 148, 150, 160, 162, 173, 174, 186, 193, 201, 207, 209, 212, 214, 218, 221, 235, 236, 239, 247, 248, 251, 256, 258, 273, 277, 278, 282, 289, 290, 293, 296, 298, 300, 303, 304, 313, 315, 316, 323, 330, 338, 349, 351, 364, 365, 366, 380, 383, 385, 392, 401, 403, 412, 425, 427, 428, 430, 432, 434, 436, 438, 442, 449, 453, 471, 480, 481, 485, 487, 489, 490, 498, 508, 511, 517, 518, 546, 552, 571, 623, 634, 671, 675, 677, 685, 687, 689. Messages to and from Assembly, 19, 98. Instructions to L. Morris, jr., 90. Order to the Sheriff of Cumberland Co., 105. Long letter to Proprietaries, 107. Treated with rudeness and insolence by members of the House, 112. Letter on transactions with Lord Loudoun, 117. Proclamation against rum, 521. Is succeeded by Governor Hamilton, 689. Speech to Assembly at New Castle, 377.

Denny, David, viii., 496. Ensign, his rank, xi., 325.

De Normandie, Dr., v., 176.

Dent, Lieutenant, a Virginia officer, xii., 274.

Department of foreign affairs to be established, xi., 599.

De Peyster, Lieutenant Colonel, A. S., on Indian negotiations, x., 86, 89.

Depositions, and Examinations, Jonah Davenport, an Indian Trader, i., 299. James Le Tort, 300. Edmund Cartledge, 304. Thomas Renick, 309. Thomas Cresap 310, 352. Respecting dams on Schuylkill, 315. Luke Mercer, 335. James Hendricks, 348, 399. John Capper, 350, 360. John Lowe, 350. William McMannick, 354. John Brabaker, 355. Joshua Lowe, 356, 363. Charles Jones, 357. Francis Ward, 357. John Patten, 358, 360. Alexander McKee, 360. Joshua Minshall, 361. Rebecca Hendricks, 361. Tobias Hendricks, 362. Abstracts of, 365-367. Samuel Thorn, 374. Jeremiah Fowler, 375. John Sullivan, 382. Richard Andrew, 382. William Andrew, 383. George Andrew, 384. John Emerson, 396. Cornelius Comages, 397. Richard Ashton, 398. William Daugherty, 400. Samuel Moncey, 401. William Glasspill, 412. Michael Dooling, 413. Henry Packard, 423. Thomas Rothwell, 424. Hugh Rainey, 433. Patrick Thomas, 440. Ann Thomas, 441. John Wright, 464. Rob. Barber, 489, 490. John Coats, 500. Jeremiah Star, 501. Wm. Miller, 501. Henry Munday, 502. John

Depositions—
Kelly, 504. On taking of Cresap —Arthur Buchanan, &c., 505, 507, 515. Robert Buchanan, 506, John Starr, 508. George Aston. 510. Samuel Scott, 510, 515, William Downard, 512. Samuel Smith, 513. David Priest, 515. Samuel Atkinson, 516. Daniel Southerland, 517. Benjamin Chambers, 519. John Ross, 521, 525, 526. Frederick Lather, 522. Balser Springler, 523. George Hornspacker, 529. Michael Tanner, 524. Thomas Coulson, 528. Joseph Evans, 555. Conrad Keller, 555. Anderson and Montgomery, 537. Riots on Schuylkill, 553. On Maryland Outrages, 555. Samuel Cartwright, 561. Sapience Harris, 562, 590. Wm. Williams, 563, 591. Thomas Rothwell, 424, 564, 590. Jno. Daneilly, 566. Matthew Donahoe, 583. Rachel Brick, (Counterfeits), 621. William Brick, do. 622. Alexander Armstrong, 643. Peter Shultz, 694. Robert Owings, 695. John Lemmon, 695. Thomas Norris, 697. J. Roberts, 698. Valentine Eyler, 699. Matthias Ulrick, 700. W. Oler, M. Kittsmiller, and J. Banker, 701. Herman Updegraef, 702. Adam Furney, 704, 726. Zachary Butcher, 707. S. White, &c., ii., 18. Samuel England, 21 Jeremiah Brown, 22. John Murray, 37. Margaret McCleary, 37. Benjamin Swoope, (riot), 50. Samuel Dickinson, 64. Martin Kittsmiller, 70. Respecting death of John Diges's son. Anthony Conley, &c., 76. John Stackers, 78. P. Coyle, 79. Leond. Kitzmiller, 80. Jacob Sheely, 81. John Seifert, 82. Patten and Montour, 123. A French deserter, 124. John Trotter, Indian Trader, 131. Peter Hogg, (Indians), 167. Francis Claw, (do.) 168. Wm. Morris and William Green, 265. James Anderson, 266. Thomas Clarke, 283. Mathias Steelman. 335. Charles Vanderford, 336. Thomas Vanderford, 337. Alexander Quillin,

Depositions—
337. Nicholas Powell, 440. Monacatootha and Montour, 452. Moravians, 459. J. Shmick and H. Fry, respecting Wyoming, 491. William Johnston, iii., 13. 16. Samuel Clifford, 44. Leonard Weeser, 45. Henry Hess, 56. John Williamson, 139. Of a Delaware prisoner, 147. D. Broadhead and E. Biddle, 244. B. Shoemaker and John Drake, 249, 254, 264. Conrad Weiser and J. McKee, 256. C. Busse and J. Orndt, 259. James Hyndshaw, 263. Michael Chavignerie, 295, 305. Francis Fevre, 363. Richard Bairds, 396. Benjamin Handy, 592. William Ellegood, 693. Abraham Ingram, 597. Andrew Collings, 597, 602. Moses Timmons, 598. Thomas Hindes, 601. John Pollock, 603. John Spicer, 603. Wm. Gray, 605. William Hayward, 606. Parker Selby, 607. John Willy, 609. Peter Dolby, 611. John Sharp, 612. Patience Wadelow Hemmons, 614. Colonel John Dennis, 615. Penington Welsh, 618. Moses Moore and Isham Bernat, 632. Barbara Lingaree and Mary Roy, 633. John Spencer, 635. Thomas Himmons, 637. Solomon Fruit, 637. Richard Coverdell, 639. Warren Burroughs, 640. James Ingram, 641. John Pettijohn, Sen., 642. Alex. West, 643. Charles Polke, 643. Magdalen Manlove, 644. Joseph Morgan, 645. Ephraim Polke, 646. Waitman Willey, 647. Jared Hitchins, 649. Robert Shankland, 652, 656. Christopher Hoskins, 677. Peter Titell, 705. Richard Davis, 705. John Loughry, 731. Depui's, Aaron, iv., 45. Sam. Sellers and Joseph Ross, respecting a French spy taken, 205. Lieutenant Charles Grant, 220. John Shelby, 222. James Wilkins, 223. Ralph Nailer, 225. J. Smith, 230. McGlashen Lt. Leond. 233, 234. Henry Prather, 237. Thomas Romberg, 23. John Jennings, 342. Wm. Sims, 387. Wm. Nimins, 387.

Depositions—
Asa Luddington, 388. Thomas Bennet, Joseph Drake, 425. Richard Brown, 430. Thomas Woods, (Sheriff,) 435. Alban Davis, 445. James McCashlin, 459. Ephraim Hunter, Sheriff, 491. George Wilson 493. Wm. Wilson, 542, John Pollock, 544. David Griffey, 555. John and James Fowler, 564. Samuel St. Clair, 565. Æneas Mackay, 566. Wm. Amberon, 568. George Ashton, 571. Arthur St. Clair, 582. Charles Foreman, 604. Samuel Whitesitt, 605. Devereux Smith, 606. Malachi Hays, 607. Frederick Fenney, 607. James Kinkead, 608. Wm. Powell, 608. Elizabeth Myers, 608. James Meyers, 608. James Smith, 610. Samuel McKenzie, 611. Æneas Mackay, 611. Peter Smith, 665. A. Cameron, Dr. Smith, and John Connolly, 682. Dewees, Col. William, v., 261. Mrs. Abigail McCay, 337. Sarah O'Brien, 339. Thomas Patterson, 420. George Kriebel, 432. Jeremiah Loughead, 452, Henry Funk, 495, 508. Riots at York, 496-508. Wm. Beckworth and A. Laughlin, 624. Robt. Galbraith, 638. Sam. McGregor, 665. Silas Burnet, vi., 7. John Sweeney, 58. Jacob Sitler, 67. Frederick Schauss, 67. Prisoners in Virginia, 75. Margaret Lederman, 117. Daniel Shelly, 95. Samuel Stewart, 217. Henry Mansin, 221. Joseph Rode, 224. Wendle Meyer, 225. James Christy, 233. Wm. Harper, 442. Col. F. Watts and S. Henry, 500. Thomas Craven, 501. Wm. Stayner, 501. Samuel Erwin, 502. R. Weston, 542. R. Weston, M. Warwick and J. Vanzant, 542. Garret and John Vanzant, 596–7. Archibald Hamilton, 679. Affey Beeth, 771. John Mitchell, vii., 207–209, 213. John Gardiner, 241. John Parker, 259. Peter Cress, 259. Thomas Pollock, 577. John Leffertie, viii., 387. Henry O'Neill, 527. D. Franks, 615. Joseph Shoemaker, 645. Respecting German Lutheran

Depositions—
Church lots, ix., 364. Sarah Keith, 501. John Robinson, 572. H. M. Breckenbridge, 572, 661. Samuel Hunter, respecting Indian murders, 658. Respecting Joseph Doane, x., 110. Mahlon Doane, 111, 112. James Oellers (1780), 161. Respecting Wyoming—Mr. Tidd, 196. Respecting escape of C. J. Longschamps, 271–274. Respecting ruins at Pittsburg, 463–464. Against Henry Carberry, 576–580. James Bell, 594. Phillip Jenkins, 594. Mark Halfpenny, 597. Robert Gibson, 598. John Boyd, 621. William Brink, 621-623. Col. J. Armstrong, 623. Respecting Wyoming, 631–638, 649-652. Taken at Wyoming, 653, 659–662, 688, 691. John Leith, on Indian robberies, 763. A. Ellicott on arrest of T. Pickering, xi., 327. Ira Manvil, Wyoming, 344. Benedict Satterlee, do., 345. Joel Whitcomb, 358. Keeny, 358. Elijah Reynolds, Joseph Earl, Martin Dudley, Jos. Kilburn, 359, Garrett Smith, 371. Wm. Smith, 393. M. Hollenbach, 394, 551. N. Kingsley, Lord Butler, T. Pickering, 551. Z. Butler, 553. Jacob Hartzell, xii., 298. Thos. Gibson, 300. James Banes, Jr., 302. Jno. Hart, 303.

Depreciation of money, ix., 77, 85, 117, 119, 129, 130, 133, 135, 136, 141, 145, 147, 171, 212; xi., 55. Of pay, Judges' opinion of, 120.

Depreciation Lands, surveys, xi., 93, 263. Sales of, 125.

Depui, see Forts, ii.

Depui's Fort, xii., 354.

Depui, Samuel, letter, iii., 423, 424.

Depui, Nicholas, ix., 105, 113.

Description of a man, singular, iv., 369.

Desertions, v., 144, 180, 196, 207, 208, 262, 648, 700.

Deserters, vi., 411, 732; vii., 356, 443, 769, 775; viii., 6, 12, 74, 77, 95, 100, 103, 184, 225, 235, 262, 263, 317, 415, 418, 510, 623; ix., 299, 503. From American regiment, x , 388.

Deshler, Col., vi., 394.

Deshler, Charles, Commissioner of magazine of provisions, vii., 17.

Deshler, David and Charles, viii., 300. (Commissioners of purchases.) 300, 517, 697, 701, 711, 721.

D'Estaing, Count, vii., 671. And his fleet in Rhode Island, 734-736. Success of fleet in West Indies, vii., 661. Respecting, 736, 747, 764, 772.

"Detector," author of, required, ix., 266.

Detroit, Governor of, by proclamation offers protection to rebels, v., 402. Gov. of, encourages Indians and Tories, vi., 460. Congress purpose an expedition against, 529. General Armstrong's views on, 657. A strong fort, above described, viii., 106. British and Indian convention at, 707. Design upon, xii., 110, 111, 118, 166, 167, 183. Governor Hamilton of, Clark's success against, 120, 131. Designs of enemy, 140, 147, 160, 184, 186, 265, 269. New fort, 188. Strength of garrison, 192, 196, 198. Fort, described, 206.

Deux Points, Count de, letter introductory, viii., 684.

De Villier, Captain, receives capitulation of Fort Necessity, ii., 146.

Dewar, David, petition respecting sailors impressed, iii., 302.

Dewees, Col. William, deposition respecting explosion of powder mills, v., 261.

De Witt, Simeon, appointed to run boundary line with N. Y., x., 450.

Diahogo, intelligence from, ii., 729.

Diary, of Pennsylvania Commissioners to Albany, ii., 195.

Dickeson, Mr. (owner of ship bringing stamps to Philadelphia), iv., 241.

Dickinson College, interest due, xi., 540, 578.

Dickinson, James, conference with Indian chiefs on survey of Donation Lands, x., 740.

Dickinson, His Excellency, John, ix., 494. Elected President of Council, 651, 731, 734. Calls attention of Judges to moral education of youth, x., 523. Ceases to be President, 527. Letter to, xii., 289.

Dickinson, Mr., house burnt by British, vi., 31.

Dickinson, Brigadier General Philemon, v., 117. Letter from, by his servant sent to Genl. W., 116, 117, 233, 244; viii., 506, 507, 736.

Dickinson, Fort, x., 184. Troops at, 189. Deep snow at, 197. Commanded by Major Moore—money wanted to pay debts, 209. Freshet at, 222.

Diemer, James, recommended as a Judge at Reading, xi., 596.

Digby, Rear Admiral, Robt., views under preliminaries of peace, x., 21.

Digges, Dudley, Gov. of Virginia, letter from, viii., 510.

Digges, John, applies for land, i., 637. Letter to R. Peters, 643. Case of, 637, 645, 681, 683, 684, 685, 686, 693, 696-710, 713, 725. Remonstrance, 693. Germans at Conewago, 709, And Kitzmiller, 713. Letter on death of his son, ii., 73. Petition of Attorney-General to Judges at York, 93.

Digges, William, letter, iv., 489.

Dill, Peter, discharge requested as a relief to Cumberl'd Co., ix., 736.

Dilworth's Spelling Book or Gand's, written for, by a member of Congress, vi., 209.

Dingey, Charles, case of, vi., 162.

Dinwiddie, Robert, Gov. of Virginia, speech on proroguing Assembly, ii., 169. Letters to and from, 177, 226, 268, 270, 273, 390, 422, 446, 454, 481, 530, 560, 581, 711; iii., 50. Proclamations about Indians, 155, 156.

Directory, first published in Philadelphia, x., 271.

Distances from Philadelphia to Ohio, ii., 133. Mouth of Wills' Creek, 134. From Harris' to Phil. Davies', 134. From do. to Logstown, 135.

Distillation of wheat and other grain to be stopped, v., 229, 710.

Distillation of liquors from grain, viii., 31.

Doane, Aaron, petition for pardon, x., 348, 716, 717. Deposition against (1784), 597. In prison, 598. Judge Bryan on, 609.

Doane, Abraham, troubles Washington county, x., 594.

Doane, Abraham and Levi, letter to C. J. McKean respecting, xi., 351. Resolution of Assembly for respite, 398.
Doane, Israel, petition for release, ix., 759.
Doane, Joseph, respecting arrest of, x., 110, 114, 152. Petition of captors, 565, 582.
Doane, Joseph, estate, xi., 725.
Doane, Mahlon, deposition respecting arrest of, x., 111, 112.
Doane, Moses, Abraham, &c., robbery of Bucks county treasury, ix., 616, 617.
Dobbs, Arthur, Governor of North Carolina, letters to and from, ii., 281, 536.
Dogs, use of, against Indians recommended, iv., 181; vii., 357.
Donaldson, Arthur, recommended to make chevaux-de-frize, iv., 774. Assists L. H. in removing chevaux-de-frize, x., 349, 350.
Donaldson, J., letter Wm. Penn to, i., 128.
Donaldson, Joseph, v., 496, 534. Riots at York, 496.
Donaldson, Joseph, &c., vi., 775.
Donation Land, lottery, proposal respecting, xi., 49.
Donation Lands, survey of, xi., 512. General Irvine's description of, 513–520.
Donnaldson, John, appointed Register-General, xi., 568. Office in State House, 509. Clerk, 570. Order, 571. Report, 722, 764. On duties of office, xii., 3.
Dongan, Gov. Thomas, deeds from, to Wm. Penn for lands on Susquehannah, i., 121, 122, 133. Letters to W. P., 74, 80, 81, 84. To Lord Baltimore, 86. To President and Council, 104.
Donnahill, John, soldiers in distress, for cash, ix., 671.
Donop, Count, wounded at Mount Holly, v., 177. Action at Red Bank, killed, 707, 709.
Donville, Monsieur, killed, ii., 620. Instructions found on him, 600.
Dorchester, Lord, Letters of Thomas Hutchins, (Geographer,) for permission to survey lands, xi., 315.
Doria, And., Brig. Capt. Robinson, takes British sloop-of-war, v., 132.
Dorsey, Thomas, v., 535, 550. Paymaster, 535.
D'Orvillier, victory over Sir C. Hardy, xii., 204.
Dougherty, Bernard, vii., 186, 297. Respecting trial at Bedford, 297. ix., 467, 538, 542, 546. Distresses of the county, 553. Indians, 558. Of Bedford, 619, 628. And D. Espy, deposition respecting M. Doane, x., 112. To send prisoners to Lancaster, 119.
Dougherty, H., enemy's ships on Reedy Island, iv., 753.
Dougherty, Capt., killed near Fort Freeland, vii., 591, 610.
Dougherty, Capt. John, viii., 369.
Doughty, Capt., v., 167.
Douglass, Capt. captures a privateer off the Delaware and takes her into Egg harbor, vii., 192.
Douglass, Commander John, judgment against, vii., 641, 647.
Douglass, Major Ephraim, on Indian negotiations, x., 62, 70, 83. Elections, 262, 696. Memorial for office in Fayette county, 118, 553. Justices, 464, 582. No sheriff in Fayette, 588. Letter from, xi., 32. Election returns, 536. On duty as surveyor, xii., 78.
Dove, R., respecting pass from New York to Virginia, ix., 625.
Dover Troops ordered to, v., 58.
Downey, Capt., leaves Billingsport, v., 430.
Downingstown, Gen. Howe's Army near, v. 606. Flour to be sent to, vi., 177.
Doyle, Sam'l, arrested, xi., 730. Acquitted, 744.
Doz, Andrew, appointed commissioner of purchases in Philadelphia, viii., 154, 169, 412. Applies, as commissioner, for the sale of State Island, 412.
Drais, Daniel, taxes on confiscated estates, x., 150.
Drake, Joseph, deposition, iv., 425.
Drayton, Wm. H. books from library, vii., 328, 335.
Drummond, Dr. George, a prisoner on parole, v., 484, 511.
Dryer, Jacob, Letter to C. J. McKean, respecting, xi., 351.
Dry lands, near Easton, Northampton Co., iii., 578, 647, 651.

Dryslow, David, vi., 336.
Duane, James, vi., 102. (M. C.) difficulty with sheriff's officer, viii., 629, 659. Committee of Congress, 694. Letter to, xii., 109.
Dubois, Abraham, Auditor of Bucks Co., ix., 11, 13, 17, 29, 36, 47, 67.
Duché, Jacob, chosen Colonel of Regiment of Phil. Co., ii., 608.
Duché, Jacob, jr., statement respect-Quakers at Easton, iii., 275.
Duché, Rev. Jacob, letter to Washington referred to, vi., 6. House to be occupied by C. J. McKean, viii., 684.
Du Coudray, Mons., Reports on Works on Del., v., 359–363, 430, 431, 526, 565.
Dudgeon, Richard, Engineer, letter, iii., 442.
Dudley, Joseph, a Wyoming rioter wounded, xi., 356, 359. Dies, 365, 367.
Duer, John, letter to F. L. Lee, vi., 277, 284.
Duffey, Patrick, letter, v., 141.
Duffield, Rev. Geo., respecting Rev. Wm. Linn, ix., 493.
Duke of York, release—deed of feoffment from, to W. Penn, for N. Castle, i., 52. Petition of Wm. Markham, to, 78; ix., 694.
Duke of Normandy, birth of, announced by Sec'y Jay, as a cause of pleasure, x., 476.
Dumas, Captain, a French Officer, copy of his instructions to Mons'r Donville, taken by English, ii., 600, 620. Claim, xi. 411.
Dunbar, Col. Thomas, letters to and from, ii., 385, 410, 412. 417. Turns back after Braddock's defeat, 383. Remarks on, 379, 383, 384, 387, 390, 391, 395, 396, 397, 400, 406, 422, 435, 440. Gov. Morris demands pay for recruits to Braddock, 401, 412.
Duncan, David, appointed Commissioner for Westmoreland County, orders to, ix., 17. Charges against, 97. Resigns, 141. Provisions, 190, 200, 305, 380, 399. And John Finley, apply for Fort McIntosh, as a place of Indian trade, x. 704.
Duncan, Stephen, resigns as Justice, being elected to Ass'y, viii., 597.
Dundas, James, v., 616. Claims against Billingsport, vii., 140, 253, 326, 333.
Dunkers opposed to militia, v., 768.
Dunlap, Col., viii., 31.
Dunlap, James, vi., 610.
Dunlap, Lt. James, vii., 488.
Dunlap John, Congress negotiate with, for continuing publication of Journals, vi., 191. Letter to, vii., 201. And J. Budden, memorial, viii., 208.
Dunmore, Earl of, dispute between Penna. and Virginia, iv., 514. Speech to White Eyes (Indian Chief), 684. Governor of Virginia, letters, 461, 482, 493, 525, 577, 579. Commissions Dr. Connolly, 477. And others, 487. Proclamation, 490. Various, 586, 612, 654–5. Has designs on Islands in Delaware River, 637.
Dunmore Fort. See Fort Pitt, iv., 521; xii., 351.
Dunwoodie, James, instructions to, Election returns, xi., 430.
Duplantain, Capt., xii., 258.
Duponceau, Peter S., applies to be Notary and Interpreter—his testimonials, &c., x., 351–353.
Du Portail, Genl., survey of Delaware River, vii., 201, 227, 229, 232, 272, 279, 280, 366, 400, 403, 409, 690. Thanks, &c., 403. On Companies of Miners and Sappers, 690. Proposals respecting Sappers and Miners, viii., 37. Money for troops, ix., 210.
Du Pui's Fort, xii., 354.
Du Quesne Fort, ii., 361, 375, 380, 390, 393, 570, 579, 582; iii., 9, 13, 59, 83, 147, 306, 527, 543, 546, 685, 693. Skirmish at, 547; xii., 355–359, 427–431.
Durham Iron Works, ii., 479. Iron-Master at, iii., 274.
Durkee, Major, John, letter, iv., 364.
Du Simitiere, translation of papers, vii., 212.
Dutch, agreement with English, on surrender of N. York, i., 25. Answer of, to Govr. of Md., 492.
Dutch, in Lancaster county, oppose the laws, and cause a riot, v., 405–408.
Dutch loan, on, ix., 563, 564, 591.
Duties on Negroes, Wines, &c., act

respecting, i., 159, 306. Orders to Govr. Gordon, 325. On Seamen, Hospital, 251. Names of Receivers, 252. Received in Philadelphia, ix., 206. Queries on, xi., 597. Answers, 601. On Tonnage, 599, 689.

Duvall, G., of Md., letter respecting Henry Carbery, x., 291. Answer of Judges of Supreme Court to, 292.

Duykinck, Col., v. 756.

Dyer, Elijah, agreement with, xi., 533.

Dyer, Ephraim, &c., Answer to Gov. Trumbull, iv., 401-408, 470. To Gov. Penn, 490.

E.

Earthquake destroys Lisbon, ii., 530. Large part of Port au Prince, iv., 371.

Eastburne, Benj., Surveyor of Boundary line, i., 611. Report. 615.

Eastburne, Captain Robert, ordered to Raystown, iii., 481. Arrived there, 489.

Easton, described by Wm. Parsons, ii., 95, 98, 305. Petition for road from, to Reading, 98. The dry lands near, 305. Road to Reading, 443. Report of Indians, 443. Deserters from, 585. Minutes of Indian Conferences at, 722-730. Of Executive Council at, 721, 730. Indians approaching, iii., 7, 36. Indians at, 53. Conduct of people at, 78. Stores at, 82. Proprietary land at, 84; no mutton or cooks at, 104. Quakers present at Treaty 1757, 205. Instructions, &c., relative to accommodations at, 205, 217, 517. Indians at, 210. Quaker presents to Indians, 214. Memorandum respecting demand of Teedyuscung for a Clerk, 235. Depositions respecting treaty at, 244, 249, 254, 256, 259, 263, 264. Quakers at, 205, 250, 262. Petition from settlers on dry lands near, 578. Treaty with Indians at, by Gov'r H., iv., 68, 78, 80, 82. Latitude and Longitude, 592. Meeting of Indians at, v., 201, 203, 208, 325. Prisoners sent to, 250, 650. Guard at, 324. Prothonotary, 332. Papers, &c., sent for safety from City to, 623. Alarm, on acccount of prisoners, &c., 650. Importance of the ferry, 651. Wagons, 652. Unguarded condition of, vi., 197. Soldiers distressed for clothing, 197. Hospitals, 198. Named as a rendezvous, 302. Tories, 342. Defenceless state of, 346. Troops ordered by Congress to, 374. No houses to be had in, 362, 381. Guards to be dismissed, 541. Difficulty in procuring a house for public papers, vii., 176. Price of Iron at, 177. Muster of Soldiers at, viii., 321. A place of deposit, ix., 263. Supplies for Genl. Sullivan, 263. Savages near, 275. Abuses in officers at, 385. Troops, 403, 426, 527. Waste on public lands, 741. Cap. Chrystie, arrives with a detachment at, x., 135. Petition of Wyoming prisoners at, 690.

Eckhart, Valentine, vii., 552. Indian murders, viii., 529. Convention prisoners, ix., 225, 230. Militia from Bucks, 433. Returns of officers in Berks Co., Militia, x., 190. Instructions to, respecting troops, xi., 203, 211.

Eden, Robert, Governor of Maryland, iv., 369, 616.

Edmonds, William, ii., 681.

Education of youth, and moral training urged on Judges by Pres. Dickinson, x., 523.

Edwards, Major, bounties, ix., 75; viii., 107, 152.

Edwards, Thomas, vi., 449. Colonel, account, viii., 237. Militia, 288.

Egg Harbour, arrival of British fleet at, v., 457. A prize brig there, vi., 736. A privateer captured by Capt. Douglass, carried into, vii., 192. Battle at, xii., 110.

Egmont, (Falkland Islands,) King of Spain disavows expedition to, iv., 387.

Eichelberger, Geo., to be arrested, vii., 193.

Eichelberger, Jacob, vii., 490, 530.

Elder, Rev. John, letters, iii., 251. Recruiting orders to, iv., 116.

Letters to or from, 127, 132, 148, 153, 714. Murder of Conestogoes, 148, 153.

Elder, Joshua, vi., 615, 616, 640; vii., 592. Election of Justices, viii., 101.

Election, return of Sheriff of Chester Co., i., 86, 115. Do., Kent Co., 116. Riot at, in York County, ii., 50. Of a Lieut. of Dock Ward, County of Philadelphia, 600. Tory in Bucks County, v., 31, 32. At Lewes, 53; vii., 97. Returns must be certified by Constable or Overseer of the Poor, x., 284. Of Matthew Irvin, as Recorder of Deeds, Philadelphia, 707.

Elizabethtown, N. J. Enemy leave, v., 178. Surprise of post at, viii., 103. Genl. St. Clair at, 103.

Ellicott, Andrew, appointed to run Western boundary, x., 452. Letters to and from, respecting boundary, xi., 140, 178, 203, 216, 429. Survey of Islands in Ohio, 583. Proposes publishing observations, 216. Describes Erie Lands, 243. Deposition on T. Pickering, 327. Purchase of Erie, 429, 537. On survey of Lake Erie, 612, 615, 704.

Elliott, Mrs., case of, vii., 247.

Elliott, Mr., Indian agent, x., 84, 85. Instructions to, xii., 222.

Elliott, Lt. Benj'n, account of his proceedings, xi., 665.

Elliott, Wm., proposal for a road, xi., 70.

Ellsworth, Oliver, conference, viii., 261.

Elmer, Jonathan, letter from, v., 7.

Elwood, John, record of proceedings in case of, for treason, vii., 59-62. He was pardoned July 15, 1779. Col. Rec., Vol., XII., p. 48.

Embargo on provisions, ii., 373, 396, 421, 500, 689, 733. Governor proposes laying at Newcastle, 396, 420. Merchants wish it removed, 709. On provisions, iii., 97, 114, 144, 148, 174, 186, 373, 393, 479; iv., 79. Deemed necessary, v., 314, 319. Ordered by Congress, vi., 585, 708, 709. Relaxation of, 732, 733, 737; vii., 78, 197, 231, 247, 315, 409, 424, 588, 639, 768, 745. Revoked, 424. Acts of Congress, 695; viii., 10, 229, 261, 263, 266, 333, 354, 432, 433, 609. Permit for provisions, ix., 38, 146. Violated by French Consul, 180. (See Holker,)

Enceinture, a good cause for staying execution, but not judgment, in opinion of C. J. McKean, viii., 298.

Enemy, intercourse with, restricted by Congress, vii., 316, 324.

England, objects to consecration of American Bishops without Test Oath, x., 434.

English vessel assumes French colors, complaint against, x., 175.

Engrossing or forestalling provisions to be prevented, vii., 85, 88, 113, 151.

Entails, in America, opinion on, i.. 281, 284.

Episcopal Church. Rev. Dr. Evans arrives, i., 134. Appointment of Rev. Mr. Campbell, 191, 236. Of Rev. Mr. Backhouse, 226. Memorial from Christ Church, 150. Dispute with Baptists, 284. Mr. Campbell to be removed, 236. Rev. Mr. Cummins to exercise jurisdiction over the Clergy of Pennsylvania, 236. Prayers for Royal Family to be altered, 225, 624. Rev. James Blair complained of, 150. Matrimonial licenses, change in the law, 236. Letter, Bishop of London, 236. Of Society for Propagating the Gospel, 191, 226. Difficulty with Keithian Baptist Church, 284. Refusal of Ministers licensed, by Bishop of London, 628. Christ Church and St. Peters, memorial on behalf of Rev. Thomas Coombe, a prisoner of war, v., 600. Reply of Council, 603. Missionary at Carlisle, land granted to, becomes tory, viii., 107. Relative to consecration of Bishops, William White consecrated, (see "Bishop of London," Vol. I., pp. x., 236, 628.) Bishop White on Marriage licenses, xii., 31, 314.

Equity Court, plan for, i., 166.

Erie, Lake, Commissioners to inquire whether any part of it is in the State, x., 129. Commis-

sioners arrive at, xi., 203. Letter to Delegates, on purchase of, &c., 237. Lands described by Col. A. Porter, 241. Estimated consideration to Indians for Triangle at, 245. Proposition of Mr. Irvine to purchase, and proceedings of Congress on, 247. Size of the tract unsettled, 251. Assembly approve of purchase, 252. Proceedings in Congress on quantity in purchase of, 308, 313. Extract from Cession of New York to United States, 309. Do. of Massachusetts. 310. Authority of Council to purchase, 313. No reservations necessary, 382. Act of Congress transferring to State, 387. Resolution of Do., 387. Report of Council on purchase of, to Assembly, 389. Estimate of Expenses of purchase from Indians, 390. Letter from Vice President to Assembly, respecting, 390. Report and Resolution of Assembly on purchase of, 395. List of Goods for Indians, 427. Letter Andrew Ellicott on purchase, 429. Obligation of Comm'rs, to deliver goods to Indians, 507. Purchase and Boundary of Indian lands, 508. Report to General Assembly, of purchase of, 528. Agreement with Gibson and Butler, and Six Nations, for purchase from, 529–533. Leave to survey to be asked of Gov. of Canada, 537, 543. Tench Coxe suggests difficulties as to title of, 539, 543. Resolution of Assembly, survey and location of, 566. John Adlum on survey of, 577. Expenses of survey, 576. Money drawn for, 589, 691. Letter of General Butler on, 591. Survey of, 612, 615, Quantity and value of, stated by Comptroller, 655. Estimate of Expenses to, 691. Deeds, 704. List of papers relating to xii., 88. Act authorizing purchase of 89. Letter Governor to Secret'y Hamilton, State ready to pay, 90. Documents to adjust account sent, 90. Causes of delay in settling, 91, 100. Deed Indian chiefs to State for, 101. Letters patent, U. S. to State, 103.

Erwin, Capt. viii., 106; xii., 203.

Erwin, Captain Joseph, state of frontiers, vii., 563.

Erwin, Col. Joseph, viii., 66, 79.

Erwin, Robert, letter, iii., 64; viii., 126, 145.

Escape, a most extraordinary, from Indians, viii., 527.

Escheats, resolution of Council respecting, ix., 341.

Escort, British and flag, vi., 217. Of Convention troops, vii., 89, 95, 99, 101, 104, 106, 107, 108, 110, 129. To Fort Lawrens, attacked, 173.

Espy, David, respecting Justices in Bedford T., viii., 102.

Estates of Tories to be seized, vi., 13. Sold, 94. Forfeited, produce money to the State, vii., 80; viii., 282, 733, 734, 736. Letter to Agents, 735. Auditors accounts, sales, &c., ix., 104. Philadelphia, Bucks, Chester, and York, 105. Terms of sale, 195.

Estherton, General Hand at, vii., 344, 510.

Estimate, cost of three battalions, 61. Current expenses of Pennsylvania, 62. Providing for four hundred men, 62. Of a continental regiment, v., 43.

Ethcart, Cap. of French vessels, viii., 546.

Ettwein, John, Moravians, vi., 751.

Ettwein, Rev'd John, orders sent to, for wafers by Council, vii., 295.

Etwein, John, account of massacre at Muskingum, ix., 525.

Eustace, J. P., v., 381.

Eustace, Capt. x., 120.

Evans, Edward, vi., 544.

Evan, Evan, resigns as Justice, being elected to Ass'y, viii., 597.

Evans, Griffith, proposals, xi., 49.

Evans, Lieut., vii., 762; xii., 137.

Evans, Lewis, proposes to publish a Map, instructions to, ii., 46, 47, 60, 309.

Evans, John, v., 246, 352, 529.

Evans, Col. John, xii., 210, 219, 225, 231, 238, 240, 253.

Evans, Rev. Mr. Evan arrives, i., 134.

Evans, Peter, lays claim to office, i., 235.

Evans, Col. Thomas, has a Tory prisoner, vi., 709.

Evans, Wm., respecting Tories, vi., 731.
Everett, Fort, xii., 359.
Evidence, act respecting, i., 155, 160.
Ewing, Genl., vi., 235.
Ewing, James, v., 298. Security for Dr. Connolly, v., 297, 298. Elected Vice-President of State, ix., 651.
Ewing, Rev. John, goes to Europe for aid to Newark (Del.) Academy, iv., 468. A Pennsylvania Commissioner to run line between Virginia, viii., 353. Commissioner on Virginia boundary, (1783) x., 171, 230, 438, 440. Resigns, 428, 443. Commissioner on Susquehanna R., 755.
Examination of Walter Winter, i., 218. Of Morgan Herbert, 219. Of James Lewis, ix., 473. Archd. Henderson robberies, 597. Jacob Miller, 600. T. Bedwel, 601.
Exchange on Moneys to France, viii., 391, 411.
Excise, amounts collected in 1752-3, ii., 85. Amount collected in Pennsylvania in 1771, iv., 2, 3, and 4, 633. Bills of credit struck on the, 634. Report of Collector, xii., 1.
Exempts from militia duty, vi., 458.
Exequator, form of, for Consul Gen. of France, ix., 390.
Expedition against Spain, orders, i., 616. Against Louisburg, 679, 688, 745, 746.
Expresses sent out, v., 693.
Eyres, Richard, letter, v., 106.
Eyre, Benjamin, v., 375.
Eyre, Benjamin G., &c., removal of vessels, vii., 644. Schuylkill bridge, viii., 144.
Eyres, Col. of Artillery, viii., 111.
Eyres, Col. Jehu, viii., 591.
Eyre, Joshua P., appointed by Governor, Commissioner on the line between Pennsylvania, Delaware and Maryland, report, iv., 37.
Eyre, Major, vi., 768.

F.

Fairfield, Conn., burned by Governor Tryon, vii., 561.
Fairlamb, N., applies for Gun locks, iv., 755.
Falconer, Nathaniel, superintendent of flour Magazine, vi., 235, 240.
Falconer, Serjeant, in battle at Sideling Hill, iii., 315.
Fallowfield, T., election, x., 364.
Farmer, Rev. Ferd., Catholic Priest, number under his care, iii., 144.
Farmer, Lewis, letter, v., 51. Estimate and price of provisions, vii., 181. Purchase of goods, 273, 755. Clothier, viii., 52, 706.
Farmer, Michael, complains of dulness of tobacco trade, vii., 453.
Fast, proclamation of Governor Morris for a, ii., 649; iii., 253. Thanksgiving, 690. Recommended by Congress, vi., 341. Proclamation of Congress, vii., 257, 261, 321. Appointed, ix., 21.
Fauntleroy, Major, ix., 752.
Fauquier, Governor Francis, of Virginia, letter to, from Governor Penn, on peace with Indians of Erie and Ohio, made by Colonel Bradstreet, iv., 207. Proclamation, 255.
Fayette, County formed from Westmoreland County, x., 118, 184. Appointments of Lieutenants not satisfactory, 265. Returns of Field officers in, 275. Memorial, 280. Troubles from Virginians, 280. Agent to, 450. No Sheriff, 588. Depositions respecting attacks on Collectors, 593, 594. J. Story opens office for adjusting claims, 742. Military Officers, xi., 702.
Fayette, Marquis de la, said to be nominated Ambassador to U. S., vi., 546, 558, 568. Expedition under, viii., 196. Orders troops from Pennsylvania and Virginia, ix., 283, 359. Compliment to, 430. Introduces Chevalier de Lambert, 627, 735. Addresses Indians at Fort Stanwix, x., 346.
Febiger, Christian, resigns as auctioneer, xi., 563. Elected Treasurer, 638. Facts, respecting Treasury department, 649. Treasurer, xii., 5.
Fees, Regulation of, act respecting, i., 158. Of officers of Customs, iv., 380.
Fenwick, John, respecting, i., 55.
Ferguson, Mrs. Elizabeth, opinion

of, by General Roberdeau, vi., 131. Letter and petition respecting her estate and husband, 617. Letter in favor of, vii., 100. Case of, in Council, 202. Petition on sale of estate, viii., 4.
Ferguson, Capt. W. his rank, xi., 240. On recruits, 590.
Ferris, Owen, arms wanted, viii., 229.
Ferrol, Capt. Thomas, xii., 163. Field Conductor of Military stores, 268, 272.
Field, N., Letter, William Penn to, i., 128.
Finances of U. S., vi., 591.
Finley, Capt., viii., 40.
Finley, James, appointed Justice, resigns—his reasons, xi., 298.
Finley, Rev. James, sent on a secret expedition to western counties, ix., 729. Sent to Westmoreland on secret expedition in relation to a new State, x., 40, 41. Instructions to, 163, (1783.)
Finley, Captain John, xii., 107, 139, 150, 181, 186, 209, 250.
Finley, Captain Joseph, xii., 181, 186, 195.
Finnie, Col., viii., 577.
Finney, Captain, marches for Fort Pitt, x., 337 ; xii., 300.
Fire, great, in Boston ; aid solicited, iii., 715. At Montreal, (ask aid,) iv., 248. Ships plan of Naticus, 666.
Fire companies in Philadelphia, revival of, recommended by Supreme Executive Council, vii., 134, 201.
Fire Rafts, D. Joy's plan for, iv., 698.
Fire Ships—object of, v., 429.
Fish, proclamation for preserving fish in rivers, iv., 347. From the Delaware, proposal to salt, for the army, vi., 380.
Fishbourne, Wm., robbery of the Treasury, i., 272-279.
Fisher, Henry, dispatches from, iv., 664, 724, 725, 732, 736, 737, 740, 743, 755, 762, 765, 769. Instructions to, 743. Guard boat sent to, 765. Letters to and from, v., 42, 47, 52, 61, 70, 99, 100, 108, 153, 263, 402, 465, 504. Instructions to, v., 42. Vessels in Delaware, vi., 706. Letters, vii., 390, 410, 705, 730. Supposed to be taken by boats in Delaware, viii., 275.
Fisher, Joshua, proposed map of Delaware Bay, Governor stops publication, ii., 592. Letter to Governor, 593.
Fisher, J. & Son, petition, ix., 645.
Fisher, Samuel R., letter from Council to C. J. McKean, respecting an intercepted letter from, vii., 225, 274, 279. To be confined, 291.
Fisher, Thomas, elections in York County, xi., 388.
Fisheries and Trade of N. E., British Acts, iv., 613.
Fishing Creek, murders by Indians, vii., 357.
Fishkill, N. Y., a place of rendezvous, vi., 302. Arms sent to by Connecticut Claimants, (1785,) xi., 456, 457.
Fitch, Thomas, Deputy Governor Connecticut, letters to and from, ii., 122, 125, 208; iv., 50, 103.
Fitzgerald, Colonel John, aid to Gen. Washington, vii., 370.
Fitzsimons, Nicholas, appointed keeper of Province Island, x., 74.
Fitzsimons, Thomas, respecting a vessel loaded by French Consul, vii., 407. Inquiry of effect of peace on goods from G. B., x., 28. Letter, 48 ; xi., 427. Appointed Commissioner on commercial regulations, 252. On loan Certificates, 595.
Flags for Galleys, v., 13, 47.
Flag, State, raised on Market street hill, x., 38.
Flag, Spanish, drawing of a, sent to the Governor, x., 743.
Flag of Truce furnished, i., 753. British, vi., 217, 232, 268, 371. From South Carolina in the Delaware, ix., 338.
Flax, worms destruc've to, viii., 281.
Fleeson, Plunket, resigns presidency of Court in favor of Ed. Shippen, x., 523.
Fleet, British, ix., 105.
Fleury, Francis, a French subject, applied for, vii., 522, 531, 532.
Flint, Royal, viii., 70, 86.
Florida, East and West, treaties with Indians, iv., 321.

Flour, large quantity ordered by Congress to be purchased, vi , 177, 256, 278, 281, 348. Magazines for provis'ns to be established, 178, 333, 377. Resolve of Congress, 377. Persons appointed to lay up, 234, 240, 241, 272. Instructions, &c., 303–314. Letters of Board of War to Congress, 316. C. and A., 333. Desist from purchase of, 422, 431, 449, 675. To be exported to procure clothing, vii., 548, 567, 685, 692. Scarce 707, 730, 733. Frauds in, 557, 558, 560, 599, 600. Assembly order flour to be distributed to poor housekeepers in Philadelphia, 740. Purchases of, 753, 766. In exchange for Salt, viii., 3. Scarcity of, 48, 51, 53, 54, 85, 86, 90, 147, 237, 359, 398, 402, 601. Conveyed to enemy, 125. Scarcity of in army, ix., 53, 54. Prize, to be inspected, 407, 408. One-third of purchases of exports to be furnished to State, 133, 162. Inspector's report, xi., 755.

Flower, Col. Benj., v., 27, 138, 181, 184, 369, 706; vi, 79, 135, 450, 463; vii., 294, 296, 385. Letters to and from, &c., viii., 26, 110. Captain Coran refuses obedience to, 468; xii., 271.

Flowertown, troops sent to, ix., 250.

Footman, Richard, Memorial of, viii., 113.

Forage, vi., 418, 738, 742, 752; vii., 101, 102, 620. Scarcity of, viii., 150, 151, 163, 175, 404, 600, 608. Master, 155, 165.

Forbes, Brigadier General, to be appointed by General Abercrombie, iii., 321. Letter from, 383. Commission to Mordecai Thompson, 398. Orders, 409. Letter, 448. Resolution of Provincial Commissioners respecting, 441. Letter from Colonel John Armstrong, 448. Letter to Rev. Mr. Barton, 452. Colonel of Regiment, 553. Death of, 579.

Fords, on Delaware, v., 375, 441.

Foreman, Charles, deposition, iv., 604.

Forestalling, vii., 85, 88, 113, 117. Of flour, 151.

Forfeited estates, Commissaries of, vii., 243. Returns to be made of, 243, 287, 540.

Forman, Brig. General, v., 435, 439.

Forman, David, viii., 332.

Forrest, Col. Thomas, v., 142. vi., 357. Major Thos., vii., 135, 254, 397. Lieutenant Col. ix., 142, 231.

Forsman, Hugh, viii., 697.

Forst, David, vi., 296.

Forsyth, Robert, purchases, viii., 577.

Fortifications at Philadelphia, i., 633, 636.

Fort Island, fortifications, &c., v., 11, 12, 23, 24, 26, 47, 61, 69, 83, 92, 98, 118, 130, 377, 432, 526. Returns of Military stores at, x., 284.

Forts:

On Ohio, French, i. 309. Allen, (see Gnadenhutten.) Augusta, (Shamokin), ii., 557, 627, 644, 646, 656, 662, 674, 700, 706, 712, 731, 739, 764, 765, 780. Above Alleminga, 677. At Armstrong's, 663, 671, 674, 686, 687, 751. (See Fort Halifax.) Brown's Fort, 738. Capt. Busse's Fort, 159. Capt. Burd's Fort, 609. Christina, curious relics discovered, 6. Croghan's Fort, 571, 623. Cumberland, (Will's Creek,) 276, 376, Dupui's or Hyndshaw, 678. Du Quesne, 361, 375, 380, 390, 393, 570, 579, 582. Franklin, 669, 678. French Forts, 240. Gap of Tolihaio, 547, 551, 554, 555. Gnadenhutten, (Fort Allen), 521, 565, 569, 638, 677, 747, 754. Granville, 743, taken [Col. Rec. 242, 278.] Archives, 556, 561, 565, 569, 603, 604, 613, 623, 631, 743, 744, 750, 753, 756. Great Cove, 462, 474. Near Great Meadow, proposed by Gov. Dinwiddie, 398. Halifax, at Armstrong's, 663, 671, 674, 686, 687, 751. Hamilton, 669, 678. Harris's Ferry, 441, 603, 635. Henry, at Tolihaio, 159, 561, 565, 570, 676. Hunter's Mill, 545, 551, 553, 554, 564, 615, 617, 686, 751. Hyndshaw, 678. Lebanon, 159, 547, 555, 565, 570, 665, 676. Lyttleton, Sugar Cabins, 556, 561,

Forts—
565, 569, 603, 604, 621, 752. McCord's, 611, 617, 623. McDowell's Mill, 575. McKee's, 634, 635, 637, 686, 751. Matchitongo, 556, (Pomfret), 561. William Henry, 585, Northkill, 159, 675. Necessity, Articles of Capitulation to Capt. De Villiers, 146. At Niagara, 579, 722. Norris, 669, 678. At Oswego, 575. Pleasant, 438, (Cumberland), Patterson's, attacked, 608, 617, 623. Pomfret Castle, 556, 565, 569, 603, 604. At Lake St. George, 437. Shirley at Augwick, 556, 561, 565, 569, 603, 604, 623, 632. Swatara, 161, 551, 554. Stockades in Cumberland, 536. In Virginia, 581. Capt. Potter ordered to build fort at, 602. A new fort, 166. Proposed by Harris. 441. Allen, iii., 5, 68, 81, 119, 152, 218, 355, 420, 424, 500, 521. Allemingle, 218, 253. Augusta, 4, 9, 12, 14, 41, 43, 79, 119, 161, 249, 277, 279, 283, 287, 326, 327, 347, 349, 374, 388, 403, 406 408, 431, 478, 480, 502, 513, 515, 521, 550, 568, 570, 574, 686, 721, 727, At Buffaloe, 13. At Carlisle, 119. Cumberland, 83. At Chambers's 12. Du Quesne, 8, 13, 59, 83, 147, 306, 527, 543, 547, 685, 693, (Fort Pitt) 696. At Mr. Everett's (Capt. Wetherhold) 355. Franklin, 32, 51, 152, 153 Frederick, 198. French and Indians building a, 79. Halifax, 6, 17, 119, 251. Hamilton, 81, 119, 139, 140, 152, 218, 222, 356. Henry, 51, 119, 194, 218, 283, 353. Hunter, 17, 52, 64, 119, 251, 277, 279, 331, 352, 489. Hyndshaw, 81, 82, 139, 140, 222. At Le Bœuf, 305. Lebanon, 31, 36, 51, 218. Ligonier, 669. Loudoun, 119, 218, 280. Lyttleton, 12, 48, 51, 58, 119. Morris, 59. At McDowell's, 29, 40, 48, 51, 58. Norris, 81, 152, 218. North Kill, 31, 36, 253, 277, 283, 354. At Presqu' isle, 13, 305, 561. At Philadelphia, 26. Ray's Town, (Stockade) 510. Shippensburg, 119. Shinglacamush, 430. Swatara, 218, 352. Venango (Machault), 305, 306, 506, 522, 561. Wyoming, 288, 297.

Forts—
William, 354. A new Fort building by Armstrong & Potter, 79. Allen, iv., 138 Augusta, 38, 82, 88, 111, 122, 123, 140, 165, 195, 214, 463. Evacuation of, 214. Dunmore, see Fort Pitt, 521, 524. Hunter, 111. Liberty Island, 764. Loudoun, 175, 209, 218, 229, 231. Mud Island, Resolution of Assembly, 474. Message to Gov. on, 475. Pitt, 210, 215, 300, 307, 337, 395, 483, 522. List of Goods and Pass for, to, 224. General Gage's opinion of, 457. Called Dunmore, 521, 524. Latitude and Longitude, 592. Redstone, old, 481. Stanwix, Treaty and purchase of lands, at, 309. Route to, from New York, 309. Fort Independence Summoned by General Heath to surrender, v., 237. Fort Lee, 66, 71. Fort Montgomery, Artillery for, 50, 671. Fort Hand, vi., 673. Fort Mercer, 21, 28. Fort Mifflin, heavy cannonading at, 11, 18. Loss of, 19, 23, 24, 27, 47. Fort at Pittsburg, plan to destroy, 507. Provisions for, 532. Respecting, 670. Fort Frederick, vii., 339, 340. Fort Freeland, (see Freeland.) Jenkins, 81, 87, 345, 357, 438, 760. Built on Ohio, by Gen. McIntosh, 132, Laurens, 173, 465, 517, 569. Fort Ligonier, 345. Fort Mifflin, cannon sent to, 298, 339. Troops for 365. Ammunition wanted, 385, 397, 720. Prices for Iron-work, 652. Fort Muncy, 5, 323, 344, 357, 512, 760. Fort Pitt, 341, 697. Fort Roberdeau, 419, 624. Fort Washington, 384. Fort Allen, viii., 286. Armstrong, (Kittaning,) 38, 106, Brady's 157. Freeland's, 157. Crawford 77, 106. At Detroit described, 606. Frederick, militia at, 5. Freeland, 637. Jenkins, 29, 40, 157, 171, 563. Mifflin, 599, 728. At Montgomery's, 29, 171. McIntosh, 531. Muncy, 29, 40, 157, 166. Pitt, 78, 109, 159, 172, 405, 441, 478, 484, 499, 552, 554, 642, 743. Rice attacked, 561. Its location, 567. Attacked, 567. Schuyler, 370. Built by English for Shawnese, 551. Allen, ix.,

Forts—
649, Armstrong, 39. Billingsport, 330. Block-house, by Col. Lochrey, 80. Crawford, 39. McIntosh, 39, 648. Miller, 596. Mud Island, 72, 330, 364. Muncy, 528. Pitt, 17, 37, 47, 55, 75, 81, 103, 111, 143, 419, 433, 521, 575, 635, 636. Reed, 596. Schuyler, 123. Smith, 522. At Wyoming, 166. Fort Island, returns of military stores at, x., 284. Billingsport, 284. Dickinson, 184, 189, 209, 222. Fort Island, 284, 509. McIntosh, 109, 391, 406, 448, 466, 704. Pitt, 53, 83, 95, 115, 140. 167, (1783) 337, 345, 462, 483. Rice, 165. Stanwix, 489 ; xi., 507. Sullivan, x., 719. McInt'h, xi. 510. Allen, xii., 70. Anderson's, 461. Armstrong, 134, 135, 139, 147, 156, 160, 161, 170, 172, 177, 192, 193, 220, 225. Men to, 215, 234, 257, 261, 327-329. Augusta, 329, 339. Bedford, at Rays town, 339, 341. Bigham, 341. Billingsport, 341, 346. Browns, 346. Burd, at Redstone, 346. Canhawa, 126, Chambers, 348. Crawford, 129, 134, 139, 172, 194, 225, 230, 261. Men to, 215. To be evacuated, 141. Capt. Stokley at, 254, 257. Descri'd, 350-352. Croghan's, 352, Cumberland, 353. Cushocken, 158. Block-houses not built, 177, Davis's 351. Detroit, Fort near old one, 184. Described, 206, 207. Dunmore, 354. (See Pitt.) Dupui's, 354. Du Quesne, 355-359, 427-431. (See Pitt.) Everett, 359. Franklin, Northampton Co., 360. Franklin, Venango Co., 361. Frederick, 362. Freeland, 362-366, Granville, 366-368. Halifax, 368-370. Hamilton, 370. Hand, 134, 172, 371. Harmar, 371. Harris's, 371. Henry, Northampton Co., 373. Henry, (at Wheeling,) 223, 231, 234, 236, 475. To be evacuated, 277. Holliday's Cove, and its garrison, to be evacuated, 277. Hunter, 375. Hyndshaw, 379-380. Jenkins, 380-382. Kittanning, 182. Named Armstrong, 134, 135, 139, 147, 156, 160, 161, 170, 177, 192, 193, 215, 220, 225. Laurens, 108, 114, 116, 125, 126, 128, 130,

Forts—
142, 148, 155. Evacuation, 141, 147. Described, 382-384. Soldier killed, 148. Lebanon, 384-387. Lehigh Gap, 388. Le Bœuf, 387, Ligonier, 389-393. Loudoun, 394-396. Lowther, at Carlisle, 348. Lyttleton, 396-398. McAlavy's, 461, McIntosh, 108, 110, 248, 250, 252, 400-404. Troops from Fort Henry, &c., 277. Capt. Brigs at, 277. Soldier killed, 148. Indians killed near, 250, 252. McKee's, 404. Machault. (See Venango.) Manaday, 405. Matchitongo. (See Pomfret Castle.) Mercer. (See Red Bank.) Mifflin, or Mud Fort, 407-412. Miller, 412. Morris, at Shippensburg, 412-415. Muncy, 415-420. Nazareth Mill, 420. Necessity, 420-423. Norris, 423. Northkill, 424-426 Patterson's, 426. Pitt, 161, 167, 182. Building, 227. Troops to, 277. Barracks in bad order, 267. Capt. Armstrong commands, 300, 431-437. Pomfret Castle, 442. Presqu'isle, 443. Red Bank, (Mercer) 445-452. Reed, 452. Rice, Northumberland Co., 453. Rice, Wash'n Co., 457. Roberdeau, 454. Robinson's, 456. Sackville, (or St. Vincent,) 120. St. Vincent, (or Sackville,) 120, 157. Shirley, 456. Standing Stone, 459. Stanwix, 112. Steele's, 461. Swartz, 461. Swatara, 462. Venango, 113, 130, 157, 463. Wallace, 464. Wiccacoa. (See Philadelphia.) William, 464. Wind Gap, 464. Wyoming, 465.

Fowler, Alexander, ix., 114. Appointed to audit acc'ts, xii., 109.

Fox, H., appointed Secretary in room of T. Robinson, ii., 490. To, iv., 80.

Fox, Ed., Commiss'rs oath, x., 103.

France, cessation of hostilities, ii., 3. Prisoners retained in, on account of nonpayment of ransom bills, iv., 201. Arrival of military stores from, for the army, vi., 108. Aid from, 173, 330. Treaty with, 466, 479, 493, 506, 521. Fleet and ambassador arrive, 638, 639. Blockade, New York, 639. King of, his birth-day

France—
celebrated in Philadelphia, vii., 648, 651. Guns, Standards, and seals, ordered in Paris, viii., 257. Minister of, Mons. La Touche, ix., 130. Papers used by the British, 152. Vessels of, import merchandise, and do not report, 176. Violation of embargo, 180. Mast-cutting on Schuylkill, 180. Supplies for, 186. Seamen of, 273. Squadron under De Barras at Newport, sailors leave, 354. Consul General, Holker, 383. Form of exequator for, 390. Recognition by Congress, 394. Birth of Dauphin, honor to, 542. Desertion of seamen, 731, 736. Mons. Marbois on storing powder for vessels of, 741. Vessel from, brings despatches respecting preliminaries of peace between Great Britain and the U. States, x., 10, 11. Colors of, on an English vessel complained of, 175. Letter to minister, interest on certificates, 223. Free ports appointed in, 267. Chev. Luzerne leaves Phila., 279–282. Minister complains of interest not paid, 355. Quarantine regulations from plague, 356. Debt to, 386. Sieur de La-Forest, Vice Consul, 735. Commercial treaty with, xi., 220–228, 287. Minister of, respecting Marbois and Longschamps, 468, 469, 470, 473, 482, 487.

Francis, Tench, Attorney General, resignation, ii., 255. Signer of bills of credit, ix., 185. Appointed Commissioner for division and sale of barrack lots in Philada., x., 240, 241, 261.

Francis, Col. Turbut, Commission, iv., 176. Instructions, 177, 194. Letter, 210.

Franklin, Benjamin, engages to procure wagons for General Braddock, ii., 294. His advertisement for them, 295. Letter to Governor on forage, 297. His success, 309. Letters to and from, 274, 344, 467, 548, 766. T. Penn's opinion of, 420. Continued as Agent for the Province in England, and Robert Charles his assistant, iii., 759. Communicates information, deemed irregular, iv., 311, 334. Letter of Congress to, 643, 644, 645. Intelligence from, respecting French, v., 283. And John Adams, letter, vi., 521. Treaty with France, 466. His opinion of Americans, 681. Introduces Mr. Van Noemer, vii., 774. Letter to Mr. Hartly, as to speaking of loyalists and their estates, ix., 670. Elected a member of Council, then president of it, and then president of the State, x., 527. Letter from, (1784) 556. Re-elected President, xi., 207. Extract from will, leaving his portrait to Council, 701. Their acceptance of it, 701 Dies. Invitation to funeral, xii., 85.

Franklin County, no marriage licences received there, x., 329. Formed, (1784), 603. Light-Horse, Election, xi., 280. Trial of W. Nugent 316. Coroner, 765.

Franklin, Fort, ii., 669, 678. iii., 32, 51, 152, 153. Northampton Co., xii., 360. Venango, 361.

Franklin and Hall, letter to Gov. on print'g letters with minutes of Assem'y, ii., 274. T. Penn's opinion of, 420.

Franklin, Colonel, John, to officers of the Garrison at Wyoming to surrender x., 621. To President Dickinson, 672. Memorial to Connecticut Assembly, 681. Resolutions of Assembly on do., 683. Letter to, from Joseph Hamilton, 751. Letters to and from, xi., 3, 14, 52, 67, 84, 94, 111, Respecting, 26, 35, 45. Issues notice for a meeting, 66. His report of proceeding in Phila. 67, Wyoming affairs, 94 Letter to William Montgomery, 111. Letter from Caleb Benton on towns on Tioga, 175. Pardoned, xii., 104. Appointed High Sheriff, 105. To Benjamin Franklin on election as president, and on Wyoming, 296.

Franklin, Governor William, New Jersey, letter on Indians passing through State, iv., 157. On Robbery of Treasury, 305. Proclamat'n against a smuggler, 381.

Franklin, Roswell, raised a party to arrest rioters at Wyo'ng, xi., 359.

Franks, David, Commissary of British prisoners, case of, vii., 76, 81, 112, 270, 395. His clerk permitted to go to New York, 173, 180. British Agent, viii., 33. Ordered to depart, 611. Depreciation of currency, 615. Deposition, 616. Reason for not departing, 617. Declared very frivolous, 617.

Franks, David S., aid to General Arnold, order to buy goods, vii., 370. Asks investigation of his conduct with Arnold, viii., 589.

Frankstown, lead mine near, vi., 293. Indians near, vii., 702. Engagement with Indians, near, ix., 202, 543. Road from to Conemach, xi., 657. Road, Report, xii., 80.

Frazer, John, and George Wood, on highway robbery near Bedford, iv., 458.

Frazer, Persifer, elected Register of Wills and Recorder of Deeds in Chester county, x., 756.

Frederick, Fort, iii., 198; vii., 339, 340; viii., 5.

Freeland, Fort, (near Muncy Hill,) Indians near, take, prisoners, vii., 346. Murders, 357, 589. Respecting, 511, 586. Destroyed, 586, 589, 590, 591, 592, 593, 596, 597, 609, 611, 619, 623. Capitulation articles, 609, 611. List of Captain Boone's party killed, 610. Location and capture, viii., 157, 637; xii., 362-366.

Freelinghuysen, Brig. Major, v., 233.

Freeman, privileges of, respecting, i., 159.

Freeman, Samuel, capture of Indian murderers, xi., 714, 721.

French and Indians, proceedings at Albany, i., 296, 298, 665. Letter to Indians about, 302. Fort on Ohio, 309. Speech of, to Shawnese, 325. And Indians, 748, 749, 750, 752, 756, 761, 770. Invasions by the, and Indians, 104. Peace with England, 127. Prisoners at New York examined, 661. War declared against, by English, ii., 635, 735. And Indians, 20, 26, 31, 50, 123, 124, 132, 167, 168,

French and Indians—170, 173, 176, 192, 213, 215, 220, 227, 229, 240, 264, 267, 290, 292, 381, 405, 411, 413, 433, 440, 446, 447, 448, 453, 471, 472, 491, 493, 495, 528, 559, 561, 565, 579, 610, 629, 689. Neutrals arrive from Canada, 513, 581. Success of Sir William Johnson over, 422, 423. In Philadelphia suffering for wood, iii., 92, 282. Cadet, orders found on a, 286, and Indians respecting, 9, 16, 151, 293, 294, 298, 305, 363, 431, 625. Neutrals, 112, 565. History of, 563. Prisoner examination, 294, 305. Commitment for, 658. Fleet sails from Brest, 677. Spy captured, iv., 205, 206. Frigate arrives in Delaware, v., 665. Prisoners at Reading, 250. Preparing to aid America, 282. Captain, accounts repecting sailors, vii., 678. Fleet, 747, 764. Fleet, (D'Estaing's 736. Frigate piloted, 12, 76. Treaties with the, 89. Gentleman supposed to have been killed by an American officer, 164, 169, 185. Fleets, flour, &c., for, 713, 720, Minister Gerard, 16, 17, 61, 62, 70, 83, 164, 169, 185, 269, 278, 532, 595, 604, 633, 648. Consul, (Holker) 137, 238, 407, 499, 503, 510, 522, 531, 536, 558, 560, 580, 599, 600, 601, 628, 641. Merchants to pay Militia fines, 499, 502, 503, 513. Army at Rhode Island, viii., 479. Fleet expected, 251, 312, 334, 347, 350, 366. Off Newport, 406. Off Virginia, 414, 416, 443, 455, 604. Search of vessels for sailors, 403, 412. Cutting masts on Schuylkill, 540, 542, 543. Correspondence relating to importation of merchandise in, 545-548, 549, 552, 571. Minister, (Luzerne,) invites President and Council to dinner, 45. Reviews Troops, 207. Letters to and from, 334. Emigrants to Scioto, ask for tents in Philada, xi., 743. Merchants complain of doing military duty, 49.

French Creek, powder works, vi., 540. Powder mill site asked for, vii., 315. Indian murder on, viii., 640. And Sugar Creeks, surveys

between, land bad near Allegheny R., x., 509. J. Hart to J. Adlum on, xi., 593. Indian towns on, xii., 167.

Freshet, heavy, at Fort Dickinson, x., 222.

Friendly, Association, address of, complaint of Conrad Weiser against, iii., 312, 313.

Frigate, Pennsylvania, Captain Sibbald, commission, iii., 190. Her sailors not to be impressed, 191. List of officers, &c., 260. Letter John Bulkley, 349. Arrives at Lewes Town, 490. Officers recommended, 657, 658. Sails, 676.

Frigate Trumbull, ix., 95, 100, 104, 239.

Frisbie, Jas., letters to, i., 38, 127.

Frisbie, Levi, Missionary passport, iv., 455.

Frontenac, French forces at, ii., 404, 423.

Frontiers, petitions from, iii., 153, 158, 159. Alarms, murders, &c., from Indians and Tories, vi., 436, 438, 447, 458, 460, 467, 469, 528. 530. Plan for support of, 526, Operations and alarms on, vii., 81, 82, 86, 192, 300, 305, 316. Five companies of Rangers for, 300; viii., 58, 65, 66, 68, 78, 106, 109, 113, 157, 158, 170, 189, 218, 246, 265, 278, 302, 305, 348, 378, 387, 393, 405, 408, 412, 418, 471, 491, 536, 558, 640, 728, 738, 742, 767. State of, ix., 23, 70, 75, 79, 115, 152, 192, 202, 232, 234, 238, 240, 275, 303, 332, 334, 369, 559, 564, 596, 620, 628, 657, 666, 742; xii., 107, 108, 109, 254.

Fry, Henry, examination respecting Wyominck, ii., 491.

Fullerton, Major Richard, asks powder for 3d Philadelphia Battalion, x., 759.

Funerals, order to attend, of Gen. Mercer, v., 222. Col. Hazlett, 223. Capt. Morris, 223.

Funk, Henry—examination—conscientious scruples, v., 495. Mitimus for, 508. Petition, 524.

Furman, Colonel, sent to Monmouth, v., 209.

Furman, Moore, vi., 439. Difficulties for provisions, money, &c., viii., 143, 146.

Furnaces, for casting cannons, v., 36, 72. Iron, 56.

Furney, Adam, case of, i., 685, 726, 727, 729, 730, 731, 737.

G.

Gaddes, Col., letter to, xii., 178.

Gage, General Thomas, iv., 137, 143, 164, 168, 170, 172, 214, 231, 240, 248, 256, 258, 276, 300, 337, 344, 379, 393, 394, 457. Ordered to return—arrives, 501.

Galbraith, Col. Bartrem, letters, iii., 277; v., 343, 353, 407, 409, 415, 457, 480, 486, 521, 532, 533, 543, 562, 573. Advanced age, 334. Lieut. of Lancaster, 353; vi.. 642, 648; vii., 370, 507, 522, 612, 679.

Galbraith, James, letter, ii., 740.

Galbraith, Col. Robert, resigns several offices, vii., 74, 99. Respecting Indian murderer, x., 466. Boundaries, 756. Distracted state of affairs in Huntingdon county, xi., 370. Road to Frankstown, 656. Road, 725. Indian chiefs, 733; xii., 301. Deposition on Records, v., 638. Letter, 730; vi., 238, 511, 550.

Galbraith, Thomas, vi., 533.

Gale, Levin, Commissioner of Maryland on boundary line, i., 603.

Galerme, John Baptiste, his relation of the history of the French Neutrals, iii., 565.

Galleys, armed, on Delaware river—names and officers, &c., v., 4. Asked for by Gen. Washington, vi., 354. Members of Congress on, 359. Dismantled, 421, 440. To be got ready, vii., 239, 240, 249. Fitting out, 314.

Galloway, Joseph, and William M., letter, iii., 160, 214; vi., 347. Memorial respecting estate of, viii., 208. Estate in Hog Island confiscated, xi., 89. Sale of estate, xii., 319.

Galloway, Mrs., through fear asks protection of Council, v., 291. His meadow on Schuylkill, 354. Respecting her property, vi., 695. The law, 675. Asks for permission to cut wood on her husband's forfeited estate, vii., 93. Reply

of Council, 95. Property to be sold, 660.
Gamble, David, trial, xii., 256. Escape, 266.
Gamble, James, petition, viii., 177.
Gap, copper mine, in Lancaster co., T. Penn interested in, ii., 311. Refuses to sell, 369.
Gap at Talihaio—Fort at, (see Forts, ii.)
Gardner, Hon. Dr., condition of Bedford county, ix.,
Gardner, John, deposition, vii., 241.
Gardner, Joseph, elected member of Congress, x., 354, 437. Letters to and from, 405, 526. Papers from Connecticut before Congress, (1785) xi., 449, 453.
Garland, Capt., George, commands a galley, vi., 737.
Garrison, at Fort Augusta, return of, iv., 122. At Fort Hunter, state of, iii., 53.
Gates, Major-General Horatio, sends a Canadian Indian, v., 153. Letter, 247. In Philadelphia, 197, 247. Appointed to command at Ticonderoga, 491. Spy taken, 639. Takes Burgoyne, 674, 676, 680, 746. Letter from, respecting capture of Burgoyne, 687. Letter to Major General John Vaughan on burning towns, 688. Answers respecting Burgoyne, vi., 108; xii., 218, 228, 230, 241, 247. Stops purchases, 233, 234.
Geddes, Capt., viii., 49.
Gehr, Captain Joseph, trial by Court Martial, ix., 362. Cashiered, 363.
Geiger, Col. Henry, his battalion, v., 253. Attacks of Indians, i., 396. Troops, 429.
Genseng, introduced, ii., 174.
George I., King, death of, i., 199.
George II., King, accession of, i., 199. Proclamation of, 200, 202. Of continuance of officers, 200. In the territories, 204. Death of, iv., 37.
George III., King, ascends the throne, iv., 37. Proclamation of, and submission to, 38. Intends marrying Princess Charlotte, iv., 58. Death of sister Princess Louisa, 300.
George, Capt., xii., 216.
George, Capt. Robert, to march his regiment to Pittsburg, xii., 142, 143. Letter to, 168.
Georges, John, appointed Commissioner to Maryland with A. H, i., 427,
Georgia, Indian treaties with, iv., 323. Citizens, driven off to Philadelphia, ix., 300, 309. Act, to comply with requisition, xi., 17, 22. Letter Governor of, 96.
Gerard, Mons., French Ambassador, arrives, vi, 638, 671. Applies for Wm. Straker, 671. His reception by Congress, 677. Claims a citizen and negroes as prisoners, vii., 16, 17. Letters to and from, 16, 17, 61, 62, 70, 83, 164, 169, 185, 269, 278, 532, 595, 604, 633, 648, 651, 653, 708. Offers a reward on captures, 120. Complaint of President to, 269, 278, 639. His commission, 655, 662. Rejoicings on King's birthday, 648, 651. Thanks, 708.
German battalion to be raised, iv., 779.
German, Lutheran, church lots, ix., 363, 364. Congregation, Philadelphia, error in their warrant, xi., 607.
German prisoners, viii., 343.
German Protestants, of Philadelphia county, address to Gov. Morris, ii., 200.
German regiment, viii., 166.
German, troops, ix., 289, 290.
Germans, in Philadelphia, complain of sufferings, ii., 217, 225. Conduct of, at York, v., 576.
Germantown, original charter of, from Wm. Penn to, i., 111–115. Arms for sale at, not to go out of province, iv., 731. Quarters for troops at, v., 206. Troops for, 225. Army at, 485. Head quarters of Gen. Washington at, 617, 645. Defeat at, 645, 714. Gen. Armstrong's letter on military movements near, vi., 70. Gen. Irwin wounded, 71. Escape of Gen. Reed, 71. Stocking weavers and tanners at work at, 128. Battle, vii., 94.
Gerry, Elbridge, v., 754. On imposts, xi., 598.
Gibbons, Lieut. C., under arrest, vii., 643.

Gibbon, Wm., vi., 530.
Gibbs, Major, journal in Rhode Island, vi., 734.
Gibson, Col. George, vi., 319, 324, 553. Commissions, xi., 607.
Gibson, John, commission to lade and unlade a Spanish vessel, iv., 105. Report, 118. Auditor-General, letter on prisoners of war, v., 65. To paymasters, 334. Letter to, on provisions, ix., 190. Commission to purchase Erie of Indians, xi., 405. Goods for, 427. Report on accounts, 588. And R. Butler, agree with Six Nations of Indians for their lands, 529–533; xii., 115. Letter to, 171.
Gibson, Col. Thomas, of Slippery Rock, deposition, xii., 300.
Gilbert, Benj., family taken prisoners by Indians, viii., 213, 222, 259.
Giles, Edward, letter, v., 437.
Gillespie, George, viii., 481.
Girty, Thomas, letter from, ix., 40.
Glass, Lieut., &c., to march Capt. Irwin's company to Fort Armstrong, xii., 172.
Gloninger, John, ix., 654.
Gloucester, riot at, i., 546. Committee of, approve of chevaux-de-frise, iv., 785.
Glover, General, vi., 31.
Gnadenhutten, massacre at, ii., 521, 549. See fort (Allen), 565; viii., 158. Fort Allen at, xii., 323, 327.
Goforth, William, Auditor of Bucks county, ix., 11, 13, 17, 29, 36, 67.
Gold, fall of, in value compared with Continental money, vii., 192.
Gonsales, Emanuel, attack on, by Indians, viii., 551.
Gooch, Gov. Wm., of Virginia, letters, i., 544, 663, 687, 756. Letter from, ii., 18.
Gordon, Adj. Court martial on deserters, xii., 165, 207, 223.
Gordon, Major James, seizure of supplies intended for Cornwallis' prisoners at Lancaster by William Henry, ix., 674.
Gordon, John, vi., 342, 344, 346, 465, 534.
Gordon, Lewis, letters, iv., 66, 67, 70, 174, 420, 423, 427. To be arrested, v., 489, 490; vi., 465, 534.
Gordon, Gov. Patrick, arrival, i., 188. Proclamation, 189. Letter to, in behalf of Swedish children, 189. Instructions to take murderers, 217. Letters to and from, 241, 243, 302, 303, 304, 313, 320, 326, 336, 340, 341, 342, 343, 347, 353, 386, 395, 403, 414, 417, 427, 437, 443, 447, 455, 547, 549, 727. Dies, 489.
Gordon, Samuel, to N. Denison respecting a Scotch emissary, xi., 213.
Gordon, Thomas, viii., 282.
Gore, Obediah, and M. Hollenbach, troops for Wyoming, xi., 216.
Gorham & Co.'s purchase of Erie lands, xi., 541.
Gourla, John, vi., 443.
Governors of States, letters to, vii., 197. Of Delaware, x., 504. Maryland, 293, 320, 324, 527, 528, 540, 542, 543, 744, 753. Mass., letter to, 354, 499, 500, 503, 504. New Jersey, 103, 366, 458, 730. New York, 413, 435, 450, 513. North Carolina, 353. South Carolina, 79. Virginia, letters to and from, 56, 72, 77, 95, 96, 145, 175, 602, 608. Of Connecticut, xi., 239, 409, 414, 447, 451, 735. Delaware, 33. Georgia, 96. Louisiana, 567. Maryland, 56. Massachusetts, 271. New Jersey, 326, 335, 336, 548, 550. New York, 96, 125, 195, 196, 326, 335, 341, 412. North Carolina, 116. South Carolina, 545. Virginia, 115, 116, 497, 499, 501, 507, 523, 557, 600.
Govett, W., & W. Geddes, viii., 73.
Græme, Thomas, M. D., to visit vessels, i., 209. Report, 210, 212. Justice of Supreme Court, 289. Visits vessels, iii., 673, 676. Report on sickly vessels, iv., 59.
Graff, Matthias, vi., 54.
Graham, Henry Hale, Justice, Del. county, xi., 638.
Grain and Salt, measurer's report, xi., 766.
Grand Jury, presentments of, Act respecting, i., 153.

Grant, Lieut., letters, iv., 229, 231, 240, 244.
Grant, Thomas, on Wyoming affairs, iii., 110.
Granville, Fort, see forts, ii.; xii., 366, 368.
Gray, Wm., and John Little, vi., 377.
Gray, William, Treasurer of North-ampton, ix., 229. Paymaster, 238.
Graydon, Lieut. Caleb, letter, iii., 728, 729; iv., 52, 88, 206, 214.
Great Britain, instructions from, to Wm. Penn, respecting wrecked treasure, i., 100. Commission and instructions to Sir R. Holmes, 97. Orders of Privy Council against pirates, 101, 102. Letter to William Penn on peace with Spain, 104. James III. born, orders respecting, 106. Commissioners of Customs to Gov'r on Navigation Act, 119. Lords Justices on peace with French, 125. Orders respecting Mediterranean passes, 177, 180, 183, 184, 439. On repeal of laws, 190. Church prayers for royal family to be altered, 225, 624. Information as to officers, &c., requested, 253, 288, 331, 332, 348, 446. On passes, 177, 180, 182, 183, 242, 256, 258, 264, 283. Duties on negroes, 306. On piratical goods, 307. On Duties, 325. Correspondence on state of affairs, (see Earl Hillsborough, Dartmouth, Fox, Pownall, Stephens, &c.)—birth of a Princess, iv., 311. Death of Princess Louisa, 300. Birth of a Prince, 414. King's speech, 355, 359. Infectious disease among cattle, 355. American affairs, 355, 357, 359. Address of House of Commons to King, 357. Do. Lords spiritual and temporal, 358. Conduct of merchants of Philadelphia, 361. Duke of Grafton appointed keeper of Great Seal after death of Mr. Yorke, 363. Ask for table of fees of officers of Customs, 380. Complains of resolutions of Philadelphia as "very strong and unbecoming," 380. Earl Dartmouth appointed Secretary, 456. Ask for information on commerce, agriculture and population, 465. Insulted by inhabitants of Philadelphia in the case of the Polly (tea ship), 480. At Hannas town, 514. Objects to Pennsylvania nominating deputies to General Congress at Philadelphia, 576, 589. Respecting Connolly and Indians, 577. Act prohibiting exportation of gunpowder, &c., 585, 616. Earl Dartmouth's letters, 588, 589, 621, 625. Earl Dunmore's letters to and from, 461, 482, 493, 525, 577, 579. On trade and fisheries of N. E., 613. Orders of, Commander-in-chief to be supreme in America, 621. People of Pennsylvania not returning to a just sense of their situation, 621. Death of his Majesty's sister, Queen of Denmark, 625. Proclamation for suppressing rebellion and sedition, 652. King's speech to Parliament, vi., 14. Burgoyne's convention to be confirmed by, 166, 176. And United States, preliminaries of peace signed x., 8. Letter of Sir Guy Carleton, 13. Rear Admiral Digby's letter respecting prisoners, 21. Inquiry respecting goods from, 28. J. Temple commissioned Consul-General, 544.
Great Cove, Indian murders at, ii., 462, 474; iv., 138.
Great Meadows, fort proposed to be built at, by Gov. Dinwiddie, ii., 398.
Green, Colonel, surprised at White Plains by De Lancey and killed, &c., ix., 155.
Greene, Gen. Nathaniel, vi., 405, 444, 483, 530. Respecting Arnold and the wagons, vii., 175, 179. Respecting forage, danger of horses starving, &c., viii., 150, 151, 163, 165, 380, 426, 475. Checked at Camden, ix., 154. Position in S. C., 283, 430. Letters to, xii., 118, 120, 145, 174, 204. Destruction of public stores, 145.
Greene, ship Gen., vii., 244, 246, 266, 309, 310, 311, 343, 397, 443. Name not to be changed for Reed,

263. Agents for, 266, 343, 344. Letters from, 266. Officers for, 266, 343, 362. Valuation, 320. Appraisers appointed, 303. Report, 320. Sale of, viii., 3.
Greenwalt, P., vii., 287, 507.
Greenwich Hospital, duties on seamen, i., 251, 403. Receivers, 251.
Greer, Joseph, vi., 395.
Grier, Lieut., viii., 642.
Gregg, Matthew, his accounts, vii., 334.
Gregory, James, v., 334, 500, 588.
Grier, Major, ix., 118.
Griffin, Col. Samuel, letter with a spy, v., 127.
Griffitts, William, iii., 92.
Griswold, Matthew, Governor of Connecticut, on rights of claimants (1784), xi., 447, 451.
Gronow, Lewis, vi., 487, 496, 722.
Growdon, Lawr., Commissioner of Pennsylvania, on boundary line, i., 601.
Grubb, Col. Curtis, vi., 174.
Grube, Rev. B. A. D., vii., 520.
Guerard, Benj., Gov. of South Carolina, asks for a list of traitors, x., 79.
Gun, a factory on French Creek, letter from P. De Haven respecting, v., 155. Memorial from gun stockers in, 733. Prices, 743; vii., 12, 133, 195, 365. Lock manufactory, iv., 712. Factory, plan for a, 767. Continental, found, xii., 262.
Gunpowder, &c., not to be exported from England, iv., 585. In Philadelp'a, inquiry concerning, vii., 146.
Guns and ammunition sent to back counties, ii., 393. Brass, cast by B. Loxley, iv., 731.
Gunsaleye, Martin's, house attacked by Indians, viii., 202.
Gurney, Francis, letter, iv., 691; v., 186. Sent to Monmouth against tories, 177. Asks for old guns to be removed from river, vii., 495; viii., 81. Resignation as warden, xii., 2.
Guthrie, illness of, xii., 151, 230.
Guyho, Captain of French vessel, on importing merchandise, viii., 546.

H.

Haberstick, Michael, vi., 362.
Hackenwelder, Rev. John, vii., 516, 524, 541. Letter, Indians, deep snow, viii., 152. Missionary, 211. Letters to and from, xii., 111, 121, 124, 132, 219, 221, 225, 227, 258, 266.
Haffa, Henry, Sheriff, viii., 704, 742.
Haffer, Henry, (see Haller,) vii., 552.
Hagner, Col. takes charge of Salt works, vii., 767.
Hagner, Will. &c., respecting Salt, vii., 677.
Hagner, Lt. Frederick, vi., 486.
Hague, Gen., ix., 641.
Hahn, Michael, Riots at York Town, xi., 97.
Haldiman, Frederick, letter, iv., 465.
Hale, Thomas, v., 203. And N. Weaver, vi., 628. Speculations with public monies, viii., 112, 115.
Hales, Gen. (Brit.) vii., 489.
"Half-King" of the Six Nations dies at Paxton, ii., 177, 178.
Half-town, (an Indian chief,) xii., 300, 322.
Half-tree, (an Indian chief, 322.
Halifax, Dunk, Earl of, letters to him, ii., 528, 657.
Halifax, Dunk, letters, iv., 192, 200, 201, 202.
HALIFAX, (Fort) see Forts. ii., Account of provisions, iii., 6, 17, 119, 251. Of no advantage—removed to HUNTER'S urged 251. xii., 368–370.
Halkett, Major, letter, iii., 450.
Hall, Charles, vii., 651. seizes land called Indian Town, viii., 118. Receipts for land, 194. Respecting trial, for lands at Lancaster, ix., 294, 321.
Hall, David, and H. Fisher, armed boats in Delaware Bay, viii., 216,
Haller, Col. Henry, vii., 483, 484, 488, 552; viii., 83, 416, 425, 426, 430. Respecting proprietary lands in Reading. ix., 237. Letter, v., 144, 250.
Hallock, Capt, Wm., Capt. Proctor's Ammunition on board the Hornet,

powder bad, iv., 750. Letter from Committee, 752.

Hamberger, John, powder works on French creek, vi., 540.

Hambright, Captain John, instructions to, iii., 42. vi., 57, 532, 570, 626; account of a murder and skirmish, 770; vii., 311, 323; viii., 370, 418. Barrack master at Lancaster, ix., 170, 335, 336.

Hamilton, Alexander, Sec. Treasury, debts, xi., 638. Answer, 641. Letters to and from, xii., 90, 100.

Hamilton, Andw., opinion on proprietary appointments, i., 129. Forbid by Wm. P. to attach the seal to a paper, 148. Letter to, on impressments, 637.

Hamilton, Andrew, and J. Georges, comrs. to Md.—notice of, to Gov. Ogle, 427. Commission, 428. Instructions, 429.

Hamilton, Fort, iii., 81, 119, 139, 140, 152, 218, 222, 356. xii., 370.

Hamilton, Hance, letters, ii., 611, 753.

Hamilton, Henry, Lieutenant Governor of Detroit, offers bribes to rebels, v., 402.—taken prisner, xii., 116, 120.

Hamilton, Gov. (an Ind'n) captured, vii., 512, 517.

Hamilton, Governor James, letters to and from, ii., 49, 60, 66, 91, 113, 120, 122, 125, 126, 130, 168. Letters to Board of Trade on Boundaries, and Claims of the State, 60, 63. Report of Privy Council on, 65. Opinion on his power to pass bills of credit, 106. Retires, 174, 180. Fort, 659, 678. Power to sell Proprietary lands, iii., 684. Succeeds Governor Denny, 689. Proclamation for a Thanksgiving day, 690. Letters to and from, 690, 693, 694, 696, 701, 702, 706, 710, 712, 714, 718, 726, 729, 732, 734. Speech to Assembly of New Castle, 721. Address of Assembly, 723, 725. Letters to, and from Amherst, Gen., iv., 37, 39, 45, 46, 50, 64, 68, 71, 73, 74, 76, 79, 87. Burd, James, 105, 125, 128. Elder, Rev. Jno., 127. Gardon, Lewis, 66. Graydon, Lt. C., 52. Hopkins, Stephen, Gov., R. I., 121. Horsfield, Timothy, 61. Indians, 60, 61. Johnson, Sir Wm., 103. Peters, R., 50. Pitt, Wm., 58. Shippen, Joseph, 82, 110. Teedyuscung, 75, 80, 81, 82. Tilghman, James, 424. Young, James, 131. Proclamation for arrest of murderers of Indians, 65.

Hamilton, James, letters to and from, ii., 447, 483, 537, 640, 731, 740. Dedimus to, to fill Commissions, 460. Orders to, 603, 604; v., 611-613, 620; vi., 372, 383, 433, 456, 468. Certificate of Dr. Shippen, 375. Pass for, 469, 486. Discharge of, 435, 456, 465, 468.

Hamilton, Joseph, to Colonel John Franklin on Wyoming affairs, x., 751. Letters to and from, xi., [illegible], 67, 84, 94, 183, 185. Apprehended, 460.

Hamilton, Major, ix., 12.

Hamilton, Wm., imprisoned, asks release, viii., 591. Report of committee, xi., 535.

Hammell, William, petition respecting Mud fort and Billingsport, ix., 330.

Hammond, Lieutenant, killed at the Compass, vi., 258, 275, 291, 326.

Hampton, John, v., 317.

Hancock, John P. C., v., 137, 179, 219, 244, 289, 352.

Hancock, John, Gov. of Massachusetts, letter from, xi., 272.

Hand, Fort, vi., 673; xii., 134, 371.

Hand, General Edward, v., 443, 488, 528, 540. Sent against Indians on frontiers, vi., 18. Recalled from Pittsburg, 69. Conference with Indians, 601; vii., 321. On his way to Wyoming, 321. Letters, 342, 345, 403, 715. Respecting, 521; viii., 134. Want of men, &c., 135. Complains of desertions, 184. His rank, 409. To, on appointments, 425, 515; ix., 244, 517. (1779), x., 159, (see Vol. VII.); xii., 118.

Hand, H., v., 382.

Hanigan, Thos., on sulphur, v., 253.

Hanna, Robert, letter, iv., 605, 625, 627.

Hanna, Major, viii., 526.
Hanna's Town, provisions to be stored at, vii., 305. Troops, 406. Troops for, viii., 50, 65. Magazine at, 69. Public records removed to, 284. Base attempt to destroy Delaware Indians near, 596. Ravages of Indians near, ix., 240. Destroyed, 596, 606. Distress of, 629. Indian murder near, x., 22. As county town of Westmoreland, 91; xii., 130, 131, 253, 254. Captain Irwin at, 170, 251.
Hannum, Col., viii., 163. To arrest murderers of Mr. Boyd, 244. Provisions, 324.
Hannum, John, Hog Island, ix., 753.
Hans, John, letter W. P. to, i., 143.
Hanson, John, appointed President of Congress, ix., 267, 444.
Harbeson, Benj., &c., vii., 102, 153.
Harden, Major John, recommendation of, x., 610.
Hardin, Mr., court martial against, xii., 152.
Hardie, Capt. Robert, petition of, vi., 259. Appeal from court martial, vii., 91. Memorial for pay for naval services, 92.
Harding, Capt. of ship Confederacy, vii., 761.
Harding, George, petition in favor of, vii., 326, 360.
Harding, Lieut., xii., 128. Attacks Indians, 156.
Harding, Nicholas, letter to, iii., 53.
Harding, Robert, Rev., Catholic priest, number under his care, iii., 144.
Hardy, Sir Charles, appointed Captain-General and Governor of New York, arrives, ii., 399. Letters to and from, 399, 405, 435, 472, 497, 526, 533, 572, 574, 585, 606, 609, 629, 646, 655, 688, 689, 695. On transports, iii., 141, 174.
Hare's Brewery, memorial respecting James Warren, vii., 113.
Hargis, Mr., keeps light-house, xii., 310.
Harmar, Col. Josiah, vii., 736, 750; viii., 305. Muster roll, 188, 220, 245, 515, 537, 539, 603. Instructions for recruiting, x., 309. Letter from, 311, 316. Returns of recruits, &c., at heights of Schuylkill, 323. Returns of troops, 337. Indian treaties, 394, 470. Troops leave for Fort Pitt, 345, 391. Returns of troops, 390, 393, 403, 431, 446, 480, 490, 492. Situation of Fort McIntosh, 406, 448. New regiment, 455. Officers willing to continue, 465. Discharges, 469, 479. Pay of officers, 484. Recruiting, 490, 509. To retain the troops, 496. Recruiting, &c., 509. Returns of troops in service, xi., 173, 174, 217, 219. His rank, 209. Arrangement of troops, 218. Re-enlistments of officers, 270. Continued in command, 282. Irregular commission to Mr. Spear, 287. Rank of officers, 325. Recruiting money, &c., 392. Troops ordered to, xii., 314.
Harmar, Fort, attacked by Indians, xi., 371, 392.
Harper, Wm., deposition, vi., 442.
Harris, David, vi., 32; vii., 638.
Harris' ferry, vii., 391.
Harris, John, letters to and from, ii., 178, 230, 232, 441, 603, 627, 635, 662. Letter from, iii., 33. Pitch and tar may be made on Susquehanna, iv., 721; v., 758. And R. Elder, 753; vi., 211, 574; viii., 23, 550.
Harris' fort, xii., 372.
Harris, James, letter to J. McLene respecting road, xi., 186.
Harris, Dr. Robert, proposals for making salt, v., 507.
Harrison, Captain, xii., 135.
Harrison. Gov. Benjamin, of Virginia, on boundary, ix., 518, 533, 549, 607. [See boundary Virginia.] On boundary, x., 56, 72, 77, 95, 96, 145, 175, 602, 608. Respecting boundaries, xi., 497, 499, 501, 507.
Harrison, Jas., commission to, i., 85.
Harrison, Lieut. John, xii., 235, 236.
Harshall, J., v., 211.
Hart, John, bounty for soldiers, impatience, viii., 750, 752; ix., 55, 128, 291, 339, 376.
Hart, Jon'a., to J. Adlum, land on French creek, xi., 593.

Hart, Col. Joseph, letter respecting troops, v., 18, 97, 237; viii., 326, 327, 356, 503, 523, 707. Robberies in Bucks and Chester, ix., 507. Letter from Geo. Wall, 529, 608-617.
Hart, Wm., vi., 396, 431, 524.
Hartford, convention at, viii., 616.
Hartley, David, letter to, from Dr. Benjamin Franklin, respecting loyalist's estates, ix., 669. Letter to Dr. Franklin on Mr. Jay's return (1784), x., 557.
Hartly, Col. Thos., v., 697; vi., 351, 497, 668, 674, 680, 682, 687, 689, 690, 691, 692, 705, 729, 770, 773. Letters, vii., 3, 10, 81, 86, 87, 258, 391, 694, 775. His operations on frontiers, 5, 117, 776. Vote of thanks to, 9. Troops in want of clothing, 336. Resignation, 366. Regiment (1779), x., 159 (see Vol. VII.), 366. To W. Bradford, on trial of York rioters, xi., 115, 156.
Hartzell, Jacob, on robbery of Tax Collectors in Bucks county, xii., 298.
Hartzell, Jonas (Sheriff), vii., 655.
Harvey, Sir Charles, victory over, xii., 204.
Haslett, Col., orders to attend funeral of, v., 223.
Hasse, John, sends petition, xi., 288.
Hatton, John, to be apprehended, v., 7.
Hauer, Samuel, letters, xi., 47, 102.
Havana, Gov. of, letter to, i., 752. Letter to, iii., 508. To Governor Penn, no foreign vessels admitted, iv., 286.
Hay, John, Sheriff of York, vii., 694.
Hay, Lieut.-Colonel, viii., 10. Pennsylvania regiment, 240.
Hayes, Col. Christ., ix., 79, 105, 141, 247, 300, 330, 354, 369, 404, 469, 637, 772. Indians murder on frontiers, &c., x., 264. Respecting appointments in Fayette co., 265. Affairs in Westmoreland, 279.
Hays, John, journal of, vii., 735-741.
Hays, Col. John, light horse in Allen township, ix., 428.
Hayes, John, viii., 317.
Haylars, Capt. of New Brunswick. captures, a cutter and her captain, R. White, a traitor, ix., 530.
Hazard, Ebenezer, petition for use of historical documents, ix., 449. Publishes two vols., 449, 450. Resolution of Congress for, 450. Reports to Congress as P. M. Gen., robbery of mail, 560.
Hazard, Sam'l, memorial to Connecticut for western lands, and their action, ii., 301.
Hazard, Samuel, appointed by Governor to arrange Archives—makes report to him, i., 17. By Legislature to superintend printing and have lithographs made, 22.
Hazelwood, John, Com'dore, orders to Captain Watkins with prisoners, v., 168. Letters, 205, 602, 620, 663, 680, 696, 721, 747. To furnish pilots, 501. Succeeds Seymour, 594. Success of fleet, 217, 746, 747; vi., 47, 121, 132, 167, 181, 234, 246, 598, 724, 749. Cannon to be sunk, 167. Facts respecting evacuation of Fort Mifflin, &c., 47-50; vii., 19, 112. Petition of, 284. Condemns purchase of provisions, viii., 653, Letters, &c., ix., 38, 54, 73, 133, 143, 425. Receiver of flour, 133.
Hazen, Col. Moses, at Brandywine, vi., 58. Petition of officers in his regiment, viii., 44. Commands Canada regiment, 17, 645. Clothing—redress, union of Canada, 105. Regiment, ix., 244. Brig.-General, 643, 648.
Heads, a Lecture on, ix., 573.
Heard, General Nathaniel, v., 262.
Heath, General William, v., 161, 162, 168. Summons, surrender of Fort Independence, 237. Respecting deserters, viii., 6.
Heinecken, J. H., Christian, recognized as Consul for U. Netherlands, at Philadelphia, x., 446.
Hellstedt, Charles, commissioned as Swedish Consul, Philadelphia, x., 362. Sends letter advising of war between Russia and Turkey, xi., 265, 293.
Henderson, Andrew, account of riotous disturbances in Huntingdon, xi., 305-307.

Henderson, Archibald, respecting robbery, ix., 601.
Henderson, Captain, v., 67.
Hendricks, James, Instructions to, iv., 112.
Henlopen, Cape, alias Cornelius, Penn's account of, i., 147.
Henlopen, Cape, Light-house, condition described by Wardens, xii., 308.
Henry, Fort, ii., 159, 561, 565, 570, 676. Garrison at, iii., 52, 119, 194, 218, 283, 353. North'n Co., xii., 373, 375. (At Wheeling,) 223, 231, 234, 236, 263. To be evacuated, 277.
Henry, George, resigns as Lieutenant of Philadelphia, v., 355.
Henry, John, asks for liberty to deliver a lecture on heads to pay off debts of Theatre, ix., 593.
Henry, Lt. George, sells public vessels, vii., 139. Respecting arms &c., 190, 239, 333, 365,
Henry, Patrick, (Gov. of Va,) on an Embargo, vii., 247. On Boundary, 441.
Henry, Patrick, Jun., v., 260, 286.
Henry, Col. Will'm, vii., 359, 416, 456, 514, 557, 599, 667. To purchase flour, 674. Proofs respecting flour, 557.
Henry, Col. William, makes large purchases of whiskey at high prices, vi., 205, 208. Letters, 558, 645 ; viii., 30, 116, 207, 309, 380, 423, 652, 667, 685, 753, 761. Return of arms &c., xi., 239 ; xii., 259 ; v., 347, 472, 543, 634, 635. Appointed Lieutenant, 355. Letters to and from, ix., 7, 154, 170, 205, 476, 575. Dragoons, 154. On paper Currency, 171. At Lancaster, seizes supplies for prisoners there from Cornwallis' army, 674. Elected member of Congress, x., 354, 437, 534. Letter, 405. ; xii., 314
Herbert, Morgan's examination, i., 219. Recommended to mercy, 225.
Hernandez, B. A., Petition for Spanish vessel to depart after Repairs, iv., 105, 118.
Hervey, Maj. George, vii., 566.
Hess, Henry, Examination of, iii., 56.
Hessian fly, importation of flour into G. Britan prohibited on acct. of, xi., 527. Information asked respecting it of Agri. Soc., 384. Reply to, 385.
Hessians embark from Staten Island, v., 45. Prisoners at Trenton, 140, 146. Sign parole, 145. Address of Council on, 146. Taken, 178. Prisoners arrived at Philadelphia, 190, 244. At Lancaster, 251. Amboy, 300. Defeated at Red Bank, 706, 709. At Middletown, vi., 549 ; viii., 95. Deserters may be enlisted in French army, 448, 449. Troops, deficiency of clothing, x., 6.
Heth, Capt. xii., 165, 167.
Hetty, Sloop, Muster Roll, v., 17.
Hewitt, Thomas, vii., 545. Expecting Indians and Tories, viii., 528.
Hibernia furnace N. J., making Cannon, &c., v., 72.
Hiester, Dan'l, Jr., viii., 697. Elected commissioner of Luzerne Co., xi., 160. Permanent seat of Government, 607.
Higgenbothan, Charles, Case of. i., 530, 535.
Higgins, Andrew, instructions to, to proceed to Cape May, ix., 413.
Highlanders, Regiments of Soldiers, arrive, iii., 440. To be located at Reading, 575.
Hill, Col. Henry, letter, v., 66, 94. Wants a new Militia Law, xi., 94.
Hillegas, Michael, vi., 538, 548, 565. (Treasurer,) 402, 492. Appointed Commr. for division and sales of barrack lots, x., 239, 241, 261.
Hillsborough, Earl of, appointed Secretary, iv., 282. Letters, 282, 283, 290, 292, 300, 302, 307, 311, 334, 361, 363, 369, 373, 375, 380, 382, 387. Secretary of Board of Trade, 301. Complains of, receiving information first from private persons, 303. Of do. through proprietaries, 306, 310. Complains of, petition of Assembly, 311. Legislative authority of Great Britain must be sustained, 340. On Conduct of Merchants

of Philadelphia, 361, 373. Appointment of Duke of Grafton, 363. Complains of Resolutions of Philadelphia, as "expressed in very strong and unbecoming terms," 380. Orders to complete the Battalions, 382.
Hiltzheimer, J., v., 354,
Hobson, Samuel, imprisoned for enlisting servants, ii., 640.
Hockley, Richard, letters to and from, ii., 475, 476.
Hodgdon, Samuel, asks for cannon, viii., 174, 453, 746. C. G. M. G. respecting arms, ix., 391; x., 39, 59. Cannon for Count de Grasse, 59. Dispatches letters to Easton, xi., 374. Arms at Carlisle, 379; xii., 314.
Hodge, Andrew, arms lent by, vii., 190. Relating to cutter Revenge, 319.
Hoffman, Stokely—traitor prisoners in jail, vii., 737.
Hog Island, right to, asserted, viii., 730, 734. Seized as confiscated, 734. Proctor's claim, 760. In Delaware river, claim, ix., 5, 42. Possession delivered, 252, 520. Claim of Caldwell and Barclay to, xi., 89. Early history involved, 90.
Hoge, Hon. Jon'a., letter to, on Indian murders, vi., 610; xi., 149.
Holdernesse, Earl of, iii., 148, 162.
Hole, Nicholas, Collector in Bucks, robbed twice, ix., 529.
Holey, Robert, case of, i., 289, 292.
Holker, Mons., Consul of France, flour stolen from, vii., 137, 238. Loads vessel, 407. Respecting two French merchants paying militia fines, 499, 503, 510. On privileges of French subjects, 510, 513, 522, 662. Applies respecting Francis Fleury, 522, 531, 532. Penrose's servant, 699, 701. Invitation to, 536. Publications, 580, 601, 630. Purchases of flour, 558, 560, 580, 599, 600, 601, 628, 632, 641, 669, 675, 679, 682, 686, 703, 713. Respecting flour, &c., viii., 11, 87, 90, 94, 134, 147, 148, 347, 350, 365, 366, 383, 396, 402, 416, 540, 545, 550, 552, 571, 614, 756. Correspondence relating to fleet neglecting regulations on importing merchandise, 545–548. Consul General of France, ix., 9, 31, 45, 153, 175, 342, 353, [illegible], [illegible], [illegible]. Detail of charges against him, 9, 175-184. Answer to, 31, 36. Answers of President Reed to, 175, 184, 342. Vessel for St. Domingo, 153. And Province Island, 298.
Holland, acknowledges independence of United States, ix., 633.
Hollenbach, M , and O. Gore, troops for Wyoming, xi., 216. Deposition respecting Capt. Schott, 394.
Holiday's Cove, troops at, xii., 108, 234, 235.
Holliday, Mr., active on frontiers, vi., 115.
Holliday, Wm., &c., petition for defence against Indians, vii., 445.
Hollingshead, Mr., service in the State, applies as master of the ship General G., vii., 365.
Hollingsworth, Henry, superintendent of flour magazine, vi., 235.
Hollingsworth, Levi, and some flour, vii., 472. And Arthur Donaldson remove chevaux-de-frise from river Delaware, x., 349. Complimentary letter to, from President Dickinson, 350. On raising chevaux-de-frise, xii., 294, 295. Report respecting Chinese, 537, 546, 548.
Holt & Kollock, privateers in Delaware, i., 763. Militia officers chosen, ii., 477.
Holt, Richard, letter for defence of Delaware, iii., 477, 509. Letter, 636.
Honeyman, Lieut., viii., 363, 378, 500.
Hooper, Col. Robert Lettis, v., 689, 756; vi., 75, 76, 187, 197, 199, 210, 240, 242, 267, 284, 286, 344; vii., 433.
Hooper, Robert Lettis, Jr., appointed to purchase flour, &c., vi., 235, 241.
Hoops. Adams, letters to and from, ii., 462, 474, 752.
Hopkins, James, order for boats for, v., 521.
Hopkins, Gov. Stephen, Rhode Island, ii., 345, 473, 500, 673. Letters to and from, iv., 121.
Hopkinson, Francis, appointed Col-

lector at New Castle, iv., 451. &c., v., 489. Appointed Judge of Admiralty Court, vii., 555, 558. Salary, viii., 241, 245, 390, 412, 658. Trial postponed, 667. Fees received in Admiralty Court, ix., 555, 567, 631, 672. Salary, 577 Judge, A. C. fees, x., 58. Escape of a vessel to Delaware—attached at Marcus Hook when launched, 355. Fees, 707. Appointed Commissioner on navigation of Susquehannah river, 755. (J. A.), case of sloop and negro brought into Delaware, xi , 55. Letters to and from, 53, 125. Resolutions of Assembly of Maryland, 77. Letter respecting, from M. Clarkson, 250. Supposed interference of British Consul with Wardens of Philadelphia, 375. On safety of admiralty papers, 634.

Horsfield, Timothy, letters to and from, ii., 289, 458, 481, 500, 512, 520, 688, 701, 713. Letters, iii., 34, 76, 142, 207, 247, 286, 350, 351, 436, 438, 741. Letters to and from, iv., 61. Recruiting orders to, 116.

Horses, number of draught and pack, in different townships of Northampton county, iii., 404. Purchase of, vi., 316, 396, 402, 415, 427, 429, 440, 443, 444, 448, 454, 525, 530, 563, 626. Purchase recommended by Com. of Congress, 316. Thieves, British, from Philadelphia, depositions respecting, 221–226, 381, 391, 396, 432, 582. Starving, viii., 169, 175, 181, 187, 309, 310, 311, 319, 496. To be branded, 417. Cost of, 483.

Hosick, Indian outrages at, ii., 167, 168.

Hospital, duties on seamen—names, i., 251. Pennsylvania, subscribers to, ii., 87. Military, Dr. Bond's opinion on nature and use of, v., 89. At Reading, 139. Articles for, viii., 496.

Hosterman, Col., viii., 513.

House of Commons, resolution on Bills of Credit, iv., 173. Respecting manufactures, 292.

House of Delegates of Virginia, resolve on boundary line, ix., 563.

House of Employment, managers of, accommodation of sick prisoners, viii., 725, 726.

Houston, Capt., of State navy, vi., 421.

Houston, Dr. J., on jail fever at Lancaster, ix., 282.

Houston, W. C., v., 366.

Howe, Gen. Sir William. army advancing to Philadelphia, v., 83. Has taken New Brunswick, 84. To Princeton, 148, 159, 163. Attempts to obtain Delaware pilots through J. Molesworth, 270, 282, 315. Movements, 438, 557. Approaching Chesapeake, 543; vi., 23, 43, 83, 129. In Chester co., 129. Proposes exchange of prisoners, 299. Letter from, to Congress, 585. Question of compelling attendance as a witness in the city as a garrison town, ix., 462.

Howe, Lord, and prisoners, correspond through Mrs. White, v., 97.

Howell, Jacob S., letters, v., 47, 55, 640. Estimate of cost of clothing Pennsylvania troops, vii., 182. Clothing, viii., 247.

Hubley, Adam, Jr., letter, v., 158, 358, 530, 533, 699. Claim of, vii., 553, 596. Sketch of Gen. Sullivan's proceedings, 721, 755. Col. in place of Col. Hartley, 366. At Sunbury, 498, 512. At Wyoming, 553. List of officers, viii., 513. Exposed state of magazine, 755. Letters to and from, ix., 8, 65, 156, 199, 211, 218, 225, 231, 235, 252, 268, 279, 292, 351, 364, 417, 422, 457, 465, 466. Daring plot discovered, 156. Goes to South Carolina, 347. Respecting Fort Sullivan and operations in New York, x., 719.

Hubley, Lieutenant Bernard, Indian murders, xi., 709, 710. Militia, 738.

Hubley, John, resigns seat in Council, v., 295. Letters, 102, 128, 295, 342, 415, 427, 505. Letter with money and papers from Philadelphia to Lancaster, 102. Public houses, 128; vi., 750. Can't attend Court at Bedford, 769. Builds a powder magazine

and storehouse at Lancaster, vii., 297. Letter, 667; viii., 84, 389, 394, 400, 586. Journal, 401. Land trial in Lancaster county, ix., 295. Burning of Court House at Lancaster, x., 278.
Hubley, Joseph, vi., 145.
Hubley, Michael, appointed president of Courts in Lancaster co., xi., 363.
Huff, Joseph, making cannon, shot, &c., at Hibernia furnace, N. J., v., 72.
Huffnagle, Michael, militia, viii., 210, 569. On supplies, ix., 397, 460, 469, 511, 596. Respecting Col. Cox, x., 125. Timber on lands opposite Pittsburg, 140, 141. Settlers on, 429. Destruction of garrison ruins, 429. Orders to, respecting Manellan township, 747. Tippling houses, &c., 186. Election at Pittsburg, 211. Sale of ruins of Garrison at Pittsburg, 462, Murder by Indians, 465, 467. On Indian robberies, 763. To, on timber, xi., 500, 501. Letter from Pittsburg on Indian affairs, xii., 300.
Hughes, Col., ix., 389.
Hugh, Ellis, letters to, iv., 647, 648.
Hughes, John, letters, iii., 288, 289, 316. Stamp officer at Philadelphia — letter to Mr. Dickeson, owner of the ship, iv., 241. Proposal to Joseph Mitchell for lands, xi., 253.
Hughes, Col., ix., 389.
Hughes, W., letter from, ii., 271.
Hugo, Lieutenant, v., 177.
Humphreys, David, Secretary of Society for propagating Gospel, letters from, i., 191, 226. Of receivers, 252.
Humphreys, Lieutenant, letters, iii., 28, 39.
Humphrey, Joshua, jr., proposes to build piers at Marcus Hook, x., 471,
Humphreys, Whitehead, contract to be made with, for steel, vi., 178.
Humpton, Col. Richard, vii., 366.
Humpton, Col. viii., 6, 539, 693; ix., 487, 505. Letter to, on soldiers, at Lancaster, x., 59.
Hunn, John, instructions, v., 450. Letters, 453, 462, 467, 468, 474, 475.
Hunt, John, remonstrance, (1777,) against treatment, by order of Council, x., 158. (see Vol. VI. 589.)
Hunter, Ephraim, Sheriff of Westmoreland, deposition, iv., 491.
Hunter, Fort, iii., 17, 52, 64, 119, 251, 277, 279, 331, 352, 489. Journal of J. Patterson, 331; iv., 111; xii., 375 379.
Hunter's Mill, ii., (see Forts.)
Hunter, Samuel, letter, v., 133, 370, 377, 415, 610, 717, 737, 762; vi., 57, 175, 191. 392, 478, 499, 537, 552, 563, 564, 570, 571, 573, 599, 615, 624, 631, 637, 666, 711, 773; vii., 116, 316, 346, 375, 438, 455, 516, 546, 574, 589, 615, 619. Attacks and murders by Ind'ns. 346. Letters to and from, viii., 29, 88, 157, 166, 173, 189, 205, 369, 393, 567, 601, 632, 633, 717; ix., 292. Discharge of Militia, 364. Frontiers, 503, 528, 637, 657, 658. Deposition respecting murders, 658.
Huntingdon, Co., disturbances in, xi., 305-307, 379 Commissioners to run Boundary lines, 571. Justices, 588. Statement of Lt. Benj. Elliott's proceedings, 665.
Huntingdon, Gen., v., 30.
Huntington, Sam'l, Elected Pres. Cong. vii., 739. Resigns as Pres. of Congress, ix., 267. Governor of Connecticut respecting John Franklin, xi., 239, 409, 414.
Huston, Capt. Jno., arrives to enlist soldiers, i., 769.
Huston, Lt. W., wounded by Indians, viii., 153.
Hutchins, Tho's, appointed Comm'r, to examine roads and rivers for internal commerce, x., 129, 130. Appointed Commrs. on Virginia Boundary, 223. Commr., 334, 438, 440. (Geographer) letters to Congress and Lord Dorchester for premission to survey lands on Erie, xi., 314, 315.
Hutchinson, Dr. James, appointed to inspect sickly vessels, vii., 408. To recommend Surgeon for Ship G. G. 343. To supply Surgeon's instruments. 547. Sur-

geon in the army, needs several articles, viii., 496. On condition of Hospital on State Island, x., 178, To Gen. Irwin, on 4 men burned at fire-works in Phila., 218. On inspector of pot and pearl ashes, xi., 679.

Hyder Ally, privateer, Capt. Barney, takes ship Gen. Monk, in Delaware River, gallant action, ix., 529. Fitted for defence of River, 621. Change of officers, 618. Sale proposed by Commissioners, granted, 672.

Hyndshaw, Fort, (see Forts,) iii., 81, 82, 139, 140, 222; xii., 379, 380.

Hyndshaw, James, deposition, iii., 263. Letter, 290.

I.

Imlay, John, vii., 264.

Imlay, Wm., a prisoner from New York, v., 597.

Immel, Mich'l, mittimus for, v., 649.

Immel, Capt., viii., 288.

Impertinent, privateer brig captured by Capt. Montgomery, vii., 476.

Imposts, resolution of Congres on, x., 582, 583. Answer of President Mifflin, 585. E. Gerry on, 598. resolution of Congress on, xi., 582, 583, Answer of President Mifflin 585. E. Gerry on, 598.

Impressments—Admiralty to Judge Hamilton on, i., 637. To Gov. Thomas on, 638, 641. Orders respecting, 640, 641. Sailors of Pennsylvania frigate exempt from, 191. Of a sailor, compl'nt against, 103.

Impressing wagons vii., 388, 427, 433, 439.

Impressments by Capt. Harding, vii., 762. Complained of Capt. Harding for, viii., 643.

Independence, Fort, summoned by Gen'l Heath to surrender, v., 237.

Independence of U. S, acknowledged by Holland, ix., 633.

Indian Trade, i., 425.

Indian Isaac, 612, 621. Certificate of, respecting battle at Sideling Hill, iii., 315.

Indians and French, i., 748, 749, 750, 752, 756, 761, 771. Reported death of Allumapees, 772.

Indians—first deed from, to Wm. Penn, i., 47. Deeds, 32, 33, 34, 35, 36, 47, 62, 63, 64, 65, 67, 88, 92, 93, 95, 117, 133, 145, 344, 374, 494, 498, 541, 641. Susquehannah, and Wm. Penn, agreement between, 144. Expenses of, 198. Expenses, resolution of H. R. respecting, 199. Complaint of George Aston against conduct of, 205. Petition from Colebrookdale against, 213. Letter, Allumapees to Governor, 214. Murder of, 215. Letter, James Le Tort to Governor on, 216. Instructions of Governor to take murderers of, 217. George Boone to governor on, 217. Examinations of Walter and John Winters and Morgan Herbert, 219. Scull and Zadusky, mission to, 220, 222. Warrant to arrest Winters and Herbert, 221. Instructions to Scull and Zaduskey, and Smith and Scholehoven, 222. Messengers to Shawnese, 223. Answer to governor, 224. Murder of an, 224. Directions to John Petty, 227. Mission of Smith and Petty to, 228, 232. Shawnese, time of their arrival, 228, Instructions to Wright and Blunston, 230. Letters from, 238, 239. Complain of encroachments on Brandywine Creek, 239. Murder of Shawnese. 241. Death of Shekalamy's son, 241. Advice to traders with, 243, 245. Delawares respecting a murder, 254. Memorial on trade with, 261. Letters from Governor to, 262, 266. Memorial on outrages by, 265. Case of J. Mattox, 266. Compl't against J. Miranda, 266. Murder of three, 267, 268. Invitation to five nations 288. Conestogoe, promise of Wm. Penn to, 295. And French proceedings at Albany, 298. Examination of Jonah Davenport, 299. Numbers of, in different tribes, 301. Message from Shawnese, 329. Outrage, 340. Delaware Chiefs to Gov. G., 341. Governor to, 347. To Gov. G., 395, 454. On Trade, 425. Release from Six Nations for Susquehanna lands, 498. Mur-

Indians, i.—
der in Virginia by, 436, 437, 439. Council with Delawares, 539, Deed for lands on Delaware, 541. Outrage at S. Bethel's 547. Resolutions respecting rum, 549, 551. Letter to Gov., 551, 552. Child claimed, 585. Power of Attorney to sell lands in New Jersey, 630. And deed for, 641. Murder of John Armstrong, &c., by 643, 646, 647. Treaty at Lancaster, present at, 656. Report of large numbers at Harris's Ferry, 657. Copy of paper given to, at Virginia, 658. Death of Tocanuwarogon an Onondago Chief, 661. Catawba respecting, 663. Letter from, to Gov. Gooch, 664. News from Oswego, 665. Shekalamy, 673

Letters from C. Weiser, respecting, ii., 8, 9, 10, 11, 15, 23, 44, 259, 316, 319, 453, 461, 503, 504, 511, 562, 563, 628, 696, 776. Expected at Lancaster, 9. Shawnese, 8, 144, 212, 570, 571, 634. Towicktowick or Twightwees, 9, 321. The praying, 11. Presents to, 11. Nantecoke, 11. Seneca, 11. Backshenoath, 634. Jagrea, 681. Traders in 1748, 14. Murders by, 16, 159–166, 363. Shekalamy, death of, 23. Tagneghdoarus, eldest son succeeds him, 23, 259, 319, 634, 647. Uneasy at settlements of whites on Juniata, &c. Deed for lands between Delaware and Susquehannah, 33. Resolutions of New York, 52. Letters on, 57, 58, 59, 113, 118, 173, 209, 229, 232, 278, 289, 394, 436, 440, 443, 444, 448, 451, 457, 462, 465, 468, 473, 478, 483, 501, 520, 535, 537, 539, 575, 620, 634, 670, 699, 701, 712, 713, 716, 720, 734, 740. 746, 748. Treatment of, by W. Penn, 109. Expenses for Indians, 111. Scaroyady, 15, 114, 220, 279, 447, 627. Monecotootha, 114, 178, 451. Traders, 118, 119, 131. French and, 123, 124, 132, 144, 167, 170, 173, 176, 276, 362, 455, 457, 580. Treaty at Albany, Commissioners to, 137-143. Make deed for lands to "Susquehannah Company," through Lydias, 147, 171. Purchase of lands from, 167, 279.

Indians, ii.—
Outrages at Hosick, 167, 168, 170. Death of the Half King, 177, 178. Six Nations, 178, 279, 299. Speech of Gov. Morris to, at Augwick, 193. Montour, Andrew, 230, 451, 627. Detail of Indian affairs, 1752–54, 233. J. Patten, a trader with, 240. Conestogos, list of, 242. Cherokees at Philadelphia, 244. Massacre at Little Meadows, 362. Arrive at Philadelphia, drunk, 389. Effect of Braddock's defeat on, 394. Conference with Shirley, 402. Do. at Lake George, 407. Near Harris's ferry, have crossed Susquehanna, letter from Gov. Morris to neighbouring Governors, 450. Alarms in Lancaster County, 450. Murders at Great Cove, 462, 464, 474. Tulpehocken murders, 503, 504. Massacre at Gnadenhutten, 524. At Mennisinks, 532. In prison at Easton, 534. Presents to, 536. Cherokees and Catawbas, 536, 558, 561, 567, 570, 571, 573, 580, 711. At Nescopeck, 558, 565. Col. Johnson's treaty with, 559. On Juniata, 566. Refugees at Bethlehem, 584. Murders in New York. 586, 610. Sent to Conestogo Manor, 595 Reward offered for scalps of, 607, 619, 625. Burn and take McCord's fort, 611, 617. Isaac brings scalp of Captain Jacobs, 612. At Bethlehem, address to Gov., 636. A bad, 645. At Burlington, 645. Captain New Castle, 682. Diahogo, account given by, of, 683. Teedyuscung, reply to Gov., 721, 722, 724. Conference at Easton, 722, 730. Captain New Castle, character of, 727. Augustus, intelligence by, from Diahogo, 729. Attack of, near Brown's fort, 738. Misconduct of a Lieutenant, 753, 766. Cumberland County, alarms in, 756. And petitions, 757, 758, 760. Murder near Fort Augusta, 764. Conversation between Conrad Weiser and Shekalamy, 776. Col. Armstrong's account of expedition to, and attack on Kittanning, with list of killed and wounded, 767, 775.

Indians, iii.—
Letters respecting, iii., 5, 8, 10, 16, 28, 29, 30, 32, 33, 34, 36, 38, 40, 48, 67, 76, 83, 107, 116, 139, 141, 142, 147, 149, 151, 173, 174, 190, 193, 201, 204, 206, 239, 246, 277, 283, 361, 420, 424, 425, 435, 453, 478, 581. Arriving at Easton, 7, 210. Teedyuscung, respecting, 8, 104, 109, 143, 193, 206, 209, 212, 235, 247, 248, 256, 286, 299. Ogaghradarika, 8. Murders, 11, 29, 30, 33, 36, 38, 40, 51, 77, 78, 139, 211, 218, 219, 241, 279, 283, 731. French and, 9, 16, 50, 79, 98, 143, 147, 151, 268–273, 293, 294, 305, 535. Weiser Conrad, letters to and from respecting, 18, 28, 31, 35, 86, 216, 221, 277. Conference, remarks on, 38, 193, 216. Gallant conduct of Lieutenant Humphreys, 28, 39. Instructions to Capt. Hambright, 42. Examination of Samuel Clifford, 44. Do. of Leonard Weeser, 45. Murder near McDowell's, 51. List of, at Bethlehem, 53. Mohicans, 52 :— Delaware, 52, 83, 98, 107, 193, 571. At Easton, 53, 78. Tokayiendisery sick, 67. Armstrong (Indian) loses a gun, 67. Mennesinks, 67. Letters of Timothy Horsfield, 34, 76. At Bethlehem, 76. Capt. Jacob's son killed, 83. Young Jacob (seven foot high) killed, 83. Sun-fish, a noted war'r, killed, 83. Shawnese, 83. Fraudulent purchase of lands from, respecting, 86. Maryred, an Indian woman, beggar, 87. Expected to attack Fort Augusta, 98. Peace with the Delawares, 98. On march to Fort Augusta, 98. Govr.'s letters on Indian affairs, 107, 117. Invited to settle at Shamoken 114. Letter from, to Gov'r of Maryland, 143. Letter from Spangenburg respecting, 141. T. Horsfield, respecting, 142. Examination of a Delaware prisoner, 147. Of a Chickasaw do. 148. Petitions for defence against, 151, 153, 159, 164, 174, 235, 238, 284. Proclamations of Gov. Dinwiddie respecting, 155, 156. Edmund Atkins superintendent of affairs with, 155. Cause of troubles with, 160. Edmund Atkins' operation at South, 174, 183. Presents to, 187. At Easton, 210. List of, killed at J. Cisney's field, 229. Journal of Van Etten, 229. Proclamation against selling rum to, 237. Abduction of a boy by four white men to the, 246. William Tatamy attended by Dr. Otto, 247. Letter of George Croghan, 248. Conference with Teedyuscung, 248. Bad policy of Gov'r inviting, 338. Conference with, in New Jersey, 341. Lands claimed by, in New Jersey, 344. Give powers of attorney to transact all future business, 346. Five on their way to Bethlehem, escort, 351. At Fort Augusta, 351. Conference of officers in Virginia on proposals from Teedyuscung, 367. Murders and alarms in Lancaster, Cumberland, &c., 377. Minutes of Meeting of Committee on Indian affairs, 382. Richard Baird's Deposition, 397. Passport for Cherokees, 405. List of names and signification, 428. Memorial of Joshua (Christian Indian), 434. Prohibition of sale of rum to, 437, 519. Conference at Philadelphia, 456–467. Memorial respecting it, 469. Presents to, 467. Certificate of delivery of, 477. Letters of Sir William Johnson, 193, 485. Letters of Capt. Orndt, 5, 51, 207, 209, 212, 350, 351, 367, 487, 491. Journal of Moses Titamy and Isaac Hill, 504-508. Moravian described, 500. Journal of Frederick Post, 521–544. King Beaver, 523, 524, 526. Delaware George, 524, 526. Cushcushking described, 525. Catawabas, 539, Speech of Ackowanothio, 548. Joshua, and other Indians to Gov'r, 575. Passport from Ohio for, 554. List of, present at treaty of Easton, 558. Conferences at Pittsburg, 560, 571, 674. Letter from Proprietaries to Delaware, 576. Commissioners of Indian affairs, letters, 382, 583, 734. Job Chillaway, 582,

Indians, iii.—
Complaint against Geo. Croghan for trading with, 665. Attack on Fort Ligonier, 669. Presents to, 675, 716, 718 Disturbances in Virginia, 694. Shekalamy, 721. Journal of John Hayes, 735-741. Conversation with, by F. Post, 742. Conference with, at Pittsburgh, by Gen. Monckton, 744.
Death of Conrad Weiser, iv., 41. Teedyuscung, respecting, 40, 44, 57, 74, 82, 85, 86. Daniel Claus, Interpreter, 41. Samuel Weiser, 26, 41. Lands from, 41, 49, 67, 86, 88, 103. Depositions, 46. Message from Gen. Amherst, 48. Tellinemut, 52, give up prisoners, 52. Letters respecting, 40, 52, 61, 62, 64, 67, 82, 103, 109, 110, 138, 142, 174, 227, 260, 317, 502. Prisoners delivered up, 52, 64. To and from Gov. Hamilton, 60. Conference, 62. Murder of, by whites, 65, 430. Henry Quamash's story, 66. Treaty with, at Easton, by Gov. Hamilton, 68. Names of, at Treaty at Lancaster, 90. Speeches, 74, 78, 80, 82, 85, 86, 497. Complain of Sir William Johnson's treatment at a Conference, 69. Allegheny, 80. Settlement at Cushetunk, 83. Names of, at Lancaster Treaty, 96. Children prisoners among, 98, 100. Delivered up, 100. Speech of Onandago Council to Susquehannah, 107. Alarm near Bedford from, 111. Murders in Cumberland Co., 117, 175. Memorial, Northampton Co, 120. Near Northampton, alarm, 125. Families, from Nain and Nazareth, 134. Job Chilliway, 138, 142, 174. Papunchay, 138. Murders at Great Cove, 138. Conestoga or Paxton, murder of, 147, 148, 151, 152. Passing through States, difficulties, 157, 158, 160, 162, 164, 167. Council at Fort George, N. Y., decide against, 167. Address of, in barracks to Gov., 170. Murders near Fort Loudoun, 175. Plan of Lords of trade for management of Indian affairs, 182, 189. Licenses to trade with, required 186. Tribes in Northern

Indians, iv.—
and Southern districts, N. A., lists of, 188. Peace made by Col. Bradstreet with, on Erie and Ohio, 207. Charge of killing, by people of New Jersey, 207. Goods, destroyed between Fort Pitt and Philadelphia, 217, 219-222, 224, 226, 228, 230. Murder by whites near Pittsburg, 217, 218. At Shamokin threatened, 217. Going to build on Great Island, 218. Murders, 249, 296, 307, 329. Letters of Sir. Wm. Johnson complaining of ill treatment of, 261. Boundaries between Colonies and, proposed, 261, 262, 281. Expenses of Conferences with, 262. Complaint from Bucks Co., against 273. Act to remove settlers on lands not purchased of, 283. Murder by Fred, Stump, 290, 296. Presents of condolence for, 294. Congress of at Sir Wm. Johnson's, 294, 307, 309. Land purchase and treaty at Fort Stanwix, 309. Trade, long report on, embracing Treaties with various Colonies, 313, 331, 349. Conference, with Six Nations at Johnson Hall, 1755, 325. Sir Wm. Johnson's speech to Six Nations, 325, 326. Boundary between Pennsylvania, &c., 329. Murder of Seneca George's son, 349. Complaint of Col Francis for land and salt springs, 349. Act of N. Y., respecting trade, 361, 369. Murderer of Indian Stephen sent from Virginia, 365. Act of Virginia on Indian trade, 371, 372. Minutes of Commissioners of Pennsylvania on Indian trade, 373, 448. Conoquieson to Sir Wm, Johnson, 373. Sir William Johnson, on proceedings at Fort Stanwix 375. Letters respecting, 411, 413, 430, 533, 539, 556, 559, 567. Murder of two, by R. Brown's servant, 430, 433. Murders near Fort Pitt, 437. Minutes of a Council held with, at Philadelphia, 438. Speech of Pipe, Chief of Delawares, 441. Gov. Penn's answer to Newcomer's message, 469. Speech of Shawanese to Geo. Croghan, 497. Letter to Six Nations

Indians, v.—
and Delawares from Arthur St. Clair, 500. Shawanese, 501, 512, 574, 583. Murder of Joseph Wipey, Indian Chief of Delawares, 503, 520. Intelligence received by messenger from Muskingum, 509. Letter from Alexander McKee, 511. And Virginians, 511, 516, 517. White Eyes, Captain, 513, 531, 539, 540, 684. Newcomer, 513. Petition from Westmoreland, 518. Murders by 519. Maclure killed by, 520, 526. Traders successful, 523. Logan (Mingo chief,) returns with scalps and prisoner, 525, 541. Minute of Conference at Pittsburg, with, 531. Depositions of W. Wilson and J. Pollock, 544. Opposed to Virginia, 551. No accommodation, 557. Speeches, 552. Message on Murders, 554. Depositions, 555. Place for Trade proposed, 557. War, accounts of the rise of, 568, Presents to, 615. Speech of Lord Dunmore to White Eyes, 684. In Northumber'd, create alarm, 789.

Canada, sent by Gen. Gates, v., 153. Col. Bull appointed to meet, at Easton, 201, 203, 208. Of Pluggy's-town commit hostilities against Virginia, 258, 260, 286, 313. Delawares, 313. Alarms and murders in Westmoreland Co., 344, 443, 540, 599. Letters, Gen. Hand, 443, 541. Capt. John Miner, 444. Capt. John Killbuck. 444. Capt. Samuel Meason, 445, D. Zeisberger, 447. Morgan Jones, 448. Wm. Cross, 449. John Corbley, 449. James Chew 449. Near Fort Augusta, 611. Joab Chillaway, 718. Condition of frontiers, 737. Murders and alarms on frontiers, 741.

On western frontiers, vi., 18. Alarms from, in Bedford county, 39, 194. Murders, 39. Westmoreland co., &c., 69, 175, 191, 194. John Harris' opinion of, 211. And tories on frontiers, 436, 447, 467, 469, 485, 487, 530, 536, 660, 662, 666, 669, 674, 682, 683, 690, 691, 692, 767. Captain Alexander McKee and others join, 445. Murders by, 485, 487,

Indians, vi.—
491, 495, 499, 515, 516, 524, 552, 559, 564, 570, 571, 573, 577, 589, 603, 610, 612, 647, 655, 661, 673, 688, 721. Commissioners to hold treaty at Pittsburg with, 578. Defence against the, 586. Gen. Hand's conference with, 601. Gen. Armstrong on warfare with, 614. At Wyoming, 626, 629, 631, 632, 634, 647, 648, 660, 662, 669, 730. General panic, 634, 635, 639, 642, 658. Defensive arrangements, 640, 645. Coshieton destroyed by, 651. Kill Captain Miller, 673. Son of Capt. Brady mortally wounded, 688, 689. Messages to Col. George Morgan, 587, 652, 714. Treaty at Fort Pitt, 717. Col. Hartley attacks, 770, 772.

On frontiers, vii., 3, 4, 5, 10, 81, 132, 173, 362, 399, 408, 419, 431, 445, 447, 505, 554, 562, 564, 569, 572, 578, 589, 603, 606, 612, 614, 615, 617, 618, 649, 650, 664, 673, 696, 710, 715, 755, 769. Chief killed, 5. Skirmishes with, 5, 6, 7, 173. Murders, 16, 173, 399, 438, 521, 524, 534, 574. Towns destroyed, 6, 81. Prisoners with, 10. Seneca chief, Great Tree, 11. Towns, 6, 11. And tories at Minnesinks, &c., 15, 63, 81. Brant at Pennipack, 63. At Wyoming and Minnesink, 63, 81. On Susquehanna, 81, 87, 117. On Chilisquaqua, 82. Escort to Fort Lawrens attacked by S. Girty and Mingoes, 173. Alarms at Ligonier and Blackleg creek, 173. Gen. Washington on expedition against, 210. State of the frontiers, 258, 268, 275, 282, 283. Arrive in Philadelphia, 292. Orders not to be waited for in emergency, 300. Massacre near Fort Ligonier—attacks and murders near Fort Jenkins, 345, 346, 357. Do. near Fort Freeland—take J. McKnight (a member of Assembly) prisoner, 346. Various massacres, 357. Use of dogs and horsemen against, recommended 357. In Philadelphia, 362, 364. Scalps, reward for, 362. In Northumberland county, 408, 574,

Indians, vii.—
606, 614, 615. Near Fort Jenkins, 438. Near Fort Laurens, 455. Speeches, 495, 505. Near Kittanning, 505, Gov. Hamilton captured, 512. Proceedings on frontiers, 516. Fort Freeland destroyed by, and British, 586, 589, 591, 592, 593, 597. Capt. Boon, &c., killed, 590, 591, 592. And Capt. Dougherty, 591, 610. Gen. Sullivan going to Tioga, 594. Arrival, 715. Letter, Jno. Van Campen, 603. Mahakamack, 603. Proceedings in Paxton, 606, 609. Shenung town burned, 667. Near Franks town, 702. Colonel Brodhead destroys towns, 702. Towns destroyed by Gen. Sullivan, 709, 721, 724. Murder of Lieut. Boyd, 723. Various tribes, 517, 518, 541. Their proceedings, 524, 526, 541. Marvellous escape of an express from, 527. In Northampton county, 572. Minnesinks, 573, 575.

Murders by, viii., 23, 140, 157, 159, 189, 203, 213, 249, 282, 341, 369, 488, 513, 514, 528, 529, 640. Delaware, murder of, 30. Scalps, James Clark, 23, 29. On frontiers, 78. Proposed mode of defence against, 114. Attack a sugar camp on Raccoon creek, 140. Letter of J. Hackenwelder, respecting, 152. Munceys, Delawares and Shawnese, 152. On Fishing and Muncey creeks, 156. Take prisoners, 157. Mingoes or Munzus, Wisndoughalends, 159 Munzey, Washnash, 159. Premiums for scalps, 167, 172, 176, 187, 283. Take Peter Bens prisoner, 171. Invasions, 176. Prisoners, 189. Incursions, 202. Attacked by Major and Capt. Westbrook and Captain Van Etten, 202. Murder of Gilbert and Peirt families, 213. Depredations by, 224, 226. In Northampton co., 238, 286. In Cumberland co., 243. In Buffaloe valley, 249. Near Augwick, 278. Near 12 M. Run, 282. Murders by, near Sunbury, 341, 513. Scalps, 369, 393. Petition from Northampton against, 387. Alarms from, 408.

Indians, viii.—
Expedition proposed against, 412. Captain Phillips and others killed by, 488. Murder by Wyandots, 513. In Kentucky, 514. Delawaretown destroyed by Colonel Church of Virginia, 515. Henry O'Niell's deposition respecting, 527. Murder between Reading and Shamokin, 529, 532. On Robinson Run, 526. Shawnese towns destroyed by Col. Clarke, 536. Incursion on Emanuel Gonsales, 558. Near Northumberland, 558. Northampton, 560. Attack on Fort Rice, 568. Scalps, 568. Base attempt to destroy Delaware, by whites near Hanna's town, 596. War between Delawares and Senecas, 640. Murder on French creek, 640. Proposed operations of, 691, 692.

Their title to Conestoga Manor, ix., 49. On frontiers, 39. Capt. Brady, 39. Delawares, 39, 97. Attack Col. Pomroy's house, 51. Murders by, 70, 107, 152, 192, 236, 240, 257. At Wills' mills, 108. Northampton county, 113, 158. In Bedford county, 152, 236. Col. Brodhead attacks towns, 161. Moravian, kindness of, 161. Near Bradford, 192. Pursued by Lieut. Morrison of Virginia regiment, 201. Engagement with Captain Moore and Lieutenant Smith near Frankstown, 202. Ravages on frontiers, 238, 559. Delawares, 247. Shawanese, 247. Wyandots, 247. Northampton co., 257, 275. George Lerne and others killed, 258. Indian town, 323. Defeated, 334. In Northumberland co., 392. Attacks, near Maconie creek, 396. Expected at Sunbury, 504. In Cumberland co., 522. Moravian massacres at Muskingum, 523, 524, 629. In Bedford county, 192, 606, 619, 629. Hanna's town, 240, 526. Expedition against, 630, 635, 636. Declined, 640, 649, 724. At and near Wyoming, 657. Deposition of Samuel Hunter respecting murder of John Martin and wife, 658. Cap. Robinson on ditto, 659. Petition of prisoners among, 733.

Indians, x.—
Murders by, x., 15, 22, 167, 265, 464. Affairs, 25, 46, 53, 83–90, 119—125, 168, 265, 294, 295, 317, 410, 554. Treaty of peace proposed, 45, 62. Hostilities on frontiers, 53. Conference at Onandago, 63. Report, E. Douglass, on negotiations with, 62, 70, 83. Captain Pipe, 83, 84, 85. Council at Detroit, 84. Various tribes, 84–90. Congress do not object to Pennsylvania holding a conference with, for purchase of lands, 105. Resolution of Assembly respecting purchase of lands from, 111. Report to Congress on Indian affairs, 119-125, 126. Treaty with, 152. In Cumberland co. (1779), 159, 161. Take Mrs. Walker and others and kill on Buffalo, and Short creeks (1783), 167. Commissioners appointed to hold treaty with, 265. Conference with Lee and Butler on treaties with, 295. Report and resolutions of Assembly on, 316. List of goods for purchasing lands from Indians, 318. Instructions to Commissioners, 320. On restoration of prisoners, 325, 326. Expenses on transportation of goods to, heavy, 332. Commissioners to treat with, arrive at Fort Stanwix, 346 La Fayette addresses, 346. Negotiations of Commissioners with Six Nations of, 357. Pine Creek, alias Tiadaughton, of treaty of 1768, 357. Answer of Six Nations, 357. Deed from, 360. Treaty at Fort McIntosh, 391, 395. Boundary with, 418. Murder by Mamaughtaquie opposite Pittsburg, 465. Indian in prison, 466. Judge Bryan, respecting his trial, 473. Commissioners for treaty with, 489. List of goods for, 497. To be delivered by W. Maclay, and explanations respecting hunting on their lands, 510. A pass requested for T. and J Killbuck, Indian hostages, returning home, 526. Speech of Sir J. Johnson, 554. Indian treaty on boundary with United States, 562. Obligation of Commissioners to deliver

Indians, xi.—
goods, &c., to, 610. Conference with "Whole Face" and "Long Hair," on survey of donation lands, 740. Segonkquas and Conhonew, 741. Indian robberies, 763.
Report to Congress on hostile intentions of, xi., 72. Purchase from, by Susquehannah county, 114. Murders by, 149, 209. Letter, Cherokee women to President, 181. Letter James Rinker, Superintendent of, to R. Butler, respecting, 206. Murders in Washington county, 209, 377. Purchase of Erie lands from, 390. Attack Fort Harmar, 392. Commissioners to purchase Erie from, 405. Outrages at Wyoming, 432. Instructions to Commissioners to, 503. Purchase of lands from Six Nations, towards Erie, 508. Obligation of Commissioners to, 507, 509. Treaty at Fort McIntosh, 510. Agreement between Gen. Butler and Gibson with Six Nations, for lands, 529. Letter of Cherokee chiefs to Pres. Mifflin, 584. Act of Congress for expense of negotiations with, 604. Defence against, 666. Troublesome in Washington county, 673, 675, 685. Col. McGillivray and chiefs of Creek Nation visit Phila., 707, 711, Murders on Pine creek, 709, 710, 714, 719, 720. Troublesome in Northumberland county, 710. Petition of prisoners among, 712. Murderers described, 721. Take horses from Plum creek, 723. Samuel Doyle arrested, 730. Cornplanter and Stiff Knee at Philadelphia, 733, 739, 740. Complaints by, 739. Against, 740. About to return from Philad'a, 740, 741. Joseph Nicholason, interpreter, 742. S. Doyle acquitted, 745.
Murders on Pine Creek, xii., 9, Cornplanter, Indian Ch'f, 32. Deed for Erie, 100. Murders, 107, 148. Mingoes, 108, 111, 114, 120, 123, 164, 179, 189, 227, 232, 233, 246, 252, 256, 269, 305. Delawares 111, 114, 120, 132, 153, 155, 156, 157, 159, 166, 182, 188, 214, 228,

Indians, xii.—
231, 233, 235, 237, 239. Shawnese, 111, 120, 132, 150, 157, 159, 163, 164, 170, 181, 180, 227, 230, 241. A town attacked by Col., Vanschaik, 112. White Eyes a Mingo chief, 119. Burn a speech of Gen. B., 120. Wyandots, 123, 131, 147, 150, 158, 159, 163, 164, 179, 184, 250, 252, 256, 259, 271. Attack fort Canhawa, 126. A Delaware murdered, 127. Tawas, 131, 147. 150, 185. Chipewas, 131, 147, 150, 184. Cherokees, 131. Pooteatomies, 131, 147, 150, 184, Mohicans, 131, 132. Nonowland, 132, 156. Affairs, 132, 153. From Coochocking, 135. Munceys, 136, 155, 159, 164. Brodhead's expedition against, 137, 153, 154, 156, 164, 165, 169. Steal horses, 139. At Fort Dillars carry off boys, 142. A prisoner taken, 147. Moses Kilbuck, 121, 147. Senecas, 147, 148, 159, 300, 321. Attacked by Lieut. Harding, Nonowland, &c., wounded, 156. Seneca towns burned, 156, 157. Huron's, 157. Yayhroonwago, 156, 165. Buckloons, 156. Mahusquechikoken, 156. Indian towns on French Creek, 157. Maquichee tribe of the Shawnese, 157, 158, 159, Col. Clarke making peace with, 157. Murder at Cheat River, 163, 164, 256. Indian lands invaded from Ohio, 176. Peckawee and Chilacoffe tribes make depredations, 179, 181. Wyandughalins, 182. Murders near Miami, 189, 210, 212, 214, 224. Council at Coshocking, 219. Lands settlers on, 220. Expedition against, 124, 125, 238. Wylandaweechan, 227. Mahingweegeesuch's letter to Council, 229. Expedition against, 229, 232. Near Logstown and Chartier's Creek, 234. Scalps, premium for, 240. Presents for, 241. Murders in Westmoreland Co., 242. Prisoners taken and killed, 243. Wyandots cross Ohio, 248. Attacked and killed near Fort McIntosh, 249, 250, 252. Take forts in the "new country," 257. Shawnese town at Chilcothe destroyed by Col., Clarke, 258, 263. Men killed

Indians—
on Robinson's Run, 261, 263. Mc Intyre's party kills, 270. Murders on Ten Mile Creek, 271. Letter of Wm. Penn to Susquehannah, 280. Slaves, 280. Purchase on Brandywine, 281. Letter of Pittsburg Committee on, 300. All-Face, a Seneca chief, 300. Half Town, 300. Capt. Harris (a warrior,) 300. Cut-Cheek, 300. Henry Kilbuck (Delaware chief) petitions for his land, 305. Charles Wilkins wishes to open a store among, 317. Murder in Northumberland Co., 318, 319, 320, 322. Cornplanter and others on their way, 321. Letter from several, 322. Sleeping Place (McConnel's Town) 461.

Ingersoll, Jared, v., 502, Council ask him to remain in the city, 503.

Ingersoll, Jonathan, ix., 643.

Innholders not to sell rum to soldiers, iii., 132.

Innes Col., at Fort Cumberland, ii., 277, 376.

Inquisition on three Indians murdered, 267, 268. At Wyoming, iv., 384.

Instructions, to commissioners to New Jersey, i., 58. To W. Penn on wrecked treasure, 140. From Great Britain, 97, 100, 102, 105. To W. Penn on birth of James III., 106. To Gov. Gordon, duties on negroes, 306. Of Governor to take murderers of Indians, 217. To proprietaries on appeals, 196. To Scull and Zaduskey, 222. Smith and Scholehoven, 223. To Hamilton and Georges, 429. To Lewis Evans about map, ii., 46. To L. Osbourne for papers from Maryland, 92. Additional, to Governor Thomas, 104. To T. & R. Penn, on appeals, 107. To Col. Shirley, 178. To General Braddock, 203. Captain Frederick Smith, 544, 552. Jonas Seely, 544, 556, 596. Adam Read, 545, 551. B. Franklin to Captain Vanetta, 546, Conrad Weiser, 517. T. McKee, 553, 563, 564. James Galbraith, 555 Jacob Morgan, 555. Captain Busse, 555. Thomas McGee, 563, 564. John Ross, 595. Col.

Instructions—ii.
Wm. Clapham, 596, 667. Of Captain Dumas, to Mons. Donville, (a French officer taken,) 600. To James Burd, 601. 603. John Steel, 601. Captain Potter, 602, 603. Edward Shippen, 603. Captains of Cumberland, 602. Elisha Salter, 603, 621. Robert Irwin, 624. Captain Miles, 687. Respecting letters of Marque, iii., 3. To Commander of Fort Hunter, 17. To Captain Hambright, 42. To Lewis Morris, Jr., 90. Privateers or letters of marque, 91. To Adjutant Kern, 334. To George Stevenson, 386. To Captain R. Walker, 409. To John Bull, 557. F. Post, 620. To officers, &c., at Fort Augusta, 727. To appraisers of transports, iv., 56. James Hendricks, 113. Colonel Armstrong, 114, 116. Rev. Mr. Elder, &c., 116. James Young, 125, 180, 192. Captain J. Schlosser, 160. Colonel Turbut Francis, 177, 195. James Webb, at Lancaster, 180. Asher Clayton, 194. Peter Bard, 210. To Sheriff, Justices and Posse of Northampton county, 421. To Comm. Caldwell, 726. To Captain Proctor, 728. To Com'r Davison, 791. To Henry Dougherty, 791. To Henry Fisher, v., 42. Captain Boyd, 43. From Councils, (volunteers,) 119. Circular, 129. For recruiting, 209. To Commodore Seymour, 233. For survey of Delaware and shore, 441. To Captain John Hunn, 450. Lieutenants of counties, 458. To escort of prisoners in Masonic Lodge, 607, 609. To Com. Hazelwood, 637. To Mr. Buchanan, 711. Letter, 771. To James Davidson, vi., 16, 186. To millers, 303–305. To superintendants, for purchase of provisions, 306, 307, 311–314. To F. Baily and Captain Laing, respecting provisions in Virginia, 404. To Sheriff, 621. To Lieutenant Stoy, 717. To James Claypoole, Sheriff, vii., 291. To Lieutenants, viii., 72. Colonel John Bull, 164. To Commissary of Supplies, 287. To recruiting officers, 290. To Colo-

33

Instructions—viii.
nel of City Battalion, 309. To Colonel Wm. Henry, 309. Capt. Samuel Morris, 310. To agents for sale of confiscated estates, 345. Captain McElhatten, 365. To L. Nicola, on enlistments, 422. To Captain Isaac Roach, ix., 96. To Andrew Higgins, 413. Of Congress to General Wm. Irvine, 419. To commissioners on boundary, 519. To Robinson and Shrawder, x., 99. To Sergeants Lee and McClure, 109. General Irvine to James Boggs, 115 To Major Moore, 127, 132. To Rev. James Finley, 163, (1783.) To Captain Shrawder, 165, (1783.) To Commissioners on boundary with Virginia, 230. To Lieutenant Colonel Harmar, 309. To commissioners to treat with Indians, 320. To Colonel Proctor, respecting H. Carbery, 323. To commissioners at Wyoming, 330. To Sheriff Antes, to arrest persons at Wyoming, 344. To William Irwine as land agent, 427. To Samuel Dale, xi., 66. To Colonel John Craig, 189, 196. To officers in Luzerne county, 204. To Commissioners, 205. To N. Denison, 212. To Balliet and Armstrong to view lands in Luzerne county, 304. To Captain Jno. Kemp, with provisions for prisoners at New York, (1782,) 497. To commissioners to Indians, 503. To Evan Owen, on Nescopec road, 585 Commissioners, on Susquehanna, 634. To commissioners to view rivers, 683. To Charles Pettit, agent, on accounts with United States, 708. Report, 749. Governor John Penn, respecting Wyoming, xii., 51.
Insurrection, Tory, in lower counties, iv., 773.
Intercourse with foreign nations, xi., 708.
Internal commerce proceedings of Ass'y, and Merch'ts, x., 128, 130.
Internal navigation, proceedings between Pennsylvania, Delaware and Maryland, respecting, xi., 25, 27, 77. Commissioners of Virginia and Maryland on, 511.

Invalid Regiment, design of, vi., 411; vii., 358. How officers are transferred to, 701. Philada., ineffective, ix., 103, 200.
Invitation of French Minister to Pres. and Council to dinner, viii., 45, 609.
Irish, Nathan, Letter to Committee of Safety, model of a boat, iv., 639.
Iron, price of at Easton, vii., 177. At Chester, 566. Furnaces, &c., in Pennsylvania, returns of, ii., 52-55. Govr's Circular respecting, iii., 275. Works at Andover, N. J., fit for steel, vi., 178. Chelsea forge, 627.
Irvine, James, letter, iii., 702.
Irvine, Col. James, Letter, iv., 138.
Irvine, Gen. James, and Col. Matthew, in behalf of prisoners of war, in N. Y., viii., 660, 663, 664.
Irvine, Hon. James, letter to, on prisoners to be discharged. x., 26. Disturbances in Washington Co., 467. Retires from V. Presidency, 527. Case of Doane and Dawson, 609.
Irvine, Col. Wm., v., 172, 340; vi., 720.
Irvine, Gen. William, viii., 74, 86, 103, 206, 225, 234, 238, 245, 409. Rank, 409. Militia, 511, 512, 540, 578, 642. Letters to and from, ix., 15, 16, 83, 240, 285, 345, 373, 458, 468, 515, 525, 552. Instructions from Congress, 419, 433. Death of Col. Lochry, 458. Massacre at Muskingum, 525. Boundary line—taxes, &c., 575. Certificates respecting engagement and wounded, 587. Destruction of Hanna's Town, 595. Expedition against Indians, 630, 635, 636, 648, 649, 724. Appoints John Irwin agent, 649. Money sent to 724. Respecting sale of Lands, x., 56, 66. At Fort Pitt, 95. Instructions to Sergts., respecting Fort McIntosh, 109. Instructions from, relative to lands opposite to Fort Pitt, 115. Agreement with Mr. Boggs, 140. Letter from Dr. Hutchinson, 218. Recommended as land agent, 425. Instructions to, 427. Surveys between French and Sugar Creeks, 509.
Irvine, William proposes in Congress, proceedings respecting Erie, xi., 247. Wyoming, 338. Timber opposite Fort Pitt, 501. Survey of the donation lands, 512. Account of donation lands, 513-520.
Irwin, Arthur, complaint against, ix., 199.
Irwin, Barclay, & Co., respecting a vessel for State, vii., 198, 246.
Irwin, Capt., vii., 39, 512.
Irwin, Mr. John, viii., 69. Appointed agent by Genl. Wm. Irvine, ix., 649. No civil magistracy in Pittsburg, x., 289.
Irwin, Gen. wounded near Germantown, and death, vi., 70, 85, 89, 90, 98, 128. Neglected by militia when he fell, 100. Letter to, from Dr. Hutchinson. Four men burned by fire-works in Phila., x., 218.
Irwin Capt. Joseph, viii., 8, 40, 68, 79; xii., 138, 160, 163, 169. A Warden, 314.
Irwin, Mr., xii., 275.
Irwin, Matthew, commiss'y, v., 587. Qr. Master, 613. Letter, 771. Fitting a privateer, vi., 166, 718. And Rob. Bridges, vii., 314. Fitting out a galley, 314. Asks for Cannon, 314; 244, 261, 265, 266, 311, 734, 765. Elected Recorder of Philadelphia, x., 707. Recorder appointed Justice of Common Pleas, xi., 136.
Irwin, R , commis'n and instruction as chief wagon master, ii., 624.
Irwin, Robert, viii., 14, 126
Irwin, Col. Samuel, viii., 637, 638.
Irwin, Tho's, &c., vii., 147. Loan of powder, viii., 138.
Irwin, Capt. enters Continental service, v., 39; vii., 512.
Irwine, Brig. Gen., letter to, v., 162, 584.
Isaac, Indian, ii., 612, 621.
Islands in Western Rivers, xi., 644, 667. In Delaware River, under jurisdiction of Pennsylvania, xii., 74. Report on claims to, 87.

J.

Jack, Capt., viii., 211; xii., 122, 139, 140, 195, 235.

Jack, James, Magistrate's Commissions, new and old differ, x., 264. Commissions, xi., 363.
Jackson, David, pay for wagons, viii., 544. Elected delegate to Congress, x., 437. Letter, 522.
Jackson, Maj. Wm., Sec'y at War, ix., 757.
Jacobs, Captain, killed and scalped, ii., 612, 621.
Jail, of Philada., prisoners for criminal offences in, ix., 249. Site of, for an exchange in Phila., x., 104.
Jamaica, fleet at, in want of provisions owing to embargo, iii., 187.
James, Abel—salt, vii., 758.
James III., (the pretender,) birth of, instructions to Wm. Penn on, i., 106.
Jameson, Lieut., Letter to, xii., 177, 186, 193. At Fort Armstrong, 177, 195.
Jamieson. David, letters, iii., 8, 413. David, vii., 490. And James Eichelberger, vii., 490, 530.
January, Thomas, letter, iii., 410.
Jay, Hon. John, elected by Congress, Secr'y of foreign affairs—his duty, &c., x., 401, 402, 557. Laws of State sent to, 407. Transmits a letter from Mons. Marbois, 409. And from John Adams, relative to consecration of American Bishops, 433. Respecting a Spanish sailor, 499. Representatives do not attend, 538. About to return from Europe, (1784,) 557. Vice Consul of France, 735. Respecting Spanish flag, 743. Inquiry, 759. xi., 171, 202, 287, 411. Letter to, xii., 163, 176.
Jeffers, Ensign, J., in favour of Cornplanter, xii., 86.
Jefferson, Thomas, Gov of Virginia, on boundary, viii., 196, 641, 707, 709. Gov. of Va., on boundary line, ix., 78, 160, 189. Secretary of State, letters from, xi., 679, 681, 685, 688, 689, 696, 700, 703, 705, 706, 707, 708, 709, 712, 713, 718, 722. Gov. of Va., Letters, to, xii., 140, 273.
Jeffries, Joseph, vi., 349.
Jenkings, Col., letter from Wm. Penn on troubles from Somerset county, Cape Henlopen, &c., i., 147.
Jenifer & Root—prices of Wagons, vii., 750.
Jenkins, Fort, vii., 29, 40, 157, 171. Burnt, 563; viii., 29, 40, 157, 171. Burnt, 563; xii., 380-382.
Jenkins, John, letter on Wyoming, x., 37, Respecting, xi., 15, 45, 52.
Jenkins, Robert, counterfeits bills of credit in England, i., 578. Arrested in N. York, 619. Delivered up to Gov. of Pennsylvania, 620. Examination of, 620. Depositions, 621. Letter, J. Ladd to J. Steele, 623.
Jenkins, Stephen, petition of, release from prison, xi , 537.
Jennings, Dr., at Sunbury, vii., 511.
Jennings, Governor, memorial to, from Salem, i., 75.
Jennings, John, deposition respecting Wyoming, iv., 343. To be arrested, xi., 328.
Jennings, Michael, vii., 311, 359.
Jewish, Congregation of Philadelphia invites President, &c., to attend consecration of Synagogue in Cherry St., (1782) x., 731.
Joel, Mr. (a tory) viii., 576, 579, 624, 657.
Johnson, Dr., Commissioner of Connecticut, iv., 470.
Johnson, Gov. Th., Letter to, xii., 166.
Johnson, Gov. of Maryland, complaint against Capt. Nicholson for contempt, v., 328. On Whiskey law, vii., 125.
Johnson, Jacob, letter on Wyoming, x., 34.
Johnson, Sir John, ix., 102. At Detroit, Indian Council, x., 84, 87. Speech to Indians, 554.
Johnson, John, robberies, ix., 603-606.
Johnson, Mr., suspected of being a British emissary on account of a proposed immigration, ix., 552.
Johnson, Mr., release of, x., 171.
Johnson, Sir William, treaty proposed at his house, ii., 279. Letters to and from, 26, 299, 393, 535. Gains advantage over French, 422, 424. Success of, 446, 531,

535. Extract from Treaty, 559. Censures Governor Morris for proclaiming war with Delaware Indians, 651. His views on declaration of war against Delaware Indians, 655; iii., 193, 485, 704; iv., 40, 44, 56, 74, 77, 78, 80, 103, 137, 165, 215, 226, 249, 260, 290, 292, 307, 349, 375. Indians complain of him, 69. Address to Six Nations of Indians, (1755,) 325.

Johnston, Col. Andrew, orders of Gov. Belcher to, ii., 481.

Johnston, Capt. Andrew, on York Co., riots, xi., 157.

Johnston, Benj., respecting lands from Virginia, x., 611.

Johnston, Col. Francis, letter, v., 125, 172. Appointed to receive and distribute clothing, vi., 181. Disabled by ill health, 250. Orders, 732. Return of 2d Brig. under, vii., 66. Letter on want of Clothing in Army, 411. Affair at Stony Point, &c., 581; viii., 373, 410, 539, 693. Appointed Receiver General of land office, ix., 67. Order for books, &c., 202, 327. Commr. to treat with Indians x., 265. On land office, 282. On restoration of prisoners, 325, 326. Counterfeit certificates, 453. Sales of depreciation lands, xi., 125. Islands in Western Rivers, 644, 667. Report, 750.

Johnston, Gen'l, of Maryland, v., 195.

Johnston, Dr. Robert, petition of, ix., 457.

Johnston, Gov. Wm. F., messages on Archives, i., 3, 16.

Jones, Rev. David, asks pay as chaplain, viii., 752. Respecting forfeited land in Northumberland, xi., 58.

Jones' Lane, turnpike, xi., 335.

Jones, Morgan, v., 448.

Jones, N., copies of deeds, Conn., ix., 677.

Jones, Owen, Jr., vi., 53-56. Operations in Continental money, 53-56, 67, 74. Resolutions of Board of War respecting, removal to Staunton, 74. Letters, 102, 106. Resol. of Congress, 79, 93, 112. Board of War requests draft, 188. Asks for pass to Elizabeth Town, ix., 521.

Jones, Samuel, Letter from, xii., 282.

Jones, Thomas, vi., 38, 69, 107, 130, 246. No flour on hand, 38.

Jones, Thomas, Jr., viii., 303.

Jordan, Capt., of Artillery artificers, x., 94.

Jordan, Jesse, respecting wagons used by Gen. Arnold, vii., 160, 179, 194, 213-220, 266, 743. Dies, murdered, 743.

Jordan, Mr., recruits, ix., 185, 191.

Joshua, (a Christian Indian,) memorial, iii., 434.

Journal from Reading to sundry forts, ii., 675. Of a visit to different forts, 159-166. Of Conrad Weiser, iii., 32. To Fort Allen, 66. Of Capt. Van Etten, 222-235. Of Jacob Morgan, 252. C. Thompson, and F. Post, 412. Moses Titamy and J. Hill, 504-508. F. Post, 521. 560. John Hayes, 735. Of Fred. Post, iv., 92. Of J. Van Campen, at Wyoming, 428. Of Major Gibbs, of operations in Rhode Island, vi., 733. Of John Hubley, viii., 401.

Joy Daniel, plan for fire rafts, iv., 698. Letters, v., 62, 121, 179. Proves cannon, 62, 121. Makes return of cannon at Forts on Del. vii., 562.

Joy, W. D., letter to, respecting cannon, iv., 738.

Judges of three lower counties appointed, iv., 339.

Judges of Common Pleas, letter from Council to, viii., 623.

Judges of Supreme Court, opinion on search of vessels for French sailors, viii., 403, 412. Letter from President Dickinson to, [1784] xi, 442, 443. On case of John Brown, 264. Wyoming and Longschamps, 415. Marbois and Do., 467, 472, 478, 488, 489, 490-494. [1784] Opinion on case of murder, 560. Answers to queries on duties, 601. Amicable suit against State for depreciation on salaries, 635, 636. Respecting a negro confined in Dauphin, 667. On tenure of offices, xii., 30.

Judicial Courts, delegates on, xi., 590.
July 4th, celebration illumination, and precautions, v., 411.
Jungman, John, petition for pay, xi., 288, 304.
Jurisdiction for trials of crimes at sea, difficulties respecting iv., 292, 301, 302. Opinion of Solicitor General, 292, 304.
Jurman, Moore, xii., 289. (Furman?)
Justices of the Peace. Wm. Penn's letter to, on the importance of the office and their duties in it, i., 143. Of Bucks County, iii., 183. Dignity of, Justice of the peace, in proportion to the curls of his wig, iv., 206. Of Berks. Co., vi., 138. Of Cumberland, Co., vii., 144. Chester Co., list of, 444. Of Phila. letters to, on nuisances, 658; viii., 101, 102. Resign, being elected to Assembly, 597. Of Northampton, letter to, respecting Rev. John Rosborough, xi., 272. Of Franklin County, trial of W. Nugent, 316. Resign, xii., 5.

K

Kackline, Andrew, vii., 775.
Kacklin, Lt. Col., viii., 176, 356.
Kannakalo, Ind'n Town, vii., 11.
Keachline, Lt. Andrew, vi., 92, 107.
Kearney, Capt., surprises Indians, vi., 722.
Kearsley's Estate, ix., 321.
Kearsley, Jonathan, on manufacture of saltpetre, iv., 727.
Keene, Lawrence, Prothonotary of Northumberland, list of Jurors recognized at Wyoming, xi., 111.
Keiser, Seck and thirty-four others, Chinese, &c., are landed sick and in destitute condition from an Indiaman named Pallas, x., 526. Their case stated to Governor of Maryland, 527. His answer, 528. Resolution of Assembly, 531. Levi Hollingsworth's report respecting them, 533, 546, 548. And other Chinese sent to Maryland xi., 57. (See Vol. X.)
Keith, Sarah, deposition—robbery in Bucks Co., ix., 501.
Keith, Gov. Sir Wm., proclamations of, i., 169, 170, 171. To Assembly, departure, 188.
Keithian, Baptist Church dispute with Christ Church, i., 285. History of, 285.
Kelley, Col., Indians, viii., 562. Defence against Indians, ix., 70.
Kelly, William, resignation required as Justice of Peace, x., 419.
Kemp, Capt, John, of Schooner Cohanzey, with provisions for prisoners at New York, (1782), instructions to, xi, 497,
Kemplen, Capt., Thomas, vii., 438, 455, 510, 547, 586, 596, 664. viii., 29.
Kendall, Jos., respecting murder of Boyd by Smiths, vii., 410.
Kennedy, Archibald, letters, ii., 702, 714, 733. Letters, iii., 477, 479.
Kennedy, David, appointed Secretary of land office, ix., 67; lots for German Lutheran congregation 363. Dry lands in Northampton Co., xi., 651. Report on land office, 757.
Kennedy, Major, killed in attempt to secure robbers, grant by Assembly to his family, x., 178, (1783.)
Kent County Del, associated military companies, iii., 23. Letter from Council of, resolutions, v., 79. Procure salt from Philadelphia, 79.
Kentucky, a new settlement, viii., 379. Murders in 514. Emigrations to, incredible, xii., 274.
Keppel, Commodore, ii., 351, 354.
Kern, Adjutant, letter to, iii., 334.
Kern, Jacob, court of inquiry ordered on, by Col. Bouquet, iv., 199.
Kern, Lt. Nicholas, Indian Murders, viii., 213, 387. Commands at Lehigh Gap, 259, 286. Col. Troops, ix., 428. To Jno. Armstrong, x., 654,
Kester, Capt., resigns, ix., 529.
Key, Geo. S., commisioner from Md. on boundary line, (1849,) iv., 37.
Kilborn, Aaron, record of Court against, xi., 546.
Kilborn, Joseph, record of conviction of, xi., 419.
Kilbuck, Henry, (Delaware Chief,) petition to Council, xii., 305.

Kilbuck, Capt. John, xii., 180, 181, 203, 258.
Kilbuck, Capt. Moses, vii., 121, 147, 262,
King of G. Britain, speech of, vi., 14.
King, Lieut., vii., 691.
Kingsbridge works levelled, vii., 636.
King's ferry, redoubt at, taken by enemy, vii., 460. March from Parkness in Jersey to, viii., 480.
Kingsley, Nathan, resigns as a justice, xi., 662.
Kirk, Samuel, appointed Serjeant at arms to H. R., ii., 100. (See Vol. III., p. 19.)
Kirkbride, Lt. Jo., v., 322, 331, 342, 368, 463, 465, 549, 567, 580. Col. vi., 96, 175, 261, 262, 280, 503. His property burned by enemy, 503; vii., 108.
Kiskiminetas, Creek, xii., 161. Scouts to be sent to, 173.
Kittanning prisoners escape, ii., 711. Account by Col. Armstrong of expedition and success, 767, 775. Killed and wounded, 773. iii., 116. Troops at, about to march in want of provisions, v., 93. Fears from removal of troops, Indian incursions, 313. Troops at, vii., 565. (Fort Armstrong,) viii., 38, 78. Authority to establish a post at, xii., 113. Fort to be built, 124, 126, 131, 132, 160.
Kitzmiller, and Digges i., 713.
Kitzmiller, Martin's, Examination, ii., 70.
Knight, John, appointed Coroner of Philadelphia, iv., 461.
Knight, Peter, v., 239.
Knox, Gen'l, respecting casting of brass cannon, v., 170. Leaves, Morristown, 192. Applies for cannon, 450. vi., 677. vii., 433. viii., 111, 193, 253, 349, 359, 406, 726. Orders shells and shot from Berks and Lancaster to head of Elk—against Cornwallis, ix., 432. Sec. of War. Letters, xi., 208, 240, 268, 281, 291, 300, 534, 555, 621, 624, 645, 685, 686, 707, 728.
Knox, John, &c., vii., 433.
Knyphausen, Gen., in N. Jersey, viii., 312.
Kollock, Jacob, jr., letter, iii., 438.
Kompeton, Capt. Commands enemy near Boon's mill, vii., 591, 596.
Kowatz, Col, vi., 705, 719.
Kreider, Conrad, viii., 435, 489.
Kriebel, Geo., deposition militia fine, v., 433. Petition, 524.
Kucher, Col. Christopher, militia, viii., 288, 289, 324.
Kuhn, Dr. Adam, viii., 585 586.
Kuhn, Ludwig, letter on troops to be raised, terms, v., 93.
Kushocton, excursion to, ix., 540, 541.
Kyasshula, (Indian,) Speech of, iv., 433.

L.

Labar, Col. Abraham, v., 320, 325.
Lacey, Capt. John, Jr., complains of ill treatment from Col. Wayne, v., 154.
Lacey, Brig. Gen. John, Jr., appointed Brigadier General, vi., 168, 170. Relieves Gen. Potter, 168. Men applauded, 97. Marches with troops near enemy's lines, 133. Respecting, 96, 168, 170, 202, 662, 663. Asks to raise a troop of militia horse, 379, 390. Skirmish, 265, 414. Account of surprise and action at Crooked Billett, 470. Depositions respecting British barbarities, 500. Commendation of, 545. Court Martial, 581. Wagons lost, 623. Letters to and from, 168, 202, 226, 240, 255, 265, 361, 379, 381, 384, 390, 398, 402, 410, 414, 470, 579, 580, 594, 595. Number of troops reduced, 202, 226, 254, 261, 265. Orders of Council, 254. Troops arrive at camp, 291, 325. Returns of troops, 297, 402, 472, 485. Remarks to General Washington about, 325. Letters to and from, viii., 178, 505, 526, 750. Letter to, respecting enemy, ix., 436, 437.
Ladd, John, letter respecting Jenkins, i., 623.
Ladies of Philadelphia, commended for their patriotic zeal, viii., 361, 384. Consult Gen. Washington as to money raised, 471.
La Fayette, Marquis de invites Gen. Wayne to dinner, viii., 587. Terms proposed by soldiers, 698.

La Lucerne, Capt., xii., 270.
Laird, Samuel, vi., 550.
Lake George, conference with Indians at, ii., 407.
Lamb, Col., his regiment, viii., 193, 253.
Lancaster, court house, report of Commissioners, i., 252. Treaty at, Indians present, 657. Treaty at, Conestogo Indians at, ii., 242. Return of iron furnaces, &c., in 1750, 53. Gap copper mine in, 311, 312, 369. Petition and alarm, 450. Ammunition sent to, 480, 613. Names of Indians at, treaty at, iv., 90. Troops rendezvous at barracks in, 180. Muster of effective men at, 195. And Pittsburg time for journey, 210. Light horse ordered to, 212. Letter of officers at, 335. Letter committee of, 697. Committee, letter from, respecting fire arms, 717. Return of Assemblymen for, 742. Saltpetre made at, sent to Philadelphia, 742. Money and papers sent to, from Philadelphia, v., 102. Governor at, 128. Letters to and from committee, 250, 266. Scarcity of salt in, 202. Magazine required at, and fears, 211. Richardson, a counterfeiter, taken to, 248. Hessian prisoners at, may be employed, 251. Riots at, 266. Inquisition for murder at, 268. Powder magazine required, 295. Wagons from, 301, 302. Advertisement for, 302. Prisoners of war to be sent to, 306. Committee's letters, 251, 266, 349, 365. Militia, 343. Magazine at, insecure, ix., 3. Convention prisoners, 5, 6, 7, 26, 234, 235, 276, 278, 282, 328, 335, 357, 345. Title to Conestoga, Manor, 48. Plot of British prisoners in barracks discovered, 156. Alarm at, 157. Affair between guards and Moylan's dragoons, 157 Capt. Hambright, barrack master, 170. Disputes between light horse and militia guards, 170. Guards, 199. Prisoners, 203. Dangerous sickness among, 204. Arrive from Reading, 204, 282. Troops at, 211, 293. In want of provisions, militia—prisoners, Colonel Wood, 225, 262, 269, 276, 345, 347. Town Major, 229, 254, 328. Guard at, too large, 262. Barracks for prisoners, 269. Militia, 270, 278. Removal of convention, troops asked for, 282, 290. Trial for land, 294, 295, 321. Capt. Scott, 335. Capt. Hambright, 336. Col. Hubley gone to South Carolina, 347, 351. Troops, 418, 456. Shot and shells from, 432. Fines, 466. Soldiers of Pennsylvania Line killed, 476. Robberies, 596, 606. Fines and militia, 654. Court of appeal on militia fines, 737. Prisoners of Lord Cornwallis' army at, supplies for, seized by W. Henry, 674. Disorderly soldiers at, x., 59. Fears of the bank being attacked, 60. Soldiers march from Philadelphia to, 62. Mutiny proposed to Gen. de Armand's and Col. Moylan's troops, 62. Prisoners to be sent from Bedford jail to, 119. Barracks, &c., care of, 233, 236. Court house burned, 278. Jno. Schreiber in charge of barracks, &c., damages to them, 309, 334. Muster rolls, 394. A pardon asked for Abraham Bare, 396. Malconduct of judges of election, 713.
Lancaster County, orders to arrest Daniel and Wm. Lowe, i., 349. Letter Justices of, to Governor, 439. Lands in, proclamation against settling on, 529. Associated military companies of, iii., 21. Number of Roman Catholics in, 144. Petitions against Indians, 159. Companies in, 389, 394. Soldiers at, 411. Proposal for a literary institution, 677–9. Want of magistrates, v., 347. Expenses of prisoners, 349. Troops ordered to Chester, 353. Difficulties in military affairs, 354. Letter of Commissioners, 364. Letter to, 762. Difficulties from Continental money, 396. Opposition to laws by the Dutch, 405, 408, 413, 427. Money sent to, 415. Search for Westmoreland Records in, 455. Militia, 480, 486, 521, 532, 534, 562. J. Morris, Jr., appointed to attend Court at, 481, 506. Session of Court at, 505, 506. Prisoners,

Lancaster Co.—
533. Troops to be stopped at, 543. To march, 571, 573. Papers removed to, 645, 749. Letters to Commissioners, 762. Quarters for militia to be provided, 758. Price of salt at, 759. Camp at, 761. Mittimus for J. Keller, &c., vi., 80. Guards for military stores, 174. Flour to be deposited at, 177. Regulations for the main guard at, 193. Controversy between an officer and tavern keeper at, 200, 206, 268. Secretary Matlack insulted at, 201. Wagon masters, 212. Letter to magistrates of, 258. Lieut. Hammond killed at "the Compass," 258. Affair of "the flag" at, 268. Traitors in, 361. Want of money to buy horses, 384. Letter of Commissioners, 531. President Wharton dies and is buried at, 493, 553. Taxes, 531. Crews from gallies arrive at, 550. Militia, 594. Illegal election in, vii., 19. C. Wirtz, respecting stores at, 220. Militia at, 230, 679. Stores, 232. Gen. Pulaski's corps, 232, 233. John Hubley builds powder magazine and storehouse at, in occupation of U. S., 297. Officers for, 306. Stores from Lebanon, 371, 469. Resolve to defend themselves, 437. Cannon, twenty-four pieces arrive from, 457. Wagons required from, 469. Flour to be purchased in, 567, 668. Prices in, 568. Martial spirit awaked, 623. Guards, 670. State lands in, viii., 30, 54, 56. Lands in Indian town seized, 118. Rein's mill, flour sent from, 125. Forage master, 155. Commissioner of, purchases horses, 187, 192. Lieut. of, 241. Fines, 324. Menonists, 329. Taxes, 380, 668. Volunteers, 389, 423. Purchases in, 398. Militia, 469, 632. Colonel Moylan's regiment going to, 604. Convention prisoners (German) to be moved from Maryland and Virginia to, 753. Complaints against Commissary, 754. Insecure magazine, 755, 761. M. Hubley appointed president of Courts, xi., 363. Turnpike, 572. Meeting

Lancaster Co.—
on improving Susquehanna river, 608.

Lancaster Turnpike, letter from R. Peters, respecting Jones' lane, xi., 335.

Lanctot, Major Godfrey, expedition against Indians, &c., viii., 557, 559; xii., 228, 246, 259, 270. To proceed to Cooshocking, 246.

Land, Samuel, letter to William Penn, i., 87.

Land Office, commission to R. Peters as Secretary, i., 545. Inquiries by officers of, viii., 307. David Kennedy appointed Secretary of, ix., 67. Francis Johnston, Receiver-General of, 67. Order for books, &c., received from E. Physic, 202, Claims, 263. Lands in Lancaster county, 294. Westmoreland and Cumberland, 409. Opening of, x., 282. Objections to the law, 283. Titles, 414, 416, 611. Counterfeit certificates, 453. Sales of lands, 536, 537, 541, 545, 547. Inquiry as to ownership of islands in the rivers, 739. Conference with Indians respecting survey of donation lands, 740; xi., 503.

Lands, grants, &c. of, in New Jersey, i., 31, 32, 33, 34, 35, 36, 37, 56, 57. Sales of, by Wm. Penn, in England, 39. Indian deeds for, 32, 34, 35, 36, 47. [See Deeds.] John Fenwicke, respecting, 56. Welsh tract, 108 to 110. On Delaware, deed for, 541. Survey of, on Susquehannah, 299, 494, 495, 498, 629. Petition of Ross and Carrol respecting, 333. Deposition, Luke Mercer, 333. On Schuylkill, deeds for, 344. At Tulpehocken, deed for, 404. Notice respecting lottery, 455. Deed for, on Susquehannah, 494. Release, 498. Lands in Jersey, 631, 641. Fraudulent purchase of Indians respecting, iii., 86, 299. Weiser's opinion, 313. Correspondence between F. J. Paris and others, 676. From Indians, iv., 40, 49, 51, 56, 66, 70, 78, 83, 88, 103, 218, 309. At Fort Stanwix, 309. Grant of, to officers of Pennsylvania regiment, 335. And

Lands—
lots, surveys of, x., 53, 56, 65, 414, 506. Purchase by T. Proctor, 420. On Alleghany river, settling, 429. Sales, 541, 602, 603. In new purchase, number of warrants issued for, xi., 121. Depreciation lands, sales at low prices, 125. Claim of S. Riddle and J. Hill, letter from land officers, 138. Virginia titles, 138, 160-162. Between northern boundary and Erie, 211. Patents for, xii., 36. Given to Cornplanter, 85. Indian invaded on the Ohio, 176. Dispute, 195. Petition of Samuel Jones, 285. Wm. Cook, respecting, 286. Western, memorial of S. Hazard for, ii., 301. Grant of, to Susquehannah Company by Connecticut, 303.

Lane, William, viii., 360.

Lanen, R., appointed Capt. ix., 529.

Lang, James, v., 396; vii., 537. Orders respecting vessels, 567.

Lanroy, Col., ix., 324.

Latima, Mrs. Charlotte, a female Tory, vii., 474, 480, 493.

Latimer, George, appointed commissioner on navigation of Susquehanna river, x., 755. Recommends J. Potter, xi., 661.

Latitude and longitude of various places in province, iv., 592.

Lauman, Ludwig, letter, v., 102.

Laumoy, Col., asks for plan of city, vi, 768.

Laurens, Fort, xii., 108, 114, 116, 125, 126, 128, 130, 132. To be evacuated, 141, 147, 155. Soldiers killed, 148. Escort Indians to, attacked and killed by Indians, vii., 173, 465. Saved by miracle, 569.

Laurens, Henry, succeeds John Hancock as President of Congress, v., 736. Letter, 735. Resolutions for a Thanksgiving, 735.

Lawrence, Gov. of Canada, letters to and from, ii., 375, 422. His success over the French, 422.

Lawrence's Island, Col. Neilson attacks and captures enemy at, v., 230.

Lawrence, Thos., vessels to be examined at Battery, iii., 675.

Laws for publishing Archives, i., 14, 22. Reasons for repealing various, 154, 156-164. Instructions on passing 184. To be proclaimed, vi., 396. Recommended by Council to Assembly, 685. respecting property, 675. Mild system, effects of, xii., 4.

Lawton, Esq., Agent for Wm. Penn in England, on various public affairs, i., 139.

Lawyers, scarcity of—but one in Carlisle, vi., 228. Not one in Reading, 245.

Lea, James, recommendation. iv., 586.

Lead, scarcity of, vi., 293. Mine near Frankstown, 293, 413. Gen. Roberdeau, undertakes working 423. Furnace at, 446. Mines, vii., 445, 446. Taken from houses in Philadelphia, 452. Pay for claimed, viii., 5.

Leaming, T. & G. Henry, vii., 422.

Leary, Capt. Dennis, attack by Indians, viii., 532.

Lebanon, Fort, described, ii., 665. (See Forts.) iii., 31; xii., 384-387.

Lebanon Town, Lancaster Co., (Quittopahella,) proposal of C. Raboteau to establish by lottery an institution of literature, iii., 677. His commission and petition, 678. 679. Recommendation, 689. Meeting at, v., 158. Number of Militia at, much reduced as guards, vi., 264, 549. Militia at, vii., 230, 232. Stores to be removed to Lancaster, 371, 459. 469, 522. Guard also discontinued, 507. Mr. Hubley objects to taking charge of stores from Lebanon, and giving up key of magazine, 509. Loan office at, viii., 51. Mr. Melshier, pastor of German Lutheran Congregation near, 123.

Lebar, Col. Abm., vi., 45, 105.

Le Bœuf, Fort, xii., 387.

Le Tort, James, letter to Governor, i., 216. An Indian Trader, examination, 300.

Ledlie, Andrew, Dep. Commissioner of prisoners at Easton, ix., 527.

Lee, Arthur, on Indian treaties, x., 294. Conference with, and R. Butler, 295. To Col. F. Johnson

respecting Indian prisoners, 326. And Butler to Council on officers, 332.

Lee, Capt., viii., 43, 57.

Lee, Francis, Lightfoot, vi., 82, 147, 277, 284.

Lee, Fort, v., 66, 71. Enemy expected to reduce, 71.

Lee, Genl., v., 45. Robbed of horses, 162. Capture, exchange, &c., 172.

Lee, Major, Henry, Jun., surprises British at Paulus Hook, vii., 661, 665. Clothing, &c., viii., 56, 67, 457, 477, 599.

Lee, Major's, party destroys vessels off New York, viii., 100. Horses and wagons, 504.

Lee, Richard Henry, applies for a pilot for a French frigate, v., 665. And M. Smith, on disputes with Virginia, vii., 73. On boundary question—operations of Cornwallis, &c., (1780,) x., 173. Elected president, 359.

Lee, Richard, Governor, Maryland, letter, iv., 538.

Lee, Major Thomas, vi., 440, 568.

Lee, Serjt. Edward, killed and scalped by Indians, ix., 659.

Lee, Thomas, Sims., Gov. of Maryland, letters to and from, ix., 12, 37; viii., 354, 432, 433.

Lee, Wm. Serj't, and McClure to take possession of Fort McIntosh, x., 109.

Leech, Thomas, iii., 676. Sails after privateers, 676. Capt. of frigate, 657.

Leffertie, John, deposition of, respecting enemies, and burning Coughenawag, viii., 387.

Lehigh Gap Fort, xii., 388. Wall on improving 292.

Lehigh, River, observations on, and roads, by S. Balliet, xi., 131, 132. Remarks on, 135. Examination, 694.

Leimback, Fred., v., 524. [See Lineback.]

Leith, John, deposition on Indian robberies, x., 763.

Lenox, David, attack on R. Smith, vii., 637. Statement of his services, x., 754. Claims depreciation of pay, xi., 55.

Leonard, Sam'l, letter Wm. Penn to, i., 129.

Lerne, Geo., wife, &c., killed by Indians in Northampton Co., ix., 257.

Lesher, John, vi., 170, 327, 346, 667, 675.

Leslie, Matthew, letter from ii., 356. Sent to purchase provisions, 316.

Letart's Spring, population of, xii., 281.

Le Tort, James, letter to Governor, i., 216. An Indian trader, examination, 300.

Letters, vol. i.—

From William Penn, 38, 49, 54, 60, 61, 67, 70, 72, 93, 126, 127, 128, 129, 131, 132, 134, 135, 136, 137, 138, 139, 142, 143, 148. To William Penn, 49, 51, 54, 55, 56, 76, 77, 79, 30, 81, 82, 83, 84, 87, 106, 129; (See W. Penn.) Gov. Markham to Lord Baltimore, 39. From the Proprietaries, 203. Indians to Governor, 214. Allumappies to Governor, 214. James Logan to R. Charles, 214. Sam'l Nutt to Governor, 215. Wm. Penn to James Frisbee, 46. From Sir Wm. Petty to Wm. Penn, 49. From Phil. Lloyd to Wm. Penn, 54. From James Nevill to Wm. Penn, 55, 56. Wm Penn to Gov. of New Jersey, 60. From Gov. Blackwell to President Lloyd, 106. James Steele to R. Shankland, 187. Gov. Keith to Assembly, 188. From Micajah Perry, 197, 206. Society for propagating the Gospel, 191, 226. Proprietaries to Trustees, 203, 236. Checochinican to Governor, 239. Gov. G. to Shekalamy, 241, 455. Admiralty to Governor, 242, 243, 253, 306. 439. Gov. G. to Traders, 243. James Logan to Traders, 245, Commissioners of Trade, 245. H. Newcastle to Gov., 246, 269, 577, 581, 594, 633, 648, 652, 679. D. Lloyd to R. Charles, 246. Commissioners of Customs to Governor, 238, 395. Greenwich Hospital to Governor, 251, 403. General Spottswood on Post Office, 264, 265. Joshua Lowe to Governor, 268. Capt. Civility to Governor, 238, 271. From Alured Popple, 245, 288, 331, 348, 433. S. Blun-

Letters—i.
ston, 295, 316, 410, 530. Rip Van Dam to Gov. G., 296. Governor to Delaware Indians, 302, 303. Edmund Cartlidge to Governor, 304. Gov. Ogle to Gov. G., 313, 320, 326, 336, 342, 343, 403, 414, 443, 727, 758. Gov. G. to Gov. Ogle, 321, 326, 337, 340, 343, 347, 417, 427, 447. Boone and Mattox to Gov. 340. Delaware Chiefs to Gov., 341. Gov. to Indians, 346, 445. Gov. to S. Blunston, 353, 437, 547. Wright and Blunston to Gov., 363, 436. Benjamin Shurmer to R. Charles, 370, 380, 390 Justices of Kent to Gov. G., 372, 389, 500. J. Ross to Gov. Ogle, 381. Gov. to Wright and Blunston, 386, 436. Lord Baltimore to Gov. G., 393, 395. Indians to Gov. G., 394, 425, 549. Abraham Wendall for Indians, to Gov., 454. James Steel to James Heath, 426. Gov. Gooch, 544, 663, 687, 756. Commissioners on Boundary Line, 556, 557, 558, 568, 574, 613. James Hamilton to R. Peters, 585. Ferd. J. Paris, 586, 628, 734. Justices of New Castle to Governor, 592. Gov. Clarke, N. Y. to Governor, 619, 620. James Ladd to J. Steel, 623. R. Peters to T. Cookson, 637. John Digges to R. Peters, 645. Between Gov. Bladen and Gov. Thomas, 645, 686, 692, 726. Conrad Weiser, 649, 650, 651, 661, 665, 671, 673. Gov. Shirley and Gov. F., 653, 667, 669, 670, 711, 746, 754 Gov. Clinton and Do., 654, 661, 678, 687, 712, 736. Thomas Cookson, 637, 646, 657, 680, 682, 684, 727, 730. D. Bush to Thos. Hopkinson, 674 Adam Furney to T. Cookson, 685. Gov. Shirley and P. Warren to Gov. Thomas, 689. R. Peters to Thos. Calder, 729, 731. Tench Francis to Do., 733. Captains at Albany, 736. Indian to President, 737, 741. Capt. John Stoddard to Gov. Shirley, 740. George Croghan to R. Peters, 742, 770. Capt. Perry to R. Peters, 745. To and from Conrad Weiser, 649, 650, 661, 665, 671, 673, 748, 749, 750, 756,

Letters—ii.
758, 761, 771, 772. Presd't P. to Gov. of Havana, 752. Do. Mons. Chastenoy, 755. Curtis and Finney to, 759. Jehu Curtis, 759. Capt. Taylor to Captain Medcalf, 760. Holt and Kollock to President, 763. President Reading of N. J., 764. Answer of President, 765. Secretary P. to Proprietaries, 768. Capt. John Huston to President, 769. Geo. Croghan to T. Lawrence, 770.

Alexander, James, ii., 465. Alexander, Wm., 170, 315, 348, 375. Allen, Wm., 362. Alricks, Hermanus, 383. Armstrong, Col. John, 451, 457, 719. Armstrong, Joseph, 247, 248. Assembly, 316, 318.

Ballett, Capt. J., ii., 7. Bard, Peter, 764. Barton, Rev. Thos., 568, 755, 756. Belcher, Gov., of New Jersey, 172, 182, 242, 243, 261, 269, 471, 478, 489, 501, 513, 527, 530, 699. Bell, John, 692. Blunston, Sam'l, 66. Board of Trade, 128, 377, 418, 467, 527, 778. Boscawen, Adm., 322, 421. Boston Selectmen, 708. Braddock, Gen., 258, 261, 263, 269, 285, 288, 290, 299, 372. Burd, James, 393, 454, 566, 631, 705. Burgesses of Wilmington, 456. Bush, D., 6.

Churchman, John, ii., 19, 25. Clapham, 596, 612, 615, 663, 669, 671, 686, 705, 739, 744, 751, 766, 778. Captains of his regiment to Commissary James Young, 703, 704, 716. Claus, Daniel, 116, 174, 645. Clinton, Gov. N. Y., 16, 26, 29, 30, 32, 65, 99. Cookson, Thomas, 9, 42. Coxe, Gov., 377. Croghan George, 13, 31, 118, 119, 132, 144, 173, 203, 209, 212, 218, 219, 483.

De Lancey, Gov., of New York, ii., 168, 179, 220, 233, 242, 243, 261, 264, 267, 270, 273, 278, 279, 280, 288, 326, 331, 338, 344, 345, 346, 350, 384, 391, 396, 398. Denny, Gov. Wm., 779. Digges, John, 73. Dinwiddie, Robert, Governor Virginia, 177, 226, 268, 270, 273, 390, 422, 446, 454. 481, 530, 560, 581, 711. Dobbs, Gov., N. C.,

Letters—ii.

281, 536. Dunbar, Col. Thos., 385, 401, 410, 417.

Edmonds, Wm., ii., 669, 681.

Fisher, Josh., ii., 592, 593. Fitch, Gov. Thos., 122, 125, 208. Fox, H., 490, 606, 659. Francis, Tench, 255. Franklin, Benj., 274, 344, 466, 548, 766. Franklin & Hall, 274.

Gage, Col., Thomas, ii., 571. Galbrath, James, 740. Gooch, Gov. 18.

Halifax, Dunk, ii., 657. Halifax, Earl of, 528, 657. Hamilon, Gov. James, 49, 60, 66, 91, 113, 120, 122. Hamilton, Hance, 611, 753. Hamilton, James, 731, 749. Hardy, Sir Charles, and Gov., 399, 435, 497, 526, 574, 585, 606, 609, 629, 646, 688. Harris, John, 178, 230, 232, 441, 627, 662. Hawkins, John, S., 117. Hendricks, Thos., 438. Hobson, Cap. Saml., 641. Hockley, Richd. 475, 476. Holt, R. and S. Kollock, 4, 477, 509. Hoops, Adam, 462, 474, 752. Hopkins, Gov. Stephen, 345, 434, 500, 673. Horsefield, Timothy, 289, 458, 481, 500, 512, 520, 688, 701, 713. Hughes, Wm., 271.

Innes, Col., ii., 217, 376. Johnson, Col. Wm., 26. Johnson, Genl., 393, 535.

Kennedy, Archd., ii., 702, 714, 733

Lawrence, Gov., ii., 375, 422. Lee, President of Virginia, 58. Lesley, Matthew, 316, 356. Logan, Wm., 479. Loudoun, Lord, 718.

McKee, Thomas, ii., 553, 563, 564, 615. Magaw, David, 39. Marshall, Capt., 29. Mercer, Capt. Hugh, 632. Mercer, James, F., 281. Morris, Gov., R. H. [See R. H. M.] Morris, Lewis, 315.

Norris, Isaac, ii., 242, 243.

Ogilvie, Wm., ii., 585. Ogle, Gov., (Md.) 40, 46, 57. Orme, Robert, 312, 325, 329. Orndt, Cap. 742.

Parsons, Wm, ii., 41, 95, 98, 305, 443, 515, 534, 539, 595, 670, 740, 742, 745, 747. Patterson, Cap., 613. Penn, Thomas and Richard, 304. Penn, Thomas, 189, 195, 252, 275, 305, 333, 366, 419, 438.

Letters—ii.

Peters, Richard, 59, 89, 172, 196, 214, 218, 232, 307, 312, 315, 345, 411, 455, 651, 660, 685. Pepperell, Wm., 329. Philadelphia, Mayor and Aldermen, 389. Phipps, Lieut. Gov., 413, 732. Polson, Cap. Wm., 246, 247, 248. Powell, B. and S. Rhoads, 3. Pownall, Sir Jno., 377, 418, 467, 527, 778.

Read, Adam, ii., 738. Read, Charles 645. Ridout, J., 734. Robinson, Sir Thos., 188, 249, 284, 291, 365, 379, 439, 440, 520, 764. Rutherford, Jno., 276, 288.

St. Clair, Sir John, ii., 567. Salter, Elisha, 611, 613, 621. Scull, Nicholas, 73. Sharp, Horatio, Governor Maryland, 113, 125, 130, 187, 192, 213, 228, 244, 274, 382, 397, 451, 490, 507, 557, 573. Shippen, Edward, 230, 358, 362, 364, 400, 455, 463, 472, 627, 634, 642, 738, 740. Shirley, Governor, 20, 26, 215, 260, 282, 298, 326, 328, 330, 338, 381, 387, 698. Shirley, General, 292, 330 405, 417, 435, 481, 493, 495, 502, 524, 569, 576, 577, 578, 579, 587, 651, 693, 715. Shirley, John, 199, 332, 402, 423. Shirley, W., 29, 293, 307, 310, 321, 346, 357. Spangenberg, Revd. Mr., 584. Spering, Lieut., 566, 587. Spry, Commod., 508. Steele, Revd. Captain John, 623. Stevenson, Geo., 442, 461, 465, 514, 749, 775. Stevenson, James, 170, 323, 411, Swaine, Charles, 360.

Tasker, Benjamin, Governor, ii., 93. Thomas, Gov., 180. Thompson, William, 752. Till, William, 464. Trent, William, 17, 50, 575.

Van Etten, Captain John, ii., 720.

Walker, Thomas, ii., 267. Washington, Colonel. George, 565, 620. Weiser, Conrad, 8, 9, 10, 11, 15, 23, 44, 259, 318, 453, 461, 503, 504, 511, 562, 563, 628, 696, 776. Wentworth, Governor, J. G., 195. West, Francis, 571. Wetterhold, Captain, 741, 753. Williams, Israel, 20. Wolcott, Governor Roger, 120, 126.

York, several persons, ii., 448.

Abercromby, Maj. General, iii., 321, 364, 366, 371, 376, 380, 392, 553.

Letters—iii.
Allen, William, C. J., iii., 64, 304. Amherst, General Jeff., 634, 694, 701, 706. 710, 712, 715, 718, 726, 734. Armstrong, Colonel John 40, 48, 51, 54, 78, 83, 146, 173, 187, 191, 201, 212, 239, 282, 289, 296, 303, 365, 446, 447, 448, 481, 551, 621, 627, 688. Atkins Edmund, 175, 183, 197, 268.
Bard, Peter, iii., 432, 499. Barton, Rev. Thos., 377, 450, 551. Beatty, Rev. Charles, 297. Belcher, Gov. J., 54, 151. Bell, John, 282. Bernard, Governor Fra., 453. Blackwood, John, 402, 403. Boscawen, Admiral, 498. Bouquet, Colonel, 82, 85, 265, 571, 670. Bulkley, John, 349. Bull, Capt. Jno. 422, 423. Bullitt, Captain Thomas, 371. Burd, Maj. James, 333, 334, 350, 367. Burk, Lawrence, 478. Bussé, Christian, 279, 425. Byers, John, 406.
Callender, Robert, iii., 29. Chauvignerie, Mons., 329. Chew, B., 397. Chief Justice, 754. Clapham, Colonel William, 9, 10, 13, 14, 38, 40, 42, 58, 64. Colden, Alex., 446. Commissioners, 93, 161, 214, 235, 258, 281, 287, 398, 498, 675. Commissioners of Lower Counties, 401. Commissioners of Customs, 546. Commissioners of Indian affairs, 583. Commissioners of Wyoming, 318. Cotes, Admiral Thomas, 186, 298. Coultas, James, 64. Council to Gov., 8. Croghan, George, 175, 247, 248, 319, 428, 544, 671, 733.
De Lancey, Governor Jas., iii., 434. Denny, Gov. William, 5, 8, 13, 18, 29, 35, 38, 40, 48, 50, 53, 54, 58, 64, 69, 76, 78, 83, 93, 95, 96, 106, 137, 138, 141, 145, 146, 148, 150, 160, 162, 173, 174, 186, 193, 201, 207, 209, 212, 214, 218, 221, 235, 236, 239, 241, 245, 247, 248, 251, 256, 258, 265, 266, 268, 273, 277, 278, 282, 289, 290, 293, 296, 298, 300, 303, 304, 313, 315, 316, 323, 330, 338, 349, 351, 360, 364, 365, 366, 370, 380, 383, 385, 392, 401, 403, 412, 425, 427, 428, 430, 432, 442, 449, 453, 471, 480, 481, 485, 487, 489, 490, 498, 508, 511, 517, 518, 546, 552, 571, 583, 584,

Letters—iii.
623, 634, 671, 675, 677, 685, 687, 689. Depui, Samuel, 423, 424. Dinwiddie, Gov. Robert, 50. Dudgeon, Richard, 442.
Elder, Rev. John, iii., 251. Erwin, Robert, 64.
Fothergill, John, iii., 667. Forbes, Gen. John, 83, 398, 448.
Galbreath, Bartram, iii., 277. Galloway, Joseph, and Wm. M., 160, 214. Gordon, Lewis, 754, 756. Governor of Havana, 508. Græme and Bond, Drs., 673, 676. Graydon, Lieut., 728, 729.
Halkett, Major, iii., 450. Hamilton, Gov. James, 690, 691, 693, 694, 696, 701, 702, 706, 710, 712, 714, 718, 726, 729, 732, 734. Harding, N., 53. Harris, John, 33. Holdernesse, Earl of, 148, 162. Holland, Nathaniel, 583. Holt, R., 636. Horsfield, Timothy, 34, 76, 142, 207, 247, 286, 350, 351, 436, 438, 741, 755. Hughes, John, 288, 289, 316. Humphreys, Lt., 28. Hyndshaw, James, 290.
Indians to Governor of Maryland, iii., 143. Irvine, James, 700.
Jameson, David, iii., 8, 412. January, Thomas, 410. Johnson, Sir William, 485, 704. Joshua, and other Indians, 575.
Kennedy, Archibald, iii., 477, 479. Kern, Adjutant, 334. Kollock, Jacob, 438.
Lawrence, Thomas, iii., 675. Leech, Thomas, 676. Lloyd, Thomas, 11, 319, 361, 411. Lords of trade, 690. Loudoun, Lord, 137, 138, 141, 145, 150, 174, 267, 277, 316, 317, 323, 338. Lyttleton, Governor William Henry, 18, 315, 398.
McClughan, John, iii., 393. McKinley, John, 381. McMichael, John 405. Masters, William and J. G., 160. Mercer, Col. Hugh, 27, 57, 571, 584, 624, 673, 685, 721, 728. Meyer, Engineer, 47, 48. Miller, John, 455, 545. Monckton, Gen. Robert, 732. Moore, Justice, 511. Morgan, Capt. Jacob, 30, 31, 39, 191. Morris, Sam'l, 635. Montgomery, Capt. Jno. 411. Nevill, Samuel, 206.
Orndt, Jacob, iii., 5, 51, 207, 209, 212, 350, 351, 367, 487, 490, 678. Os-

Letters—iii.
wald, Thomas, 298. Otto, Dr. M., Jno. 247, 251.
Paris, F. J., iii. 666. Parsons, Wm., 5, 7, 35, 81, 84, 104, 139, 142, 163, 211. Pemberton, Israel, 37, 555. Peters, Richard, 7, 11, 33, 37, 51, 80, 84, 86, 92, 104, 157, 206, 217, 239, 245, 251, 283, 288, 297, 298, 377, 381, 384, 386, 389, 390, 393, 397, 402, 406, 409, 422, 428, 438, 450, 455, 471, 475, 478, 484, 488, 500, 510, 514, 516, 544, 546, 551, 552, 555, 571, 575, 580, 621, 627, 636, 660, 662, 673, 675, 677, 698, 727, 733, 741, 754. Peters, William, 299, 312, 547. Pitt William, 94, 96, 106, 301, 330, 519, 753, Post, Fred'k, 580, 698, 700, 702, 705-709. Pownall, John, (secretary,) 97, 759. Pownall, John, Gov. Mass., 693, 714. Price, G., 488. Price, Lieut. Samuel, 429, Proprietaries, 106, 157, 193, 576, 668, 683.
Quamas, Capt. Henry (Indian,) iii., 758.
Quinby, Jonathan, iii., 681.
Raboteau, C. C., iii., 677. Read, Chas., Jr. 546. Read, Jas, 36, 245. Reading, alarms at, 36. Reading, Philip, 699. Reed, Adam, 426. Reynolds, George, 5. Ridout, J., 660, 662. Rebertson, Maj. James, 291.
St. Clair, Sir Jno., iii., 266, 661. Shackerly, Mr., agent, 137. Shankland, William, 3 62. Sharp, Horatio, Gov. 143, 183, 197, 585, 697, Shippen, Jos. 333, 389, 409, 410, 42[illegible], 449, 470, 510. Shippen, Edward, 8, 304, 394, 409, 427. Sibbald, Capt. Jno. 490. Spangenberg, Rev. Mr., 69, 141, 434, 500. Stanwix, Col. John, 220, 239, 241, 288, 301, 438, 517, 668, 687, 693, 696, 710, 713. Stevenson, George, 384, 386, 390, 391, 395, 400, 411. Stevenson, Surgn., James, 82. Stephen, Col. Adam, 83, 668. Swain, Charles, 424. 516, 686.
edyuscung, iii., 385, 509, 623, 704. Tennent, Rev. William, 514. Thomson, Charles, 256, 422. Till, William, 471, 475. Trent, Wm., 1[illegible]9. Trump, Levi, 408, 425, 430, 480, 582, 699. Turner, J., 442.

Letters—iii.
Van Etten, Cap. iii., 139. Vining, T., 635.
Walker, Capt., Richard, iii., 409. Washington, Col. George, 300. Weiser, Conrad, 19, 28, 31, 35, 86, 207, 217, 221, 277, 283, 293, 312, 313, 425, 428, 439, 500, 571, 699, 701. Weiser, Samuel, 10. Wentworth, Gov., 5. West Francis 707, 732. Wetherhold, Lieut. Jacob, 211.
Young, James, iii., 12, 49, 57, 455, 484, 488.
Allen, Andrew, iv., 702. Allen, Jno. 680. Allison, R. and J. Worrell, 764, 784. Atlee, Col., 772. Amherst, Gen. Jeffrey, 37, 39, 45, 46, 48, 50, 64, 68, 71, 73, 74, 76, 79, 87. Anonymous, 156. Apty, Thos., 157. Armstrong, John, 108, 135, 136, 146, 152, 154, 174, 193, 203, 205. Attorney-General, S. G. B. 302.
Ball, Joseph, iv., 761. Bard, Peter, 210. Barnsley, Capt. Thos. 209, 212. Barry, John, 750. Barton, Rev. Thos., 133. Bayard, Major John, 707. Beatty, R. and J. Miller, 151. Bedwell, Thomas, 719. Belton, Joseph, 650, 654. Berks county Committee, 679. Bernard, Gov. F., Mass, 162. Biddle, Owen, 765, 789. Blaine, Ephraim, 590. Boone, Gov. Tho's, 67. Borden, Joseph, 753. Botetourt, Lord Governor, 365, 368, 371. Boudinot, Elias, 720, 727. Bouquet, Col. Henry, 166, 198, 204, 206, 208. Bradshaw, Thos. 297, Bryan, George, 777. Burd, Capt. James, 88, 111, 124, 128, 140, 165. Burd, Mark, Chairman of Bucks county, 697. Butler, Z., Capt., 364, 643, 647, 648.
Cadwalader, Col. John, iv., 757. Caldwell, Commodore, 706, 717, 726. Callender, Robert, 411, 413. Capts. of Pennsylvania armed vessels, 707. Carleton, Gov. Guy, 364. Carnahan, John, 603. Carpenter, E. 160. Cavet, James, 622. Chambers, Benjamin, 535. Chew, Benjamin, 494. Clayton, Ashur, 138, 142, 174. Colden, Gov. Cadwalader, 167, 364, 562, 563, 579. Collins, Major Luke,

Letters—iv.
454. Commissioners of Bedford county, 712. Commissioners of Carlisle, 706, 713. Commissioners of Connecticut, 470, 471. Commissioners of Customs, Boston, 289, 305, 311. Commissioners of Trade, 174, 182, 189. Commissioners of Westmoreland county, 489. Committee of Chester county, 718, 730. Committee of Frederick county, Md., 681. Committee of Lancaster county, 717. Committee on Naval affairs, 692. Committee of Reading, 757. Committee of Safety, 635, 638, 642, 651, 654, 656, 664, 666, 668, 679, 680, 696, 697, 702, 703, 704, 706, 708, 711, 712. 713, 714, 717, 718, 720, 721, 722, 723, 726, 727, 729, 730, 731, 733, 734, 736, 737, 738, 740, 742, 743, 744, 745, 746, 747, 750, 751, 757, 760, 761, 762, 763, 765, 768, 769, 770, 773, 774, 775, 777, 779, 790. Committee of Secresy of Congress of North Carolina, 733. Congress, 640, 643, 644, 645, 680, 728, 732, 760, 773, 778, 782. Congress of North Carolina, 734. Connolly, John, 548, 695, 703, 770. Connolly, Mrs., 778, 780. Conway, H. S., Sec'y, 244. Cooper, Guy, Sec'y, 250. Coxe, John, 757, 762. Crawford, Wm. 424. Croghan, G., 452, 482, 506.
Dartmouth, Earl of, iv., 456, 460, 464, 480, 538, 576, 579, 585, 588, 613, 614, 621, 625. Davison Commodore, 791. De Haven, Peter, 731. Dickeson, Mr 241. Dickinson, John, 784. Digges, Wm., 489. Dougherty, H., 753, 778, 791. Durkee, John, 364. Dunmore, Earl of, 460, 482, 493, 525. Dyer, Eliphalet, &c., 394, 401.
Eden, Robert, Gov. of Maryland, iv., 369. Edmondstone, Chas. 433. Elder, Rev. John, 127, 128, 132, 135, 148, 153, 714.
Fairlamb, N., iv., 753. Fisher, Henry, 664, 724, 725, 732, 736, 737, 740, 743, 755, 762. Instructions, 686, Fitzsimons. T., and J. Moulder, 763. Fox, Mr., 80. Francis, Col. Turbutt, 210. Franklin, William, Gov'r, N. J., 157, 305. Frazier, J., and George Wood, 458.

Letters—iv.
Gage, Gen. Thomas, iv., 137, 143, 144, 164, 168, 170, 172, 214, 217, 231, 240, 248, 256, 260, 276–300, 337, 344, 377, 393, 394, 457. Gordon, Lewis, 66, 67, 70, 143, 174, 420, 423, 427. Governor of Havana, 286. Grant. Lieut. Chas., 229, 231, 240, 246. Graydon, Lieut. Caleb, 52, 88, 207, 214. Gurney, Francis, 691.
Haldiman, Frederick, iv., 465. Halifax, Dunk. 192, 200, 201, 202. Hallock, Captain William, 751. Hamberger, Thomas, 795. Hanna, Robert, 605, 625, 627. Harris, John, 721, 789. Hazelwood, Commodore, 765. Hamilton, Gov'r James, 37, 39, 45, 46, 50, 52, 58, 60, 64, 67, 68, 71, 73, 74, 76, 79, 80, 82, 86, 103, 105, 110, 124, 128, 130, 419, 424. Hendrick, James, 346. Hillsborough, Earl of, 282, 283, 290, 292, 295, 297, 299, 300, 302, 306, 309, 311, 334, 340, 361, 363, 364, 375, 380, 382, 387, 414. Hopkins, Governor Steph., 121. Horsfield, Thomas, 61. Howell, John L., 765. Hughes, Ellis, 647, 648. Hughes, John, 241.
Indians, iv., 60, 61, 170, 450, 500. Irish, Nathan, 638. Irvine, Col. James, 138.
Johnson, Sir William, iv., 40, 44, 56, 74, 77, 78, 80, 103, 137, 162, 165, 215, 226, 249, 260, 290, 292, 307, 309, 349, 375. Johnson, William Samuel, 475. Joy, Capt., 738.
Kearsley, Jonathan, iv., 727.
Lancaster, officers at, iv., 335. Lancaster Committee, iv., 697. Ledlie, Doctor, 427, Lee, Richard, 538. Logan, William, 62, 530.
Macbean, Angus, iv., 731, Mackay, Æneas, 484, 494, 516, 517, 540. McKinley, John, 746, 749, 764. Maclay, William, 462, 660. Maul, James, 680. Miles, Colonel Samuel, 748, 783, 787. Montgomery, John, 505, 506, 530. Moore, Sir Henry, Governor of New York, 337. Morris, Robert, 750, 752, 768, 773. Morris, Samuel, 787. Morton, John, 772. Moylan, Stephen, 774.

Letters—iv.
Nicola, Lewis, iv., 635, 726. New York Commissioners, 150, 168, 337.
Old, James, iv., 721.
Penn, Governor John, iv., 135, 136, 138, 140, 143, 144, 146, 148, 150, 153, 155, 157, 158, 160, 163, 164, 166, 168, 170, 172, 174, 182, 192, 198, 201, 203, 206, 208, 210, 214, 217, 226, 231, 243, 244, 248, 250, 256, 258, 260, 262, 274, 276, 280, 290, 295, 297, 299, 300, 302, 305, 307, 309, 311, 334, 337, 339, 340, 344, 349, 361, 363, 365, 369, 377, 380, 387, 411, 414, 431, 449, 573, 576, 578, 585, 586, 588, 603, 604, 612, 614, 616, 620, 622, 625, 627, 629, 652, 659, 688. Penn, Governor Richard, 448, 450, 456, 460, 465, 466, 476, 480, 484, 494, 506, 521, 526. Peters, Richard, 40, 44, 50, 56, 62, 64, 66, 70, 77, 80, 530. Phelps, Richard, 297, 300. Pilots restricted, 777. Pitt, William, 58. Plunket, William, 109. Pollard, William, 787. Pownall, John, 309, 368, 415, 486, 629, 652. Proctor, Thomas, 729, 753, 790. Provincial Commissioners, 142.
Read, Captain Thomas, iv., 745, 747, 750, 751, 753, 769. Reed, Joseph, 679. Reese, William, 653. Reid, Colonel John, 246. Reilley, Richard, 783. Richard, James, 721. Roberdeau, Colonel, 719, 760, 786.
St. Clair, Arthur, iv., 426, 437, 452, 471, 476, 481, 494, 500, 506, 530, 573, 583, 586, 589, 622, 624, 628, 637, 659. Sample, David, 481. Schlosser, Captain J., 158. Seely, Jonas, 141. Sharpe, Gov'r of Maryland, 207, 262, 277. Shelburne, Earl of, 274, 276, 280, 281. Shippen, Edward, 62, 64, 154. Shippen, Joseph, Jr,, 82, 88, 102, 108, 110, 128, 132, 154, 175, 209, 212, 298, 412, 419, 420, 437, 471, 481, 488, 540, 546, 550, 557, 558, 560, 564, 583, 618, 624, 637, 650. Sluman, J. and W. Judd, 661. Smith, Daniel, 498. Smith, Devereux, 511, 515, 612, 630. Smith, James, 228, 641. Smith, Robert, 776, 783. Smith, Thomas,

Letters—v.
488, 618. Smith, Rev. Dr. Wm., 475, 511. Smith, William, 229, 245. Spear, J., 481. Stedman, Charles, 685. Stephens, Sec'y of Admirality, 243, 331, 623. Stevenson, George, 102. Stewart, Charles, 383, 384, 416, 417, 428, 689. Stuart, John, 189.
Teedyuscung, iv., 74, 78, 80, 82. Thompson, John, 415, 416. Thompson, William, 521, 526, 680. Tilghman, James, 335, 346, 416, 417, 419, 420, 424, 427, 428, 462, 488, 535, 591. Trumbull, Governor Jonathan, of Connecticut, 394, 401. Tryon, William, Governor of New York, 467.
Van Campen, John, iv., 415, 416, 417. Vining, John, 338, 341. Virginia, Governor, 207.
Washington, General, George, iv., 644, 645-6, 775. Webb, James, 213. Westmoreland County, Trustees of, 449. Wickes, Capt. Lambert, 758, Wilkins, Colonel, 395. Williamson, Dr. Hugh, 364. Willson, George, 426, 455, 466. Wilson, Thomas, 108. Wynkoop, Henry, 702, 792.
Yeates, Abm., Cha'n, iv., 646. Young, James, 208, 210.
Alexander, Charles, v., 626. Anderson, Patrick, 26. Armstrong, Gen. John, 164, 229, 324, 558, 560, 563, 568, 572, 581, 587, 598, 636, 641, 645, 653, 672, 684. Arndt, John, 421. Arnold, Benedict, 367, 376. Assembly, 179, 264, 491, 681. Atlee, Col. S. J., 6, 10. Atlee, William, 248, 301, 327, 365, 376.
Bache, Richard, v., 409. Bailey, John, 405, 413. Bailey, William, 349. Bancroft, Daniel, 231, 246. Baxter, Lieutenant-Colonel, Wm., 31, Bayard, Capt. Jno., 106, 148. Becker, Lieutenant-Col., Henry, 485. Benezet, James, 469. Bensell, C., 11. Berks County, Committee, 111, 112, Biddle, Clement, 140, 145, 170, 197, 721, 739, 744. Biddle, Owen, 3, 11, 80, 105, 117, 148, 158, 182, 192, 249, 267, 301, 315. Bird, Mark, 9. Blaine, Col. Ephraim, 299, 677, Blair, James, 24, 50. Blewer, Jos,

Letters, v.—
120, 464, 713. Board of War, 268, 292, 306, 314, 320, 399, 583, 585, 683, 751, 756. Boggs, Major, 232. Bond, Phineas, 578. Bond, Dr. Thos., 78, 89, 383. Boudinot, Elias, 313, 443. Bowen, Capt. J. B., 114. Boyd, Alexander, 49. Boyd, Col. Andrew, 712, 748. Boger, Richard, 31. Bradford, William, 401, 430, 557, 575, 582, 615, 644, 648, 649, 663, 668, 707, 740, 745. Brodhead, Daniel, 21, 29, 158, 283, 345. Brown, Wm., 37, 106, 135. Bryan, Geo. V. P., 352, 463, 490, 514, 529, 530, 543, 574, 610, 661, 682. Buchanan, Wm., 552, 667, 677, 690, 711, 742, 744. Budden, James, 590, 591. Bull, Col. John, 59, 102, 201, 203, 208, 255, 304, 306, 709. Butler, Anthony, 553, 557.

Cadwalader, John, v., 95, 136, 160, 161, 178, 180, 186. Caldwell, Andrew, 261. Cameron, Allan, 383. Campbell, George, 269. Carothers, John, 634, 639. Casdorp, Thomas, 200. Chambers, David, 113. Chambers, Col. James, 364. Cheney, Col. 732. Chester County, Lieutenants, 475, 582, 629. Chew, James, 449. Christ, H. &c., 605, 633, 734. Clark, John, 699. Clark, Michael, 712. Clarkson, Dr. Gerardus, 165. Clinton, Gen. George, 676. Coats, Col. Wm., 158, 528, 766. Coleman, Robt., 39. College of Philadelphia, 198. Committee of Berks, 111, 112. Committee for driving off cattle, 473, 512, 545, 567, 610, 630. Committee of inspection, Cumberland, 79. Committee of Fifty, 473, 630. Com. of Lancaster, 251, 266, 349, 365. Committee of New York, 40. Committee of Safety, [which see.] Committee at Trenton, 69. Committee of Westmoreland, 313. Committee of Yorktown, 151. Congress, 137, 179, 217, 219, 244, 289, 290, 372, 411, 413, 435, 439, 471, 491, 575, 586, 592, 593, 599, 626, 627, 681, 688, 738, 768. Connolly, John, 101, 130, 242, 245, 297, 298. Connor, Colonel Morgan, 315. Conway, Gen. T., 522, 530. Cooke, William, 84. Corbley, John, 449. Council of Safety, [which see.] Council of Safety of Kent, 79. Creigh, John, &c., 628. Crispin William, 114, 681, 706, 748. Cross, William, 449. Cumberland County, 12, 77.

Davis, Col. v., 292. Davison, Commodore, Saml., 378. De Haven, Hugh, 569. De Haven, Peter, 155, 255, 606, 607. Delegates in Congress, 537. De Normandie, Dr. J. A. C., 176. Dewees, Thomas, 266. Dickinson, Gen. Philemon, 116, 117, 233, 244. Donaldson, &c., Joseph, 496, 534. Dorsey, Thomas, 534, 550. Downey, Capt. 431. Drummond, Dr. George, 511. Dundas, James, 616.

Elder, Robert, v., 753. Elmer, Jona'n, 7. Episcopal Churches, 600, 603. Eustace, J. P., 381. Evans, John, 246, 353, 529. Ewing, James, 146, 298. Eyers, Richard, 106. Eyre, Benjamin, 375. Eyers, Col. Jehu, 591.

Farmer, Capt. Lewis, v., 51. Fisher, Henry, 42, 47, 52, 61, 70, 99, 100, 108, 153, 263, 402, 465, 504. Flowers, Col. Benjamin, 27, 138, 181, 184, 369, 716. Forman, Brigadier-General, David, 435, 439.

Galbraith, Lieuten't-Col., Bartrem, v., 343, 353, 407, 409, 415, 457, 480, 486, 521, 532, 533, 543, 562, 573. Galbraith, Robert, 730. Gates, Major-General Horatio, 247, 687, 688. Gerry, E., 754. Gibson, John, 65. Giles, Edward, 437. Gregory, James, 334, 500, 588. Griffin, Col. Samuel, 127. Griffith, Capt. 328. Gronow, Lewis, 487, 732. Gurney, Col. Francis, 186.

Hale, Thomas, v., 203. Haller, Henry, 144, 250. Hamilton, James, 611, 613, 620. Hampton, John, 316. Hancock, John, P. C., 137, 179, 219, 289, 352, 491, 539, 544, 574, 586, 592, 589, 626, 627, 681. Hand, General Edward, 443, 540. Hand, H., 382. Hanni-

Letters, v.—
gan, Thomas, 253. Harris, John, 753, 758. Harshall, J., 211. Hart, Joseph, 18, 97, 237. Hartley, Thomas, 697. Hayes, Capt. 704. Hazelwood, Commodore John, 205, 602, 620, 663, 680, 696, 721, 747. Heard, Gen. Nathaniel, 262. Henry, Patrick, Jr., 260, 286. Henry, Col. William, 347, 472, 543, 634, 635. Hill, Col. Henry, 66, 94. Hiltzeimer, J., 354. Hodge, Andw., 148. Hooper, Robert Lettis, 689, Hopkinson, Francis, 489. Howell, Jacob S., 47, 55, 641. Hubley, Adam, Junr., 158, 358, 530, 533, 666, 698. Hubley, John, 102, 128, 295, 347, 415, 427, 505. Huff, Joseph, 72. Hunn, John, 450, 453, 462, 467, 468, 474, 475. Hunter, Lt. Samuel, 133, 244, 370, 377, 415, 610, 717, 737.

Ingersoll, Jared, v., 502. Irwin, Matthew, 613, 771.

Johnston, Francis, v., 125, 172. Jones, Morgan, 449. Joy, Daniel, 62, 121, 179.

Kirkbride, Joseph, v., 322, 331, 342, 368, 463, 465, 549, 567, 580. Knight, Peter, 239. Knox, Gen., 170. Kuhn, Ludwig, 93.

Labar, Colonel Abm., v., 320, 325. Lacey, Captain John, Jr., 154. Lancaster, Committee of, 251, 266, 365, 571, 762. Lang, James, 396. Lauman, Ludwig, 102. Laurens, Henry, 735. Lee, Richard Henry, 665. Leimback, Frederick, 524. Levers, Robert, 332, 618, 622, 623, 645, 650, 653, 717. Lieutenants of Counties, 297, 365, 379, 380, 424, 475, 521, 541, 545, 556, 582, 592, 615, 629, 660, 694. Livingston, Governor William, 238, 243, 251, 267, 294, 296, 301, 320, 328, 346, 348, 614, 621. Lochry, Archibald, 344, 488, 741. Lochry, W., 135. Loughead, James, 485. Lyon, Wm., 416.

McCalister, Richard, v., 330, 333. 335, 369, 412, 558, 633, 640, 767. McClean, Archd., 514, 536, 575, 661, 682, 704. McIlvaine, Wm., 509. Mackay, Æneas, 59, 92. McKinley, General, 34, 309, 456. Magistrates, 411, 421, 473, 504,

Letters, v.—
553, 599, 633. Marten, James, 436. Matlack, Timothy, 254, 323, 332, 337, 355, 357, 364, 469, 485, 487, 507, 602, 612, 616, 620, 659. Meade & Co., 61. Mease, James, 193. Mease & Caldwell, 104, 120. Meason, Captain Samuel, 445. Melchor, Colonel Isaac, 178, 206, 507, 527, 584, 653. Mercer, Hugh, General, 41, 67, 71. Mifflin, Jona., 86, 584, 594, 596, 597. Mifflin, General Thomas, 125, 375, 381, 490, 554, 720. Miles, S., 5. Minor, Captain John, 444. Mitchell, John, 62. Montgomery, Hugh, 37, 120. Moor, John, 66, 135. Morgan, George, 286, 313, 447. Morgan, Jacob, 299, 313, 322, 341, 407, 447, 466, 530, 608, 632, 756, 761. Morris, John, Jr., 161, 294, 481, 482, 506, 749. Morris, Lewis, 351. Morris, Rt., 28, 31, 126, 132, 138, 173, 174, 190, 216, 255, 379, 382, 626, 759, 760. Morris, Captain Samuel, 204. Morris, Samuel C., 108, 132.

Navy Board, State, v., 293, 346, 402, 425, 429, 446, 475, 488, 491, 501, 505, 510, 521, 538, 542, 590, 594, 602, 663, 696, 722. Navy Board, Continental, 319, 491. Nevill, John, 286. Nevell, Thomas, 64. Nelson, Thomas, 167. Nesbitt, Alexander, 240, 628. New York Committee, 40. Nice, Captain John, 427. Nicola, L., 7, 29, 71, 75, 78, 90, 92, 121, 148, 200, 354, 364, 410, 417, 600, 604, 608, 612, 619, 631. Nixon, John, 489.

Officers of the Army, v., 188. Old, James, 179, 398.

Paca, William, v., 635. Paine, Thomas, 659. Parke, Lieutenant Colonel Jno., 181. Patten, Major John, 40. Pennell, Joseph, 143, 197. Peters, Richard, 14. Philadelphia county, letter to, 660. Pintard, Lewis, 196. Piper, John, 149, 436. Potter, David, 86, 218, 305. Potter, General James, 433, 436, 440, 460, 511, 551, 570, 571, 718, 719, 738, 752, 755, 768. Potts, Jonathan, 350. Prisoners in Masonic Lodge, 604. Proctor, Colonel Jno., 202. Proctor, Thos., Major, 11, 33, 45, 50, 52, 97, 118,

Letters, v.—
130, 134, 141, 189, 192, 207, 234, 236, 249, 455. Putnam, General Israel, 118, 127, 163, 168, 170, 176, 196, 208, 215, 230, 232, 247, 282, 300, 676. Putnam, Daniel, 215.

Read, James, v., 20, 68, 138, 204, 258, 323, 463, 602. Read, John, 12, 21, 23, 24, 26, 47, 60, 68. Reed, Joseph, 109, 151, 289, 379, 692, 701, 702. Richards, Wm., 13, 47, 62, 166, 169, 242. Richardson, Joseph, 254. Rittenhouse, Benj., 743. Rittenhouse, David, 10, 62, 264, 357. Roberdeau, Daniel, 639, 659, 673, 726, 728, 735, 757, 770, 772. Ross, George, Jr., 704, 758. Rouget, Stephen Joseph, 569. Rush, Benjamin, 3, 38, 59.

Savadge, Thomas, v., 55, 194, 216, 217, 228, 418, 540, 763. Searle, James, 216. Seymour, Commodore, 67, 83, 104, 401, 577. Shee, Colonel John, 417. Shippen, Wm., 768. Simmons, Leeson, 538. Skinner, B. G. Cortland, 367. Smith, Robert, 8, 9, 37, 324, 426. Smyth, Hugh, 703. Sprogell, Ludick, 230. Stansbury, Jos., 94, 98. Stephens, General, 175. Stevenson, George, 68, 635. Stewart, Col. Walter, 401, 713. Stillwell, Nicholas, 453. Stirling, Lord, 157, 166, 170, 173, 174, 194. Stockton, Richard W., 317. 367. Sutter, James, 750. Supreme Executive Council, [which see.]

Tallman, Peter, v., 64. Taylor, George, 49. Thomson, Charles, 68. Thorne, Wm., 143. Tilghman, James, 156, 174, 502, 641. Tilghman, Tench, 674. Treasury, U. S., 334. Trenton, Committee at, 69. Trumbull, Jona'n, 657. Tyler, John, 731.

Vaughan, Major General John, (British,) v., 688. Virginia, delegates in C., 413. Virginians, 14.

Walters, John, v., 182, 245. War Office of Pennsylvania, 268, 281, 282, 283, 292, 294, 306, 314, 315, 319, 325, 328, 342, 345, 346, 348, 350, 355, 358, 364, 377, 382, 396, 398, 401, 409, 418, 427, 428,

Letters, v.—
434, 451, 471, 485, 540, 674, 683. War Office, Continental, 290, 382, 399, 430, 434, 439, 450, 502, 512, 535, 675, 683, 685, 686. Washington, General George, 113, 117, 253, 290, 373, 419, 431, 439, 452, 482, 510, 526, 617, 619, 624, 664, 669, 678, 691, 697, 710. Way, Nicholas, 315. Wayne, Colonel Anthony, 89. Weedon, Colonel G., 241. Wetzell, Lieutenant John, 85, 544. Wells, Richard, 189. Wetherill, Samuel, Jr., 342, 355. Wharton, John, 489. Whilldén, J., 382. Williams, Ennion, 34, 39, 51, 53, 80, 103, 105, 107, 112, 115, 117, 126, 204, 209, 212. Wirtz, Christian, 202, 208. Witman, Christopher, 111. Wood, Colonel Joseph, 87. Wynkoop, Henry, 32.

Adams, John & B. F., vi., 521. Antes, William, 456. Armstrong, Gen. John, 30, 43, 53, 60, 70, 84, 90, 100, 122, 148, 149, 230, 238, 293, 412, 489, 516, 612, 613, 635, 657, 661, 669, 680, 715, 717, 744. Arndt, John, 336. Arnold, Gen. Benedict, 687, 708, 748, 749. Assembly, 153, 369, 518, 685, 709. Attlee, Mr., 212. Auditor-Gen'l U. S., 591.

Bailey, Francis, and Capt. Lang, vi., 404. Bailey, James, 766. Bayard, Col. John, 60. Beaton, John, 494. Bedford Co., freeholders, 577. Berks Co. Commissioners, 521. Berks Co. Justices, 138, 722, Biddle, Col. Clement, 92, 104, 123, 139, 187, 220, 299, 321, 540, 738. Blaine, Eph., D. C. G., 252. Blewer, Capt. Joseph, 671. Board of War, Continental, 35, 42, 52, 63, 79, 84, 86, 93, 118, 127, 174, 184, 188, 192, 194, 205, 208, 214, 216, 234, 268, 281, 286, 339, 351, 360, 369, 393, 402, 429, 444, 454, 492, 515, 526, 533, 549, 556, 558, 576, 581, 586, 593, 605, 608, 643, 644, 646, 648, 649, 654, 655, 667, 668, 676, 684, 688, 727, 745, 749, 758. Bondfield, John, 172, 330. Boudinot, Elias, 89, 162. Boyd, Andrew, 355, 432, 483, 582, 646. Boyd, Colonel J., 596. Bradford, Colonel Wm., 11, 24, 27, 80, 204.

Letters, vi.—
Bradford, Wm. C., 451. Bridges, Robert, 718. Brodhead, Colonel Daniel, 462, 492, 660, 772. Bryan, Geo., V. P., 10, 108, 109. Buchanan, Arthur, 485, 487, 603. Buchanan, William, 34. Bull, Colonel John, 128, 133, 190, 746. Butler, Colonel Richard, 252, 386, 404. Butler, Colonel Zebulon, 690.

Cadwalader, Col. Lambert, vi., 655. Caldwell, Charles, 502. Carothers, John, 436, 438, 446, 467, 487, 491, 539, 559, 609, 719, 700. Chaloner, John, 320, 321. Chaloner & White, 761, 762. Chambers, John, 504. Circulars, 65, 88, 124, 179, 240, 294, 392, 431, 452, 638, 650. Clark, Abraham, &c., 367, 389. Clarke, John, Jr., 23. Claypoole, James, 624. Clymer, Daniel, 104. Coats, Colonel Wm., 227. Collectors of Clothing, 33. Commissioners for collecting Clothing, 179. Commissioners for collecting provisions, 278, 294, 329, 418, 431. Commissioners for seizing Estates, 13, 644. Commissioners of Bucks Co., 395. Commissioners of Chester Co., 561. Commissioners of Lancaster County, 531. Commissioners for Western Department, 386. Committee of Congress, 316. 363, 367, 384, 389, 677. Congress, to and from, 3, 9, 12, 30, 31, 41, 116, 136, 153, 158, 161, 176, 207, 208, 210, 211, 248, 249, 284, 298, 316, 318, 327, 340, 350, 351, 364, 394, 403, 448, 460, 485, 488, 493, 507, 523, 524, 589, 507, 607, 613, 657, 670, 671, 672, 708, 710, 712, 713, 726, 727, 737, 741, 754, 775. Combe, Rev. Thomas, Jr., 626. Council of Safety, 3, 4, 41. Cowell, Ebenezer, 51. Cox, John, 16, 29. Craig, Capt., 746. Craig, Robert, 41. Craig, Col. Thomas, 412. Crispin, Wm., 151, 174, 203, 440. Culbertson, Colonel Robert, 448.

Dana, Francis, vi., 318, 384. Davidson, James, 16. Davison, Hugh, 504. De Haas, J. P., 648. De Haven, Hugh, 58. De Haven, Peter, 52, 453, 474, 632. Delegates, of

Letters, vi.—
Penn'a in Congress, 4, 116, 136, 207, 231, 242, 269, 279, 299, 380, 455, 535, 577. Deshler, Colonel, 394. Donaldson, Joseph, &c., 775. Duane, James, 102. Duer, John, 276. Dunlap, James, 610.

Edwards, Thomas, vi., 449. Elder, Joshua, 615, 616. Ettwein, John, 751. Evans, Edward, 544. Evans, Colonel Thomas, 709. Evans, Wm., 731.

Ferguson, Mrs. Elizabeth, vi., 617. Fisher, Henry, 706. Flowers, Colonel B., 79, 135, 450, 463. Forrest, Major, 357. Forst, David, 296. Franklin, Benjamin, and Jno. Adams, 521. Furman, Moore, 439.

Galbraith, Lt. Bartrem, vi., 642, 648. Galbraith, Robert, 238, 511, 550. Galbraith, Thomas, 532. Galloway, Mrs. Joseph, 675. Garland, Captain George, 737. Gates, Gen. Horatio, Pres. B. of W., 205. Gerard, Mons., French Minister, 638, 671. Gibbon, Col. William, 530. Gibson, Colonel George, 319, 324, 553. Gourla, John, 443. Gray, Wm., and John Little, 377. Graeff, Matthias, 55. Greene, General Nathaniel, 444, 482, 530. Greer, Joseph, 395. Gronow, Lewis, 496. Grubb, Colonel C., 647.

Harberstick, Michael, vi,, 362. Hagner, Lt. Fred'k, 486. Hale, Thos., 628. Hambright, Captain John, 57, 532, 570, 626, 770. Hamilton, James, 372, 433, 456, 468, 469. Hand, General, 601. Harris, John, 211, 574. Harris, David, 32. Hart, William, 396, 431, 425. Hartley, Colonel Thomas, 351, 497, 674, 688, 690, 691, 612, 705, 729. Hazelwood, Commissioner, John, 47, 121, 132, 167, 181, 235, 246, 598, 724, 749. Henry, William, 558, 645. Hillegas, Michael, 538, 548, 565. Hoge, Jonathan, 610. Houston, Captain Thomas, 736. Hubley, John, 769. Hubley, Joseph, 145, 750. Hunter, Lt. Samuel, 57, 175, 191, 393, 478, 499, 537, 552, 564, 570, 571, 593, 599, 615, 524, 631, 637, 711, 773.

Letters, vi.—
Irvin, Matthew, vi., 156, 718, 726. Irvine, Colonel William, 726.
Jeffries, Joseph, vi., 349. Johnston, Colonel Francis, 732. Jones, Owen, Jr., 53, 54-56, 102, 106. Jones, Thomas, 38, 69, 107, 130, 247.
Keachline, Lieutenant, vi., 92, 107. Kirkbride, Colonel Joseph, 96, 175, 261, 262, 280, 503. Knox, Robert, 736.
Lacey, Brigadier-Gen., vi,, 168, 202, 226, 255, 265, 361, 381, 384, 390, 398, 402, 410, 414, 470, 579, 580, 594, 595. Laird Samuel, 550. Lancaster county commissioners, 531. Lebar, Colonel Abraham, 44. Lee, Francis Lightfoot, 82, 147, 276. Lee, Major, 440. Lesher, John, 170, 327, 347, 667, 675. Levan, Abraham, 406, 449, Levers, Robert, 5, 76, 140, 141, 341, 344, 346, 362, 381, 435, 464, 486, 534, 626, 719, 721. Levis, Thomas, 651. Lewis, William, 641. Lieutenants, 157, 169, 426, 452, 501. Livingston, Gov. Wm., 133, 453, 599, 604, 728. Lochrey, Colonel Archibald, 143, 459, 495. Lutterloh, Colonel, 210, 283, 322, 348, 352. Lyon, William, 228.
McCalister, Colonel Richard, vi., 22, 171, 196, 244, 369, 463, 479, 547, 706. McClean, Archibald, 294, 376. McDowell, Alexander, 572. McHenry, Captain, 732. Mackay, John, 400. McKean, Thomas, 266, 555, 566, 569. Maclay, Wm., 634. McGee, John, 38. Magistrates, 258. Marsteller, Philip, 264. Matlack, Timothy, 5, 10, 76, 82. Mease, James, 22, 426, 428. Melchor, Col. Isaac, 676, 699. Mitchell, John, 762, 763, 764. Morgan, Col. George, 587, 652, 714. Morgan, Jacob, L. B. C., 14, 47, 119, 288, 418, 522, 542, 563, 630. Morgan, Col. Jacob, 119. Morgan, Jacob, Jr., 382, 399, 441, 568, 575, 638. Morris, R., 45. Musser, John, 55.
Navy Board, State, vi., 24, 38, 110, 243, 332, 355, 421, 434, 517, 554, 696, 706, 745. Nesbit, John M., 652. Nicola, Col. Lewis, 179, 213, 358, 411, 656, 742.

Letters, vi.—
O'Neal, Dennis, vi., 498.
Patterson, Capt. Alex'r, vi., 432. Penn, John, 10. Peters, Richard, 72, 493. Pettit, Charles, 366, 513, 525, 620, 623, 738, 742. Phila. Co., Lieutenants of, 500. Pickering, Timothy, 173, 237, 528, 546. Piper, Col. John, 34, 36, 115, 138, 194, 229, 469, 505, 682. Pleasants, Samuel, 524. Porter, Captain Andrew, 574. Potter, General James, 51, 83, 89, 97, 98, 141, 150, 167, 169, 516, 517, 521, 603, 665, 729. Potts, Samuel, 595. Price, Philip, 695. Proctor, Col. John, 445, 458, 516, 659, 722. Proctor, Colonel Thomas, 676, 712.
Ralston, John, &c., vi., 747, 772. Rice, Robert, 722. Rea, Samuel, 611, 672. Read, Jas., 234, 245, 473. Recruiting Officers, 248, 280, 287, 288. Reed, Gen. Joseph, 120, 218, 712, 733, 739. Reigart, Ab'r., 626. Rittenhouse, David, 184, 643. Roberdeau, General Daniel, 10, 18, 130, 134, 144, 183, 207, 209, 214, 273, 287, 295, 359, 374, 422, 436, 446, 567, 583, 585, 609. Ross, George, 69. Ross, Col. Geo., Jr., 319, 324. Rudolph, Lt. John, 454. Rush, Jacob, 752. Russell, William, 286.
Sanders, William, vi., 716. Savadge, Thomas, 17, 159, 182, 236, 398, 401, 417. Scott, Abraham, &c., 647. Scott, Thomas, 673. Sergeant, Jonathan, D., 496, 630, 683, 740. Seymour, Comm'r Thos., 97. Shippen, Edward, 682. Shippen, Dr. Wm., 688. Skinner, Lt. Abraham, 625. Slough, Matthias, 53, 55. Smith, James, 270. Smith, Jonathan B., 109, 124, 160, 191, 232, 292, 303, 314, 350, 357, 359, 365, 371, 403, 420, 429, 466, 545. Smith, Lt , 92. Smith, Matthew, 632. Smith, Lt. Colonel Samuel, 4, 92, 107. Smith, Thomas, 39. Smith, Dr. Wm,, 621. Sprogel, Lodick, 678. Spyker, Henry, 391. Stevenson, George, 94. Stevenson, R., 653. Stewart, Lt. Col. George, 485, 517, 603. Stewart, Colonel Walter, 285, 343, 717. Stiles,

Letters, vi.—
Capt. Joseph, 480. Stoddart, Benj., 608. Stoy, Lieut., 717. Stroud, Col. Jacob, 651, 748. Sweers, Cornelius, 473.
Tilghman, Jas., vi., 96. Tilghman, Tench, 407. Thompson, J., 299.
Van Campen, John, vi., 767.
Wagon Masters, vi., 124, 212, 763, 765. Wallis, Samuel, 664, 787. Washington, Gen. George, 9, 30, 153, 156, 180, 188, 200, 201, 235, 241, 250, 254, 255, 263, 274, 277, 288, 291, 325, 333, 338, 353, 354, 357, 401, 405, 409, 410, 416, 425, 430, 445, 480, 490, 498, 522, 529, 546, 557, 558, 604, 742, 752. Watkins, Jos., 368. Watson, John, Jr., 769. Wayne, Gen. Anthony, 86, 142, 248, 251, 387, 397, 408, 411, 419, 429, 451, 474, 746. Weaver, N., 628. Wetzel, Lt. John, 270, 541, 551, 629, 651. Wharton, Pres. Thomas, 11, 12, 13, 14, 17, 18, 22. White Eyes, Capt., 587, 652. Wilcocks, John and Alexander, 740, 754. Wirtz, Major, 201. Wise, Frederick, 415. Woods, George, 39. Wynkoop, Henry, 600.
Young, Jas., vi., 75, 218, 259, 276, 282, 289, 320, 321, 322, 330, 337, 343, 357, 366, 519, 676, 761, 762, 763, 764, 765, 766.
Zantzinger, Paul, vi., 23.
Achilles, Brig, owners of, vii., 308. Adams, Samuel, 14, 763. Admiralty, Judge of, 694. Allen, Mrs., 452. Allison, Francis, Jr., 589, 591. Armstrong, Gen. John, 18. Arnold, Gen. Benedict, 256, 370. Artillery officers, 254. Assembly, 64, 77, 94, 100, 120, 142, 191, 202, 472, 693, 712, 720, 738. Atlee, Will'm, 674. Avery, John, Jr., of Mass., 477.
Baltimore, to Magistrates of, vii., 391. Barge & Tyng, 728. Bayard, John, 189, 311, 693. Baahm, Philip, 13. Blaine, Col. Ephraim, 403, 707. Bland, Col. Theo'd, 99, 107. Blythe, Col. Benjamin, 496. Board of War, 89, 90, 98, 99, 101, 201, 202, 227, 229, 230, 232, 233, 256, 282, 284, 286, 287, 289, 292, 305, 308, 312, 329, 332, 339, 340, 375, 385, 387, 397, 404,

Letters, vii.—
418, 420, 421, 424, 437, 442, 450 454, 456, 459, 460, 469, 480, 492, 493, 508, 539, 627, 640, 649, 676, 677, 681, 691, 696, 709, 710, 713, 719, 727, 730, 731. Boyd, Col. Andrew, 97, 471. Boys, Capt. Nathan, 201, 248, 566. Bradford, Thomas, 560. Bradford, W. C., 556. Brodhead, Col. Dan'l, 465, 505, 516, 521, 524, 541, 569, 710, 771. Brown, Capt. Alex'r, 515, Brown, John, 226, 240, 271. Bucks Co., Militia—Circular, 104. Bull, Col John, 240, 544, 635. Burke, Thomas, 170, 172. Butler, Col. Richard, 65, 482, 514. Butler, Col. Zebulon, 283. Buyers, John, 591. Campbell, Capt. Thomas, 301, 447. Carson, John, 437, 470, 637, 659, 699. Carothers, Col. John, 405, 618. Chesney, Will'm, 599. Circulars, 104, 105, 183, 304, 747. Clarkson, Matthew, 554. Claypoole, James, Sheriff, 252, 291, 360, 630, 765. Clingham, W. 158. Cluggage, Capt. Thomas, 512, 624, 659, 742. Coats, Lt. Col. William, 376, 377, 763, 764. Commercial Comm'e of Congress, 579, 605. Commissaries of purchases and issue, 304. Commissary Gen'l. of Issues, 587. Commissioners for procuring Salt, 769, Commissioners of forfeited Estates, 243. Commissioners for purchase of flour, 753, 766. Committee of City, 461. Congress, 13, 14, 75, 81, 89, 102, 106, 120, 127, 152, 243, 246, 261, 265, 270, 273, 304, 312, 313, 324, 347, 369, 374, 396, 417, 507, 513, 522, 532, 536, 552, 631, 647, 662, 664, 673, 695, 716, 738, 757, 761, 765. Delegates in, 134, 140, 141, 160, 162, 174, 181, 184, 189, 192, 478, 557, 639. Delegates from Virg'a, 184. Committee of, 84, 85, 88, 159. Marine Comm'ee, 12, 76, 120, 187, 235, 241, 588, 657. Connor Col. Morgan, 336. Conyngham, Capt. G., 319. Cook, Col. John, 593. Council of Massachusetts. 138. Cox, Col. John, 749. Craig, James, &c., 717. Crawford, James, &c., 760. Crispin, Wm., 200, 314. Cushing, Thomas, 250.

Letters, vii.—
Davis, Caleb, vii., 444. Deane, Jas. 11. De Haas, Gen. J. P. 330. De Haven, Peter, 133, 175, 195. Delaney, John, 94. Delany, Sharp, 762. Delapt, Rich'd, &c., 702. Delaware, Gov'r, of, 199. Delegates in Congress, 134, 140, 160, 162, 174, 181, 184, 189, 422, 551, 557, 639. Delegates in Congress from Virg'a, 184. Deshler, Charles 17. Dougherty, Bernard 186, 297. Drayton, Wm. H., 328, 335. Dundas, James, &c., 140, 253, 326, 333. Dunlap, John, 201. Du-Portail, Brig. Gen. Le Ch., 272, 279, 280, 366, 399, 403, 409, 690. Du Simitiere, 212.
Eckert, Valen'e, vii., 552. Edwards, Major, 107, 152. Eichelberger, Jacob, 491, 530. Elder, Joshua, 592. Erwin, Capt. Joseph, 563. Ettwein, Rev'd John, 295. Eyre, Benj. G. &c., 644. Eyre, Col. Jehu, 457.
Farmer, Col. Lewis, vii., 273, 689, 754, Farmer, Michael, 453. Fire Companies, 134. Fisher, Henry, 390, 410, 705, 730. Fitzsimons, Thos 407. Flower, Col. Benj. 294, 296, 385. Franklin, Benj., 774.
Galbraith, Colonel Bartrem, vii., 370, 507, 522, 611, 699. Galbraith, Col. Rob't, 18, 74, 99. Galloway, Mrs. Joseph, 93, 95. Gerard, Mons'r, Fr. Min., 16, 17, 61, 62, 70, 83, 164, 169, 185, 269, 278, 595, 604, 633, 648, 651, 653, 708. Governors of States, 152, 197. Greene, Major, Gen. Nath'l, 175, 179. Greenwalt, P. 287. Gregg, Matthew, 334. Grube, Rev'd B., A. D., 521. Gurney, Francis, 495,
Hackenwelder, John, vii., 516, 524. 541. Hagner, Will. &c., 677, Hagner, Col. 777. Hale, Thos. 688. Hall, Charles, 651. Haller, Col. Henry, 488. Hambright, John, 311, 323, 519. Hand, Gen. Edward, 321, 344, 715. Harbeson, Benj'n, &c., 102, 154. Hardie, Robert, 91, 92. Harding, Capt. 761. Harris, David, 638. Harmar, Lt. Col. Joseph, 750. Hartley, Col. Thomas, 3, 5, 9, 81, 86, 87, 91, 258, 391, 694, 776. Hay, John, 694. Hazelwood, Comm'r, John,

Letters, vii.—
19, 112. Henry, George, 139, 190, 239, 333, 365, 423. Henry, Gov. Patrick, 247, 441. Henry, Col. William, 359, 416, 456, 514, 557, 599, 600, 667, 710. Hertzel, Jonas, Sh'ff, 655. Hervey, Maj. George, 566. Hewitt, Thomas, &c., 545. Hodge, Andrew, 319. Hoffman, Stokely, 737, Holker, Mons. 137, 238, 498, 502, 503, 510, 513, 531. 532, 558, 560, 580, 601, 628, 641, 669, 675, 678, 682, 683, 686, 699, 701, 703, 713. Hopkinson, Francis 558, 694. Hubley, Lt. Col Adam, 366, 498, 553, 596, 721, 755. Hubley, John, 297, 667. Hunter, Lt. Samuel, 116, 316, 346, 375, 438, 455, 510, 536, 546, 574, 589, 590, 594, 615, 619. Hutchinson, Dr. James, 408.
Imlay, John, vii., 264. Irwin, Barclay, &c., 198, 246, 263, 265, 266. Irwin & Bridges, 314. Irwin, Matthew, 246, 261, 265, 311, 734, 765. Irwin, Thomas, 147.
James Abel, vii., 758. Jameson, David, 491, 529, 652. Jameson, D. & J. Eichelberger, 529. Jennings, Michael, 311, 359. Jennifer & Root, 750. Johnson, Gov. of Md., 125. Johnston, Col. Francis, 411, 581. Jordan, Jessie, 191. Joy, Capt. Daniel, 562. Judges of Supreme Court, 773.
Kackline, Andrew, vii., 775. Kendall, Jos., 410. Kirkbride, Joseph, 108. Knox, John, 433.
Lang, Capt. James, vii., 537, 538, 567. Leaming, T. & G., Henry, 422. Lee, Richard, Henry, 73. Levan, Dan'l, 610. Levers, Robert, 15, 176,. Lieutenants, 267, 275, 486, 650, 747. Livingston, Gov. Wm. 260, 474, 480, 492. Lochery, Col. A., 173, 362, 363, 430, 564, 754, 769. Lowell, Hon. James, 477. Louden, Sam'l, 206. Loughhead, James, 531, 673, 764. Lyon, William, 144, 399.
McAlester, Col. Rich'd, vii., 110, 115, 367, 399, 414, 427. McCalla, William, 620. McCulloh, Capt. John, 371, 506. McClenachan, B. & C. 248, 252, 267, 281, 285, 288, 309, 310, 318, 322, 343, 364, 397, 442, 768. McElheney, George, 315.

Letters, vii.—
McGinley, Capt. John, 652. McHenry, Capt. Matthew, 384. McKean, Thomas, C. J., 21, 225, 274, 279, 328, 637, 644, 699, 703, 732, 735, 744. Maclay, William, 192, 357, 586, 590, 591, 593, 597, 598, 621. McPherson, Capt. John, 180. Marine Committee of Congress, 12, 76, 120, 187, 235, 241, 588, 657. Marshall, Christopher, 668. Marsteller, Col. Phillip, 567, 716. Martin, Col. 416. Maryland, Gov. of, 197. Massachusetts, Council of, 138, 231. Maxwell, Gen. Wm. 178. Miller, H. & J. Clark, Jr., 609. Mitchell, John, 160, 189, 213, 248, 262, 345, 412, 474, 527, 746. Montgomery, Capt. James, 454, 476, 487, 521, 532, 706, 755. Moore, Thomas, 543. Morgan, Col. Jacob, Jr., 483, 484, 559. Morris, A. James, 760. Morris, J. Jr., 120, 309, 310. Morris, Robert, 125, 386, 417, 608. Murray, William, 432. Myers, Jacob, &c., 745.

Navy Board, vii., 695. Neilson, Captain John, 74. Nesbit, J. M., 210, 228, 234, 247. New Jersey, Delaware and Virginia, 152, 197. Nicholson. Captain, 488. Nicola, Major Lewis, 72, 190, 203, 255, 358, 362, 364, 387, 484, 489, 492, 509, 519, 523, 526, 548, 549, 561, 562, 574, 625, 632, 635, 641, 643, 646, 648, 663, 674, 682, 698, 701, 767, 769, 775. Northampton County, Colonels of, 616.

Officers at Billingsport and M. I., vii., 409, 424, 502, 720, 745, 747. Orndt, John, 625. Owners of Brig Achilles, 308.

Patterson, Alexander, vii., 527. Patterson, William Augustus, 167. Peale, Charles Wilson, 384. Pearson, John, 70. Pettit Chas., A. Q. M. G., 196, 335, 399, 420, 421, 433, 460, 481, 495. Philadelphia Justices, 658. Phyle, Dr. F., (Naval Officer) 185. Pickering, Timothy, 656. Piper, Col. John, 578. Pitcairn Captain, P., 374. Pomroy, Ralph, 312. Potter, General James, 418. Printers of Newspapers, 136, 201, 206. Proctor Thomas, 121, 123, 125, 146,

Letters, vii.—
260, 270, 290, 298, 405, 423, 440, 476, 485. Pulaski, General Count, 233. Purchasers of flour, 548, 692. Purchasers of Salt, 728.

Read, James, vii., 289. Read, John, 272. Reading, Geo., 345. Recruit'g Officers, 300. Reed, Bowes, 262. Reed, President J., (see Supreme Executive Council). Risberg, Gustavus, 550. Rittenhouse, Benjamin, 142. Rittenhouse, David, 302. Roberdeau, General Daniel, 100, 137, 159, 167, 181, 184, 192, 195, 197, 236, 296, 299, 643. Rogers, Rev. William, 253, 273, 449. Root, Hon. Jesse, 774. Ross, Geo., 212, 451, 468. Rush, Dr. Benj., 408. Rush, Joseph, and J. Craig, 303. Ryan, Philip, 541.

St. Clair, General Arthur, vii., 237, 291, 355, 452, 491, 500, 582, 607, 665, 736. Savadge, Thos., 96, 109, 111, 116. Scammell, Alex., 649. Scott, Thomas, 434. Scott, Wm., 118, 206. Schuyler, Philip, 11, 75. Scull, Major, Sec. B. W., 469. Searle, Hon. James, 141. Sergeant, Jona. D., 267, 275, 395, 743. Sheriff, High, of Philadelphia, 252. Shippen, William, 209. Shoemaker, Lieut. Jacob, 632, 688. Smith, George, 164. Smith, Colonel Matthew, 280, 306, 472, 574, 589, 606, 609, 614, 747. Smith, Merriweather, 73. Smith, Thomas, 696. Sprogel, Lodick, 129, 550. Stanley, Dr. Valentine, 165. Steuben, Baron, 199, 325. Stevenson, R., 206. Stewart, Colonel Walter, 9, 660. Stiles, Captain Joseph, 141, 238, 358. Straker, William, 71, 72. Stroud, Colonel Jacob, 63, 613. Sub-Lieutenants, 105. Sullivan, Gen. John, 94, 120, 211, 388, 427, 439, 450, 457, 473, 568, 593, 594, 756, 768.

Thompson, Hon. James, vii., 632. Thompson, William, vii., 65.

Urie, Thomas. vii., 534.

Van Campen, John, vii., 573, 574, 603. Virginia, Delegates, in Congress, 184. Governor of, 197. Wade, Captain, vii., 12. Wade, Francis, 412. Wadsworth, Jere-

Letters, vii.—
miah, 159, 672. Wall, Colonel Geo., Jr., 103, 104, 660. Walker, Captain Andrew, 323. Wardens of Philadelphia, 627. Washington, General George, 89, 95, 119, 127, 129, 161, 188, 211, 225, 236, 293, 327, 337, 341, 351, 377, 407, 447, 479, 535, 555, 626, 670, 671, 684. Wayne, General Anthony, 64, 142, 255. Westbrooke, Major Samuel, 63. Wetherill, Samuel, Jr., 172. Wetzel, Colonel, John, 299, 572, 579, 617. Whiteside, Thomas, 19. Wilcocks, Alex'r and John, 122, 148, 721, 725, 727. Will, William, &c., 759. Wilkinson, General J., 449, 744. Woods, George, 534.

Young, James, vii., 98, 148, 151.

Zeigler, Captain David, vii., 368.

Active, agents of sloop, viii., 209. Adams, John, 399, 563. Admiralty, 542. Agents of Confiscated Estates, 735, 760. Allen, Ira, 88. Amberson, Wm., 487. American Philosophical Society, 136. Antes, Frederick, 219. Armstrong, Major General John, 31, 152, 241, 636. Armstrong, Major William, 34, 311, 599. Assembly, 262, 280, 609, 625, 656, 658, 663, 687, 693, 737, 758. Atlee, Colonel Samuel J., 216, 241, 250, 305, 311, 333, 335, 351, 423, 437, 438, 469, 484, 524, 580, 673. Atlee, Hon. Wm., (Judge) 56, 124. Auditors of soldiers' accounts, 762.

Bailey, James, viii., 390. Baker, Hilary, Jr., 720. Balliet, Lieut. Colonel Stephen, 564. Battalions, Colonels of, 111. Bayard, Hon. J., 247. Bedford, inhabitants of, 749. Beelor, Colonel Joseph, 583. Bell, Major, 287. Berks County, Commissioners of Taxes, 124, 133, 138. Biddle, James, 136. Biddle, Owen, 151, 169, 223. Blaine, Ephraim, 13, 260, 304, 479, 480, 494, 565, 579, 603, 631, 646, 703. Blythe, Benjamin, 96. Board of War, 5, 8, 38, 40, 43, 57, 62, 74, 96, 98, 110, 122, 132, 141, 153, 159, 161, 165, 171, 175, 181, 224, 248, 269, 308, 343, 425, 433, 434, 435, 436, 442, 453, 456,

Letters, viii.—
471, 478, 485, 498, 502, 505, 506, 507, 508, 509, 549, 552, 554, 573, 575, 579, 580, 581, 600, 601, 611, 632, 689, 704, 722, 727, 728, 739, 747. Boyd, Colonel A., 12, 322. Boys, Captain Nathan, 228, 254, 728. Bradford, Thomas, 97, 502. Bradford, William, Jr., Attorney General, 621, 666, 725, 730, 760. Bradford, William, (Pres. of H. C.,) 616. Brady, Capt., Samuel, 565. Brodhead, Colonel Daniel, 21, 22, 38, 42, 50, 65, 66, 68, 89, 106, 108, 119, 120, 140, 149, 152, 158, 197, 210, 218, 246, 249, 300, 378, 513, 515, 536, 558, 565, 583, 584, 585, 588, 595, 596, 640, 641, 743, 766. Bull, Colonel John, 164. Butler, Colonel Richard, 607, 741, 748. Butler, Lieut. Colonel William, 747. Butler, Colonel Zebulon, 601, 632.

Campbell, Captain Thomas, viii., 36. Caswell, Richard, Governor, N. C., 191. Chaloner & White, 248. Circulars, 20, 111, 145, 202, 251, 277, 292, 441, 447, 454. Clarke, Capt. John, 68. Clarkson, Matthew, 498, 500. Claypoole, James, Sheriff, 117, 321. Clinton, George, Governor of New York, 132, 179. Cluggage, Maj. Robert, 278. Coats, Colonel William, 42. Colonel of City Battalions, 309. Commissaries Gen'l of purchases, 240, 720. Commissary of supplies, 287. Commissioners for procuring flour, 84. Commissioners of Philadelphia County, 80. Commissioners of purchases, 277, 441. Commissioners for salt, 4, 24, 28. Commissioners of Taxes of Berks County, 124, 133, 138. Commissioners of Taxes, 125. Commissioners of Virginia, 91. Committee of Assembly, 694, 737, 758. Committee of Congress, 694. Committee of co-operation of Congress, 266, 315, 337, 338, 355, 356, 414. Committee of merchants of Philadelphia, 306. Congress, 20, 75, 85, 87, 98, 99, 135, 143, 199, 202, 203, 229, 251, 263, 277, 299, 325, 334, 340, 343, 348, 375, 395, 417, 429, 458, 515, 517, 529, 534, 535, 560, 583, 590,

Letters, viii.—
606, 609, 635, 639, 657, 685, 702, 703, 719, 722, 723, 724, 744, 751. Congress—Delegates of State in, 9, 46, 61, 160, 191, 392, 494, 643, 703, 722, 744, 757. Committee of, 53, 239, 266, 281, 293, 312, 314, 338, 404. Delegates of Connecticut in, 111, 112, 351. Marine Committee of, 231. Connecticut Delegates in Congress, 111, 112, 351. Conolly, Dr. John, 104. Convention at Hartford, 616, Cox, John, 406.

Davis, David, viii., 382, 458. Dean, Joseph, 712, 734. De Corny, Mons., 383, 406, 416. De La Fayette, Major General, 587. De La Luzerne, Chev., 448, 449. Delegates in Congress, 9, 46, 61, 160, 191, 392, 494, 643, 703, 711, 722, 744, 757. Delegates of Connecticut in Congress, 111, 112, 351. Denny, David, 496. Deshler, David and Charles, 300, 517, 699, 702, 711, 721. Digges, Lieut. Gov. of Virginia, 510. Dickinson, Philemon, 507, 736. Doz, Andrew, 154, 169, 412. Duane, James, 629, 659. Duncan, Stephen, 597. Du Portail, Mons., 37.

Eckhart, Valentine, viii., 529. Edwards, Colonel Thomas, 237, 288. Elder, Joshua, 101. Elliot, Andrew, 620. Ellsworth, Oliver, 261. Erwin, Captain, Joseph, 79. Espy, David, 102. Ethcart, Captain, (French) 546. Eyre, Major Benjamin G., 144.

Farmer, Colonel Lewis, viii., 52, 704. Fayette, Marquis De La, 587. Ferguson, Elizabeth, 4. Ferris, Owen, 229. Fisher, Henry, 216. Flint, Royal, 70. Flower, Colonel Benjamin. 26. Forman, David, 332. Forsman, Hugh, 697. Forsyth, Major, 510, 577. Franks, David S., 589, 611, 615, 619. French Consul, 90. French Minister, (Luzerne,) 45, 615, 628. Furman, Moore, 143, 146.

Gamble, James, viii., 177. Geddes Captain, 49. Gillespie, George, 481. Govett, William, and W. Geddes, 73. Greene, Major Gen. Nathaniel, 150, 151, 165, 381, 426, 475. Guyho, Capt., (French) 546.

Letters, viii.—

Hackenwelder, John, viii., 152, 770. Haffa, Henry, 704. Hale, Thomas, 112, 115. Hall, Charles, 54, 118, 194. Hall, David, and H. Fisher, 216. Haller, Henry, 83, 416, 430. Hamilton, William, 591. Hand, General Edward, 135, 184, 425. Hannum, Colonel John, 244, 324. Harmar, Colonel Joseph, 188. Harris, John, 550. Hart, John, 750. Hart, Colonel Joseph, 326, 327, 356, 503, 523, 717. Hayes, John, Jr., 317. Hazen, Colonel Moses, 105, 645. Hazelwood, John, 653. Heath, William, 6. Heister, Daniel, Jr., 697. Henry, Colonel William, 30, 116, 207, 309, 380, 423, 652, 667, 685, 730, 754, 761, 769. Hewitt, Thomas, 528. Hillegas, Michael, 402, 492, 493. Hodgdon, Samuel, 174, 746. Holker, Mons., 11, 87, 90, 94, 134, 147, 148, 347, 350, 365, 366, 396, 402, 540, 545, 546, 550, 552, 571, 750. Hopkinson, Francis, 241, 245, 390, 412, 500, 667. Howell, Jacob S., 247. Hubley, Colonel Adam, 512, 755, Hubley, John, 83, 389, 394, 400, 586. Huffnagle, Michael, 569. Hunter, Colonel Samuel, 29, 157, 166, 189, 205, 369, 392, 567, 601, 632, 717. Huston, Lieut. and Adjutant W., 153.

Irvine, General James, viii., 660, 663, 664. Irvine, General Wm., 74, 103, 206, 225, 232, 238, 245, 409, 511, 512, 540, 578, 642. Irwin, Captain John, 771. Irwine, Captain Joseph, 68. Irwin, Colonel Samuel, 637. Irwin, Thos., &c., 137. Jackson, David, 541. Jefferson, Thomas, Governor of Virginia, 196, 641. Col. Francis Johnston, 410. Rev. David Jones, 752. Jones, Thomas, Jr., 303.

Kern, Lieutenant Nicholas, viii., 213. Knox, General H., 253, 349, 358, 726. Kryder, Conrad, 433, 489. Kucher, Christopher, 288, 289, 324. Kuhn, Dr. Adam, 585.

Lacey, General, viii., 178, 505, 508, 526, 750. Lanctot, Godfrey, 551. Land office to be opened, 94. Land Officers, 307. Lane,

Letters, viii.—
William, 360. Leary, Dennis, 531. Lee, Major Henry, Jr., 56, 67, 457, 479, 599. Lee, Thomas Sim, (Governor of Maryland,) 330, 354, 432, 433. Lewis, William, 231. Lieutenants, County, 72, 387, 454, 476, 519. Livingston, William, Governor of New Jersey, 138, 314, 576, 624, 634, 636, 648. Lochry, Colonel Archibald, 42, 50, 65, 66, 69, 77, 282, 290, 318, 405, 518. Loughead, James, 567. Lutz, Nicholas, 201, 301, 313, 342, 357, 367, 399, 417, 438, 474. Luzerne, Chev. de la, 45, 334, 368, 448, 449, 540, 543, 615, 629. Lyndermood, Colonel Michael, 230, 236. Lyon, Samuel, 439, 715.

McCalister, Richard, viii., 16. McCalla, William, 212, 661. Maclay, William, 156, 172. McClean, Archibald, 14, 126, 144, 280, 731, 745. McClenachan, Blair, &c., 3. McElroy, Archibald, 323. McGuire, Matthew, 756. McKean, C. J. Thomas, 14, 178, 234, 298, 331, 403, 597, 649, 650, 654, 657. McLane, Captain Allen, 258. McLeery, William, 584. McLene, James, 61. McMullin, William, (Agt.) 282. McPherson, Major W., 617. Mahingwegeesuch, 769. Managers of House of Employment, 725, 726. Marine Committee of Congress, 231. Marsteller, Colonel Philip, 50, 155, 328, 362, 371, 383. Mason George, 287. Mason, John, 373. Massachusetts, Council of, 522. Matlack, Colonel Timothy, 60, 112, 502, 503. Matthews, Colonel G., 660. Melchor, Colonel Isaac, 65. Merchants of Philadelphia, 266, 306, 703. Miles, Col. Samuel, 533, 600, 608, 618, 699, 718, 719. Militia Officers, 265. Miller, Rev. Peter, 606. Minister of France, 615. Miralles, Don Juan, &c., 174. Mitchell, John, 186, 334, 500, 501, 716. Montgomery, Rev. Joseph, 170. Morgan, Col. Jacob, 238, 344, 368, 369, 449, 544, 594, 702. Morgan, Lieutenant Jacob, 273. Morris, Robert, 372, 415. Morris, Samuel, 699.

Letters, viii.—
Morris, Captain Samuel, 310. Morris, Samuel (Register), 228. Morris, Samuel, Jr., 308. Moylan, Colonel Stephen, 183. Muhlenberg, F. A., 123.

Navy Board, viii., 346, 553. Nicholson, John. 73. Nicola, Colonel Lewis, 12, 95, 100, 108, 181, 262, 316, 358, 363, 376, 378, 389, 391, 415, 423, 469, 510, 516, 669-682, 724, 750.

Officers of Militia, viii., 265. Of land office, 307. To Assembly, 693. Oster, (French V. Consul,) 604.

Paine, Thomas, viii., 21, 226. Patton, John, 502. Peale, Chas. Wilson, 319. Penet, P., 257. Peters, Rich'd, 119. Pettit. Chas., 104, 143, 146, 197, 211, 223, 320, 342, 406, 614. Philadelphia Co. Commissioners, 80. Philadelphia Library Company, 183. Philadelphia merchants, 266, 306. Phyle, Dr., 547. Physic, Edmund, 113. Pickering, Colonel Timothy, 499, 503, 604. Piper, Colonel John, 234, 278, 297, 302, 319, 349, 489, 530. Potter, Gen. James, 484, 561, 689, 710. Potts, Dr. John, 96. Powell, Jeremiah, President of Mass. Bay, 254. Powell, Col. Leven, 767. Presidents of Council of C. P., 622, 658. Prisoners of war at New York, 619, 620, 626. Proctor, Colonel John, 217, 284. Proctor, Colonel Thomas, 710. Prothonotaries, County, 58. Purchasers of flour, 3. Purviance, Samuel, Jr., 644.

Quemahoning, Inhabitants of, viii., 531.

Rea, Samuel, viii., 213, 221, 222, 227, 259, 286, 320, 386, 560, 592, 640, 683, 729. Recruiting officers, 290. Reid, Major James, 44. Revol, Captain (French), 546. Reynolds, John, 690. Rice, Patrick, 33. Riche, Mrs. Anne, 141. Risberg, Gustavus, 210. Rittenhouse, David, 657, 662. Roach, Isaac, 254, 339. Roberdeau, General Daniel, 5. Roberts, Jehu, 296. Rodney, Governor of Delaware, 10. Rowan, William, 23.

Letters, viii.—
Ryan, Lieut. Colonel, Michael, 371, 582, 656.
St. Clair, General Arthur, viii., 168, 374. 397, 515, 537, 669, 672, 690, 691, 701, 721, 723. Schott, Captain John Paul, 24. Scott, Hon. Thomas, 63, 280, 569, 713. Scott, Colonel William, 365, 379, 382, 408, 434, 524, 531, 623. Scull, Major Edward, 368, 655. Scull, William, 94. Searle, Jas., 515, 532. Sergeant, Jona. D., 6, 498, 613. Shippen, Joseph, Jr., 200. Shippen, Dr. William, 643. Smith, Mr., 311. Smith, Lieutenant Colonel Abraham, 443, 491, 522. Smith, Colonel George, 52. Smith, Colonel Matthew, 23, 249, 417, 513, 691. Smith, Richard, 740. Smith, Lieut. Robert, 455, 535. Smith, Thomas, 113. Smith, Wm., 415. Steel, Archibald, 21. Steuben, Baron, 270. Stevenson, George, 50, 107, 141. Stewart, Charles, 698. Stiles, Joseph, 139. Stroud, Colonel Jacob, 9, 176, 188. Swaine, Francis, 34, 76, 117, 428, 431, 433.
Thomson, Charles, viii., 550. Thompson, John, 413. Treasurers, County, 58. Treasury, U. S., 92, 185.
University of Pennsylvania, viii., 246, 643.
Van Campen, John, viii., 262, 683. Vankemp, John, 551. Vanderen, John, Jr., 594. Virginia Commissioners, 91.
Wade, Francis, viii., 274. Wadsworth, General Jeremiah, 205. Wagonmasters, 444, 447. Wall, George, 178. Waln, Nicholas, 81, 100. Washington, General George, 35, 36, 43, 48, 54, 70, 74, 75, 117, 128, 145, 155, 163, 180, 193, 214, 240, 267, 292, 312, 314, 338, 339, 356, 361, 373, 377, 414, 470, 474, 482, 486, 525, 577, 598, 682, 687. Watts, Colonel Frederick, 558. Wayne, Gen. Anthony, 450, 451, 587, 593, 680. Wetzel, John, 602. Weltner, Col. Lund., 40, 57, 62, 161, 171, 233, 341. West, William, Jr., 631. Westmoreland Representatives, 709.

Letters, viii.—
Wharton, James, 766. Wilkinson, James C. G., 269. Will, Wm., 638. Willet, Augustin, 305. Williams, Benseller, 63. Wilson, James, 541, 542. Wirtz, Christian, 187, 192, 304, 311, 328, 398, 575, 602, 632, 653, 667. Witman, Adam, 129, 264, 303, 742. Wynkoop, Henry, 557, 572.
York County, Lieutenants of, viii., 444.
Zeigler, Captain David, viii., 59, 209. Zeisberger, David, 158.
Admiralty, Board of, ix., 95, 100, 106. Agnew, John, 135. Anderson, Thomas, 175. Antes, Wm., 381. Arbuthnot, Capt. Alexander, 574. Armstrong, John, Jr., 650. Arndt, John, 53, 109, 136, 175. Ashman, George, 154, 202. Assembly, 5, 16, 51, 61, 188, 197, 219, 221, 231, 241, 248, 412, 425, 447, 459, 461, 463, 467, 501, 509, 510, 513, 620. Committee of, 14, 62, 415, 515. Atlee, William, 170, 203, 335, 347, 596. Auditors of Bucks county, 11, 13, 17, 29, 36, 67. Chester county, 12. Of State, 104. York county, 18.
Bailey, Jas., ix., 160. Baker, Hilary, Jr., 195. Balliott, Stephen, 649. Barclay, Thomas, 563. Barras, Mons. De, 353, 354. Beatty, John, 125. Biddle, Clement, 129. Blaine, Col. Ephraim, 54, 72. Blair, Rev. Samuel, 111. Board of Admiralty, 95, 100, 106. Board of War, 3, 7, 14, 19, 23, 24, 26, 31, 53, 57, 58, 96, 103, 111, 124, 150, 167 186, 187, 198, 206, 290, 291, 391, 526, 527. Board of Wardens of Philadelphia, 101. Boys, Capt. Nathan, 175, 416. Bradford & Hall, 266. Bradford, Thomas, 338, 380. Bradford, William, Jr., Att. G., 199, 266, 272, 407, 408, 515, 526, 553, 576, 656, 659, 676, 690, 695, 631, 750. Brodhead, Col. Daniel, 39, 51, 52, 57, 169, 365, 379. Brown, William, 641. Bryan, V. P., 279, 288, 299, 305, 309, 384, 422. Bucks county Auditors, 11, 13, 17, 29, 36. Butler, Col. Richard, 561, 664. Buchanan, Arthur, 192.

Letters, ix.—
Caldwell, A., ix., 480. Caldwell, S., 520. Campbell, Captain Thomas, 435. Carrington, Lieut. Edward, 487. Cessna, Charles, 467. Chambers, Col. Maxwell, 292. Christ, Henry, 80, 133, 196, 237, 347. Christie, Capt. Jacob, 385. Circulars, 226, 252, 548. Clarke, Brig. Gen. G., 23, 137, 189, 331. Clark, Walter, 381. Clarkson, John L., Sec. Treasurer, 226, 229. Claypoole, Capt. James G., 278, 376. Coats, Col. William, 250, 272, 325, 358, 377, 535. Commissioners for defence of Delaware, 531, 586, 618, 621, 625, 647, 672. On Connecticut claim, 624, 683, 686, 688, 689, 691, 692, 693. Commissioners of Northumberland, 440. Cumberland county, 737. Commissioners of taxes Philadelphia county, 116, 139, 328, 478. Committee of Assembly, 14, 62. Of Congress, 281. Congress, Pres. of, 20, 43, 54, 71, 75, 76, 81, 83, 84, 94, 102, 108, 110, 112, 124, 151, 162, 163, 194, 210, 242, 267, 273, 284, 309, 370, 395, 400, 416, 423, 433, 441, 448, 463, 475, 479, 518, 523, 548, 560, 561, 686, 757. Delegates to, 103, 163, 306, 420. Delegates of Virginia, 260, 266, 269, 274, 763. Congress circular, 252. Connecticut, agent, 681, 682, 683, 685, 686, 691. Connecticut, Gov. of, 629. Cook, Col. Edward, 629. Cook, William, 411. Cooper, Leonard, 424. Cooper, Ensign William, 750. Craig, Capt. Isaac, 497. Craig, Capt. Thomas, 503. Crispin, Wm., 437. Cummins, Lieut., 28. Cummins, Major J. R., 20, 24. Cunningham, Hon. James, 495, 606.
Dalley, Gifford, ix., 274. Dean, Wm., 358. De Barras, Mons., 353, 354. Delegates of State in Congress, 103, 163, 306, 420, 434, 763. Delegates of Virginia in Congress, 260, 266, 271, 274. Depui, Nicholas, &c., 105, 112. Dickinson, John, Gov. Del., 494, 731, 734. Donnahill, John, 671. Dougherty, Bernard, 467, 539, 543, 546, 553, 557, 619, 628. Dove, R., respecting a pass, 625. Dubois, Abraham, 48, 67. Duffield, Rev. George, 493.

Letters, ix.—
Duncan, D., ix., 17, 97, 190, 200, 305, 380, 606. Du Portail, Brig. General, 210. Dyer, Eliph., & J. Root, 683.
Eckart, Valentine, ix., 225, 230, 433. Edwards, Major, 75.
Fayette, Marq's de la, ix., 626. Field officers, 187. Forrest, Lieut. Col. T. 231. Fowler, Alexander, 114. Franklin, Dr. Benj., 669.
Gardner, Dr., ix., 628. Geiger, Col. Henry, 396. Gibson, John, 190. Girty, Thomas, 40. Glonenger, John, 655. Goforth, William, 48, 67. Gordon, Major James, 673. Governor of New York, 629. Connecticut, 626.
Hall, Charles, ix., 294, 321. Hattie, Henry, 237. Hambright, John, 336. Hammell, William, 330. Hannum, John, 758. Harrison, Gov. Benj., of Virginia, 518, 533, 549, 562, 607. Hart, John, 55, 128, 291, 338, 376. Hart, Colonel Joseph, 507, 529. Hartley, Mr., 639. Hayes, Christopher, 141, 300, 354, 368, 404, 469, 631. Hays, Col. John, 428. Hazard, Ebenezer, 449. Hazelwood, John, 38, 133, 425. Hazen, Brig. General Moses, 643. Henry, John, 573. Henry, William, Esq., 6, 138, 139, 154, 171, 205, 476, 574. Higgins, Andrew, 413. Holker, Mons. (Fr. Cons.) 9, 31, 45, 153, 175 342, 353, 354. Hopkinson, Francis, 555, 567, 577, 631, 672. House of Delegates of Virginia, 562. Houston, Dr. J., 282. Howe, Major Gen., 462. Hubley, Col. Adam, 8, 65, 156, 199, 211, 218, 224, 231, 235, 252, 269, 278, 292, 351, 360, 364, 417, 422. 456, 465, 466. Hubley, John, 295. Huffnagle, Michael, 410, 469, 511, 596. Hughes, Capt. John, 533. Hunter, Col. Samuel, 292, 364, 503, 528, 657. Hutchinson, James, 327. Ingersol, Jonathan, 643. Irvine, Gen. William, 83, 240, 285, 345, 373, 458, 468, 515, 525, 552, 575, 595, 630, 635, 648, 724, 731.
Jackson, Maj. Wm. (Sec'y.), ix., 757. Jefferson, Thos., Gov. of Virginia, 78, 160, 189. Johnston, Francis, 263, 327. Johnston, Dr. Robert,

Letters, ix.—
457. Jones, N., 677. Judges of Sup. Court, 634. Justices of Gloucester, 544.
Keith, Sarah, ix., 501. Kennedy, D., 263, 363. Kern, Col. Nicholas, 428.
Lacey, Gen., ix., 437. Ledlie, And'w, 527. Lee, Thomas S., Gov. of Md., 13, 37. Levan, Daniel, 38. Levers, Capt. Robert, 227, 257, 268, 275, 321, 338, 348, 377, 403, 426, 428, 578, 742. Lewis, Col., 421. Lieutenants, County, 226, 337, 387, 407, 425. Lincoln, B., Sec'y at War, 549, 627. Livingston, Hon. R. R., 493, 506, 544, 545, 633. Livingston, Wm., Gov. of N. J., 82, 287, 388, 392, 404, 437, 530, 531, 608, 617, 618, 621, 622, 623, 651. Lochrey, Col. Archibald, 18, 28, 51, 79, 115, 246, 307, 333. Loughead, James, 436. Lukens, John, 61. Lux, George, 45. Luzerne, Chev. de la, 547.
McCalla, William, ix., 136, 423. McDowell, John, 729. McFarlane, A., 55. Maclay, William, 640. Maclean, Alexander, 564, 585, 588, 772. McClean, Archibald, 58, 352, 359, 370, 402. M. McConnell, 326, 371, 424. McKean, C. J. Thomas, 42, 125, 735, 751. Marbois, Mons., 734, 741. Marsh, Col. Joseph, 396, 440. Marshall, Col. James, 193, 233, 304, 343, 367, 444, 484. Marsteller, Philip, 638, 639, 641. Maryland, Gov. of, 13. Mason, Isaac, 238, 303. Massachusetts, Rhode Island and Maryland, 474. Matthews, Wm., 551. Mentges, Lieut. Col. P., 216, 299. Merchants of Philadelphia, 731. Mersereau, Joshua, 287. Miles, Col. Samuel, 80, 95, 127, 150, 153, 280, 324, 346, 357, 432. Miller, Rev. Peter, 27, 313, 314, 751. Minister of France, 130. Miralles, Don Juan, 196. Mitchell, Capt. Alexander, 165, 166. Montgomery, William, 640. Morgan, Col. Jacob, Jr., 127, 236, 326. Moore, James, 62. Morris, Gov., 308. Morris, Robert, 244, 245, 250, 251, 262, 264, 280, 281, 286, 287, 291, 310, 376, 383, 387, 395, 397, 398, 414, 416, 417, 418, 419,

Letters, ix.—
435, 446, 454, 474, 477, 481, 487, 488, 505, 512, 513, 544, 636, 668, 739, 740. Morris, Capt. Sam, 221, 415. Moultrie, Brig. Gen., 215. Moylan, Col. Stephen, 267, 321. Muhlenberg, F. A., 60. Muhlenberg, M., 241.
Nevill, Thos., ix., 76, 283. New York, Gov. of, 629. Nicholson, Capt., 239, 664. Nicholson, John, 48, 118, 131, 154, 174, 212, 216, 243, 663, 664, 677, 737, 738, 747, 749, 755, 758. Nicola, Col. Lewis, 198, 254.
Officers of Land Office, ix., 409. On removal of Records, 412. Officers of Westmoreland, 189. Orth, Adam, 187, 460, 737. Osborne, H., 252, 341, 390, 563, 639, 642, 643, 681, 682, 685, 688, 689. Oster, Mons. F. C., 730.
Parr, James, ix., 327. Parr, William, 263. Pemberton, John, 551. Penet, A. P., 430. Pentecost, Dorsey, 315, 540, 541, 545, 556, 661. Perry, John, 55, 248. Peters, Richard, 454. Pettit, Col. Charles, 129, 159. Philadelphia Co. Light Horse, 230. Pickering, Timothy, 389, 577. Perry, James, 52. Pixley, Thos., 364, Porter, Major Andrew, 327, 632. Postlethwaite, Samuel, 192. Potter, Gen. James, 70, 184, 528, 641. Prisoners on prison ships, 668. Prudden, T., 480.
Randolph, Lt. Asher, ix., 436. Rea, Lieut. Col. Samuel, 107, 108, 158. Read, James, 191. Reed, Joseph, 517, 526, 563, 691. Reichel, John Frederick, 265. Rittenhouse, David, 117, 119, 229. Roach, Isaac, 96, 112. Roberts, Joseph, 745. Robins, Ezekiel, 674, 677, 756. Robinson, Capt. Thomas, 208, 228, 237, 334, 392, 659. Rogers, Rev. Wm., 3. Root, Jesse, and Eliph. Dyer, 683.
St. Clair, Gen. Arthur, ix., 27, 37, 60, 386, 735, 752. Schlosser, G., 299. Scott, Hugh, &c., 771. Scott, Col. Thomas, 20, 324, 354, 374, 438, 496, 644, 646. Scott, Lieut. Wm., 228, 232, 302, 319, 341, 350, 426, 455, 556, 632. Searle, Hon. Jas., 519, 589, 591. Secretary at war, 549. Sergeant, Jon. D., 526.

Letters, ix —
Shiell, H. N., 520. Shrawder, Capt. Philip, 388, 660, 761. Smith, Col. Abraham, 234, 400, 514. Smith, Dr., 643. Smith, George, 42, 358. Smith, James, 459. Smith, Lt. Col. Robert, 421, 434. Smith, Hon. Thomas, 652. Sterret, Sam'l., 676. Stewart, Charles, 675. Stirling, Lord, 675. Stokely, Thomas, Capt., 330, 406. Stroud, Jacob, 108, 259.
Thome, J'n, ix., 118. Thomson, Chas., 267. Thompson, Jas., 228. Treasury, Board, 226, 229. Trumbull, Governor of Connecticut, 639, 642, Trustees of University, 461.
Van Campen, Jno., ix., 106, 123, 522, 693. Van Staphorst, N. and J., 591, 593. Virginia delegates in Congress, 260, 266, 269, 274.
Wagon masters, ix., 421. Wall, Geo., Jr., 529, 628. War, Secretary at, 483, 549, 757. Wardens of Philadelphia, 126. Washington co., inhabitants, 355. Washington, Gen. George, 39, 54, 66, 71, 75, 84, 98, 102, 111, 120, 124, 141, 195, 197, 207, 242, 254, 284, 293, 320, 481, 485, 486, 501, 505, 509, 536, 550, 626, 642, 653, 656, 661, 674. Wayne, Gen. Anthony, 15, 66, 74, 123, 124, 137, 138, 139, 155, 173, 283, 359, 366, 430. Weiss, Lewis, 298, 523. Westmoreland county, officers of, 189. Willing, Thomas, 497. Wilson, James, 526. Wirtz, Christian, 379. Wood, Col. James, 24, 236, 262, 276, 289, 328, 357, 382. Wylie, Capt. Thomas, 191, 665.
York county, Auditors, ix., 18.
Zantzinger, Paul, ix., 282.
Adams, John, x., 384, 386, 433, 434, 746, Agents of Confiscated Estates, 154. Allison, James, 167. Antes, Henry, Sheriff Northumberland, 344, 482, 650. Armstrong, John, Jr., Secy., 46, 53, 56, 63, 65, 78, 341, 147, 187, 199, 211, 238, 286, 327, 330, 339, 343, 345, 525. Armstrong, Lt. Col. John, 307, 315, 317, 319, 361. Arm- Gen. John, 430, 653, 654, 655, 658, 669, 677, 679, 685, 686, 688, 692, 694. Armstrong, Capt. Wm. 12. Assembly, 126, 195, 199, 223,

Letters, x.—
226, 407, 427, 428, 692, 696, 697. Atlee, Samuel J., 333, 346, 360. Atlee, William, 394.
Barclay, Thomas, x., 267. Bartholomew, Edward, 442. Baynton, John, (Collector of Tonnage,) 511. Blaine, Ephraim, 609. Board of Treasury, 527, Boggs, Matthew, 699. Boudinot, Elias, 74, 98. Bowdoin, James, Gov. of Massachusetts, 500, 503, 504. Bowen, E. F. & E. Beatty, 437, 596, 604, 605. Boyd, Hon. John, 307, 330. Boyd, and Armstrong, 591, 627, 630, 662, 664. Bradford, Wm. Jr., 202, 494, 655, 713, 743. Brodhead, Col. Daniel, 160. Brussine, De, and N. Garrison, 144. Bryan, George, 16, 73, 609. Bryan, Saml. (Secy.) 327. Butler, Col. Richard 69, 294, 332. Butler, William, 421.
Caldwell, Samuel, x., 185, Carleton, Gen. Guy, 13, 101, 131. Carleton, Joseph, Sec. War Office, 314. Carmathen, Secy, 746. Censors, Council of, 153, 302, 306, 333, 336, 596, 604, 655. Christie, Cap. Jas., 135, 209. Circulars, 284. Clinton, George, Gov. of New York, 205, 413, 422, 435, 450, 513. Coats, Lt. Col. William, 758 Commissioners for sale of Barracks, 239, 240, 241, 261, 276, 737. Commissioners of Boundary Line, 233, 236, 416, 438, 454, 489, 506. Commissioners, (Boyd, &c.) 307, 330, 339. Commisioners of Cumberland Co., 79. Commissioners for defence of Delaware, 26. Commissioners of Lands, 541, 545. Commissioners for treating with Indians, 265, 325, 332, 333, 346, 357, 395, 410, 489, 496. Commissioners of Roads, 533. Commissioners on Navigation of Susquehanna, 755. Commissioners of Taxes, 238. Commissioners of Taxes, Bucks Co., 75. Commissioners of Taxes, Lancaster, 82. Commissioners of Taxes, of Northampton, 92. Commissioners of Taxes, Philadelphia Co., 51, 104, 222, 224. Commissioners of Philadelphia Co., 307. Commissioners of Washington Co., 136, 564, 584.

Letters, x.—
Commissioners of Westmoreland Co., 98, 593. Commissioners to Wyoming, 661, 660, 677. Committee of Merchants, 210, 212, 219, 221. Congress, 60, 61, 74, 98, 135, 193, 206, 231, 234, 263, 358, 368, 397, 417, 424, 433, 440, 442, 457, 461, 473, 489, 493, 494, 499, 507, 530, 535, 537, 539, 543, 564, 732, 736, 745, 754. Circular, 424. Congress, Delegates in, 7, 25, 27, 38, 45, 52, 55, 69, 72, 101, 126, 151, 154, 155, 156, 183, 184, 204, 210, 223, 358, 368, 397, 398, 410, 440, 457, 477, 511, 549, 556, 563, 575, 576, 581, 592, 601, 697, 705, 715, 759. Connecticut, Gov. of, 147, 148. Council of Censors, 153, 302, 306, 333, 336, 596, 604, 655. Cox, Gabriel, 125. Craig, Thomas, 296, 303, 305. Crawford, Edward, Jr., 392. Creveceur, Mons., 195. Cummins, Lt. John, 22.
Delaney, Sharp, x., 97, 442, 715. Delegates in Congress, 7, 25, 27, 38, 45, 52, 55, 69, 72, 101, 126, 151, 154, 155, 156, 183, 184, 204, 210, 223, 358, 368, 397, 398, 410, 440, 457, 477, 511, 549, 556, 563, 575, 576, 581, 601, 697, 705, 715. 759, 768. De Marbois, Mons., 311, (See Marbois.) Depeyster, Col. A. S. 62. Dickinson, James, 740. Dickinson, John, 77. Digby, Rear Adml. Robert, 21. Donaldson, Arthur, 350. Donaldson, John, 565, 583. Dougherty, Barnard, 114, 119. Douglass, Ephr'm, 62, 70, 71, 262, 553, 564, 581, 588, 696, Duponceau, Peter S. 352. Duval, Hon. Gabriel, 291.
Ellicott, Andrew, x., 452. Espy, David, 114, 119. Ewing, Rev. Dr. John, 428, 443.
Filbert, Peter, Sheriff B. C., x., 67. Finley, Rev. James, 40, 41, 163. Fitzsimons, Thomas, 28, 48. Fleeson, Plunket, 523. Francis, Tench, 240, 261, 276. Franklin, Benjamin, 386, 556, Franklin, John, 621, 629, 672, 681, 751. Fullerton, Major, Richard, 758.
Galbraith, Robert, x., 466. Gardner, Joseph, 404, 516, 698. Gov. of Connecticut, 147, 148, 213. Gov. of Delaware, 540. Gov. of Maryland, 292, 320, 324, 526, 528, 540, 542, 543, 744, 753. Gov. of Massachusetts, 354, 500, 503, 504. Gov. of New Jersey, 103, 366, 458, 730. Gov. of New York, 205, 353, 412, 450, 513. Gov. of North Carolina, 353. Gov. of South Carolina, 79. Gov. of Virginia, 57, 145, 175, 602. Grand Inquest, Philadelphia, 347, Guerard, Benj., Gov. South Carolina, 79. Gurney, Francis, 144.
Hamilton, Joseph, x., 751. Harmar, Lt. Col. Josiah, 309, 311, 316, 322, 337, 345, 391, 394, 406, 430, 448, 455, 465, 469, 479, 483, 490, 508. Harrison, Gov. Benj., 57, 145, 175, 602, 608. Hartley, David, 557. Hays, Christopher, 264, 279. Hellstedt, Charles, Min. N. Nether'd, 350, 362, 408. 435. Henry, Wm., 405. Hillegas, Michael, 238, 261, 276. Hodgdon, Samuel, 39, 59, Hollingsworth, Levi, 350, 533, 546, 548. Hopkinson, Francis, 58, 355, 707, 755. Howe, Maj. Gen., 66. Hubley, Col. Adam, 718. Hubley, John, 278. Huffnagle, Michael, 125, 140, 141, 147, 186, 211, 429, 462, 464, 467, 763. Humpton, Col. Richd, 59. Hutchinson, Dr. James, 178, 218.
Inhabitants of Wyoming, x., 670. Irvine, Hon. James, 26, 458, 467, 609. John, Irwine, 289. Irvine, Gen. Wm., 56, 66, 218, 509.
Jacks, James, x., 264. Jackson, Hon David, 522. Jay, Hon. John, Secy. F. A., 401, 407, 433, 446, 499, 538, 735, 743, 759. Jefferson, Thomas, &c., 386. Jenkins, John, 33. Johnston, Benj., 611. Johnston, E. & W. Baldwin, 679. Johnson, Col. Francis, 282, 325, 326, 333, 453. Johnson, Jacob, 34. Judges of Supreme Court, 448, 460, 523. Justices of Northumberland, 628, 629, 630. Justices of Wyoming, 662.
Kern Nicholas, x., 654.
Land Office, x., 536, 537, 739. Lee, Arthur, 294, 326, 332. Lee, Richard Henry, 173. Levers, Robert, 341. Lieutenants, (County,) 286, 345, 410, 419. Livingston, R. R.,

Letters, x.—
Secy, 9, 13, 21. Livingston, Gov. Wilm. of N. J., 103, 713. Loan, Office, 57, 168, 169, 174, 514. Longschamps, 742. Luce, Benjn., 679. Lukens, John S. G., 53, 65, 95, 451, 458, 506, 540, 678. Luzerne, Chev. de la, 27, 28, 72. Lyon William, 285.
McClean, Alexander, x., 294, McClean, Brig. Gen., Allen, 70, 71. McDowell, Surgeon John, 343. McKean, C. J. Thomas, 176, 285, 290, 292, 396, 448, 739, 766. Maclay, William, 46, 346, 418, 444, 510. Magistrates and Sheriffs of North'ld Co., 295, 304. 344, 347, 460. Managers of State Lottery, 362, 372, 400, 468, 474, 513. Marbois, Mons. Barbe de, 175, 277, 283, 350, 351, 356. Marbois, Mons. de, 311, 351 354, 362, 367, 368, 409, 430, 440, 447, 471. Massachusetts, Gov. of, 354. Matlack, Timothy, 226. Mead, David, 222, 404, 482, 663, 707. Merchants, Committee of, 210, 212, 219, 221, 406, 409, 418. Mifflin, Thos., 183. Milligan Robert, 755. Milligan, James, 426. Minister of France, 223, 409 Minister of Holland, 415. Minister of United Netherlands, 350, 362, 408, 435. Montgomery, Hon. John, 206, 220. Montgomery, Joseph, Ch'n, 30, 32, 444. Montgomery, William, 765, 766, 767. Moore, Lt. Col., 286. Moore, Major James, 132, 185, 187, 197, 207, 222, 232. Moore, William, 93. Morales, Francis, 476. Morgan, George, 526. Muhlenberg, F. A., 153. Murray, Lt. Francis, 679.
New Jersey, Gov. of, x., 103, 366, 458. New York, Gov. of, 205, 353, 435, 450. Nicholson John, 6, 16, 28, 46, 48, 50, 52, 53, 93, 95, 96, 97, 481, 529, 750. Northumberland Magistrates and Sheriffs, 295, 304, 344, 347. North Carolina, Gov. of, 350.
Officers of Pennsylvania Line, x., 425, 592. Okeley, John, 330, 339, 696. Owen, Griffith, 563.
Paca, John, x., 292 Paca, William, Gov. of Maryland, 320, 324. Parker, Wm., 167. Patterson, Alex.,

Letters, x.—
Ch'n, 30, 32, 35, 208, 574, 617, 619, 624, 626, 627, 675. Peale, Charles W., 162. Pearson, James, 373, 420, 426, 442, 535, 547. Pentecost, Dorsey, 167, 181, 262, 413, 757. Pettit, Charles, 208, 497. Phile, Frederick, 240. Phipps, Paul, 359. Pierce, John, 536, 539. Porter, Andrew, 372, 760, Potter, Gen. James, 47, 159, Proctor, Thos., Sheriff, Philadelphia, 286, 323, 324, 327, 420, Prothonotaries, 268, 439. Prothonotary of Washington County, 78.
Read, Jas., x., 330, 339. Receiver Gen. of Land Office, 546. Redick, David, 416. Reed, Joseph, 157, 159, 160, 163, 719, (1779-80). Reynolds, John, 277, 327. Rittenhouse, David, 241, 269, 439, 454, 455, 456, 458, 730. Robins, Ezekiel, 26, 213. Robinson, Capt. Thomas, 14, 48, 99. Rosencrone, Count de, 434. Rush, Hon. Jacob, 292. Ryan, Michael, 308.
St. Clair, Gen. Arthur, x., 49, 260, 483. St. Saphorin, de, 434, Schrieber, John, 309, 334. Scott. Thomas, 65, 78, 80, 364. Scott, Lt. William, 591. Seely, Jonathan, 650, 677, 678, 692. Secretary of Foreign Affairs, 9, 13, 21, 401, 407, 433, 446, 475, 499, 538, 735, 743, 759. Shaw, William, 764. Shoemaker, B., 93. Shrawder, Capt. Philip, 23, 24, 99, 104, 131. Slough, Mathias, 237. Smallwood, Gov. of Maryland, 542, 543, 744, 753. Smith, Thomas, 57, 78, 168, 170, 174, 190, 447, 461. Smith, W. and W. Kelly, 419. Smith, Wm. Hooker, 760. Smyser, Jacob, 77. South Carolina, Governor of, 79. Sproat, David, 68. Sproat, Rev. James, 720. Stanhope, Henry, (Brit. Capt.) 503, 504. Steuben, Baron, 352. Story, John, 450, 451, 742. Street Commissioners, Philadelphia, 55. Surveyor Gen., 53, 65.
Taylor, Timothy, x., 432. Trumbull, Gov. Jon. of Connecticut, 147, 148, 213. Trustees of Loan Office, 481, 532, 545. Trustees of Provence Island, 75. Trustees of

Letters, x.—
Westmoreland Co., 91. Turnbull, Marmee, & Co., 281.
Van Berckal, P. J., x., 415. Van Campen, John, 24. Vancouver, Charles, 712. Virginia, Gov. of, 57, 145, 175, 602.
Wardens of Philadelphia, x., 93, 281, 349, 456, 571, 580, 584, 585, 588, 589, 606, 607. War Office, 27, 302, 459, 460, 479, 495, 497, 525, 529. Washington, Gen. Geo., 150, 151. Weitzel, John, 99, 109, 232, 343. Wilkinson, Gen. James, 610. Williamson, Hon. Hugh, 397. Wilson, James, 202, 399, 471. Wilson, Joseph, 152. Wilson, William, 304, 654. Wynkoop, Henry, 211.
Atlee, Wm. T., (Judge) xi., 233, 485. Adlum, John, 576, 693, 620. Agricultural Society, 527, 384, 385. Anstey, John, 149. Antes, Frederick, &c., 439. Armstrong, John, Jr., 137, 407, 436, 447. Armstrong, Major William, 214, 242, 460. Ascheraden, Shultz Von, 295. Assembly, 87, 103, 187, 206, 390, 397, 398, 402, 409, 521, 529, 547, 669, 673, 674, 675.
Baker, Hilary, xi., 604. Balliet, Stephen, 177, 179, 460. Barclay, Jno., 89. Bartholomew, Ewd., 767. Bayard, John, 28, Benton, Caleb, 175. Biddle, Clement, 236, 573, 743. Bingham, Wm., 308. Board of Treasury, (see Treasury Board.) Board of War, 208, 240, 268, 281, 291, 300, 534, 555. Bond, Phineas, (British Consul,) 255, 381. Bradford, Wm., Jr., 58, 114, 122, 232, 234, 250, 260, 273, 310, 415, 419, 431, 445, 446, 467. Breckenridge, H., 732. Brearly, David, (C. J. N. J.) 548. Brison, James, 422, 624. Brodhead, Daniel, S. G., 641, 660, 663, 758. Brown, Andrew, 412. Brown, John, (prisoner,) 264. Bryan, George, (Judge) 264, 283, 286, 490. Burd, Edward, 765. Butler, Lord, 330. Butler, Gen. Richard, 427, 562, 591, 715, 723. Butler, Col. Zebulon, 179, 192, 330, 351, 356, 381, 414, 459, 619, 676. Buyers, John, &c., 439, 440.
Caldwell, Sam'l., xi., 89, 594. Canan, Col, John, 588. Caswell, Richard,

Letters, xi.—
Gov. N. C., 116. Chaloner, John, 680, 761. Cherokee Chiefs, 584. Cherokee Indian Women, 181. Churchman, John, 718. Cincinnati, Society of, 726. Circulars, 379, 746. Clarkson, Matthew, 250. Clinton, George, Governor New York, 96, 125, 187, 196, 197, 326, 335, 341, 412. Coats, Lieut. Colonel William, 273, 274. Commander of Spanish Frigate, 100, 101, 102. Commissioners for western boundary, 26, 52, 69, 178. Northern boundary, 203. On Connecticut claims, 159. To commercial Convention, 60. To Indians, 503, 507, 508, 509, 510. Of Luzerne Co., 205, 302, 332. Of Maryland, 61. For improving inland navigation, 77. To examine rivers, 622, 634, 637, 681, 683, 690, 750. Of taxes, 499, 593, 603. Of Virginia and Maryland, 511. Committee of Assembly, 547. Of Congress, 583, 585. Comptroller Gen., 33, 34, 90, 97, 139, 142, 198, 229, 234, 249, 259, 323, 404, 561, 589, 655, 658, 731, 729, 739, 742, 747. Congress, 4, 15, 50, 51, 57, 70, 71, 79, 121, 122, 132, 143, 145, 168, 171, 173, 175, 180, 190, 191, 214, 239, 285, 293, 311, 314, 323, 339, 353, 375, 387, 432, 451, 472, 483, 562, 583, 739. Delegates in, 4, 27, 37, 41, 106, 188, 189, 207, 237, 251, 252, 266, 280, 308, 342, 350, 352, 365, 373, 382, 383, 408, 482, 456, 457, 459, 504, 505, 537, 543, 590, 685. Committee of Ways and Means, 259, 583, 585. Committee of States, 446, 483. Connecticut, to and from Governors, 238, 409, 414, 447, 451, 735. Cornplanter, (Indian Chief,) 739, 740. Correy, Jona., 104. Cowperthwaite, Jos., (Sheriff,) 330. Coxe, Tench, 61, 539, 543. Craig, Lieutenant Col., John, 196, 236, 305. Craig, Thomas, 276. Crawford, Edward, Jr., 690. Cunningham, James, 263. Curwen, John, 572.
Dale, Samuel, xi., 66. Davis, Benj., Jr., 766. Delany, Sharp, 259, 597, 601, 603. Delaware, Governor of, 33. Delegates in Congress, 4, 27, 37, 41, 87, 106, 188, 189,

Letters, xi.—
207, 237, 251, 252, 266, 280, 308, 342, 350, 352, 365, 373, 382, 383, 456, 457, 460, 504, 505, 537, 543, 685. Denison, Nathan, 212, 213, 326, 619. Donaldson, John, 569, 570, 722, 763. Dorchester, Lord, 315. Douglas, Ephraim, 32, 535.
Eckert, Val'ne, xi., 203, 211. Ellicott, Andrew, 134, 140, 178, 216, 243, 326, 429, 583, 613, 615, 705. Elliott, Lieutenant Benjamin, 665.
Falconer, N., xi., 737, 747. Febiger, Christian, 563, 649, 758. Ferguson, Captain William, 590. Finley, James, 299. Fisher, Thomas, 388. Fitzsimons, Thomas, 427, 595. Franklin, Benj., 701. Franklin, Col. John, 3, 14, 52, 67, 84, 94, 111, 175, 182, 183, 185, 549, 556. Freeman, Samuel, 714, 721. Fullerton, Richard, 726.
Galbraith, Rob., xi., 379, 656, 725, 733. Gardner, Hon. Joseph, 451, 453. Gerry, Elbridge, 598. Gettig, Christian, 439. Gibson, Geo., 606. Gibson, John, 427. Gordon, Samuel, 213. Gore, Obadiah, 192, 216. Governor, of Connecticut, 238, 409, 414, 447, 451, 735. Of Delaware, 33. Of Georgia, 96. Of Maryland, 56. Of Massachusetts, 271. Of New Jersey, 73, 326, 550. Of New York, 96, 125, 187, 196, 326, 412. Of North Carolina, 116. Of South Carolina, 545. Of Virginia, 115, 116, 212, 249, 256, 284, 290, 497, 501, 523, 557. Graham, Henry Hale, 638. Grant, Thomas, 110. Griswold, Matthew, Governor of Connecticut, 447, 451. Gurney, Col. Francis, 768.
Hahn, Michael, xi., 97. Hamilton, Alex., (Sec. Treas.,) 638, 639, 641, 654, 663. Hamilton, Dr. Joseph, 3, 67, 84, 94, 182, 185. Hancock, (Gov. John, of Mass.,) 271. Hand, General Edward, 505 Harmar, Lieutenant Colonel Josiah, 173, 217, 270, 286, 325, 391. Harris, James, 186. Harrison, Benjamin, Governor of Virginia, 497, 499. 501, 507. Hart, Jonathan, 593. Hartley, Colonel Thomas, 114, 156. Hasse, John, 288. Health Officer, 737, 747. Hellstedt, Charles,

Letters, xi.—
(Swed. Cons.,) 265. Hiester, Daniel, Jr., 607. Henderson, Andrew, 305. Henry, Wm., 238, 453. Hollenbach. Mathias, 216. Hodgdon, Samuel, 205, 374, 379. Hoge, Honorable Jonathan, 149. Hopkinson, Francis, 53, 77, 125, 375, 634. Houer, Samuel, 47, 102. Hubley, Adam, 755. Hubly, Lt. Bernard. 709, 710, 739. Huffnagle, Michael, 500. Huntington, Gov. Samuel, of Connecticut, 238, 409, 414. Hutchins, Thomas, (Geographer,) 314, 315.
Ingels, George, xi., 767 . Irvine, General Wm., 501, 512. 513. Irwin, Matthew, 749.
Jacks, Jas., xi., 363. Jefferson, Thos. Secretary of State, 679, 688, 689, 696, 700, 703, 705, 706, 707, 708, 709, 712, 713, 718, 720, 722. Jenkins, John, 52. Johnston, Capt. Andrew, 157. Johnston, Colonel Francis, 125, 139, 245, 589, 644, 645, 668, 750. Jones, David, 58. Jay, John, 74, 171, 201, 287, 293, 411. Judges of Sup. Court, 233, 264, 283, 295, 441, 442, 443, 472, 478, 484, 488, 490, 601, 667. Justices of Berks County, 286. Justices of Franklin County, 316. Justices of Northampton, 272.
Kemp, Capt. J., xi., 497. Kennedy, David, 139, 651, 757. Keene, Lawrence, 111. Kingsley, Nathan, 662. Knox, Gen. H., (Sec. War,) 208, 268, 281, 290, 301, 524, 555, 621, 624, 707, 711, 728.
Land Officers, xi., 138, 757. Latimer, George, 661. Lenox, David, 55. Levan, Daniel, 63. Lewis, William, 273, 727. Lianes, Thos. de Ugarte, Y., 100, 102. Lieutenants of Counties, 379, 619. Livingston, Governor William. 93, 336, 550. Lloyd, Peter Z. 729. Loan Office, Trustees of, 170. Lukens, John, 32, 37, 98, 139, 427. Luzerne, Chevalier de la, 462, 464, 465, 466, 468, 470, 475, 476, 482, 487. Lyon, Wm., 731.
McKean, (C. J.) Thos., xi., 264, 276, 283, 295, 351, 366, 485, 661. McLean, Alexander, 71, 642. McClean, Captain James, 229, 230, 231, 406. McLene, James, 186. Magis-

Letters, xi.—
trates, Wyoming, 440. Managers, of State Lottery, 89, 118. Marbois, Mons. Barbe de, 49, 461, 471, 479, 481, 484, 494. Marshall, Lt. James, 209, 377. Martin, Robert, &c., 438. Maryland, Governor of, 57. Maryland, Commerce Commissioner of, 61. Massachusetts, to and from, Gov.. 271. Mead, David, 454, 455. Melcher, Col. Isaac, 523. Mentges, Col. Francis, 78. Mercantile Society of Philadelphia, 103. Mifflin, John, 646. Mifflin, Thomas, 505. Milligan, Robt, 27. Minister of France, 462, 464, 465, 466, 468, 470, 473, 476, 482, 487. Minister of United Netherlands, 469, 470, 475, 477, 479, 480. More, Brigadier General, 567. Mitchell, Joseph, 253. Montgomery, Thos., 505. Montgomery, Wm., 35, 108, 111. Moore, Colonel James, 434, 435, 436, 443. Moore, Thomas, 99. Morris, Richard, (C. J. N. Y.,) 413. Morris, Robert, 505. Muhlenberg, General Peter, 133, 135, 231.

Nesbitt, John Maxwell, xi., 520. New Jersey, to and from, Governor, 93, 326. New York, to and from Governor, 125, 187, 196, 326. Nicholason, Joseph, 742. Nicholson, John, 33, 34, 90, 97, 139, 142, 198, 229, 234, 249, 259, 323, 404, 561, 589, 655, 658, 729, 731, 739, 742, 747. Nicola, Lewis, 536.

Officers of Militia, of Philadelphia, xi., 57. Officers, Commanding in Luzerne County, 204. Officers, of Military, of Luzerne County, 299. O'Hara, James, 228. Owen, Evans, 585. 643. Oxenstierna, F. G., 266.

Patterson, Alexander, xi., 457. Pennel, Joseph, 506. Perin, Joseph, 288. Peters, Richard, 335, 432, 572, 636. Pettit, Charles, 37, 41, 87, 106, 266, 708. Phila., Agricultural Soc'y., 384, 385, 527. Phila., Company, 428. Pickering, Col. Timothy, 133, 134, 159, 176, 177, 179 180, 205, 208, 256, 281, 295, 296, 312, 346, 353, 356, 363, 365, 366, 399, 424, 541. Pinckney, Thomas, Gov. of S. C., 545.

Letters, xi.—
Pine, R. E., 95. Porter, Colonel Andrew, 156, 178, 203, 214, 241, 502. Potter, James, 661. Powel, Samuel, (Pres. Agricul. Soc'y,) 384, 385, 527. Practitioners of Law, Phila., 425. Proctor, Thos., (Sheriff,) 469, 477, 664. 719, 740, 741, 763. Prothonotaries Circular, 591, 765.

Randolph, Bev., Gov. Va., xi., 557. Randolph, Edmund, Gov. of Va., 115, 116, 212, 249, 256, 284, 290, 523, 525. Read, Jas, 757. Receiver, Gen., 667, 693, 696, 750. Redick David, 149, 197, 244, 338, 410, 414, 432, 459, 593. Reed, Hon. James R., 283, 308. Reed, Lieut. Samuel, 435. Register Gen., 569, 570, 722, 763. Rinker, James, 206. Rittenhouse, David, 203, 337, 743. Robins, Ezekiel, 495. Robinson, John, 719. Robinson, Capt. Thos., 432. Ross, James, 458, 730. Rush, Dr. Benjamin, 427, 540, 578. Rush, Judge, Jacob, 295, 485. Ruston, Thomas, 632. Ryerson, Thomas, 666.

St Clair, Hon. Arthur, xi., 127, 189, 393, 716. Schott, Capt. John P., 297, 298, 397, 663. Scott, Thos., 215, 568. Secretary of Foreign Affairs, 75, 171, 201, 287, 293, 413. Secretary of State, U. S., 679, 688, 689, 696, 700, 703, 705, 706, 707, 708, 709, 712, 713, 718, 720, 722. Secretary of Treasury, 638, 641, 654, 663, 664. Sec'y of War, 208, 240, 268, 281, 291, 300, 645, 685, 686. Sellers, John, 623. Shannon, Wm., 748. Sheriff of Philada., 469, 477. Shippen Ewd. 91. Simms, Charles, 160, 169. Skinner, John, 92, 143, 158. Smith, Francis, 195. Smith, Jonathan, B. 423. Smith, Robt., Editor, 126. Smith, Thos Duncan, 305. Smith, Wm. Hooker, 45, 102, 104, 108, 193, 330. South Carolina, Gov. of, 545. Sprague, Joseph, 93. Stiles, John, 202. Stroebell, John C., 651. Sullivan, Prest., John, of N. H., 122. Surveyor Gen., 758. Swaine, Francis, (Sheriff,) 267.

Talbot, Lt. Jere., xi., 280. Tax, Commissioners, 499, 593, 603. Telfair,

Letters, xi.—
Edward, (Gov., Georgia,) 96. Thomas, Jos., 725. Todd, Wm., 645. Traill, Hon. Robert, 288, 289, 446. Treas'r., 563, 649, 743, 758. Treasury, Board of, 15, 64, 79, 86. 155, 382, 383. Trimble, James, 679. Trustees of Loan Office, 170. Trustees of Washington Academy, 215. Turnbull, William, 623. University of Penn'a, xi., 613.
Van Campen, John, xi., 26. Vandyke, Gov. Nicholas, 33. Vaughan, Samuel, 675. Virginia, to and from, Govs., 115, 116, 249, 256, 284, 290, 497, 507, 523, 557.
War, Board of, xi., 208, 240, 268, 281, 291, 300, 534, 555, 621, 624, 707, 711, 728. Wardens of Philadelphia, 99, 100, 101, 543. Washington, Gen. George, 496. Washington, President U. S., 587, 596, 599, 600, 601, 602, 604, 605, 611, 615, 616, 673. Westbrook, Abraham, 47, 102. Will, William, 417, 713. Willett, Col. Marinus, 711. Williamson, Hon. Hugh, 449. Wilson, James, 445, 453. Wilson, Col. William, 192.
Armstrong, Col. John, M. G., xii., 109, 285. Attorney Gen., 99.
Bayard, Col. Stephen, xii., 117, 133, 134, 139. Beall, Capt Thomas, 23. Beck, Ensign John, 142, 276. Biddle, Col. Clement, 314. Biggs, Capt. Benj., 195, 235. Blaine, Col. E., 278. Brady, Capt. Samuel, 213, 276. Brodhead, General Daniel, 105–279.
Campbell, Lt. Col., xii., 135, 141, 154. Campbell, Capt. Thomas, 160, 171, 179, 187, 194. Carlton, Joseph, 267. Carnaghan, Captain James, 193, 254. Chambers, Benj., 281. Clarke, Col. George Rogers, 143, 216, 238. Clarke, Captain Jno., 174, 276. Clinton, Gov. N. Y., George, 32. Coleman, Ensign, 138, 141. Commissioners of Washington county, 288. Cooke, William, 286. Cornplanter, 322. Council, 287, 289, 290, 293, 294, 296, 300, 302, 304, 306, 314, 317, 319, 320, 322. Council at Coochocking, 228. Craig, Capt., 233.
Dallas, Alex. J., Secretary, xii., 99.

Letters, xii.—
Davis, Col. John, 117, 152. Dawson, Capt. Samuel, 145, 151. Douglass, Ephraim, 78. Duane, James, 109. Duncan, David, 247.
Evans, Colonel John, xii., 213, 219, 231, 238, 240, 253.
Flowers, Col. Benjamin, xii., 271. Franklin, John, 296.
Gaddes, Colonel, xii., 178. Gates, Major General, 218, 228. George, Capt. Robert, 142, 168. Gibson, Colonel John, 171. Glass, Lieut. 172. Greene, Major General, 118, 120, 145, 174, 204.
Hamilton, Alex., S. T., xii., 90, 100. Harrison, Lieutenant John, 236. Heckenwelder, John, 111, 121, 124, 221, 227. Hollingsworth and Donaldson, 291, 292. Huffnagle, M., 300.
Indians, Susquehanna, xii., 250. Ingersoll, Jared, Atty. Gen., 99. Irwine, Captain Joseph, 138, 169.
Jameson, Lieut. John, xii., 177, 186, 193.
Jay, John, xii., 163, 176. Jefferson, Gov. Thos. of Virginia, 140, 273. Johnson, Th., Gov., 166. Jones, Samuel, 282.
Lanctot, Major, xii., 246, 259. Lt's of Counties, 137, 246, 275. Livingston, Gov. Wm., N. J., 71. Lochrey, Col. Archibald, 122, 123, 130, 139, 169, 202, 214, 215, 219, 225, 239, 257, 260, 261, 264. Lukens, John, S. G. 79.
M'Ilvaine, Francis, xii., 161, 170. M'Intyre, Capt. Thos., 208, 212. M'Kean, Thos., C. J., 79, 299.
Mifflin, Gov. Thomas, xii., 8, 31, 32, 90, 93, 95, 100. Mitchell, David, 250, 260. Mitchell, Col. John, 148. Moore, James F., 144. Moore, Wm., V. P., 71. Moorehead, Capt. Samuel, 129. Morgan Capt., 173, 208. Morgan, Col. Geo., 116, 153, 159, 191.
Nicholson, John, xii., 7, 90, 93, 95, 97.
Page, Hon. John, xii., 167. Peery, Col., 262, 265. Pendleton, Col., 201. Penn, William, 280. Peters, Richard, 207, 210, 224, 234, 271, 274, 281, 282. Peters, Rev. William, 284. Pettit, Chas., 7. Peyton, Col., 201. Pickering,

Letters, xii.—
Timothy, 106, 113, 128, 133, 149, 158, 179, 183, 190, 237, 241, 244, 248, 255, 258, 263.
Rawlin, Col., xii., 272. Reed, President Joseph, 107, 159, 163, 180, 186, 251. Robeteau, Thomas C., 284. Rogers, Captain John, 217. Ross, V. P., 317, 318.
Scammel, Col. Alex., xii., 185, 226, 268. Secretary at War, 292. Shepherd, Col. David, 167, 270, 277. Shippen, Doctor Wm., 191. Shrawder, Captain Philip, 70. Slaughter, Major, 232. Smith, Col. T., 152. Smyth, Thomas, 112. Springer, Ensign, 195. Springer, Capt. Uriah, 274, 279. Steele, Col. Archibald, 115, 136, 153, 161, 223, 230, 245. Stiles, Joseph, 317. Stoddard, Benjamin, 266. Stokely, Capt. Thos., 254. Sullivan, Major General, 154, 165. Susquehannah Indians, 280.
Taylor, Major, xii., 182, 188, 192, 194, 197, 200. Tilghman, James, 285, 286. Treasury, Comptroller of, 97, 99. Treasury, Secretary of, 95.
Valandigham, Colonel George, xii., 261. Van Campen, John, 70. Vernon, Major Frederick, 121.
Wall, George, Jr., xii., 289, 290, 293, 319. War, Secretary at, 32, 292. Wardens of Philadelphia, 287, 290, 291, 292, 294, 304, 306, 308. Washington county Commissioners, 289. Washington, President, George, 8. —— General, 113, 120, 125, 131, 146, 155, 164, 176, 184, 188, 197, 206, 212, 223, 233, 242, 243, 252, 256, 258, 265, 269. White, John, 302, 304. White, Bishop William, 31, 314. Whitehead, J., 314. Williams, Adj. William, 295. Williams & Engle, 295. Wilkins, Charles, 316. Wilkins, Dr. John, Jr., 321, 322. Wilkinson, James, 199, 209, 226, 250. Wilson, Col. William, 319, 320, 322. Wolcott, Oliver, S. T., 91, 94, 97. Wynkoop, Henry, 299, 302.
Zëisberger, Rev. David, xii., 192, 196, 203, 214, 221, 231.
Letters of Marque. granted, ii., 660. Orders of the government respecting, 684. Orders respecting, iii., 3, 91, 162.
Letts, Ezekiel, petition for captaincy, v., 57.
Levan, Abraham, vi., 406, 449.
Levan, Daniel, letter to Council, vii., 611. Council ask for Continental money, ix., 38. A Justice required at Reading, xi., 63.
Levers, Robert, v., 332. Prothonotary, &c., 333, 618, 622, 623, 645, 717; vi., 5, 76, 140, 141, 341, 344, 346, 362, 381, 435, 464, 486, 534, 626, 719, 721. Letters, vii., 15, 176. Can't find house at Easton, 176. Lieut., ix., 64. Convention prisoners, militia, 227, 323, 348, 403, 426. Indian murders, 257. Provisions, savages, 268, 275. Trial of Col. Stroud, 339. Taxes, 377. Light horse in Allen township, 428. Complaint against, 527. Militia, frontiers, &c., 579, 742. Letter on election in Northampton county, x., 341. Death of, xi., 289.
Levis, Thomas, vi., 651.
Levy, Miss, pass to, by Arnold, vii., 223, 224.
Lewes, Delaware, Collectors appointed, i., 196. Vessels captured off, ii., 4. Notice to be given of enemy, 5. Signal guns and flag described, 5. Collector of Customs at, iii., 546; iv., 76. Privateers, 676. Tory election at, v., 53. Riotous conduct, 54. Signals, &c., at, 167.
Lewis, Col., letters sent to, ix. 421.
Lewis, General, at Fort Pitt, vi., 717.
Lewis, James, examination, servant of Col. Conolly, and taken with him, ix., 473.
Lewis, Thomas, appointed by Virginia Commissioner on boundary, x., 146.
Lewis, William, letter, vi., 641. To defend a suit, viii., 231, 236. And Attorney General, case of Niess and Rheiner, xi., 273. Infractions of treaty, 727.
Lianes, Thomas de Ugarte, Y. Commander of Spanish frigate at Marcus Hook, correspondence with, xi., 99, 192.

Libling, Andrew, prisoner in jail, and others, revolt, x., 327-329.
Library Co., Philadelphia, books arrived at New York, viii., 183.
Licenses, marriage and tavern, iv., 110. For Indian trade required, 186; vii., 611; xi., 69. Rev., Wm. Linn, ix., 893. Marriage, Bishop White on, xii., 31, 314.
Lieutenants, hints for, v., 265. Circulars to, 297, 365, 379, 380, 424, 459, 475, 523, 541, 545, 556, 582, 592, 615, 660, 694. Letters to, vi., 157, 169, 193, 500, 650. Circular letters to, vii., 105, 267, 275, 486, 650, 747; viii., 72, 453, 476, 519. County, circulars to fines, ix., 226, 387, 407, 425. Circular to, xi., 379. Of Luzerne, to N. Dennison on militia laws, 619; xii., 137, 246, 275.
Lightfoot, Sam'l., petition of, against William Moore, iii., 328.
Light Horse, ordered out, ix., 556.
Light-house at Cape Henlopen, xii., 308.
Ligonier, Fort, Indians attack, iii., 669. Defence of, vi., 532. Murders at, by Indians, vii., 345. In danger, 518; xii., 389-393.
Ligonier Valley, ravages of Indians, ix., 240
Lincoln, Gen., v., 281. Wounded at Ticonderoga, 675; vii., 736.
Lincoln, Gen. B., Secretary at War, ix., 526, 527. Fayette introduced Chevalier de Lambert, 627. Requests a guard for prisoners in the new jail, 549, 618; xii., 149.
Lindsay, Dr. Alexander, viii., 518.
Lineback, Frederick, relates respecting massacre of Moravian Indians at Muskingum, ix., 523, 524. [See Leimbach. Vol. V.]
Liquor, soldiers demand, ix., 437. Regulations respecting sale of, x., 439.
Lisbon, destroyed by earthquake, ii., 530.
Little, John, signs article of capitulation at Fort Freeland, vii., 611.
Liturgy, prayers for the Royal family directed to be altered, i., 225, 624.
Livingston, R. R., Secy. of foreign affairs, Number, of Servants, ix., 465. Resolutions of Congress, 493, 506. Boundaries, 494. Birth of Dauphin of France, 544. Holland acknowledges independence, 632. Secy. of Foreign Affairs, letters to and from, x., 9, 13, 21.
ivingston, William, Gov., of N. J., v., 238, 243, 251, 267, 294, 296, 301, 320, 328, 346, 348, 614, 621. vi., 133, 453, 599, 604, 728. vii., 260, 475, 480, 492. viii,, 139, 314, 576, 624, 634, 636, 648. Cruelty of the Enemy, ix., 81. Deserters, 287. Fears Enemy, 388, 393. Cartridges, Clinton &c., 404. Letter, 411. Movements of enemy, 437. Capture of a Traitor, 530, 531. Bucks Co. robbery, 608, 616, 617. Enemy, 618. Passes, 619, 621, 622, 623, 651. Letters to and from, x., 103, 366, 458, 730; xi., 73, 326, 338. Demands, Wm. Allen, a counterfeiter 550. Letter from, xii., 71
Lloyd, David, letter from, i., 246.
Lloyd, Peter, Z., address, xi., 728.
Lloyd, Philemon, letter to Penn, i., 54.
Lloyd, Thomas, proposed subscription to publication of debates, xi., 213.
Lloyd, Cap. Thomas, ii., 759. Letters to and from, iii., 11, 319, 361, 411.
Loan Office, report on, i., 457. Income of, ii., 86. Continental, to receive bills of Credit of States v., 183. Thos. Smith, Commissioner of, 183. On opening, to receive Bills of Credit, vi., 184. Certificates, 421, 427, 545, 565, 566. At Lebanon, viii., 51. Respecting, x., 57, 169, (1783,) 170, 174, 190, 223, 447, 453, 514, 532. Counterfeit certificates in circulation, 447. Letter of trustees of, 481. On scarcity of bills, 481, 545. Trustees apply for bills, 532. Respecting, xi., 33, 659. Report of Trustees on nonpayments, 170, Clement Biddle, on exchange of loan, 573, 659. Certificates, 747. Interests on Loans, to be paid in bills on Paris, v., 602. Office to be removed 617. Authorized by Assembly, viii., 7, 276.
Lochry, Archibald, v., 344, 488,

741. Call on by Gen. Hand for militia, 488; vi., 68, 143, 459, 495. vii., 173, 362, 363, 430, 754, 770. Opinion on reward for Indian Scalps, 362. State of frontiers, 564. Letters to and from, &c. viii., 42, 50, 65, 66, 69, 77, 109, 282, 290, 318, 405, 518. Letters to and from, ix., 18, 28, 51, 79, 115, 246, 301, 307, 336. Clarke's expedition, 332, 336, 405. Capture and death of, 458, 468; xii., 107, 163, 172. Letters to, 122, 123, 130, 139, 169, 202, 214, 215, 219, 225, 239, 257, 260, 261, 264. To order men to Fort Pitt, 169, 215, 255.

Lochry, Wm., v., 135.

Lodge, Mr., case of vii., 546.

Logan, (Mingo chief,) raises a party to cut off Shawnee Town traders, v., 513. Return with scalps, 525.

Logan, James, letter from, i., 245. Letter to R. Charles, 215. Resigns as member of Council, 730.

Logan, Wm., letters to and from iv., 63, 530. Letter, ii.,

Loganian Library to be used by Soldiers, v., 399.

Logstown, Indians near, xii., 234.

Loller, Robert, candidate for office, xi., 618.

Long, Andrew, petition, viii., 548. Memorial, ix., 762.

Long Island, Battle of, movement of troops, v., 21.

Longschamp, C. J. depositions respecting his escape, x., 271–274. Mons. Marbois respecting, 277. Retaken, 277. Proceedings, 350, 351, 358. Anonymous letter to Mons. Marbois respecting, 409. He demands him, 706. Asks leave of absence to select a plantation, 742. And Mons. Marbois, respecting attack on, xi., 442, 461–495 Letter to Judges, respecting, 442. Arrested, 466, 469, 470, 477. Claimed, as a French subject, 467, 468. Certificate, 471. Letter, to Judges, 472, 478, 485, 488. To Congress, 472. Case, 485, 489, 490. Sentence, 491.

Lottery, Land, notice respecting, i., 455. Managers of the State, sale of tickets, &c., x., 362, 372, 400, 468, 475, 513. Donation land, xi., 49. State, 89, 118.

Louden, Samuel, printer, vii., 206

Loudoun, Fort, iii., 119, 280. Conference of a Council of officers at, in Virginia, 367. murders near, iv., 175, 209, 219, 229. Light horse expected at, 209. Letter from, 218, 226, 231; xii., 394–396.

Loudoun, Lord, appointed Commander in Chief, ii., 647. Earl of, introduction of, 657. Letters to and from, 691. His appointment and arrival, 718; iii., 137, 138, 141, 145, 150, 174, 267, 278, 316, 317, 323, 338. Asks loan of Cannon, 267. Hints at a plot discovered by intercepted letters, 325.

Loughead, James, v., 485; vii., 531. 673, 764; ix., 436.

Loughead, Jeremiah, deposition respecting Records of Westmoreland County, v., 452.

Loughery, John, deposition respecting Indian Murders, iii., 731.

Lousia, Princess, death of, iv., 300.

Louisburgh, expedition against, i., 667–670, 679, 689, 692, 711. Distress at, ii., 391. Papers respecting operations at, iii., 442, 446.

Louisiana, demand on Gov. Miro, for a Negro, xi., 567.

Lovelace, Francis, succeeds Governor Nicolls, i., 28. Grants island in Delaware to Peter Cock, 29.

Lovell, Hon. James, of Mass., letter to, vii., 477.

Lowe, John, deposition, i., 350.

Lowe, Joshua, letter on murder of Indians, i., 268.

Lowther, Fort at Carlisle, xii., 348.

Loxley, Benj., for casting brass guns, iv., 731.

Loyalists, Dr. Franklin's advice respecting, ix., 668.

Loyalsock, Indian murders at, vi., 576, 599. Indian murders, vii., 357.

Luce, Benj., warned to depart from Wyoming, x., 679.

Ludwig, Christopher, Superintendent of Bakers, sent by Gen. Washington to Philadelphia for hands, v., 439.

Lukens, John, elected Surveyor

Gen. ix., 66. Comm. to run Virginia line, 20. On survey of donation lands, x., 451, 459. Appointment by, 458. Returns of surveys, 506. Letter of James Dickinson on survey of donation lands—conference with Indians, 740. Letters and instructions to, 53, 56, 65, 95, 756. Appointed commissioner, on Virginia boundary, 223. Letters to and from, xi., 32, 93, 139, 427. His death, 631. D. Brodhead succeeds, letter, xii., 78, 630.

Lumber, report of, inspector, xii., 1.

Lumber, inspection at Philadelphia, memorial of merchants, iv., 263.

Lutheran Churches, address to Gov. Morris, ii,, 183, 184. Phila., petition for a brief to raise funds for Zion Church, iv., 253. Of Berks county, petition, 279. Missionaries to Georgia, 563.

Lutheran (German) congregation at Lebanon, an old dispute among, viii., 123.

Lutterloh, Col. J. H., vi., 210, 250, 283, 323, 343, 348, 352.

Lutz, Nicholas, appointed commissioner of purchases in Berks Co., viii., 201, 301, 313, 342, 356, 367, 399, 417, 438, 474.

Luzerne, Chevalier de la, reception of by Congress as French minister, viii., 9. Letters, 334, 368, 448, 540, 543, 609, 614, 628. And Mons. Holker, charges, ix., 180. Birth of Dauphin, to, honors, 543, 544, 545, 547. Dispatches respecting peace between Great Britain and the Uuited States, x., 12. Valedictory, on leaving, 279. Answer of Council to, 282. Mons. Marbois on, 283. Respecting attack on Mons. Marbois by Longschamp, xi., 461, 462, 464, 465, 466, 468, 469, 470, 473, 476, 482, 487.

Luzerne County, deluge in, xi., 85. Gen. Muhlenberg resigns as Commissioner, 136. Want the laws, 159. Daniel Heister elected and resigns; W. Montgomery elected, 160. Disturbances in, 207. Officers of Military companies in, 299. Commissioners appointed to view the land in, 304. Commissioners on capture, 332. Disturbances in, 363, 365. Field Officers elected, 384. Memorial for division of land, 386. Militia Laws, 619. N. Kingsley resigns as Justice, 662. Difficulties in collecting militia, 676. (See Col. Rec.)

Lycoming Creek, Indn. murders, vi., 552, 599, 603.

Lydius, John, purchase of land from Indians for Susquehanna Company, ii., 60, 171, 174, 176, 273, 279, 298, 303, 323. And his purchase of lands for Connecticut, iv., 41, 51, 57, 66, 70, 83, 88, 103.

Lyndermood, Col. Michael, viii., 230, 273.

Lyon, Samuel, viii., 439, 715.

Lyon, William, v., 416; vi., 228; vii., 144, 399. Return of Sheriffs on Cumberland county, x., 285. Offices in different Counties, xi., 731.

Lyttleton Fort, ii., (see Forts) iii,, 12, 99; xii., 396-398.

Lyttleton, Governor William H., of South Carolina, letters, iii., 19, 315, 399. Asks for ammunition, 315. For Pilots, 399.

M.

McAlister, Jno., depositions respecting him as commissary, vii., 490, 513, 529, 550, 652.

McAlavy's Fort, xii., 461.

McCalester, Col. Richard, letter, v., 330, 333, 335, 369, 412, 558, 633, 640, 692, 768; vi., 22, 171, 196, 244, 369, 463, 479, 547; vii., 110, 115, 367, 401, 414, 425. Wishes to resign, 415, letter from, viii. 16.

McCalester, Contract, xii., 208.

McCall, Samuel, appointed Commissioner to settle accounts for wagons for Gen'l Braddock, ii., 598.

McCall, Capt. Wm., ix., 554.

McCalla, Wm., vii., 620; fines, viii., 212, 557, 661. Commissioner of Bucks Co., ill-treated, ix., 199. Supplies, 423.

McCay, Abigail, examination of, v., 337.

McClean, Alexander, going on Gen. Clarke's expedition, ix., 352. Boundary line, 353, 402, 563, 566, 585, 588, 772. Appointment of Lieut. Beal—in favor of conduct of Virginians in Westmoreland Co., x., 293. On boundary, xi., 26, 69, 71. Bond as Surveyor, 642. Road to Pittsburg, 642.
McClean, Archibald, v., 514, 536, 575, 661, 682, 704; vi., 294, 376. Letters to C. J. McKean, on foul practices, vii., 14. To and from, 127, 145. New state, 280. Appointed a commissioner to run line between Virginia, ix., 20. Alexander McClean, his substitute, 20. Commission 301, 304. Town lands, 371.
McClean, Capt, James, instructions from Comptroller to arrest smuggled goods, xi., 229. His letter to President Franklin, asking his advice, 230. President Franklin's answer, 230. Letter to Muhlenberg on, 231. Wants of the Invalid Guards, 406.
McCleery, Wm., viii., 584.
McClenachan, Blair, &c., respecting Cutter Revenge, vii., 248, 252, 281, 285, 288, 309, 343, 364, 397. Notice to, respecting sale of Ship Gen. Greene, viii., 3.
McClenachan & Irwin, agents of Gen. Greene, vii., 263, 265, 309, 310, 318, 322, 442. Sale of Minerva's cargo of fish, 768.
McCleery, Col , xii., 278.
McClughan, John, letter, iii., 393.
McConnell, Major Matthew, ix., 254, 346, 371, 424.
McConnels Town or Sleeping Place, xii., 461.
McCord's Fort, attack on, ii., 617; xii., 399.
McCulloh, Captain John, vii., 370. Arrives at Billingsport to relieve Col. Proctor's Artillery, 371.
McDonald, Cap., takes Fort Freeland, vii., 591.
McDowell, Alexander, vi., 572.
McDowell's Fort, iii., 51. At, xii., 398.
McDowell, John, applies to Rev. Mr. Finley, to visit western frontiers, ix., 729.
McElhatton, Cap., instructions to, viii., 365.
McElheney, Geo., vii., 315. Orders 537.
McElroy, Archibald, commands a Battalion, viii., 323, 326.
McFarlan, Lt., viii., 594.
McFarlane, A., ix., 55.
Magee, John, vi., 38.
McGillivray, and Chiefs of Creek nation of Indians visit Philada., xi., 707.
McGinley, Capt. John, vii., 652.
McGlasken, Sergt. Leonard, warrant to arrest, iv., 224. Letter from Wm. Smith respecting, 229. Deposition, 233, 234.
McGowan, Capt., viii., 209.
McGuire, Matthew, applies for money for Penna. Line, v., 756.
McHenry, Capt., Matt., vii., 384.
McIllvaine, Francis, xii., 161. Letters to, 170, 172.
McIlvaine, Wm., v., 509.
McIntosh, Fort, ix., 648. Instructions to Sergts. Lee and McClure to take possession of, x., 109. Situation of, 391. Facts respecting, 406, 448, 466. To be vacated, 704. Troops at, xii., 108, 277, 300. Design in building, 110. Has preference of General W., 125, 126, 168. Described, 400-404. Soldier killed, 148. Provisions, 174, Capt. Clarke at, 174, 234, 247. Indians cross Ohio near, 248—killed, 250, 252.
McIntosh, General Lach, of Geo., proposed to succeed Gen. Hand, vi., 467. Arrives at Lancaster, 564. His movements, 646, 651, 662; vii., 131, 173, 342. Operations on Ohio, 132, 565. Respecting, 431. Unfortunate, 465; xii., 109, 119, 146. Designs on Detroit—building of Fort McIntosh, 110, 118. Appoints officers, 113. Provisions, 114. Not on good terms with General Morgan, 116. To go south, 118.
McIntyre, Capt., viii., 40, 106.
McIntire, Captain Thomas, xii., 158, 159, 209, 212, 216, 235, 237, 243. Attacks and kills Indians, 249, 250, 252, 270.
McKean, Thomas, opinion of, attainder on a free-holder's removal

to another State, v., 400. Qualification and oath as Chief Justice, 621; vi., 266, 555, 566, 569. Opinion respecting Treasurer, 566. Asked for notes in trial of Roberts & Carlisle, vii., 21. His notes in case of Ab'm Carlisle, 44-52. Proceedings in Congress respecting him and General Thomson, 137. Prisoners in jail, 699, 703, 773. Letter from Council respecting D. Lenox and R. Smith, 637. Intercepted letter from S. R. Fisher, 225, 274, 279. Favor of George Hardy, 326. Letter to on forfeited estates, 328. Riot at Fort Wilson, 732, 735, 744. Opinion on Traitors and when Government began, 645. Respecting Sheriffs, Justices, &c., 699. Letters, viii., 14, 178, 234, 298, 330, 406, 597, 649, 650, 657. Bailing of Griswold, &c., 649, 650. Statement of attorney general, 666. Correspondence with President Reed, on bailing Griswold, 649-651, 654, 666. To occupy Duchés house, 685. Letters, ix., 42. Elected President of Congress, 267. J. Thomas, persons under sentence of death, 125. Can he, being delegate to Congress, legally act as Judge of Supreme Court of the State? 163. Proposes a pardon, 634. Passport for R. Logan, 751. Letter of French minister on Seamen, 734. Answers to Council on Justices of peace, x., 19-21. Case of Dr. Wm. Moland, 176. Commission expires—is re-elected C. J., 285. Respecting Henry Carberry, 290, 291. Asks for a pardon for A. Bare, 396. Letter to, on disturbances in Northumberland Co., 448, 460. Opinion on claim of Messrs. Penn to interest, 730. Opinion on depreciation of pay, xi., 120. On Brown's case, 264. On powder magazine, 276, 283. Letter to, respecting A. and L. Doane and J. Dryer, 351. Jones and McElroy, 366. Recommends J. Potter, 661. On price of affixing great seal, xii., 78. Letter to, on robbery in Bucks County, 299.

McKee's Fort, vi., 404.

McKee, Capt. Alex., joins Indians, vi., 445.

McKee, Capt. Thos., (McGee) Commission, to iii., 219. Letters to and from, 563, 564, 615, 684. Instructions, 533; x., 86.

McKinley, John, letter from, iii., 381. Vessels of war near mouth of Christiana, iv., 746. Despatches from Wilmington, men of war off creek's mouth, 746. Engagement with the Roebuck and Liverpool, 749.

McKinley, Brig. General John, letters, v., 34, 309, 456.

McKinney, David, resigns as Justice to enter Assembly, viii., 597.

McKnight, James, an Assemblyman, captured by Indians, vii., 346.

McLane, Captain Allen, clothing, viii., 56. Applies for an appointment, 258.

McLaughlin, Captain James, agreement with his Company, ii., 541. His orders, 543.

McLean, Moses, a commissioner to examine rivers, x., 330.

McLean, Brig. Gen., on Indian affairs, 70, 71, 88. Invites to dinner, 79.

McLean, Col., viii,, 555.

McLene, James, taxes, viii., 61. Letter from James Harris, on a road, xi., 186.

McMichael, John, petition, iii., 405.

McMillan, Rev. W., ix., 572.

McMillan, Rev. John, (1783,) x., 169.

McMullen, Wm., viii., 282.

McPherson, Capt. John, on defence of Del. River, vii., 180.

McPherson, Major W., application for adoption into the State, viii., 617.

McWilliams, Richard, appointed Judge, iv., 580.

Mackay, Æneas, letters, iv., 484, 494, 516, 517, 540. Deposition, 611. Letters, v., 59, 92. Insolence of officers, 59. On march from Kittanning—provisions scarce, 93, 135.

Mackay, Alex'r, notice to inhabitants west of Alleghany mountains, iv., 251.

Mackay, John, vi., 400. Required to attend Council, 400.
Maclay, William, letter on gaol, &c. at Sunbury, iv., 463. On Connecticut, 660; vi., 634; vii., 192, 357, 586, 590, 591, 593, 597, 598, 623. Recommends use of dogs against Indians, 357. Respecting Indians, viii., 156, 172. ix., 611. Letters to and from, x., 46. Commissioner to treat with Indians, 265. To examine roads and rivers, 129, 130. Indian boundary, 418, 444. Appointed commissioner, 334. To deliver goods to Indian chiefs, 510. And to explain certain expressions, 510.
Macclure, David, missionary passport, iv., 455.
Maconie Creek, attacks of Indians, ix., 396.
Madison, James, a Virginia commissioner, to run line between Pennsylvania, viii., 353.
Madison, Rev. James, appointed by Virginia, commissioner to run line, ix., 78, 233, 402, 439, 445. Appointed by Virginia as commissioner on boundary, x., 146. On trade of United States, 738.
Magazine required, v., 382. For provisions to be established, vi., 178. At Lancaster unsafe, ix., 36. At Wyoming, 166.
Magistrates, &c.—Qualifications.—Act respecting, i., 155. Complaint against a, 191. Recommended, iv., 409; v., 322, 347, 411, 421, 473, 504, 553, 581, 599; vi., 258. Conduct towards soldiers complained of, viii., 391.
Mahakimack settlements, distress of, vii., 603.
Mahingweegeesuch, Indian, xii., 229. Letter to Council at Coochocking, 230.
Mahusquechikoken, an Indian town on French Creek, xii., 157.
Mail packets between England and Halifax to be established, ii., 467.
Mail, robbery, of U. S. resolve of Congress on letter of P. M. Gen'l, ix., 560.
Mamachtagwin, Indian prisoner for murder—opinion of Judge Bryan as to his trial, x., 473.
Manaday Fort, xii., 405.
Manchash taken by Spaniards, xii. 216.
Manners, Rev. Mathias, Catholic priest, number under his care, iii., 144,
Mansin, Henry, examination, vi., 221.
Manufactures, inquiries respecting, iv., 292. Pennsylvania Society for encouraging cotton, subscription to, by the State, xi., 569.
Manvil, Ira, deposition, xi., 344. Commitment, 345. In gaol, 347.
Map of Delaware Bay and River, Fisher's, ii., 592, 593. Of Pennsylvania proposed by Lewis Evans, 47, 60, 309.
Marbois, Mons., letter on desertion of French seamen, ix., 734. Storing of powder, 741. Respecting plague supposed to exist at Marseilles, and regulations, x., 356. Letter from, 362. Appeal respecting duties on a box arriving for him, 367. Collector tenders the box—he declines, 368. Relinquished by Council—question reserved, 368. On resolution of Congress—settlement of accounts, 369. Anonymous letter to, respecting Longschamp, 409. Going to New York with Congress, 432. A French criminal, 440. L. Collinet released at his request, 447. Appoints his brother Vice-Consul, 471. Demands Longschamp, 706. Respecting English vessels assuming French colors, 175, (1783.) Respecting Longschamp, 277, 350. On Chev. Luzerne's departure, 283. Correcting a former letter, 311. At Fort Stanwix, 346. Thanks to Council in case of Longschamp, 351. Complains of interest not paid, 355.
Marbois, St. Pierre Francois Barbe de, Vice Consul at Philadelphia, x., 470, 478.
Marbois, Mons. Barbe de, letters to and from, xi., 461, 471, 479, 481. Certificate, [1784] 461. Complains of French merchants having to perform military duty, 49. Various documents, [1784] relating to affair with Longschamp, 461–495.
Marcus Hook, vessel launched, at-

tached under writ of Admiralty—escapes to Wilmington—letter of Judge Hopkinson respecting, x., 355. Piers at, 407, 471, 713. Spanish frigate in danger at, xi., 99–102.

Marine Committee of Congress, vii., 12, 76, 120, 235, 587, 637. On shipments of flour, 588; viii., 231.

Market Clerk of Reading, persons recommended, iii., 658. In Philadelphia ruined by enemy, vi., 369.

Markham, Gov. William, chooses first Council at Upland, and takes obligation of members, i., 37. Letter to Lord Baltimore, 39. Letter to, from Robert Wade, & J. S., 46. Negotiates first Indian purchase for Penn, 47. Recommended by William Penn, 69. Goes to England—petition to Duke of York, 78. Grants certificates of naturalization, 118. Letter William Penn to, respecting his bond, 126.

Marriage licenses, iv., 102, 175; xi., 690. Bishop White on, xii., 31, 314.

Marsh Creek, account of affairs at, i., 625, 634.

Marsh, Col. Joseph, orders to, ix., 396. Flag-staff on Market street hill to be repaired, 440.

Marshall, Christopher, to assist in procuring flour, vii., 668.

Marshall, Colonel James, disputes boundary line, &c., ix., 304, 315–319, 367.

Marshall, Lt. James, militia, ix., 192. Conduct of Penticost, 193, 233, 317, 343. Affairs in Washington Co., 343, 444, 484, 575. On defence of frontiers, xi., 377.

Marsteller, Philip, vi., 264. To purchase flour, vii., 567, 716. Respecting flour, viii., 51. Forage master, 155, 328, 362, 371, 383. Supplies for expedition, ix., 638, 641.

Martial, Courts, v., 384, 396.

Martial law, opinion of, xii., 127.

Martin, Col. Sub. Lt. of Bedford Co., vii., 446.

Martin, Henry, intercession for, ix., 751.

Martin, John, and wife murdered and scalped by Indians, ix., 658, 659.

Martin, Thomas, petition of, xi., 69.

Maryland, an Indian trader murdered by Indians, ii., 16. Depositions relating to, 18, 81, 22, 37, 64, 76, 82, 265, 266, 283, 335, 440; (see depositions.) Letter J. Churchman, 19, 25. Care of Joseph England, 21, 25. Digge's choice, petition, 28. Correspondence between Governors of, and Pennsylvania, 40, 46, 57, 91, 93, 113, 125, 130, 187, 192, 213, 228, 244, 274, 382, 397, 451, 504, 540, 557, 573. Boundary line between Pennsylvania, 40, 41, 49, 73. Examination of Martin Kitzmiller, 70. Letter John Digges on the death of his son, 73. Depositions respecting, 76–82. Letter to Geo. Stevenson, forbidding a levy on certain lands, 89. List of Taxes, 94. Governor of Pennsylvania sends for copies of public papers, 92. Granted, 93. Petition of Henry Darnall, Attorney-General, to Judges at York, respecting death of Digge's son, 92. Letter John S. Hawkins, 117. Commissioners to Indian treaty at Albany, 138. Wm. Morris and Wm. Green, depositions, 265. James Anderson, 267, 283. Watman Sipple's case, 335, 337, 440. Petition to Governor Morris from sufferers by Maryland, 432. Grant of £10,000 by Assembly, 685. Statement of Wm. Johnson, a prisoner, iii., 16. Letter from Indians to Governor of, 143. Letters to and from Governor Sharpe, 143, 183, 197, 585, 662. Depositions, (which see.) Death of Outten, 585, 660. Minutes of Council, 586. Proceedings in Worcester County Court, 609. Agreement between Lord Baltimore and T. & R. Penn, to appoint commissioners to run boundary line between Maryland and Pennsylvania, 1760, iv., 1–36. Commissioners appointed by Maryland, Delaware and Pennsylvania, respecting State lines,

1849, George S. Key appointed, 37. Letter of Gov. Penn to Gov. Sharpe, on peace made with Indians by Bradstreet, 207 Frontier inhabitants removing over mountains, 217. Letter, Gov. Sharpe, 262, 277. Petition from S. Kennedy, &c., of New Castle county, against rioters from, 331. Case of Saml. Galloway, convicted at Dover, 341. Letter Gov. Eden on convention on Indian trade, 368. On proclamation, 616. Letter from Wm. Digges, respecting Digges' choice, 489. From Benj. Chambers, 535. From Gov. R'd Lee, 538. Examination of Connolly, &c., by Committee on Frederick County, 680. Regiment under Colonel Richardson, v., 177. Troops from, expected under General Johnston, 194. Arrive in Philadelphia, 196. Expected attack by British, 289. Contempt of Capt. Nicholson, to Gov. Johnson, 328. Gen. Howe in Chesapeake, 543. Lands in, 557. Offers troops for Phila., vi., 183. Provisions for Cheaspeake, 442, and men from gallies, 442. Law respecting distillation of grain, vii., 125. Letter to Gov., 197. To Magistrates of Baltimore, 390. Wheat carried into, 688. Price, 688. Gov. Lee's letters, on Embargo, viii., 329, 354, 432, 433. Signs, articles of confederation, 749, 751. Convention, prisoners to be removed from, to Pennsylvania, 753. Convention prisoners, ix., 5. Letters of Gov. Lee, 12, 37. Letter R. Morris to, 474. Mason & Dixon's line, 549. Line of soldiers, x., 55. Passes an Act on restrictions of British on American commerce, 155. Correspondence respecting Henry Carberry, 290–293. Letter to Gov., 320. From, 324, 744. Chinese recommended to Gov. of, 527, 528. Inland navigation commissioners, 538, 540. Act respecting claims, 753. Act to comply with requisitions, xi., 16, 23. Letters to Governor respecting sick Chinese, 56. Resolution of Assembly, 77. Inland navigation, 77. And Virginia on internal navigation, 511. On commerce, 521.

Maryland and Pennsylvania. — Depositions (which see) Letters to and from Gov. Calvert, i., 289, 292. Conference with Willam Penn, 74. Case of Wherry and Holey, 289, 292. Thomas Cresap, 311, 313, 316, 320, 321, 326, 336, 338, 352, 398, 410, 412, 415, 417, 419, 462, 464, 475, 476, 489, 501, 556. Warrant to arrest, 489. Depositions, 504, 528. Correspondence between Gov. Ogle and Gov. Gordon, 313, 320, 326, 330, 427, 434, 442, 447, 461, 466, 471, 479, 486. Relative to Boundary Line, 336, 342, 461, 556, 557, 558, 595, 616. Agreement received, 342. Petition of Ross and Carroll, 333. Case of Daniel and W. Lowe, 349. Titles of various documents, 369, 376, 402. Abstract of Newton's deed, 374. Justices of Kent to Justices of Maryland, 376. Answers, 376, 387, 388. Lord Baltimore to Gov. G., 393, 395. Case of James Heath and J. Steele, 426, 433. Hamilton and Georges appointed by Pennsylvania Commissioners to, 427. Their commission, 428. And instructions, 429, 435. Case of T. & J. Rothwell, 433, 561, 584, 590, 592. Historical sketch by Gov. G., 479. Mittimus for prisoners, 529, 530, 533. Case of Charles Higginbotham, 530, 534. Canon's case, 534. Answer of Dutch to Governor, 492. Miles Foy in jail at Philadelphia, 547. Outrages, 555 Notice to, of meeting of Commissioners in Philadelphia, 623. Affairs at Marsh Creek, 625, 535. Case of John Digges, 637, 643, 681, 683, 684, 685, 686, 693, 696, 710, 719. Letters to and from Gov. Bladen and Gov. G., 645, 686, 692.

Mason and Dixon—agreement on which they afterwards ran the boundary line, 1760, iv., 1-36. Line to be extended to fix a boundary, between Virginia and

Pennsylvania, viii., 353, 570. Allowance to Commissioners for extending, ix., 4. Commissioners to extend, 78, 190, 304, 519, 549; x., 224.
Mason, George, declines building a house, his reasons, vi., 287.
Mason, John, militia, vi., 373.
Mason, Isaac, ravages of Indians, ix., 238, 303.
Massachusetts Assembly, Resolutions, i., 666. Correspondence with Governors, ii., 20, 26, 181. Commissioners to Indian treaty at Albany, 137. Wants provisions from Philadelphia, 412. Embargo on provisions asked by Assembly, 283. Asks for provisions, 732. Gov. Pownall describes great fire in Boston and asks for aid, iii., 714. Commissioners of, claim share of parliamentary grant, iv., 159. Letter Gov. Bernard, 163. Assembly circular to the Colonies, 286. Send letters from Franklin and Adams, vi., 521. Letter to President of Council respecting Mr. Temple, vii., 138. Letter to President of, respecting embargo on flour, 231. Asks for flour—recommendation of Congress, 315, 324. Representation, 763. Troops, viii., 44. Letter to Pres. Powell, of, 254. Asks provisions, 522. Letter from Robert Morris to, ix., 474. Letter to Gov., demand of fugitives, x., 354. Insult to, by Capt. Stanhope, 499. Acts of, complained of by British, 745-747. Act to comply with requisitions, xi., 16, 23. Proclamation against Daniel Shays, &c., 119. Annulled, 271. Extract from deed of cession of Erie, 310.
Master of Rolls, iii., 703.
Masters, William and Joseph Galloway, letter, iii., 160.
Masts, for French Fleet, being cut on Schuylkill, viii., 545, 548, 549, 552, 578. Cut on Schuylkill for French navy, ix., 10, 181.
Matchitongo, ii., 556, 561.
Matlack, Timothy, v., 254, 323, 332, 337, 355, 357, 364, 469, 485, 487, 507, 602, 612, 616, 620. Letters, vi., 5, 10, 56, 76, 82, 106. Insulted by guards at Lancaster, 201. Letter to Arnold, vii., 223. Answer, 224. Letter, viii., 60. Memorial, x., 198-202. Letters of Attorneys for State, 202, 364, 367. Respecting his case, 9, 363, 365. Report on, 365. Memorial, xi., 150. Warrant to arrest, 154.
Matthews, Colonel George, on behalf of prisoners of war, at New York, viii., 660.
Matthews, Dr. Hugh, to be arrested in Philadelphia, iii., 64.
Mattox, John, Indian outrages on, i., 266.
Maul, James, instructions to, iv., 680.
Maxitawny, murders by Indians, iii., 219.
Maxwell, General, v., 177. Proceedings of Congress in case of, 328; vii., 119, 129, 178. Report to Congress respecting, 138.
May, Cape, Channel, v., 425, 429. Guns for, 346. Beacon at, xi., 93.
Mead, David, on Wyoming affairs, v., 207, 222, 404, 482, 663, 707, On Wyoming affairs, [1785] vi., 455.
Meade, George, & Co., v., 61. Vessel loaded by French Consul, vii., 407.
Mease, James, appointed Clothier General, v., 193.
Mease and Caldwell, letter, v., 104, 120.
Mease, James, vi., 22, 426, 428. Clothier, viii., 639.
Mease, John, elected auctioneer for Philadelphia, x., 206, 209.
Meason, Captain Samuel, v., 445.
Measurement of Vessel, instructions respecting, iv., 56.
Medicines, list of, for army, viii., 519.
Mediterranean, passes, orders respecting, i., 177, 180, 183, 184.
Meeker, Major, (of New York) vii., 573.
Meens, Lieut., prevents a rescue, vii., 299.
Melchor, Colonel Isaac, v., 178, 206, 507, 527, 584; vi., 676, 699;

viii., 65. Map of boundary, xi., 423.

Melsheimer, Mr., a British chaplain, recommended, viii., 123.

Memorial to Governor Jennings, from Salem, i., 75. Inhabitants of Welsh Tract, 108, 110. Of Christ Church, 150. On Indian trade, 261. On Indian outrage, 265. S. Hazard to Connecticut, for Western lands, ii., 301. Of Joshua, a Christian Indian, iii., 434. Of Synod against plays, 656. Of John Bayard and Rd. Peters, on troops in City, iv., 17. Of Committee for driving cattle, 461. Of Gun stockers, 733. Commander Seymour, 434. Northampton county, for defence, iv., 120. Of pilots of Philadelphia, 262. Wardens, 264. Merchants, 270. L. Weiss, 472. Northumberland and Northampton, 669, 685. To Congress, from prisoners at Winchester, vi., 111. Of recruiting officers to Council, 280. Of Council and Assembly to Congress, 333. In cases of John Roberts and Abm. Carlisle, vii., 21-24. In favor of John Roberts, 24-44. In favor of Abm. Carlisle, 52-58. Of Justices of Northumberland, 72. Respecting James Warren, 113. Of widow, &c., of John Roberts, 122. Of first company of artillery of Philadelphia, 392. B. Flower to Assembly, viii., 27. Of Hazen's regiment to General W., respecting Canada regiment, 17. Of Dunlap and Budden, 208. Of officers of militia, 264. From Colonel Proctor's artillery, ix., 74. Of Col. Butler's regiment of artificers, 105. Captain Thomas Robinson, 228. Of Virginia delegates, 266. Of second battalion, 429. Prisoners in Clarke's expedition, 574. Overseers of poor of N. L., 739. Andrew Long, 762. Of Major M. Ryan, x., 91, 308. Of Ephriam Douglass, 118. Against theatres in Philadelphia, 141-143. Of T. Matlack, 198, 226, 363, 365. Of Merchants of Philadelphia, 208, 411. Fayette county, 280. John Franklin to Assembly of Connecticut, 681. Of Merchants, on Barbary powers, 411, 418, 705. Light infantry of Philadelphia, xi., 30. Of Northumberland co., 123. Of T. Matlack, 150. Of Charles Sims, 160. Inhahitants of Luzerne county for division of lands, 386.

Menonists or German Quakers, iii., 194. Opposed to militia, v., 768. Complain of oath, vi., 572. Of Lancaster Co., have many cattle, viii., 329.

Mentges, Colonel Francis, military parade in Philadelphia. xi., 78. His pay, 103.

Mentges, Lieutenant Colonel P., sales of confiscated estates at Reading, ix., 216, 299.

Mercantile Society of Philadelphia, thank Council for use of room, xi., 103.

Mercer, Fort, vi., 21. Evacuated, 21, 28. xii., (See Red Bank.)

Mercer, Widow, pension, xi., 679.

Mercer, Captain Hugh, orders to, ii., 603. Letter, 632; iii., 57, 571, 624, 673, 685, 721.

Mercer, James H., recruiting in Pennsylvania, ii., 281.

Mercer, Brigadier-General, cannons sent for, by Council, v., 41, 67. Letters, 41, 67, 71. Orders to attend funeral, 222.

Mercer, Colonel James, commanding a battalion at Lancaster, ix., 654.

Merchants complain against duty on tobacco, i., 149. Petition on size of barrels, 203. New York, complain of embargo, ii., 702. Of Philadelphia—memorial, inspection of lumber, iv., 270. Complaints against, 361, 373, 380. Of Philadelphia, letter to, on embargo, viii., 266. Aid, 704. Of Philadelphia, petition on seizure of sugars, ix., 534. On French seamen, 731. Of Philadelphia, conference of Assembly with, on internal commerce, x., 128. Letter to, in answer to memorial, 208, 210. Letter from, to Council, regulations, &c., 212. Advice asked by President Dickinson, 219. Their answer, 221. Letter to, on piers in Delaware River, 407. Memorial respecting Barbary

powers, 411, 418, 705. Apprized of war between Algiers and United States, xi., 522.
Meridian, &c., N. Scull, on mode of ascertaining, ii., 73.
Merlin, British man-of-war, blown up in Delaware, v., 721, 722.
Mersereau, Joshua, letter to Gov. Livingston on a supposed British deserter, ix., 287.
Messages, Governor Johnston, respecting publication of Records and Archives, i., 3. Shawnese, to Governor, 329. To and from Assembly, iii., 19, 90, 99, 112, 710, 718. Teedyuscung to Governor, 509. From Assembly at New Castle, 379, 384. Gen. Amherst to Indians, iv., 48. Governor to Assembly of New Castle, 72, 585. Teedyuscung, 78. Assembly, 250, 474. Governor to Assembly, 685. Of Council to Assembly, vii., 738. &c., of Gov. Mifflin, xii., 29, 85.
Methodists, persecuted by a magistrate, who considers them Tories, viii., 740.
Meyer, Isaac, murdered—proclamation, iv., 376.
Meyer, Engin'r, letters, iii., 47, 48.
Meyer, Wendle, examination, vi., 225.
Miami Indians, x., 85. On trade, 744.
Middletown, New Jersey, action at, v., 158. Guards at, vi., 549. Escort of stores from, vii., 458.
Mifflin, Fort, attack on, v., 699, 701. Heavy cannonading at, vi., 11. Loss of, 19, 23, 24. Complaints against fleet, 24. Commodore Hazelwood's account, 47-50; vii., 240, 270, 339, 365, 369, 562, 652. Or Mud Fort, xii., 407-412.
Mifflin, John, dry lands in Northampton county, xi., 646.
Mifflin, Jona., making lumber into rafts on Delaware, v., 86. Letters, 86, 584, 594, 596, 597. Appointed superintendent of flour magazines, vi., 235, 240, 289.
Mifflin, Colonel Samuel, orders to, v., 44.
Mifflin, General Thomas, addresses a town meeting at State House, v., 77. Letter to, 125. At Lancaster, 128. Return to army—arrival at Monmouth, 158. Announces to Congress that General Washington thinks British intend starting for Phila., 358. Appointed with Mons. Du Coudray, to complete works on Delaware, 359. Letters, 125, 375, 381, 490, 554. Attacks Tories at Monmouth, 168. At Morristown, 192. Letters, 125, 375, 381, 490, 720. Announces resignation of Washington, x., 183. Elected President, xi., 411.
Mifflin, Gov. Thos., on Indian murders, xii., 9 Certifi'te of election as Gov'r, 28. First message as Governor, 29. Letters to and from, 31, 32, 90, 93, 95, 100. To Speaker on communication between two houses, 33. Address before Legislature, 34, and their answer, 44. Approves acts, and appoints A. J. Dallas, Secretary of State, 46. Messages, 29, 85. Invitation to funeral of Benjamin Franklin, 85.
Miles, Colonel Samuel, letter from, v., 5. Appointed Dep. Q. M. by T. Pickering, viii., 499, 533, 600, 608, 618. Applies for authority to cut wood for soldiers, over Schuylkill, 618. Furnish a horse, 699. Quarters for soldiers in Philadelphia, 718, 719; ix., 80, 95, 150, 153, 280, 324, 346, 357, 389, 432. Shot and shells to be sent to head of Elk, 432. Certificate of Supreme Court in case of, xi., 547.
Military affairs, iv., 37, 40, 45, 47, 51, 73, 74, 114, 124, 129, 132, 141, 143, 145, 147, 166, 171, 172, 176, 179, 181, 193, 195, 196, 199, 203, 206, 210, 212, 259, 377, 393, 639, 642, 656, 693, 702, 710. Court of Inquiry on Jacob Kern, 199; v., 3, 5, 10, 12, 13, 14, 17, 18, 27, 33, 34, 43, 52, 58, 63, 80, 102, 104, 107, 113, 114, 115, 119, 170, 265, 267, 304, 322, 326, 330, 333, 343, 345, 364, 369, 384-396, 425, 432, 482, 483, 485, 491, 492, 522, 530, 556; x., 14, 15, 22, 23, 39, 53, 190, 284, 436, 449, 450.
Military School, vi., 411.
Military trophies, to be collected by order of Congress, viii., 68.
Military stores in Pennsylvania, xi.,

699. A conductor to be appointed xii., 268.

Militia Law, passed, ii., 513, 531, 561. Noticed, v., 200. Of Bucks County, 322.

Militia, Associated Companies of Philadelphia City, iii., 19. Of Bucks County, 19. Of York Co., 20. Of Lancaster County, 21. Of New Castle County, 21, 22. Kent County, 23. Sussex, 23. Estimate cost of three battalions, 61. Of New Castle, Kent, and Sussex, 87. List of officers in Province pay and dates of Commissions, 88, 89. Number of blankets, &c., sent west of Susquehanna, 95. Number of men, 99. Act for forming and regulating the, 107, 112, 117, 120. Rights of Conscience protected in, 128. Respecting, 150. Killed &c., at Ticonderoga, 203. Fines, cases of Quakers at Wilmington, Del., 154, 165, 170. Remarks on Law, 309. List of officers in pay with date of Commiss'ns, 336; vi., 34, 57, 59, 85, 86, 89, 100, 119, 149, 155, 157, 166, 169, 172, 174, 176, 180, 196, 200, 229, 241, 244, 263, 275, 277, 288, 296, 301, 302, 350, 361, 369, 370, 374, 379, 389, 391, 392, 398, 413, 416, 426, 445, 452, 464, 472, 478, 481, 490, 494, 540, 556, 579, 582, 586, 594, 619, 644, 649, 654, 667, 687, 691, 700, 711, 727, 745, 756. Complaints against, 85, 89. Law, Gen. Wayne's of, 86. Neglect of, in case of Gen. Irwine, 100. Soldiers to be free from Ruptures &c., 248; vii., 18, 64, 66, 69, 74, 77, 80, 82, 98, 99, 104, 106, 110, 115, 116, 122, 142, 146, 202, 230, 260, 280, 282, 341, 354, 355, 365, 367, 369, 375, 393, 401, 404, 406, 415, 426, 430, 435, 455, 496, 499, 519, 535, 546, 553, 564, 612, 615, 640, 677, 679, 681, 741, 763, 764. Baron Steuben, views of, 325. Laws respecting delinquents, President Reed's views, 359. Laws good, 508; viii., 5, 16, 21, 26, 27, 39, 50, 52, 62, 68, 69, 96, 103, 109, 119, 120, 149, 189, 207, 243, 250, 264, 265, 268, 270, 271, 292, 293, 305, 309, 315, 321, 333, 337, 338, 344, 351, 374, 376, 378, 382, 386, 389, 401, 443, 454, 484, 491, 503, 507, 509, 531, 535, 549, 623, 633, 640, 645, 667; ix., 7, 8, 30, 47, 52, 62, 65, 69, 71, 149, 184, 186, 198, 202, 205, 209, 210, 211, 218, 220, 221, 225, 226, 228, 231, 241, 253, 276, 288, 303, 338, 348, 364, 382, 397, 400, 407, 410, 418, 419, 421, 429, 433, 434, 457, 514, 539, 632. Law, difficulties, 381, 382. Fines, 186, 200. Companies in Berks Co., and officers, x., 190. Of Cumberland Co., returns, xi., 605, Fines, 669. Lieut. Hubley respecting, 738, Ordered out, xii., 215.

Miller, Capt. 8th Penn. Regt., killed by Indians with seven others, vi., 673.

Miller, Rev. Frederick Cosemer, recommended for chaplain, iii. 362.

Miller, Fort, xii., 412.

Miller, Henry, and John Clark, Jr., vii., 609.

Miller, John, letters, iii., 455, 545.

Miller, Rev. Peter, intercedes for John Rein, viii., 606. Applies in behalf of John Rein, ix., 27. Intercedes for John Rein, 313. Reply to, 314. For Menonists 751.

Millers, Instructions to, vi., 303.

Milligan, James, nominates John Story as commissioner to settle accounts, x., 426, 427. Commissioner on Susque'na River, 755.

Milligan, Robert, on internal navigation, xi., 27.

Mills, Francis, oath of allegiance, v., 15.

Miners and Sappers, companies to be formed, vii., 690.

Mines at Sinking Spring Valley, vii., 305.

Mingo Indians, number of, i., 301; xii., 108, 111, 114, 119, 120, 123, 127, 181, 233.

Minister of France, French Squadron expected, calls for American troops, promised, viii., 334. Asks President and Council to dinner, 45, 609. Affairs of Mr. Holker, 614, 628.

Minnesinks, Tories and Indians burning and destroying at, vii., 15. Distress at, 573, 575.

Minor, Captain John, v., 444.
Mintzes, Francis, Adjutant, v., 6.
Minutes of Council, not in Colonial Records, ii , 166. Of a meeting at Sugar Cabins, on Braddock's road, 321. Of Executive Council at Easton, 721, 730, 743. Of Provincial Commissioners, iii., 454, 476. Of Council at New Castle, on bills of credit, 630. Of Council at Fort George, New York, iv., 167. Of Board of Commissioners for defence, 195. Of Commissioners of Pennsylvania on Indian trade, 372. Of conference with Indians at Pittsburg, 531. Of Committee of Berks, 649. Of committee for erecting powder mills, 709.
Miralles, Don Juan De, asks permission to ship flour, viii., 174. Dies, 228. Will defective, 228. Rent of house in Market street demanded, ix., 196.
Miranda, J., complaint against by Indians, i., 267.
Miro, Brigadier-General, Governor of Louisiana, letter to, respecting a negro, xi., 566.
Missionaries, passports for, iv., 455. Journal of, 495.
Mitchell, David, xii., 250, 260.
Mitchell, Captain Alexander, provisions, ix., 165. Return of troops, 166.
Mitchell, John, letter on provisions for troops, v., 62; vi., 762, 763, 764 ; vii., 160, 189, 345, 412, 474, 527. Respecting Arnold's affair, 160, 175, 179, 207, 213, 220, 262. Wagons, 248, 746. Money for Schuylkill bridge, viii., 187. Horses, 334. Command at Wyoming, 716, 721. On militia, 500, 501. Letters to, xii., 148, 152.
Mitchell, Joseph, purchase of lands from William Penn through John Hughes, xi., 253.
Mittimus for two Maryland prisoners, i., 529. For Joseph Richardson, v., 249. Henry Funk, 508. M. Immel, 649. For John Brown, vi., 25. For several persons, 80.
Mohican Indians, xii., 131, 132.
Moland, Dr. Wm., case of, x., 176.
Molesworth, James, British spy, depositions, John Eldridge, v., 270, 271. Andrew Higgins, 270, 272, 336. John Snyder, 271,272, 336. Abigail McCoy, 275, 278, 290, 336. Examination of J. Molesworth, 277. His confession, 280. Sarah O'Brien, 277, 290, 337. War office to General Lincoln, respecting, 281. Accomplices, 281, 282, 315. Board of war to General Putnam, 282. To Executive Council, 290. Executed, 283. Opinion respecting his estate, ix., 659.
Molyneaux, ——, killed, x., 73.
Monckton, Gen. Robert, letter, iii., 732. Conference with Indians at Pittsburg, 744. Brigadier-General, iv., 39, 45.
Monk, British ship of war General, captured by Hyder Ally, Captain Barney, ix., 532. Purchased for defence of Delaware river, 531. Name changed, 530. Captures by the Washington, 586. To be sold, 621. Sale of, 624.
Money, rates of, Act respecting, i., 156. Continental, resolves of Congress on, v., 126. Scarcity, vi., 81, 384, 391. Scarcity of, viii., 133. Rate of, 302, 304. Depreciation, 350, 383, 385, 396. Plan to appreciate, xi., 416. Depreciation great, xii., 146, 248.
Monmouth C. H., v., 158. Mifflin attacks tories at, 169. Gurney, do., 177.
Montgomery county, no prison there, x., 408. Dispute between magistrates and commissioners respecting fees, 743.
Montgomery, Mrs. Dorcas, pass for to Europe, vi., 84.
Montgomery, Fort, artillery for, v., 50. Taken, 671.
Montgomery's fort, viii., 29, 171.
Montgomery, General, oration on death of, to be delivered before Congress, iv., 714.
Montgomery, Hugh, v., 57, 120.
Montgomery, Capt. James of Ship, Gen. Greene, vii., 311. Ordered to join Boston frigate, 454, 487. Takes privateer Brig Impertinent, 476. Cruizes with Capt. Nicholson, 533. Takes privateer Brig Bayard, 706. Takes prizes, 609, 623, 664, 755.

Montgomery, James, T., warden, xii., 314.
Montgomery, John, letters, iv., 505, 506, 533.
Montgomery, Hon. John, letter respecting Court decided on by Congress, x., 216 Representation in Congress, 220.
Montgomery, Joseph, letter on Wyoming, x., 31. A commissioner, 330, 444. Elected commissioner to examine rivers, 312. Asks for a transit instrument, 416.
Montgomery, Revd. Joseph, respecting Frontiers, viii., 170.
Montgomery, William, history of, vi., 62. Trial, 239.
Montgomery, Wm., ix., 641; appointed to exam'e rivers, x., 130. Resigns, 312. Appointed comm'r, 335. Elected member of Congress, 354. To Council, 765, 766. Letters to and from, xi., 35, 108. Letter from Colonel John Franklin, to, 111, Appointed commissioner to Luzerne, 177.
Montgomery, ship, and other continental vessels burned in the Delaware for safety, v., 740.
Montour, Andrew, ii., 9. Wants a house built for him, 12. Respecting, 230, 454; xii., 196.
Montreal, Great fire at, asks aid, iv., 248.
Moore, Captain, resigns, viii., 288; Engagement with Indians, ix., 202.
Moore, Cap. J. F., resigns, xii., 144.
Moore, James, ix., 62.
Moore, Major, James, ix., 285; Recruiting instructions, x., 127. Commands Pennsylvania, Line, 131. Instructions, 132. On Wyoming affairs, 183, 187, 197, 209, 222, 232, 286.
Moore, Lt. Col. James, on Wyoming, xi., 434, 435, 436, 443.
Moore, John, appointed collector of Philadelphia, i., 195; Letter from Fort Lee, v., 66, 135, &c.; petition setting forth the great scarcity of provisions, vii., 186.
Moore, Robert, a murderer, proclamation against, i., 170.
Moore, Thomas, vii., 543; Respecting danger to piers from Spanish frigate at Marcus Hook, xi., 99
Moore, William, Confession of, iii., 324. Petition against, 328. Commitment of, 332. Flattering letter to and from Governor, 512. Elected, V. P. vii., 745. Elected President of State, ix., 447. Term expires as President of Council, 651. Letter to, respecting corporation papers, x., 93.
Moorehead, Cap. of Indep. Co., viii., 78; xii., 127, 129, 165.
Morales, Francis, case of a sailor, x, 476, 499.
Moravian Indian Towns, general war expected, viii., 766. Indians, kindness of, ix., 167. Massacre at Muskingum, 523, 524, 629.
Moravians, Examinations of ii., 459. Settlements destroyed, 521, 525, 526, 527, 549, 565. List of, at Bethlehem, iii., 69, 76, 242. Letters respecting, 141. Indians, 500. Missionaries—Journal, to Muskingum, iv., 495. Letter from D. Zeisberger, 498. Ask for relaxing of the Test, vi., 541, 551; viii., 551.
Morden, Ralph, convicted of Treason letter, C. J. McK. respecting, viii., 597.
Morgan, Dr., arrives at Pittsburg, xii., 117, 191.
Morgan. Col. George, v., 286, 313, 447. Honorable acquittal, vi., 386 587, 652. Message from Indians 652, 714; ix., 17. Respecting J. and T. Kilbuck, Indian hostages—asks for a pass for them to Pittsburg, x., 526; xii., 115, 129, 146, 206, 208. Letters to 116, 153, 159, 190, 208, 249. Not on good terms with Gen. McI., 116.
Morgan. Cap. Jacob, letters, iii., 30, 31, 39, 191. Journal, 252.
Morgan, Col. Jacob, v., 299, 313, 322, 341, 407, 447, 466, 530, 608, 632, 756, 761, 767; vi., 14. 47, 119, 288, 419, 441, 522, 706; viii., Indians arms, 238. Appoint-for Philad., 448, 552, 594, 702.
Morgan, Lt. Jacob, respecting militia of Berks county, viii., 273, 345. Provisions, 344. Militia, 369, 545, 655.
Morgan; Lt. Jacob, Jr., vi., 47, 119, 128, 382, 399, 543, 568, 575, 638. Appointed Quarter Master, resigns

as Council, 399; vii., 3, 483, 484, 559. Accounts, ix., 127. Lands of proprietary, 231. Letter to, on Indian murders, 236. Provisions, 326.
Morgan, Lt. B. C., vi., 562, 630 Q. M. G., viii., 83.
Morgan, Capt. Simon, xii., 173, 208.
Morocco, signals agreed upon between, and United States, xi., 171.
Morris, Colonel Anthony, wounded, v., 162. Order to attend funeral of, 223. Recommended as an officer, vi., 99.
Morris, Col. (British), v , 158.
Morris, Cadwalader, elected member of Congress, x., 354. Resigns, 354.
Morris, fort, at Shippensburg, xii., 412–415.
Morris, A. James, troops, vii., 760.
Morris, John, Jr., letter, v., 160, 294, 481, 482, 506, 749. To attend courts, 481, 506.
Morris, Lewis, letters to and from, ii., 314; v., 351.
Morris, Lewis, Jr., instructions to, private vessels for soldiers, iii., 90.
Morris, Robert, letters to and from, v., 28, 31, 126, 132, 138, 173, 174, 189, 191, 216, 255, 379, 382, 627, 759, 760. Asks for a pilot, 28. For a surgeon, 254. Asks leave of absence from Congress to attend to his private affairs, 759. Granted, 760. Respecting Jno. Brown, vi., 45. Letter respecting arms imported, vii., 125, 387, 417, 608. Arms for state, viii., 373, 415. Submits to Congress a plan for a National Bank of North America, ix., 172, 477. Letters to and from, 244, 245, 250, 251, 263, 264, 280, 281, 285, 286, 287, 291, 310, 373, 376, 383, 387, 395, 397, 398, 414, 416, 417, 418, 419, 435, 446, 454, 474, 477, 481, 487, 488, 505, 512, 513, 544, 636. To provide supplies, 262, 285. Respecting, 346. Superintendent of finance, 244, 254. Tents, 386, 387. His advice requested by President Reed, 416. Writes to States, 474. Views of Finances, prospects of peace, &c., 488–492. Report of Committee on, 499. Captain Van Heer, 505. Public accounts, 513. Appoints agent to settle accounts between Pennsylvania and United States, 668. President Dickinson asks state of revenue, 739. Answer to, 740. Letters to, on refusing to pay troops, x., 312. Answer to, 313. Letter from War Office, 314. Answer, 315. Letters to and from, 53. Copies of accounts sent to Council by Comptroller General, 481. On accounts, xi., 505. Commissioners on Commerce, 522.
Morris, Governor Robert Hunter, arrives, ii., 172. R. Peter's letters to, 172. Letters from, 177, 186, 192, 203, 216, 220, 223, 226, 231, 232, 244, 249, 261, 262, 267, 268, 270, 272, 276, 279, 280, 284, 298, 325, 328, 331, 335, 345, 356, 358, 361, 365, 372, 375, 376, 379, 382, 389, 391, 395, 396, 397, 401, 405, 412, 432, 440, 447, 450, 454, 461, 469, 470, 472, 475, 480, 498, 500, 506, 508, 512, 520, 524, 526, 528, 530, 540, 556, 560, 562, 564, 566, 569, 572, 574, 576, 582, 592, 596, 602, 606, 612, 616, 618, 621, 622, 625, 626, 629, 637, 638, 643, 647, 648, 665, 672, 674, 684, 688, 694, 711, 714, 733, 739. Addresses to, from churches, &c., 183, 184, 185, 186, 191, 200, 223, 251. Speech to Indians at Augwick, 193. On bills of credit, 221, 223. Letters to Proprietaries, 223, 229, 286, 311. From Proprietaries, 189, 195, 252, 253, 275, 304, 305, 333, 366, 419, 438. To Committee of Assembly, 271, 272. Controversy with Franklin and Hall, about printing minutes of Assembly, 274. Orders to Secretary to inspect their Journals, 276, 284, 286. Hears of Braddock's defeat, 382. Complaint for not writing to Board of Trade, 438. Complaint of Commissioners respecting a sentence in the order for scalps, 620. Message to Assembly, 750. Expects a successor, 712. Ceases to be Governor, succeeded by Wm. Denny, 760.
Morris, Governeur, letter to, vii., 472; ix.. 308.
Morris, Samuel, appointed Com-

missioner to settle accounts for wagons for General Braddock, ii., 598. Register, Miralle's will defective, viii., 228.
Morris, Captain Samuel, Jr., troops, viii., 308, 310. Light horse ordered out, 699. Troops ordered out, ix., 221, 415.
Morris, Samuel C., letters, v., 109, 133. In battle at Trenton, 162.
Morrison, Ensign, takes a prisoner, xii., 147.
Morrison, Lieut. of Virginia regiment in pursuit of Indians, ix., 200.
Morris town, Washington at, v., 177. Army at 192, 215. Enemy marching for, viii., 356. Pennsylvania Volunteers at, 394.
Mortality, in Philadelphia, i., 769.
Mortars, imported by Virginia, xii., 189.
Moultrie, Brig. Gen. Wm., stopped at Billingsport, asks pass to City, ix., 215.
Mountfort, Count, introduced by Col. Brodhead, vi., 462, 492, by J. Read, 473. His plan for regulating Militia, 489.
Mount Holly, skirmish at, v., 177.
Mountjoy, Camp at, vi., 251.
Moylan, Stephen, iv., 774.
Moylan, Col. Stephen's regiment to guard magazine at Lancaster, ix., 7. His dragoons in want, 137, 139, 150. Affair with Guards at Lancaster, 157. Resolution of Congress, 209. Lieutenants in regiment, 321. Leaves Lancaster, 267. Troops, 752.
Moylan, Colonel, regiment, x., 62.
Moylan, Colonel, vii., 666.
Moylan's Regiment, Return of, viii., 129. Returns of 4th Regiment, 183. Which he commends, 184. Going to Lancaster county, 605.
Mud Fort, or Mud Island, or Fort Mifflin, v., 11, 23, 24, 26, 47, 61, 92, 584, 595, 639, 679, 732, 733, 750, 755, 766.
Mud Island, purchase of Island, iv., 474. Resolution of Assembly, 474. Message to Governor, 475. Banks to be repaired, vii., 240. Fort, Troops for, 270, 339, 365, 369, 395, 397, 652, 745, 747. Cannon for, 290, 410, 562. Ammunition wanted, 385. Officers relieved. 502. Persons not to visit, 587 Fortifications, viii., 599. Arms to be returned, 728; ix., 72, 330. Chart of river near, mentioned, 255, 364. Lease of, xi., 139, 142. Condition of, 198, 404, 560, 562. Report, 586, 617. Or Fort Mifflin, xii., 407-412.
Muhlenberg, F. A., recommends a British Chaplain, viii., 123; ix., 60. Speaker of Assembly, 241.
Muhlenberg, Henry A., Report on publishing Colonial Records and Pennsylvania Archives, i., 4.
Muhlenberg, Rev. Henry, letter to Rev. Richard Peters, on his secular employment, iii., 80. Passport to Ga., as Missionary, iv., 563.
Muhlenberg, General Peter, resigns as Commissioner to Luzerne Co., xi., 136. Successor elected, 160. Elected Vice President, 207.
Muncey Fort, vii., 5, 10, 323, 344, 346, 357, 512; viii., 29, 40, 157, 162, 166; ix., 528; xi., 29, 40, 157, 166; xii., 415-420.
Muncy Hill, viii., 619.
Muncey Indians, xii., 155, 157, 261.
Murders by Indians, i., 254, 643, 647; ii., 16, 159-166, 571, 613. [See Indians.] A, vi., 771. Of Mr. Boyd by the Smiths, vii., 410. Jesse Jordan, 743. In Washington county, xi., 209.
Murphy, Capt., brave action with boats from British vessels, v., 504. Opinion of Council respecting, 510.
Murran, Mr. Commission for, vii., 420.
Murray, Lieut. Francis, difficulties in raising troops, x., 679.
Murray, Colonel James, vi., 774. Indians near, ix., 657.
Murray, Major, carried off by Tories, vi., 291.
Murray, William, letters for, vii., 432.
Murrow, Captain, vii., 3. Skirmish, 8, 10.
Muskingum, massacre of Moravian Indians at, ix., 523, 524, 525, 629. River and Ohio, proposed settlement at, (1783,) x., 168. Severe

cold at, 244. Delawares behave well at, xii., 237.
Musser, John, vi., 55. Purchases Conestoga manor, viii., 30, 54, 56, 118, 195.
Mustard, memorial from Philadelphia, xi., 684.
Muster Roll of Sloop Hetty, v., 16.
Mutiny of Pennsylvania line, ix., 188.
Mutton, none at Easton, or cooks to dress it, iii., 104.
Myers, Lieut. Jacob, vii., 745, 747.
Myers, Godfrey, Lieut., prisoner exchanged, ix., 389.

N.

Nagle, Sergeant of 3d Pennsylvania Regiment, Orders to arrest, x., 63, 67, 69, 72.
Nail Factory, near Philadelphia, Proposal to employ Hessian prisoners at, v., 206.
Nailer, Ralph, statem't of, respecting highway robbery of goods, &c., for Fort Pitt, iv., 225.
Nain, Indian Families from, iv., 134.
Nancarrow, Mr., on air furnaces, viii., 456.
Nanfan, J., letter W. P. to, i., 128, 148.
Nantucket in want of provisions, viii., 522.
Nash, Genl., to proceed with troops to Billingsport, v., 419. Wounded at Germantown, 646 ; vi., 544.
Natchez, taken by Spaniards, xii., 216.
National and party distinction. What ? vi., 383.
Naturalization certificate from W. Markham, i., 118. Certificate of, to Swedish Clergyman, iii., 692. Certificate of J. Shippen to a list of persons, who, having taken the sacrament, make oath, &c., iv., 242.
"Nauticus," plan for fire-ships, iv., 666.
Naval Service of Pennsylvania, No. of men in actual service, iv., 739. Officers, payments to, x., 114. Stores, Commissioners of Trade on, i., 634.
Navigation Act, orders respecting, i., 117.
Navigation, Inland, report, x., 538, 541.
Navy, American, sale of ship Gen. Greene, viii., 3. J. Gamble applies to be received into, 177. To be fitted for sea, 273, 277. Galley officers to be discharged, 728.
Navy, Continental, the Trumbull frigate going on a cruise, ix., 95. Letter to Capt. Nicholson on manning, 239. Relating to, 95, 100, 106, 239, 338. Ship Gen. Washington, captures by, 586.
Navy Board of State, appointed, v., 252. Letters, 293, 402, 425, 429, 465, 501, 504, 510, 521, 538, 542, 590, 594, 602, 746. Of State, vi., 110, 227. 243, 332, 333, 355, 421, 434, 517, 554, 696, 745. Washington asks the men from the Gallies, 421. Men from Gallies to serve as guards, &c., 434, 440, 454, 460, 492, 493. The Gallies, &c., sunk, 517. Crews arrived at Lancaster, 550. Pay of, 598. Rations, 656, 657. Brig Convention asked for use of State, 695. Prize taken by Guard boats, questions about it, 696. A Galley to be placed in Cape May channel, 702, 749. Armed boat to go to Chester, 724. Captain Garland commands a galley, and makes his selection, 737. Damages claimed, 770. Attempt to muster 678. Continental, v., 319, 346, 489, 491. Continental, apply for cannon, vi., 695. Ship Confederacy, 761. Letters, viii., 346, 552. Sale of negroes, 346. Iron ballast, 552.
Navy, British, fleet sail from N. Y., vii., 385, 390; 63, 77, 100, 181, 332, 339.
Navy, French, fleet, viii., 251, 312, 342. Squadron expected, 334.
Navy of Pennsylvania, No. of men, &c., in, v., 3. Pay of, 30. Respecting, 106, 118, 119, 126, 132, 138, 169, 205, 293, 346, 378, 402, 425, 429, 465, 488, 491, 501, 504, 510, 521, 538, 542, 590, 594, 602, 663, 680, 696, 721, 722, 723, 740, 746. Vessels burned for safety, 740. Council of War on Board, vi., 20. Complaints against, 24, 121, Several vessels burnt for safety,

28, 81. Letters, 38. List of fleet that passed Philadelphia, 50. Laid up, 110, 421. Letters respecting, 121, 132, 133, 243, 246, 354, 451. Gun boats asked for, 204, 243, 247. Want money, 227, 262. State of, 235. Case of Robert Hardie, 259. Washington's advice respecting the Galleys, 332, 333, 354. Dismantled, 421, 440. Court-Martial at Trenton, 527. Galleys asked for by comm'e, vii., 11, 19. Appeal from Court-Martial by Capt. Hardie, 91. His memorial for pay, 92. Vessels to be sold, 100, 112, 139. Dr. Stanley claims pay as Surgeon, 165. Deane frigate, 198. Vessels to be purchased, 199, 210, 228, 234, 235. Guarda Costa, Capt. Conyngham's vessel for, 235. Gallies to be got ready, 239. 240, 249. Ship Greene, 244, 246, 261, 265, 266, 303, 308, 309, 311, 320. Cutter Revenge, 167, 241, 266, 281. 285, 308, 310, 318, 319, 322. Dragon Boat, 730. Claims of Wm. Rush against Gallies, 277. Vessels to be hired, 269. Petition of Com. Hazelwood, 284. Terms proposed by Agents, 285. Men of gallies put on the line, 291. Officers of ship Gen. Greene, 310, 311. Return of officers and men in, 373, 389, 528, 706. Seamen taken to Balt.—difficulty of manning, 390. Capt. Montgomery joins Boston frigate, 454, 487. Capt. Montgomery takes Brig Impertinent privateer, &c., 476. Chases others, 521. May enlist prisoners, 488. Capt. M. cruizes with Capt. Nicholson in Deane Frigate and Confederacy, 533. Letter, T. Pickering on severe discipline in, 656.

Nazareth, Indian families from, iv., 134.

Nazareth Mill, fort at, xii., 420.

Necessity Fort, capitulates to Capt. De Villiers, ii., 146. Articles of Capitulation to Capt. De Villiers, 146; xii., 420-423.

Negroes, &c., duty on, Act respecting, i., 159, 160, 306. Sent to Havana to be tried, 752, 755. Manumission of, recommended, vii., 79. Claimed by French minister, 16, 17, 61, 62, 70, 83. Sale of, belonging to continental sloop of war Florida, viii., 346. Captured by British, xi., 75. A slave claimed, 249, 256. Slave, letter V. P. Muhlenberg to Gov. Randolph respecting, 249, 256. Judges of Supreme Court, 667. A free, demanded of Louisiana, 567.

Neilson, Capt. John, respecting militia, vii., 74. Attacks and captures enemy under Stockton at Lawrence's Island, v., 230.

Nelson, Thomas, Jr., applies for guard for Loan Office certificates for Connecticut, v., 167.

Nemos & Valliant, French merch'ts, refuse to pay militia fines, vii., 510, 513, 514.

Nesbitt, Jno. M., v., 240; vi., 652. Letter respecting purchase of vessels by State, vii., 211, 228, 234, 246. Letter to merchants on war with Algiers, xi., 522.

Nescopec Indians at, ii., 558, 561, 565. Settlements on N. E. branch destroyed, vii., 81, 87.

Nescopec Creek, road to Lehigh proposed, xi., 133. To E. Owen, 585, 643, 669.

Netherlands, United, attack on Marbois and Longschamps, xi., 468, 470, 475, 477, 479, 480.

Nets, for fishing, ordered, xii., 115, 116, 152, 160, 245.

Neutrals, French, History of, iii., 565.

Nevill, James, letters from, i., 55, 56, 83.

Nevell, John, letter, v., 286.

Nevell, Samuel, iii., 206.

Nevell, Thomas, letter on gun carriages, v., 64. Respecting State House steeple, Philadelphia, xii., 76, 283.

Newark (Del.) Academy, seeks aid, iv., 468.

Newark, N. J., surprise of post at, viii., 103.

New Castle, grant of, to Penn, i., 52. Call of Council and Assembly of, 126. Proclamation of King George II., at, 204. Memorial for County officers, 224. Justices of, letter to Gov., 592. Embargo proposed at, ii., 396. Call of Council,

William Penn's letter to Justices of, i., 142. County associated Military Companies of, iii., 21, 22. Order to pay workmen at Battery at, 317. Governor's speech to Assembly at, 377. Message from do. to Governor, 379. Letter from Commissioners, 401. Embargo, 471. Minutes of Council, 631. Common, message of Governor respecting, 688. Speech of Governor, 723. Address from, 723. Recommendation of a Clerk of market at, iv., 53. Share of Parliamentary grant, 72. Message from Gov. to Assembly at, 72. Collector of Customs appointed, 254, 451. Rioters from Maryland, 331. Judges appointed, 339. Captain, an Indian Chief, directions, ii., 682. His daughter brought to Philadelphia, 684. Letter to Mr. Taafe, 685. Letters, 726, 727.

Newcastle, Holles, letters from, i., 246, 247.

New Hampshire, Commissioners to Indian treaty at Albany, ii., 138. Correspondence between, and Gov. Pennsylvania, 186. Acts to comply with requisitions, xi., 16, 23. Deputies to Convention in Philadelphia, 123.

New Haven, Connecticut, expedition against, vii., 561. Burned, 561.

New Jersey, deeds for lands in West, i., 29, 31, 32, 33, 34, 35, 36, 630, 641. Proceedings of a Court in Salem, 37. Letter James Nevill, respecting lands in, 55. Commissioners appointed by Penn to treat with, for river, &c., 58. East, Minutes of a Council of the Proprietors, ii., 75. Board of Trade on paper money of, 128. Correspondence with Governors of, and Pennsylvania, 172, 182, 433. Address to Gov. Belcher in 1757, on State of affairs, iii., 171. Regiment, list of killed, &c., 203. Conference with Indians in, 341. Lands claimed by them, 343. Power of attorney to transact business, 366. Letter Gov. Bernard, 453. Letter Gov. Franklin, respecting Indians passing through his State, iv., 157. People of, fire on Indians, 206. Opinion respecting an Act of, 295. Treasury, 305. Boundary between, and New York, 337, 339, 340. Proclamation of Gov. Franklin against a smuggling vessel, 381, 445. Cartridges sent to troops in, 786. Petition for ammunition from city, v., 30. Salt sent to, 64. Hibernia furnace casting shot, cannon, &c., 72. River craft to be removed from, to Pennsylvania, 84. Bridges on Burlington road to be destroyed, 95, 238. Monmouth C. H., 158. Middletown, action at, 158. Counterfeits, 239, 240, 327. Militia ordered to join Gen. W., 240. Respecting prisoners, 243, 251, 267, 296, 320, 329, 346. Water craft collected in, 321. Guns for, 346. Respecting slaves captured with prisoners, 348. Militia called out, 359. Act exempting men at salt works from enlisting, 764. Governor applied to in behalf of Navy laid up, vi., 133. Andover iron, only suitable for steel, 178. Pittstown, 421, 435. Letter to, vii., 152, 197. Letters to and from Gov., viii., 63, 139, 314, 576, 624, 634, 637. Col. Bond of, attacks a party of tories at Del. Water Gap, 259. Enemy near Springfield, 308. Gen. Knyphausen in, 312. Enemy at Elizabethtown point, 314. Enemy leaves, 361. Army marches from Parkness to Kings's ferry, 480. Tories, 637. Letters from Gov. Livingston, ix., 82. To raise troops, 394. Sent to Congress, 411. Advices of enemy, 412. [See Governor L.] Letters to and from Gov., x., 103, 366, 458, 730. Commissioners to inquire what islands in Delaware river, above Falls, are in each State, 130, 366, 458. Resolution of Pennsylvania on jurisdiction of islands, 611, 710. Respecting Captain White, 730. Acts to comply with requisitions, xi., 16, 23. Ground for beacon at Cape May, 93. Capture of T. Pickering, 327. To Governor, 326, 335, 338. C. J. Brearly, on demand of prisoners, &c., 548. Governor asks for a

counterfeiter, 551. Letter to Governor, xii., 71.

New London, enemy's vessels alarmed, vii., 636. Burned by Arnold, ix., 404.

Newport, Del., head quarters at, v., 598.

Newport, R. I., flour sent to, viii., 125. French fleet arrive off, 406. French squadron at, ix., 353, 354.

Newspapers ordered by S. E. Council, vii., 136, 201, 206.

Newton, Bucks co., British soldiers to be escorted to, v., 96. Cloth carried off by tories, vi., 291. Return of officers and privates in artillery, settled with at, ix., 30, 55. Troops, 278, 291, 423, 437. Demand for liquor by soldiers, 437.

New York, articles of agreement between Dutch and English on surrender of, i., 25. Letters to and from Gov. Dongan, 74, 80, 81, 84, 104. Efforts of, against the French and Indians, 104. Letter, Gov. Rip Van Dam to Gov. G., 296. From Commissioners at Albany to Gov. Van Dam, 297. Minutes of Commissioners at Albany, 297 Proceedings of Assembly at, relative to French and Indians, 298. Letter of Gov. Clarke, &c., relating to Jenkins, 619. Gov. Clinton, letters from, 654, 661, 678, 687, 712, 736, 766. Letter from Gov. Clinton respecting a prisoner, ii., 16. Resolutions on Indian affairs, 52. Correspondence between Governors of, and Pennsylvania, 16, 26, 29, 30, 32, 65, 99, 168, 179, 220, 233, 433. (See De Lancey, Hardy.) Depositions respecting Indian outrages at Hosick, 168. Independent companies of, condition of, 256. Opposes levies, 298. Controversy between Shirley and De Lancey, about cannon for Cape Breton expedition, 338, 354. Scarcity of sailors at, 352. Governor Sir Charles Hardy appointed and arrives, 399. Gen. Shirley at Oswego and operations, 381. At Oneida, 388. Fort at Oswego, 575, 629, 646. Murders in, 586, 610. Operations on Lake George and Ontario, 693. Minutes of a Council at, 694. Embargo, 694. Merchants against embargo, 702, 733. Regiment attack Ticonderoga, list of killed and wounded, &c., iii., 203. Letter Governor De Lancey, 691. Letter Gov. Tryon, iv., 467. Act of Assembly claiming share of parliamentary grant, 149. Letter of Commissioners to Gov. Penn, 150, 168, 337, 368. Oppose Indians passing through, 157, 167. Council at Fort George, 167. Boundary between, and New Jersey, 337, 339. Act on Indian trade, 361. Boundary between, and Pennsylvania—proposal of G. Colden on settlement of, 562, 576, 578. Minute of Council on, 576. British expected at, 645. Committee sends prisoners to Philadelphia, v., 40. Large number of houses secured for British army, 72. British fleet leaves, 351, 352. French fleet arrives, vi., 638, 639. Attack on, meditated, 645. British about leaving, vii., 18. Abandonment of, by British, 77. Evils of intercourse with enemy at, 176. Major Meeker of, 573. Alarmed, 636. With Vermont, controversy, viii., 88. Letter Gov. Geo. Clinton, 132, 179. British fleet at, 339. Ill treatment of prisoners at, 619, 620, 660, 663, 664. Provisions for, 621, 626. Intercourse of tories with, 636. Fear of Fort Schuyler being abandoned, ix., 123. Invested by Gen. Washington, 301. Papers asked from, 629. Number of prisoners in prison-ships at, 667. Supplies for, 674. Copies of Records obtained, 730. Prisoners at, in want, x., 68. Demand for fugitives, 101, 131. Boundary with, 412, 413, 422. Letters to and from Gov., 413, 422, 435, 513. Act respecting boundary, 422, 435. Commissioners, 422, 450, 454, 711. Acts complained of by British merchants, 747. Acts to comply with requisitions, xi., 16, 23. Division line, 125, 140, 156, 178, 187. Complete, 214, 216. And Wyoming affairs, 196, 199. Extract from deed of cession of Erie,

309. To Governor on arrest of T. Pickering, 326, 335, 338. C. J. Morris issues a warrant against Wyoming insurgents, 340, 341. Supplies for prisoners at, [1782] 495. Boundary, 522, 526. Enemy evacuate, xii., 262. Attack on, 269.

Niagara Expedition, ii., 349, 353, 355, 357, 423, 425, 427, 579.

Nice, Capt. John, v., 427. Promoted, viii., 515.

Nichalson, Jno., plan for a Gun factory, iv., 767.

Nicholason, Joseph, Indian interpreter, vi., 742.

Nicholson, Capt. of Deane frigate may enlist prisoners, vii., 488. Commands fleet, 521, 533.

Nicholson, Capt. of Trumbull frigate, ix., 239.

Nicholson, Capt. James, complaint of Gov. Johnson of Maryland, against, for contempt, he is dismissed by Congress, v., 328.

Nicholson, John, viii., 73. Letters, ix., 48, 118, 131, 154, 174, 212, 747, 749, 753. Instructions to, 174. Account, 216, 243. Expenses of office, 663. Funds, 664, 677, 678, 737, 738, 758. Compt. Gen., x., 6, 16, 28, 29, 46, 48, 50, 52, 53, 93, 94, 96, 529, 750. On Claims on traitors' estates, 96. On James Searle's claim, 97. Asks for a guard, 750. Letters, xi., 33, 34, 90, 96, 139, 142, 198, 228, 249, 258, 328, 404, 635, 693, 695, 702, 728, 739, 742, 747. Buys depreciation lots, decision respecting them, 702. Letters to and from, xii., 7, 91, 93, 95, 97.

Nicola, Lewis, letter from on defence of the Delaware, iv., 635. Plan for powder magazine, 715. Letters to and from, v., 7, 29, 71, 75, 78, 90, 92, 121, 130, 148, 200, 354, 364, 410, 417, 600, 604, 608, 612, 619, 631. Orders, 96, 121, 122–124, 131, 184, 201, 219–228. Applies for rations as Town Major, while enemy was in city, vi., 174. Letters, 197, 213. Unsafe condition of Easton, 197. Rations, 213, 358, 411, 656, 657. Arrest of Dr. Berkenhaut, 742. Letters, vii., 77, 190, 203, 255, 358, 362, 364, 387, 484, 489, 492, 509, 519, 523, 526, 548, 560, 561, 562, 576, 625, 634, 635, 642, 643, 646, 648, 663, 674, 682, 697, 701, 767, 769, 775. Recruiting in Philadelphia useless, 501, 549. On defence of River and City, 190. Letters, viii., 12, 77, 95, 100, 108, 181, 262, 316, 358, 363, 378, 389, 391, 415, 469, 510, 516, 724, 750. Instruction, 422. Correspondence on recruiting, 669–682. Plan proposed to render militia for guards, ix., 299. Leaves city—appoints successor, 254. Respecting condition of jail, xi., 536. List of prisoners in the workhouse, 648.

Nichols, Gov. Richard, enters into agreement with Governor of New York, on its surrender, i., 25. Grants lands on Delaware, 27. Succeeded by Governor Lovelace, 29.

Niser, George, massacre at Muskingum, ix., 525.

Nixon, John, chosen Lieutenant of a Company in Philadelphia, ii., 600.

Noemor, M. Van, introduced by Franklin, vii., 774.

Nonowland, (a Delaware Chief,) xii., 132. Wounded in attack on Indians, 156.

Norris, Fort, xii., 423.

Norris, Isaac, letter to and from, ii., 244, 245, 345. Fort, 669, 678.

North, Colonel Caleb, viii., 610.

North America, Bank of, Resolutions of Congress approving establishment of, as a national bank, ix., 172. Charter of, 471, 477. Letter to T. Willing, 496.

Northampton county, petition for road, ii., 98. Alarms from Indians, 515. Number of Roman Catholics in, iii., 144. Petitions from, for defence, 151, 174, 237, 284, 321, 357, 360. Ammunition wanted, 163, 164. Position of Troops in, 325. Number of wagon and horses in, 404. Memorial for defence, iv., 120 669. Military Company formed, 124. Alarm from Indians, 125. Petition of Roman Catholics 279. Instructions to Sheriff, &c., 421. Troops to join Washington, v., 115, 523.

Prisoners from, 139. Letter to Sheriff, 489. Wagons in, 421. Sheriff to arrest prothonotary, 489, 490. Records, 654. Wagon masters, vi., 212. Militia, 406. Tories, 551. Instructions to Sheriff, 621. Situation of, 719, 721. Militia, vii., 13, 613, 688. Petition from ——, alarms from Indians, proceedings against spies, 360. Constitutional Society of 4th battalion of, 384. Indians, 572, 613, 616, 617, 689. Letter to Colonels of, 616. Executions, 655. Indians in, viii., 238, 500. Commissioner of purchases, 300, 317. Petition from, 387. Petition from, respecting defence against Indians, ix., 40. Distress in, 106, 238. Murders by Indians, 107, 123, 158. Convention prisoners ordered to, 227, 234. Treasurer, 229. Plan of defence against Indians, 238. Estimate of damages sustained by the inhabitants from the British, 765. Collection of taxes in, x., 92. Letter of Council to Lieut. Craig, respecting Wyoming, 296, 303, 305. Election, writ for, 339. Letter Robert Levers respecting, 311. Letter to Prothonotaries respecting Wyoming, 749. Taxes, xi., 603. Dry lands, 644, 647, 651. Nescopec road, 585, 643, 669.

North Carolina, Indian treaties with, iv., 323, 324. Prisoners to be distributed, 733. List of those sent to Philadelphia, 734. Troops to go to Billingsport, v., 418. Offers troops for Philadelphia, vi., 183. Rendezvous in, 302. Letter to Governor Caswell respecting a prisoner, viii., 191. Letter to Governor, demand for fugitive, x., 353. Acts to comply with requisitions, xi., 17, 23. Gov. Caswell sends acts for delegates to convention, 116. Proposes amendment to Constitution United States, 674. Act appointing delegates to Convention in Philadelphia, 117. Cession to United States of eastern territory accepted, 681. Cession of lands to United States, 688.

Northern Boundary, estimate of necessary stores for 1787, xi., 104. Letter A Ellicott, 134.

Northern Liberties of Philadelphia, petition to have streets regulated, iv., 312.

North Kill, ii., 159, 675.

North Kill, Fort at, iii., 31, 253; xii., 424-426.

Northumberland county, petition of officers against Connecticut settlers, ii., 240. Memorial for defence, iv., 669, 685. Condition of troops at, v., 85. Militia, 158. Militia, vi., 169, 499. Indian murders in, 499, 575. No flints, 500. Arms for, 522. Supplies for, 539. Defenceless state of, 577. Murders in, 590. Waste of ammunition, 593. Distressing condition, 609, 631, 633, 634, 637, 642, 692, 729. Case of Mr. Lodge, vii., 546. Distresses of, 586. Sheriff to be sued for escapes, 700. Forts Muncey and Jenkins, 760. Memorial of Justices respecting Courts, want of District Attorney, &c., 72. Long suspension of justice has rendered people licentious, 73. Indians and Tories, 117, 574, 593, 614. Officers for troops at, 317, 341. Justices discharge a deserter, 356. Petition, 519. Orders to Justices respecting officers, 545. Distress of, 593, 596, 598, 604, 618. Fort Freeland destroyed, 586, (See Freeland Fort.) Much exposed, viii., 88. Troops, 97. Condition of, 156, 157, 167, 249, 558. Scarcity of provisions at, 270. Council at, deferred on account of trial of F. Hopkinson, 658. Condition of, ix., 208. Magistrates, 229. Taxes, 381, 440. Indians in, 392. New Board of Commissioners, 440. Records, 440. Letter of Council to magistracy and Sheriff, &c., of, respecting Wyoming, x., 295, 303, 304. Sheriff to arrest insurgents, 344. Magistrates to aid, 344, 347, 460. Field Officers elected, 404. Militia Officers, 444, Disturbances in, 448. Justices of, to Alexander Patterson, &c., to keep peace, 628. To John Franklin, &c., demanding arms,

&c., 629. Answer of John Franklin, 629. Letter to prothonotaries respecting Wyoming, 749. Claim for forfeited land in, xi., 58. Letter from L. Keene, Prothonotary of, 111. Recording of deeds, 123. Returns of officers, 416. Pension of Widow Mercer, 677. Indians in, 710. Murders on two Indians in, xii., 318, 319, 320.

O.

Oaths, and Affirmations, Act respecting, i., 158. Dedimus to administer, iv., 40. Or test law, opposition to, v., 427. Taken by C. J. McKean, 621. Of allegiance to be taken, vi., 433, 434. Form of Certificate, 679. To be taken by Soldiers, viii., 291. By several young men, 333. Of Edward Fox, x., 103. Act of Congress respecting, xi., 600.

O'Bail, Cap., (Indian,) xii., 300.

Obligations, J. Smith and J. Owens, iv., 245. Jonathan Smith, 246. For appearance, v., 695.

O'Brien, Mrs. Sarah, examination of, v., 337.

Odgers, William, an officer of customs, murder of, iv., 297. Demand of murderer at New York, 297.

Office, claimed by Peter Evans, i., 234.

Officers of Pennsylvania Regiment in Prov'ce, pay and dates of Commissions, iii., 88. Quarters at Philadelphia, 558. Of the Province in 1773, showing their salaries, &c., iv. 600—603. In Army and Navy appointments, &c., v., 33, 39, 90, 114, 124, 235, 265, 284, 293, 303, 355, 356, 395, 401, 551, 738. Exchange of, 165. Rank, 172, 241, 371, 483. List of in Penn. State Reg., 318, 341, 528, 595. Insolence of, 59. In pay of U. S., 176, 345. Address of respecting Militia of Penn., 186, To Assembly, 724. Charges against, 756. Non Commissioned, vi., 159. Inconvenience of too many, 151. Instructions to recruiting, 248. List of recruiting, 249, 251. They ask more pay, 280, 287, 288, 327. May be suspended by the States, 356. Promotion of, 357, 677. An increase of, recommended, 387, 397. Appointed, 461. Gen. McIntosh, 467. In Army, rank of, appeal to Congress on, &c., vii., 162, 607, 660, 691. Washington on, 188. European, to divest themselves of European ideas—letter to Gen. Pulaski, 233. Recruiting, letter to, 300. Appointments, 306, 512, 607. Petition of, of Penna. line on rank, 306. Men in State Navy, 373, 389. At Billingsport and Mud Island, letters to, 409, 424. Resolutions of Congress respecting, 436, Necessary, 452. Recommended, 501, 553, 565, 597. At Mud Island and Billingsport relieved, 502. Conduct to be inquired into, 542. Authority vested in the State, 552. Half pay, 582. Mr. Brodhead, 583, 606. Who have broken parole, 626. Only in the Army to receive articles, 627. In hospitals, 649. Insolence of, on Continental vessels, 657. Decision in case of Lt. Brodhead, 660. And in 1st Penn. Regiment, 726. In St. Clair's division, 752. Petition for provisions, viii., 8, 35, 45, 67, 111, 290, 389, 410, 512, 522, 569, 599, 610. Appointments, 290 310, 607. At Fort Pitt, misunderstanding between, 405. And prisoners of war in charge of T. Bradford, Comm'y, 93. Names of Cols. Battalions, 111. Respecting clothing, petition, 17, 116. Congress recommend suspending appointments of, 142, 206. Rank of, 153, 409. Duty of Col., 154. Sells clothing, 161, 162, 165. Surgeons propose resigning, 168. Clothing for, of hospital and medical staff, 185. Pay too small, 207, 722. Rank, 232, 238, 729. Promotions, 245, 248, 264, 515. Memorial of Pennsylvania Line, 264, 265. Recruiting instructions to, 290. Petition of officers in favor of prisoners, 610. Rank of Governors in the field, 535. Captured, petition in favor of, 610. In favor of prisoners at New York, 619,

Officers—
620. To Assembly, 693. Galley officers to be discharged, 728. Depreciation of pay, ix., 3, 6, 13, 77, 112, 133. How to be appointed, 27. returns of those paid, 30. Pay of captive, 78. Of Col. Proctor's artillery, and a memorial, 98, 142; accounts of officers with prisonr's, 111. Names of, required, 123, 124. Adjutant and Inspector General required, 125. Charges against, 135. Respecting several, 142, 143, 529. Of Bedford Co., 149. Resolutions of Congress—confederation and petition of Penn. regiment of artillery, 168. Letter to field officers of Westmorland Co., 189. Of Philada. Co. Light Horse Co., 230. In Moylan's regiment, 321. Petition of, 327. Col. Stroud's, 268, 339, 365. Of land office, 409. Return of non-commissioned, serving in Southern army, 517. Returns of Pennsylvania line, 725—729. Rank of, x., 49. Pay of, 113, 114, 179. Commutation by Congress, 179. Of troops in Philada. Co., 218, 219, 225. In Fayette Co., 275. Westmoreland Co., 275, 276. In Washington Co., 287—289. Required by war office for defence of western posts, 296, 302. Of Berks Co. militia, 191, 331. To be appointed, 332, Returns of, &c., 338. Field, elected for Northumberland Co., 404, 444. Recommend William Irvine, 425. Of Washington Co., 436. Philada. Co., 443. Militia elected under law, 453. Of Penn. Line, willing to continue in service of United States, 466. Privates and officers of state in federal regiments, 511. To command regiment of federal malitia required from this state, 525. of Penn. Line, 593. Of militia in Cumberland Co., (1784,) 599-600. Of Penna. line, (1781,) 721, 728. Naval, return of payments to, 114. Of Philadelphia Militia invite Governor, &c., to attend review, xi., 57. Instructions to, in Luzerne county, 204. Rank of, 204. In Luzerne County, 300. Returns of, elected in Philadelphia, under militia law, 302, 378 561. Returns of Luzerne county, 384. Of Westmoreland Co., 402. Of Northumberland county, 416. And offices, public Gov. to, on tenure of, xii., 32.

Ogden, Col., of Elizabethtown, advises of enemy, ix., 412.

Ogden, Nathaniel, killed at Wyoming, iv., 383. Inquisition on, 384. Depositions, 386—392.

Ogle, Gov., Letters between, and Gov. G., i., 320, 326, 330, 336, 421, 427, 434, 443, 447, 461, 471, 479, 488. Letters from, ii., 40, 46, 57.

O'Harra, Capt., xii., 126, 165, 167, 198, 300.

O'Hara, James, claims for pay, xi., 58, 228.

Ohio River, French Fort on, i., 309. Settlements, ii., 31. Distances from various places to, 141. A party proposes to form a settlement on, at mouth of Muskingum, unusually low, (1783), x., 168. Survey of Islands in, xi., 583. Falls of, xii., 164, 168.

Okely, J., brings Canadian Indian from Genl. Gates, v., 153. Appointed commissioner to Wyoming, x., 330. Applies to be commissioner on jurisdiction of islands in the Delaware, 696.

Old, James, casts a 24 pound cannon, iv., 721. Cast shot, v., 179, 398.

Old Town, xii., 117, 136, 263.

Oneida carrying place, Gen. Shirley at, ii., 388. Indians, x., 88.

O'Neill, Dennis, vi., 498.

O'Neil, Henry, deposition respecting attack of Indians, viii., 527.

Onondago, council, at speech to Indians, iv., 107.

Opinion of D. Ryder, King's attorney, on several acts of Assembly, ii., 100. Of Thomas McKean, allegiance and rights of a freeholder, v., 400. Of C. J. McKean, on traitors, when the Government began, &c., vii., 645. J. D. Sergeant, on concealing taxable property, viii., 49. Nicholas Waln on do., 81. Commissioners of Phila. Co., 80. Of James Biddle, 136. J. D. Sergeant on British Commissions to Cruizers, 395. Of Judges

of Supreme Court on search of vessels for French sailors, 403, 412. J. D. Sergeant on right of Marshal to sell in certain cases, 498. Of Chief Justice M'Kean on Penna. claim to interest, x., 739. Of Wm. Bradford on fees in Montgomery Co., 743. Of W. Bradford, (A. G.) on case of James O'Haras' claim, xi., 58. Of Judges McKean and Bryan on depreciation of pay, 120. Of Att'y Gen'l on appeals, 122. On claim of Chas. Sims to Lands, 162. Of judges, &c., on a point submitted by Att'y Gen'l, 233–234. On Citizenship, 260. On Admiralty case, 383. Of Judges on a case of Murder, 560. W. Bradford, on Health Office fees, 619. On Weights and Measures, 734. Of Judges of Supreme Court on tenure of Officers, xii., 32. On contempt of Court, 83.

Oppakhassits, (Indian,) Answer to Govenor, i., 224.

Ord, Captain, ii., 346, 356, 358. Orders to Captains Martin and Craig, 541. Captain Isaac Wayne, 543.

Order to affix great Seal, iii., 318. To Saml. Mifflin, v., 44. To Commodore Seymour, 83. Of L. Nicola, Town Major, 96, 121, 122, 124, 131, 184, 201, 219–228, 547. Of Council for intelligence of enemy, 157. Commo're Hazelwood to Capt. Mathews with prisoners, 168. Of Genl. Gates for quarters for troops at Germantown, 207. To Col. Melcher to examine and clear houses occupied by troops in Phila., 215. To Capt Mullen with prisoners, 235. To Col. D. Brodhead, 283. Lieutenants, 297, 321, 364, 371, 379, 380, 404, 424, 541, 545. To Col. Nicola to collect wagons, 364. To S. Hunter, 370. To Militia to be ready, 404. General, 384–396. The Northampton troops, 544. To Gen. Armstrong, vi., 53. Of Council of Safety, 93. Of Board of War, 199. To Jacob Morgan, 385. Of General Wayne to Capt. Craig, recruits, 746. From Executive not to be waited for in cases of emergency, vii., 300. Disobedience of, 515. Respecting Mud Island, 537, 720. Billingsport, 538, 720. General, from Head Quarters, viii., 696. Of Gen. St. Clair, ix., 60. Lieut. Cummins, 29. For Books, &c., of land office, 202. To Pres't Quarter Sessions, 323. To officers on removal of records, 412. To Andrew Higgins, 413. To wagon masters, 420. Lieutenants, 425.

Ordinance of Congress respecting capture and condemnation of prizes, ix., 43., 478. Bank of North America, 471, 477, 478. For Government of N. W. Territory, xi., 162–168, 604.

Orme, Robert Captain, introduction of, to Gov. Morris, ii., 195. Letters to and from, 312, 325, 329. Wounded in Braddock's defeat, 379, 400. Going to England, 400.

Orndt, Captain, letter, ii., 742. Letters, iii., 5, 51, 207, 209, 212, 350, 351, 367, 487, 491, 670.

Orndt, John, vii. 625. Power of Justices of Sup. Court, tenure of Sheriff's office, &c., 701.

Orth, Col. Adams, ix., 186, 461, 654, 737.

Osborne, Henry, Escheator, Gen'l, ix, 341. Illumination of city, 390. On Connecticut claim, 563. To Gov. Trumbull, for papers, &c., 639, 642, 643, 681, 682, 685, 686, 687, 730.

Osborne, Joseph, sent to Maryland for public papers, ii., 92.

Oster, Mons. French Consul, case of, viii., 390. Asks pass for French Vessels, 604. Sailors from French ships, ix., 372.

Osterhout, Gideon, Petition, xi., 553.

Oswald, Eleazer, Trial for contempt of Court, &c., xi., 348. And'w Brown vs., 349.

Oswald, Thomas, iii., 298.

Oswego, Gen. Shirley's arrival, and operations at, ii., 381. Minutes of Council of War at, 413, 427. Fort at, 574. Gen. Ross commands at, x., 89.

Otsego, Gen. Clinton arrives from, at Fort Sullivan, x., 719.

Ottendorf, Major, corps commanded by, viii., 62.

Otto, Dr. Matthew, report on Wil-

liam Tatamy, (an Indian,) wounded, iii., 247, 251.
Ottawa Indians, x., 86.
Outten, death of, iii., 589, (see depositions,) iii., 661.
Owen, Evan, instructions to, on Nescopec Road, xi., 585.
Owens, Samuel, obligaton to disperse, &c., iv., 245.

P.

Paca John, respecting Henry Carberry, x., 293.
Paca, William, applies in behalf of J. Tilghman, v., 635. Of Maryland, letters to and from, x., 293, 320, 324.
Pack-horses, xii , 213, 245, 272.
Page, Lt. Gov., of Virginia, xii., 165, 167.
Page, John, appointed by Va., commissioner on boundary, x., 146.
Paine, Thomas, selected to correspond with Assembly on state of affairs, v., 659. Resolutions of Assembly, viii., 226.
Pamphlets respecting Quakers, ii., 257.
Paper, want of, to be seized, vi., 355.
Paper money, Wm. Henry's plan to raise value of, ix., 171, 665.
Papists, to be deprived of arms, ammunition, &c., iii., 130. (See Roman Catholics.)
Papley, Cap., viii., 97.
Pardon, petition for, iv., 102. Of prisoners under Test-laws, vii., 130 Prerequisites to, 651. Of John Franklin, xii., 101.
Paris, Ferd. J., Letters, i., 526, 628. Letters to and from, respecting purchase of lands from Indians, iii., 666.
Parke, Lt. Col. John, vii., 181.
Parker, John Deposition, vii , 259.
Parker, Wm., letter respecting prisoners taken by Indians, (1783) x., 167.
Parks, David, Conviction of, xi., 419.
Parliament of G. B., King's speech, vi., 14.
Parliamentary Grants, claims for, iv., 72, 121, 159.
Parmiter, John. Letter W. P. to, i., 127.
Parole of Hougonere, &c., v., 18. Not to be taken in certain cases, vi., 381.
Parr, Major William, ix., 256, 263, 371.
Parsons, Wm., Letters from, ii., 41. Description of Easton, 95, 98, 305, 443, 515, 534, 596, 670, 714, 741, 742, 745, 747. Letters to and from, iii., 5, 7, 35, 81, 84, 104, 139, 142, 163, 211.
Party Walls, in Philada, Act respecting, i., 159.
Passes, Mediterranean, Orders respecting, i., 177, 180, 182, 183, 242, 256, 258, 264, 282, 439; iv., 243, 622.
Passport for Cherokees, iii., 405. For F. Post, 578, 689. For Teedyuscung, 692. For a showman, iv., 164. For express to Col. Bouquet, 173. F. Post, 277. To missionaries, 455, 563. Dr. Ewing, &c., 468; xii., 71.
Patents and Grants, Act respecting, i., 159. For Erie, from U. S., xii., 103.
Patterson, Alexander, Narrative of a most extraordinary escape of an express from Indians, vii., 527. Letters on Wyoming, x., 31, 32, 207, 208, 574. Conference with, 207. To Judges of Supreme Court, 617. To Council, 619. Commissioners, 625, 626, 627. Justices of Northumberland bound to keep peace, &c., 628. Letter to, (1786,) on arms sent to Fishkill, xi., 457. Orders to, ii., 603. Letters, 613; vi., 432.
Patterson's Fort—See Forts, ii.
Patterson's Fort, xii., 426.
Patterson, James, Journal at Fort Hunter, iii., 321.
Patterson, Lt., controversy at Lancaster, vi., 201, 206, 228.
Patterson, Mr., xii., 135.
Patterson, Wm. A., vii., 167. Account of his services in the Army 167.
Patton, Major John, letter, v., 41.
Patton, Col. John, Superintendent of flour magazine, vi., 235.
Patton, John, cast-iron shot, viii., 502.

Paules Hook, Surprise of British at, by Major Lee, vii., 661.
Paxton, or Conestoga, Indians, Murder of, Inquest on, iv., 147. Letters John Elder, 148, 153. From agents, 151. Sir Wm. Johnson, 162, 165; vii., 606, 609. Upper, difficulty respecting election of Justices, viii., 101.
Pay of Soldiers, &c., v., 3, 9, 31, 43, 267. Navy, 500. Of Officers and Soldiers of American Army, 113.
Peace between Great Britain and U. States, preliminaries signed, x., 10, 11. Letter of Sir Guy Carleton, 13 From Rear-Admiral Digby on, 21. Letter Ezekiel Robbins respecting prisoners, 26. Respecting goods imported from Great Britain since, 28. proclamation of Congress for Thanksgiving, 134. Treaty ratified, 193, 549. Rejoicings for, 149, 428. Negotiations, 185.
Peale, Charles Wilson, vii., 384; Presents a portrait of Prest. Wharton, viii., 319; And other citizens—invitation to attend delivery of an eulogium on the brave men who fell in the revolution, by Mr. Breckenridge, (1779) x., 162; Tenders to council a portrait of Pres. Wharton, painted by him, (1780) x., 163.
Pearson, James, repairs on State House, Philada. x., 373, 420, 426, 442, 535, 547. Trees for State House yard, 420.
Pearson, John, letter, vii., 70.
Peculations, viii., 74.
Peery, Col., xii., 262, 265.
Piers at Marcus Hook, x., 407, 471, 713.
Peirt, Benjamin, family taken prisoners, viii., 213, 222.
Pemberton, Israel, proceedings against, i., 585; Letters, to and from, iii., 37, 555. Respecting, 249, 250, 255, 262, 264, 275, 319; &c., remonstrance (1777) against treatment of them by order of Council, x., 158. See Vol., VI., page 509.
Pemberton, John and William Matthews, on a religious visit to Europe, make their intentions known to President and Council, ix., 551.
Pendleton, Col., xii., 201.
Penet, P., agent in France, fusees, flag and seal, viii., 257; A. P., discovery of a metal and mastic for ships' bottoms, ix., 430.
Penn, John, letters from, i., 203, 237. Dies, 734. Proceedings about his will, 734; Appointed Governor, iv., 119. Proclamation on preserving fish in Delaware, 347. Against murderer of J. Meyer, 376. On Western riots against Dunmore, 580. Letters to and from; Admiralty, board of, 622. Apty, Thomas, 157. Armstrong, Col. John, 135, 136, 146, 155, 174, 192, 203. Bard, Peter, 210. Belton, Joseph, 652. Bernard, Gov. F., Mass., 163. Bouquet, Col. H., 166, 199, 206, 208. Botetourt, Lord, Governor Virginia, 365, 368, 371. Burd, Col. James, 140, 144, 164. Callender, Robert, 411. Carnahan, John, 603. Clayton, Asher, iv., 139, 174. Colden, Gov. Cadwalader, 167, 562, 578, Commis'rs of Connecticut, 471. Commissioners of customs, Boston, 289, 305, 310. Commissioners of Customs, London, 253. Commissioners of New York, 150. Commissioners of Westmoreland County, 487, 579. Conway, S. H. Secretary, 244. Cooper, Guy, Secretary, 250. Dartmouth, Earl of, 464, 480, 539, 579, 585, 589, 613, 614, 621, 625. Eden, Robert, Governor of Maryland, 368, 616. Edmonstone, Charles. 433. Elder, Rev. John, 135, 148. Fauquier, Gov. Francis, of, Virginia, 207. Francis, Turbutt, 210. Franklin, Gov. Wm. N. J. 156. Gage, Gen. Thomas, 142, 144, 156, 164, 168, 170, 172, 214, 217, 219, 231, 248, 256, 258, 260, 300, 337, 377, 393, 394, 410. Gordon, Lewis, 143. Graydon, Lieut. C., 207, 214, 218. Haldeman, Frederick, 465, 501. Halifax, Dunk, 192, 200, 201, 202. On stamps, 202. Post office, 203. Hanna, Robert, 605, 625, 627. Governor of Havana, 286. Earl of Hillsborough, 282, 283, 290,

292, 295, 297, 299, 300, 302, 307, 309, 311, 334, 340, 361, 363, 369, 380, 382, 387. Irvine, Col. James, 138. Johnston, Samuel, 378. Johnson, Sir William, 162, 164, 214, 226, 249, 268, 290, 307, 309, 349. Knox, W., letter, 505. Lee, Richard, 538. McFarlane, Andrew, 487. Mackay, Æneas, 484, 494, 514, 517. Message to Assembly, 290. Montgomery, John, 505, 507, 533. Moore, Sir Henry, Gov. New York, 337. New York Commissioners, 150, 168, 337. Phelps, Richard, 300. Pownall, John, 307, 368, 370, 410, 465, 535, 616, 620, 629, 652. Robinson, John, 379. St. Clair, Arthur, 476, 501, 504, 509, 510, 514, 519, 523, 530, 539, 542, 545, 550, 557, 558, 560, 564, 573, 583, 586, 589, 628, 659. Schlosser, Capt., 158, 160. Seely, Jonas, 141. Sharpe, Governor, of Maryland, 207, 262, 277. Shippen, Joseph, Jr., 298. Earl of Shelburne, 274, 276, 280. Smith, Devereux, 515, 612. Stephens, Phillip, Secretary, of Admiralty, 243, 331, Stewart, Charles, 382, 384, 689. Trade, Lords Commissioners, 174, 182, 281. Thompson, William, 521, 526. Trumbull, Jonathan, Gov. Connecticut, 408. Tryon, William, Governor of New York, 467. Vining, John, 338, 341. Williamson, Dr. Hugh, 366. Young, James, 208, 210; Jno., late Govr., priso'r of war, escort, for, v., 478, 484, 511; sends for clover seed, vi., 10, request in favor of, 61, removal of, 85. Release, 364, 367, 378, 380, 389, 507, 523; Receives papers of Secretary's office, viii., 200; Instructions respecting Wyoming, xii., 51.

Penn, John, Jr., and John Penn, statement of their claim to the province, and opinion of the judges, on it, x., 485. Opinion of do. as to interest, 739.

Penn, Richard, letter from, i., 236.

Penn, Thomas, and others to be, arrested, for riot, at Gloucester, i., 546. Commission to Governor, Thomas, 625. Letters to and from, 203, 237, 410; Letters to, ii., 223, 229, 286, 311. From, 189, 195, 252, 253, 275, 304, 305, 333, 366, 419, 438. On instructions, Connecticut, 254. Introduces Captain Orme, 194. Respecting his interest in Gap Copper mine, 311, 369.

Penn, Thomas and Richard, petition to the King respecting laws, i., 716. Suit against E. Jersey, minutes of a Council, ii., 75. Instructions to, from King, respecting appeals, 107. Answer to Assembly on various subjects, 108. Revenue of Province, 110. Right to purchase lands, 111. On taxation of estate, 112. Letters, 304; iii., 107, 157, 193, 576. Agreement with Lord Baltimore about running the boundary line, 1760, iv., 1–36. Message from Assembly, 248. Intervention of proprietaries in communicating information, irregular, 307, 310.

Penn, Richard, appointed Governor, iv., 447. Proclamation against Connecticut intruders, 453. Answer to new comers message, 469. Message, 555. Passport to missionaries, 455. Letters to and from—Dartmouth, Earl, 456, 460. Dunmore, Earl, 461. Frazer, John, and G. Wood, 458. Indians, 450, 451. Tryon, Gov., New York, 447. Westmoreland Trustees, 449. Gage, Gen., 457. Galloway, Joseph, &c., 448.

Penn, William, Letters from, to James Frisbie, i., 38, 127. To Governor and Council of N. Jersey, 60, 61. Henry Savell, 68. Thos. Taylor, 70. Jno. Tucker, 72. Philemon Lloyd, 72. Council, 93. W. Markham, 126. John Parmiter, 127. Luke Watson, 127. J. Donaldson, 128. N. Field, 128. J. Nanfan, 128, 148. Saml. Leonard, 129. Wessel Alricks, 131. Jno. Birch, 131. Circular, to persons to serve in Council, 132. Robert Asheton, 134. Gov. Blackiston, 135. Owners of ship Providence, 136. Joseph Coysgarne, 136. Col. Quarry, 137. Commissioners of Customs, 138, 149. Esquire Lawton, his agent in England on various public

affairs, 139. Justices of New Castle, good advice to, 142. John Hans, 143.

Letters—
To, from Sir Wm. Petty, 49. Thos. Culpepper, 51. Philemon Lloyd, 54. James Nevill, 55, 56, 83. Governor Dongan, 76, 80, 81, 84. Wm. Clark, 77. John West, 79. John Richardson, 81. William Welch, 82, and T. Lloyd, 84. Samuel Land, 87. Council at Whitehall, on birth of a Prince, 106. Andrew Hamilton, 129. Sales of land by, in England, 39.
Indian Deeds—
For land between falls of Delaware and Neshaminey, 47. Between Pennepack and Neshaminey, 62, 63, 64. West side of Schuylkill, 65. Between Schuylkill and Chester, 65. Between Schuylkill and Pemapecha, 66. Between Susq. and Del., 67. Land on Perkiomen, 88. Pennepack, 92. Deeds to, from Gov. Thos. Dongan, 121, 122. On Pemapecha, 91. Between ditto and Chester, 92. Between Duck Creek and Chester, 95. Neshaminey and Poequessing, 116. For Susquehannah confirming Dongan's, 133. Calls Court at Upland, 51. Appoints Commissioners to treat with New Jersey on boundaries and satisfaction, 58. Feoffment from Duke of York for New Castle to, 52. Letter to Governor of New Jersey, claim to Del. river, &c., 60. Proclamation against dealing with Thomas Matthews for lands, 68. Recommends W. Markham, 69. Conference with Charles Calvert 74. Commission to Wm. Welch, &c., 85. Declaration against Lord Baltimore, 88. Letter to the Council, 93. Proclamation against cutting timber in Philadelphia, 97. His conduct to Indians, 302. Instructions to, respecting wrecked treasure, 100. Charter of Germantown, 1689, 111-115. Asks persons to assist in Council, 132. Agreement with Susquehannah Indians respecting conduct to each other, &c., 144. Complains of trouble from Somerset county, Cape Henlopen, also Cornelius, of the Dutch, 147. Forbids Gov. Hamilton to affix the seal to a paper, 148. His will established, 203. His powers under charter to make laws, ii., 101. His treatment of Indians, 109. Warrants for Welsh tract, xii., 279, 280. Letter to Susquehannah Indians, 280.

Penn's Valley, Indian murders in, vi., 515, 516, 517.

Pennell, Joseph, letter, v., 143, 197. Accounts, xi., 506.

Pensions, list of, ix., 588; xi., 624, 679.

Pensioners, payment of, xi., 545. List of, sent to War Office, 645, 729. Pensions, 728, 729, 730, 731.

Pennnsylvania, its future greatness predicted by Sir Wm. Petty, i., 49. Memorial, &c., from Welsh tract, 108, 110. W. P.'s description of 1683, 68. Deeds for, see Deeds. African trade of, 152. Proclamation of Governor Keith for continuing the Government, 69. Commission to Hamilton and Georges, 428, 429. Do. to Gov. Thomas from T. Penn, 625. Correspondence between Governors of, and Maryland, ii., 40, 46, 57, 91, 93. Boundary line between Maryland, 40, 41, 49, 64, 73. Map of, by Lewis Evans, 46, 60, 309, 583. His instructions, 47. Returns of Iron and Steel Furnaces, Slitting Mills, Tilt Hammers in 1750, 52-55. Letter of Governor Hamilton on boundaries of, and claims of French, Virginia, &c., 60, 63. Report of Privy Council on, 65. N. Scull, on mode of finding Meridian, Tangent line and running the Circumference of the Circle, 73. Statement of Excise collected, 85. Income of Loan Office, 86. Governor sends to Maryland for copies of public papers, 92. Answer, 93. Proprietary revenue, 110. Connecticut settlers on land in, 120 to 127, 196. Commissioners to Indian Treaty at Albany, 142. Their Diary, 145. Governor Hamilton retires, succeeded by Robert Hun-

Pennsylvania, iii.—
ter Morris, 180. An account of the state of the province referred to, 225. Supplies expected from, 249, 293, 305, 306, 579. Letter, Committee of Assembly to Governer Morris on £5000, 271. Answer, 272. Purchase of land from Six Nations, 279. Bond given for arms to King, 300. Grant by Connecticut to Susquehannah Company, 303. Commissioners of Trade and Plantations send interrogatories for information respecting, 378, 418, 527, 778. Account of guns and ammunition delivered to back counties, 392. Representation of citizens of Philadelphia to General Assembly demanding defence, 485. General Shirley sends ammunition to, 502. And arms, 654. Assembly granted £55,000 and Proprietary £5000, 513, 529, 530, 536. Gov. Shirley's troops ordered from, 577. Murder by mob for enlisting servants, 578. Map of Delaware bay and river by Joshua Fisher, 592, 593. Commissioners offer rewards for Indian prisoners and scalps, 606. Officers at Shamokin complain of pay, 700. Commissioners decline further payments, 742. Message to Assembly from Governor, state of province, 750. William Denny arrives and succeeds Morris as Governor, 760. Addresses to him, 760, 762, 763.
Account of arms and ammunition purchased, iii., 25. Estimated annual expense, 62. Cost of three battalions, 62. Of provisions for four hundred men, 63 Proprietary land at Easton, 84. List of officers in pay of the province and dates of commissions, 88. Secretary Pitt urges Assembly to provide forces, 95, 96. Plan of protection by Major Burd, 99. Number of men in pay of province, 99, 341. Squadron from England, 96. Quarters for troops in city, 110. Letters to and from Proprietaries, 106, 157, 193, 576. Number of Roman Catholics in, 144. Opinion of Proprietaries' right to pay out bills of credit, 157. Frigate,

Pennsylvania, iv.—
190. Guarantee against impressment of sailors of, 191. List of officers, 260. Troops making forts at Wyoming, 303. Address of Assembly of lower provinces, 308. Intercepted letters and a plot discovered, 324. List of officers in pay of the province and dates of commissions, 336. Regiment, their stations, 337. Forces between Delaware and Susquehanna, 340. Number in pay of the province, 341. Troops, 449. Depositions respecting Maryland, (which see). Warrant to survey land, 663. Proceedings of Court against John Willey, 664. Letters between Ferd. J. Paris and others respecting fraudulent purchase of lands from Indians, 666. Power of Attorney from Thomas and Richard Penn to sell lands, 685.
Agreement betw. Lord Baltimore and T. and R. Penn, respecting boundary line, 1760, iv., 1–36. Commiss'ers appointed by Pennsylvania, Delaware and Maryland on the line between those states, J. P. Eyre appointed, 37. Military affairs in, 37, 40, 45, 47, 51, 73, 74. Claims for distributive share of moneys allotted by parliamentary grants in 1758. Three lower counties, 72. Rhode Island, 121. New York, 149, 169. Massachusetts, 159, 163. John Penn appointed Governor, 119. Insurrections in back counties, 155. Claims of Carlisle, 168, 170. Letter from Indians in barracks to Governor, 170. Col. T. Francis to raise troops, 176. Equipment of, 179. Musters of effective men at Lancaster, 195. Do. of second battalion at Carlisle, 196. Orders to, 198. Draught of warrant for enlisting troops, 197. Orders to battalions of Pennsylvania regiment, 198. Peace with Indians on Erie and Ohio granted by Col. Bradstreet, 207. Proclamation of Col. Fauquier, respecting settlers on western lands, 255. Account of certificates granted to pay public debt, 257. Return of royal regiments stationed in, 259. Re-

Pennsylvania, v.—
port of Attorney and Solicitor General on certain acts, 274, 276, 280, 281. Earl Hillsborough asks for information, 283. Act to remove settlers from Indian lands, 283. Communications not to pass through proprietaries, 307, 310. Governor not to communicate public letters to Assembly, 309. Complains of petition of Assembly, 311, 334. Boundary of lands with Six Nations, 329, 424. Estimate of debts due from, 333, 345. Officers of Pennsylvania regiment ask for grant of land on Susquehanna, 335. Permission granted to survey on, of boundary line between New York and New Jersey, 339, 340. Western boundary, 346, 426, 430. Proclamation respecting fish, 349. Agreement between proprietors and Connecticut settlers, 350, 352. Minutes of Commissioners on Indian trade, 372. Claim on Gen. Gage for pay of carriages used by Lieut. Col. Wilkins, 377. Letters to and from A. St. Clair [see St. Clair.], depositions, &c., respecting western boundary, 430, 435, 455. Messages to and from Assembly, 436. Richard Penn appointed Governor, arrives, 446. Reasons of Commissioners, appointed to meet at New York, for not attending, 448. George Croghan on western boundaries, 452. Highway robberies near Bedford, 456. Counterfeits, 461, 466. Proclamation for apprehending counterfeiters, 466. Westmoreland county Courts, &c., 467, 471, 487, 492. Dr. John Connolly's proceedings, 476, 478, 484, 528. Jurisdiction extended to Pittsburg, 479, 481, 483, 489, 525. Lord Dunmore's letter, &c., on jurisdiction, 483, 514. Letter William Digges respecting Digges' choice, 490. Proclamation of Earl Dunmore, 490. And Virginia dispute, 511, 514. Letter Benj. Chambers, 536. Assembly resolves to pay a certain number of Rangers, 548, 559. Message, 554. Governor Colden on settlement of boundary with New York, 562.

Pennsylvania, vi.—
Minute respecting, 577. Great Britain objects to sending deputies to general Congress at Philadelphia, 576. New Assembly not to meet till further orders, 579. Proclamation of Gov. Penn against Lord Dunmore, &c., 580. Answers to queries from Great Britain, respecting statistics of, showing commerce, manufacture, population, offices, salaries, occupants, boundaries, &c., 591-603. Gov. Eden requests suspension of issue of proclamation, 616. Earl Dartmouth thinks she is not returning to a sense of her situation, 621. Duties on peltries to be collected, 628. Amount of Excise for 1771, 2, 3 and 4, 633. State of the bills of credit struck on the Excise, 634. A. St. Clair recommends temporary line, 659. Number of men in actual pay in naval service, 739, 781. Also in military, 780.

Men in pay in service of; in army and navy of; salaries, v., 3. Troops, clothing, 13. Furnaces for casting cannon, and quantity cast, 31. Quotas of grain to be furnished by each Co., 182. Loan offices to receive bills of credit of, 183. Militia, important services of, 186. Address of officers, 186. Gallant affair at Lawrence's Island, 230. Thomas Wharton, Junior, elected President, and George Bryan, V. P., 252. Finances, 264. Call for troops, 319, 461, 523, 539. Transfer of, to Continental service, 357. Debtors not to depart from, 356. State of the treasury, 357, 372, 378, 381, 409. Joseph Reed appointed Chief Justice, 289, 379. Declines, 379. Proposal to Virginia on subject of boundary, 413. Militia ordered to Ticonderoga, 492. T. McKean, Chief J., 621. Militia to be ready, 583. Return of, belonging to State, 595.

Claims Wm. Straker, from French Minister, as a citizen of the State, vii., 61, 62, 70, 72, 83; and Virginia, relative to disputes between, 73. Three Co's to be enlisted, 76.

Pennsylvania, vii.—
Council ascribe victory to God, 77. Benefits in prospect from, 77. Gradual abolition of slavery proposed, 79. Marriage licenses liable to abuse in, 79. Differences between Connecticut and Virginia and this State to be brought to a settlement, 79. State of military affairs, owing to redemption of old paper money, 80. Tax of, 5s. assessed in different Co's, 80. Taxes recommended towards paying off paper money, 80. Money received from forfeited estates, 80. Guard for Convention troops to be called from different counties, 90. Act to prohibit distillation of grain, 125, 152. Supreme Executive Council asks for a portrait of Washington, 127. Quota not to be increased, 141. Quota of taxes ordered by Congress, 157. Advance of money from Congress, 160. Cost of clothing the troops, 182. Circular from Council to the other States, respecting abuses of power by Congress. Gen. Arnold, &c., 183. Great scarcity of provisions for want of hard money, 186. State of finance, 87. Propose buying a vessel, 199. Surveys of Susquehannah, 210. On defence, 238. Grant from Congress of two millions, 269. Resolutions of Congress in favor of, 288. Members of Council called to form a quorum, 389. Complimentary resolutions passed by Assembly on President and Executive Council, 295. Do. by Congress of the State of, 312. Similar resolutions of the Legislature and Executive of the State, 313. Correspondence respecting Genl. Arnold, 325, 327, 337, 347, 351, 380. Military position, 342. Washington disclaims partiality to any State, 353. Men and means furnished by, during the War, 378. Is this State a separate Department? 256, 339, 385, 387. Death of Judge George Ross, 554. Rangers and riflemen, 568. Opinion of C. J. McKean when the Government of, began—traitors and treason, 645. Not exceeded by any State in supply of militia, 681. Prisoners expected, 731. Quota of assessment by Congress, 733. Report on salaries of officers, 739. Return of General St. Clair's division of army, 753. Thanksgiving Day, 757.

Pennsylvania, viii.—
Boundary between, and Virginia, viii., 46, 56, 63, 91, 191, 285, 352, 488, 516, 570, 713, 744, 746. Lands belonging to, 56, 91. Troops surprised at Elizabethtown and Newark, 103. Drafts for money by Congress, 104, 122, 197, 252, 256, 320, 342, 402, 492. Returns of troops, 110, 111. Demand on Edmund Physic for books, records, &c., respecting proprietary estates now vested in, 113. Lands seized in Manor T., Lancaster County, said to have been purchased by Mr. Penn at Fort Stanwix, 118. Soldiers of, in Moylan's regiment, 128. Colonel Moylan commands Fourth regiment of light dragoons, 184. Account of taxes from Treasurer U. S., 185. Intrusions by Virginia, 191. Return of troops under General St. Clair, 220. Colonel Hay of 10th regiment, 240. Captain Alexander of 7th regiment, 248. Loan of field-pieces, 253. Quotas of ten millions, 255. Guns, standards and seal ordered in France by agent Penet, 257. State of Pennsylvania regiments, 271. A loan authorized by Assembly, 276. New State proposed, 280. Call for militia, 294, 306. Quota of provisions, 294. Agreement between Virginia and Pennsylvania on boundary question, 352, 570. Commissioners on, 353, 569. Embargo, 10, 229, 261, 263, 266, 333, 354, 433, 452, 609. Congress furnish exchange on minister to France, 391. Money asked of Congress, 392, 395. Volunteers at Morristown, 394. Asks a bill of exchange from French Consul, 397. James Searle sent to France as agent to procure loan, &., 399, 514, 532. President Reed complains against Committee of Con-

Pennsylvania, ix.—
gress—statement of facts, 420. Too great a dependence on, for supplies, 426. President Reed's statement to Congress of State proceedings and demands on her from first to last, 458-468. Quota of supplies demanded by Committee of Congress, 472. Virginia confirms line run in 1779, 488, 516, 583, 713, 744, 746. To draw in Continental bills by taxes, 534. Rank of governors in the field, 535. Loan office certificates for bills of exchange to be sold, 555. Congress call for cattle, 556, 560. Revolt of Pennsylvania line, 603, 718, 721, 722, 723, 724, 729, 731, 734, 736, 737, 744, 761. Thos. Smith and Rd. Bache, appointed by Congress to sign bills, 635, 639. Proprietary lots of, wrong opinion respecting, 636. Returns of artillery under General Wayne, 647. Names of officers under government asked for, 658. State of treasury, 657, 662. State of account with Congress, 694. Names of officers in Captains Porter and Simon's companies, 696. Troops of Pennsylvania line to join army in Virginia, 737. Against bringing convention prisoners to, 745. Assembly grant money for raising troops, 752. Resolution of Congress respecting convention prisoners from Maryland and Virginia to, 753, 757, 758. Resolution of Congress calling in Continental money—Committee of Assembly, 757. Estimate of expense of convention prisoners to the State, 758. Estimate of sums necessary for payment of bounties to general officers, &c., 758. Colonel Proctor and others claim Hog Island, 730, 734, 760. Allowance to commiss'ers for extending Mason and Dixon's line, &c., ix., 4, 78, 161. Exhausted state of treasury, 15. Comparison with other States as to supplies, 16. Commissioners to run line between Virginia, 20. Rifles requested from Board of War, 26, 31. Commissioners appointed by Virginia, 78. Board of War tender muskets to the State, 96. State of affairs, 130. President's letter to General Washington respecting, 141-149. Question as to legality of trial before Supreme Court, Judge being member of Congress, 163. Cannot comply with requisitions of Congress, 187. Mutiny of Pennsylvania line, 188. Proceedings of Pentecost and Cannon, 193. Case of seizure of merchandise in Pennsylvania, belonging to Virginia, to pay a private debt—correspondence with delegates in Congress, &c., respecting, 260, 266, 271, 272, 274. Corps of three hundred riflemen to be raised, 280. La Fayette orders troops from, to South Carolina, 283. Accounts with United States, 288. Boundary with Virginia, 233, 234, 301, 304, 315, 344, 352, 356, 402, 444, 506, 562, 607. Finances, 310. General Clarke's expedition, 357. James Searle, agent to Holland, 367. To raise three thousand men, 395, 397, 398. Removal of records, 413. E. Hazard applies for access to documents for history, 449. Publishes a collection, 447. Supplies for prisoners in New York, 470. And Connecticut, 447, 510, 526, 563, 568, 629. Wm. Moore elected President, and J. Potter, Vice President, 447. Troops at Fort Pitt, 521. Instructions, &c., to commissioners on boundary with Virginia, 518, 533, 549, 562, 566, 585, 772. President Moore's term expires—John Dickinson elected President, and Jas. Ewing, Vice President, 651. State of the paper money, 665. B. Stille, of Rhode Island, appointed agent to settle accounts between Pennsylvania and United States, 668. Various papers—proceedings at Trenton on Connecticut claim, 679-724. Claim stated, 700, 701, 710, 713. Deeds produced at Trenton, 715-724. Rev. Mr. Jas. Finley's secret expedition to Western counties, 730. Copies of records of Connecticut and New York obtained, 730. Proclama-

Pennsylvania, x.—
tion respecting decree at Trenton, 732.
Boundary between Virginia, x., 8, 56, 72, 81, 95, 96, 125, 145, 171, (1783) 175, 181, 223, 231, 233, 236, 269, 280, 336, 372, 373, 413, 414, 416, 428, 438, 439, 489, 506, 573, 602, 611, 705. Confirmation of line run by Nevill and McClean, 8. Wyoming affairs, 147, 148, 711. [See Wyoming] New state threatened on frontiers — Rev. James Finley sent to counteract it—correspondence, 40, 41. Instructions to, 163. Pennsylvania line of soldiers, 55. Letters of Governor Harrison, of Virginia, on boundary (1783), 56, 65, 72, 77, 78, 95, 96, 145, 175. Resolutions of Congress on purchase of lands from Indians, 105, 119, 124, 126. Resolutions of Assembly respecting purchase of lands from Indians, 111. Lands opposite Fort Pitt, 115. Report to Congress on Indian affairs, purchase of lands, &c., 119-125, 126. Affair of Colonel G. Cox, and boundary of, 81, 86, 96, 125. Proceedings of Assembly and merchants on internal commerce —by roads and rivers, 129, 130, 312. To inquire what islands above Falls belong to this State and New Jersey, 130. Captain Chrystie reaches Easton with a detachment, 135. Letters from Gov. Trumbull, 147, 148. Resolutions of Assembly, intentions towards Connecticut settlers, 196. Commissioners appointed by, on Virginia boundary, 223. Instructions to Commissioners on, 230. Apportionment of $636,000, 238. Exhausted treasury, 241. Alphabetical list of persons attainted of high treason under the laws of, 250-260. Commissioners to treat with Indians appointed—letter, 265. Affairs in Fayette county, 280. Opening of land office, 282. Objections to the law for, 283. Chief Justice McKean re-elected, 285. Offic rs required for defence of western posts, 303. Pine Creek means Tiadaughton of,

Pennsylvania, xi.—
1768, 357. Vote of, on settlement of accounts, 369, 370. Report of Commissioners on boundary, 373, 374. Pennsylvania troops in service of United States, 393, 394, 403, 431, 443. Claims of State on United States, 397, 398, 422. Purchase of land from Indians, 412. Boundary with New York, 412, 413, 422, 435, 450, 454, 711. Commissioners, 422. James Milligan and J. Story, Commissioners to settle accounts with United States, 426. Western boundary described, Commissioners, 452. Penn, John, and John, Jr., their claim to the province, and judge's opinion on it, 485-488. Quota of State, 517, 529, 530, 531. Land claims under Virginia titles, 611. Surveys of lands received from Virginia, 705. Inquiries from land office, whether islands in the rivers belong to the proprietaries or the State, 739. Opinion of judges of Sup. Court, on claim of Messrs. Penn to interest, 739. Acts complained of by British merchants, 747. Western boundary, 760.
Acts to comply with requisitions, xi., 17, 23. Appoints Commissioners to commercial convention, 60, 61. Her present system, 62. Requisitions on, 74. Inland navigation, 25, 27, 77. Report of Treasury on claim of, 79, 82, 87, 234, 235. Connecticut proposed cession of lands W. of, 5, 107. Boundaries, 140, 169, 187, 214, 216, 310, 497, 499, 501, 507, 522. Accounts between, and United States, 146. Troops in service of United States, 174, 175. Requisitions, 198, 214. North line completed, 214. Amount of claim against United States, 234, 235. Description of lands around Erie, by Porter, Armstrong and Ellicott, 241, 243. Respecting the finances, 258. Authority of Council to purchase Erie, 313. Respecting Erie, 203, 237, 241, 245, 247, 251, 252, 308, 309, 310, 313. Rights of State supposed to be infringed by British Consul,

Pennsylvania, xii.—
375. Letter from P. Bond on, 381. Opinion of judges on, 383. Campbell's and Simpson's claims, 501. Boundary with New York, 522, 526. Commercial Regulations proposed by Virginia, 523–526. Resolutions in Assembly to call State Convention, 565. Respecting survey of Erie lands, 566. Subscribers to Society for Encouraging cotton manufactures, 569. Committee of Congress ask information on imposts, 583. Answer to, 585. Congress calls for statement of public debts, 613, 638. C. Febiger elected Treasurer, 638. Cession of lands from North Carolina to United States, 681, 688. Accounts between United States and, 698. Return of military stores in, 699. Benjamin Franklin leaves his portrait, by Martin, to Executive Council, 701. They accept of it, 701. Charles Pettit appointed to settle accounts with United States, 708. Asks of Connecticut aid in arresting a fugitive debtor, 73. Opinion of Attorney General, 737.
Constitution of 1776, xii., 54–68. 1790, 12–27. Thomas Mifflin, election as Governor, 28. A. J. Dallas, Secretary of State, 46. Islands in the Delaware over which she has jurisdiction, 74. Letter to Congress on infractions of treaty with Great Britain, 76. Fee for affixing Great Seal, 79. Ratifies Constitution of United States, 82. Seal established, 88. Virginia boundary line, 179, 182, 195. Premium offered for scalps, 240. John White to settle United States accounts, 303, 304.

Pennsylvania and Maryland, disputes depositions. (See deposition.) Letters between Gordon and Calvert, i., 282, 289. Thomas Cresap, 311, 313, 320, 321, 336, 352, 398, 412, 415, 417, 419, 462, 476, 489, 501, 534. Letters, J. Blunston, 316. Letters between Governor Gordon and Ogle, 320, 326, 330, 336, 427, 434, 443, 447, 461, 471, 479, 488, 489. Petition, Ross and Carrol, lands on Susquehanna, 333. Boundary line, 336, 342, 556, 557, 558, 595–615. Agreement received, 342. Case of Daniel and William Lowe, 349. Titles of various documents, 369, 376, 402. Newton's deed, abstract, 374. Justices of Kent to Justices of Maryland, 376, 387. And answer, 379, 388. Lord Baltimore to Governor Gordon, 393, 395. James Heath and J. Steele, 426. Hamilton & Georges, appointed Commissioners to Maryland, 427. Commission, 428. Instructions, 429, 435. Case of T. and J. Rothwell, 433. Mitimus for Maryland prisoners, 529, 530, 532. Case of Higenbotham, 530. Warrant to arrest rioters, 538.

Pennsylvania Board of War, v., 281, 282, 283, 290, 294. (See also Board of War.)

Pennsylvania Frigate, iii., 190, 191, 260.

Pennsylvania Hospital, list of first subscribers and amounts, ii., 87–89.

Pennsylvania Invalid Guards, Philaadelphia returns of, xi., 418.

Pennsylvania Line, petition of Captains of, vii., 306. Return of officers, 494. Account of recruits for, 548. Colonel Atlee, 583. Return of Captains, &c., of 1st Regiment, 726. Revolt of, viii., 603, 718, 721, 724, 729, 731, 734, 736, 737, 744, 761. Memorial of officers of, 264. Answer to, 265. Thanks of President, 265. Respecting, 603. Defection, ix., 39, 143, 147, 175, 188. The flower of the army, 143. Causes of mutiny, 147. Mutiny, 188. Soldiers killed, 4[illegible]6. Returns of officers, 725–729. State of, 747, 759. Commanded by Major J. Moore, x., 131. Instructions, 132. Resolution of Assembly respecting officers, 179. Certificates of final settlement distributed to, by Bowen and Beatty, 437. Letter of officers to Council—pay and land, 593. Arrangement of officers in, (1781) 721–729. Plan and Instructions for recruiting, 728–730.

Pennsylvania Rangers, ix., 228.
Pennsylvania Regiment. one and two battali'ns officers in Province, pay and dates of Commissions, iii., 88. List of officers in pay of United States, v., 176. Who want commissions, 318. Cash paid for recruiting service, 335. Continental, 357. Clothing distributed, vi., 47. State of Treasury, 81. Boundary between Virginia and, 82. Congress order grain to be threshed. or paid for as straw, 82. Recovery of debts, and punishment of crimes, 84. Council and Assembly remonstrate with Congress against cantonment of army, 104, 107, 111. Petition to Congress from Council and Assembly, 154, 160. Resolutions of Assembly, 64, 66, 73, 84, 155. Inquiry respecting magazines for provisions, 178. Recommendation of Assembly on military affairs, 180. Approval of Congress for recapturing Philadelphia, 184. Attorney General attacked at Reading, 267. Militia returns, 297. Troops ordered to several places, 383. Drafts of militia in, 301. Council concur in confederation, 455. R turns of State troops now in service of United States, 476. Of artillery, claim of, Officers under Resolutions of Congress, ix., 168. Troops, return of, at Fort Pitt, 521.
Pentecost, Colonel Dorsey, seditious conduct of, ix., 193, 233. Depositions respecting, 572. In General Clarke's Camp. Virginia boundary, state of affairs, J. Marshall, &c., 315-319, 540, 541, 545, 556, 661. Refutes charges by Breckenridge against him, 662. On Indian murders, (1783) x., 167, 181. Deposition, 362. On boundary, 413. Attack on excise officers in Washington county, 757.
Pepperell, Sir Willliam, letters, ii., 329, 353, 365.
Perkin, Joseph, return of arms, &c., xi., 238.
Perry, Col., ix., 79, 331.
Perry, Col., James, purchases, ix., 200. Respect'g ravages of Indians, 210. Accounts, 247,306; xii., 261.
Perry, Micajah, letter from, i., 197, 206.
Perry's Mills, xii., 130.
Pest house, on Province Island, sick from vessels, removed to, iv., 59. On State Island, repairs of, x., 52. Letter from Health Officer, xi., 737.
Peters, Richard, Commissioner of Pennsylvania on Boundary Line, i., 601. As secretary of land office commission, 545.
Peters, Richard, letters, ii., 59, 89, 172, 196, 214, 218, 232, 307, 316, 345, 441, 443, 449, 455, 651, 654, 685; Letters to and from, iii., 7, 11, 33, 37, 51, 80, 84, 86, 92, 104, 157, 206, 217, 239, 245, 251, 283, 288, 297, 298, 381, 384, 386, 389, 390, 393, 397, 402, 406, 422, 428, 438, 450, 455, 471, 475, 478, 484, 488, 500, 510, 514, 516, 544, 546, 551, 552, 555, 571, 575, 580, 621, 660, 662, 673, 675, 677, 698, 727, 733, 741, Memorandum, respecting deed of (1718,) 262; Letters to and from, iv., 40, 44, 62, 64, 66, 70, 77, 80, 530. Dedimus to, 40; Letter, disputes among soldiers, v., 14. Memorial respecting troops in City, 17; vi.. 72, 493; ix., 454; On Turnpikes, xi., 335, 572. On Trial of Judges, 636. xii., 207, 210, 224, 234, 271, 274, 281, 282.
Peters, Rev. Richard, claim for lands, viii., 50.
Peters, William, statement respecting Quakers at Easton, iii., 274, 299, 312, 547; Dedimus to, iv., 40; Letter to, xii., 284.
Peterson, Lieut. xiii., 139.
Petition, of the Swedes, Report on, i., 172. Of merchants in Philada. on size of barrels, 203. Of frontier inhabitants against, Indians, 209. Of Eight members of Assembly, respecting privileges, 211. Answer to, 212. Inhabitants of Colebrookdale against Indians, 213. Miles Foy, &c., prisoners in Philada. Jail, 546. From Phiadelphia relative to road to Gloucester, 436, Against powder house in Philada. 675. From Conestoga, 681. From Chester Co., respecting bridges and road, 767. Of George Gray,

Petitions—
&c., road to New Castle, 768. Inhabitants near Digge's choice, ii., 28. Henry Darnell, 93. For a Road in Berks and Northumberland Counties, 98. Of officers of Northumberland County, 240. Of Susquehanna Company, 303. From Cumberland County, 385. To Governor, from sufferers by Maryland, 432. Lancaster Co. 450. York, 461. Cumberland Co. 758. John Hughes, 638. Chester Co., for defence, 656. Capt. Jacob Morgan, iii., 31. From Northampton County for defence, 151, 153, 164, 174. Lancaster County, 159. York County 235. Northampton County, 238, 284, 321, 357, 360. David Dewar, 302. Against William Moore by S. Lightfoot, 329. Berks County, 361. J. McMichael, 405. Settlers on dry lands near Easton, 578. Against plays, &c., 659: Jacob Hockstetter, iv., 99. Catharine McKey, 99. John Martin, 100. Pardon for negro Joe, 102. F. and M. Ennis, 106. B. A. Hernandez, 118. Thos. Romberg, 239. Bucks county against Indians, 273. Roman Catholics of Northampton, 279. Lutherans in Berks, 253, 279. Of Assembly complained of by Lord Hillsborough, 311. Of Northern Liberties to have streets regulated, 312. Samuel Kennedy, 331. For improvement of Schuylkill 360. For road from Schuylkill to Susquehannah, 362. For aid to Port au Prince, 371. Respecting Conedogwinet creek, 392. For road in Northern Liberties, 442. Of Christian Lehman to be appointed notary public, 444. John Knight for coroner, 461. Westmoreland county, 518, 520, 535. Pittsburg, 526. Laurence Birnie, 777. Northumberland Co. for protection from Indians, 788. From N. J. for powder, v., 30. Of Capt. D. Woelpper, for office, 48. Ezekial Letts, 57. Stephen J. Rouget for commission to arm, 569; From Council and Assembly to Congress on recovery of Philadelphia, vi., 154, 160. Robert

Petitions—
Hardie, 259. Prisoners to Virginia, 510; Of R. Hardie, vii., 92. For guns and amunition, 102. John Moore and others on provisions, 186. William Rush, 277. Of Captains of Pennsylvania Line, 306. Favor George Harding, 326, 360. Of inhabitants of Northampton Co. 360. Wm. Holliday, &c. against Indians, 445. Of M. Jennings for clothing, 359. From Philadelphia, 416, 422. Congress will hear, 439; Elizabeth Ferguson, on sale of estate, viii., 4. Captain Irwin, 8. Officers in Col. Hazen's Regiment, 44. Lieut. W. Huston, 153. Of inhabitants of Northampton Co. 387. Andrew Long, 548, James Rowan, 573. Officers in behalf of the prisoners at New York, 619; Of Northampton County, ix., 40. Officers of Pennsylvania Regiment of Artillery, 168. Of Philadelphia County, Light Horse, 230. From York, for Clerk of Market, 256. Of non-commissioned Officers of 8th Pennsylvania Regiment, 365. Of Richard Rundle, 443, 448. Of Owen Jones, Jr., 521. William Brown, from Cumberland County, 522. Of Merchants of Philadelphia, 534. Of prisoners on Clarke's expedition, 574. Joshua Fisher & Sons, 644. Prisoners by Indians, 733 Wikoff & Clarke. 740. Isarel Doane, 759; Robert Turner, x., 39. Of John Reynolds, jailor, at Philadelphia, 119. From York, against Armand's legion, 133. Of Daniel Drais, 150. Aaron Doane, 348, 716, 717. P. S. Duponceau, 352. Of captors of Joseph Doane, 565. Of Zebulon Butler, &c., 559, 580, 613, 716. Of prisoners at Easton, 690. Inhabitants of Wyoming, 699. Of D Duncan and J. Finley, for Fort McIntosh, 704. Of Philadelphia road, near Master's estate, (1773,) 718; Respecting acknowledgment of deeds, xi., 136. Of Thos. Lloyd to print debates, 213. John Brown, 264. John Jungman, 288, 304. Of Quakers against Theatres, 342, Stephen Jenkins, 537. Gideon

Petitions—
Osterhout, 553. University of Pennsylvania ask for use of State-House bell, 613. Granted, 614. Robert Loller, 619. Northampton County, on Nescopec road, 669. From Westmorel'd Co., on excise on liquors, 670. Mustard in Phila. 684. Thomas Martin, Lands, 697, Indian prisoners, 712; Samuel Jones, lands xii., 182. Henry Kilbuck, (Del. Chief,) 305.

Petit, Charles, vi., 366, 513, 525, 620, 623, 738, 742. A. Q. M. G., vii., 196, 219, 335, 399, 420, 421, 433, 460, 481, 495. Plan of finance, 481. Letters to and from, viii., 104, 143, 146, 342, 406, 614. Defendants on State, 197, 211, 223, 224, 320, 614. Money, ix., 129, 159. Memorial of merchants, x., 208, 211. Elected delegate to Congress, 437, 534. Claims of Turnbull, M., & Co., for land, 497. Letters, xi., 37, 41, 87, 106, 266, 456. Respecting his pay as member, 266. Instructions and appointment as agent to settle accounts with United States, 708. On accounts, xii., 6. Letter to, 7.

Pettit, Daniel, collector of Bucks, ix., 206. Robbed, 459.

Petty, John, mission to Indians, i., 229. Letter from, 232.

Petty, Sir William, writes to Wm. Penn on future greatness of Pennsylvania, i., 49.

Pixley, Thomas, at Mud Island, ix., 365.

Peyton, Colonel, xii., 201.

Phelps, Richard, letter iv., 300.

Philadelphia, petition from owners of meadows, respecting road to Gloucester, i., 437. Council with Delawares at, 539. Meeting of commissioners of Maryland and Pennsylvania, 623. Report on fortifications, 633, 650. And petition of merchants, 636. Powder house, petition against, 675. Proclamation of W. P. against cutting timber in, 97. Proceedings of Provincial Court at, on quit rents, 98. Governor Blackwell arrives at, 106. Searcher of customs, 117. Merchants complain against duties on tobacco, 149. Memorial

Philadelphia—
of ministers and vestry of Christ Church in favor of Governor Nicholson, 150. Party walls in, Act respecting, 150. Act for better government of, respecting, 160. Act for raising money in, 161. Lower ferry on Schuylkill, Act, 161. Collectors, &c., of customs appointed, 195, 196, 199, 385, 389. King George II. proclaimed, 202. Petition of merchants on size of barrels, 203. Physicians to visit vessels, 208. Courts of business in, 279. Difficulty between Christ Church and Baptists, 285. Great mortality in, 769. Names of several persons who died, 769.
Cleansing and walling the dock, and improving swamp between Budd's buildings and Society Hill, ii., 4. Arch under Dock street to Third, 4. Name given to it, 4. Proprietary called on for his share of expense, 4. Presents to Captain Ballet of ship Otter, 5. Account of steel furnaces in 1750, 53. An extraordinary writing master arrives, 170. Addresses to Governor Morris, 183, 185, 191, 200. Petition of Germans in, sufferings, 217, 224. Cherokee Indians at, 244. Sheriff warned not to discharge King's soldiers, 296. Letter to committee for provisions, 354. Embargo on provisions, 263, 283, 373, 375. Indians arrive in liquor, lodge in State House Square, citizens to be kept from them, 389. Colonel Dunbar's and Sir Peter Halket's regiments expected, Governor asks Mayor to provide quarters for them, 395. Demand of Governor on Sheriff for carriages, 432. Representation of citizens to General Assembly demanding means of defence, 485. Address of Quakers to Assembly, 487. Fisher's map of Delaware Bay, 592, 593. Election for lieutenant of company of Dock ward, John Nixon chosen in place of Thomas Willing, resigned, 600. Legality of, doubted, 600. Officers chosen by regiment of the county, 607. New Castle's daughter

Philadelphia—
brought to, 685. Merchants of, petition for removal of embargo, 709. Address of Unitas Fratrum to Governor Denny, 760. Of ministers, &c., of Christ Church, 763. Of regiment of county, 760, and reply, 763.
Associated military company, iii., 19. Guns and stores belonging to fort at, 26. Estimate of cost of garrison at Wiccacoa, 27. Do. of vessels of war at, 27. Letter, William Allen to Sheriff to arrest Dr. Matthews, 64. Potash made at, 53. Small-pox prevails among soldiers, 82. Return of beds for soldiers in, 85. Demands of Col. Bouquet of Mayor, for quarters for soldiers, 85, 111. Soldiers ordered by General Shirley to, and instructions to L. Morris, Jr., to provide vessels for them, 90. French in, suffering for wood, 92, 282. Quarters for troops in, 110. City watch, 113. French neutrals, 92, 114. May form a company, 126. Provisions of bodies scrupulous to bear arms, 126. Number of Roman Catholics in, 144. Lieut. Col. Bouquet in, 146. Barracks, 282. Indian conference at, 456, 469. Memorial of, 28. Quakers respecting, 469. Presents to Indians, 467. Ordinance and stores at, 492, 497. Return of officers quartered at, 559. Judges of Courts, iv., 42. Thomas Coombe, health officer, to exam'e sickly vessels, 59. Petition for a pardon, 102. Proceedings respecting a Spanish vessel in distress, 105. Mayor of, commissioned to impress wagons, 108, 117. Indians under protection of, threatened by rioters—attempts to send them through New York, opposed, 167. Letter from Indians in barracks to Gov., 170. Goods from, to Fort Pitt, destroyed, 215, 229, 230, 241. Stamps arrive at, letters respecting, and other proceedings, 241. Lutheran Church, (Zion,) in want of funds, asks for a brief, 253. Searcher of Customs appointed, 253, 305. Memorial—of pilots, 263. Of

Philadelphia—
Wardens, 265–269, 271. Of Merchants, 270. Report on trial of prisoners at, 298, 299, 302, 304, 307. Troops under Lieutenant Colonel Wilkins, to march from, to Fort Pitt, 300. Life of searcher at, threatened, 310. Petition of Northern Liberties to have streets regulated, 313. Troops to depart for Ireland, 344. Complaint against merchants of, 361, 373, 380. Resolutions of Inhabitants of, expressed "in very strong and unbecoming terms," 380. Council with Indians at, 437. Petition for road through Widow Masters' land, 443. Rob't Bayard, Collector of Customs at, 449. John Knight appointed Coroner, *vice* Caleb Cash, deceased, 461. Troops to be stationed in, 465. British insulted by, in the case of the Polly, (Tea Ship,) 480. Tea Ship at, 480. Congress, general, at, objected to by Great Britain, 576, 589. Latitude and longitude, 592. Plan of Lewis Nicola, for defence of the Delaware, 635. Expense of converting old jail into barracks, 715. Prisoners from North Carolina, 734. Heavy cannon asked from Congress, 735. State of the Barracks, v., 7, 71, 75. Troops in city, 17. Plan for protection of, 17, 38. Petition of Cumberland county, New Jersey, for ammunition, 30. Prisoners sent from New York, 40. Attack expected, 72. Minutes of Meeting at Indian Queen respecting tories, 73. Names of suspected persons, 74. Town Meeting at State house, 77. Barracks, 78, 184. Sick sent from Brunswick to, 79. General Howe's army expected, families to prepare for removal, 81. Resolutions of Council of Safety, 82. No person to pass Delaware river without a pass, 82. Resolutions of "Real Whigs," all persons to arm for defence, 83. Guards and officers appointed, and districts laid off, 90, 92. Troops, German-terms, 93. Orders of L. Nicola, Town Major, 96, 201. British soldiers escorted to Newtown, 96. State

Philadelphia—
prisoners to be removed, 99. Vessels of war in the Delaware, 42, 47, 52, 61, 70, 99, 100, 108, 153. Letters, Dr. Jno. Connolly, from prison, 101, 130. Money and papers sent, for safety, to Lancaster, 102. Shops, closing and opening, 115. Orders of Town Major, 96, 121, 122–124, 131, 184, 201, 219–228. Major Stockton and prisoners taken at Lawrence's Island sent to, under Major Bogg's 232. Prisoners sent to, 232, 235, 247, 300. Hessian prisoners sent to, 244 General Gates in, 197, 247. Condition of old jail, 266. Enemy expected, 268, 305. Prothonotary Campbell inquires about oath, 269. F. Phyle, naval officer, 298. Remonstrance of Council and Assembly on withdrawal of troops from, 307. Embargo proposed, 314, 319. Attempt to bribe Delaware pilots through J. Molesworth, his trial and execution, &c., 270–282, 335. Contract for manufacture of woolens in, by S. Wetherill, 342, 355. George Henry declines as Lieut., and William Henry appointed, 355. Ephraim Bonham Sub-Lieutenant, 356. Also Wm. Simple, 356. Enemy expected at, 358, 457, 469, 471, 472. Report on works on Delaware, by Du Coudray, 359. Wagons required, 364. Gen. Arnold appointed to command of militia, 366. Magazine required, 382. General orders, 384–396, 547. Old Loganian Library to be cleared for soldiers, 399. Celebration of July 4th, illumination, &c., 411 Measures for preserving order for, 12. Wood for officers' use, 417. Persons to take account of flour, &c., in, 477. Time of militia expiring, 485. Gen. Howe approaching, via. Chesapeake, 543. Tories to be arrested, houses searched, 551. Warrants to Lieutenants to search for arms, 563. Representation of Christ Church, and St. Peter's, in behalf of Rev. Thomas Coombe, then a prisoner of war, 600. Proceedings against, 556, Bakers to have furloughs, 570. Wagons,

Philadelphia—
581. Removal of Congress, 132. Hessian prisoners sent to, from Trenton, 141, 190, 206. Complaint against guards extorting money, 148. More wagons not required, prospects better, 150. Prisoners sent from Lewes, 152. Protest of James Tilghman, on behalf of proprietaries against cutting woods from Commons, 156, 174. Associators, bravery of, 159. Lord Sterling sends prisoners to, 170. Rich'd Penn's house suitable for a store for furniture, 178. Number of militia in, 178, and sick, 178. Cannon in State house yard, 180. Arms sent to be repaired in, 184. Standing orders for the garrison in, 184. Important services rendered by militia of, 186. Maryland troops arrive in, 196. Address of College, &c., of, on interruptions by soldiers, 198. Houses where troops are, to be daily visited, 201, 215. Report on buildings at air furnace, 206. Exorbitant prices at, 209. Funeral of Gen. Mercer, 222. Col. Haslett and Capt. Morris, 223. Wagons, 490. Foundry in Southwark, 583. Enemy expected, 592. Continental soldiers not to be entertained in, 619. Valuable public papers removed from to Easton, 623. Blankets, shoes, &c., to be impressed, 623, 626. Provisions, &c., to be removed, 627, 630. Military Court martial on prisoners, 631. Enemy leave Philadelphia, 692. Records removed to Lancaster, 749.
On recapture of, vi., 31, 120, 154, 183, 273. L. Nicola asks for rations, while enemy was in, 174. Committee of Congress on recapture, 183, 218. Troops offered by different States, 183. Congress approves of attempt at regaining, 184. Inquiry respecting officers with prisoners for, 216. Horse thieves from, 221, 225, 226. Insolence of Tories, 291. J. Simons asks permission to enter, 299. Counterfeiter to be arrested, 359. Insults of enemy, 361. Prospect of evacuation of, 366, 557, 579,

Philadelphia—
580. Nightly watch, 369. Stalls in the market, 369. Right of corporation to rent ferries and landings, 369. Bridge at Schuylkill, 370. Supply of marketing to the city by Tories, 384, 412, 414, 521. Whipped, 521. Measures to prevent disorders in, after evacuation, 557, 558, 579. British shipping drop down, 568. General Arnold to command in, 568. Defence, evacuation by British army, 604, 630. Proclamation of Genl. Arnold in, 606. Council remove to, 608. Tory property, &c. in, 628, 659, 663. Committee of Congress to inquire into property in, 659. Bridge over Schuylkill, 685, 768. Demolishing of military works, 687. Report of Committee of Congress on property in Philadelphia, 703. Salt seized of J. and A. Wilson, 703, 754. Continental troops going to, Gen. W. asks for militia, 708. Recruiting in, 722. Chains to be set across Chestnut street and State House square, 741.
Gen Armstrong called to command in, vii., 18. Militia, 98. Salt seized in, 122. Fire Companies in, revival of, recommended by Supreme Executive Council, 134, 201. State House can't be used by Congress owing to election, 140. Powder magazine, 141. Danger from gunpowder, 146. Capt. McPherson on defence of, 180. Arnold's command in, 181. Wagons not to stop before State House, 189. L. Nicola on defence of, 190. Conference between Assembly and Council on, 191. Warrants to Sheriff, 149, 192. Bridge over Schuylkill, terms of Army, 196. Propose buying a vessel, 199. Indians arrive in, 292. Memorial of first Artillery Company of, 392. Old library room in State House—key asked for to accommodate Indians, 362. Refused, 364. Drs. Rush and Hutchinson to inspect sickly ves'ls, 408. Petition respecting currency, 416. Do, respecting Court of Appeals—privateers, 422. Embargo, 78,

Philadelphia—
197, 231, 247, 315, 409, 424. Mrs. Allen asks pay for lead taken from her house in, 452. Tobacco trade in, dulness complained of, 452. Letters, committee of city to dealers in flour and importers, 461. Two large guns in river, 495, Recruiting in, by Col. Nicola, useless, 501. Death, and residence of Judge Ross, 554. Hudson square or orchard, 554. Ferries, 627. Plan adopted by Town meeting for improving currency, 621, 643. Bells to ring, and fireworks on birth-day of King of France, 748. Power of Wardens over nuisances in the markets, 658. Guards for prisoners, &c., at, 676, 677, 689. Salt at, 677. Clerk of market, 708. Militia from forts on Delaware ordered up to, 719, 720. Riot at J. Wilson's, 732, 735. Flour distributed by Assembly to poor housekeepers, 740. Embargo, 78, 197, 231, 247, 315, 409, 424, 588, 639, 745.
Dinner by French minister to Pres. and Council, viii., 45. Barracks in used by U. S. out of repair, 61. Troops expected for quarters, 65. Letter of Comm'rs to Council on concealing property from taxation, 80, 81. Commissioner's letter on taxes, 80. Wardens to remove watch from Court House to guard prison, 117. Schuylkill Bridge secured, repairs to, 144, 186. Andrew Doz appointed Comm'r of purchases in, 154, 164. Barracks, 61, 161. Library Co. ask to bring books from New York, 183. City Battalions, 309. Patrols of Light horse, 310. Forage yard in, 311. Sheriff's office, 321. Embargo, 330. Quantity of Salt on hand, 85. Prize brought into, 262. President to Merchants on Embargo, 266. Washington, &c., commends patriotic spirit of the Ladies, 361, 384. Taxes, 381. City Light horse to march, 470. Amount raised by Ladies of—letter Pres. Reed to Gen. Washington, 471. Mrs. Washington on

Philadelphia—
her way to City, 471. Of N. Rowan as Vendue Master, 573. Sketch of duty of a police officer in, 582. Frauds at grate of the gaol, 691. Merchants of, reject application of Pres. for aid, 704. Quarters for Soldiers in, 718, 719. Prisoners in Gaol, 723. Sick prisoners in House of Employment, 725. Board of War apply for use of west wing of State House, 727.
Estimate of taking down St. house steeple, ix., 46, 283. Resolution of Assembly to pull down, 52. T. Nevill on, 76. Wardens on sale of lots, 101. Prisoners and stores in danger, 103. Account of sales of forfeited estates, 105, 126. Taxes, 116, 139. Removal of fence from lot, now Girard square, by Wardens, 150. Rent of house in Market street demanded of Don Juan Miralles, 196. Plan of L. Nicola for dispensing with militia as guards, 198. Duties received in, 206. Light Horse company, petition, 230. Prisoners for criminal offences in jail of, 249. L. Nicola leaves, names Capt. McConnell in his place, 254. Capt. Cooper inspector of barracks, 255, 424. Quarters sought for citizens of South Carolina and Georgia in, 274, 281, 300, 309, 323, 324. Counterfeit half-pence discovered, 279. One hundred city lots to be laid off for sale, 299, 305, 422. Barracks, 255, 326, 424. Taxes, City lots, 329. Lead spouts taken in war to be valued, 366. Reasons for deferring illumination, 390. Removal of Records, 413. Light Horse to be ready, 415. Prisoners from York, 426. Flag-staff on Market street hill to be repaired, preparatory to news from Cornwallis, 440. News of capture of Cornwallis reaches, 454. Federal troops expected, barracks to be put in order, 455. Criminals in jail, 469. Bank North America chartered by Congress, 471. Taxes, 478. Action of Gen. Monk and Hyder Ally in the Delaware, 529, 530. Petition of merchants on

Philadelphia—
seizure of sugars, 534. Guard asked for prisoners in new jail, 549. Debts of theatre, proposal to pay off by a lecture on heads, 573. Prisoners taken in Clarke's expedition in distress in, 574. Isaac Snowden, treasurer, 587. Merchants addressed by Council respecting French seamen, 731. Memorial of Overseers of Poor of N. L., respecting taxes, 739. List of City lots purchased, 748, 749.
Flag on Market street hill, x., 39. Taxes in, 51. Congress ready to deliver up new prison at, 53. Street Commissioners, letters to and from, 55. Troops expected from S. C., sick, 55. Mutiny of troops, 63. Combination formed in, 65. Proposals to appropriate site of old jail for exchange—objections by City Commissioners, 104. Jailor at, petitions postponement of execution of sentence, on account of weather, 119. Conference with merchants on internal commerce, 128. Removal of seat of government of U. S.—proceedings in Congress respecting, 136. Memorial against theatres in, 141. Removal of chevaux-de-frises from river, 93, 144–146, 349, 350, 565. Resolution of Assembly—preparations for rejoicing for peace, 149, 428. Congratulatory letter or address to Gen. Washington, on his safety and return, 150. His answer, 151. Government mansion, 166. Condition of hospital on State Island, 179. Auctioneers elected by Assembly for, 206. Memorial of merchants, 206. Four men burned by fire-works, 218. Returns of troop of light horse, 218. Of officers of first battalion, 219. Advice asked of merchants respecting commercial interests, 219. Their answer, 221. Tax on billiard tables, 222, 224. Purchasers of city lots, 225. Returns of fourth battalion, 235. Commissioners for division and sale of barrack lots, 239, 241, 261, 268, 276, 737. Call on persons collecting moneys, 260. Proposals for "labelling" and numb'ng houses

Philadelphia—
in, 269. Directories first published in, 271. Chevalier de la Luzerne leaves, 278, 282, 283. Powder magazine full, 281. Number of persons confined in jail for felony, 286, 296-302. Account of public arms, &c., required, 286. Commissioners inquire about the iron in old jail, &c.—law for sale, &c., 307. Revolt in the jail, 327, 329. Repairs on executive mansion, 333. Report on repairs of State House, 335, 348, 372, 420, 426, 442, 493, 535, 542, 547, 563. Grand jury present the want of room in magazine for powder, 347. Charles Hellstedt, Swedish Consul, appointed, 362. Disposal of old prison work house, 407. Allowance to prisoners, 407. Trees planted in State House yard, 420. French Consul-General leaves for New York with Congress, 432. Militia officers, 442. J. H. C. Heinecken, Consul at, from United Netherlands, 446. Piers contracted for, 457, 713. Chinese, &c., land, sick and in want, 527. State House clock and G. Owen (1784), 563. Wardens want money to proceed with improvements in river (1784), 571. Removal of buoys by ill-disposed persons, 580. Beacon placed on Cross Ledge (1784), 586. Chevaux-de-frise, 589. Aaron Doane in jail at, 598. Memorial of merchants and traders respecting Barbary powers, 705. Matthew Irwin elected Recorder of Deeds, 707. Petition for a road near Master's lands, 718. Invitation of Jewish congregation to Supreme Executive Council to attend consecration of synagogue in Cherry street (1782), 731. Sieur de la Forest, vice-consul of France, 735. Comptroller asks for a guard at State House, 750. Act to ascertain number of taxables in Philadelphia, 750. Major Fullerton asks for powder for third battalion, 759. City lots which have reverted to the State, 762.
Memorial of light infantry to, offer of service, xi., 36. Franklin and

Philadelphia—
Jenkins, agents from Wyoming, arrive, 52. Officers of Militia, invite Governor to attend a review, 57, 78. J. Franklin's report of proceedings in, 67. Wardens purchase ground at Cape May for beacon, 93. R. E. Pine, paints portraits in Assembly room, 95. Danger to piers at Marcus Hook, from Spanish frigate, 99-102. Mercantile Society thank Council for committee room, 103. Act of North Carolina, appointing delegates to convention, 117. Do., New Hampshire, 123. The "Evening Chronicle" established, 126. Matthew Irwin, Recorder, appointed Justice of Common Pleas, 136. Power of recorders to acknowledge deeds, 136. Phineas Bond, British Consul, 145. Larger powder magazine required, 202. Militia artillery stores in, 257. Opinion of C. J. McKean on powder magazine, 276, 283, 546. Returns of officers elected under militia laws, 302, 378, 561. Wardens interfered with by British Consul, 375, 381. Opinion of Judges on, 383. Resolution of Assembly to purchase a powder magazine, 393, 546. Contested election of a Sheriff, James Ash elected, 410. Returns of invalid guards, 418. Jona. B. Smith resigns as Prothonotary, 423. Lawyers recommend James Biddle for Prothonotary, 426. Attack on Mons. Marbois by Longschamps, 461-495. Barrack lots, sale of, 506, 589, 590. Commercial convention proposed at, 523. L. Nicola, on condition of the prison, 536. Expense of watching public buildings, 543, 575. Repairs of State House, 558. Febiger resigns as auctioneer, 563. Register General opens office in State House, 569, 570. Burial ground for strangers, 570, 571. Memorial of Controller on city lots, 571, 588, 590. Of Receiver General, do., 572. James Read, flour inspector, 573. Tonnage duties, 594. Tavern licenses, 604. Error in warrants of German Lutheran

Philadelphia—
Congregation, 607. Regulation of water courses in Southwark, 611. Commissioners to examine Delaware river, 622. Prisoners in work-house, 648. Trees for State House yard, 674. Inspector of pot and pearl ash, 679. John Chaloner appointed auctioneer, 680. Powder magazine, 682. Memorial on mustard, 685. Of William Semple, sub-lieutenant, 687. Solitary cells in jail to be erected, 706. Creek Indian chiefs visit, 707, 711. Daily Advertiser established by B. F. Bache, 713. District Court, United States, to sit in Philadelphia, 723. Cornplanter and Stiff-Knee arrive, 733. Committee room in State House, 739. Indians are going home, 740. City lots, 742. University corner-stone laid, 742. French emigrants to Scioto, 748. President's arrival to be celebrated, 763.
Resignation of F. Gurney as warden, xii., 2. Accommodations for President U. S., 37. Warden's report on Delaware river, 287. On piers, 294. On improving Delaware, 294. Wardens purchase lot at Cape May for a beacon, 294. Proposals for repair of State House, 295. Complaints on loss of arms, 295. Wardens ask for a burying ground for strangers, 304. Paper money—oil for lighthouses, 306. On state of the river, 307, 308, 314. As respects lighthouse, buoys, piers, winter harbors, &c., 308–314. Powder magazines full, a history of, 317. Fort Wiccacoa, or Association battery at, 437. Potter's field, or Washington square, 468.
Philadelphia Library Company, ask to bring books from New York, viii., 183.
Philadelphia Company for promoting manufactures, &c., propose a road, xi., 428.
Philadelphia County Commissioners to erect cells, xi., 706.
Philadelphia County Light Horse Company, petition, ix., 230.
Philips, Captain, and eleven men killed by Indians in Bedford co., viii., 488.
Philips, General, reported junction with Lord Cornwallis in Virginia, ix., 173.
Phips, Lieutenant-Governor P., asks to load provisions at Philadelphia, ii., 412. Letter, 732.
Phipps, Paul, letter from President Dickinson to, on his polite attentions, x., 360.
Phyle, Doctor Frederick, naval officer at Philadelphia, v., 298; vii., 185. On merchandise in French vessels, viii., 547. Naval officer, x., 240.
Physic, Edmund, order on, iv., 418. Demand for the public books, respecting proprietary estates, viii., 113.
Pickering, Timothy, vi., 173, 237, 546. On ill usage on board a public vessel, vii., 656. Appoints Colonel Samuel Miles deputy quarter-master, viii., 499, 503; ix., 262, 281, 389, 577. Appointed Register, &c., in Luzerne, xi., 84. Letters to and from, 133, 135, 159, 176, 177, 179, 180, 205, 208, 256, 281, 295, 296, 312, 346, 353, 359, 363, 365, 399, 424, 541. Capture of, 326. Proclamation, 329. Certificates, &c., respecting, 551–555. On roads, 133, 135. To be advised with respecting Franklin, 189. Militia officers and justices at Wyoming, 312. Proclamation, to arrest persons, 329. Letters to Governors New York and New Jersey, respecting, 338. Depositions respecting, 345, 358, 371. Restored to liberty, captors, 346, 353, 363, 399, 552. Views respecting old settlers, &c., 353. Applies as Surveyor-General, 630. Indian murders, xii., 8. Letters to and from, 106, 113, 128, 133, 149, 158, 179, 183, 190, 237, 241, 244, 248, 255, 258, 263.
Pierce, John, certificates, x., 536, 538.
Piers at Marcus Hook; x., 407, 471, 713; xii., 2.
Pierry, James, letter, ix., 52, 55.
Pilots asked for by South Carolina, iii., 399. Of Delaware river, memorial, iv., 265; memorial of War-

dens, 265, 271. Of H. Fisher, 664. Regulations for, 680, 686. Restricted, 731, 743 ; v., 28, 47, 270–283, expense of Chevaux de frise, 426, 501. Attempt of Molesworth to bribe, 270–282, 315.

Pinckney, Gov. Tho., of S. C., applied to for public papers, as evidence, xi., 545.

Pine Creek, murders by Indians, vi., 552. Alias Tiadaughton, x., 357. Indian murders on, xi., 709, 710, 714. Indian murders on xii., 318.

Pine, R. E., paints portraits of Revolutionary heroes, xi., 95.

Pintard, Lewis, letter, xi., 196.

Pipe, Col., (Indian chief,) x., 83, 84.

Pipe, Capt., xii., 197, 203.

Piper, John, Col., letter, v., 149, 436, vi., 34, 36, 115, 138, 141, 194, 229, 469, 505; vii., 578; viii., 235, 278, 297, 302, 319, 349, 488, 530. Attacks of Indians near his house; ix., 152, 554.

Pirates, orders, &c., respecting, i., 97, 99, 101, 102, 207. Letter, Privy Council on, 269, 306.

Piratical Goods, orders respecting, i., 307.

Pitcairn, Capt. P., prisoner at Reading, asks to remain there, vii., 374.

Pitch and Tar, manufacture of, iv., 410.

Pitt, Fort, iv., 210, 298, 300, 307, 337, 395, 483, 511. Conference with Indians at, 298. Troops to march from Philadelphia for, 300. Letter, &c., Colonel Wilkins, 395. Gen. Gage in, 456. Latitude and longitude, 592. Called Dunmore, 521, 524; ix., 17, 37. A tory paper found in a powder horn near, 39. Washington's letter respecting, 81. Has never wanted flour, 143. Gen. Irvine ordered to, 419, 433. Boundary line, taxes, &c., 575 ; x., 53, 83, 95, 115, 167, (1783,) 337, 345; instructions relative to lands opposite to, 115; timber on—agreement Gen. Irvine and Boggs, 140, 141, 699 ; Col. Bayard commands at, (1783) 167 ; ruins of garrison at, 421, 462, 464 ; depositions respecting—bill of sale, 463 ; ejectment against Capt. Lucket, 466 ; to be given up to certain persons, 477, 498 ; sale at, 483 ; Turnbull, Marmie & Co., claim the land, 497 ; xii., 161, 167, 182, 431–437.

Pitt, William, Secretary of State iii., 94, 96, 106, 321, 518 ; notices of King George's intention to marry Princess Charlotte, iv. 58.

Pittsburgh,—Journal of F. Post to, iii., 560. Return of provisions at, 579. No. of garrison at, 580. Conferences at, 560, 571, 674, 744. Fort at, 685, 693. Fort Pitt, 696. Military post near, iv., 39, 45, 210, 484. To Lancaster, journey to, 210. County town of Westmoreland, 449, 471. Petition against Connolly, 526. Troops marching from Virginia to, 530. Minutes of Indian conference at, 531. Thoughts of abandoning, 550. Gen. Hand recalled from, vi., 461. Fort at, threatened, 507. Provisions for, 532. Col. Brodhead's regiment marches for, 700. An agent from Virginia at, vii., 79. Troops, 341. Delaware Indians at, viii., 22. Troops thrown into private dwellings at, by Col. Brodhead, 22, 119, 120. Fort Pitt, a serious concern, 440. Garrison in distress, 554. election at, x., 211. State of, for want of acting civil magistrates, 289. Printing office proposed, 421. Gen. Gage orders works to be demolished, 429. Ruins, 462. Ejectment against Capt. Lucket, 466. To be taken possession of for the State, as soon as relinquished by the U. S., 498. Road to, 533. Road to, proposed, xi., 70. Severe cold at, 244. Lands opposite described, 244. Timber on, 500, 501. Road from Bedford to, 560, 643 ; xii., 150. Boat-builders employed, 112. Want of provisions, 112. Colonel Rawlins's detachment arrives at, under Capt. Beal, 120. Fort encroached on, 133, 190. Letter of committee on Indians, 300. Capt. Armstrong commands, 320. Forts at, 355–359, 427–431.

Pittstown, N. J., powder sent to, vi., 421. Arms at, 435, 439.

Plays, Games, and Sports, reasons for repealing Act against, i., 155, 159. Memorial against, iii., 657.

Pleasants, Samuel, vi., 524. Re-

monstrance (1777) on treatment, x., 158. See Vol. VI., p. 509.
Pluckamin, Gen. Washington at, v., 168, 171.
Pluggy's town, Indians attack Virginia, v., 258, 260.
Polson, Capt. William, letters to and from, ii., 246, 247, 248. On recruiting service, 247, 248.
Pomfret Castle, (see Forts, ii.)
Pomroy, Col., house attacked by Indians, ix., 51.
Poor, overseers of N. Liberties, memorial ix., 739.
Pooteatomies, xii., 131, 147.
Popple, Alured, Letters from, i., 245, 288.
Population of State in 1775, iv., 597.
Port au Prince, earthquake at, petition for aid, iv , 370.
Porter, Capt. Andrew, vi., 574; viii., 57 ; ix., 257. Major Andrew, ix., 632. Col., letter respecting his rank, x., 49. Andrew, commissioner on W. boundary, x., 444, 455, 760. Asks advice respecting wagons, &c., 372. On boundary, xi., 26, 69, 156, 178, 215, 241. Commis'er, 502. N. line complete 214. Describes Erie lands, 242.
Porter, Capt. Stephen, appointed commissary to commissioners on boundary with Virginia, x., 438. Asks pay to be raised, 737.
Post, Fred., Journal with C. Thomson, iii., 412. Journal, 412, 422, 520, 524, 560-565. Character of, 578. Letters, 581, 698, 700, 702, 706, 709. Instructions, 621. Relation of conversation with Indians, 742. Journal, iv., 92-98. Passport, 277.
Postage, franking privilege, xi., 142.
Post Office, A. Spotswood, letter on, i., 264. Answer, 265. Facilities recommended by Dunk Halifax, iv., 202.
Postlethwaite, Capt. Samuel, letters, Indian murders, ix., 192.
Pot and pearl ash Inspector, xi., 679.
Potash works at Philadelphia, iii., 53.
Potomac Fall as seat of government of United States, x., 138.
Potters' Field, Philadelphia, patent, &c , xii., 304, 468.
Potter, David, asks for Salt for Bridgetown, New Jersey, v., 86. Letters, 86, 218, 305, 433, 436, 440, 460, 511, 551, 570, 571, 584, 718, 719, 730, 752, 755, 768.
Potter, Gen. James, letters, vi., 51, 70, 83, 89, 97, 98, 150, 166, 169, 231, 516, 517, 521, 603, 665, 729. His operations west of Schuylkill, 98. Skirmish at Blue Bell, 32. Near Barren Hill Church, 70, 98. Wishes to retire, 123. Near Darby, 141. Asks leave of absence, 167. Relieved by Gen. Lacey, 168. Clamor against, 231. Skirmishes near Germantown, 70. Respecting, 662, 681, 684; vii., 342, 418. Recommended, 448, 473; viii., 484, 561, 567, 689, 699, 710. State of frontiers.—Indian murders, ix., 70. Soldiers, 128. Recruits, 184. Elected Vice President, 447. Expedition declined, 640. Arms for Wyoming, x , 47. Letter to President Reed, (1779. See Vol. VII.,) militia, Indians, &c., 159. Death of, xi., 660.
Potter, James, appointed Surveyor, xi., 661, 663.
Potts, Jonathan, v., 350.
Potts, Samuel, vi., 595.
Potts, Dr. John, letter to on clothing, viii., 96.
Potts Grove, flour to, be deposited at, vi., 177.
Powder, agreement for, by Congress Committee, iv., 696. Offer of, by Berks county, 679. Scarcity of, viii., 434, 442. For celebrating President's arrival, xi., 763.—Required for thirty-nine discharges, xii., 9. Magazines at Philadelphia, 317. Magazine, plan of a, by Lewis Nicola, iv., 715; vii., 141. Waste of, 398, 404. Philadelphia presented by Grand Jury as not capable of containing all the powder, x , 347. Too small for all the powder, xi., 202. Advice asked of C. J. McKean, 276. Opinion, 283. Described, 546. Powder magazine at Philadelphia, to be purchased, 393, 682.
Powder-mills, erected, iv., 745. Committee for erecting, 709. Location of several, 709. Report on, 765. R. Morris asks for, 768.

Explosion of State, letter P. De Haven, v., 255. Testimony respecting, 256, 257, 261. Magazine at Lancaster, 295. Merchants apply for, 319. Hemberg's vi., 139, 540. Discovered, 544. Property on French Creek desired, vii., 315.

Powell, Jeremiah, President of Massachusetts, prisoner carried into, viii., 254.

Powell, Col. Leven, letter from Kentucky, viii., 766.

Powel, Samuel, (Prest. of Philadelphia Agricultural Society,) information requested on Hessian fly, xi., 527, 384, 385.

Pownall, Sir John, letters, ii., 377, 467, 527, 778.

Pownall, Secretary, John, letters, iii., 97, 759; iv., 309, 368, 465, 535, 616, 617, 620, 629.

Pownall, T., Governor of Massachusetts,—Account of great fire in Boston, solicits aid, iii., 714. Granted by Assembly, 715.

Prather, Henry, Deposition, iv., 237.

Prayers, for the Royal family, to be altered, i., 225, 624.

Presbyterian, Synod, Address to Gov. Thomas, i., 743. Second Church, do., 744.

President and Council have power to discharge soldiers, viii., 110.

President and V. President, election of, xi., 635.

Presqu'isle, fort at, iii., 13, 563. xii, 443.

Price, G., letter, iii., 488.

Price, Lt., Samuel, letter, iii., 429.

Prince, birth of a, iv., 414.

Princess, Louisa, death of, iv., 300.

Princess, a, born, iv., 311.

Princeton, Enemy advancing to, v., 148, 157, 158. Washington has, 159. Battle at, 159, 163, 168, 171, 215.

Prison, (new,) at Philadelphia, x., 52.

Prisoners, delivered up by Indians, iv., 100. At Philadelphia, on trial of, opinions, iv., 298, 299. Taken at St. John's, and Chamble, sent to interior, 688: v., 77, 99, 168, 170, 232, 233, 234, 241, 243, 244, 249, 267, 294, 296, 306, 317, 320, 329, 371, 383, 442, 469, 471, 502, 511, 513, 534, 604, 609. Relief of, 442, 585, 600, 620, 632, 647. In Masonic Lodge, 582, 584, 586, 593, 604, 607, 609. Of war—in Reading, 21. Pay of officers, 31. In Bristol, 61. Care of, 65. At Carlisle, 77. At Philadelphia, to be removed, 99. From Com. Hazelwood, 169. Sent to Philadelphia, 232; vi., 105, 127, 216, 261, 263, 410, 427, 519, 680, 709. Exchange of, proposed by Gen. Howe, 300, 318. From Philadelphia in Virginia, 74, 75, 102, 104, 106, 111, 158, 210, 365, 367, 401, 402, 404, 453, 509, 510, 524. Memorial to Congress, 111, 158. Remonstrance, 509. Petition, 511. Exchange not exempt from military duty, vii., 496. Who have broken parole, 626. Expected, 731; viii., 5, 43, 93, 157, 163, 180, 188, 191, 343, 368, 555, 723, 725, 726, 745, 753. Of war at N. York, distress of, 619, 620, 660, 663. Provisions, 620. Regulations respecting supplies, 626. The Convention, to be removed from Maryland and Virginia, to Yorktown and Lancaster, 753. Convention, letters to Assembly on, ix., 5, 6, 7, 24, 37, 38, 158, 203, 341, 357, 515. Plot discovered at Lancaster, 156. In Clarke's expedition, memorial, 574. Confined for criminal offences in Philadelphia jail, 249. In prison ships at New York, 667. Ships, British, at New York. Suffering on board, ix., 656. At N. York, number of prisoners, 667. Letter of Council to prisoners, 668. Described, 757, 763. War, ix., 561. In prison ships at New York, number, 667. Letter of Council to, 668. Provisions for, 669, 674. At New York, supplies for (1782,) xi., 495. In workhouse, Philadelphia, 648. Letter, Gen. Washington respecting, (1782,) 496.

Privateers, Spanish, on Delaware, i., 759, 763, 765, 766. King's orders respecting, iii., 91, 162. Commissioned, v., 569. Commissions granted by Congress for, vi., 327, 378, 670, 705, 726, 727. Commissions for, vii., 127, 224, 536. Commissions for, viii., 603.

Prize money, Commissioners, for distributing, appointed, i., 654, 655. And prize money, viii., 262. Act for capture and condem'ion of, ix., 43.

Proceedings of a General Court Martial, ix., 361.

Proclamation, William Penn against Thomas Matthews, i., 68. Against cutting timber in Philadelphia, 97. Of Gov. Keith to continue the Government, 169. Of do. reward for a murderer, 170. Of Gov. Gordon, 189. Of King George II, 200, 220, 204. Of Gov. Thomas against settling on lands in Lancaster county, 629. Of Gov. Gordon, 189. Of Gov. Morris for a fast, ii., 649. Of Gov. Dinwiddie, of Virginia, respecting Indians, iii., 155. Against selling rum to, 237, 519. And submission of inhabitants to George III., iv., 38. Gov. Hamilton for murderers, 65. Gov. Fauquier, 255. For preserving fish in Delaware river, &c., 347. Against murderer of Isaac Meyer, 376. Of Gov. Franklin, New Jersey, against a smuggler, 381, 445. Gov. Penn, against Dunmore's 580. Fleming Elliott, 665. Of Gen. Washington, v, 700. On threshing out grain, vi., 116. For pardon to tories recommended, 434. Of Gen. Arnold after the evacuation, 606. For pardon of prisoners under Test laws, vii., 130. Of Congress for a Fast day, 257, 261, 321. For apprehending deserters, 448. By Congress for Thanksgiving, 757. Respecting Virginia boundary, viii., 63. Of Congress for a Fast, 130. For apprehending J. & R. Smith, murderers of Mr. Boyd, 244. Respecting counterfeits in Philadelphia, ix., 279. Of Congress for a Thanksgiving, 650. Respecting the money and credit, 131. For Thanksgiving by Congress, victory over Cornwallis, 443. Respecting decree at Trenton, 732. Congress for Thanksgiving for peace, x., 134. Of Governor of Connecticut, on Wyoming lands, 146. Of Massachusetts for arrest of Daniel Shays, &c., xi., 119. On arrest of Col. Pickering, 329. For Indian murders, xii., 318.

Proctor's Col., regiment, xii., 223.

Proctor, Col. John, v., 202; vi, 445, 458, 506, 659, 722; viii., 193, 217, 253, 284, 710.

Proctor, Captain Thomas, to return bedding, &c., from Province Island, iv., 728, 729. On the Barracks, 729. Has proved cannon, &c., 790. Return of stores, 754.

Proctor, Major Thomas, letters to and from, v., 11, 33, 45, 50, 52, 97, 118, 130, 134, 141, 189, 192, 207, 234, 236, 249, 451, 455. Orders prisoners to jail, and arrest of Mrs. White, 97. Appointed a Regiment of Artillery, 234. On joining the Continental service, 189.

Proctor, Col. Thomas, vi., 676, 712, 732. Letters, vii., 121, 123, 135, 146, 261, 270, 290, 298, 405, 423, 440, 476, 485. Objects to uniform, 292, 293. Companies, 339, 340, 387, 397. Letters, viii., 43, 57, 76, 193. Claims Hog Island, 730, 734, 760. Threats, complaints against, ix., 11, 17, 120. Resignation, 142, 511.

Proctor, Thomas, Sheriff, instructions to, respecting H. Carberry, x., 323, Revolt in jail, 327. Purchase of land, 420.

Proctor, Gen. Thomas, proposes celebration of President Washington's birth day, xi., 664. Indian murders, 719. Respecting Indians, 740, 741.

Proctor's Col., regiment, xii., 223.

Proposals for raising an army at westward, iv., 654.

Proprietaries, notice respecting land lottery, i., 455. To trustees, letter from, 236. Appointments, Andrew Hamilton's opinion on, 129. Land at Easton, iii., 84. Letters of government, 107, 157, 193, 576, 668. Power to Gov. Hamilton to sell, 685. Lands in Reading, ix., 231, 237.

Prothonotaries must reside within their counties, vii., 638. County, viii., 58. Of Washington county, letter from Governor of Virginia, x., 78. Circulars to, 268, 439, 749; xi., 591. Of Supreme Court, 765.

Providence Ship, letter W. P. to owners, on seizure, i., 136.

Province Island, first house on for sick, iv., 59. And Mr. Holker, ix., 298. Lots, 384, 385. University, &c., 385. Hospital, keeper appointed, x., 75. Purchasers of lots, 225.

Provincial forces refuse to do duty for want of pay, iii., 98. Number in pay, 99. Proposed dress of, 101. Commissioners' letter, iv., 142.

Provisions—Embargo on, ii., 263, 283, 373, 375, 500. Gen. Shirley remits to Gov. Morris for, 357. Requested for Bermuda, 661. For soldiers, bad, iii., 48, 54. Estimate cost of, 62. Commissioners on, 92, 214. Ammunition at fort Augusta, 79. At different forts, 81. Embargo on, 97, 114, 144, 148. High prices of, v., 667, 676, 690, 721, 739, 742, 744, 748. Cost of liquor, 742; vi., 34, 38, 104, 107, 129, 130, 135, 143, 207, 269, 271, 277, 281, 284, 286, 289, 294, 296, 306, 307, 348, 377, 378, 552, 667. Resolutions of Assembly respecting, 66. Great want of, in the Army, 38, 107, 263, 329, Large quantity of flour, &c., ordered by Congress, 177, 256. Inquiries by Board of War respecting, 165. Prospects of a supply, 231, 240. Commissioners for purchasing, 294, 329. Instructions, &c., 303–314. Letter of Board of War to Congress on, 315. Letter of Council to Commissioners, 327. Memorial of Council and Assembly to Congress on the causes of delay and difficulty respecting, 333–336. Purchases to be desisted from, 427, 435, 441, 449; vii., 85, 88, 128, 159, 181, 186, 391, 432, 514, 555, 570, 586, 605, 670, 671, 685, 692, 727, 730. Prices of, 181, 192, 245. Resolution of Congress for supply of 245. Magazines for, 305; viii., 8, 48, 55, 66, 69, 70, 74, 75, 85, 86, 90, 94, 97, 146, 178, 198, 240, 248, 251, 255, 260, 277, 285, 295, 300, 301, 305. Great scarcity in Army, 122, 132, 260. Places of deposit, 170, 260, 270, 287, 313, 317, 325, 328, 330, 342, 354, 362, 364, 367, 371, 379, 382, 383, 399, 425, 430, 432, 438, 439, 441, 458, 471, 475, 477, 479, 480, 485, 494, 505, 515, 522, 525, 526, 539, 548, 556, 558, 560, 565. Quota of supplies demanded of all States, 472, 572, 601, 603, 611, 629, 635, 652, 653, 661, 697, 719, 720, 739. Rendezvous for, 720. Estimate of, necessary at different posts, 631; ix., 15, 16, 17, 53, 54, 55, 57, 58, 66, 71, 73, 81, 83, 84, 99, 102, 103, 111, 124, 137, 143, 151, 161, 165, 167, 175, 186, 190, 201, 207, 250, 262, 265, 277, 285, 290, 303, 327, 345, 348, 359, 381, 399, 400, 410, 411, 417, 419, 423, 425, 459, 470, 529, 744; x., 105, 109, 118; xii., 112, 114, 116, 117, 121, 125, 132, 134, 135, 136, 154, 160, 161, 164, 172, 173, 179, 183, 186, 208, 218, 229, 230, 231, 234, 236, 241, 247, 253, 254, 256, 257, 259, 260, 262, 264, 266, 272, 273, 274, 277. Destroyed, 145, 200, 263.

Provost, Rev. Samuel, consecrated Bishop, x., 434.

Provost, Gen., (British,) vii., 736.

Prudden, T., and A. Caldwell, ix., 480.

Prussia, treaty with, xi., 5–14. Rights of conscience, worship and burial secured by, to United States, 8.

Prussian merchants, certificates in favor of, ix., 361.

Public Records, report on, securing, xi., 545.

Pulaski, General, his legion, vi., 705, 719. Complaints against his corps, vii., 230, 232, 233, 353, 378. Letter from Board of War, 233.

Punishment, in Army, v., 119.

Purchasers of flour, vii., 548, 674, 692, 718, 753, 766. Of salt, 728, 769. Of flour to exchange for salt, viii., 3, 51.

Purdie, Col., viii., 562, 567.

Purviance, Samuel, Jr., complaint of conduct of seamen on Delaware, viii., 644.

Putnam, Daniel, letter, v., 215.

Putnam, Gen. Israel, orders lumber on Delaware R., to be made into rafts, v., 86. Visits Fort Island, 130. At Crosswicks, 181. Letters, 163, 168, 170, 177, 196, 208, 215, 230, 232, 247, 282, 300.

Q.

Quarry, Col., letter W. P. to, i., 136.
Quakers—pamphlets respecting, ii., 257. Address to General Assembly on present state of affairs, 487. A deputation at Easton desire to make presents to Indians, 728. Governor's objections, 729.
Present at Easton at Treaty, iii., 265, 250, 262, 263, 264, 274, 319, Memorial respecting Conference at Philadelphia, 469.
Resolutions, and other acts of Congress against v, 551, 574, 580, 589, 593, 596, 600. Of Council against, 555, 574, 582, 584, 586, 590, 591, 593, 600, 604, 608, 609, 612, 632.
Proceedings against, vi., 4, 74, 75, 401, 402, 404, 432, 509–510, 572, 709.
Representation of, for not illuminating houses, ix., 450. John Pemberton and William Mathews make known their intentions to go to Europe on a religious visit, 551. Petition against theatres, xi., 342.
Quamash, Henry, (a lame Indian,) story about sale of lands, iv., 66.
Quarter Master, department to be regulated, vii., 84, 85.
Quarters for soldiers in Philadelphia, iii., 85, 111, 112.
Quemahoning, T., petition from, letter Colonel Piper, answer to, viii., 530.
Quinby, Jonathan, land on Delaware, iii., 681.
Quit-rents, proceedings of court on, i., 99.
Quittapahilla, iii. (See Lebanon.)

R.

Raboteau, C. L., proposes a lottery to raise funds for a Literary Academy, iii., 677. His commission, 678. Petition, 679, 680.
Raccoon Creek, Indians attack a Sugar Camp on, viii., 140, 159. Boys taken, xii., 148, 210, 214.
Radiere, Col. de la, vii., 400.
Rain deluges Luzerne Co., xi., 85.
Ralston, John, &c., to investigate cause of distress, vi., 647. Reports, 772.
Randolph, Beverly, Governor of Virginia, call of a convention, xi., 557. Indians, 600.
Randolph, Edmund, Governor Virginia, memorial of Charles Simms, xi., 115, 116. Resolutions of Virginia, 212. Respecting a negro slave claimed, 249, 256. Laws requested, 284. Laws—Joseph, Elam, 290. Commercial regulations, (1786,) 523, (1784,) 525.
Randolph, Lieut. Asher, information of enemy, ix., 436.
Rangers, armed boat to Committee of Safety, iv., 704. For provisions, 704. Complain of ill treatment, 705. Five companies to be raised, vii., 300, 301.
Rank, antedated commissions not to give, v., 371. Arrangement of, 483. Of officers, appeal to Congress respecting, vii., 162, 447, 607, 691. Washington on, 188.
Ransom bills unpaid, prisoners held in France on account of, iv., 201.
Rattan [Ruatan ?] Isl'd, to be settled, i., 659, 660.
Ratification of Constitution of U. S., xii., 82.
Rations, in Continental army, iv., 679. What constitutes a, vi, 247, 272, 657. Value of, vii., 302, 515. Act of Congress respecting, furnished inhabitants on frontiers, 673.
Rawlings, Col., regiment, vii., 339, 340; viii., 5, 38; xii., 115, 147, 272. His detachment arrives at Pittsburg, 120.
Ray's Town, Stoc'de fort at, iii., 510.
Raystown, Fort Bedford at, xii., 339–341.
Razer, Peter, appointed Collector of Customs at Lewestown, iii., 546; iv., 76.
Ratzer, Capt. Bernard, Surveyor of boundary between New York and New Jersey, protection asked for him, iv., 336, 337, 339. Commission of Governor Penn to him, 339.
Rea, Samuel, vi., 611, 672. Attack of Indians on Gilbert and Piert, viii., 221. Savages, 222, 227. Tories at Water Gap, 259. Militia, Indians, 286, 560. Troops, 320, 386, 592, 640, 683, 729; ix., 581.

Murders by Indians, 107, 108, 158. Militia, 743.
Read, Captain Adam, orders to, ii., 545, 551. Letter to, 738.
Read, Charles, letter, iii., 546.
Read, James, iii., 36, 245. Letter respecting prisoners of war, v., 20. Special messenger, 68. Letters, 20, 68, 138, 204, 258, 323, 463, 602. Prothonotary, 323; vi., 234, 235, 245, 473; vii., 289. Appointment as Register of Court of Admiralty of Berks Co., ix., 191. Appointed commissioner to Wyoming, x., 330. Flour Inspector, xi., 573.
Read, John, letters to and from, respecting Mud Fort, v., 12, 23, 24, 26, 47, 60, 64, 91.
Read, Captain Thomas, on the naval affairs of the river, iv., 745, 747. Complains of want of seamen, bad powder, &c., 750, 751, 753. Resigns, 769.
Reading, Berks County, water obtained at, ii., 45. Guard for, 544, 596. Public stores at, 660. Jour. from, by Captain Young, to sundry forts, 674. To receive Highland soldiers, iii., 575. Recommendations for Clerk of Market, 659. Committee respecting arms, &c., iv., 757. Uneasiness respecting prisoners of war, v., 20, 250. Furnace, cannon cast at, 31. Letter from, 139. Hospital at, 139. Quantity of arms in, 341. Prisoners at, 467. J. Morris to attend court at, 481. Fear from powder, 633. Places of worship used as barracks, 653. Troops sent from, vi., 14. Flour to be deposited at, 177. Clothing at, 250. Attacks on Attorney-General, 267. No lawyer, 245. Troops ordered to, 374. Guards dismissed, 542. Request of prisoners to remain at, vii., 374. Disturbance by prisoners at, 450, 454, 480. Tory letters, 488. Prisoners, and scarcity of provisions at, viii., 425. Sales of confiscated estates at, ix., 216. Convention prisoners arrive at, 225, 230, 236, 289, 290. Proprietary land, 231, 237. Quarters to Troops, refused at, 299. Respecting, 346, 347. Commissioners appointed to examine Roads, &c., between Susquehanna, and improving communications between Schuylkill and Susquehanna rivers, x., 129. Case of Big Spring tracts, 712. A justice of peace required, xi., 63. Election of Burgesses, 275. Recommendation of J. Deimer as Judge, 597.
Reading, George, murders, &c. near Fort Ligonier, vii., 345.
Reading, John, President of New Jersey—death of John Hamilton—demands a counterfeiter, i., 764.
Reading, Philip, letter, iii., 699.
Reasons for not building a house viii., 287.
Receiver General, islands in Ohio, xi., 667. Report, 750. Report on certificate, xii., 47.
Recorders to have power to acknowledge deeds, xi., 136.
Records of Bucks county, v., 237. Westmoreland, 452, 455. Chester county, 462. Bedford, 638. Northampton county, 654. To Lancaster, 749. And papers, public, Richard Peters' letter respecting, vi., 72. Circular of Council on, 88. To be removed to Northampton county, 88, 140. Public, viii., 318. Removal of, ix., 412. Of Court against Kilborn and Parks, xi., 419. A. Kilborn, 546. S. Miles, 547. Report on securing public, xi., 575.
Recruiting, service of twelve Pennsylvania regiments, cash paid for, v., 335, 483. Col. Hartley on, vi, 321. Wayne on, 408. Officers' memorial to Council, 280, 397. Letter to General Washington, 287, 288, 292. Plan of Congress for, vii., 442. Accounts, 500; viii., 72, 351, 363, 368, 382, 422, 437, 439, 669, 682, 730, 732, 744, 745, 753; ix., 69, 136, 187, 191, 196, 221. Rendezvous for, 484. Instructions to Maj. Moore, x., 127. Suspended, 529. Ordered by Secretary of War, xi., 555.
Recruits, respecting, vi., 410, 411, 433, 451, 659, 746; vii., 64, 65, 70, 105, 442, 476, 500, 659, 667, 711. 742.
Red Bank, attack on, v., 118, 130.

State of, 362, 663, 699, 701, 703, 706, 707, 709, 719, 745, 746. Count Donop killed, 699. Commodore Hazelwood account of action, 721, 722; vi., 21, 24, 28, 31, Visit of President, &c. to, vii., 199, 200. Fort (Mercer), battle, &c. at, viii., 445-452.

Redick, David, difficulty in surveys in Washington county, x., 416. Account of Indian murders, xi., 149. Intelligence from N. Y., 197, 339. Elected Vice President, 411. Describes lands opposite Pittsburg, 244. Asks letters from Gov. Clinton, of J. Franklin and Dr. Hamilton, 412. Hamilton and Benton (1787), 459. Justices, 592.

Redstone,—people against Captain Springer, xii., 278.

Reed, Adam, letter, iii., 426.

Reed, Bowes, vii., 262.

Reed, Fort, xii., 452.

Reed, Joseph, letter, iv., 679. Arms to be taken from soldiers leaving army, v., 108. Sends prisoners from Trenton, 151. Appointed C. J., 289, 379. Letters to and from, 109, 151, 289, 379, 692, 701, 702. Has horse shot under him and narrowly escapes, vi., 71. Recommended for Brigadier General by General Armstrong, 91. Appointed on committee of Congress on memorial of Councils and Assembly, 160, 183, 218. Letters, 120, 218, 712, 733, 739. Asked to assist Attorney General, 712. Gen. Armstrong's opinion of, 662, 681. Gibb's journal in R. I., 733. Presence required, 739. Letters to and from. (See Sup. Executive Council.) Affidavits respecting, before Congress, by Clarkson and Franks, vii., 270. Complimentary resolutions of Assembly, 295. Correspondence respecting Arnold, 162, 283, 327, 337, 347, 351, 380. Views on militia laws, 359. Letters to Gen. Washington, 377-383. Compliment to, 582, 584, 665. His private position, 712. Wrong impressions of Board of War, 713. Correspondence with J. Wilcox, 721, 725, 727. Sickness, 744. Proposes to command troops in person, 760. Letter to Congress on dispensing with part of the sentence of Court Martial respecting Gen. Arnold, viii., 99. Letter to Nicholas Waln on oppressive execution of law, 106. On power with Council to discharge soldiers, 110. Gen. Brodhead proposes a purchase of manor lands, 120. President declines being concerned, 150. Thanks to officers of militia, 265. Asks meeting of merchants, 266. [See Sup. Executive Council.] Replies at length to Mons. Holker, ix., 175-184. Reply to field officers, 187. Letters, 517. To H. Osburne, on Connecticut claim, 563, 691. Account as counsel in Connecticut case, 738. Letters to, from Council (1777) respecting office of Chief Justice, x., 157. Letters to and from (1779), 157, 159, 160. Elected member Congress, 254; xii., 106. Letters to, 150, 163, 180, 186, 251.

Reed, Leonard, wagon master, resigns, vi., 290.

Reed, Major, viii., 116.

Reed, Lieut. Samuel, operations at Wyoming, xi., 435.

Reese, William, letter, iv., 653.

Reformed German Clergy, address to Gov. Morris, ii., 185.

Regiment, Pennsylvania, how stationed, iii., 339. State of the forces between Delaware and Susquehannah, 340. Number in pay of province, 341.

Regiment of Philadelphia county, address to Gov. Denny, ii., 763. His reply, 763.

Register General appointed, xi., 568. Opens office in State House, 569. Appoints Thomas Smith, clerk, 570. Order, 571. To Comptroller General, 693, 696. Report on finances, 722. On duties of office, xii., 3.

Reichel, John, Frederick, Moravian missionary, applies for passport, ix., 265.

Reid, James, R. &c., letter, viii., 45. Delegate in Congress, xi., 308. Pay as member, 280.

Reigart, Adam, vi., 626.

Reilly, Capt., vii., 691.

Rein, John, viii., 606.
Rejoicings for peace, resolutions of Assembly, x., 149.
Religious liberty and rights secured by treaty between U. S. and Prussia, xi., 8.
Religious societies, holding lands, &c., respecting, i., 160.
Remonstrance of Council and Assembly to Congress on the withdrawal of Continental troops from Philadelphia, v., 307. Of Council and Assembly to Congress against army going into winter quarters, vi., 104, 107, 111. Of prisoners in Masonic Lodge, 509. Jas. Pemberton, John Hunt and Samuel Pleasants (1777) against treatment by order of Council, x., 158. [See vol. VI., p. 509.]
Rendezvous, plans of, proposed, vi., 302.
Repeal of various laws, reasons for, i., 155, 191.
Reports, of Senate, &c., committee respecting Colonial Records and Archives, i., 3, 10. Of S. Hazard, respecting Archives, 17. To be printed in English and German, 21. On petition of the Swedes, 172. Of Drs. Græme and Zachary, 210. Commissioners on Lancaster, C. H., 252. On passes, 256. On Loan Office, 457. On public accounts, 459. On fortifications at Philadelphia, 633, 636. Of Board of Trade on laws, 721. Of C. Thomson and F. Post, of journey to Indians, iii., 412. Of committee on Commissioners' accounts, 452. Of Drs. Græme and Bond, iv., 59. Of John Gibson, 118. To Commissioners trade and plantations respecting certain acts, 275, 281. Of Solicitor General, on trial of prisoners at Philadelphia, 298, 299, 300, 304, 307. On salt works, 771. Of barrack master on dirty houses left by soldiers, v., 265. Of De Coudray on defences on Delaware, 360, 565. To Congress respecting Burgoyne, vi., 163. Respecting Wm. Straker, 701. On property in Philadelphia, 706. Committee on Congress, 753. To Congress, respecting Gen. Maxwell, vii., 138. Ass'y on salaries of officers, 739. Of comm'e of Congress on public debt, ix., 85–93. Of committee on letter from Superintendant of finances, 499. To Assembly on boundary line between Virginia and Pennsylvania, x., 8, 72, 95. In case T. Matlack, 9. Ephraim Douglass to Sec'y of War, 83. To Congress on Indian affairs, 119–125. On internal commerce, 128. To Congress on full representation, 139. On interest on debt, 242–250. T. Matlack, 365. On national debt, 514–520. On State House, 335, 375. Council censors, 383. Of Commissioners on boundary, 373, 374, 506. On arrears of imposts, 378. Of Commissioners on boundary between Pennsylvania and Virginia, 506. To Congress on revenue system, U. S., 732–735. To Assembly (1784), on Wyoming, 541.
Of Treasury, xi., 15 On Western boundary, 69, 308. On commerce, 75. On cession of lands by Connecticut, 107. Proceedings of landholders, at Wyoming, 246. To Assembly on Erie, 252. Of Attorney General, on citizenship, 259, 260, Report, to Congress on letter of Commissioners of Virginia, 317. Of Council on Lake Erie, 389. Of commissioners on boundary between N. York, and Pennsylvania, 522, 526. Of Council to General Assembly, on purchase of Erie, 528. On claim of Wm. Hamilton, 535. On securing public records, 544, 575. On rewards of Captors, 554, 577. On J. Adlum's letter on surveys, Comptroller General, on accounts, 587–582, 590. On Mud Island accounts, 586, 617. On accounts of General Gibson, and Butler, 588. On attorney's fees, 647. On account, 695. Health officer, 747. of auctioneers, 748, 755, 761. Master of Rolls, 748. Receiver General, 750. Commissioners viewing rivers, 751. Flour inspector, 755. Secretary of land office, 757. Surveyor General, 758. of treasurer, 758. Register General, 763. Prothono-

tary of Supreme Court, 765. Measurer of grain and salt, 766. Collector of Excise, xii., 1. Inspector of Lumber, 1. Treasurer's, 4. Charles Pettit on accounts 6. Of Receiver on Certificates, 47. Of Commissioners to Wyoming, 73, 296. On Frankstown Road, 80. Of Wardens on state of river, 308.
Representation of Quakers, for not illuminating houses, ix., 450.
Representation in Congress, state of, xi., 122, 132, 168, 175, 180, 214, 263, 275, 298.
Requisitions by Congress on the States, xi., 15, 23, 30, 73, 198,
Resignations in favor of persons not allowable, vii., 99; viii., 597, 612; Of F. Gurney as Warden, xii., 2. Of Justices, 5.
Resolutions of Assembly of Massachusetts i., 666; Of N. Y. Assembly, ii., 52; Of House of Commons on Bills of Credit, iv., 173. Of Council at New York on Indians passing through New York, 172. House of Commons on Manufactures, 292. Of Philadelphia, complained of by Earl Hillsborough, as "in very strong and unbecoming terms," 380 Of Assembly relative to Fort at Mud Island, 474. Of Assembly 548; Of Congress, v., 25, 62, 124, 137, 183, 268, 283, 304, 309, 310, 319, 325, 328, 366, 418, 461, 469, 470, 492, 513, 528, 539, 551, 552, 554, 575, 580, 583, 589, 596, 604, 606, 616, 623, 627, 647, 649, 675, 678, 736. Of Council of Safety, 80, 84, 115, 124, 317. 699. Of meeting of "Real Whigs" at Philadelphia, 83. Of Cumberland, Co., 340. Of Assembly, 617; Assembly, vi., 64. 66, 73, 84, 155, 396, 694, 733, 741. Congress, 9, 59, 79, 83, 111, 145, 150, 162, 177, 184, 215, 256, 273, 286, 299, 300, 323, 341, 356, 358, 364, 365, 374, 375, 377, 382, 388, 398, 422, 433, 442, 458, 461, 507, 508, 557, 578, 585, 586, 602, 659, 672, 702, 705, 732, 733, 755, 758. Council, 64. Board of War, 74; Of Congress, vii., 15, 20, 75, 76, 83, 87, 101, 129, 154, 158, 173, 204, 221, 249, 251, 263, 287, 293, 315, 316, 365, 374, 413, 436, 439, 500, 519, 542, 641, 732, 734, 741. Of Assembly, 187, 192, 237, 244, 269, 278, 284, 294, 295, 718, 740, 741. Board of War, 256. Of House of Delegates of Va., 441; viii., 86, 142, 173, 175, 185, 195, 255, 256, 261, 272, 285, 332, 346, 352, 391, 448, 519, 520, 553, 603, 629, 635, 649, 687, 699, 700, 724, 737, 749, 753, 761. Assembly, 8, 14, 21, 276, 569, 570, 646, 657, 685, 728, 729, 733, 734, 736, 738, 639, 751, 752, 759, 761. General Assembly of Virginia respecting western boundary, 352. Of Council, 608; Of Assembly, ix., 4, 5, 11, 22, 53, 66, 68, 69, 202, 464, 476, 483, 506, 509, 666, 754, 762, Congress, 73, 77, 109, 134, 152, 164, 168, 185, 188, 209, 243, 273, 300, 309, 366, 383, 391, 394, 411, 446, 450, 483, 484, 493, 506, 548, 560, 582, 608, 645, 741, 756. Of Council, 341. House of Delegates of Virginia, 562; x., 8, 111, 129, 130, 149, 166, 177, 178, 179, 184, 195, 196, 203, 204, 209, 233, 315, 316, 333, 334, 335, 336, 365, 367, 369, 412, 420, 488, 531, 559, 695, 710, 711, 749, 750, 756.
Of Assembly of Connecticut, x., 116, 117, 633.
Of Congress, x., 27, 36, 90, 105, 136, 139, 194, 209, 241, 507, 508, 511, 520, 528, 536, 543, 544, 549, 550, 561, 562, (1784,) 566-572, 590, 716.
Of Council of Censors, x., 149, 153, 302, 326, 327, 332.
Of House of Delegates, of Maryland Commissioners on trade, x., 744.
Of House of Delegates of Virginia on boundary, (1783,) 171. Commissioners on trade, 738; Of Assembly, xi., 84, 207, 211, 252, 393, 395, 398, 406, 523, 564, 565, 614; 635, 636, 665, 669, 682, of Maryland, 77; Of Congress, 38, 50, 64, 73, 74, 75, 128, 129, 141, 142, 282, 316, 352, 387, 555, 582, 586, 612, 613, 616, 665, 677; Of Council of Virginia, 291; Of Executive Council, on purchase of Erie, 313. Lake Erie relinquished by Congress, 387. Powder Magazine, 393. Purchase of Erie, 395, Respite of Doanes, 398. Accounts, 406, Commissioners to Virginia

and Maryland, 523. Call of State convention, 564. Sale of Erie lands, 566; Of Wyoming settlers, 83.
Returns of Assemblymen, for Chester county, iv., 739. For Lancaster, 742. Of troops, vi., 484. Of 2d Brigade of Foot under Colonel Johnston, vii., 66. Pennsylvania Brigade under Col. Stewart, 69. Of Gen. St. Clair's division, 752. Of non-comm'd officers, serving in Southern army, ix., 517. Of troops at Fort Pitt, 521. Of deserters from American regiment, x., 390. Of Pennsylvania line, 390. Of Military, 22, 390, 393, 436. Of officers of Troops in Philadelphia Co., 218, 219, 235. Of military stores at Fort Island and Billingsport, (1784,) 284.
Revel, Capt., of French vessel, on importing merchandise, viii., 546, 547.
Revenge, Cutter, vii., 187, 241, 266, 281, 285, 289, 300, 310, 318, 322.
evenue system of U. S., report to, Congress on, x., 732.
Reynolds, Jno., frauds at the grate of the jail, viii., 690. Jailer, petition to postpone execution of sentence on account of weather, x, 119. Longschamp retaken, 277. Revolt in jail, 327.
Rheiner, John, forfeiture of flour to D. Niess, submitted to Judges, xi., 273.
Rhode Island Commissioners to Indian Treaty at Albany, ii, 141. Act appointing Commissioners to meet General Shirley, 442. Request provisions, 672. Letters of Governor, 434, 500. Claim for share of parliamentary grant, iv., 121. Journal of Major Gibbs of, military and naval operations there, vi., 733–736. Enemy quitting, 387. Letter, Robert Morris to, ix, 474. Troops to march for the Highlands, 549. B. Stille, of, appointed to settle accounts of Pennsylvania and United States, 668. Act to comply with requisitions, xi., 16, 23. Act to establish judicial courts, U. States, in, 707.
Rice, Capt. viii., 161, 162.
Rice, Fort, attacked by Indians, viii., 561, Where located, 567. Attacked, 567; x., 165; xi., 453, 454.
Rice, Patrick, clerk of D. Franks, allowed to go to New York to settle accounts, vii., 173. Pass for, 180. Letter, viii., 33.
Rice, Robert, recruiting in Philadelphia, vi., 722.
Riche, Mrs. Anne, pass to New York refused, viii., 141.
Richards, James, a prisoner to be removed, petition, iv., 722.
Richards, William, letters, v., 13, 47, 62, 166, 169, 242.
Richardson, Col., v., 177.
Richardson, Joseph, letters, v., 254. Counterfeits, 239, 248, 254, 327, 525. In Lancaster, 248. Mittimus for, 249.
Richardson, John, to W. Penn., i., 81.
Riddle, Geo. Read, appointed by Delaware on boundary line, 1849, iv., 37.
Ridout, J., Letters, ii., 734.
Ridout, Sergeant, letter to, iii., 660, 662.
Rinker, James, respecting the disposition of Indians, xi., 207.
Riot at Gloucester, warrant, i., 546. On Schuylkill, 553. At election in York county ii., 50. At Lancaster. Danger to Mr. Wirtz from, v., 266. At J. Wilson's in Philaphia, vii., 732, 735, 744.
Rioters, seize goods on way to Fort Pitt from Philadelphia, iv., 217, 219, 222, 224, 226, 228, 230, 244, 246. In New Castle county, 331. At Wyoming, 385.
Risberg, Gustavus, vii., 550. Flour wanted, viii., 200.
Rising Sun Inn, burned, vi., 71.
Rittenhouse, Benjamin, to superintend Gun Lock factory, iv., 712; v., 743. On gunlock factory, vii., 142. Appointed commissioner, to examine Schuylkill, xi., 623.
Rittenhouse, David, letters, v., 10, 62, 264, 357. Presides at Town Meeting, v., 77; vi., 184, 643. Report on state of Treasury, vii., 118, 302. A Pennsylvania Commissioner to run line between Virginia, viii., 353. State of Trea-

sury, 657, 662. Treasurer on paper currency, &c., ix., 117, 119, 229. Appointed Commissioner to examine roads and rivers for internal commerce, x., 129, 130. Commissioner (1783,) of boundary with Virginia, 171, 223. Treasurer, 241, 456, 534. Commissioner, 334, 444, 454, 455, 736. Instruments, 454. Asks for a quadrant, it would be useful, 458. Commissioner on Susquehanna river, 755. Treasurer, on taxes, xi., 337. Indemnifying bond, 743.

Rivers, examination of, xi., 681, 683, 690, 694, 756.

Roach, Isaac, boats in Delaware Bay, viii., 254. Prisoners taken by, 339. Sent to Capes to watch British fleet, ix., 80. Instructions to, 96. Vessels seen, 112. To return, 189.

Roads and bridges, i., 767.
Petition respecting, from Philadelphia through Wiccaco to Gloucester, 436; ii., 98. Condition of various, iii., 279. From Schuylkill to Susquehanna, petition for, iv., 362. In bad order to be repaired, vi., 441, 450, 482. Proposed, &c., xi., 70, 91, 131, 133, 135, 143, 149, 186, 262, 560, 643, 656, 725. Frankstown, report, xii., 80.

Robbery, highway, near Bedford, iv., 458. In Bucks and Chester counties, ix., 459, 501, 507, 529. Of Bucks tax collectors, xii., 299.

Roberdeau, D., explanations, v., 658. Letters, 639, 659, 673, 726, 728, 735, 756, 772; vi., 10, 18, 130, 134, 144, 183, 206, 209, 214, 273, 287, 295, 359, 374, 422, 436, 446, 567, 583, 584, 609. Speaks favorably of Mrs. Ferguson, 131. Of books, 583. Proceeds to the lead mine, 423. Proposes to build a fort there, 424. And furnace, 446; vii., 100, 137, 159, 167, 184, 192, 194, 198, 236, 296, 299, 643. In favor of Mrs. Ferguson, 100. Of Lieutenant Meens, 299. Claims payment for lead, viii., 5.

Roberdeau, Fort, vii., 419, 446; xii., 454.

Roberts, John, memorials, &c., in favor of his pardon, vii., 21–44. Memorial of widow, &c., respecting dower, 122. Respecting estate of John R., viii., 206.

Roberts, Joseph, petition for pardon, ix., 745, 764.

Roberts, Jonathan, respecting execution of John Brown, xi., 279.

Robertson, James, iii., 291.

Robeson, Captain, eldest Continental officer in the navy, vi., 21.

Roberteau, Thomas C., letter from, xii., 284. Reasons for leaving service, 284.

Robinson, Andrew, Register of Berks, death of, ix., 191.

Robins, Ezekiel, agent for relieving wants of prisoners at New York, ix., 675, 677. His proceedings, 756. Letter on orders to discharge prisoners, x., 26, 213. Supplies for prisoners at New York, (1782,) xi., 495.

Robinsons, Fort at, xii., 456.

Robinson, Captain Isaiah, takes a British sloop of war, v., 32.

Robinson, John, deposition respecting D. Penticost, ix., 572. Indian murders, xi., 719.

Robinson's Run, (Youghioghany Co.,) men killed at, xii., 261, 263.

Robinson, Samuel, letter, ii., 480.

Robinson, Captain Thomas, ix., 184, 228, 237, 334, 393, 504, 528, 657, 659. Memorial, 228. Murder by Indians, 659. On military affairs, x., 14, 99. Indian murders, 15. On Wyoming affairs, 47, 48. Instructions to, 99. On Indian outrage, xi., 432.

Robinson, Sir Thomas, letters to and from, ii., 188, 249, 284, 291, 365, 379, 439, 440, 491, 764. Resigns as secretary, 491.

Rode, John, examination, vi., 224.

Rodney, Cæsar, appointed Judge of Supreme Court, iv., 581.

Rodney, Governor, of Delaware, letter to, viii., 10.

Roebuck, and Liverpool, British men-of-war in the Delaware, iv., 748, 749. In Lewestown Roads, 753. Gone, 762. Engagement with, 749. Man-of-war, in Delaware river, v., 99, 100, 108, 118, 190, 453, 668, 721, 722.

Rogers, Captain John, letter to, xii., 201, 217.

Rogers, Rev. William, (Chaplain,) asks for clothing, vii., 253. Further supplies, 273, 277. Half pay in advance, 449. Respecting pay as chaplain, ix., 3.
Rolls, Master of, report, xi., 748.
Roman Catholics, suspicions of, ii., 114, 176, 228, 423, 646, 690, 694. Mass house, iii., 16. Deprived of arms, &c., (see Papists,) 131. To pay military fines, 132. Number in Pennsylvania, 144. Of Northampton, petition for a church, iv., 279.
Romberg, Thomas, deposition, iv., 238. Petition, 239.
Root, Hon. Jesse, respecting flour, vii., 774.
Roots, George, deposition respecting ruins of Fort Pitt, x., 463.
Ropewalk, J. Wharton's, v., 94.
Rosborough, Rev. John, killed at Trenton, his family recommended by council for pay, xi., 272.
Rosencranze, Colonel, ix., 106.
Ross, Alexander, sells lands to Charles Sims, Virginia titles, xi., 160.
Ross, Colonel, ix., 351.
Ross, Major, commands at Oswego, x., 89.
Ross, Colonel George, vi., 69, 319, 324. Appointed Judge of Admiralty—Letter accepting, vii., 212. Asks for a Register, 451. Claims of Sloop Active, 463. Death of, 554. His successor, 558. Elected Vice-Pres., xi., 411.
Ross, Lieut. James, order on, for arms, (1787,) xi., 458.
Ross, John, instructions to take Indians to Conestoga, ii., 595.
Ross, William, claims for captors of T. Pickering, xi.
Rotfong, Captain, ix., 360.
Rothwell, Thomas and Garret, their case, i., 567, 583. Petition, 567. Depositions, 583.
Rouget, Stephen J., petition for privateer, v., 569.
Roupe, Colonel, ix., 349.
Rous, Rev. Lucas, address in Latin to Gov. Morris, ii., 251.
Route of Royal American Regiment in Pennsylvania, iii., 267.
Rowan, James, petition to be vendue master, viii., 573.
Rowan, Wm., Sheriff, instructions respecting executions, viii., 23.
Rudolph, Lieut. John, vi., 454.
Rum, Indian, resolutions respecting, i., 549, 551. Not to be sold by Inn holders, to soldiers, iii., 132. Proclamation, 237. Advertisement against, 437. Proclamation, 519. Charge of selling, at Fort Augusta, iv., 88.
Rumford, ——, of Wilmington, purchase of flour, vii., 558, 560, 600, 601, 629.
Rundle, Richard, petition of, ix., 444, 448.
Rush, Dr. Benjamin, Letter to Owen Biddle. His salary, v., 3. Letters, 3, 38, 59.
Rush, Dr. Benjamin, appointed to inspect sickly vessels, vii., 408. Dickinson College, xi., 427, 540, 578.
Rush, Jacob, vi., 752. Judge of Supreme Court, respecting H. Carberry, x., 291.
Rush, Joseph & J. Craig, appointed to appraise Ship General Greene, vii., 303. Report, 320.
Rush, William, petition, respecting work, at Gallies, vii., 277.
Russell, Ensign, William, who lost a leg at Brandywine, applies for promotion, vi., 214, 286. Loses leg at Brandywine, vii., 609.
Russia, war with Turkey, xi., 265.
Ruston, Dr. Thomas, claims seat in council, for Chester county, xi., 633. C. Willing declared in possession, 633.
Rutherford, John, letter on General Braddock's affair, ii., 277, 299.
Ryan, Lieut. Colonel, his pay, viii., 656.
Ryan, Capt. Michael, viii., 371, 582.
Ryan, Major, Michael, memorial, services of, x., 92. Memorial respecting certificates received for pay— for payment of which he is in the hands of the Sheriff, his services, &c., x., 308.
Ryan, Philip, vii., 541.
Ryder, D., King's Attorney General, opinion on several Acts of Assembly, ii., 100.
Ryerson, Thomas, defence against Indians, xi., 667.

S.

Sacrament of Lord's Supper to be partaken of previous to naturalization, iv., 242.
Saddles, scarce, vi., 363.
Sailors of frigate Pennsylvania guaranteed against impressment, iii., 191.
Sailors, jurisdiction for trial of, for crimes at sea, iv., 292, 301, 362. Opinions of Attorney and Solicitor General, 292, 304, 307. Elope from French vessels, viii., 347, 350, 366.
St. Clair, Sir John, reviews soldiers, ii., 276. Displeased with Gov. Morris, 293. Introduction to Gov. Morris, 188. Respecting, 315. Letters, iii., 266, 661.
St. Clair, Arthur, letters, iv., 426, 437, 452, 471, 476, 481, 500, 504, 509, 510, 514, 519, 523, 530, 539, 542, 545, 546, 547, 573, 583, 586, 589, 625, 637, 659. Conduct at Ticonderoga, to be inquired into, v. 491; vii., 237, 291, 355, 452, 607, 736. Receives a cask of wine from President, 292. Wishes to purchase a forfeited estate, 491. Letter on army, 583. Opinion of victory at Stony Point, 585. Major Lee's success, 665. Return of his division, 752; viii., 76, 103, 168, 297, 374, 397, 515, 537, 608, 670, 671, 672, 673, 674, 675, 676, 678, 680, 690. At Elizabethtown, 103. Return of Pennsylva- troops under him, 220. Unsuccessful with the mutineers, 701, 721, 723. Letters to and from, ix., 27, 36, 61, 386. Respecting de Lambert, 735, 752. Resp., 142, 256. On rank of Colonel Porter, x., 49. Sale of Fort Pitt, 485. Elected auctioneer of Phila., 205, 209, 261. Elected to Congress, 534. Asks time on payment of auction duties, xi., 127. Advanced, successor appointed, 129. Wyoming, 189. Attack on Fort Harmar by Indians, 392. Letter from, 529. To Gen. Butler on Indians, 746. Ask troops for Western Territory, 716.
St. Peter's Church, Philadelphia, petitions for Rev. Thos. Coombe, v., 600, 603.
St. Vincent, post at, prisoners taken, xii., 116, 157.
Salaries of public officers of United States, xi., 129, 615.
Salt, bill respecting, 197, 206. Made on Tom's river, v., 55. Sent to New Jersey, 64, 69. Kent Co., Delaware, applies for, 79. Scarcity of, 202, 758. Dr. Harris's proposal for making, 507. New Jersey, Act exempting men from enlisting, 764. Seized in Philadelphia, vii., 122, 149, 759, 765. In exchange for flour, 674, 675, 678, 682, 693, 769. Scarcity of, 709, 728, 729, 734, 759. For flour, plan of Assembly, 718. Scarcity of, viii., 4, 13, 24, 28, 84, 85. Seized in the hands of Mr. Wilcox, decision in his favor, ix., 750.
Salt Petre, person sent from York to manufacture, iv., 668. H. Wynkoop on, 702. Manufacture of, 706, 727, 742.
Salt Works, report on, iv., 771. At Tom's River, v., 55, 194, 216, 217, 228, 418, 427, 540, 614, 753, 758, 763. In danger from enemy, 56. Visits from, 194, 217. Seen from, 217. Attacks, 228. Workmen exempt as militia, 614, 621. On Tom's river, instructions to J. Davidson, vi., 16, 181, 186, 236. Purchase of land at, 16, 29, 237. Men leave, 160. Men sent to from fleet, 182. At Squan, &c., destroyed, 398, 400. Council refuse more money for, 417. Seized in Philad'a, 703, 724, 740, 753. On Tom's River, vii., 96, 109, 111, 116. Colonel Hagner takes charge of, 766.
Saltar, Elisha, Commissary General's orders, ii., 604. Letters to and from, 611, 613, 618, 621.
Sample, Samuel, visits Connolly in jail, iv., 728.
Samptown or Quibble. Skirmish at, v., 249.
Sanderlane, James, writes to Governor Markham, i., 46.
Sanders, William. vi., 716.
Sandusky, Expedition to, under Col. Crawford, ix., 366. Failure of,

556, 576, 637, 649. Upper, xii., 120, 121, 164, 242. Indians, x., 84.
Saphorin, M. de St., on consecration of American Bishops by Denmark, x., 434.
Sappers and Miners Co. proposed, viii., 37.
Saratoga. Capture of Burgoyne, relating to, v., 675, 676, 680, 684, 687, 726–729.
Sasoonan, &c., deed from, 1732, i., 344.
Satterlee, Benedict, deposition, xi., 344. Commitment, 345. In gaol, 347.
Savadge, Thomas, letters relating to enemy, and Salt works at Tom's River, v., 55. 194, 216, 217, 228, 418, 540, 763. Purchase of land, 763. Letters to, vi., 17, 159, 182, 236, 398, 400, 417. Part owner of salt works, 186. Objects to J. Davidson's appointment, 236. Letters, vii., 96, 109, 111.
Savell, Henry, letter to, from Wm. Penn, describing the country, i., 69.
Scalps, premium offered by commissioners for, ii., 619. Minutes respecting, 619. Letter of Governor Morris to commissioners, 620, 625, 629. Brought in, 639, 641. Opinions on, iii., 185, 199. Of Indians, inquiries respecting a reward for, vii., 362, 569. Premiums, &c., offered for Indian, viii., 167, 172, 176, 189, 283, 301, 369, 393, 568, 592. Supreme Executive Council offer premium for, xii., 240.
Scammell, Alexander, vii., 649; xii., 185, 226, 268.
Scarroyady, ii., 15, 114.
Schlatter, Rev. Michael, pass for, ii., 67.
Schlosser, Captain J., conducts Indians to Amboy, iv., 158. Instructions to, 160.
Schlosser, George, to lay off city lots, ix., 299.
Schneider, Rev. Theodore, Catholic priest, number under his care, iii., 144.
Schools, public, for education of youth, urged to attention of Judges of Supreme Court, by President Dickinson, x., 523.
Schott, Captain John Paul, letter and history of, viii., 24, 153, 161. Raising a troop of light dragoons, xi., 297, 298, 397. Censured, 393, 394. Troops, &c., 663.
Schreiber, John, in charge of barracks, &c., at Lancaster, damage to them, x., 309, 334.
Schropp, Matthew, account of Moravians at Bethlehem, iii., 242.
Schuyler, Fort, viii., 370. Fear of its abandonment, ix., 123.
Schuyler, General, conduct at Ticonderoga, to be inquired into, v., 491.
Schuyler, Philip, vii., 11, 75. Commissioner on New York line, x., 450.
Schuylkill River, lower ferry on, Act respecting, i., 161. Lands on, deed for, 344. Dams on, 315. Riots on, 553. Ferry, application for, ii., 648. Petition for improvement of, iv., 361. Road from, to Susquehanna, 362. British erect a battery at, v., 663. Army west of, vi., 91, 254. Cornwallis crosses, 23. General Potter's proceedings, 98. Washington's views of troops, necessary on, 153, 156. Ordered to, 169. Magazine for provisions at, 347. Ferry and bridge, Philadelphia, 370. Survey of, with a view to transportation of supplies, 513, 525. List of fords on, 514. Bridges over, 685, 768. Bridge on, vii., 94. Sullivan's, 94, 107, 152. Bridge secured, repairs to, viii., 144, 186. Men engaged in cutting masts on, for French fleet, 540. Order of Monsieur Holker, 540–543, 550, 571. Wood, 618. Toll at bridge, 618. Respecting masts cut for French navy, ix., 10, 34. And Susquehanna river, communication between, x., 129, 130. Commissioners to examine, xi., 623, 677. Falls, observations on, by John C. Stroebel, 651. Examination of, 677, 694. Little, murders by Indians, viii., 529, 532.
Scioto, banks of, xii., 111.
Scott, Abraham, &c., vi., 647.
Scott, Hugh, &c., court-house and

prison, Washington county, ix., 771.
Scott, Thomas, vi., 673; vii., 434; viii., 63, 81, 280, 713. Letters to and from, ix., 20, 324, 355, 374, 438, 497, 646; x., 65, 78, 80. Election in Fallowfield township, 364. In behalf of Washington academy, xi., 215. On his way to Congress, 568.
Scott, William, vii., 118. And R. Stevenson, respecting election in York county, 206; viii., 365, 379, 382, 408, 444, 524, 531, 623. Of York county, arms in Philadelphia. ix., 228, 232, 302, 319, 341, 350, 426, 455, 556, 632. Arms at York, x., 591.
Scull, Nicholas, on method of finding the meridian, &c., ii., 73. Surveyor-General, viii., 95.
Scull, Major Edward, Secretary of Board of War, vii., 469; viii., 369, 655.
Scull, William, surveyor, applies, viii., 94.
Sea, letters granted by Congress to vessels, xi., 239.
Seal, the great, order to affix, iii., 318. For Admiralty Court, vii., 694. Representing the arms of the State, ordered in Paris, viii., 257. The great, fee for affixing, xii., 78. Of the State established, 88.
Seamen, shipwrecked, order of Admiralty, i., 234. Hospital, duties on, 251.
Searle, James, v., 216; vii., 141. Agent to Europe for loans, &c., introduced to John Adams, viii., 399. Letter at sea, 514. From Brest, 532. To be sustained, 625. Agent to Europe, recall proposed, reasons against, ix., 62, 311. Object of mission, 311. Coming home, 367, 520. Loans, 565. Death of wife, 520. Respecting loans in Europe, 589. Agent to Europe claim for compensation, x., 97.
Seat of Government, proceedings in Congress respecting removal from Philadelphia, x., 136, 139.
Secret Committee to Committee of Safety sends ammunition, iv., 773.
Secretary of Commonwealth, resolution of Ass'y, respecting, ix., 762.
Secretary of foreign affairs, letters to and from, x., 9, 13, 21, 735; xi., 74, 202, 293, 411, 599.
Secretary of Treasury, xi., 655, 663.
Security, officers to give, i., 395.
Seditious papers from British, action of Cong. against, vii., 14, 15.
Seely, John, to H. Antes, x., 650, 677, 678.
Seely, Jonas, Recruiting orders to, iv., 116, 141. Orders to, ii., 544.
Seely, Col., ix., 404.
Seidel, Christian, examination of, ii., 459.
Selin, Capt., viii., 153, 161, 171.
Sellers, John, resigns as commissioner on Schuylkill, xi., 623.
Sellers, Nathan, appointed Commissioner to examine roads and rivers with a view to internal commerce, x., 129, 130, 334.
Semple, Wm., Sub. Lt. of Phila., memorial, xi., 687.
Seneca Indians, ii., 11. Expedition against, xii., 147, 150, 154, 155. Towns burned, 156, 300,
Sergeant, Jona. D., Attorney General, attacked at Easton, vi., 267. Resigns as Att'y. Gen., 740. Letters to and from, 496, 630, 683, 740, vii., 267, 275, 395, 743. Arnold's trial, 743. Lett's to and from, viii., 5. Opinion on concealing taxable property, 49, 303. British Commissions to cruisers, 395. Sale of articles, 498. Resigns as Attorney General, 612. Form of Commission, 613. Account as counsel against Connecticut, ix., 738.
Servants and Apprentices, on enlisting, ii., 417, 572, 576, 582, 587. Murder by mob, 576. Indented, proceedings of Board of War, respecting enlisting of, v., 328. Resolutions of Cumberland county, respecting, 340. Enlisted to be paid for, viii., 730. Number of R. R. Livingston, ix., 467.
Sewickly, xii., 131.
Seymour, Commodore. Order, not to let vessels pass Chevaux-de-friese, v., 67. To send up Galleys, 83. Enemy, 104. Letters, 67, 83, 104, 401, 577. Memorial, 434. Instructions, 233. Demand for pay, 577. Superceded by Commodore Hazelwood, 594; vi., 97.

Shackerly, Mr., Agent, letter to, iii., 137.
Shadow of Death, xii., 461.
Shamokin, house built at, for Shekalamy, i., 660. Minutes of a Council at, respecting officers' pay, ii., 700. Fort Augusta at, xii., 329–339.
Shannon, Doctor, to be arrested, vi., 53.
Shannon, Capt. John, commission and instructions to enlist, i., 688.
Sharpe, Horatio, Gov. Maryland, letters to, and from, ii., 113, 125, 130, 187, 192, 216, 228, 244, 274, 382, 397, 451, 468, 490, 507, 520, 556, 557, 573, 685. Governor of Maryland, iii., 143, 183, 197, 585, 662, 697. Of Maryland, letter to, from Gov. Penn, on peace made by Col. Bradstreet with Indians of Erie and Ohio, iv., 207, 262, 277.
Sharpe, W., orders in Council respecting Privateers, iii., 91.
Shaw, William, Wyoming affairs, x., 764. Answer of President Dickinson, 761; xi., 109.
Shawanese, message from, i., 223. Time of their arrival in the State, 228. Indians, number of, 302. Letter of Governor to, Wm. Penn's conduct to, their arrival, &c., 302. Speech of the French to, 324. Message to Governor, 329; iv., 501, 511, 513, 540, 543, 583; ix., 247; x., 83, 86, 161; xii., 111, 119, 120, 157, 158, 179, 181, 227, 238, 241. Town destroyed, 258, 263.
Shawnee Town in possession of Butler, vii., 6.
Shays, Daniel, proclamation of Massachusetts to arrest, &c., xi., 119.
Shee, Colonel John, v., 417.
Shekalamy, letter Governor to, i., 241, 455. Death of his son, 241. At Shamokin, 673. Indian Chief, 757. Death noticed, his son succeeds as Chief, ii., 23. Presents to his family, 24.
Shelburne, Earl of, letters, iv., 274, 276, 280, 281.
Shepherd, Lieut., xii., 137.
Shepherd, Colonel David, letter to, xii., 167, 225, 238, 270, 277.
Sheriff of Cumberland county, orders to arrest B. Chambers and Cannon, iii., 105. High, of Philadelphia—to re-place whipping post, &c., vii., 252. Warrants to, 149, 193. Letters to, x., 63. List of, in Cumberland Co., (1777 to 1783, 285.)
Sherman's Valley, time of settlement, xii., 285.
Shiel, H. N., Hog Island, ix., 520.
Shingass, iii., 531.
Shinn, Bertliss, (a suspicious person,) viii., 638.
Shippen, Edward, letters to and from, ii., 230, 358, 362, 364, 400, 455, 463, 472, 576, 603, 608, 634, 738, 740. Commission to settle accounts for wagons for Braddock, 598; iii., 8, 304, 394, 409, 410, 427. Letters to and from, iv., 62, 64, 154. Prothonotary, vi., 682. Resigns as Justice, xi., 91.
Shippen, Joseph, appointed Captain, ii., 622. Letter, 636.
Shippen, Joseph, Jr., letters, iii., 333, 389, 409, 410, 426, 449, 470, 510. Letters to and from, iv., 82, 88, 102, 108, 109, 110, 128, 132, 154, 175, 209, 212, 298, 412, 423, 437, 471, 481, 488, 530, 539, 542, 545, 550, 557, 558, 560, 564, 583, 586, 618, 625, 637. Dedimus to, 101, 104. Books and papers belonging to Secretary's office, viii., 200.
Shippensburg, Road to Clarke's Gap, xi., 143.
Shippen, Doctor William, Director General of Military hospitals, v., 223. To Congress, 768. To furnish medicines for the army, vi., 688. Lectures on Anatomy, viii., 643; xii., 191.
Shippen, William, letter to, respecting Matthew Clarkson, vii., 209.
Shirley, Governor William, letters, i., 746, 754. (of Mtts.) letters from, ii., 20, 26, 181, 215, 231, 260, 298, 326, 328, 338, 345, 348–355, 357, 361, 381, 395, 698. General appointment as Colonel, and instructions to, 178, 442, 447. Letters to and from, 495, 498, 501, 502, 569, 576, 577, 578, 579, 582, 587, 638, 715. Sends ammunition, 502. Death of his son, 524. Plan of operations, 524.

Ordered to England, 606. Fort, (See Forts.)
Shirley, General William, orders soldiers to Philadelphia, iii., 90. Letters to and from, ii., 292, 293, 307, 310, 317, 321, 334, 346, 357, 361. Secretary to Braddock, 307. Shirley, John, letters to and from, ii., 199, 332, 381, 387, 422. Death of, 524, 531.
Shmick, John, examination respecting Wyominck, ii., 491.
Shoemaker, B., letters respecting corporation papers, x., 93.
Shoemaker, Henry, convicted of riot, removed as a Justice, x., 695.
Shoemaker, Lieutenant Jacob, vii., 655, 688.
Shoemaker, Joseph, deposition of, viii., 645.
Shoes for army, v., 670.
Showman, obtains a passport, iv., 164.
Short creek, prisoners taken by the Indians on, (1783,) x., 167.
Shrawder, Captain Phil., viii., 161; ix., 349, 388. Takes up march from Gnaddenhutton, 649. Soldiers sick, 660. Troops at Wyoming, 761. Respecting Wyoming, x., 23, 24, 99, 104, 131. Appointed Capt., 131. Letter from, xii., 70.
Shrewsbury, New Jersey. Express to, for intelligence of enemy, v., 43, 49. Ships of war passing, 49. Colonel Gurney at, 186.
Shurmer, Benjamin, letters to and from, i., 370, 380, 390
Sibbald, Capt. John, of Pennsylvania Frigate, commission, iii., 190, 350. Letters, 490. Recommendations, 657, 658, 660. Leaves frigate—succeeded by T. Leech, 658.
Sideling Hill, battle at, iii., 315.
Signals agreed upon with Morocco, xi., 171.
Simcock, John, commiss'n to, i., 85.
Simmons, Leeson, v., 538.
Simonds, Captain, ix., 120.
Simsbury, Connecticut, convention prisoners sent to, ix., 25.
Sims, Charles, memorial respecting lands under Virginia title, xi., 160. Opinion of W. Bradford, Jr., 162. Letter to Vice President, 169.
Sims, Major or Captain, charge, against by William McIlvaine v., 509. General Washington respecting, 509.
Sinking Spring Valley, provisions to be stored at, vii., 305.
Sipple, Watman's case, ii., 335.
Six Nations of Indians, agreement for purchase of lands from the, by Generals Butler and Gibson, xi., 529-533.
Skelton, Captain, xii., 126, 250.
Skinner, Lieut. Archibald, vi., 625.
Skinner, Courtland, B. G., v., 367.
Skinner, John, proposes a road, xi., 91, 92, 143, 158.
Skipton, xii., 117, 230, 241.
Skirmishes, v., 211, 232, 234, 249; vi., 32, 70, 97, 98, 134, 141, 265, 285, 414, 673, 688, 770; vii., 7.
Slaughter, Major, xii., 232, 238.
Slavery, gradual abolition of, in the State—bill furnished to Assembly for, vii., 79. Act for abolishing, passed, viii., 720.
Slippery Rock, near Pittsburg, xii., 300.
Slough, Matthias, vi., 53, 55.
Smallman, Thomas, purchases Island below Fort Pitt, viii., 596.
Small-pox, prevails among soldiers at Philadelphia, iii., 82. At Marcus Hook, iv., 783. Among soldiers, ix., 660.
Smallwood, General, takes a brig, vi., 161.
Smallwood, Governor, of Maryland, internal navigation, x., 542, 543. Delegates on trade, 744. Claims, 753.
Smith, Colonel, vi., 31, 32. Abraham, viii., 443, 491, 522; ix., 203, 234, 400, 514; xii., 119.
Smith, Devereux, letters, iv., 512, 515, 612, 630. Deposition, 606. Victualler of troops at Kittanning, v., 313.
Smith, Captain Frederick, orders to, ii., 544.
Smith, Garrett, deposition respecting Wyoming, xi., 371.
Smith, George, vii., 164. Respecting bounty, viii., 52.
Smith, Henry, mission to Indians, i., 229. Letter from, 232.
Smith, James, passes given by, for sundry goods destroyed, iv., 219.

Depositions respecting, 220. Letter to, escorting party, 229. Obligation, 245. M. C., vi. Purchases ix., 459.
Smith, Dr. John, examination and history of, in Maryland, iv., 682. Deposition, 230.
Smith, Jonathan, obligation, iv., 246.
Smith, Jon. B., presides at meeting of "Real Whigs," v., 83; vi., 108, 109, 124, 160–191, 232, 292, 303, 314, 350, 357, 359, 365, 371, 403, 420, 427, 466, 545. Resigns as prothonotary of Philadelphia, xi., 423.
Smith, Lieutenant, engagement with Indians, ix., 202.
Smith, Matthew, vi., 633; vii., 280, 306, 472, 574, 589, 594, 606, 609, 614. With troops at Sunbury, 609. Elected vice-president, 745. On Indian murders, viii., 23, 249, 370, 417, 513, 671.
Smith, Meriwether, and R. H. Lee, on disputes with Virginia, vii., 73.
Smith, Richard, complains of a magistrate, inimical to the Methodists, viii., 740.
Smith, Robert, state of Billingsport, v., 8. Letters, 8, 9, 37, 324, 426. Attack on, vii., 637. Militia fines, viii., 535.. Lieutenant of Chester county, ix., 421, 434.
Smith, Lieutenant-Colonel Samuel, vi., 4, 92, 107.
Smith, Thomas, letter, iv., 488, 618. Commissioner of loan office of United States, v., 183; vi., 39; vii., 696–7. On state of frontiers, proposes mode of defence, viii., 114. Appointed by Congress to sign bills, 635, 639. Bills of credit, ix., 185. Troops from Wyoming, 652. Loan officer, letters to and from, x., 57, 169, (1783,) 170, 174, 190, 447, 461. Loan officer, xi., 33, 34.
Smith, W. Hooker, to Corporal Montgomery, on Wyoming affairs, x., 760. Letters, xi., 45, 102, 104, 105, 108.
Smith, William, second letter, iv., 244.
Smith, William, muskets arrived, viii., 415. As Justice of the peace, resignation, required, x., 419. Deposition respect'g J. P. Schott's Company, xi., 393 394. Memorial of, &c., 400. Passes given by, for sundry goods, iv., 219. Deposition respecting, 220. Letter to Lieut. Grant, 229.
Smith, Rev. Dr. William, iv., 475.
Smith, Dr. William, vi., 621. Depositions respecting, vii., 259.
Smith, William, (a tory,) to be confined to his house, v., 106. Obligation of, 145.
Smiths, murder of Mr. Boyd by, vii., 410.
Smith, William Moore, vii., 488. Respecting execution of John Brown, xi., 277.
Smith's fort, ix., 522.
Smithfield, prisoners taken at, vi., 402.
Smyser, Jacob, x., 77.
Smyth, Hugh, v., 703.
Smyth, Colonel Thomas, letter to, xii., 112, 152.
Snodgrass, —— collector in Bucks, robbed, ix., 507.
Snow, deep at Fort Dickinson, x , 197.
Snows, deep on mountains, viii., 120, 152, 156.
Snowden, Isaac, Treasurer, viii., 567. Treasurer, ix., 587.
Snowden, Jedediah, wishes to be clerk of the market, vii., 708.
Snyder, Captain John, appointed to command armed schooner for defence of the Delaware, ix,, 672.
Society for Propogating Gospel, appoint Rev. Mr. Campbell minister of Apoquinimy, i., 191. Rev. Mr. Backhouse at Chester, 226. Letters from Secretary of, 191, 226.
Soldiers, distressed condition of, i., 712, 724. Desertion of, 745. Articles of agreement with officers, ii., 541, 547. At Fort Augusta disposed to mutiny, iii., 686. In want, 688. Pay of, 140, 687, 688. Want of provisions, &c., v., 3, 9, 12, 14, 37, 58, 79, 80, 104, 105, 115, 132, 142. Absenting themselves, names of, 110. Desertions, 144, 166. Wants of, 160, 161, 165, 345, 674. Pay of, 533, 550, 575. Good effects of good clothing on, vi., 26. Great scarcity of pro-

visions, &c., 38, 61, 343, 354, 386, 408, 419. Number of, 159. Distress of, 189, 253. Regulations of main guard at Lancaster, 193. Consumption of liquor, 203. British, depositions respecting, 217, 225. Enlisted, to be sound, 248. Bounty from Congress, 508. Shot by another, 718. Distress of families of, vii., 482, 637, 666. And seamen, disabled, provided for, vii., 89. Bounties to, 355, 748. Oath to be taken, viii., 291. Raised by subscription, 689. Pay of, 739. Bounties and gratuities, ix., 18. Disorderly at Lancaster, x., 59. At Philadelphia, attack on Congress, submission, 61.

Solitary cells in Philadelphia to be erected, xi., 706.

Solomons, Captain, ix., 70.

Somerset, C. H., Army at, v., 162. Enemy at, 367.

Soundings of Delaware river, xii., 69.

South Carolina asks for ammunition and stores, iii., 315. For pilots, 399. Indian treaties with, iv., 323. Accommodation of Citizens driven from, to Philadelphia, ix., 274, 281, 300, 309, 323, 324. Position of affairs in, 283, 430. Flags of truce from, 338. Letter from Governor asking list of traitors, x., 99. Operations of Lord Cornwallis, (1780,) 173. Act to comply with requisitions, xi., 17, 23. Governor applied to for public papers as evidence, 545.

Spain acknowledges independence, xii., 111. Offers a loan, 111.

Spain and Portugal, treaty with, vi., 173.

Spalding, Captain, skirmishes with Indians, vii., 8.

Spangenberg, Rev. Mr. letters, ii., 584, 715. Catalogue of Moravians, iii., 69. Letters to and from, 69, 141, 435, 500.

Spaniards, conduct of privateers towards, complained of, iii., 162.

Spanish flag, a drawing sent to the Government, x., 743.

Spaniards take Natchez, &c., xii., 216.

Spanish frigate at Marcus Hook in danger from ice, correspondence with Commissioner Lianes, xi., 99 102.

Spanish ship puts in in distress, proceedings, iv., 105. Attacked by privateers, 192.

Spearing, Lieutenant, letters, ii., 566, 587.

Speeches of Governor Morris at Augwick, ii., 193. Governor Belcher's, iii., 98. Indians, 204. Of Governor to Assembly at New Castle, 379. Teedyuscung, iv., 85, 86. Governor Hamilton, 86. Conoquieson (Indian) to Sir William Johnson, 373. Kyasshula, 433. Of Pipe, a Delaware Chief, 441. Of Shawanese, 497. Lord Dunmore to White Eyes, 684. King Great Britain, vi., 14.

Spelling books required in Congress, vi., 209.

Spies, viii., 598.

Spirituous Liquors, on use of, in Army, v., 560, 673, 720. Cost of for the Army, 743; vi., 203, 205, 240, 247, 395, 689. Act against distillation from grain, vii., 125, 152. In army, 550.

Spouts, leaden, in Philadelphia, taken during war, to be appraised, ix., 366,

Sprague, Joseph, on Wyoming affairs, xi., 93.

Springer, Ensign, xii., 195.

Springer, Capt. Uriah, xii., 274, 278.

Springfield, N. J., enemy near, viii., 308.

Sproat, David, on prisoners at New York, x., 68. Major, ix., 244.

Sproat, Rev'd James, chaplain asks for clothing, x., 720.

Sprogel, Lodick, v., 230; vi., 678. Escort of troops, vii., 129, 552.

Spry, Commodore, ii., 508.

Spy, British, taken by Gen. Clinton, v., 639.

Spyker, Benj., Jr., deposition respecting H. Carberry, &c., x., 577.

Spyker, Henry, vi., 391.

Stamps, proposed for Colonies, iv., 202. Arrive at Philadephia, 241. Letter J. Hughes to Mr. Dickeson respecting, 240.

Standard ordered in France, viii., 257,
Standing Stone, Town, Inhabitants, driven, off, and murders, vi., 438, 603, 610, 650. Account of, ix., 546. Fort, xii.,458-460.
Standley, Dr. Valentine, vii., 165.
Stanhope, Capt. Henry, British sends insulting letters to Gov. of Massachusetts, x., 499-506.
Stansbury, Joseph, suspected, v., 74. Letters from jail, 94, 98. To be confined to his house, 106. Obligation of, 145.
Stanwix, Fort, Congress and purchase of lands at, iv., 309, 375. Arrival of Comm'rs at x., 346. Marquis Fayette addresses Indians at, 346. Mons. Marbois at, 346. Purchase of land at, xi., 508.
Stanwix, Col., John, iii., 150, 173, 188, 191, 196, 220, 239, 241, 288, 301, 439, 517, 628, 668, 687, 693, 696, 710, 713.
State House steeple, estimated cost of taking down, ix., 46. Resolution of Assembly to pull down, 52. T. Nevill on, 76. (Philad'a,) reports on repairs, x., 335, 348, 372, 420, 425, 442, 493, 535, 542, 547. Trees planted in, 420. Guard asked for, by Comptroller, 750. Repairs of clock, 563. Repairs, xi., 558. Trees for, 675.
State (or Province) Island, repairs of Pest-houses at, x., 53.
State Island, repairs wanted, xi., 286.
"State rights," case of between Pennsylvania and Virginia, ix., 260, 266, 270, 272.
Staunton, Phil., prisoners sent to. vi., 74, 75.
Stedman, Alex., appointed Comm'r to settle accounts for wagons furnished General Braddock, ii., 598.
Stedman, Charles, announcing arrival of fleet at Boston, vi., 685.
Steel, contract for, vi., 178. Iron of only Andover Works, New Jersey, suitable for, 178.
Steele, Archib'd, letter to, viii., 41 Letters, &c., to xii, 115, 116, 119, 136, 145, 148, 153, 160, 161, 174, 204, 223, 230, 244, 249, 262, 263.
Steele's, Fort at, Rev. Mr., xii., 461.
Steele, James, letter from, on call of Assembly, i., 187, 426.
Steele, Rev'd Capt. John, letters, ii., 623,
Steelman, James, viii., 634, 648.
Stephen, Col. Adam, letters, iii., 83, 668.
Stephens, Mr., makes Potash at Philadelphia, iii., 53.
Stephens, Philip, Secretary of Admiralty, letter to Gov., iv., 243.
Stephenson, Col., death of, vii., 401.
Stephenson, Lieut., xii., 137.
Sterret, Samuel, copies of acts of lands for benefit of University of Pennsylvania, ix., 676.
Steuben, Baron, reviews troops, vi., 568. Invited to examine defences of Delaware, vii., 199. Militia, 325. Book on military discipline, 643. Military plans of, viii., 225, 270, 642. To Pres. Dickinson in behalf of P. S. Duponceau as notary, &c., x., 352.
Steuben, Fred., Wm., De, accounts settled, xi., 703.
Stevens, Gen. Said to be slain, v., 160. Extract of letter from, 175.
Stevenson, George, letters to and from, ii., 89, 449. Letter, iii., 384, 390, 395, 400, 411; iv., 102. Letter, Circular of Councils, v., 68. Chairman, 97; vi., 94, Letters to and from, viii., 50, 107, 141. Lays claim to town land in York, 732.
Stevenson, Surgeon James, letter, iii., 82.
Stevenson, James, account, ix., 221.
Stevenson, R., vi., 653.
Stewart, Charles, letters, iv., 383, 384, 416, 417, 689. Provisions, viii., 578, 698. Letter to, from Lord Sterling, ix., 675.
Stewart, Lieut. Colonel George, vi., 217, 485, 517, 603.
Stewart, John, letter from Commissioners on Indian trade to, iv., 189.
Stewart, Lazarus, capture and escape, iv., 378.
Stewart, Colonel Walter, v., 401, 713. Loss at Brandywine, 714; vi., 285. Skirmish, 285, 343, 717. Letters, vii., 9, 660. Return

of Pennsylvania Brigade under, 69.
Stiff-Knee, Indian Chief, arrives in Philadelphia, xi., 733.
Stiles, Captain Joseph, vi., 480. On powder magazines, vii., 141. On arms, 238, 358. Repairs of arms, viii., 139. Powder magazine too small, xi., 202. Describes it, 546. Keeps powder magazine, at Philadelphia, xii., 317.
Stillwell, Nicholas, v., 453.
Stirling, Lord. Brigade on way to Brunswick, v., 66. Clothing for, 80, 105, 112. Letter respecting movements in New Jersey, 157, 162, 170. 173, 174, 194. Letters, 157, 166, 170, 173, 174, 195; viii., 314, 698. Recovering from sickness—wants a pipe of wine, ix., 675. Commission to examine, 694.
Stock, Live, &c., to be removed on appearance of enemy, v., 317, 404, 456, 461, 473, 512, 545. Plan and persons for, 424.
Stockton, Major Richard—(British.) Captured and defeated by Colonel Neilson, at Lawrence's Island, v., 230. Sent to Philadelphia, 232. A noted Tory, 237. John Norris, taken with, 301. Exchange proposed, 316.
Stockton, Richard W., v., 367.
Stoddard, Benjamin, vi., 608. Letter to, xii., 266.
Stoddart, Captain, skirmish with Indians, vii., 8.
Stokeley, Captain, viii., 210; x., 22, 262
Stokely, Captain Thomas, xi., 107, 122, 254. Stationed at Fort Crawford, 255. Death of, in General Clarke's expedition, ix., 369, 458. Under Colonel Lochry, 330, 333, 405, 406. Letters to and from, 330, 446.
Stony Brook. Engagement at, v., 162.
Stony Point, Wayne's victory, vii., 581, 585. Enemy at, 636. Resolution of thanks to Gen. Wayne, 741.
Stores, Return of, at Fort Augusta, iv., 122.
Story, John, appointed with James Milligan Commissioner, to settle accounts between United States and Pennsylvania, x., 427, 450, 451, 742.
Stoy, Lieutenant, vi., 717.
Straker, Wm., captured by French, with his negroes, Mr. Gerard applies to Congress for his imprisonment, vi., 671. Facts respecting, 678. Report of Board of War, 701. Resolution of Congress, 702. With several negroes claimed by Mons. Gerard, French Minister, (See Vol. VI.) vii., 16, 17, 61, 62, 70, 83. Letters, 71, 72.
Strangers, Burial ground reserved in Philad'a, xi., 571, 570.
Strettell, Robert, letters to and from, ii., 648.
Strobogh, Lieut., death of. vii., 135, 146.
Stroebel, Jno. C., on Schuylkill Falls, xi., 651.
Strong, Captain Solomon, xi., 108.
Strong, Commissioner of Connecticut, iv., 470.
Stroud, Colonel Jacob, vi., 748. Letters, &c., vii., 63, 572, 573, 613. Respecting battalion, viii., 9. Indians, 176, 188; ix., 108, 113, 250, 268. Court martial, 268, 339.
Stroud, Samuel, vi., 651.
Stump, Frederick, murders Indians, iv., 290, 296.
Style, Act for changing Old to New, 1752, ii., 68.
Sub-Lieutenants—circular to, vii., 105.
Substitutes, v., 487, 672. Discontinuance of, vi., 59, 251. Expense of, 65, 96, 171; vii., 401.
Sugar Cabins, minutes of a meeting at the, ii., 320.
Sugar Camp, murders at, xii., 210, 212.
Sullivan, Capt., xi., 201.
Sullivan, Fort, when and where erected, x., 719.
Sullivan, Gen., complained of, vi., 37, 97.
Sullivan Gen. John, respecting the bridge built by him on Schuylkill, vii., 94, 120. Letter respecting papers, 211. Impressing wagons, 388, 427, 433, 439. Guard for stores, 451. On ranging Co.'s,

455, 568. Respecting Quarter Masters. Escort for stores, 405, 418, 424, 447, 457, 473. Respecting, 473, 512, 535. Movements, 553, 554, 555, 585, 590–594, 597, 620, 640, 649, 667, 686, 709, 715, 721–724, 756, 768. Complained of, 590, 593. Letters from, 593, 594. Going to Tioga, 594. Destroys Indian Towns, 721–724, 756. Is complained of for making appointments, viii., 425. Expedition, ix., 263; xii., 119, 138, 148, 154, 165, 175.

Sullivan and Carberry, mutiny, xi., 27.

Sulphur, refining of, iv., 719, 752. Discovered near Susquehanna, 719. Near Elizabeth Town, New Jersey, 720. In Bristol, 723. Near Bordentown, 753; v., 182, 245, 253.

Sunbury, troops, &c., Jail proposed, iv., 463; vii., 341, 344, 375, 499, 553, 574, 593, 609, 619. Flour ordered to, viii., 310. Murders by Indians, 341. German battalion called from, 474. Indian murders near, viii, 513, 529. Distress of, 611. Troops at, ix., 293. Supplies for, 411. Fort Augusta, at, xii., 329, 339.

Sunderland, Earl of, orders, &c., from him, i., 97, 100, 102, 105.

Supersedeas, of Thomas Yorke, a Judge, iv., 42.

Supreme Court, plan for, i., 166. At York, letter from Judges, viii., 773.

Legality of trial and sentence when the Judge is a delegate to Congress, ix., 163.

Judges, requested by President, to recommend importance of moral training of youth, public schools, &c., x., 623.

Prothonotaries' Reports, xi., 765.

Opinion of Judges on tenure of offices, xii., 30.

Supreme Executive Council organized, v., 252. Call of, 312.

Letters to and from, Armstrong, Colonel John, 324, 558, 561, 568, 570, 572, 581, 587, 598, 636, 641, 645, 655, 672, 684, Arndt, John, 421. Arnold, Benedict, 376. Assembly, 586. Atlee, William, 327.

Bailey, John, v., 405, 413. Bailey, Wm., 349. Bryan, George and J. Evans, 352. Biddle, Colonel Clement, 721, 739. Biddle, Owen, 267, 268, 301. Blaine, Ephraim, 299, 677. Blewer, Joseph, 464. Bond, Phineas, 578. Boudinot, Elias, 313, 442. Boyd, Colonel Andrew, 712. Bradford, Colonel William, 430, 557, 582, 615, 644, 648, 649, 663, 668, 707, 740. Buchanan, William, 552, 667, 677, 690, 711, 742, 744. Budden, James, 591. Bull, Colonel John, 304, 306, 709. Butler, Anthony, 557.

Campbell, George, v., 269. Carothers, John, 639. Cheney, Colonel, 732. Christ, H., &c., 605, 623, 734. Clark. Mich., 712. Coats, Lieut. Colonel William, 766. Committee for driving off cattle, 473, 512, 545, 567, 610. Committee of Lancaster, 266, 349, 571. Committee of fifty, 473, 631. Congress, 289, 352, 366, 372, 411, 471, 536, 574, 586, 593, 626, 630, 638. Connolly, John, 297. Conway, Brig. Gen. T., 523, 530. Crispin, Wm., 706.

DeHaven, Hugh, v., 569.

DeHaven, Peter, 606, 607. Dewees, Thomas, 266. Downey, Capt., 431. Donaldson, Joseph, 497, 534. Dorsey, Thomas, 535, 550. Dundas, James, 616.

Episcopal Church, v., 600, 603.

Eyre, Joshua, 591.

Flower, Benjamin, 369, 706.

Galbraith, Bartrem, v., 343, 353, 407, 409, 415, 457, 480, 486, 521, 532, 533, 543, 562, 573. Galbraith, Robert, 730. Gerry, E., 754. Gregory, James, 334, 500, 588. Gronow, Lewis, 487, 732.

Hamilton, James, v., 611, 613, 620. Hancock, John, President, 289, 574. Hand, Brig. General Edward, 443, 540. Hazelwood, John, 602. 620, 680, 696, 721. Henry, Colonel, William, 473, 543. Henry, William, and J.

Supreme Executive Council—v. Hubley, 347. Hooper, Robert, Lettis, 689. Hopkinson, F., &c., 489. Howell, Jacob S., 640. Hubley, Adam, 531, 533, 667. Hubley, John, 295, 415, 427, 505. Hunn, John, 453, 462, 467, 468, 475. Hunter, Lieutenant Samuel, 370, 377, 414, 737. Hunter, Col. Samuel, 610, 717.
Ingersoll, Jared, v., 503. Irwin, Matthew, 613, 771.
Kirkbride, Jo., v., 322, 331, 342, 368, 463, 465, 549, 567, 580.
Laurens, Henry, v., 735. Lee, Richard Henry, 665. Leimback, Frederick, 524. Levers, Robert, 618, 622, 623, 645, 650, 654, 717. Lieutenants of Counties, 365, 379, 380, 424, 474, 523, 541, 545, 556, 582, 593, 615, 694. Livingston, Governor William, 267, 294, 296, 301, 321, 329, 614, 621, Lochry, Archibald, 344, 488, 741. Lyon, William, 417.
McCaliister, Richard, v., 330, 333, 335, 369, 412, 559, 633, 640, 692, 767. McIlvaine, William, 509. McKinley, Jno., 309, 456. McLean, Archibald, 514, 536, 575, 682, 704. Magistrates, 421, 473, 504, 553, 580, 598. Melchor, Isaac, 527, 653. Mifflin, Jonathan, 584, 594, 595, 597. Mifflin, General Thomas, 554, 720. Morgan, Jacob, 299, 322, 341, 406, 466, 530, 632. Morris, J., Jr., 294, 481, 506, 749.
Navy Board, v., 293, 425, 429, 501, 511, 521, 538, 540, 542, 590, 594, 600, 722. Navy, Continental, 491. Nicola, L., 600, 619, 630.
Paca, William, v., 635. Potter, General James, 305, 433, 437, 440, 461, 511, 551, 570, 718, 719, 738, 768. Proctor, Col. Thomas, 455.
Read, James, v., 323, 602. Reed, Joseph, 289, 379, 693, 701, 702. Rittenhouse, Benj., 743. Roberdeau, Daniel, 639, 659, 669, 726, 728, 735, 770, 772.
Savadge, Thomas, v., 763. Seymour, Commodore, 577. Sheriffs, Magistrates, &c., 291. Sheriff of Northampton Co., 489. Shippen, William, 768. Smith, Robert,

Supreme Executive Council—vi. 324, 426. Smyth, Hugh, 703. Stewart, Colonel Walter, 713. Stillwell, Nicholas, 453. Sutter, James, 750.
Tilghman, James, v., 502, 641. Tilghman, Tench, 674. Treasury, United States, 334. Trumbull, Jonathan, 657. Tyler, John, 731.
Virginia, Delegates in Congress, 413.
War Office, v., 290, 296, 301, 306, 371, 398, 430, 439, 450, 502, 512, 535, 570, 583, 584, 675, 685, 686, 751. War Office of Pennsylvania, 409, 428, 451, 471, 683. Washington, General George, 419, 431, 482, 510, 617, 618, 624, 664, 669, 678, 697. Weitzell, Lieutenant John, 268, 544.
Young, James, v., 336, 337, 411.
Antes, William, vi., 456. Armstrong, General John, 30, 43, 53, 60, 70, 85, 91, 100, 122, 148, 149, 230, 238, 293, 413, 489, 612, 613, 635, 660, 669, 680, 715, 717, 744. Arndt, John, 338. Arnold, General Benedict, 687, 706, 748. Assembly, 104, 369, 518, 685. Auditor-General, United States, 591.
Bailey, Francis, and Captain Lang, 405. Bayard, Colonel John, 61. Beaton, John, 494. Berks county justices, 138, 722. Biddle, Colonel Clement, 92, 104, 122, 139, 187, 220, 540. Blaine, Ephraim, D. C. G., 252. Blewer, Captain Joseph, 671. Board of war, (Continental,) 35, 42, 52, 63, 84, 86, 92, 118, 127, 174, 185, 188, 192, 195, 205, 208, 214, 216, 234, 268, 280, 339, 351, 359, 369, 402, 429, 444, 454, 492, 517, 526, 533, 540, 549, 556, 576, 581, 586, 593, 604, 608, 643, 644, 647, 649, 654, 655, 667, 668, 684, 727, 745, 758, 768. Bondfield, John, 172, 330. Boudinot, Elias, 89, 162. Boyd, Lieutenant Andrew, 355, 432, 482, 582, 647. Boyd, Colonel J., 596. Bradford, Colonel William, 11, 24, 27, 80, 204. Bradford, William C., 451. Brodhead, Daniel, 462, 492, 772. Buchanan, William, 34. Bull, Colonel John, 129, 133, 190, 746. Butler, Col. Richard, 253, 386, 404.

Supreme Executive Council—vi.
Cadwalader, Lambert, vi., 655. Caldwell, Charles, 502. Carothers, Lieutenant John, 438, 447, 466, 491, 539, 559, 609, 619, 700. Chambers, John, 504. Circulars, 65, 88, 124, 179, 240, 294, 427, 431, 452, 638, 650. Claypoole, James, 624. Clymer, Daniel, 105. Coates, Colonel William, 227. Collectors of clothing, 33. Commissioners of Berks county, 327, 520. Commissioners of Chester county, 560. Commissioners for Lancaster, 531. Commissioners of clothing, 27, 179. Commissioners for seizing estates, 13, 644. Commissioners for collecting provisions, 278, 294, 329, 418, 431. Commissioners for Western department, 386. Committee of Congress, 316, 362, 367, 384, 389, 677. Congress, 12, 104, 136, 152, 153, 158, 161, 176, 207, 208, 210, 248, 249, 284, 298, 318, 327, 340, 350, 364, 378, 394, 403, 448, 460, 485, 488, 493, 507, 522, 524, 589, 592, 607, 670, 675, 708, 710, 713, 726, 727, 737, 775. Coombe, Rev. Thomas, Jr., pass for New York, 626. Cowell, Ebenezer, 51. Coxe, John, 16, 29. Craig, Robert, 41. Craig, Colonel Thomas, 412. Crispin, William, 151, 174, 203, 441. Culbertson, Colonel Robert, 448.
Dana, Francis, vi., 316. Davidson, James, 16. Davis, John, 562. Davison, Hugh, 504. DeHaven, Hugh, 58. De Haven, Peter, 52, 475, 633. Delegates in Congress, 116, 124, 137, 207, 231, 242, 269, 277, 298, 359, 380, 455, 535, 577. Deshler, Colonel, 394. Dickinson, Jonathan, 496.
Edwards, Thomas, vi., 449. Elder, Joshua, 616. Ettwein, John, 751. Evans, Edward, 544. Evans, Colonel Thomas, 709. Evans, William, 731.
Ferguson, Mrs. Elizabeth, vi., 617. Flower, Colonel Benjamin, 135, 450, 463. Forst, David, 296. Freeholders at Bedford county, 577. Furman, Moore, 439.
Galbraith, Bartrem, vi., 643, 648.

Supreme Executive Council—vi.
Galbraith, Colonel Robert, 238, 511, 550. Galloway, Mrs. J., 674. Garland, Captain George, 737. Gates, General Horatio, President B. W., 205. Gibbon, Colonel William, 530. Gibson, George, 319, 553. Gourla, John, 443. Gray, William, and Jno. Little, 377. Greene, Major-General Nathaniel, 444, 483, 530. Greer, Joseph, 395. Gronow, Lewis, 496.
Haberstack, Michael, vi., 362. Hagner, Lieutenant Frederick, 486. Hale, Thomas, and N. Weaver, 628. Hambright, John, 770. Hamilton, James, 372, 383, 433, 456, 468. Harris, David, 32. Harris, John, 211, 574. Hart, William, 396, 431, 525. Hartley, Thomas, 497, 674, 691, 692, 720. Hazelwood, Commodore John, 47, 121, 132, 167, 180, 246, 599, 724, 749. Henry, William, 645. Hilegas, Michael, 538, 548, 565. Hubley, John, 750, 769. Hubley, Joseph, 145. Hunter, Lieutenant Samuel, 175, 191, 392, 478, 499, 536, 552, 563, 564, 571, 573, 599, 624, 636, 711, 773.
Irvine, Matthew, vi., 166. Irvine, Colonel William, 726. Irwin, M., and R. Bridges, 718.
Jeffries, Joseph, vi., 349. Jones, Thomas, 107, 130.
Kirkbride, Joseph, vi., 96, 175, 261, 262, 280, 503.
Lacey, Brig.-Gen., vi., 168, 202, 226, 240, 255, 265, 361, 378, 381, 384, 390, 398, 402, 414, 470, 579, 580, 594, 595. Laird, Samuel, 550. Lebar, Colonel Abraham, 44, Lee, Francis Lightfoot, 82, 147. Lee, Major Thomas, 440. Lesher, John, 170, 327, 347, 667, 675. Levan, Abraham, 406, 449. Levers, Robert, 140, 141, 341, 344, 346, 362, 381, 435, 464, 486, 533, 626, 719, 721. Levis, Thos., 651. Lewis, William, 641. Lieutenants, 156, 169, 426, 452, 500, 650. Livingston, Governor William, 133, 453, 599, 604, 728. Lochrey, Archibald, 68, 142, 459, 495. Lutterloh, Colonel, 210, 348, 352. Lyon, William, 228.

Supreme Executive Council—vi.
McCalester, Colonel Richard, vi., 22, 171, 197, 244, 369, 463, 479, 517. Maclay, William, 634. McClean, Archibald, 294, 376, 750. McDowell, Alex., 572. Mackay, John, 401. McKean, Thomas, 266, 555, 566, 568. Magistrates, 258. Mease, James, 22, 426, 428. Marsteller, Philip, 264. Melchior, Colonel, 676, 699. Morgan, Colonel George, 714. Morgan, Jacob, L. B. C., 14, 288, 418, 441, 522, 542, 562, 630, 706. Morgan, Jacob, commissioner, 47, 382. Morgan, Jacob, Jr., 128, 399, 568, 574, 639. Morris, Robert, 45.
Navy Board, State, vi., 24, 38, 110, 243, 332, 333, 355, 421, 434, 517, 696, 745. Nesbit, John M., 652. Nicola, Lewis, 197, 213, 358, 411, 656, 742.
O'Neal, Dennis, vi., 498.
Patterson, Captain Alexander, vi., 432. Peters, Richard, 72, 493. Pettit, Charles, 366, 513, 525, 620, 623. Pickering, Timothy, 173, 237, 546. Piper, Colonel John, 34, 36, 115, 138, 194, 229, 469, 505, 682. Pleasants, Samuel, 524. Porter, Captain Andrew, 594. Potter, General James, 51, 83, 89, 97, 98, 141, 150, 169, 521, 665, 729. Potts, Samuel, 595. Price, Philip, 695. Prisoners in Masonic Lodge, 509, 511. Proctor, Colonel John, 445, 458, 506, 659, 722. Proctor, Col. Thomas, 676.
Ralston, John, &c., vi., 747, 772. Rea, Samuel, 611, 672. Read, James, 234, 245, 473. Recruiting officers, 280. Reed, Joseph, 120, 218, 712, 739. Rice, Robert, 722. Rittenhouse, David, 643. Roberdeau, General Daniel, 10, 131, 134, 144, 183, 206, 209, 216, 273, 287, 295, 359, 374, 422, 446, 567, 583, 584, 609. Rudolph, Lieutenant John, 454. Rush, Jacob, 752.
Sanders, Wm., vi., 716. Savadge, Thomas, 159, 182, 236, 398, 400, 417. Scott, Thomas, 673. Sergeant, Jonathan D., 630, 683, 740. Seymour, Commodore Thos., 97. Shippen, Edward, 683. Shippen, Dr. William, 688. Skinner, Abraham, 625. Smith, Lieutenant Colonel, 4. Smith, James, 270. Smith, Jonathan, B., 160, 191, 232, 293, 303, 314, 350, 357, 359, 365, 369, 403, 420, 427, 466, 545. Smith, Matthew, 632. Smith, Thomas, and Edward Woods, 39. Smith, Dr. William, 621. Smith, and Keachline, lieutenants, 92, 107. Sprogel, Lodick, 678. Spyker, Henry, 391. Stevenson, George, 94. Stevenson, Robert, 653. Stewart, Colonel Walter, 285, 343. Stiles, Captain Jos., 480. Stoddart, Benjamin, 608. Stroud, Col. Jacob, 748. Sweers, Cornelius, 473.
Tilghman, James, vi., 96. Tilghman, Tench, 407.
Van Campen, &c., John, vi., 767.
Wagon masters, vi., 212. Wallis, Samuel, 666, 687. Washington, General George, 153, 156, 180, 189, 200, 201, 241, 250, 254, 255, 263, 274, 277, 291, 325, 338, 353, 354, 357, 401, 405, 409, 416, 425, 431, 445, 480, 490, 498, 522, 546, 557, 558, 604, 752. Watkins, Joseph, 368. Watson, John, 769. Wayne, Anthony, 25, 86, 142, 251, 381, 387, 397, 408, 411, 419, 428, 451, 474. Weitzel, Lieutenant John, 271, 541, 551, 629. Wirtz, Major, 201. Wynkoop, Henry, 600.
Young, James, W. M., vi., 75, 218, 259, 276, 282, 289, 321, 330, 337, 343, 366, 519, 674.

Supreme Executive Council—vii.
Adams, Samuel, vii., 14, 763. Admiralty, Judge of, 558, 694. Allen, Mrs., 452. Allison, Francis, Jr., 589. Armstrong, General John, 18, Arnold, Major General Benedict, 370. Artillery, officers, 254. Assembly, 64, 77, 100, 142, 191, 202, 472, 693, 712, 720, 738. Atlee, William, 674, 773.
Baltimore, magistrates, vii., 390. Barge, and Tyng, 728. Bayard, John, 189. Beahm, Philip, 13. Blaine, Ephriam, 707. Bland, Colonel Theodore, 107. Blythe, Colonel Benjamin, 496. Board of war, (Continental,) 90, 98, 101, 201, 202, 227, 229, 230, 232, 256,

Supreme Executive Council—vii. 282, 284, 286, 287, 289, 292, 308, 312, 329, 339, 340, 375, 385, 389, 397, 404, 418, 420, 421, 424, 437, 442, 450, 454, 456, 459, 460, 469, 480, 495, 496, 507, 627, 640, 649, 676, 677, 681, 691, 696, 709, 710, 713, 719, 727, 730, 731. Boyd, Colonel Andrew, 97, 471. Boys, Captain Nathan, 200, 240, 248, 566. Bradford, Thomas, 560. Bradford, W. C., 556. Brodhead, Colonel Daniel, 465, 505, 569, 710, 771. Brown, Lieutenant-Colonel Alexander, 515. Brown, Lieutenant-Colonel John, 226, 271. Bull, Colonel John, 240, 544, 635. Burke, Thomas, 170, 172. Butler, Colonel Richard, 482, 514. Butler, Colonel Zebulon, 283.

Campbell, Captain Thomas, vii., 301, 447. Carothers, Col. John, 405, 618. Carson, John, 437, 470, 637, 659, 691. Chesney, William, 599. Circulars, 104, 105, 183, 304, 486. Clarkson, Matthew, (Marshal,) 554. Claypoole, Jas., Sheriff, 252, 291, 360, 631, 765. Clingham, W., 158. Cluggage, Captain Thomas, 512, 624, 659, 742. Coats, Lieutenant-Colonel William, 376, 377, 764. Commercial Committee of Congress, 579, 605. Commissaries of purchases and issues, 304. Commissary General of issues, 587. Commissioners for collecting flour, 753, 766. Commiss'ers of forfeited estates, 243. Commissioners for procuring salt, 769. Committee of City, 461. Committee of Congress, 84, 85, 88, 170. Congress, 5, 12, 13, 14, 81, 89, 102, 106, 127, 162, 241, 246, 261, 265, 270, 274, 304, 312, 313, 324, 347, 369, 396, 417, 479, 490, 507, 513, 521, 532, 536, 552, 631, 647, 662, 664, 673, 695, 716, 738, 756, 765. Connor, Colonel Morgan, 336. Conyngham, Captain G., 320. Council of Massachusetts, 138. Coxe, Colonel John, 749. Craig, James, &c., 717. Crawford, Jas., 760. Crispin, William, 200, 314. Cushing, Thomas, 250.

Davis, Caleb, vii., 444. De Haas, General J. P., 330. De Haven,

Supreme Executive Council—vii. Peter, 133, 175, 195. Delaney, John, 94. Delaney, Sharp, 762. Delapt, Richard, 702. Delegates in Congress, 134, 137, 140, 141, 160, 174, 181, 184, 192, 422, 478, 551, 557. Delegates in Congress from Virginia, 184. Deshler, Charles, 17. Dougherty, Bernard, 186, 297. Drayton, William H., 328, 335. Dundas, James, &c., 140, 253, 326, 333. Dunlap, John, 201. Du Portail, Brigadier-General, ch., 272, 279, 280, 3[illegible]6, 399, 403, 409, 690. Du Simitiere, 212. Edwards, Major, 107, 152. Eckhard, Valentine, 552. Erwin, Captain Joseph, 563. Ettwein, Rev. John, 295. Eyre, Col. Jehu, 457. Eyre, Benj., G., &c., 644. Farmer, Colonel Lewis, 273, 689, 754. Farmer, Michael, 453. Fire companies, 134. Fisher, Henry, 390, 410, 705, 730. Fitzsimons, Thomas, 407. Flower, Colonel Benjamin, 294, 296, 385. Franklin, Benjamin, 774.

Galbraith, Colonel Bartrem, vii., 370. 507, 522, 611, 679. Galbraith, Colonel Robert, 18, 74, 99. Galloway, Mrs. Grace, 93, 95. Gerard, Mons., 16, 17, 61, 62, 70, 83, 164, 169, 185, 269, 278, 595, 604, 632, 648, 651, 653, 708. Governors of States, 197. Greene, Gen. Nathaniel, 175, 179. Greenwalt, P., 287. Gregg, Matthew, 334. Gurney, Francis, 495.

Hagner, Will., &c., vii., 671, 767. Hale, Thomas, 688. Hall, Chas., 651. Haller, Captain Henry, 488. Hambright, John, 519. Hand, General Edward, 321, 344, 403, 408, 715. Harbeson, Benjamin, &c., 102, 153. Hardie, Captain Robert, 91, 92. Harding, Capt., 761. Harmar, Colonel Joseph, 750. Harris, David, 638. Hartley, Colonel Thomas, 3, 10, 71, 86, 87, 258, 391, 776. Hazelwood, Com. John, 19, 112. Henry, George, 139, 190, 239, 333, 365. Henry, Governor Patrick, 247, 441. Henry, Col. William, 359, 416, 456, 514, 557, 599, 600, 667, 711. Hervey, Major George, 566. Hewitt, Thomas, 545. Hodge,

Supreme Executive Council—vii.
Andrew, 319. Hoffman, Stokely, 737. Holliday, William, 445. Holker, Monsieur (Consul), 137, 238, 499, 502, 503, 510, 513, 531, 532, 536, 558, 560, 580, 601, 628, 641, 669, 675, 678, 682, 683, 686, 699, 701, 703, 713. Hopkinson, Francis, 758, 694. Hubley, Lieut. Colonel Adam, Jr., 366, 498, 553, 596, 721, 755. Hubley, John, 297, 667. Hunter, Lieut. Col. Samuel, 116, 316, 346, 375, 438, 455, 510, 546, 615, 619.
Imlay, John, vii., 264. Irwin, Barclay & Co., 198, 244, 246, 263, 265, 266, 734. Irwin & Bridges, 314. Irwin, Matthew, 244, 261, 263, 311, 734, 765. Irwin, Thos., &c., 147.
James, Abel, vii., 758. Jameson, David, 529, 652. Jameson, D., and J. Eichelberger, 490, 530. Jennifer & Root, 750. Jennings, M., 311, 359. Johnson, Colonel Francis, 411, 581. Jordan, Jesse, 194. Joy, Captain Daniel, 562. Judges of Supreme Court, 773.
Kackline, Andrew, vii., 775. Kendal, Joseph, 410. Kirkbride, Joseph, 108. Knox, John, 433.
Lang, Captain, James, vii., 537, 567. Leaming, T., & George Henry, 422. Levan, Daniel, 610? Levers, Robert, 15, 176. Lieutenants, 267, 275, 486, 650, 747. Livingston, Governor William, 260, 474, 480, 492. Lochry, Lt. Col. Arch'd, 173, 362, 363, 430, 564, 754, 770. Loudon, Samuel, 206. Loughead, James, 531, 673, 764. Lyon, William, 144, 399.
MacAlester, Colonel Richard, vii., 110, 115, 367, 399, 414, 426. McCalla, William, 620. McClenachan, B. & Co., 248, 252, 281, 285, 288, 309, 310, 318, 322, 343, 364, 442, 768. McCulloch, Capt. John, 371, 506. McGinley, Capt. John, 652. McIlheney, George, 315. McIntosh, Gen. Lachn., 131. McKean, Thomas, C. J., 21, 225, 274, 279, 328, 637, 644, 699, 703, 732, 735, 744, 773. Maclay, Wm., 192, 357, 586, 593, 597, 598, 623. McPherson, Captain John, 180. Marine Committee, of Congress,

Supreme Executive Council—vii.
76, 120, 187, 235, 241, 588, 657. Marshal, Christopher, 668. Marsstoller, Colonel Philip, 567, 716. Massachusetts, President of Council of, 231. Maxwell, General William, 178. Martin, Colonel, 446. Meade & Co., George, 407. Miller, H., & Jno. Clark, Jr., 609. Mitchell, John, 160, 189, 213, 248, 262, 345, 474, 527, 746. Montgomery, Captain James, 455, 476, 487, 521, 533, 706, 755. Moore, Thomas, 543. Morgan, Colonel Jacob, Jr., 484, 559. Morris, A. James, 760. Morris, John, Jr., 120, 309, 310. Morris, Robert, 125, 386, 417, 608. Murray, William, 432. Myres, Jacob, 745.
Navy Board, vii., 695. Neilson, Captain John, 74. Nesbitt, J. M., 210, 228, 234, 246. New Jersey, Delaware and Virginia, 152. Newspaper Printers, 136, 201. Nicholson, Captain, 488. Nicola, Lewis, 77, 190, 203, 255, 358, 362, 364, 387, 484, 489, 492, 509, 519, 523, 526, 548, 549, 561, 562, 574, 625, 634, 635, 641, 643, 646, 648, 663, 674, 682, 698, 701, 767, 769, 775. Northampton county, inhabitants of, 360. Colonels of, 616.
Officers at Billingsport and M. Isl., vii., 409, 424, 502, 720, 745. Orndt, John, 625. Owners of brig Achilles, 308.
Patterson, William A., vii., 167. Persons on forestalling, 113. Pettit, Charles, 196, 335, 399, 403, 420, 433, 460, 481, 495. Philadelphia Justices, 658. Phyle, Dr. F. (Naval Officer), 185. Pickering, Timothy, 656. Piper, Lt. John, 578. Pomroy, Ralph, 312. Potter, General James, 419. Proctor, Colonel Thomas, 121, 123, 135, 146, 260, 270, 290, 298, 405, 423, 440, 476, 485. Purchasers of flour, 548, 692, 766. Purchasers of salt, 728.
Read, James, vii., 289. Read, John, 272. Reading, George, 345. Recruiting officers, 300. Reed, Bowes, 262. Risberg, Gustavus, 550. Rittenhouse, Benjamin, 142. Rittenhouse, David, 302. Rober-

Supreme Executive Council—vii. dean, Gen. Daniel, 100, 137, 159, 167, 184, 192, 198, 236, 296, 299, 643. Roberts, widow, &c. of John, 122. Rogers, Rev. Wm., 253, 273, 449. Root, Hon. Jesse, 774. Ross, George, 212, 451, 468. Rush & Hutchinson, Drs., 408. Rush, Jos., and James Craig, 330. Ryan, Philip, 541.
St. Clair, Gen. Arthur, vii., 237, 291, 355, 452, 491, 500, 582, 607, 665, 736. Savadge, Thomas, 96, 109, 111, 116. Scammell, Alex., 649. Scott, Thomas, 434. Scott, W. & R. Stevenson, 206. Scull, Major, 469. Searle, Hon. James, 141. Sergeant, Jonathan D. 267, 275, 395, 743. Sheriff, High, of Philada., 252, 291, 360. Shippen, Wm. 209. Shoemaker, Lt. Jacob, 688. Smith, George, 164. Smith, Col. Matthew, 280, 306, 607, 609, 614, 747. Smith, Meriwether, & R. H. Lee, 73. Smith, Thomas, 695. Snowden, Jedediah, 709. Sprogel, Lodick, 129. Standley, Dr. Valentine, 165. Steuben, Baron, 199, 325. Stewart, Col. Walter, 9, 660. Stiles, Capt. Joseph, 141, 238, 358. Straker, William, 71, 72. Stroud, Col. Jacob, 63, 613. Sullivan, Gen. Jno. 211, 388, 427, 439, 450, 457, 473, 756, 768.
Thompson, Hon. James, vii., 652.
Van Campen, John, 573, 574, 603.
Wall, Gen. Geo., Jr., vii., 103, 104, 660. Wardens of Philada., 627. Washington, Gen. George, 119. 127, 129, 161, 188, 210, 236, 293, 327, 337, 341, 351, 377, 407, 447, 479, 535, 555, 626, 670, 671, 672, 684. Wayne, Gen. Anthony, 142. Wetherill, Samuel, Jr., 172. Wetzel, Col. John, 299, 572, 579, 617. Whitesides, Thomas, 19. Wilcox, Alexander and John, 122, 148, 721, 725, 727. Wilkinson, Gen. J., 449, 744. Will, William, 729, 759. Young, James, 98, 151. Zeigler, Capt. David, 368.
Active Agents of sloop, viii., 209. Adams, John, 399, 563. Admiralty, 542. Agents for confiscated estates, 735, 760. Allen, Ira, 88.

Supreme Executive Council—viii. Amberson, William, 487. Amer. Philosophical Society, 136. Antes, Frederick, 219. Armstrong, Gen. John, 31, 152, 243, 599, 636. Armstrong, William, 34. Assembly, 280, 609, 655, 656, 685, 687, 758. Atlee, Col., Samuel J., 216, 241, 220, 305, 333, 335, 351, 423, 437, 438, 469, 484, 524, 580. Atlee, Judge William, 56, 124. Auditors of soldiers' accounts, 762.
Baily, James, viii., 390. Baker, Hilary, Jr., 720. Balliet, Lt. Col. Stephen, 564. Bayard, Hon. J., 247. Bedford, Inhabitants of, 749. Blaine, Ephraim, 13, 260, 304, 478, 480, 494, 565, 577, 603. 630, 646. Blythe, Benj., 96. Board of War, 5, 8, 38, 39, 43, 57, 74, 98, 110, 122, 132, 141, 153, 159, 161, 165, 175, 181, 224, 248, 269, 308, 343, 425, 432, 434, 435, 436, 442, 453, 457, 471, 478, 485, 498, 505, 506, 507, 508, 509, 549, 552, 554, 573, 576, 579, 580, 581, 600, 601, 611, 632, 689, 722, 727, 728, 739, 747. Boyd, Col. A., 12, 323. Boys, Capt. Nathan, 228, 728. Bradford, Thomas, 97, 503. Bradford, William, Jr., 621, 666, 725, 730, 760. Brodhead, Colonel Daniel, 22, 38, 106, 109, 120, 140, 149, 197, 210. 217, 246, 249, 300, 378, 513, 515, 536, 558, 565, 588, 596, 640, 743, 766. Bull, Col. John, 164. Butler, Col. Richard, 607, 741, 748. Butler, Lt. Col. William, 747. Butler, Col. Zebulon, 633.
Campbell, Thomas, viii., 36. Caswell, Richard, Gov. N. C., 191. Chaloner and White, 248. Chambers, Col. John, 320. Circular of Congress, 277. Clarkson, Matthew, (marshal) 498, 500. Claypoole, James, 117, 321. Clinton, Gov. George, 132, 179. Cluggage, Major Robert, 278. Coats, Col. William, 43. Colonels of Battalions, 111. Colonel of City Battalion, 309. Commissioners for procuring flour, 84. Commissioners of Philada., 80. Commissioners of purchases, 277, 441, 720. Commissioners for purchase of

Supreme Executive Council—viii. salt, 4, 24, 28. Commissaries of supplies, 287. Commissioners of Taxes of Berks county, 124, 133, 138. Commissioners of Virginia, 91. Committee of Assembly, 737, 758. Committee of Congress at Camp, 266, 293, 315, 355, 404. Congress, 20, 85, 87, 96, 99, 135, 142, 199, 202, 203, 229, 263, 299, 325, 340, 343, 349, 375, 419, 429, 458, 517, 529, 560, 583, 590, 606, 608, 635, 639, 657, 702, 719, 722, 723, 744, 751. Congress, Committee of, 53, 239, 281, 337, 338, 355, 356. Conolly, Dr. John, 104. Cox, Col. John, 406.

Davis, David, viii., 382, 458. Dean, Joseph, 712, 734. De Corny, Mons. E., 383, 416. Delegates in Congress, 9, 47, 61, 160, 191, 351, 392, 494, 643, 703, 722, 745, 757. Delegates of Connecticut in Congress, 111, 112, 711. Denny, David, &c., 496. Deshler, D. and C., 300, 535, 697, 711, 721. Dickinson, Gen. Philemon, 736. Doz, Andrew, 154, 413. Duane, James, 628, 659. Du Portail, Genl., 37.

Eckart, Valentine, viii., 529. Edwards, Col. Thomas, 237, 288. Elder, Joshua, 101. Ellsworth, Hon. Oliver, 261. Erwin, Capt. Joseph, 79. Espy, David, 102. Eyre, Major Benj. G., 144.

Farmer, Col. Lewis, viii., 52, 706. Ferguson, Elizabeth, 4. Ferris, Owen, 229. Flower, Col. Benj., 26. Franks, David S., 611, 617.

Geddes, Capt., 49. Gillespie, George, 481. Govett, Wm., & Wm. Geddes, 73. Greene, Genl. Nathaniel, 150, 165, 381, 426, 475.

Haffa, Henry, viii., 704. Hale, Thomas, 112, 115. Hall, David, and H. Fisher, 216. Hall, Charles, 54, 118, 194. Haller, Henry, 83, 417, 426, 430. Hamilton, William, 590. Hand, General, Edward, 155, 184, 425. Hannum, Colonel John, 244, 324. Harmar, Colonel Joseph, 188. Hart, John, 750. Hart, Joseph, 326, 327, 356, 503, 523, 717. Hayes, John, Jr., 317. Hazelwood. John, 652. Hazen,

Supreme Executive Council—viii. Colonel Moses, 105, 645. Heisler, Daniel, Jr., 697. Henry, Colonel William, 30, 207, 309, 380, 423, 652, 667, 685, 730, 654, 761. Hewitt, Thomas, 528. Hillegas, Michael, 403, 492, 493. Hodgdon, Samuel, 174, 746. Holker, Mons., F. C. 11, 90, 94, 134, 147, 148, 347, 350, 365, 366, 396, 402, 545, 550, 552, 571, 756. Hopkinson, Francis, 241, 245, 490. 667. Howell, Jacob S, 247. Hubley, Col., Adam, 512, 755. Hubley, John, 83, 395, 586. Huffnagle, Michael, 569. Hunter, Colonel Samuel, 29, 157, 166, 189, 205, 369, 393, 567, 632, 717. Huston, Lt., W. 153.

Irvine, General James, viii., 663, 664. Irvine, General William, 103, 206, 225, 232, 238, 245, 409, 511, 512, 570, 578, 643, Irwin, Captain John, 771. Irwin, Colonel, Samuel, 637. Irwin, Thomas, &c., 137.

Jackson, David, viii., 544. Jefferson, Thomas, Gov. of Virginia, 196, 641. Johnston, Col. Francis, 410. Jones, Rev. David, 752. Jones, Thomas, Jr., 303.

Knox, General, H. viii., 253, 349, 359, 726. Krieder, Conrad, 435, 489. Kucher, Christopher, 289, 324. Kuhn, Adam, 585.

Lacey, General John, viii., 505, 508, 526. Lanctot, Godfrey, 551, Lane, William, 360. Leary, Dennis, 531. Lee, Major Henry, Jr., 56, 67, 457, 477, 599. Lee, Thomas Sim, Governor, of Maryland, 330, 354, 432, 433. Lewis, William, 231. Lieutenants of counties, 72, 387, 454, 476, 519. Livingston, Governor William, 139, 374, 576, 624, 635, 636, 648, Lochrey, Colonel Archibald, 42, 77, 282, 290, 318, 405. Loughead, James, 567. Lutz, Nicholas, 201, 301, 313, 342, 357, 367, 399, 417, 438, 474. Luzerne, Chevalier de la, 358, 448, 540, 542, 614. Lyndermood, Col. Michael, 230, 236. Lyon, Samuel, 439, 715.

McCalester, Colonel Richard, viii., 16. McCalla, William, 212, 661, McClean, Archibald, 14, 126, 144,

Supreme Executive Council—viii. 731, 745. McClenachan, Blair, 3, McGuire, Matthew, 756. McLane, Capt. Allen, 258. McLene, James, 61. McKean, C. J. Thomas, 178, 234, 298, 331, 403, 597, 649, 650, 654, 657. McMullin, Wm. 282, McPherson, Major, W. 617, Maclay, William, viii., 156, 172. Managers of House of Employment, 725 726. Marsteller, Col. Philip, 51, 155, 328, 362, 371, 383. Mason, John, 373. Massachusetts, Council, 522. Matlack, Colonel Timothy, 60. Melchor, Colonel Isaac, 65. Merchants of Philadelphia, 266, 306, 704. Miles, Colonel Samuel, 533, 600, 608, 618, 699, 718, 719. Miller, Rev. Peter, 606. Miralles, Don Juan de, 174. Minister of France, 614, 628. Mitchell, John, 186, 334, 500, 501, 716. Montgomery, Rev. Joseph, 170. Morgan, Lt. Jacob, 273. Morgan, Colonel Jacob, 238, 344, 369, 449, 544. Morris, Robt. 372. Morris, Captain Samuel, 310, 699. Morris, Samuel, Jr., 308. Morris, Samuel, (Reg,) 228. Moylan, Colonel Stephen, 183. Muhlenberg, F. A. 123.
Navy Board, viii., 346, 543. Nicholson, John, 73. Nicola, Col. Lewis, 12, 77, 95, 100, 108, 181, 262, 316, 358, 363, 376, 378, 391, 415, 422, 460, 510, 516, 724.
Officers of land office, viii., 307. Oster, Mons. (F. C.) 604. Officers of militia, 265.
Paine, Thomas, viii., 21, 226. Peale, Charles Wilson, 319. Penet, P. 257. Pettit, Charles, 104, 197, 211, 224, 342, 406, 614. Philadelphia Library Co., 183. Physic, Edmund, 113. Pickering, Colonel Timothy, 499, 604. Piper, Colonel John, 234, 297, 302, 319, 349, 488, 530. Potter, General James, 485, 561, 689, 710. Powell, Jeremiah, Pres. of Mass. Bay, 254. Presidents, of Common, Pleas, 622, 658. Proctor, Col. John, 217, 284. Proctor, Thomas, 710. Prothonotaries of Counties, 58. Purchasers of flour, 3. Purviance, Samuel, Jr., 644.
Rea, Lieutenant Samuel, viii.,

Supreme Executive Council—viii. 221, 222, 227, 259, 286, 386, 560, 640, 683, 729. Reid, Major James, 44. Reynolds, John, 690. Rice, Patrick, 33. Riche, Mrs. Annie, 141. Risburg, Gustavus, 200. Rittenhouse, David, 657, 662. Roberdeau, General Daniel, 5. Roberts, Jehu, 296. Rodney, Gov. of Delaware, 10. Rowan, William, (Sheriff,) 23. Ryan, Michael, 371, 582, 657.
St, Clair, General Arthur, viii., 168, 374, 397, 515, 537, 701, 721, 623. Schott, Captain John Paul, 24. Scott, Hon. Thomas, 63, 713. Scott, Colonel William, 365, 379, 382, 444, 524, 580, 623. Scull, Edward, 655. Scull, William, 94. Searle, James, 514. Sergeant, Jonathan D., 395, 498, 613, Shippen, Joseph, Jr., 200. Smith, Colonel Ab'm, 443, 491, 522. Smith, Colonel George, 52. Smith, Colonel Matthew, 23, 249, 417, 513, 706. Smith, Richard, 740. Smith, Lieutenant, Robert, 445, 535. Smith, Tho's, 113. Steuben, Baron, 270. Stevenson, George, 50, 107, 141. Stewart, Charles, 699. Stiles, Joseph, 139. Stroud, Col. Jacob, 9, 176, 188. Swaine, Francis, 34, 76, 117, 428, 431, 433. Treasurers of Counties, 58. Treasury, U. S. 92, 185.
University, of Pennsylvania, viii., 246.
Van Campen, Jon. viii., 222. Vankemp, John, 551.
Wade, Francis, viii., 274. Wadsworth, Jeremiah, 205. Wagon Masters, 447. Waln, Nicholas, 100. Washington, Gen. George, 35, 36, 43, 48, 54, 70, 74, 75, 116, 128, 145, 155, 161, 180, 193, 214, 240, 267, 292, 314, 332, 339, 361, 377, 470, 474, 482, 486, 525, 534, 535, 577, 599, 684. Watts, Colonel Frederick, 558. Wayne, General Anthony, 450, 451, 587, 593. Weltner, Colonel Lund, 161, 233, 341. West, William, Jr., 631. Westmoreland representatives, 709, Wharton, James, 766. Wilkinson, James, C. G., 269. Will, Colonel William, 628. Willet

Supreme Executive Council,—ix. Augustin, 305. Williams, Bensiller, 63. Wirts, Christian, 187, 192, 304, 310, 328, 398, 575, 602, 653, 668. Witman, Adam, 129. 264, 303, 742. Wynkoop, Henry, 557, 572. Zeigler, Capt. David, 59, 209.
Admiralty, Board of, ix., 94, 100, 106. Agnew, John, 135. Antes, William, 381. Armstrong, John, Jr., 650. Arndt, John, 53, 109, 137. Ashman, George, 152, 202. Assembly, 5, 16, 51, 61, 188, 197, 219, 221, 232, 241, 248, 412, 447, 459, 463, 467, 501, 509, 510, 513, 620. Atlee, William, 170, 203, 335, 347, 596. Auditors of Bucks county, 11, 13, 17, 29, 36, 47, 67, 105, 113. Auditors of Chester county, 42. Auditors of Philadelphia county, 104. Auditors of York county, 18.
Bailey, James, ix., 160. Baker, Hilary, Jr., 195. Balliott, Stephen, 649. Barclay, Thomas, 563. Beatty, John, 124. Biddle, Clement, 129. Blaine, Colonel Ephraim, 72. Blair, Rev. Samuel, 110. Board of War, 3, 8, 16, 19, 23, 26, 31, 57, 58, 96, 103, 111, 150, 167, 186, 187, 198, 206, 290, 291, 391, 526, 527. Board of Wardens of Philadelphia, 101. Boys, Captain Nathan, 175, 416. Bradford and Hall, 266. Bradford, Thomas, 338, 380. Bradford, William, Jr., Attorney General, 199, 266, 272, 407, 408, 515, 526, 553, 576, 656, 659, 676, 690, 750. Brodhead, Colonel Daniel, 39, 57, 161, 365, 379. Bryan, Vice-President, 279, 288, 299, 305, 309. Butler, Colonel Richard, 561.
Caldwell, Samuel and H. A. Shiell, ix., 520. Campbell, Capt. Thomas, 435. Carrington, Lieut. Edw'd, 487. Cessna, Capt. Chas., 236, 467. Christ, Henry, 81, 133, 196, 237, 347. Circulars, 226, 337, 387, 407, 425. Clarke, General G., 23, 137, 331. Clarke, Walter, 381. Claypoole, Captain A. G., 278, 378. Coats, Colonel William, 250, 272, 325, 358, 377, 535. Commissioners on Connecticut claim, 624, 683, 688, 689, 690, 692, 693. Comm'rs of Cumberland Co., 736. Comm'rs for defence of Delaware, 586, 618, 621, 625, 647, 672. Commissioners of Northumberland, 440. Commissioners of Taxes, Philadelphia county, 116, 139, 328, 478. Committee of Assembly, 14. 62, 415. Committee of Congress, 281. Congress, 21, 43, 76, 81, 83, 94, 102, 108, 110, 112, 151, 162, 163, 194, 210, 242, 252, 267, 273, 309, 395, 400, 416, 423, 433, 441, 448, 463, 475, 479, 486, 518, 523, 548, 560, 561, 757. Congress, delegates, in, 103, 163, 306, 420, 768. Connecticut, Governor of, 629. Cook, Colonel Edward, 629. Cook, William, 410. Cooper, Leonard, 424. Cooper, Ensign William, 750. Counsel in Connecticut, claim, 526. Craig, Captain Isaac, 497. Craig, Captain Thomas, 503. Cummings, J. R., Major, 20, 24. Cummins, Lieutenant, 28. Cunningham, Hon. James, 495.
Dalley, Gifford, ix., 274. De Barrass, Monsieur, 353, 354. Delegates in Congress, 103, 163, 306. Delegates of Virginia in Congress, 260, 266, 271, 274. Depui, Nicholas, &c., 105, 113. Dickinson, Governor, John, Delaware, 494. Dickinson, President, John, 731, 734. Donnahil, John, 671. Dougherty, Bernard, 467, 539, 543, 546, 553, 557, 619. Dove, R., 625. Dubois, Abraham, 47, 67. Duffield, Rev. George, 493. Duncan, David, 17, 97, 200, 305, 380. Du Portail, Brigadier General, 210.
Eckhert, Lieut. Valentine, ix., 225, 230.
Edwards, Major, ix., 75.
Field officers, ix., 187. Forrest, Lieut. Col. T., 231. Fowler, Alex., 114.
Gloninger, John, ix., 654. Goforth, William, 47, 67. Gordon, Major James, 673. Governor of Maryland, 12, 37.
Hall, Charles, ix., 294, 321. Hambright, Colonel John, 336.

Supreme Execntive Council,—ix. Hommel, Wm., 330. Hannum, John, 753. Harrison, Governor Benjamin, 518, 533, 549, 562, 607. Hart, John, 54, 128, 291, 338, 376. Hart, Joseph, 507. Hayes, Christopher, 141, 300, 354, 368, 404, 637. Hazard, Ebenezer, 449. Hazelwood, John, 38, 133. Hazen, Col. Moses, 643. Henry, John, 573. Henry, Wm., 7, 154, 171, 205, 476. Higgins, Andrew, 413. Holker, Monsieur, (F. C.,) 9, 31, 45, 153, 175, 342, 353, 354. Hopkinson, Francis, 555, 567, 577, 631, 672. Howe, Major General, 462. Hubley, Colonel Adam, 8, 65, 156, 169, 211, 218, 224, 231, 234, 252, 268, 278, 292, 295, 351, 360, 364, 417, 422, 456, 465. 466. Huffnagle, Michael, 410, 511, 596. Hughes, Capt. John, 533. Hunter, Col. Samuel, 503, 528, 657.

Irvine, Gen. William, ix., 83, 240, 285, 345, 373, 458, 468, 515, 525, 552, 575, 595, 630, 635, 648, 724.

Jefferson, Thomas, Governor of Virginia, ix., 78, 160, 189. Johnston, Dr. Robert, 457. Johnston, Col. Francis, 263, 327. Jones, N., 677. Judges of Supreme Court, 634. Justices of Gloucester, 544.

Keith, Sarah, ix., 501. Kennedy, D., 263, 363.

Lee, Thomas, S., ix., 12, 37. Levan, Daniel, 38. Levers, Robt., 227, 257, 268, 275, 321, 339, 348, 377, 426, 463, 578, 742. Lewis, Colonel, 421. Livingston, Hon. R. R., 493, 506, 544, 545, 633. Livingston, William, Governor of New Jersey, 82, 388, 393, 404, 437, 530, 531, 608, 617, 618, 621, 622, 623, 651. Lochrey, Colonel Archibald, 18, 28, 79, 115, 246, 307, 333. Loughead, James, 436. Lukens, John, 61, Lux, George, 45. Luzerne, Chevalier de la, 542.

McCalla, Wm., ix., 136, 423. Maclay, Wm., 640. McClean, Alex., 564, 585, 588, 772. McClean, Arch'd., 59, 352, 359, 370, 402.

Supreme Executive Council,—ix. McConnel, Major Matthew, 327, 371, 424. McDowell, John, 729. McKean, Thos., C. J., 42, 125, 751. Marbois, Mons., 741. Marsh, Colonel Joseph, 396, 440. Marshall, James, 193, 233, 304, 343, 367, 444, 485. Marsteller, Philip, 639. Mason, Isaac, 238, 303. Mentges, Lieutenant Colonel P., 216, 299. Merchants of Philadelphia, 731. Miles, Colonel Samuel, 80, 95, 127, 150, 153, 280, 324, 346, 357, 432. Miller, Rev. Peter, 27, 313, 314, 751. Minister of France, 542. Miralles, Don Juan, 196. Mitchell Alexander, 165, 166. Montgomery, Wm., 641. Moore, James, 62. Morgan, Col. Jacob, Jr., 127, 326. Morris, Governor, 308. Morris, Robert, 244, 245, 250, 251, 262, 264, 280, 281, 286, 287, 291, 308, 310, 376, 383, 387, 395, 397, 398, 414, 416, 417, 418, 419, 435, 446, 474, 477, 481, 487, 488, 505, 512, 513, 544, 637, 668, 739, 740. Morris, Capt. Samuel, 221, 414. Moultrie, Brigadier General, 215. Moylan, Colonel Stephen, 267, 321. Muhlenberg, F. A., 60.

Nevill, Thomas, ix., 76, 283. New York, Governor of, 629. Nicholson, Capt., 239. Nicholson, John, 49, 118, 131, 154, 174, 212, 216, 243, 663, 664, 677, 678, 737, 738, 747. Nicola, Colonel Lewis, 198, 254.

Officers on removal of Records, ix., 112. Officers of land office, 409. Orth, Adam, 188, 470, 737. Osborne, H., 252, 341, 390, 688, 689, 730. Oster, French V. C., 372.

Pemberton, John, and William, Matthews, ix., 551. Penet, A. P., 430. Pentecost, Dorsey, 315, 540, 541, 545, 556, 661. Perry, James, 240. Peters, Richard, 454. Pettit, Col. Charles, 129, 159. Pickering, Timothy, 389, 577. Porter, Andrew, 327, 632. Postlethwaite, Samuel, 192. Potter, Gen. James, 70, 184, 641. President of Quarter Sessions, 323. Prisoners in Prison ships, 668. Prudden, T., and A. Caldwell, 480.

Supreme Executive Council,—xi.
Rea, Colonel Samuel, ix., 107, 158. Read, James, 191. Reed, Joseph, 517, 526. Reichel, John Frederick, 265. Rittenhouse, David, 117, 119, 229. Roach, Isaac, 96, 112. Roberts, Joseph, 745. Robins, Ezekiel, 674, 677, 756. Robinson, Thomas, 208, 237, 334, 392, 659. Rogers, Rev. William, 3.
St. Clair, General Anthony, ix., 27, 36, 386, 735. Scott, Hugh, &c., 771. Scott, Thos., 20, 324, 354, 374, 438, 496, 646. Scott, Lt. William, 228, 232, 302, 319, 341, 350, 455, 556, 632. Searle, Hon. James, 519, 589, 591. Secretary at War, 483, 549, 757. Shrawder, Captain Philip, 761. Smith, Col. Abraham, 234, 400, 514. Smith, George, 42. Smith, James, 459. Smith, Lieutenant Col. Robert, 421, 434. Smith, Hon. Thomas, 652. Sterrett, Samuel, 676. Stokely, Captain Thomas, 330, 406.
Thome, John, ix., 118. Treasury Board, 226, 229.
Van Campen, John, ix., 105, 123, 522. Van Staphorst, N. & J. 591, 593.
Wagon Masters, ix., 421. Wall, George, Jr., 628. Washington, Co., Inhabitants of, 355. Washington, General George, 54, 98, 102, 120, 141, 195, 197, 207, 242, 254, 284, 293, 320, 481, 485, 486, 501, 505, 509, 536, 550, 626, 642, 653, 656, 661, 674. Wayne. Gen. Anthony, 15, 74, 123, 124, 137, 155, 173, 283, 359, 366, 430. Weiss, Lewis, 298. Willing, Thomas, 496. Wilson, James, &c., 526. Wirtz, Christian, 379, Wood, Colonel James, 236, 262, 276, 289, 328, 357, 382. Wylie, Captain Thomas, 191, 665. Zantzinger, Paul, ix., 282.
Agents of Confiscated Estates, x., 154. Antes, Henry, Sheriff, Northumberland, 344, 482, 694. Armstrong, Br. Gen. John, 686, 688. Armstrong, Lt. Col. John, 307, 315, 317, 319, 361. Armstrong, Capt. William, 12. Assembly, 195, 198, 223, 407, 427, 428, 692, 694.

Supreme Executive Council,—x.
Atlee, Samuel J., 333, 346, 360. Atlee, William, 004.
Barclay, Thomas, x., 267. Bartholomew, Edward, 442. Baynton, Jon, 511. Blaine, Ephraim, 669. Boggs, Matthew, 699. Boudinot, Elias, 74. Bowen, F. B. and E. Beatty, 437, 596, 604, 605. Boyd, Hon. John, 307, 330, 339. Boyd and Armstrong, 591, 627, 630, 662, 664–669, 670, 676. Bradford, William, Jr., Attorney General, 494, 655, 712, 743. Brodhead, Col. Daniel, 160. Brussine and Garrison, 145. Bryan. Hon. Geo., 16, 73. Bryan, Samuel. (Sec'ry,) 327. Butler, Col. Richard, 69, 294. Butler, William, 421.
Caldwell, Samuel, x., 185. Carleton, Gen. Guy, 101, 131. Christie, James, (Capt.) 135, 209. Circulars, 284. Clinton, Gov. Geo., of New York, 205, 412, 422, 435, 450, 513. Commissioners for sale of barracks, 239, 241, 261, 268, 276. Commissioners of boundaries, 233, 234, 416, 438, 454, 489, 506. Commissioners of Cumberland county, 79. Commissioners on defence of Delaware, 26. Commissioners for treating with Indians, 265, 325, 332, 333, 346, 357, 392, 395, 410, 489. Commissioners on lands, 541, 545. Commissioners of Philadelphia, 104, 307. Commissioners of roads, 533. Commissioners of Taxes, 238. Commissioners of Taxes of Bucks county, 75. Commissioners of Taxes of Lancaster county, 82. Commissioners of Taxes of Northampton Co., 92. Commissioners of Taxes of Philadelphia, 51, 222, 224. Commissioners of Washington county, 136, 584. Commissioners of Westmoreland county, 98, 593. Congress, 60, 62, 74, 98, 135, 193, 206, 231, 233, 263, 359, 369, 397, 410, 417, 440, 442, 457, 461, 473, 489, 493, 494, 499, 507, 532, 535, 537, 539, 543, 544, 736, 745, 754. Council of Censors, 153, 302, 306, 333, 336, 596, 604, 655. County Lieuts., 286, 345, 410, 419. Craig, Thomas, 296, 303, 305. Crevecour, Mon., 195. Cummins, Lt. John 22.

Supreme Executive Council,—x.
Delany, Sharp, x., 97, 441, 715. Delaware, Gov. of, 540. Delegates in Congress, 7, 25, 27, 28, 38, 45, 48, 52, 69, 72, 101, 151, 154, 155, 156, 183, 184, 204, 210, 213, 358, 369, 397, 398, 449. 456, 477, 511, 549, 556, 563, 575, 576, 581, 592, 601, 705, 715, 759. Dickinson, John, 77. Dougherty, Bernard, 114, 119. Douglass, Ephraim, 262, 553, 564, 581, 588, 696. Donaldson, Arthur, 350. Donnaldson, John 565, 583. Duval, Hon. Gabriel, 291.
Ellicott, Andrew, x., 452. Espy, David, 114, 119. Ewing, Rev. Dr. John, 428, 443.
Finley, Rev. James, x., 41, 163. Fitzsimons, Thomas, 28, 48. Fleeson, Plunket, 523. Francis, Tench, 240, 261. Franklin, John, 672. Fullerton, Richard, 758.
Galbraith, Robert, x., 466. Gardner, Hon. Joseph, 405, 526. Gov. of Connecticut, 147, 148, 213. Gov. of Delaware, 540. Gov. of Maryland, 292, 320, 324, 526, 527, 540, 542, 543, 744, 753. Gov. of Massachusetts, 354, 500, 503, 504. Gov. of New Jersey, 103, 366. Gov. of New York, 205, 412, 422, 435, 450, 513. Gov. of North Carolina, 353. Gov. of South Carolina, 79. Gov. of Virginia, 56, 145, 175. Grand Inquest, 347. Guerard, Gov. Benjamin, of South Carolina, 79.
Harmar, Lt. Col., Josiah, x., 309, 311, 316, 322, 337, 345, 398, 394, 406, 430, 448, 455, 465, 468, 479, 483, 490, 508. Harrison Gov. Benjamin, 56, 145, 175, 608. Hays, Christopher, 264, 279. Hellstedt, Charles, Minister of Uni'd Netherlands, 350, 362, 409. Henry, William, and G. Gardner, 405. Hillegas, Michael, 239, 261. Hodgdon, Samuel, 39, 59. Hollingsworth, Levi, 350, 533, 546, 548. Hopkinson, Francis, J. A., 58, 355, 707, 735. Howe, Major General, 66. Hubly, John, 278. Huffnagle, Michael, 125, 140, 141, 147, 186, 211, 429, 462, 464, 467, 763. Humpton, Col., Richard, 59. Hunter, Samuel, 47. Hutchinson, Dr., James, 178.

Supreme Executive Council,—x.
Irvine, Gen. William, 56, 67, 509. Irvine, John, 289.
Jacks, James, x., 264. Jackson, Hon. David, 522. Jay, John, Secretary of Foreign Affairs, 401, 407, 409, 475. Johnston, Benjn., 611. Johnston, Col., Francis, 282, 325, 326, 333, 453. Judges of Supreme Court, 448, 460, 523.
Land Office, x., 536, 537, 739. Lee, Arthur, 295. Lee, Richard Henry, 173. Levers, Robert, 341, Livingston, R. R., Secretary, &c., 9. Livingston, Gov. William, 103, 366, 458, 730. Loan Office, 57, 168, 169, 174, 190, 481, 515. Longschamp, John, 742. Lukens, John, S. G., 53, 65, 95, 451, 458, 506. Luzerne, Chev. de la, 278, 282. Lyon, Wm., 285.
McClean, Alex., x., 293. McDowell, Surgeon, 343. McKean, Thomas, C. J., 19, 176, 284, 290, 291, 730. Maclay, William, 46, 346, 418, 444, 510. Magistrates and Sheriff of Northumberland, county, 460. Managers of State Lottery, 362, 372, 400, 468, 474, 513. Marbois, Mons. 175, 223, 277, 283, 311, 350, 351, 354, 356, 362, 367, 368, 409, 432, 440, 445, 471. Mead, David, 404, 483, 707. Merchants, committee of, 210, 212, 219, 221, 406. Mifflin, Thomas, 183. Milligan, James, 426. Milligan, Robert, 755. Minister of Holland, 415. Minister of United Netherlands, 350, 362, 409, 415, 435. Montgomery, John, 216, 220. Montgomery, Joseph, 444. Montgomery, William, 765, 767. Moore, Lt. Colonel, 286. Moore, Major, James, &c., 183, 186, 197, 207, 222, 232. Morales, Frc's. 476. Morgan, George, 526. Morris, Robert, 53, 312. Muhlenberg, Frederick A., Pres. C. C., 153.
Nicholson, John, x., 6, 16, 28, 46, 48, 50, 52, 53, 93, 94, 96, 97, 481, 529, 750. Northumberland, Mag. and Sheriffs, 295, 304.
Officers of Pennsylvania Line, x., 425, 592.
Parker, William, x., 167. Patterson, Alexander, 208, 574, 617, 619, 623, 626, 627, 675. Peale, Chas.

Supreme Executive Council,—x.
W., 162, (1779,) 163, (1780.) Pearson, James, 373, 420, 426, 443. Pentecost, Dorsey, 167, 101, 262, 413, 757. Pettit, Charles, 208, 497. Phile. Fredk., N. O., 249. Phipps, Paul, 359. Peirce, John, 536. Porter, Andrew, 372, 762. Potter, Gen. James, 47, 159, Proctor, Thomas, Sheriff, 286, 323, 420. Prothonotaries, 78, 268. Prothonotary of Washington county, 78.
Receiver Gen. of Land Office, x., 547. Redick, David, 416. Reed, Joseph, 157, 159, 160, 163. Reynolds, John, 277. Rittenhouse, David, Treasurer, 241, 269, 439, 454, 455, 456, 458, 736. Robbins, Ezekiel, 213. Robinson, Captain Thomas, 14, 48. Ryan, Michael, 308.
St. Clair, Gen. Arthur, x., 49, 260, 483. Schreiber, John, 309, 334. Scott, William, 591. Scott, Thos., 65, 78, 80, 364. Secretary of Foreign Affairs, 9, 401, 407, 432, 446, 499, 538, 735, 743, 759. Shaw, William, 764, 767. Sheriffs, 63, 67. Shrawder, Capt. Philip, 23, 104. Slough, Mathias, 237. Smyser, Jacob, 77. Smith, Wm., and W. Kelly, 419. Smith, Thomas, Land Office, 57, 168, 169, 174, 192, 447, 461. Sproat, Rev. James, 720. Sproat, David, 68. Stanhope, Henry, Captain, 503, 504. Steuben, Baron, 362. Story, John, 450, 451, 742. Street Commissioners of Philadelphia, 55. Surveyor Gen., 53, 65, 95, 451, 458, 506.
Taylor, Timothy, x., 432. Trumbull, Gov. Jonathan, Connecticut, 147, 148, 213. Trustees of Loan Office, 481, 532, 545. Trustees of Westmoreland county, 91. Turnbull, Marmee & Co., 281.
Van Berkel, P. J., Minister of Holland, x., 476. Vancouver, Chas., 712.
Wardens of Philad., x., 93, 281, 349, 456, 571, 581, 584, 585, 588, 589, 606, 607. War Office, 27, 302, 459, 460, 479, 495, 497, 525, 529. Washington, Gen. George, 150, 151. Weitzel, John, 99, 109,

Supreme Executive Council,—xi.
222, 343. Wilkinson, Gen. James, 610. Williamson, Hon. Hugh, 397. Wilson, James, 399, 471. Wilson, Wm., 304. Wilson, Jos., 153. Wynkoop, Henry, 211.
Adlum, John, xi., 576, 629. Agricultural Society, 327, 384, 385. Anstey, John, 148. Armstrong, John, Jr., 137, 407. Brig. Gen. John, 447. Armstrong, William, 215, 242. Assembly, 87, 103, 187, 206, 390, 397, 398, 402, 409, 529, 669, 673, 674, 675.
Bache, Benjamin F., xi., 713. Baker, Hilary, 604. Balliet, Stephen, 177, 179, 460. Barclay, John, 89, Bartholomew, Edward, 767. Bayard, John, 28. Biddle, Clement, 236, 573, 743. Board of Treasury, 155. Board of War, 208, 240, 268, 281, 291, 300, 534, 555, 645, 685, 686, 707. Bond, Phineas, 255, 381. Bradford, William, Jr., Attorney General, 122, 232, 234, 250, 260, 273, 310, 415, 419, 431, 445, 446, 467. Brearly, David, C. J., New Jersey, 548. Brison, Jas., 422, 624. Brodhead, Daniel, 641, 661, 662, 663, 758. Brown, Andrew, 412. Bryan, Geo., (Judge.) 264, 283, 286. Burd, Edward, 765. Butler, Lord, 331. Butler, Gen. Richard, 427, 563, 591, 715. Butler, Col. Zebulon, 179, 192, 330, 351, 356, 381, 414, 459, 676. Buyers, John, &c. 438, 440.
Caldwell, Samuel, xi., 89, 594. Canan, Col. John, 588. Caswell, Richard, Gov. North Carolina, 116. Chaloner, John, 762. Cherokee Chiefs, 584. Cherokee Indian woman, 181. Clarkson, Matthew, 250. Clinton, George, Gov. New York, 96, 187, 326, 335, 341, 412. Coats, Lt. Col. William, 273, 274. Commander Lianes of Spanish Frigate, 101, 102. Commissioners of Commercial Convention, 60. Commissioners on Connecticut Claims, 159. Commissioners to Indians, 503, 507, 508, 509, 510. Commissioners for improving Inland navigation, 77. Commissioners of Luzerne county, 304, 332. Commissioners of Northampton county, 603. Commis'rs on Rivers, 622,

Supreme Executive Council,—xi. 634, 637, 681, 683, 690. Commissioners of Taxes, 499. Commissioners of Virginia and Maryland, 511. Commissioners of West. Boundary, 26, 52, 69, 178. Committee of Assembly, 103, 547. Committee of Ways and Means, Congress, 285, 545. Committee of Congress, 583, 585. Congress, 4, 50, 51, 56, 70, 71, 79, 121, 122, 128, 143, 145, 168, 171, 173, 180, 191, 214, 239, 285, 293, 311, 314, 323, 339, 353, 375, 387, 432, 543, 562. County Commissioners, 593, Cowperthwaite, Joseph, 330. Coxe, Tench, 5, 9, 542. Craig, Lt. Col. John, 196, 236, 305. Craig, Thomas, 276. Crawford, Edward, 690. Cuningham, J., 263. Curwen, John, 572.
Dale, Samuel, xi., 66. Davis, Benjamin, Jr., 766. Delany, Sharp, 259, 602. Delegates to Congress, 4, 27, 37, 87, 106, 188, 207, 237, 251, 252, 266, 280, 308, 342, 351, 352, 364, 373, 382, 383, 408, 433, 456, 457, 460, 504, 505, 537. Denison, Nathaniel, 212, 327. Douglass, Ephraim, 32, 535. Donaldson, John, 569, 570, 722, 763. Dunwoodie, James, 430.
Eckert, Valentine, xi., 203, 211. Ellicott, Andrew, 134, 140, 178, 216, 243, 326, 429, 583, 612, 615, 705. Elliott, Lt. Benjamin, 665.
Falconer, Nathaniel, xi., 737, 747. Febiger, Christian, 563, 649, 761. Ferguson, Capt. W., 590. Finley, Rev. James, 299. Fisher, Thos., 388. Fitzsimons, Thos., 426, 595. Franklin, Dr. Benj., Executors, 701. Franklin, John, 14, 52, 94, 111, 175, 182, 183, 185, 549, 556. Freeman, A., 714.
Galbraith, Robert, xi., 379, 656. Gardner, Hon. Joseph, 451, 453. Gibson, George, 606. Gore, Obediah, 192, 216. Gov. of Delaware, 33. Of Connecticut, 238, 409, 447, 451. Of Georgia, 96. Of Maryland, 57. Of Massachusetts, 271. Of New Jersey, 93, 550. Of New York, 96, 125, 187. Of North Carolina, 116. Of South Carolina, 545. Of Virginia, 115, 116, 212, 256, 284, 290, 497, 501,

Supreme Executive Council,—xi. 523, 525, 557. Graham, Henry Hale, 638. Grant, Thomas, 110. Griswold, Gov. of Connecticut, 447, 451. Gurney, Francis, 768.
Hollenbach, Mathias, xi., 216. Hamilton, Alex., Secretary Treasury, 638, 641, 654, 663, 664. Hancock, Gov. John, of Massachusetts, 272. Harmar, Lieut. Col. Josiah, 173, 217, 270, 286, 325, 391. Harrison, Governor Benjamin, of Virginia, 497 (1783), 499, 501, 507. Hartley, Colonel Thomas, 156. Hellestedt, Chas. (Swe. Cons.), 265. Hiester, Daniel, Jr., 607. Hodgdon, Samuel, 374, 379. Hopkinson, Fra's, 53, 77, 125, 375, 634. Houer, Samuel, 47, 102. Hubley, Adam, 755. Hubley, Lieut. Bernard, 709, 710. Huffnagle, Michael, 500. Huntington, Governor of Connecticut, 238, 409, 414.
Indian prisoners, xi., 712. Ingels, Geo., 767. Irvine, Gen. Wm., 501. 512, 513. Irvine, Matthew, 749.
Jacks, James, xi., 361. Jay, John, 171, 202, 287, 293, 300, 411. Jefferson, Thomas, Secretary State, 679, 688, 689, 696, 700, 703, 705, 706, 707, 708, 709, 712, 713. Jenkins, John, 15, 52. Johnston, Captain Andrew, 157. Johnston, Francis, 644, 750. Jones, David, 58. Judges of Supreme Court, 233, 264, 283, 295, 441, 442, 451, 472, 478, 484, 488, 490, 601, 667. Justice of Berks co., 286. Justices of Franklin co., 316. Justices of Northampton co., 273.
Keene, Lawr., xi., 141. Kemp, Captain John, 497. Kennedy, David, 651, 757. Knox, Gen. H. (Sec'y War), 208, 268, 269, 281, 290, 301, 524, 555.
Land Officers, xi., 138. Latimer, George, 661. Lenox, David, 55. Levan, Daniel, 63. Lieutenants of counties, 379. Light Infantry Company of Philadelphia, 36. Livingston, Wm., Gov. N. J., 93, 336, 350. Loan Office, trustees, 170. Lukens, John, 32, 93, 427. Luzerne, Chevalier de la, 462, 464, 465, 466, 468, 470, 473, 482, 487.

Supreme Executive Council,—xi.
McKean, C. J., Thos., xi., 264, 276, 283, 295, 351-366, 661. McLean, Alex., 71, 642. McLean, Capt. James, 229, 230, 231, 406. Magistrates of Wyoming, 440. Managers of State Lottery, 89, 118. Marbois, Mons. Barbe de, 49, 461, 471, 481, 494. Marshall, James, 209, 377. Mead, David, 454, 455. Melchor, Isaac, 523. Mentges, Col. Francis, 78. Mercantile society of Philadelphia, 103. Mifflin, John, 647. Milligan, Robert, 27. Minister of United Netherland, 468, 470, 475, 477, 479, 480. Miro, Brig. Gen., 567. Mitchel, Joseph, 253. Montgomery, Wm., 35. Moore, Col. James, 434-436-443. Moore, Thomas, 99. Morris, Richard, (C. J., of N. Y.), 413. Morris, Robt., 505. Muhlenberg, Peter, V. P., 231.
Nesbitt, John Maxwell, xi., 520. Nicholason, Joseph, 742. Nicholson, John, 33, 34, 90, 139, 142, 198, 234, 249, 259, 322, 404, 561, 589, 655, 658, 702, 731, 739, 742, 747. Nicola, Lewis, 536.
Officers commanding in Luzerne, xi., 204. Officers of Militia of Philadelphia Co., 57. O'Hara, James, 228. Owen, Evan, 585, 643.
Patterson, Alex., xi., 457. Peters, Richard, 335, 432, 572, 636. Pettit, Charles, 28, 37, 41, 167, 266, 708. Philadelphia Agricultural Society, 384-385, 527. Pa. Company, 428. Philadelphia County Comm'rs, 706. Pickering, Timothy, 159, 177, 178, 179, 180, 208, 256, 281, 295, 296, 312, 346, 353, 359, 363, 365, 366, 399, 424, 541. Pinckney, Gov. Thomas, of South Carolina, 545. Pine, R. E., 95. Porter, Col. Andrew, 156, 178, 214, 241-502. Powel, Samuel, 527, 384, 385. Proctor, Thomas, (Sheriff,) 469, 477, 664, 719, 740, 741, 763.
Randolph, Beverly, Gov. of Virginia, xi., 557, (1784.) Randolph, Edmund, Gov. Virginia, 115, 116, 212, 249, 256, 284, 290, 523, 525. Read, James, 757.

Supreme Executive Council,—xi.
Receiver Genl., 667, 696. Redick, David, 149, 197, 244, 338, 410, 459, 592. Register Genl., 569, 570, 722, 763. Rittenhouse, David, 203, 337, 743. Robbins, Ezekiel, 495. Robinson, Capt. Thos., 432. Ross, James, 458. Rush, Dr. Benjamin, 437, 540, 578. Rush, Jacob, (Judge) 295. Ruston, Thomas, 632. Ryerson, Thomas, 666.
St. Clair, Hon. Anthony, xi., 127, 189, 393. Schott, John P., 297, 298, 397, 663. Scott, Thomas, 215, 569. Secretary of Foreign Affairs, 171, 202, 287, 290, 300. Sellers, John, 623. Shannon, Wm., 748. Sheriff of Philada, 469, 477, 664, 719, 740, 741, 763. Shippen, Edward, 91. Skinner, John, 92, 143, 159. Simms, Charles, 169. Smith, Francis, 193. Smith, Jona. B., 423. Smith, T. D., and A. Henderson, 305. Smith, Wm. Hooker, 14, 45, 102, 192, 330. Sprague, Joseph, 93. Stiles, Joseph, 202. Sullivan, Pres. John, 125. Swaine, Francis, 269.
Talbot, Lieut. Jeremiah, xi., 280, Telfair, Edward, Gov. of Georgia, 96. Torrence, Lieut. Joseph, 702. Trail, Robert, 446. Treasury Board, 64, 79, 86. Trinble, James, 679. Trustees of Loan Office, 170. Trustees of Washington Academy, 215. Turnbull, Wm., 623.
University of Penns., xi., 613, 704, 742.
Van Campen, John, xi., 26. Vandyke, Gov. Nichs., of Delaware, 33. Vaughan, Sam., 674.
War, Board of, xi., 208, 240, 268, 281, 291, 300, 534, 555, 621, 624, 645, 685, 686, 707, 711. Wardens of Philadelphia, 99, 101, 543. Washington, Gen. George, 496. Washington, President, 587. 596, 599, 600, 601, 602, 604, 605, 611, 615, 616, 673. Westbrook, Abraham, 47, 102. Wilson, Jas., 445, 453. Wilson, William, 192. Will, William, 413. Willet, Col. Marinus, 711. Williamson, Hon. Hugh, 449.

Supreme Executive Council,—xii. Zeigler, Captain David, xi., 284, 290, 301.
Congress, xii., 76. Cornplanter and other Indians, 322. Franklin, John, &c., 296. Huffnagle, M., 300. Gov. Livingston, N. J., 71. Secretary of War, 292. Wall, George, jr., 293, 319. Wardens of Philadelphia, 287, 294, 304, 306, 307. White, John, 304. Wilkins, Dr. John, jr., 321. Wilson, James, 294. Wilson, William, &c., 318, 319, 320, 322. Offer premiums for scalps, 240.
Surgeons wanted in the army, iii., 57. Excuse for one, 265. For the army, ix., 238.
Surveyor General, appointed, i, 310, 326. John Lukens elected, ix., 66. Instructions to, respecting lands and lots, x., 53, 56, 65. Meeting at, on survey of lands received from Virginia, 705. Office, xi., 32, 93, 660, 663.
Surveys of Erie, John Adlum on, xi., 576. Report on, 577.
Susquehanna Company, deed for lands from Indians, (supposed fraudulent), ii., 147, 175. Grant of land to, by Connecticut, 303.
Susquehanna Co. meeting and resolutions respecting lands purchased of natives, xi., 114.
Susquehanna—Lands, people settling on, iv., 218. Officers of Pennsylvania Regiment ask for, grant of Land on, 335. Road from Schuylkill to, 362. Deed for lands between, and Delaware, ii., 33, 36. List of inhabitants west of, in 1748, 38. Lands granted by Connecticut, 303. Sulphur discovered near, iv., 719. Pitch and tar may be made on, 721. Settlements on N. E. branch burned and destroyed, vii., 81. Survey of, by State, 210. Commissioners appointed to examine river, x., 129. And opening a Communication between, and Schuylkill, 129, 312. Proposal for building a Town on east bank of, 129. Commissioners appointed, 130, 334. Heavy freshet, 222. Tiadaughton, means Pine Creek, 357. Proceedings at Lancaster to examine and clear, xi., 608, 611. J. Adlum, recommended, appointed, 621, 629. Meeting of counties to improve, 625–629. Instructions to Commissioners, 635, 637, 682. Letters from, 637, 694. Examination, 679, 694. Estimate of expenses to view, 694.
Susquehanna Indians, letter William Penn to, xii., 280.
Sussex county—associated military companies, iii., 23.
Sutter, James, v., 759.
Sutter, Captain to be arrested vii., 632.
Swaine, Chas., ii., 361. Letter on making provision at Easton for Governor, &c., iii., 517. Wagons, 686.
Swaine, Francis, letters to and from, viii., 34, 78, 117. Tried and convicted by Court Martial, 397, 429, 431, 433. (Sheriff) explains difficulty charged on execution of John Brown in Montgomery Co., xi., 269.
Swartz, Fort, xii., 461.
Swatara Fort, xii., 262.
Swearingen, Captain viii., 210, 559; xii., 121.
Swanwick, Richard, forfeited estate, vii., 328.
Swedes, report on a petition of the, i., 173.
Swedes-ford, to be fortified, v., 615, 617. Howe, expected to cross at, 664.
Swedish minister at Wilmington naturalized, iii., 692.
Swedish Consul, Charles Hellstead appointed, x., 362. Advises of War between Russia and Turkey, xi., 265, 292.
Swedish Envoy sends papers on barratry of a Captain of a vessel, xi., 295.
Sweeney, Lieutenant, skirmish with Indians, vii., 7.
Sweeney, John, taken at Brandywine, vi., 58.
Sweers, Cornelius, letter, vi., 473. Charged with frauds, 672.
Swenkfelders, ask for relaxing of the Test, vi., 541, 551.
Swift, Captain, Capture of, vi., 261.

T.

Taghneghdoarus, Shekelamy's son, succeeds him as chief, ii., 23.
Tait's brigade, xii., 260.
Talbert, Major, ix., 135.
Talbot, Colonel George, proceedings on part of Maryland, i., 87.
Talbot, Lieutenant Jeremiah—election of troop of light horse in Franklin county, xi., 280.
Tallman, Peter, respecting salt sent to New Jersey, v., 64.
Tannehill, Captain A., xii., 225, 226.
Tarleton, Colonel, advances towards South Carolina, ix., 283.
Tavern licenses, xi., 604.
Taxes, assessed or laid, vii., 80, 118, 157. Quota of each State, 157. On land, viii., 54, 61, 124, 125, 132, 136, 138, 185, 302, 303. Grain to be received for, ix., 16, 53, 59. Heavy amounts outstanding, 82. In Philadelphia county, 116, 139. Ought to be in specie, 171, 233; x., 51, 52, 75, 79, 82, 222, 224. Commissioners of, xi., 498, 593, 603.
Taylor, Frederick, collector of Chester county, robbed, ix., 459.
Taylor, George, letter, v., 49.
Taylor, Major Richard, xii., 167, 182, 188, 192, 194, 197, 200, 201.
Taylor, Captain Polycarp, of ship Fancy, off Capes, letter, i., 760.
Taylor, Silas, deposition, respecting Wyoming, ix., 622.
Taylor, Timothy, respecting Solomon Vickers, x., 432, 433.
Teedyuscung, ii., 715. Reply to Gov., 721, 722. Always drunk, 724. At Easton, iii., 8. At Fort Allen, 104, 109. Respecting, 143, 193, 206, 209, 212, 235, 247, 248, 256, 286, 318, 319, 346, 350, 367, 376, 425, 435, 464, 509, 521, 576, 692, 717, 735. His demand for a clerk, 235. Requests houses to be built at Wyoming, 385, 412–422. Behaves badly, iv., 40, 44. Respecting, 40, 74. Letters, &c., 74, 78, 80, 82, 85, 86. Denies charge of land fraud. 86.
Telfair, Edward, Governor Georgia, letter from, xi., 96.
Temple, Lieutenant-Colonel, viii., 053.
Temple, John, Consul-General from Great Britain, x., 544.
Tenbrook, Dereck Wassel, appointed Ensign, ix., 529.
Ten-mile Creek, murders on, xii., 271.
Tennent, Reverend William, recommends an Indian interpreter, iii., 514.
Tents, wanted for Southern army, viii., 575. Proposals of R. Morris for, ix., 386, 387; xii., 162.
Tenure of office, Judge's opinion on, xii., 30.
Test Act, effects of, v., 661. The relaxation of, asked for by Moravians, &c., vi., 540, 551. Refuse it, 751. Pardons for prisoners under, vii., 130.
Thanksgiving Day, proclamation for, iii., 690. Ordered by Congress, v., 736. Appointed by Congress, vii., 89, 757. Proclamation of Congress for, ix., 441, 443, 518, 650. For peace, proclaimed by Congress, x., 134.
Theatres and plays, petitions against, iii., 656, 659. And other amusements recommended by Congress and Assembly to be suppressed, vii., 78. Their evil effects, 78. Philadelphia, petition for a lecture on heads, to pay off debts of, ix., 573. In Philadelphia, memorial against, x., 141. Petition of Quakers against, xi., 342.
Thomas, Governor George, proclamation, i., 629. Commission from T. Penn, 625. Letters to and from. [See Letters.] Additional instructions on bills of credit, ii., 104. Letter to Governor Morris, 180.
Thomas, Joseph—Doan's estate, xi., 725.
Thome, John, ix., 118.
Thompson, Captain, at Brandywine, vi., 58.
Thompson, General, proceedings in Congress respecting, and C. J. McKean, vii., 137.
Thompson, Colonel James, ix., 228.

Thompson, General, x., 483.
Thompson, Hon. James, purchases flour, vii., 632.
Thompson, Jesse, scalped, petition, vii., 308.
Thompson, William, letter on recruits, vii., 65.
Thompson, John, iv., 415, 416 ; vi., 299. Expedition to Indian towns, viii., 413.
Thompson, Mord'i, appointed wagon master of Chester county, iii., 398.
Thomson, Charles, clerk to Teedyuscung, iii., 256. Reports of journey with F. Post to Indians, 412–422; viii., 550.
Thorne, Wm., letter, v., 143.
Tiadaughton, Creek, of treaty of 1768, explained by Indian as Pine Creek, x., 357.
Ticonderoga, list of killed and wounded, &c., of party sent towards, iii., 203. Statement of operations at, 472, 477, 479. Lead found at, iv., 646. Condition of troops at, v., 87, 350. Inquiry into conduct of Generals at, 491. Militia ordered to, 492. Gen. Horatio Gates to command at, 492, 494. Resolutions of Congress respecting, 492, 494. Wounded at, 675, 676. Captured by Gen. Gates, Burgoyne, &c., prisoners at, 657.
Tidd, Martin, deposition respecting Wyoming, x., 196.
Tilghman, James, Letter, iv., 335, 346, 416, 417, 423, 488, 535, 590, 590. Protests against cutting wood from commons of Philadelphia, v., 156, 174, 502. Refuses to take parole, 502. Applies to be in Maryland, 635, 641 ; vi., 96. Letter to, xii., 285, 286.
Tilghman, Tench, accounts of Ticonderoga Battle, v., 675 ; vi., 407.
Till, Wm., letter, iii., 471, 475.
Tin, block, required, vi., 368.
Tinicum Island, a part of the estate of Joseph Galloway, viii., 208.
Tioga burned, vii., 6. Kannakaloo, 11. Gen. Sullivan, marching for, 594.
Tioga, River, towns on. Caleb Benton to Col. John Franklin, xi., 175. Military post to be at, 369.
Titamy, Wm., (an Indian) wounded, iii., 246, 251.
Tobacco, complaints of merchants against duties on, i., 149, 203. Trade in Philadelphia, dullness of, complained of, vii., 452.
Todd, Wm., counterfeits money, vi., 359.
Todd, William, Islands in Western Rivers, xi., 645.
Tom's River, salt works established by Council at, v., 55.
Tomlins, Joshua, proposals for making Gun Barrels, iv., 771.
Tonnage duties, xi., 599, 691.
Tories, embodying in New Jersey, Troops to be sent there, iv. 782. Meeting at Philadelphia respecting, v., 72. Taken, 113. At Monmouth, 169, 177, 209. Col. Furman sent to, 209. Election in Berks Co., 31, 32. Sent prisoners from N. Y., 40. Election at Lewes, 53. Confined, 106. Obligation of, 145. Attacked at Monmouth by Mifflin, 169, 177. Major Stockton, 230, 232, 237. Colonel Duyckings, 241. Sent to Phila., 247, 420. To be arrested, 478, 481, 502, 511, 513, 555, 624, 665. Escort for 512. At Yellow Springs, 606. Proceedings against, vi., 4, 5, 13, 44, 51, 75, 77, 83, 94, 117, 118, 144, 170, 210, 242, 342, 344, 345, 346, 347, 359, 361, 362, 434, 443, 445, 453, 498, 533, 534, 542, 551, 555, 596, 602, 611, 615, 621, 625, 641, 644, 651, 653, 663, 672, 680, 683, 695, 709, 715, 721, 728, 731, 742, 744, 750, 752. Action of Congress respecting, 210. Insolence of, 291; vii., 3, 6, 15, 112, 130, 164, 225, 236, 260, 387, 488, 493, 563, 589, 651, 737. A female, 474, 486, 492; viii., 84, 107, 125, 127, 129, 178, 259, 282.
Tory papers, list of, sent to Governor of New Jersey, 625, 707.
Torrence, Lieutenant Joseph, military officers, xi., 702.
Town Meetings, &c., at Philada., v., 73, 77, 83.
Trade, Admiralty on, i., 253, 331, 332. Indian, 261, 304. Board

of, inquiries respecting African trade of Pennsylvania, i., 152, 288. Letter from customs on, 185. Board of, on Bills of credit, 186. Indian, 327. Depredations by enemy on, vii., 235.

Trade, Lords Commissioners of, iii., 690. To Governor Penn, iv., 174, 182. Plan for management of Indian trade, 182, 313. Letter to John Stuart on, 189. Illicit, Dunk Halifax to Governor Penn, 280. Report of Lords of, on Indian boundary, 281. Ditto of Commissioners of, respecting acts of New Jersey relative to vessels stranded, 295. Lord Hillsborough, Secretary of, 301. Report of Commissioners on Indian Trade, 313-31, 447. Commissioners on Indian, to meet at New York, 361, 363, 368, 371, 372, 448. Sir William Johnson, on trade with, 375. Arthur St. Clair on, 557.

Trail, Hon. Robert, letter from, xi., 288. Death of R. Levers, 289—resigns in council, and applies for his place, 289. Prisoners in Easton jail, (1784,) 446.

Traitors, confiscated estate, Controller Nicholson on, x., 96. List of, 250. Certified list of, applied for by J. Anstey, a British Agent, xi., 148.

Transports employed in King's service not subject to Custom-house regulations, iii., 137, 138, 146. Fraud attempted on Custom-house, 291. General Amherst on, iv., 46, 87. Commission to appraisers of, 53. Their report on, as to value, &c., 55. Instructions to appraisers respecting measuring, 56. Difficulties about a, 87.

Treason, opinion of Jon. D. Sergeant, vii., 396.

Treasury, robbery of the, i., 278-279. Of New Jersey, robbed, iv., 305. U. S., v., 334, 373. State of, vi., 81. U. S., to be organized and provided with a house, vii., 89. Of State, balance in, 118; viii., 58, 92. Of Bucks co., robbed, ix., 609. Judges advise some pardons, 634. Board, 226, 229. Letters to and from loan officer, to give bonds, x., 527. Letters to and from, xi., 15, 64, 79, 86, 155, 382, 383, 663, 664. Report to Congress, 15, 50. Resolutions of Congress respecting, 64. Rsservations at Erie, 382. Department, facts respecting, 649.

Treasurer, U. S., tax of Pennsylvania, viii., 185. County, 58. Report of, xii., 4.

Treaties, reference to, i., 168. At Lancaster, Indians present at, 656. Indian, at Lancaster, 656. With Indians, ii., 559. With France, vi., 466, 479, 493, 521. Infractions with G. B., xi., 72. Commercial, with France, 220-228.

Trees, elm, presented by Col. George Morgan, for State House yard, thanks of Council for, x., 420.

Trent, William, account of a murder by Indians, ii., 16, 50, 575. Letter, iii., 149.

Trenton, Council send salt to, v., 69. Battle, prisoners, &c., 140, 141. Letters respecting, 140-142, 146, 159, 161, 168. Troops rendezvous at, vii., 764. Troops at, viii., 523. Troops at, ix., 18, 82. Provisions at, 113.

Trimble, James, widow Mercer's pension, xi., 677. Variation charts, 719.

Trophies, military, to be collected, viii., 99.

Trumbull, frigate, going on a cruise, ix., 95, 100, 106, 229. In the Del., 338.

Trumbull, Jonathan, Gov. of Connecticut, letter to E. Dyer, &c., iv., 394. Answer, 401. Letter to Gov. Penn, 408. Governor of Connecticut, papers requested, ix., 639, 642. Of Connecticut, proclamation on Wyoming, x., 146. Letters to and from, 147, 148.

Trumbull, Gen. Joseph, commissary, death of, vii., 374. Resolutions of Congress respecting settlement of his accounts, 374, 396.

Trumbull, William, proposals for a magazine of provisions, iv., 760.

Trump, Levi, letter, iii., 403, 425, 430, 480, 582. 699.

Trustees of general loan office, x., 431, 514, 545.
Tryon, William, Gov. of New York, answer to queries, iv., 467. Burns Fairfield, Connecticut, vii., 561.
Tulpehocken, deed for lands, i., 404. Murders at, ii., 503, 504, 511, 525.
Turkey and Russia, at war, xi., 265.
Turnbull, Marmie & Co., on storing powder in magazine, x., 281. Claim for land on which fort stands at Pittsburg, 497.
Turner, Joseph, letter to, from a merchant at Halifax, iii., 442.
Turner, Robert, raises flag on Market street hill, x., 39.
Turnpike, Rh'd Peters on Lancaster, xi., 335.
Tuscarawas, xii., 142.
Tyler, John, (armourer), v., 731.

U.

Unander, Rev, Erick, Swedish minister at Wilmington, certificate of naturalization iii., 692.
Uniform of Troops, Colonel Proctor objects to color of, vii., 292. Views of General Washington, respecting, 293.
Union of Colonies suggested i., 678; Draft of a plan for, ii., 197. At Albany, 199. Plan of Governor Morris's views of, 499. Meeting proposed at New York, 498. Gov. Morris to Earl of Halifax on, 529. Colonel Washington desires an, 621.
Unitas, Fratrum, address of, to Gov. Denny, ii., 760; Exempt from militia duty, iii., 134. (see Moravians.) Passport for F. Post, 578, 989.
United Netherlands, letter from Pres. Dickinson to minister of, respecting Longschamp, x., 351. Extract of letter from, 108. Letter from P. J. Van Berekel, respecting, 415. Pres. Dickinson to the minister of, 435. J. H. Christian Heinecken, consul of, for Philadelphia, 446.
United States, of America, the confederation completed by Maryland signing the articles, viii., 749, 751; Independence acknowledged by Holland, ix., 633; And Great Britian, preliminaries of peace between, signed, x., 10. Seat of Government, proceedings in Congress on, 136, 139. Returns of Pennsylvania troops in service of 393, 403, 431, 449. Claims of Pennsylvania on, 397, 398. John Jay elected secretary of foreign affairs, 401, 402. J. Milligan and J. Story, Commissioners to settle accounts between, and Pennsylvania, 426. Will barely relinquish Pittsburg, 498. National debt, 514–20, 260. Loan office, 520, 522. Report to Congress on Revenue system of, 732. Commissioners appointed by Virginia on trade of, 738. do. by Maryland, 734; Report of treasury to Congress, on acts passed by the States, to meet the requisitions, xi., 15. Account of receipts and expenditures, 30. Finances, 15, 23, 30, 33, 50, 86. Uniformity of commercial systems in the States, proposed, 61. Requisitions, 73. Ordinance for settling accounts between, and States, 146, 154, 317, 323. Algiers, war between, 522. Statement of quantity and value of Erie, 685. Amendments to constitution, proposed by N. Carolina, 674. Census, 679. Accept cession of Western territory from N. Carolina, 681, 688. Accounts with Pennsylvania, 698. Gov. of Western territory, 703. Courts, 703. Charles Pettit, appointed to settle accounts between Pennsylvania and, 708; Patent for Erie, xii., 103.
University of Pennsylvania, laws of College, viii., 246. Shippen's anatomical lectures at, 643. Fund arising from sales of estates, for the charity schools, ix., 385. Sale of confiscated estates, 461, 676; Estates allotted to, x., 195; Ask for use of State House bell, now meeting at Philosophical Society's Hall, xi., 613. Granted by Assembly, 614. Invitations to commencement, 704, 711.
Upland, first Council at, i., 37. Court called at, 51.
Urie, Thomas, vii., 535.

V.

Valandigham, Col. George W., letter to, vii., 261.
Valley Forge, winter quarters at, vi., 122.
Van Berekel, P. J., respecting a publication in a newspaper, x., 413.
Van Campen, John, letter to, iv., 70; vi., 767. Distress at Minnisinks, vii., 573, 575, 603. Incursions of Indians, viii., 202, 551, 683. Distress of inhabitants, ix., 106, 123, 522. Sick soldiers, 660. Connecticut claim, 693. Letter of Capt P. Shrawder, to, 24. Letter, xi., 26; xii., 70.
Vance, Capt., xii., 183, 187.
Vancouver, Chas., patronage, for a book, x., 712.
Van Dam, Gov. Rip, letter to Gov. Gordon, on Indian affairs, i., 296.
Vanderen, John, Jr., wheat and flour in Delaware, viii., 594.
Vandyke, Gov. Nicholas, of Dela., letter from, xi., 33.
Van Etten, Capt. Jno., instructions to, ii., 546. Letter, 720. Letters to and from, vii., 139. His Journal, 222–235. Encounters Indians, viii., 303, 321.
Vanfleck, Henry, suspicions against, vi., 57. Deposition respecting, 67, 77.
Van Hur, Capt., viii., 539.
Van Heer, troop of Marechause, ix., 486, 505, 506.
Van Horn, Capt., ix., 300.
Van Lier, Mr., xii., 115, 134, 162.
Van Noemer, M. introduced by Franklin, vii., 774.
Vanschaick, Col., commands at Fort Stanwix, and attacks an Indian town, xii., 112.
Van Staphorst, N. and J., on Dutch loans, ix., 564. Loans, 591.
Vanzant, Garret and John, examination respecting robberies, vi., 596, 599, 600, 604.
Varnum, Gen., vi., 31, 121.
Varnum, Major and his company have hard fare, vii., 465.
Vaughan, Col., iv., 39.
Vaughan, Maj. Gen. John, Gates's letter to, on burning towns, v., 688.
Vaughan, Gen. (British) commands expedition to Conn., vii., 561.
Vaughan, Samuel, on trees for State House yard, xi., 674.
Venander, George, ix., 529.
Venango, Fort at, iii., 13. Authority to establish a post at, xii., 113, 130, 131. Indian towns near, 157. Fort at, 463.
Veness, Jerome, noble conduct, of, vi., 689.
Vermont and New York, controversy between, viii., 89.
Verner, Frederick, proceedings in his case, vi., 713. Exchange of, proposed, vii , 246.
Vernon, Major Frederick, xii., 108. Letter to, 121. Want of provisions, 121, 125.
Vessels—Rules for measuring transports, iv., 56. Sickly to be examined, 59, 374. Difficult to obtain, for transports, 79. A Spanish, in distress, proceedings, 105, 118. Ransom bills unpaid, prisoners detained in France on account of, 200. Law of New Jersey respecting stranded, 295. Memorial of L. Weiss, on sickly, 472. Purchased, 764. Not to pass chevaux-de-frise, v., 67. Order respecting, in Delaware, vii., 747. Substitute for copper discovered, for sheathing of, ix., 431.
Vickers, Jesse, robbery of Treasury of Bucks county, confession, ix., 609.
Vickers, Sol., confession, respecting robbery, ix., 614, 615. Case of, on charge of robbery in Bucks Co., x., 432.
Vining, John, letter, iv., 336, 341. Appointed Judge, 337. Case of Galloway, at Dover, 341.
Virginia, murder by Indians, i., 436. Letters of Governor Gooch, ii., 18. Pres't Lee, 58. Gov. Dinwiddie's speech on proroguing assembly, 169. Correspondence with Governor of Pennsylvania, 18, 58, 177, 226, 268. Provisions for, 268, 449. Forts in, 581. French neutrals in, 581. Grant of men and money, 621. Council of officers at Fort Loudoun in, iii., 367. Indian affairs in, 694. Letter to Gov. Fauquier from Governor Penn, on peace with Indians made by Col. Bradstreet, iv., 207. Frontier in-

habitants moving over Allegheny mountains, 217. Murder in Augusta county, 218. Proclamation of Gov. Fauquier, 255. Lord Botetourt, Letter from, 365. Act on Indian trade, 372. On Western boundaries, 455. Counterfeits, 461, 462. Act of, against counterfeits, 462. Papers, &c., relating to Dr. John Connolly's proceedings, 476, 479. Muster at Redstone, old Fort, 481. Boundary with Pennsylvania, 481, 483, 490, 515, 516. Lord Dunmore's Letters, &c., 460, 482, 493, 522. Proclamation of Earl Dunmore, 490. Advertisement of Dr. Connolly, 521. Letter, 526. Remarks on Connolly's proceedings, 528. Troops marching from, to Pittsburg, 530. Indians aim at, 550. Cap. Crawford, President of Court, 551. Depositions, 582, 603, 705, 607–612. Letters respecting dispute, 586, 587, 589, 612. Minutes of Council of, on Indian hostilities at Pluggy's Town, appoints, Geo. Morgan and Col. Nevill to confer, and chastise them, v., 258. Letter, P. Henry, Jr., 260, 286. Letters to delegates in Congress, 413. Proposition for settlement of boundary between, and Penn., 413, Troops to go to Billingsport, 418. Quakers, &c., to be sent to, 580, 582, 584, 586, 600, 604, 632. Boundary unsettled, vi., 69, 82. Volunteers expected from, 120. Act of, for clothing their troops, 125. Consents to confederation, 144, 232. Offers troops for Philadelphia, 183. Rendezvous, in, 302. Letter from, on disputes with Pennsylvania, vii., 73. An agent from, in Pittsburg, 79. Circular to, 152. From Delegates of, in Congress, 73, 184. Resolves of General Assembly of, 185. Letter to Governor, 197. Letter from Patrick Henry on Embargo, 247. Papers respecting boundary called for, 309, 310, 441. Resolutions of House of Delegates on boundary line, 441 Enemy land at Portsmouth, 412. Boundary between, and Pennsylvania, viii., 46, 56, 63, 91, 191, 285, 352, 488, 516, 570, 583, 641, 713, 744, 746. Intrusions by, 191. Letter from Gov. Jefferson on, 196, 641. Suit against Col. Brodhead by, 202. Congress sustain him, 195, 202. Resolution of General Assembly of, respecting agreement and boundary between, and Pennsylvania, 352, 570. Commissioners, 353. Looked to for provisions, 471. Confirms line run in 1779, &c., 488, 516, 570, 583, 641, 713, 744, 746. Obtaining more territory, 707. Convention prisoners to be moved from, to Pennsylvania, 753. Convention prisoners, ix., 5, 25. Line between Pennsylvania Commissioners, 20, 78, 189, 301. Rev. Jas. Madison and Rev. Robert Andrews, Commissioners to extend Mason & Dixon's line, 78, 233, 234. Instruments required, 78. Gov. Jefferson's letters, 78, 160. Reported junction of Lord Cornwallis and Gen. Phillips in, 172. Proceedings of Pentecost and Cannon, 193. Lt. Morrison of 9th Virginia regiment in search of Indians, 201. Movements of enemy in, 210. Delegates of, in Congress on seizure of merchandise belonging to State for a private debt, letters respecting, 260, 266, 271, 272, 274, Troops ordered to South Carolina by Fayette, 283. Boundary with Pennsylvania, 233, 234, 301, 304, 315, 344, 352, 356, 374, 402, 439, 445. Position of Lord Cornwallis in, 301, 337, General Clarke's expedition, 325, 343, 352, 355, 356, 561. Boundary line, 468, 506, 513, 519, 533, 562, 566, 585, 607, 772. Letters of Gov. Harrison, 518, 533, 549. Resolutions of House of Delegates, 562. Boundary line between, and Pennsylvania, x., 8, 56, 72, 77, 95, 96, 145, 146, 171, 175, 181, 223, 232, 233, 236, 269, 280, 293, 336, 372, 373, 374, 413, 414, 428, 438, 439, 489, 506, 573, 602, 611, 705. Letters of Gov. Harrison, 56, 65, 72, 77, 78, 95, 145, 175, (1783.) Case of Col. Cox, 81, 96, 125, 172, (1783.) Commissioners appointed by, 146, Resolution of House of Delegates, 1783, 171. Commis-

sioners of Pennsylvania, (1783.) 171, 223. Case of John Campbell, 172, Rejects finance plan of Congress, 153, (1780.) Agreement at Baltimore, 223, Letter A. McClean, respecting Westmoreland, 293. Report of Commissioners on Boundary, 373, 374. Difficulties on surveys, 414. Report of Commissioners, 506, Titles in Washington Co., 414, 417. Meeting at Surveyor General's respecting surveys of Land, obtained from, 705. Resolution of House of Delegates, appointing Commissioners on Trade of U. S. 738. Act to comply with requisition, xi., 17, 23. Letter from land officers, on claims under titles of, 138, 160. Memorial of Charles Simms, 160, 169. Letters, Gov'r Randolph, 212, 284. Laws requested, 284. Proceedings of Council, respecting titles, 291. Report to Congress, on letter of Commissioners of, 317. Letters to and from Govr. Harrison (1783), on boundaries, 497, 499, 501, 507. Campbell and Simpson's claim, 501. Copy of laws asked for, 507. And Maryland, on internal navigation, 511. Commissioners to be appointed by Penn'a, 521. Act of, on commerce, 523-526. Letter to Gov. Randolph on calling convention, 557. Arrival of Indian chiefs in, 600. Clothing for troops, xii., 106. Militia Law, 127, 147. Letter to Gov. Jefferson, 140. Pay to soldiers, 150. Troops of, 165. Letter to Gov. Page, 167. Troops sent to Col. Clarke, 177. Boundary line, 178, 182, 195. Import mortars, 189. Provisions, 263. Troops and officers—Capt. Berry and Lieut. Dent, 274.

Virginians, copy of paper given to Indians by, i., 658. Letter from, respect'g accusation against them, v., 14.

W.

Wade, Captain, pilots a French frigate, vii., 12.

Wade, Francis, letter to J. Mitchell relative to landing of enemy in Virginia, vii., 412. Enemy's boats in Delaware, viii., 274.

Wade, Robert, & J. S., letter to Governor Markham, respecting Lord Baltimore, i., 46.

Wadsworth, Gen. Jeremiah—fears a want of flour for the army, vii., 159, 672. Asks copy of a letter respecting flour, viii., 205.

Wagoners, deserted, vi., 320, 337. Drowned, 321, 322, 337. Counterfeit bills found on, 200, 206, 215.

Wagon Masters, circular to, vi., 124, 212, 330, 337, 338, 357, 763, 765.

Wagons, number of, in Northampton county, iii., 404. Advertised for by Colonel Stanwix, 629, 660. To be impressed in Philadelphia, iv., 108, 116. Required, v., 171, 186, 292, 301, 364, 490, 553, 554, 594, 596, 599, 605, 618, 622, 689, 717, 734, 771. Scarcity of, vi, 41, 65, 69, 77, 107, 116, 124, 130, 137, 139, 141, 179, 200, 210, 212, 218, 220, 252, 276, 282, 289, 298, 319, 320, 324, 328, 330, 334, 338, 343, 348, 353, 362, 366, 371, 377, 405, 416, 450, 483, 513, 519, 546, 608, 621, 623, 676, 699, 761-767; &c., vii., 81, 98, 101, 151, 160, 175, 194, 207, 248, 266, 335, 388, 402, 420, 421, 424, 427, 433, 439, 460, 469, 474, 478, 483, 484, 485, 495, 523, 746, 749, 750, 768; viii., 84, 319, 323, 339, 351, 390, 405, 415, 416, 417, 430, 435, 482, 489, 504, 544, 705; ix., 153, 160, 357, 412, 420.

Waldechers made prisoners, v., 178.

Walk, Indian, on lands, iv., 85.

Walker, Captain Andrew, to J. Hambright, vii., 323.

Walker, Captain Richard, instructions, iii., 409.

Wall, Geo., respecting tories, viii., 178.

Wall, Colonel George, Jr., vii., 103, 104, 660. Officers resigned and appointed, ix., 529. Doan's estate, 628. On improving the Delaware River, xii., 289, 293. On sale of J. Galloway's estate, 319. Letter from, 289.

Wallace, Fort, xii., 464.

Wallis, Samuel, vi, 664, 687.

Waln, Nicholas, letter to, on oppressive execu'n of laws, viii., 101.

Walter, John, letter on Sulphur, v., 082, 244.
Wampum, quantity of, left with Secretary, by Conrad Weiser, ii., 17.
War, declared between England and France, ii., 735. Indian, account of the rise of the, iv., 569. Board of, letters to and from, xi., 240, 268, 282, 290, 301, 531, 555, 621, 624, 645, 685, 686, 729, 730. Council of, held, vi., 21. Office, Continental. [See Board of War.] v. Of Penn. [See Board of War.] v. Secretary at, ix., 483, 526. Office, letters to and from, x., 27, 302, 314, 315, 459, 461, 479, 494, 497, 529. Corps, under Colonel Harmar, necessary to protect lands, 495. With Algiers, xi., 522. Secretary at—Cornplanter, xii., 32. Quota of Penns., 292.
Ward, Mr., xii., '035.
Wardens of Philadelphia, memorial of, respecting pilots, iv., 265–269, 271. Letter to, respecting ferries, vii., 627. On sale of lots, ix., 101, 126. Removal of fence, 150. Removal of Chevaux-de-frise from river, x., 93, 349, 350, 606, 607. On storing of powder, 281. Piers, 407. Contract for piers, 456. Removal of Buoys, &c., 580. J. Donnaldson resigns, 583, 584. Joseph Bullock, elected, 583. Expenditures, 585. Beacon on Cross Ledge, 589. Purchased ground for beacon, at Cape May, xi., 93. Danger to piers, at Marcus Hook, from Spanish frigate, 99. Correspondence with commander, &c., 99–102. Supposed interference of British Consul, with, 375. Expense of watching public buildings, 543. Resignation of, xii., 2. Report on Delaware river, 287, 289, 291, 292, 293, 294. Public burying ground, 305.
Warminster, Collector of, robbed, ix., 508.
Warrant to arrest rioters, i., 538, 546. For enlisting troops, iv., 197. To arrest Sergt. McGlasken, 224. To arrest tories, v., 478, 479, 480, 484. For Lieut's of City and County, Philadelphia, v., 563. To arrest, vi., 12, 53, 65. To Sheriff, to seize salt, vii., 149. George Eichelberger, 193. For sale of a cargo, viii., 491. For lands in new purchase, number of, issued, xi., 121. Against Wyoming insurgents, xi., 340. William Penn, for Welsh Tract, xii., 279, 280.
Warren, James, memorial in favor of—as interested in Hare's brewery, vii., 113.
Warwick, English man-of-war taken by the French, ii., 630.
Warwick furnace, cannon cast at, v., 31.
Washington Academy, lands for, xi., 215.
Washington, Col., Geo., charged by T. Penn, with imprudence, ii., 255. Desires union of Colonies, 621. Decided to resign, 620. Letters, 541, 565, 620; iii., 300.
Washington county, letter of Dorsey Pentecost respecting, ix., 315, 540, 541. Gen. Clarke's expedition, 325, 343, 354. Affairs in, 343, 355, 367, 435, 484. Inhabitants of, letter, 356. Election of Justices, 405, 496. State of parties, 438, 444. Letter Capt. Hughes, 533. Expedition to Sandusky, 556. State of affairs, 564, 646, 666. Site for Court house and prison selected, 772. New State threatened, Rev. J. Finley sent to, x., 40, 41, 163. Letter of Prothonotary, 78. Case of Col. Cox, 81, 96, 125. Taxes, 136, 593. Laid out, 181, (1783.) D. Pentecost on affairs, 262. Return of militia, officers in, 287. Difficulties from Virginia titles, 416. Return of public stores, in, 436. And officers of militia in, 436. John Story, agent on accounts, 451. Disturbances in, 467, 554, 585. Doane gives trouble in, 582, 584. Commissioners of, 584, 587, 593. J. Story opens office for adjusting claims, 742, Attack on Excise office of, 757. Indian murders in, xi., 209. Application from, for defence, 377. Danger from Indians, 686. Divided, 640. Indian troubles in, 673, 675, 685, 686. Secretary of

War to Lieutenants of, 686. Petition on taxes, xii , 288.

Washington, General George, Letter sent from Congress to Committee, iv., 644, 645. From Committee, relative to works on Delaware—asking for an engineer, 775. Movements, v., 84, 113, 367, 373, 451. Retreats from New Brunswick before Gen. Howe, 84. Letters to and from, 113. Council recommend to open shops, 115. Bucks and Northampton to join, 115. Letter Gen. Dickinson, sent to, 116, 117. In possession of Princeton, 159. At Somerset, 162. At Pluckamin, 168, 171. Letters to and from, 113, 117, 253, 290, 373, 419, 431, 439, 452, 482, 510, 526, 617, 619, 624, 664, 669, 678, 691, 697, 700, 710. Asks for maps of country, 419. At Morristown, 177, 215. Important services rendered by militia of Pennsylvania to, 186. To be reinforced, 616. Head-quarters at Germantown, 617. Orders Continental soldiers not to be entertained in city, 619; vi., 9, 30, 43, 153, 154, 180, 189, 200, 201, 235, 241, 250, 254, 255, 263, 274, 277, 287, 288, 291, 325, 333, 339, 353, 354, 357, 401, 405, 409, 410, 416, 425, 430, 445, 480, 490, 498, 522, 529, 546, 557, 558, 604, 742, 752. His movements, 91, 122. Affair at Chestnut Hill, 100. Takes winter quarters in Chester county, 61. Proclamation on threshing grain, 116. Distress of the Army, 189, 328. On clothing, 200, and party with clothing for prisoners at Lancaster, 216 Address to citizens, 277, 326. Asks for Gallies, 354. Empowered to call out 5000 Militia, 399, 409, 446. Introduces Gen. Greene, 405. Letter to Gen. Lacey on prisoners with marketing, 410. Respecting wagon law, 416. Men from Gallies, 421. Militia, 490. Arms, 498, 522. May empower persons to obtain provisions, 66. Distress for provisions, &c., 263, 326, 328. On evacuation of Fort Mifflin, 47. Takes measures in case of evacuation, 558. Evacuation of Philadelphia, 604. Letters to and from,

Washington, Gen.—vii., 89, 90, 95, 119, 127, 129, 161, 187, 225, 293, 327, 337, 341, 351, 377, 406, 447, 479, 555, 738. His movements and designs on Susquehanna, 86. Escort of Convention troops, 95, 99, 101, 104, 106, 107, 110, 112. On intercourse with enemy, 119, 127. Reply to request to sit for his portrait for Council, 127. On clothing, 129, 161. On rank of officers, 188. Respecting Arnold, 188. Asks for survey of Susquehanna—Expedition against Indians, 210. Respecting Tories going within enemy's lines, 225, 236. Survey of Delaware by Du Portail, 229. Views of, respecting uniform of troops, 293. Wafers ordered from Bethlehem, 295. Court Marshal on Arnold, 327, 337. Orders troops for secret expedition, 329. Pres. Reed, to, in relation to Gen. Arnold, 337, 341, 351, 380, 406. Correspondence with Pres. Reed, 351, 377, 555, 684. Extract of letter to Congress on situation of enemy, 479. On partiality to particular States, 353. On Militia, 354. Col. John Fitzgerald to, 370. Respecting Gen. Sullivan, 535, 555. Col. Lochry tenders thanks to, 565. Writes for Pennsylvania Rangers and Riflemen, 568. On evacuation of Fort Laurens, 569. Officers who have broken parole, 626. On clothing the Army, 670. Anticipated want of flour, 671, 685. Co-operation with French fleet, 736. Supply of Militia, 741. Embargo laid to aid in supplies, 745. French fleet to co-operate with, 748. Makes an effort to close war, 748. Letters to and from, viii., 35, 36, 43, 48, 54, 70, 74, 75, 128, 145, 154, 163, 180, 193, 240, 267, 332, 338, 339, 348, 356, 369, 373, 375, 412, 470, 474, 482, 486, 525, 577, 598, 682, 686. Memorial of Col. Hazen to, 17. Remarks on, 116, 155. Circular respecting supplies, 145. Appoints places of deposit for provisions, 180. Respecting Magazines. 193. Army, 267. Opinion of militia, 268. State Militia, call

Washington, Gen.—viii.
for, 292. Prospects, 312. Militia, 314. Army in danger, 314. Reduction of Charlestown, 316. Writes alarming letters about enemy, 333, 336, 337. Expects French fleet—calls for troops, 338. Arrival of Admiral Arbuthnot at New, York, 339. Wagons, 351, 356. Distress for provisions and men, 355. Enemy marching to Morristown, 356. Enemy leaves New Jersey, 361. Commends the patriotic spirit of the ladies of Philadelphia, 361. Militia unnecessary, 377. Want of forage, 404. French fleet between Virginia and Delaware—our troops not ready, 414. His situation, 417. Calls German Battalion from Sunbury, 474, 486. In want of provisions, 525, 577, 719. Reduces Regiments, 595. Respecting several spies, 598. On Wyoming, 682. To post garrison at Wyoming, 717. Letters to and from, ix., 39, 54, 66, 75, 84, 98, 102, 111, 120, 124, 141, 195, 197, 207, 242, 255, 284, 293, 320, 481, 485, 486, 501, 505, 509, 513, 536, 550, 626, 642, 653, 656, 661. To Gen. Wayne, on critical situation of Southern affairs, 66. Frontiers, 75. Respecting Fort Pitt, 81, 102. Want of provisions, 84, 124. Respecting officers, 98. Removal of stores from Delaware, 101. Fears Fort Schuyler will be abandoned, provisions, army, 123. Artillery officers of Col. Proctor's regiment, 141. Requisition of troops, 195, 197. Confinement of prisoners, 205. Militia, prospects of, 207. Provisions, 207. Riflemen wanted, 242. Robert Morris appointed to procure supplies, 254. Appoints places of deposit, 262. Supplies, promotions, want of troops at King's bridge, 285. Encouragement from President Reed, 293. Invests New York, 301. Rifle corps, 320. Operations, 387. Finances, 481, 485. Captain Van Heer's troops, 486, 505. Future operations, 509, 513. Views and prospects of affairs, 536–539. Recruits, 550. Indians, 626, 642.

Washington, Gen.—ix.
Withdrawal of troops from Wyoming, 652, 653, 656, 858. Passes, 661. Declines expedition against Indians, 640, 642. Appoints Dobbs' Ferry as rendezvous for persons having passes, 661. Passport requested of, and granted by Sir Guy Carlton, 674. Address of Council, congratulatory on his safety, &c., x., 150. His reply, 151. Letters of Pres. Dickinson, to Delegates, suggesting an annual sum to meet expenses arising out of his position, 152, 185, 575. Answer from Delegates, in Congress, 155. Suggests uniformity of arms in the States, 154. Renounces his commission to Congress, 183, (1783.) To, respecting prisoners at New York, (1782.,) xi., 496. Letters to, xii., 113, 120, 125, 131, 146, 155, 164, 176, 184, 188, 197, 206, 212, 223, 233, 242, 243, 252, 256, 258, 265, 269.

Washington, Geo., President United States, circular on mode of communication with executives, xi., 587. Sends Acts, 596, 599, 601, 602, 603, 604, 611, 615, 616. Celebration of birth-day, 664. Letters on Indian murders, 8.

Washington, Fort, Andrew Boyd taken prisoner at, vii., 384.

Washington, Geo., (an Indian,) xii., 214.

Washington, ship, (formerly General Monk,) captures by, ix., 586. To be sold, 621. Sale, 624, 625.

Washnash, a noted Indian warrior, viii., 159.

Wasock, Capt. Strong's town, at, xi., 69.

Water Gap, meeting of tories at, attacked by Capt. Bond, of New Jersey, viii., 259.

Watkins, Joseph, vi., 368.

Watson, John, Jr., claims damages done by galley men, vi., 769.

Watson, Luke, letter W. Penn to, i., 127.

Watts, Frederick, viii., 558.

Way, Nicholas, v., 315.

Wayne, Col. Anthony, on a supposed fraud, v., 88. Dreadful condition of troops at Ticonderoga, 88. Complained against by Capt. John

Lacey, Jr , for ill treatment, 154. Brigadier General, letters, vi., 25, 86, 251, 387, 397, 408, 411, 419, 428, 451, 171. His opinion of well-clad soldiers, 26. Exertions to clothe soldiers, 61, 408. On Militia and clothing, 142, 419. On substitutes, 251. Recruiting orders, 248, 397, 408, 411, 419, 746. Return of troops, 476. Letters, vii., 64, 142, 255. Brilliant victory at Stony Point, 581, 585. Resolution of thanks by Assembly and Supreme Executive Council to, his victory at Stony Point, 741; viii., 223, 450, 587, 681, 737. Attack on Bergen, 450. Orders of, 451. Invited by La Fayette to dinner, 587. Expedient to make soldiers comfortable, 593. Return of Artillery under him, 647. Letters to and from, ix., 15, 66, 74, 123, 124, 137, 138, 139, 148, 150, 155, 173, 283, 358, 366, 430. Destined for Yorktown, 74, 359. Respecting, 142, 148, 154, 155. Goes to meet Cornwallis, 359.

Wayne, Captain Isaac, orders to, ii., 542.

Weather, very severe at Muskingum and Pittsburg, xi., 244.

Weaver, Capt. Wendle, viii., 288.

Webb, James, instructions to, iv., 180, 213.

Weed, Captain Elijah, instructions respecting fugitives to New York, x., 102.

Weedon, Col. G., letter, v., 241.

Weights and Measures, opinion, xi., 734.

Weiser, Conrad, letters to and from, i., 649, 650, 661, 665, 671, 673, 748, 749, 750, 756, 758, 761, 771, 772. Proceedings at Onondaga, 649. Builds a house for Shekilamy at Shamokin, 661. Letters from, ii., 8, 9, 10, 11, 15, 23, 44, 259, 319, 453, 461, 503, 504, 511, 547, 550, 562, 563, 628, 696, 776. Purchases land, 10. Journal of distances to Ohio, 12. Quantity of Wampum left with Secretary, 17. Letters, iii., 18, 28, 31, 35, 86, 207, 217, 221, 277, 283, 293, 312, 313, 425, 428, 439, 500, 571, 699, 701. Memorandum of conference with Indians, 216. Deposition, 256. Respecting Sower's papers, 440. Journals of, 32, 66. On purchase of lands from Indians fraudulently, 86. Respecting a horse sold Indians, 86. Complains of an address of Friendly Association, 313. Death of, iv., 41. His son Samuel, interpreter, 41.

Weiser, Samuel, account of expenses to Augusta, iii., 713. Proposed as Interpreter, x., 266.

Weiss, Lewis, memorial respecting infectious diseases and impositions on passengers, iv., 472. Respecting Mr. Holker and Province Island, ix., 298. Massacre of Moravian Indians at Muskingum, 523.

Weitzel, John, in want of hemp, v., 85, 544; viii., 602. Letter to, x., 99, 109, 232, 343.

Welch, William, to Wm. Penn, i., 82. Commission to, 85.

Well, Colonel, viii., 111.

Wells, Richard, a Tory, v., 108. Reasons for declining a seat in Council, 189.

Welsh Tract, Memorial of inhabitants to Commissioners, i., 108. Proceedings of Commissioners, 108. Paper from, 108. Reply to by Commissioners, 110. Warrant, William Penn for, xii., 279, 280.

Weltner, Colonel Lund, viii., 40, 42, 57, 62, 153, 161, 166, 171, 206, 214, 233, 270, 341, 369, 377.

Wentworth, Governor, of New Hampshire, letters to and from, ii., 186, 195, 200. Letters to and from, iii., 5.

West, Francis, iii., 706.

West, William, Jr., viii., 631, 639.

Westbrook, Major Samuel, respecting Brandt, &c., at Minisinks, vii., 63. Captain, do., viii., 202. Major, attacks Indians, 203.

Westbroek, Abraham, letters, xi., 47, 102.

West Florida, continental sloop, viii., 346.

Western boundary, xi., 26, 52, 69, 71.

Western Lands, suggestions respecting Cession of, x., 152.

Western and north-western terri-

tory, sale of townships in, xi., 141. Ordinance for government of, 162. Ceded by N. Carolina, 681.

Western territory, Act of Congress respecting, xi., 332, 339. Defence of, 621. Act of Congress for, 621, 715, 716.

West Indies, action in, vii., 636. Success of Count D'Estaing's fleet in, 661.

Westmoreland County—difficulty about courts, &c., iv., 467. Letter, A. St. Clair, about Pittsburg as County town, 471. Assessors can't collect the taxes, 487. Deposition of Sheriff Hunter, 491. Of George Wilson, 492. Letter, J. Montgomery, on affairs, 505, 506. G. Croghan, 507. Men raising, 509. Men killed, 510. Petition from, 518, 520, 536. Death of Maclure, 526. Depositions, 492, 526, 564, 568, 571, 582, 603–605, 607–612, 624, 627, 628, 630, 647, 648, 659. Trustees on County seat, 579. Letter respecting, 589, 605, 618, 623. Trustees fix on Pittsburg as County seat, 449, 471. Opposed, 471. Troops, leave, v., 202. Com. letters respecting Indians, 313, 443. Alarms, 344. Records, 452. Search for, in Lancaster, 455. Militia, 488. Aid asked for Gen. Hand, 529, 540, 541, 542. Indians in, 599. Indian affairs in, vi., 3, 68. Mr. Holliday, 115. Alarm from Indians and Tories, 438, 458, 460. Number of arms in, 495. Indian murders, 495. Supplies for, 538. Troops for, vii., 305, 341, 404, 406, 424, 515, 569. Condition, owing to boundary question with Virginia, viii., 47. Col. Lochry, Lieut. of, 109. Colonel Brodhead, &c., 198, 250. New State proposed, 280. Lieut. of, 290. Troops, sent to—alarms from Indians, 408, 766. Letter, Representatives of, 709. David Duncan, appointed Commissioner of purchases, ix., 17. Militia, 18, 28, 57. Col. Lochry commands, 18, 28. New County proposed out of, 36. A prothonotary recommended, 36. Provisions, 55. Blockhouse or Magazine, built by Col. Lochry, 80, 115. Letter to officers of, 189. Pentecost and Cannon, 193. Claims for land, 263. Disputes in, 300, 596. State of, 666. Gen. Clarke's expedition, inquiries into, 325, 332, 344, 355. State of money, troops, &c., 331. Disputes on Virginia boundary, 344, 439. Lieut. for, 354, 356. Respecting lands in, 409. Militia, 410. Affairs in, 468, 511. Minutes of a meeting in, for defence of county, 559. Memorial of prisoners in Clarke's expedition, 574. Condition of, 2. Counties, 637. Received Mr. Finley's mission to, 730. New State proposed, 730. Troops, 750. New State threatened, Rev. J. Finley sent to, x., 40, 41, 163. Hanna's Town, as County seat, 91. Commissioners interfered with, by Virginians, 98. Fayette, Co. formed from, 118, 181. Alarming state, of Manallen T., 147, 553. Rangers, Captain Stokely, 262. Returns of Field officers, 275, 276. State of affairs, 279. Letter, Alexander McClean, exculpatory of the Virginians, 294. John Story, agent on accounts, 450. Road to Pittsburg, 533. County Commissioners on attacks on Collectors in Springhill Township, 594. Franklin Co. formed, 603. J. Story opens office, for adjusting claims, 742. James Hamilton elected Register of Wills, Recorder of Deeds, 750. Returns of militia officers, xi., 402, 403. And arms, 404. Excise on liquors, 661. Petition from, 670. Indian murders in, xii., 107, 242, 355. Troops raising, 108. Times of troops expire, 157. Infested with Mingos, 232, 234. To furnish flour, 278.

Westmoreland, town, (See Wyoming,) vi., 371.

Weston, Richard, examination of, vi., 142. Wetzel, Lt. John, 271, 383, 541, 551, 629, 651.

West Point in danger, viii., 339. Flour for, 349.

Wetherill, Sam'l, Jr., v., 342, 355.

Invitation to funeral of James Young, vii., 172.
Wetherhold, Lieut. Jacob, letters, iii., 211.
Wharton, Thomas, Jr., elected President of the State, v., 252; Letters, vi., 11, 12, 14, 17, 18, 22, 25. Death of, 493, 546, 558, 569, 625. Funeral at Lancaster, 552; Portrait of, viii., 319.
Wheat, distillation of, and other grain to be stopped v., 229; To be threshed or taken for straw, vi., 83; High price of, vii., 399, 717. Destruction of crops, 401, 426. Purchase of, 559; Cheaper than flour, viii., 363.
Wheeling, troops at, xii., 108. Boys killed, 148.
Wheeling, Captain xii., 216.
Wherry, David, case of, i., 281, 282, 289, 292.
"Whigs, Real," resolutions of meeting of, at Philadelphia, v., 83.
Whilldin, James, v., 382.
Whiskey to be allowed soldiers, v., 372; Large purchases, at high prices, by an officer, vi., 205, 208.
White, Mrs., to be seized, with her papers, for giving intelligence to Lord Howe, v., 97; vi., 63, 239.
White Eyes, speech of Lord Dunmore to, iv., 684; Captain (Indian,) message to Colonel Morgan, vi., 587, 652, 714; A (Mingo Chief,) xii., 119.
White, John, to settle accounts with U. S., xii., 303, 304.
White Marsh, camp at, v, 767.
White Plains, Col. Green, surprised and killed at, by De Lancey, ix., 155.
White, Cap. Robert, a traitor captured in a cutter, by Cap. Hylars, ix., 530, 531; Letter from Gov. of New Jersey respecting, x., 730.
White, William, consecrated American Bishop, x., 434.
White, Bishop William, on Marriage Licenses, xii., 31, 314.
Whitehead, J., letter, xii., 314.
Whiteside, Thomas, vii., 19.
Whitesitt, Samuel, deposition iv., 604.
"Whole Face," and "Long Hair," Indian Chiefs, conference with, x., 740.
Wiccacoa, estimate of cost of garrison, iii.,
Widows, at Letart Spring, xii., 281.
Wig, importance of a, to a justice of the peace iv., 206.
Wilcocks, J. and A., claim salt seized in Philadelphia, vi., 703, 724, 740, 754; Alexander and John respecting salt seized, vii., 122, 148. Currency, 721, 725, 727.
Wilcocks, John, salt decision in favor of, ix., 750.
Wilkins, Charles, letter on Indian store, xii., 317.
Wilkins, Captain John, xii., 300.
Wilkins, Dr. John, xii., 321.
Wilkins, Lieutenant Colonel, to march with troops from Philadelphia to Fort Pitt, iv., 300. Pay for carriages used by, 377. Explains his course against charges at Fort Pitt, 395.
Wilkinson, J. complaint against Gen. Arnold, vii., 449; J., vii., 736, 744; Commissioner to examine Rivers, x., 129, 130, 334. Resigns, his commission as Brigadier, Gen. 610; xii., 199, 209, 226, 250; C. G., viii., 269.
Will, William, &c., salt, vii., 729, 759; viii., 638; Contests election of Sheriff Ash, xi., 410, 413.
Willett, Augustin, viii., 305.
Willet, Col. Marinus, accompanies Indians, to Philada., xi., 707, 711.
Willey, John, proceedings, of Court of Sussex, against, iii., 665.
Williams, Amos, case, of, x., 713.
Williams, Major Ennion, letters v., 34, 35, 39, 51, 52, 80, 103, 105, 107, 112, 115, 117, 127, 204, 209, 212. Resigns his commission, reasons for, 212.
Williams & Engles on State-House, xii., 295.
Williams. Benseller, viii., 63.
William, Fort, xii., 464.
Williams, Adjutant William, on loss of arms, xii., 295.
Williamson, Dr. Hugh, letter on affairs at Wyoming, iv., 365. Goes to Europe, 468; To, in answer, a member of Congress x., 397; On memorial, &c., from Conn., (1785,) xi., 449.
Williamson, Capt. Ralph, collector in Bucks Co., robbed, ix., 508.

Willing, Capt. exchange of, ix., 111; Company, xii., 143
Willing, Thomas, President of Bank North America, ix., 496.
Wills, mills, ix., 108.
Wilmington, (Del.) Fort and battery erected by D. Bush, &c., ii., 6. Letter from Burgesses of, alarm at, 456. Complaints against D. Bush about militia fines, iii., 154, 165-170. Rev. Erick Unander, Swedish minister at, 692. Enemy's vessel near Creek's mouth, iv., 746. Engagement with the Roebuck, 748. Troops at, v., 586.
Wilson, G., letter, iv., 426, 455, 466.
Wilson, James, riot at (Fort Wilson) in Philadelphia, vii., 732, 735, 744. On cutting masts for French fleet on Schuylkill, viii., 541, 542. Attorney for State, in case of T. Matlack, x., 202. Thorough knowledge of Wyoming affairs, 204. Agent on disputed lands, 399. Elected delegate to Congress, 437, 534. Wyoming affairs in Congress, (1785,) xi., 453. As agent on Wyoming, xii., 294.
Wilson, Joseph, claim for arrest of Joseph Doane, x., 152.
Wilson, William, Lieutenant of Northumberland county, respecting Wyoming, x., 304. To J. A., 654. Bearer of ammunition to Wyoming, xi., 192. Provisions at Skipton, xii., 230. Indian murders, 318, 319, 320.
Winchester, Virginia, prisoners from Philadelphia at, vi., 74, 75, 102, 104, 106, 111, 158, 210, 364, 367, 509, 510, 524. Remonstrance from prisoners, 509. Petition, 510.
Windgap, Fort, xii., 464.
Wine, a cask of, sent by President to General St. Clair, vii., 292.
Winter, John, examination of, i., 219.
Winter, Walter, examination of, i., 219.
Wipey, Joseph, a Delaware Indian, murdered, iv., 503.
Wirtz, Christian, v., 202, 208. Regulations of guards at Lancaster, vi., 193, 201. T. M., respecting stores at Lancaster, vii., 220. Respecting purchase of horses, &c., viii., 187, 192, 304, 310, 328, 398, 574, 602, 653, 668.
Wirtz, Major, ix., 226, 229, 379.
Wise, Frederick, vi., 415.
Wistar, Dr. Caspar, Jr., on inspector of pot and pearl ashes, xi., 679.
Witherspoon, Major, wounded at Germantown, v., 646.
Witman, Adam, Taxes, viii., 129, 264, 303. Classing inhabitants of Berks county, 742.
Wetterhold, Captain, ii., 618, 741, 753.
Wetzel, Lieut. Colonel, complaints against, vii., 195. Respecting orders, 299, 572, 578, 617; viii., 602.
Woelpper, John David, a soldier in the Indian war, v., 48.
Wolcott, Roger, Governor Connecticut, letters to and from, ii., 120, 126.
Woman, a, in distress in the army, vi., 716, 772.
Wood, purchase and price of, v., 507.
Woods near Philada., v., 156, 174.
Wood, Colonel James, letters to, respecting desertions of Convention prisoners, ix., 25, 225, 328, 357. Militia, Law, 382. Letters, 262, 276, 345. Removal of Convention prisoners, 203, 225, 236, 262, 289.
Wood, Colonel Joseph, dreadful condition of soldiers at Ticonderoga, v., 87.
Woods, George, vi., 39; vii., 504.
Woods, Thomas, Sheriff, deposition, iv., 435.
Wool recommended to be purchased and manufactured, vi., 41.
Woolens manufactured in Philadelphia, v., 342, 355.
Wrangel, Rev. Charles Magnus, certificate of Governor to, iv., 251.
Wright, John, Deposition, i., 464. Instructions to, 279.
Writ for call of Assembly, i., 504.
Writing master, an extraordinary, arrives at Philadelphia, ii., 710.
Wyalusing, Captain Hartley attacks Indians near, vi., 773. Arrives at, vii., 7.

Wyandot Indians, murders by, viii., 159; 513; ix., 247; x., 86. Forsake the English, xii., 123, 127, 128, 131, 147, 181, 186, 188, 248, 252, 259, 260. Cross Ohio, 248, 270, 271.

Wykoff, P., appointed auctioneer in place of General St. Clair, xi., 128.

Wykoff, W. & L. Clarke, ix., 740.

Wylandaweecham, (Indian,) xii., 227.

Wylie, Capt. Thomas, recruits, ix., 191. A return of Pennsylvania Corps of Artillery artificers, 665. Captain of Artillery artificers, x., 94.

Wynkoop, Henry, letter on sa'tpetre, iv., 702. Letter, v., 32; vi., 600, viii., 557, 572. Letter to, on vacancy in magistracy, x., 211. Letter on robbery, xii., 298, 302.

Wyoming, examinations respecting, ii., 491, 500; iii., 248, 288, 297, 301, 303, 304, 318, 412, 422, 582. Houses for Teedyuscung at, 385. (See Connecticut.) N. E. settlers at, iv., 105, 127, 343. Agreement with rioters, 350, 352. List of residents, 354. Letter, John Durkee to Capt Butler, 364. Letter, Dr. H. Williams on situation of affairs, 364 Letter, Saml. Johnston, respecting Lazarus Stewart and his escape, 378. Inquisition, 384 List of rioters at, 385. Deposit'ons and examinations, 386, 387, 888, 391, 425. Nathen Ogden killed by Lazarus Stewart, 385. Letters, Charles Stewart, respecting, 383, 384. Letter, Governor Trumbull, 3 4. E. Dyer, &c., answer, 395–408. Respecting, 416, 420, 427, 430. Condition of things, 419, 420. Directions to sheriff, 421. Surrender of b ockhouse, 427. J. Van Campen's minutes of proceedings at, 428. Treatment of Simpson and Forster, owing to connection with the Ogdens, 430. Proclamation of R. Penn, Governor, 453. Letters, Comm'sr of Connecticut, 470, 471. Letter Wm Johnston to Dr. Smith, 475. Letter, Z. Butler, 647. P. Sluman and W. Sudd, 661. Depositions, Peter Smith,

Wyoming—vi.

665. Obligation of sett'ers, 688, 689. Petition for troops, supply by Congress, vi., 371. Threatening appearances, 621. Cut off, 626, 628, 631, 632, 634, 643, 647, 664, 686. Company, from, 674. Colonel Brodhead ordered to, 660, 662. Rendezvous, at, 680, 691, 721, 730, 772. Danger from Indians, vii., 3, 8. Murders by Indians, 16, 340, 357. Alarms about, 63. Invested by Indians, &c., 81, 82, 87, 344, 384. Express from, 284. In want of ammunition, 286. Jesse Thompson scalped near, 308. General Hand on his way to, 321, 344. Stores for, 408, 450. Boats for, 438. Guards for stores, 450. Colonel Hubley and Gen. Sullivan at, 553, 620. Head Quarters at 568, 596. Letters to delegates from Connecticut respecting lands, viii., 111; Indians take prisoners, 157, 171, 189; Indians and tories, 528; Col. Z. Butler, 600, 601, 611, 633; reasons for stopping provisions destined for, 611, 632, 633, 682; Indian operations, 692; Act of Congress for relief of, 649, 657, 717. Return of rations to troops at, under Colonel Zebulon Butler, ix., 166. Fort and magazine at, 166. Stores at, 167. Silas Taylor's deposition. Zebulon Butler, 622. Withdrawal of troops from, 652. Attacks of savages, 657. Resolutions of Assembly, 754. Troops at, 761. Act relative to suits at, x., 5. Return of Stores, 14. Letters of Cap. P. Shrawder, 23, 24, 104. Return of Stokely's company, 22. Letter of, Alexander Patterson, 30, 32, 35. Joseph Montgomery, 31, 34. Jacob Johnson, 34. List of persons at, who wish to support the laws, 37. Capt. Robinson at, 47. Ammunition sent to, 47. Provisions to be sent to, 99. Provisions for, 104. Returns of Captains Robinson, and Shrawders, Companies of Pennsylvania Rangers at, 105. Provisions for, 104, 109, 131. Resolutions of Assembly of Connecticut, 116, 117. Reports of Assembly,

Wyoming—x.
224. Proposals for supplying troops with provisions at, 118. P. Shrawder appointed Captain at, 131. Major Moore, commands Pennsa. line, 131, 132. Captain Chrystie, reaches Easton, with a detachment, 135. Proclamation of Gov. of Connecticut, respecting lands, 146. Letters to and from Gov. Trumbull, 147, 148. Decision against Connecticut unexpected, 148. Instructions to Cap. Shrawder, (1783,) 165. Letter, J. Moore, 183, 187, 286. Troops at Fort Dickinson, 189, 197. Resolution of Congress, for a Court to determine right of soil, 194. Resolutions of Assembly, intentions of State towards, Connecticut settlers, 196. Deposition of Martin Tidd, 195. Deep Snow, 197. Condition of settlers, 197. Papers asked for by Council, 198. Pennsylvania, opposed to revision of decision, at Trenton, 204, 210, 216. Letter to Gov. Clinton, of N. Y., 205. Behaviour of Settlers, 207, 208. Letter, President Dickinson, to Governor T., 213. J. Montgomery, on the court, 216. Provisions, 222, 232. Time of withdrawing troops from, 224. Letter of Congress on Court, 231. Letter of Council, to Magistracy and Sheriffs of Northumberland Co., respecting, 296, 304. To Thomas Craig, Lieut. of Northampton Co., on, 296, 303. Letters, of Council to Lieut. Wilson, of Northumberland Co., 304. Council, to Boyd and Armstrong, 307. Wheat reaped on disputed lands, how disposed of, 317, 337. Letter of Pres. to Col. Armstrong, measures respecting lands, &c., 319. Men shut up in the garrison at Fort Dickinson, 321. Commissioners appointed, 330. Instructions to, 330, 339. Provisions, 343. Sheriff to arrest certain insurgents, 344. Troops to march from Bucks and Berks Cos. for, 345. Order to magistrates of Northumberland, 347. Letter to delegates on claims, 399. James Wilson appointed to manage, 399.

Wyoming—x.
David Mead, letter on state of affairs at, 404. Plundering, 399. To judges on disturbances in Northumberland Co., 448, 460. Report of Committee of Assembly, 460, 471. Sheriff Antes charged with not executing his duty, 481. Letters of D. Mead, 207, 222, 401, 482. Resolution of Congress, (1784,) on court, 550. Report to Assembly, (1784). petition of Shepherd, &c., (1784,) 551, 552, 557. Proceedings of Assembly, (1784,) 557-561. Proceedings in Congress, 563. Letter Alexander Patterson to Council (1784,) proceedings, 574. Resolutions of Assembly, (1784,) 575. Petition of Zeb. Butler, &c., 559, 580. Letter to Boyd and Armstrong, commissioners, 591. Various documents respecting, 615–710. Petition of Z. Butler, &c., to Congress, 613–617. Alex. Patterson to Judges of Supreme Court, 617. Do. to Council, 619. John Franklin, &c., to officers of the garrison to surrender, 621. Deposition of John Boyd, 621. Wm. Brink, 621, 623. Colonel J. Armstrong, 625. Commissioners to Alex. Patterson, 624. Answer, 624. Commissioners to Alexander Patterson, 625. Answer, 626. Commissioners to Alexander Patton, 626. Answer, 626. Thomas Hewett, &c., to Alex. Patterson, 627. Answer, 627. Boyd and Armstrong to President Dickinson, 627. Justices of Northumberland at, ready to execute the laws, 628. Justices of Northumberland to A. Patterson, &c., demanding bond to keep peace, 628 Justices of Northumberland to Jno. Franklin, &c., demanding arms, &c., 629. Answer of John Franklin, 629. Justices of Northumberland Co., 630. Boyd and Armstrong respecting, 630. Depositions respecting, 631–638, 639-650, 651, 652. Persons who bore arms, 638. Jona. Seely to H. Antes, 650. List of affidavits taken at, 652. Letter J. Armstrong, 653. 654, 669. William Wilson to J.

Wyoming—xi.
Armstrong, 652. Deposition, 655. 656. Act of Assembly restoring certain lands, 657. Depositions, 659-662. Question to magistrates by commissioners as to safety, 662. Answer, 663. Depositions, 665-668. Escape of prisoners from Easton jail, 663-666. Advertisement of commissioners at, 669. John Franklin to President Dickinson, 672. Deposition, &c., of Capt. Shoemaker, 674. Alex. Patterson to Col. Armstrong, 675. Commissioners to Pres. Dickinson, 676. Claimants disposed to violence, 676. Letter J. Armstrong to J. Seely, 677, 678. Connecticut claimants warning to Benj. Luce to depart, 679. Lieut. Francis Murray to Brig. Gen. Armstrong, difficulty in raising troops, 672. Memorial of John Franklin to Assembly of Connecticut, 681. Resolutions of Assembly on do., 683. Brig. Gen. Armstrong to inhabitants of, 685. Letter to President Dickinson, 686. Depositions, 688, 691, 693. Petition of prisoners at Easton, 690. Brig. Gen. Armstrong to President, recommending defensive measures, 694. Henry Shoemaker convicted of riot, and removed as a justice, 695. Petition of inhabitants, 699-704. No motion in Congress by delegates from Connecticut, 706. Letter David Mead, depositions, 707-710. Resolution of Congress, Z. Butler, 716. Sec. Armstrong to prothonotaries relating to, 749. Report to Assembly read and recommitted, 749. Joseph Hamilton to Col. John Franklin, 751. Cession proposed by Connecticut, 759. W. Hooker Smith, &c., to Corporal Montgomery, 760. Wm. Shaw to Council, 764. Answer, 766. Wm. Montgomery to Council, 765. Ethan Allen, &c., 765, 766.
Letters, &c., to and from Colonel John Franklin, xi., 3, 14, 45, 47, 52, 67, 84, 94, 111, 182, 238. Letters to and from Joseph Hamilton, 3, 67, 84, 94, 182, 183. Congress accept cessions of Con-

Wyoming—xi.
necticut, 3, 107. Proceedings in respect, to Connecticut, 5, 107. Safety of agents from, secured, 15, 52. William Hooker Smith, letters to and from, &c,, 15, 45, 102, 104, 105, 108. John Jenkins, letters to and from, &c., 15, 45, 52. John Van Campen, on, 26. Meeting at, 47. Montgomery, William, on, 35, 108, 111. Susquehanna Co., 45, 114. Westbroek and Hauer, 47. Obed. Gore, 48. Franklin and Jenkins in Philadelphia, 52, 67. Instructions to Samuel Dale, 66. Notice issued by J. Franklin, 67. Report of proceeding of F. and J., in Philadelphia, 67. Capt. Strong's town at Wasock, 69. Resolves of settlers, 83, 114. T. Pickering Register, &c., 84. Deluge in, 85. Letter, Joseph Sprague, on affairs at, 93. Dr. Benton—Captain Bortle,—town of Putnam—Capt. Strong,—Hagaboom settlers, 94. Letter, Governor New York, Ethan Allen and S. Strong, 96. W. H. Smith, &c., to council, 102. Do. to Jona. Correy and Mr. L., 104. A serious address to inhabitants, by W. H. Smith, 105. W. Montgomery to Council respecting E. Allen, Captain Strong and Col. Franklin, &c., 108. Thos. Grant, to Council, 110. Lawrence Keene to do, on recognizances, 111. J. Franklin to William Montgomery, 111. Meeting of the proprietors of Susquehanna Co. 114. Report on cession, proposed by Commissioner of lands west of Pennsylvania, 107. List of land-holders, 124. Letters to and from T. Pickering, 133, 135, 159, 176, 178, 179, 180, 195, 205, 208, 256, 281, 295, 296, 312, 359, 363, 365-371, 399, 424, 541. Roads, 133, 135. Letter from Commissioners on Connecticut claims, 159. Commissioners elected, 160. Letter, Benton to John Franklin on Tioga towns, 175. Council, to Pickering and Balliet, 179. Instructions to Colonel John Craig, to take Franklin, 189. Letter from Delegates in Congress, 189. Arms,

Wyoming—xi.
&c., sent, to, 192. Disturbances at, 192. Combination of settlers, 194. Right to dispossess in a Federal Court, 194. Respecting T. Pickering, in letter F. Smith, 195. Instructions to officers, 204. To commissioners, 205. Council ask Assembly to apply to Congress for men, 206, 207. Arms for, 212. Instructions for N. Dennison, 212. Letter, Gore and Hollenbach, troops, 316. Letter to Governor of Connecticut, 238. Report and proceeding of landholders, 246. Courts held quietly, 256. Bill respecting, introduced, 260. Complaint against justices, 281, 312. Recognizance, for John Franklin's appearance, 295. Letter, L. Myers, respecting F., 296. Half-share men taking lands at Tioga, 296. John P. Schott raising a troop, 297, 298. Officers of light dragoons, in Luzerne Co., 299. Commis'ners appointed to view lands in, 304. Election of militia officers, 312. Justices, 313. Letters to Gov'rs. of New York and New Jersey, on capture of Timothy Pickering, 326. N. Denison, on insurgents, 327. Deposition of A. Ellicott relative to T. Pickering, 327. Proclamation, 329. John Jenkins, &c., 329. Directions to sheriff respecting John Franklin, 330. Z. Butler, &c., to Pres., riot, 332. From commrs., on capture of, T. Pickering, 332. Letter to Gov. of N. Y., 326, 335. N. J., 336, 338. From D. Redick, 338. Warrant against insurgents, 340, 345. Depositions of Ira Manvil and B. Satterlee, for capture of T. Pickering, 345, 347, 353, 358, 399. T. Pickering restored to liberty, 346. Congress applied to for troops. 350, 352, 353. Letter to Z. Butler commanding officers of government, 351. Views of T. Pickering respecting old settlers, &c., 353. From Zeb. Butler, capture of rioters, J. Dudley, wounded, 356, 349. Roswell Franklin raises a party to arrest rioters, 359. Letter, T. Pickering, detailing occurrences, 359. Capt. Ross wounded, 361. Letter of V. P. Muhlenberg to T. Pickering, on release, &c., 363, 364, 366. Military post at Tioga, to be fixed, 369. Deposition, Garret Smith, 372. Letters, Z. Butler; election of officers, 381, 414. Memorial from Luzerne for divisions of lands as Connecticut claimants, 386. Captain Scott's movements, 393, 394, 397. Memorial of William Smith, 400. Claims of rewards, 399, 402. Governor Huntington, respecting John Franklin. 409, 414. Papers respecting, &c., 415. Conviction of Kilbourne and Parks, 419. B. & A. Abbott, 420. Zeb. Cade, 421, 424. John Franklin sent to Phila., by Captain Ross, 424. John Jenkins not to be favored, 425. Various documents respecting, (1782 to 1788,) 431-461. Wm. Bradford, at Trenton, (1782,) 431. R. Peters summoned, to do. (1782,) 432. Defence from Indians, 432. Lands, address by Jenkins, &c., (1784,) 434. Letter to Col. J. Moore at, withdrawal of arms, &c., from, 434. Lieutenant James Reed, at Abram's plains, (1784,) 435, 436. Letter, J. Buyers, &c., 439. Pres. D., writes to magistrates at, 440. To judges, 441, 442, 443. Wilson and Bradford, on private right of soil, 445, 446. Prisoners in Easton jail, 446. Dispatches from General Armstrong. 447. Governor of Connecticut to J. Franklin, rights of settlers, &c., 447, 451. Letter, Hugh Williamson, (1785,) on Memorial from Conn. claimants, 449. J. Gardner, respecting, &c., 451. Gov. Conn. to Congress, (1784,) 451, 453. James Wilson, (1785,) to Pres. D. 453. David Mead to Do., (1785) 455. Delegates to do. (1785,) arms, &c., to Fishkill, 456. Answer, (1785,) 456. To Alexander Patterson (1786,) on do., 457. Arms to M. Hollenbach, (1787,) 458. Arms sent to Lieut. Butler, (1787,) 459. To D. Redick, (1787,) respecting

Wyoming—xii.
Hamilton and Benton, 459. President to delegates, (1787,) apprehension of Hamilton and his papers, 460. President to Balliet and Armstrong, (1788.) Lands, 461. Agreement with E. Dyer, (1780,) 533. Petition of Stephen Jenkins, for release from prison, 537. Appointment of justices of, proposed, 541. Record of Court against A. Kilborn, 546. Certificates respecting capture of T. Pickering, 551-554. John Franklin asks for supplies in prison, 548. Report of committee on letter, T. Pickering, 552. Petition, Gideon Osterhout, for rewards for captures, 553. Reports of Committee on rewards, 554. Lieutenants to N. Denison, on militia laws, 619. Petition of Thomas Martin for lands, 697. Instructions of John Penn, xii., 51. Report of Commissioners to, 73, 296. Troops raised, 126. Letter of inhabitants to Council, 296. Fort at, 465.

Y.

Yahrungwago, Indian town, xii., 156, 165.
Yeas and nays to be required by Delegates in Congress in certain cases, vii., 174.
York, Colonel, (Brit.) vii., 561. Wm. Chesney, agent of, letter on confiscated estates, 599. Criminals at, 773.
York county, riot at election in, ii., 51. Petition of attorney-general of Maryland to Judges at, respecting Digges, 93. Letter from sundries at, and great alarm at, 448, 514. Associated Military Companies, iii., 20. Number of Roman Catholics in, 144. Petition for protection, 235, 236. Companies in, 395, 400. Return of officers at, 410. Committee, letter respecting manufacture of arms, ix., 708. From inhabitants of, on military affairs, 710. Resolutions of, 711. Companies may be raised, 711. Minutes of Com-
York Co.—
mittee of officers of militia, 639. Letter to delegates in, 641. Do. to Committee of Safety, 642. Address from inhabitants to Committee of Safety, 657. Military Associations in, 656. Rules for associators, 657. Letter from, 668. Militia, vi., 169, 379. Determined not to march, 196. Court at, 238, 294, 511. Application from, 376. Lieutenants, 426. Scarcity of money. Recruits, 497. Elections, 775. Salaries, complained of, 776. Colonel Galbraith resigns several offices in, vii., 74. Militia, 115, 367. Elections, 193, 206. Letter from Scott and Stevenson, 206. Affairs in, 401, 415. Town major inquired about, 456, 459. Embezzlement of public stores at, 490, 513, 529, 550, 551, 652. Is a Commissary necessary? 530. Martial spirit in, 623. Counterfeiters in prison, 694. Malpractice in staff department, viii., 141. Prisoners escape from gaol, 178. Volunteers to be raised, 413. Militia of, 524. Claim to the "Town Land," 732. Recommendation respecting, 746. British convention, prisoners to be removed from Maryland and Virginia to, 753. Convention prisoners, ix., 5, 232, 234, 236, 319, 337, 341, 345, 350, 426. Auditors of, 18. Troops ordered to, 60. Sales of forfeited estates in, 105. Clerk of Market, 256. Troops for, 346. Light Horse, 455. Mildew and hail destroy grain, x., 77. Petition of inhabitants against Armand's legion, 133. Report of arms at, 591. Riots in, xi., 98, 115, 156, 157. Elections, 387.
York, Duke of, release from, ix., 694.
York, Mr., death of, keeper of the great seal, iv., 363.
York, Mr., to be confined, v., 471.
York, Thomas, Judge *supersedeas*, iv., 42.
Yorktown—troops from, v., 151. At, in want of provisions, 198. Military election, 330, 333. Riot at, 496-500. Affairs at, 514-520,

534, 536, 570, 558, 661, 682, 692, 704, 730, 752, 767. Warrant to arrest, 520. Conduct of Germans, 576, Tories sent from to Carlisle, 588. Plot discovered, 634, 635. Letter from D. Roberdeau on, 659. Prices at, 677. Gen. Wayne destined for, ix., 74. Riots at, xi., 99, 115, 156.

Youghioghany county, murders at Robinson's run, xii., 263.

Young, Commissary James, ii., 703. Captains of Clapham's regiment complain, 702. His letter to Governor Morris respecting pay of soldiers, 704, 716. Commissioner of musters, Journal to different forts, 681. Letters, iii., 12, 49, 57, 455, 484, 488. Instructions to, iv., 125, 129, 180, 192. Musters men at Lancaster and Carlisle, iv., 195, 196. Letters, 209, 211, 213; v., 336, 337, 411. Letters, vi., 218, 259, 276, 282, 289, 320, 321, 329, 343, 357, 366, 519, 676, 761, 762, 763, 764, 765, 766; vii., 98, 146, 151. Death and invitation to funeral of, 172.

Young, Captain James, pursued Indians, ix., 202.

Youngman, (Jungman?) John, petition militia fines, xi., 304.

Z.

Zachary, Lloyd, M. D., to visit vessels, i., 209. Report, 210.

Zadusky, Anthony, instructions to, i., 220. Letter from, account of a murder, 227.

Zantzinger & Kuhn, manufacture saltpetre at Lancaster. iv., 742.

Zantzinger, Paul, v., 699; vi., 23. Respecting convention troops at Lancaster, ix., 282.

Zedirtz, Herman, vi., 5.

Zeigler, Capt. David, vii., 368; viii., 59, 209. Capt., x., 322, 509. Respecting his rank, xi., 241. Commands, 268. Respecting his company, 284. From Secretary of War, 290, 300, 301. Respecting his Company, 338.

Zeisberger, David, examination of, ii., 459. Letter from, iv., 498; v., 446. His life in danger, and saved by savages, vii., 542. Letter respecting Indians, viii., 159. Missionary, 211; ix, 57; xii., 192, 196, 203, 214, 221, 231, 243, 244. To ascertain the strength of garrison at Detroit, 192, 196, 203, 221. Letter from Council at Coochocking, 219.

Zuber, David, recommended for a pardon, viii., 331.